Business Studies for A Level

4th Edition

Ian Marcousé
Malcolm Surridge
Andrew Gillespie

Orders: please contact Bookpoint Ltd, 130 Milton Park, Abingdon, Oxon OX14 4SB. Telephone: (44) 01235 827720. Fax: (44) 01235 400454. Lines are open from 9.00 to 5.00, Monday to Saturday, with a 24 hour message answering service. You can also order through our website www.hoddereducation.co.uk
If you have any comments to make about this, or any of our other titles, please send them to educationenquiries@hodder.co.uk

British Library Cataloguing in Publication Data
A catalogue record for this title is available from the British Library

ISBN: 978 1444 12275 6

First edition published 1999
Second edition published 2003
Third edition published 2008
This edition published 2011
Impression number 10 9 8 7 6 5 4 3 2 1
Year 2014 2013 2012 2011

Hachette UK's policy is to use papers that are natural, renewable and recyclable products and made from wood grown in sustainable forests. The logging and manufacturing processes are expected to conform to the environmental regulations of the country of origin.

Cover photo from VGL/amanaimagesRF/Getty Images.
Typeset by Fakenham Prepress Solutions, Fakenham, Norfolk NR21 8NN.
Printed in Italy for Hodder Education, An Hachette UK Company, 338 Euston Road, London NW1 3BH by Printer Trento.

CONTENTS

SECTION 5 INTRODUCTION TO MANAGING OPERATIONS

SECTION 6 CORPORATE OBJECTIVES AND STRATEGIES

SECTION 7 ADVANCED ACCOUNTING AND FINANCE

SECTION 8 ADVANCED MARKETING

SECTION 9 ADVANCED PEOPLE IN ORGANISATIONS

SECTION 10 ADVANCED OPERATIONS MANAGEMENT

SECTION 11 ADVANCED EXTERNAL INFLUENCES

SECTION 12 MANAGING CHANGE

SECTION 13 EXAM TECHNIQUE FOR A LEVEL

ACKNOWLEDGEMENTS

Every effort has been made to trace the copyright holders of material reproduced here. The authors and publishers would like to thank the following for permission to reproduce copyright illustrations:

Fig. 1.2 courtesy of Naked Pizza; fig. 4.2 source *esp@cenet* service/EPO; fig. 5.2 © Rohit Seth/Alamy; fig. 6.1 © PA Archive/Press Association Images; fig. 7.1 © Nick Hawkes – Fotolia; fig. 9.1 © Red Cover/Alamy; fig. 10.2 © fotolincs/Alamy; fig. 12.1 © Skogas – Fotolia; fig. 13.1 © Wolfgang Zintl – Fotolia; fig. 15.1 © Dino Hrustanovic – Fotolia; fig. 16.2 © PA Archive/Press Association Images; fig. 18.1 © Imagestate Media; fig. 19.2 © Tyler Olson – Fotolia; fig. 21.1 © Save the Children; fig. 21.3 © AP/Press Association Images; fig. 22.1 © Jacek Chabraszewski – Fotolia; fig. 23.1 © Yuri Arcurs – Fotolia; fig. 24.3 courtesy Taisun Foods & Marketing Co Ltd; fig. 25.2 image courtesy of Waitrose; fig. 26.1 © AP/Press Association Images; fig. 27.6 © Mackie's of Scotland; fig. 28.3 © Bernardo De Niz/Bloomberg via Getty Images; fig. 29.2 © Richard Naude/Alamy; fig. 30.1 © imagebroker/Alamy; fig. 32.1 © Ray Tang/Rex Features; fig. 32.2 © Gareth Byrne/Alamy; fig. 33.1 © Peter Baxter – Fotolia; fig. 38.2 © Beatrice Prève – Fotolia; fig. 39.1 © Daniel Krylov – Fotolia; fig. 40.2 © Philippe Minisini – Fotolia; fig. 42.1 © Monkey Business – Fotolia; fig. 44.2 © Liv Friis-larsen; fig. 46.1 © Alex Segre/Alamy; fig. 49.1 © www.gerardbrown.co.uk/Alamy; fig. 49.2 © Eye Ubiquitous/Rex Features; fig. 49.4 © Patti the Architect; fig. 50.1 © Rex Features; fig. 52.3 © Alex Segre/Rex Features; fig. 53.1 © Ralph125/iStockphoto.com; fig. 54.1 courtesy Innocent Drinks; fig. 54.2 © ABACA/Press Association Images; fig. 55.1 © Marion Divis – Fotolia; fig. 56.6 © Mark Penny – Fotolia; fig. 57.2 © British Retail Photography/Alamy; fig. 58.1 Martin Lee/Rex Features; fig. 29.1 © PA Archive/Press Association Images; fig. 60.2 AP/Press Association Images; fig. 61.1 © mediablitzimages (UK) Limited/Alamy; fig. 61.4 courtesy H. J. Heinz Company Limited; figs 62.1 and 64.5 © AP/Press Association Images; fig. 65.1 © Vittorio Zunino Celotto/Getty Images; fig. 67.1 © Patrick Lane/Somos Images/Corbis; fig. 68.3 © iphoto – Fotolia; fig. 70.1 © Daily Mail/Rex Features; fig. 70.2 © David Hoffman Photo Library/Alamy; fig. 71.2 © INSADCO Photography/Alamy; fig. 72.2 © Jonathan Hordle/Rex Features; fig. 73.3 © Robert Stainforth/Alamy; fig. 73.4 © AP/Press Association Images; fig. 74.2 © Neale Haynes/Rex Features; fig. 75.2 © PA Archive/Press Association Images; fig. 77.1 © Lou Linwei/Alamy; fig. 78.2 © Monkey Business – Fotolia; fig. 79.3 © PA Archive/Press Association Images; fig. 80.2 © Lou Linwei/Rex Features; fig. 83.2 © Imagestate Media; fig. 84.1 © Mirek Hejnicki – Fotolia; fig. 85.1 © Alex Segre/Rex Features; fig. 86.4 © Stockbyte/Photolibrary Group Ltd; fig. 89.4 © Leonid Shcheglov – Fotolia; fig. 90.1 © Olly – Fotolia; fig. 91.1 © Kadmy – Fotolia; fig. 96.2 © Angie – Fotolia.

Enterprise and entrepreneurs

UNIT 1

Enterprise is the combination of attitudes and skills that helps an individual turn an idea into reality. Many people think 'if only ...' but do nothing about it; **entrepreneurs** show the enterprise to stop dreaming and get working.

1.1 INTRODUCTION

Most entrepreneurs see the opportunities that others see, but they also have the courage and initiative to act quickly. The past ten years have seen two clear trends: an increasing desire for travel and more and more thrill-seeking, such as extreme sports. Many people could see that both trends pointed to a gap for a new service: space tourism, that is, individuals going into outer space – just for the fun of it. Richard Branson saw the same opportunity and started Virgin Galactic, which plans to charge £150,000 per trip. It hopes to make its first flight before 2012.

A successful entrepreneur needs the following characteristics.

- Understanding of the market – to know what customers want and to see how well or badly current companies are serving them
- Determination – to see things through even if there are difficulties
- Passion – not just to make money, but to achieve something, such as to design a more efficient solar panel, or to transform rooms from shabby into bright and freshly painted ones
- Persuasive abilities – entrepreneurs need to persuade others to do things like provide planning permission, supply goods on credit or work harder/faster to get things completed on time; they also may need to persuade staff to take a chance by joining a brand new, risky venture
- The ability to cope with risk.

A-grade application

From 6th Form College to Squillionaire

Aged 17, Andrew Michael turned an A-Level project into an internet business start-up. He recently sold the company, receiving a cheque for just over £46 million. His business was Fasthosts, which provides email and other services for small companies. It grew rapidly, earning a listing in *The Sunday Times* as the second fastest-growing technology company in Britain.

Fasthosts was famous for the parties Andrew threw for his staff. At different Christmases he has hired Girls Aloud, The Darkness and The Sugarbabes. Now he's sad to have sold his business, but looking forward to achieving a lifetime ambition of owning a helicopter.

1.2 RISK-TAKING

Business decisions are always about the future. Therefore they always involve uncertainty, because no one can be sure about the future. The oil giant BP's management had a wonderful reputation until it was damaged by safety issues in America in 2005 and 2006. Then in 2010 there was the Gulf Oil catastrophe, resulting in 11 deaths and America's worst-ever oil spill. Similarly, phone companies such as '3' forecast huge growth from person-to-person video phoning, yet this has not happened.

Good entrepreneurs consider not only what they think will happen, but also what could happen differently. Someone opening a restaurant may expect 60 customers a day, each spending £25. In fact, one month after opening, there may just be 40 customers spending £20 each. Receiving just £800 instead of £1,500 may make it hard for the restaurant to survive financially; there may be a risk of closure. This possibility should have been foreseen so that plans could be made.

An entrepreneur looks at the risks, compares them with the possible rewards and makes a considered decision. If there's a good chance of making £1,000 a week, but also a (small) chance of losing £500 a week, it is worth carrying on. Risk-takers accept that sometimes they will take a loss; that is part of business. See Table 1.1 for details of what makes a good entrepreneur.

Table 1.1 Characteristics of good and bad entrepreneurs

People who aren't entrepreneurs	Bad entrepreneurs	Good entrepreneurs
Are very cautious – never want to take any risks	Ignore risks – assume that their own charisma/skill will guarantee success	Take calculated risks, weighing up the potential risks and rewards
Assume that things are the way they have to be	Rush to bring in something new or make huge changes	Launch new ideas in response to changing consumer tastes or attitudes
Like to be sure of next month's pay cheque – and the one after, until retirement	Trust that things will go as planned, spend freely at the start as they're sure the cash will start flowing tomorrow	Accept that the early days of a new business may be very tough, so try to spend as little as possible

1.3 MOTIVES FOR BECOMING AN ENTREPRENEUR

Although 20 per cent of entrepreneurs have money as their prime motive, most are looking for more than financial gain. Typically they are looking for 'a challenge' or 'to prove myself'. In other words people are looking for greater satisfaction than they can get from a regular job. A recent Natwest survey of 1,400 entrepreneurs names the top start-up motive as 'to gain more control and avoid being told what to do'. Just 6 per cent said that they started their venture 'to make money'. Some of the key motivators for entrepreneurs are set out in Figure 1.1.

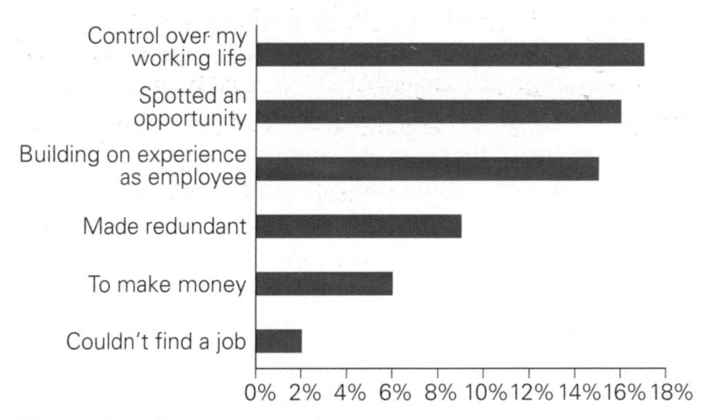

Figure 1.1 Key motivators for entrepreneurs
Source: Natwest Bank, IFF Research

In some cases, starting a business can be hugely challenging, satisfying, absorbing and profitable. An example is Matteo Pantani, whose passion for ice cream led him to start 'Scoop' in 2007, opening his second London outlet in 2010 and third in spring 2011. Yet some people deceive themselves about enterprise. They assume it's more satisfying, glamorous and profitable than it often is. Many shopkeepers work very long hours for quite poor rewards. Many small builders speak bitterly about their experiences in dealings with customers, suppliers and employees; they feel it would be easier to just earn a wage. Furthermore, government figures show that 30 per cent of new businesses fail within their first three years.

1.4 GOVERNMENT SUPPORT FOR ENTERPRISE

Novice entrepreneurs believe that the government will be behind them all the way. They will soon find out that life is not like that. Over 40 per cent of those thinking about starting a business believe that they will get a grant; in fact only 2 per cent get funding in this way, that is, 1 new business in 50.

The government's main expenditure to support new business has been funding the Business Link network. This offered advice for all those starting up, plus a free consultation with an expert nominated by Business Link. Unfortunately, the quality of the advice was very variable. Accordingly, the new coalition government decided in 2010 to replace Business Link with an online-only advice service. This decision to cut expenditure on business start-up was criticised by some organisations representing owners of small businesses.

The new government wants to continue the long-standing policy to encourage an 'enterprise culture'. In effect, create a spirit among young people that being enterprising is 'cool'. The argument runs that if lots of people want to start their own businesses, perhaps the British economy will develop as dynamically as America – the heart of the enterprise culture.

A-grade application

From £40 million to £80 million

In the 1980s the government operated an 'Enterprise Allowance' worth £40 a week to any young person starting their own business. Julian Dunkerton used this allowance to start up a market stall in Cheltenham. Later he was able to open his first shop, called Cult. The business built up steadily until he saw the opportunity to launch a new range of clothing aimed at young, fashionable men. 'Superdry' took off when David Beckham started to wear its jeans and jackets. In March 2010 Dunkerton's business floated on the London stock market, yielding him a cheque for £80 million. It also employed more than 1,000 staff. Not a bad return on a government investment of £40 a week.

ISSUES FOR ANALYSIS

- Some people think that real entrepreneurs are born that way, that is they have the right skills, self-confidence and attitudes from birth. Others say that all the skills can be learnt – sometimes quite late in life. Research points clearly to the second argument – that the skills can be learnt.
- A second important issue is whether entrepreneurs tend to be school underachievers whose success comes from their reaction against their school 'failure'. Businesspeople such as Richard Branson and Duncan Bannatyne were dyslexic and did badly at school. Countering that, however, is any glance at Britain's Rich List. Most of the business multi-millionaires came from wealthy families and had good educations.

1.5 ENTERPRISE AND ENTREPRENEURS – AN EVALUATION

Perhaps the most important issue of all is whether the government does enough to help entrepreneurs. Business representatives like to suggest that 'red tape' (government regulation) makes it hard to start up. This is largely nonsense; Britain is one of the easiest, quickest and cheapest places in the world to start up a new firm. It comes as a shock to many, though, to find how little help is available. Overwhelmingly, people starting a new business need to use their own savings and plenty of their own time. Government rarely provides a magic wand.

Key Terms

Entrepreneur: someone who makes a business idea happen, either through their own effort, or by organising others to do the work.

Innovations: new ideas brought to the market.

Mentor: an experienced advisor, to be there when needed.

WORKBOOK

A REVISION QUESTIONS

(25 marks; 25 minutes)

1 Why is 'initiative' an important quality in an entrepreneur? (2)

2 Section 1.1 lists the characteristics needed to be a successful entrepreneur. Which two from this list seem of greatest importance to:

 a) a new firm facing a collapse in demand due to flooding locally (2)

 b) a 19-year-old entrepreneur wanting to start her own airline? (2)

3 Section 1.2 mentions a restaurant that expects to receive 60 customers per day spending £25 each, but actually gets 40 customers spending £20. Calculate the shortfall in revenue that will result from these changes. (3)

4 Explain two actions the government could take to encourage more people to become entrepreneurs. (4)

5 Briefly explain one argument for and one against saying that entrepreneurs are born, not made. (5)

6 Having read this chapter, explain briefly how successful or unsuccessful you think you would be as an entrepreneur. Take care to explain your reasoning. (7)

B REVISION EXERCISES

B1 DATA RESPONSE

Travis Sporland is a surfer who believes he has created a revolutionary design for surfboards. His father was made redundant from a Devon boatyard two years ago, so Travis thinks they can start up a small manufacturing business together. The Travis surfboard is designed for children up to the age of 11. He believes the size of the world market may be as high as 1.5 million units. Some of his forecasts about the business are set out in Table 1.2.

Table 1.2 Forecasts for new business

	Year 1 figures (surfers under 11)		
	UK market only	US market only	Rest of the World
Surfer population	22,000	580,000	460,000
Forecast year 1 sales	2,200	29,000	23,000
Surfboard selling price	£120	$200	$150

Questions

(20 marks; 20 minutes)

1 If you were asked to advise Travis, identify four questions you would like to ask him about his business plans. (8)
2 Explain your reasoning behind *one* of those questions. (3)
3 Discuss two main factors you think he should also consider before going ahead. (9)

B2 CASE STUDY

Naked Pizza

In 2006 a pizza takeaway opened in New Orleans. It was called 'The World's Healthiest Pizza'. It attracted attention but, as co-founder Jeff Leach puts it, 'people thought it would taste like the side of a tree'. The business struggled. Then a local advertising specialist advised a name change. He recommended 'Naked Pizza'. Since then, sales have risen dramatically and – in 2009 – two wealthy backers invested in making the business grow.

In a country obsessed by food, Naked Pizza's message is 'keep buying the pizza you love, but buy ours because it's better for you'.

The thinking behind the business was to do 'an Activia' in the pizza market. In other words, create probiotic pizza dough that can be friendly towards stomachs. Leach and partner Randy Crochet said they spent $750,000 on research and experimentation to find the perfect dough. It is made from 12 different whole grains and contains probiotic bacteria – just like Activia. Leach says that until Naked Pizza was introduced the usual American pizza was 'nothing more than a doughnut with tomato sauce'. Sceptics have questioned whether these friendly small bacteria can survive a 400^0 pizza oven, but Leach is sure they can.

In August 2010 the first Naked Pizza outlet opened in Florida, one of 50 planned for that United State alone. The race is on to open 400 Naked Pizza (franchise) stores between August and December 2010. After that there will be a big push for worldwide distribution. Eventually the founders hope for as many outlets as Papa John's, with 2,500 stores in America alone.

Figure 1.2 Naked Pizza

The Naked Pizza website suggests that an investment of $250,000 is required per franchisee, but it is not clear what fee and royalty Naked Pizza will demand. In its day, many early franchisees in McDonalds became millionaires. The same hopes will be true in this case.

Soon enough Naked Pizza will come to a city near you. There may be a huge rush to become a franchisee. Recent years have seen the rise of Subway. Perhaps it is time for something new on the High Street.

Questions

(40 marks; 45 minutes)

1 Outline three characteristics of successful entrepreneurs shown by the founders of Naked Pizza. (6)
2 Examine Jeff Leach and Randy Crochet's probable motives for setting up and building their Naked Pizza business. (6)
3 By Autumn 2010 the business was developing rapidly. Examine two possible risks that may undermine the success of this expansion. (8)
4 In Britain, Domino's charges £10.49 for a medium pizza such as the Meat Combo and Papa John's charges £12.49. Discuss the prices that Naked Pizza should set for delivered pizzas in the UK market. (10)
5 Do you think Naked Pizza will be a super-sized success or not? Justify your view. (10)

B3 DATA RESPONSE

Tips for start-up success

The following tips from the US website www.entrepreneur.com focus on people starting a business from home.

1 Begin with a plan. Not all home businesses need an official business plan, but every home business owner must spend some time planning. Sit down and determine how much money you need to invest, your goals (short- and long-term), your marketing plan and all those 'pesky' details.

2 Find a mentor. You may know someone who has successfully created a home business and feel comfortable asking for advice. Seek help from other small businesses, professionals, government agencies, employees and trade associations. Be alert, ask questions, and learn everything you can.

3 Money in the bank. Don't give up your day job just yet. For those of you considering the full-time freelance plunge, set up a savings account with enough funds to cover at least six months' worth of bills. This will give you a buffer to help with your budget. While hunger might be a good motivator, it's easier to work when you have electricity and your house isn't being repossessed.

4 Keep competitive. Even if you think your business is unique, you need to conduct a competitive analysis in your market, including products, prices, promotions, advertising, distribution, quality and service. Be aware of the outside influences that affect your business. Know what the difference is between you and your competitors. Is it service, price or expertise?

5 All systems grow. Word of mouth is the best way to grow your business. Ask your satisfied clients for referrals, offer free consultations to new referrals, and consider a referral or finder's fee. Get your name out to build your brand.

Source: www.entrepreneur.com/article/207270 with permission of Entrepreneur Media Inc.

Questions

(20 marks; 20 minutes)

1 Outline two pieces of advice that attempt to reduce the risks of start-up. (4)
2 Explain why 'every business owner must spend some time planning'. (4)
3 Explain the risks involved when an entrepreneur wrongly thinks that the business is unique. (6)
4 The text suggests ways to exploit 'word of mouth'. Explain how it can be created among customers of a new pizza takeaway business. (6)

UNIT 2

Identifying business opportunities

Business opportunities must be spotted and acted upon before someone else gets there first.

2.1 GENERATING BUSINESS IDEAS

At the heart of successful entrepreneurship is spotting a good business idea. This is usually based on a good understanding of consumer tastes and/or the needs of the retail trade. Both qualities were shown by Martyn Dawes, who spotted the opportunity for machines that could automatically make high quality coffee. His 'Coffee Nation' machines in motorway service stations and Tesco Express stores have made him a millionaire.

The main sources of business ideas are set out below.

- Observation: Martyn Dawes had seen similar machines in New York delis, and saw their potential use in Britain.
- Brain-storming can be useful; this is where two or more people are encouraged to come up with ideas, without anyone criticising other ideas, no matter how bizarre; the appraisal process comes later.
- Thinking ahead: perhaps about the new opportunities that will arise if the weather continues to get warmer (for example, air conditioning, ice cream, and so on).
- Ideas from personal or business experience: for example, 'there are no ice cream parlours for miles around' or 'in my company we need quality sandwiches delivered at lunchtime'.
- **Innovations:** these may come from new science, such as Pilkington's self-cleaning glass (used in skyscrapers worldwide), or from clever reworkings of existing knowledge, such as the Apple iPad.

2.2 SPOTTING AN OPPORTUNITY

It would be easy to become gloomy and to think that all the great business ideas and opportunities have already gone: the hamburger chain, the fizzy cola, and so on. In fact, this is completely wrong. Society changes constantly, with different attitudes or fads marking out the generations. In the 1990s most people went on 'packaged holidays' such as, for example, trips to Spain run by big holiday companies. Today far more people do things independently, giving opportunities for new discount airlines, independent hotels and small car hire companies. If people want a packaged holiday, it is more likely to be a specialist one, such as diving in Egypt; it will probably be run by a small, independent travel company.

The keys to spotting new business opportunities are as follows.

- Think about changes to society: for example, is there now more concern about the body beautiful? If so, what effect will this have on the demand for cosmetic surgery, anti-ageing creams and fashion clothing?
- Think about changes to the economy: will a continuing boom in China give opportunities for British brands such as Burberry, Cadbury and Superdry?
- Think about the local housing market: are people moving into or out of your area? Are prices moving up or down? Many local business opportunities may rise or fall depending on these factors
- Use the techniques outlined below: small budget research and careful market mapping.

2.3 SMALL BUDGET RESEARCH

Even before using market research (see Chapter 4) good entrepreneurs take the time to gain a general understanding of the market. Someone thinking about buying into a Subway franchise for Brighton, for example, may do the following.

- Walk around the town, mapping where sandwich bars and other fast food outlets are located (this is called **geographical mapping**). See Figure 2.1 to see how plotting the existing suppliers can help to identify a suitable place to start up
- While doing so, check on prices, special deals, student discounts, and so on
- Arrange to spend a day with Subway at their franchise in a nearby town, to help understand the customer and the way the service is provided
- Based on the knowledge gained by the above, produce a **market map** of fast food in Brighton; this will help to identify whether Subway will have a **market niche** to itself.

Small budget research may also point towards new business opportunities. *The Grocer* magazine provides many useful insights. Each week it highlights one consumer marketplace. For example, the 19 December 2009 issue highlighted that sales of Cadbury's Trident gum had fallen by 27 per cent in its third year on the UK market. This awful performance by Trident fruit-based chewing gums encouraged the company to go back to basics and the launch of Trebor Extra Strong gum with its strong mint flavour.

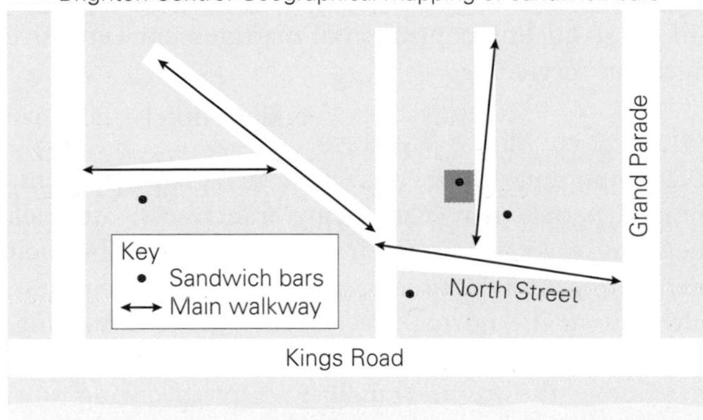

Figure 2.1 Geographical mapping of sandwich bars in Brighton centre

2.4 MARKET MAPPING

Market mapping is carried out in two stages.

1 Identify the key features that characterise consumers within a market; examples in the market for women's clothes would be: young/old and high fashion/conservative
2 Having identified the key characteristics, place every brand on a grid such as that shown in Figure 2.2; this will reveal where the competition is concentrated, and may highlight some gaps in the market.

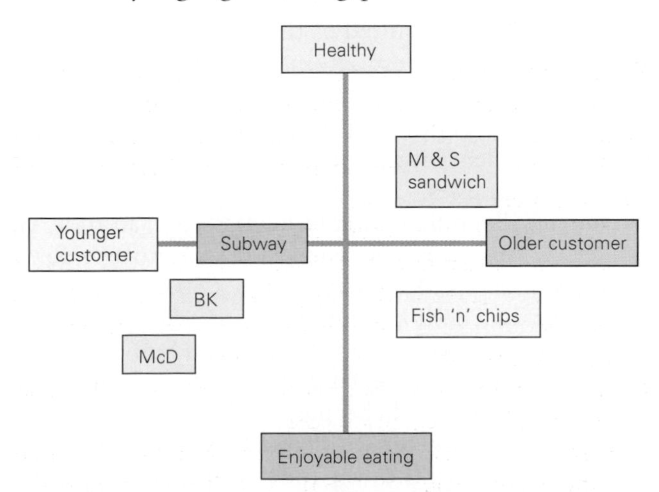

Figure 2.2 Example of a market map for fast food

Using this approach could help in identifying a product or market niche that has not yet been filled. In the market map shown in Figure 2.2 there appears to be an available niche for healthy eating for younger customers within the fast food sector. The market map points to this possibility; then it would be up to the entrepreneur to investigate further. In particular, the niche may be present, but too small to provide an opportunity for a profitable business.

2.5 FRANCHISES

Starting a new business with a new idea requires a huge amount of planning, skill and perhaps luck on the part of the businessperson. Government figures suggest that only 70 per cent will survive for three years. The reasons for a failure rate of nearly one third are easy to see.

- The business idea may not be good enough.
- Even a good idea can be copied by other firms rushing into the market.
- A good idea can be wrecked if the product or service disappoints the customer, for example slow service, late delivery, inconsistent product or poorly trained staff.

Many of these problems can be avoided if entrepreneurs go for a situation that is a 'half-way house' towards running their own business: a franchise. Natwest Bank suggests that 93 per cent of franchises survive their first three years; that is, the failure rate is only 7 per cent.

For example, if you start up an independent optician service, you have to:

- Design and decorate a store that will create the right customer image.
- Create systems for staff training, stock control and accounting.
- Do your own advertising to bring in customers and to make them willing to pay the high prices charged by opticians.

Alternatively, you could start up your own, 100 per cent independent limited company, and then sign up for a Specsavers franchise. This would mean, for example, access to the specially written Specsavers store management software. From a scan of a sold pair of glasses, the software ensures that all the necessary stock ordering and accounting actions are taken. The franchise owner (Specsavers) also provides full training for the **franchisee** (the entrepreneur), plus advice and supplier contacts for store decoration and display and, of course, the huge marketing support from a multi-million pound TV advertising campaign. If you start up J. Bloggs Opticians, how many people will come through the doors? If you open up Specsavers, customers will trust the business from day 1.

A-grade application

Specsavers

Specsavers was started by Doug and Mary Perkins in Guernsey in 1984. They opened branches in Devon and Cornwall, each run by a manager within their own Specsavers chain. In 1988, the company decided to speed up its growth by getting individuals to open their own Specsavers franchise outlets. The finance needed to open each new branch (approximately £140,000) would come from the franchisee, not Doug and Mary. Also, the founders would no longer have to manage each store on a day-to-day basis. Each franchisee has every incentive to run his or her store well, because all the outlet's revenues are kept locally – apart from the royalty rate of 5 per cent that must be paid to Specsavers Head Office. Doug and Mary also receive a start-up fee from each new franchisee, which is a sum of between £25,000 and £50,000 depending upon the location.

This approach has allowed Specsavers to develop into the largest privately owned optician in the world, with more than 1,500 branches. Annual turnover for 2010 is estimated at more than £1,300 million.

Founding a franchise

It only becomes possible to start selling franchises in your own business when its success is clear and quite long-established. Seventeen-year-old Fred deLuca borrowed $1,000 in 1964 to open a sandwich shop. He built his business up to a chain of successful stores and then, in 1975, started offering franchises to others who wanted to buy into his Subway business. By 1995 there were 11,000 Subway outlets and in 2010 there were over 33,000 (2,000 in the UK).

The franchise owner (also know as the **franchisor**) then needs to establish:

- a training programme so that franchisees learn to do things 'the Subway way'
- a system of pricing that is profitable without putting off potential franchisees; usually the franchise rights are bought for £10,000 to £100,000, then the franchisee must buy all store fittings and equipment via the franchise owner (this may cost £50,000 to £250,000) and then buy all supplies from the franchise owner; on top of this, a 5 per cent royalty is usually paid on all income and a fee of 3 per cent to 5 per cent to contribute towards the national advertising campaign
- a system of monitoring, so that poorly run franchises do not damage the reputation of the brand.

Becoming a franchisee

For those starting their first business, full independence means the freedom to make all decisions, including making many mistakes. Buying into a franchise makes the start-up much safer. Instead of struggling to establish a local reputation, the business has a national reputation from day 1, such as, for example, KFC, Subway or Specsavers. All marketing decisions will be handled by head office, not by the franchisee.

The franchisee will be an independent business, but working within the rules laid down by the franchise owner. These will cover the store decoration, the staff uniforms, the product range, the product pricing and much else. Yet the franchisee will still have to manage: staff recruitment, training and motivation; stock ordering; quality control and management; effective customer service.

Pitfalls of running a franchise

It is important to be clear that really independent-minded people may hate being franchisees; after all, they may want to start their own business to 'be their own boss'. A franchisee is the boss of the business, but without the normal freedoms of decision making. This could be very frustrating. It will also be important to choose the right franchise. On the fringes of franchising are some dubious businesses that sell the promises of training and advertising support, but supply very little after they have pocketed the franchise fee. As with anything in business, careful research is essential; better franchise operators are members of the British Franchise Association, the BFA. It should also be borne in mind that the franchise owner's slice of your income may make it difficult to make good profits from 'your' business.

Benefits of running a franchise

A young businessperson could treat being a franchisee as a wonderful training towards becoming a full entrepreneur. 'Today I'll open a Subway; in five years I'll sell it and open my own restaurant.' Very few people have the range of skills required of the independent business owner. Who is expert at: marketing, buying, store design, window display, staff management, sales, stock control and accounting? This is why the failure rate for new independent businesses is so much higher than for franchise businesses.

Due to the different failure rates, the attitude of bankers is very different when you seek finance for a franchise start-up. Ask Natwest for £50,000 to start J Bloggs sandwich shop, and the door will quickly be closed; ask for £50,000 to help finance a Subway outlet and the response will be far more positive. Franchisees find finance easier and cheaper to get. The interest rate charged by a bank for a potential Subway franchisee will be lower than the rate they would charge to the founder of an independent business start-up.

ISSUES FOR ANALYSIS

When thinking of a new business idea, it is important to not only think about its unique features and the response of customers, but also how easy is it to copy? Opening the first Polish restaurant in Luton may look like a licence to print money, but how will the business fare when the second and then the third Polish restaurants are opened further down the road?

Buying into a franchise can be seen as business-made-easy. The difficulties should not be underestimated, though. Above all else, most entrepreneurs gain most of their satisfaction from the challenge of creating and marketing a unique business idea. What they least look forward to is the everyday slog of running a shop or managing semi-interested part-time staff. The life of a franchisee is a long way from the life of a full entrepreneur; it will only suit a certain type of person.

2.6 ENTERPRISE – AN EVALUATION

Every aspect of starting a business is challenging. If something looks easy, it is probably only due to naivety. Therefore anyone who has started a successful business deserves respect. If their start-up seems to have been smooth, probe and question whether the whole story is being told. If it is, then the entrepreneur(s) were probably incredibly well organised and perhaps a bit lucky. Most entrepreneurs are willing to accept that luck plays its part, for instance in how intelligently competitors react to their start-up. Starting a business is fascinating precisely because not all the factors can be controlled; every start-up is a bit of a stab in the dark.

Key Terms

Franchisee: a person or company who has paid to become part of an established franchise business (such as Subway or Specsavers).

Franchisor: the owner of the holding company and franchise, for example KFC.

Geographical mapping: plotting on a map the locations of all the existing businesses in your market, in order to show where all your competitors are.

Market map: a grid plotting where each existing brand sits on scales based on two important features of a market; for example, in the car market: luxury/economy and green/gas guzzling.

Market niche: a gap in the market, that is, no one else is offering what you want to offer.

WORKBOOK

A REVISION QUESTIONS

(30 marks; 30 minutes)

1 Explain how 'observation' could help a business-minded person to come up with a great new idea for starting a firm. (3)
2 The UK population is growing older, with a rising proportion of over 60s. Outline two business opportunities that may arise as the population gets older. (4)
3 Explain in your own words the purpose of geographical mapping. (3)
4 Identify three markets where age is a crucial factor in drawing up a market map. (3)
5 Examine two reasons why a successful, growing business may choose not to sell franchises in the business. (6)
6 Why are good franchise owners keen to inspect their franchisees regularly, even though they have no ownership stake in the franchisee businesses? (3)
7 Why should a potential franchisee be very careful to research fully the background of the franchise owner? (4)
8 Section 2.6 talks about the importance of luck in business start-ups; outline how bad luck could damage the start of a small bakery. (4)

B1 DATA RESPONSE

Cara Phelps has worked in Sainsbury's Personnel department for eight years and is getting bored. She owns her own flat in Leeds, has managed to save £18,000 and wants to start her own business. Her passion is shoes (she has 70 pairs!) so she wants to start a shoe shop. She has been eyeing a site close to Harvey Nichols, as she wants to target those willing to pay £50–£200 a pair. She was going to start up an independent shop, but her father has asked her to look at the franchise opportunities being offered by an upmarket London shoe shop.

Figure 2.3 shows a profile of Cara, drawn up by a friend who is a business consultant.

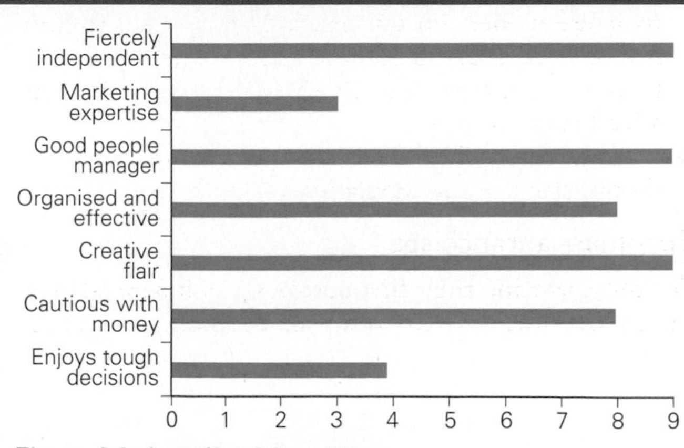

Figure 2.3 A profile of Cara Phelps

Questions

(25 marks; 25 minutes)

1 Outline two pieces of small budget research Cara should carry out before taking things any further with her upmarket shoe shop in Leeds. (6)

2 Consider the following.

  a) Outline one possible benefit to Cara of opting to become a franchisee. (3)

  b) Outline one aspect of the London shoe shop franchise that Cara should examine more carefully before signing any agreements. (4)

3 Use the text and Figure 2.3 to discuss whether Cara is better suited to running a franchise or an independent shoe shop. (12)

B2 DATA RESPONSE

Why franchise?

After many years as a call centre manager, Malachy Miller looked into starting his own business. He quickly decided that franchising would be the right route for him:

'Unless you have an idea or product that will turn everything upside down then this is better than simply going it alone ... Franchises allow you to minimize the risk and you're buying into something that's already there.'

When Mal went to a franchising exhibition in Birmingham he was impressed by the O'Brien's stand. This chain of 300 franchise sandwich bars has been trading for over 15 years. The exhibition stand was being run by existing franchisees who were very happy with their relationship with O'Briens.

O'Briens required an investment of £80,000, of which half had to be from Mal's own pocket. This would pay for all the shopfitting on new premises in Northampton. In addition to this initial outlay, O'Briens takes 9 per cent of the weekly turnover in fees and advertising support charges. As it can be hard to charge high prices for sandwiches, will there be enough profit for Mal to make a good living? By Googling 'O'Briens' it soon becomes clear that quite a few of the franchise sandwich bars are up for sale, including one in Glasgow on sale for £50,000. Should Mal proceed?

Not everyone has had good experiences with franchising. Mark Simmonds was a franchisee of the restaurant chain Pierre & Victoire, when it went into liquidation. He has this advice for potential franchisees:

- Don't rely on financial information given; get it checked out.
- Speak to other franchisees to validate the information given, especially that relating to profits.
- Make sure the revenue statistics are achievable.
- Validate start-up costs.
- Make sure the location is good if it is a food franchise.

Adapted from Working Lunch (BBC)

Questions

(30 marks; 30 minutes)

1 Explain why Mal wanted to start a franchise, not an independent, business. (4)

2 Examine why the views of the franchisees at the exhibition may not have been typical of those of all O'Brien's franchisees. (5)

3 Apart from the franchise fee, suggest three other business costs Mal would have to pay to run the sandwich shop. (3)

4 Consider the list of advice given by Mark Simmonds. Discuss which aspects of that would be especially useful for Mal. (9)

5 Recommend whether Mal should proceed or not with the O'Brien's franchise. Explain your thinking. (9)

Building demand and managing supply

UNIT 3

'Demand' measures the level of interest customers have in buying a product. To be 'effective', that interest must be backed by the ability to pay. 'Supply' is the quantity of a product that producers are able to deliver within a specific time period, for example one week.

3.1 WHAT MAKES A MARKET?

The traditional market took place in a street or square. It was a place where buyers and sellers came together. Today the word 'market' usually means all the buyers and all the sellers across the country, for example 'the car market'. Such a market has a physical element (car showrooms, garages and so on) and a virtual element, such as www.autocar.co.uk.

The common factor among all markets is that they rely on cash or credit to enable the sales to take place. In the housing market, virtually no one pays in cash; the common currency is credit from a bank or building society. This, in turn, means debt for the buyer. Markets that rely a great deal on credit can collapse if credit becomes more difficult or more expensive to obtain. Examples of different types of cash and credit markets are given in Table 3.1.

Table 3.1 Examples of cash and credit markets

Cash markets	Credit markets
• Food and drink	• Cars
• Newspapers and magazines	• Houses
• Cinema, football and other leisure	• Carpets and furniture

Ideally, a market would be made up of lots of buyers and lots of sellers. The sellers would compete with each other, so that none could make an easy living by charging greedily. In a busy street market, if one seller is charging 20p extra per pound of potatoes, the buyers will go elsewhere. In effect, the buyers will force the seller to cut the price back to the level charged by the competitors.

In a market with fierce competition, the rules are simple.

- High demand pulls prices up.
- Weak demand (not many customers) forces firms to cut prices.
- If there is a supply shortage, prices tend to rise.
- If supply is plentiful, prices will fall.

By no means all markets work in this way. The situation in the diamond market is quite the opposite. The South African diamond giant De Beers has control over 50 per cent of the world's diamonds. It uses this control to keep prices high (diamonds were quite cheap, readily available jewels until De Beers decided that 'Diamonds Are Forever'). With one company monopolising such a big slice of the world market, individual shops have to pay De Beers' prices if they want to have a full range of diamond-based jewellery.

A-grade application

On 30 October 2010 many adult tickets to the Premier League match at Fulham were available for £5. Two weeks later tickets cost a minimum of £35. Why was there a sevenfold difference in price? On 30 October the opposition was Wigan, and the expectation of the Fulham ticket office was that it would be a struggle to sell the 26,000 tickets. Two weeks' later, the visitors would be Tottenham, and the 26,000 seats could be sold easily. So, with low demand expected for 30 October the price was cut sharply, whereas the in-demand Tottenham game led to high ticket prices.

3.2 WHAT SHOULD FIRMS SUPPLY?

In some cases, this is an easy question to answer. When Fulham play Wigan, the 26,000 seats will provide more than enough supply. The ticket office will sell to whoever is willing to pay the price. The available supply will be 26,000; the demand may be around 20,000, leaving a surplus of 6,000.

In other cases, the supply may be harder to plan for. A farmer planting a field with apple trees knows that the first fruit crop will begin in 2 to 5 years' time. So the actual supply in 3 years' time is very uncertain. This is important because the big supermarket chains will only deal with suppliers who promise to deliver the right quantity at the right time.

Profit-focused firms will want to supply at the level that makes as high a profit as possible. This is known as the profit-maximising point. In the example shown in Table 3.2 the profit maximising point occurs when the business supplies 40,000 units per week.

Table 3.2 Example to show the profit maximising point for a business

Supply	Profit per unit	Total profit
10,000	£3.20	£32,000
20,000	£3.60	£72,000
30,000	£3.50	£105,000
40,000	£3.20	£128,000
50,000	£2.50	£125,000

There are several factors that affect the quantity of product a firm would want to supply.

1 The operating costs, such as the cost of materials, rent, fuel, salaries, advertising and so on. The higher are the costs, the lower the incentive to supply. This is because the higher the costs, the lower the profit per unit.
2 The price that can be reached within the marketplace. If the product is attractive enough to customers, they will be willing to pay a high price. This will result in higher potential profit per unit, in which case the business would be delighted to offer further supplies, if it is able to do so.

> **A-grade application**
>
> **Lady Gaga's UK tour**
>
> On Thursday 16 December 2010 Lady Gaga played a concert at London's O2 arena. The tickets originally went on sale at prices ranging from £50 to £100. The demand was so huge that tickets sold out within five minutes. By 1 October 2010 pairs of seats were available from ticket 'resellers' (touts) for around £400. At the time of writing, Lady Gaga's management is attempting to put extra dates onto her UK tour; that is, to benefit from the high demand by adding extra supply.

3 Physical constraints. Some businesses are not able to change one or more of the key factors determining supply. Between January 2004 and August 2008, the world price for copper rose from $2,500 to $8,000 per ton. A key factor was that the world's copper mining companies struggled to increase supply, even though there was plenty of demand from China. Quite simply, the mines were working to full capacity, and no new copper mines were discovered and opened during this time. Even though the 2008/2009 recession pushed prices down, by the end of 2010 the copper price was back up to $8,000 per ton.

3.3 DRAWING A SUPPLY CURVE

A **supply curve** can be drawn to show how supply increases when customers are willing to pay more for the product. In the example shown in Figure 3.1, companies are willing to supply 20,000 tons when the price is $4,000. If the price were to rise further, to $6,000, suppliers would be delighted to offer 30,000 tons of supply.

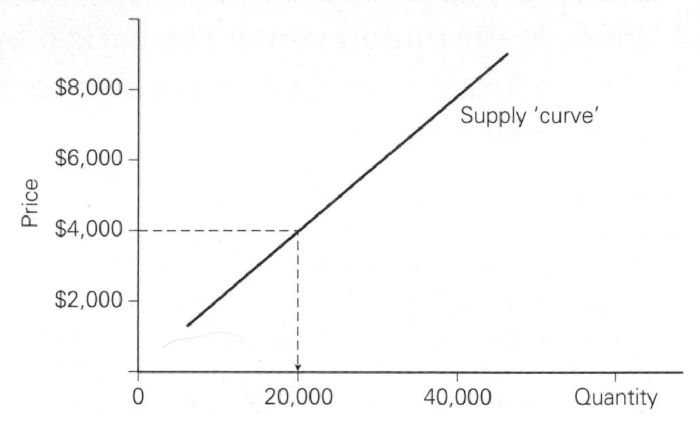

Figure 3.1 A supply curve

The supply curve is drawn on the assumption that suppliers can respond quickly to changes in demand. This would be possible if plenty of the product was kept in storage, or if the production process is speedy and flexible enough to be increased at will.

3.4 FACTORS AFFECTING DEMAND

Every business needs to learn about the key factors that affect the level of demand for its products. For producers of soft drinks and ice creams, nothing depresses demand more than a wet summer. A long, hot summer can treble the sales of Coke, Fruit Shoot and Walls Solero.

Important factors affecting demand:

- Price: the price set by the supplier is a crucial part of the consumer equation:

$$\frac{\text{Quality}}{\text{Price}} = \text{Value for money}$$

  it should be remembered, though, that price also affects the image for quality, so it is as much a matter of psychology as maths.
- Competitors' prices: if the price of a direct substitute is set relatively low, the rival will probably steal market share from your own product; on 3 May 2010 the price in Spain of the Xbox 360 was cut from €199 to €169; the impact was felt immediately by rivals Sony and Nintendo.
- Fashion/taste: what is fashionable at one time is often unfashionable soon afterwards; consumer trends such as anti-obesity or pro-organic can also fade in and out of importance; well-run businesses respond to changing consumer attitudes and desires.

- The state of the economy: if consumers fear that the future looks bleak, they will tend to save more and spend less, thereby causing the economic slowdown they feared. High interest rates and hikes in personal taxation are ways in which consumer spending may be forced downwards by people's lack of confidence in their future.
- Other factors may be hugely important in specific business circumstances, such as seasonality (toys; greetings cards; perfumes), weather (beer; soft drinks; gloves) and marketing spending, for example the amount spent on advertising.

3.4 DRAWING A DEMAND CURVE

A **demand curve** can only be drawn after gathering evidence about the likely level of sales at different prices. If you had the rights to a one-off 'Evening with J.K. Rowling', in which Harry Potter's creator was to speak for the first time about 'Harry's Greatest Adventure', what would you charge for the tickets? Ideally, you would try to work out what the demand would be at different prices (see the demand curve shown in Figure 3.2). Then you could find out the cost of hiring differently-sized venues, to create a supply curve. From that you would be able to work out the most profitable combination of price and demand.

The graph shown in Figure 3.2 is based on (assumed) research findings given in Table 3.3.

Table 3.3 Research findings of demand for tickets

Price	Demand for tickets (in Manchester)
£40	40,000
£50	38,000
£60	36,000
£70	34,000
£80	32,000

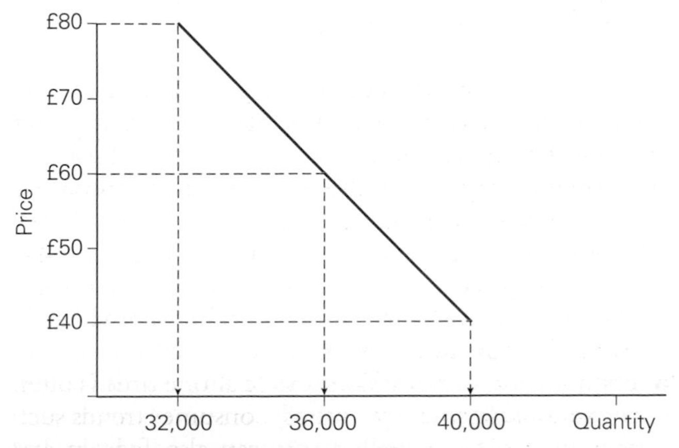

Figure 3.2 Demand curve for J.K. Rowling tickets

Once the curve has been drawn up, you can use it to work out, for instance, the right price to charge if you hire the City of Manchester stadium, which would be able to seat 35,000 people for the evening 'show'.

3.5 INTERACTION OF SUPPLY AND DEMAND

In the above example, if you found that there were three venues in Manchester capable of holding this level of audience (including Manchester United football stadium, which could easily take 40,000), you could draw a supply curve on the same graph as the demand curve.

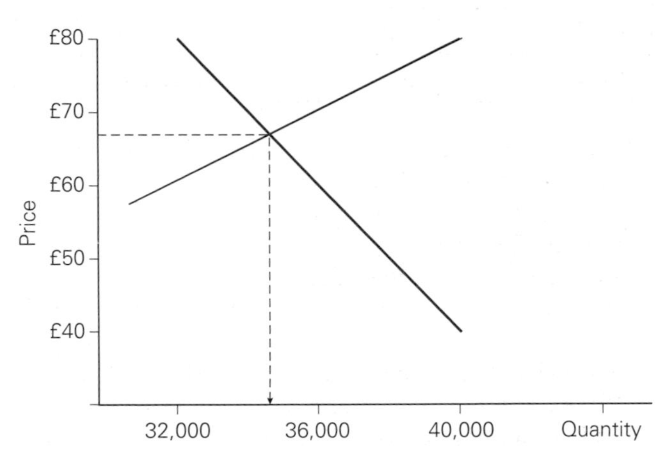

Figure 3.3 Supply and demand curves for a one-off evening with J.K. Rowling

Figure 3.3 shows that the most sensible outcome would be to hire the City of Manchester stadium and price the tickets at £68 in order to fill the 35,000 seats. The price at which supply equals demand is known as the **market price**.

The interaction of supply and demand is an important factor in many business decisions. In this case, the focus is on the price of tickets. Globally, the world oil price has an enormous effect on firms. This is also determined by supply and demand. In early 2008 the supply of oil was restricted by the difficulty of extracting it safely in major oil countries such as Iraq. Meanwhile the demand for oil was kept high by the booming, massive economies of China and India. As a result, the world oil price rose to $120 per barrel (quadruple the figure from three years before). By 2010, a rise in supply and (recession-influenced) slippage in demand allowed the oil price to fall back to $75 per barrel.

Table 3.4 shows the impacts of different supply and demand conditions upon the price of oil (or any other commodity).

Table 3.4 The impacts of different supply and demand conditions on price

	THE IMPACT OF SUPPLY UPON PRICE		
	Supply down	Supply the same	Supply up
Demand up	Price up sharply	Price up	Price unchanged
Demand stays the same	Price up	Price stays the same	Price down
Demand down	Price stays the same	Price down	Price down sharply

3.6 BENEFITS OF MARKET ORIENTATION

A well-run business is sensitive to demand. Its managers realise that demand is a complex, ever-changing factor. Running a hotel is a good example. Demand for hotel rooms is weakest on a Sunday night, so room-rates are at their lowest. For city centre hotels, Saturday night may be a good night for bringing in wealthy night-clubbers, but business customers from Monday to Thursday are the biggest 'money-spinners'. Look at the room rates shown in Table 3.5 for a Leeds hotel in October 2010.

Table 3.5 Room rates for a Leeds hotel in October 2010

Date	Executive Room (for 2)
Tuesday 5 Oct	£119
Wednesday 6 Oct	£109
Thursday 7 Oct	£109
Friday 8 Oct	£79
Saturday 9 Oct	£119
Sunday 10 Oct	£69
Monday 11 Oct	£109

Source: www.laterooms.com. Hotel: Crowne Plaza, Leeds.

What the room prices show is a business that is well-enough tuned into its customers to know that the rates need to be different on different days. A really well-run hotel would also know that the breakfast service on a Sunday should be different from the fast-paced approach taken from Monday to Friday.

Most businesses not only face daily sales variations but also seasonal ones. Carpet and furniture sales rise in the spring, as people see the wear and tear more clearly in the spring sunshine. Swimwear and holiday sales peak in the summer, while toy and perfume businesses can take 50 per cent of their year's sales in the five weeks leading up to Christmas. Businesses that are close to their customers make sure that seasonal sales cause no surprise.

The key to meeting varying demand is to anticipate it by varying supply. The toy shop buys in extra supplies and hires extra, temporary staff in September. The stock is in place and the staff are trained comfortably before the Christmas rush. Cadbury's starts making pre-Easter Creme Eggs from summer in the previous year to ensure that plenty of stock is available for the amazing peak sales of this major UK brand.

ISSUES FOR ANALYSIS

- It is essential to be able to analyse supply and demand in different circumstances and with application to different businesses or markets. It will not work to simply memorise phrases such as 'demand up, price up', and so on. Understanding is the key. Therefore you must make sure to test yourself on the Section A and B questions in the Workbook.
- All businesses operate in a world in which the forces of supply and demand provide pressure on business decisions. Nevertheless, some companies get close to the business ideal of dictating to the market instead of having market forces dictate to the business. For example, for 50 years Chanel has kept its 'No 5' brand the 'must have' perfume among 20- to 50-year-old women. Its advertising creates the demand and its distribution policy controls supply, allowing Chanel No 5 to always be expensive and exclusive. In this time no other brand has come close to the image of Chanel No 5.
- In many other markets, competition is a central factor in every day's decisions. In Britain's newspaper market, the publisher of *The Daily Mirror* knows that tomorrow's sales of the newspaper would fall sharply if *The Sun* cuts its cover price to 20p. The sharp business analyst is the one who understands the circumstances of different businesses.

3.7 BUILDING DEMAND AND MANAGING SUPPLY – AN EVALUATION

The cleverest judgements to be made in business come from the ability to separate what is from what could be. For 20 years Britain's *Financial Times* (business) newspaper was priced at a small premium to the other 'quality' papers, *The Times* and the *Guardian*. Then, between 2007 and 2009, the price of the *Financial Times* was increased until – at £2 – it became double the price of its rivals. Astonishingly, sales were virtually unaffected. A clever executive had spotted the opportunity to make considerably more profit from the paper. Such good judgement is usually based upon market orientation; that is, a really fine understanding of what customers think, feel and want. Good judgement is, of course, the same thing as good evaluation.

Key Terms

Demand curve: a line showing the demand for a product at different prices (the higher the price, the lower the demand).
Market price: the price of a commodity that has been established by the market; that is, where supply equals demand.
Supply curve: a line showing the quantity of goods firms want to supply at different price levels (the higher the price, the more enthusiastic the supply).

WORKBOOK

A REVISION QUESTIONS

(35 marks; 35 minutes)

1 Choose one of the following terms, and explain what it means:
   a) stock market
   b) labour market
   c) foreign exchange market. (4)
2 State the probable impact on price of:
   a) falling demand, while supply remains unchanged
   b) rising supply at a time when demand is unchanged
   c) rising demand at a time of falling supply. (3)
3 When a shortage of Lady Gaga tickets allows touts to charge £400, only wealthy people can get to the concerts. Most people would not worry about this. But why might people be concerned about a high 'market price' if there was a shortage of water at a time of drought? (4)
4 Identify two possible physical constraints that could stop a railway company from completing engineering works on time. (2)
5 Consider the following.
   a) Draw a supply curve for Cadbury's Creme Eggs, based on the data shown in Table 3.6. (5)
   b) Why may Cadburys be unwilling to supply any Creme Eggs at a price of 20p each? (2)

Table 3.6 Data for Cadbury's Creme Eggs

Price	Supply
20p	0
25p	1m
30p	6m
35p	15m
40p	32m
45p	65m
50p	80m

6 Use your knowledge of **one** of the following to explain the two factors you believe are the most important in determining the demand for:
   a) Arsenal season tickets
   b) Vittel bottled water
   c) *Vogue* magazine
   d) Kit Kat 4-finger pack. (3)
7 Suggest one way in which a business could try to estimate the future demand for its brand-new product. (3)
8 Examine Figure 3.3 (supply and demand for JK Rowling in Manchester) and explain:
   a) Why £68 is the right price to charge for the tickets. (4)
   b) What the effect would be of setting a price of £80 for the tickets. (5)

REVISION EXERCISES

B1 DATA RESPONSE

Kylie in demand

In February 2008 a London pop fan could have chosen three different concerts to take a loved-one to. All were to take place in the 20,000-seater O2 Arena and all the tickets were available on a well-known second-hand ticket website. Table 3.7 shows the prices of tickets for the concerts.

At first glance, the ticket prices seem to reflect differing demand for the three artistes. In fact, though, the situation is more complicated. Kylie has six nights booked at the O2 Arena. Therefore, there is a supply of 120,000 seats in London in August. Rihanna has only one night, so the supply is 20,000, whereas Girls Aloud has two nights, that is, 40,000 capacity.

What does this tell us about the fan base for each artiste?

Table 3.7 Prices of tickets for three different concerts in February 2008

Date	Concert	Price of reserved seats
7 March 2008	Rihanna	£93.50 each
17 May 2008	Girls Aloud	£86.90 each
1 August 2008	Kylie	£132.00 each

Questions

(30 marks; 35 minutes)

1 Explain why higher demand leads to higher prices. (4)
2 Examine the evidence and discuss whether Rihanna or Girls Aloud is the more popular artiste. (9)
3 **a)** Assuming all the Kylie seat capacity is sold at the price of £132 each, calculate the total revenue generated over her six days in London. (3)
  b) If Kylie's managers decided to put on an extra two nights at the same stadium in August, what could be the effect on the price of second-hand Kylie tickets for the other concerts? (5)
4 Discuss whether it should be illegal for websites to openly 'resell' concert tickets at prices that may be much higher than the original price decided on by the artiste. (9)

B2 DATA RESPONSE

Supply, demand and the entrepreneur

By the edge of Lake Victoria, Tanzania, is a village with 2,000 people. It is poor, but has its own fishing boats, boatbuilder, vegetable field and (tiny) street market. The villagers work together, but individuals can keep any money they make. One villager, Pembo, noticed that – year after year – the villagers planted tomatoes in the ideal growing conditions of the rainy season.

But when the tomatoes were ripe the price in the local market town was too low to make a profit. Fewer people wanted to buy them (they grew their own) and far more growers brought tomatoes to the marketplace.

In August 2008 Pembo marked out a large patch of sandy earth by the side of the lake, and sowed tomato seeds. As the rainy season was over, he had to water by hand. Every day he spent hours collecting water in a bucket from the lake and watering each plant. He marked his patch out carefully and replanted each seedling to give it the space to grow. He tied them, tended them and eventually was able to harvest them and take them to the market. Whereas the villagers' tomatoes usually fetched $2 per bushel, Pembo's made $5. As he had done all the work himself, the villagers accepted that he kept all the money: this proved to be just over $100 for two months' work (about 6 times the average income). He used the $100 to buy a second hand motorbike with a trailer.

Others in the village soon copied the method for growing tomatoes, though Pembo was already onto his next idea. He paid two 12-year-olds to look after his own patch, while he talked to a hotel in the Serengeti National Park about delivering all their fruit and vegetables.

Questions

(25 marks; 30 minutes)

1 Outline two possible motives for Pembo's business start-up. (4)
2 Examine the understanding of supply and demand shown in Pembo's start-up of his tomato patch. (8)
3 Comment on whether this business idea of out-of-season tomato-growing will continue to succeed. (6)
4 Examine the signs suggesting that Pembo may prove to be a really successful businessman in the longer term. (7)

Figure 3.4 Pembo growing tomatoes by Lake Victoria

UNIT 4

Protecting business ideas

An idea cannot be protected, but patents and copyright are methods of preventing others from copying an actual invention or piece of creative work.

4.1 INTELLECTUAL PROPERTY

Intellectual property (IP) is the general term for assets that have been created by human ingenuity or creativity. These would include music, writing, photographs and engineering or other inventions. Around the world, governments are keen to protect intellectual property because otherwise there would be no financial incentive to create anything. Why should J.K. Rowling spend years writing about Harry Potter if others could simply photocopy the books? She is protected by copyright. To get fully up-to-date information, go to www.ipo.gov.uk; this is the Intellectual Property Office (IPO), formerly the Patent Office.

4.2 PATENT

The *Patents and Designs Journal* lists a series of patent applications that have recently been granted. One is by a British inventor Michael Reeves, for a 'Lightning Protected Golf Cart'. It is easy to see that if this invention works (and can be produced at reasonable cost), it should sweep every other golf cart off the market.

The purpose of a patent is to provide a window of up to 20 years in which the work of an inventor cannot be copied by anyone else. The 20-year period starts from the moment the patent is applied for. The IPO itself admits that applications take at least two and a half years to process, and can take up to five years! In Michael Reeves' case, he probably has about 17 years after the patent has been granted to get his Lightning-Protected Golf Cart to the market.

The patent system acts as an incentive to the inventor; nevertheless it can mean higher prices for the consumer. Mr Reeves' golf cart could prove to be significantly more expensive than its rivals, just because Mr Reeves has the **monopoly power** that comes from the patent.

For a small firm, obtaining a patent can be expensive, perhaps costing between £1,000 and £4,000 for the UK alone. Then, if the product has worldwide potential, patent applications will be required in America, Japan, China, and so on. The total cost could be £50,000+. Worse may come later, if a competitor breaks your patent. This is because breaking a patent is not a criminal offence, so you cannot call the police. It is a civil offence, so the patent owner has to sue the competitor. If a small firm is to take a giant such as Nike to court, there is a real risk that the cost of the court proceedings may ruin the minnow's finances.

A-grade application

In September 2010 the Chief Executive of Sentec, a British company specialising in metering technology, said 'If you go to court in a patent case, then effectively you need to have £1 million in your back pocket to be able to finance (the legal costs), which of course most small companies cannot afford to do'.

At the same time a partner in Notion Capital (venture capital firm) said 'The process of filing for a patent is complicated, expensive, time-consuming and very frustrating. The whole area is not a level playing field ... successfully protecting your IP is dependent on how much you can afford'.

Despite the shortcomings, the system of patents has proved to be an excellent way to give inventors the incentives they need. Figure 4.1 shows how patent applications are leaping ahead in China (up by 30 per cent in 2009). It also shows Britain slipping back (down 4 per cent in 2009) and the continuing dominance of the United States and Japan.

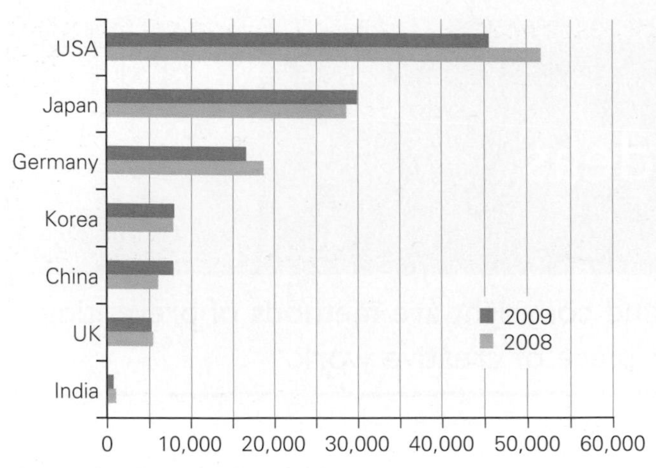

Figure 4.1 Patent applications by country per year
Source: WIPO Statistics Database

4.3 COPYRIGHT

Copyright applies to original written work such as books, newspaper articles, song lyrics, and so on. Unlike patents, it occurs automatically, so there is no need to spend time and money applying for it. Copyright in a literary work lasts for the lifetime of the author plus 70 years.

Clearly copyright is at the heart of the publishing and music industries. Less obvious is that it is also at the heart of computing and the internet. The imaginative prices charged by Microsoft for its Office software are bound up in the copyright protection it enjoys. If Microsoft catches anyone breaking its copyright it will sue immediately. As with patents, it can be argued that this is crucial to the development of the industry. Whereas the cost of developing a Playstation 1 game was said to be around £500,000 and Playstation 2 around £5 million, today the cost of a PS3 game is approximately £20 million. To justify such huge expenditure, the software producer needs to be confident that the game will sell millions of copies; if it is copied by millions it will affect the software producer's ability to pay the bills!

4.4 TRADEMARKS

The Intellectual Property Office describes a trade mark as:

> 'Any sign that can distinguish the goods and services of one trader from those of another'

It goes on to say that 'These signs can include words, logos, pictures, sounds, smells, colours … or any combination of these'. This makes a trademark a 'badge of origin', a way to spot one product or brand in a herd of competitors.

To have any force in law, a trademark must be registered at the IPO. In order to be registered, the mark must be truly distinctive and original. You would not get 'Coffee Shop' registered just because the font is bright purple, but 'Zaydor Coffee Shop' could be registered. Magners Cider was launched in 2005 with the brilliant image of cider poured over ice; the company asked whether advertising cider poured over ice could be trademarked, and was told no. By 2009 Magners' sales were slumping because Bulmer's had unashamedly stolen the Magner's 'over-ice' approach.

The importance of trademarks becomes most obvious when you think of the iconic ones such as the Coca-Cola logo, the Lloyds Bank horse, the Heinz Salad Cream label and Cadbury's 'glass and a half' (of milk).

Registering a trademark costs relatively little, perhaps £1,000–£2,000. It is not something that a small business would think much about until it starts to succeed. For businesses such as UK-based Innocent Drinks, however, early registration of their trademarks was crucial to the company's success.

ISSUES FOR ANALYSIS

- Consumers often ignore intellectual property. They will download music tracks without paying, or photocopy an article without paying the author. Many businesses rely hugely, though, on tightly regulated IP. The problem is that everyone can see the potential benefits of IP in the long term, but no one wants to pay higher prices in the short term.
- Business success relies on building a distinctive market position and consumer image. The more that patents, copyright and trademarks can help a firm to achieve this, the more secure it will become compared with its rivals. BMW, for example, does not want its products called cars; they are 'the ultimate driving machine'.

4.5 PROTECTING BUSINESS IDEAS – AN EVALUATION

Fifty years ago, most people bought products and services with little thought for who had made them. In today's brand and fashion-conscious world, the logo on the back pocket of a pair of jeans can double its selling price, as can a tick on a pair of trainers (Nike even calls it a 'Swoosh' to try to differentiate it). With products and services making ever-greater appeals to our senses, trademarks become ever more important. The only time when trademarks matter less is when a firm has made a genuine technical breakthrough, perhaps from a patented product. If golfers want a Lightning Protected Golf Cart, they will quickly move away from the company that has supplied them in the past. Intellectual property is a huge twenty-first century business issue.

Key Terms

Copyright: this makes it unlawful for people to copy an author's original written work.
Monopoly power: is the ability to charge high prices because you are the sole supplier of a product.
Patents: provide the inventor of a technical breakthrough with the ability to stop anyone copying the idea for up to 20 years.
Trademark: any sign that can distinguish the goods and services of one trader from those of another.

WORKBOOK

A REVISION QUESTIONS

(20 marks; 20 minutes)

1 Briefly explain why Mr Reeves should be able to build a very successful business based on the patent explained in Section 4.2. (4)
2 Explain why an entrepreneur may struggle if the success of new business relies on a patented invention. (4)
3 See Figure 4.1 and identify:
  a) Two countries where the number of patent applications rose in 2009 (1)
  b) Two countries where the number of patent applications fell in 2009 (1)
4 Briefly explain why it may disappoint the British Government to see that the number of patent applications in Britain has been falling. (3)
5 For each of the following, identify whether the IP issue relates to patent, copyright or trademark:
  a) Galaxy has designed a new pack for its Celebrations brand. (1)
  b) Burberry has come up with a new way to get solar power from a tartan cap, sufficient to keep an iPod powered all day long. (1)
  c) Lacoste has developed a new, completely distinctive scent for men. (1)
  d) You have just copied a tennis game from your friend's Wii console. (1)
6 Why may intellectual property be more important today than 50 years ago? Briefly explain your answer. (3)

B REVISION EXERCISES

B1 DATA RESPONSE

In its fourth annual Digital Music Survey, research consultancy Entertainment Media Research found that just under half of the 1,700 people it questioned were illegally downloading music tracks. This was a third more than in 2006 and 40 per cent more than in 2005. Legal downloading was found to be in decline.

Young people were found to be the worst culprits with twice as many 18- to 24-year-olds admitting to illegally downloading music as those aged between 25 and 34. The price of legal downloads was cited as the key factor for this after 84 per cent of those questioned said that older digital downloads should be cheaper to buy than new releases.

John Enser, head of music at law firm Olswang, agreed. He said: 'As illegal downloading hits an all-time high and consumers' fear of prosecution falls, the music industry must look for more ways to encourage the public to download music legally.'

However, the British Phonographic Industry (BPI), the record industry's trade association, disagreed with the research claiming that both legal and illegal downloads had risen within the past year as a result of a 25 per cent growth in broadband penetration.

A spokesman for the BPI told *Computeractive*:

'Consumers must also understand that by downloading songs free they are denying an artist of money and rights which could cause the industry to collapse.'

Source: *Computeractive*, 31 July 2007

Questions

(25 marks; 25 minutes)

1 Explain whether the above issue is about breaking copyright or trademark law. (4)
2 Outline two possible reasons why 18- to 24-year olds may be the 'worst culprits'. (4)
3 Discuss whether John Enser is right to urge the music industry to cut its prices for officially downloaded music. (8)
4 Evaluate whether young people are likely to listen to the appeal by the BPI spokesman against 'downloading songs free'. (9)

B2 DATA RESPONSE

The transport sensation of the late Victorian period was the bicycle. A practical problem, though, was that 'ladies' wore long dresses, not trousers (or jeans). Therefore a bicycle was difficult to ride, with risks ranging from dirtied dresses to tangled spokes and sudden stops. British inventors set to work on this problem, with more than 50 patents registered with reference to 'ladies' and 'cycling'. An example of these patents includes a lady's rational or divided skirt for cycling, by Oretta Bywater of Glamorgan, in 1903. The main drawing is shown in Figure 4.2.

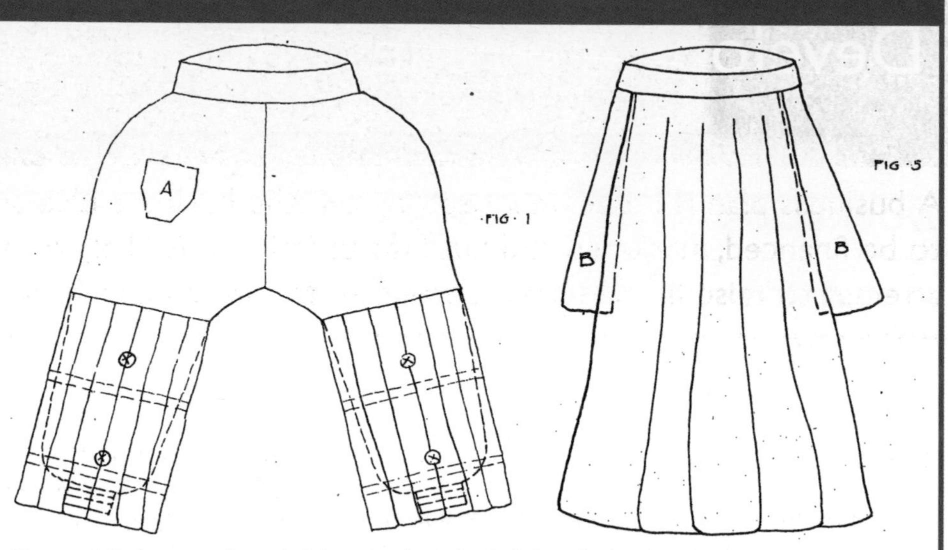

Figure 4.2 A patent for a lady's rational or divided skirt for cycling

The drawing labelled 'Fig. 1' is the harness for bunched up skirts; 'Fig. 5' is the 'overdress' to protect the wearer's modesty. It is not known whether Bywater had a commercial success with the cycling skirt, because although a patent grants monopoly rights for up to 20 years, it does not guarantee that people will buy the product.

Questions

(20 marks; 20 minutes)

1 Explain in your own words the meaning of the word patent. (3)
2 Examine the likely reasons why Oretta Bywater applied for a patent on the technical innovations within the bicycle dress. (7)
3 Discuss whether Oretta was likely to lose out as a result of focusing on the patent application rather than her target market. (10)

UNIT 5

Developing business plans

A business plan is a document setting out the business idea and showing how it is to be financed, marketed and put into practice. It is likely to be a crucial part of an attempt to raise finance from outside sources such as a bank.

5.1 PURPOSE

Starting a business is quite complex, as it requires a lot of different tasks to come together in a coordinated way at the right time. For example, if you are opening your first restaurant, all the following tasks must be completed before your opening night: building work; decoration; kitchen equipment bought and fitted; staff hired and trained; menu chosen and printed; wines chosen, delivered and wine list printed; food supplies bought; tills and credit card-reading equipment in place. For this to work without a clear plan is asking for the impossible. Therefore a business plan seems essential for start-up success. Yet most entrepreneurs treat a business plan as something banks ask for; that is, something for others, not for themselves.

Government figures show that, on average, new business entrepreneurs are white, male, in their mid-30s and have a university degree. As a consequence, many have built up the capital to start up without needing any external finance. Therefore they do not *need* a full business plan. As a result, the same government figures show that most businesses start up without a formal plan.

For a young entrepreneur, this would be virtually impossible. The need to find the capital to start up would make it crucial to have a plan that is persuasive enough to obtain funding. For most, the sole purpose of the plan is to obtain capital. This is a pity, because a good plan can steer the novice businessperson towards her or his goals.

5.2 THE CONTENTS OF A GOOD PLAN

A good plan should be persuasive to an outside investor and useful to the entrepreneur. It should explain what makes the business special and help the entrepreneur to never lose sight of what she or he is trying to achieve. Despite this, it is clear that a business that needs capital will concentrate mainly on the outside investor. This might be a bank or (less likely) a 'Dragon' type of investor who will buy an ownership stake in the business. A bank's main concern is that the start-up will be a safe investment whereas a 'Dragon' is mainly interested in the upside potential, that is, the chance of making a huge profit.

The heart of the business plan should be based around **competitive advantage**; this means identifying the features of your own product or service that will make it succeed against competitors. This may be based on a unique idea, a better product or service or the protection provided by a patent or copyright. On the other hand, a business may decide to strip a product or service down, to make it possible to be the cheapest in the market. Ryanair's competitive advantage is based on being Europe's lowest-cost airline; this allows it to charge the lowest prices, yet still make a profit.

Every business plan should contain the following sections:

1. **Executive summary**: this should be short, but compelling enough to persuade the busy banker to want to read on. It should say who you are, what the customer's 'pain' is and how you will 'relieve' it, why your team is ideal for the task, how much capital you need for the start-up, and how much you are putting in yourself.
2. The product/service: explain it from the customer's point of view; for example, when describing smoothies, do not say 'we'll crush fruit and put it in bottles', but 'it'll provide busy people with two portions of fruit in an enjoyable, unmessy way'. If others already offer the service, you must explain what is different about your idea.
3. The market: focus on market trends rather than market size, such as whether the market is growing and, if so, how rapidly. Also there is a need to provide a brief analysis of key competitors.
4. Marketing plan: how do you plan to communicate to the customers you are targeting? How expensive will this be? Within this section there should be an explanation and justification for the prices you plan to set plus a forecast of likely sales per month for the first two years.

5 Organisational plan: to explain who will be in the team and how they will be managed and organised; CVs should be provided for all key managers.
6 Operational plan: how will the product or service be produced and delivered. This could involve production in China, in which case you will need to have already made contacts with willing suppliers.
7 Financial plan: the heart of this will be a cash flow forecast, that is, a prediction of monthly cash out and cash in from the start of the business until at least two years after the firm has started trading. This will give an idea of the bank balances over the start-up period, and therefore the financing needs.
8 Conclusion: this will include some idea of the longer-term plans for the business, including any 'exit strategy', for example a plan to sell the business within five years.

A-grade application

Estimating financial needs

Tom Doyle worked as a motor auctioneer for ten years before, at the age of 28, he decided to set up his own car dealership. He would specialise in German cars, especially BMWs, Audis and Volkswagen. He knew all the local garages and felt confident that he could get cars serviced, painted and valeted in order to maximise the value added. The business model was simple: buy slightly run-down German cars at the auction, make them look good to potential purchasers and then sell them at a higher price. He thought that he could make £300–£500 net profit per car.

Tom wrote-up his plans with care, using a blank business plan from Natwest Bank. He made his sales forecasts, his cash flow projections and committed himself to putting in half of the £100,000 to start up the business. When he went to see the regional business bank manager, the conversation went well until it came to the financial needs. The bank manager thought Tom had underestimated the finance needed to run the business day by day. Tom was turned down because he had asked for £20,000 too little!

Table 5.1 The business plan: benefits and problems

Benefits	Problems
Forces the entrepreneur to think carefully about every aspect of the start-up, which should increase the chances of success	Making a forecast (e.g. of sales) doesn't make it happen; entrepreneurs sometimes confuse the plan with reality; poor sales can come as a terrible shock
May make the entrepreneur realise that she or he lacks the skills needed for part of the plan, and therefore try harder to employ an expert or buy in advice	Problems arise if the plan is too rigid; it is better to make it flexible, so that you are prepared for what to do if sales are poor (or unexpectedly high)
If the plan is well received by investors, they may compete to offer attractive terms for obtaining capital	Plans based on high sales will include lots of staff to meet the demand; risks are lower if the business starts with a low-cost/low-sales expectation
Many entrepreneurs have the whole plan in their head, not on paper; if illness or accident strikes, others will only be able to keep things going with a paper plan	Business success is often about people, not paper. An over-focus on a perfect plan may mean too little time is spent visiting suppliers or talking to shoppers

5.3 BENEFITS AND PROBLEMS OF BUSINESS PLANS

The benefits and problems associated with business plans are given in Table 5.1.

The key thing to remember is that the business plan is only as good as the information inside. As much of this will have to be estimated or guessed, it is clear that no one should treat a business plan as a factual document. It may help steer the business in the right general direction, but it may be an exaggeration to see it as a 'Sat-nav'.

5.4 SOURCES OF INFORMATION AND GUIDANCE

Government agencies

At the time of writing, Britain's new coalition government has decided to scrap most of the agencies that have supported small businesses. Their view that they were poor value for money was shared by many. The key government agencies for the future are set out below.

1 The Department for Business, Innovation and Skills (BIS, formerly the DTI) runs the Small Firms **Loan Guarantee Scheme**, which encourages high street banks to lend to high-risk small firms. If the firm collapses, the government guarantees to pick up the bill. Any firm using this method of borrowing capital will have to pay an extra 2 per cent interest per year on the loan. Up to 75 per cent of a loan can be borrowed in this way; that is, a high street bank has to be willing to put up 25 per cent.
2 Local Enterprise Partnerships, which are a local version of the previous Regional Development Agencies, such as the North-West RDA. The partnerships between local councils and local businesses will be charged with providing advice and help for new firms starting up. It is too early to be sure how effective this structure will be.

Banks

Banks claim to provide great help to new small businesses, but rarely do. The only thing they are all keen to help with is to provide a business plan toolkit. After all, they want you to open your business banking account with them. Just Google 'bank business plan' and you'll be able to choose from at least six options from the different major banks. New firms need a bank account, so banks are essential; it would be wrong to think, though, that small-scale entrepreneurs spend hours talking things through with their bank advisor or manager.

Accountants

For those with no business knowledge it may be helpful to get cash flow and profit forecasts checked by an accountant. For those who have studied Business Studies, this would be an unnecessary expense. The only aspect of a business start-up that an accountant would be invaluable for is advice on tax issues. Should the business buy a van or lease it? Should the business start as a limited company or as a sole trader? These are technical questions that an accountant will know more about than you ever will.

Small business advisors

Local Enterprise Partnerships should help to put entrepreneurs in touch with a local advisor. Especially for a young person it is invaluable to have a mentor: someone to turn to when the unexpected happens. Consider the following scenario. You have opened a phone shop in the High Street and a Carphone Warehouse opens next door six weeks later? It would be ideal to talk about what to do with a more experienced businessperson. The problem is that good people will not come cheap.

Prince's Trust

The Prince's Trust works with unemployed or disadvantaged people up to the age of 30. It can lend up to £4,000 to a new business start-up, but probably more important is that the Trust insists that you regularly attend sessions with a (free) mentor. Due to the royal connections of the Trust, the mentors are often quite high-powered businesspeople, whose advice is invaluable. To find out more, go to www.princes-trust.org.uk.

ISSUES FOR ANALYSIS

- Even if there is no point in having a business plan, it may still be valuable to have created one. For most, the business plan is likely to gather dust after it has served its purpose of raising finance. That may well be all right because the key thing is preparing the plan.
- Putting the plan together forces the entrepreneur to think about every aspect of the business and perhaps start to see a few potential problem areas. Solutions may be put into place before the business actually starts up. When the business starts, the figures in the plan will probably soon look silly, either too high or far too low.

5.5 DEVELOPING BUSINESS PLANS – AN EVALUATION

In order to start a great new business an entrepreneur needs to have a good idea based on a strong understanding of the customer and the competition. Then the entrepreneur needs to have the personal qualities to build effective relationships with suppliers, retail buyers and staff. If drawing up a business plan helps in that process, that's fine. The worry is that if entrepreneurs bury their heads in paper plans it may divert them from the important tasks associated with starting a new business. A business plan can help to get investment from outsiders and may help a disorganised entrepreneur to make fewer mistakes, but it is no substitute for having strong enterprise skills.

Key Terms

Competitive advantage: features of a product or service that make it stronger in the marketplace than its competitors.
Executive summary: brief highlights of a report, placed at the front, so that top executives can glance at the main points without having to read the whole thing.
Loan Guarantee Scheme: a government scheme that encourages High Street banks to lend to small firms. The government takes on 75% of the risk that the loan will not be repaid.

WORKBOOK

A REVISION QUESTIONS

(30 marks; 30 minutes)

1. Explain in your own words the meaning of the term 'business plan'. (3)
2. Why may young entrepreneurs need a business plan more than middle-aged ones? Briefly explain your answer. (3)
3. Some people think that a business plan aimed at 'Dragon' investors should be different from one aimed at bankers. Outline two ways in which a plan aimed at investors may be different from one aimed at a banker. (4)
4. Why may an entrepreneur find it easier to write a business plan for a second business start-up than for his or her first? (4)
5. Re-read the table of benefits and problems in Section 5.3 and decide whether the following entrepreneurs should

take time to write out a full business plan. Explain your reasons.

a) A 30-year-old, previously a teacher, who needs to borrow a small sum to help finance the launch of a night club. (3)

b) A 50-year-old, previously an accountant, who can personally finance the start-up of a business producing digital radios. (3)

6 How may an accountant help someone to draw up a good business plan? (3)

7 If you were to open your own business after completing your A levels, do you think you would complete a business plan? Explain your answer with reference to your own strengths and weaknesses. (7)

REVISION EXERCISES

B1 DATA RESPONSE

Extract from business plan for opening a Thai restaurant in Swindon

An extract from a business plan, showing Sections 3.3 and 3.4 is given below.

Section 3.3 Cash Flow Forecast for first 12 months

A cash flow forecast for the first 12 months is shown in Figure 5.1.

Section 3.4 Financing Requirement

The business will need £80,000 of start-up capital. The directors are investing £40,000 of their own funds, so we wish to borrow £40,000. As shown in the cash flow table, we will be able to repay the sum in full by the end of the first year of trading.

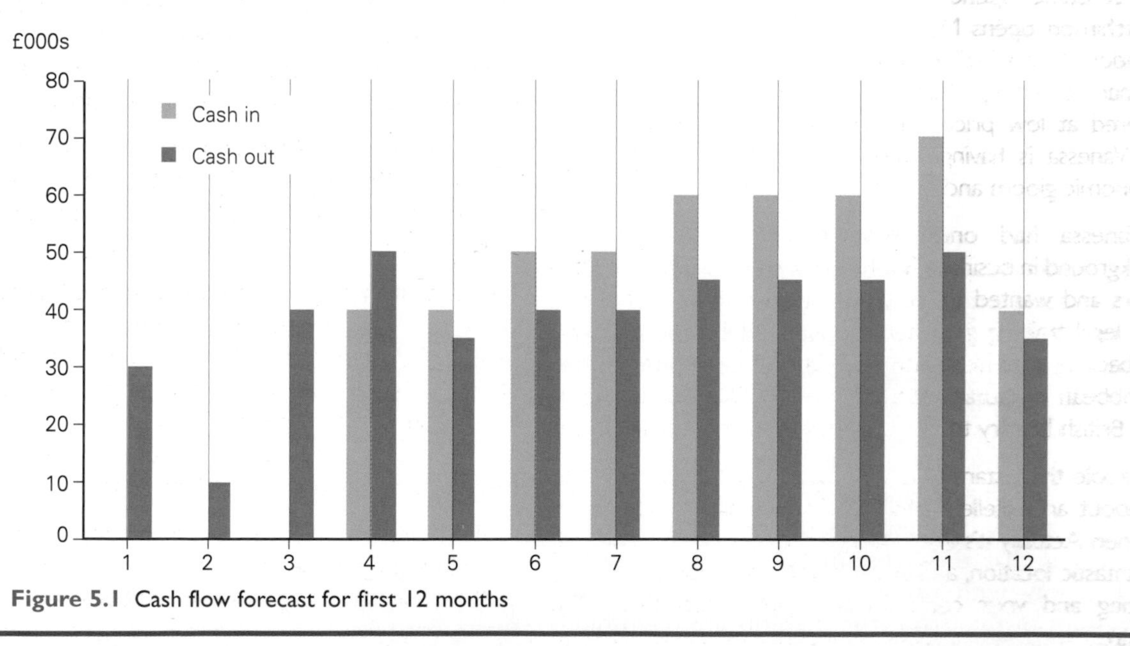

Figure 5.1 Cash flow forecast for first 12 months

Questions

(20 marks; 20 minutes)

1 Look carefully at the graph for the first four months of the life of the business. Are the directors borrowing the right sum of money? Explain your answer. (4)

2 If the cash flow forecast proves correct, are the directors right to say that the £40,000 can be repaid by the end of the first year? Explain your answer. (4)

3 Discuss why a banker might be concerned to read 'As shown in the cash flow table, we will be able to repay the sum in full...'? (7)

4 Explain why the directors may be wise to borrow rather more capital than they believe they will need to finance the first year of the business. (5)

B2 DATA RESPONSE

The launch of Mahoe Café

Figure 5.2

It's August 2008. In the middle of a recession that is about to get much worse (Autumn 2008 was the worst time for consumer spending for more than 50 years). Vanessa Hutchinson opens Mahoe bar/café in Bow Lane, Central London. Mahoe offers Caribbean food in a casual but upmarket setting. Usually in London, Caribbean food is offered at low prices in cafés that are very very basic. So Vanessa is having to break through two constraints: economic gloom and possible price resistance.

Vanessa had one other important weakness: no background in business. She had worked as a lawyer for ten years and wanted to do something different. Fortunately, her legal training gave her a focus on facts and evidence to back up her ideas. So when she was thinking about a Caribbean restaurant, she went to the business centre at the British Library to do some crucial secondary research.

People think starting a business in the restaurant sector is about an excellent chef or a lot of experience in the kitchen. Actually it's about researching your market, finding a fantastic location, and making sure you understand your pricing and your competitors.' Vanessa also found the centre's business plan clinics invaluable: 'If you need to raise finance as I did, then you'll want to have a really sensible business plan that allows people to understand what you're proposing. The centre pointed me in the right direction.'

Later, Vanessa added: 'The right location has also been a key driver of success. A good location is vital in the restaurant trade, so I spent hours combing the streets of London. Bow Lane was ideal because it was in the hub of the City and while there was lots of competition, they were mainly sandwich bars and formal restaurants. I felt Mahoe, with its exotic food and vibrant colours would be a big hit.'

Vanessa signed up for a lease on the Bow Lane property in March 2008, which was on the market for £150,000. She also had to sign up to an annual rent of £50,000. Between March and August she had to plough further capital into turning the premises into a sleek, upmarket bar.

With the economy in such a weak position, Mahoe started up with a cleverly pitched menu. It included low-cost, casual items such as wraps and sandwiches. At around £5, this was a low pricing point in central London.

Trade built up quickly, but Vanessa is very realistic about how hard it can be to make a business successful: 'Cash flow can be a problem. Setting up a restaurant is expensive and you need a substantial amount of money to get the venture off the ground. If you are booked to host a party, then all alcohol and food must be paid for ahead of the event and sometimes people can take their time settling their bills.'

She continued: 'Restaurants are costly to run, business rates have gone up in recent months and bills often come in faster than invoices get paid.' (Source: the *Financial Mail* www.fmwf.com)

Despite launching with a value-for-money menu, Vanessa was always clear on her target market. With menu options such as Krug champagne at £130 a bottle and sirloin steak at £15.95, business customers could easily see Mahoe as an unusual but still posh option. Although reggae music will be playing and rum punches are on offer, the interior of the restaurant is London posh, not Jamaican.

Now, with the restaurant fully established, the Mahoe website highlights the team effort involved in the success of the business. A section on 'Our people' pays tribute to the unsung heroes such as kitchen manager Urmilla. In her understanding of how to succeed in business, Vanessa takes some beating. No wonder she has won a string of business awards, including 'Best Business of the Year 2009'.

Source: Topical Cases, A-Z Business Training March 2010.

Questions

(30 marks; 35 minutes)

1 Outline three characteristics of a successful entrepreneur shown by Vanessa. (6)
2 Discuss the difficulties Vanessa would have had in estimating the revenues, costs and therefore profit for Mahoe's first year. (12)
3 Research by Warwick University's Business School has shown that black entrepreneurs in Britain are four times more likely to be refused a bank loan than white entrepreneurs. Discuss the reasons why Vanessa was able to beat that statistic. (12)

Choosing the right legal structure

UNIT 6

The legal structure of a business is crucial in determining how serious the financial impact will be for the owners if things go wrong. It also has an impact on the taxation levels to be paid by the business and its owners.

6.1 BUSINESSES WITH UNLIMITED LIABILITY

Unlimited liability means that the finances of the business are treated as inseparable from the finances of the business owner(s). So if the business loses £1 million, the people owed money (the creditors) can get the courts to force the individual owners to pay up. If that means selling their houses, cars, and so on, so be it. If the owner(s) cannot pay, they can be made personally bankrupt. Two types of business organisation have unlimited liability: sole traders and partnerships.

Sole traders

A **sole trader** is an individual who owns and operates his or her own business. Although there may be one or two employees, this person makes the final decisions about the running of the business. A sole trader is the only one who benefits financially from success, but must face the burden of any failure. In the eyes of the law the individual and the business are the same. This means that the owner has **unlimited liability** for any debts that result from running the firm. If a sole trader cannot pay his or her bills, the courts can allow personal assets to be seized by **creditors** in order to meet outstanding debts. For example, the family home or car may be sold. If insufficient funds can be raised in this way the person will be declared **bankrupt**.

Despite the financial dangers involved, the sole trader is the most common form of legal structure adopted by UK businesses. In some areas of the economy this kind of business dominates, particularly where little finance is required to set up and run the business and customers demand a personal service. Examples include trades such as builders and plumbers, and many independent shopkeepers.

There are no formal rules to follow when establishing a sole trader, or administrative costs to pay. Complete confidentiality can be maintained because accounts are not published. As a result many business start-ups adopt this structure.

The main disadvantages facing a sole trader are the limited sources of finance available, long hours of work involved (including the difficulty of taking a holiday) and concern with respect to running the business during periods of ill health.

Partnerships

Partnerships exist when two or more people start a business without forming a company. Like a sole trader, the individuals have unlimited liability for any debts run up by the business. Because people are working together but are unlimitedly liable for any debts, it is vital that the partners trust each other. As a result this legal structure is often found in the professions, such as medicine and law. If the partners fail to draw up a formal document, the 1890 Partnership Act sets out a series of rules which govern issues such as the distribution of profits.

The main difference between a sole trader and a partnership is the number of owners. The key advantages and disadvantages of forming a partnership are set out below.

Advantages gained from forming a partnership

The advantages of forming a partnership include:

- *Additional skills*: a new partner may have abilities which the sole trader does not possess. These can help to strengthen the business, perhaps allowing new products or services to be offered, or improving the quality of existing provision.
- *More capital*: a number of people together can inject more finance into the business than one person alone. This, plus the extra skills, makes expansion easier.
- *Shared strain*: the new partner will help to share the worry of running the business, as well as taking on a share of the workload. This should help to reduce stress and allow holidays to be taken.

Disadvantages of forming a partnership

The disadvantages of forming a partnership include:

- *Sharing profit*: the financial benefits derived from

running the business will have to be divided up between the partners according to the partnership agreement made on formation. This can easily lead to disagreements about 'fair' distribution of workload and profits.

- *Loss of control*: multiple ownership means that no individual can force an action on the business; decision making must be shared.
- *Unlimited liability*: it is one thing to be unlimitedly liable for your own mistakes (a sole trader); far more worrying, surely, to have unlimited liability for the mistakes of your partners. This problem hit many investors in the Lloyds insurance market in the 1990s. Certain partnerships (called syndicates) lost millions of pounds from huge insurance claims. Some investors lost their life savings.

6.2 BUSINESSES WITH LIMITED LIABILITY

Limited liability means that the legal duty to pay debts run up by a business stays with the business itself, not its owner/shareholders. If a company has £1 million of debts that it lacks the cash to repay, the courts can force the business to sell all its assets (cars, computers, etc). If there is still not enough money, the company is closed down, but the owner/shareholders have no personal liability for the remaining debts.

To gain the benefits of limited liability, the business must go through a legal process to become a company. The process of **incorporation** creates a separate legal identity for the organisation. In the eyes of the law the owners of the business and the company itself are now two different things. The business can take legal action against others and have legal action taken against it. Each owner is protected by limited liability and their investment in the business is represented by the size of their shareholding. Limited liability sounds unfairly weighted towards the shareholders, but it encourages individuals to put forward capital because the financial risk is limited to the amount they invest.

In order to gain separate legal status a company must be registered with the **Registrar of Companies**. The following two key documents must be completed.

1. The **Memorandum of Association** governs the relationship between the company and the outside world. This includes the company name, the object of the company (often recorded simply as 'as the owners see fit'), limitation of liability and the size of the authorised share capital.
2. The **Articles of Association** outline the internal management of the company. This includes the rights of shareholders, the role of directors and frequency of shareholder meetings.

The key advantages and disadvantages which result from forming a limited company are set out below.

Advantages of forming a limited company

The advantages of forming a limited company are:

- Shareholders experience the benefits of limited liability, including the confidence to expand.
- A limited company is able to gain access to a wider range of borrowing opportunities than a sole trader or partnership. This makes funding the growth of the business potentially easier.

Disadvantages of forming a limited company

The disadvantages of forming a limited company are:

- Limited companies must make financial information available publicly at Companies House. Small firms are not required to make full disclosure of their company accounts, but they have to reveal more than would be the case for a sole trader or partnership.
- Limited companies have to follow more, and more expensive, rules than unlimited liability businesses, for example audited accounts and holding an annual general meeting of shareholders; these things add several thousands of pounds to annual overhead costs.

A-grade application

One Water

In 2003, Duncan Goose quit his job and founded One Water. He wanted to finance water projects in Africa from profits made selling bottled water in Britain. The particular water project was 'Playpumps': children's roundabouts plumbed into freshly dug water wells. As the children play, each rotation of the roundabout brings up a litre of fresh, clean water.

Duncan thought of forming a charity, but felt that the regulations governing charities might force them to be inefficient. So, for the sum of £125 he founded a limited company, Global Ethics Ltd. This enabled him to set the rules, for instance that the shareholders receive no dividends and the directors receive no fees. But, of course, it ensured that he and other volunteers who put time into One Water are protected, should something go wrong and big debts build up. Today One Water is a major business trading internationally. It has funded more than 600 Playpumps, giving clean water to 1 million people, permanently.

6.3 PRIVATE LIMITED COMPANIES

A small business can be started up as a sole trader, a partnership or as a private limited company. For a private limited company, the start-up capital will often be £100, which can be wholly owned by the entrepreneur, or other people can be brought in as investors. The shares of a private limited company cannot be bought and sold without the agreement of the other directors. This means the company cannot be listed on the stock market. As a result it is possible to maintain

Table 6.1 Factors influencing choice between starting a new business as a sole trader or private limited company

Sole trader	Private limited company
When the entrepreneur has no intention of expanding (e.g. just wants to run own restaurant in Warwick)	When the entrepreneur has ambitions to expand quickly, therefore needs it to be easier to raise extra finance
When there is no need for substantial bank borrowing (i.e. start-up costs are low)	When large borrowings mean significant chances of large losses if things go wrong
When the business will be small enough to mean that one person can make all the big decisions	When the business may require others to make decisions (e.g. when the entrepreneur is on holiday or unwell)

close control over the way the business is run. This form of business is often run by a family or small group of friends. It may be very profit focused or, like Global Ethics Ltd., have wholly different objectives than maximising profit.

A legal requirement for private companies is that they must state 'Ltd' after the company name. This warns those dealing with the business that the firm is relatively small and has limited liability. Remember, limited liability protects shareholders from business debts, so there is a risk that 'cowboy' businesspeople might start a company, run it into the ground and then walk away from its debts. Therefore the cheques of a limited company are not as secure as ones from an unlimited liability business. This is why many petrol stations have notices saying 'No company cheques allowed'.

Some of the factors that may determine when a business should start up as a sole trader and when as a private limited company are outlined in Table 6.1.

6.4 PUBLIC LIMITED COMPANIES

When a private limited company expands to the point of having share capital of more than £50,000, it can convert to a public limited company. Then it can be floated on the stock market, which allows any member of the general public to buy shares. This increases the company's access to share capital, which enables it to expand considerably. The term 'plc' will appear after the company name, for example Marks and Spencer plc or Tesco plc.

The principal differences between private and public limited companies are:

- A public company can raise capital from the general public, while a private limited company is prohibited from doing so.
- The minimum capital requirement of a public company is £50,000. There is no minimum for a private limited company.
- Public companies must publish far more detailed accounts than private limited companies.

Almost every large business is a plc. Yet the process of converting from a private to a public company can be difficult. Usually, successful small firms grow steadily, perhaps at a rate of 10 or 15 per cent a year. Even that pace of growth causes problems, but good managers can cope. The problem of floating onto the stock market is that it provided a sudden, huge injection of cash. This sounds great, but it forces the firm to try to grow more quickly (otherwise the new shareholders will say: what are you doing with our cash?). See the A-grade application on Sports Direct.

A-grade application

Sports Direct

On 28 February 2007 Mike Ashley made over £900 million when he floated Sports Direct onto the London stock market. Ashley had owned 100 per cent of Sports Direct, and sold 43 per cent of his shares at 300p a share. Within a few months City analysts were troubled by the way Ashley was spending his money. He bought 3 per cent of the shares in Adidas and then made a takeover bid for Newcastle United. He also seemed desperate to spend Sports Direct's money, as it went on a shopping spree making purchases that included Blacks Leisure, Field & Trek and the Everlast boxing equipment company. With so much activity, it seemed that no one was paying enough attention to the company's trading position. Revenues and profits dropped back and within six months of the float the shares had halved in value. By July 2010, three-and-a-half years after floating, the shares were 110p, giving shareholders a 63 per cent loss. By coincidence, Ocado was being floated onto the stock market at the same time. Having never made a profit, this business was being valued at £800 million. Some analysts noted that this 'might be another Sports Direct'.

Other problems associated with public limited companies

Profit becomes the only objective

When a firm becomes a plc, it becomes hard to hold on to any objective other than profit. This is because City analysts and business journalists criticise heavily any business that is not making more money this year than last. This pressure may have been the underlying problem that led BP to underspend on safety measures in America, leading to disaster in Texas in 2005 and in the Gulf of Mexico in 2010.

Maintaining control of an organisation is limited

The extent to which any one individual, or group, can maintain control of an organisation is severely limited by the sale of its shares on the stock exchange. For example, a family may find their influence on a business diminished when a listing is obtained. In turn, this means that publicly quoted companies are always vulnerable to a takeover bid. In 2009 the one-time family business Cadbury was swallowed up by a multi-billion pound takeover bid from the US giant 'Kraft'.

Figure 6.1 Cadbury: protests against the Kraft take-over

Divorce of ownership and control

Shareholders are the owners of public limited companies, but they do not make decisions on a day-to-day basis. Many have little detailed knowledge of the firm's operations. Nor can they know the directors who, theoretically, they vote onto and off the Board. In fact it is usually the chairman and chief executive who 'run the show'. They have control, though the shareholders supposedly have the power. This situation is known as the divorce of ownership and control, and it may lead the directors to pursue the interests of their own careers and bank balances rather than the best interests of the business and its staff.

Short-termism

A separate problem that may be caused by the divorce of ownership and control is short-termism. In private companies, where shareholders and directors are usually family members, the desire is to build a successful business to hand over to the next generation. This is how the great retail firms such as Sainsbury's and Marks and Spencer were built. In plcs the lack of concern about the long-term future of the shareholders may lead directors to focus too much on the short term. Much research has shown that British managements are more likely than others to focus upon short-term issues, possibly to the neglect of long-term investment in Research and Development (R&D) or staff training.

6.5 OTHER FORMS OF BUSINESS ORGANISATION

Cooperatives

These can be worker-owned, such as John Lewis/Waitrose, or customer owned, such as the retail Co-op. Cooperatives have the potential to offer a more united cause for the workforce than the profit of shareholders. Workers at John Lewis can enjoy annual bonuses of 20 per cent of their salary, as their share of the company's profits. The Co-op has been less successful, though its focus on ethical trading has made it more relevant to today's shoppers.

Not-for-profit organisations

Mutual businesses

Mutual businesses, including many building societies and mutual life assurance businesses, have no shareholders and no owners. They exist solely for the best interests of members: its customers. In the 1980s and 1990s traditional mutual societies such as Abbey National and the Halifax were turned into private companies. Not one of these businesses survived the 2007–09 Credit Crunch without being bailed out or taken over. Nationwide now says it is 'proud to be different', as it is still a true building society in that it has no shareholders pressuring for profits.

ISSUES FOR ANALYSIS

When analysing which type of organisation is the most suitable for a business, consider the factors outlined below.

- The financial risks involved. Manufacturing businesses require heavy investment in plant and equipment before anything is available for sale. Therefore a great deal of capital is put at risk. This suggests limited liability is essential. Some service businesses such as tax advisors or dry cleaners require relatively little capital outlay. If the owner intends to finance the start-up without any borrowings, there is no need to seek limited liability.
- The image you wish to portray. Although cautious businesses may refuse company cheques, most people think *M. Staton Ltd.* sounds more established and professional than *Mervin Staton*. In the same vein, a small software production company called T.I.B. Ltd. changed its name to T.I.B. plc. They rightly thought it sounds bigger and more impressive. What's in a name? Ask Coca-Cola.
- An organisation considering a move to public company status and a stock market listing has far bigger issues to consider. It must weigh the benefits to be gained, particularly in terms of raising additional finance, against the costs incurred and the loss of control. Many business questions can be analysed fruitfully by considering the short versus the long term. Private (family) versus public (stock market investor) ownership is a classic case in point.

Charities

Many important organisations have charitable status. These include pressure groups such as Greenpeace and Friends of the Earth. They also include conventional charities such as Oxfam and Save The Children Fund. Charitable status ensures that those who fund the charity are not liable for any debts. It also provides significant tax benefits.

6.6 CHOOSING THE RIGHT LEGAL STRUCTURE – AN EVALUATION

Business organisation is a dry, technical subject. It does contain some important business themes, however, three of which are particularly valuable sources of evaluative comment.

1. The existence of limited liability has had huge effects on business. Some have been unarguably beneficial. How could firms become really big if the owners felt threatened by equally big debts? Limited liability helps firms to take reasonable business risks. It also, however, gives scope for dubious business practices. For example, it is possible to start a firm, live a great lifestyle, then go into liquidation leaving the customers/creditors out of pocket, and then start again. All too often this is the story told by programmes such as the BBC's *Watchdog*. Companies Acts try to make this harder to do, but it still happens. Such unethical behaviour is why government intervention to protect the consumer can always be justified.
2. Bill Gates and Richard Branson are worth billions of dollars. How can such wealth be justified for people who do not save lives (doctors) or help build them (teachers)? The answer lies in the risks involved in business. For every Richard Branson there are hundreds of thousands of small entrepreneurs who sunk their life savings into a business and saw the savings sink. Sadly, there are thousands every year who end up personally bankrupt. In other words, in a business world in which risk is ever-present, rewards for success should be accepted.
3. Short-termism is a curse for effective business decision making. There is no proof that a stock exchange listing leads to short-termism, only the suspicion that in many cases it does. Of course, massive companies such as Unilever, Nestle and Shell are likely to be above the pressures for short-term performance. In many other cases, though, it seems that British company directors focus too much on the short-term share price. Could this be because their huge bonuses depend on how high the share price is? Worries about shareholder pressures or takeover bids may distract managers from building a long-term business in the way that companies such as BMW and Toyota have done.

Key Terms

Bankrupt: when an individual is unable to meet personal liabilities, some or all of which can be as a consequence of business activities.

Creditors: those owed money by a business, for example suppliers and bankers.

Incorporation: establishing a business as a separate legal entity from its owners, and therefore giving the owners limited liability.

Limited liability: owners are not liable for the debts of the business; they can lose no more than the sum they invested.

Registrar of Companies: the government department which can allow firms to become incorporated. It is located at Companies House, where Articles of Association, Memorandums of Association and the annual accounts of limited companies are available for public scrutiny.

Sole trader: a one-person business with unlimited liability.

Unlimited liability: owners are liable for any debts incurred by the business, even if it requires them to sell all their assets and possessions and become personally bankrupt.

WORKBOOK

A REVISION QUESTIONS

(25 marks; 25 minutes)

1. Explain two differences between a sole trader and a partnership. (4)
2. In your own words, try to explain the importance of establishing a separate legal entity to separate the business from the individual owner. (4)
3. You can start a business today. All you have to do is tell HM Revenue & Customs (the taxman). Outline two risks of starting in this way. (4)
4. Briefly discuss whether each of the following businesses should start as a sole trader, a partnership or a private limited company.
   a) A clothes shop started by Claire Wells with £40,000 of her own money plus £10,000 from the bank. It is located close to her home in Wrexham. (3)
   b) A builders started by Jim Barton and Lee Clark, who plan to become the number one for loft extensions in Sheffield. They have each invested £15,000 and are borrowing £30,000 from the bank. (3)
5. Explain the possible risks to a growing business of making the jump from a private limited company to 'going public', then floating its shares on the stock market. (5)
6. In what way may the type of business organisation affect the image of the business. (2)

REVISION EXERCISES

B1 DATA RESPONSE

(20 marks; 20 minutes)

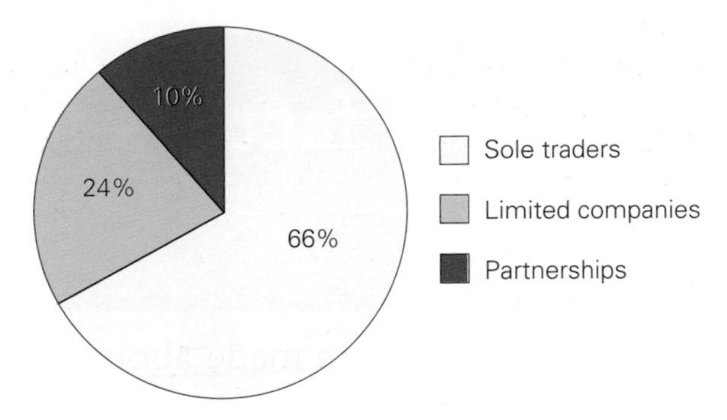

Figure 6.2 UK business organisations
Source: S Fraser, *Finance for Small and Medium Sized Enterprises: The United Kingdom Survey of SME Finances* (Warwick Business School, 2005)

1 **a)** Calculate the number of sole traders in the UK; then calculate the number of limited companies. (3)
   b) Explain two possible reasons why there are so many more sole traders than companies. (6)
2 What proportion of British businesses operate with unlimited liability? (1)
3 Dr Fraser's research also shows that 1 in 5 businesses is principally owned by a woman and 93 per cent are owned by white and 7 per cent by non-white ethnicity.
   a) Examine two possible reasons why women are so much less likely to own a business than men. (6)
   b) The percentage figures for non-white business ownership are slightly below the number of non-whites in the population (between 8 per cent and 9 per cent). Outline two reasons that may explain this. (4)

B2 DATA RESPONSE

Starting a new business

Forming a limited company can be time-consuming. According to the World Economic Forum, the number of actions required to get started varies from 1 in New Zealand to 13 in India. As a result of the different processes, the number of days it takes to start up varies from 1 day in New Zealand (the world's quickest) to 141 days in Venezuela (the world's slowest).

Figure 6.3 provides data selected from the World Economic Forum's 2010–11 'Global Competitiveness Report'.

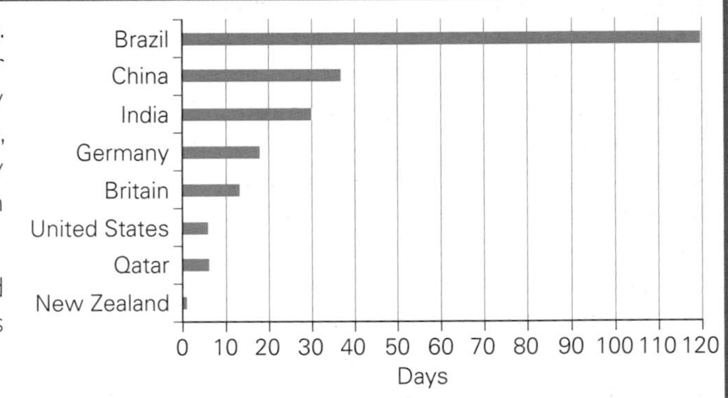

Figure 6.3 Time required to start a business

Questions

(20 marks; 20 minutes)

1 Explain the implications for starting a business in Brazil upon the following two factors in business start-up:
   a) Cash flow, that is, the daily flows of cash into and out of the business. (4)
   b) Hiring and training new staff. (4)
2 A sole trader can start a business straight away, whereas forming a limited company takes the time shown in Figure 6.3. To what extent should an entrepreneur be influenced by this data in deciding whether to form a company or act as a sole trader? (12)

31

Technology and choice of location

The role of technology has had a major influence on a firm's choice of location. Technology and the ease of communication that this facilitates has enabled some firms to become more 'footloose'. This means that they are not tied to any location and can operate anywhere without considering any of the influences previously discussed. However, the ability to be footloose will always be determined by the nature of the business.

ISSUES FOR ANALYSIS

You demonstrate the skill of analysis every time you use theory or business logic to develop a solution to a business problem. Good analysis acknowledges that short-term solutions may have long-term implications. For example, if a firm chooses a location because it attracts government finance this may be a good decision in the short term, but it may not be the best location in the long term if the firm needs to expand its premises or access a wider geographical market.

7.5 LOCATION FACTORS FOR A BUSINESS START-UP – AN EVALUATION

You demonstrate the skill of evaluation when you make judgements based on assessing and weighing up different evidence. Good evaluation is also demonstrated when you assess the quality, reliability and relevance of the evidence. For example, it is important to remember that new start-ups do not have access to the same financial resources as well-established firms and they are also more likely to focus on a smaller and more local market. Therefore, influences such as national transport links may not be as important in their choice of location as the cost of rent. It is therefore critical that you demonstrate your evaluation skills in relation to location by recognising that the factors that sway new entrepreneurs in the real world are not always the factors that influence well-established firms. Many new businesses start out in spare rooms, garages and garden sheds until success enables them to expand their operations and locate in other places. Furthermore, it is also important to distinguish between theory and practice. For example, in theory we assume that all service businesses want to locate near to their market whereas, in practice, proximity to the market may be important, but it may not be vital. This is because an increasing number of firms' contact with the marketplace is made via telephones and the internet using call centres.

Key Terms

Bulk reducing/bulk increasing: a firm that uses large bulky materials to produce smaller end products/a firm that uses small materials to produce larger end products.

Footloose: a firm that is not tied to a particular location as it relies on technology and communication links.

Infrastructure: the network of utilities such as transport links, telecommunications systems, health and education services.

Just-in-time: a manufacturing system that aims to minimise costs of holding stocks of raw materials, components and work in progress by producing goods in response to a definite order. It requires efficient ordering and delivery systems.

Labour intensive/capital intensive: a process in which labour costs represent a high proportion of the total costs. Small firms and firms in the service sectors are likely to be labour intensive. By contrast, a capital intensive process relies more on machinery in the production of its products.

Least-cost location: a business location that allows a firm to minimise its costs.

WORKBOOK

A REVISION QUESTIONS

(30 marks 30 minutes)

1 Explain what is meant by the 'quantitative' factors that may influence a firm's choice of location. (3)
2 Describe one factor that would be important to a manufacturing firm but not a retail firm when choosing a location. (2)
3 Explain why a firm relying on mail order may not locate in a high rent area. (2)
4 How could the use of just-in-time production influence the location of a business? (3)
5 State two factors that would influence the location of a firm that employs a labour intensive process. (2)
6 How may selecting the least-cost location improve a firm's competitive ability? (4)
7 Explain two reasons why a firm may decide to choose a location near to its supplier. (4)
8 Identify two qualitative factors that may influence a firm's choice of location. (2)
9 Explain how a cheap location for a new service industry may represent a 'false economy'. (4)
10 What is meant by the term footloose? Identify two factors that may prevent a business from being footloose. (4)

REVISION EXERCISES
B1 ACTIVITY

Choosing the right location for a pizza takeaway.

Leona and Seun want to open a Domino's pizza franchise outlet in a medium-sized town in Bedfordshire. It will offer pizza to takeaway or for delivery. After some weeks of research, they have narrowed their choice down to two locations, details of which are shown in Table 7.2. Which should they go for?

Table 7.2 Potential locations for a pizza franchise outlet

	Martin Way	Dame Alice Street
Road details	Busy main road from town to M1; near big housing estate	Busy high street near station; next to Primark
Accommodation	3 bed flat above premises in good order; access from back of shop; rental value up to £100 per week	2 flats, each with 2 beds; separate access from street; rental value £200 per week each
Leasehold details	Lease 15 years; price £55,000	Lease 12 years: price £220,000
Rent per year	£12,500 per year	£68,000 per annum
Parking	Plenty at the back of premises	NCP car park, 200 metres away

1 Discuss the pros and cons of each location, bearing in mind the type of business.
2 Write a three-slide presentation on:
   1 Strengths of Martin Way location
   2 Strengths of Dame Alice Street location
   3 Which you recommend and why.

B2 DATA RESPONSE

(20 marks; 20 minutes)

John Michaels set up a business producing wind-up radios 14 months ago. He produces the radios in his garage and sells them via a national mail order company specialising in organic, 'green' products. Since starting up his business, the sales of his radios have increased by 18 per cent. He is now considering renting a small industrial unit which would enable him to increase the number of radios he could produce.

Questions

1 What factors should John take into account before moving his production into the industrial unit? (6)
2 Explain how John's profits could be affected by his decision to move to the industrial unit. (4)
3 What are the benefits of selling the radios via a mail order company? (5)
4 What qualitative factors may be behind John's decision to relocate production from the garage to the industrial unit? (5)

B3 CASE STUDY

Metro's banking revolution

Metro Bank – the first brand new bank on the British high street for more than 100 years – opened on 29 July 2010. US-owned Metro Bank planned a new customer-focused experience, with longer opening hours and seven-days-a-week counter service. The first branch opened in Holborn. The location was brilliant, at an extremely busy junction at the entrance of Holborn tube station. It not only has a vast number of commuters and tourists passing by; there are also lots of people who live nearby.

Most new banks would tend to locate in the City of London, to establish their good name. The decision to go to Holborn shows the owner's focus on the customer, for example making it easy for busy commuters to go to their bank in the early evening.

It seems that Metro is targeting small businesses, which often have to pay fees for everyday banking facilities such as depositing coins. 'The location is interesting as there are lots of small businesses in the locality and the opening hours – till 8.00 p.m. – and the ability to deposit coins in large quantities easily and without charge will really appeal to these customers,' said David Black, a banking analyst.

The tradition in service businesses has been to say that location is critical. In these days of online banking, has Metro made a mistake in setting itself up in a very expensive central London location?

Source: adapted from *The Independent*, 25 July 2010

Questions

25 marks; 30 minutes

1 Examine one strength and one weakness of Metro Bank's start-up location. (8)
2 Explain why location may be especially critical for a business start-up in the service sector. (5)
3 Discuss whether location still matters in a sector such as banking, where online is taking a rising market share. (12)

UNIT 8

Employing people

An employee is someone who works for an organisation under a contract of employment in return for a salary or wage.

8.1 INTRODUCTION: TAKING ON NEW STAFF

Many entrepreneurs are obliged to carry out a number of different tasks and roles when they start out in business. Not only are they responsible for decision making and creative input, but they are also required to carry out all the day-to-day activities needed to keep the business going. However, as the business expands, this approach may act as an obstacle to further growth. Most entrepreneurs will have an area of expertise that led them into business in the first place, but it is highly unlikely that they will have all of the skills needed to run a business successfully. In addition, working around the clock may be necessary initially but, in the long term, can lead to stress and poor decision making. Eventually, any ambitious entrepreneur will have to employ new staff.

8.2 FACTORS TO CONSIDER

Recruitment can be an expensive process, and has to be considered in relation to the wider objectives of the firm. Therefore, before spending time and money hiring staff, there are a number of factors to think about.

The business should start by identifying the skills, qualities and experience that are needed to continue to operate successfully. This requires a clear understanding of the exact nature of the firm's product and the market in which it operates. A detailed analysis of the market-place usually forms a major part of a firm's business plan (see Unit 4).

The next step would be to pinpoint current skill strengths and weaknesses so that gaps in expertise can be filled. For example, trying to get the books to balance without the financial skills required to do so can use up a great deal of time. This could be spent more profitably promoting products, dealing with customers and managing suppliers.

Another factor to consider is the length of time that workers are likely to be needed. For instance, additional staff may be taken on in order to respond to an increasing workload. Is this increase likely to be temporary or permanent? How many extra hours of work will be needed each week?

Once a business has developed a clear understanding of its workforce needs, it will be in a position to choose from a number of employment options.

8.3 EMPLOYMENT OPTIONS

The firm may wish to consider a number of possible options before deciding on the best way of taking on additional workers (see Figure 8.1). This should help to ensure that the extra help can be acquired without creating unaffordable labour costs.

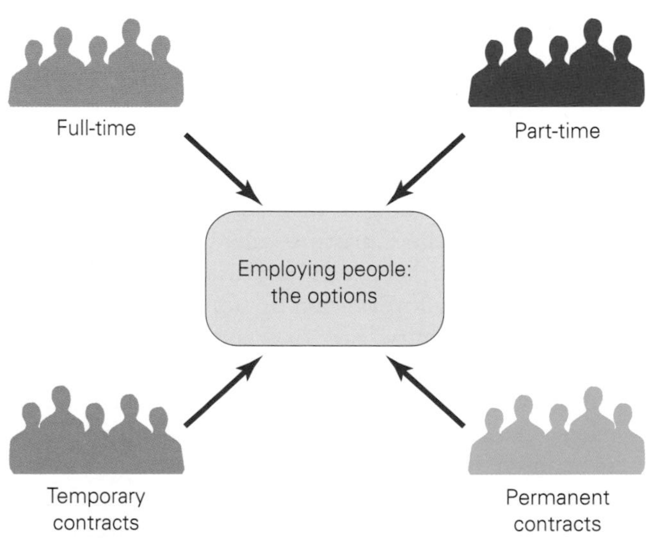

Figure 8.1 Employment options

Part-time versus full-time employees

Employer surveys generally classify jobs as being part-time if the contracted period of work is equal to or less than 30 hours per week. Approximately 7.63 million, or just over 25 per cent, of employees were employed on a part-time basis within the UK in 2010. Employing part-time rather than full-time employees can offer a business a number of benefits.

- It can be a more efficient way of meeting labour requirements, especially for small businesses, by keeping costs down when there is no need for full-time cover.
- Employing part-timers can also help to increase the degree of workforce flexibility, allowing firms to cater for predicable fluctuations in demand..
- Offering part-time contracts to staff may also help to improve the quality and productivity of the workforce. It may attract more applicants for job vacancies, including women with small children. The option of working part-time may also lead to a more motivated workforce, reduced absenteeism and labour turnover.

However, relying too heavily on part-time employees may mean additional induction, training and administration costs for a firm. It may also lead to a deterioration in communication, if staff see very little of each other, making it difficult to coordinate activities.

Temporary versus permanent employees

A temporary employee is employed for a limited period of time by a business. Such workers are often hired on fixed-term contracts (i.e. a contract of employment based on a definite period of time, such as three months). Employment is terminated once the contract expires and no notice is required from the employer, although the contract can be ended sooner if either side does give notice. The advantages of employing staff on a temporary basis include the following.

- A more flexible workforce can be created to cope with changes in demand over certain periods of time. For example, a retailer may choose to recruit sales assistants on a temporary basis to help deal with increased demand and maintain customer service standards over the Christmas sales period.
- Temporary workers can be used to cover for permanent employees such as, for instance, during maternity/paternity leave or secondment to another area of the business.
- Employing workers on fixed-term contracts allows even small businesses to gain access to highly specialised skills, such as IT or marketing, without having to bear the costs of having to permanently hire what are likely to be expensive employees.

The level of commitment of temporary employees to the business is, however, likely to be much lower than that of workers on permanent contracts. Lack of job security may mean that workers move to permanent jobs elsewhere as and when such positions arise, resulting in increased labour turnover. This, in turn, could lead to higher recruitment costs and lower productivity while new workers familiarise themselves with their duties.

8.4 USING EMPLOYMENT AGENCY STAFF

One possibility for businesses looking to hire staff on a temporary basis is to use an employment agency. Although the workers supplied carry out duties within the business, they are paid by the agency. This means that the business has a contract with the agency, rather than individual workers, and pays a fee for its services.

Agency staff are often used to cover for short-term holiday or sickness absence, or in situations where there is a high labour turnover, such as in the hotel and catering industries. The main advantage to a business of using agency workers is that the agency is the employer; this makes the agency responsible for the recruitment and administration functions involved in employing staff. This is very useful if the job is something like a security guard or an office cleaner. Topshop wants to be good at selling attractive, fashionable clothes; it does not want its store managers worrying about recruiting new cleaners.

8.5 EXTERNAL ADVISERS, CONSULTANTS AND CONTRACTORS

A business in need of expert skills over a specific period of time may decide to use a business adviser, consultant or contractor. These individuals or organisations provide agreed services, such as accountancy or human resources functions, for a set time and fee.

Advisers, consultants and contractors can provide a cost-effective means of completing one-off projects or accessing skills and expertise to improve the performance of the business. They avoid the need for the potentially costly recruitment and training of permanent workers who may be under-utilised, especially in small firms. However, consultants and advisers can be very expensive, and their frequent or lengthy use may actually end up costing the business more than taking on permanent employees. These 'outsiders' may also fail to understand the special character of an individual business, and may lack commitment to its long-term success.

8.6 LEGAL RESPONSIBILITIES

Regardless of whether workers are employed on a full- or part-time, temporary or permanent basis, firms must be aware of the responsibilities involved in taking on additional staff. Employers have a number of obligations, including the need to provide a safe and secure environment, to treat workers fairly and avoid discrimination. All workers must be given a written statement of the terms and conditions of their contract of employment, and have a number of legal entitlements, including:

- the right to receive the National Minimum Wage
- minimum levels of rest breaks
- paid holidays and statutory sick pay.

Employers are required to register with HM Revenue & Customs (HMRC) and establish a payroll in order to deduct income tax and National Insurance contributions from employees' pay.

Part-time and fixed-term employees have the same employment rights as their full-time colleagues. This means that, by law, employers must treat staff in the same way, regardless of the basis for their employment. Therefore part-time staff should receive, pro rata, the same terms and conditions, including rates of pay, holidays and access to training, promotion and redundancy. Failure to treat staff fairly could result in an employee making a complaint to an employment tribunal, potentially leading to the firm having to pay compensation.

A-grade application

Small firms fear changes to the law

Changes to UK employment law in recent years could be discouraging small businesses from hiring new staff, according to some commentators. New regulations designed to provide agency workers with greater protection and bring UK employment law in line with the European Union's Agency Workers Directive, were laid before Parliament in January 2010 and are due to be implemented across the country by October 2011. However, Russell Lawson of the Federation of Small Businesses in Wales claimed that this legislation, together with recently increased provision for maternity leave and the extension of flexible working rights to adult carers, had all added to small business fears about employing workers. A poll conducted by the FSB in 2009 indicated that 99 per cent of its members were less likely to recruit temporary workers once the agency workers' legislation was implemented.

Source: www.walesonline.co.uk

ISSUES FOR ANALYSIS

Opportunities for analysis using this topic are likely to focus on the following areas:

- the reasons for and against a small business expanding its workforce
- the advantages and/or disadvantages to a firm of employing staff on a part-time or full-time basis
- the benefits and drawbacks of employing staff on a temporary or full-time basis
- the suitability of using consultants or contractors to a firm in given circumstances.

8.7 EMPLOYING PEOPLE – AN EVALUATION

Taking on extra workers is one of the hardest decisions that an entrepreneur is likely to face. This is the point in the firm's development where the individual is forced to admit that she or he cannot do everything. There may also be a reluctance to hand over some control to others: people who may have different opinions and challenge the way the business is run. Employing someone with strongly opposing views is likely to lead to conflict and, unless everyone is moving in the same direction, the business will not move forward. However, a successful firm requires a range of skills and experience. Refusing to bring in additional support and expertise can seriously damage the potential of the business to continue to survive and thrive.

Key Terms

Contract of employment: a legal document setting out the terms and conditions of an individual's job. These include the responsibilities of the employee, rates of pay, working hours, holiday entitlement, and so on..

Employment agency: an organisation that supplies workers with particular skills, on a short- or long-term basis, to other businesses, in return for a fee.

Employment tribunal: an informal courtroom where legal disputes between employees and employers are settled.

Full-time employees: staff who are under contract to work the normal basic full-time hours of a business.

National Minimum Wage: the lowest hourly wage rate that an employer can legally pay to an employee.

Part-time employees: staff who are contracted to work for anything less than what is considered the normal basic full-time hours of a business.

Permanent employees: workers with a contract of employment with a business that is open-ended (that is, there is no time given at which the contract is due to end).

Temporary employees: employees on fixed-term contracts of employment, either for a predetermined time or until a specific task or set of tasks is completed.

WORKBOOK

A REVISION QUESTIONS

(40 marks; 40 minutes)

1 Outline three reasons why a small business may need to take on additional staff. (6)

2 Suggest two reasons why the owner of a small business might be reluctant to employ more staff. (2)

3 Explain why a business should consider any plans to expand the workforce in relation to its wider objectives. (4)

4 Examine two advantages of employing part-time staff to a small, expanding business. (6)

5 Suggest two reasons why an over-reliance on part-time staff could, in fact, increase the costs of a business. (4)

6 Briefly explain what is meant by a fixed-term contract. (2)

7 Analyse the main advantages and disadvantages of using temporary workers for a domestic cleaning business. (6)

8 Suggest one suitable method of dealing with the following staff shortages:

a) providing cover for a receptionist on two weeks' holiday (1)

b) providing extra sales assistance at a delicatessen on Saturdays (1)

c) providing additional waiters and kitchen staff at a restaurant over the busy Christmas period. (1)

9 Suggest one benefit and one drawback to a small business of using consultants to provide specialist skills. (4)

10 Briefly explain the main risks for a small business from failing to adhere to legislation regarding the employment of workers. (3)

B REVISION EXERCISES
B1 ACTIVITY

Flexible working at City Sightseeing Glasgow

City Sightseeing is a company set up to provide visitors to Glasgow with guided sightseeing tours. Its double-decker buses operate 362 days a year between 8.00 a.m. and 6.00 p.m., with tour guide services available for almost 24 hours per day. The nature of the business means that the company is required to adopt a flexible approach to its workforce. The company employs 70 people in the summer, falling to around 20 people in the winter. The business deliberately targets those who are not interested in working a full '9 to 5' week, including students, workers over the age of 40 and women returning to the labour market. At the beginning of both the summer and winter, each employee is required to indicate the number of hours they would like to work in the forthcoming season. Staff typically work between two and six days a week and job sharing is common.

Making sure that all shifts are covered and standards of service are maintained requires careful management and staff are encouraged to give as much notice as possible about changes in their work schedule. However, adopting a flexible approach to the workforce has also led to a number of benefits. The company does not need to advertise job vacancies, absenteeism is low and the staff retention is over 90 per cent.

Source: British Chamber of Commerce.

Questions

(15 marks; 20 minutes)

1 Explain two reasons why the nature of City Sightseeing's business requires it to employ a large percentage of part-time and temporary workers. (6)

2 Analyse the main implications for City Sightseeing of employing part-time and temporary staff, rather than full-time, permanent staff. (9)

B2 ACTIVITY

The Gourmet Chocolate Pizza Company

Helen Ellis took the decision to set up her own business in 2006. Her job as a part-time administrator had come to an end after the company employing her had closed down. Supported by her family, and keen to continue to work from her Nottingham home, Helen surfed the internet, looking for inspiration. She came across the concept of chocolate pizzas from an American website and was confident that, by putting her own twist on the idea, she had a successful venture on her hands. The result was the Gourmet Chocolate Pizza Co – a business producing and selling chocolate-based pizzas, covered with a selection of mouth-watering toppings, to order online and over the telephone.

Working from home for 18 months had proved to Helen that she had many of the skills and qualities required to run her own business: hard working and dedicated, with good organisational skills and an ability to deal with suppliers and the general public. Helen decided to pay a professional designer in order to get the business's website up and running quickly, and carried out her own research to see how other similar businesses marketed themselves.

Getting the business up and running required Helen to put in a lot of hours, including evenings and weekends. However, despite doing this and receiving a great deal of unpaid help from her mother, the increasing workload made it difficult to run the business effectively. Although Helen was managing to meet the growing number of orders, she was unable to cope with all the other jobs involved in expanding the business. In particular, the need for additional production staff to help box up the pizzas persuaded Helen to hire an extra worker.

Her search focused on finding someone who was flexible and reliable, could show initiative and shared a similar approach to the business. After taking advice on employment terms and conditions, the new employee was hired on a six-month temporary contract initially, before being appointed on a permanent basis.

According to Helen, 'employing another member of staff was the best thing I did ... a bit daunting, but one of those things you need to do to push the business forward, so really you take a deep breath and do it.' By 2010, the company's workforce had increased to five, consisting of three production workers, one dispatch worker and an assistant manager. Only one worker is employed on a part-time basis. This expansion means that Helen is no longer directly involved with production, allowing her to focus on growing the business.

Source: Gourmet Chocolate Pizza Company

Questions

(35 marks; 40 minutes)

1 **a)** Identify two qualities possessed by Helen Ellis that helped her to establish her business. (2)
  b) What is meant by the term 'temporary contract'? (2)
  c) What is meant by the term 'part-time basis'? (2)

2 Explain one advantage and one disadvantage to Helen's business of employing new staff. (6)

3 Examine the benefits of appointing a new member of staff on a temporary contract initially. (9)

4. Assess the possible consequences for the Gourmet Chocolate Pizza Co from Helen's decision to no longer be directly involved in the production process. (14)

UNIT 9

Opportunity cost and trade-offs

Opportunity cost is the cost of missing out on the next best alternative when making a decision. For example, the opportunity cost of not going to university may be to risk missing out on massive extra lifetime earnings (in general, graduates are much better paid than non-graduates). Similarly, trade-offs look at what you have to give up in order to get what you want most. They may not easily be expressed as a 'cost' (that is it may not be possible to quantify them).

9.1 INTRODUCTION TO OPPORTUNITY COST

This concept will be useful throughout the A-level Business Studies course. It is at the heart of every business decision, from small to multinational companies. It can usefully be explained with reference to football club management. In 2010 new manager Roy Hodgson was given a budget of £10 million to buy new players for Liverpool FC. As he also sold Javier Mascherano for £20 million, he had £30 million to spend. He could have spent it all on one top player, such as David Villa. Instead he spent it on five players, including Raul Meireles and Paul Konchesky. The opportunity cost of buying these five was missing out on buying David Villa. The £30 million could only be spent once, so it was vital to spend it wisely. As with every football manager, the wisdom of this decision will affect Hodgson's job security.

Every business faces the same issue: limited resources mean that hiring a marketing manager leaves less money to spend on a marketing campaign. For a start-up business, spending lots of money on a flash opening party means there is less money to pay for staff training.

For a new business the two most important resources are money and time. Both have an opportunity cost. Time spent by an entrepreneur in creating a pretty website could mean that too little time is left for recruiting and training staff, or too little time to sit back to reflect on priorities. The same issue arises with money: it can only be spent once.

It follows that every business decision has an opportunity cost, measured in time, money, and often both. The same is true in other walks of life. A prime minister focused on foreign adventures may lose sight of the key issues affecting people at home. A chancellor who spends an extra £10 billion on education may have to cut back on healthcare.

For a new business start-up, the most important opportunity cost issues are as follows.

- Do not tie up too much capital in stock, as this cash could be used more productively elsewhere in the business.
- Do not overstretch yourself: good decisions take time, so make sure you are not doing too much yourself.
- Take care with every decision that uses up cash; at the start of a business it is hard to get more of it, but more is always needed.

9.2 OPPORTUNITY COSTS IN DEVELOPING A BUSINESS IDEA

Personal opportunity costs

Starting your first business is likely to be tough. Long hours and highly pressured decisions may cause stress, but the biggest problems are beyond psychology. A difficult cash flow position is quite normal, yet places a huge strain on the business and its owner(s).

The owner of a first business will probably have come from a background as a salary earner, possibly a very well-paid one. So the first opportunity cost is missing out on the opportunity to earn a regular income. As it could take six months or more to get a business going, this is a long period of financial hardship.

Then comes the investment spending itself, such as the outlay on a lease, on building work, on fixtures and fittings, on machinery and then on the human resources (staff) to make everything work with a human face. All this is using money that could otherwise be used on the proprietor's house, holidays, and so on. The personal opportunity costs add up massively.

Business writers often use the term 'stakeholders', which means all those with a stake in the success or failure of a business. Usually, the key groups are those within the business ('internal stakeholders'), such as staff, managers and directors, and outside groups ('external stakeholders'), such as suppliers, customers, bankers and shareholders. In the case of a business start-up, however, there is a whole extra consideration: the wear and tear on the family. Starting a business is a hugely time-consuming and wholly absorbing activity. The restaurant owner might easily spend 80 hours a week on site in the early days, then take further paperwork home. An American business psychologist has said that, 'even when you are home, you're still thinking about the business – it's easy for a spouse to feel neglected, even jealous'.

Despite this, research by a US investment business has shown that, although 32 per cent of new entrepreneurs said that the experience had caused marriage difficulties, 42 per cent of chief executives in fast-growing new firms said that the pressures and exhilarations made their marriages stronger.

The opportunity costs of developing one business idea as opposed to another

When 30-year-old Mike Clare opened his first Sofabed Centre in 1985 he could raise only £16,000 of capital, even though his estimates showed that £20,000 to £25,000 was needed. Fortunately, hard work plus a great first month's sales brought in the cash he needed to get the business going properly. At that time, none of the banks would lend him any money. Now, the renamed Dreams is Britain's biggest bed retailer, with 150 outlets and a sales turnover of more than £160 million. Mike Clare remains the main shareholder and the boss.

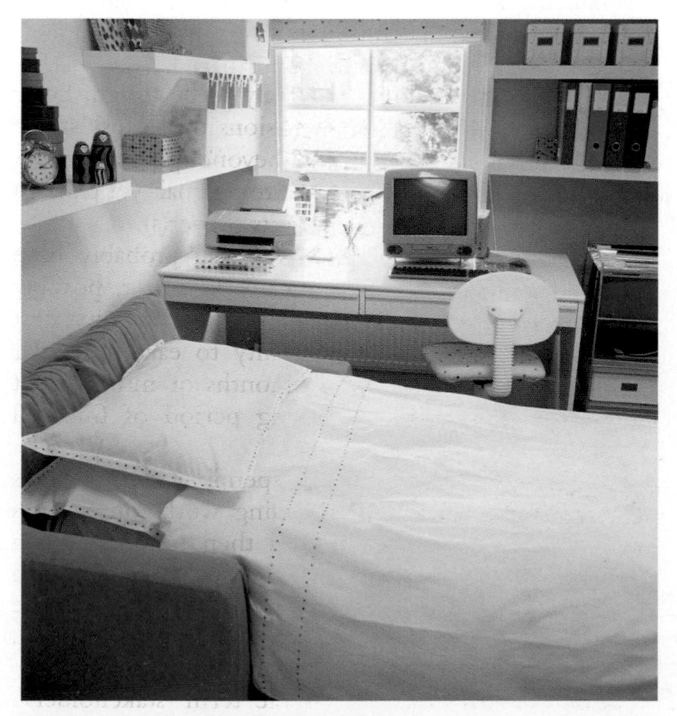

Figure 9.1 Dreams is Britain's biggest bed retailer and still sells sofabeds

The fact is, though, that it would have been impossible for Mike to have chosen to launch two different businesses at the same time; he had to choose one. Fortunately, he chose wisely.

Given the need to focus on the opportunity, the main circumstance in which opportunity cost arises is when an entrepreneur has two ideas. One should be chosen and one rejected. This is possible if the entrepreneur is ruthless. After evaluating the two options carefully, the weaker of the two should be stopped completely. The reason is simple: opening one business is tough enough; two would be impossible.

In the lead-up to Mike Clare's first store opening, he spent time organising public relations events (to get coverage in the local paper), helping with the building work, wrangling with suppliers over credit terms and making decisions about pricing and display. When the store opened, he spent 18 hours a day there 'doing everything'. When the first store took £30,000 in month 1, he also started looking for a second location. It was open in November 1985, six months after the first store had opened. Quite clearly, there was no possibility of starting more than one business at a time.

9.3 DECIDING BETWEEN OPPORTUNITIES

Successful business people are those who can make successful decisions. The three founders of Innocent Drinks wanted to start a business together, but had no idea what type of business to start. As friends at university they had already run nightclub events together, and two ran an annual music festival in west London. They could have developed their skills as showmen into a successful festival business, but stumbled upon the idea of a business that made all-fruit smoothies. On finding an investor, in 1999, who could help turn their dream into a reality, they left their salaried jobs, gave up their other business opportunities and concentrated on building the Innocent brand. The 2010 sale of a majority of the Innocent shares to Coca-Cola for £75 million showed the success of this start-up.

When deciding between business start-up opportunities, certain factors are crucial.

Estimating the potential sales that could be achieved by each idea

This is hugely difficult, both in the short term and – even more – in the longer term. Innocent's first-year sales were £0.4 million. Who could have guessed that, eight years later, its sales would be more than 300 times greater? Yet estimates must be made, either by the use of market research, or by using the expertise of the entrepreneur. For instance, Mike Clare of Dreams had previously worked as an area manager for a furniture retailer, so he had a reasonable idea about what the sales might be. Inside knowledge is, of course, hard to beat.

Considering carefully the cash requirements of each idea

The Innocent trio were very lucky to find an American investor who put £250,000 into the start of the business in return for a 20 per cent stake. Some new businesses are very hungry for cash (such as setting up a new restaurant in London, which costs over £1 million); other new business ideas (such as a new website) can be started from a back bedroom, keeping initial costs very low.

Deciding whether the time is right

Innocent's 1999 launch fitted wonderfully with a time of luxury spending plus growing concern about diet. In the same year, a small business started in west London, focusing on customising cars: 'souping up' the engines to make the cars go faster and give the engines a 'throaty roar'. As rising fuel prices became a greater concern, the business was squeezed out. Five years before, it might have made a lot of money, but it no longer did so.

> **A-grade application**
>
> **Cobra Beer**
>
> Cobra Beer has become the standard lager to be found in Indian restaurants throughout the UK. Its origins date back to when the owner and founder Karan Bilimoria came from India to study at a British university. He found British lagers too gassy for comfort. After completing his degree, Karan and a family friend spent their time importing items from India to Britain; this included polo sticks, towels and silk jackets. They were planning to start importing seafood and visited a supplier that also had a small, privately owned brewery. Karan (now Lord) Bilimoria explained the less gassy style of beer that he wanted, and the brewery helped out.
>
> The pair of friends had very little money, but managed to get a £7,000 overdraft to pay for the first beer imports to Britain. To keep focused, they decided to drop all their other import businesses. Today Cobra Beer has annual sales of over £100 million. Lord Bilimoria's stake in the business is worth well over £50 million (he bought out his friend's stake along the way). Several times over, Lord Bilimoria made the right decision.

Deciding whether the skills needed fit your own set of skills

Running a restaurant requires a mix of organisational skills, discipline and meticulous attention to detail. Does that describe you? Or are you better suited to running an online business that can be handled in a relaxed way behind the scenes?

9.4 TRADE-OFFS

In business there are many occasions when one factor has to be traded off against another. An entrepreneur might get huge help at the start from friends, yet realise that these same friends lack the professionalism to help the business grow. The needs of the business may have to be traded off against the friendships. Can a softie be a real business success? Probably not: some inner toughness is clearly important.

Other trade-offs may include:

- when starting in the first place, trading off the start-up against a year's international travel (perhaps with friends); or trading the start-up against going to university
- trading off the aspects of the business you most enjoy doing against those that prove most profitable for the business; the chef/owner may love cooking, yet find the business works far better when she or he has the time to mix with the customers, motivate the waiting staff and negotiate hard with suppliers
- trading off time today and time tomorrow; the entrepreneur's ambition may be to 'retire by the time I'm 40'; that may sound great in the long term but, in the short term, the family may feel neglected.

Overall, the key to success will be to be clear about what you and your family want from the business. It may be to become outrageously rich, no matter what, or – more likely – to find a balance between the freedom and independence of running your own business and the need to find time for the family. Books on business success assume that success can be measured only in millions of pounds. Many people running their own small businesses would tell a different story; the independence alone may be the key to their personal satisfaction.

WORKBOOK

A REVISION QUESTIONS

(20 marks; 20 minutes)

1 Explain in your own words why time is an important aspect of opportunity cost. (3)
2 Give two ways of measuring the opportunity cost to you of doing this homework. (2)
3 Outline one opportunity cost to a restaurant chef/owner of opening a second restaurant. (3)
4 Explain the trade-offs that may exist in the following business situations. Choose the two contexts you feel most comfortable with.
  a) Levi's pushes its workers to produce more pairs of jeans per hour.
  b) A chocolate producer, short of cash, must decide whether to cut its advertising spending or cut back on its research and development into new product ideas.
  c) A football manager decides to double the number of training sessions per week.
  d) A celebrity magazine must decide whether or not to run photos that will generate huge publicity, but probably make the celebrity unwilling to cooperate with the magazine in future. (6)
5 Re-read the A-grade application on Cobra Beer. Outline the trade-offs involved in Karan Bilimoria's decision to start his beer business. (6)

B REVISION EXERCISES

B1 DATA RESPONSE

James Sutton had a job as a marketing manager, paying £55,000 a year. His career prospects looked very good, yet he handed in his notice to start up his own online business. He knew that it would take him away from 9 to 5 work and towards the dedication of 8.00 a.m. until 9.00 p.m. If he took on a member of staff, the wage bill would rise by £16,000.

Questions

(10 marks; 15 minutes)

1 Outline three opportunity cost issues within this short passage. (6)
2 Outline the possible impact on James of the increase in the workload. (4)

B2 DATA RESPONSE

In 2002 a cooperative agreement between coffee farmers in 250 Ugandan villages broke down. It had taken years to put together, but disagreements made it collapse. The prize for a successful cooperative was to produce organic coffee beans grown to Fairtrade standards for partners such as Cafédirect. This would ensure getting significantly higher prices for the raw coffee beans and also much better credit terms (being paid quickly to help with cash flow).

Over the next two years countless hours of work were put into forming a new cooperative. In early 2004 the new 'Gumutindo' coffee cooperative was Fairtrade certified. By 2010 7,000 farmers had joined the Gumutindo cooperative. They receive a guaranteed price of $1.26 per pound of coffee beans, whereas the world price has been as low as $0.80 over the last eight years. The extra (and stable) income should help the farmers, of whom only 25 per cent have running water and 79 per cent live in mud huts with iron sheet roofing. The Fairtrade organisation has supported the cooperative in starting up its own production plant, converting the raw coffee into packs of coffee ready for sale.

Source: based on www.fairtrade.org.uk

Questions

(25 marks; 30 minutes)

1 What would be the opportunity cost of the farmers who put 'countless hours of work into forming a new cooperative'? (4)
2 Outline one risk for the farmers and one risk for the Fairtrade organisation in forming a new cooperative with high guaranteed prices for coffee beans. (6)
3 Some commentators have suggested that Waitrose should make all its coffee 'Fairtrade', therefore getting rid of brands such as Nescafé Gold Blend. Outline the trade-offs Waitrose management would have to consider before making any such decision. (6)
4 Discuss whether producing coffee ready for sale would definitely increase the income levels of the 7,000 members of the cooperative. (9)

Economic factors affecting business start-up

UNIT 10

Economic factors deal with the economy as a whole (sometimes known as the 'macro' economy). These include interest rates and exchange rates, either of which could affect the success of a new small business start-up.

10.1 WHAT IS 'THE ECONOMY'?

Each of us goes about our business in our own way. A teacher receives a monthly salary paid directly into the bank, and draws out the cash needed to buy the shopping, buy petrol and give the children some pocket money. The children may spend this on chocolate, Coca-Cola and packets of crisps.

Although, as individuals, we 'do our own thing', the actions and decisions taken by millions of people and businesses make up 'the economy'. Collectively, chocolate purchases in Britain add up to £3,000 million per year. This, in turn, provides the income for chocolate producers and shopkeepers, who employ tens of thousands of staff.

If the value of all spending on all products bought in the UK is added together, it comes to an annual figure of over £1.3 trillion (a million million). So the spending on chocolate makes up just 0.25 per cent of all spending on all goods sold in Britain in a year. This spending provides the vast revenues companies need in order to pay for Britain's 28 million workers, and they still need enough profit to pay for business growth.

The key thing to remember is that the economy is intertwined. Cadbury is successful only if families have enough cash to be able to buy chocolate bars. So, if there was a big cutback in consumer spending, perhaps in the wake of government spending cutbacks, many firms would struggle, including Cadbury.

When times are bad, almost every business suffers; this, in turn, can lead to job losses. When the economy is recovering, things get better for almost all firms.

10.2 CURRENT ECONOMIC CLIMATE

Business thrives on confidence. Confident consumers are willing to dip into their savings for a holiday, or to borrow to buy a new carpet or car. Confident investors are willing to put more money into businesses in return for shares. And the companies themselves will spend to invest in their future: new factory buildings, new machinery and new computer systems. All this spending can create an upsurge in economic activity.

The reverse also applies: gloom can spread doom. Therefore the **economic climate** is important. The sections that follow give an idea of the factors that help to create an economic climate, either of optimism, or pessimism. These factors include:

- changes in interest rates
- changes in the exchange rate
- the consequences for business of unemployment and inflation
- the effect of government spending or taxation.

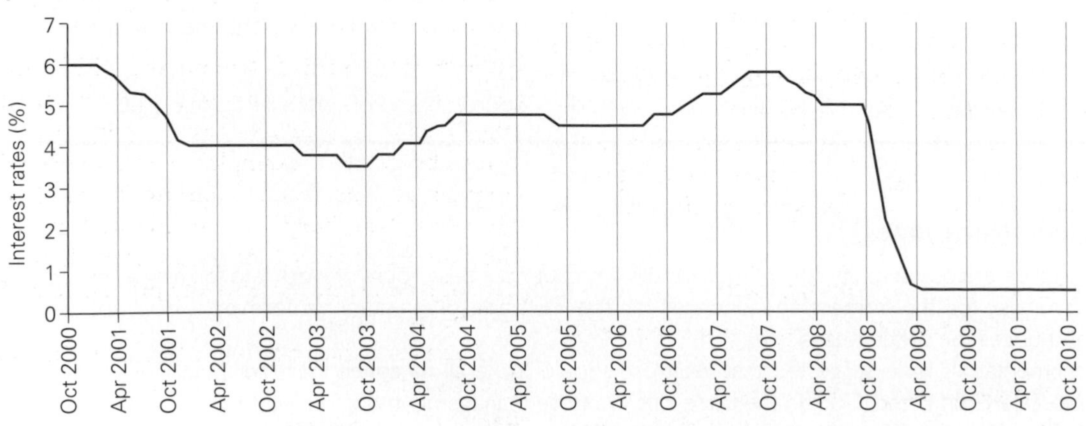

Figure 10.1 UK bank interest rates, 2000–10
Source: Bank of England

10.3 CHANGES IN INTEREST RATES

The interest rate is the price charged by a bank per year for lending money or for providing credit. Individual banks decide for themselves about the rate they will charge on their credit cards or for the overdrafts they provide. But they are usually influenced by the interest rate that the central bank charges high street banks for borrowing money: the bank rate. In Britain, this is set each month by a committee of the Bank of England.

The Bank of England committee is asked to set interest rates at a level that should ensure UK prices rise by around 2 per cent per year. If the committee members decide that the economy is growing so strongly that prices may rise faster than 2 per cent, it will increase interest rates. Then people will feel worried about borrowing more (because of the higher repayment cost) and may cut their spending. This should help to discourage firms from increasing their prices.

For firms, the level of interest rates is very important because:

- it affects consumer demand, especially for goods bought on credit, such as houses and cars; the higher the rate of interest, the lower the sales that can be expected
- the interest charges affect the total operating costs (that is, the higher the interest rate, the higher the costs of running an overdraft, and therefore the lower the profit)
- the higher the rate of interest, the less attractive it is for a firm to invest money into the future of the business; therefore, there is a risk of falling demand for items such as lorries, computers and factory machinery.

If interest rates fall, the opposite effects occur, to the benefit of both companies and the economy as a whole.

10.4 EXCHANGE RATES

In Britain the currency used for selling goods and services is the pound sterling (£). In America goods and services are sold in US dollars ($). The exchange rate measures the quantity of foreign currency that can be bought with one unit of domestic currency. Movements in the exchange rate can dramatically affect profitability because the exchange rate affects both the price of imported and exported goods.

The pound's rate of exchange against the US dollar is determined by the supply and demand for the pound on international currency markets. Exchange rates affect firms in different ways.

The impacts of a high exchange rate

The impacts of a high exchange rate are set out below.

On firms with large export markets

UK firms that sell a high proportion of their output overseas will prefer a low exchange rate (that is, a weak pound). Why is this so? The best way of explaining is via a numerical example.

America is an important export market for Morgan Cars. Morgan charges its UK customers £18,000 for a basic two-seater Roadster.

Figure 10.2 Morgan Roadster

To achieve the same profit margin in America, Morgan has to charge a price in US dollars that will convert into £18,000. At the beginning of 2007 the exchange rate against the US dollar was £1 = $1.90. To obtain £18,000 from the exported car, Morgan had to charge its American customers:

£18,000 × $1.90 = $34,200

By November 2007 the exchange rate had gone up to £1 = $2.10. To generate the same £18,000 of export revenue per car sold, Morgan had to charge its American customers:

£18,000 × $2.10 = $37,800

In other words, Morgan had to increase the price of its car in America by $3,600 in order to maintain the current profit made on each car sold. That price increase would, of course, be off-putting to car buyers. So sales would be likely to fall.

On firms that import most of their raw materials or stock

Supermarkets such as Sainbury's, which import much of their stock, will prefer a high exchange rate. A high exchange rate reduces the cost of buying goods from abroad. For example, Jack Daniel's whiskey is a popular product with Sainsbury's British consumers. However, Sainsbury's has to import this product from the American firm that produces it. If the price of a case of Jack Daniel's is $50, the price paid by Sainsbury's will be as follows.

If the exchange rate is £1 = $1.90, the case will cost Sainsbury:

$50/1.90 = £26.30.

However, if the exchange rate goes up to £1 = $2.10 the same case of Jack Daniel's will now cost Sainsbury's £23.80 ($50/2.10 = £23.80). A high exchange rate will benefit Sainsbury's because it will be able to make more profit on each bottle of Jack Daniel's that it sells to UK customers.

The impacts of a low exchange rate

The impacts of a weak exchange rate are the reverse of the impacts of a strong exchange rate. Firms such as Morgan that were damaged by a strong currency find life easier when the exchange rate falls. Between November 2007 and November 2010 the pound had fallen from $2.10 to $1.50. This weakening of the pound made UK exports seem cheaper to foreign consumers, helping Morgan to sell more of its cars in America.

On the other hand, firms such as Sainsbury's are damaged by a low exchange rate because it costs them more in pounds to buy in their imported stock. If Sainsbury's reacts to the falling exchange rate by raising its prices the company could lose customers. If the company does nothing it will make less profit on each unit of imported stock sold.

10.5 THE CONSEQUENCES FOR BUSINESS OF UNEMPLOYMENT AND INFLATION

Unemployment

Unemployment is created when the number of jobs (the demand for labour) falls in comparison to the number of people looking for work (the supply of labour). Therefore there are just two things to consider: the demand for labour and the supply.

Demand for labour

The demand for labour in Britain is mainly affected by two things.

1 *The demand for goods in general and therefore the number of jobs available:* if the economy is booming, firms need plenty of full-time, part-time and seasonal staff, so there are plenty of jobs around. In an economic downturn, jobs are far less plentiful. In America, the number of jobs available increased by 95,000 a month during 2007, but by less than 20,000 a month during 2009, at a time of recession.
2 *The demand for jobs in Britain compared with overseas:* in 2010 Cadbury switched chocolate production from Britain to Poland; many banks have switched their call centres from Britain to India. Despite this, the number of jobs available in Britain reached record levels in 2010, so the fear of 'outsourcing' is exaggerated.

Supply of labour

The supply of labour in Britain is affected by two things:

1 demographic factors affecting the number of people of working age (roughly 28 million) plus the number of EU migrants available within the workforce (approximately half a million)
2 the willingness of employable people to look for work, which may be weighed down by benefits such as free rent for those out of work, but is boosted by rising minimum wage rates, which help to provide a better financial incentive to work; over the ten years to 2010 the number of people employed in Britain grew by more than 2 million.

Long- and short-term factors in unemployment

In the long term, the above are key factors. In the short term the main single factor is likely to be the number of jobs on offer. Firms squeezed hard by an economic downturn will stop recruiting and may start to look for redundancies, to cut back on the workforce. This could push unemployment up sharply. In the past, as much as 20 per cent of the workforce has been unemployed in Britain. In such an event, the impact on people's lives is very severe, especially if the unemployment lasts for several years, as in the '**recessions**' of the early 1980s and 1990s.

What is inflation?

Inflation measures the percentage annual rise in the average price level. It reduces the internal purchasing power of money. For consumers, inflation increases the cost of living. The impacts of inflation on a firm's finances are mixed. There are some advantages created by inflation but there are also disadvantages created too.

Advantages of inflation to a business

The advantages of inflation to a business are as follows.

1 Inflation can boost the recorded profitability of a business. For example, suppose that firm X made the following profit this year:

Total revenue	£100m
Total cost	£80m
Profit	£20m

During the following year inflation is 10 per cent. Even if the firm's sales volume remains unchanged, its revenue can be increased. Inflation encourages the firm to increase its prices by 10 per cent. It is also likely that the firm's costs will also rise by 10 per cent. If the above turns out to be true, the firm's profit for the year will increase by £2 million.

Total revenue	£110m
Total cost	£88m
Profit	£22m

The firm could also claim that it had achieved a £10 million increase in revenue during the year. However, the increase is merely an illusion created by inflation. The firm still sold the same amount of product as it did in the previous year. There has been no increase in sales in **real terms** (taking into account the effects of inflation). Inflation has made the business look more profitable simply because it has made the revenue and cost figures larger.

2 Firms with large loans also benefit from inflation because inflation erodes the real value of the money owed. Firms with high borrowings typically find that the fixed repayments on their long-term borrowings become more easily covered by rising income and profits (after five years of inflation the repayments on a £1 million loan no longer seem so difficult to repay, because the business is enjoying higher revenues).

Disadvantages of inflation to a business

The disadvantages of inflation to a business are as follows.

1 Inflation can damage profitability, especially for firms that have fixed-price contracts that take a long time to complete. For example, a local building company might agree a £5 million price for an extension to a local private school, which is expected to take three years to finish. If inflation is higher than expected, profit could be wiped out by the unexpectedly high cost increases created by the unexpectedly high rates of inflation.

2 Inflation can also harm a firm's cash position because it pushes up the price of new assets that need to be bought, such as machinery. This can penalise manufacturers such as Ford that need to replace their machinery regularly in order to stay internationally competitive.

3 If costs in Britain are rising faster than prices elsewhere, UK companies will find that they are losing their ability to compete effectively with foreign firms. Renault is planning to make a new small car for India, to be launched in 2013. It is likely to be priced at £2,200, which would hardly pay the labour costs if the car was produced in Britain.

10.6 THE EFFECT OF GOVERNMENT SPENDING OR TAXATION

In addition to economic change, businesses can be affected by economic policy decisions taken by government. If worried about sharply rising prices, a government could decide to increase income tax. This would take spending power out of the pockets of consumers, softening the upward pressure on prices, but cutting demand for the products and services produced by businesses. What might be right for the economy as a whole could be damaging for individual businesses.

Why would any government take actions that could damage businesses and therefore threaten jobs? The answer is simple: because ministers may believe that short-term pain may be necessary for long-term gain. This might be correct, but it will be no consolation to any business squeezed out of business by an unexpected tax rise.

The other main weapon government can use to achieve its policy goals is to change the level of government (known as 'public') spending. At present, just over 40 per cent of the British economy is generated by public spending. The rest is mainly generated by private consumers (you and me). The government spends huge sums on the health service, defence, roads and much else. If the government was concerned about rising prices, it could consider cutting back on its own

Table 10.1 The impact of a change in spending and taxation

	Government spending up	Government spending down	Government puts taxes up	Government puts taxes down
To help reduce the level of unemployment	Extra spending on road-building, health and other services with big workforce			Reduce income tax to enable families to keep and spend more of the money they earn
To cut the growth rate when it's rising too fast		Cut the spending on health, education and defence, to take a bit of spending from the economy	Increase income tax to force people to think harder and more carefully about what they buy	
To improve the competitiveness of British firms	Extra spending on education			Cut company taxation (Corporation Tax)
To cut the rate of imports, especially of consumer goods		Cut benefits (e.g. state pension) to cut people's ability to buy imports	Increase VAT on all goods other than food and drink	

spending. This would reduce the income of businesses involved in education, road-building, and so on. They, in turn, may have to make redundancies, thereby dampening down consumer spending, which should help to keep prices from rising so sharply.

It follows, therefore, that sensible businesspeople keep an eye on government activity. Years ago, the government announced its tax and spending plans in the Spring Budget, which was always kept secret until the government announced it. Today, an 'Autumn Statement' announces, six months in advance, the government's public spending plans. This ensures that firms can anticipate the tax decisions that will be announced in the spring.

Table 10.1 shows how a government could use its power over taxation and spending to tackle different economic problems.

ISSUES FOR ANALYSIS

The key to successful analysis of the effect of economic factors on business is to keep things simple. The best way to do this is to make a clear, direct link between the economic factor and the business featured in the exam question. Beware of drifting towards complicated sequences of: 'this affects this, which affects that, which has a knock-on effect on that', and so on. For example:

- higher interest rates hit the demand for goods bought on credit, such as cars and houses
- a rising pound will hit XXX Co, because it exports to 15 countries and will now face pressure to increase its overseas selling prices
- rising inflation may damage the XXX Co's competitiveness, by forcing the company to increase its prices.

Good analysis will take the answer quickly from the economics to the business reality.

10.7 ECONOMIC FACTORS AFFECTING BUSINESS START-UP – AN EVALUATION

Judging the importance of different economic factors is made much easier if you have a full grasp of the business context (what the firm does, how it does it, what its strengths and weaknesses are, and so on). For example, a 20 per cent increase in the value of the pound would cause serious problems for the UK car industry (as most UK-produced cars are exported), but would make little difference to a small corner shop.

As is true in every other part of the course, good judgement comes from breadth of experience. This can be helped by watching business TV, and reading *Business Review* and the A-grade application entries in this textbook.

Key Terms

Consumer demand: the levels of spending by consumers in general (not just the demand from one consumer).

Economic climate: the atmosphere surrounding the economy (for example, gloom and doom or optimism and boom).

Exchange rate: the price of a currency, measured by the amount of a foreign currency it will buy (for example, £1 = $1.90).

Real terms: changes in pounds totals (for example, for household income) excluding the distorting effect of inflation.

Recession: a downturn in sales and production that occurs across most parts of the economy, perhaps leading to six months of continuous economic decline.

WORKBOOK

A REVISION QUESTIONS

(25 marks; 25 minutes)

1 Explain why a fall in spending in London could have a knock-on effect on the economy in Bradford, Plymouth, Norwich or anywhere else in the country. (3)

2 Explain how a business such as Alton Towers could be affected by a recession in America. (6)

3 Identify whether the Bank of England should raise or cut interest rates in the following circumstances:
  a) a sharp recession has hit the UK economy (1)
  b) inflation is predicted to rise by 3 per cent over the coming months (1)
  c) house prices have risen by 16 per cent in each of the last two years. (1)

4 A British detective agency has been hired by a French woman to tail a man. The fee is €500 per week. After four weeks the sum of €2,000 is due to be paid, but the rate for the pound against the euro has fallen from 1.45 to 1.25.
  a) What sum will the detective agency receive in pounds for this two weeks' work? (3)
  b) What may stop the firm from simply putting the euro price up? (4)

5 Outline why an economic downturn could affect the level of unemployment. (6)

B REVISION EXERCISES

B1 DATA RESPONSE

Is confidence enough?

In February 2008 the economic news in America was grim. Employment and the stock market were falling and the service sector (70 per cent of the economy) was reporting a sharp slowdown. Yet although company chief executives reported 'concern at the prospect of a darkening economic picture', few admitted to seeing any problem with their own business or industry. Procter & Gamble, the world's largest household goods firm, reported no switch to own-label products. Consumers were still willing to pay the price premiums for brands such as Pampers and Gillette. Data for January 2008 showed that small firms were still taking on more staff and awarding pay rises. No sign of recession there, then.

Yet, according to an article in the prestigious *Harvard Business Review*, research over a 20-year period shows that, 'As evidence gathers that a downturn is likely, executives often continue to radiate confidence about the future. They don't want to frighten the troops [staff], which will only make matters worse ... Some contend that their industries are safe. Others believe that their own company's ability to weather a downturn is superior to that of competitors.'

Chief executives could point to the interest rate cut from 4.25 per cent to 3 per cent as a clear sign that things were looking up. But financial analysts worried that optimism was 'preventing companies from planning for a downturn'.

Source: adapted from the *Financial Times*, 13 February 2008, p. 11.

Questions

(20 marks; 25 minutes)

1 Explain why the experience of Procter & Gamble might not be typical of all firms. (4)

2 a) Explain why chief executives might want to 'radiate confidence about the future'. (4)
   b) Outline two possible disadvantages to a business of excessive confidence on the part of a chief executive. (4)

3 The chief executives were pinning their hopes on the impact of the 1.25 per cent cut in interest rates. Choose two of the following businesses, then analyse the effect of the fall in interest rates on each, in turn.
   a) Procter & Gamble
   b) Coca-Cola
   c) A small building firm
   d) Gucci, supplier of luxury clothes and accessories. (8)

B2 DATA RESPONSE

Boom times for manufacturing

In late 2010 and early 2011 there was a wave of optimism about the prospects for UK manufacturing. In the fourth quarter of 2010, manufacturing was 5 per cent up on 2009, despite an overall fall in GDP. A closely watched survey by the Chartered Institute of Purchasing and Supply gave the highest figures for manufacturing growth in 16 years. Export sales were especially strong. Figure 10.3 shows an index of manufacturing output for the whole of Britain.

One company benefiting from these conditions was Cotswold Manufacturing, a medium-sized producer of wood products such as doors, doorframes and internal glazed screens. Based in the north-east of England, Cotswold was proud to boast a move to new premises, taking it from 29,700 to 53,000 square feet of factory space. With 27 staff and a sales turnover of £3 million, this huge growth in capacity showed great faith in the upward trend.

Cotswold sells extensively to public sector organisations such as schools, universities, hotels, hospitals and army barracks. In January 2011 Ken Napper, commercial director of Cotswold Manufacturing, said, 'We are delighted with the success of the business. We have a fantastic team who all focus on getting the product right and ensuring customer satisfaction. We have developed a unique system in our machinery which sets us apart from our competitors. These are very exciting times for Cotswold Manufacturing.'

With ISO 9001 certification and robot-controlled production machinery, Cotswold is confident that it is in a strong position to compete effectively. The only worry might be that 2011 will see the start of the government's deficit-reduction plans to cut public spending.

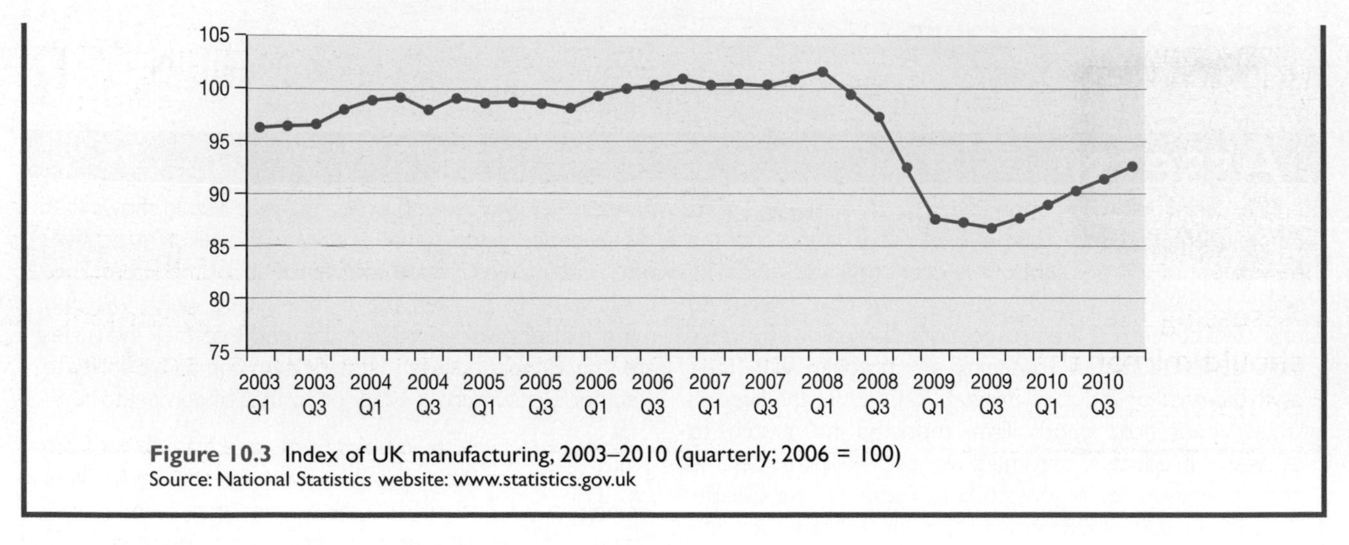

Figure 10.3 Index of UK manufacturing, 2003–2010 (quarterly; 2006 = 100)
Source: National Statistics website: www.statistics.gov.uk

Questions

(25 marks; 30 minutes)

1 Examine one reason in favour and one reason against the optimism shown by the management at Cotswold Manufacturing. (10)
2 Discuss the impact on the British economy as a whole of a sustained boom in manufacturing output. (15)

Assessing business start-ups

UNIT 11

Assessing means weighing up, in the sense of making a judgement. This assessment should mirror the ways in which entrepreneurs need to decide: should I go ahead or not?

11.1 INTRODUCTION

Social entrepreneur Duncan Goose had, by mid-2010, established One Water as a £2 million brand. It was funding the building of a new water pump in Africa every eight days, and he was able to focus the six staff on his primary objective: one new water pump built every day.

Yet he was already looking towards a new project, One Toilet Tissue. The profits from selling the tissue would fund hygienic toilet blocks in schools in Africa. But launching a new idea takes time and money; and he was short of both. If One Toilet Tissue drained Duncan's energies and those of his staff, what might be the effect on One Water? Duncan had to make a careful assessment of whether or not to start up his next project.

Although he could see the reasons against doing so, Duncan decided to go ahead. His objective in giving up a comfortable job and salary to start One was to make a difference. How could he stop now? The opportunity was there for building on One Water's success, so it would seem wrong to stop. The risks of failure only made it more of a challenge. Duncan made an assessment of the risks, costs and benefits of starting One Toilet Tissue, but was motivated mainly by his personality. He wanted the challenge.

How should one assess whether or not a business start-up is worthwhile? There are four issues to consider:

1 the business objectives
2 the business plan
3 the risks involved
4 the possible causes and consequences of failure.

11.2 SUMMARISING START-UP OBJECTIVES

There are three main types of objective when starting a business: financial, personal and social.

Financial

Some entrepreneurs consciously set out to get rich. They may hope to make enough money to retire by the age of 45 or even 25. For them, the ideal is to start up and build a business so that it can be sold or **floated** on the stock market. Either way, they will turn hard work into lots of capital. Mike Ashley started Sports Direct as a teenager and, at the age of 42, floated it on the stock market. He sold 43 per cent of the business for more than £900 million, keeping the remaining 57 per cent of the shares. He then used his personal cash to buy Newcastle United FC.

The other financial goal is not to get rich, but simply to make a living. People who open a small grocery store or sweet shop want to earn enough for the family, but may not be especially ambitious. Their financial goals may be no more than to make £25,000–£40,000 per year from the business.

Personal

Many people start up their own business because they want to prove that they can succeed. Perhaps they are disappointed with their own career and feel: 'this'll show them'. Or they are trying to prove something to themselves.

Among the key personal goals are to:

- be my own boss
- show what I can do
- get out of a boring career
- be able to build something
- avoid later regrets (if failing to take advantage of a business opportunity)
- build something for my family.

Social

As in the case of Duncan Goose, some people are true **social entrepreneurs**. The way they achieve their personal goals is through an enterprise that has a purpose other than profit-making. Yet it would be wise to be sceptical. For every one person who is a true social entrepreneur, there are probably ten who cover their financial ambitions in green or charitable clothing. If 'carbon neutral' is a message that sells, many will adopt the slogan as a way to boost profit. Despite this, the fact that true social entrepreneurs exist means that it would be simplistic to suggest that all business start-ups are about making money.

11.3 ASSESSING START-UP OBJECTIVES

The success of a new organisation can only be measured in relation to the objectives of its founder. A London pizza business called Pizza Euforia was started eight years ago with the ambition of creating a chain of 20 restaurants within three years. Today there are two outlets, one of which is barely breaking even. Clearly this is not a success. Yet government statistics show that restaurant start-ups have one of the lowest survival rates of all businesses: 40 per cent fail within three years. So Pizza Euforia failed in relation to the founders' objectives, but not compared with national data.

The reason for setting an objective is to give a target to strive for, in order to provide motivation. The clearer the objective the better; a good example is provided by the One Water objective of building one water pump per day. Some new firms start without a clear objective. The entrepreneur may just be looking for survival in year 1 'and then let's see where we get to'. Woolly objectives such as this may interfere with the firm's progress. The problem will be most acute if the business employs several staff. Ideally, every staff member would treat every customer as precious: the future of the business. This would be easier to establish if everyone had a clear sense of purpose and direction.

11.4 ASSESSING THE STRENGTHS AND WEAKNESSES OF A BUSINESS PLAN

The business model

There are two issues to consider here. A business plan is a detailed look at why and how a business idea could become successful. To raise capital from investors, there is an earlier stage that must be mastered: the **business model**. Investors want the business idea summed up briefly, so that they can try to picture how the business can succeed. Examples could include:

- 'Chocolate': a chain of High Street outlets offering varieties of hot chocolate, chocolate shakes, chocolate ice creams and chocolate bars; mainly takeaway but with bar stools for eating in; start with one outlet, build to four or five and then use franchising for further growth.
- 'Eggxactly': patent-protected waterless cookers for the perfect 'boiled' egg, selling for around £30. Start by manufacturing in Britain and selling direct on the internet; once the business has built up, distribute more product to retailers, moving production to China when sales volumes are high enough.

A good business model must have the potential to become profitable and – for venture capital investors – have significant growth prospects.

Developing the business model into a working document

The business plan should develop the business model into a working document. It should show what needs to be done, by when and at what cost. A strong business plan will not necessarily be very long, but it will cover all the key aspects of the specific business being looked at. For example, a business plan for Eggxactly will need to set out the following.

- The track record of the manufacture chosen to supply the products; whether there is a back-up company in case of supply problems.
- The relationship between internet orders and supply. Will there be a big warehouse of stock or will each item be produced, packed and posted per order?
- The supply cost per machine. What gross profit will that generate compared with the £30 selling price?
- The method used to attract customers to the website. If a marketing campaign is needed, how big is the budget and how will it be spent?
- How a Chinese supplier will be selected and monitored. Will there be an Eggxactly employee in China permanently to carry out quality checks?

These and many other issues must be tackled fully. If an important aspect of the business seems poorly thought through, investors may look elsewhere.

11.5 WHY START-UPS CAN BE RISKY

The future is uncertain therefore every business decision is risky. Latest research shows that only one in seven new products is successful. And these products are the high-profile ones from companies such as L'Oreal or Cadbury, launched in a blaze of publicity. Table 11.1 shows how old the Cadbury product portfolio is. Between these years of success there have been countless new product flops, most of which are now forgotten. So, if big companies with big market research and advertising budgets struggle, how can a small business start-up be anything other than risky?

The risks come from many directions; all are based on uncertainty. A small business cannot know how high or low sales will be; nor can it know for certain what all its costs will be. Hiring staff may prove far harder than expected, and keeping good staff may be the hardest thing of all. The big risk at the start is that teething troubles may hit the cash position of the business, forcing it to close. Figure 11.1 shows what might happen to a restaurant with a set-up cost of £140,000 that has fewer customers than forecast in its first year. Instead of making profits in the months after opening, it is losing money. Its bank could close it down at any time after month 6.

Table 11.1 Cadbury brands – successes and flops

Cadbury's big-sellers		Cadbury's flops	
Brand	**Launch date**	**Brand**	**Launch date**
Cadbury's Dairy Milk	1905	Cadbury Strollers	1995
Cadbury's Milk Tray	1915	Fuse Bar	1996
Cadbury's Flake	1920	Cadbury's Marble	1998
Crunchie Bar	1929	Cadbury Spira	1999
Cadbury's Fudge	1949	Cadbury's Brunch bar	2001
Cadbury's Creme Egg	1971	Dream with Strawberries	2004
Double Decker	1976	Double Decker with Nuts	2005
Cadbury's Heroes	1999	Melts	2006
Cadbury's Wispa (relaunch)	2009		

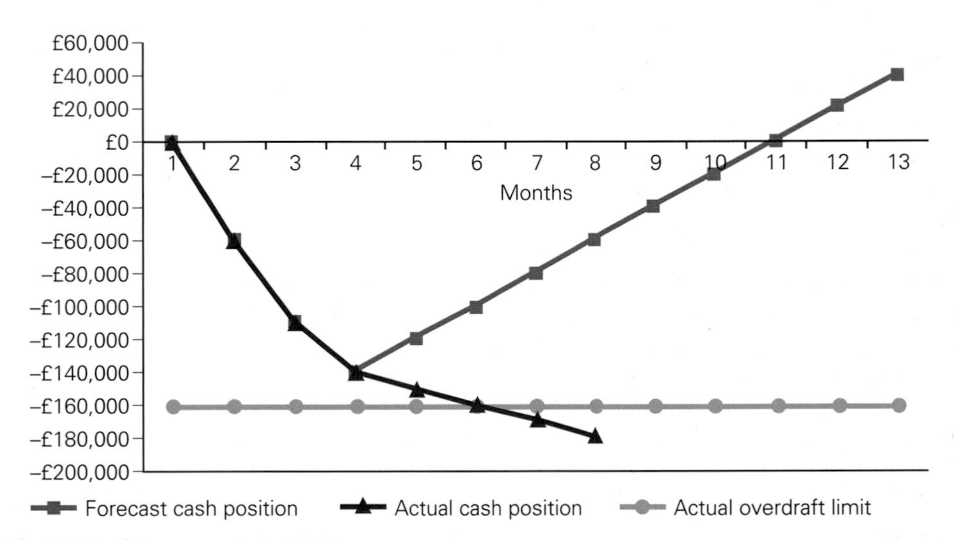

Figure 11.1 Cash flow crisis for a new restaurant

11.6 WHY START-UPS MAY FAIL

There are three main types of reason for start-up failure:

- poor analysis of the market (that is, the opportunity did not exist)
- right idea, but poor execution of the plan (that is, put into practice badly)
- right idea, but bad luck (for example, fierce competitor opens nearby or something unexpected happens)

Poor market analysis

China Fang opened in Cheshire in 2009. Its location was on a busy main road in a beautiful corner building. There was a side-road for parking and enough room for a kitchen and a restaurant seating 40 people. It opened to good customer numbers as local residents were curious to try it. There were no other restaurants nearby, just a pizza takeaway. Early customers were very pleased with the quality of the food and service, though they found the prices 'a little high'. All seemed well set, but after a month or two customer numbers steadily fell away. The problem was that locals preferred to go into the town centre, where there was a 'bit of a buzz' in the evenings. A visit to China Fang was too low-key and quiet. It was a good restaurant in the wrong location. The restaurant closed in early 2011.

Right idea, wrong execution

A good business idea might be poorly carried out. There are an enormous number of mistakes that can be made, including the following.

- Poor staff recruitment and/or training and/or supervision: staff may enjoy joking with each other in a way that irritates or insults customers.
- Faulty purchasing: a young entrepreneur may set up a stylish clothes shop but prove poor at selecting

and buying stock from suppliers such as the fashion houses (that is, right shop but wrong stock).

- Too desperate: any business needs to establish itself and the process is hard to rush; over-hasty 'Buy One Drink Get One Free' offers can make a bar busy without building brand loyalty; when another bar makes a better promotional offer, the customers desert the first one.
- Failure to control cash flow: the business operation may be going well, but if the finances are poorly managed, the bank may close down a business with a great future.

Right idea, bad luck

You may produce a well-considered plan for a new cinema in a town that does not have one. You spend £15,000 on the research into whether this would be a worthwhile project and you are sure it is 'a winner'. Then, just as you sign the papers to buy a good site, you hear that someone has the same idea, but is a month ahead of you. You could carry on and fight it out, or pull out altogether; either way you have been unlucky. The worst outcome would be to carry on the fight but end up with a failed business.

An entrepreneur should respond to bad luck with undimmed confidence and the determination to try again. Unfortunately, it may not be that easy. Established hoteliers Barry Hancox and Andrew Riley opened Russell's – a restaurant and hotel – in Worcestershire, having borrowed 80 per cent of the £1.5 million set-up costs from the bank. An entrepreneur with a business start-up failure to his or her name would not have the opportunity to borrow so much. Worse still, losses made from one failure – however unlucky – make it harder to find the personal capital to start again.

A-grade application

In September 2010 German property company ACI Real Estate filed for bankruptcy for four of its seven property developments in Dubai. Investors who had put in $75 million in 2004 stood to lose everything. In 2004 the Dubai growth story seemed endless, backed by the fabulous oil wealth of the United Arab Emirates. Newspapers daily featured the property purchases by stars such as Tiger Woods and Michael Owen. Unfortunately, before the four property developments were ready, the 2008–09 recession hit Dubai. Property prices fell by 50 to 60 per cent in 18 months. Was this bad luck or bad judgement?

Key Terms

Business model: the precise way in which profit will be generated from a specific business idea.

Floated: making a public company's shares widely available for purchase on the stock market.

Social entrepreneurs: strictly speaking, this should mean people who start up an organisation in pursuit of purely social objectives; but some profit-seekers dress themselves in social or environmental clothing.

ISSUES FOR ANALYSIS

When tackling the issue of business start-up in an exam, bear the following in mind.

- Awareness of risk and potential failure is a thoroughly good thing; fear of failure could easily become a serious problem; the good entrepreneur tries to anticipate possible problems and allow for them in the cash flow forecast – but does not treat possible problems as impossible hurdles.
- Therefore a good business plan will be based on realistic objectives and will allow for real life proving tougher than expected; every new business should press for a generous overdraft limit from the bank – to give a satisfactory cushion in the event of experiencing difficulties.
- Despite the risks, the personal and financial rewards from entrepreneurship can be massive. How else would a fan on the terraces be able eventually to buy Newcastle United? A Saturday Lottery win would not usually provide a sufficient gain to buy a player!

11.7 ASSESSING BUSINESS START-UPS – AN EVALUATION

Every new business is unique, as each one depends upon the personality, character and motives of the founder, plus the specific market, competitive and economic context. Timing is another vital factor, in which luck plays a particularly important part. An ice cream parlour opening in May one year may be blessed with a hot summer; opening the following year may be cursed with rain and gloom.

It is because of these factors that it is hard to be sure whether a business plan will succeed or not. Whenever assessing a business start-up, it is very unwise to sound too certain about whether it will succeed or fail.

WORKBOOK

A REVISION QUESTIONS

(20 marks; 20 minutes)

1 Identify two entrepreneurial qualities shown by Duncan Goose. (2)
2 Explain in your own words why it is wise to have doubts about some of the businesses that call themselves 'social enterprises'. (4)
3 Outline two ways to assess whether a business start-up has been a success. (4)
4 Explain why potential investors would want to hear about the business model before reading a business plan. (4)
5 Outline two possible reasons why an established firm such as Cadbury can achieve no better than a 1 in 7 success rate when launching new products. (4)
6 Look at Figure 11.1. If the entrepreneur had thought hard about the risks of starting a new restaurant, how might she or he have done things differently? Identify two points. (2)

B REVISION EXERCISES

B1 DATA RESPONSE

In 2005 Michael Birch started up a social networking site, Bebo, that became the British rival to Facebook. In 2008 he sold Bebo to AOL for an astonishing $850 million. Still in his 30s, he never had to work again. Yet far from making him relax, within nine months he was undergoing open heart surgery. After recovering, he began to look for new online enterprises to start up or to invest in.

In 2005 Birch had seen the opportunity for a broad social networking site, but now the space is taken entirely by Facebook. So he is looking at a niche market: 'Jolitics', which is a sophisticated social networking site for people who are interested in or active in politics. This is planned to open in early 2011.

A June 2010 *Financial Times* article reported him as saying: 'I don't understand why you wouldn't want to set up a new start-up. Not many entrepreneurs really want to retire. You don't start up a company to sell it and make money. There is a great satisfaction in achieving something'.

Birch is open about the importance of risk-taking and of making mistakes. He says that his own success-rate has been 50–50, with three start-up flops and three successes. He agrees with the widespread view that Britain is tougher on 'failures' than America. There, a start-up failure is a badge of honour. In Britain people see a business failure as a personal failure. Birch believes that real entrepreneurs see a business flop as something to be learnt from.

Questions

(30 marks; 35 minutes)

1 Explain why an entrepreneur could benefit from involvement in a failed start-up. (6)
2 Facebook is the mass-market social networking site.
   a) Outline the case for and the case against a niche site such as 'Jolitics'. (6)
   b) Do you think 'Jolitics' could be a business success? Justify your view. (8)
3 Discuss whether entrepreneurs are looking for 'satisfaction in achieving something' or planning to become very rich. (10)

B.2 DATA RESPONSE

Glasses Direct

In 2004 22-year-old Jamie Murray-Wells used the last of his student loan to start a business: Glasses Direct. Puzzled that two pieces of glass and some plastic frames could cost £250 in a high street optician, Jamie researched the industry with care. When he approached manufacturers, he was greeted with suspicion; they worried that he might jeopardise their profits. But eventually he persuaded them to supply him. In September 2004 he started selling pairs of glasses over the internet for £15 a pair. Although he had no money for advertising, journalists were keen to write about his story, so he had terrific free public relations (PR). In the first year he sold 22,000 pairs, generating revenues of more than £300,000. By 2006 sales were heading towards £3 million, helped by a growing reputation for great customer service from the 17 staff.

From the start Jamie made it clear that he wanted to 'Get very big very fast'. He realised that this would require outside finance. Since 2004 his family had helped provide the capital to grow; now it was time for serious investment by a venture capital fund. It took until July 2007 to achieve the right package. Two venture capital companies invested £2.9 million with the intention of using the capital on marketing, in order to make Glasses Direct a household name. It is not clear what percentage of the shares have been retained by Jamie and his family, but it is believed to be around 50 per cent. In 2009 Jamie suggested that his aim was to make the business a £1 billion company.

Questions

(25 marks; 25 minutes)

1 a) Identify the business objective at Glasses Direct. (1)
   b) Explain why this objective may have helped encourage staff to provide 'great customer service'. (5)
2 Look at the six personal objectives within Section 11.2. Outline which one of them you believe was most important for Jamie when starting Glasses Direct. (5)
3 Glasses Direct seems to have enjoyed a relatively untroubled start-up. Outline two risks that the company faced, even though things turned out well. (6)
4 As Glasses Direct was growing satisfactorily, discuss whether Jamie was right to sell around 50 per cent of the shares in exchange for the £2.9 million of fresh capital. (8)

Introduction to finance

UNIT 12

Finance has two main aspects: it can provide the numbers that help managers to make better decisions, and it can count what is happening and what has happened. Here the focus is on finance for decision making.

12.1 THE FINANCIAL BASICS

Of the 60 per cent of new restaurants that close within three years, almost all die because the business has run out of cash. As the crisis point starts to draw near, the staff will notice irate suppliers 'dropping by' to demand payment. Key supplies may not arrive, as the suppliers get increasingly tough about payment. So it is crucial to keep cash spending under tight control.

The main underlying problem is that people get starry-eyed about the process of business start-up. They start to believe their own publicity, and assume that their restaurant is going to be 'hot' from day one, or their nightclub is going to be 'cool'. The consequence of this is that too much of the start-up capital is tied up in fixed assets such as interior design and equipment. Far too little is left for the day-to-day running of the business: the working capital.

The problem is an obvious one. To be an entrepreneur you have to be an optimist; but optimists do not look for the downside. They expect business to be fantastic from week one, ignoring the evidence that most businesses find it hard to establish a loyal base of customers at the start. For most new businesses it is wise to set aside half the start-up capital as working capital. That will be the money used in the early weeks of operation, to pay the wages, pay the rent and pay upfront when suspicious suppliers demand to be paid with cash, not credit. Once the weekly takings are high enough, the money coming in will pay for all the costs that have to be paid out, but that may take time.

Look at Table 12.1; among small business start-ups in south London, this shows how long it took until weekly cash in started to exceed weekly cash outflows.

12.2 WORKING CAPITAL

The key is to keep on top of the working capital. The top priority is to keep an everyday check on costs, credit transactions and cash payments. This can be hard if you have several people working for you. Each could expect to be given the authority to make a decision, such as to buy a pizza oven from supplier X rather than supplier Y. But if lots of people are spending your money, it will be virtually impossible to keep track of everything.

New entrepreneurs often choose one person to be the 'moneybags', the person with sole control over spending. Clever entrepreneurs make sure to give the job to someone else. Then even the business owner has to work at justifying why exactly he wants gold washbasin taps instead of ordinary ones, or brand new kitchen equipment instead of second-hand.

In addition to keeping a check on a firm's day-to-day finance – its working capital – managers need to:

- identify the costs involved in making a product; this can be the first step in deciding the selling price
- work out how many products they need to sell to make a profit
- find out how much capital they will need in the coming months, and then decide on the best way to obtain this extra finance

Table 12.1 Small business start-ups in south London: weeks until cash drain ceased

Type of business	Location	Weeks until cash drain ceased
Barber	Near tube station	26 (i.e. 6 months)
Pizza restaurant	Residential area	10 weeks
Sports trophy shop	Local shopping street	156 (i.e. 3 years) (that was 15 years ago, so it was worth it)
Sweet shop	High street	6 weeks

- keep tight control over the way in which the firm's money is spent.

12.3 KEY FINANCIAL CONCERNS FOR NEW BUSINESS START-UPS

The starting point is to work out the following three things.

1 How much it will cost to get from a business idea to opening its doors on the first day (the start-up costs). For a new clothes shop, this will include a huge range of items (see the A-grade application) and could reach a figure such as £40,000.

2 How much the running costs will be (the costs week by week when the business is operating fully). These will come in two parts: the costs that will be fixed, no matter whether the business is going well or badly, such as the rent, heating and lighting and staff salaries; in addition, there will be costs that vary in line with sales, such as the cost of purchasing the items you are selling (the dress sold for £40 may cost you £20 to buy from the dress designer). Every entrepreneur needs a solid understanding of the firm's fixed costs and variable costs. (Fuller coverage of this topic is provided in Unit 13.)

3 How much revenue can you expect from the customers you serve? Broadly this is a simple calculation of customers served multiplied by the amount they spend. Although the calculation is simple, it is very hard to anticipate what the figures will be. In August 2010 there were rumours that Microsoft was starting to research the Xbox 720, to be launched in 2014/2015. So many years in advance, who could know the likely selling price or how many would be sold? Market research could help in making a sales forecast, but as only one in seven new products proves a success, six out of every seven new products must come with an incorrect sales forecast (no one would launch a new product that was forecast to flop, so presumably there was a faulty forecast). For new small businesses the problem is always the same: how can we forecast the number of loyal customers we can expect? This issue is tackled in Unit 63.

Figure 12.1 A new business

A-grade application

A costly start-up

Raza and Sujagan opened a new grocery shop on a busy Wimbledon road last December. It was an unusually big shop, as they were buying a lease from a furniture business that had closed down. The four-year lease cost £25,000 to purchase, and there were additional monthly payments of £1,500. The fixtures and fittings (fridges, shelving, lighting, and so on) cost £32,000, and building and decorating added a further £9,000. Two tills plus a scanning system and a CCTV security system added a further £8,000. Because the shop floor space was so big, stocking the shop was very expensive, requiring a further investment of £28,000.

Once it was operating fully, it proved to be that, on average, for every £1 taken through the till, 72p had to be paid to suppliers. In other words, they were making a profit of 28p in the pound (though that is before paying the monthly bills). Those monthly bills, including the £1,500 to the landlord, came to £4,800.

Wretchedly, in early January as Raza opened the shop at 6 o'clock one morning, a bulldozer was their first warning that a 20-week roadworks operation was to start right outside the shop. By mid-February, the shop was still taking nowhere near the amount needed to pay the £4,800 of monthly fixed costs, let alone provide some profit.

Having worked out these things, a business can use them in different ways.

- To calculate the profit level that can be expected: it is wise to do this at three different sales levels, based on what you believe to be the worst case (for example, only ten customers a day), the best case (fully booked at 50 a day) and a midway point (such as 30 a day); this is wiser than simply looking at one forecast sales level.
- To estimate the cash inflows and outflows (that is to work out, month by month, what the firm's bank balance will look like in the future): this might identify, for example, that a new toy shop's cash position in early autumn looks very bleak, as lots of money is paid out on stock, but cash is not yet coming in from Christmas shoppers. Careful forecasting of cash flows can identify problems such as this, and enable the business to make the necessary arrangements (for example a temporary bank overdraft). Cash flow is covered in Unit 15.
- To estimate how much finance the business needs to raise.

12.4 RAISING FINANCE

When a business is operating fully and successfully, cash coming in from customers will provide all the finance necessary for effective operation. Until then, raising finance is an important issue, especially for young entrepreneurs with little personal capital. Table 12.2 lists the sources of finance available to firms.

Table 12.2 Sources of business finance

Short term (under 1 year)	
Bank overdraft	Allowing the firm's bank account to go into the red up to an agreed limit Flexible and easy to arrange but interest charges are high
Trade credit	Suppliers agree to accept cash payment at a given date in the future Failure to pay on time can present problems for future orders
Medium term (2–4 years)	
Bank term loan	Banks lend sums of capital, often at a fixed rate of interest, to be repaid over a fixed period Makes financial planning easy but interest rates can be high, particularly for small firms
Leasing	Firms sign a contract to pay a rental fee to the owner of an asset in return for the use of that asset over a period of two to four years (usually) Expensive, but avoids large cash outflows when buying new assets
Long term (5+ years)	
Owners' savings	Most small businesses are set up with the owners' savings They are 'interest free' but will be lost if the business fails Banks will not provide a loan or overdraft unless the owners are sharing the financial risk
Sale of shares	Private and public limited companies can sell shares in the ownership of the company In return, shareholders gain a say in how the firm is run, and are entitled to a share of profits
Reinvested profits	Profits are the most important source of long-term finance This form of finance is good because there are no interest payments to be made
Venture capital loans	These specialist providers of risk capital can provide large sums The finance is usually partly loan capital and partly share capital
Government loans	Although much paperwork is involved and only some firms are eligible, national government and the EU do offer grants and loans for firms Less than 3 per cent of business finance stems from this source

A-grade application

Financing Facebook

Facebook was started in February 2004 by college student Mark Zuckerberg. That summer he was introduced to a wealthy co-founder of PayPal, who invested $500,000 in establishing Facebook as a limited company. Within a month Zuckerberg was offered $10 million for the business, but turned it down. Two years later, in 2006, Yahoo offered $1,000 million, but was also rejected!

In Facebook's early years, there was no doubting the growth in users, but lots of doubt about how to turn users into cash. Fortunately for Zuckerberg, people kept investing. A big break came in 2007 when Microsoft handed over $240 million for just 1.6 per cent of the share capital. This valued Facebook at an amazing $15 billion.

By late 2010 Facebook had more than 500 million users worldwide and had a total of $830 million of capital investment from many different venture capital businesses. Zuckerberg's share stake is unknown, but assumed to be enough to keep him in full control. When and if Facebook floats as a public company, the young founder will be a multi-billionaire.

ISSUES FOR ANALYSIS

- The difference between cash and profit can lead to excellent analytical comment. Without cash, bills go unpaid and stocks are not bought. So it is possible for profitable firms to run out of cash and go out of business. In examinations, many students treat cash flow and profit as if they are the same thing. Distinguishing clearly between the two is a helpful starting point for strong analysis of a financial issue. This is covered fully in Unit 19.
- It is also important to place any financial question firmly in the context of the business. Are its founders novice investors or experienced and well advised? Is it largely dependent on just one product or customer? Is its marketplace fast-moving and fiercely competitive?

12.5 INTRODUCTION TO FINANCE – AN EVALUATION

Reliability is a key issue when looking at any financial statement. Management accounts, such as cash flow forecasts, are predictions. In other words, they are not statements of fact but educated guesses. This means that they should be used only as a guideline. Questions need to be asked, such as who drew up the figures and do they have an interest in making the accounts point in a particular direction? For example, have forecasts been produced to try to persuade outsiders to invest, or are they produced by managers for their own use? In the first case, it may be that the desire to squeeze finance out of a bank or venture capital firm encourages an excessively optimistic set of forecasts.

A second key point to remember is how finance fits into the big picture of Business Studies. Feel the weight of this book. There are several units dedicated to finance, but many more covering other areas of business activity. Accounts are good at dealing with financial, quantitative information, but qualitative factors may be more important, such as whether the business is building strong customer loyalty. Today's high sales may collapse tomorrow if they are based only on special offers, not on customer loyalty.

Key Terms

Fixed costs: those that do not change as the number of sales change (for example, rent or salaries).

Variable costs: those that change in line with the amount of business (for example, the cost of buying raw materials).

Working capital: the finance available for the day-to-day running of the business.

WORKBOOK

A REVISION QUESTIONS

(25 marks; 25 minutes)

1 Outline two possible reasons why a newly started restaurant could run out of cash. (4)

2 Explain what is meant by working capital. (3)

3 Give two examples of situations in which a small bakery business could use the following sources of finance:
 a) short-term
 b) medium-term
 c) long-term. (6)

4 Reread the A-grade application 'A costly start-up'.
 a) Calculate the founders' total start-up costs. (2)
 b) Outline one factor that may have made the business struggle, even without the bad luck of the roadworks. (3)

5 Explain one advantage and one disadvantage to a firm of having large sums of cash for a long period of time. (6)

B REVISION EXERCISES
B1 DATA RESPONSE

Starting up Moneysupermarket.com

Moneysupermarket.com was started in 1999 by 32-year-old Simon Nixon. The site was designed to provide people with up-to-date, easy-to-compare information on, for example, the interest charges on different credit cards. The start-up costs were 'around £100,000', all of which came from the sale of an earlier online business. Nixon's earlier experience made sure that he pursued a 'no frills' policy to his start-up, focusing most of the start-up capital on public relations (PR). He employed a City of London PR firm that ensured it contacted financial journalists regularly. The journalists came to use the site as an easy source of data, referencing all their articles to 'Source: Moneysupermarket.com'. Spreading the name in this way encouraged increasing usage by ordinary customers, providing a hit rate of 50,000 customers a month by the end of its first year.

Nixon built the business up steadily, launching Travelsupermarket.com in 2004. By 2006, he could for the first time afford to run a TV advertising campaign. Since then, the firm's spending on TV has escalated hugely, as it brought huge additional numbers of customers and income. In the first half of 2007, visitors to the group's websites rose by 58 per cent, helping sales revenue to rise from £48 million to £78 million. So although the advertising spending rose from £2.7 million to £9.8 million between 2006 and 2007, overall operating profits went up by £14 million.

Although Nixon managed to build the business largely through internal finance (reinvested profit), by 2007 he decided to sell up by floating the shares on the London stock market. On 31 July 2007, shares in Moneysupermarket.com were floated at 170p. This netted Nixon over £100 million in cash, though he still retains over 50 per cent of the shares in the business he started. That seemed to provide the cash to be able to finance a growth future, not only in Britain but overseas. Unfortunately for Nixon, recession plus ferocious competition halved the value of the shares by 2010. Moneysupermarket has had to focus on survival, not growth.

Questions

(25 marks; 30 minutes)

1 Explain why Simon Nixon was able to limit the start-up costs of Moneysupermarket.com to £100,000. (3)
2 Outline two ways in which Nixon might have been helped in the Moneysupermarket.com story by the fact that he could finance the whole thing without outside sources of finance. (4)
3 **a)** Calculate the percentage increase in sales revenue between the first half of 2006 and the first half of 2007. (3)
b) Consider what factors may have led to this sales increase. (6)
4 In 2007 Nixon became fabulously rich. Discuss whether the entrepreneurial skills he showed justified becoming that rich. (9)

UNIT 13

Calculating revenue, costs and profit

Revenue is the value of total sales made by a business within a period, usually one year. Costs are the expenses incurred by a firm in producing and selling its products. This is likely to include expenditure upon wages and raw materials. Profit is the difference which arises when a firm's sales revenue exceeds its total costs.

13.1 BUSINESS REVENUES

The revenue or income received by a firm as a result of trading activities is a critical factor in its success. When starting up, businesses may expect relatively low revenues for several reasons:

- their product is not well known
- they are unlikely to be able to produce large quantities of output
- it is difficult to charge a high price for a product which is not established on the market.

Entrepreneurs start their financial planning by assessing the income or revenue that they are likely to receive during the coming financial year. Businesses calculate their revenue through use of the following formula:

Sales revenue = volume of goods sold × average selling price

You can see that there are two key elements which comprise sales revenue: the quantity of goods that are sold and the prices at which they are sold. A firm seeking to increase its revenue can plan to sell more or aim to sell at a higher price. Some firms may maintain high prices even though this policy depresses sales. Such companies, often selling fashion and high-technology products, believe that this approach results in higher revenue and ultimately higher profits.

To sustain high revenues from relatively few sales, a business has to be confident that consumers will be willing to pay a high price for the product and that direct competition will not appear – at least in the short term. This is only possible if the start-up business has a product or service that is really special and different, unique even. An additional advantage of a low output strategy is that it keeps down the cost of producing the goods or services; this is important in the early stages of running an enterprise.

A-grade application

Farmers operate lost cost system

Trials at Harper Adams University College have established new, lower cost methods of looking after cattle over the winter months. The trials revealed that leaving young cattle in the field over the winter months (out-wintering), feeding on root crops such as turnips can cut costs by almost 50 per cent when compared with keeping them indoors. Cattle kept indoors gained the same amount of weight as those kept outdoors but cost more in feed and labour.

Harper Adams researcher Simon Marsh said that fixed and variable costs were cut by 48 per cent using the out-wintering system.

Looking after cattle during the winter months is expensive partly due to the high cost of animal feed. Any system that can reduce costs by such a figure (and thereby boost profits) is likely to be of interest to farmers at a time of rising costs.

Figure 13.1 Leaving cattle outside in winter

Source: Adapted from *Farmers Guardian*, April 2009

The other way to boost revenue is to charge a low price in an attempt to sell as many products as possible. In some markets this may lead to high revenues and profits. Firms following this approach are likely to be operating in markets in which the goods are fairly similar and consumers do not exhibit strong preferences for any brand. This is true of the market for young holidaymakers in Spain or Thailand. Price competition is fierce as businesses seek to maximise their sales and revenue.

Some businesses adopt a revenue-orientated approach for different reasons. If the company experiences circumstances where few of its costs vary with the level of its output then it will seek to maximise revenue. Because its costs are not sensitive to the level of its sales, then maximising sales will result in maximum profits. This is the position for the operators of both theme parks and football clubs. Whereas making and selling a Mercedes creates revenue but also a lot of costs, the theme park's costs are largely fixed. Attracting extra customers on a day adds few costs. Similarly, football clubs have the same costs whether their stadium is full or half empty. So when playing a less attractive team, many Premier League teams set children's ticket prices as low as £5. Alternative ways to maximise revenue are shown in Figure 13.2.

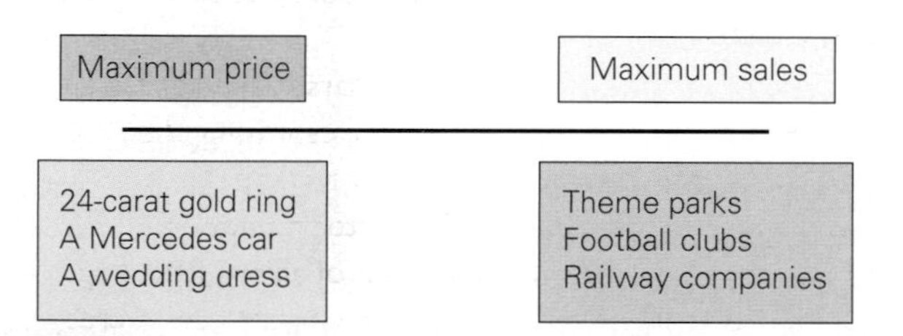

Figure 13.2 Alternative ways to maximise revenue

The new venture

In September 2010 Hotel Verta was opened, as Europe's first hotel built alongside a heliport. Situated on London's South Bank, the 5 star hotel has little competition nearby, either for the hotel rooms or for luxury dining. Every year there are 6,000 helicopter landings at the site, including Madonna and former US President Clinton. The hotel has 70 rooms, but the general manager is hoping that half the income will come from food and drink sales. There is also scope for revenue to be generated from hosting business meetings and celebrity press conferences.

You will have realised from the analysis so far that price, cost and volume are all important elements of a firm's planning and success. Each of these factors affects the others and all of them together determine the profitability of a business.

If a business cannot control its costs, then it will be unable to sell its products at a low price. In turn this will mean a low sales volume. This will mean that overhead costs such as the rent of a factory will be spread over a low output, causing further pressure on costs of production.

It is to the costs of production that we now turn our attention.

13.2 THE COSTS OF PRODUCTION

Costs are a critical element of the information necessary to manage a business successfully. Managers need to be aware of the costs of all aspects of their business for a number of reasons.

- They need to know the cost of production to assess whether it is profitable to supply the market at the current price.
- They need to know actual costs to allow comparisons with their forecasted (or budgeted) costs of production. This will allow them to make judgements concerning the cost-efficiency of various parts of the business.

Fixed and variable costs

This is an important classification of the costs encountered by businesses. This classification has a number of uses. For example, it is the basis of calculating break-even, which is covered in a later unit.

Fixed costs

Fixed costs are any costs that do not vary directly with the level of output. These costs are linked to time rather than to level of business activity. Fixed costs exist even if a business is not producing any goods or services. An example of a fixed cost is rent, which can be calculated monthly or annually, but will not vary irrespective of whether the office or factory is used

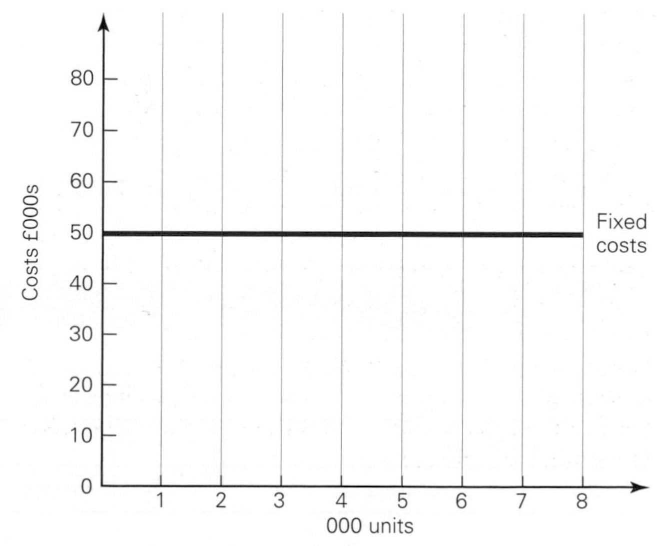

Figure 13.3 Fixed costs of £50,000

intensively to produce goods or services or is hardly utilised at all.

If a manufacturer can double output from within the same factory, the amount of rent will not alter, thus it is a fixed cost. In the same way, a seaside hotel has mortgage and salary costs during the winter, even though they may have very few guests. Given that fixed costs are inevitable, it is vital that managers work hard at bringing in customers to keep the fixed costs covered.

In Figure 13.3, you can see that the firm faces fixed costs of £50,000 irrespective of the level of output. How much would the fixed costs per unit of production be if production were (a) 1,000 units a year and (b) 8,000 units a year? What could be the implications of this distinction for the managers of the business?

Other examples of fixed costs include the uniform business rate, management salaries, interest charges and depreciation.

In the long term, fixed costs can alter. The manufacturer referred to earlier may decide to increase output significantly. This may require renting additional factory space and negotiating loans for additional capital equipment. Thus rent will rise as may interest payments. We can see that in the long term fixed costs may alter, but that in the short term they are – as their name suggests – fixed.

Variable costs

Variable costs are those costs which vary directly with the level of output. They represent payments made for the use of inputs such as labour, fuel and raw materials. If our manufacturer doubled output then these costs would double. A doubling of the sales of Innocent Strawberry Smoothies would require twice the purchasing of strawberries and bananas. There would also be extra costs for the packaging, the wage bill and the energy required to fuel the production line.

The graph in Figure 13.4 shows a firm with variable costs of £8 per unit of production. This means that variable costs rise steadily with, and proportionately to, the level of output. Thus a 10 per cent rise in output will increase total variable costs by the same percentage.

However, it is not always the case that variable costs rise in proportion to output. Many small businesses discover that as they expand, variable costs do not rise as quickly as output. A key reason for this is that as the business becomes larger it is able to negotiate better prices with suppliers. Its suppliers are likely to agree to sell at lower unit prices when the business places larger orders.

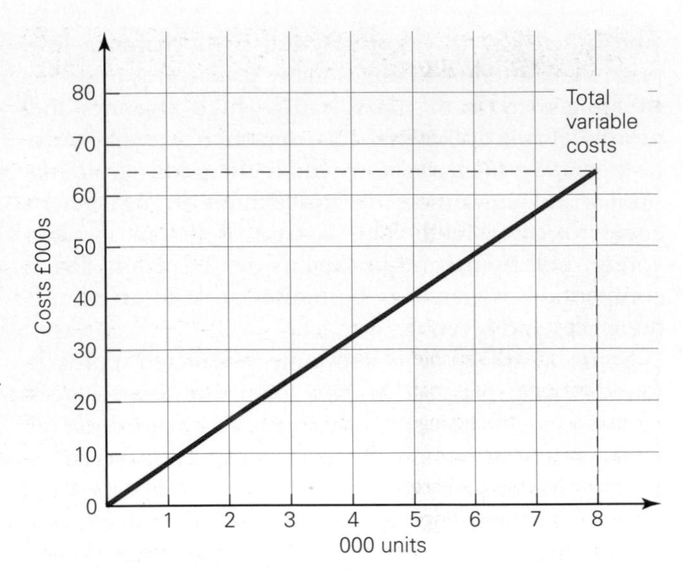

Figure 13.4 Variable costs of £8 per unit

Examples of some variable, fixed and hard-to-classify costs are given in Table 13.1.

Total costs

When added together, fixed and variable costs give the total costs for a business. This is, of course, a very important element in the calculation of the profits earned by a business.

The relationship between fixed, variable and total costs is straightforward to calculate but has some important implications for a business. If a business has relatively high fixed costs as a proportion of total costs, then it is likely to seek to maximise its sales to ensure that the fixed costs are spread across as many units of output as possible. In this way, the impact of high fixed costs is lessened. For small businesses, it is often variable costs that are high, for example high food costs at a restaurant. This may make them push their prices up to a level that makes customers reluctant to come regularly. This can be the start of a slippery slope downwards for the business.

Table 13.1 Some costs are easy to classify, some are hard

Variable costs	Fixed costs	Hard to classify
• Raw materials	• Rent	• Delivery costs
• Packaging	• Heating and lighting	• Electricity
• Piece-rate labour	• Salaries	• Machine maintenance costs
• Commission (percentage on sales)	• Interest charges	• Energy

A-grade application

Paying the costs

In 2010 Scoop opened its second London ice cream parlour. The company intended to continue making all the ice cream at the original Covent Garden store, but deliver ice cream daily to the new branch near Piccadilly Circus (one mile away). This meant that all the fixed production costs would remain unchanged (rent on the floor space, the machinery and the professional ice cream maker's salary). Variable costs would double, as long as the new parlour's sales matched the Covent Garden one. These costs would be the ingredients, especially milk, cream and sugar; plus the cost of the electricity to run the ice cream-making machines. There would also be some brand new fixed costs: the refridgerated van plus the rent and the staff at the new premises. Overall, owner Matteo Pantani knew that he could increase his revenue by 100 per cent while total costs increase by 75 to 80 per cent. This should boost profit considerably.

13.3 PROFITS

Having considered revenues and costs it is now appropriate to focus upon a prime motive for businesses: profits. Profit is a comparison of revenues and costs. This comparison determines whether or not an enterprise makes any profit. As we saw at the beginning of this unit the key formula is:

Profit = total revenue − total costs

However, it is worth remembering that some businesses are not established with the objective of making profits. Not-for-profit businesses, also known as social enterprises, operate with other objectives. For example, Katie Alcott from Bristol received an entrepreneurship award in 2007 for her social enterprise 'Frank Water'. Katie's business sells bottled spring water in the UK, and uses the proceeds to provide clean, safe water for villages in India and Africa. Her aim is to support others, not to make a profit.

Calculating profits

Although the profit formula is simple (revenue − costs), it is easy to make mistakes when calculating the figures. The problems rarely come from calculating revenue; the hard part is getting total costs right. The following example may help:

The types of profit

Although profit is always revenue minus costs, there are different profit figures which are used. Managers frequently refer to operating profit. This is the amount remaining once all fixed and variable costs have been deducted from total revenue, but before tax has been paid.

Perhaps a more important measure is profit after tax since this is the profit which the business can decide how to allocate. The most important uses to which these profits can be put are:

- payments to the owners of the business, to partners or to shareholders in the form of dividends
- reinvestment into the business to purchase capital items such as property and machinery.

A-grade application

Shopfitting company to cut costs

Employees at the shopfitting firm Havelock Europa have been warned that the company will have to cut costs due to a 'dire' trading year in 2009. The company, which employs 800 people mainly in Scotland, recorded a £5.9 million loss in 2009 compared with a profit of £7 million in 2008.

David Hurcomb, Havelock Europa's acting chief executive, said that the plan was to increase sales (and therefore revenue) as well as cutting costs and that success in finding new business will shape the extent of cost cutting. The company has not said how many jobs are at risk and David Hurcomb commented 'The focus is on every cost in the business, including warehousing, transport and suppliers'.

Source: adapted from BBC News, June 2010

Gwen and John's pasta restaurant charges £10 for three courses and has an average of 800 customers per week. The variable costs are £4 per customer and the restaurant has fixed costs of £3,400 per week. To calculate profit:

1 Calculate revenue:
   Price × No. of customers
   £10 × 800 = £8,000
2 Calculate total costs:
   Fixed costs + Total variable costs
   (No. of customers × variable costs per meal)
   £3,400 + (800 × £4 = £3,200)
3 Calculate profit:
   Total revenue − Total costs
   £8,000 − (£3,400 + £3,200) = £1,400 per week

See the Workbook section for exercises to practise this very important skill.

13.4 THE IMPORTANCE OF PROFIT

Undeniably profits are important to the majority of businesses. Profits are usually assessed in relation to some yardstick, for example the amount invested or sales revenue. We will consider how to measure profits in relation to other variables in Unit 18.

Profits are important for the following reasons:

- They provide a measure of the success of a business (important for a new business)
- They are the best source of capital for investment in the growth of the business, for example to finance new store openings or to pay for new product development
- They act as a magnet to attract further funds from investors enticed by the possibility of high returns on their investment.

However, it is not uncommon for a new business to fail to make profits in the first months – or even years – of trading. The need to generate profits becomes more important as time passes. A business ultimately needs to make profits to reward its owners for putting money into the enterprise.

ISSUES FOR ANALYSIS

Forecasting costs and revenues can be tricky for an entrepreneur starting a new business. It is not possible to look back at trading records for guidance and therefore the likelihood of inaccuracy is greater. At this stage of a business's history all cost and revenue figures are forecasts and therefore not necessarily correct. It is possible that entrepreneurs will underestimate fixed and variable costs and overestimate revenues, thereby suggesting higher profits (or lower losses) than proves to be the case.

A key element with respect to the revenues earned by a business is the relationship between the price charged and the volume of sales achieved. Choosing the right price is an exercise requiring considerable judgement on the part of the entrepreneur. Simply raising price will not necessarily provide more revenue for a business. If a 10 per cent price rise causes customer numbers to fall by 15 per cent, the business will have lower revenues than it started with. Factors influencing consumers' decisions will include the quality of the products in question and how strong the competition is.

You may like to consider circumstances in which firms could earn higher revenue by raising prices, and when the opposite could be true. Do you think a firm could earn more revenue by *lowering* its price?

13.5 CALCULATING REVENUE, COSTS AND PROFITS – AN EVALUATION

One important issue for evaluation in relation to costs, revenues and profits for a new enterprise is to judge the likely accuracy of the forecast figures and the degree of reliance that can be placed upon them. This is an important judgement for a number of stakeholders who may have an interest in the new business. Investors will obviously look closely at any forecast figures before committing money to the enterprise, and suppliers will want to be assured of payment before agreeing to supply any raw materials.

It is also worth thinking about whether profits are the best measure of success for a new business. A successful first year of trading may see an enterprise gain a customer base and repeat orders by supplying at competitive costs. This may result in small profits initially while the business builds a reputation. Profits may become a more important measure of success in the longer term.

An assessment of the true worth of a business's performance as measured by its profits would also take account of the general state of the economy. Are businesses in general prospering, or is it a time of recession? They would also take into account any unusual circumstances such as, for example, the business being subject to the emergence of a new competitor.

Key Terms

Fixed costs: these costs do not vary as output (or sales) vary.

Piece-rate labour: paying workers per item they make, that is without regular pay.

Total costs: all the costs of producing a specific output level, that is fixed costs plus total variable costs.

Total variable costs: all the variable costs of producing a specific output level, that is variable costs per unit multiplied by the number of units sold.

Variable costs: the costs of producing one unit (can be known as unit variable costs).

WORKBOOK

A REVISION QUESTIONS

(27 marks; 25 minutes)

1 Why may a business initially receive relatively low revenues from a product newly introduced to the market? (3)
2 State two circumstances in which a company may be able to charge high prices for a new product. (2)
3 For what reasons may a firm seek to maximise its sales revenue? (3)
4 If a business sells 4,000 units of Brand X at £4 each and 2,000 units of Brand Y at £3 each, what is its total revenue? (4)
5 State two reasons why firms have to know the costs they incur in production. (2)
6 Distinguish, with the aid of examples, between fixed and variable costs. (4)
7 Explain why fixed costs can only alter in the long term. (3)
8 Give two reasons why profits are important to businesses. (2)
9 State one advantage and one disadvantage that may result from a business deciding to lower the proportion of profits it distributes to its owners. (2)
10 State two purposes for which a business's profits could be used. (2)

B REVISION EXERCISES
B1 CALCULATION PRACTICE

(30 marks; 25 minutes)

1 During the summer weeks Devon Ice Cream has average sales of 4,000 units a week. Each ice cream sells for £1 and has variable costs of 25p. Fixed costs are £800.
   a) Calculate the total costs for the business in the summer weeks. (3)
   b) Calculate Devon Ice Cream's weekly profit in the summer. (3)
2 a) If a firm sells 200 Widgets at £3.20 and 40 Squidgets at £4, what is its total revenue? (3)
   b) Each Widget costs £1.20 to make, while each Squidget costs £1.50. What are the total variable costs? (3)
   c) If fixed costs are £300, what profit is the business making? (3)
3 'Last week our sales revenue was £12,000 which was great. Our price is £2 a unit, which I think is a bit too cheap.'
   a) How many unit sales were made last week? (2)
   b) If a price rise to £2.25 cuts sales to 5,600 units, calculate the change in the firm's revenue. (4)
4 BYQ Co has sales of 4,000 units a month, a unit price of £4, fixed costs of £9,000 and unit variable costs of £1. Calculate its profit. (4)
5 At full capacity output of 24,000 units, a firm's costs are as follows:

managers' salaries	£48,000
materials	£12,000
rent and rates	£24,000
piece-rate labour	£36,000

   a) What are the firm's total costs at 20,000 units? (4)
   b) What profit will be made at 20,000 units if the selling price is £6? (1)

B2 CASE STUDY

Cleaning up

Mary Ruffett saw the building of a large new housing estate across the road from her home as an opportunity, not an eyesore. The estate contained 500 new homes and was nearing completion with only a few houses left to sell. Most were large detached houses and Mary had noticed that there were no window cleaners offering their services on the estate. Although she had no experience as an entrepreneur or a window cleaner, Mary was interested.

Mary did some sums and researched local window cleaners in Yellow Pages; there was only one listed. She could take out a loan to purchase a van, a ladder and the other equipment needed. She estimated that this would cost her £350 each month to repay. Her variable costs per house cleaned would be minimal; she estimated 50 pence per house. The tricky bit was the price to charge, but eventually she estimated £4 per household. Limited research amongst the new occupants of the estate suggested that she may be able to clean the windows of 125 houses each month. At a price of £5 per household she forecast that she would have 100 customers monthly.

Questions

(25 marks; 25 minutes)

1 Which of Mary's two prices would provide her with the higher monthly revenue? (3)
2 Calculate Mary's monthly profits (or losses) in each case. (6)
3 Analyse two possible reasons why Mary's financial forecasts may not prove to be accurate. (7)
4 Analyse the case for and against Mary charging £5 per household for her window-cleaning service. (9)

B3 CASE STUDY

Chalfont Computer Services Ltd

Robert has decided to give up his job with BT and to work for himself offering computer services to local people. He has paid off his mortgage and owns his house outright, so feels this is the time to take a risk. Robert has no experience of running a business, but is skilled in repairing computers and solving software problems. In the past Robert has repaired computers belonging to friends and family and is aware of the costs involved in providing this service. He believes that with the increase in internet usage there will be plenty of demand for his services. Robert has spoken to a few people in his local pub and this has confirmed his opinion. Robert needs to raise £10,000 to purchase equipment for his business and to pay for a new vehicle and intends to ask his bank for a loan.

The work Robert has already done allows him to forecast that the average revenue from each customer will be £40, while the variable costs will be £15. His monthly fixed costs will be £1,000. Table 13.2 gives Robert's estimates of the number of customers he expects to have.

Table 13.2 Estimates of number of customers

Month	Number of customers
January	40
February	50
March	60
April	82

Questions

(25 marks; 25 minutes)

1 What is meant by the term 'variable costs'? (2)
2 Calculate Robert's forecast profits for his first three months' trading. (5)
3 Robert estimates that if he cut his prices by 10 per cent he would have 20 per cent more customers each month. Calculate the outcome of these changes and whether this would benefit Robert. (8)
4 Examine the case for and against a bank lending Robert £10,000 on the basis of his forecast profits. (10)

C Essay questions

(40 marks each)

1 Discuss whether a new ethnic restaurant, trading in a very competitive market, should aim to maximise its revenue, rather than its profits, during its first year of trading.
2 For all new enterprises it is vital to sell at the right price; this is the most important determinant of profits. Discuss whether this view is always correct.

UNIT 14

Break-even analysis

Break-even analysis compares a firm's revenue with its fixed and variable costs to identify the minimum level of sales needed to cover costs. This can be shown on a graph known as a break-even chart.

14.1 INTRODUCTION

The starting point for financial management is to know how much goods or services cost to produce. This was covered in detail in Chapter 13. Businesses also benefit from knowing how many products they have to produce and sell in order to cover all of their costs. This is particularly important for new businesses with limited experience of their markets. It is also of value for established businesses that plan to produce a new product.

Look at Table 14.1, which shows forecast revenue and cost figures for Burns and Morris Ltd – a business that is planning to start manufacturing silk ties.

Table 14.1 Forecast revenue and cost figures for Burns and Morris Ltd

Output of ties (per week)	Sales income (£ per week)	Total costs (£ per week)
0	0	10,000
100	4,000	11,500
200	8,000	13,000
300	12,000	14,500
400	16,000	16,000
500	20,000	17,500
600	24,000	19,000

You can easily identify that 400 is the number of sales that Burns and Morris Ltd must achieve each week to break-even. Note what happens to its profits if sales are lower – or higher.

To calculate the break-even point we need information on both costs and prices. A change in costs or in the firm's pricing will change the level of output at which the firm breaks even.

Break-even can be calculated and shown on a graph. The calculation of break-even is simpler and quicker than drawing break-even charts.

14.2 CALCULATING BREAK-EVEN

Calculating the break-even point for a product requires knowledge of:

- the selling price of the product
- its fixed costs
- its variable costs per unit.

Fixed costs are expenses which do not change in response to changing demand or output. Fixed costs have to be paid whether or not the business is trading; examples include rent, business rates and interest charges. On the other hand, variable costs will alter as demand and output adjust. An increase in output will require greater supplies of fuel and labour, for example, and the costs of these items will rise. A doubling of demand will double variable costs.

The break-even output level can be calculated by the following formula:

$$\text{Break-even output} = \frac{\text{Fixed costs}}{(\text{Selling price per unit} - \text{variable cost per unit})}$$

The following example – Sue's guided tours – shows how to use this formula to calculate break-even as part of the planning for a new enterprise.

Example: Sue's guided tours

Sue Pittman is planning to offer an open-top bus tour in London during the summer months to take tourists on sightseeing tours of the capital. The bus will conduct four trips each day and Sue estimates that the cost of each trip will be £400 in fuel, food and wage costs for the driver and courier. The trip will include a snack and soft drinks for all the passengers, as well as a London guidebook. She estimates that these items will cost £10 for each passenger on the bus. The maximum number of passengers Sue is allowed to take on each trip is 40. Sue intends to price the day trips at £30 per passenger.

The first thing we should note is that the fixed cost of each tour is forecast to be £200. Sue will have to pay for the fuel for the bus and the wages of her employees as well as depreciation on the vehicle, irrespective of how many passengers she has. So it is easy to fill in the top of the formula we set out above. Fixed costs per tour are £400.

Calculating the bottom half of the formula is only a little more difficult. We know that she will charge each passenger £30 per tour and that the variable costs associated with each passenger will be £10. This is to pay for the snacks and drinks and the guidebook given to each passenger. The amount left (the contribution) will be £20 for each customer. So the formula will look like this:

$$\text{Sue's break-even output} = \frac{\text{Fixed costs}}{(\text{Selling price per unit} - \text{variable cost per unit})}$$

$$= \frac{£400}{(£30 - £10)}$$

$$= \frac{£400}{£20}$$

$$= 20 \text{ passengers.}$$

In other words, Sue will need 20 passengers on each of her tours if she is to break even.

As we have seen, break-even level of output can be calculated using the simple equation shown above, but more understanding of the sensitivity of the relationships between costs, sales revenue and production can be achieved through the use of break-even charts.

14.3 BREAK-EVEN CHARTS

A break-even chart is a graph showing a business's revenues and costs at all possible levels of demand or output. The break-even chart is constructed on a graph by first drawing the horizontal axis to represent the output of goods or services for the business in question. The vertical axis should represent costs and sales values in pounds. The horizontal axis shows output per time period; this is usually output per month or year.

Example: Berry & Hall Ltd

Berry & Hall Ltd are manufacturers of confectionery. The company is planning to launch a new line called Aromatics, a distinctive sweet with a very strong fragrance. The company intends to sell these sweets for £1 per kg. The variable cost of production per kg is forecast at 60 pence and the fixed costs associated with this product are estimated to be £50, 000 a year. The company's maximum output of Aromatics will be 250,000 kg per year.

First, put scales on the axes. The output scale has a range from zero to the company's maximum output; this will be 250,000 kg. The vertical axis records values of costs and revenues. Since revenue is usually the higher figure we simply multiply the maximum output by the selling price and then place values on the axis up to this figure. In this case it will have a maximum value on the axis of £250,000 (£1 × 250,000).

Having drawn the axes and placed scales upon them, the first line we enter is fixed costs. Since this value does not change with output it is simply a horizontal line drawn at £50,000.

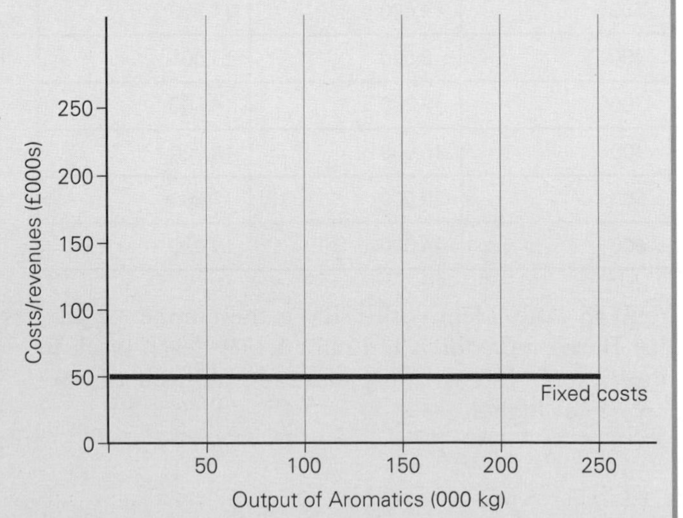

Figure 14.1 Fixed costs for Aromatics

These costs cover rent and rates for the factory that will be used to produce Aromatics and also interest paid on loans taken out by Berry & Hall Ltd to establish production of the new sweet.

Next, add on variable costs to arrive at total costs. The difference between total costs and fixed costs is variable costs. Total costs start from the left hand of the fixed costs line and rise diagonally. To see where they rise to, calculate the total cost at the maximum output level. In the case of Aromatics this is 250,000 kg per year. The total cost is fixed costs (£50,000) plus variable costs of producing 250,000 kg (£0.60 x 250,000 = £150,000). The total cost at this level of output is £50,000 + £150,000 = £200,000.

This point can now be marked on the chart; that is, £200,000 at an output level of 250,000 kg. This can be joined by a straight line to total costs at zero output: £50,000. This is illustrated in Figure 14.2.

Finally, sales revenue must be added. For the maximum level of output, calculate the sales revenue and mark this on the chart. In the case of Aromatics the maximum output per year is 250,000 kg; multiplied by the selling price this gives £250,000 each year. If Berry & Hall does not produce and sell any Aromatics it will not have any sales revenue. Thus zero output results in zero income. A straight diagonal line from zero to £250,000 represents the sales revenue for Aromatics (see Figure 14.3).

This brings together costs and revenues for Aromatics. A line drawn down from the point at which total costs and sales revenue cross shows the break-even output. For Aromatics, it is 125,000 kg per year. This can be checked using the formula method explained earlier.

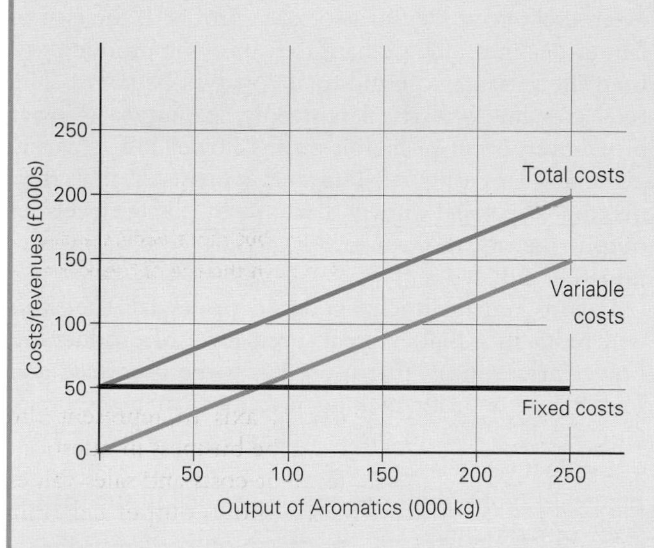

Figure 14.2 Fixed, variable and total costs for Aromatics

Figure 14.3 Break-even output for Aromatics

14.4 USING BREAK-EVEN CHARTS

Various pieces of information can be taken from break-even charts such as that shown in Figure 14.3. As well as the level of break-even output, it also shows the level of profits or losses at every possible level of output. Many conclusions can be reached, such as:

- Any level of output lower than 125,000 kg per year will mean the product is making a loss. The amount of the loss is indicated by the vertical distance between the total cost and the total revenue line. For example, at an output level of 90,000 units per year Aromatics would make a loss of £14,000 for Berry & Hall Ltd. This is because sales are worth £90,000 but costs are £104,000 (£54,000 + £50,000).
- Sales in excess of 125,000 kg of Aromatics per year will earn the company a profit. If the company produces and sells 150,000 kg of Aromatics annually, it will earn a profit of £20,000. At this level of output total revenue is £150,000 and total costs are £130,000. This is shown on the chart by the vertical distance between the total revenue line (which is now the higher) and the total cost line.
- **The margin of safety.** One feature of a break-even chart is that it can show the margin of safety. This is the amount by which demand can fall before the firm starts making losses. It is the difference between current sales and the break-even point. If annual sales of Aromatics were 175,000 kg, with a break-even output of 125,000 kg, then the margin of safety would be 50,000 kg.

Margin of safety = 175,000 – 125,000 = 50,000 kg

That is, output could fall by 50,000 units before Berry & Hall incurred a loss from its new product. The higher the margin of safety the less likely it is that a loss-making situation will develop. The margin of safety is illustrated in Figure 14.4.

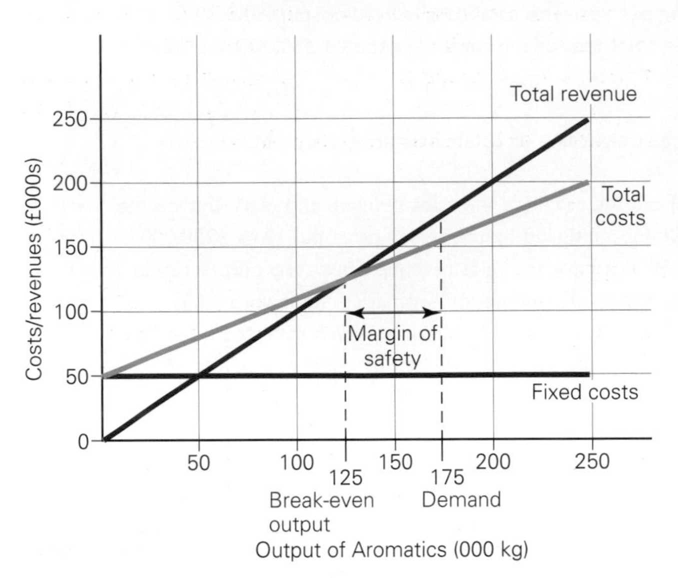

Figure 14.4 Margin of safety

14.5 CHANGE AND BREAK-EVEN ANALYSIS

The application of break-even analysis to the planned production of Aromatics shows how the technique operates. But it assumed a very stable (and therefore unrealistic) business environment. Competitors might have reacted to the introduction of Aromatics by producing similar products if it was a genuinely new idea, or was generating high profits. This competition may have forced Berry & Hall to reduce the price of Aromatics even before they are entered onto the market. Alternatively, competitors' actions may have generated the need for more advertising, raising Berry & Hall's costs. In either case the break-even point and the break-even chart would change.

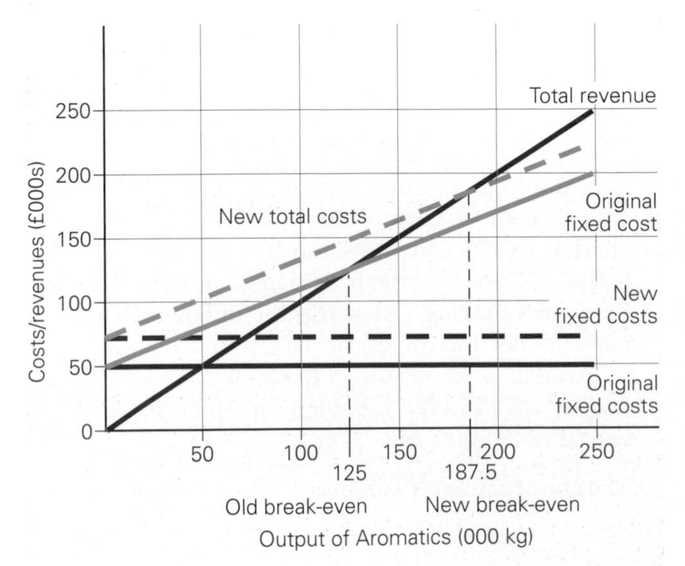

Figure 14.5 A rise in fixed costs

Suppose that Berry & Hall did have to carry out additional advertising for the launch of Aromatics and that this advertising cost £15,000 over the first year. What impact would this have upon the break-even point and the break-even chart? The extra costs would require a higher output (and income) to break even. The rise in marketing costs can be regarded as a fixed cost because this cost must be borne whatever the level of output. This is shown in Figure 14.5.

The break-even chart shows the increased fixed cost and total cost lines which create a higher break-even output. This also has the effect of reducing the level of profit (or increasing the loss) made at any level of output. Any factor leading to a fall in fixed costs will have the opposite effects.

Other external factors can impact upon the break-even level of output and associated profits. If the cost of labour declines, due perhaps to improving productivity, then the variable cost and total cost will be lower. The total cost line will rise less steeply, leading to a lower break-even point of higher profits (lower losses) at any given level of output. The curve pivots (rather than making a parallel move) because at lower levels of output the saving from lower variable costs is proportionately reduced.

If costs remain unchanged and prices fall then this will result in a higher break-even level of production. Lower prices mean that more has to be produced and sold before a profit-making position can be reached. Conversely, a rise in price will result in a lower level of production necessary for break-even to be attained. Figure 14.6 illustrates the impact of a fall in the market price of a product.

Summary of possible changes to the break-even chart to look out for in an exam

1 Prices can go up or down. If a price is increased, the revenue line starts in the same place but rises more steeply.
2 Fixed costs can rise or fall, so you may have to draw a new horizontal line. But remember that a change to fixed costs will also affect the total cost line.
3 Variable costs can rise or fall. An increase will make the variable cost line rise more steeply, though it will still start at the same point – at the fixed cost line. A change in variable costs will change the total costs line as well.

Note that each of these three changes will alter the break-even point.

14.6 THE VALUE OF BREAK-EVEN ANALYSIS

Strengths

Break-even analysis is simple to understand; it is particularly useful for small and newly established businesses, where the managers may not be able to employ more sophisticated techniques. Businesses can use break-even to:

- estimate the future level of output they will need to produce and sell in order to meet given objectives in terms of profits
- assess the impact of planned price changes upon profit and the level of output needed to break even
- assess how changes in fixed and/or **variable costs** may affect profits and the level of output necessary to break even
- take decisions on whether to produce their own products or components or whether to purchase from external sources
- support applications for loans from banks and other financial institutions – the use of the technique may indicate good business sense as well as forecast profitability.

Weaknesses

The weaknesses of break-even analysis are set out below.

- The model assumes that costs increase constantly and that firms do not benefit from bulk buying. If, for example, a firm negotiates lower prices for purchasing larger quantities of raw materials, then its total cost line will no longer be straight. It will in fact level out at higher outputs
- Similarly, break-even analysis assumes the firm sells all its output at a single price. In reality, firms frequently offer discounts for bulk purchases
- A major flaw in the technique is that it assumes that all output is sold. This may well not be true and, if so, would result in an inaccurate break-even estimate. In times of low demand, a firm may have difficulty in selling all that it produces
- Break-even analysis is only as good as the data on which it is based: poor quality data can result in inaccurate conclusions being drawn.

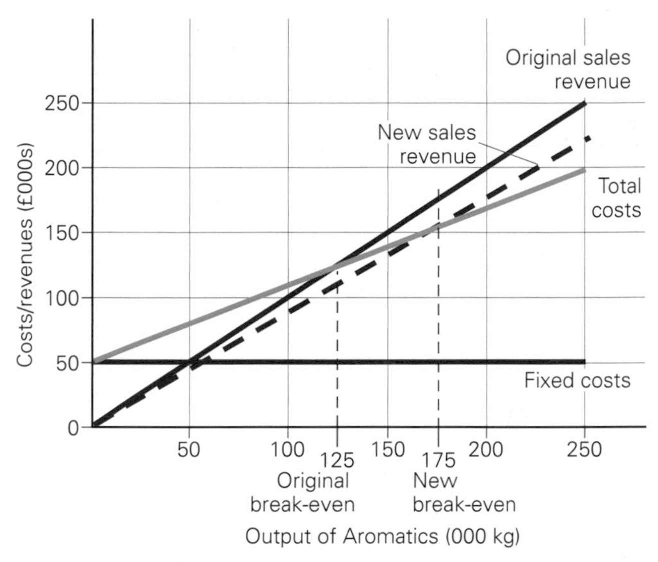

Figure 14.6 The effects of a fall in price

A-grade application

Recently launched carbon neutral food market closes

A £1.5 million carbon neutral food market in Devon has gone into administration only three months after it started trading. Foodeaze was a food market with associated restaurants operating with the objective of sustainability. The business, based in Exeter, sold locally produced products and ran its delivery vehicles on bio-diesel. The closure of the market has resulted in the loss of 60 jobs.

Foodeaze owner Nick Hess said it could not compete with the new £220 million Princesshay retail development in Exeter. Mr Hess said the development had a huge impact on Foodeaze's sales and its financial position. He said that within five weeks of opening they were close to their break-even point, but then the opening of the new retail development had a bigger impact than originally forecast.

'We put a percentage into our business plan for the effect we thought it was going to have but unfortunately it was far greater than what we actually forecasted', he said. 'The new development is stunning and I'm not criticising it – it's just unfortunately one of those things of bad timing.'

Source: Adapted from BBC News, May 2007

A-grade application

English football clubs fail to break even

The annual review of football finance from Deloitte (one of the world's largest accountancy and auditing businesses) has shown that recent seasons have been challenging in financial terms for English football clubs.

The Editor of 2010 report, Dan Jones, argues that football faces a number of financial issues including rising wage bills for players. 'It is a real game of two halves with Premier League finances', he says, referring to the season 2008/09, which the report covers.

'On the revenue side, things are still very successful and continuing to grow, and getting closer to that £2 billion revenue target across the Premier League. But it is the cost control side of things where the problem is.'

Portsmouth Football Club failed to break even in 2010 because it failed to control its costs and a high level of spending on players' wages was one factor which took the Club into administration. However, unexpected declines in revenues can also contribute to failure to reach break-even; relegation or failure to qualify for European competitions are obvious examples.

Football clubs are preparing for a future where revenue growth is likely to be lower and controlling costs will become more important. Even wealthy and high spending clubs such as Chelsea are moving towards '... a break-even model' says Dan Jones 'Although they are not there yet their losses have slimmed considerably.'

Source: Adapted from BBC News, June 2010

Table 14.2 How changes in business circumstances affect the break-even chart

	Cause	Effect
Internal factors	• Extra launch advertising • Planned price increase • Using more machinery (and less labour) in production	• Fixed costs rise, so total costs rise and the break-even point rises • Revenue rises more steeply; break-even point falls • Fixed costs rise while variable costs fall; uncertain effect on break-even point
External factors	• Fall in demand • Competitors' actions force price cut • Fuel costs rise	• Break-even point is not affected, though margin of safety is reduced • Revenue rises less steeply; break-even point rises • Variable and total cost lines rise more steeply; break-even point rises

Figure 14.6 shows the effects of a fall in prices. When using break-even analysis a business may draw several charts using different prices to assess the impact of various prices for a new product. This approach is particularly useful in markets where prices may be volatile.

Table 14.2 shows how changes in business circumstances affect the break-even chart.

ISSUES FOR ANALYSIS

- Analytical issues in relation to break-even centre upon the effective use of break-even charts. It is important to appreciate how changes in the business environment may affect the break-even position of a business. Any analysis of break-even should recognise that changes in revenues or costs will impact upon the level of break-even output.
- As an example, you should be able to state whether, in the following circumstances, break-even output will rise or fall:
- wage negotiations result in a 4 per cent pay rise
- the business rate levied upon a firm's premises is increased
- the market price for the business's product increases
- a change in the price of oil means that fuel prices fall by 5 per cent.
- A break-even chart shows the level of profit or loss at any level of output. If the business's circumstances change it is important to be able to quantify the extent to which profitability changes at any level of output.

14.7 BREAK-EVEN ANALYSIS – AN EVALUATION

There is a risk in exams of assuming that break-even charts tell you 'facts'. Break-even analysis seems simple to conduct and understand. It appears to be cheap and quick to carry out. That assumes, of course, that the business knows all its costs and can break them down into variable and fixed. Tesco certainly can, but not every business is as well managed. Football clubs such as Sheffield Wednesday, Portsmouth and Darlington have hit financial problems partly because of ignorance of their financial circumstances. Similarly, few NHS hospitals could say with confidence how much it costs to provide a heart transplant.

Break-even analysis is of particular value when a business is first established. Having to work out the fixed and variable costs will help the managers to make better decisions, for example on pricing. It also shows profit and loss at various levels of output, particularly when presented in the form of a chart. Indeed it may be that financial institutions will require this sort of financial information before lending any money to someone aspiring to run a business.

As long as the figures are accurate, break-even becomes especially useful when changes occur, such as rising raw material costs. The technique can allow for changing revenues and costs and gives a valuable guide to potential profitability.

Key Terms

Break-even chart: a line graph showing total revenues and total costs at all possible levels of output or demand from zero to maximum capacity.

Fixed costs: fixed costs are any costs which do not vary directly with the level of output, for example rent and rates.

Variable costs: variable costs are those costs which vary directly with the level of output. They represent payments made for the use of inputs such as labour, fuel and raw materials.

Contribution: this is total revenue less variable costs. The calculation of contribution is useful for businesses that are responsible for a range of products.

Margin of safety: the amount by which current output exceeds the level of output necessary to break even.

Key formulae

Break-even output: $\frac{\text{Fixed costs}}{\text{Contribution per unit}}$

Contribution per unit: Selling price – Variable costs per unit

Margin of safety: Sales volume – Break-even output

Total contribution: Contribution per unit x unit sales

WORKBOOK

A REVISION QUESTIONS

(25 marks; 25 minutes)

1 What is meant by the term 'break-even point'? (2)
2 State three reasons why a business may conduct a break-even analysis. (3)
3 List the information necessary to construct a break-even chart. (4)
4 How would you calculate the contribution made by each unit of production that is sold? (2)
5 A business sells its products for £10 each and the variable cost of producing a single unit is £6. If its monthly fixed costs are £18,000, how many units must it sell to break even each month? (3)
6 Explain why the variable cost and total revenue lines commence at the origin of a break-even chart. (3)
7 What point on a break-even chart actually illustrates break-even output? (2)
8 Explain how, using a break-even chart, you would illustrate the amount of profit or loss made at any given level of output. (2)
9 Why might a business wish to calculate its margin of safety? (2)
10 A business is currently producing 200,000 units of output annually, and its break-even output is 120,000 units. What is its margin of safety? (2)

REVISION EXERCISES

B1 DATA RESPONSE

An entrepreneur's first hotel

Paul Jarvis is an entrepreneur and about to open his first hotel. He has forecast the following costs and revenues:

- Maximum number of customers per month: 800
- Monthly fixed costs: £10,000
- Average revenue per customer: £110
- Typical variable costs per customer: £90

Some secondary market research has suggested that Paul's prices may be too low. He is considering charging higher prices, though he is nervous about the impact this might have on his forecast sales. Paul has found his break-even chart useful during the planning of his new business, but is concerned that it might be misleading too.

Questions

(45 marks, 50 minutes)

1 a) Construct the break-even chart for Paul's planned business. (9)
  b) State, and show on the graph, the profit or loss made at a monthly sales level of 600 customers. (4)
  c) State, and show on the graph, the margin of safety at that level of output. (4)
2 Paul's market research shows that in his first month of trading he can expect 450 customers at his hotel.
  a) If Paul's research is correct, calculate the level of profit or loss he will make. (5)
  b) Illustrate this level of output on your graph and show the profit or loss. (3)
3 Paul has decided to increase his prices to give an average revenue per customer of £120.
  a) Draw the new total revenue line on your break-even chart to show the effect of this change. (3)
  b) Mark on your diagram the new break-even point. (1)
  c) Calculate Paul's new break-even number of customers to confirm the result shown on your chart. (6)
4 Paul is worried that his break-even chart may be 'misleading'. Do you agree with him? Justify your view. (10)

B2 DATA RESPONSE

The Successful T-shirt Company

Shelley has recently launched the Successful T-Shirt Company. It sells a small range of fashion T-shirts. The shirts are available in a range of colours and contain the company's logo, which is becoming increasingly desirable for young fashion-conscious people.

The shirts are sold to retailers for £35 each. They cost £16.50 to manufacture and the salesperson receives £2.50 commission for each item sold to retailers. The distribution cost for each shirt is £1.00 and current sales are 1,000 per month. The fixed costs of production are £11,250 per month.

The company is considering expanding its range of T-shirts and has approached its bank for a loan. The bank has requested that the company draw up a business plan including a cashflow forecast and break-even chart.

Questions

(30 marks, 40 minutes)

1 What is a break-even chart? (4)

2 Calculate the following:
  a) the variable cost of producing 1,000 T-shirts
  b) the contribution earned through the sale of one T-shirt. (6)

3 Shelley has decided to manufacture the shirts in Poland. As a result, the variable cost per T-shirt (including commission and distribution costs will fall to £15 per T-shirt. However, fixed costs will rise to £12,000.
  a) Calculate the new level of break-even for Shelly's T-shirts.
  b) Calculate the margin of safety if sales are 1,000 T-shirts per month. (10)

4 Should Shelley rely on break-even analysis when taking business decisions? Justify your view. (10)

B3 CASE STUDY

US: Saab lowering break-even point

Newly reorganised car maker Saab is steadily reducing its break-even point and has more than enough cash to survive as it begins to rebuild sales, its chief executive officer has said. After near-liquidation by former owner General Motors, Saab must rebuild its sales from a new start and is focused on restructuring its operations, president and CEO Jan Ake Jonsson told news agency AFP.

'We had been closed down for seven weeks,' Jonsson told reporters in Detroit. 'We couldn't order any material or do any advertising because we were in liquidation,' he said. 'Now we have about 4,500 cars in stock. We're completely focused on getting our products out as quickly as possible.'

The company is currently living on reserves, including loans from the European banks and a US$200 million technology deal with Beijing Auto, according to AFP, though Jonsson said Saab should be able to break even in the second half of 2011. He hopes to reduce operating costs to the point where Saab can break even with annual sales of 80,000 to 85,000 vehicles, though potential sales are significantly higher. Jonsson is confident Saab could sell as many as 125,000 units annually 'at which point we would be quite profitable.' 'These are very conservative estimates,' he told AFP, noting that Saab had sold 98,000 cars in 2008 when it was still owned by GM.

Source: www.just-auto.com, 13 May 2010

Questions

(25 marks; 30 minutes)

1 Explain why Saab's management might have wanted to 'steadily reduce its break-even point'. (6)

2 a) If Jonsson achieves his sales expectations for Saab, what would be the company's margin of safety? (4)
  b) Explain the possible importance of that safety margin to a business like Saab. (6)

3 In May 2010 Jonsson said Saab 'should be able to break even in the second half of 2011'. Discuss the threats to Saab's survival in the period up until it reaches its break-even point. (9)

C Essay questions

(40 marks each)

1 'Break-even is the most vital part of a business plan for a new enterprise'. Do you agree with this statement? Justify your view.

2 'Break-even analysis is of limited value to a start-up business because it ignores the market'. To what extent do you agree with this statement?

Cash flow management and forecasting

UNIT 15

Cash flow is the flow of money into and out of a business in a given time period. Cash flow forecasting is estimating the flow of cash in the future.

15.1 THE IMPORTANCE OF CASH FLOW MANAGEMENT

Managing cash flow is one of the most important aspects of financial management. Without adequate availability of cash from day to day, even a company with high sales could fail. As bills become due there has to be the cash available to pay them. If a company cannot pay its bills, suppliers will refuse to deliver and staff will start looking for other jobs. Cash flow problems are the most common reason for business failure. This is particularly true for new businesses. It is estimated that 70 per cent of businesses that collapse in their first year fail because of cash flow problems.

Businesses need to continually review their current and future cash position. In order to be prepared and to understand future cash needs, businesses construct a **cash flow forecast**. This sets out the expected flows of cash into and out of the business for each month. In textbooks cash flows are normally shown for six months, but they can be done for any period of time. Most firms want to look 12 months ahead, so the cash flow forecast is constantly updated.

A-grade application

In 2010 Portsmouth Football Club became the first Premier League Club to become bankrupt. In spite of getting into the FA Cup Final the club was unable to pay its debts. The administrator, Andrew Andronikou, estimated that the club owed around £119 million. There has been much discussion about how this level of debt had built up, but it seems that the size of the wages bill was a major problem. It was estimated that the wages bill over the previous three years was at least 10 per cent higher than the revenue going into the club. The administrator pointed out that over a five-year period the wages bill was £247 million and total revenue was £221 million.

15.2 WHO NEEDS TO USE A CASH FLOW FORECAST?

All businesses can benefit from using cash flow forecasts, but they are particularly useful for business start-ups. A carefully planned cash flow forecast will help to ensure that the business has enough finance to keep afloat during the early months. This is the most difficult period for a business as sales may be slow. There will be little income but bills still need to be paid.

Figure 15.1 A seaside hotel is affected by seasonal factors

Existing businesses also need to be aware of their cash position. In many cases there are seasonal factors that make cash hard to manage. Every year a seaside hotel has to cope with winter months when cash flow will almost certainly be negative; in other words, cash out will be higher than cash in. A cash flow forecast will help to ensure that the business plans for future cash needs and that it can cope if unexpected events happen. If a business is growing, cash flow forecasts can be particularly useful. They enable the business to ensure that any growth is backed by sufficient funding.

15.3 PREPARING A CASH FLOW FORECAST

To prepare a cash flow forecast businesses need to estimate all the money coming into and out of the business, month by month. These flows of money are then set onto a grid showing the cash movements in each month.

Cash in

In the example shown in Table 15.1 the business is a new start-up. The business will receive an injection of capital of £30,000 in March. The business will start production in April and will only receive cash when sales start in May. Cash inflows are expected to increase each month until reaching a maximum of £15,000 in August.

It is important that the income from sales is shown when the cash is received not when the sale is made.

Cash outflow

In the example shown in Table 15.2 in March the firm will buy machinery for £23,000. Materials will cost £6,000 each month. The first delivery in April must be paid for on delivery. After that the supplier will give the firm two months' credit so the next payments do not need to be made until July. Rent for the building costs £2,000 per month but the owner requires two months' rent in advance. Wages are estimated to be £2,000 per month and there are other expenses of £1,000 per month.

When these figures have been entered onto the grid the total expenditure can be calculated.

Cash flow

The cash flow forecast can now be completed by calculating the following.

Monthly balance

This is cash inflow for the month minus cash outflow. It shows each month if there is a positive or a negative movement of cash. In the examples shown in Tables 15.1 and 15.2 inflow is greater than outflow except in April. When outflow is greater than inflow the monthly balance will be negative. This is shown in brackets to indicate that it is a minus figure.

Opening and closing balance

This is like a bank statement. It shows what cash the business has at the beginning of the month (opening balance) and what the cash position is at the end of the month (closing balance). The closing balance is the opening balance plus the monthly balance. For example, the business starts with £1,000 in the bank in August; another £4,000 flows in during the month, so the closing bank balance is £5,000.

The closing balance shows the business's expected net cash position each month.

The completed cash flow forecast will be as shown in Table 15.3.

Table 15.1 Example of cash inflow (March to August)

MONTH £s	March	April	May	June	July	August
Cash inflow						
Capital	30,000					
Sales			7,000	10,000	13,000	15,000
Total inflow	**30,000**	**0**	**7,000**	**10,000**	**13,000**	**15,000**

Table 15.2 Example of cash outflow (March to August)

MONTH £s	March	April	May	June	July	August
Cash outflow						
Equipment	23,000					
Materials	0	6,000			6,000	6,000
Rent	4,000	2,000	2,000	2,000	2,000	2,000
Wages		2,000	2,000	2,000	2,000	2,000
Other expenses		1,000	1,000	1,000	1,000	1,000
Total outflow	**27,000**	**11,000**	**5,000**	**5,000**	**11,000**	**11,000**

Table 15.3 Example of a cash flow forecast

MONTH £s	March	April	May	June	July	August
Cash inflow						
Capital	30,000					
Sales			7,000	10,000	13,000	15,000
Total inflow	**30,000**	**0**	**7,000**	**10,000**	**13,000**	**15,000**
Cash outflow						
Equipment	23,000					
Materials	0	6,000			6,000	6,000
Rent	4,000	2,000	2,000	2,000	2,000	2,000
Wages		2,000	2,000	2,000	2,000	2,000
Other expenses		1,000	1,000	1,000	1,000	1,000
Total outflow	**27,000**	**11,000**	**5,000**	**5,000**	**11,000**	**11,000**
Monthly balance	3,000	(11,000)	2,000	5,000	2,000	4,000
Opening balance	0	3,000	(8,000)	(6,000)	(1,000)	1,000
Closing balance	**3,000**	**(8,000)**	**(6,000)**	**(1,000)**	**1,000**	**5,000**

This shows that there is a negative cash balance for the months of April, May and June. Only in July does the business start having a positive cash flow.

As there is no such thing as negative money this cash flow forecast shows the business that it must take action if it is to avoid problems in the early months. The easiest remedy for a cash flow problem such as this is a bank overdraft.

15.4 BENEFITS OF CASH FLOW FORECASTS

A cash flow forecast will enable a business to carry out the following.

- Anticipate the timing and amounts of any cash shortages. In the example shown above, the business can find out from the cash flow forecast whether it has sufficient cash. In fact, this business does not have enough cash for three months (April, May and June). There is no such thing as negative money, so the business will not be able to make some of its payments. It will not be able to pay wages or the rent. This would mean that although the business looks cash rich in the longer term – by July they will have a positive cash flow – they may not survive.
- Arrange financial cover for any anticipated shortages of cash. Having information about when the business will have a cash shortage means that the business can take measures to ensure that it has cash available. In the example shown above, the business needs to find additional finance for the three months when it has a cash shortage.
- Review the timings and amounts of receipts and payments.
- Obtain loans (if the problems are long term) or overdrafts (if the problems are short term).

If a firm wants to take out a loan the bank will always request a cash flow forecast. Banks do this in order to ensure that the business:

- has enough cash to enable it to survive
- is able to pay the interest on the loan
- will be able to repay the loan
- is aware of the need for cash flow management.

A-grade application

Blockbuster warns that it is in danger of bankruptcy

The DVD rental chain Blockbuster warned early in 2010 that it was facing the possibility of bankruptcy. The USA-based company is facing a double squeeze on its cash flow. High interest payments on its huge debt are one burden, but it is also generating lower revenue because of a change in the way its customers view films. The market has changed from focusing on store-based rentals to focusing more on mail order operations. The new technology that allows films to be downloaded or streamed directly has also affected the revenue of the business. In the UK the company is trying to reduce costs by renegotiating the leases on its 630 stores.

How reliable are cash flow forecasts?

In order to prepare a cash flow forecast, businesses need to make assumptions about the future, though some actual figures may be used such as, for example, the monthly rent agreed with the landlord.

When looking at cash flow forecasts it is useful for the firm to be aware that the figures are estimates and to build in some safety margins. Companies should ask what would happen if:

- sales are lower than expected
- the customer does not pay up on time
- prices of materials are higher than expected?

Using spreadsheets enables companies to look at some of these possibilities. With the use of spreadsheets it is possible to adjust both the timings and amounts. This enables a business to evaluate the most likely and the worst-case situations. The business also needs to be aware that the figures are based on current assumptions about the market and the economic climate. If changes are detected it looks at how these will affect the cash flow position.

15.5 MANAGING THE DAY-TO-DAY FINANCES

Even when the high set-up costs have been completed, new businesses can be shocked by the amount of capital needed to run the business day-by-day. To operate, the business needs money to buy stock, to pay wages and the day-to-day bills such as electricity and telephone bills. If the bills cannot be paid on time there are serious consequences. In the worst situation the business may fail.

The cash cycle

Managing the day-to-day finances is a continuous process. When a business starts up it takes time to generate income. Money to pay for stock and the running costs will need to be found from the initial capital invested in the business. As the business cycle gets going, income from customers will be available to pay for expenditure. The firm needs to ensure that there is always enough cash to meet daily requirements. If the business is expanding, extra care needs to be taken (see Figure 15.2).

Each business will have its own distinct cycle. Businesses may also suffer unexpected shocks and need the cash to be able to cope with these.

Problems caused by insufficient cash flow

Problems caused by insufficient cash flow include the following.

- With suppliers: a firm with too little cash will struggle to pay its bills on time. It may resort to delaying payments. Unpaid suppliers may refuse credit for a future order.
- Banks are quick to sense a cash flow crisis: and equally quick to reduce the bank's risk by calling in any overdrafts. As they can insist on being repaid within 24 hours, the speed of repayment can put firms in terrible difficulties.
- Opportunities may be missed: the business may not be able to buy supplies in bulk. This removes the advantage of lower prices. Even more importantly it may have to refuse a large order because it cannot finance the extra cash requirement.

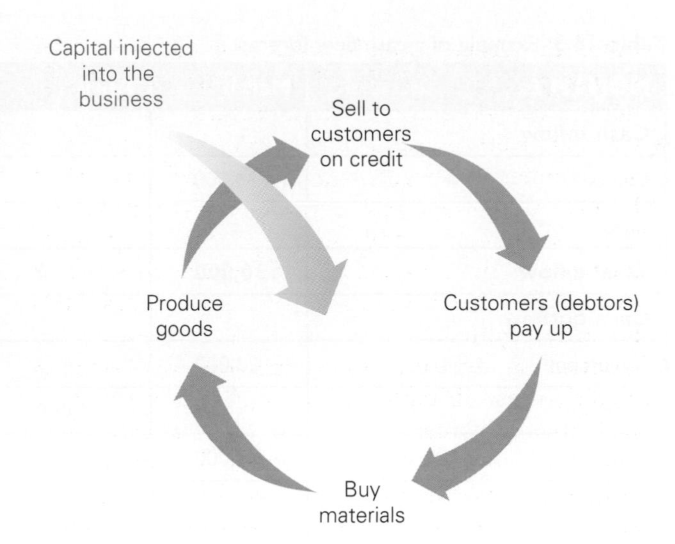

Figure 15.2 The cash cycle

In the longer term, shortage of cash means insufficient funds are available for development. The business will not be able to grow as rapidly as its rivals. This may make it hard to stay competitive.

> **A-grade application**
>
> **Late payments woes**
>
> A survey from RBS and Natwest, published in April 2010, found that 71 per cent of SMEs (small and medium enterprises) had been affected by late payments in the past year. The study estimates that in the last year a total of £62 billon was owed to businesses in bills paid beyond agreed deadlines. Around £15 billion was more than 120 days overdue. Another survey from the Forum of Private Businesses, found that small businesses currently have an average of £47,000 tied up by late payments. This is around 35 per cent of turnover.
>
> Stephen Alambritis, head of public affairs at the Federation of Small Businesses, said: 'Poor payment practices can drastically affect cash flow for small firms at a time when business owners are doing their best to hold on to precious funds.'
>
> Source: Smallbusiness.co.uk (15 April 2010)

15.6 IMPROVING CASH FLOW INTO THE BUSINESS

The business can improve the flow of cash into the business in several ways. These are set out below.

- Getting goods to the market in the shortest possible

time: the sooner goods reach the customer, the sooner payment is received. Production and distribution should be as efficient as possible.
- Getting paid as quickly as possible: the ideal arrangement is to get paid cash on delivery. Most businesses, though, work on credit. Even worse, it is interest-free credit, so the customer has little incentive to pay up quickly. Early payment should be encouraged by offering incentives such as discounts for early payment.
- Controlling debtors: confusingly this is known as credit control. If customers do not pay on time this will obviously mean that the cash does not come into the business when expected. Businesses can reduce the likelihood of non- or late payment by ensuring the debtor is creditworthy before granting credit (by obtaining a bank reference).
- Factoring: it may be possible to speed up payments by factoring money owed to the business. The company is able to receive 80 per cent of the amount due within 24 hours of an invoice being presented. The factor then collects the money from the customer when the credit period is over and pays the seller the remaining 20 per cent less the factoring fees. These depend on the length of time before the payment is due, the credit rating of the creditor and current rates of interest. The fees are usually no more than 5 per cent of the total value of the sale.

15.7 REDUCING CASH OUTFLOWS FROM THE BUSINESS

The other way of improving cash flow is to manage the outflow of cash from the business. This can be done by:
- Obtaining maximum possible credit for purchases. Delaying payment of bills will keep cash in the business for longer.
- Controlling costs. This can be done by keeping administrative and production costs to a minimum. Efficient production reduces costs. Savings may be possible by upgrading machinery to replace labour. This will benefit the firm's profit as well as its cash flow.
- Keeping stocks of raw materials to a minimum. Good stock management such as a just-in-time system means that the business is not paying for stocks before it needs them for production. Controlling stock losses means that less is spent on replacements for lost or damaged stock.

Keeping cash in the business

Cash flow can also be improved by keeping cash in the business. Minimising short-term spending on new equipment keeps cash in the business. Things that the business can do include:
- Lease rather than buy equipment. This increases expenses but conserves capital.
- Renting rather than buying buildings; this also allows capital to remain in the business.
- Postponing expenditure, for example on new company cars.

15.8 FINDING ADDITIONAL FUNDING TO COVER CASH SHORTAGES

If the business is unable to keep a healthy cash flow by internal management it may need to look outside to cover cash shortages. This can be done by:
- Using an overdraft; this is arranged with a bank. It allows the business to overdraw up to an agreed limit negotiated in advance. Overdrafts usually incur interest rates as high as 6 per cent over base rate. However, an overdraft ensures the firm only borrows money on the days it really needs it. It is a very flexible form of borrowing. This makes it suitable for small or short-term shortages of cash. Although it should only be used to fund short-term problems, a recent study of firms in Bristol found that 70 per cent of small firms had a permanent overdraft. A risky aspect of an overdraft is that the bank can withdraw the facility at any time and demand instant repayment. So, when a firm needs it most, such as in a recession, it may not be available.
- Taking out a short-term loan; this incurs a lower rate of interest than an overdraft. Although less flexible than an overdraft, short-term loans offer more security and may have fixed interest charges (whereas on an overdraft they are variable).
- Sale and leaseback of assets; if a business has fixed assets it may be possible to negotiate a sale and leaseback arrangement. This will release capital and give an immediate inflow of cash. The equipment will be paid for through a leasing arrangement. This will be a regular and ongoing cost that must be budgeted for.

A-grade application

Tesco's sale and leaseback deals

In April 2010 Tesco announced plans to continue its expansion plans. Included in this were 2.4 million sq ft of retail space, the equivalent of 80 superstores, in Britain and 8.5 million sq ft overseas, not including ambitious plans to open nine large shopping centres in China. How is it funding this? Of course its huge annual revenue gives it cash to invest, but for many years it has been following a policy of releasing capital from its massive property portfolio. It has done this by organising sale and leaseback deals. As an example, in 2009 it carried out a deal worth £514 million, which involved 15 stores and 2 distribution centres. By doing this it continues to have use of the property but has use of the capital raised to help fund its expansion plans.

Some methods that maybe used to improve cash flow are set out in Table 15.4.

Table 15.4 Ways to improve cash flow

Measure	Result	Drawbacks
Discounting prices	Increases sales Reduces stock Generates cash	May undermine pricing structure May leave low stocks for future activity
Reduce purchases	Cuts down expenditure	May leave business without means to continue
Negotiate more credit	Allows time to pay	May tarnish credit reputation
Delay payment of bills	Retains cash	Will tarnish credit reputation
Credit control – chase debtors	Gets payments in and sooner	May upset customers
Negotiate additional finance	Provides cash	Interest payments add to expenditure Has to be repaid
Factor debts	Generates cash A proportion of the income is guaranteed	Reduces income from sales Costs can be high
Selling assets	Releases cash	Assets are no longer available
Sale and leaseback	Releases cash Asset is still available	Increases costs – lease has to be paid Company no longer owns asset

ISSUES FOR ANALYSIS

When answering a question on cash flow management and forecasting, it is important to understand that the figures are only the starting point for analysis and decision making. Consideration needs to be given to:

- The validity of the figures: who constructed the forecast? Are the figures reliable and unbiased?
- What the figures show: a careful analysis of the position month by month.
- The need to take full account of the circumstances of the business. If sales are to a foreign country, payment may not be certain and even if it arrives, changes in currency values may make cash inflows worth fewer pounds than forecast.
- The differences between cash flow and profitability (see Unit 19).
- Especially for small firms, cash flow is the equivalent of blood circulating round the body. If the cash dries up, the firm dies. When looking at how the firm can improve its cash flow, consideration must be given to the type of firm and its market situation. There is no point suggesting that the firm should demand cash payment if it is supplying large businesses in a highly competitive market.
- When looking at solutions to cash flow problems it is important to consider what is causing the problem and how long the problem could exist. There is a lot of difference between a problem caused by poor payment and one that is caused by poor sales.

15.9 CASH FLOW MANAGEMENT AND FORECASTING – AN EVALUATION

There is no doubt that cash flow management is a vital ingredient in the success of any small business. For a new business, cash flow forecasting helps to answer key questions:

- Is the venture viable?
- How much capital is needed?
- Which are the most dangerous months?

For an existing business the cash flow forecast identifies the amount and timing of any cash flow problems in the future. It is also useful for evaluating new orders or ventures.

Nevertheless, completing a cash flow forecast does not ensure survival. Consideration needs to be given to its usefulness and limitations. It must be remembered that cash flow forecasts are based on estimates. These estimates are not just amounts but also timings. The firm must be aware that actual figures can differ wildly from estimates, especially for a new, inexperienced firm. When preparing cash flow forecasts, managers need to ask themselves 'what if?' A huge mistake is to look at only one forecast. It is far better to look at **best case** and **worst case** possibilities. Spreadsheets allow for easy manipulation of data. It is easy to see the impact of single and multiple changes to the forecast figures. This should help to reduce the risks. It does not guarantee results. Having completed a cash flow forecast and taken the necessary steps to ensure financing also does not guarantee success. The firm needs to be continually aware of the economic and market climate and its current cash position.

Improving cash flow will often uncover problems elsewhere in the business. Perhaps the reason there is poor stock control is that the person in charge is demotivated. In this respect, managing cash flow is an integrated activity involving each aspect of the company. Efficient production keeps costs to a minimum and turns raw inputs into finished goods in the shortest possible time. Effective management of stock can have considerable impact on cash needs. Effective marketing ensures that the goods are sold and that demand is correctly estimated. This avoids wasted production. Cash then flows in from sales.

A business with plenty of cash flowing in and out is a healthy business.

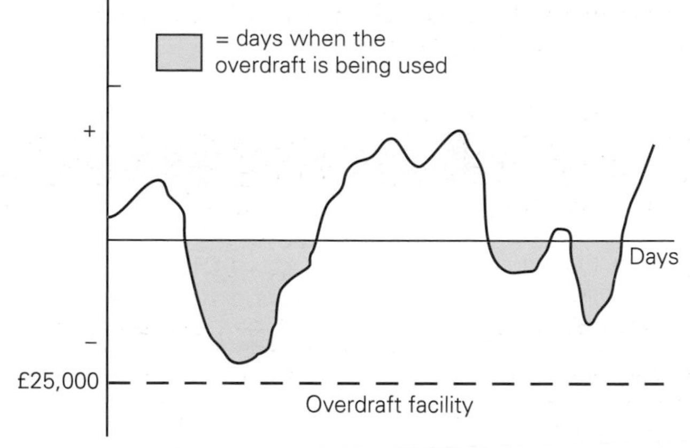

Figure 15.3 Daily cash balances for a firm with a £25,000 overdraft

Key Terms

Best case: an optimistic estimate of the best possible outcome, for example if sales prove much higher than expected.
Cash flow forecast: estimating future monthly cash inflows and outflows, to find out the net cash flow.
Factoring: obtaining part-payment of the amount owed from a factoring company. The factoring company will then collect the debt and pass over the balance of the payment.
Negative cash flow: when cash outflows are greater than cash inflows.
Overdraft: short-term borrowing from a bank. The business only borrows as much as it needs to cover its daily cash shortfall.
Sale and leaseback: a contract that, at the same time, sells the freehold to a piece of property and buys back the leasehold.
Worst case: a pessimistic estimate assuming the worst possible outcome, for example sales are very disappointing.

WORKBOOK

A REVISION QUESTIONS

(50 marks; 50 minutes)

1 What is meant by 'cash flow'? (2)
2 Why is it important to manage cash flow? (4)
3 What is a cash flow forecast? (3)
4 Explain two limitations of cash flow forecasts. (4)
5 Give two reasons why a bank manager may want to see a cash flow forecast before giving a loan to a new business. (2)
6 How could a firm benefit from delaying its cash outflows? (3)
7 What problems could a firm face if its cash flow forecast proved unreliable? (3)
8 How could a firm benefit from constructing its cash flow forecasts on a computer spreadsheet? (4)
9 Outline the probable cash cycle for a small sandwich shop. (4)
10 Explain why 'good management of cash flow starts with good forecasting'. (3)
11 Outline two problems that may arise if a firm is operating with very poor cash flow. (4)
12 How could a small producer of shelf fittings benefit from factoring? (4)
13 Outline three ways in which a business can improve its cash flow situation. (6)
14 What internal factors could affect a firm's cash flow? (4)

B REVISION EXERCISES
B1 CASH FLOW

(20 marks; 20 minutes)

A business is to be started up on 1 January next year with £40,000 of share capital. It will be opening a designer clothes shop. During January it plans to spend £45,000 on start-up costs (buying a lease, buying equipment, decorating, and so on). On 1 February it will open its doors and gain sales over the next five months of: £12,000, £16,000, £20,000, £25,000 and £24,000 respectively. Each month it must pay £10,000 in fixed overheads (salaries, heat, light, telephone, and so on) and its variable costs will amount to half the revenue.

Complete the cash flow table below (Table 15.5) to find out:

1. the company's forecast cash position at the end of June (18)
2. the maximum level of overdraft the owners will need to negotiate with the bank before starting up. (2)

Table 15.5 Cash flow table (all figures in £000s)

	Jan	Feb	Mar	Apr	May	June
Cash at start						
Cash in						
Cash out						
Net cash flow						
Opening balance						
Closing balance						

B2 DATA RESPONSE

Merlin Construction has planning permission to convert an old office block into four flats. The directors managed to borrow £130,000 from the bank in January. They used £100,000 to buy the building that month. The work will start in January and take nine months to complete. The plan is to build and sell the two upstairs flats in June and then complete the ground-floor flats. These will be sold in September. The flats should sell for £60,000 each. Materials are estimated to cost about £10,000 a month with one month's credit. Wages and salaries will be £4,000 a month. Interest charges will be £1,000 a month. Other expenses will be £1,000 a month.

Questions

(30 marks; 30 minutes)

1. Construct a cash flow forecast for the business for January to September. (10)
2. Outline two significant features of this cash flow forecast. (6)
3. Discuss two possible courses of action. (8)
4. Examine two ways in which the cash flow forecast may be unreliable. (6)

B3 CASE STUDY

From cocoa to cash

Joe Callery and David O'Doherty started Celtic Chocolates in 1990 in a converted cottage in County Meath, Ireland. It cost about £50,000 to get the chocolate business started.

'It took about two years to get a marketable product together,' says Joe Callery. 'For the first two years, we were really selling nothing'. Only in 1995 did the business start to generate a positive cash flow. Now annual turnover is above €1.5 million and the business has 20 full-time staff. A factory built behind the cottage has since been extended. 'In food manufacturing, you have to invest constantly to stay ahead.'

The product portfolio is based on three product ranges: purely seasonal products such as Easter Eggs; seasonal luxury after-dinner mints and truffles; and a range of 'free-from' chocolates, including diabetic and dairy-free chocolates. They are all at the luxury end of the market, though they can be bought at supermarkets such as Tesco as well as at speciality food stores.

'This whole business revolves around Christmas and Easter. We have just finished Easter production and will close for two weeks. Then from May to September we will be preparing for Christmas. Single days, such as St Valentine's Day or Mother's Day, are not significant.'

For this reason, Celtic Chocolates has worked hard to build up its specialist lines. 'The real difficulty is cash flow during down times. Specialist lines will sell all year round. In Ireland, we have 700 to 800 retail customers all buying at Christmas and Easter. About 200 customers buy all year round. That's what keeps us going.'

A long time ago, the company learnt about the risks of relying on one big customer. In 1999, Boots was its main client, accounting for about 40 per cent of turnover. Then Boots decided to cut back all products that were not central to its business and Celtic Chocolates was dropped. The sales slump forced the firm to make redundancies.

Starting a business is about surviving the first five years, according to Callery. 'We had borrowed money to finance investment; then rates went through the roof,' he said. 'At the end of the first year interest rates were so high that we owed more money to the bank than we had at the beginning – even though we had paid back 20 per cent of the amount borrowed. We just kept going; that's all you can do. Sometimes you just have to wait it out.'

In 2008 Celtic Chocolates celebrated winning a coveted Gold award at Britain's 'Great Taste Awards' for its new Organic Fairtrade mint products. In 2010 the company received further awards for its 'Free From' range. Twenty years after its start-up, Celtic Chocolates is a perfect example of how a small business can find a profitable niche in a big marketplace.

Questions

(30 marks; 35 minutes)

1 Analyse why a new business such as Celtic Chocolates may struggle with cash flow in the early stages of its start-up. (8)

2 Explain why it is risky for cash flow for a business such as Celtic Chocolates to rely 'on one big customer'. (6)

3 **a)** Explain the seasonal cash flow problem faced by Celtic Chocolates. (6)

b) Discuss whether Celtic Chocolates should decide to put an end to its seasonal cash flow problems by scrapping the production of lines such as Easter Eggs. (10)

B4 CASE STUDY

Tescopoly power

With the Credit Crunch underway, many manufacturers were already concerned about their cash flow. Then there was a big shock. Tesco announced that it would be changing its payment terms to suppliers of non-food items such as TVs, books, clothing and gardening supplies. Starting this autumn, Tesco would be switching from paying its suppliers within 30 days to paying within 60 days. So, with hardly any warning, the cash flow forecasts of hundreds (Tesco says 300) of manufacturers will have to be torn up and redone.

The attraction for Tesco is clear. As it spends more than £3,000 million per month (!) on supplies, a one month delay in paying could boost the firm's cash position by hundreds, even thousands, of millions of pounds. With the world economy entering recession, what could be cleverer than that? For a small manufacturer supplying Tesco, though, this would be especially infuriating. It would almost mean the 'mighty' Tesco raiding the small firm's bank account to boost its own.

Despite their anger, no small supplier came out in public to complain about the change in terms. The *Financial Times* newspaper suggested this was because they feared 'retribution from the retailer'. On 30 October 2008, though, they found a surprising defender in the form of the chief executive of the huge Reckitt Benckiser company (Nurofen, Airwick, Cillit Bang and many other brands). Bart Becht warned that it could 'push some smaller players out of business'. Smaller suppliers will certainly have been outraged to hear that Reckitt had *not* been approached by Tesco to make any changes to its credit terms.

Tesco's defence is that it is only asking for 60 days' credit from suppliers of slower-moving stock such as books and kettles. Even if there is justification for doubling the credit period, three reasons make it especially hard to forgive Tesco's action:

1. The threat to small producers posed by banks' current difficulties
2. The fact that Tesco has such a hugely strong financial position itself
3. The very short notice given; suppliers needed plenty of warning so that they could plan for the vicious hit to their cash flow represented by this move. Did Tesco's executives simply not understand the implications for its suppliers? Or did they not care?

In tough times like these, Tesco appears to be showing the worst side of big business. We can all understand a business being tough on its competitors. But these are not competitors, they are suppliers. In the past, Tesco has often boasted of its pride in working with suppliers and forming strong long-term relationships. It is showing how hollow these warm words can be.

Source: Topical Cases, A-Z Business Training.

Questions

(40 marks; 45 minutes)

1 Explain the impact of Tesco's action on a small supplier, assuming that 75 per cent of its output is being sold to Tesco. (6)

2 a) Assume that this same small supplier has the cash flow forecast shown in Table 15.6. Rework the cash flow assuming that Tesco's new payment rules begin on 1 November. Draw out Table 15.7 for your answer. (12)

Table 15.6 A small supplier's cash flow forecast

	October	November	December	January
Cash in	£200,000	£260,000	£270,000	£140,000
Cash out	£180,000	£220,000	£230,000	£170,000
Net cash	£20,000	£40,000	£40,000	(£30,000)
Cumulative cash	(£10,000)	£30,000	£70,000	£40,000

Table 15.7 A small supplier's cash flow forecast assuming Tesco's new payment rules begin on 1 November

	October	November	December	January
Cash in	£200,000			
Cash out	£180,000			
Net cash	£20,000			
Cumulative cash	(£10,000)			

b) Discuss the best way for the small firm to overcome this cash flow problem. (10)

3 Discuss whether large firms such as Tesco should be forced by law to pay their bills within 30 days. (12)

UNIT 16

Sources of finance

All businesses need money. Where the money comes from is known as 'sources of finance'.

16.1 THE NEED FOR FINANCE

Starting up

New businesses starting up need money to invest in long-term assets such as buildings and equipment. They also need cash to purchase materials, pay wages and to pay the day-to-day bills such as water and electricity. Inexperienced entrepreneurs often underestimate the capital needed for the day-to-day running of the business. Generally, for every £1,000 required to establish the business, another £1,000 is needed for the day-to-day needs.

Growing

Once the business is established there will be income from sales. If this is greater than the operating costs, the business will be making a profit. This should be kept in the business and used to help the business to grow. Later on, the owners can draw money out of the business, but at this stage as much as possible should be left in. Even so, there may not be enough to allow the business to grow as fast as it would like to. It may need to find additional finance and this will probably be from external sources.

Other situations

Businesses may also need finance in other circumstances. They may have a cash flow problem caused by changes in market conditions. A major customer may refuse to pay for the goods, causing a huge gap in cash inflows. Or there may be a large order, requiring the purchase of additional raw materials. In all these cases businesses will need to find additional funding.

16.2 INTERNAL AND EXTERNAL SOURCES OF FINANCE

Finance for business comes from two main sources:

1. inside the business: known as internal sources of finance
2. outside the business: known as external sources of finance.

Internal sources

Existing capital can be made to stretch further. The business may be able to negotiate to pay its bills later or work at getting cash in earlier from customers; the average small firm waits 75 days to be paid (two and a half months); if that period of time could be halved, it would provide a huge boost to cash flow.

Nothing soothes a difficult cash situation better than profit. It is also the best (and most common) way to finance investment into a firm's future. Research shows that over 60 per cent of business investment comes from reinvested profit.

External sources

If the business is unable to generate sufficient funds from internal sources then it may need to look to external sources. There are two sources of external capital: loan capital and share capital.

Loan capital

The most usual way is through borrowing from a bank. This may be in the form of a bank loan or an overdraft. A loan is usually for a set period of time. It may be short term – one or two years; medium term – three to five years; or long term – more than five years. The loan can either be repaid in instalments over time or at the end of the loan period. The bank will charge interest on the loan. This can be fixed or variable. The bank will demand collateral to provide security in case the loan cannot be repaid.

An overdraft is a very short-term loan. It is a facility that allows the business to be 'overdrawn'. This means that the account is allowed to go 'into the red'. The length of time that this runs for will have to be negotiated. The interest charges on overdrafts are usually much higher than on loans.

Share capital

Alternatively if the business is a limited company it may look for additional share capital. This could come from private investors or venture capital funds. Venture capital providers are interested in investing in businesses with dynamic growth prospects. They are willing to take a risk on a business that may fail, or may do spectacularly well. They believe that if they make ten investments, five can flop, and four do 'OK' as long as one does fantastically. Peter Theil, the original investor in Facebook, probably turned his $0.5 million investment into $200 million or more, making a profit of 39,900 per cent!

Once it has become a public limited company (plc), the firm may consider floating on the stock exchange. For smaller businesses this will usually be on the Alternative Investment Market (AIM).

A-grade application

Financing growth

How do rapidly growing small firms finance their growth? By venture capital? By loans? To find an answer to this question, Hamish Stevenson from Templeton College, Oxford, looked at 100 of the fastest growing UK firms. One of these is R Frazier, a firm which recycles computers. Its sales grew from £294,000 to £7,400,000 in just three years. In common with the majority of the firms, R Frazier's early growth was self-funded, in other words from reinvested profits and trade credit. 'These are the real entrepreneurs,' says Stevenson. 'They grab money where they can. It is fly-by-the-seat-of-their-pants finance.' The 54 firms which used this method were doing so 'through default not by design', according to the research. In other words they had no alternative.

Twenty-one of the firms received external finance from share capital: 15 from venture capital houses and 6 from business angels. Just 10 used long-term bank debt. Having survived, even thrived, through these hectic early years, as many as 40 of the firms are looking at, or in the process of, floating their firms on the London stock market. This would secure the finance for the next stage of growth.

16.3 HOW MUCH FINANCE CAN THE BUSINESS OBTAIN?

The type and amount of finance that is available will depend on several factors, which are set out below.

The type of business

A sole trader will be limited to the capital the owner can put into the business plus any money he or she is able to borrow. A limited company will be able to raise share capital. In order to become a plc, it will need to have share capital of £50,000+ and have a track record of success. This will make borrowing easier.

The stage of development of the business

A new business will find it much harder to raise finance than an established firm. As the business develops it is easier to persuade outsiders to invest in the business. It is also easier to obtain loans as the firm has assets to offer as security.

The state of the economy

When the economy is booming, business confidence will be high. It will be easy to raise finance both from borrowing and from investors. It will be more difficult for businesses to find investors when interest rates are high. They will invest their money in more secure accounts such as building societies. Higher interest rates will also put up the cost of borrowing. This will make it more expensive for the business to borrow.

16.4 ADVANTAGES AND DISADVANTAGES OF SOURCES OF FINANCE

Internal sources

The advantages and disadvantages of internal sources of finance are set out below.

Reinvested profit

The profit generated by the business will provide a return for the investors in the business and can be ploughed back into the business to help it to grow.

The advantage of reinvested profit is that it does not have an associated cost. Unlike loans it does not have to be repaid and there are no interest charges.

The disadvantage is that it may be limited so will constrain the rate of business expansion.

Cash squeezed out of day-to-day finances

By cutting stocks, chasing up customers or delaying payments to suppliers, cash can be generated. This has the advantage of reducing the amount that needs to be borrowed. However this is a very short-term solution and if the cash is taken from working capital for a purpose such as buying fixed assets, the firm may find itself short of day-to-day finance.

Sale of assets

An established business has assets. These can be sold to raise cash. The business loses the asset but has the use of the cash. It makes good business sense for businesses to dispose of under-used assets. They can finance development without extra borrowing. If the asset is needed, it may be possible to sell it, but immediately lease it back. In this way, the business has use of the money and the asset. This is known as sale and leaseback.

External sources

The advantages and disadvantages of external sources of finance are set out below.

Bank overdrafts

This is the commonest form of borrowing for small businesses. The bank allows the firm to overdraw up to an agreed level. This has the advantages that the firm only needs to borrow when and as much as it needs. It is, however, an expensive way of borrowing, and the bank can insist on being repaid within 24 hours.

Trade credit

This is the simplest form of external financing. The business obtains goods or services from another business but does not pay for these immediately. The average credit period is two months. It is a good way of boosting day-to-day working capital. A disadvantage could be that other businesses may be reluctant to trade with the business if they do not get paid in good time.

Venture capital

This is a way of getting outside investment for businesses that are unable to raise finance through the stock markets or loans. Venture capitalists invest in smaller, riskier companies. To compensate for the risks, venture capital providers usually require a substantial part of the ownership of the company. They are also likely to want to contribute to the running of the business. This dilutes the owner's control but brings in new experience and knowledge. The term 'Dragon' became a well-known term for a venture capital provider, thanks to the BBC TV series 'Dragons' Den'.

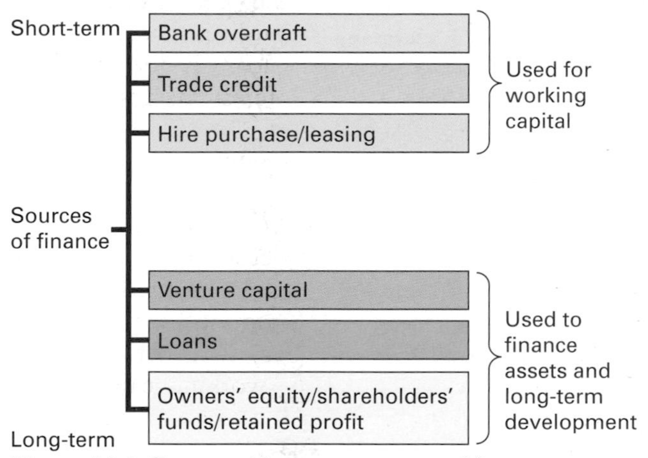

Figure 16.1 Short- and long-term sources of finance

16.5 FINANCE SHOULD BE ADEQUATE AND APPROPRIATE

Having adequate funding means ensuring the business has sufficient access to finance to meet its current and future needs. This is a major issue for new firms and for those that are expanding rapidly. When a business expands without sufficient finance it is known as overtrading.

Appropriate financing means matching the type of finance to its use. A distinction is made in company financing between short- and long-term finance (see Figure 16.1). Short-term finance is usually considered to be for less than one year. Medium-term is one to five years. Long-term finance is longer than five years.

Short-term finance should not be used to finance long-term projects. Using short-term finance such as overdrafts puts continual pressure on the company's cash position. An overdraft should only be used to cope with ups and downs in cash flows. By its very nature, growth is a long-term activity, so appropriate long-term finance should be sought to fund it.

A-grade application

The banking crisis: Northern Rock

The effects of the banking crisis in 2007–08 are still being felt in 2010 and will continue to affect many economies for a number of years to come. Banks have long been seen as organisations that give financial advice to business and private customers. It was ironic that not only had they made rash decisions regarding investments but that they proved in some cases to be incapable of managing their own affairs. Northern Rock was a prime example. In September 2007 it became the first British bank in 150 years to suffer a 'run on the bank', as savers feared for the bank's solvency. Northern Rock had expanded rapidly, financing its long-term growth with short-term finance; when the finance dried up, the bank collapsed. The business proved to have neither adequate nor appropriate finance. The crisis was averted only when the Bank of England guaranteed that no customer would lose their money.

Figure 16.2 Queues outside Northern Rock

ISSUES FOR ANALYSIS

When analysing or suggesting appropriate sources of finance, ask yourself the following questions.

- Why is the business seeking finance? The key here is to ensure that the finance is suitable for the business in its particular circumstances. A new business will have very different needs to a growing business. Remember the finance should be adequate and appropriate.
- Is the business stable or risky? If risky, the form of financing should be as safe as possible. Remember that financial institutions are unlikely to lend to risky or unproven enterprises.
- What is the owners' attitude to sharing the business? If the owners are reluctant to lose control of the business it is not a good idea to suggest raising finance by selling more shares. Financing growth by borrowings may be more appropriate.

A-grade application

Philippines Planters Bank: a model for small business banking

There has been much talk following the 'credit crunch' of the difficulties that small businesses face in getting loans from the banks. The government has tried to force banks to increase lending to this important part of the economy.

Jesus Tambunting, the former Philippines ambassador to the UK, has suggested that the UK should look to the Philippines for a banking model that lends effectively to small businesses. Mr Tambunting is the chairman of Planters Bank, which lends to the owners of small and medium-sized businesses (SMEs) in the Philippines.

He said that banks had to get back to 'basic banking' and that more dedicated small business banks should emerge so that customers could be better served.

'It's not viewed as commercially viable by the banks,' he said. 'You need an institution like us that's totally focused on SMEs. If you have a regular bank it is not going to work.'

'Admittedly it is not easy to lend to SMEs. We charge a higher rate but it's to compensate for a lot of the work. We are doing a lot of hand-holding. They may be first time borrowers. We try to educate them about what you need in a bank to approve a loan.'

Planters loans typically range in size from $10,000 to $1 million. Where businesses do not have collateral, Planters makes use of loan guarantee schemes run by the Philippines Government, which are similar to the UK's Enterprise Finance Guarantee.

Source: *Daily Telegraph*, 10 June 2010. © Telegraph Media Group Limited 2010

16.6 SOURCES OF FINANCE – EVALUATION

Finding finance may involve balancing conflicting interests. Internal sources of finance may be too limited to provide opportunities for business development. Obtaining external finance increases the money available, but has its downsides. Borrowing too much can be risky. Raising extra share capital dilutes the control held by existing shareholders.

Having adequate and appropriate finance at each stage in the firm's development will ensure it stays healthy. Decisions about where to obtain the finance will be a matter of considering the business objectives, the stage of development of the business and the reasons for the funding requirement.

Key Terms

Collateral: an asset used as security for a loan. It can be sold by a lender if the borrower fails to pay back a loan

Overtrading: when a firm expands without adequate and appropriate funding.

Public limited company (plc): a company with limited liability and shares, which are available to the public. Its shares can be quoted on the stock market.

Share capital: business finance that has no guarantee of repayment or of annual income, but gains a share of the control of the business and its potential profits.

Stock market: a market for buying and selling company shares. It supervises the issuing of shares by companies. It is also a second-hand market for stocks and shares.

Venture capital: high-risk capital invested in a combination of loans and shares, usually in a small, dynamic business.

WORKBOOK

A REVISION QUESTIONS

(30 marks; 30 minutes)

1 Describe the problem caused to a company if a major customer refuses to pay a big bill. (3)
2 Why do banks demand collateral before they agree to provide a bank loan? (2)
3 Outline two ways in which businesses can raise money from internal sources. (4)
4 What information may a bank manager want when considering a loan to a business? (4)
5 Read the A-grade application on Northern Rock. Explain the two mistakes made by the bank. (4)
6 Outline two sources of finance that can be used for long-term business development. (4)
7 Explain why a new business could find it difficult to get external funding for its development. (5)
8 Outline one advantage and one disadvantage of using an overdraft. (4)

B REVISION EXERCISES

B1 ACTIVITY

Indian in China?

Hi everyone, I am from India and wish to open a quick takeaway and a small restaurant or café but with Indian snacks and food in Nanjing, near the International University. I would like to know about:

1 the rules and regulations
2 the approximate budget
3 the minimum area requirement
4 the real estate prices in an area like Shanghai Lu, Nanjing.

Please contact me by leaving a comment here.

Thank you, Karishma

Hi Karishma,

You have to know that the life expectancy of a new foreign restaurant on Nanjing Road is between three and six months, in 50 per cent of cases. Many foreigners open restaurants without complying with all the rules ... Be ready to have enough funds to survive for one year minimum without any revenues. If you want I could give you contacts with very good companies that could help you for all legal aspects. Good luck, and I will come to your restaurant!

Paul Martin

Source: discussion at www.chinasuccessstories.com

Questions

(25 marks; 30 minutes)

1 Explain the implications of Paul Martin's reply for the financing of Karishma's start-up. (6)
2 Analyse the circumstances in which Karishma should proceed with her idea, if she were able to obtain the start-up finance. (7)
3 Assuming this information is widely known, discuss the probable attitude of any Chinese banks Karishma approaches. (12)

B2 ACTIVITY

Odd Jobs Ltd

Jeff Hale was made redundant from his job in the printing industry at the age of 51. Having worked with the firm since he was 15, he received a small pension that would be paid straightaway and a lump sum redundancy payment of £30,000.

He decided to set up a business called Odd Jobs Ltd. The idea was to fill the gap in the market between the DIY enthusiast and general builders. He knew from experience that it was often very difficult to get a builder to come and do the smaller jobs.

He set up the business as a limited company with a friend, Malcolm Baines, who had also been made redundant. They each invested £20,000 of their redundancy money. The remainder they used to reduce their mortgages to take some financial pressure off them whilst the business was becoming established. They rented a small office and a van and bought tools and office equipment. After making their purchases they were confident that they had sufficient working capital to finance the business until it became profitable. Their policy was to charge a reasonable rate for the job. They had a fixed scale of charges for run-of-the-mill jobs and gave a detailed estimate for any more complicated work.

They soon got a reputation for good quality work and after six months they found that they no longer needed to advertise. They resisted the temptation to do larger jobs, preferring to keep to their original idea. Most jobs took less than half a day to complete. Seven years later they now employ two office staff and a team of four other workers. They have bought three vans with the help of a £40,000 bank loan. Each van is equipped with a full set of tools. The business is prospering and they can look back with satisfaction. Even during a period of recession they were mostly unaffected.

Jeff and Malcolm feel that there is no more room for expansion in their hometown. They have been looking at setting up another branch in another town 35 km away. They feel that this is near enough to keep control of both businesses and to gain some advantage from the good reputation of the business.

They have prepared a business plan and feel that to make the venture work they will need to get a loan or some other external funding. They estimate that they will need around £40,000. Of this, £10,000 will be spent on office equipment and tools and £15,000 on the purchase of a new van. The remainder will be used as working capital to fund office rental and wages.

Questions

(25 marks; 30 minutes)

1 Acting as a bank manager, make a list of questions that you would want to ask Jeff and Malcolm before considering their loan. Explain why you want the information. (8)
2 If the bank will not provide the loan, consider how else the business could obtain the £40,000 needed for the expansion. (6)
3 Assuming that they can get the funding, do you consider that Jeff and Malcolm should go ahead with the expansion? Explain your decision. (11)

B2 DATA RESPONSE

Fair trade fashion: Bobelle

In early 2008 Claire Watt-Smith launched a Fair-trade fashion business called Bobelle. Its main product line is a series of handbags and purses made from super-smooth eel-skin leather. The skins used to be thrown away when eels (a delicacy in the Far East) were cooked. Now the skins are, in effect, recycled by turning them into soft leather.

Claire started the business with just £6,000. Most was from her student loan, but there was also a small investment made by her mother. At the time, she reflects: 'We were at the start of a recession. Banks didn't want to lend.'

In 2009–10, the second year of trading, Bobelle had a turnover of £65,000. It also had a small bank overdraft facility, which Claire rarely used. With distribution expanding to include 60 stores and a thriving e-commerce website, future growth looks likely. Claire is not sure that she can continue to finance growth through reinvested profits; she may need some outside capital investment. If so, she will turn her sole trader business into a private limited company.

Questions

(20 marks; 20 minutes)

1 How much external finance did Claire raise to start up Bobelle? (3)
2 Explain the difference between an overdraft and an overdraft facility. (4)
3 Outline two reasons why a small business that's growing rapidly may need 'outside capital investment'. (6)
4 Explain how Claire may be able to raise fresh capital after turning the business into a private limited company. (7)

UNIT 17

Budgets and budgeting

A budget is a target for costs or revenue that a firm or department must aim to reach over a given period of time.

17.1 INTRODUCTION

Budgeting is the process of setting targets, covering all aspects of costs and revenues. It is a method for turning a firm's strategy into reality. Nothing can be done in business without money; budgets tell individual managers how much they can spend to achieve their objectives. For instance, a football manager may be given a transfer expenditure budget of £20 million to buy players. With the budget in place, the transfer dealing can get under way.

A budgeting system shows how much can be spent, and gives managers a way to check whether they are on track. Most firms use a system of budgetary control as a means of supervision. The process is as follows:

1. Make a judgement of the likely sales revenues for the coming year.
2. Set a cost ceiling that allows for an acceptable level of profit.
3. This budget for the whole company's costs is then broken down by division, department or by cost centre.
4. The budget may then be broken down further so that each manager has a budget and therefore some spending power.

In a business start-up, the budget should provide enough spending power to finance vital needs such as building work, decoration, recruiting and paying staff, and marketing. If a manager overspends in one area, she or he knows that it is essential to cut back elsewhere. A good manager gets the best possible value from the budgeted sum.

17.2 WHAT IS BUDGETING FOR?

Budgeting is used:

- To ensure that no department or individual spends more than the company expects, thereby preventing unpleasant surprises.
- To provide a yardstick against which a manager's success or failure can be measured (and rewarded). For example, a store manager may have to meet a monthly sales budget of £25,000 at a maximum operating cost of £18,000. As long as the budget holder believes this target is possible, the attempt to achieve it will be motivating. The company can then provide bonuses for achieving or beating the profit target.
- To enable spending power to be delegated to local managers who are in a better position to know how best to use the firm's money. This should improve and speed up the decision-making process and help to motivate the local budget holders. Management expert Peter Drucker refers to 'management by self-control'. He regards this as the ideal approach. Managers should have clear targets, clear budgets and the power to decide how to achieve them. Then they will try everything they can to succeed.
- Budgeting can motivate the staff in a department. If budget figures are used as a clear basis for assessing their performance it becomes clear to staff what they must achieve in order to be considered successful.

17.3 BUDGETS AS A MEANS OF DELEGATING SPENDING POWER

Once a business grows beyond a simple one-person operation, there will be times that the boss is not around to authorise spending money – even small amounts like ordering a little extra stock or paying the window cleaner. To make sure the business can run smoothly, the boss needs to find a way to give staff the power to make spending decisions themselves. However, the boss will want to ensure that these decisions are not going to bankrupt the firm. Budgets can be used to allow employees to decide what money to spend within the limits specified by the budget. If an entrepreneur who has successfully opened a beauty salon wants to open a second branch, she or he will need to appoint a manager of the second branch. The entrepreneur can then agree budget targets for the income and expenditure of the second branch, knowing that the manager will be working hard to hit the budget targets.

The budgets for costs should help to avoid any unexpected financial surprises, since the manager would be expected to discuss any budget overspend with the entrepreneur before they are incurred. The manager can run the shop on a day-to-day basis, spending whatever money needs to be spent without checking with the boss all the time, yet the boss will be happy that the costs of the second branch are being controlled within the limits set by the budget.

This principle applies to huge multinational companies as well as businesses that have just started growing. In a huge firm, there will be many more budget holders and many more separate budgets; however, the concept is the same, as shown in the simple example in Figure 17.1.

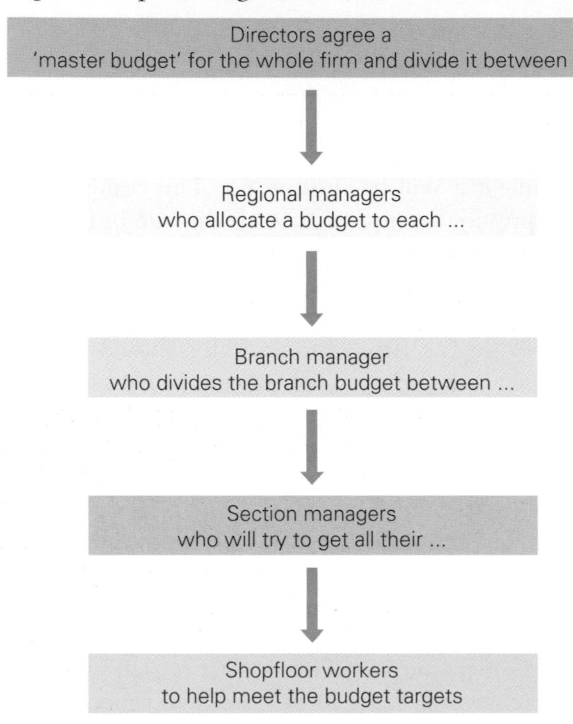

Figure 17.1 Budget holders

17.4 BUDGETS AS A METHOD OF MONITORING BUSINESS PERFORMANCE

With budgets in place for each department, the management has criteria against which success can be measured. Budget holders will try to exceed revenue budgets or stay under cost targets. The implication, of course, is that budgeted figures will be compared with what actually happens to make a judgement on performance. It is this process of comparison that allows budgets to be used as a method of monitoring business performance.

17.5 TYPES OF BUDGET

Income budget

The income budget sets a minimum target for the desired revenue level to be achieved over a period of time. If a manager knows, halfway through the year, that sales figures have not been strong enough to achieve the target, she or he might decide to run a price promotion or a 'buy one get one free' (BOGOF) offer. When buying a new car it is clever to wait for the last day of the month, as showroom managers are often trying desperately to achieve their monthly sales target: their incentive may be a salary bonus or a monthly prize such as a trip to the Caribbean for the month's top-performing sales manager; your incentive is a cheaper car!

Expenditure budget

The expenditure budget sets a maximum target for costs; for example, the manager of the Derby McDonald's may have a staff budget of £2,100 for the month of November. Spending beyond an expenditure budget occasionally will be tolerated, but a manager who persistently overspends is likely to get a stern talking-to. An intelligent boss will also question expenditure underspending (for example, not spending the budget for safety training) as this may cause major problems later on.

Profit budget

The profit budget is a function of the previous two budgets: the higher the income budget and the lower the expenditure, the higher the profit. Senior managers should look with care at how a profit budget has been met or beaten. For example, the profit achievement may have been a result of cost-cutting that threatens health and safety. Of course, managers are supposed to meet their profit targets, but there is more to running a business successfully than simply getting the numbers right.

> **A-grade application**
>
> **The BP Disaster**
>
> On 23 March 2005 a huge explosion at BP's Texas oil refinery killed 15 people and injured more than 180. Most were the company's own staff. The refinery, America's third biggest, had previously suffered safety problems. In 2004 two workers died when scalded by super-heated water that escaped from a high-pressure pipe and, in a separate incident, BP was fined $63,000 for safety breaches at the plant.
>
> After an inquiry, the chairwoman of the US Chemical Safety Board reported that 'BP implemented a 25 per cent cut on fixed costs from 1998 to 2000 that adversely impacted maintenance expenditures at the refinery'. The report stated that 'BP's global management' (the British Head Office) 'was aware of problems with maintenance spending and infrastructure well before March 2005'. Yet they did nothing about it. The chairwoman delivered the final critique:
>
> 'Every successful corporation must contain its costs. But at an ageing facility like Texas City, it is not responsible to cut budgets related to safety and maintenance without thoroughly examining the impact on the risk of a catastrophic accident.' BP confirmed that its own internal investigation had findings 'generally consistent with those of the CSB'.
>
> In 2010, there was an echo of this disaster when an explosion on a BP well in the Gulf of Mexico killed 11 people and caused the biggest oil spill in American history.
>
> Source: Adapted from Topical Cases, www.a-zbusinesstraining.com

17.6 SETTING BUDGETS

Setting budgets is not an easy job. How do you decide exactly what level of sales are likely next year, especially for new businesses with no previous trading to rely on? Furthermore, how can you plan for costs if the cost of your raw materials tends to fluctuate? Most firms treat last year's budget figures as the main determinant of this year's budget. Minor adjustments will be made for inflation and other foreseeable changes. Given the firm's past experience, budget-setting should be quite quick and quite accurate.

For start-ups, setting budgets will be a much tougher job. The entrepreneur will need to rely on:

- a 'guesstimate' of likely sales in the early months of the start-up
- the entrepreneur's expertise and experience, which will be better if the entrepreneur has worked in the industry before
- the entrepreneur's instinct, based on market understanding
- a significant level of market research.

A-grade application

Budgeting helps but is not easy for start-ups

Stanford University research into 78 business start-ups showed that firms with budgeting systems were more likely to survive and experience significant growth rates. They reported that budgeting systems allowed senior staff access to the information needed when making decisions. However, they acknowledged the difficulties in setting budgets for new start-ups. They point out that, for a new company, predicting the future is hugely unpredictable and setting 12-month budgets is likely to be unrealistic.

An alternative approach is zero budgeting. This sets each department's budget at zero and demands that budget holders, in setting their budget, justify every pound they ask for. This helps to avoid the common phenomenon of budgets creeping upwards each year.

The only serious drawback to zero budgeting is that it takes a long time to find good reasons to justify why you need a budget of £150,000 instead of £110,000. As it is so time-consuming for managers, it is sensible to use zero budgeting every four to five years, rather than every year. Figure 17.2 shows the benefits of this approach.

The best criteria for setting budgets are:

- to relate the budget directly to the business objective; if a company wants to increase sales and market share, the best method may be to increase the advertising budget and thereby boost demand
- to involve as many people as possible in the process; people will be more committed to reaching the targets if they have had a say in how the budget was set.

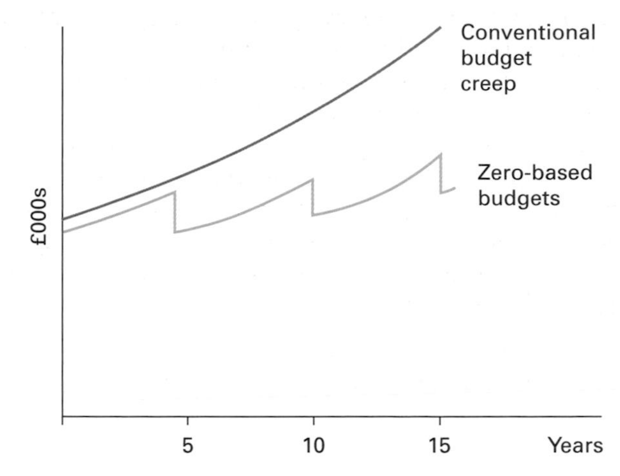

Figure 17.2 The benefits of zero budgeting

Simple budget statements

A simple example of a budget statement may look like that shown in Table 17.1.

Table 17.1 Example of a budget statement

	January	February	March
Income	25,000	28,000	30,000
Variable costs	10,000	12,000	13,000
Fixed costs	10,000	10,000	11,000
Total expenditure	20,000	22,000	24,000
Profit	5,000	6,000	6,000

This information is only of value if it proves possible for a manager to believe that these figures are achievable. Only then will she or he be motivated to try to turn the budgets into reality.

17.7 PROBLEMS IN SETTING BUDGETS

The main problem is that individual managers want as much spending power as possible (a high budget). This will help them do their job successfully and more enjoyably (for example a big expense account). The bosses, though, want to keep costs as low as possible among junior managers (to set low budgets). A senior Cadbury's manager might feel sure that an advertising budget of £2 million will be enough for Creme Eggs this year. Yet the brand manager for Creme Eggs may have a convincing argument for why £3.5 million is needed. (And no one knows the 'right' figure.)

The main problems in setting budgets occur when:

- a new firm or new manager lacks experience in knowing what things really cost
- a senior manager is too arrogant to listen to his or her staff, and just sets a budget without discussion (successful budgets should be agreed, not set)
- the type of business makes it hard to set budgets in a meaningful way (meaning that managers struggle

to take them seriously); see the description of the research carried out by Stanford University in the A-grade application box above.

A-grade application

Chessington World of Adventures

In April 2010 Chessington World of Adventures opened up for its summer season. The newly appointed merchandise manager (in charge of all non-food sales) was given his sales budget for the year, which had been set 6 per cent higher than for 2009. He thought the budget was quite ambitious, especially when a cold April and May meant that there were fewer visitors. Then the period June to August saw hot, dry weather and the turnstiles were 'buzzing' again. As a hot day at Chessington can boost crowds by 50 per cent, he did not need to make any effort to meet his budget. Do budgets have a purpose in a business such as this?

Budgetary variances

Variance is the amount by which the actual result differs from the budgeted figure. It is usually measured each month, by comparing the actual outcome with the budgeted one. It is important to note that variances are referred to as adverse or favourable – not positive or negative. A **favourable variance** is one that leads to higher than expected profit (revenue up or costs down). An **adverse variance** is one that reduces profit, such as costs being higher than the budgeted level. Table 17.2 shows when variances are adverse or favourable.

Table 17.2 Adverse or favourable variance?

Variable	Budget	Actual	Variance	
Sales of X	150	160	10	Favourable
Sales of Y	150	145	5	Adverse
Material costs	100	90	10	Favourable
Labour costs	100	105	5	Adverse

The value of regular variance statements is that they provide an early warning. If a product's sales are slipping below budget, managers can respond by increasing marketing support or by cutting back on production plans. In an ideal world, slippage could be noted in March, a new strategy put into place by May and a recovery in sales achieved by September. Clearly, no firm wishes to wait until the end-of-year profit and loss account to find out that things went badly. An early warning can lead to an early solution.

A-grade application

A wiser dragon

Rachel Elnough was one of the original dragons on the BBC TV series *Dragons' Den*. As founder of the gift company Red Letter Days, she was making a £1 million profit on a turnover of £10 million at the height of the firm's success. Once she stepped back from day-to-day control of the company, however, things started to go wrong. The major lesson she reports is that although budgets had been set, there was a lack of monitoring of those budgets and therefore problems in reaching targets became clear to her only once the firm was in too much trouble to save.

ISSUES FOR ANALYSIS

- Especially relevant to a small business owner will be deciding whether designing and implementing a budgeting system will cost more in terms of time and money than it could save. In other words, she or he must decide on the opportunity costs involved. In the often chaotic world of a small business start-up, it is easy to see how time spent talking to customers and suppliers would be more valuable. It is harder to appreciate how time spent in front of a computer spreadsheet estimating revenues and costs will help to enhance profit and the chances of survival.
- Variances are the key to analysing budgets. Once a variance between budgeted and actual figures has been identified, the analysis can begin. The important step is to ask why that variance occurred. Does the person responsible know the reason? Is it a one-off, or does this same person offer a different excuse each month for poor performance?
- Variance analysis is a means of identifying symptoms. It is down to the user of the variance figures to make a diagnosis as to the exact nature of any problem, and then to suggest the most appropriate cure.

Key Terms

Adverse variance: a difference between budgeted and actual figures that is damaging to the firm's profit (for example costs up or revenue down).
Criteria: yardsticks against which success (or the lack of it) can be measured.
Delegated: passing authority down the hierarchy.
Expenditure budget: setting a maximum figure on what a department or manager can spend over a period of time; this is to control costs.
Favourable variance: a difference between budgeted and actual figures that boosts a firm's profit (for example revenue up or costs down).
Income budget: setting a minimum figure for the revenue to be generated by a product, a department or a manager.
Profit budget: setting a minimum figure for the profit to be achieved over a period of time.
Zero budgeting: setting all future budgets at £0, to force managers to have to justify the spending levels they say they need in future.

17.8 BUDGETS AND BUDGETING – AN EVALUATION

The sophistication of budgeting systems is usually directly linked to the size of a business. Huge multinationals have incredibly complex budgeting systems. For a small business start-up, any budgeting system is likely to be far more simplistic. Most will rely on a rough breakdown of how the start-up budget is to be divided between the competing demands. There is, however, no doubt that budgeting provides a more effective system of controlling a business's finances than no system at all.

Budgets are a management tool. The way in which they are used can tell you a lot about a firm's culture. Firms with a culture of bossy management will tend to use a tightly controlled budgetary system. Managers will have budgets imposed upon them and variances will be watched closely by supervisors. Organisations with a more open culture will use budgeting as an aid to discussion and empowerment.

Whatever the culture, if a manager is to be held accountable for meeting a budget, she or he must be given influence over setting it, and control over reaching it. Although budgets are set for future time periods, analysis of actual against budgeted performance can take place only after the event. This is true of all financial monitoring and leads to doubts as to its effectiveness as a planning tool. Other measures may be far more reliable in predicting future performance; market research indicating growing levels of customer complaints, for instance, may well be more useful in predicting future performance.

WORKBOOK

A REVISION QUESTIONS

(45 marks; 45 minutes)

1 Explain the meaning of the term 'budgeting'. (2)
2 List three advantages that a budgeting system brings to a company. (3)
3 Why is it valuable to have a yardstick against which performance can be measured? (3)
4 What are the advantages of a zero-based budgeting system? (3)
5 Briefly explain how most companies actually set next year's budgets. (3)
6 Why should budget holders have a say in the setting of their budgets? (4)
7 Complete the budget statement shown in Table 17.3 by filling in the gaps: (8)
8 How could a firm respond to an increasingly adverse variance in labour costs? (4)
9 Explain what is meant by a 'favourable cost variance'. (3)
10 Look at Table 17.4, then answer the following questions.
 a) Calculate the budgeted and actual profit figures for both months (2)
 b) Identify a month with:
  i) a favourable revenue variance
  ii) an adverse fixed cost variance
  iii) an adverse variable cost variance
  iv) a favourable fixed cost variance
  v) an adverse total cost variance
  vi) an adverse revenue variance
  vii) a favourable total cost variance
  viii) an adverse variable cost variance
  ix) an adverse profit variance
  x) a favourable profit variance. (10)

Table 17.3 A budget statement

	January	February	March	April
Income	4,200	4,500	4,000	
Variable costs	1,800		2,000	1,800
Fixed costs	1,200	1,600		1,600
Total costs		3,600	4,100	
Profit				600

Table 17.4 Budgeted and actual figures for May and June

	May		June	
	Budgeted	Actual	Budgeted	Actual
Revenue	3,500	3,200	4,000	4,200
Variable costs	1,000	900	1,200	1,500
Fixed costs	1,200	1,200	1,300	1,100
Total costs	2,200	2,100	2,500	2,600
Profit				

B REVISION EXERCISES
B1 DATA RESPONSE

The partnership began in the Atlantic Ocean. Kurt and Brian were both windsurfing fanatics and got to know each other one winter in the Canary Isles. Looking for a way to fund ever more expensive winter watersports trips, they pooled their savings to buy the lease on a flooded former gravel pit in the UK. The location, just outside London, gave them access to a large market of affluent watersports enthusiasts. KB Wetsports could provide this market with their fix of windsurfing, dinghy sailing or kayaking. In addition to the fees for use of the lake and tuition fees for beginners, a shop would also feature at the centre, selling specialist watersport supplies that were hard to find inland. Both Kurt and Brian had studied management at university and knew that budgeting would be important. They could use it to control expenses and to motivate their small team of staff. They drew up the budget statement shown in Table 17.5.

Table 17.5 Budget statement for KB Wetsports

	Jan–Mar	Apr–Jun	Jul–Sep	Oct–Dec
Shop sales	200	3,000	5,000	2,000
Lake fees	0	22,000	25,000	2,800
Stock	2,500	1,000	2,500	1,000
Wages	1,000	5,000	5,000	1,000
Overheads	1,000	4,000	6,000	4,000
Profit				

Questions

(30 marks; 30 minutes)

1 Complete the budget statement by filling in the gaps. (4)
2 Adjust the budget to show the effect of a 50 per cent increase in shop sales in the third quarter and a 25 per cent increase in wages in the fourth quarter. (4)
3 Explain why a budgeting system might help KB Wetsports to:
  a) control expenses (6)
  b) motivate staff. (6)
4 To what extent is budget-setting a crucial element of a successful small business start-up such as KB Wetsports? (10)

B2 Data analysis

Table 17.6 Variance analysis

	January			February		
	B	A	V	B	A	V
Sales revenue	140*	150	10	180	175	?
Materials	70	80	(10)	90	95	?
Other direct costs	30	35	(5)	40	40	0
Overheads	20	20	0	25	22	?
Profit	20	15	(5)	?	18	?

*All figures in £000s

Questions

(20 marks; 20 minutes)

1 What are the five numbers missing from the variance analysis shown in Table 17.6? (5)
2 Examine one financial strength and two weaknesses in this data, from the company's viewpoint. (9)
3 How may a manager set about improving the accuracy of a sales budget? (6)

B3 Data response

Table 17.7 Budget data for Clinton & Collins Ltd (£000s)

	January		February		March		April	
	B	A	B	A	B	A	B	A
Sales revenue	160	144	180	156	208	168	240	188
Materials	40	38	48	44	52	48	58	54
Labour	52	48	60	54	66	62	72	68
Overheads	76	76	76	78	76	80	76	80
Profit	(8)	(18)	(4)	(20)	14	(22)	34	(14)

Questions

(25 marks; 25 minutes)

1 Use the data given in Table 17.7 to explain why February's profits were worse than expected. (5)
2 Why may Clinton & Collins Ltd have chosen to set monthly budgets? (5)
3 Explain how the firm could have set these budgets. (4)
4 The directors of Clinton & Collins Ltd knew that the recession was causing problems for the firm but were unsure as to whether things were improving or worsening. To what extent does the data suggest an improvement? (11)

B4 DATA RESPONSE

Cutting work trip hotel costs

According to new research, UK organisations are overspending by £1.3 billion every year on unnecessarily extravagant business trips. Nearly half of all organisations fail to produce an official business travel policy. Therefore many employees admit to booking what they want and 88 per cent claim not to be influenced by cost.

Stephen Alambritis, chief spokesman of the Federation of Small Businesses, comments: 'Business owners understand the importance of face-to-face meetings and consider personal contact with customers an essential part of generating new sales. But well-run firms control the cost of business travel, setting budgets for both transport and accommodation. Controlling costs across the business underpins future growth and success.'

The findings were alarming: UK businesses simply don't maintain financial control over employee business trips.

The wastage facts

- Nearly half (48 per cent) of all organisations never set a business trip budget. This figure rises to 59 per cent when relating to small to medium-sized businesses.
- Over 40 per cent of employees make their own individual business trip arrangements and claim that they can spend what they like on trips.
- An overwhelming 88 per cent say they aren't influenced by cost.
- Almost a third (30 per cent) of 18 to 29 year olds exploit business trips as perks.
- Only 12 per cent of employees believe their organisations are interested in cost-cutting.

This clear lack of control has left employees free to squander up to £1.3 billion of their employers' money every year.

Source: www.workingbalance.co.uk

Questions

(20 marks; 25 minutes)

1 Identify and explain three pieces of evidence from the text that demonstrate the problems for firms that operate without a budget. (9)
2 Explain how a small business might benefit from setting expenditure budgets for its business travel. (5)
3 Outline two problems a business could have in setting a travel budget. (6)

UNIT 18

Measuring and increasing profit

Net profit is the profit left after all the operating costs have been deducted from revenue. Net profit margins look at the percentage profit compared with the sales revenue of the business.

18.1 MEASURING PERFORMANCE

The performance of organisations may be measured in many ways, such as:

- sales or sales growth
- market share
- the job satisfaction of its employees
- its track record on environmental issues
- the quality of its relationships with suppliers
- customer satisfaction.

The most appropriate measure(s) will depend on the nature of the organisation; a hospital may look at the number of successful operations, a university may measure the number and class of the degrees of its students, and a sports club may measure the number of matches played and won. Organisations will often have several different measures to assess their performance in different areas. However, one of the most common measures of success for organisations is net profit.

Net profit measures the profit left after all the operating costs of the business have been deducted. These costs may include the costs of producing and marketing the products, as well as fixed costs (such as rent). Net profit is the lifeblood of the organisation because unless the business makes a profit, it cannot finance growth. In a growing economy, with new opportunities arising all the time, a business that cannot grow is condemned to a slow death. The perfect example of this is Woolworths. In its 2007 financial year it made a net profit that was less than 1 per cent of its sales. In other words, of every £1 taken through a Woolworths till, less than 1p was the company's net profit. Not surprisingly the company ultimately failed and its stores closed in January 2009.

18.2 NET PROFIT AND NET PROFIT MARGIN

The net profit of a business is an absolute number that is measured in value terms. For example, a business may earn a net profit of £10,000. Is this a good level of profit or not? To find out, the profit is measured in relation to the total value of sales. This is known as the net profit margin:

$$\text{Net profit margin} = \frac{\text{Net profit}}{\text{Sales} \times 100}$$

For example, if the net profit is £10,000 and the sales are £50,000 the net profit margin is:

$$\frac{£10{,}000}{£50{,}000} \times 100 = 20\%$$

This means that 20 per cent of the firm's revenue is actually profit (of every £1 of sales, 20p is net profit). Notice that the net profit margin is a percentage.

A-grade application

Dell computers

In 2010 Dell, the world's largest computer maker reported a 6 per cent fall in overall profits despite an increase in sales due to its falling profit margins. The company saw sales of its personal computers rise by 29 per cent over the first three months of 2010, but consumers were choosing to buy the less profitable, cheapest models. Influenced by the recession and a lack of demand generally in the economy, customers looked for better deals and bargains leading to lower profit margins on sales. Even though more computers were sold by Dell its total profits fell.

What is a good net profit margin?

The typical net profit margin in an industry will vary from one sector to another. Net profit margins from selected 2009 company accounts are shown in Table 18.1. The food retail market, for example, is very competitive and the profit per sale (the profit margin) is likely to be quite low (for example, 5 per cent). However, provided you can sell a high volume of items your overall net profits can still be high. You may make relatively little profit per can of beans, but provided you sell a lot of beans your overall profits may still be high.

In the case of luxury items such as Ted Baker clothes or Rolex watches the profit margin is likely to be much higher. However, although the profit per sale is relatively high, this does not automatically mean the profits are high – that depends on how many items you sell.

Table 18.1 Net profit margins from selected 2009 company accounts

	Net profit (£ million)	Sales (£ million)	Net profit margin (%)
Tesco	2,954	354,327	5.44
Sainsbury's	466	18,911	2.46
Ted Baker	17.7	152	11.4

18.3 THE RETURN ON CAPITAL

Profitability measures profit in relation to some other variable. As we have seen, the net profit margin measures profit in relation to sales. We may also want to measure the net profit in relation to the amount invested in a project. The money invested is often called 'capital'.

If, for example, a business invests £20,000 into a project and this generates a profit of £5,000 then the return on the capital invested (known as **return on capital**) is 25 per cent:

$$\text{Return on capital} = \frac{\text{Net profit}}{\text{Capital invested} \times 100}$$

$$= \frac{£5{,}000 \times 100}{£20{,}000} = 25\%$$

The return on capital is an important indicator of the success of a project or business. Imagine a business proposal is expected to earn a return on capital of 25 per cent; this is very good compared to the return you are likely to get if you invest your money in a bank. The opportunity cost (the return you could get elsewhere) is probably lower than 25 per cent, which makes the project attractive.

If, however, you expected to invest £20,000 and generate profits of only £500:

$$\text{Return on capital} = \frac{\text{Net profit}}{\text{Capital invested}} \times 100$$

$$= \frac{£500}{£20{,}000} \times 100 = 2.5\%$$

In this case, the return on capital is only 2.5 per cent and you would probably expect to earn more if you saved your money in a bank instead.

18.4 RETURN ON CAPITAL AND THE NET PROFIT MARGIN

Obviously the return on capital is linked to the net profit margin. The overall returns will depend on how many units are sold and on the profit per sale (the net profit margin).

If the firm can sell the same amount of products but with a higher profit margin, the overall return on capital will increase. Alternatively, if the net profit margin remains the same but more units are sold this will also boost the overall return on capital.

Figure 18.1 Consider the marketing mix

18.5 METHODS OF IMPROVING PROFITS

To increase profits a business must:

1 increase revenue
2 decrease costs
3 do a combination of 1 and 2.

To increase revenue a business may want to consider its marketing mix. Changes to the product may mean that it becomes more appealing to customers. Better distribution may make it more available. Changes to promotion may make customers more aware of its benefits. However, the business needs to be careful that rising costs do not swallow up the rise in sales revenues.

To reduce costs a business may examine many of the functional areas (such as marketing, operations, people and finance):

- Could the firm continue with fewer staff?
- Could money be saved by switching suppliers?
- Do the firm's sales really benefit from sponsoring the opera?
- Are there ways of reducing wastage?

A-grade application

Vietnam as a production base

Average wages in Vietnam are lower than those of two of its neighbours: Thailand and China. Vietnamese factory workers earn just two thirds of what their colleagues in China take home.

Companies such as Foxconn, which assembles consumer electronics and phones for big-brand companies like Apple and Sony, operate on very low profit margins and so try to find the lowest cost location they can. This makes Vietnam very attractive as a production base. The toy industry is another low-cost, high-volume industry which is why you will find many well-known brands now being produced in Vietnam rather than China. Wages in China's coastal manufacturing areas have risen between 15 and 20 per cent per year recently; this has significantly reduced producers' profit margins so they have decided to relocate to Vietnam.

Essentially, a business should look for ways of making the product more efficiently (for example, with better technology) by using fewer inputs or paying less for the inputs being used. However, a business must be careful that when it reduces costs, the quality of service is not reduced. After all, this might lead to a fall in sales and revenue. Cutting staff in your coffee shop may cut costs, but if long queues form it may also reduce the number of customers and your income. Managers must weigh up the consequences of any decision to reduce costs.

18.6 METHODS OF INCREASING PROFIT MARGINS

To increase net profits in relation to sales a business could do the following.

Increase the price

Increasing the price would boost the profit per sale, but the danger is that the sales overall may fall so much that the overall profits of the business are reduced. (Notice the important difference again between the net profit margin and the overall level of profits; you could make a high level of profit on one can of beans relative to its price, but if you only sell one can your total profits are not that impressive!) The impact of any price increase will depend on the price elasticity of demand; the more price elastic demand is, the greater the fall in demand will be, and the less likely it is that a firm will want to put up its prices. On the other hand, a price-elastic demand may mean it is worth cutting price. Although less profit may be made per item (there is a lower profit margin) the overall profits may increase due to the boost in sales.

Cut costs

If cutting costs can be done without damaging the quality in any significant way then this clearly makes sense. Better bargaining to get the supply prices down or better ways of producing may lead to high profits per sale. However, as we saw above, the business needs to be careful to ensure that reducing costs does not lead to a deterioration of the service or quality of the product, as this may damage sales.

18.7 PROFITS AND THE FUNCTIONS OF BUSINESS

As we can see, the profits and the profitability of a business depend on all its different functions. The operations management may determine how much can be produced and sold. Human resources management may affect how many people need to be employed and the costs of staff. Marketing decisions will affect the sales and revenue earned. To boost profits you may consider each and every one of these functions to look for ways of increasing revenue and/or cutting costs.

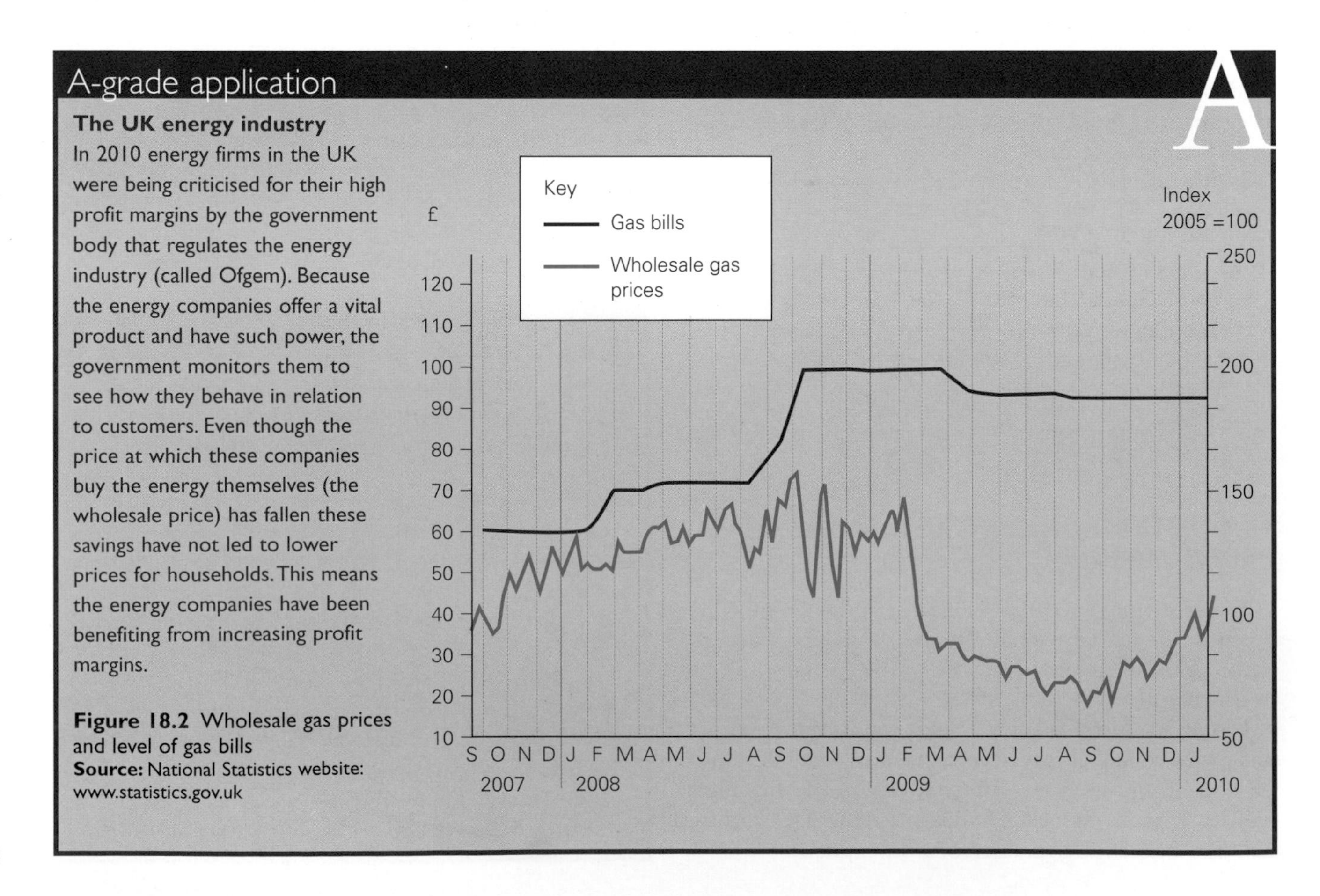

A-grade application

The UK energy industry

In 2010 energy firms in the UK were being criticised for their high profit margins by the government body that regulates the energy industry (called Ofgem). Because the energy companies offer a vital product and have such power, the government monitors them to see how they behave in relation to customers. Even though the price at which these companies buy the energy themselves (the wholesale price) has fallen these savings have not led to lower prices for households. This means the energy companies have been benefiting from increasing profit margins.

Figure 18.2 Wholesale gas prices and level of gas bills
Source: National Statistics website: www.statistics.gov.uk

ISSUES FOR ANALYSIS

Many organisations survive without profit, but largely because of government or private charity. This unit is largely about business organisations that need profit to survive and, especially, to grow. If a business is as unprofitable as Woolworths it is hard to understand how it survives.

In exams there are various questions to ask yourself about a loss-making firm:

- What has caused the losses: **internal reasons** or external ones? Internal ones would include poor decision making.
- What may be the downsides to any new approach? Will staff cutbacks cost more from damaged morale than they provide from lower wage costs?
- Finally, what is the timescale of the decision making? Is the business forced to take action immediately to boost profit, or can it wait to see if today's poor circumstances ease off.

18.8 MEASURING AND INCREASING PROFIT – AN EVALUATION

A difficulty with questions about poor profits is that many suggestions made in exams are too obvious. As shown in Table 18.1, Sainsbury's has only half the profit margin of Tesco. But is it worth pointing out to Sainsbury's that it could look for bulk-buying discounts on its supplies? Of course not. A good exam answer will show the maturity to see that Sainsbury's managers will already be doing all they can to tackle the problem.

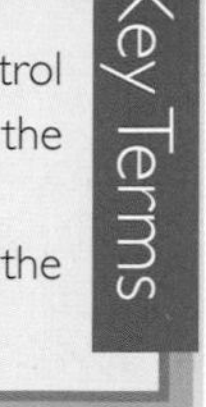

Internal reasons: these come within the control of the management (for example, the quality of the materials used in production).

Return on capital: profit as a percentage of the capital a firm invests in a project.

WORKBOOK

A REVISION QUESTIONS

(25 marks; 25 minutes)

1. What is meant by 'revenue'? (2)
2. What is meant by 'net profit'? (2)
3. Does an increase in price necessarily increase revenue? Explain your answer. (3)
4. How can revenue increase without an increase in cash inflows? (2)
5. Is profitability measured in pounds or percentages? (1)
6. What is the equation for the net profit margin? (2)
7. How can the net profit margin increase and yet the return on capital fall? (2)
8. Explain two ways of increasing profits. (4)
9. Why may cutting costs end up reducing profits? (3)
10. In what ways do the different functions of a business affect its profits? (4)

B REVISION EXERCISES

B1 DATA RESPONSE

SOFA-SOGOOD Ltd is a retailer of sofas. It had been experiencing a 'very slow' summer. Revenues had been falling but costs had been pushed up by pay increases, higher rent costs and higher interest payments on debts. As a result, net profits had fallen by 20 per cent on last year. Renis, the managing director, was very disappointed that revenue had fallen because he had cut prices by 5 per cent and had expected customer numbers to increase sharply. Once it became clear that this discounting policy was not working, he imposed a pay freeze on everyone in the company and a policy of non-recruitment. If any staff member left, she or he would not be replaced.

Questions

(30 marks; 30 minutes)

1. Distinguish between revenue, costs and net profit. (3)
2. Explain why a fall in price might not have led to an increase in revenue. (5)
3. Apart from the methods mentioned in the text, analyse two other actions SOFA-SOGOOD could take to improve its profitability. (8)
4. Discuss the advantages and disadvantages to the business of the staffing cost-saving actions taken by Renis. (14)

B2 DATA RESPONSE

Farmoor College

Farmoor College is a private sixth-form college based in London that charges students to study for their A-levels. The fees are £15,000 a year. The college is proud of its small classes (average size five students) and its excellent examination results. This year it has 200 students studying with it, which is about its present capacity in terms of the number of classrooms available. The college has a core of key staff but employs other teachers and support staff depending on the levels of demand in any year. The college's net profit margin is 12 per cent and the capital invested in the business is £15 million.

Questions

(40 marks; 40 minutes)

1 Calculate the likely net profits for the college this year. (3)
2 Calculate the college's likely return on capital this year. Comment on your findings. (4)
3 Outline two costs the college is likely to have. (4)
4 Explain one factor that could cause a change in demand for the college. (4)
5 Explain how the net profit of the college may be used. (5)
6 Analyse how you could measure the performance of the college apart from looking at its financial results. (8)
7 Discuss the ways in which the college could increase its profits. (12)

Cash flow versus profit

UNIT 19

Cash flow is the movement of cash into and out of a firm's bank account. Profit is when revenue is greater than total costs.

19.1 INTRODUCTION

A year ago a busy bar in Wimbledon closed down. Regulars were surprised, shocked even, that such a successful business had failed. The business was operating profitably, but the owners had become too excited by their success. Their investment into two new bars elsewhere in London had drained too much cash from the business, and the bank had panicked over the mounting debts. It forced the business to close. A profitable business had run out of cash.

To understand how cash differs from profit, the key is to master profit. On the face of it, profit is easy: total revenue *minus* total costs. Common sense tells you that revenue = money in and costs = money out. Unfortunately that's far too much of a simplification.

19.2 DISTINGUISHING REVENUE FROM CASH INFLOW

Revenue is *not* the same as money in. Revenue is the value of sales made over a specified period: a day, a month or a year. For example, the takings at a clothing outlet last Saturday: £450 of cash sales, £2,450 on credit cards and £600 on the store card (£3,500 in total). Note that the cash inflow for the day is just £450, that is, revenue is not the same as 'cash in'.

Whereas revenue comes from just one source (customers), cash inflow can come from many sources.

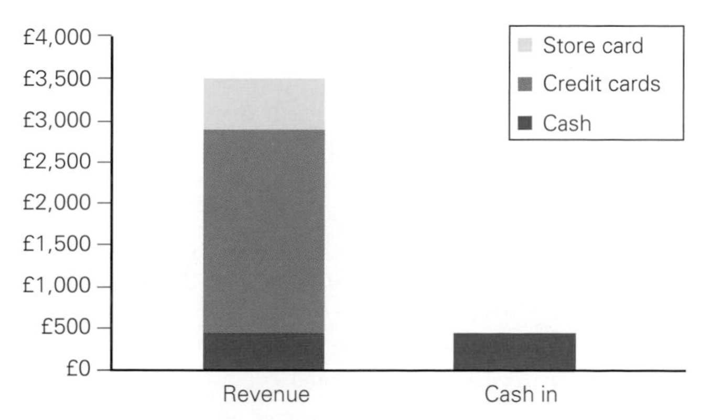

Figure 19.1 Saturday takings at a clothing outlet

It is not limited to trading. Selling an old warehouse for £600,000 does not generate revenue, but it does bring in cash. Similarly, taking out a bank loan could not be classed as revenue, but it does put cash into your bank current account.

So cash inflows *can* be part of the revenue, but they do not have to be. Therefore cash and revenue are not the same. Examples of differences between cash inflows and revenue are given in Table 19.1.

Table 19.1 Differences between cash inflows and revenue

Financial item	Cash inflow	Revenue
Cash sales made to customers	✓	✓
Credit sales made to customers	✗	✓
Capital raised from share sales	✓	✗
Charge rent on flat upstairs	✓	✓
Take out a £20,000 bank loan	✓	✗
Carry out a sale & leaseback	✓	✗

19.3 DISTINGUISHING COSTS FROM CASH OUTFLOW

The same distinction applies to costs and cash outflows. There are many reasons why a firm might pay out cash. Paying the business costs is only one of them. For example, the firm may pay out **dividends** to its shareholders, or it may repay a bank loan, or it may buy a piece of land as an investment.

In the case of the Wimbledon bar, the £200,000 annual profit gave the owners the confidence to buy leases on two new premises. They put together a business plan for expansion and received a £90,000 bank loan plus an £80,000 overdraft facility from a high street bank. They then hired architects and builders to turn the premises into attractive bars. Unfortunately, building hitches added to costs while delaying the opening times. The first of the new bars opened without any marketing support (there was no spare cash) and with the second of the bars still draining the business of cash, the bank demanded to have its overdraft repaid. As there was no way to repay the overdraft, the business went into liquidation.

So, a profitable business may run out of cash, simply because it expands too ambitiously, perhaps unluckily. There are other reasons why a profitable business might run into **negative cash flow**. These are set out below.

Seasonal factors

A firm that is generating sufficient revenue to cover its costs over a 12-month period might still hit short-term cash flow problems. This is a particularly difficult problem for new small firms. A new bicycle shop opens in the spring and may enjoy an excellent first 6 months' trading. The owners may get quite excited at the good profit level, buy a new van and have a much-needed holiday. They would have expected the winter half-year to be fairly poor for bike sales, but may be shocked by the level of decline. By February they may run out of cash and be unable to pay their staff. If only they had known the pattern of demand, the owners could have saved money in the first half of the year; but a fundamentally profitable business may close down due to a cash flow crisis.

Problems with credit periods

If a firm gives credit periods to its customers, there is risk from a serious delay to a credit payment. For example, a builder who has put a great deal of money into renovating a large house finds that the client keeps delaying the final payment. The more serious the builder's cash flow problems become, the stronger the position of the client. So a profitable business may be thrown into a cash crisis that could threaten its survival. Examples of differences between cash outflows and costs are given in Table 19.2.

Table 19.2 Differences between cash outflows and costs

Financial item	Cash outflow	Costs
Cash payments to suppliers	✓	✓
Purchases from suppliers on credit	✗	✓
Paying out wages	✓	✓
Repayment of bank loans	✓	✗
Tax bill received but not yet paid	✗	✓
Buying freehold property*	✓	✗
Paying the electricity bill	✓	✓

*Because a £500,000 property is worth £500,000, an accountant would not treat it as a cost.

19.4 CASH-RICH FIRMS CAN BE UNPROFITABLE

It is also possible for a cash-rich business to be unprofitable. This has given rise to several business scandals in the past. A classic situation is as follows. A new insurance company is started up, and builds a customer base through extensive TV advertising. New customers pay in their insurance premiums, which helps to pay for the advertising and a rapid build-up of staff. As extra customers join, the business finds itself awash with cash. In fact, because there are few if any insurance pay-outs yet, the business may be barely profitable (it may be operating at no more than its true break-even point). Yet because the cash inflows arrive before the cash outflows, the business is cash-rich. An honest and well-run business will be aware of this, and make sure to save the cash rather than spend it. There have been many cases, though, where the proprietors have paid out large sums (to themselves, perhaps) and later been unable to pay out to the policy holders. The legal protection provided by limited liability can ensure that the owners enjoy pay-outs from 'profits' that prove to be an illusion.

A-grade application

Collapse of the Ponzi Scheme

On 28 June 2009 there were cheers as Bernie Madoff was sentenced to 150 years in prison. The 71-year-old was convicted for running a $65 billion 'Ponzi Scheme', defrauding tens of thousands of people out of their life savings. Those looking to retirement gave it to Madoff to invest, as he promised high, stable dividends and had the credibility of a former chairman of the New York NASDAQ stock exchange.

In fact, Madoff invested little of the money that savers gave him. He used new cash to pay dividends to older investors and to fund a lavish lifestyle. The Ponzi Scheme collapsed in December 2008 when recession-hit investors tried to withdraw their savings. Madoff had been cash-rich, but there were no underlying profits to provide a fall-back position.

19.5 WHAT DOES ALL THIS IMPLY FOR MANAGERS?

The key is to appreciate that cash flow and profit are different aspects of the same thing. Cash flow and profit are linked, but they are not the same. Good financial planning requires an estimate of the likely profitability of a course of action. It then requires a careful forecast of the flows of cash in and out of the business. Profitability shows the long-term value of a financial decision; cash flow shows the short-term impact of that decision on the firm's bank balance.

Cash versus profit: an example

Trish decides to open a beauty salon. She estimates that annual fixed overheads will be £160,000 and annual revenues £300,000 offset by variable costs at 20 per cent of revenue (£60,000).

In other words annual profit should be: £300,000 – (£160,000 + £60,000) = £80,000

The start-up costs of opening the salon are expected to be £60,000, so the business will be profitable from year 1.

However, there are some important cash flow issues to consider: first, how long will it take before the salon opens its doors (and cash starts flowing in)? Second, will the business *really* start at a revenue level equivalent to £300,000 per year (£25,000 per month), or will it take many months before sales rise to a satisfactory level?

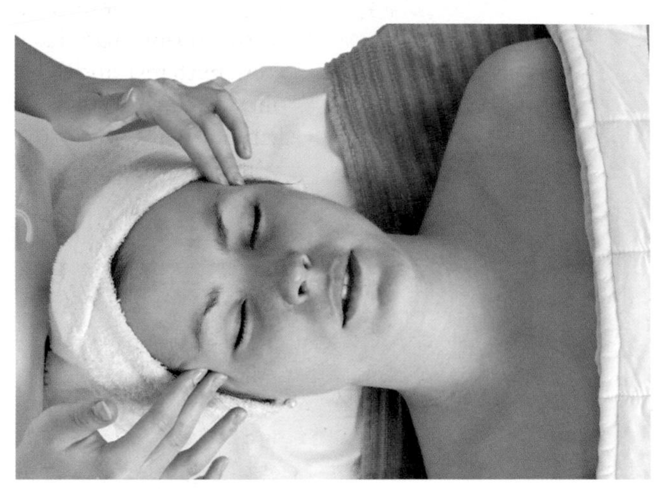

Figure 19.2 The beauty salon

Table 19.3 shows the cash flow position of the business, assuming that it takes three months to prepare the beauty salon (building work, decoration, and so on) and that it will take four months before regular custom has built up fully. The forecast is for the first eight months.

As you can see, even after eight months the business still has a serious cash flow problem. If the figures remain the same, it will be another six months before cumulative cash flow (the bank account) becomes positive. So the 'profitable' first year (and any accountant would confirm that the year is profitable) ends in the red.

The reason is simple. The cash investment to set up the business all takes place at the start, before the salon can generate a penny of cash inflow. The cash flow problem is because the cash outflow occurs before the cash inflows arrive. Therefore, the bank must be kept informed, so that it is willing to keep the business afloat. Unless the overdraft requirements are clear, and predicted, the bank manager may lose faith and demand all loans to be repaid.

ISSUES FOR ANALYSIS

- A key difference between cash flow and profit is time. Starting a vineyard may prove hugely profitable – eventually. But experts warn that it takes 10 years to recover the initial costs of starting up (that is, cash flow will be negative for 10 years). Cash flow measures today's money in and money out; profit is a more long-term calculation.
- The other key factor is the type of business. Most new business start-ups are vulnerable to cash flow problems, but which are in the toughest position? It is hardest by far for manufacturers, especially if they have an innovative new product. They have to spend months, perhaps years, developing the product, then building, equipping and staffing a factory. Only then (after all that cash outflow) can they start producing a product and start to sell it on to retailers. Even when they have made a sale and delivered the goods, many retailers take 60 days to pay their bills. The impact on cash flow is awful, even for a product that later proves to be highly profitable.

19.6 CASH FLOW VERSUS PROFIT – AN EVALUATION

Especially for small firms, every significant decision needs to be assessed in terms of cash flow as well as profit. The cash flow forecast predicts the impact on the bank balance, and may show the need for extra overdraft facilities to be negotiated. Or, if the firm's cash position is already weak, it may be safer to postpone the proposal.

Yet cash flow is no substitute for calculating profit. A cash-rich business idea (such as insurance) may

Table 19.3 Cash flow forecast for new beauty salon

All figures in £000s	1	2	3	4	5	6	7	8
Cash at start	0	(20)	(40)	(60)	(64)	(64)	(59)	(51)
Cash in	0	0	0	10	15	20	25	25
Cash out	20	20	20	14	15	15	17	17
Net cash	(20)	(20)	(20)	(4)	(0)	5	8	8
Cumulative cash*	(20)	(40)	(60)	(64)	(64)	(59)	(51)	(43)

*This is the firm's bank balance at the end of each month.

inevitably lead to **insolvency**, if the business is not profitable. Getting cash inflows at the start seems great, but will turn into a nightmare if the cash outflows eventually start flooding in.

Remember, then, that cash flow and profit are not the same. Cash flow measures the short term; and profit shows the longer-term financial result of a decision. Clever managers look at both before they proceed.

Key Terms

Dividends: annual payments to shareholders from the profits made by the company. It is the equivalent of the interest paid to those who lend money.

Insolvency: inability to pay the bills, forcing closure.

Negative cash flow: when cash outflows outweigh cash inflows.

Sale and leaseback: selling the freehold to a piece of property then simultaneously leasing it back, perhaps for a period of 20 years. The owner gives up tomorrow's valuable asset in exchange for cash today.

WORKBOOK

A REVISION QUESTIONS

(20 marks; 20 minutes)

1 Explain in your own words why cash inflow is not the same thing as revenue. (3)
2 Look at Table 19.1. Explain why taking out a £20,000 bank loan generates cash inflow but not revenue. (3)
3 Give two reasons why a profitable business could run out of cash when it expands too rapidly. (2)
4 Look at Table 19.2. Explain why 'purchases from suppliers on credit' is treated as a cost, yet not as a cash outflow. (3)
5 Identify whether each of the following business start-ups would be cash-rich or cash-poor in the early years of the business.
   a) A pension fund, in which people save money in return for later pay-outs. (1)
   b) Building a hotel. (1)
   c) Starting a vineyard (grapes only pickable after 3 to 5 years). (1)
6 Look at Table 19.3. Use it and the accompanying text to explain why the cash flow of the beauty salon is different from its profit. (4)
7 Why is it important for a small business to look both at profit and cash flow? (2)

REVISION EXERCISES
B1 DATA RESPONSE

Collapse of Independent Insurance

On 23 August 2007 the former boss of a £1 billion insurance company broke down in tears at Southwark Crown Court. Michael Bright led the stock market flotation of Independent Insurance in 1986. Rapidly expanding the business, the company's market value soared to £1 billion in 2000. It had 500,000 personal policy holders and 40,000 business customers. A year later the business was bankrupt, after underestimating the cost of claims and overseas expansion. About 1,000 employees were out of work. Serious Fraud Office investigators were called in to examine the collapse. It was six years, though, before the case against three leading executives was brought to trial. Eventually Bright was sentenced to seven years in jail and, in February 2009, Bright and other leading executives each had £1 million confiscated by the courts.

Questions

(15 marks; 20 minutes)

1 Outline three groups of people (stakeholders) who would have lost out in the collapse of Independent Insurance. (6)
2 Explain how a fast-growing insurance business could be cash-rich, yet unprofitable. (9)

B2 DATA RESPONSE

Investment Dragon Peter Jones on cash and profit

Managing your cash in a focused manner is fundamental to survival, let alone success. Businesses are more likely to fail because they run out of cash – not because they're unable to generate a profit. You can have a lorry load of orders with the promise of untold profits in the pipeline, but if you don't have the cash to make and sell your products in the first place, and you are unable to pay your immediate bills, your business will fold.

Cash flow is a common hurdle for small and start-up enterprises. For that reason, it is important to *strengthen cash flow* from the outset.

Monitor profit and *avoid over-commitment*. One common mistake entrepreneurs make is that they see a run-rate of business and immediately start to incur costs. They'll rent an office, take on new lease commitments, buy a new car. These monthly payments can result in losing sight of the real cash that's generated through the business.

Grow the business organically and *keep costs down,* especially if you can't access bank finance. Focus on keeping costs to a bare minimum. Forget the office; work from home. Forget the car; use public transport. Grow the business, grow a pot of cash and then invest in the business. Using that money to reinvest is vital.

Reinvest profits wisely. It is important to:

- Understand what your start-up and ongoing costs are. Be realistic. It is better to overestimate expenditure and time and underestimate revenue than fall short of revenue and overspend.
- Evaluate and monitor profit continually.
- Reinvest your profit. That way, you'll scale the business far quicker than if you use the profit to rent another office building or buy a car. It's how you spend the profit that's important. Entrepreneurs always spend profit on the business. Successful entrepreneurs invest that profit on the right areas to maximise growth and enhance existing offerings.

Source: www.peterjones.tv

Questions

(20 marks; 25 minutes)

1 Explain why, in the first paragraph, Peter Jones seems to be suggesting that cash flow is more important than profit for a small business. (4)

2 By 'run-rate' Peter Jones means the revenue generated by the business once it is up and running. Why does he think an entrepreneur should wait before spending at this rate? (5)

3 Growing 'organically' means from within; that is, not rushing to buy up other businesses. Organic growth is usually at a slow enough pace to cope with cash flow pressures. Examine why rapid growth can cause big cash flow problems. (6)

4 Explain why it is 'better to overestimate expenditure and time and underestimate revenue'. (5)

UNIT 20

Managing working capital

Working capital is the finance available for the day-to-day running of the business.

20.1 WHAT IS WORKING CAPITAL?

All businesses need money; it is required for the purchase of machinery and equipment. This expenditure on fixed assets is known as capital expenditure. The business also needs money to buy materials or stock and to pay wages and the day-to-day bills such as electricity and telephone bills. This money is known as working capital.

Managing working capital is about ensuring that the cash available is sufficient to meet the cash requirements at any one time. If the bills cannot be paid on time there are serious consequences. In the worst situation, the business may fail. Insufficient working capital is the commonest cause of business failure. Managing working capital is therefore a vital business activity.

20.2 THE WORKING CAPITAL CYCLE

Managing working capital is a continuous process. When a business starts up it takes time to generate income. Money to pay for stock and the running costs will need to be found from the initial capital invested in the business. As the business cycle gets going, income from customers will be available to pay for expenditure.

The firm needs to ensure that there is always sufficient cash to meet daily requirements. If the business is expanding or takes on a special order, extra care needs to be taken. Sufficient funds are needed to pay for the additional expenditure until the revenue arrives. This continuous process is shown in Figure 20.1, which also shows why working capital is sometimes referred to as circulating capital.

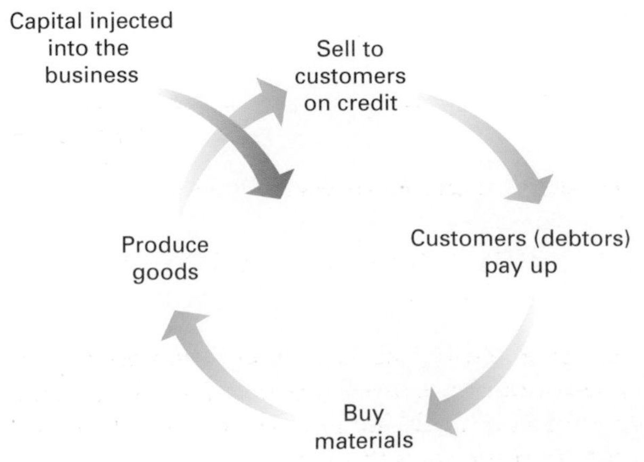

Capital injected into the business
Sell to customers on credit
Customers (debtors) pay up
Buy materials
Produce goods

Figure 20.1 The working capital cycle

As can be seen from Figure 20.1, managing working capital is about two things:

1 ensuring the business has enough finance to meet its needs
2 keeping cash moving rapidly through the cycle, so there's enough to meet future orders.

Each business will have its own distinct cycle. Businesses will also be subject to unexpected events and need to be able to cope with these. Therefore it is helpful to have a generous overdraft limit, which can be drawn upon when needed.

Examples of unexpected events include the following.

- A major customer gets into financial difficulties and is therefore unable to pay its bills on time.
- The cost of materials rises quickly, as with the trebling in the price of copper between January 2009 and January 2011.

20.3 PROBLEMS CAUSED BY INSUFFICIENT WORKING CAPITAL

With suppliers

A firm with too little working capital will struggle to pay its bills on time. It has no spare cash. It may resort to delaying payments. It may need to borrow more money. Delaying payment means that suppliers are not paid on time. They may reduce the **credit period** or refuse credit for a future order.

With banks

If the business is resorting to borrowing it will have the additional cost of interest charges. If the bank is concerned about the financial situation it may impose higher charges. The business will find it more difficult to get loans. Any lender will want to be assured that the company is managing its working capital effectively.

Opportunities may be missed

The business may not be able to buy supplies in bulk. This removes the advantage of lower bulk-buying prices. Even more importantly, it may have to refuse a large order because it cannot finance the extra working capital requirement.

In the longer term, shortage of cash means that no funds are available for development. The business will not be able to grow. In extreme cases, creditors may ask for the business to be declared insolvent. A sole trader or partnership will be declared bankrupt. Most creditors will take this action only if they feel that there is little hope of being paid. They will look at the future prospects and past performance of the business.

20.4 HOW MUCH WORKING CAPITAL DO BUSINESSES NEED?

The working capital requirement varies from business to business. It depends on the following factors.

The length of the business process

There are huge variations in the length of the **working capital cycle** for different businesses. A fruit stall market trader buys supplies, using cash, from a wholesaler in the morning and sells everything (for cash) by late afternoon; the cycle takes less than a day. By contrast, for a small construction firm building four houses, it may take a year from starting the project to receiving cash paid by a new home owner.

The amount of stock the firm holds

Self-evidently, 'stock' is the fundamental part of every clothes shop and every supermarket; without stocked shelves, there would be no business. So every shop needs to have a great deal of working capital invested in stock. Nevertheless, some shops carry more stock than they need, often due to poor buying (too many size 16 dresses, or too much ice cream during the winter). Incompetence leads such shops to tie up more money in working capital than is necessary.

The credit given to customers

Most shops get paid very promptly by their customers. Many pay in cash and even credit card payments come through within three or four days (from the credit card companies). By contrast, manufacturers usually have to give long credit periods of perhaps 60 days. This means that they have to wait for 60 days, and even then may find they have to chase payment if a customer has not paid on time. The longer the credit period you give to customers, the more working capital your business will need. As capital is always costly (and has a high opportunity cost), this is damaging to the firm's profitability.

The credit given for purchases of materials or stock

Most businesses obtain credit for their purchases. The length of time allowed before payment depends on:

- how established the firm is: an established firm can negotiate longer credit than a new firm
- its credit record: a firm with a good record of paying can negotiate longer credit
- the size of the order: larger orders may get longer credit
- regular orders: regular customers expect longer credit than occasional customers.

The business needs to take into account both the timing and the amounts involved when working out its working capital requirements. It also needs to include an allowance for uncertainty. An extra 10 per cent on top of the expected cash requirement would be the very minimum required. For a new small firm such as a new restaurant, though, a bigger safety net can be wise. It can take months for word to spread sufficiently to push a business above its break-even point.

Figure 20.2 shows the need for **contingency finance;** in other words, the financial back-up to allow for the unexpected. June 2007 was the wettest in 100 years, with Hull the worst-hit town; more than 10,000 homes had to be evacuated. Think about the double hit that would have been inflicted on small businesses in the flooded areas. Completely unpredictably, they could have faced sales revenue down by, perhaps, 30 per cent as residents moved away to temporary accommodation. For a new business with little cash in the bank, the position would have threatened its survival. Figure 20.2 shows the role of contingency finance such as an agreed overdraft facility.

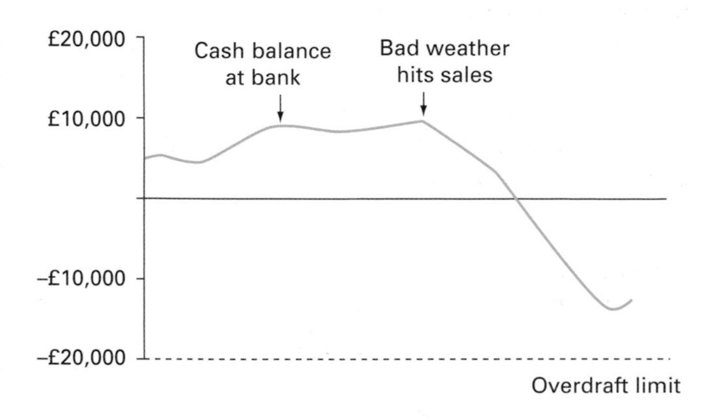

Figure 20.2 The need for contingency finance

20.5 CAN A BUSINESS HAVE TOO MUCH WORKING CAPITAL?

In America and Britain it is thought important that a business should not have too much working capital. The term 'too much' implies that the capital would be wasted. In some ways this is true. There is no point in having too much capital tied up in stock or giving too much credit to customers. There is a problem, though, in defining what 'too much' actually means.

Japanese and German firms have always tended to adopt a very cautious approach to their finances. In the period 2005 to 2009, City of London analysts questioned why firms such as Toyota had billions of dollars of cash lying idle in their accounts. Why did they have so much working capital? In fact, this level of caution proves very helpful when uncertainty strikes, as in early 2010 when concern about Toyota quality problems hit sales worldwide.

It should always be remembered that whereas you can have too much stock or too many debtors, you can never have too much cash!

A-grade application

General Motors

For 80 years, General Motors was the world's biggest car manufacturer. In 2008 that changed when Japan's Toyota became number one. In 2003 a London newspaper poked fun at the cautious finances of Japanese firms such as Toyota. It suggested that they 'had no idea how to look after their shareholders'. The complaint was that Toyota held nearly £8,000 million of cash in its accounts. The newspaper journalist saw the money as a wasted asset; Toyota saw it as a form of contingency finance.

In February 2008 General Motors announced a record £19 billion loss (that is more than 15 times the annual revenues of Real Madrid, Manchester United, Barcelona, Chelsea and Arsenal Football Clubs put together). At the same time Toyota announced profits of £12 billion for the 12 months of 2007. Toyota's cash kitty had enabled the business to invest in successful new cars such as the hybrid Prius. You can never have too much cash!

20.6 HOW SHOULD A BUSINESS MANAGE ITS WORKING CAPITAL?

Intelligent working capital management is centred on the following aspects.

Control cash used

Examples of ways in which a business can control the amount of cash used includes: minimising stock levels, keeping customer credit as low as possible (without pushing customers away) and trying to get as much credit from suppliers as you can. It is also important to get goods to the market in the shortest possible time. The sooner goods reach the customer the sooner payment is received. Production and distribution should be as efficient as possible.

Minimise spending on fixed assets

Minimising spending on fixed assests keeps cash in the business. The business must balance its need for cash and its need for fixed assets. A compromise is to lease rather than buy equipment. This increases expenses but conserves capital.

Plan ahead by estimating cash needed

Planning ahead by estimating the amount of cash needed next month and beyond means that cash shortfalls can be anticipated and planned for. If the next two months look problematic, perhaps that purchase of the boss's new BMW should be delayed for a while.

Seek long-term solutions to short-term issues

Thinking carefully about possible long-term solutions to short-term working capital issues is what Michael Dell did when he set up his hugely successful Dell Computers.

A-grade application

The cash whirlpool

The 2009 recession knocked 9.5 per cent off the revenues at kitchen equipment giant Whirlpool. To preserve cash, the business slashed its working capital usage. Factory stock levels were cut by 15 per cent and payments to suppliers were delayed sharply. These two actions alone saved $700 million of working capital, thereby boosting short-term cash flow by the same amount. Of course, this financial tactic can only be done once, but that may be long enough until sales start to recover.

ISSUES FOR ANALYSIS

To analyse working capital management in a business case study or data response question it is important to remember:

- that, for small firms especially, the working capital cycle is the equivalent of blood circulating around the body – if the cash dries up, the firm dies
- the problems caused by too little or too much working capital.

It would be nice if there was a perfect, 'right' level of working capital, but there isn't – so the key issue is: can the firm fund the short-term actions it would like to take? Is it safely in a position to pay its bills? And is its working capital position improving or worsening?

20.7 MANAGING WORKING CAPITAL – AN EVALUATION

Managing working capital is very important for every business. As in many other areas of business, it is about getting the balance right. Too much may be wasteful; too little can be disastrous. Businesses need to consider working capital requirements right from the outset. Most new businesses underestimate their working capital needs. Typically, firms allow only £20 of working capital for every £100 of fixed capital (assets). Accountants usually advise a £50:£50 ratio.

Managing working capital is not just about managing cash flow. The timing and amounts of cash flow are important, but working capital management goes beyond that. It is about managing the whole business. In this respect it is an integrated activity. It involves each aspect of the company. Efficient production keeps costs to a minimum and turns raw inputs into finished goods in the shortest possible time. Effective management of stock can have considerable impact on working capital requirements. Effective marketing ensures that the goods are sold and that demand is correctly estimated. This avoids wasted production. Cash then flows in from sales. Efficient distribution gets the goods to the customer quickly. The accounting department can help to control costs. Effective credit control improves cash flow. Each of these can reduce the need for cash and/or ensure that cash is available to the business.

Key Terms

Contingency finance: planning how to cope if there are extra, unexpected financial requirements.

Credit period: the length of time allowed for payment.

Working capital cycle: how long it takes for a complete cycle from cash out (buying stock) to cash back in from a customer payment. It may be one day (for example, for a fruit and veg stall) or one year (for example, for a house builder).

WORKBOOK

A REVISION QUESTIONS

(40 marks; 40 minutes)

1 What is working capital? (3)
2 What is capital expenditure? (3)
3 What is working capital used for? Give two examples. (5)
4 What problems could arise if a firm is operating with very low working capital? (4)
5 Why may a business be unable to get a loan or overdraft if it has working capital difficulties? (4)
6 On 1 February, JG Co received an order for £20,000 worth of office furniture. Between 15 February and 20 March the company spent £11,000 on materials and labour. Between 20 March and 31 March a further £4,000 was contributed to fixed costs such as quality control. The finished order was delivered on 1 April, together with an invoice requiring payment in 60 days. On 1 June, the payment of £20,000 was received. How long is JG Co's working capital cycle? (3)
7 Explain two factors that influence the amount of working capital required by a firm. (4)
8 Outline three ways in which a business can improve its working capital situation. (6)
9 How does better stock management help a firm to control its working capital requirements? (5)
10 List three ways in which stock levels can be reduced. (3)

B REVISION EXERCISES

B1 DATA RESPONSE

Life and death

Managing cash flow effectively is really a matter of life and death for a new business. Government figures show that small businesses are owed as much as £17 billion from customers at any one time, and that 10,000 UK businesses fail each year because of late payment from customers.

Ironically, one of the reasons for cash-flow problems is that small, growing businesses can find themselves 'overtrading' (i.e. sales may be strong, but the company lacks the cash to buy more stock or pay its bills).

A previous client of mine was worth over £1 million, yet was at the end of its bank overdraft limit simply because one customer was too large for its business. It used all its working capital supplying this one customer! In addition, though the client was paying its own bills immediately, it wasn't being firm about collecting money from its own customers.

To put the situation right, the firm first had to walk away from its large customer and focus on smaller ones, and then actively chase late payments. Chasing invoices is perfectly acceptable, and in fact some businesses will never pay until chased. Finally, the company also negotiated better terms with its own suppliers.

I recommend a number of important cash flow rules.

- Make payment terms a central part of the contract and enforce them.
- Invoice as soon as possible.
- Chase invoices the moment they become due.
- Walk away from bad payers.
- Do a cash-flow forecast and re-forecast regularly – at least every month.
- Cash cheques as soon as you receive them.

Source: adapted from an article by Jeff Maplin at www.startups.co.uk

Questions

(20 marks; 25 minutes)

1 Why could late payment from customers be such a serious matter? (3)
2 Explain the difficulties that may arise for a business that uses 'all its working capital supplying' one customer. (6)
3 Outline one advantage and one disadvantage involved in chasing late payers. (5)
4 Sum up what you see as the three main themes that come through from the 'important cash flow rules'. (6)

B2 DATA RESPONSE

Unilever turns the screw on small suppliers

Unilever has joined the rush of big businesses putting the squeeze on suppliers. The consumer products giant has ruled it will take 90 days to pay instead of 30, starting within weeks.

A small business, which did not want to be named, told *Financial Mail* it had received a letter from Unilever warning that, from 15 July, invoices would be settled within 90 days. Previously the business had agreed terms of 30 days.

Martin Williams of credit reference agency Graydon UK said: 'Far too often, smaller suppliers accept terms imposed by big customers for fear of losing the business.' Unilever said: 'By working with suppliers to release cash, we provide funds for Unilever to invest in further growth, which is in the long-term interests of us and our suppliers.'

Financial Mail Editor Lisa Buckingham says:

Bullying is never acceptable. That is why the swathe of big companies extending the time they take to pay small suppliers is so unpalatable, not to mention dangerous, as it risks draining the lifeblood of the economy at a delicate time.

That these companies claim to subscribe to the Government's prompt payment scheme is ridiculous. 'Yes, we have extended our payment deadline from 30 days to 120 days', they say, 'but we pay on time at the end of that period'. This is baloney and utterly against the spirit of the guidelines, which encourage payment within 30 days.

Companies such as Unilever, which prides itself on being a good corporate citizen, should be ashamed of such tactics; shoring up its own cash flow while applying a tourniquet to others.

Source: *Financial Mail*, 4 July 2010

Questions

(30 marks; 35 minutes)

1 a) Explain the impact of this move by Unilever on the working capital position of its small suppliers. (6)
   b) Outline the possible impact of this on a supplier's cash flow. (6)
2 Re-draw Figure 20.1 to show the impact of Unilever's actions on a supplier's working capital cycle. (6)
3 Discuss whether Unilever's actions can be said to be 'in the long-term interests of us and our suppliers'. (12)

C ESSAY QUESTIONS

(40 marks each)

1 Managing working capital is vital for the future of any business. Discuss.
2 In periods of economic downturn it is even more important to control working capital in the business. Do you agree with this statement?
3 To what extent do you agree with the following statement? 'Managing working capital is not just the business of the finance department; it is the responsibility of everyone in the business.'

Effective marketing objectives and strategy

UNIT 21

Effective marketing achieves the firm's sales and profit targets by convincing customers to buy the firm's products again and again.

21.1 MARKETING OBJECTIVES

A marketing objective is a marketing target or goal that an organisation hopes to achieve, such as to boost market share from 9 to 12 per cent within 2 years. Marketing objectives steer the direction of the business. Operating a business without knowing what your objectives are is like driving a car without knowing where you want to go. Some businesses achieve a degree of success despite the fact that they choose not to set marketing objectives; stumbling across a successful business model by accident. But why should anyone rely on chance? If firms set marketing objectives the probability of success increases because decision making will be more focused.

Marketing objectives should be compatible with a business's overall company objective; they cannot be set in isolation by the marketing department. Achieving the marketing objective will help the firm to achieve its company wide objective. For example, boosting market share from 9 to 12 per cent will help the business to achieve its overall objective of growth.

To be effective, marketing objectives should be quantifiable and measurable. Targets should also be set within a time frame. An example of a marketing objective that fits this criterion, which Nestlé could set, is: 'To achieve a 9 per cent increase in the sales of Kit-Kat by the end of next year.'

Examples of marketing objectives

Increasing sales

A car manufacturer, such as BMW, could set the following marketing objective: 'To increase the number of BMW 3 Series cars sold in China from 150,000 to 200,000 over the next 12 months'. Setting sales volume targets can be particularly important in industries such as car manufacturing because of the high fixed costs associated with operating in this market. If sales volume can be increased, the high fixed costs of operating will be spread across a greater number of units of output, reducing fixed costs per unit. Lower unit costs will help BMW to widen its profit margins. Higher profit margins will give BMW the opportunity to increase its research and development budgets, raising the likelihood of success for BMW's next generation of new car models.

Nike has benefited from a slightly different way of looking at sales volume. In 1996 chairman Phil Knight set Nike's sights on being the number 1 supplier of football boots and kit. At the time, Nike was a minor player in the football sector of the sportswear business, compared with Adidas. Nike's approach has clearly paid off. In 1994 Nike generated sales of just $40 million from football. In 2010 Nike set, and then subsequently beat, a sales target for its football division of $1,500 million!

To enhance, or reposition a brand's image

Although some brands stay fresh for generations (Marmite is over 100 years old) others become jaded due to changes in consumer tastes and lifestyles. At this point the firms need to act and take measures to refresh the brand image to keep the products relevant to the target market. A clear objective must be set. What brand attributes do we want to create? What do we want the brand to stand for?

Repositioning occurs when a firm aims to change a brand's image, so that the brand appeals to a new target market. Kellogg's wanted to reposition Cornflakes, as sales had been sliding for years. At the time, consumers thought that Cornflakes were just one among many breakfast cereals. The company wanted consumers to rethink the brand as being a quick and healthy snack food to be eaten at any time of the day as a meal substitute, which would help aid weight-loss. In the longer term, repositioning should help to boost sales. When repositioning a brand it is important to have a clear objective. Who is our new target market; how old are they; which social class do they belong to; what is their lifestyle, and so on?

> **A-grade application**
>
> **Marketing objectives in the non-profit sector**
>
> 
>
>
> **Figure 21.1** The Save the Children logo
>
> Charities such as Oxfam and Save the Children need marketing to keep their brands alive and donations coming in. Typical marketing objectives that a charity may set could include the following.
>
> - **Raise brand awareness**. Brand awareness is the percentage of the market that know of your brand; that is, they can recognise it from a list of brand names, or they can quote it unaided. Raising brand awareness could be a very important marketing objective for a smaller charity that is yet unknown. If a greater percentage of the general public is aware of a charity's existence and its activities, donations may increase, enabling the charity to expand its work.
> - **Brand loyalty**. Brand loyalty exists when consumers repeat-purchase your brand rather than swapping and switching between brands. A charity could set a marketing objective to improve brand loyalty. If existing donors can be persuaded to set up a direct debit to the charity the charity's cash-flow will improve.
> - **Corporate image**. A scandal-hit charity could set a marketing objective of trying to improve its reputation, in order to protect its income stream from donors.

21.2 EFFECTIVE MARKETING STRATEGY

Marketing strategy is the medium- to long-term plan for how to achieve your marketing objectives. The process of thinking it through requires rather more, though, than simply writing down a plan. In his book *Even More Offensive Marketing* Hugh Davidson says that effective marketing strategy requires POISE: see Table 21.1.

It is easy to see that Nintendo showed all these features in their brilliant development and marketing of the Wii games console. While Sony and Microsoft focused on even better and faster graphics for the core 'shoot-em-up' gamer market, Nintendo led the market towards a huge number of new users. The Wii was a huge risk because it was really innovative, but its huge following among older people (busily 'brain-training'), young children (playing 'Nintendogs') and young families (using the interactive facility) are all testimony to Nintendo's market leadership. Nintendo sales doubled between 2006–07 and 2008–09 and profits rose nearly as fast. POISE is clearly profitable.

The most effective marketing strategies are not necessarily the most obvious ones. Unit 25 shows how firms think their strategies through using the marketing mix, carefully combining the four main marketing levers: product, price, promotion and place. Later on in this unit, we focus on underlying issues that must be planned with care, before a strategy can be put into action. These are:

- identifying the target market
- market segmentation
- market orientation
- identifying the right brand image.

21.3 WHAT IS EFFECTIVE MARKETING?

The term 'marketing' is widely misunderstood by people who have not studied business and management. Many people still think that 'marketing' is just another interchangeable term for selling, advertising and other forms of promotion (for example, sponsorship). Some people even think that marketing is about persuading consumers to buy or use a product they do not want. So, if marketing isn't just about designing glitzy advertising, or aggressive high-pressure 'selling', what is it?

Marketing is the business function that aims to identify, influence and then satisfy consumer wants profitably. Effective marketing starts with identifying an opportunity, just as Nintendo did with its Wii console. Instead of assuming that all consoles had to target players of shoot-em-up games, Nintendo identified other opportunities among girls (*Nintendogs*) and older people (*Brain Trainer*).

In many small businesses, the owner will come into regular contact with customers. This allows the

Table 21.1 POISE

P	Profitable	A proper balance between the firm's need for profit and the customer's need for value
O	Offensive	Get on the attack, leading the market, taking risks and force competitors to be followers
I	Integrated	The marketing approach must flow through the whole company, from directors to telephonists
S	Strategic	Probing analysis of the market and your competitors leading to a winning strategy
E	Effectively executed	Strong and disciplined teamwork in carrying the strategy through effectively

Source: Adapted from *Even More Offensive Marketing*, H Davidson, Penguin Books

owner to hear first-hand about the needs and wants of the target market. In large businesses, formal market research is undertaken because head office managers cannot feel sure that they know what customers think and want. Once consumer wants have been identified, products and services will need to be designed to match consumer preferences. Finally, a launch marketing mix must be decided. This involves decisions such as setting price, choosing an appropriate distribution channel and setting a promotional strategy.

21.4 WHY IS EFFECTIVE MARKETING IMPORTANT?

Consumers tend to be quite rational. They will seek out fairly priced products that satisfy their needs. In a competitive market firms stand or fall according to their ability to satisfy the needs of the consumer. Generally, firms that fail will lack customer loyalty and be punished automatically by the market. These firms will lose market share and profit. Firms with products and services that offer genuine consumer benefits will attract revenue and profit.

Consumer tastes do not tend to stay the same for very long. Therefore, a key aspect of effective marketing is the ability to respond, quickly, to any change in consumer tastes. Firms that fail to adapt their business model, at a time when consumer tastes are changing, are normally forced out of business. In recent years, UK retail chains such as KwikSave, Unwins and the Gadget Shop have collapsed.

A-grade application

Fopp

In June 2007 the music retailer Fopp announced that it was closing down all 105 of its UK stores. The management of Fopp had failed to react fast enough to a change in consumer preferences for buying music. In the last five years there has been a growing trend towards purchasing music via internet downloads. Fopp tried to respond by lowering its prices. Unfortunately for Fopp, this tactic failed to generate the revenues required by the company to break even, proving that low prices alone cannot save a business from closure, especially if consumers no longer wish to purchase the product that the business concerned sells.

21.5 THE CHARACTERISTICS OF EFFECTIVE MARKETING

Identifying the target market

When a business creates a new market (as Richard Branson is attempting currently with space tourism) it can aim its product at everyone who can afford the product. Some time later competitors will arrive, and usually focus on one segment of the market. In space tourism, perhaps some firms will focus on thrill-seekers, while others target wealthy, older travellers seeking a super-safe, luxury version of the same thrill.

To succeed at marketing you need to know and understand the customers within your target market: what do they *really* want from your product? Is it the satisfaction of using/having the product, or the satisfaction of showing it off to friends? What are their interests and lifestyle?

Having a clear idea of the age, sex, personality and lifestyle of the target market enables the business to do the following things.

Focus market research

A business may focus market research by interviewing only those who make up the target market. This should make the findings far more reliable. If the target market is clearly defined, the firm's market research budget can be spent with greater effect. Quota sampling could be used instead of a wide random sample; only those who meet the specific criteria for the target market will be interviewed, saving the firm time and money.

Focus advertising spending

A business may focus advertising spending on the people most likely to buy the product. One national TV commercial can cost £500,000; it will reach millions of people, but how many are really in the target market? Men do not need to know that 'Maybe it's Maybelline'. A product targeting young women would be advertised far more cost-effectively in magazines such as *More* or *Look*.

Segment markets

Most markets are not made up of identikit consumers who all want exactly the same product. In practice, consumer preferences can vary greatly. Firms that market their products effectively in this situation produce a range of products, each targeted at specific market segments.

A good example of a company that has used market segmentation to great effect is British Sky Broadcasting (BSkyB); in 2010 the company made an operating profit of £1,096 million.

Before Sky joined the market, the choice of what to watch on TV was limited. The BBC, ITV and Channel 4 tried in vain to produce a range of programmes in an attempt 'to be all things to all men'. Today Sky offers subscribers a choice of over 800 different channels. Among the target segments are 'kids', sports fans (men), ethnic minorities and fans of different music types; for example, MTV Base and Performance (classical music). The output of each channel is carefully matched to a particular consumer interest or hobby. Many of these channels attract additional charges, which has helped BSkyB to increase its monthly income (see Figure 21.2).

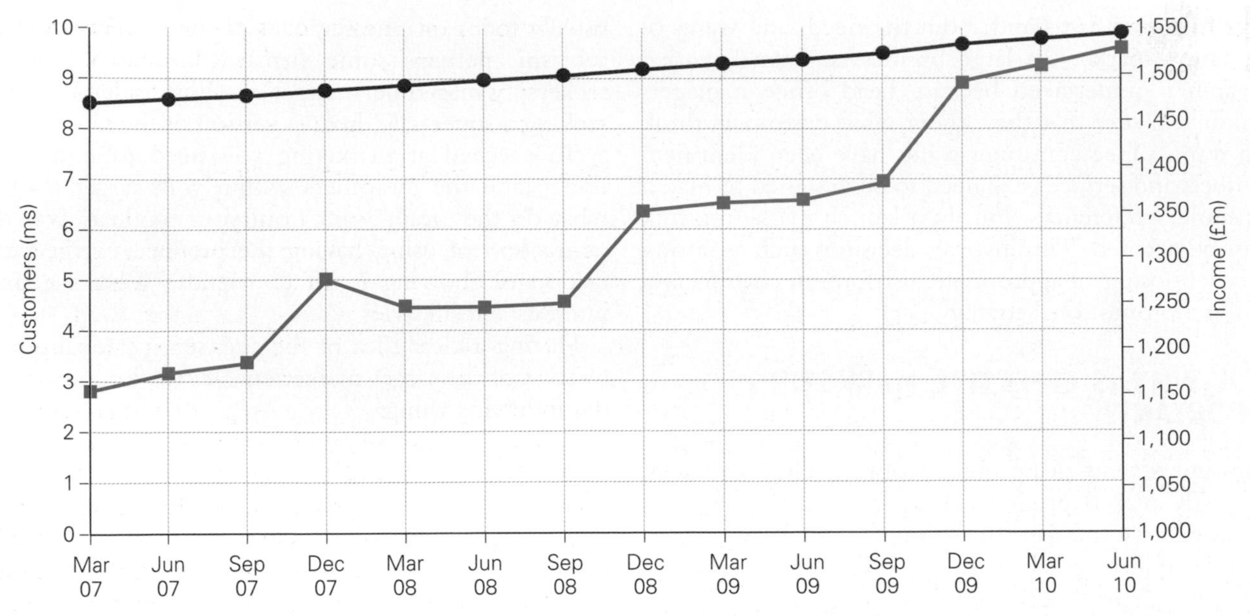

Figure 21.2 BSkyB growth 2007–10

Market-orientated marketing

Effective marketing is usually based around an approach that is market-orientated, rather than production-orientated. In a market-orientated business, managers take into account the needs of the consumer before making any decision. They put the customer at the heart of the decision-making process.

Some firms still use a production-orientated approach to marketing. Production orientation leads managers to focus on what the firm does best; internal efficiency comes before consumer preferences. The production-orientated approach to marketing may lead the business towards the following approaches.

- *The hard sell:* employing a large salesforce to go out and convince consumers that they should buy your product. Individualised sales targets, low basic salaries and high rates of commission ensure that sales staff will be 'motivated' to hit their targets, ensuring that the firm sells the products that it has already produced.
- *Cutting costs and prices:* if a production-orientated firm's products are not selling very well, managers tend to respond to this crisis by cutting costs. If costs can be cut, retail prices can also be cut without any loss of profit margin.

On the other hand, there are some weaknesses in market orientation. The death of Rover Cars (once one of the world's biggest car producers) was partly due to this. Rover management seemed convinced that customers could be attracted by marketing gimmicks such as 'special edition' cars, or cars with angular steering wheels. A greater focus on the quality and reliability of the product would have been far more effective. The ideal approach is that of a firm such as BMW, which is hugely proud of its products, but always makes sure that it understands what its customers really want from them.

A-grade application

Gap

Figure 21.3 Gap

By 2010, Gap's chief executive, Patrick Robinson, had seen sales fall by 14 per cent since his appointment in 2007. And the American clothes retailer had been overtaken by Zara as the world's number one clothing retailer.

Gap has suffered from falling sales and market share because it has failed to keep up to date with changes in fashion. Gap built its reputation around selling 'preppy' clothes. Consumer tastes have moved on, but Gap has not. To survive, Gap will probably have to abandon its 'preppy' clothes and instead switch to a more market-orientated approach. Market research needs to be given a bigger role. Focus groups could be carried out to identify popular contemporary style and fashion. New lines of clothing can then be designed that will have a better chance of appealing to Gap's target market.

A coherent brand image

Firms that market their products successfully use the marketing mix in an integrated manner to create a coherent and attractive brand image that appeals to the target market. Marketing success depends upon getting all four marketing mix decisions right. A good product that is properly priced and promoted will still fail if distribution is poor. Firms use the marketing mix to create an attractive and coherent brand image for each of the products that they sell. Creating the right brand image is important. If the brand image created by the marketing mix appeals to the target market there should be an increased chance that the product will succeed.

The most important thing to remember is that all four elements of the mix must be coordinated. If the marketing mix is not coordinated, mixed product messages will be sent out to the target market. This could create confusion, leading to disappointing sales. The key, then, is to think through the brand image that you want to create *before* making any other decisions on your product: how you might want to price it, promote it and distribute it.

Marketing is everyone's job

Many Japanese firms do not have a marketing department. Firms that adopt this approach believe that every employee has a part to play in marketing their business. Marketing should not be the preserve of a specialised marketing department; it is everyone's responsibility. To be successful the management has to create the right culture. Every member of staff must see their role as to better serve the needs and wants of the consumer.

21.6 SHORT-TERMIST MARKETING = INEFFECTIVE MARKETING

Short-termism describes a business philosophy whereby a firm pursues strategies that could boost profit in the short run, even if these strategies damage the firm's long-run profitability. Some examples of short-termist marketing strategies are given below.

High prices designed to exploit consumer loyalty or a dominant market position

In the short run, firms that operate in a market where there is little competition may be tempted to raise their prices to boost revenues and profits. In recent years, both Manchester United and Chelsea have tried to exploit the loyalty of football fans by raising ticket prices. In the short run this can work; however, in the longer term fans may rebel against the price increases and drift away from the game completely. There are signs that this has already started to happen. For example, in September 2009 Chelsea sold fewer than 25,000 tickets for a Champions League game.

A decision to exploit consumers by charging high prices is definitely not a good example of effective marketing. High prices can also encourage new competitors to join the industry.

Short-run sales-driven marketing

Some managers believe that their employees can only be motivated to work hard if they are set targets that are linked to bonuses and other performance-related payments. An over-reliance on targets and performance-related pay can create a ruthless and dishonest culture that can affect a firm's marketing. For example, a recent BBC investigation suggested that staff at a high-street bank were encouraged by their supervisors to lie to the bank's customers, in order to hit their personal sales targets. Mis-selling inappropriate financial products to customers can improve a bank's profitability in the short run; however, if the unethical marketing practices are exposed, the resulting wave of bad publicity may hit demand for the firm's products.

ISSUES FOR ANALYSIS

- Weak exam answers present marketing as a set of simple tools: the 4Ps. In fact, effective marketing is remarkably difficult, even for the biggest and best companies. A survey by *The Grocer* magazine placed Coca-Cola as Britain's most valuable brand. Yet Coca-Cola has been responsible for some dreadful new product flops in this country recently, including Dasani water, Coke Blak (coffee-flavoured Coke!) and Vanilla Coke. Good exam answers acknowledge that marketing is difficult because it is based on judgements about the future: future competition, future consumer tastes and future consumer attitudes.
- Achieving success depends on devising a genuinely new type of product that meets an actual consumer need or desire. Apple's iPhone did exactly that, as did Innocent Drinks when they made smoothies an everyday drink for wealthy young adults.

21.7 EFFECTIVE MARKETING OBJECTIVES AND STRATEGY – AN EVALUATION

To judge the likely effectiveness of a firm's marketing plans requires a full understanding of the market. Therefore, just as the marketing manager must research into the market, so you must take care to study the evidence available within the case material. An exam question based on Cadbury might lead to very different answers to the same question based on Mars or Nestlé, even though they all make chocolate. Good judgement comes from good application to the market and to the company.

WORKBOOK

A REVISION QUESTIONS

(30 marks; 30 minutes)

1 In your own words, explain the meaning of the term 'marketing'. (3)
2 Explain why some firms choose not to carry out market research. (3)
3 Why do you think most firms decide to review their marketing strategy at fairly regular intervals? (3)
4 What is meant by the phrase 'target market'? (2)
5 Outline two reasons why it is important for firms to be able to identify their target market. (4)
6 **a)** Distinguish between a production-orientated and a market-orientated approach to marketing. (3)
b) Outline whether a production-orientated or market-orientated approach would be better for ***one*** of the following companies:
i) Manchester United FC
ii) easyJet
iii) Topshop. (4)
7 Explain how market segmentation has helped companies such as BSkyB to improve their profitability. (4)
8 What are the marketing advantages of *not* having a specialised marketing department? (4)

B REVISION EXERCISES

B1 DISCUSSION POINT

The role of chance/luck

Effective marketing usually comes about as a result of careful planning and market-orientated decision making. However, in some cases, firms stumble across a successful marketing strategy by chance. Morgan cars is a conservatively run private business. The production methods used by the company have hardly changed at all in 40 years. Cars are still made largely by hand. Morgan's best-selling cars are based on designs that have not been changed for decades. In most industries this approach would be a recipe for disaster. Fortunately for Morgan, the cars continue to sell well within a tiny niche comprised of customers that want to purchase a hand-built British sports car, built in the Brooklands tradition. Morgan has not deliberately engineered its niche market position, it has just happened accidentally; the company has just been fortunate.

Discussion questions

1 From your reading of the text, is it really true that all Morgan's success is down to luck?
2 What marketing problems could the business face if it attempts to expand?

B2 CASE STUDY

Wimbledon Quality Cars

Wimbledon Quality Cars (WQC) sells second-hand cars. The business was set up five years ago when the economy was still booming. The owner of the business, Roger Raymond, believes that most businesses over-complicate their marketing. According to Roger, 'marketing is just a set of tools to sell more products, in my case, cars'. The marketing mix of WQC could be summarised as follows.

- *Price:* according to Roger, the bulk of second-hand car buyers are interested in only one thing: low prices. Most of the cars sold by WQC are sold for less than £2,000 – an important psychological pricing point.
- *Promotion:* Roger spends £300 per week advertising his cars in the south London press. He also employs two salesmen, Andy and John, who are paid a basic wage of £200 per week and a flat rate commission of £250 per car sold.
- *Product:* Roger believes that the bulk of his customers are not fussy about the make or model of car that they buy. 'Most of my punters want a cheap runaround. The majority of them don't know a good car from a death trap. In our market, quality always comes second to a low price.' Roger buys most of his cars from car auctions.
- *Place:* WQC has an old, run-down car showroom, just opposite Wimbledon dog track.

Last year WQC enjoyed its most profitable year yet: sales were up 40 per cent on the previous year. Unfortunately, events took a dramatic turn for the worse last month. To Roger's horror WQC was the subject of a TV documentary investigating sharp practice in the second-hand car market. The programme alleged that WQC sold cars that were not roadworthy. The implication was that Roger was happy to put the profits of WQC before his customers' safety. Ex-customers of WQC claimed that they had been tricked into buying poor-quality cars by WQC salesmen who failed to disclose faults with the cars.

Questions

(30 marks; 30 minutes)

1 According to Roger, 'Marketing is just a set of tools to sell more products.' Explain the possible drawbacks of this approach. (7)
2 How would you describe WQC's marketing philosophy? Is it production orientated or is it market orientated? (7)
3 Using the example of WQC, explain why an unethical approach towards marketing can often yield profitable results in the short term. (8)
4 Outline two internal and two external factors that might affect the effectiveness of WQC's marketing. (8)

Market research

UNIT 22

Market research gathers information about consumers, competitors and distributors within a firm's target market. It is a way of identifying consumers' buying habits and attitudes to current and future products. Market research data can be numerical (such as what proportion of British 16 to 24 year olds buy *The Sun* newspaper every day?) or psychological (for example, why do they buy *The Sun*?).

22.1 CONDUCTING START-UP MARKET RESEARCH

Where do you start? What do you need to know first? And how do you find it out?

The starting point is to discover the marketing fundamentals: how big is the market you are thinking about (market size), what is its future potential and what are the market shares of the existing companies and brands?

Market size means the value of the sales made annually by all the firms within a market. For example, in 2009 the UK market for yoghurts and pot desserts was worth £1,974 million. Market potential can be measured by the annual rate of growth. In the case of yoghurt, this has been at a rate of 4.5 per cent per year, by value. This implies that, by the year 2015, the potential market size will be over £2,550 million.

When looking at a completely new market, these statistics will not be available. So research may be needed into other indicators. For example, the producer of an innovative, new fishing rod would find out the number of people who go fishing regularly.

Market shares are also of crucial importance when investigating a market, as they indicate the relative strength of the firms within the market. In 2009, 27 per cent of the yoghurt market was held by Müller, making it the leading brand by far. A benefit it received for its strong market share was a distribution level of almost 100 per cent: nearly every grocery store stocked Müller. If one firm dominates, it may be very difficult to break into the market.

So how can firms find out this type of information? The starting point is secondary research: unearthing data which already exists.

Figure 22.1 The UK market for yoghurt is growing

22.2 METHODS OF SECONDARY RESEARCH

Internet

Most people start by 'Googling' the topic. This can provide invaluable information, though online providers of market research information will want to charge for the service. With luck, Google will identify a relevant article that can provide useful information.

Trade press

All the above data about the yoghurt market came from an article in *The Grocer* magazine. Every major market is served by one or more magazines written for people who work within that trade. Spending £2.40 on an issue of *The Grocer* provides lots of statistical and other information. Many trade magazines are available for reference in bigger public libraries.

Government-produced data

The government-funded National Statistics produces valuable reports such as the 'Annual Abstract of

Table 22.1 The pros and cons of primary and secondary research

	Secondary research	Primary research
PROS	• often obtained without cost • good overview of a market • usually based on actual sales figures, or research on large samples	• can aim questions directly at your research objectives • latest information from the marketplace • can assess the psychology of the customer
CONS	• data may not be updated regularly • not tailored to your own needs • expensive to buy reports on many different marketplaces	• expensive, £10,000+ per survey • risk of questionnaire and interviewer bias • research findings may only be usable if comparable *backdata* exists

Statistics' and 'Labour Market Trends'. These provide data on population trends and forecasts; for example, someone starting a hair and beauty salon may find out how many 16 to 20 year old women there will be in the year 2015.

Having obtained background data, further research is likely to be tailored specifically to the company's needs, such as carrying out a survey among 16 to 20 year old women about their favourite haircare brands. This type of first-hand research gathers primary data. Some of the pros and cons of primary and secondary research are given in Table 22.1.

22.3 METHODS OF PRIMARY RESEARCH

The process of gathering information directly from people within your target market is known as primary (or field) research. When carried out by market research companies it is expensive, but there is much that firms can do for themselves.

For a company that is up and running, a regular survey of customer satisfaction is an important way of measuring the quality of customer service. When investigating a new market, there are various measures that can be taken by a small firm with a limited budget.

- Retailer research: the people closest to a market are those who serve customers directly – the retailers. They are likely to know the up-and-coming brands, the degree of brand loyalty and the importance of price and packaging, all of which is crucial information.
- Observation: when starting up a service business in which location is an all-important factor, it is invaluable to measure the rate of pedestrian (and possibly traffic) flow past your potential site compared with that of rivals. A sweet shop or dry cleaners near a busy bus stop may generate twice the sales of a rival 50 yards down the road.

For a large company, primary research will be used extensively in new product development. For example, if we consider the possibility of launching Orange Chocolate Buttons, the development stages, plus research, would probably be as shown in Table 22.2.

Table 22.2 Primary research used in new product development (Orange chocolate buttons)

Development stage	Primary research
1. The product idea (probably one of several)	1. Group discussions among regular chocolate buyers (some young, some old)
2. Product test (testing different recipes, different sweetness, orangeyness etc.)	2. A taste test on 200+ chocolate buyers (on street corners, or in a hall)
3. Brand name research (testing several different names and perhaps logos)	3. Quantitative research using a questionnaire on a sample of 200+
4. Packaging research	4. Quantitative research as in item 3
5. Advertising research	5. Group discussions run by psychologists to discover which advertisement has the strongest effect on product image and recall
6. Total proposition test: testing the level of purchase interest, to help make sales forecasts	6. Quantitative research using a questionnaire and product samples on at least 200+ consumers

A-grade application

The Toyota MR2

When Toyota launched the MR2 sports car, sales were higher than expected. The only exception was found in France, where sales were very poor. The Japanese head office asked the executives of Toyota France to look into this. Why had it been such a flop? Eventually the executives admitted that they should have carried out market research into the brand name MR2 prior to the launch. Pronounced 'Em–Er-Deux' in France, the car sounded like the French swear word *merdre* (crap).

22.4 QUALITATIVE RESEARCH

This is in-depth research into the motivations behind the attitudes and buying habits of consumers. It does not produce statistics such as '52 per cent of chocolate buyers like orange chocolate'; instead it gives clues as to why they like it (is it really because it's orange, or because it's different/a change?). Qualitative research is usually conducted by psychologists, who learn to interpret the way people say things, as well as what they say.

Qualitative research takes two main forms, as described below.

Group discussions (also known as focus groups)

These are free-ranging discussions led by psychologists among groups of six to eight consumers. The group leader will have a list of topics that need discussion, but will be free to follow up any point made by a group member. Among the advantages of group discussions are the facts that they:

- may reveal a problem or opportunity the company had not anticipated
- reveal consumer psychology, such as the importance of image and peer pressure

Depth interviews

These are informal, in-depth interviews that take place between a psychologist and a consumer. They have the same function as group discussions, but avoid the risk that the group opinion will be swayed by one influential person. Typical research questions are shown in Table 22.3.

A-grade application

Researching Morrisons

Following its successful relaunch in 2007, Morrisons held group discussions among customers. An individual in one group mentioned Tesco's 'Computers For Schools' initiative and discussion turned towards 'Seeds for Schools', which encourages primary schools to have vegetable patches. Morrisons turned this idea into a nationwide 'Let's Grow' campaign, which 85 per cent of primary schools joined in with. Thirty-nine million vouchers were redeemed and Morrisons generated £21 of sales for every £1 spent on the promotion. The whole marketing approach won a gold medal at the 2009 Advertising Effectiveness competition.

22.5 QUANTITATIVE RESEARCH

This asks pre-set questions on a large enough sample of people to provide statistically valid data. Questionnaires can answer factual questions such as 'How many 16 to 20 year olds have heard of Chanel No 5?' There are three key aspects to quantitative research:

- sampling, ensuring that the research results are typical of the whole population, though only a sample of the population has been interviewed
- writing a questionnaire that is unbiased and meets the research objectives
- assessing the validity of the results.

Sampling

The two main concerns in sampling are how to choose the right people for interview (sampling method) and deciding how large a number to interview (sample size). There are three main sampling methods.

Random sample

A random sample involves selecting respondents to ensure that everyone in the population has an equal chance of being interviewed. This sounds easy, but is not. If an interviewer goes to a street corner one morning and asks passers-by for an interview, the resulting sample will be biased towards those who are not in work, who do not own a car and have time on their hands (the busy ones will refuse to be interviewed). As a result, the sample will not be representative. So achieving a truly random sample requires careful thought.

Table 22.3 Typical research questions

Qualitative research	Quantitative research
• Why do people *really* buy Nikes?	• Which pack design do you prefer?
• Who in the household *really* decides which brand of shampoo is bought?	• Have you heard of any of the following brands? (Ariel, Daz, Persil, etc.)
• What mood makes you feel like buying Haagen Dazs ice cream?	• How likely are you to buy this product regularly?
• When you buy your children Frosties, how do you feel?	• How many newspapers have you bought in the past 7 days?

Research companies use the following method:

1 Pick names at random from the electoral register, for example every fiftieth name
2 Send an interviewer to the address given in the register
3 If the person is out, visit up to twice more before giving up (this is to maximise the chances of catching those who lead busy social lives and are therefore rarely at home).

This method is effective, but slow and expensive.

Quota sample

This method involves selecting interviewees in proportion to the consumer profile within your target market. An example of quota sampling is given in Table 22.4.

Table 22.4 An example of quota sampling

	Adult Chocolate buyers (%)	Respondent quota (sample: 200)
Men	40	80
Women	60	120
16–24	38	76
25–34	21	42
35–44	16	32
45+	25	50

This method allows interviewers to head for busy street corners, interviewing whoever comes along. As long as they achieve the correct quota, they can interview when and where they want to. As this is a relatively cheap and effective way of sampling, it is the one used most commonly by market research companies.

Stratified sample

This method involves interviewing only those with a key characteristic required for the sample. For example, the producers of Oil of Olay might decide to interview only women aged 30 to 45, the potential buyers of the future. Within this stratum/section of the population, individuals could be found at random (a *stratified random* sample) or by setting quotas based on factors such as social class and region.

Sample size

Having decided which sampling method should be used, the next consideration is to determine how many interviews should be conducted. Should 10, 100 or 1,000 people be interviewed? The most high-profile surveys conducted in Britain are the opinion polls, in which people are asked how they will vote in a general election. These quota samples of between 1,000 and 1,500 respondents are considered large enough to reflect the opinions of the electorate of 45 million. How is this possible?

Of course, if you only interviewed ten people, the chances are slim that the views of this sample will match those of the whole population. Of these ten, seven may say they would definitely buy Chocolate Orange Buttons. If you asked another ten, however, only three may say the same. A sample of ten is so small that chance variations make the results meaningless. In other words, a researcher can have no statistical confidence in the findings from a sample of ten.

A sample of 100 is far more meaningful. It is not enough to feel confident about marginal decisions (for example, 53 per cent like the red pack design and 47 per cent like the blue one), but is quite enough if the result is clear cut (such as, 65 per cent like the name 'Spark'; 35 per cent prefer 'Valencia'). Many major product launches have proceeded following research on as low a sample as 100.

With a sample of 1,000, a high level of confidence is possible. Even small differences would be statistically significant with such a large sample. So why doesn't everyone use samples of 1,000? The answer is because of the cost of doing so: money. Hiring a market research agency to undertake a survey on 100 people would cost approximately £10,000. A sample of 1,000 people would cost three times that amount, which is good value if you can afford it but not everyone can. As shown in the earlier example of launching Orange Buttons, a company might require six surveys before launching a new product. So the amount spent on research alone might reach £180,000, if samples of 1,000 were used.

Writing a questionnaire

Quantitative research is expensive and its results may influence major decisions, such as whether to launch a new product. So making a mistake in writing the questionnaire may prove very costly. For instance, the wording may influence respondents to sound more positive about a new product than they really feel. The key features of a good questionnaire are as follows.

1 There should be clearly defined research objectives. What exactly do you need to find out?
2 Ensure that questions do not point towards a particular answer.
3 Ensure that the meaning of each question is clear, perhaps by testing (piloting) questions before putting them into fieldwork.
4 Mainly use closed questions; that is, ones with a limited number of pre-set answers that the respondent must tick. Only in this way can you ensure quantifiable results.
5 It is useful, though, to include a few open questions to allow respondents to write a sentence or two, providing more depth of understanding.
6 Ensure that the questionnaire finishes by asking full demographic and usership details; that is, respondents'

sex, age, occupation (and therefore social class) and buying habits. This allows more detailed analysis of sub-groups within the sample.

22.6 OTHER IMPORTANT CONSIDERATIONS IN PRIMARY RESEARCH

Response rate

If a company sends out 2,000 questionnaires and only 200 people send back a response, the question must be asked: are those who respond typical of those who do not respond? Or is there a bias built into the findings as a consequence of the low response rate?

Face to face versus self-completion

In the past, most surveys were conducted by interviewers who asked the questions face to face. This had drawbacks such as cost and the risk of bias (a bubbly young interviewer may generate more positive responses). Clear benefits of such an approach, however, included a high response rate and the assurance that the interviewer could help to explain an unclear question. Today, self-completion questionnaires are increasingly common.

22.7 MARKET RESEARCH TODAY

Market research is increasingly influenced by technology. Instead of standing on windy street corners, interviewers are more likely to be sat in a telephone booth in an office. There are also more and more internet opinion polls, in which a pop-up questionnaire appears on the screen. For instance, someone looking at the Amazon.com shopping site may be asked to answer questions about book-buying.

An even stronger trend is towards database-driven research. Instead of finding the right people by trial and error, client firms supply research companies with database information on current or ex-customers. Retailers such as Tesco and Sainsbury's have millions of customer names on their databases, gained from customers' membership of 'Loyalty Card' schemes such as Clubcard. Shoppers are grouped into categories such as regular/irregular shoppers, petrol buyers, disposable nappy buyers, and so on. If Tesco wants to survey customer satisfaction with their baby products section, they know exactly who should be contacted.

The future of market research is clearly bound up in technology. However, the basics will remain crucial: the avoidance of bias in the wording of questions, large enough sample sizes to provide valid data and intelligent analysis of the research findings.

ISSUES FOR ANALYSIS

When developing an argument in answer to an exam question, market research offers the following main lines of analysis.

- The key role of market research in market orientation; that is, basing decisions upon the consumer, rather than the producer's needs or opinions.
- The need for a questioning approach to data: when presented with a research finding one needs to know: was the sample size large enough? Who paid for the research? Businesspeople learn to ask questions about every 'fact' shown by research.
- The importance of market knowledge: large, established firms have a huge advantage over newer, smaller firms because of their knowledge of consumer attitudes and behaviour, built up from years of market research surveys.

Key Terms

Bias: a factor that causes research findings to be unrepresentative of the whole population, for example bubbly interviewers or misleading survey questions.
Primary research: finding out information first-hand, for example Coca-Cola designing a questionnaire to obtain information from people who regularly buy diet products.
Secondary research: finding out information that has already been gathered, for example the government's estimates of the number of 14 to 16 year olds in Wales.
Sample size: the number of people interviewed; this should be large enough to give confidence that the findings are representative of the whole population.
Sampling method: the approach chosen to select the right people to be part of the research sample; for example, random, quota or stratified.

22.8 MARKET RESEARCH – AN EVALUATION

In large firms, it is rare for any significant marketing decision to be made without market research. Even an apparently minor change to a pack design will only be carried out after testing in research. Is this overkill? Surely marketing executives are employed to make judgements, not merely do what surveys tell them?

The first issue here is the strong desire to make business decisions as scientifically as possible; in other words, to act on evidence, not on feelings. Quantitative research, especially, fits in with the desire to act on science not hunch. Yet this can be criticised, such as by John Scully, former head of Apple Computers, who once said 'No great marketing decision has ever been made on the basis of quantitative data'. He was pointing out that true innovations such as the Apple iPad were the product of creativity and hunch, not science.

The second issue concerns the management culture. In some firms, mistakes lead to inquests, blame and even dismissal. This makes managers keen to find a let-out. When the new product flops, the manager can point an accusing finger at the positive research results: 'It wasn't my fault. We need a new research agency.' In other firms, mistakes are seen as an inevitable part of learning. For every Sinclair C5 (unresearched flop) there may be an iPod (unresearched moneyspinner). In firms with a positive, risk-taking approach to business, qualitative insights are likely to be preferred to quantitative data.

WORKBOOK

(35 marks; 35 minutes)

A REVISION QUESTIONS

1 State three ways in which a cosmetics firm could use market research. (3)
2 Outline three reasons why market research information may prove inaccurate. (6)
3 Distinguish between primary and secondary research. (3)
4 What advantages are there in using secondary research rather than primary? (3)
5 Which is the most commonly used sampling method? Why may it be the most commonly used? (3)
6 State three key factors to take into account when writing a questionnaire. (3)
7 Explain two aspects of marketing in which consumer psychology is important. (4)
8 Outline the pros and cons of using a large sample size. (4)
9 Identify three possible sources of bias in primary market research. (3)
10 Why may street interviewing become less common in the future? (3)

B REVISION EXERCISES

B1 MARKET RESEARCH ASSIGNMENT

Hampton is a medium-sized producer of health foods. Its new company strategy is to break into the £400 million market for breakfast cereals. It has created three new product ideas that it wishes to test in research before further development takes place. They are:

- *Cracker*: an extra-crunchy mix of oats and almonds
- *Fizzz*: crunchy oats which fizz in milk
- *St James*: a luxury mix of oats, cashews and pecan nuts.

The research objectives are to identify the most popular of the three, in terms of product trial and regular usage; to identify price expectations for each; to find what people like and dislike about each idea and each brand name; and to be able to analyse the findings in relation to consumers' demographic profile and current usage patterns.

Questions

(30 marks; 30 minutes)

1 Write a questionnaire based upon the above details, bearing in mind the advice given in the text (12)
2 Explain which sampling method you would use and why. (6)
3 Interview six to eight people using your questionnaire; then write a 200-word commentary on its strengths and weaknesses. (12)

B2 DATA RESPONSE

Each year more than £1,000 million is spent on pet food in the UK. All the growth within the market has been for luxury pet foods and for healthier products. Seeing these trends, in early 2008 Town & Country Petfoods launched 'HiLife Just Desserts', a range of pudding treats for dogs. They contain Omega-3 but no added sugar and therefore have no more than 100 calories per tin.

Sales began well, especially of the Apple & Cranberry version. Now sales have flattened out at around £1 million a year and the company thinks it is time to launch some new flavours. Three weeks ago they commissioned some primary research that was carried out using an online survey linked to pet care websites. The sample size was 150.

The main findings were as shown in Table 22.5.

Table 22.5 Findings of online survey

1 Have you ever bought your dog a pet food pudding?				
Ever bought:	**Never**	**Just once But no longer do**	**Yes in past**	**Yes, still**
%	61	13	12	14
2 Which of these flavours may you buy for your dog?				
May try:	**Never (%)**	**May try (%)**	**May buy monthly (%)**	**May buy once a week+ (%)**
Muesli yoghurt	61	19	15	5
Rhubarb crumble	43	33	22	2
Apples and custard	52	34	12	2

The marketing director is slightly disappointed that none of the new product ideas has done brilliantly, but happy that there's one clear winner. She plans a short qualitative research exercise among existing HiLife customers, and hopes to launch two new flavours in time for the annual Crufts' Dog Show in three months' time.

Questions

(20 marks; 30 minutes)

1 Outline whether the sample size of 150 was appropriate in this case. (4)

2 Examine the marketing director's conclusion that 'none of the new product ideas has done brilliantly, but happy that there's one clear winner'. (7)

3 **a)** Explain one method of qualitative research that could be used in this case. (3)

b) Analyse two ways in which qualitative research may help the marketing director. (6)

C Essay questions

(40 marks each)

1 'Market research is like an insurance policy. You pay a premium to reduce your marketing risks.' To what extent do you believe this statement to be true?

2 After ten years of rising sales, demand for Shredded Wheat has started to slip. Discuss how the marketing manager could make use of market research to analyse why this has happened and help to decide the strategy needed to return Shredded Wheat to sales growth.

3 Steve Jobs, boss of Apple, once said that he ignored market research in the early stages of the iPod. He believes that research is useful in relation to existing products, but does not work with innovative new products.

a) Why may this be?

b) How could research be used to best effect for assessing new innovations?

Understanding markets

UNIT 23

A market is where buyers meet sellers; examples include eBay or Smithfield meat market. The key elements within every market are its size (how much is spent by customers in a year), the extent to which it can be subdivided, for example the confectionery market into chocolate, sugar-based sweets and chewing gum; and the extent to which the market is dominated by one or two companies or brands.

23.1 TYPES OF MARKET

Local versus national

Most new small firms know and care little about the size of the national market. If you have just bought an ice cream van that you intend to operate in Chichester, it does not matter whether the size of the UK market for ice cream is £500 million or £600 million per year. Your concern is the level of demand and the level of competition locally. And you will probably be delighted if you achieve annual sales of £0.1 million (£100,000).

In the case of the market for ice cream in Chichester, there are several things to consider:

- How do locals buy ice cream at the moment? (Multipacks from supermarkets? Individual cones from ice cream stalls or vans?)
- How many tourists come to the city? Do they come all year round? What type of ice cream do they buy? Where do they buy it?
- How much competition is there? What do competitors offer and charge at the moment? Are there gaps in the market that you can move into?

Other firms are focused more on the national market. For example, Klein Caporn is a small food company that started in 2005. It produces high-quality, high-priced ready-to-eat meals. It started by targeting small grocers, but soon found that the sales volumes were too low to cover their costs. A sales breakthrough in Waitrose supermarkets was followed in 2007 by acceptance by Sainsbury's. This enables the company to deliver to just two warehouses, cutting the business costs dramatically. Then Waitrose and Sainsbury's distribute to their local shops. So Klein Caporn has a national presence, even though sales remain well below 1 per cent of the market for ready meals.

To deal on the national level, Klein Caporn has to deal professionally with the supermarket buyers, and produce eye-catching packaging that can compete effectively with national and multinational competitors.

Physical and electronic (virtual)

Once, all markets were physical. The London Stock Exchange was a place where buyers met sellers and face-to-face agreements took place. Similarly, auctions were physical, with bidders having to catch the eye of the auctioneer.

Today an increasing number of markets are electronic (or virtual). The stock market exists only on computer screens, and the likes of eBay are transforming auction and other markets worldwide.

Figure 23.1 Bidding on eBay

From a business point of view the key factors about electronic markets (for example for finding hotel rooms or flights) are as follows.

- They are fiercely price competitive, so the companies supplying services have huge pressure to keep their costs as low as possible.
- They do not rely on physical location, for example a business can easily be run from a bedroom, such as selling Wii computer games.

- The market is easy and quite cheap to enter, so new competitors can arrive at any time.
- They provide a 'long tail' of competitive, profitable small businesses, able to carve their own little niche in markets; this is very difficult to achieve in the high street, where rents are so high that only big firms can afford them.

23.2 FACTORS DETERMINING DEMAND

Demand is the desire of consumers to buy a product or service, when backed by the ability to pay. It is also known as 'effective demand' (that is, only when the customer has the money is demand effective). Several factors determine the demand for a specific product/service.

Price

This affects demand in three ways.

1. You may want an £80,000 Mercedes convertible, but you cannot afford it; the price puts it beyond your income level. The higher the price, the more people there are who cannot afford to buy.
2. The higher the price, the less good value the item will seem compared with other ways of spending the money. For example, a Chelsea home ticket costing £48 is the equivalent of going to the movies six to eight times. Is it worth it? The higher the price of an item, the more there will be people who say 'it's not worth it'.
3. It should be remembered that the price tag put on an item gives a message about its 'value'. A ring priced at 99p will inevitably be seen as 'cheap', whether or not it is value for money; so although lower prices should boost sales, firms must beware of ruining their image for quality.

Incomes

The British economy grows at a rate of about 2.5 per cent a year. This means that average income levels double every 30 years. Broadly, when your children are aged about 16–18, you are likely to be twice as well off as your parents are today. Economic growth means we all get richer over time (and lazier, and fatter and spend more time in traffic jams).

The demand for most products and services grows as the economy grows. Goods like cars and cinema tickets are 'normal goods', for which demand rises broadly in line with incomes. In some cases it grows even faster; for example, if the economy grows by 3 per cent in a year, the amount spent on foreign holidays can easily rise by 6 per cent. This type of product is known as a luxury good.

Still other goods behave differently, with sales falling when people are better off. These products are known as inferior goods. In their case, rising incomes mean falling sales. For example, the richer we get, the more Tropicana we buy and the less Tesco Orange Squash. As Orange Squash is an inferior good, a couple of years of economic struggle (and perhaps more people out of work) would mean sales would increase as people switch from expensive Tropicana to cheap Squash.

Actions of competitors

Demand for British Airways (BA) Heathrow to New York flights does not only depend on their price and the incomes of consumers. It also depends on the actions of their rivals. If Virgin Atlantic is running a brilliant advertising campaign, demand for BA flights might fall as customers switch to Virgin. Or if American Airlines pushes its prices up, people might switch to BA.

The firm's own marketing activities

Following the same logic, if British Airways is running a new advertising campaign, perhaps based on improved customer service, it may enjoy increased sales. In effect, its sales will rise if it can persuade customers to switch from Virgin and American Airlines to BA. One firm's sales increase usually means reduced sales elsewhere.

Seasonal factors

Most firms experience significant variations in sales through the year. Some markets such as ice cream, soft drinks, lager and seaside hotels boom in the summer and slump in the winter.. Other markets, such as sales of perfume, liqueurs, greetings cards and toys boom at Christmas. Other products that have less obvious reasons for seasonal variations in demand include cars, cat food, carpets, furniture, TVs and newspapers. The variation is caused by patterns of customer behaviour and nothing can be done about that. A well-run business makes sure it understands and can predict the seasonal variations in demand; and then has a plan for coping.

23.3 MARKET SIZE AND TRENDS

Market size is the measurement of all the sales by all the companies within a marketplace. It can be measured in two ways: by volume and by value. Volume measures the quantity of goods purchased, perhaps in tons, in packs or in units. Market size by value is the amount spent by customers on the volume sold. So the difference between volume and value is the price paid per unit.

Take, for example, the figures shown in Table 23.1 for the UK market for butter and spreads.

Table 23.1 UK market for butter and spreads

2009–10 market by value	£1,093 million
2009–10 market by volume	415 million kg
Average price per kg	263.3 pence (£1093/415)

Source: *The Grocer* magazine 3 July 2010.

Market size matters because it is the basis for calculating market share (the proportion of the total market held by one company or brand). This, in turn, is essential for evaluating the success or failure of a firm's marketing activities. Market size is also the reference point for calculating trends. Is the market size growing or declining? A growth market is far more likely to provide the opportunities for new products to be launched or new distribution initiatives to be successful.

Recent figures and forecasts for the car market in China help to show the importance of market trends. In 2001 the UK car market was four times bigger than that in China. In 2005 China accelerated past Britain. And look at the forecasts for the coming years, shown in Table 23.2.

Table 23.2 Sales of new passenger cars (actual and forecast)

Year	China	Britain
2007	6,000,000	2,400,000
2008	6,700,000	2,100,000
2009	10,300,000	2,000,000
2012 (forecast)	15,000,000	2,100,000
2020 (forecast)	25,000,000	2,400,000

Source: Forecasts by industry experts.

In 2009 China became the world's biggest car market. Clearly these figures show that success in China will be far more important to car firms than success in Britain.

23.4 MARKET SHARE

Market share is the proportion of the total market held by one company or product. It can be measured by volume, but is more often looked at by value. Market share is taken by most firms as the key test of the success of the year's marketing activities. Total sales are affected by factors such as economic growth, but market share only measures a firm's ability to win or lose against its competitors. As shown in Table 23.3, rising market share can also lead to the producer's ideal of market leadership or market dominance. Cadbury's Dairy Milk has market leadership among confectionery brands. Walkers has market dominance among crisps and snacks. Pampers and Actimel have even stronger positions within their sectors.

There are many advantages to a business in having the top selling brand (the brand leader). Obviously, sales are higher than anyone else's, but also:

- The brand leader gets the highest distribution level, often without needing to make much effort to achieve it. Even a tiny corner shop stocks Whiskas, as well as a 'Happy Shopper' own-label cat food. Success breeds success.
- Brand leaders are able to offer lower discount terms to retailers than the number two or three brands in a market. This means higher revenues and profit margins per unit sold.
- The strength of a brand-leading name such as Walls Magnum makes it much easier to obtain distribution and consumer trial for new products based on that brand name.

23.5 MARKET SEGMENTATION

Most markets can be subdivided in several different ways. If you go to WH Smith and look at the magazine racks, you will see the process in action. There are magazines for men and (many more) for women. Within the women's section there are magazines for 'kids', teens, young adults, those who are middle-aged and some for the elderly. Then there are magazines that target different interests and hobbies, from football to computer consoles to gardening.

Market segmentation is the acknowledgement by companies that customers are not all the same. 'The market' can be broken down into smaller sections in which customers share common characteristics, from the same age group to a shared love of Manchester United. Successful segmentation can increase customer satisfaction (if you love shopping and 'celebs', how wonderful that *Look* magazine is for you!) and provide scope for increasing company profits. After all, customers may be willing to pay a higher price for

Table 23.3 Brands with the highest UK market share

Leading brand in its market	Sales of leading brand (£ million)	Market size (by value) (£ million)	Market share (%)	Share of nearest competitor (%)
Walkers Crisps*	497	2,171	22.9	6.2
Cadbury's Dairy Milk	371	3,069	12.1	6.2
Pampers	277	467	59.3	21.5
Actimel	114	248	45.9	15.8
Magnum Ice Cream	88	437	20.1	7.4

*Not including Sensations, Potato Heads or other Walker brands.

Source: *The Grocer* 19 December 2009 quoting from Nielsen.

a magazine focused purely on the subjects they love, instead of buying a general magazine in which most of the articles stay unread.

The keys to successful market segmentation are as follows.

- Research into the different types of customer within a marketplace, for example different age groups, gender, region and personality types.
- See if they have common tastes/habits; for example, younger readers may be more focused on fashion and celebrities than older ones.
- Devise a product designed not for the whole market, but for a particular segment; this may only achieve a 1 per cent market share, but if the total market is big enough, that could be highly profitable.

Key Terms

Inferior goods: products that people turn to when they are hard up, and turn away from when they are better off (for example Tesco Value Beans instead of Heinz).

Luxury goods: Products that people buy much more of when they feel better off (for example, jewellery, sports cars, and holidays at posh hotels).

Normal goods: Products or services for which sales change broadly in line with the economy; that is, if the economy grows by 3 per cent, sales rise by 3 per cent (for example, travel and sales of fast food).

ISSUES FOR ANALYSIS

- The key to analysis is precision. Terms such as inferior goods and normal goods have to be understood so well that you spot where they are relevant and are able to use them to develop your answer. Every student would recognise that a Mercedes sports car is a luxury product. Few could continue by saying that its sales will therefore grow especially fast when times are good, but may slump when the economy is struggling.
- To analyse the market that a business is operating in, make sure to consider the market size, trends and share, the degree of segmentation, the factors determining demand and the type of market, for example local versus national. This is a powerful combination of concepts that should provide a lot of scope for analytic answers.

23.6 UNDERSTANDING MARKETS – AN EVALUATION

Almost every large business carries out detailed market analysis on a regular basis. They buy 'retail audits' to find out how retail sales are doing. It can be said, though, that some managers suffer from 'paralysis by analysis'. In other words they gather so much data (some of it conflicting) that they end up unable to make a decision. Contrast this approach with that of Apple. Boss Steve Jobs focuses on understanding customers, not analysing the market as it stands at present. He believes that Apple can always stay one step ahead, by thinking about what customers will want in future. Given Apple's success, it is hard to argue with him.

WORKBOOK

A REVISION QUESTIONS

(35 marks; 35 minutes)

1. Outline three features of the market for fast food near to where you live. (6)
2. Section 23.2 lists five factors determining the demand for a product: price, incomes, actions of competitors, marketing activities and seasonality. Identify which two of these would most heavily affect sales of:
   a) Strawberries
   b) EasyJet tickets to Barcelona
   c) Tickets to see Newcastle United
   d) DFS furniture. (8)
3. Explain in your own words the difference between market size by volume and market size by value. (2)
4. a) Look at Table 23.2. Toyota's share of the UK car market is about 6 per cent. If it continues with that share, how many UK car sales would that amount to in 2020; and how many Toyota cars would be sold in China in 2020, assuming the same market share? (4)
   b) Outline two ways in which Toyota could respond to that sales difference? (4)
5. Why may a shoe shop focusing on 'Little Feat' be able to charge higher prices per pair than a general shoe shop? (2)
6. Explain in your own words how the market for shoes could be segmented. (3)
7. Look at Table 23.3. Discuss which business should be happier with its market position: Walkers or Pampers. (6)

REVISION EXERCISES
B1 DATA RESPONSE

In late August 2007 entertainment retailer ChoicesUK called in the receivers. It was unable to continue trading after losing money consistently during 2007. As many as 1,700 jobs were threatened at ChoicesUK's 200 branches.

This came on top of the collapse of Fopp music retailers earlier in the year. At the same time, industry giant HMV suffered a halving of its profits. The reason was the same: the collapse in the total market for CDs and DVDs, compounded by a switch to buying online or downloading. The UK CD market, for example, fell by 10 per cent in the first half of 2007.

Questions

(15 marks; 15 minutes)

1 Outline two reasons why a whole market may shrink in size, as happened to CD sales in the first half of 2007. (4)
2 ChoicesUK collapsed as the market declined. Explain two ways in which it might have set about boosting its market share (to combat the decline in the market as a whole). (6)
3 In the past, more than half the annual sales of ChoicesUK have taken place in the three months before Christmas. Should the Directors have kept the business going a few months more? (5)

B2 DATA RESPONSE

Lidl and Aldi winning grocery wars

Discount grocers are the big winners in 2007, TNS Worldpanel figures show. The grocery market grew by 4 per cent year-on-year in the 12 weeks to 16 July 2007. Tesco, Sainsbury's and Asda all grew slightly faster than the total market, while Somerfield sales actually fell by 6 per cent. Lidl and Aldi bucked the trend with sales growth of 13 per cent and 11 per cent respectively. Iceland also performed well, growing by 12 per cent. Perhaps these three low-cost grocers benefited from the collapse of Kwik-Save.

The changes leave Tesco as the market leader with 31.5 per cent (unchanged on 2006), while Asda's share grew from 16.6 to 16.7 per cent and Sainsbury's from 16 to 16.2 per cent. Morrison's suffered a fall in market share, from 11.3 to 11.1 per cent. A decline of 0.2 per cent may seem trivial, but as the value of the UK grocery market is £128.2 billion per year, 0.2 per cent market share represents sales of £256.4 million! See Figure 23.2.

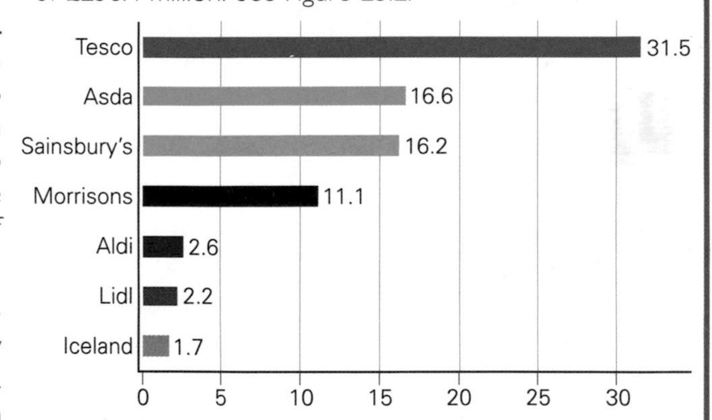

Figure 23.2 UK grocery market share 2007
Source: TNS World Panel and Nielsen, quoted in *The Grocer* 28 July 2007.

Questions

(30 marks; 30 minutes)

1 a) What was the grocery market size and market growth in 2007? (2)
  b) Identify three possible reasons why sales at Somerfield actually fell in 2007. (3)
2 a) Show the workings to calculate that a 0.2 per cent share of the UK grocery market equals £256.4 million. (3)
  b) Use the figures and the bar chart to work out the value of the UK 2007 sales of Lidl. (2)
  c) Examine two possible reasons why Lidl enjoyed the biggest sales growth within the grocery market in 2007. (6)
3 a) Outline two ways in which Tesco may benefit from being the grocery market leader. (4)
  b) Ten years ago, Sainsbury's was the UK grocery market leader. Discuss whether it could return to that position within the next ten years. (10)

Niche versus mass marketing

UNIT 24

Mass marketing means devising products with mass appeal and promoting them to all types of customer. Niche marketing is tailoring a product to a particular type of customer.

24.1 MASS MARKETING

Mass marketing is the attempt to create products or services that have universal appeal. Rather than targeting a specific type of customer, mass marketing aims the product at the whole market. The intention is that everyone should be a consumer of the product. Coca-Cola is a good example of a firm that uses mass marketing techniques. The company aims its product at young and old alike. Its goal has always been to be the market leader and it still is today. The ultimate prize of mass marketing is the creation of generic brands. These are brands that are so totally associated with the product that customers treat the brand name as if it was a product category. Examples include 'Hoover' (vacuum cleaner) and 'Bacardi' (white rum).

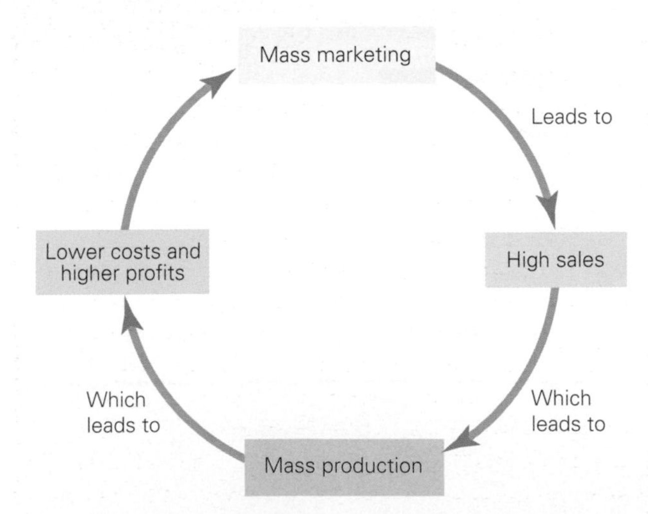

Figure 24.1 Mass marketing

As shown in Figure 24.1, when mass marketing is carried out successfully it can be highly profitable. Firms such as Ryanair set out to be high-volume, mass-market operators and achieve handsome profits. However, it is important to note that mass marketing does not have to go hand in hand with low prices. For example, Apple, when it launched the iPod, decided to become *the* MP3 player. Its brilliant launch advertising and – most importantly – the development of iTunes meant that it achieved mass market sales while keeping its prices high. Even now, with its sales entering the decline phase of its product life cycle (see Figure 24.2), it remains the dominant brand in its market. The brilliant marketing of the iPod provided the necessary product differentiation to sell high sales volumes without the need to cut prices.

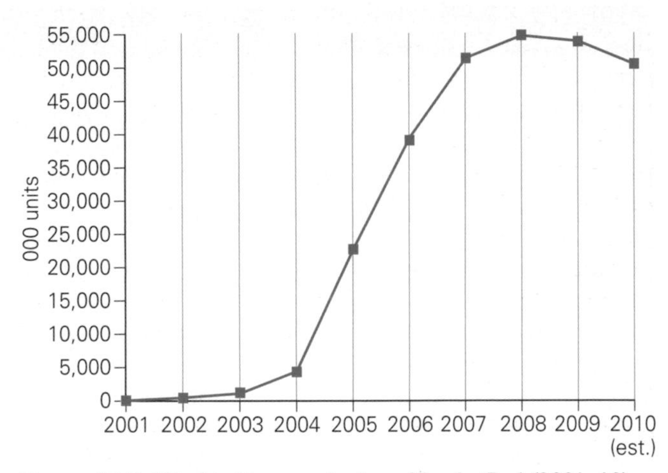

Figure 24.2 Worldwide annual sales of Apple iPod (2001–10)
Source: Apple annual accounts

24.2 NICHE MARKETING

A niche market is a very small segment of a much larger market. Niche marketing involves identifying the needs of the consumers that make up the niche. A specialised product or service is then designed to meet the distinctive needs of these consumers. Niche-market products tend to sell in relatively low volumes. As a result, the price of a niche-market product is usually higher than the mass market alternative. Niche-market operators often distribute their products through specialist retailers, or directly to the consumer via the internet.

An entrepreneur wanting to set up a niche-market business must first identify a group of people who share a taste for a product or service that is currently unsatisfied. A product or a service must then be designed that is capable of meeting this unsatisfied need. To stand a good chance of success, the new niche product will need to be superior to the mass market equivalent that is currently available. Finally, the niche must be large enough to support a profitable business. Many new niche-market businesses fail because the revenue generated from their niche-market business is not high enough to cover the costs of operating.

A good example is provided by a small neighbourhood restaurant called 'Bajou' that tried, unsuccessfully, to make a business out of selling Cajun food in south Croydon. At the weekend the restaurant was never completely empty, proving that a gap in the market did exist. Unfortunately, this gap in the market was not large enough to cover the overheads of running a restaurant. The restaurant was never full enough to operate above a break-even level. Six months after 'Bajou' opened it was forced to close down. In niche markets entrepreneurs must manage their overhead costs with care if the business is to operate above its break-even point.

Small niche operators lack the economies of scale required to compete on price with larger, established operators. Instead, the small firm could try to find a small, profitable niche. The amount of profit generated by this niche needs to be high enough for the small firm, but too trivial for the big business. In Birmingham's City Centre, 'Rubicon Exotic' is a profitable line of soft drinks; but with a market share of less than 1 per cent Coca-Cola will not 'crash this party' (or attempt to enter this niche market). The profit generated is enough to satisfy the requirements of Rubicon Drinks, with its low overheads. Small, niche-market businesses survive on the basis that they occupy a relatively unimportant, low-profit market niche. Larger firms operating in the mass market are happy to ignore the niche businesses because they pose no threat.

Niche-market businesses sell specialised, differentiated products that are designed to appeal to their very specific target market. Firms selling niche-market products can exploit the low price sensitivity created by product differentiation by raising price. Total revenue will rise after the price increase because, in percentage terms, the fall in sales volume will be less than the price increase.

Successful niche marketing in practice

Until recently catalogue retailing has suffered from a down-market image. Operators such as Argos based their success on selling mass-market products at budget prices. However, in the last few years internet retailing has seen a host of new niche-market players entering the market. Companies such as 'Nordic Kids' sell a highly differentiated range of niche-market premium quality designer clothes that are not available on the high street. In this case the niche market is affluent middle-class parents seeking, according to the company's website, 'effortless Scandinavian cool': http://www.nordickids.co.uk/

24.3 ARE NICHE MARKETS SAFE HAVENS FOR SMALL BUSINESSES?

In the past many large companies focused on mass markets and ignored small market gaps and the small companies that filled them. To fill lots of small niches would require lots of short production runs (for example, 90 minutes on the printing press producing the Hartlepool FC fanzine, and 60 minutes producing the Darlington one). This has always been expensive, because it takes a long time to reset machinery.

This has changed due to technology. As production lines are increasingly set up by computer, they can be reset almost instantly. So large firms can build the sales volumes they need by producing a large variety of low-volume niche-market products. Small scale producers are coming under threat from larger companies that have begun to target their niches.

Fortunately, small firms are often 'quicker on their feet', so when a large firm 'lumbers' towards the market, the smaller one may still be able to win the competitive war. When the multi-billion dollar PepsiCo bought the smoothie business PJ's, Innocent Drinks thought that the market might become very difficult for them. In fact, Innocent kept its market share rising within the small smoothie niche within the soft drinks market.

A-grade application

Flares nightclub chain

A good example of a successful business that uses the niche marketing approach is the 'Flares' nightclub chain. It targets a niche market comprised, mostly, of ageing clubbers in their forties who want a 1970s retro night out. Each Flares nightclub tends to be relatively small, so even a comparatively small number of customers will make the club look reassuringly busy. The small capacity also helps to reduce overheads, decreasing the number of customers required each week to break even. The interior design is deliberately garish; an exaggerated version of what a typical nightclub looked like in the 1970s, complete with features such as mirror-balls and an under-lit glass dance floor. The music policy holds no surprises either; 1970s funk and other kitsch retro classics such as ABBA, which are likely to appeal to the ageing clubber.

Source: Flares

ISSUES FOR ANALYSIS

- It is useful to analyse niche marketing in relation to price elasticity. Niche-market products are invariably designed to meet the needs of customers looking for something different. This means that buyers of niche-market goods are likely to be less price sensitive than consumers of mass market brands. This is especially true for the first brand to open up a niche market. Consumers may regard the originator of the market segment as 'the real thing'. An example would be Marmite, in the relatively tiny market for savoury spreads (most people prefer sweet things on their toast, for example honey or jam). This allows Marmite to charge extraordinarily high prices such as £4 for a jar that is the same size and weight as a £1 jar of honey.
- Fundamentally there are two approaches to making profit. The first is to be a high-volume, low-profit margin operator, such as Ryanair. The second is to charge higher prices and be a low-volume, high-profit margin business, such as Marmite. This is the route taken by those who adopt niche marketing tactics.

24.4 NICHE VERSUS MASS MARKETING – AN EVALUATION

Which is better? Is it mass or niche marketing? The answer is that it depends. In the bulk ice cream market, large packs of vanilla ice cream have become so cheap that little profit can be made. It is better by far, then, to be in a separate niche, whether regional (Mackie's Scottish ice cream) or upmarket such as Rocombe Farm or Haagen Dazs. The latter can charge ten times as much per litre as the mass-market own-label bulk packs.

Yet would a film company prefer to sell a critic's favourite or a blockbuster, smash hit? The answer is the latter, of course. In other words, the mass market is great, if you can succeed there. Businesses such as Heinz, Kelloggs and even Chanel show that mass marketing can be successful and profitable in the long term.

Key Terms

Economies of scale: factors that cause costs per unit to fall when a firm operates at a higher level of production.

Generic brands: brands that are so well known that customers say the brand when they mean the product (for example, 'I'll hoover the floor.').

Price elasticity: the responsiveness of demand to a change in price.

Product differentiation: the extent to which consumers perceive your brand as being different from others.

WORKBOOK

A REVISION QUESTIONS

(20 marks; 20 minutes)

1 Identify two advantages of niche marketing over mass marketing. (3)
2 Give three reasons why a large firm may wish to enter a niche market. (3)
3 Why may small firms be better at spotting and then reacting to new niche-market opportunities? (3)
4 Give two reasons why average prices in niche markets tend to be higher than those charged in most mass markets. (2)
5 Outline two reasons why Information Technology has made niche marketing a more viable option for large firms. (4)
6 Explain why it is important for a large firm to be flexible if it is to successfully operate in niche markets. (2)
7 In your own words, explain why the price elasticity of niche-market products may be lower than for products in the mass market. (3)

B REVISION EXERCISES

B1 DATA RESPONSE

The return of mass marketing to the car industry

For many years car manufacturers such as Toyota and Nissan have sought out market niches in an attempt to improve profitability. Cars such as the Toyota Prius, a hybrid electric powered vehicle, are not intended to sell in high volumes. Instead, niche market cars sell for high prices, delivering a higher profit margin per car than more conventional mass market models.

However, in the last couple of years, there are signs that car manufacturers have sought a return to conventional mass marketing, particularly in Asia where rapid rates of economic growth have created a growing middle class. At present both the Indian and the Chinese car markets are unsaturated. For example, in India car ownership is only 8 per 1,000, whereas in the US and the UK the corresponding figure is 477 and 373 respectively. Income per head, whilst increasing rapidly, is still low by American and

European standards, and so far this has limited the demand for new cars in India.

Now car manufacturers have spotted a gap in the market for a basic, low cost car. The first company to fill this gap in the market was the Indian car manufacturer, Tata Motors. It sells its basic 'People's car' for less than 100, 000 rupees (£1,500). Multinationals such as Renault and General Motors are now opening their own Indian factories to produce similar mass market cars sold at ultra-low prices. The challenge for these producers will be to manufacture the cars cheaply enough to make the low prices profitable.

Environmentalists have expressed their concerns that these new cheap cars will add to the problem of global warming and climate change. This year Tata Motors expects to sell a quarter of a million new cars in India.

Questions

(38 marks; 45 minutes)

1 **a)** What is a niche-market product? (2)
  b) Explain why the Toyota Prius is a good example of a niche-market product. (2)
2 Explain two reasons why the Indian car market has grown. (4)
3 **a)** What is a mass-market product? (2)
  b) Explain why the Tata Motor's 'People's car' is a good example of a mass- market product. (4)
4 Analyse two advantages and two disadvantages for European car manufacturers, such as Renault, of mass marketing £2,000 cars in India. (8)
5 £2,000 cars can be profitably made in India. Explain why UK consumers are unlikely to benefit from similar low prices. (4)
6 Discuss whether companies such as Tata Motors should take into account the concerns of environmentalists when making their business decisions. (12)

B2 DATA RESPONSE

Winter melon tea

Mass market soft drinks like Coca-Cola and Pepsi are very popular in countries such as Hong Kong and Singapore. In an attempt to survive against the imported competition, local producers of soft drinks have managed to establish a flourishing niche market for traditional Asian drinks sold in 33 cl cans. Sales of these niche-market products have been rising but from a very low level.

Consumers that make up this niche market are encouraged to believe, through advertising, that traditional drinks such as winter melon tea and grass jelly drink are healthier than their mass market alternatives. Other firms use economic nationalism to sell their drinks, using slogans such as 'Asian heritage' in their advertising.

However, producers of traditional drinks could now become a victim of their own success. Foreign multi-nationals have noticed the rapid growth of this market niche, and in response, they have launched their own range of traditional drinks.

Figure 24.3

Questions

(26 marks; 35 minutes)

1 a) What is a niche-market product? (2)
   b) Explain why Asian traditional drinks are examples of niche-market products. (2)

2 Explain two ways in which the producers of traditional drinks, such as winter melon tea and grass jelly drink, created product differentiation. (4)

3 Niche-market products are normally more expensive than most mass-market products. Using the example of traditional Asian drinks, explain why this is usually so. (6)

4 Discuss whether the local producers of Asian traditional drinks will be able to survive in the long term given that their products now have to compete against me-too brands produced by foreign multinationals such as Coca-Cola and Pepsi. (12)

Designing an effective marketing mix

UNIT 25

The marketing mix is the balance between the four main elements of marketing needed to carry out the marketing strategy. It consists of the '4Ps': product, price, promotion and place.

25.1 COMPONENTS OF THE MARKETING MIX

When working out how to market a product successfully, there are four main variables to consider (the **marketing mix**).

Product

The business must identify the right product (or service) to make the product both appealing and distinctive; to do this, it needs to understand fully both its customers and its competitors. No product will have long-term success unless this stage is completed successfully.

Price

Having identified the right product to appeal to its target market, the business must set the right price. The 'right' price for a Versace handbag may be £1,200; it is a great mistake to think that low prices or special discounts are the path to business success.

Promotion

Marketing managers must identify the right way to create the right image for the product and present it to the right target audience. This may be achieved best by national TV advertising, but specific markets can be reached at far lower cost by more careful targeting (for example, advertising lawnmowers in magazines such as *Amateur Gardening*). 'Promotion' includes both media advertising (TV, press, cinema, radio) and other forms of promotion (including special offers, public relations, direct mail and online).

Place

For products, 'place' is how to get your product to the place where customers can be persuaded to buy; this may be through a vending machine or on a Tesco shelf, or positioned just by the till at a newsagent (the prime position for purchases bought on impulse); for service businesses, place may be online, or in the location of a retail outlet (for example, Tesco Direct and Tesco stores).

The units that follow this one deal with each of these factors in turn.

A-grade application

Both McVitie's Jaffa Cakes and Burton's Jammie Dodgers are well-known biscuit brands, but the former is distributed in 90 per cent of retail outlets, whereas the latter is in only 64 per cent. Clearly this restricts sales of Jammie Dodgers, because few customers would make a special journey to find them. Both companies have a similar view of the right outlets for their products (for example,. supermarkets, corner shops, garages, canteens and cafés), so why may Burton's be losing out to McVitie's in this particular race? Possible reasons include the following.

- Jaffa Cakes have higher consumer demand; therefore retail outlets are more willing to stock the product.
- Jammie Dodgers may have more direct competitors; high product differentiation may make Jaffa Cakes more of a 'must stock' line,
- if Jaffa Cakes have more advertising support, retailers know customers will ask for the product by name while the advertising campaign is running,
- McVitie's has a much larger market share; therefore the company is in a stronger position to cross-sell (persuade a shopkeeper to buy a range of McVitie's brands).

25.2 HOW IS THE MARKETING MIX USED?

The marketing mix can be used by a new business to develop ideas about how and where to market a product or service. A very small business start-up may look no further than leaflets to be handed out or posted in neighbouring front doors. In a larger business, a senior manager is likely to set a maximum budget; then the individual marketing managers will look at each of the ingredients in the mix. They then decide what marketing actions need to be taken under each of the headings. If marketing activity is to be effective, each ingredient needs to be considered.

For each market situation, managers are trying to set the ideal combination of the ingredients based on a balance between cost and effectiveness. The ingredients need to work with each other. A good product poorly priced may fail. If the product is not available following an advertising campaign, the expenditure is wasted. A successful mix is the one that succeeds in putting the strategy into practice (Figure 25.1).

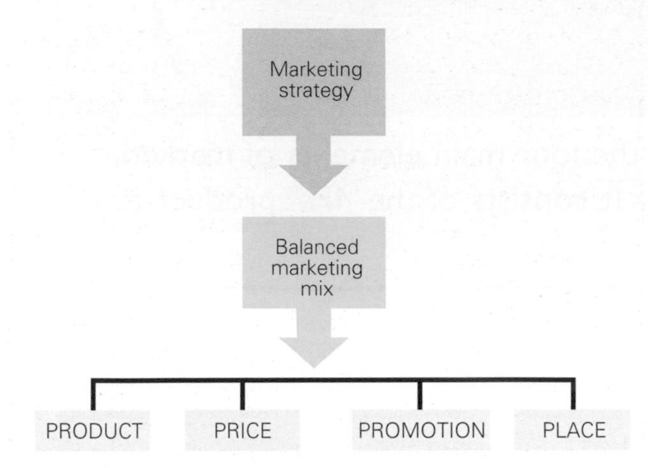

Figure 25.1 A balanced marketing mix

For each market situation there will be a different mix

The focus of the marketing mix will vary according to the market in which the firm is operating. Careful market research should reveal the attitudes and tastes of the target market. An important issue will be whether the goods are:

- regular purchases
- impulse purchases
- emergency purchases.

Impulse purchases (such as chocolate brands) are interesting because they require strong branding, great distribution and display, and eye-catching packaging. In other words, the mix focuses on place and promotion. Price is much less important and the quality of the product may not be hugely important. See Table 25.1.

Table 25.1 Different types of purchasing and the marketing mix

Type of purchasing	Most important elements of the mix
Regular purchases	Product, promotion and price
Impulse purchases	Place and promotion (including packaging)
Emergency purchases	Place and product

Within each market there may be many different segments

The differences in customers and buying habits result in many 'markets within markets'; these are known as market segments. Each segment will require its own marketing mix. The fashion industry is an example. At one end, cheap, cheerful with mass availability is the key; at the other end exclusivity, quality workmanship and a famous brand name are important.

The ingredients are not equally important

In most cases the product is the vital ingredient. No amount of marketing effort will make a poor product succeed. When selling to other businesses, reliability and quality will probably be far more important than brand image. However, a good product without good support may also fail. The balance will vary. In a price-sensitive market, pricing will be important. This is seen in the petrol market. If one company reduces its price the others follow rapidly.

25.3 INFLUENCES ON THE MARKETING MIX

Finance

Every marketing director is attempting to achieve the best mix of marketing factors to enable the marketing strategy to be a success. She or he must decide how big

A-grade application

Waitrose bucks the trend.

High-end stores like Waitrose are not expected to do well in a recesssion. Business theory would expect it to lose customers to other supermarkets offering lower prices. However profit is up by 25 per cent and the company is planning to expand by building ten new supermarkets per year and to continue to roll out convenience stores. So how has it bucked the trend? One major factor has been the introduction of its essential range; this includes 1,400 new 'everyday' products specifically designed for shoppers on a budget. It has created £500 million of sales in the first year and Waitrose estimates that it is getting 400,000 more customers each week. The introduction of the essential range was a change in marketing strategy. Previously marketing had been brand-based. The new 'essential' campaign emphasised price and coupled it with the company's reputation for quality. The strapline 'Quality you'd expect at prices you wouldn't' sums up the message. The whole campaign was backed by considerable advertising on TV, posters, direct mail and online.

Figure 25.2 The Waitrose Essential range

a budget is needed to market the product successfully, and then how to divide the budget between the 4Ps. If £1 million is available, should it all be put into a TV advertising campaign, or should half the budget be kept for offering special discounts to retailers who stock the product for the first time?

If the budget is big enough, the company will be able to do all the things it wants. Yet even Cadbury, with a £12 million marketing budget for its Dairy Milk brand, cannot do everything. This is not surprising, given that a single week of strong TV advertising nationally would cost more than £1 million.

If the budget is very tight, the business may have to be clever about setting the right marketing mix. Small, upmarket food producer Klein Caporn started with a strategy based on advertising in classy magazines, and distribution through small, independent food shops. After 12 months it became clear that this would never be profitable because of the costs of delivery to lots of small shops. So bosses Paddy Klein and Ed Caporn changed approach, cutting their price level and targeting the main supermarkets. Waitrose provided distribution in its London stores and then, the company made a breakthrough into Sainsbury's outlets nationally. They also changed their promotional strategy, hiring a public relations company to get them features in the press instead of spending on advertising. The new approach is working well.

Technology

Years ago, a peak-time advertisement on ITV could reach 33 per cent of the population. Now it would reach only 15 per cent, and less than 10 per cent of the key market of 15 to 24 year olds. Fewer and fewer families sit together through a night's television: grannies are on Google, while the 15 to 24 year olds may be in their bedroom on Facebook, playing *Halo 3* or swapping digital files with WiFi-connected friends.* Long-term success in marketing requires that firms keep up with changes and invest in technology. Tesco showed the sharpness of its management by going into online sales and delivery in the 1990s. Now almost every retail outlet makes its goods available online. Online sales are estimated to be 8 per cent of total sales and they are growing at a faster rate than store-based sales. Amazon.com make considerable investment in technology to ensure that their sites are customer friendly.

A new retailer, such as Superdry, will ensure from the start that their website creates as powerful an image as their stores. With e-commerce (online purchasing), they can make their products available worldwide, even if they only have a handful of retail outlets.

*By definition this sentence will probably be out of date by the time you read it.

> **A-grade application**
>
> **Amazon success due to customer focus**
>
> Amazon.com has been ranked the 'financially healthiest' retailer in the US for the second year in a row by an investment advice firm. A 2009 survey found that Amazon was the UK's favourite music and video retailer, and third overall retailer. Sales in 2009 were 15 times higher than ten years ago. So what is the secret of the undoubted success of this business? Its 2009 letter to shareholders makes interesting reading.
>
> It says 'The financial results for 2009 reflect the cumulative effect of 15 years of customer experience improvements: increasing selection, speeding delivery, reducing cost structure so we can afford to offer customers ever-lower prices. This work has been done by a large number of smart, relentless, customer-devoted people across all areas of the company. We are proud of our low prices, our reliable delivery, and our in-stock position on even obscure and hard-to-find items. We also know that we can still be much better, and we're dedicated to improving further'.
>
> Source: Extracted from Amazon.com INC 2009 Letter to shareholders, 14 April 2010.

Market research

If finance and technology are important to a successful marketing mix, market research is vital. Note that this does not have to be formal research (questionnaires, group discussions, and so on). All firms are in daily contact with their customers, but it is usually only small firms that can capture this information. If a Pizza Hut customer complains that a pizza is too greasy, the head office manager for pizza supplies is very unlikely to ever hear the bad news. At a small Italian restaurant, the chef should hear straight away and think hard about whether the dough has too much oil in it.

Medium-sized and large firms need primary research to keep the senior managers in touch with the customers they rarely see. Small firms should constantly listen to what customers say – in praise or in criticism. There is no better form of market research, because getting the product right is the key to all marketing success.

25.4 WHERE DOES THE MARKETING MIX FIT INTO MARKETING PLANNING?

In marketing planning, the marketing mix should follow on from the marketing strategy. Managers need an excellent understanding of the market if they are to mix the ingredients effectively.

Statistical analysis should highlight trends. Investigation will reveal the reasons for them.

Market research should provide:

- an understanding of the product's place in the market, the market segments and target customers
- customers' views on the product

- reasons for the success or failure of the product
- an understanding of competitive activity.

The marketing strategy should follow from this analysis. The marketing mix will put the strategy into practice (see Figure 25.3).

Figure 25.3 Where do the 4 Ps fit into market planning?

ISSUES FOR ANALYSIS

When answering questions on the marketing, mix consideration should be given to the following points.

- How well the mix is matched to the strategy; only if every aspect of the mix is coordinated and focused will it be effective.
- The relative importance of the ingredients in the marketing mix. Although the product is likely to be the most important element of the mix, every case is different. Taste tests show Coca-Cola to be no better than Pepsi; yet Coke outsells its rival by up to 20 times – in nearly every country in the world.
- How each of the mix ingredients can be used to achieve effective marketing. The mix elements must be tailored to each case. One product may require (and afford) national television advertising. In another case, small-scale local advertising might be supported by below-the-line activity to increase distribution. There is never a single answer to a question about the marketing mix. The best approach depends on the product, its competitive situation, the objectives and the marketing budget.

25.5 DESIGNING AN EFFECTIVE MARKETING MIX – AN EVALUATION

The concept of the marketing mix has remained unchanged since it was first introduced in the 1950s. It has proved to be a useful marketing tool. However, many believe that there are strong arguments for adding a fifth ingredient: people. Many also feel that it should not be presented as a list of equally important parts but that the mix should be seen with the product at the core, supported by the other ingredients.

With the growing importance of customer service and of good sales staff, it is legitimate to extend the marketing mix to include people. A customer who feels the salesperson is rude or lacks knowledge will go elsewhere. The type of people employed, and their attitude, can be used to build the company's image. Disney employees have to be smart, without facial hair, and be 'upbeat'. Particularly in service businesses, people matter. Good exam answers do not simply repeat a theory, they show a willingness to criticise it. It is worth remembering that not everyone agrees that the mix should have only 4Ps.

Although the 4Ps are presented as a list, there is no doubt that in almost every case the product is the most important ingredient. A successful marketing mix should be matched to the marketing strategy. And that strategy is rooted in how well the product is matched to the segment of the market being targeted.

Key Terms

Marketing budget: the sum of money provided for marketing a product or service during a period of time (usually a year).

Marketing mix: the elements involved in putting a marketing strategy into practice; these are product, price, promotion and place.

Marketing planning: producing a schedule of marketing activities based on decisions about the marketing mix. This will show the when, what and how much of a product's advertising, promotions and distribution drives over the coming year.

Marketing strategy: the medium- to long-term plan for meeting the firm's marketing objectives.

WORKBOOK

A REVISION QUESTIONS

(30 marks; 35 minutes)

1 Briefly outline each of the four ingredients of the marketing mix. (8)
2 Pick the marketing mix factor (the 'P') you think is of most importance in marketing any **two** of the following brands. Give a brief explanation of why you chose that factor.
  a) *The Sun* newspaper
  b) The iPod
  c) Cadbury's Creme Eggs
  d) A top-of-the-range BMW. (6)
3 Outline how the marketing mix for Mars Bars may affect their level of impulse sales in a small corner shop. (4)
4 What is meant by a market segment? (3)
5 Explain why new products are so important to businesses. (3)
6 List three different ways of promoting the product. (3)
7 Explain why it might be difficult for a new, small firm to get distribution in a supermarket chain such as Sainsbury's. (3)

B REVISION EXERCISES
B1 DATA RESPONSE

Cadbury planning new cafe chain

Chocolate-maker Cadbury is planning to open a national chain of branded cafes. The cafes – reportedly to be branded Cadbury Cocoa House – are expected to offer afternoon tea, along with a range of Cadbury-themed goods. One novelty on offer could be chocolate-building demonstrations of giant versions of well-known bars such as Curly Wurly and Flake. Cadbury says it has been planning the move for some time, well before its recent takeover by US firm Kraft.

Negotiations are already underway for sites and the first outlets – in London – could be open for business before the end of the year. However, Cadbury stressed that it was 'very early days' for the plans. Cadbury would not run the venture – called Cadbury Cocoa House – itself; instead it will be run under licence by a separate team, led by former Harrods director, David Morris.

Mr Morris told *Property Week* magazine, 'We want to build on the Cadbury heritage and the British heritage of Cadbury. All food will be sourced from the UK where possible, and we will really develop that heritage of the brand – from fireplaces and fireside chairs to traditional English afternoon teas.'

'Affordable' afternoon tea is promised, which is currently something of an expensive luxury at up-market hotels. Mr Morris said Cadbury Cocoa House planned to sell afternoon tea for less than half the prices charged by hotels, at £14.50.

Hannah Prevett, section editor at *Management Today*, said,

> Cadbury has come full circle – after all, it started out selling comforting hot drinks. It is no surprise the company has chosen to do this. Mid-priced coffee chains have been star performers throughout the downturn – on top of that this means Cadbury is selling the product direct – cutting out the middle-man.

Cadbury aims to have an edge over successful rivals such as Starbucks and Pret A Manger. It intends to sell alcohol alongside its more traditional beverages.

Story from BBC News: 9 April 2010.

Questions

(25 marks; 30 minutes)

1 Using the marketing mix, analyse the proposal to open the Cadbury Cocoa Houses. (10)
2 Do you think it is a good idea? Explain your reasons. (15)

B2 CASE STUDY

The battle for customers

A leading UK supermarket chain is considering expanding into India. It sees this as a relatively untapped market. The home market is saturated, and price wars and loyalty cards have reduced profit margins. In the UK, the supermarkets have been blamed for the disappearance of the corner shop. In India the situation is very different. A recent survey by an Indian market research firm concluded that small grocery shops will continue to dominate the food retailing market for the foreseeable future. Several firms, which have been lured to India by its rapid economic growth and over 1 billion mouths to feed, have not been successful in their attempts to establish supermarkets in India's largest cities. Neither of the two main contenders has managed to break even since opening in the early 1990s. They are continuing to expand and hoping that, eventually, economies of scale will permit lower prices and hopefully improve their standing and their profitability.

These new supermarkets have faced several problems.

- The local stores do not stock as many brands as the supermarkets, but they will stock an item if a customer wants it. If they do not have what the customer wants they will get it.
- The local stores offer a free delivery service and allow customers credit.
- The supermarkets cannot match the cost base of the local store. The poor transport infrastructure makes operational costs very expensive.
- Government laws limiting urban development mean that property prices are high. The smaller stores have often been in the family for generations, and so the initial cost of the site has long since been forgotten.

To try to gain customers, one of the supermarket chains has introduced promotions such as coupons, and has advertised in local newspapers. Another has teamed up with local manufacturers. It obtains staples such as lentils and rice locally. These are then packaged and branded by local manufacturers. This has helped to lower prices for customers and improve margins. A recent entrant into the market is trying to stay ahead of the competition. It has invested in air-conditioning and additional telephone lines to ensure that customers do not have to wait when they call.

The UK chain has looked at the existing market in India and feels it can succeed. However, the managers know they will do this only after a struggle to change customer attitudes.

Questions

(30 marks; 35 minutes)

1 What is meant by 'the home market is saturated'? (2)
2 What are the marketing implications for a business in a saturated market? (6)
3 Why could expansion allow economies of scale? (4)
4 What problems could a British retailer have in marketing its product in India? (6)
5 Using the marketing mix, analyse the existing market and evaluate the UK firm's chances of success. (12)

Product and product differentiation

UNIT 26

A product is a good or service that is bought and sold within a market. Products are developed so that they satisfy a specific consumer need or want that has been targeted by the business.

26.1 A PRODUCT'S ACTUAL AND PSYCHOLOGICAL BENEFITS

Successful products are normally bought by consumers for more than one reason. Products such as Coca-Cola and Stella Artois deliver both physical and psychological consumer benefits. Both products taste good, delivering a fairly obvious physical benefit for the consumer. In addition, both brands also offer consumers psychological benefits: both products have brand images that consumers want to buy into.

The key to having a good product is achieving consumer satisfaction. A restaurant can improve the quality of its product in many ways. The most obvious method would be to improve the quality of food sold. Purchasing new superior tables and chairs could also improve the 'product'. However, the restaurant's product could also be improved by providing waiting staff with better training so that customer service improves. For service-sector businesses, such as hotels, a major element of the 'product' is the staff. Motivating employees so that they provide high standards of customer care is vital in terms of producing a high-quality product.

26.2 INFLUENCES ON THE DEVELOPMENT OF NEW PRODUCTS

Technology

Technological advances can provide firms with opportunities to produce new products that offer consumers new benefits. According to 'Moore's law' computer speed and capacity doubles every two years. Advances in computer technology have enabled firms to develop new and improved mobile phones and laptop computers that offer consumers new features. These new features enable the firm that was first to the market with these new products to steal market share away from its rivals.

Rapid technological advances in computing have major implications for computer and mobile phone producers. Product life cycles are very short in both

A-grade application

The iPad

Netbooks, portables and tablet computers had been around for years before Apple introduced its iPad. Observing the many previous flops in this sector, many analysts suggested that iPad would struggle to make an impact. Yet people queued to get their hands on the new computer and within six months it had achieved an amazing 84 per cent market share within its sector of the US market.

The explanation for its success has been as much to do with marketing as technical excellence. Apple created a remarkable buzz about the product before it was unveiled in early 2010, and then ran expensive advertising campaigns in Europe and America. This was surprising because the product was often sold-out as production struggled to keep up with demand. Of course, the beautiful product design was a huge help, especially the good looks and the pin-sharp screen. The highly differentiated package allowed Apple to price it markedly higher than its rivals.

By late July 2010 analysts were suggesting that the iPad's sales would achieve double the launch expectations, at 13 million units, with sales of 50 million expected for 2012.

Figure 26.1

markets. As a consequence, component suppliers face tremendous timescale pressures to launch new components before they become technologically obsolete. Even a delay of just a month could be the difference between a successful new product and a failed launch.

A-grade application

Mercedes-Benz: innovative technology at your service

Sleeping at the wheel is one of the major causes of road fatalities. To combat this problem Mercedes-Benz is trying to develop the technology necessary to detect driver fatigue. Teams of engineers, computer scientists and psychologists at Mercedes are working on the idea of installing an infra-red camera directed at the driver's eye. If eye-blink frequency drops below a critical level, indicating the onset of sleep, an audible alarm will sound inside the car to re-awaken the driver.

Competitors' actions

Firms operating in competitive markets may try to emulate a successful new product produced by one of their rivals by launching their own 'me-too' version of the successful new product. A me-too is a new brand that is largely an imitation of an existing product. Me-toos normally sell at a price discount compared to the original product.

The entrepreneurial skills of managers and owners

Most firms use market research findings to help them identify profitable new gaps in the market. Once these gaps in the market have been found, firms will then try to design new products that possess the characteristics required by the target market. Entrepreneurs need to be good at spotting gaps in the market; they also need to develop systems within their business that enable it to react first to changes in market trends.

Entrepreneurial managers can launch their new products quickly enough to benefit from 'first-mover advantage'. Firms that can launch their new products before their rivals have the opportunity to charge premium prices until competition arrives. In most markets brand loyalty tends to be established at a very early stage. Businesses run by managers with weaker entrepreneurial skills, which launched their new products late will probably find it very difficult to gain a foothold in the market.

A-grade application

Zara's fast fashion revolution

Zara is one of Europe's fastest-growing fashion retailers. The company has based its success on fast fashion. The aim of this strategy is to launch new lines of cheap clothing that replicate exclusive designs, shown just a week earlier at major fashion shows. To make this strategy possible, the founder of Zara, Amancio Ortega, used lean production techniques first developed by the car maker Toyota to reduce new product development times.

26.3 PRODUCT DIFFERENTIATION AND USPs

Product differentiation is the degree to which consumers perceive that your brand is different from its competitors. A highly differentiated product is one that is viewed as having unique features, such as Marmite or the iPhone. A highly differentiated product may have substitutes. However, if differentiation is strong enough, consumers will not even bother looking at these other brands when making their purchasing decisions. The substitutes available are not acceptable to the consumer. A product's point of differentiation is often described as a unique selling point, or proposition (USP).

Creating product differentiation

Product differentiation can be created in two ways.

Actual product differentiation

This is actual differentiation that creates genuine product advantages that benefit the consumer in some way. Actual product differentiation can be created by:

- a unique design that is aesthetically pleasing to the eye (for example Scandinavian furniture from IKEA)
- a unique product function (for example a mobile phone with a new feature)
- a unique taste (for example Dr Pepper)
- ergonomic factors (for example a product that is easier to use than its rivals)
- superior performance (for example a Dyson vacuum cleaner).

A-grade application

Shopping for luxuries in New Delhi

In New Delhi's most upmarket shopping mall, global luxury brands such as Cartier and Armani are on the ground floor. But many wealthy shoppers go to the second floor, where luxurious boutiques offer local designs from fashion houses that include Bajaj and Valaya. These customers want the style and quality of the western companies but with more flamboyant Indian designs. The 'little black dress' may impress westerners, but these customers want something that everyone notices. The design must be unique, but with luxury that is apparent and differentiation that is obvious.

Imagined differentiation

This type of differentiation involves creating differences that exist only in the mind of the consumer. A product can be differentiated by psychological factors, despite the fact that it is not physically different from a similar product produced by the competition. Imaginary product differentiation can be created via persuasive advertising, celebrity endorsements and sponsorship. When a product is consumed it is not just the product itself that is consumed; buyers also enjoy 'consuming' the brand's image too. Many people are prepared to pay a price premium for a product that has a brand image that appeals to them.

ISSUES FOR ANALYSIS

When developing an argument in answer to an exam question, product differentiation offers the following main lines of analysis.

- Firms operating in competitive markets need to sell products that have strong USPs if they are to hold on to market share.
- Product differentiation reduces consumer price sensitivity. The brand loyalty created by the differentiation means that prices can be increased without having to worry about a substantial fall in sales volume. Total revenue should rise when prices are increased because highly differentiated products tend to be price inelastic.
- Product differentiation boosts value-added because it makes premium prices possible.

26.4 PRODUCT AND PRODUCT DIFFERENTIATION – AN EVALUATION

Product differentiation is rarely permanent. Changes in consumer tastes and technological advances can make a product's point of differentiation ineffective. Can the idea be easily copied? Is there patent protection?

Which is more effective, imagined differentiation or actual differentiation? It could be argued that imagined differentiation, created by persuasive advertising, might be more long-lasting than actual differentiation because it might be harder for a me-too to replicate a brand's distinctive personality. Magners' original differentiation was relatively weak. Competitors quickly realised that they could also package their premium ciders in pint bottles, promoting the brand to be drunk over ice. If Magners is to hold on to its market share it must identify a new USP.

Globalisation has increased the availability of products to consumers. As a result firms now face increased competitive pressure. In order to survive, firms must continually develop new, ever more powerful USPs for their products. Will small firms with modest research and development resources be able to compete against their larger rivals?

Key Terms

Brand loyalty: the desire by customers to stick with one brand; perhaps to always buy that brand (for example always buying Galaxy instead of Cadbury's).

First-mover advantage: the benefits of being the first business into a new market sector (as Coca-Cola once was – in 1886!).

Unique selling point: one feature that makes a product different from all its rivals (for example Bounty is the only mass-market chocolate bar featuring coconut).

WORKBOOK

A REVISION QUESTIONS

(40 marks; 40 minutes)

1. Outline two reasons that might explain the success of products such as Coca-Cola and Stella Artois. (4)
2. Analyse how training could be used to improve the quality of the product produced by a service-sector business such as a supermarket. (3)
3. Explain how technological advances can influence the direction of new product development. (3)
4. What is first-mover advantage? State two benefits firms receive if they can achieve first-mover advantage. (4)
5. What is a me-too product and why do some firms choose to launch them? (4)
6. Explain the meaning of the term product differentiation, using your own example. (4)
7. Outline two ways in which a clothes shop might differentiate itself from its competitors. (6)
8. Explain two benefits a firm can gain from selling a differentiated product. (4)
9. Why is it particularly helpful to have a product that is differentiated by a USP? (4)
10. Outline two examples of USPs in current products or services you buy. (4)

B REVISION EXERCISES

B1 DATA RESPONSE

San Paulo is a highly successful Brazilian company that runs over 2,000 coffee bars across South America. The idea for the business came ten years ago when the founder of the business, Roberto Carlos, visited Italy for a family holiday. During his holiday Carlos was impressed by the décor and ambience of the traditionally styled Italian coffee shops that he visited.

On his return to Brazil, Carlos decided to set up his own Italian-styled coffee bar. To ensure authenticity and a strong unique selling point, Carlos imported all the fixtures and fittings for his café from Italy. The business was an overnight success. At the time nothing like it existed in his home town of Campo Grande, and the business quickly expanded by opening up new franchised outlets in other cities across Brazil and Argentina. Over time, trading conditions have become tougher as new competitors have entered the market. Most of these competitors have sought to replicate San Paulo's original unique selling point: classic Italian interior design. Today, San Paulo is still the market leader; a significant percentage of customers see San Paulo as being the original coffee bar of its type. However, in an attempt to grow market share Carlos recently took the decision to reduce San Paulo's price premium.

The company now has plans to enter the UK market. The first bar will be set up in Croydon. The management of San Paulo believe that they will have to charge their UK consumers substantially more than their South American customers to overcome higher European wages and rents. The UK coffee bar market is extremely competitive. Will San Paulo be able to survive against companies such as Costa, Caffè Nero and Starbucks?

Questions

(25 marks; 30 minutes)

1 a) Define the term 'unique selling point'. (2)
   b) Identify the original unique selling point that made San Paulo a successful business in South America. (2)
2 Using the data in the case as a starting point, discuss whether constant innovation is required to maintain product differentiation. (12)
3 You have been hired to manage the new bar in Croydon. Despite your concerns about the strength of the competition locally, your English boss wants you to charge high prices. Outline three ways that could be used to create the high product differentiation required for your coffee bar. (9)

B2 DATA RESPONSE

Absolut vodka

Absolut vodka was developed by the Swedish state-owned monopoly provider of strong alcohol, Systembolaget, in the late 1970s. The government's goal was to create a premium-priced product that would sell well in America. Blind product tests showed that consumers were not able to tell the difference between one brand of vodka and another. The challenge, then, was to create a consumer preference for Absolut vodka where there was no real difference.

To create the product differentiation required, the advertising agency appointed to market Absolut had to create a unique image for the brand that would appeal to consumers. The first step was to create a distinctive award-winning bottle that reflected the brand's Scandinavian origins. The second step was more controversial. A brand heritage for Absolut was required to convince American consumers that the brand was authentic. Advertisements claimed that the brand was over 400 years old. Unfortunately, this was not true: Absolut was first sold in Sweden in 1879 and, for many years, the brand had been withdrawn and was unavailable for sale; production of Absolut only restarted in 1979, just before the brand's relaunch. Less controversially, differentiation was also built up by the decision to use world-famous artists such as Andy Warhol to promote the brand. In America the company also sponsored arts and cultural events to enhance the image of the brand. The strategy worked. Today, Absolut holds over 30 per cent of the American vodka market.

Questions

(40 marks; 45 minutes)

1 What is a premium-priced product? (3)
2 Explain why product differentiation can create premium prices. (6)
3 Outline two factors that could influence the direction of new product development in the alcoholic drinks industry. (6)
4 Analyse two ways in which product differentiation was created for the Absolut brand. (10)
5 Discuss the ethics of the marketing of Absolut vodka. (15)

UNIT 27

Product life cycle and portfolio analysis

The product life cycle is the theory that all products follow a similar pattern over time, of development, birth, growth, maturity and decline.

27.1 WHAT IS THE PRODUCT LIFE CYCLE?

The product life cycle shows the sales of a product over time. When a new product is first launched sales will usually be slow. This is because the product is not yet known or proven in the market. Retailers may be reluctant to stock the product because it means giving up valuable shelf space to products that may or may not sell. This involves a high risk. Customers may also be hesitant; many may want to wait until someone else has tried it before they purchase it themselves.

If the product does succeed, then its sales will grow and it enters the growth phase of the product life cycle. However, at some point sales are likely to stabilise; this is known as the maturity phase. This slowing down of the growth of sales might be because competitors have introduced similar products or because the market has now become saturated. Once most households have bought a dishwasher, for example, sales are likely to be relatively slow. This is because new purchases will mainly involve people who are updating their machine, rather than new buyers.

At some point sales are likely to decline. This may be because new technology means the product has become outdated. An example is the way CD sales have fallen due to the rise of downloading. A decline in sales may also be because competitors have launched a more successful model or the original creator has improved its own product; for example, the iPad drawing sales from the iPhone.

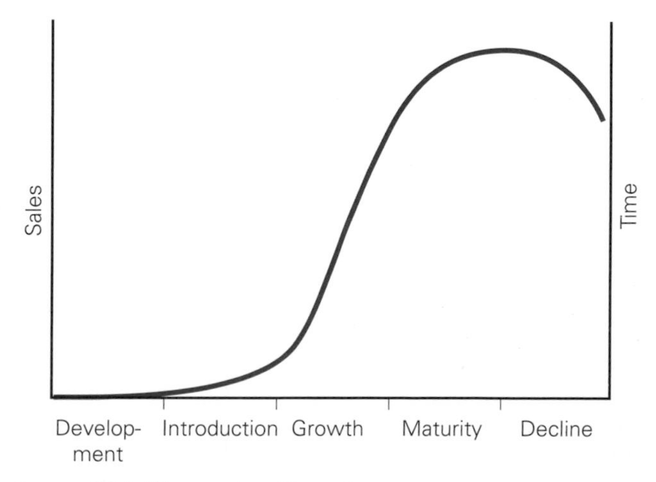

Figure 27.1 The product life cycle

The five key stages of a product's life cycle are known as: development, introduction, growth, maturity and decline. These can be illustrated on a product life cycle diagram. The typical stages in a product's life are shown in Figure 27.1.

Do remember that many products never make it as far as being launched. Many would-be entrepreneurs have what they think are great ideas. Unfortunately, it turns out they are not financially viable or they cannot find a way of successfully getting them to market. Just think how many ideas are rejected during each series on the BBC TV show *Dragons' Den*, because the investors do not think demand is going to be high enough.

Even well-established firms will find that many of their new ideas do not prove commercially viable. Cadbury rejects 20 new product ideas for every one that reaches the market. Apple's iPod may have been a great success but its internet software Cyberdog lasted about a year, and its first phone – launched with Motorola in 2005 and called the ROKR – was a flop. (Its second effort, the iPhone, did rather well!) Thousands of products are taken out of production each year because they fail to hit their initial sales targets and have not reached the growth stage of the life cycle.

27.2 WHAT USE IS THE PRODUCT LIFE CYCLE?

The product life cycle model helps managers to plan their marketing activities. Marketing managers will need to adjust their marketing mix at different stages of the product life cycle, as outlined below.

- In the introduction phase the promotion may focus on making customers aware that a new product exists; in the maturity phase it may focus more on highlighting the difference between your product and competitors that have arrived since its introduction.
- At the beginning of the life cycle, a technologically advanced product may be launched with a high price (think of the iPhone); over time the price may fall

as newer models are being launched. By considering the requirements of each stage of the life cycle, marketing managers may adjust their marketing activities accordingly.

Managers know that the length of the phases of the life cycle cannot easily be predicted. They will vary from one product to another and this means the marketing mix will need to be altered at different times. For example, a product may be a fad and therefore the overall life of the product will be quite short. Many fashions are popular only for one season and some films are popular only for a matter of weeks. Other products have very long life cycles. The first manufactured cigarettes went on sale in Britain in 1873. By chance, sales hit their peak (120,000 million!) exactly 100 years later. Since 1973 sales have gently declined.

It is also important to distinguish between the life cycle of a product category and the life cycle of a particular brand. Sales of wine are growing, but a brand that was once the biggest seller (Hirondelle) has virtually disappeared as wine buyers have become more sophisticated. Similarly, confectionery is a mature market but particular brands are at different stages in their life cycles: Mars bars are in maturity while Maltesers are in the growth stage, even though the brand is 80-years-old!

Table 27.1 Examples of how the marketing mix may vary at different stages of the product life cycle

	Development	Introduction	Growth	Maturity	Decline
Sales	Zero	Low	Increasing	Growth is slowing	Falling
Costs per unit	High; there is investment in product development but only a few prototypes and test products being produced	High, because sales are relatively low but launch costs are high and overheads are being spread over a few units	Falling as overheads are spread over more units	Falling as sales are still growing	Still likely to be low as development costs have been covered and reduced promotional costs are needed to raise awareness
Product	Prototypes	Likely to be basic	May be modified given initial customer feedback; range may be increased	Depends – may focus on core products and remove ones in the range not selling well; may diversify and extend brand to new items	Focus on most profitable items
Promotion	As development is nearly finished it may be used to alert customers of the launch	Mainly to raise awareness	Building loyalty	May focus on highlighting the differences with competitors' products	Probably no spending at all
Distribution	Early discussions with retailers will help in finalising the product packaging	May be limited as distributors wait to see customers' reactions	May be increasing as more distributors willing to stock it and product is rolled out to more markets	May focus on key outlets and more profitable channels	Lower budgets to keep costs down
Price	Not needed	Depends on pricing approach, e.g. a high price if skimming is adopted (if demand is high and not sensitive to price); a low price if penetration is adopted to gain market share	Depends on demand conditions and strategy adopted; e.g. with a skimming strategy the price may now be lowered to target more segments	May have to drop to maintain competitiveness	Likely to discount to maintain sales

A-grade application

Most companies leave profitable brands in maturity for as long as possible. They love the high profits to be gained from a brand that is selling well, but going nowhere (and therefore needs no investment). The genius of Apple has been to launch newer, better, killer products before the competition. iPhone2 killed the first iPhone before Nokia managed to launch a serious competitor. Therefore Apple stays on top.

Figure 27.2 shows the amazing sales of the iPhone in its first three years. By the second quarter of 2010 iPhone sales were worth more than $5 billion for that three-month period alone. Apple has shown the benefits of a highly active approach to the product life cycle. Most marketing companies sit back and watch; Apple makes things happen.

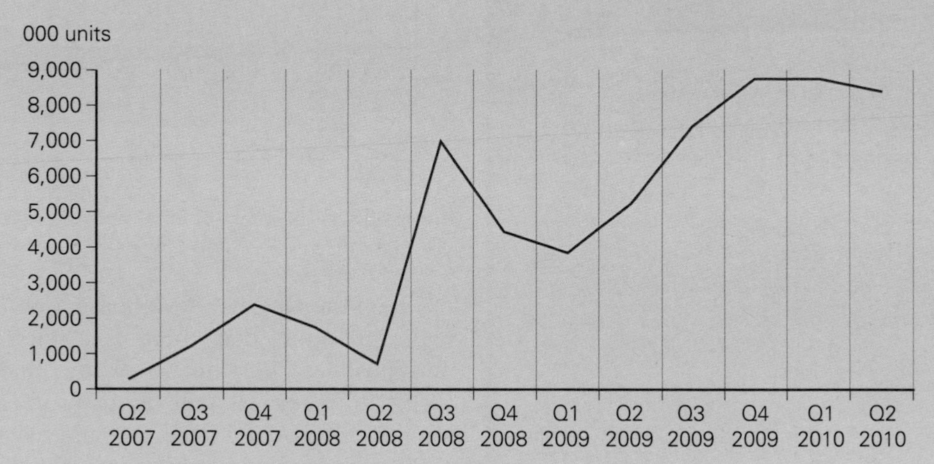

Figure 27.2 Quarterly iPhone sales, 2007–2010
Source: Apple Inc. (official filings to SEC)

27.3 THE PRODUCT LIFE CYCLE AND CAPACITY

When considering the future sales of the business, managers will need to link their forecasts to their plans for the firm's capacity. The capacity of an organisation is the maximum it can produce given its existing resources. If managers choose a capacity level that is relatively low this means that a sudden increase in sales (for example, if the product enters the growth phase quickly) may mean customers have to be turned away. On the other hand, if the chosen capacity level is high, if the product is not successful the business will have invested in facilities that are not required; this is inefficient and expensive. Trying to match the capacity of the business to the likely sales is a difficult challenge for managers.

27.4 CASH FLOW AND THE PRODUCT LIFE CYCLE

In the development phase before a product is launched, cash flow will be negative. The firm will be spending money on research and development, market research and production planning, but no revenue is yet being generated. Prototypes and models are being made (Dyson produced 5,000 prototypes of the Dyson vacuum cleaner before launching it) but income is zero. The business may also decide to test-market the product, which again costs money.

Once the product is on sale, cash should begin to come in. However, at this stage, sales are likely to be low and the firm will still be promoting the product heavily to generate awareness. Overall cash flow may continue to be negative for some time. In many cases, the cash flow will not become a positive figure until some way into the growth stage of the life cycle. It may only be at that stage that the firm reaches operational break-even. Cash flow should then continue to improve until the decline stage, when the volume of sales and the amount of cash coming in begin to fall.

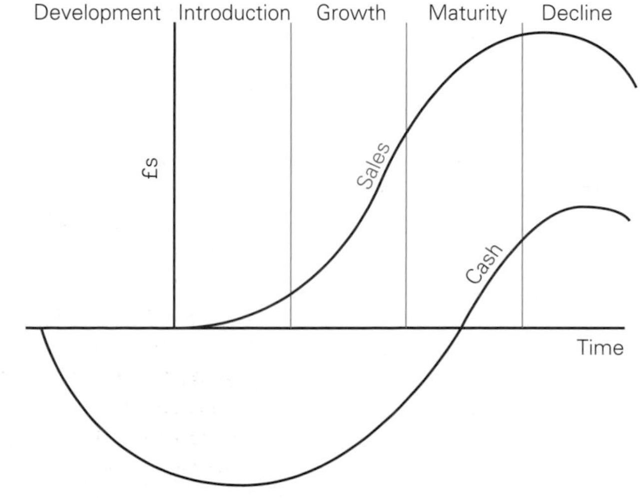

Figure 27.3 The product life cycle and cash flow

It is important, therefore, for firms to manage their cash flow effectively during the life cycle, and to plan ahead. Although a product may prove successful in the long term it may also cause the firm to experience severe cash flow problems in the short term unless its finances are properly managed. Careful budgeting is important at this stage, to avoid overspending.

A-grade application

Ocado

Ocado is an online grocer that is in partnership with the supermarket Waitrose. Ocado was established in 2001 and, within its first six years, had gained sales of £300 million per year. Even so, it was still not making a profit because of the huge costs of establishing the business. For example, Ocado has invested in an enormous central warehouse, where the products are stocked and packed. This is the size of seven football pitches and six storeys high. By 2007 the warehouse was still operating at 35 per cent capacity.

In 2010 Ocado floated on the stock market to become a public limited company. The firm raised about £200 million from the share sale to build a second depot for fulfilling customer orders. Its sales at this stage were £427.3 million, but it had still not made a profit! Investors were willing to bet that the huge cash investment would eventually pay off.

27.5 EXTENSION STRATEGIES

The aim of an extension strategy is to prevent a decline in the product's sales. There are various means by which this can be achieved, as noted below.

- *By targeting a new segment of the market:* when sales of Johnson & Johnson's baby products started to fall, the company repositioned the product and aimed it at adults. Alternatively, a new geographic market may be targeted.
- *By developing new uses for the product:* the basic technology in hot-air paint strippers, for example, is no different from that in a hairdryer.
- *By increasing the usage of a product:* Actimel's 'challenge' was for consumers to eat one pot a day for a fortnight – a wonderful way to encourage increased consumption.

The continued success of products such as Coca-Cola and Kellogg's cornflakes is not just due to luck; it is down to sophisticated marketing techniques, which have managed to maintain sales over many years despite fierce competition. The Kellogg's logo is regularly updated, new pack sizes are often introduced, and various competitions and offers are used on a regular basis to keep sales high. The company has also tried to increase the number of students and adults eating its products. It has run advertising campaigns to encourage people to eat the product throughout the day as well as in the morning.

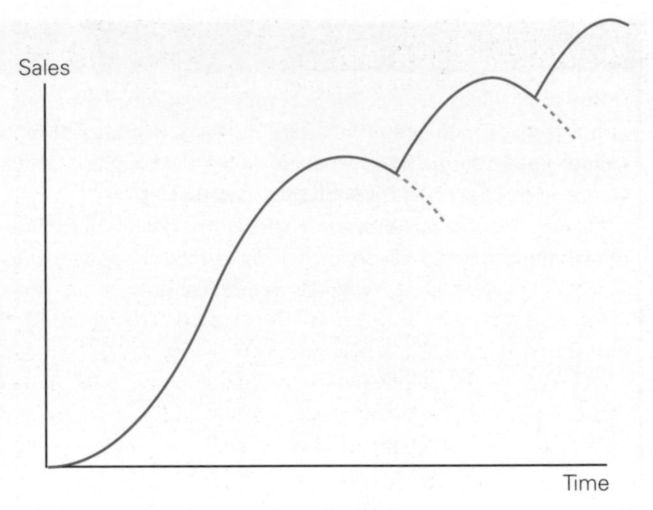

Figure 27.4 The effect of extension strategies

Given the fact that developing a product can involve high costs and that there is a high failure rate of new products, it is not surprising that if a product is successful managers will try to prolong its sales for as long as it is profitable. Who would have thought, in the 1880s, that a frothy drink would still be a huge seller more than 125 years later? Clever Coke.

27.6 IS A DECLINE IN SALES INEVITABLE?

In the standard product life cycle model it seems as if a decline in sales is inevitable. This may be true in some situations. For example, developments in technology may make some products obsolete. On the other hand, the decline in sales may be the result of poor marketing. Effective extension strategies may ensure that a product's sales are maintained. The long-term success of products and services such as Monopoly and Kit-Kat shows that sales can be maintained over a very long period of time. Creative marketing can avoid the decline phase for a substantial period of time, but only if the product is good enough to keep buyers coming back for more.

One of the reasons for sales decline may be that some managers assume the product will fail at some point and so do not make enough effort to save it. This is known as 'determinism': managers think sales will decline and so sales do fall because of inadequate marketing support. Instead of adapting their marketing strategy to find new ways of selling the product, they let it decline because they assume it cannot be saved.

It is important to remember that a life cycle graph only shows what has happened; it is not a prediction of the future. Top marketing managers try to influence the future, not just let it happen. They try to shape the product life cycle not let it shape their success.

A-grade application

Drinks

The soft drinks market in the UK is worth about £13 billion. In this market, new product development is critical. Soft drinks have increasingly come under attack for their impact on children. The sugar content can lead to obesity, and artificial additives can lead to hyperactivity. These criticisms might have led to a decline in sales in the market. However, producers have responded by developing products with a healthier image, to keep sales growing. Claims about the lack of additives, preservatives and low/no/reduced sugar drinks are now almost essential. Retail value sales of soft drinks are expected to grow by 17 per cent between 2009 and 2014.

27.7 THE PRODUCT PORTFOLIO

Product portfolio analysis examines the existing position of a firm's products. This allows the firm to consider its existing position and plan what to do next. There are several different methods of portfolio analysis. One of the best known was developed by the Boston Consulting Group, a management consultancy; it is known as the Boston Matrix.

The Boston Matrix shows the market share of each of the firm's products and the rate of growth of the markets in which they operate. By highlighting the position of each product in terms of market share and market growth, a business can analyse its existing situation and decide what to do next and where to direct its marketing efforts. This model has four categories, as described below.

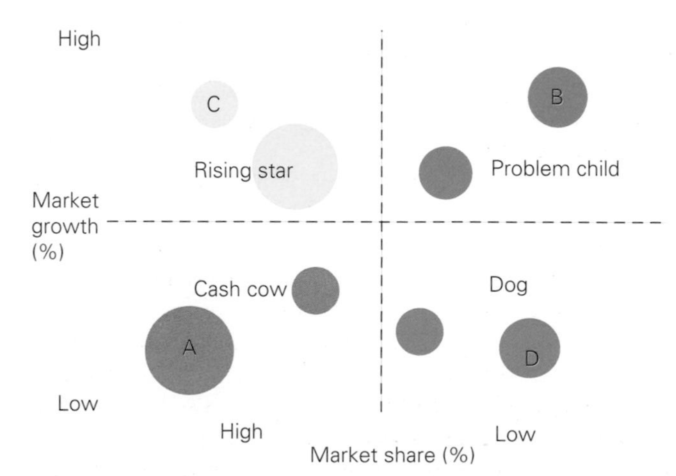

Figure 27.5 Product portfolio: the Boston Matrix

Cash cow: a high share of a slow-growing market

In Figure 27.5, product A has a high market share of a low-growth market. The size of the circle depends on the turnover of the product. This type of product is known as a cash cow. An example of a cash cow may be Heinz Baked Beans. The overall market for baked beans is mature and therefore slow growing. Within this market, the Heinz brand has a market share of more than 50 per cent. This type of product generates high profits and cash for the company because sales are relatively high, while the promotional cost per unit is quite low. Consumers are already aware of the brand, which reduces some of the need for promotion. High and stable sales keep the cost per unit relatively low. Heinz can therefore 'milk' cash from baked beans to invest in newer products such as Heinz Organic Ketchup.

Problem child: a low share of a fast-growing market

Product B, by comparison, is in a high-growth market but has a low market share. This type of product is known as a problem child (also called a 'question mark'). A problem child may well provide high profits in the future; the market itself is attractive because it is growing fast and the product could provide high returns if it manages to gain a greater market share. However, the success of such products is by no means certain and that is why they are like problem children: they may grow and prosper or things may go wrong. These products usually need a relatively high level of investment to promote them, get them distributed and keep them going. A new Heinz recipe may be in this position.

Rising star: a high share of a growing market

Rising stars such as product C have a high market share and are selling in a fast-growing market. These products are obviously attractive; they are doing well in a successful market. However, they may well need protecting from competitors' products. Once again, the profits of the cash cows can be used to keep the sales growing. Heinz Organic Soups are in this category. They are very successful, with fast-growing sales, but still need heavy promotion to ensure their success.

Dogs: a low share of a stable or declining market

The fourth category of products is known as dogs. These products (like product D in Figure 27.5) have a low share of a low-growth market. They hold little appeal for a firm unless they can be revived. The product or brand will be killed off once its sales slip below the break-even point.

The purpose of product portfolio analysis

Product portfolio analysis aims to examine the existing position of the firm's products. Once this has been done the managers can plan what to do next. Typically this will involve four strategies.

1 Building: this involves investment in promotion and distribution to boost sales and is often used with problem children (question marks).

2 Holding: this involves marketing spending to maintain sales and is used with rising star products.
3 Milking: this means taking whatever profits you can without much more new investment and is often used with cash cow products.
4 Divesting: this involves selling off the product and is common with dogs or problem children.

The various strategies chosen will depend on the firm's portfolio of products. If most of the firm's products are cash cows, for example, it needs to develop new products for future growth. If, however, the majority are problem children then it is in quite a high-risk situation; it needs to try to ensure some products do become stars. If it has too many dogs then it needs to invest in product development or acquire new brands.

Both the product life cycle and product portfolio analysis are marketing tools to help firms with their marketing planning. By analysing their existing situation they can identify what needs to be done with the marketing mix to fulfil their objectives. However, like all planning tools, simply being able to examine the present position does not in itself guarantee success. Firms still have to be able to select the right strategy and implement it successfully.

ISSUES FOR ANALYSIS

When analysing the importance of the product life cycle and portfolio model it may be useful to consider the following points.

- Portfolio analysis examines the position of all the firm's products, and helps managers to decide what to do with each of them (for example, invest more or milk them).
- The models do not in themselves tell the firm what to do; managers must interpret their findings and decide on the most effective course of action.
- Managers must avoid letting these models become self-fulfilling (for example, deciding the product is in decline and so letting its sales fall).
- Product life cycles are generally becoming shorter due to the rapid developments in technology and the increasing levels of competition in most markets.
- As well as the life cycle for a particular product it can be useful to study the life cycle of a category of products (for example, examining the life of Flora margarine and the life cycle for the whole margarine market).

27.8 PRODUCT LIFE CYCLE AND PORTFOLIO ANALYSIS – AN EVALUATION

The product life cycle model and portfolio analysis are important in assessing the firm's current position within the market. They make up an important step in the planning process. However, simply gathering data does not in itself guarantee success. A manager has to interpret the information effectively and then make the right decision. The models show where a business is at the moment; the difficult decisions relate to where the business will be in the future.

Product portfolio analysis is especially useful for larger businesses with many products. It helps a manager to look critically at the firm's product range. Then decisions can be made on how the firm's marketing spending should be divided up between different products. By contrast, the product life cycle is of more help to a small firm with one or two products. A company called Filofax made a fortune in the 1990s marketing a paper-based 'personal organiser'. When people switched to electronic products such as the BlackBerry, Filofax wasted years (and many millions of pounds) by persisting with its paper product. The business needed to acknowledge when a life cycle decline was unstoppable.

Key Terms

Cash cow: a product that has a high share of a low-growth market.

Dog: a product that has a low share of a low-growth market.

Extension strategy: marketing activities used to prevent sales from declining.

Portfolio analysis: an analysis of the market position of the firm's existing products; it is used as part of the marketing planning process.

Problem child: a product that has a small share of a fast-growing market.

Rising star: a product that has a high share of a fast-growing market.

WORKBOOK

A REVISION QUESTIONS

(35 marks; 35 minutes)

1 Identify the different stages of the product life cycle. Give an example of one product or service you consider to be at each stage of the life cycle. (4)
2 Explain what is meant by an 'extension strategy'. (4)
3 Outline the likely relationship between cash flow and the different stages of the life cycle. (4)
4 How is it possible for products such as Barbie to apparently defy the decline phase of the product cycle? (6)
5 What is meant by 'product portfolio analysis'? (3)
6 Distinguish between a cash cow and a rising star in the Boston Matrix. (4)
7 Explain how the Boston Matrix could be used by a business such as Cadbury. (4)
8 Firms should never take decline (or growth) for granted. Therefore they should never take success (or failure) for granted. Explain why this advice is important if firms are to make the best use of product life cycle theory. (6)

B REVISION EXERCISES

B1 DATA RESPONSE

Fire Angel

Sam Tate and his partner have developed an innovative smoke detector called Fire Angel. This product is placed in a light fitting and its energy supply is automatically recharged when the light is turned on. This way the danger of your smoke detector failing to work because of flat batteries should be reduced and, because it recharges itself, customers do not need to buy new batteries. Fire Angel is now stocked in around 6,000 stores.

Before launching Fire Angel, Sam did lots of market research. He spoke to the Fire Brigade and the government office responsible for fire safety, to ensure that there was a need for this sort of product, and to estimate the market size and market growth. He then interviewed people in the street to see what they thought, as well as analysing competitors' products. He also examined different ways of getting the product to market and eventually decided that selling through the supermarkets was the key to achieving a high volume of sales.

The average price of smoke detectors is between £15 and £20 but Sam felt he could charge a premium price because his product does not need a battery and lasts for up to ten years, so he set the price of the Fire Angel at £30. He felt it was better to go in with a higher price than a lower one because it is more difficult to lower the price than increase it later on. It took three years to get the Fire Angel from the idea stage to the launch stage; most of this time was spent on design and testing, but it did take many months to convince some of the retailers to stock it.

Source: adapted from Business Link

Questions

(30 marks; 35 minutes)

1 What is meant by 'market growth'? (2)
2 Outline the unique selling point of the Fire Angel, and explain how this can benefit the business. (6)
3 Analyse the possible benefits to Sam of undertaking market research before launching the Fire Angel. (7)
4 Explain why Sam might have had cash flow problems in the first few years of his business. (6)
5 At the moment the Fire Angel is still in its growth phase. Discuss the ways in which the marketing mix of the Fire Angel could change as it enters the maturity phase. (9)

B2 DATA RESPONSE

Mackie's ice cream

Mackie's is a luxury ice-cream maker based in Scotland.

All Mackie's ice cream is made at its farm in Aberdeenshire. Its production chain includes the wind that provides the business with renewable energy, its own crops that feed its cattle and its own cows that produce the milk and cream for the ice cream. 'It's a real plough to plate – or cow to cone story,' says the company.

Mackie's employs 70 people and produces over 7 million litres of luxury ice cream a year.

Mackie's ice cream is well established as the brand leader in the luxury ice-cream market in Scotland; it has an increasing market share in England and is being exported to Seoul, South Korea and Norway.

The Mackie family have been farming at Westertown farm since the turn of the century, but it was only in 1986 that it started pilot trials for an ice cream. In 1993 some of the farm's facilities were converted to a modern ice cream dairy, capable of producing more than 10 million litres a year. In 1996 the new product development kitchen was added. In 2006 production machinery was added to raise capacity in the ice cream dairy to 6,000 litres per hour. It sells through shops, restaurants and ice cream parlours.

Its luxury ice cream products include: traditional vanilla (this is its cash cow), raspberry, honeycomb, strawberry and cream, chocolate mint and absolutely chocolate. These are available in a variety of sizes; the company also produces 100 per cent fruit frozen smoothies, sorbets and organic ice cream.

Figure 27.6 Mackie's ice cream – a team product

Source: Mackies

Questions

(30 marks; 35 minutes)

1 What is meant by the term 'market share'? (2)
2 Explain the factors that Mackie might have considered before expanding its capacity. (5)
3 Explain how the promotion of a new Mackie's ice cream could vary at different stages in its life cycle. (5)
4 Examine the possible benefits to Mackie of having a portfolio of products. (8)
5 Consider whether new product development is likely to be essential for success in the ice cream market. (10)

Pricing

UNIT 28

Price is the amount paid by the customer for a good or service.

28.1 HOW IMPORTANT ARE DECISIONS ABOUT PRICE?

Price is one of the main links between the customer (demand) and the producer (supply). It gives messages to consumers about product quality and is fundamental to a firm's revenues and profit margins. As part of the marketing mix it is fundamental to most consumer buying decisions. The importance of price to the customer will depend on several factors, as discussed below.

Customer sensitivity to price

Consumers have an idea of the correct price for a product (see Figure 28.1). They balance price with other considerations. These include the factors set out below.

The quality of the product

Products seen as having higher quality can carry a price premium; this may be real or perceived quality.

How much consumers want the product

All purchases are personal; customers will pay more for goods they need or want.

Consumers' income

Customers buy products within their income range; consumers with more disposable income are less concerned about price. Uncertainty about future income will have the same effect as lower income. If interest rates are high, hard-pressed home-buyers will be much more sensitive to price; they need to save money and so they check prices more carefully and avoid high-priced items.

Figure 28.1 The 'right' price

Table 28.1 Price sensitivity in practice

Products, services and brands that are highly price sensitive	Products, services and brands that are not very price sensitive
No-frills air travel	Business-class air travel
Fiat and Ford cars	BMW and Mercedes cars
Children's white school shirts	Babies' disposable nappies
Monday-night cinema tickets	Saturday-night cinema tickets

The level of competitive activity

The fiercer the competition in a market, the more important price becomes. Customers have more choice, so they take more care to buy the best-value item, whereas a business with a strong monopoly position is able to charge higher prices.

The availability of the product

If the product is readily available, consumers are more price-conscious. They know they can go elsewhere and find the same product – perhaps cheaper. Scarcity removes some of the barriers to price. This is why perfume companies such as Chanel try to keep their products out of supermarkets and stores like Superdrug; they want to avoid shops price-cutting brands such as Chanel No 5.

A-grade application

John Lewis

In October 2010, London's John Lewis department store was out of stock of only one leather handbag. It could sell you an LK Bennett Luna bag for £295, or a Lulu Guinness Romilly bag for £395, or perhaps a Mulberry Hayden bag for £495? But despite a price tag of £695, the Mulberry Alexa bag was sold out. Named after celebrity Alexa Chung, its price seemed to present no barrier to demand.

28.2 PRICE DETERMINES BUSINESS REVENUE

Pricing is important to the business. Unlike the other ingredients in the marketing mix it is related directly to revenue through the formula:

Revenue = Price × Units sold

If the price is not right the business could:

- lose customers: if the price is too high, sales may slump and therefore revenue will be lost; it will depend on the **price elasticity** of the product (see Unit 29); if goods remain unsold, the costs of production will not be recovered
- lose revenue: if the price is too low, sales may be high, but not high enough to compensate for the low revenue per unit.

Pricing involves a balance between being competitive and being profitable.

28.3 HOW DO BUSINESSES DECIDE WHAT PRICE TO CHARGE?

At certain times during a product's life cycle pricing is especially important. Incorrect pricing when the product is launched could cause the product to fail. At other stages in the product's life, pricing may be used to revive interest in the brand.

There are two basic pricing decisions: pricing a new product and managing prices throughout the product life. Both decisions require a good understanding of the market: consumers and competitors.

Pricing decisions require an understanding of costs. These costs must include purchasing, manufacturing, distribution, administration and marketing. Cost information should be available from the company's management accounting systems.

The lowest price a firm can consider charging is set by costs. Except as a temporary promotional tactic (a loss leader), businesses must charge more for the product than the variable cost. This ensures that every product sold contributes towards the fixed costs of the business.

The market determines the highest price that can be charged. The price that is charged will need to take account of the company objectives. The right price will be the one that achieves the objectives.

There are several ways that businesses obtain market information. These are set out below.

- Market research can provide consumer reactions to possible price changes.
- Competitive research tells the company about other products and prices.
- Analysis of sales patterns shows how the market reacts to price and economic changes.
- Sales staff can report on customer reactions to prices.

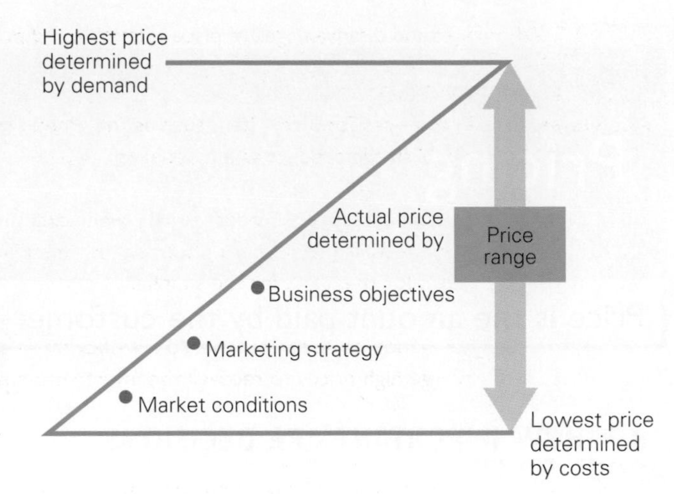

Figure 28.2 Determining the price

When making changes to product prices the business needs to understand the relationship between price changes and demand. Demand for some products is more sensitive to price changes than for others. Price elasticity of demand measures how sensitive demand is to price changes. If demand for a product is sensitive to price changes an increase in price could cut total revenue.

> **A-grade application**
>
> **London's Hoxton Hotel**
>
> If you put '£1 hotel rooms' into Google, London's Hoxton Hotel pops up in front of you. This 200-room hotel sells five rooms per night at £1 and another five at £29. The other 190 are at the 'normal' rate of £189! The Hoxton uses this device to get customers to register as members of the Hoxton Fan Club. Only they are told when the sale is taking place of £1 rooms (to cover the next three months). The website boasts that in each sale, 1,000 rooms are sold in 20 minutes. So this pricing trick makes sure that Hoxton has a terrific emailing list of people interested in hotel rooms.

28.4 PRICING STRATEGIES

A pricing strategy is a company's plan for setting its prices over the medium to long term. In other words it is not about deals such as 'This week's special: 40% off!' Short-term offers are known as tactics. Medium- to long-term plans are called strategies.

For new products, firms must choose between two main pricing strategies:

1 skimming
2 penetration.

Some advantages of price skimming and price penetration are shown in Table 28.2.

Skimming

This is used when the product is innovative. As the product is new there will be no competition. The

Table 28.2 Advantages and disadvantages of price skimming and price penetration

	Price skimming	Price penetration
Advantages	High prices for a new item such as the iPhone help establish the product as a must-have item Early adopters of a product usually want exclusivity and are willing to pay high prices, so skimming makes sense for them and for the supplier Innovation can be expensive, so it makes sense to charge high prices to recover the investment cost	Low-priced new products may attract high sales volumes, which make it very hard for a competitor to break into the market High sales volumes help to cut production costs per unit, as the producer can buy in bulk and therefore get purchasing costs down Achieving high sales volumes ensures that shops will provide high distribution levels and good in-store displays
Disadvantages	Some customers may be put off totally by 'rip-off pricing' at the start of a product's life When the firm decides to cut its prices its image may suffer Buyers who bought early (at high prices) may be annoyed that prices fell soon afterwards	Pricing low may affect the brand image, making the product appear 'cheap' It may be hard to gain distribution in more upmarket retail outlets, due to mass-market pricing Pricing on the basis of value for money can cause customers (and therefore competitors) to be very price sensitive

price can therefore be set at a high level. Customers interested in the new product will pay this high price. The business recovers some of the development costs, making sure that enthusiasts who really want the product pay the high price they expect to pay. For example, the first DVD players came onto the UK market at a price of around £1,000. Firms use the initial sales period to assess the market reaction. If sales become stagnant the price can be lowered to attract customers who were unwilling to pay the initial price. The price can also be lowered if competitors enter the market.

Penetration

Penetration pricing is used when launching a product into a market where there are similar products. The price is set lower to gain market share. Once the product is established the price can be increased. It is hoped that high levels of initial sales will recover development costs and lead to lower average costs as the business benefits from bulk-buying benefits.

Pricing strategies for existing products

For existing products the key is to be clear about where your brand stands in the market. Pricing strategy on the latest Mercedes sports car will be based on the confidence of the company in the strength of its brand name. Mercedes will not worry about what Ford or Mazda charge for a sports car, nor even the prices of its BMW or Lexus rivals. The Merc will be a 'price leader': where it sets prices, others will follow. Weaker brands, such as Chrysler or Fiat, are the followers.

A-grade application

After years of dominance by Nike and Adidas, local sports footwear manufacturers made some inroads into the Chinese market in 2010. Local brand Li Ning pulled alongside Adidas as the industry number 2 (market share by volume). To push further, Li Ning announced a new, higher-priced product range to sit 15–20 per cent below its foreign rivals. The head of JWT, China (advertising agency) said, 'The moment that a local brand can command the same price as a multinational brand is the day that a breakthrough has been made'.

Figure 28.3 A Li Ning promotion

They are 'price takers' (that is, they have to take the lead set by the strong brands, usually pricing their own products at a lower level).

Price leader

This is where the price is set above the market level. This is possible when the company has strong brands, or there is little effective competition. In Britain the accepted price of chewing gum is set by Wrigley's, which has a 90 per cent market share. Other brands have little choice but to charge at or below the level set by Wrigley's.

Price taker

This is when the price is set at the market level or at a discount to the market. This happens in highly competitive markets, or in markets where one brand dominates. When Branston Baked Beans were launched in 2006, they were priced at 41p, compared to the 44p charged by the price leader, Heinz. By 2010 the price of Branston was 62p to the 64p of Heinz, implying that Branston is still a price taker, but in a slightly stronger position now than then.

Choosing a pricing strategy

The choice of pricing strategy will depend on the competitive environment. Figure 28.4 shows how the choice of pricing strategy will vary according to the level of competition.

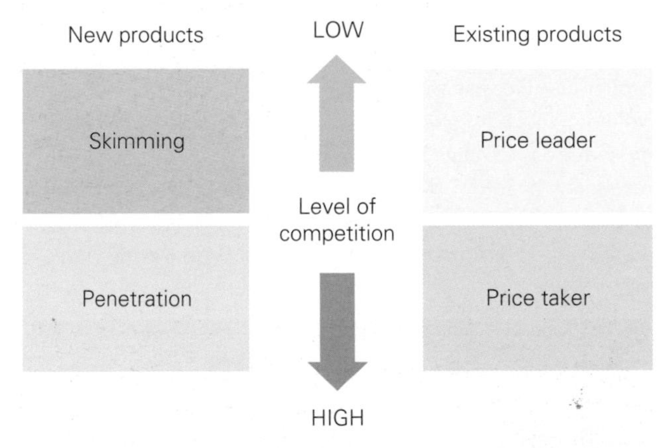

Figure 28.4 Factors affecting choice of pricing strategy

28.5 PRICING TACTICS

Whichever strategy has been selected, there are tactics that should also be considered. They can be part of normal pricing or used as one element in the firm's promotional tactics. They include the following.

Loss leaders

Prices are set deliberately low – so low that the firm may make a loss on every unit sold. The idea is to encourage customers to buy other products or complementary goods that generate profit. Supermarkets commonly use this approach. At Christmas they may attract custom by selling tree lights for 49p, confident that shoppers will end up with a full trolley of other goods. Children's sticker albums may also be offered very cheaply; but the packs of stickers to go inside are often expensive.

Psychological pricing

Prices are set at a level that seems lower to the customer. Without thinking about it, customers see a price of £9.99 as quite significantly lower than £10.50. The loss of 51p per item is more than made up for by higher sales.

Special offer pricing

This includes, for example, buy one get one free; or offers made for a period of time or to clear stocks.

ISSUES FOR ANALYSIS

When answering a question on pricing it is important to understand the following points.

- The relationship between price and demand: in other words, a change in price will almost always affect the demand for a product.
- The role of pricing as one part of the overall marketing mix: the price should match the image suggested by the product design, advertising, branding and distribution outlets; an expensive-looking perfume displayed in Harrods would have its image undermined if it were priced at £4.99.
- The influence of price upon profitability: many products have profit margins of only 20 per cent; therefore a 10 per cent price cut will halve the profit per unit. It would take a huge increase in demand to compensate.
- The factors influencing pricing: for example, cost, customer psychology and competitors.

28.6 PRICING – AN EVALUATION

Economists think of price as a neutral factor within a marketplace. Its impact upon demand can be measured, predicted and captured in the concept of price elasticity (see Unit 29). Many businesses would disagree, especially those selling consumer goods and services. The reason is that consumer psychology can be heavily influenced by price. A '3p off' flash makes people reach for the Mars bars, but if they are half price people wonder whether they are old stock or have suffered in the sun; they are *too* cheap.

When deciding on the price of a brand new product, marketing managers have many options. Pricing high may generate too few sales to keep retailers happy to stock the product. Yet, pricing too low carries even more dangers. Large companies know there are no safe livings to be made selling cheap jeans, cheap cosmetics or cheap perfumes.

If there is a key to successful pricing, it is to keep

it in line with the overall marketing strategy. When Häagen-Dazs launched in the UK at prices more than double those of its competitors, many predicted failure. In fact, the pricing was in line with the image of adult, luxury indulgence and Häagen-Dazs soon outsold all other premium ice creams. The worst pricing approach would be to develop an attractively packaged, well-made product and then sell it at a discount to the leading brands. In research, people would welcome it, but deep down they would not trust the product quality. Because psychology is so important to successful pricing, many firms use qualitative research, rather than quantitative, to obtain the necessary psychological insights.

Key Terms

Complementary goods: products bought in conjunction with each other, such as bacon and eggs, or Gillette shavers and Gillette razors.

Early adopters: consumers with the wealth and the personality to want to be the first to get a new gadget or piece of equipment; they may be the first to wear new fashion clothes, and the first to get the new (and expensive) computer game.

Monopoly: a market dominated by one supplier.

Price elasticity: a measurement of the extent to which a product's demand changes when its price is changed.

Price sensitive: when customer demand for a product reacts sharply to a price change (that is, the product is highly price elastic).

WORKBOOK

A REVISION QUESTIONS

(35 marks; 35 minutes)

1 Explain why price 'is fundamental to a firm's revenues'. (3)
2 Look at Figure 28.1. Outline two factors that would affect the 'psychologically right price range' for a new Nokia phone. (4)
3 Explain how the actions of Nike could affect the footwear prices set by Adidas. (4)
4 Look at Table 28.1, on the price sensitivity of products, brands and services. Think of two more examples of highly price-sensitive and two examples of not-very-price-sensitive products, services or brands. (4)
5 Explain the difference between pricing strategy and pricing tactics. (2)
6 For each of the following, decide whether the pricing strategy should be skimming or penetration. Briefly explain your reasoning.
   a) Richard Branson's Virgin group launches the world's first space tourism service (you are launched in a rocket, spend time weightless in space, watch the world go round, then come back to earth). (4)
   b) Kellogg's launches a new range of sliced breads for families who are in a hurry. (4)
   c) The first Google phone is launched (called G-Fone) with free, instant WiFi access to Google. (4)
7 Is a cash cow likely to be a price maker or a price taker? Explain your reasoning. (3)
8 Identify three circumstances in which a business may decide to use special offer pricing. (3)

B REVISION EXERCISES

B1 DATA RESPONSE

On 1 August 2010, Tesco Pricecheck provided the information given in Table 28.3 on the prices of shampoo brands. Study the table then answer the questions that follow.

Table 28.3 Prices of shampoo brands in August 2010

Product description	Tesco price (£)	Asda price (£)
Tresemme Fresh Start 200 ml	2.99	4.28
Pantene Volume & Body 250 ml	2.27	1.00
Head & Shoulders 250 ml	2.39	2.38
Elvive Anti-Breakage 250 ml	2.40	2.40
John Frieda Sheer Blond 250 ml	5.00	5.00
Own-label* Kids/Baby 250 ml	1.00	0.98
Own-label* Budget Shampoo 400 ml	0.80	0.80
Bob Martin Dog Shampoo 300 ml	2.62	2.62

*Own-label means the supermarket's own brand.

Questions

(25 marks; 25 minutes)

1 Briefly explain why it may be fair to describe Pantene Volume & Body shampoo as a price-taker. (3)
2 John Frieda shampoo is priced at more than 10 times the level of supermarket budget shampoos (per ml). Explain why customers may be willing to pay such a high price. (6)
3 Examine the position of the long-established brand Head & Shoulders within the UK market for shampoo. What pricing strategy does it seem to be using and why may it be possible to use this approach? (7)
4 Discuss whether dogs should have 'better' shampoo than kids. (9)

B2 DATA RESPONSE

The price of a milkshake

ShakeAway is a chain of milkshake shops that grew from 1 to 64 outlets between 1999 and 2011. 27 of those stores opened in the scary recession year of 2009. In quite a crowded market for milkshake shops, ShakeAway is the undisputed leader.

The product is a made-to-order milkshake made of milk, ice cream and any of hundreds of possible ingredients, from fresh fruit through to jam doughnuts or Ferrero Rocher chocolates. The menu covers more than 150 recipes, but customers are free to think up their own. The stores offer water, juices and coffees as well. There are a few tables and chairs (and a free football table, where there's space) but most customers take their shake away. Co-founder Rob Hazell feels that the personality of the stores and the brand is a key part of the product. ShakeAway stores are noisy, bright and fun – as a matter of company policy.

ShakeAway started on the south coast, and still has most of its stores in the south of England. Nevertheless it does have some franchise outposts in cities such as Leeds and Manchester.

Prices are set by head office: £2.80 for a regular shake and £3.80 for a large. Optional extras can take the prices a little higher. ShakeAway shakes are more expensive than most ice creams, but most customers accept that 'made-to-order' costs money – the value for money seems high. ShakeAway prices are the same throughout the country.

Among ShakeAway's competitors is Shakeaholic, which opened its first store in Newcastle in 2007. By early 2011 it had 7 branches, all in the north-east of England. In Leeds its branch competes directly with ShakeAway. Shakeaholic's prices are £2.60 for regular shakes and £3.30 for large.

Location is an enormously important factor for the business. The main target age group is 14–21, with university students especially big fans. Therefore, university towns such as Brighton and Kingston are ideal. Within a town, the right place is where people are walking around; for example, a car-free shopping zone. High rents are worth paying if the location is good enough.

Questions

(30 marks; 35 minutes)

1 Does it seem likely that ShakeAway is a 'price leader' or a 'price taker'? Briefly explain your reasoning. (4)
2 Explain two factors that may have affected ShakeAway's decision on the prices of its milkshakes. (8)
3 In Leeds, people have the choice between a ShakeAway shake and a lower-priced one from Shakeaholic. Explain why they might choose ShakeAway. (8)
4. ShakeAway's founders believe that 'high rents are worth paying if the location is good enough'. Analyse the possible impact of store location on the price of a milkshake. (10)

Price elasticity of demand

UNIT 29

Price elasticity measures the extent to which demand for a product changes when its price is changed.

29.1 INTRODUCTION

When a company increases the price of a product, it expects to lose some sales. Some customers will switch to a rival supplier; others may decide they do not want (or cannot afford) the product at all. Economists use the term 'the law of demand' to suggest that, almost invariably:

Price up	⟶	Demand down
Price down	⟶	Demand up

Price elasticity looks beyond the law of demand to ask the more subtle questions, 'When the price goes up, by how much do sales fall?', 'Do they collapse or do they fall only slightly?'

Elasticity measures the extent to which price changes affect demand.

29.2 PRICE ELASTICITY OF DEMAND

In the short term, the most important factor affecting demand is price. When the price of the *Guardian* newspaper increased from 70p to 80p in 2007 sales fell by 8 per cent, whereas a 30p increase in the price of the *Financial Times* newspaper in the same year cut sales by just 1.5 per cent. Readers of the *Guardian* proved much more price sensitive than readers of the *Financial Times*, therefore the owners of the *Financial Times* could feel delighted with their pricing decision. Selling 1.5 per cent fewer papers but receiving 30 per cent more for each one sold meant that revenue rose by more than a quarter.

The crucial question is how much will demand change when the price is changed? This question can be answered by calculating the price elasticity of demand. Price elasticity is not about whether demand changes when price changes, it is about the degree of change. Consequently, price elasticity is a unit of measurement rather than being a thing in itself. A price cut will not cause price elasticity to fall; instead the price elasticity figure explains the effect the price cut is likely to have on demand. Will demand rise by 1 per cent, 5 per cent or 25 per cent following the price cut? The answer can be known only by referring to the product's price elasticity of demand. Price elasticity measures the responsiveness of demand to a change in price.

Some products are far more price sensitive than others. Following a 5 per cent increase in price the demand for some products may fall greatly, say by more than 20 per cent. The demand for another type of product may fall by less than 1 per cent.

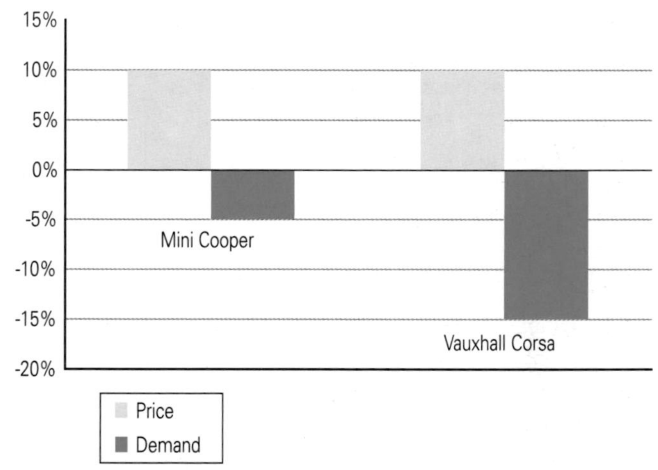

Figure 29.1 The impact of a 10 per cent price rise on car sales, when price elasticity is −2

$$\text{Price elasticity} = \frac{\%\ \text{change in quantity demanded}}{\%\ \text{change in price}}$$

Price elasticity measures the percentage effect on demand of each 1 per cent change in price. So if a 10 per cent increase in price led demand to fall by 20 per cent, the price elasticity would be 2. Strictly speaking, price elasticities are always negative, because price up pushes demand down, and price down pushes demand up. For example:

$$\frac{-20\%}{+10\%} = -2$$

The figure of −2 indicates that, for every 1 per cent change in price, demand is likely to change by 2 per cent. All price elasticities are negative. This is because there is a negative correlation between price and quantity demanded. In the short term, a price cut will always boost sales and a price rise will always cut sales.

may be that much more sensitive about eating fatty foods, making a price rise a reason to stop buying KitKats altogether.

The price elasticity of a brand is a complex combination of its fashionability, the number of direct competitors it faces and the loyalty of its existing customers. All these things can change over time, causing the elasticity to go up or down. It is also possible that elasticity changes over a product's life cycle. It may be highly price elastic at the start, when people are suspicious of a new product. In its growth phase it may become trendy, making it less sensitive to price. In its decline phase people may hang on to the product only if the price is attractive, making it price elastic again.

In conclusion, it is unwise to talk about a product's price elasticity as if it is a fact. Firms make decisions using their assumptions or estimates about the price elasticity of their products. These assumptions are usually based on data that may now be out of date.

29.7 STRATEGIES TO REDUCE PRICE ELASTICITY

All businesses prefer to sell price-inelastic products. Charging more for a price-inelastic product guarantees an increase in short-term profit. If a firm has price-elastic products it will always feel vulnerable, as a rise in costs may be impossible to pass on to customers. And if a firm is tempted to cut the price of a price-elastic product, sales will probably rise so sharply that competitors will be forced to respond. A price war may result.

It is important to realise that the price elasticity of a brand is not set in stone. Price elasticity is not an external constraint. The most important influence on a brand's price elasticity is substitutability. If consumers have other brands available that they think deliver the same benefits, price elasticity will be high. So, to make a brand price inelastic, the firm has to find ways of reducing the number of substitutes available (or acceptable). How can this be done?

Increasing product differentiation

Product differentiation is the degree to which consumers perceive that a product is different (and preferably better) than its rivals. Some products are truly different from others, such as Britain's only business newspaper, the *Financial Times*. Others are successfully differentiated by image, such as Versace Jeans or Coca-Cola. The purchasers of highly differentiated products like Versace Jeans often remain brand-loyal despite price rises. The reason for this low price elasticity is that wearing Versace Jeans makes a statement about the wearer, even if the cloth itself is no different from that used by Levi's or Wrangler.

Predatory pricing

Predatory pricing is a deliberate attempt to force a competitor out of a market by charging a low, loss-making price. Once the competitor has been forced out of the market, the consumer has one less source of supply. The reduction in the number of substitutes available to the customer allows the predator to raise prices successfully. If there are no cheaper substitutes available the customer is forced to pay the higher prices or go without. The same effect can be achieved by takeover bids (for example, the purchase by Adidas of Reebok footwear).

ISSUES FOR ANALYSIS

In examinations, elasticity of demand is a key discriminator between good and weak candidates. Really weak candidates never bring the concept into their answers at all. Better candidates apply it, but imprecisely. Top-grade students see where it is relevant and show a clear understanding of the concept and its implications. Here are two ways to use price elasticity for business analysis.

- Whenever answering any question about pricing, elasticity is a vital factor. Even if a firm faces severe cost increases, a price rise will be very risky if its products have a high price elasticity. Pricing decisions must always start with careful consideration of price elasticity.
- People naturally assume that marketing (especially advertising) is always about trying to increase sales. In fact, most firms are far more interested in their image; a glance at any commercial break will confirm this. Companies focus upon their image because that is the way to differentiate themselves from others. That, in turn, is the way to reduce price elasticity and therefore give the company stronger control over its pricing.

29.8 PRICE ELASTICITY OF DEMAND – AN EVALUATION

For examiners, elasticity is a convenient concept. It is hard to understand, but very easy to write exam questions on! But how useful is it in the real world? Would the average marketing director know the price elasticities of his or her products?

In many cases the answer is no. Examiners and textbooks exaggerate the precision that is possible with such a concept. The fact that the price elasticity of the *Financial Times* appeared to be −0.05 in 2009 does not mean it will always be that low. Price elasticities change over time, as competition changes and consumer tastes change.

Even though elasticities can vary over time, certain features tend to remain constant. Strong brands such as Apple and Coca-Cola have relatively low price elasticity. This gives them the power over market pricing that ensures strong profitability year after year. For less established firms, these brands are the role models: everyone wants to be the Coca-Cola of their own market or market niche.

Key Terms

Correlation: the relationship between one variable and another.
External constraint: something outside the firm's control that can prevent it achieving its objectives.
Predatory pricing: pricing low with the deliberate intention of driving a competitor out of business.
Price-elastic product: a product that is highly price sensitive, so price elasticity is above 1.
Price-inelastic product: a product that is not very price sensitive, so price elasticity is below 1.
Price war: when two or more companies battle for market share by slashing prices, perhaps selling at or below cost.

WORKBOOK

A REVISION QUESTIONS

(35 marks; 35 minutes)

1 a If a product's sales have fallen by 21 per cent since a price rise from £2 to £2.07, what is its price elasticity? (4)
  b Is the product price elastic or price inelastic? (1)
2 Outline two ways in which Nestlé could try to reduce the price elasticity of its Aero chocolate bars. (4)
3 A firm selling 20,000 units at £8 is considering a 4 per cent price increase. It believes its price elasticity is −0.5.
  a) What will be the effect upon revenue? (5)
  b) Give two reasons why the revenue may prove to be different from the firm's expectations. (2)
4 Explain three ways a firm could make use of information about the price elasticity of its brands. (6)
5 Identify three external factors that could increase the price elasticity of a brand of chocolate. (3)
6 A firm has a sales target of 60,000 units per month. Current sales are 50,000 per month at a price of £1.50. If its products have a price elasticity of −2, what price should the firm charge to meet the target sales volume? (4)
7 Why is price elasticity always negative? (2)
8 Explain why the manager of a product with a price elasticity of −2 may be reluctant to cut the price. (4)

B REVISION EXERCISES
B1 DATA RESPONSE

A firm selling Manchester United pillow cases for £10 currently generates an annual turnover of £500,000. Average variable costs are £4 per unit and total annual fixed costs are £100,000. The marketing director is considering a price increase of 10 per cent.

Questions

(20 marks; 25 minutes)

1 Given that the price elasticity of the product is believed to be −0.4, calculate:
  a) the old and the new sales volume (3)
  b) the new revenue (3)
  c) the expected change in profit following the price increase. (6)
2 If the firm started producing mass-market white pillow cases, would their price elasticity be higher or lower than the Manchester United ones? Why is that? (8)

30.3 DISTRIBUTION CHANNELS

There are three main channels of distribution; these are described below.

Traditional

Small producers find it hard to achieve distribution in big chains such as B&Q or Sainsbury's, so they usually sell to wholesalers who, in turn, sell to small independent shops. The profit mark-up applied by the 'middleman' adds to the final retail price, but a small producer cannot afford to deliver individually to lots of small shops.

Modern

Tesco, B&Q and WH Smith do not buy from a wholesaler. They buy direct from producers and then organise their own distribution to their outlets. Their huge selling power gives them huge buying power. Therefore, they are able to negotiate the highest discounts from the producers.

Direct

Using this channel of distribution the producer sells directly to the consumer. Manufacturers can do this through mail order or – far more likely today – through a website. This ensures that the producer keeps 100 per cent of the product's selling price. Often a manufacturer receives only half the shop-selling price of an item after the retailer and the wholesaler have taken their cut. So the benefit of the direct distribution channel is that the producer's higher profits can finance more spending on advertising or on new product development.

> **A-grade application**
>
> **Tesco Online**
>
> In 2009–10, Tesco Online enjoyed a 12 per cent rise in its sales revenue, which compared with a 4 per cent sales increase in Tesco's UK stores. This repeats a growth pattern typical within the company in the last few years. Interestingly, Online is more profitable for Tesco than its normal shop business. The figures in Table 30.1 show that Tesco Online gives higher net profit margins than the traditional business. No wonder Tesco has extended its internet business by launching Tesco Direct, which will deliver Tesco clothes and other non-food items direct to the consumers' door.

Table 30.1 Tesco stores versus Tesco Online, year to February 2010

	Tesco plc	Tesco.com
Sales	£56,910m	£2,100m
Operating (net) profit	£3,412m	£136m
Net profit margin	6.0 per cent	6.5 per cent

Source: Tesco plc, 2010 Annual report and accounts.

30.4 HOW DOES A SMALL FIRM OBTAIN GOOD DISTRIBUTION?

To obtain distribution for the first time, a small firm producing organic biscuits would have to take the following steps.

Distribute product samples

The small firm would need to announce, display and hand out free samples of the product at a trade exhibition, and/or use direct mail to send advertising messages and product samples to trade buyers. (But does it have a good mailing list? McVitie's will know every key decision maker in the grocery retail trade.)

Advertise in the trade press

A example of a suitable trade publication for a firm producing organic biscuits is *The Grocer* magazine. The advertisement will show the attractiveness of the packaging and will emphasise the market gap that has been identified, the generous trade profit margins available, the heavy consumer advertising support and the package of point-of-sale (POS) display materials that are being provided to increase the level of **impulse purchasing** within the store.

Identify and agree distribution and sales targets

There would be a need to identify and agree distribution and sales targets for each area of the country, and type of outlet. A major company such as McVitie's is likely to be confident of achieving distribution targets as high as 80 per cent. A new small firm may find it very difficult to gain distribution at 15 per cent of stores. Having set distribution targets, it should send sales representatives to visit each of the main wholesale and retail buyers. A possible way to break into major multiples is to agree on an exclusive arrangement (for example, that the new product will be stocked only at Tesco for its first six months). This gives the retailer the possibility of a worthwhile benefit: Tesco scores a minor triumph in its competitive battle against Sainsbury's and the others.

> **A-grade application**
>
> Even the biggest firms can struggle to keep their products on the shelves. In July 2010 Pepsi had to admit that low sales of its Pepsi Raw brand had led to several major retailers withdrawing it from distribution. In the year to 26 June 2010 its total UK retail sales were £704,000, a pinprick in the huge market for soft drinks. When it was launched into the retail sector in October 2008 Pepsi had said it would 'rejuvenate' the £400 million cola market. Instead it has become too small a niche to be worth allocating precious shelf space.

30.5 WHAT IS PROMOTION?

Promotion is a general term that covers all the marketing activity that focuses on letting customers know about a product and persuading them to buy that product. It is not just about advertising. The different elements of promotion can be grouped into two broad categories: those that stimulate short-term sales and those that build sales for the long term.

30.6 TYPES OF PROMOTION FOR BUILDING LONG-TERM SALES

These include those described below.

Branding

One of the best forms of promotion is branding. Branding is the process of creating a distinctive and lasting identity in the minds of consumers. Establishing a brand can take considerable time and marketing effort, but once a product brand is established it becomes its own means of promotion. The brand name is recognised and this makes it more likely that the customer will buy the product for the first time. If the experience is satisfactory the customer is very likely to continue to choose the brand. Once established, branding has many advantages, such as the following.

- It enables the business to reduce the amount spent on promotion.
- Customers are more likely to purchase the product again (repeat purchases).
- It is easier to persuade retailers to put the products in their stores.
- Other products can be promoted using the same brand name.

Persuasive advertising

Persuasive advertising is designed to create a distinctive image. A good example is BMW, which has spent decades persuading us that it produces not a car but a 'Driving Machine'. Advertising of this kind has also helped to create clear consumer images for firms such as Tesco and L'Oréal (see Table 30.2).

Table 30.2 Examples of persuasive advertising

Company	Slogan	Meaning
Tesco	'Every little helps'	We understand your needs and we try to help (we're not just a great big, greedy business)
L'Oréal	'Because you're worth it'	Go on, spoil yourself; you can afford that bit extra, so buy our products, not our competitors'
Innocent Drinks	'Nothing, but nothing, but fruit'	Our products are pure (whereas others are not)

A-grade application

Social advertising – Nike

Social networks are the latest trend in getting your products in front of potential consumers. Social network sites such as Facebook, Twitter and YouTube are increasingly being used to promote products. Coca-Cola and IKEA are two of the big brands that use Facebook. During the 2010 World Cup Nike scored a major goal. An advertising video originally shown on TV was then shown on YouTube. The number of hits, over 16 million after a few months, showed that this reached a much greater audience than the original TV ad.

Figure 30.1 Corporate sponsorship may be used as a form of promotion

Public relations

This is the attempt to affect consumers' image of a product without spending on media advertising. It includes making contacts with journalists to try to get favourable mentions or articles about your product. It would also include activities such as sponsorship of sport or the arts. The London Olympic Games in 2012 has Lloyds TSB as one of its main sponsors. This allows the business to advertise and use its logo alongside the Olympic logo.

30.7 TYPES OF PROMOTION FOR BOOSTING SHORT-TERM SALES

These include those described below.

Sales promotions

These range from on-pack competitions to in-store offers such as buy one get one free (BOGOF). These can be very effective at boosting sales, but there are risks involved, such as: customers may stock up at (in effect) half price, then not need to buy more items in the weeks following the offer; special offers may undermine the brand image (what would it say to consumers if Apple started offering 'buy one iPhone

to safety was called into question, especially within its vast North American operation. BP executives must have wished they truly were Beyond Petroleum, but the reality had always been that BP was a huge oil company with a very minor interest in alternative forms of energy.

31.3 ENVIRONMENTAL TRENDS AND THE MARKETING MIX

In 2007, £1,500 million was spent on organic food, marking a rise of 70 per cent since 2002. This was a sign that people were starting to take seriously long-held concerns about animal welfare plus the need to eat purer food. Yet when recession hit in 2008, sales of organic foods were among the first to suffer. Simply to survive, yoghurt-maker Rachel's Organic became Rachel's because the association of 'organic' with 'high price' made it a handicap during tough times. In 2009 the market for organic foods slipped by more than 10 per cent in the UK. When sales of organic foods were growing, producers assumed that the sales upturn represented a permanent choice away from processed, chemical foods. In hindsight it was more of a lifestyle choice; a luxury that people quickly dropped when recession came.

Other environmental factors affecting shoppers, and therefore being taken seriously by food manufacturers and retailers, are described below.

Recyclable packaging

Waste materials can be disposed of in one of only three ways: burn them, bury them or reuse them. Burning them directly increases greenhouse gas emissions and burying them is not only destructive of the environment, but can also cause air pollution. The ideal solution is therefore recycling, meaning to reuse as much as possible of the original materials. There are simple solutions to this that shoppers seem uninterested in; for instance, getting milk from a milkman who collects, washes and refills glass milk bottles; people are sufficiently ill-focused to make a fuss about recycled plastic when there is a much better solution available.

Nevertheless, individual businesses cannot concern themselves with re-educating the public; their duty is to attract custom. Innocent Drinks is now proud to proclaim a world first, in that all its bottles are now made from recycled plastic. At the same time, they have asked their supplier to make them slightly thinner, saving 20 per cent on the weight of the plastic; this is cheaper for Innocent, and better for all of us. Innocent's website promotes this move enthusiastically, seeing it as a matter of great interest to many of its customers.

Food miles

The term **food miles** is used to criticise shoppers who buy food thoughtlessly. Britain grows wonderful cherries, but the eating season is early summer, so for nine months of the year there are no fresh British cherries. Campaigners criticise supermarkets for flying in supplies of cherries from California or Spain, pointing out the impact on CO_2 emissions of all the 'food miles' concerned.

When an issue such as this is raised, clever marketers can sometimes seize opportunities to build it into their marketing mix. So Walkers now advertises that all its potato supplies are British. From a marketing point of view, that is very clever. It makes Walkers seem socially responsible. Does it make the planet a better place to live? Well, only if Walkers changed its buying practices to stop buying from abroad. In fact it was already buying almost entirely from British farmers, making it an easy claim to make.

Sourcing sustainable materials

Sustainability means that the purchase you make will not affect long-term supplies of the product, because it is automatically replenished. For example, although cod is an endangered fish, with a serious risk that supplies will dry up, there are plenty of supplies of other fish available, such as pollock. Birds Eye has given in to pressure to reduce the amount of cod in its fish fingers, using pollock instead. Pollock and chips, anyone?

Other environmental factors

At the time of writing, another key environmental concern was the 'carbon footprint' created by products. This is a measurement of all the CO_2 emitted by the materials used, delivery miles, manufacturing and office costs (especially energy) involved in producing, packing and delivering a product. Walkers has done a detailed analysis of the carbon emissions involved in producing a single, standard pack of its Cheese & Onion crisps. It has worked out that each 35 g pack generates 75 g of carbon! This can be broken down in the way illustrated in Figure 31.1.

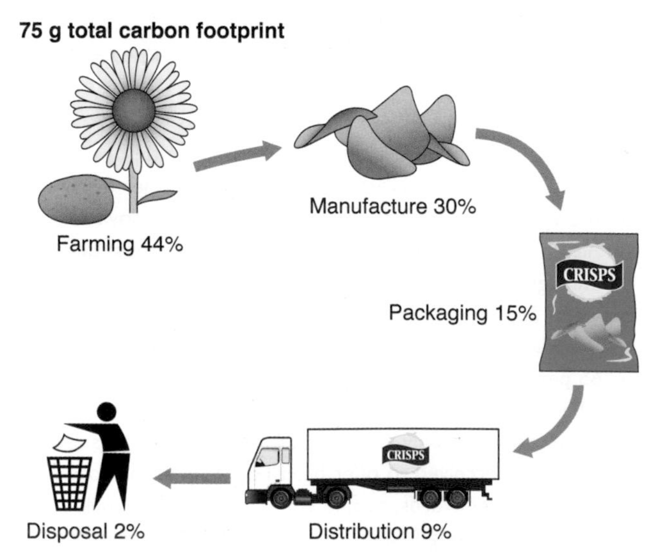

Figure 31.1 Carbon footprint for a standard 35 g pack of Walkers Cheese & Onion crisps

1 Our raw materials: potatoes, sunflowers and seasoning.
2 Manufacture: producing crisps from potatoes.
3 Packaging our crisps.
4 Distribution: bringing our crisps to you.
5 Disposal of the empty packs.
Source: www.walkerscarbonfootprint.co.uk

An intelligently run business will try to avoid being the butt of media jokes about pollution. Walkers is clearly being very clever in keeping one step ahead of its rivals. Nevertheless, if a competitor were able to claim a 50 g carbon footprint for the same-sized pack of crisps, there may be an interesting new form of competition in future.

31.4 ONLINE RETAILING AND THE MARKETING MIX

Traditionally, location was a key factor for retailers. For online retailers that is clearly not a concern. Yet there are many other potential pitfalls. James Murray-Wells started Glasses Direct at the age of 21, just after completing a degree. He offered pairs of glasses for £15 instead of the £150 paid in the high street.

James designed the website himself, but – with no money and no publicity – sales in the first month averaged just one or two pairs a day. The only expense he could afford was to get some leaflets printed. This is often a weak form of advertising, but with his incredibly strong offer (£15 instead of £150) his leaflets proved highly effective. He took a train from Bristol, handing out flyers to people who would be stuck on a train with nothing else to do but read them. Within days sales started coming through from people living in Bristol. Shortly afterwards came emails of thanks, with people clearly surprised that the glasses were every bit as good as those available on the high street. By the end of the summer, word of mouth had spread and the first articles started appearing in papers. Orders were received for up to 100 pairs a day and the business was booming. Within two years turnover hit £3 million and rising.

In this case, an outstanding price offer combined with a good product, good service and a small investment in advertising to create a highly successful mix. In effect, it was the original idea (high-street glasses at non-rip-off prices) that was the key. In other cases this will not work, because the offer has to be similar to the competition. If you are selling skateboards online, your prices will not be much different to those of other suppliers. This will make it much more important to identify a winning marketing strategy.

Here are some that work well.

- *The saturation approach*: as used by Moneysupermarket.com to make sure that everyone thinks of you first; the downside, of course, is the huge cost of the TV advertising.
- *Google search optimisation:* that is, design your website so that it comes very high on the list when people are Googling for something you want to sell. This takes time and a small amount of money, but is much, much cheaper than a multi-million-pound advertising campaign.
- *Build a website people will talk about:* some good examples are those of Innocent Drinks and Ted Baker. A fun website can provide strong support to a brand image, and get the brand written about in the media, which provides extra, free promotion.

31.5 RETAILER PURCHASING POWER

By 2008 four retailers controlled more than 75 per cent of Britain's grocery market, with Tesco alone accounting for more than 30 per cent. As the pie charts in Figure 31.2 show, Britain's shopping habits have been transformed in the ten years to 2008. The four majors (Tesco, Sainsbury's, Asda and Morrisons) all make sure that their marketing and advertising messages emphasise their wish to help the customer. Tesco's slogan 'Every Little Helps' may prove to have been Britain's most successful advertising slogan ever.

Yet there are many critics who feel that the supermarkets hide some questionable practices behind their slogans. In February 2008 the Competition

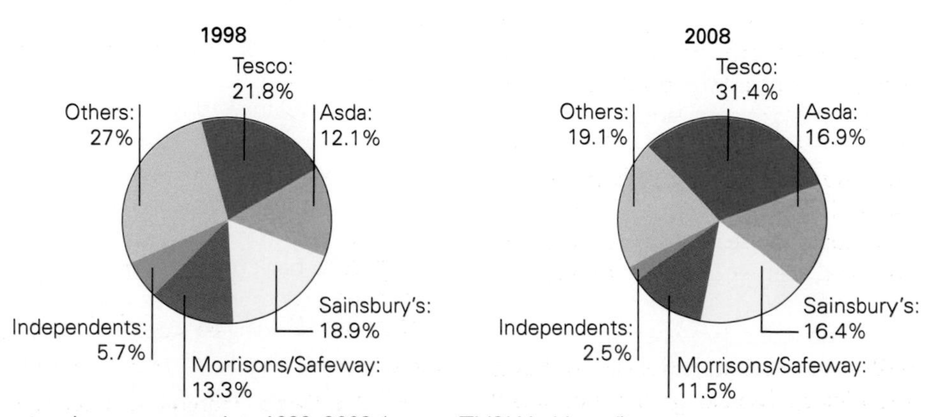

Figure 31.2 Comparing the grocery market, 1998–2008 (source: TNS Worldpanel)

Commission announced that suppliers to supermarkets would be able to complain (confidentially) to an independent 'ombudsman' if they were unhappy about their treatment. The concern was that farmer suppliers to the supermarkets can be forced to accept terms that make it impossible to operate profitably without cutting corners. If Tesco decides to run a promotion of '2 chickens for £5', it may be the birds that suffer for the customer's (and Tesco's) benefit.

The supermarkets retort that an ombudsman will add more bureaucracy without affecting customers or suppliers. This may well be true, as the only long-term solution is for customers to show the shops that they really care about where products come from and how they were made or grown. The reality is that many shoppers like to have it both ways: to sound shocked about poor conditions at the supplier end, yet still pick up a £1.99 chicken and a £3 school shirt on the way to the checkout.

ISSUES FOR ANALYSIS

- The key is to analyse the real intent of the company. Is there a true commitment to a social purpose (the environment, or people's health, or to poorly paid staff working for suppliers) or is the motivation purely to cash in on a trend? Some people may argue that it doesn't matter and that, as long as companies are doing the 'right thing', it doesn't matter about their motives. The BP example shows, however, that just because a company says the right things it does not mean that it is really doing them.
- Analytically, it is easiest to see why companies such as Innocent Drinks will almost always be trying to align their marketing mix to the right social purpose. This is because Innocent's brand image is entirely associated with 'being innocent/good', and its brand image and company image are inseparable. The situation is more complex for a business such as Walkers (owned by PepsiCo). There is no doubt that the business has tried hard to act with social responsibility in relation to this key brand. The saturated fat content of the crisps has been reduced, yet potato crisps are unarguably bad for a population suffering rising obesity. For example, the Walkers brand Wotsits proudly proclaims 'NOW 25 per cent less fat', yet the product still contains 33 g of fat per 100 g of crisps, which is about half the daily recommended allowance for an adult woman. Unfortunately for Walkers it cannot escape questions about whether its packaging and promotion are really responsible.

31.6 THE MARKETING MIX AND SOCIAL TRENDS – AN EVALUATION

The most important judgement concerns the extent to which firms can be relied upon to act responsibly in their marketing. The government has doubts, as it tries to put pressure on firms to conform to rules such as pack labelling in relation to diet, or the way firms act in relation to the threat of global warming. If companies are left to their own devices, they may act responsibly (to avoid bad publicity) but could do the absolute minimum. A well-run business will probably see the opportunity to motivate staff and customers by taking a forward-looking approach to social obligations. Then, if the business has done all it can to minimise any environmental or health damage caused by its products, it can honestly build its marketing mix on a positive social message.

Key Terms

Food miles: a calculation of how much travelling is involved in making and delivering a product (for example, raspberries flown 2,000 miles from Israel, then driven 300 miles to a supermarket).

Sustainability: whether the supply source can be continued indefinitely into the future (if not, it is unsustainable).

WORKBOOK

A REVISION QUESTIONS

(35 marks; 35 minutes)

1 Outline two possible reasons why Maltesers is still selling successfully over 75 years after the brand's birth. (4)

2 Explain why it is important to distinguish between a trend and a fad. (4)

3 Reread the A-grade application feature 'Selling soya'. Why does the writer question 'whether [soya] is making people healthier'? (3)

4 Reread section 31.2 and consider whether BP's Lord Browne was right to rebrand British Petroleum as Beyond Petroleum. (5)

5 Consider the following:
   a) In February 2008, Cadbury announced the launch of a range of Easter eggs that would not have any outer packaging (they would just be sold in a foil wrapper). Outline one advantage and one disadvantage of this. (4)
   b) Do you think this approach will be successful for Cadbury? Explain your reasoning. (5)

6 Explain whether you believe these businesses are pursuing a profitable marketing approach or a good social purpose. Choose two from the following:
   a) HSBC bank running a 'January sale', based on linking its products to improving the environment
   b) B&Q deciding to stop selling outdoor patio heaters
   c) Coca-Cola sponsoring the London Marathon. (4)

7 Should shoppers see it as their personal responsibility to think about how a shop is able to sell a new suit for £25 or a chicken for £1.99? (6)

B REVISION EXERCISES
B1 DATA RESPONSE

Food companies police themselves on junk food

Diane Abbott, the shadow public health minister, is calling for the health select committee to launch an inquiry into government moves to put McDonald's, PepsiCo, Unilever and Kellogg's at the heart of writing policy on obesity, diet-related disease and alcohol misuse in the UK.

Abbott said she was 'shocked' by revelations in the *Guardian* that Andrew Lansley, Secretary of State for Health in the 2010 coalition government, has set up five networks dominated by the food, alcohol and retail industries to write 'responsibility deals' between business and government to tackle the crises of public health. She is writing to the select committee asking it to investigate. Leading public health experts joined Abbott in expressing deep concern about the government's strategy of inviting industry to volunteer measures on public health instead of taking the lead with mandatory action.

Professor Simon Capewell, of Liverpool University, was on the public health commission Lansley set up before the election to make recommendations to the Conservatives on diet-related diseases and alcohol abuse, but said that he now believes the commission was set up to suit business interests.

Capewell is gagged by a confidentiality undertaking from describing the detailed discussions of the commission. However, he said that 'after calm reflection' he felt the process had been 'carefully stage-managed' – the health representatives on the group were always in a minority, and those individuals were put under intense pressure to support the party line when it came to the wording of the final report.

Specifically, he says, describing foods high in fat, salt or sugar as junk food was brusquely ruled out. The strong scientific evidence that traffic light food labelling was much more effective than industry's Guideline Daily Amount scheme that Lansley has supported was repeatedly ignored.

Commenting on Lansley's new responsibility deals with business, he said: 'This sort of talking shop is essentially a waste of time. It's a cynical public relations smokescreen for industry interests. It flies in the face of extensive scientific evidence about the most effective and cost-effective interventions to promote public health. Consistent lessons from the UK and internationally demonstrate that the most powerful policy levers are: legislation, regulation, and taxation of harmful substances, plus subsidies for healthy options.'

There is extensive published evidence, Capewell says, that population-wide regulatory approaches reduce health inequalities.

Source: Felicity Lawrence, *Guardian*, 15 November 2010.

Questions

(30 marks; 35 minutes)

1 Explain what Diane Abbott is 'shocked' about. (6)
2 Explain how a hamburger chain might adapt its marketing mix if it had to label its products 'junk food'. (10)
3 The government's plan is to allow food companies freedom from marketing regulations. Examine the possible effect on the marketing mix used by a company such as Kellogg's. (14)

Marketing and competitiveness

UNIT 32

Competitiveness measures a firm's ability to compete (that is, compares its consumer offer to the offers made by its rivals).

32.1 INTRODUCTION: WHAT IS A COMPETITIVE MARKET?

In the past, markets were physical places where buyers and sellers met in person to exchange goods. Street markets are still like that. Today, some buyers and sellers never meet each other, a good example being eBay.

Some markets are more competitive than others. In general, a competitive market could be described as one where there is intense rivalry between producers of a similar good or service. The number of firms operating within a market influences the intensity of competition; the more firms there are, the greater the level of competition. However, the respective size of the firms operating in the market should also be taken into account. A market consisting of 50 firms may not be particularly competitive, if, for instance, one of the firms holds a 60 per cent market share and the remaining 40 per cent is shared between the other 49 firms. Similarly, a market composed of just four firms could be quite competitive because the firms operating within this market are of a fairly similar size.

Consumers enjoy competitive markets. However, the reverse is true for the firms that operate in these markets. In competitive markets, prices and profit margins tend to be squeezed. As a result, firms operating in competitive markets try hard to minimise competition, perhaps by creating a unique selling point (**USP**) or using **predatory pricing**.

It could be argued that marketing is vital no matter what the level of competition is within the market. Firms that fail to produce goods and services that satisfy the needs of the consumers making up their target market will find it hard to succeed in the long term. Ultimately, consumers will not choose to waste their hard-earned cash on products that fail to meet their needs.

32.2 THE DEGREE OF COMPETITION WITHIN A MARKET

One dominant business

Some markets are dominated by one large business. Economists use the word 'monopoly' to describe a market where there is a single supplier, and therefore no competition. In practice pure textbook monopolies rarely exist; even Microsoft does not have a 100 per cent share of the office software market (though it does have a 90 per cent share).

Monopolies are bad for consumers. They restrict choice, and tend to drive prices upwards. For that reason most governments regulate against monopolies and near monopolies that exploit consumers by abusing their dominant market position. The UK government's definition of a monopoly is somewhat looser. According to the Competition Commission, a monopoly is a firm that has a market share of 25 per cent and above.

Deciding whether or not a firm has a monopoly is a far from straightforward task. First of all, the market itself has to be accurately defined. For example, Camelot has been granted a monopoly to run the National Lottery; however, it could be argued that Camelot does not have a dominant market position because there are other forms of gambling, such as horse racing and the football pools, available to consumers in the UK. Second, national market share figures should not be used in isolation because some firms enjoy local monopolies. In 2007 the Competition Commission accused Tesco of abusing its market position in towns such as Inverness and Slough by occupying sites previously occupied by its rivals. In both towns, consumers had to travel more than 15 minutes by car to reach another supermarket chain.

Firms implement their marketing strategy through the marketing mix. In markets dominated by a single large business, firms do not need to spend heavily on promotion because consumers are, to a degree, captive. Prices can be pushed upwards and the product element of the marketing mix should be focused on creating innovations that make it harder for new entrants to break in to the market. Apple spends millions of dollars on research and development in order to produce cutting-edge products such as the iPhone 4 (see Figure 32.1). To ensure that Apple maintains its dominant market position new product launches are patented to prevent me-too imitations from being launched by the competition.

Figure 32.1 iPhone 4

Competition amongst a few giants

The UK supermarket industry is a good example of a market that is dominated by a handful of very large companies. Economists call markets like this **oligopolistic**. The rivalry that exists within such markets can be intense. Firms know that any gains in market share will be at the expense of their rivals. The actions taken by one firm affect the profits made by the other firms that compete within the same market.

In markets made up of a few giants, firms tend to focus on **non-price competition** when designing the marketing mix. Firms in these markets tend to be reluctant to compete by cutting price. They fear that the other firms in the industry will respond by cutting their prices too, creating a costly price war where no firm wins.

The fiercely competitive market

Fiercely competitive markets tend to be fragmented, made up of hundreds of relatively small firms, each of which competes actively against the others. In some of these markets competition is amplified by the fact that firms sell near-identical products, called commodities. Commodities are products such as flour, sugar or blank DVDs that are hard to differentiate. Rivalry in commodity markets tends to be intense. In markets such as this, firms have to manage their production costs very carefully because the retail price is the most important factor in determining whether the firm's product sells or not. If a firm cannot cut its costs, it will not be able to cut its prices without cutting into profit margins. Without price cuts market share is likely to be lost.

In fiercely competitive markets firms will try, where possible, to create product differentiation. For example, the restaurant market in Croydon, Surrey, is extremely competitive. There are over 70 outlets within a two-mile radius of the town centre. To survive without having to compete solely on price, firms in markets like this must find new innovations regularly because points of differentiation are quickly copied.

A-grade application

Are you thinking about taking a holiday in Barcelona? There are many different airlines that will fly you there. The three main UK ones are Ryanair, British Airways and easyJet. In August 2010 it was possible to book return flights for March 2011 from Gatwick Airport to Barcelona for the prices shown in Table 32.1.

Table 32.1 Prices for return flights from Gatwick Airport to Barcelona in March 2011

Airline	Price
British Airways:	£103.90
easyJet:	£60.98
Ryanair:	£49.58

This is a ferociously competitive market, because many airlines offer a very similar service on exactly the same route. Here, the traveller has a choice based on price and on the customer service image of each airline. It will be hard for any of these three airlines to make a profit on such low prices. By contrast, Virgin Rail can use its monopoly position to charge £200 for a return fare from London to Birmingham.

32.3 DETERMINANTS OF COMPETITIVENESS

The key to competitiveness is customer satisfaction. If consumers are satisfied with quality and value for money, the firm concerned should be competitive. Competitive firms find it easier to hold on to, or even gain, market share. Competitiveness is a function of internal factors that are within the firm's control, and external factors, which are not.

Efficiency

Ryanair is a highly efficient company that manages its costs very effectively. The company's business model focuses on cost minimisation, by:

- avoiding airports that have high take-off and landing charges; instead, Ryanair prefers to fly from secondary airports, some of which actually pay it for using them
- operating only one type of aircraft: the Boeing 737; staff employed to pilot or service Ryanair's aircraft need only be trained on one plane, minimising staff training and stock holding costs (for plane components)
- cutting out free food, drinks and newspapers; passengers that wish to consume these items have to pay for them; charging for food and drink has converted a cost into an important source of revenue.

Cost-efficient businesses such as Ryanair can charge lower prices than their less efficient rivals, yet make the same or more profit per unit supplied. In highly competitive commodity markets, such as low-cost air travel, price cutting is a highly effective way of gaining market share.

Design

Some firms are highly competitive because they sell products that have been differentiated by their design. In countries such as the UK, where wage rates are relatively high, manufacturers cannot compete on price alone. Production costs are too high, compared with rivals in countries where wage rates are lower. By using design as a USP, British manufacturers can compete on quality rather than price, making them less vulnerable to competition from China and India. Good-looking design can add value to a product. For example, the BMW Mini relies upon its retro 1960s styling to command its price premium within the small car market.

Brand image

In many markets brand image is crucial. The results of blind tests indicate that, in many cases, consumers are unable to tell the difference between supermarket own-label products and premium-priced brands. Clever branding and advertising may be the only thing ensuring that Stella Artois carries on outselling Tesco's Premium Lager.

External factors

Competitiveness is also partially determined by external factors that are beyond the firm's control. The going wage rate in a country is an excellent example of an external factor that is beyond any single firm's control. High wages tend to drive up costs, making a firm less competitive. On average, factory workers in the USA get paid somewhere in the region of $15 to $30 per hour. In China the corresponding figure is less than $1 per hour. Firms try to improve their competitiveness by making internal changes to help compensate for factors, such as labour costs, that are beyond their control. European car manufacturers such as VW and Mercedes have decided to close down some of their European factories and re-open them in low-cost countries such as China in an attempt to improve their competitiveness.

32.4 METHODS OF IMPROVING COMPETITIVENESS

Training

Some firms aim to improve their efficiency by increasing the amount they spend on staff training. Well-trained staff create the following competitive advantages.

Lower costs

Training tends to increase the productivity of labour because trained staff can work faster and make fewer mistakes; if output per worker increases, unit labour costs will tend to fall.

Improved product quality

Trained staff know what they are doing, improving the build quality of the finished product, which could give the firm concerned a competitive advantage in the market.

Better customer service

Effective training can dramatically improve customer service; for example, in some supermarkets untrained staff are still sent straight to the checkouts to learn how to use the till on the job; this can lead to queues and irritated customers.

Management

The quality of management has an important impact on the competitiveness of a business. For many years newspapers blamed British workers for the decline of UK car producers such as Rover. Yet, today, the Nissan plant in Sunderland is the most productive car factory in Europe. This implies that British management methods were at fault, as the Nissan plant's workforce is British. Improving the quality of management within an organisation is notoriously difficult, requiring a change in an organisation's culture.

Modernisation and investment

Some firms try to improve their competitiveness by purchasing new machinery and technology designed to improve efficiency. For example, a car manufacturer could drive down unit costs by replacing labour with the latest CAM (computer-aided manufacturing) technology. It is hoped that the new machinery will boost efficiency by driving up productivity, while at the same time reducing the firm's wage bill.

ISSUES FOR ANALYSIS

- Every firm is different, and so is every market. It is always essential to think hard about the structure of the market, as this can affect every aspect of management within individual firms. Facing the same opportunity (for example, for robot window-cleaners), a small firm may react very differently from a large one.
- It is then necessary to remember the huge difference between what firms do and what is right. Many firms try to improve their competitiveness by cost-cutting, such as the attempt by McDonald's to operate a 'zero training' policy. From a marketing point of view that was a poor idea, as it would inevitably affect customer service.

32.5 MARKETING AND COMPETITIVENESS – AN EVALUATION

Competitiveness is a much wider issue than marketing. It is affected by the quality of the design and build of the products, and by the enthusiasm of the staff. These are clearly operations and personnel issues. Nevertheless, marketing is at the heart of competitiveness for many firms. Mars knows how to produce Galaxy chocolate, so the key to the firm's success next year is how well the brand can be marketed. The managers must understand the customers, and then have the wisdom and the creativity to find a way to make the product stand out.

Key Terms

Non-price competition: rivalry based on factors other than price (for example, advertising, sales promotions or 'new improved' products).

Oligopolistic: a market in which a few large companies have a dominant share (for example, the UK chocolate market with a 70 per cent share divided between Cadbury, Nestlé and Mars).

Predatory pricing: when a large company sets prices low with the deliberate intention of driving a weaker rival out of business.

USP: a point of genuine difference that makes one product stand out from the crowd (for example, the Toyota Prius 'hybrid synergy drive').

WORKBOOK

A REVISION QUESTIONS

(35 marks; 35 minutes)

1 What is a competitive market? (3)

2 Explain how the marketing mix of Virgin Trains could be affected by a decision by government to allow other train-operating companies to compete on Virgin's routes. (3)

3 Describe the main features of an oligopolistic market. (3)

4 Consider the following:
 a What is a price war and ... (3)
 b why are they rare? (3)

5 Explain why product differentiation becomes more important as competition within a market increases. (3)

6 Identify four factors that could be used to identify whether or not a business is competitive. (4)

7 How could the size of an organisation affect its efficiency? (3)

8 Why may a firm that is struggling to be competitive increase its training budget? (3)

9 Explain how the quality of management can impact upon an organisation's efficiency. (4)

10 Apart from market research, how may a firm achieve its goal of attempting to get closer to the consumer? (3)

B REVISION EXERCISES

B1 DATA RESPONSE

At the beginning of the 1960s Indian food was a niche market business: there were just 500 Indian restaurants in the whole of the UK. As Table 32.2 illustrates, in the two decades that followed, the UK Indian restaurant market grew at a spectacular rate. In more recent times the market has continued to grow; however, the rate of growth has declined. Today, the Indian restaurant market is firmly established. The industry is one of Britain's largest, employing over 60,000 people.

Table 32.2 Number of Indian restaurants in UK

Year	No. of restaurants	Market growth rate (%)
1960	500	–
1970	1,200	140
1980	3,000	150
1990	5,100	70
2000	7,940	56
2004	8,750	10
2010	8,900	2

The Indian restaurant market is extremely decentralised. The market is made up of thousands of small, independent operators. In most British high streets there are several Indian restaurants that compete aggressively against one another. Indian food is very popular: over 23 million portions of Indian food are sold in restaurants each year. In the 1960s and 1970s, the growing affluence and cosmopolitan nature of the British public boosted takings at most Indian restaurants, and they began to make a lot money from the industry. Most owners chose to use some of the profit made to upgrade their facilities. Gradually, Indian restaurants became more sophisticated (for example, luxurious-looking tables, chairs and tablecloths, piped Indian music, air conditioning, dinner-jacketed waiters and flock wallpaper). Some 30 years ago, Indian restaurants tended to look the same. Most had fairly similar menus too. As a result Indian restaurants were forced into competing against each other on price. Unfortunately, intense price competition led to falling profit margins. Indian restaurateurs began to realise the importance of product differentiation as a competitive weapon. The first real attempt to create differentiation occurred in the early 1960s when a handful of forward-looking Indian restaurants, such as the Gaylord in Mortimer Street, London, imported tandoors. A tandoor is a special type of oven made from clay that gives the food cooked inside it a distinctive taste. Restaurants using tandoor ovens found that they could charge slightly higher prices without emptying their restaurants. Today, Indian restaurants use a variety of tactics to compete including those listed below.

- *Décor and design:* in recent times several now famous London-based Indian restaurants, such as the Cinnamon Club, opened in 2001 at a cost of £2.6 million in the Old Westminster Library, ditched the old-style traditional Indian restaurant décor in favour of a more upmarket-looking modern minimalistic interior design style. This change inspired many other Indian restaurants up and down the land to upgrade their fixtures and fittings in the hope that they too could charge Cinnamon Club-style premium prices (for example, smoked rack of lamb with Rajasthani corn sauce and pilau rice for £22.00).
- *Exotic-sounding premium-priced menu items:* for example, Seabass Kaylilan prepared with fenugreek and tamarind.

Figure 32.2 A contemporary Indian restaurant

Other restaurants have adopted a different approach. For example, the Khyber in Croydon has tried to win customers by emphasising its authenticity. The restaurant's website informs the reader that 'Our success is based on more traditional recipes.' The slogan 'Its just how mum would cook it back home' also features prominently on its internet menu. It also offers:

- balti cooking, including the super-sized big-as-your-table Nan breads!
- a prestigious imported German lager on draught, or a selection of fine wines
- flying in celebrated curry chefs from the Indian subcontinent for a limited period to cook up special food for a Curry Festival; this is the equivalent of a nightclub flying in a celebrity DJ.

Questions

(35 marks; 40 minutes)

1 Using the table, explain what has happened to the degree of competition within the UK Indian restaurant market over the last 50 years. (6)

2 Giving your reasons, discuss whether the Indian restaurant market in the UK is an example of a fiercely competitive market. (6)

3 a Explain how efficiency could affect the competitiveness of an Indian restaurant. (4)

b How may an Indian restaurant go about improving its efficiency? (4)

4 Identify and explain three internal factors that could affect the competitiveness of an Indian restaurant. (6)

5 Product differentiation is essential if an Indian restaurant is to survive in the long run. Discuss. (9)

B2 CASE STUDY

Tesco's £9 toaster

The prices of consumer electronics, including toasters, satellite TV set-top boxes and MP3 players, have tumbled in recent years. Supermarket chains such as Tesco now sell DVD players that previously cost hundreds of pounds for under £10. So, why have the prices of these goods fallen? In part, the price falls reflect the falling price of the components that go into consumer electronics. Low prices also reflect the fact that there is now more competition in the market. In the past, consumers typically bought items such as TVs and computers from specialist retailers such as Currys and Dixons. Today, the situation is somewhat different: in addition to these specialist retailers, consumers can now buy electrical goods over the internet and from supermarkets. Industry analysts also believe that some of the supermarket chains are using set-top boxes and DVD players as loss leaders.

In today's ultra-competitive environment, manufacturers of consumer electronics face intense pressure from retailers to cut costs so that retail prices can be cut without any loss of profit margin. To cut prices without compromising product quality, manufacturers such as the Dutch giant Philips have transferred production from the Netherlands to low-cost locations such as China.

Questions

(35 marks; 40 minutes)

1 Describe three characteristics of a highly competitive market. (6)
2 Why has the market for consumer electronics become more competitive? (4)
3 Explain three factors that would affect the competitiveness of a manufacturer of consumer electronics. (6)
4 What is a loss leader and why do supermarkets sell them? (3)
5 How could the degree of competition impact upon the marketing mix used by a Chinese manufacturer of own-label toasters? (6)
6 In today's increasingly competitive market for consumer electronics, firms must constantly cut costs and prices if they are to survive. Discuss. (10)

People, productivity and performance

UNIT 33

Productivity is a measure of efficiency; it measures the output of a firm in relation to its inputs.

33.1 PRODUCTIVITY: WHAT IS IT?

Productivity is a measurement of a firm's efficiency. It measures output in relation to inputs. A firm can increase its efficiency by producing more with the same inputs or producing the same amount with fewer inputs.

The most common measure is **labour productivity**. This measures the amount a worker produces over a given time. For example, an employee might make ten pairs of jeans in an hour. Measuring productivity is relatively easy in manufacturing where the number of goods can be counted. In the service sector it is not always possible to measure anything tangible. Productivity in services can be measured in some cases: the number of customers served, number of patients seen, and the sales per employee. But how can the productivity of a receptionist be measured?

When considering a firm's efficiency it is important to distinguish between productivity and total output. By hiring more employees the firm may increase the total output, but this does not necessarily mean that the output per employee has gone up. Similarly it is possible to have less total output with higher productivity because of a fall in the number of workers. Imagine, for example, 20 employees producing 40 tables a week in a furniture company. Their productivity on average is 2 tables per week. If 5 employees make 15 tables the overall output has fallen, but the output per worker has risen. This situation of falling output but rising productivity happened in manufacturing companies around the world in the 2008–09 recession. Faced with falling demand many companies were forced to **rationalise** their organisations. This led to high levels of redundancies and extra work for those who still had a job. The result was that there were fewer people working, but at the same time there was often higher output per person.

A-grade application

Each year the Harbour Report provides feedback on the productivity of the US car industry. Published in 2009, the figures shown in Table 33.1 are for 2007 production of midsize cars. Productivity is shown not as output of cars per person, but in terms of the time taken to produce each car; the lower the figure the better.

Table 33.1 Production of midsize cars in USA in 2007

Producer and location	Actual production 2007	Production hours per vehicle	Percentage over benchmark
Toyota, Georgetown	358,077	18.69	Benchmark
General Motors, Fairfax	188,432	19.34	3.5
Ford, Hermosillo	213,458	20.78	11.2
Chrysler, Sterling Heights	238,106	33.29	19.3
General Motors, Orion	153,416	26.74	43.1

Source: Oliver Wyman. © 2009 Oliver Wyman

In its report, Harbour says that 'Toyota is the best in the industry. It is not a matter of spending more than competitors, but of effective kaizen improvement activities and the flexibility that comes with well-coordinated engineering.' The report also suggests that the highest productivity factories are increasingly the highest quality plants as well. It seems that well-managed staff will succeed at both together.

Table 33.2 Shoe factory productivity and wage costs

	Daily wage rate (£)	Productivity rate (per day)	Wage cost per pair (£)
Factory 1	50	5	10
Factory 2	50	10	5

33.2 WHY DOES PRODUCTIVITY MATTER?

The output per employee is a very important measure of a firm's performance. It has a direct impact on the cost of producing a unit. If productivity increases then, assuming wages are unchanged, the labour cost per unit will fall. Imagine that in one factory employees make five pairs of shoes per day, but in another they make ten pairs per day; assuming the wage rate is the same this means the labour cost of a pair of shoes will be halved in the second factory (see Table 33.2). With lower labour costs this firm is likely to be in a better competitive position.

By increasing productivity a firm can improve its competitiveness. It can either sell its products at a lower price or keep the price as it was and enjoy a higher profit margin. This is why firms continually monitor their productivity relative to their competitors and, where possible, try to increase it. However, they need to make sure that quality does not suffer in the rush to produce more. It may be necessary to set both productivity and quality targets.

33.3 HOW TO INCREASE PRODUCTIVITY

Increase investment in modern equipment

With modern, sophisticated machines and better production processes, output per worker should improve. Many modern factories have very few production workers. Mechanisation and automation are everywhere. However, firms face financial constraints and should be cautious about assuming that mechanisation guarantees higher profits.

Many managers call for new technology when in fact more output can be squeezed out of the existing equipment. It may prove more efficient to run the machines for longer, spend more on careful maintenance to prevent breakdowns and discuss how to improve working practices. Firms can often achieve significant productivity gains without new equipment. This is the reason for the success of the *kaizen* approach taken by many firms. Important benefits can be achieved from what seem to be relatively small changes to the way the firm operates, rather than large scale investment in technology.

Improve the ability level of those at work

To increase productivity a firm may need to introduce more training for its employees. A skilled and well-trained workforce is likely to produce more and make fewer mistakes. Employees should be able to complete the task more quickly and will not need as much supervision or advice. They will be able to solve their own work-related problems and may be in a better position to contribute ideas on how to increase productivity further.

However, firms are often reluctant to invest in training because employees may leave and work for another firm once they have gained more skills. Training also involves higher costs in the short run, which the business may not be able to afford, and the actual training period may cause disruptions to the normal flow of work. There is also a danger that the training will not provide sufficient gains to justify the initial investment and so any spending in this area needs to be properly costed and researched. Simply training people for the sake of it is obviously of limited value. However, in general UK firms do not have a particularly good record in training and more investment here could probably have a significant effect on the UK's productivity levels.

It should also be remembered that elaborate training may not be necessary for a firm that recruits the right people. Great care must be taken in the selection process to find staff with the right skills and attitudes. A firm with a good reputation locally will find it much easier to pick the best people. This is why many firms take great care over their relations with the local community.

Improve employee motivation

Professor Herzberg once said that most people's idea of a fair day's work was less than half what they could give if they wanted to. The key to success, he felt, was to create the circumstances in which people wanted to give all they could to the job. His suggestions on how to provide job enrichment are detailed in Unit 34.

There is no doubt that motivation matters. A motivated sales force may achieve twice the sales level of an unmotivated one. A motivated computer technician may correct twice the computer faults of an unmotivated one. And, in both cases, overall business performance will be affected.

A-grade application

Motivation on the pitch

When Fulham Football Club appointed a new groundsman, few people even noticed. The fans had always been proud of the pitch, but newly appointed Frank Boahene was not impressed. He thought it needed a dramatic improvement before the start of the new season in August. With no time to reseed the pitch, he decided the best way to strengthen the grass was to cut it three times a day (!). Doing so, first thing in the morning and last thing in the afternoon was not a problem. But he also chose to 'pop back' from his home in Reading (an hour's drive) to do the third cut at 11.00 at night. Every day! That's motivation.

Figure 33.1

The role of management

The management's style and ability can have a significant impact on motivation and on how effectively resources are used. Good managers can bring about substantial productivity gains through well-organised work, the effective management of people and the coordination of resources. Bad managers can lead to wastage, inefficiency and low productivity.

Perhaps the key management role is to identify increasing productivity as a permanent objective. For example, the Japanese bulldozer company Komatsu set a target of a 10 per cent productivity increase every year, until the world-leading American producer Caterpillar had been overhauled. In many firms, productivity is not a direct target. The focus, day by day, is on production, not productivity. After all, it is production which ensures customer orders are fulfilled. An operations manager, faced with a 10 per cent increase in orders, may simply ask the workforce to do overtime. The work gets done; the workforce is happy to earn extra money; and it's all rather easy to do. It is harder by far to re-organise the workplace to make production more effective. Managers whose main focus is on the short term, therefore, think of production not productivity.

ISSUES FOR ANALYSIS

When answering a case study or essay it may be useful to consider the following points.

- Productivity is an important determinant of a firm's ability to compete in this country or overseas because it can have a significant impact on unit costs.
- High productivity does not in itself guarantee that a firm is competitive, as this also depends on other factors including the cost of materials, product quality, product design, good marketing and external factors such as the exchange rate.
- The productivity within an industry will depend on a combination of factors such as training, capital equipment and production techniques; the main single factor is the quality of management.

33.4 PEOPLE, PRODUCTIVITY AND PERFORMANCE – AN EVALUATION

Greater labour productivity can lead to greater efficiency and higher profitability. This is because, other things being equal, it lowers the labour cost per unit. However, productivity is only one factor that contributes to a firm's success. A firm must also ensure it produces a good quality product, that it is marketed effectively and that costs are controlled. There is little point increasing productivity by 20 per cent if at the same time you pay your staff 30 per cent more. Similarly, there is no point producing more if there is no actual demand. Higher productivity, therefore, contributes to better performance but needs to be accompanied by effective decision making throughout the firm.

The importance of productivity to a firm depends primarily on the level of value added involved. Top price perfumes such as Chanel have huge profit margins. Production costs are a tiny proportion of the selling price. Therefore a 10 per cent productivity increase might have only a marginal effect on profit and virtually none on the competitiveness of the brand. For mass market products in competitive markets, high productivity is likely to be essential for survival. A 5 per cent cost advantage might make all the difference. Therefore, when judging an appropriate recommendation for solving a business problem, a judgement is required as to whether boosting productivity is a top priority for the business concerned.

Key Terms

Labour productivity: output per worker.

Kaizen: a Japanese term meaning continuous improvement. Regular, small increases in productivity may achieve more (and be less disruptive) than major changes to working methods.

Rationalise: increase efficiency by cutting out unnecessary activities or resources (for example, staff cutbacks).

WORKBOOK

A REVISION QUESTIONS

(40 marks; 40 minutes)

1 What is meant by the term 'productivity'? (3)
2 Why may it be hard to measure the productivity of staff who work in service industries? (4)
3 How does productivity relate to labour costs per unit? (4)
4 Explain how a firm may be able to increase its employees' productivity. (4)
5 How can increased investment in machinery help to boost productivity? (3)
6 Identify two factors which help and two factors which limit your productivity as a student. (4)
7 Outline the likely effect of increased motivation on the productivity of a teacher. (5)
8 Calculate the change in productivity at BDQ Co (see Table 33.3) since last year. (4)

Table 33.3 Productivity at BDQ Co

	Output	Number of staff
Last year	32,000	50
This year	30,000	40

9 Explain how motivation and productivity may be linked. (4)
10 Explain how productivity can be linked to unit labour costs. (5)

B REVISION EXERCISES
B1 DATA RESPONSE

Productivity in recession

When the recession hit in 2008, businesses were surprisingly reluctant to make people redundant. So the fall in output affected the efficiency of production (that is, productivity). As output per worker fell, unit wage costs rose, even though wage increases were modest. Look carefully at the graph shown in Figure 33.2 before answering the questions.

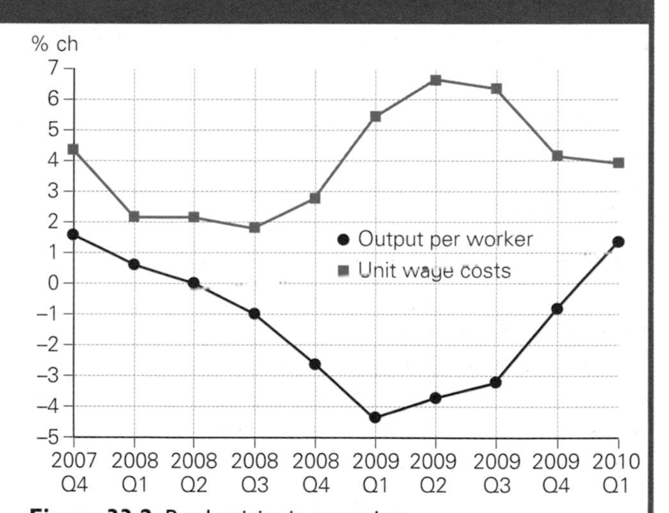

Figure 33.2 Productivity in recession
Source: National Statistics website: www.statistics.gov.uk

Questions

(30 marks; 35 minutes)

1 Explain how a fall in the productivity of UK firms could affect UK exports. (6)
2 Briefly explain why unit wage costs were stable in the first quarter (Jan to March) of 2010. (6)
3 Spartax Ltd produces widgets for washing machines. It chose to cut its workforce by 20 per cent in Autumn 2008 in response to a 10 per cent fall in its sales.
Explain how its productivity would be affected by this staff cut. (6)
4 Discuss the possible reasons why most UK firms were willing to allow productivity to fall during the recession instead of cutting back sharply on staff numbers. (12)

B2 CASE STUDY

Going potty

Farah Stewart was trying to explain the need to boost productivity to the employees at her ceramics factory, FS Ltd. Relations between Farah and her staff had not been good in recent years. The company was not doing well and she blamed the workers. 'On average you work 8 hours a day at £8 an hour and produce around 160 pots each. Meanwhile at Frandon, I am told, they produce 280 pots a day. Can't you see that this makes it cheaper for them and if things go on like this we'll be out of business? You need to work much harder to get our unit costs down! I know you are expecting to get a pay rise this year, but I cannot afford it until you produce more; then we'll think about it.'

Jeff Battersby, the spokesperson for the employees, was clearly annoyed by Farah's tone. 'Firstly Ms Stewart have you ever considered that if you paid us more we might produce more for you? I'm not surprised productivity is higher at Frandon – they get about £80 a day. There's no point demanding more work from us if you are not willing to pay for it – we're not slaves you know. If you paid us £10 an hour, like Frandon, I reckon we could increase productivity by 50 per cent. However that's not the only issue: they've got better equipment. It's not our fault if the kilns don't work half the time and take an age to heat up. Sort out the equipment and our pay and you'll soon see productivity improve. Why not ask us next time instead of jumping to conclusions?'

Questions

(60 marks; 60 minutes)

1 **a)** FS Ltd employs 50 pot makers whilst Frandon Ltd employs 30 people in production. Calculate the total output for each of the two companies. (4)
  b) With reference to FS Ltd and Frandon Ltd explain the difference between 'total output' and 'productivity'. (6)
2 **a)** Calculate the average labour cost per pot at FS Ltd if employees are paid £8 an hour and their daily output is 160 pots each. (4)
  b) What is the wage cost per pot at Frandon? (assume an 8 hour day) (3)
  c) Analyse the short- and long-term benefits to Frandon of its lower labour costs per unit. (12)
  d) Jeff Battersby claims that if the employees at FS Ltd. were paid £10 an hour their productivity would increase by 50 per cent. What would the unit wage cost be then? (5)
3 Would you recommend Farah increases the pay of her employees to £10 an hour? Justify your answer. (12)
4 Discuss the possible gains from involving employees in discussions about how to improve productivity. (14)

Motivation in theory

UNIT 34

One key theorist (Professor Herzberg) believes motivation occurs when people do something because they *want* to do it; others think of motivation as the desire to achieve a result. The difference between these two definitions is important and should become clear in this unit.

34.1 INTRODUCTION

A recent study by the Hay Group found that just 15 per cent of UK workers consider themselves 'highly motivated'. As many as 25 per cent say they're 'coasting' and 8 per cent admit to being 'completely demotivated'. In the same survey, employees felt they could be 45 per cent more productive if they were doing a job they loved, and 28 per cent more productive with better training. Poor management is part of the problem, as 28 per cent say they would be more productive with a better boss.

The Hay Group calculates that if the under-performance was tackled successfully, the value of UK output would rise by more than £350 billion a year. So motivation matters. This is why it merits a unit to itself and is the reason why many consider motivation theory to be the most important topic within Business Studies.

34.2 F W TAYLOR AND SCIENTIFIC MANAGEMENT

Although there were earlier pioneers, the starting point for the study of motivation is F W Taylor (1856–1917). As with most of the other influential writers on this subject, Taylor was American. His influence over the twentieth-century world has been massive. Much business practice in America, Europe, Japan and the former Communist countries is still rooted in his writing and work.

A recent biography of Taylor is titled *The One Best Way*; this sums up neatly Taylor's approach to management. He saw it as management's task to decide exactly how every task should be completed, then to devise the tools needed to enable the worker to achieve the task as efficiently as possible. This method is evident today in every McDonald's in the world. Fries are cooked at 175 degrees for exactly three minutes; then a buzzer tells employees to take them out and salt them. Throughout every McDonald's is a series of dedicated, purpose-built machines for producing milkshakes, toasting buns, squirting chocolate sauce, and much else. Today, 100 years after his most active period working in industry, F W Taylor would feel very much at home ordering a Big Mac.

So, what was Taylor's view of the underlying motivations of people at work? How did he make sure that the employees worked effectively at following 'the one best way' laid down by managers?

Taylor believed that people work for only one reason: money. He saw it as the task of the manager to devise a system that would maximise efficiency. This would generate the profit to enable the worker to be paid a higher wage. Taylor's view of human nature was that of 'economic man'. In other words, people were motivated only by the economic motive of self-interest. Therefore, a manager could best motivate a worker by offering an incentive (a 'carrot') or a threat (the 'stick'). Taylor can be seen as a manipulator, or even a bully, but he believed his methods were in the best interests of the employees themselves.

Taylor's influence stemmed less from his theories than his activities. He was a trained engineer who acted as a very early management consultant. His methods were as follows.

- Observe workers at work, recording and timing what they do, when they do it and how long they take over it (this became known as time and motion study).
- Identify the most efficient workers and see how they achieve greater efficiency.
- Break the task down into small component parts that can be done quickly and repeatedly.
- Devise equipment specifically to speed up tasks.
- Set out exactly how the work should be done in future; 'each employee', Taylor wrote, 'should receive every day clear-cut, definite instructions as to what he is to do and how he is to do it, and these instructions should be exactly carried out, whether they are right or wrong'.
- Devise a pay scheme to reward those who complete or beat tough output targets, but that penalises those

who cannot or will not achieve the **productivity** Taylor believed was possible; this pay scheme was called **piece rate** – no work, no pay.

As an engineer, Taylor was interested in practical outcomes, not in psychology. There is no reason to suppose he thought greatly about the issue of motivation. The effect of his ideas was profound, though. Long before the publication of his 1911 book *The Principles of Scientific Management*, Taylor had spread his managerial practices of careful measurement, monitoring and – above all else – control. Before Taylor, skilled workers chose their own ways of working and had varied, demanding jobs. After Taylor, workers were far more likely to have limited, repetitive tasks; and to be forced to work at the pace set by a manager or consultant engineer.

Among those influenced by Taylor was Henry Ford. His Model T was the world's first mass-produced motor car. By 1911 the Ford factory in Detroit, USA, was already applying Taylor's principles of high **division of labour**, purpose-built machinery and rigid management control. When Ford introduced the conveyor belt in 1913, he achieved the ultimate Taylorite idea: men's pace of work dictated by a mechanical conveyor belt, the speed of which was set by management.

Eventually workers rebelled against being treated like machines. **Trades union** membership thrived in factories run on Taylorite lines, as workers wanted to organise against the suffocating lives they were leading at work. Fortunately, in many western countries further developments in motivation theory pointed to new, more people-friendly approaches.

34.3 ELTON MAYO AND THE HUMAN RELATIONS APPROACH

Elton Mayo (1880–1949) was a medical student who became an academic with a particular interest in people in organisations. Although an Australian, he moved to America in 1923. Early in his career, his methods were heavily influenced by F W Taylor. An early investigation of a spinning mill in Pennsylvania identified one department with labour turnover of 250 per cent, compared to 6 per cent elsewhere in the factory. His Taylorite solution was to prescribe work breaks. These had the desired effect.

Mayo moved on to work at the Hawthorne plant of Western Electric Company in Chicago. His investigations there are known as the Hawthorne Experiments.

He was called in to Hawthorne to try to explain the findings of a previous test into the effects of lighting upon productivity levels. The lighting conditions for one work group had been varied, while those for another had been held constant. The surprise was that whatever was done to the lighting, production rose in *both* groups. This proved that there was more to motivation and efficiency than purely economic motives.

Between 1927 and 1932 Mayo conducted a series of experiments at Hawthorne. The first is known as the Relay Assembly Test. Six volunteer female assembly staff were separated from their workmates. A series of experiments was carried out. The results were recorded and discussed with the women. Every 12 weeks a new working method was tried. The alternatives included different:

- bonus methods, such as individual versus group bonuses
- rest periods
- refreshments
- work layout.

Before every change, the researchers discussed the new method fully with the operators. Almost without exception productivity increased with every change. At the end, the group returned to the original method (48-hour, 6-day week with no breaks) and output went up to its highest level yet! Not only that, but the women claimed they felt less tired than they had at the start.

The experiments had started rather slowly, with some resistance from the operatives. Progress became much more marked when one member of the group retired. She was replaced by a younger woman who quickly became the unofficial leader of the group.

Mayo's conclusions

Mayo drew the following conclusions from experiments:

- The women gained satisfaction from their freedom and control over their working environment.
- 'What actually happened was that six individuals became a team and the team gave itself wholeheartedly and spontaneously to cooperation in the experiment' (Mayo, 1949).
- Group norms (expectations of one another) are crucial and may be influenced more by informal than official group leaders.
- Communication between workers and managers influences morale and output.
- Workers are affected by the degree of interest shown in them by their managers; the influence of this upon motivation is known as 'the Hawthorne effect'.

The consequences of Mayo's work were enormous. He influenced many researchers and writers, effectively opening up the fields of industrial psychology and industrial sociology. Many academics followed Mayo's approach in what became known as the human relations school of management.

Businesses also responded to the implications of Mayo's work for company profitability and success. If teamwork, communications and managerial involvement were that important, firms reasoned that they needed an organisational structure to cope. In Taylor's era, the key person was the engineer. The winners from Mayo's work were personnel departments. They grew throughout America and Britain in the 1930s, 1940s and 1950s as companies tried to achieve the Hawthorne effect.

34.4 MASLOW AND THE HIERARCHY OF NEEDS

Abraham Maslow (1908–70) was an American psychologist, whose great contribution to motivation theory was the 'hierarchy of needs'. Maslow believed that everyone has the same needs, all of which can be organised as a hierarchy. At the base of the hierarchy are physical needs such as food, shelter and warmth. When unsatisfied, these are the individual's primary motivations. When employees earn enough to satisfy these needs, however, their motivating power withers away. Maslow said that 'It is quite true that humans live by bread alone – when there is no bread. But what happens to their desires when there is bread?' Instead of physical needs, people become motivated to achieve needs such as security and stability, which Maslow called the safety needs. In full, Maslow's hierarchy consisted of the elements listed in Table 34.1.

Ever since Maslow first put his theory forward (in 1940) writers have argued about its implications. Among the key issues raised by Maslow are the following.

- Do all humans have the same set of needs? Or are there some people who need no more from a job than money?
- Do different people have different degrees of need; for example, are some highly motivated by the need for power, while others are satisfied by social factors? If so, the successful manager would be one who can understand and attempt to meet the differing needs of her/his staff.
- Can anyone's needs ever be said to be fully satisfied? The reason the hierarchy diagram (see Figure 34.1) has an open top is to suggest that the human desire for achievement is limitless.

Maslow's work had a huge influence on the writers who followed him, especially McGregor and Herzberg. The hierarchy of needs is also used by academics in many subjects beyond Business Studies, notably Psychology and Sociology.

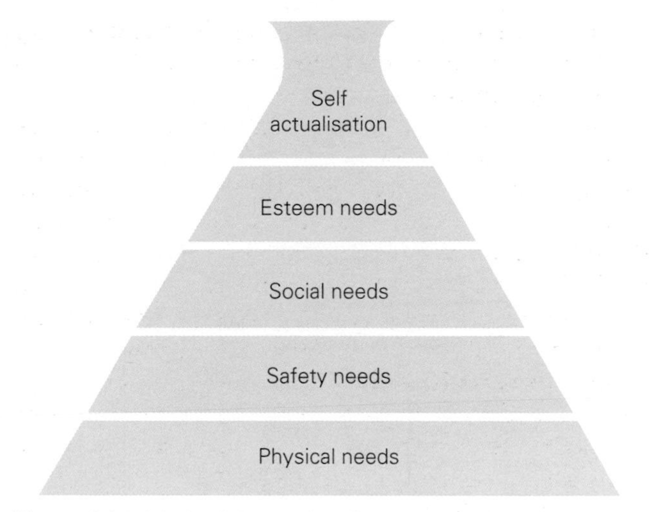

Figure 34.1 Maslow's hierarchy of needs

34.5 HERZBERG'S TWO FACTOR THEORY

The key test of a theory is its analytic usefulness. On this criterion, the work of Professor Fred Herzberg (1923–2000) is the strongest by far.

The theory stems from research conducted in the 1950s into factors affecting workers' **job satisfaction** and dissatisfaction. It was carried out on 200 accountants and engineers in Pennsylvania, USA. Despite the limited nature of this sample, Herzberg's conclusions remain influential to this day.

Herzberg asked employees to describe recent events that had given rise to exceptionally good feelings about their jobs, then probed for the reasons why. 'Five factors stand out as strong determiners of job satisfaction,' Herzberg wrote in 1966, 'achievement, recognition for achievement, the work itself, responsibility and advancement – the last three being of greater importance for a lasting change of attitudes.' He pointed out that each of these factors concerned the job itself, rather than issues such as pay or status. Herzberg called these five factors 'the motivators'.

Table 34.1 Maslow's hierarchy of needs: implications for business

Maslow's levels of human need	Business implications
Physical needs, e.g. food, shelter and warmth	Pay levels and working conditions
Safety needs, e.g. security, a safe structured environment, stability, freedom from anxiety	Job security, a clear job role/description, clear lines of accountability (only one boss)
Social needs, e.g. belonging, friendship, contact	Team working, communications, social facilities
Esteem needs, e.g. strength, self-respect, confidence, status and recognition	Status, recognition for achievement, power, trust
Self-actualisation, e.g. self-fulfilment; 'to become everything that one is capable of becoming,' wrote Maslow	Scope to develop new skills and meet new challenges, and to develop one's full potential

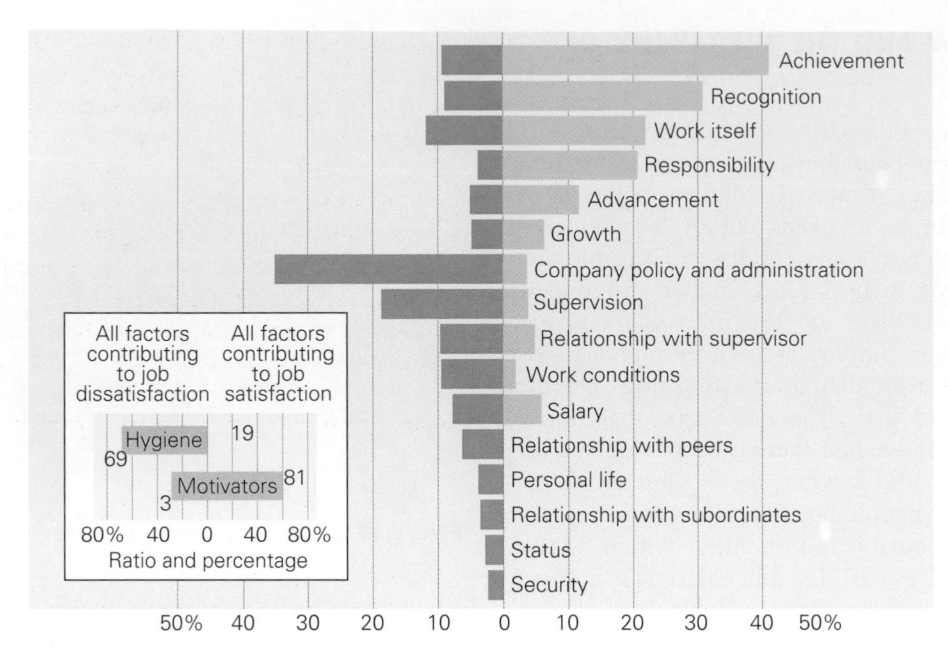

Figure 34.2 Comparison of satisfiers and dissatisfiers

The researchers went on to ask about events giving rise to exceptionally bad feelings about their jobs. This revealed a separate set of five causes. Herzberg stated that 'the major dissatisfiers were company policy and administration, supervision, salary, interpersonal relations and working conditions'. He concluded that the common theme was factors that 'surround the job', rather than the job itself. The name he gave these dissatisfiers was '**hygiene factors**'; this was because fulfilling them would prevent dissatisfaction, rather than causing positive motivation. Careful hygiene prevents disease; care to fulfil hygiene factors prevents job dissatisfaction.

To summarise: motivators have the power to create positive job satisfaction, but little downward potential; hygiene factors will cause job dissatisfaction unless they are provided for, but do not motivate. Importantly, Herzberg saw pay as a hygiene factor, not a motivator. So a feeling of being underpaid could lead to a grievance; but high pay would soon be taken for granted. This motivator/hygiene factor theory is known as the 'two factor theory' (see Table 34.2).

Movement and motivation

Herzberg was keen to distinguish between movement and motivation. Movement occurs when somebody does something; motivation is when they *want* to do something. This distinction is essential to a full understanding of Herzberg's theory. He did not doubt that financial incentives could be used to boost productivity: 'If you bully or bribe people, they'll give you better than average performance.' His worries about 'bribes' (carrots) were that they would never stimulate people to give of their best; people would do just enough to achieve the bonus. Furthermore, bribing people to work harder at a task they found unsatisfying would build up resentments, which might backfire on the employer.

Herzberg advised against payment methods such as piece rate. They would achieve movement, but by reinforcing worker behaviour, would make them inflexible and resistant to change. The salaried, motivated employee would work hard, care about quality and think about – even welcome – improved working methods.

Job enrichment

The reason why Herzberg's work has had such an impact on businesses is because he not only analysed motivation, he also had a method for improving it. The method is job enrichment, which he defined as

Table 34.2 Herzberg's two factor theory

Motivators (can create positive satisfaction)	Hygiene factors (can create job dissatisfaction)
Achievement	Company policy and administration (the rules, paperwork and red tape)
Recognition for achievement	Supervision (especially being over-supervised)
Meaningful, interesting work	Pay
Responsibility	Interpersonal relations (with supervisor, peers, or even customers)
Advancement (psychological, not just a promotion)	Working conditions

'giving people the opportunity to use their ability'. He suggested that, for a job to be considered enriched, it would have to contain the following.

A complete unit of work

People need to work not on just a small repetitive fragment of a job, but a full challenging task; Herzberg heaped scorn upon the 'idiot jobs' that resulted from Taylor's views on the merits of high division of labour.

Direct feedback

Wherever possible, a job should enable the worker to judge immediately the quality of what she or he has done; direct feedback gives the painter or the actor (or the teacher) the satisfaction of knowing exactly how well they have performed. Herzberg disliked systems that pass quality inspection off onto a supervisor: 'a man must always be held responsible for his own quality'. Worst of all, he felt, was annual appraisal, in which feedback is too long delayed.

Direct communication

For people to feel committed, in control and to gain direct feedback, they should communicate directly – avoiding the delays of communicating via a supervisor or a 'contact person'. In itself, it is hard to see the importance of this. For a student of Business Studies, it leads to an important conclusion: that communications and motivation are inter-related.

Conclusion

Herzberg's original research has been followed up in many different countries, including Japan, Africa and Russia. An article he wrote on the subject in the *Harvard Business Review* in 1968 (called 'Just one more time, how do you motivate employees') has sold more than 1 million reprinted copies. His main insight was to show that unless the job itself was interesting, there was no way to make working life satisfying. This led companies such as Volvo in Sweden and Toyota in Japan to rethink their factory layouts. Instead of individual workers doing simple, repetitive tasks, the drive was to provide more complete units of work. Workers were grouped into teams, focusing on significant parts of the manufacturing process, such as assembling and fitting the gearbox, and then checking the quality of their work. Job enrichment indeed. Some key quotes from Professor Herzberg are given in Table 34.3.

ISSUES FOR ANALYSIS

- In an exam context, the starting point is to select the most appropriate theory to answer a question. If a case study context suggested poor relations between management and workforce, Elton Mayo's would be very suitable. If motivation was weak, Herzberg's theory provides a comprehensive analysis.
- When applying a theory, the analysis is strengthened by using a questioning approach. Herzberg's theory is admirable, but it is not perfect. It provides insights, but not necessarily answers – and certainly not blueprints. A job enrichment programme might be highly effective in one situation, but a disappointment in another.
- This leads on to another key factor: the success of any new policies will depend hugely on the history of trust – or lack of it – in the workplace. Successful change in the factors involved in motivation may be very difficult and slow to achieve. There are no magic solutions.
- Accordingly, when a firm faces a crisis, changes in factors relating to motivation will rarely provide an answer. A crisis must be solved in the short term, but human motivation requires long-term strategies.

Table 34.3 Key quotes from Professor Herzberg

On the two factor theory	'Motivators and hygiene factors are equally important, but for different reasons'
On movement	'If you do something because you want a house or a Jaguar, that's movement. It's not motivation'
The risks of giving bonuses	'A reward once given becomes a right'
The importance of training	'The more a person can do, the more you can motivate them'
The importance of always treating staff fairly	'A remembered pain can lead to revenge psychology ... They'll get back at you some day when you need them'
On communication	'In industry, there's too much communication. And of course it's passive ... But if people are doing idiot jobs they really don't give a damn'
On participation	'When participation is suggested in terms of control over overall goals, it is usually a sham'

34.6 MOTIVATION IN THEORY – AN EVALUATION

Most managers assume they understand human motivation, but they have never studied it. As a result they may underestimate the potential within their own staff, or unthinkingly cause resentments that fester.

The process of managing people takes place in every part of every organisation. By contrast, few would need to know the financial concept of 'gearing' in their working lives. So lack of knowledge of motivation theory is particularly unfortunate and has exceptionally widespread effects. In some cases, ignorance leads managers to ignore motivation altogether; they tell themselves that control and organisation are their only concerns. Other managers may see motivation as important, but fail to understand its subtleties.

For these reasons, there is a case for saying that the concepts within this unit are the most important in the whole subject.

Key Terms

Division of labour: subdividing a task into a number of activities, enabling workers to specialise and therefore become very efficient at completing what may be a small, repetitive task.

Hygiene factors: 'everything that surrounds what you do in the job', such as pay, working conditions and social status; all are potential causes of dissatisfaction, according to Herzberg.

Job satisfaction: the sense of well-being and achievement that stems from a satisfying job.

Piece rate: paying workers per piece they produce (for example, £2 per pair of jeans made).

Productivity: output per person (that is, a measure of efficiency).

Trades union: an organisation that represents the interests of staff at the workplace.

FURTHER READING

Herzberg, F. (1959) *The Motivation to Work*. Wiley International.

Maslow, A. H. (1987) *Motivation and Personality*. HarperCollins (1st edn 1954).

Mayo, E. (1975) *The Social Problems of Industrial Civilisation*. Routledge (1st edn 1949).

WORKBOOK

A REVISION QUESTIONS

(35 marks; 35 minutes)

1. Which features of the organisation of a McDonald's could be described as Taylorite? (3)
2. Explain the meaning of the term 'economic man'. (3)
3. Explain how workers in a bakery may be affected by a change from salary to piece rate. (3)
4. Give a brief outline of Mayo's research methods at the Hawthorne plant. (4)
5. How may 'group norms' affect productivity at a workplace? (3)
6. Explain the meaning of the term 'the Hawthorne effect'. (2)
7. Which two levels of Maslow's hierarchy could be called 'the lower-order needs'? (2)
8. Describe in your own words why Maslow organised the needs into a hierarchy. (3)
9. State three business implications of Maslow's work on human needs. (3)
10. Herzberg believes pay does not motivate, but it is important. Why? (3)
11. How do motivators differ from hygiene factors? (3)
12. What is job enrichment? How is it achieved? (3)

B REVISION EXERCISES
B1 DATA RESPONSE

Look back at Figure 34.2. It shows the results of Herzberg's research into the factors that cause positive job satisfaction and those that cause job dissatisfaction. The length of the bars shows the percentage of responses. Their width indicates how likely the respondent was to say that the effect was long term.

Questions

(20 marks; 20 minutes)

1 Which of the factors had the least effect on satisfaction or dissatisfaction? (1)
2 One of Herzberg's objectives was to question whether good human relations were as important in job satisfaction as claimed by Elton Mayo. Do you think he succeeded? (6)
3 Responsibility had the longest-lasting effects on job satisfaction. Why may this be the case? (5)
4 Discuss which of the factors is the most important motivator. (8)

B2 CASE STUDY

Tania was delighted to get the bakery job and looked forward to her first shift. It would be tiring after a day at college, but £52 for eight hours on a Friday would guarantee good Saturday nights in future.

On arrival, she was surprised to be put straight to work, with no more than a mumbled: 'You'll be working packing machine B.' Fortunately, she was able to watch the previous shift worker before clocking-off time, and could get the hang of what was clearly a very simple task. As the 18.00 bell rang, the workers streamed out, but not many had yet turned up from Tania's shift. The conveyor belt started to roll again at 18.16.

As the evening wore on, machinery breakdowns provided the only, welcome, relief from the tedium and discomfort of Tania's job. Each time a breakdown occurred, a ringing alarm bell was drowned out by a huge cheer from the staff. A few joyful moments followed, with dough fights breaking out. Tania started to feel quite old as she looked at some of her workmates.

At the 22.00 meal break, Tania was made to feel welcome. She enjoyed hearing the sharp, funny comments made about the shift managers. One was dubbed 'Noman' because he was fat, wore a white coat and never agreed to anything. Another was called 'Turkey' because he strutted around, but if anything went wrong, got into a flap. It was clear that both saw themselves as bosses. They were not there to help or to encourage, only to blame.

Was the bakery always like this, Tania wondered? Or was it simply that these two managers were poor?

Questions

(25 marks; 30 minutes)

1 Analyse the working lives of the shift workers at the bakery, using Herzberg's two factor theory. (8)
2 If a managerial follower of Taylor's methods came into the factory, how might she or he try to improve the productivity level? (7)
3 Later on in this (true) story, Tania read in the local paper that the factory was closing. The reason given was 'lower labour productivity than at our other bakeries'. The newspaper grumbled about the poor attitudes of local workers. Consider the extent to which there is some justification in this view. (10)

UNIT 35

Motivation in practice

Assessing how firms try to motivate their staff and how successful these actions appear to be. In this context, companies take 'motivation' to mean enthusiastic pursuit of the objectives or tasks set out by the firm.

35.1 INTRODUCTION

There are four main variables that influence the **motivation** of staff in practice:

1 the financial reward systems
2 job design
3 empowering the employees
4 working in teams.

All four will be analysed with reference to the theories outlined in Unit 34.

Motivation: famous sayings

'The worst mistake a boss can make is not to say well done.' *John Ashcroft, British executive*

'Motivation is everything. You can do the work of two people, but you can't be two people. Instead, you have to inspire the next guy down the line and get him to inspire his people.' *Lee Iacocca, successful boss of Chrysler Motors*

'I have never found anybody yet who went to work happily on a Monday that had not been paid on a Friday.' *Tom Farmer, Kwik-Fit founder*

'Motivating people over a short period is not very difficult. A crisis will often do just that, or a carefully planned special event. Motivating people over a longer period of time, however, is far more difficult. It is also far more important in today's business environment.' *John Kotter, management thinker*

'My best friend is the one who brings out the best in me.' *Henry Ford, founder of Ford Motors*

Source: Stuart Crainer: *The Ultimate Book of Business Quotations*, Capstone Publishing.

35.2 FINANCIAL REWARD SYSTEMS

Piecework

Piecework means working in return for a payment per unit produced. The payment itself is known as piece rate. Pieceworkers receive no basic or shift pay, so there is no sick pay, holiday pay or company pension.

Piecework is used extensively in small-scale manufacturing; for example, of jeans or jewellery. Its attraction for managers is that it makes supervision virtually unnecessary. All the manager needs to do is operate a quality control system that ensures the finished product is worth paying for. Day by day, the workers can be relied upon to work fast enough to earn a living (or a good) wage.

Disadvantages of piecework

Piecework has several disadvantages to firms, however, including the following.

- Scrap levels may be high, if workers are focused entirely on speed of output.
- There is an incentive to provide acceptable quality, but not the best possible quality.
- Workers will work hardest when they want higher earnings (probably before Christmas and before their summer holiday); this may not coincide at all with seasonal patterns of customer demand.
- Worst of all is the problem of change; Herzberg pointed out that 'the worst way to motivate people is piece rate ... it reinforces behaviour'; focusing people on maximising their earnings by repeating a task makes them very reluctant to produce something different or in a different way (they worry that they will lose out financially).

Performance-related pay

Performance-related pay (PRP) is a financial reward to staff whose work is considered above average. It is used for employees whose work achievements cannot be assessed simply through numerical measures (such as units produced or sold). PRP awards are usually made after an appraisal process has evaluated the performance of staff during the year.

On the face of it, PRP is a highly attractive system for encouraging staff to work towards the organisation's objectives. The usual method is outlined below.

1 Establish targets for each member of staff/management at an appraisal interview.
2 At the end of the year, discuss the individual's achievements against those targets.

3 Those with outstanding achievements are given a Merit 1 pay rise or bonus worth perhaps 6 per cent of salary; others receive between 0 per cent and 6 per cent.

Lack of evidence for benefits of PRP

Despite the enthusiasm they have shown for it, employers have rarely been able to provide evidence of the benefits of PRP. Indeed the Institute of Personnel Management concluded in a report that:

'It was not unusual to find that organisations which had introduced merit pay some years ago were less certain now of its continued value ... it was time to move on to something more closely reflecting team achievement and how the organisation as a whole was faring.'

This pointed to a fundamental problem with PRP: rewarding individuals does nothing to promote teamwork. Furthermore, it could create unhealthy rivalry between managers, with each going for the same Merit 1 spot.

Other problems for PRP systems

Other problems for PRP systems include the following.

- *Perceived fairness/unfairness:* staff often suspect that those awarded the maximum are being rewarded not for performance but out of favouritism; this may damage working relations and team spirit.
- *Whether they have a sound basis in human psychology:* without question Professor Herzberg would be very critical of any attempt to influence work behaviour by financial incentives; a London School of Economics study of Inland Revenue staff found that only 12 per cent believed that PRP had raised motivation at work, while 76 per cent said it had not; Herzberg would approve of the researchers' conclusion that 'The current system has not succeeded in motivating staff to any significant degree, and may well have done the reverse.'

As the last point illustrates, a key assumption behind PRP is that the chance to be paid a bit more than other employees will result in a change in individual behaviour, in increased motivation to work. A survey for the government publication *Employment in Britain* found that 'pay incentives were thought important for hard work by fewer than one in five, and for quality standards by fewer than one in ten.

Why do firms continue with PRP?

So why do firms continue to pursue PRP systems? There are two possible reasons:

1 to make it easier for managers to manage/control their staff (using a carrot instead of a stick)
2 to reduce the influence of collective bargaining and therefore trades unions.

A-grade application

Performance-related pay does not encourage performance

The clue ought to be in the name. Performance-related pay is pay for performance, and the better performance you turn in and the harder you work the more you will get to take home. Except, academics are now suggesting, more often than not the opposite may be the case.

New research by the London School of Economics has argued that, far from encouraging people to strive to reach the heights, performance-related pay often does the opposite and encourages people to work less hard.

An analysis of 51 separate experimental studies of financial incentives in employment relations found what the school has described as 'overwhelming evidence' that these incentives could reduce an employee's natural inclination to complete a task and derive pleasure from doing so.

The findings are, of course, deeply controversial, given the depths of anger still felt by many over the role of performance-related pay in causing or contributing to the current economic crisis.

'We find that financial incentives may indeed reduce intrinsic motivation and diminish ethical or other reasons for complying with workplace social norms such as fairness,' argued Dr Bernd Irlenbusch, from the LSE's Department of Management.

'As a consequence, the provision of incentives can result in a negative impact on overall performance,' he added.

Companies therefore needed to be aware that the provision of performance-related pay could result in a net reduction of motivation across a team or organisation, he suggested.

Source: www.management-issues.com, 25 June 2009

Profit sharing

A different approach to financial incentives is to provide staff with a share of the firm's annual profit. This puts staff in the same position as shareholders as, in effect, they are paid an annual dividend. This offers clear psychological benefits, as outlined below.

- Staff can come to see profit positively. Before, they may have regarded it as an unfair way of diverting pay from their own pockets to those of shareholders.
- Herzberg and other theorists warn that financial incentives distort behaviour. For example, if you pay a striker £500 per goal, 'wave goodbye' to passing in the penalty area. Profit sharing, however, is more of a financial reward than an incentive. It may encourage people to work harder or smarter, but should not stop them working as a team.
- If paid to staff in the form of free shares, the employees may develop a strong sense of identity with the company and its fortunes.

Profit sharing can represent a substantial bonus on top of regular earnings. For instance, the John Lewis Partnership pays an annual bonus that can be worth

plenty of others used to dealing with the job. Therefore there is no disruption. Team working also gives scope for motivating influences such as job enrichment and quality circles.

Professor Charles Handy suggests in his book *Inside Organisations* that 'a good team is a great place to be, exciting, stimulating, supportive, successful. A bad team is horrible, a sort of human prison.' It is true that the business will not benefit if the group norms within the team discourage effort. Nevertheless, team working has proved successful in many companies in recent years. Companies such as Rolls-Royce, Trebor, Rover and Komatsu have reported major improvements in absenteeism and labour turnover, and significant shifts in workforce attitudes.

A-grade application

Motivation at the RNLI

How do you motivate 4,500 unpaid staff, especially when you require them to put you before everything else, including family? This is the task of Ali Peck, human resources director for the RNLI, the Royal National Lifeboat Institution. If a boat capsizes in stormy weather, the lifeboatmen must stop whatever they are doing, put out to sea, and risk their own lives to save someone else's.

Peck's task is made more difficult because the 230 lifeboat stations are, of course, dotted around the coast. So the only way to bring people together is through training. Every lifeboatman has to go through a retraining programme every three to five years. This takes place at a purpose-built college. This is also where new volunteers are trained. Peck explains that the RNLI spends 50 per cent more per head on training than any comparable organisation. It is crucial, because if the volunteers drifted away from the job, the organisation would fold. In the case of the RNLI, the staff motivations come from the teamwork and from a real sense of personal achievement and pride. The lifeboatmen are certainly not motivated by money.

ISSUES FOR ANALYSIS

The key ways to analyse motivation in practice are as follows.

- To select and apply the relevant motivation theory to the method being considered: good analysis of methods such as performance related pay or job rotation require a critical eye.
- To question the publicly stated motives of the organisation or manager concerned: businesses can be very loose in their use of words such as motivation or empowerment. They can be euphemisms for tougher targets and greater pressure. If the recent history of a firm makes employees sceptical of the goodwill of managers, students should be equally questioning.
- As John Kotter has said, 'Motivating people over a short period is not very difficult.' The key test of a new approach to motivation is over a two- to five-year period, not the early months of a new initiative. So always consider the timescale.

35.6 MOTIVATION IN PRACTICE – AN EVALUATION

There are many aspects of business studies that point solely towards money. How profitable is this price or that? What is the forecast net cash flow for April? And so on. In such circumstances it is understandable that human implications may be forgotten. A high price for an AIDS cure may be profitable, but life-threatening to those who cannot afford the medicine. April's positive cash flow may be achieved only by sacking temporary staff.

When covering motivation in practice, there is little excuse for ignoring the implications for people. Exaggerated commissions or performance-related pay can lead sales staff to oversell goods or services, which may cause customers huge difficulties later on, such as cosmetic surgery or questionable investments. Also, within the workplace, serious problems can arise: bullying to 'motivate' staff into working harder, or creating a culture of overwork which leads to stress.

Fortunately, there are many businesses in which the management of motivation is treated with respect: companies which know that quick fixes are not the answer. Successful motivation in the long term is a result of careful job design, employee training and development, honesty and trust. It may be possible to supplement this with an attractive financial reward scheme, but money will never be a substitute for motivation.

Key Terms

Division of labour: subdividing a job into small, repetitive fragments of work.

Group norms: the types of behaviour and attitude seen as normal within a group.

***Kaizen* (continuous improvement):** moving productivity and product quality forward in regular, small steps.

Motivation: to Professor Herzberg, it means doing something because you want to do it; most business leaders think of it as prompting people to work hard.

Zero defects: production that is right first time, therefore requiring no reworking; this saves time and money.

FURTHER READING

Charles Handy (1990) *Inside Organisations,* BBC Books.

WORKBOOK

A REVISION QUESTIONS

(40 marks; 40 minutes)

1. 'Job design is the key to motivation.' Outline one reason why this may be true, and one reason why it may not. (4)
2. Look at the famous saying by Lee Iacocca on page 202. Explain in your own words what he meant by this. (3)
3. How *should* a manager deal with a mistake made by a junior employee? (4)
4. State three reasons why job enrichment should improve staff motivation. (3)
5. Distinguish between job rotation and job enrichment. (4)
6. How does 'empowerment' differ from 'delegation'? (4)
7. Identify three advantages to an employee of working in a team. (3)
8. State two advantages and two disadvantages of offering staff performance-related pay. (4)
9. What could be the implications of providing a profit share to senior managers but not to the workforce generally? (5)
10. What problems may result from a manager bullying staff to 'motivate' them? (6)

B REVISION EXERCISES
B1 DATA RESPONSE

In July 2010 Channel 4 showed a programme called 'Undercover Boss'. The chief executive of hotel chain 'Best Western' grew a tatty beard, left his suit at home, and worked on the shop floor for a week. He saw some awful things, but was delighted by breakfast supervisor Leona at the Castle Green hotel in the Lake District. Even though she had to work hard, at quite a low wage, she was welcoming, warm and enthusiastic. Each breakfast service can involve 120 breakfasts in three hours, which means intensive, pressured work. Yet she found time for all 'her' staff – and for the customers. When asked why, she said: 'They're so good to you here. You can have an overnight stay, and leisure club membership.' It was clear that she loved working there. Unsurprisingly, the first entry on the online hotel site 'Tripadvisor' suggested that 'the hotel (Castle Green) must be one of the friendliest in the country'.

Questions

(25 marks; 30 minutes)

1. Why do some managers assume that working people are motivated by money? (6)
2. Analyse two possible reasons why Leona is so well motivated. (8)
3. Evaluate the likely business benefits to the Castle Green hotel of having a well-motivated staff. (11)

B2 ACTIVITY

Write a questionnaire for self-completion by full-time employees. Your research objectives are to discover:

- whether there are any policies in place for encouraging workplace involvement/consultation
- whether job enrichment or job rotation measures exist (and what their effect is)
- how your respondents would describe the workplace culture
- whether there are any financial bonuses available, such as piece rate or performance-related pay, and what is their effect on motivation
- how highly motivated they feel themselves to be
- how highly motivated they believe their colleagues are.

This questionnaire should be conducted with at least ten respondents. It is preferable for the questionnaire to be conducted face to face, but if that is not possible, self-completion is acceptable.

When the research is completed, analyse the results carefully and write a summary of them in report form.

Leadership and management styles

UNIT 36

Management involves getting things done through other people. Leadership, at its best, means inspiring staff to achieve demanding goals. According to Peter Drucker, a manager does things right; a leader does the right thing.

36.1 INTRODUCTION TO LEADERSHIP STYLES

The way in which managers deal with their employees is known as their management style. For example, some managers are quite strict with workers. They always expect deadlines to be met and targets to be hit. Others are more relaxed and understanding. If there is a good reason why a particular task has not been completed by the deadline, they will be willing to accept this and give the employee more time. Although the way in which everyone manages will vary slightly from individual to individual, their styles can be categorised under three headings: autocratic, democratic and paternalistic. See Table 36.1.

Autocratic managers

Autocratic managers are authoritarian: they tell employees what to do and do not listen much to what workers themselves have to say. Autocratic managers know what they want doing and how they want it done. They tend to use one-way, top-down communication. They give orders to workers and do not want much feedback.

Democratic managers

Democratic managers, by comparison, like to involve their workers in decisions. They tend to listen to employees' ideas and ensure people contribute to the discussion. Communication by democratic managers tends to be two-way. Managers put forward an idea and employees give their opinion. A democratic manager would regularly delegate decision-making power to junior staff.

The delegation of authority, which is at the heart of democratic leadership, can be approached in one of two main ways: management by objectives and laissez faire.

Management by objectives

In this situation the leader agrees clear goals with staff, provides the necessary resources, and allows day-to-day decisions to be made by the staff in question; this approach was advocated by management guru Peter Drucker and by Douglas McGregor (see below) in his support for what he called the Theory Y approach to management.

Laissez-faire

Meaning let it be, this occurs when managers are so busy, or so lazy, that they do not take the time to ensure that junior staff know what to do or how to do it. Some people may respond very well to the freedom to decide on how to spend their working lives; others may become frustrated. It is said that Bill Gates, in the early days of Microsoft, hired brilliant students and told them

Table 36.1 Assumptions and approaches of the three types of leader

	Democratic	Paternalistic	Autocratic
Style derived from:	belief in Maslow's higher-order needs or in Herzberg's motivators	Mayo's work on human relations and Maslow's lower- and middle-order needs	a Taylorite view of staff
Approach to staff	Delegation of authority	Consultation with staff	Orders must be obeyed
Approach to staff remuneration	Salary, perhaps plus employee shareholdings	Salary plus extensive fringe benefits	Payment by results, e.g. piece rate
Approach to human resource management	Recruitment and training based on attitudes and teamwork	Emphasis on training and appraisal for personal development	Recruitment and training based on skills; appraisal linked to pay

no more than to create brilliant software. Was this a laissez-faire style or management by objectives? Clearly the dividing line can be narrow.

Paternalistic managers

A paternalistic manager thinks and acts like a father. He or she tries to do what is best for their staff/children. There may be consultation to find out the views of the employees, but decisions are made by the head of the 'family'. This type of manager believes employees need direction but thinks it is important that they are supported and cared for properly. Paternalistic managers are interested in the security and social needs of staff. They are interested in how workers feel and whether they are happy in their work. Nevertheless, it is quite an autocratic approach.

36.2 McGREGOR'S THEORY X AND Y

In the 1950s Douglas McGregor undertook a survey of managers in America and identified two styles of management, which he labelled Theory X and Theory Y (see Table 36.2). Theory X managers tend to distrust their subordinates; they believe employees do not really enjoy their work and that they need to be controlled. In McGregor's own words, many managers believe that 'The average human being has an inherent dislike of work and will avoid it if he can.' Note that McGregor is not putting this forward as a theory about workers, but about managers. In other words, Theory X is about the view managers have of their workforce.

Theory Y managers, by comparison, believe that employees do enjoy work and that they want to contribute ideas and effort. A Theory Y manager is, therefore, more likely to involve employees in decisions and give them greater responsibility. The managerial assumptions identified by McGregor as Theory Y included those set out below.

It is clear that Theory Y managers would be inclined to adopt a democratic leadership style. Their natural approach would be to delegate authority to meet specific objectives.

Table 36.2 Theory X versus Theory Y managers

Theory X managers ***believe:***	**Theory Y managers** ***believe:***
Employees dislike work and will avoid it if they can	Putting some effort into work is as natural as play or rest; employees want to work
Employees prefer to be directed, want to avoid responsibility and have little ambition	Employees want responsibility provided there are appropriate rewards
Employees need to be controlled and coerced	Employees are generally quite creative

The Theory X approach is likely to be self-fulfilling. If you believe people are lazy, they will probably stop trying. Similarly, if you believe workers dislike responsibility, and fail to give them a chance to develop, they will probably stop showing interest in their work. They will end up focusing purely on their wage packet because of the way you treat them.

In his book *The Human Side of Enterprise,* McGregor drew upon the work of Maslow and Herzberg. It need be no surprise that there are common features to the theories of these three writers. McGregor's unique

Managerial assumptions identified by McGregor as Theory Y

'Commitment to objectives is a function of the rewards associated with their achievement.'

'The average human being learns, under proper conditions, not only to accept but to seek responsibility.'

'The capacity to exercise a relatively high degree of imagination, ingenuity and creativity in the solution of organizational problems is widely, not narrowly, distributed in the population.'

McGregor, D. (1987) *The Human Side of Enterprise*. Penguin Books (first published 1960).

A-grade application

Liverpool Football Club

On 19 February 2008, Liverpool manager Rafa Benitez was under intense pressure. A bright start to the season had descended into patchy league form and an embarrassing FA cup defeat to Barnsley. Now it was make or break, with a Champions League game against the mighty Inter Milan. A defeat would surely lead to a Benitez resignation; a victory would give a small amount of breathing space (until the second leg, at least).

Among Liverpool supporters there had always been faith in Benitez, and criticism of the club's American owners, but this match would be a huge test of leadership. Could he inspire the players to give everything for him and for the club?

Unlike the Premiership's best managers, Wenger and Ferguson, Benitez had always seemed rather distant. Wenger and Ferguson practise a management style that is simultaneously paternalistic and autocratic. Benitez seemed only autocratic, making decisions on team selection that baffled everyone, yet never feeling the need to explain.

Cometh the hour, cometh the man?

(Ninety minutes after this was written, Liverpool had won 2–0 and Rafa was the hero. But within two years he was fired, after repeated disappointments on the field.)

contribution was to set issues of industrial psychology firmly in the context of the management of organisations. So whereas Herzberg's was a theory of motivation, McGregor's concerned styles of management (and thereby leadership).

So, which is the 'right' approach? Clearly a Theory Y manager would be more pleasant and probably more interesting to work for. A Theory X approach can work, however, and is especially likely to succeed in a business employing many part-time, perhaps student workers, or in a situation where a business faces a crisis.

36.3 CHARISMATIC LEADERSHIP

Gordon Brown is a highly intelligent man, whose leadership (as Chancellor) of the British economy between 1997 and 2006 was brilliant. Yet he had no charisma; people were not inspired by him or warmed to him. He therefore had an enormous difficulty in communicating his ideas in a way that made people want to follow his lead. When he became Prime Minister in 2007, his performance was largely disastrous. There is a strong case for saying, therefore, that personal charisma is an important quality in a leader.

Yet it is important to remember that some charismatic historical leaders have led people to disaster, such as Napoleon and Hitler. Perhaps some charisma is good, but too much is dangerous. In Britain, the most charismatic recent leader was BP's Lord Browne. On 25 July 2006, the *Guardian* ran a leader article that began 'Lord Browne, the chief executive of the BP group, is the nearest thing British business has to a rock star.' The paper went on to describe Richard Branson as a 'mere pygmy' compared with the leader of 'one of the world's largest companies'. The *Guardian* also said that 'the 96,000 people employed by BP around the world all have cause to admire Lord Browne's achievements'. Within six months Lord Browne had resigned from BP in a personal scandal. Those looking back today at Lord Browne's leadership are largely critical, especially of the company's approach to safety and the environment.

Some famous saying about leadership are given below.

Leadership: famous sayings

'As for the best leaders, the people do not notice their existence. The next best, the people honour and praise. The next, the people fear; and the next, the people hate ... When the best leader's work is done the people say, "We did it ourselves."' *Lao-Tsu, quoted in Townsend, R. and Joseph, M.,* Further up the Organisation

'... the capacity to create a compelling vision and translate it into action and sustain it'. *Warren Bennis*

'Leadership is a potent combination of strategy and character. But if you must be without one, be without the strategy.' *General Norman Schwarzkopf, US soldier*

'You do not lead by hitting people over the head – that's assault, not leadership.' *Dwight Eisenhower, US President*

Source: Stuart Crainer (1997) *The Ultimate Book of Business Quotations*, Capstone Publishing

36.4 WHAT IS THE BEST STYLE OF LEADERSHIP?

Each style of management can work well in different situations. If there is a crisis, for example, people often look for a strong leader to tell them what to do. Imagine that sales have unexpectedly fallen by 50 per cent, causing uncertainty, even panic, within the organisation. The management needs to quickly take control and put a plan into action. An autocratic style might work well at this moment. In a stable situation where employees are trained and able to do their work successfully, a more democratic leadership style might be more appropriate. It is often said that countries elect very different types of leaders when there is a threat of war or economic instability than when the country is doing well. Similarly, think about how people react when they are learning to drive. For the first few lessons they are uncertain about what to do and are grateful to be told. Once they have passed their test and have driven for several years, they will no doubt resent anyone telling them how to drive better!

The best style of management at any moment will depend on an enormous range of factors such as the personalities and abilities of the manager, and the workers, and the nature of the task. Imagine a confident manager who knows her job well but is faced with an unusually difficult problem. If the staff are well trained and capable, the manager would probably ask for ideas on what to do next. If, however, the manager was faced with a fairly routine problem she would probably just tell the employees what to do because there would be no need for discussion.

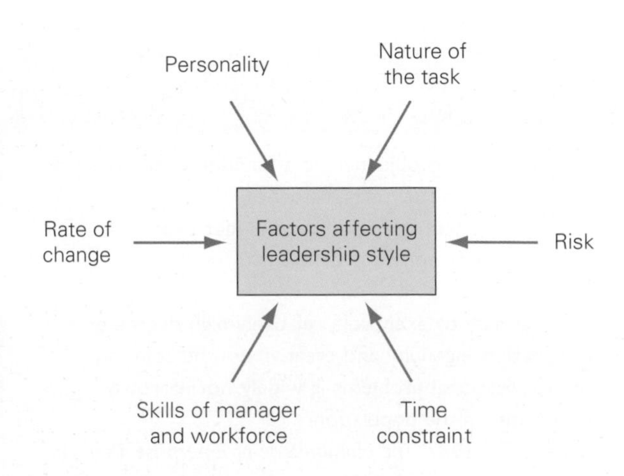

Figure 36.1 Factors affecting leadership style

A manager's style should, therefore, change according to the particular situation and the people involved. It will also vary with the time and degree of risk involved. If a decision has to be made urgently and involves a high degree of risk, the manager is likely to be quite autocratic. If there is plenty of time to discuss matters and only a low chance of it going wrong, the style may well be more democratic.

36.5 DOES THE STYLE OF MANAGEMENT MATTER?

The way in which a manager deals with his or her colleagues can have a real impact on their motivation and how effectively they work. An experienced workforce that is used to being involved in decisions may resent a manager who always tries to tell them what to do. This might lead to a reduction in the quality of their work, a fall in productivity and an increase in labour turnover. If, however, these employees were involved in decision making, the firm could gain from better ideas and a more highly motivated workforce. This does not mean that everyone wants to be involved, or indeed that it is appropriate, as employees may lack the necessary training or experience. Therefore, a democratic approach may simply mean that it takes longer for management to reach the decision it was going to make anyway.

What is the most common style of management?

The style of management people adopt depends on many factors, such as their personality, the particular circumstances at the time and the culture of the organisation. Although we have discussed three main styles, the actual approach of most managers is usually a combination of all of them, depending on the task or the nature of the situation. If an order has to be completed by tomorrow and time is short, for example, most managers are likely to be autocratic to make sure it gets done. If, however, there is plenty of time available the manager may be more democratic. No one is completely autocratic or completely democratic; it is simply a question of degree. However, some managers do tend to be more autocratic than others. This often depends on their own experiences (What was their boss like? What worked well when they were being trained?) and their personality (Do they like to be in control of everything? Are they willing to delegate? Do they value the opinions of others?).

In general, the move has been towards a more democratic style of management in the UK in recent years. This is probably because employees expect more from work than they did in the past. They are better educated, have a higher basic standard of living and want more than just money in return for their efforts. Having satisfied their lower-level needs they are now looking to satisfy their higher-level needs. The growth of democratic management and greater participation has also increased with the move towards lean production and the emphasis on techniques such as total quality management (TQM). These methods of production require much more involvement on the part of employees than in the past. Employees are given control over their own quality, given the authority to make decisions over the scheduling of work and are expected to contribute ideas on how to improve the way they are working. This approach requires much more trust in employees than was common many years ago. It has to be matched with a more democratic leadership style.

ISSUES FOR ANALYSIS

Management style can have a significant impact on the way people work. By adopting the right approach employees are likely to be more motivated and show greater commitment. Therefore, effective analysis of leadership should be rooted in the theories of writers such as Mayo and Herzberg.

- The 'correct' management style will depend on factors such as the task, the people involved and the amount of risk. There is no one style that is always appropriate. Therefore the context of the business case is always relevant.
- It may not be easy for managers to change their style. There may be situations in which managers should be more democratic; this does not necessarily mean they will be. Effective management training could be a useful way to persuade managers to be flexible.
- There is some debate about the extent to which you can train people to become effective managers or leaders. One extreme view is that good managers and leaders are born that way; if this is true, companies have to put their resources into finding the right sort of person. It is more likely that a good leader is the result of a combination of training and personal characteristics.

36.6 LEADERSHIP AND MANAGEMENT STYLES – AN EVALUATION

All firms seek effective managers. Good managers make effective use of the firm's resources and motivate staff; they provide vision and direction, and are therefore a key element of business success. Look at any successful company and you will usually find a strong management team. The problem is knowing what it is that makes a good manager and what is the 'best' management style. Even if we thought we knew the best style, could we train anyone to adopt this approach, or does it depend on their personality?

There are, of course, no easy answers to such questions. The 'right' style of management will depend on the particular circumstances and the nature of the task, and while it is possible to help someone to develop a particular style it will also depend on the individual's personality. As employees have benefited from a higher standard of living in the UK, and have higher expectations of work, managers have generally had to adopt a more democratic style in order to motivate people. However, there are plenty of autocratic managers who also succeed.

FURTHER READING

McGregor, D. (1987) *The Human Side of Enterprise.* Penguin Books.

Crainer, Stuart (1997) *The Ultimate Book of Business Quotations*, Capstone Publishing.

Key Terms

Autocratic manager: autocratic managers keep most of the authority to themselves; they do not delegate much or share information with employees. Autocratic, or authoritarian, managers tend to tell employees what to do.

Democratic manager: democratic managers take the views of their subordinates into account when making decisions. Managers discuss what needs to be done and employees are involved in the decision.

Paternalistic manager: a paternalistic manager believes he or she knows what is best for employees. Paternalistic managers tend to tell employees what to do, but will often explain their decisions. They are also concerned about the social needs of employees.

WORKBOOK

A REVISION QUESTIONS

(40 marks; 40 minutes)

1 Distinguish between autocratic and paternalistic management. (4)
2 Identify two features of democratic management. (2)
3 Outline one advantage and one disadvantage of an autocratic management approach. (4)
4 Distinguish between McGregor's Theory X and Theory Y. (4)
5 Why is it 'clear that Theory Y managers would be inclined to adopt a democratic leadership style'? (4)
6 Is there one correct leadership style for running a football team or a supermarket chain? (4)
7 Explain why autocratic managers may be of more use in a crisis than democratic ones. (4)
8 Explain a circumstance in which an authoritarian approach to leadership may be desirable. (4)
9 Many managers claim to have a democratic style of leadership. Often, their subordinates disagree. Outline two ways of checking the actual leadership style of a particular manager. (4)
10 Analyse the leadership style adopted by your teacher/tutor. (6)

B REVISION EXERCISES
B1 DATA RESPONSE

Leading Tesco's rise

Sir Terry Leahy became Tesco's Chief Executive in 1997. He stepped down in early 2011. In those 14 years he built Tesco into the world's third largest grocer. An article in *Management Today* once probed him on his approach to leadership.

> When you meet Leahy, you're not confronted with some huge presence ... Blink and you would miss him.
>
> What's his leadership style? 'I spend a lot of my time working on how I manage ...'. He meets with his executive committee every Monday and Wednesday morning for two hours, but what makes Leahy different is the extraordinary degree to which he chats with junior staff and absorbs their views, and the attention he pays to customers.
>
> In Leahy's Tesco, the two – staff and customer – have become blurred. Tesco, he says, has always prided itself on being an 'egalitarian organisation'. It's a philosophy he's scrupulously followed. 'There are only six levels between me and a check-out assistant.' Every member of staff has the opportunity to train and rise up the ladder. This year, 10,000 Tesco staff will undergo training to move upwards.
>
> 'There's no officer class at Tesco, we don't have a graduate elite intake, there's no fast-track.' So speaks the chief who followed a girlfriend to London, got a casual job stacking shelves in the local Tesco and never left. There can't be a store he hasn't visited, a job he doesn't know.
>
> The people he started out with back then in 1979 are his friends still today, many of them at senior levels in the business. 'I must have spoken to thousands of staff – I've grown up with many of them,' he says.
>
> In June, he went to a store in Royston and mucked in

as a general assistant. Come on, this sort of thing – it's all for show, isn't it? 'Not at all, I enjoy it, I find it very satisfying. I'm learning as well. I want a better understanding of how these jobs are done.' Leahy makes all his senior staff do it. Last year, 1,000 store managers worked in other stores and 1,000 staff from head office did the same.

Source: 'The MT Interview: Sir Terry Leahy', Chris Blackhurst, *Management Today*, 1 February 2004

Questions

(25 marks; 30 minutes)

1 Analyse how Terry Leahy's approach compares with that of a charismatic leader. (6)
2 Explain which leadership style is closest to (Sir) Terry Leahy's leadership of Tesco. (8)
3 Discuss whether it is a good use of senior managers' time to spend a day working on the shop floor. (11)

B2 ASSIGNMENT

An investigation into a leader

1 Arrange to interview an employee. Preferably this person should be a full-timer who has worked for at least a year. The employee could be a manager but should not be a director.
2 Your objective is to gain a full understanding of the leadership style prevailing at the employee's workplace, and the style employed by the individual's own manager.
3 Devise your own series of questions in advance, but make sure to include the following themes.
   a) How open are communications within the business?
   b) Are staff encouraged to apply a questioning or critical approach?
   c) Are there any forums for discussion or debate on important policy issues affecting staff?
   d) What does the organisational hierarchy look like? Where is your employee on that diagram? How powerful or powerless does she or he feel?
   e) How exactly does the employee's boss treat him or her? Is there delegation? Is there consultation? How effective is communication between the two of them?

Write at least 600 words summarising your findings and drawing conclusions about how well the experience conforms to the leadership theory dealt with in this unit.

C ESSAY QUESTIONS

(40 marks each)

1 'A good leader can always turn an ineffective business into a successful one.' To what extent can good management make a difference to the success of a firm?
2 'Management is no longer about leading others; it is about working with them.' Critically assess this view.
3 Consider the view that autocratic management has no place in today's business world.
4 'Good managers are born, not made.' Discuss this view.

Organisational structure

UNIT 37

Organisational structure is the formal and systematic way the management of a business is organised. When presented as a diagram, it shows the departmental functions and who is answerable to whom.

37.1 INTRODUCTION

As organisations became larger and more complex, early management thinkers such as F W Taylor and H Fayol considered how to structure an organisation. Both saw the function of organisations as converting inputs, such as money, materials, machines and people, into output. Therefore, designing an organisation was like designing a machine, the objective being to maximise efficiency. Early managers wanted to be told the best way to manage. And the organisational structure which would work best.

Taylor and Fayol based their thoughts largely on the way an army is organised. The key features of the hierarchy would be:

- To break the organisation up into divisions with a common purpose: in business, this was usually the business functions: marketing, finance and so on
- Every individual would answer to one person: their **line manager**
- No manager would be overloaded with too many subordinates, so the **span of control** was kept low
- To achieve low spans of control, it was necessary to have many management layers. Examples of management layers are shown in Table 37.1.

Table 37.1 Examples of management layers

Military	Business
Captain	Senior manager
Lieutenant	Manager
Sergeant	Team leader
Corporal	Supervisor
Foot-soldier	Shop-floor worker

37.2 THE GROWING BUSINESS

In the early stages of a new business, there are often only one or two people involved. When the business is so small the day-to-day tasks are carried out by the owner/s. It is not necessary to have a formal organisation structure as communication and coordination will be carried out on an informal, face-to-face basis. However, as the business grows and more people become involved, the firm will need to develop a more formal organisational structure. This will show the roles, responsibilities and relationships of each member of the firm. This is often illustrated through an organisational chart. This is a diagram that shows the links between people and departments within the firm. They also show communication flows/channels, lines of authority and layers of hierarchy. Each of these terms will be explained later in the chapter.

When Matteo Pantani founded Scoop ice cream in Covent Garden in 2007, he only employed part-time staff at the counter to serve the ice cream and take the money. Matteo made the ice cream and ran the business. He did not need to think about a 'hierarchy' or a 'structure'. But the organisational structure that existed in 2007 is shown in Figure 37.1.

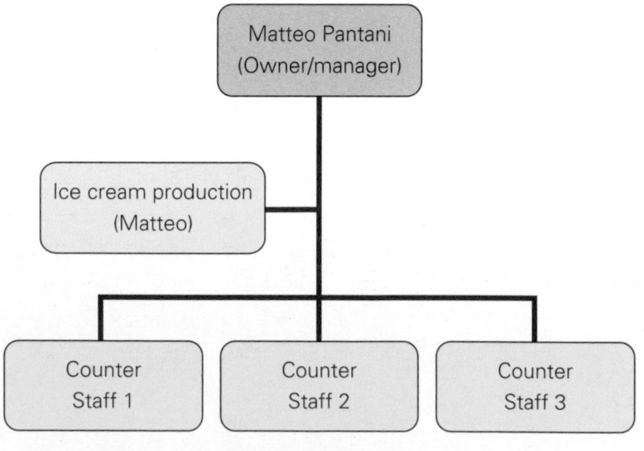

Figure 37.1 Scoop: old organisational structure

As the business grew, he opened a second outlet in 2010, in Brewer Street, Soho. This meant he needed a manager to run the Soho outlet, while Matteo was largely at Covent Garden (he also needed time to look for the third Scoop outlet). By mid-2010, the

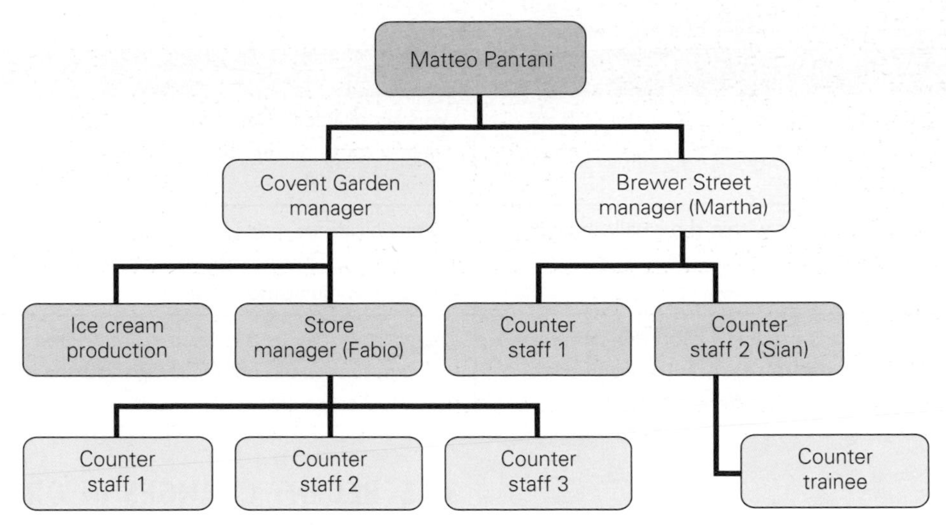

Figure 37.2 Scoop: new organisational structure

organisational hierarchy looked like the one shown in Figure 37.2.

The point, of course, is to appreciate how much more complex a hierarchy becomes as the business grows.

37.3 THE ROLES AND RELATIONSHIPS

This section will describe the different roles and relationship within organisations and will illustrate these with references to the above chart.

Roles

These describe the different tasks that the individuals are responsible for. At this point it is important to define responsibility, authority and accountability. Responsibility means carrying the burden of blame, even if an error is made by a subordinate. After all, if Alex Ferguson plays his reserve goalkeeper in a football match, it is Ferguson who will be blamed if the keeper lets in a soft goal. Authority means having the power to make a decision or carry out a task. However, if the Covent Garden manager delegates authority to Fabio to carry out a particular task, the senior manager still retains the overall responsibility for that task. This shows how important it is for a manager to consider carefully who they delegate tasks to. Accountability is the extent to which an individual is held responsible for her or his decisions and actions.

Directors

Directors are members of 'the Board', that is the board of directors who handle the most senior appointments and set out the main aims and objectives of the business. There are two types of director: executive director and non-executive director.

Executive directors

Executive directors are appointed to the Board because they head up important divisions or departments, for example the marketing director.

Non-executive directors

These are part-time directors from outside the business; their job is to take an independent view of the shareholders' best interests.

Manager

A manager is a person responsible for organising others to carry out tasks. A line manager is the person immediately above someone in the organisational chart. For example, Figure 37.2 shows that Sian's line manager is Martha.

Team leader

This role will usually arise in firms that organise themselves in a **matrix management** structure. This is where the firm allocates its workers into project teams rather than departments and a team leader will manage the workers involved in a particular project. Project teams will be made up people with different skills; for example, in a typical team there will be financial, marketing and operations specialists. This will enable them to make integrated decisions for the project. Building and engineering firms usually adopt this matrix approach in which the team leader is responsible for the management of the tasks and people involved.

37.4 ORGANISATIONAL STRUCTURE: OTHER KEY TERMS

Levels of hierarchy

These show the number of different supervisory and management levels between the bottom of the chart and the top of the hierarchy. Figure 37.2 shows that at Scoop there are now four levels of hierarchy.

Table 37.2 Advantages and disadvantages of a narrow span of control

Advantages	Disadvantages
Allows close management supervision; this is vital if staff are inexperienced, labour turnover is high or if the task is critical, e.g. manufacturing aircraft engines	Workers may feel over-supervised and therefore not trusted; this may cause better staff to leave, in search of more personal responsibility
Communications may be excellent within the small, immediate team, e.g. the boss and three staff	Communications may suffer within the business as a whole, as a narrow span means more layers of hierarchy, which makes vertical communications harder
Many layers of hierarchy means many rungs on the career ladder, i.e. promotion chances arise regularly (though each promotion may mean only a slightly different job)	The narrow span usually leads to restricted scope for initiative and experiment; the boss is always looking over your shoulder; this will alienate enterprising staff

Span of control

This describes the number of people directly under the supervision of a manager. Fabio has the biggest span of control, as he has three workers directly under him. If managers have very wide spans of control, they are directly responsible for many staff. In this case they may find that there are communication problems, or the workers may feel that they are not being given enough guidance. The ideal span of control will depend upon the nature of the tasks and the skills and attitude of the workforce and manager. (See Table 37.2 for information about the advantages and disadvantages of a narrow span of control.)

Chain of command

This shows the reporting system from the top of the hierarchy to the bottom; that is the route through which information travels throughout the organisation. In an organisation with several levels of hierarchy the chain of command will be longer and this could create a gap between workers at the bottom of the organisation and managers at the top. If information has to travel via several people there is also a chance that it may become distorted.

Centralisation and decentralisation

This describes the extent to which decision-making power and authority is delegated within an organisation. A centralised structure is one in which decision-making power and control remains in the hands of the top management levels. A decentralised structure delegates decision-making power to workers lower down the organisation. Many organisations will use a combination of these approaches, depending upon the nature of the decision involved. For example, in many schools and colleges, the decisions concerning which resources to use will be decentralised, that is, taken by teachers as opposed to the senior management team. Other decisions, concerning future changes in subjects being offered, may be centralised, that is taken by senior managers.

37.5 RECENT CHANGES IN ORGANISATION STRUCTURES

In the past some firms had very tall hierarchical structures, which meant there were many layers of management, often with quite narrow spans of control. This made them expensive to run, because of the management salaries that had to be paid. Tall structures also resulted in longer chains of command, which could have a negative impact on communication. More recently, companies have liked to announce that they are becoming flatter, meaning fewer layers of management with each manager having a wider span of control. Although some managers dislike this increased responsibility, their workers may thrive under the increased independence that is gained. Furthermore, the firm will have reduced overhead costs, which should mean greater efficiency.

Why is organisational structure so important?

As a firm grows, more people will become involved and, to ensure that the different tasks are fulfilled, it will be vital that every person is clear about what the role involves and who they are answerable/accountable to and responsible for. Poor organisational structures will lack coordination and the following problems could result:

- poor communication leading to mistakes
- duplication of tasks
- tasks being overlooked
- different departments failing to work together effectively.

In the longer term, these problems will create a sub-standard service and this will have an impact on the firm's sales, revenue and profit. As a firm expands, it must ensure that its organisation structure accommodates the growth.

ISSUES FOR ANALYSIS

- When discussing the topic of organisation structure, it is important to recognise that the structures are not static and they should adapt to the environment in which they operate. If more people enter the firm, then changes should take place and this may have an impact on the roles and relationships of the existing workers.
- The key to a top exam answer is to think about the match between the structure and the type of organisation. When Google started up it had virtually no structure; brilliant people were hired and told to do brilliant things; the structure was deliberately loose. Today Google is a vast business, needing a tighter structure, but probably not so tight as to strangle innovation.

37.6 ORGANISATION STRUCTURE – AN EVALUATION

There is no 'ideal' organisational structure or span of control. What works for one business may fail in another, even if both are the same size. In exams there will usually be hints about whether the structure is working. A flat hierarchy may be at the heart of an innovative business, or there may be signs that staff lack direction and morale. A tall hierarchy may be at the centre of a focused, career-orientated workforce, or it may be bureaucratic and incapable of a quick decision. The judgement is yours.

Key Terms

Line manager: a manager responsible for meeting specific business targets, and responsible for specific staff.
Matrix management: where staff work in project teams in addition to their responsibilities within their own department. Therefore, staff can be answerable to more than one boss.
Span of control: the number of staff who are answerable directly to a manager.

WORKBOOK

A REVISION QUESTIONS

(30 marks; 30 minutes)

1 What is meant by the chain of command? (2)
2 Define span of control. (2)
3 Some theorists believe that the ideal span of control is between three and six. To what extent do you agree with this? (5)
4 Explain two implications of a firm having too wide a span of control. (4)
5 Explain what an organisational chart shows. (4)
6 Why is it important for a growing firm to think carefully about its organisational structure? (4)
7 State three possible problems for a business with many levels of hierarchy. (3)
8 What is meant by the term 'accountable'? (2)
9 What do you think would be the right organisational structure for a hospital? Explain your answer. (4)

REVISION EXERCISES
B1 DATA RESPONSE

These questions are based on the Scoop organisation charts (Figures 37.1 and 37.2)

Questions

(20 marks; 25 minutes)

1 Explain why communication might be harder in the larger Scoop of 2010. (6)
2 Should the Brewer Street counter staff be allowed to contact ice-cream production directly: for example, if they see they are running out of vanilla ice cream? Explain your reasoning. (6)
3 Examine two ways in which Matteo may find his management responsibilities more difficult when he opens his third Scoop outlet. (8)

B2 DATA RESPONSE

Span of control in call centres

Span of control measures the ratio of supervisors to sales agents. For example, a call centre with 160 agents and 10 supervisors has a span of control of 16 to 1. If you have too many supervisors, your costs will be higher than necessary. If you have too few supervisors, then service quality may degrade and staff turnover may increase among your agents.

A customer service centre with a tight span of control (low number of agents per supervisor) will have a hierarchical organisation. In contrast, a loose span of control (large number of agents per supervisor) correlates with a flat organisation. Hierarchical companies have many layers of staff, supervisors and managers. Typically, there are clear boundaries and policies governing how work is performed. In contrast, a flat organisation has a minimum number of levels and emphasises staff ownership and empowerment. There are benefits and drawbacks to both types of call centre structures as shown in Tables 37.3 and 37.4

So is there a 'right' number for span of control at call centres? This will depend on the type of call centre and the management practices within the centre. According to benchmarking results from 'Prosci's Call Centre Study', span of control ranges from 16:1 to 8:1 depending on industry and type of centre. This range is significant. A call centre with 250 agents would save more than half a million dollars per year by moving from a span of control of 8:1 to 16:1.

Adapted from www.call-centre.net/tutorial-measuring-span-of-control.htm

Table 37.3 Benefits and drawbacks of a call centre with a tight span of control

Benefits	Drawbacks
Stronger quality monitoring programme	Multi-layered organisation that inhibits information sharing
More one-on-one supervision	Less flexibility
Better control over customer service	Micro-management
Improved reporting	Higher overhead costs
Clearly-defined procedures and policies	

Table 37.4 Benefits and drawback of a call centre with a loose span of control

Benefits	Drawbacks
Streamlined information flow throughout the organisation	Poor call quality
Agents are authorised to make customer-impacting decisions and take ownership of calls	Supervisor stress due to excessive workload
Reduced overhead costs	Less reported information about performance levels
	Less one-on-one agent feedback

Questions

(25 marks; 30 minutes)

1 Outline the meaning of the terms:
   a) flat organisation (3)
   b) staff ownership. (3)
2 Explain why moving from a span of control of 8 to 16 could save a call centre a large amount of money. (7)
3 One benefit of a loose span is that 'agents are authorised to make customer-impacting decisions and take ownership of calls'. Discuss the possible impact of this upon the motivation of call centre staff. (12)

B3 DATA RESPONSE

Chicken Little

Peter (known as 'Paxo') Little set up his free range chicken farm in the early 1990s. At the time it was an unusual move, especially on the grand scale envisaged by 'Paxo'. His farm had the capacity to produce 250,000 chickens every 45 days; that is, 4 million birds a year. Since then the business has grown enormously, to a turnover of £25 million today.

But Paxo is getting concerned that his business is not as efficient as it used to be. As managing director, he finds that he rarely hears from junior staff; not even the quality manager's five staff, who used to see him regularly. As he said recently to the operations director, 'the communication flows seem like treacle today, whereas they used to be like wildfire'.

Fortunately, the boom in demand for free range and organic produce has helped the business. So even though the team spirit seems to have slipped away, profits have never been higher. Unfortunately, the marketing director repeatedly talks about rumours that a huge Dutch farming business is about to set up poultry farms in Britain. That could 'set the cat among the chickens'; in other word, provoke quarrelling and dissention.

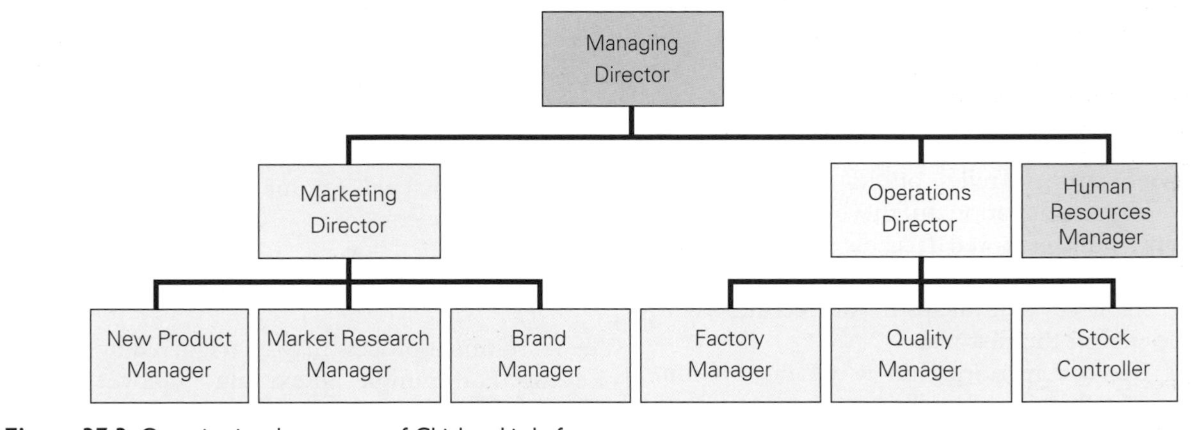

Figure 37.3 Organisational structure of Chicken Little farms

Questions

(25 marks; 30 minutes)

1 **a)** What is the managing director's span of control? (1)
 b) Comment on the strength and weaknesses of this organisational structure. (6)
 c) How important does Human Resources seem within this business? (3)

2 Explain why vertical communications may not be as effective today as they used to be in the past at Chicken Little. (5)

3 Discuss the ways in which the factory manager may benefit or suffer from the organisational structure shown in Figure 37.3. (10)

UNIT 38

Recruitment and training

Recruitment (and selection) is concerned with filling job vacancies that may arise within a business. The process involves a number of activities, including defining the job, attracting suitable candidates and selecting those best suited to fill it. Training is a provision of work-related education, where employees learn new skills or develop the skills they already possess.

38.1 THE NEED FOR EFFECTIVE RECRUITMENT

Every service business relies on its staff to present the face of the organisation to the customer. It can be a gloomy, perhaps bored face, or it can be lively and smiling. Many factors are involved in this stark difference, but it certainly helps if you recruit bright, enthusiastic staff in the first place.

In 2011, Tesco is recruiting for its Graduate China programme. Staff selected will be on a fast-track route to management, specialising in Buying, Store Management or Marketing. Tesco already has 70 stores in China and is planning a huge expansion programme. The lucky graduates will have terrific career prospects.

A-grade application

Ryanair and easyJet compete for qualified pilots

The rapid growth of low-cost airlines has forced Ryanair and easyJet to compete fiercely for the scarcest resource: qualified pilots. Table 38.1 shows what each airline was offering in summer 2010 to attract potential recruits.

Table 38.1 Terms and conditions of employment

	easyJet	Ryanair
Annual salary:	£81,509	'Up to £100,000'
Days off a year	137 days	162 days
Extra remuneration	7 per cent pension contribution	Share option scheme
Extra attraction	Share options	Home every night

Source: easyjet.com and ryanair.com

Despite the expenses involved, businesses like Tesco recognise the importance of committing sufficient resources to recruitment. Hiring the right people with the right skills is vital if company objectives are to be achieved.

38.2 THE RECRUITMENT PROCESS

The recruitment process may be triggered by a number of events. For example, an existing employee may have chosen to leave his or her job, perhaps as a result of retirement or after finding employment elsewhere. At this point, it would be worth analysing the vacant job role. Do all of the responsibilities associated with the vacant job still need to be carried out or are some redundant? Could the remaining duties be reorganised amongst the existing employees? Alternatively, additional workers may need to be recruited in order to support a firm's expansion strategies, or employees with new skills may be required to help develop new products or new markets.

Once the firm has established its human resources requirements, the next step is to consider the nature of work and workers required in order to draw up a job description and a person specification.

Both documents have an important influence on both recruitment and selection; not only can they be used to draw up job adverts, but also to assess the suitability of candidates' applications and may also form the basis of any interview questions.

Job description

A job description relates directly to the nature of the position itself, rather than the person required to fill it. Typically, a job description would contain the following information:

- the title of the post
- details of the main duties and tasks involved
- the person to whom the job holder reports and any employees for whom the job holder is responsible.

Person specification

A person specification identifies the abilities, qualifications and qualities required of the job holder in order to carry out the job successfully. The main features of a person specification include:

- any educational or professional qualifications required
- necessary skills or experience
- suitable personality or character, for example ability to work under pressure or as part of a team.

A-grade application

Graduates looking for jobs in the retail sector were targeted by a Waitrose recruitment drive during summer 2010. The retailer aimed to take on eight graduates who would be placed in store-based retail management roles and have the opportunity to become a department manager within 12 to 24 months.

Competition for places was expected to be tough, with Waitrose receiving some 2,500 applications for just 12 vacancies during its last recruitment campaign, and it has developed a new online system to help it to identify the highest quality candidates. Applicants fill out an online form and personality questionnaire before sitting an online test, which helps the retailer to filter out less suitable candidates.

The test assesses a graduate's judgement and decision-making abilities based on typical workplace situations. The test will help to whittle down the thousands of applicants to some 150 who then attend an assessment at one of Waitrose's selection centres before going forward to interview.

Source: www.graduate-jobs.com, 21 July 2010.

38.3 INTERNAL RECRUITMENT

A business may choose to fill a vacancy internally, that is from the existing workforce. This could be done either by redeploying or promoting a worker from elsewhere in the business. Although internal recruitment can have a number of benefits, it also has a number of disadvantages and is obviously of no use when a business needs to expand its workforce in order to respond to an increase in demand. See Table 38.2.

38.4 RECRUITING EXTERNAL CANDIDATES

Firms can choose from a range of methods to attract external candidates to fill a job vacancy. The advantages and disadvantages of external recruitment are set out in Table 38.2.

Methods of recruitment

Methods of recruiting external candidates include those set out below.

Media advertising

Firms may place job adverts in newspapers or specialist magazines, on the radio, TV or by using dedicated employment websites such as www.monster.co.uk.

Job centres

These are government-run organisations which offer a free service to firms and tend to focus on vacancies for skilled and semi-skilled manual and administrative jobs.

Commercial recruitment agencies

Examples of commercial recruitment agencies include Alfred Marks or Reed, which will carry a number of human resources functions, including recruitment, on behalf of firms in return for a fee.

Executive search consultants

Executive search consultants are paid to directly approach individuals – usually those in relatively senior positions. (This is known as poaching or headhunting.)

Firm's own website

In addition, many businesses have careers pages on their own websites, which are used to advertise vacancies.

Factors influencing choice of method

The choice of recruitment method or methods used by a business will depend on a number of factors, including:

- the cost of the recruitment method
- the size of the recruitment budget
- the location and characteristics of the likely candidates.

Table 38.2 Internal recruitment: advantages and disadvantages

Advantages	Disadvantages
It is likely to be quicker and cheaper than external recruitment	Existing workers may not have the skills required, especially if the business wants to develop new products or markets
Greater variety and promotion opportunities may motivate employees	Relying on existing employees may lead to a stagnation of ideas and approaches within the business
It avoids the need (and cost) of induction training	It may create a vacancy elsewhere, postponing external recruitment, rather than avoiding it
The firm will already be aware of the employee's skills and attitude to work	

Table 38.3 External recruitment: advantages and disadvantages

Advantages	Disadvantages
It should result in a wider range of candidates than internal recruitment.	It can be an expensive and time-consuming process, using up valuable resources.
Candidates may already have the skills required to carry out the job in question, avoiding the need for (and cost of) training.	It can have a de-motivating effect on members of the existing workforce, who may have missed out on promotion.

38.5 SELECTING THE BEST CANDIDATE

Once a number of suitable candidates have applied for the vacancy, the selection process can begin. This will involve choosing the applicant who most closely matches the criteria set out in the person specification for the job. A number of selection techniques exist, including those set out below.

Interviews

This is still the most frequently used selection technique; an interview may consist of one interviewer or a panel. Interviews are relatively cheap to conduct and allow a wide variety of information to be obtained by both sides, but are often susceptible to interviewer bias or prejudice. They are, therefore, considered to be an unreliable indicator on their own of how well a candidate will carry out the job in question.

Testing and profiling

Aptitude tests measure the level of ability of a candidate such as, for example, the level of ICT skills. Psychometric profiling examines personality and attitudes, for example whether the candidate works well under pressure or is an effective team player. Profiling is commonly used as part of management and sales consultancy recruitment, but it is questionable as to whether recruiting a 'personality type' for a particular job is desirable. Recruiting a wider range of personalities may lead to a more interesting and creative environment.

Assessment centres

These allow for a more in-depth assessment of a candidate's suitability by subjecting them to 'real-life' role plays and simulations, often over a number of days. Although assessment centres are considered to be an effective selection method, they can be expensive and tend, therefore, to be reserved for filling more senior, management positions. See Figure 38.1 for an illustration of the stages in the recruitment process.

Although a firm can only be certain that the right person has been recruited once he or she starts work, effective recruitment and selection will reduce the risk involved. There are a number of methods that can be used to evaluate the process, including calculating the cost and time involved in filling a vacancy, the percentage of candidates who actually accept job offers and the rate of retention of staff once employed.

Figure 38.1 Stages in the recruitment process

> **A-grade application**
>
> **Poor recruitment procedures can damage retailers' brand image**
>
> A survey of job applicants in the retail sector in 2010 found that almost half (49 per cent) had formed a negative view of the company concerned following an unsuccessful application for a job vacancy, and almost a fifth (18 per cent) had taken their custom elsewhere as a result. The research, carried out by SHL, a leading talent assessment organisation, found that the biggest issue for job seekers was the lack of communication provided by retail firms. According to the survey respondents, the greatest concern was not being told whether their job application had been successful (46 per cent), followed by a lack of feedback about applications (39 per cent), as well as not acknowledging receipt of an application (36 per cent).
>
> Source: SHL

38.6 TRAINING

The purpose of training is to help employees to develop existing skills or gain new ones. The benefits and costs of training are given in Table 38.4. Types of training include those set out below.

Induction training

Induction training aims to make newly appointed workers fully productive as soon as possible by familiarising them with the key aspects of the business. Induction would typically include:

- information on important policies and procedures, such as health and safety
- a tour of the organisation and an introduction to colleagues
- details of employment; for example, payment arrangements, holiday entitlement, and so on, and basic duties.

On the job training

For this method of training employees are not required to leave their workplace but actually receive instruction while still carrying out their job. This means that workers can receive training while remaining productive to some extent. Common methods include mentoring, coaching and job rotation.

Off the job training

For off the job training employees leave their workplace in order to receive instruction. This may involve using training facilities within the firm, for example seminar rooms, or those provided by another organisation, such as a university, college or private training agency. Although this will inevitably involve a temporary loss of production, it should allow the trainee to concentrate fully on learning and perhaps allow access to more experienced instructors than those available within the workplace.

Table 38.4 Training: benefits and costs

Benefits	Costs
It increases the level and range of skills available to the business, leading to improvements in productivity and quality.	It can be expensive, both in terms of providing the training itself and also the cost of evaluating its effectiveness.
It increases the degree of flexibility within a business, allowing it to respond quickly to changes in technology or demand.	Production may be disrupted while training is taking place, leading to lost output.
It can lead to a more motivated workforce by creating opportunities for development and promotion.	Newly-trained workers may be persuaded to leave and take up new jobs elsewhere (known as **poaching**), meaning that the benefits of training are enjoyed by other businesses.

38.7 LABOUR MARKET FAILURE

Like any market, the labour market is made up of supply (labour services provided by those who wish to work) and demand (firms in need of workers to produce goods or provide services). An efficient labour market would require firms to provide training for their workers in order to improve their skills and knowledge. However, the danger of poaching may create a general disincentive for firms to invest in training, for fear that the short-term costs and disruption of training may not be recouped if newly-trained employees are enticed to work elsewhere. In such circumstances, the government may become involved in training provision, in order to ensure the economy remains competitive.

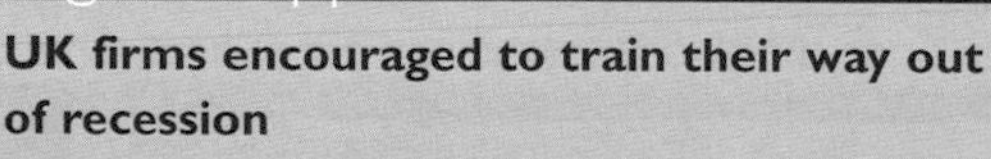

UK firms encouraged to train their way out of recession

Research carried out by Cranfield School of Management has claimed that training existing staff can be more effective than external recruitment. The findings of the research were published in a report entitled 'Nurturing Talent'. Nearly 1,200 firms took part in the study. Three quarters of the respondents felt that training their own staff was more beneficial to their businesses than recruiting people from outside. Half the businesses had discovered that training made staff more likely to stay. One third of the businesses found it increased employee motivation, while almost one half said they saved money by doing so. The research findings have been used by both union leaders and senior business figures, including the chairmen of BT and Marks and Spencer, to encourage firms to maintain their spending on training during the recent recession.

38.8 TRAINING AND THE GOVERNMENT

Like any market, the labour market is made up of supply (labour services provided by those who wish to work) and demand (firms in need of workers to produce goods or provide services). An efficient labour market would require firms to provide training for their workers in order to improve their skills and knowledge. However, the danger of poaching may create a general disincentive for firms to invest in training, for fear that the short-term costs and disruption of training may not be recouped if newly trained employees are enticed to work elsewhere (**labour market failure**). In such circumstances, the government may become involved in training provision, in order to ensure the economy remains competitive.

The UK government uses a number of methods to support and encourage firms to train their workers, including those set out below.

The 2010 UK coalition government seems more likely to leave training initiatives to 'the free market' than to intervene directly.

Modern apprenticeships

These are structured programmes aimed at improving the level of technical skills within the workforce. Apprentices receive a combination of on-the-job

Questions

(25 marks; 30 minutes)

1 Explain why Tesco may want all candidates to have a 'Psychometric test'. (6)
2 Consider whether the programme seems likely to attract high-calibre applicants. (6)
3 Does this programme seem attractive to you personally? Explain your views. (13)

B3 CASE STUDY

Solving skills shortages at Mulberry

Mulberry is a leading manufacturer of luxury handbags and leather goods, based in the south-west of England. Its reputation depends to a great extent on maintaining a highly skilled workforce, trained to handle valuable materials and use a variety of leatherworking techniques, such as cutting and stitching. These techniques are complicated to teach, requiring lengthy training periods before workers can become productive.

With an ageing workforce and a chronic shortage of workers with the appropriate manufacturing skills across the UK textile industry generally, Mulberry was faced with a dilemma. If it recruited and trained workers in-house, it would not qualify for public funding available for employees undertaking recognised qualifications. However, the courses offered by external training providers were too general and, therefore, failed to address the company's specific training needs.

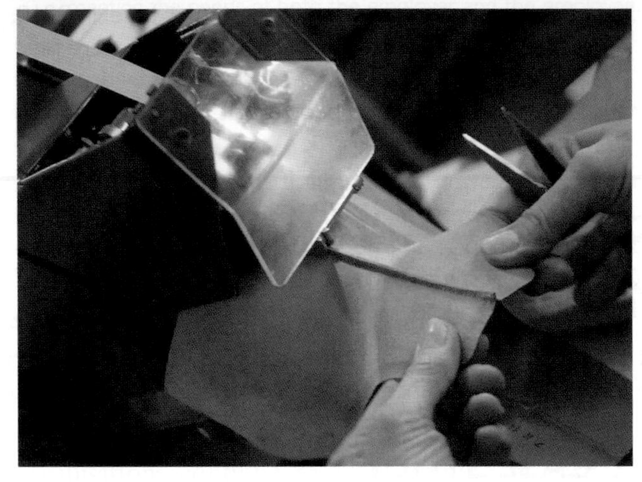

Figure 38.2

The company's solution was to set up a partnership with Bridgwater College, a further education institution with a reputation for supporting local employers. The collaboration resulted in a new two-year apprenticeship qualification, designed precisely to meet Mulberry's training needs. Apprentices spend the majority of their time at the company's industrial plant in Somerset, training 'on the job' and learning a range of techniques. The apprentices also spend half a day each week at the college learning about the leather industry and developing skills such as teamwork and communication. The scheme allows Mulberry to control the content of the training and, because the scheme is recognised by the relevant awarding bodies, the company receives £2,500 of public funds for each apprentice trained.

Source: Skillfast UK

Questions

(25 marks; 30 minutes)

1 Briefly explain, using examples, the difference between 'on-the-job' and 'off-the-job' training. (4)
2 Analyse one benefit and one drawback to a company such as Mulberry from its new apprenticeship scheme. (9)
3 To what extent do you agree that the reputation and, therefore, success of UK manufacturers like Mulberry depends on maintaining a highly skilled workforce? (12)

C ESSAY QUESTIONS

(40 marks each)

1 Stamford Software Solutions, a medium-sized IT company based in the south-east of England, needs to recruit a new sales manager. Consider how the company should do this.
2 According to the Leitch Report, UK employers spend an estimated £33 billion in total each year on training, yet one third of employers provide no training at all. Evaluate the main consequences for firms who choose not to train their staff.

Measuring the effectiveness of the workforce

UNIT 39

Staff costs are usually between 25 and 50 per cent of a firm's total costs. So firms try to measure the performance of their people objectively (that is, in an unbiased way). Calculations such as staff productivity can be used to measure the success of initiatives such as new methods of working or payment.

39.1 THE NEED TO MEASURE PERFORMANCE

Managers require an objective, unbiased way to measure the performance of personnel. The firm needs to be able to see several things:

- Is the workforce fully motivated?
- Is the workforce as productive as it could be?
- Are the personnel policies of the business helping the business to meet its goals?

It is not possible to measure these things directly. How, for example, can the level of motivation of workers be measured accurately? Instead, a series of indicators are used which, when analysed, can show the firm if its personnel policies are contributing as much to the firm as they should.

There are two main performance indicators used to measure the effectiveness of a personnel department. They are:

1 labour productivity
2 labour turnover.

39.2 LABOUR PRODUCTIVITY

Calculating labour productivity

Labour productivity is often seen as the single most important measure of how well a firm's workers are doing. It compares the number of workers with the output that they are making. It is expressed through the formula:

output per period/number of employees per period

For example, if a window cleaner employs ten people and in a day will normally clean the windows of 150 houses, then the productivity is:

$$\frac{150}{10} = 15 \text{ houses per worker per day}$$

At its simplest, the higher the productivity of the workforce, the better it is performing. Any increase in the productivity figure suggests an improvement in efficiency. The importance of productivity lies in its impact on labour costs per unit. For example, the productivity of AES Cleaning is 15 houses per worker per day; MS Cleaning achieves only 10. Assuming a daily rate of pay of £45, the labour cost per house is £3 for AES but £4.50 for MS Cleaning. Higher productivity leads to lower labour costs per unit. And therefore leads to greater competitiveness both here and against international rivals.

Figure 39.1 Window cleaning

Productivity is covered in more detail in Unit 33. Remember that productivity is just one way to measure staff performance. There are others, including labour turnover.

39.3 LABOUR TURNOVER

Measuring labour turnover

This is a measure of the rate of change of a firm's workforce. It is measured by the ratio:

$$\frac{\text{Number of staff leaving the firm per year}}{\text{Average number of staff}} \times 100$$

So a firm which has seen 5 people leave out of its staff of 50 has a labour turnover of:

$$\frac{5}{50} \times 100 = 10\%$$

As with all of these figures, it would be a mistake to take one figure in isolation. It would be better to look at how the figure has changed over a number of years. And to look for the reasons why the turnover rate is as it is.

Causes of labour turnover

If the rate of labour turnover is increasing, it may be a sign of dissatisfaction within the workforce. If so, the possible causes could be either internal to the firm or external.

Internal causes

Internal causes of an increasing rate of labour turnover could be:

- A poor recruitment and selection procedure, which may appoint the wrong person to the wrong post. If this happens, then eventually the misplaced workers will wish to leave to find a post more suited to their particular interests or talents.
- Ineffective motivation or leadership, leading to workers lacking commitment to this particular firm. They will feel no sense of loyalty or ownership to the business, and will tend to look outside the firm for promotions or new career opportunities, rather than looking for new ways in which they could contribute to 'their' firm.
- Wage levels that are lower than those being earned by similar workers in other local firms. If wage rates are not competitive, workers will feel dissatisfied by their position. They may look elsewhere to find a better reward for doing a similar job.

External causes

External causes of an increasing rate of labour turnover could be:

- More local vacancies arising, perhaps due to the setting up or expansion of other firms in the area
- Better transport links, making a wider geographical area accessible for workers. New public transport systems enable workers to take employment that was previously out of their reach.

Consequences of high labour turnover

Negative effects

A high rate of labour turnover can have both negative and positive effects on a firm. The negative aspects would be:

- the cost of recruitment of replacements
- the cost of retraining replacements
- the time taken for new recruits to settle into the business and adopt the firm's **culture**
- the loss of productivity while the new workers adjust.

Positive effects

On the positive side, labour turnover can benefit the business in several ways:

- new workers can bring new ideas and enthusiasm to the firm
- workers with specific skills can be employed rather than having to train up existing workers from scratch
- new ways of solving problems can be seen by workers with a different perspective, whereas existing workers may rely on tried and trusted techniques that have worked in the past.

On balance, then, there is a need for firms to achieve the right level of labour turnover, rather than aiming for the lowest possible level.

> ### A-grade application
>
> **Labour turnover at Red Carnation Hotels (RCH)**
>
> Liz McGivern joined the RCH luxury hotel chain just after a terrorist attack had hit air travel. Business was soon down by 20 per cent as American tourists disappeared. Yet she noticed a shocking detail about RCH; its labour turnover was 80 per cent. This would be poor for any hotel, but luxury hotels have to offer good service, which would always be tricky if new, inexperienced staff were dealing with guests. Nothing could be done about nervous flyers, but the high labour turnover was inexcusable.
>
> Liz carried out some internal research which revealed high levels of staff dissatisfaction due to poor management and strained internal relationships. Her solution was to implement a company-wide training programme focusing on improved customer service. The cost per person was in the order of £1,000 so, with a staff of more than 500, this was a substantial investment by the directors. Fortunately it went well, resulting in improved repeat business from guests and fall in labour turnover to 29 per cent. Even more importantly for the business, the revenue received per room rose by 11 per cent at a time when the market trend was towards falling room rates.
>
> Source: based on www.people1st.co.uk

39.5 EVALUATING THE SUCCESS OF PERSONNEL MANAGEMENT

Productivity and labour turnover data provides the firm with a commentary on its performance. Poor productivity and high labour turnover might be a commentary on poor management in the workplace. For the most effective comparisons, good managers analyse the figures to identify:

- changes over time (this year versus last)
- how the firm is performing compared with other similar firms
- performance against targets, such as a 20 per cent improvement on last year.

Each of these comparisons will tell the firm how it is performing in relation to a yardstick. This will indicate to the firm where it is performing well and where it may have a problem. The firm must then investigate carefully the reasons for its performance before it can judge how well its personnel function is operating.

For example, labour productivity may have fallen since 12 months ago. Closer investigation may show that the fall was due to the time taken to train staff on new machinery installed at the start of the year. Figures may show that productivity in the last six months was actually higher than at any time in the past, and the firm could be confident that future productivity will continue to increase. An apparent problem was actually masking an improvement for the firm.

39.6 DOWNSIDES OF PERSONNEL MANAGEMENT: REDUNDANCY AND DISMISSAL

Redundancy occurs when a job is no longer needed; therefore the business has no further need for the person doing the job. For instance, an automated voice recognition system could replace the job of a telephonist. A well-run business will have anticipated this situation, and discussed with the telephonist what to do next. Options may include retraining, perhaps, as a personal assistant or as a telephone salesperson? Or perhaps the telephonist would rather take the opportunity to leave. A redundancy package for a 32-year-old who has spent ten years at the firm would probably be no more than the government minimum figure of ten weeks' pay. This might amount to £3,000 to £3,500, which may do no more than tide the person over until a new job emerges. For each year's employment, workers receive the following amounts of statutory redundancy pay:

- a worker aged 18 to 21 – half-a-week's pay
- a worker aged 22 to 40 – one week's pay
- a worker aged 41 to 65 – one-and-a-half weeks' pay.

Clearly, then, if a struggling business needs to make people redundant, selecting young adults to leave will be the cheapest option by far.

Dismissal concerns the person, not the job. The business has decided (rightly or wrongly) that everyone will be better off without that person. By implication, she or he should never have been employed in the first place, so the recruitment staff ought to discuss how or why this happened. Dismissal will always be unpleasant, but may sometimes be essential. Football managers Arsene Wenger and Alex Ferguson both needed to clear 'boozy' players (that is, those who drank alcohol to excess) out of their dressing rooms before they achieved real success. One incompetent member of a team can spoil the atmosphere (and, perhaps, the bonuses) for many.

Dismissal can be 'fair' or 'unfair'. It is 'fair' if the member of staff has had two verbal warnings about poor performance, followed by a written warning. If she or he fails to improve, dismissal is legally 'fair'. It is 'unfair' if dismissal is due to reasons that include:

- joining a trade union
- becoming pregnant
- refusing to work on Sundays.

Overall, a good leader would ensure that staff take great care over recruitment, to ensure that there are no 'rotten apples' (that is, bad persons taken on to join other good people). Then the personnel staff should work together to ensure that redundancies and dismissals are kept to the absolute minimum.

ISSUES FOR ANALYSIS

There are several important business issues relating to personnel performance indicators:

- Business success comes from being the best and staying the best. This is always hard but is the only way to be sure of staying at the top. Football managers may say all that counts is what happens on the pitch, but lateness or absence from training is often a good indicator of problems to come. Every manager should be alert to early warning signs, find out the reasons and tackle them straight away.
- Personnel issues are considered 'soft' by some employers. Who cares about labour turnover or health issues, they say, as long as the job gets done and profits are high? This may be true in the short term. For firms pursuing long-term growth, however, the quality and involvement of staff is crucial. So morale matters. As does absence and lateness.

39.7 MEASURES OF PERSONNEL EFFECTIVENESS – AN EVALUATION

Performance ratios such as labour turnover raise questions. They do not supply answers. Follow-up staff surveys or chats may be needed to discover the underlying problems. Figures such as these give the firm an indication of what issues need addressing if the firm is to improve its position in the future, but this must be taken within the context of the business as a whole. A high labour turnover figure may have been the result of a deliberate policy to bring in younger members of staff who may be more adaptable to a changing situation at the factory.

Measures of personnel effectiveness are merely indicators for a firm to see where it may be facing problems. The measures may indicate poor performance, or reflect the short-term effect of a change in business strategy.

It must be remembered that these figures are all looking to the past. They tell the firm what has happened to its workforce. Although this has a strong element of objectivity, it is not as valuable as an indication of how the indicators may look in the future.

Culture: the accepted attitudes and behaviours of people within a workplace.
Labour productivity: output per person.
Labour turnover: the rate at which people leave their jobs and need to be replaced.

Key Terms

WORKBOOK

A1 REVISION QUESTIONS

(20 marks; 20 minutes)

1 Define the following terms:
  a) Labour productivity
  b) Labour turnover. (4)

2 Why could an increase in labour productivity help a firm to reduce its costs per unit? (3)

3 In what ways could a hotel business benefit if labour turnover rose from 2 to 15 per cent per year? (4)

4 Some fast food outlets have labour turnover as high as 100 per cent per year. What could be the effects of this on the firm? (4)

5 How might a firm know if its personnel strategy was working effectively? (5)

B REVISION EXERCISES
B1 DATA RESPONSE

Personnel effectiveness

A firm has the data shown in Table 39.1 on its personnel function.

Table 39.1 Data held by a firm on its personnel function

	Year 1	Year 2
Output	50,000	55,000
Average no. of workers	250	220
No. of staff leaving the firm	12	8
Working days per worker – possible	230	230
Average no. of staff absent per day	4	3

Questions

(25 marks; 25 minutes)

1 Calculate the following ratios for both years:
a) Labour productivity (5)
b) Labour turnover. (5)

2 Explain what questions these figures could raise in the minds of the firm's management. (15)

B2 DATA RESPONSE

Monitoring personnel performance at Best Motors

James West, the new personnel officer at Best Motors, the manufacturer of the world-famous, hand-made sports cars of the same name, sat down at his desk and considered the figures in front of him. (See Table 39.2.) He would need to report on the existing position of the business to Elizabeth Best, the chief executive, on Friday.

James knew the company operated for 50 weeks of the year (only closing down for the annual works holiday), and that all employees worked full time, five days each week. He opened his briefcase and got out a calculator. 'The first thing to do is determine the key human resource indicators' he thought to himself as he started to work.

Table 39.2 Best Motors

	4 years ago	3 years ago	2 years ago	Last year	This year
Number of leavers	3	2	4	8	7
Working days lost due to absence	124	102	145	169	204
Total annual output	780	803	805	790	811
Number of shop floor accidents	5	3	7	2	4
Average number of employees	23	25	25	24	26

Questions

(25 marks; 30 minutes)

1 Calculate labour turnover and labour productivity at Best Motors for all five years. (10)
2 Using your results, evaluate the effectiveness of Best Motors' personnel management. (8)
3 What additional information would you seek to help James gain a better understanding of how staff have been managed at Best Motors? Explain your reasoning. (7)

B3 CASE STUDY

Turner's Butchers is a chain of three shops in a large town in the North of England. The shops are all supplied with prepared and packaged produce from Turner's Farm, owned by the same family.

The management is particularly concerned at present by the differing performance of the three shops. In particular, they feel there may be a problem with the personnel management in the chain. The concerns were highlighted recently in a report looking at various indicators of personnel effectiveness.

The key section of the report is shown in Table 39.3.

Table 39.3 Key section of a report on indicators of personnel effectiveness

Workforce performance data per shop	Grayton Road	St. John's Precinct	Lark Hill
Staff (full-time)	8	6	7
Labour turnover (%)	25	150	0
Absence rate (%)	5	12	1
Sales per employee (£000s)	28	30	36

Questions

(30 marks; 35 minutes)

1 Briefly outline your observations on each of the three shops in terms of their personnel management. (12)
2 Give possible reasons for the factors you described in question 1. (9)
3 Taking the business as a whole, make justified recommendations as to how any problems could be tackled by the management. (9)

Introduction to operations management

UNIT 40

Operations management turns a customer order into a delivery.

40.1 INTRODUCTION

Operations management is the central business function of creating the product or service and delivering it to the customer (that is, meeting the customer requirement). Operations management at Ford means designing the cars and the machinery for making them, ordering the supplies, manufacturing the products, delivering them to the car showrooms and handling customer service issues such as warranty claims. Marketing creates the demand; operations management creates the supply to meet the demand. To achieve this, it requires human and financial resources.

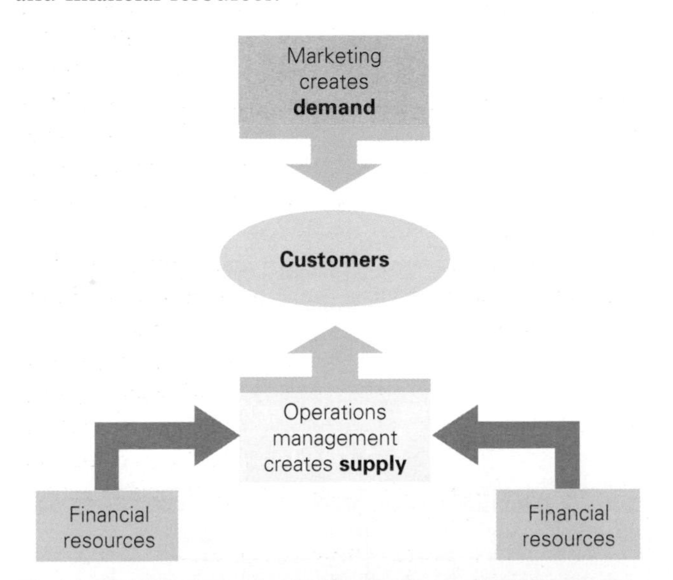

Figure 40.1 The central role of operations management

The importance of operations management is especially clear in the car industry. Rover Cars once commanded more than a 50 per cent share of the British car market. Its cars were well designed but poorly made. In 2005 the business ceased to exist as a British producer. In the years of Rover's decline, Toyota moved from being outside the top 20 world car producers to its current position as number one. Toyota has never been famous for producing stylish cars, but their quality and reliability have built its reputation worldwide. Toyota's business success has been built not on marketing but on operations management. By 2007, this success brought it annual profits of around £10 billion, more than the rest of the world's car makers put together. Even though Toyota had quality problems in 2010, the fundamental strength of the business (and its customer loyalty) keeps it motoring.

Figure 40.2

40.2 WHAT IS OPERATIONS MANAGEMENT?

Step 1: design

The process starts by designing a product or service to meet the needs or desires of a particular type of customer (see Table 40.1 for examples). The key at this, and every other, stage is to be clear about the customer and his/her requirements. If an airline's target customer is a student, the design of the plane interior must be simple, economical and effective, in order to help keep costs low enough to provide the low prices the student traveller wants.

Step 2: establishing the supply chain

In a manufacturing process, the heart of the operation will be the factory. This is where a collection of materials and parts will be turned into a finished product. In the case of a car, literally thousands of parts are involved in making each vehicle. Components that may cost little to produce, such as metal fixings for seat belts, all combine to turn £4,000 worth of parts into a car worth £10,000.

Table 40.1 Examples of designs that aim to meet customer requirements

Market	Type of customer	Customer needs or wants	Outline operational design
Hotels	Busy traveller and busy worker	Low-cost but comfortable hotel room in city centre	Well-located building with small but very well-equipped rooms; all food and drink from vending machines
Car market	Family with young children	A car to make family journeys more pleasant	Spacious car with good entertainment (seat-back monitors, etc.) and a small refrigerated drinks unit
Mortgages	University students	Students wanting to buy a flat on a joint mortgage – to stop relying on landlords	Flexible, low-cost mortgage, which is easy to get into and out of; available online to students with limited financial histories

This does not mean, though, that the car maker receives £6,000 of profit for every car sold; £6,000 of value has been added to the components, but at what cost? The most obvious cost is labour (that is, the staff needed to organise and run the factory). This will typically cost about 20 to 25 per cent of the value of the output. There are other factors that are a clear waste of money for the business, such as those listed below.

- *Production line errors leading to 'wastage':* if a car reaches the end of the production line and, when tested, fails to start, labour time is wasted finding the fault, and more time and components involved in correcting the problem. Modern companies try to eliminate all activities that waste time, but failing to take care over quality can never make sense for any company that wants to build a long-term future.
- *Breakdowns, perhaps due to faulty maintenance, or just due to wear and tear:* a well-run business uses preventative maintenance – checking machinery and replacing worn parts before a breakdown occurs.

Having established a well-run factory, the business can establish the other key parts of the **supply chain**, as indicated in Figure 40.3.

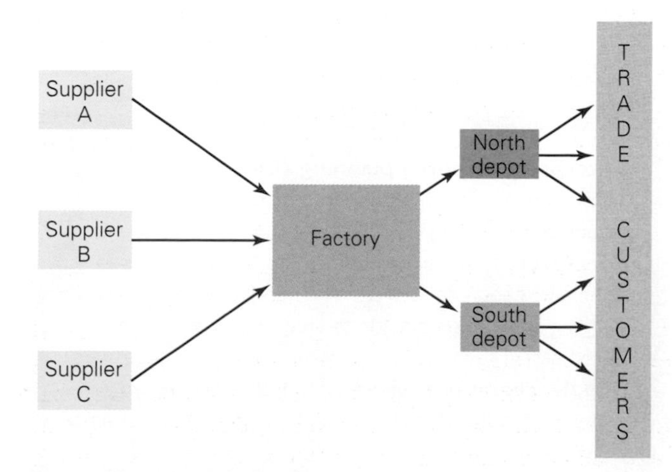

Figure 40.3 The supply chain

Step 3: working with suppliers

Very few businesses produce 100 per cent of a product or service. Almost all use suppliers. In some cases suppliers may do most of the operational work. Companies that 'bottle' Coca-Cola buy in: the aluminium cans, already printed with the can design; the water; the carbon dioxide used to create the fizz; and the secret Coke syrup (sent from the Coca-Cola factory in America). They may also get a distribution company such as Exel to make all the deliveries to wholesale and retail customers. So what does the Coca-Cola bottler actually do? Well, not a huge amount, clearly. But it must still be responsible for the coordination of all the suppliers and the quality of their work. If Waitrose ordered a container load of Coke Zero to reach its Bracknell depot at 10.00 on a Tuesday morning, did it turn up on time? If not, why not?

For many companies, working with suppliers is a key to success. A homemade ice cream parlour may do all the production operations on-site, but it still relies on suppliers of: fresh fruit, fresh milk and cream; grocery items such as sugar; wafer biscuits and cones; paper cups and plastic spoons, and so on. To run the parlour successfully all the operations have to be carried out successfully. If you have run out of cones, the best ice creams can remain unsold.

A company must therefore select suppliers that can deliver the right goods reliably; and must negotiate low enough prices for the supplies to make it possible to run the business economically.

Step 4: managing quality

Quality is not easy to define. It is a combination of real factors plus psychological ones. A haircut may be carried out very expertly, yet the customer may go away and cry! A less expert hairdresser may produce a technically worse cut, yet the effect may be just what the customer wants. In this case, providing quality means providing what the customer wants (that is, delivering customer satisfaction).

Yet what if the customer wants the 'wrong' thing? The traveller may only care about getting to work on time, yet if the train company has safety concerns, the train should be slowed down or stopped. The traveller may get to work, cursing the train company's poor-quality service; but in reality the company has done the right thing.

Ten years ago few shoppers worried about healthy eating, so McDonald's and others made their money 'supersizing' their customers. Were the companies providing a high-quality service? Perhaps not.

Effective operations management requires certain quality objectives, though.

- The product/service must do what the customer has been promised
- It must arrive on time, in good condition
- It must last at least as long as the customer expects
- Customer service should be effective (for example, phones answered quickly)
- After-sales service should also be effective (for example, speedy repair if something goes wrong).

These are the basics; on top of these should come the psychological factors that can mean a huge amount (e.g. service with a warm smile, with staff showing warmth towards the customers). Modern business theory suggests that, to stand out, a company needs to achieve 'customer delight' not just customer satisfaction. The easiest way to delight a customer is to be genuinely welcoming; a fake smile is worse than none at all.

Step 5: using technology effectively

Twenty years ago it required a room full of computers to do what a laptop can do today. In ten years there will probably be more computing power in a mobile phone than today's PC. At a time of dramatic change, some firms have come unstuck when upgrading their whole IT system; still more have struggled to make the best use of the internet.

Within the operations department of a business, the key requirement has been to find software that will satisfactorily manage the day-to-day process, from supplies through to delivery. For example, if fashion retailer Zara of Spain suddenly orders 4,000 'Glastonbury' jackets from your clothing factory, you need instantly to know:

- how many metres of cloth to order from your suppliers, and how many metres of lining
- how many buttons and zips to order
- when is the earliest date that all the above can be received, and therefore the job can begin
- how many hours of machine time will be needed
- how much overtime will be needed from staff, if the factory is already busy
- how many extra delivery vehicles will be needed and when
- when Zara can expect delivery of all 4,000 items to its Spanish headquarters.

This should all be available at the touch of a button using **enterprise resource planning** (ERP) software. This software has all the details of the business operation and provides not only the planning but will also monitor on a day-to-day basis whether things are working to schedule.

ISSUES FOR ANALYSIS

There are several concepts within operations management that are perfect for analysis:

- The idea that the heart of every business is the interface between marketing (demand) and operations (supply); and that operations relies on human and financial resources; only if all these departments work in harmony can the operation succeed
- Success in managing operations requires a true understanding of what the customer really wants: a car to get from A to B, or an 'ultimate driving machine' to impress the neighbours?
- A well-run operation should be able to capture all its key information in the form of an ERP software package; in fact, most firms who buy this software find that they lack much of the information they need; without accurate data it can be 'garbage in, garbage out'. Exactly this problem happened with Sony in its much-delayed development of the PS3.

40.3 INTRODUCTION TO OPERATIONS MANAGEMENT – AN EVALUATION

Every business is different, especially in the status given to operations staff. In Toyota or BMW, top engineers are the stars of the business and the operations department will be at the heart of all major decisions. In a business such as Innocent Drinks, the marketing people lead the business, with the operations changing to suit the market. Usually the importance and power of operations staff will reflect the needs and history of the business. In some cases, though, career politics will have intervened. A company that should be based on strong operations may actually be dominated by marketing and finance people, in which case, key decisions about the future may be taken wrongly. The A-grade student not only analyses the precise circumstances of the business, she or he is also willing to make a judgement on whether the business is being run well or badly.

Key Terms

Enterprise resource planning (ERP): logs all of a firm's costs, working methods and resources (machinery, labour, stocks of materials) within a piece of software; this provides a model of the business that can be used to answer questions such as 'When do we need to start working to get stocks made in time for delivery before Christmas?'

Supply chain: the whole path from suppliers of raw materials through production and storage on to customer delivery.

WORKBOOK

A REVISION QUESTIONS

(25 marks; 25 minutes)

1 Why may the quality of product design be less important for some businesses than others? (3)

2 Explain two key elements of operations management for:
  a) a children's shoe shop (4)
  b) a new, all-business-class airline. (4)

3 Choose one of the examples in Table 40.1 and outline one strength and one weakness of that business idea. (4)

4 Identify three ways in which staff might be at fault in production line errors that cause wastage. (3)

5 Examine the possible effects on a firm such as Coca-Cola of being unreliable in delivering to a big customer like Waitrose. (5)

6 Outline one possible benefit to a business from 'delighting' rather than 'satisfying' its customers. (2)

B REVISION EXERCISES

B1 DATA RESPONSE

Lean, green, efficient operations

Recent years have been great for Toyota, largely due to one car: the Prius. It is the car beloved of Hollywood stars due to its green technology – part electric, part petrol engine. The car has sold 'only' 2 million units, but its impact has been much greater. It has made the Toyota brand stand out in the crowded mass market in America, and helped Toyota become the world's number one car maker. Without doubt it is the world's richest, with more than £8,000 million of cash in its bank account. Now Citroën wants to 'muscle in' on Toyota's green success.

Of course, it is not enough to simply copy a rival. Citroën decided to tackle the main weakness of the Prius: its price. As the Prius has two engines (one electric, one petrol), its production costs are higher, forcing it to be priced at £2,000 to £3,000 more than comparable cars. Citroën's new car is called the C-Cactus and is priced at the level of the comparable petrol-only Citroën C4 model. This is because the C-Cactus has been made with dramatically fewer parts than a normal car. The car's interior, for example, has half the usual number of 400 separate components. That saves time and money in building the car. The C-Cactus therefore is less costly on parts and much less costly on labour than the C4.

Citroën's designers have questioned the need for every component in the car. Where possible they have cut back and simplified – but without risking passenger comfort. The car doors have two parts instead of the 12 on a normal car. The dashboard has gone, with most controls on a touch-screen indicator in front of the driver.

According to Citroën, the C-Cactus will not only drink less fuel, it will also use few fewer labour hours. There is no doubting that it is a designed to be lean and efficient; the only worry is whether customers will accept the very different look and feel of the car. It certainly will not have the luxury touches that some car buyers expect.

Source: www.scoop.co.nz

Questions

(30 marks; 35 minutes)

1 **a)** Outline two features of the C-Cactus that could prove to be appealing to car buyers. (6)
  b) Outline one reason why buyers of large family cars may not buy the C-Cactus. (4)

2 **a)** On average, Prius cars have sold for £12,000. How much revenue, therefore, has the brand generated for Toyota? (3)
  b) Product development on the Prius took eight years and cost an estimated £850 million. Was it worth it? Explain your answer. (5)

3 This unit sets out five important elements of operations management. Discuss which one of the five proved to be the most important in the development of the C-Cactus. (12)

B2 DATA RESPONSE

Insourcing: bringing jobs back home

Insourcing means bringing a service back in-house, to be operated by the firm's own personnel. In other words it means reversing the process of outsourcing (to countries such as India).

Insourcing seems to have been an increasing trend in America, especially in functions such as customer service and technical support. Why has this pattern occurred? Delta Airlines recently announced that it would no longer handle customer service calls from India and confirmed that these would be handled in-house in the US. 'Customer acceptance of call centre representatives in other countries was low and our customers are not shy about letting us have that feedback.'

According to mycustomer.com, the airline has cancelled its contract with offshore services provider Wipro, following negative customer feedback received after routing calls to India. The initial outsourcing was expected to save the company £15 million a year. The customer reaction was a less positive side-effect.

Other companies to go down the road of insourcing include United Airlines. Originally it was not clear to Indian outsourcing organisations whether these moves were due to customer backlash or an effort on the part of these companies to bring jobs back home to help to stimulate the economy. A source at United Airlines EMEA revealed that 165 jobs were made available in the US in April, to be split between Chicago and Hawaii as part of a 'change to the way customer relations are handled'.

Despite the cost-cutting times, the need for quality service to sell a quality product will endure and put firms in a strong position for coming out of the recession. And this quality, many companies find, often begins at home.

Source: Ben Lobel, *Supply Chain Digital*, 15 March 2010, with permission of White Digital Media.

Questions

(25 marks; 30 minutes)

1 Explain why a business could benefit from bringing its customer service function 'in-house'. (6)
2 From the article, analyse whether Delta Airlines has helped the efficiency of its operations by bringing the customer service and technical support functions back in-house. (8)
3 It is possible that the trend to insource is due to the availability of (cheap) unemployed staff in the US. Discuss whether it would ever be wise for a customer-focused business to outsource its customer service personnel. (11)

Invention, innovation and design

UNIT 41

An invention occurs when a new product or process is created; inventions will earn money only if they are put into practice – in other words, innovation takes place. Innovation means using a new idea in the marketplace or the workplace. Design involves developing both the physical appearance and the internal workings of a product. Design is used by firms to ensure that their products are attractive and practical.

41.1 INTRODUCTION

At the heart of any business is the product it sells. That product is the key to success. Invention, innovation and design are the processes by which interesting, new or unique products enter markets. As illustrated by the business example in the A-grade application, inventions can increase the total value of a market, or can lead to the birth of totally new markets.

A-grade application

How inventions can affect the market

For over 20 years, scuba divers were kept under water by the same type of 'open' oxygen system. They breathed in from their oxygen tank and breathed out through a tube that sent a stream of air bubbles to the surface. With the technology unchanged, suppliers' market shares were also stable. In recent years, however, closed 'Rebreather' systems have been developed and marketed.

Exhaled oxygen is recycled, enabling the diver to stay under water for two to three times as long. The system also avoids the streams of bubbles, which could frighten away the fish or whales the diver is trying to observe.

Although the cost of around £2,500 is far more than that of open diving equipment, Rebreathers have sold well in places like Florida and the Bahamas. This new technology has added value, changed market share and increased total spending within the marketplace.

41.2 INVENTION

The very activity of inventing new products is somewhat hit and miss. Many new products have been invented by accident. The Post-it note was the result of the discovery of a seemingly useless glue, which wasn't very sticky. Apple's iPod was largely the **invention** of company outsiders, but Apple added key design features and saw the need to link it with the music distribution system it called iTunes. When it made its press debut in 2001, the iPod wasn't particularly well-received. It was the public that saw the big opportunity, not the press 'experts'. Other products have been invented in order to fulfil a particular purpose, such as stairlifts for the elderly and disabled.

Invention is not limited to products (**product invention**). Production processes have been invented that have led to great competitive advantages (**process invention**). See Table 41.1. The glass manufacturer Pilkington plc developed the self-cleaning glass process (branded and patented as Pilkington Activ). This has a coating that breaks down dirt particles so that they do not stick to the glass (and therefore are washed away by normal rainfall). This has earned the firm significant sums in licensing revenues from foreign manufacturers.

Table 41.1 Product and process invention

Type of invention	Description	Examples
Product invention	Devising a new type or category of product, i.e. opening up a new market	• the Blu-Ray HD DVD • digital radios • real fruit smoothies
Process invention	Devising a new way of producing or manufacturing (which may allow new products to be made, or improve the efficiency of making existing products)	• self-cleaning glass • soft ice coating (Walls Solero) • robotic welding

Although many inventions come from lone inventors such as James Dyson, most are the result of big company research programmes. An individual may come up with an idea that can be produced and marketed under licence by a larger firm that has greater facilities. Or the inventor may set up his or her own firm, if the product idea is good enough and sufficient capital can be raised. Yet most of our lives are dominated by big corporate inventions such as the science behind the iPhone, iPad or Xbox Kinect.

Having come up with an invention, a vital step is to patent it. This means registering with the Patent Office that the new technical process is a genuine step forward from previous patents. If a patent is granted, no other firm has the legal right to use your new process for at least 20 years. This provides a long period in which the inventor enjoys exclusive rights to sell the new product or process. This allows the inventor to gain high rewards from selling at a high price due to the product's uniqueness. In October 2010 observant bloggers noted that Apple had taken out patents in China for key developments that are likely to add a video-conferencing facility to the 2011 iPad2. This will help maintain the price premium that iPad already enjoys due to its external design and cult status.

A-grade application

Plug-In Prius?

Toyota's 1990s development of 'hybrid synergy drive' has become one of the biggest innovation success stories in business history. Not only had Prius sales amounted to more than £15,000 million by early 2008, but also the car had transformed the whole company image. In the huge US market, 'Toyota' came to mean environmentally responsible and technically advanced (though its 2010 safety scandals dented this).

The only weakness of the Prius is that, unless the driver goes on long journeys, the battery is not charged up enough to operate as an electric car in town. So although the car is great for someone who drives 30 miles to work (in town), it is less effective for someone who crawls 2 miles to work in heavy traffic.

So, in autumn 2010 Toyota launched a 2-year trial of 600 Plug-In Prius cars. It has the same petrol plus electric engine, but with a plug-in facility that recharges the battery in 90 minutes. This enables the car to use its electric motor for a much higher percentage of each journey, generating over 100 miles per gallon of fuel. After a 2-year trial, Toyota plans to launch the Plug-In Prius in 2012.

41.3 INNOVATION

As with invention, **innovation** can be based on products or processes. However, successful innovation requires business skill in addition to inventive talent. The inventive idea must be honed into a marketable product. Meanwhile the method of production must be developed and finance found. Successful innovation is vital for the long-term survival of a firm. Innovation allows the firm to update its product portfolio by replacing products at the end of their life cycle.

It is particularly important to continue to innovate in markets where competition is strong, product life cycles are low and the rate of innovation is high. Computer manufacturers seek to launch a new innovation every few months, in an attempt to gain a competitive advantage over rivals. In industries such as this, innovation is essential for survival. A computer firm selling three-year-old technology is unlikely to be able to add much value or sell high volumes.

A-grade application

The robot vacuum

In 2002 iRobot – a company formed in 1990 by three MIT research scientists – launched the Roomba vacuuming robot. Between 2002 and 2010 more than 4 million have been sold worldwide, at prices of around £200 each. The Roomba lives on a recharging pod, gets itself up, can clean up to four rooms, then finds its way back to its pod and settles down to recharge its batteries. If you have a cat or dog (so that pet hair is a constant problem) a daily clean by Roomba is ideal. And this is the perfect present for older relatives who may struggle to keep their homes clean.

The latest Roomba can be programmed for the week, and include information about when to clean. iRobot is soon to launch a 'Wash and Go' version that will wash and dry a kitchen floor!

Radical innovations such as the robot cleaner described in the A-grade application are rare. In most markets, the term 'innovation' means nothing so dramatic. In the salad cream market, the first squeezable bottle was called an innovation by Heinz. Breweries were equally thrilled to announce the first 'widget' canned beer. The reason is that, in large, established markets, quite small product innovations can have a major impact on market share. Heinz hopes that its 2010 innovation of a resealable baked bean can will give it an advantage over its rivals.

41.4 DESIGN

The design of a product is not just about its appearance and shape. It is also about the product's function, quality and durability. Designers work to a design brief, which tells them the criteria for looks, cost and quality. All must be considered in designing the finished product. Larger firms may have their own design teams on the payroll. Smaller firms may rely on design consultants to turn a product idea or requirement into a finished product.

A useful way to consider design is through the design mix. As Figure 41.1 indicates, every designer must consider the following three factors.

1 *Aesthetics:* the look, feel, smell or taste (that is, the appeal to the senses).
2 *Function:* does it work? Is it reliable? Is it strong enough or light enough for the customer's purpose?
3 *Economic manufacture:* is the design simple enough for it to be made quickly and efficiently?

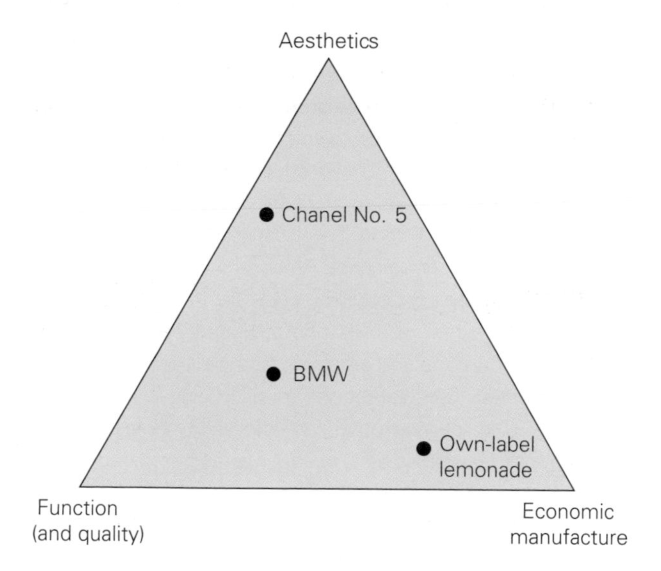

Figure 41.1 The design mix

In some cases, all three factors will be of equal importance. In most, there will be a clear priority. As Figure 41.1 shows, with own-label lemonade, cheap production would be the overwhelming priority. Therefore cheap design, using low-cost materials that are easy to manufacture, will be required. For BMW, design for function would be important, as would the car's appearance. Firms decide on their design priorities after careful market research to identify the purchasing motivations of existing and potential customers.

A-grade application

Designing the Post-It note

Offices throughout the world are likely to have three brand names in common. Intel-based computers, Microsoft software and .... Post-It notes. These yellow pads of sticky paper have made many millions of dollars for the American company 3M. They were invented by 3M employee Art Fry in the 1960s. He had been shown a 'failed' development of a glue; it simply didn't stick well. He realised that the glue's 'problem' was that it stayed quite sticky for a long time, instead of being very sticky at one time. He tried it on pads of paper, found that yellow had the most impact – and the Post-It note was born. The Post-It was an innovation that stemmed from a research and development programme.

Market research on consumer's needs and state of the market

↓

Identify gap in the market

↓

Original idea developed

↓

Design brief prepared

↓

Approach designers (in-house or consultants)

↓

Chose design from initial submissions

↓

Models or prototypes made up

↓

Working samples made up and tested

↓

Consumer trials on target group

↓

Tooling up for manufacture

↓

Organise supplies of raw materials

↓

Full scale production

Figure 41.2 The design process

41.5 INVENTION AND INNOVATION IN BUSINESS

Invention and innovation in marketing

Many would argue that the most important element of the marketing mix is the product itself. Successful product development keeps a firm one step ahead of the competition. This usually means keeping one step ahead in pricing as well. Whether you are introducing a new drug, such as Viagra, or a new football management computer game, you have the opportunity to charge a premium price. Innovative new products are also very likely to get good distribution. Sainsbury's is very reluctant to find space on its shelves for just another ('me-too') cola or toothpaste, but if the new product is truly innovative, the space will be found.

Invention and innovation in finance

Invention, innovation and design all require significant amounts of long-term investment. Innovation takes time, and that time is spent by highly paid researchers. The result is that firms who are unwilling to accept long payback periods are unlikely to be innovators. Short-termist companies are far more likely to copy other firms' successes. In fact, much of the money spent by firms on invention and innovation provides no direct payback. Ideas are researched and developed before discovering that they will not succeed in the marketplace. The result is that innovation is something of a hit-and-miss process. There are no guaranteed rewards, but there is the possibility of a brand new, market-changing product. It is these successes that can radically alter the competitive conditions within a marketplace, allowing an innovative company to claim a dominant position.

Invention and innovation in people

Inventors are sometimes caricatured as 'mad scientists' working alone in laboratories with bubbling test tubes. This is far from the truth. For many years, firms have realised that teamwork provides many of the most successful innovations. As a result, research teams are encouraged to share their breakthroughs on a regular basis in the hope that the team can put their ideas together to create a successful product. These research teams are often created by taking specialists in various fields of operation, from different departments within an organisation. This means that a team may consist of several scientists, an accountant, a production specialist and someone from the marketing department. This blend of expertise will enable the team to identify cost-effective, marketable new ideas that can be produced by the company, without the need for the new idea to be passed around the different departments within an organisation.

Invention and innovation in operations management

As previously mentioned, the terms 'invention' and 'innovation' are not limited to describing finished products. New production processes can be invented or developed. These can lead to more efficient, cheaper or higher-quality production. Furthermore, new products often need new machinery and processes to be developed for their manufacture. Returning to the Post-it note – its lack of successful imitators is because no other firm has been able to replicate successfully 3M's machine for sticking the glued pad together. Design is also important in production. The process needs to be clearly thought through so that every machine and activity has a logical place in the production system.

ISSUES FOR ANALYSIS

- Invention should not be confused with innovation. The British have a proud record as inventors. The hovercraft, television, penicillin and many more products were British inventions. In recent years, however, there has been less success in this country with innovation. The Japanese have been the great innovators in electronics, the Americans in computers and the Swiss in watches. British firms have failed to invest sufficiently to develop ranges of really innovative new products.
- Major innovation can completely change a firm's competitive environment. The market shares of leading companies may change little for years; then an innovation comes along that changes everything. The firm that has not prepared for such change can be swept aside. This may happen to bookshops that do not establish a major presence on the internet.
- Good management means looking ahead, not only to the next hill but the one after that. Anticipation makes change manageable. It may even ensure that your own firm becomes the market leader due to the far-sightedness of your own innovation. In turn, that would ensure high product differentiation and allow relatively high prices to be charged.
- Innovation can happen in management procedures, attitudes and styles. A management that is progressive and adventurous may well find that an empowered workforce generates the new ideas that seemed lacking before. It would not be wise to assume that invention and innovation is all about scientists and engineering. It is about people.

41.6 INVENTION, INNOVATION AND DESIGN – AN EVALUATION

The fundamental theme for evaluating any question involving design, invention and innovation is the contrast between long- and short-term thinking. Invention and innovation are clearly long-term activities. It could be argued that design is the same. Part of the brilliance of Mercedes engineering is that, although the cars develop year by year, there are design themes that keep a Mercedes completely recognisable. Companies whose objective is short-term profit maximisation are unlikely to spend heavily on invention, innovation or design. The key is to take a long-term view, then stick to it. This is what Pilkington did with its self-cleaning glass, which took ten years to perfect. The Toyota Prius took more than ten years to become profitable. As a past Guinness advertisement once said: 'Good things come to those who wait.'

Key Terms

Innovation: bringing a profitable new product or process to life.
Invention: drawing up a new way of making a product or process.
Process invention: devising a new way of making things (production process).
Product invention: devising a new product to make.

WORKBOOK

A REVISION QUESTIONS

(40 marks; 45 minutes)

1 Distinguish between innovation and invention. (3)
2 Why is it important to reduce the time taken to develop new ideas? (4)
3 Distinguish between product and process innovation. (3)
4 Why is it 'vital' to patent an invention? (3)
5 What marketing advantages does good design bring to a firm? (4)
6 Where, on Figure 41.1 would you plot the following?
  a) An iPhone (3)
  b) The packaging of a Cadbury £4 Easter egg? (3)
  Briefly explain your answers.
7 Why could product-orientated firms produce more inventions than market-orientated ones? (4)
8 How are the concepts of short-termism and innovation linked? (4)
9 Many businesses are concerned at the fall in the number of students taking science A-levels. How may this affect firms in the long term? (5)
10 What effect would a lack of innovation have on a company's product portfolio? (4)

B REVISION EXERCISES
B1 DATA RESPONSE

Tide Coldwater

Procter & Gamble (P&G) is the world's biggest household products company. Its company website says that 'Innovation is the company's lifeblood'. If so, it has worked well, as P&G's annual sales in 2007 were $76.5 billion and profits exceeded $15 billion. In 2005, it launched the innovative Tide Coldwater in America after a long development phase that had been conducted in strict secrecy. Tide had long been America's top-selling detergent, and now P&G wanted to persuade US customers that clothes could be washed perfectly well in cold water. The prize for P&G could be increased market share, and at slightly higher prices. After all, cold-water washing would save the householder money, so therefore the product would be worth more (that is, it would have higher value added). P&G would not miss the opportunity to increase its profit margins.

The biggest prize, though, would be the huge goodwill that P&G could enjoy by basking in the warm, green glow of social responsibility. According to the company, 85 per cent of the energy used when washing clothes comes from the water temperature (as opposed to the production of the detergent). As 7 million US households use Tide Coldwater, the energy saving represents millions of tonnes of carbon emissions per year.

Questions

(35 marks; 40 minutes)

1 Outline the market research that P&G would have needed to do before launching an innovative product such as Tide Coldwater. (8)
2 **a)** Calculate the percentage profit margin being made by P&G in 2007. (2)
  b) In 2001, the company's profit margin was 10.9 per cent. Examine two possible actions the management may have taken to increase the margins over recent years. (6)
3 Explain the possible impact on P&G's marketing managers of the company's proud boast that 'Innovation is the company's lifeblood'. (5)
4 Explain why the development of a product as ordinary as a detergent might be kept so secret. (6)
5 Examine the possible benefits to P&G of the environmental 'green glow' involved in the launch of Tide Coldwater. (8)

C ESSAY QUESTIONS

(40 marks each)

1 To what extent does an innovative product guarantee success?
2 'Any business has two, and only two, basic functions. Marketing and innovation.' Discuss whether there is value in this statement by Peter Drucker.
3 'Luck is the most important factor in successful innovation.' Discuss the validity of this statement.
4 Spending on research and development is wasted money since many firms find success through copying other firms' products. Discuss this statement.

UNIT 42

Customer service

Customer service describes the range of actions taken by a business when interacting with its customers. Effective customer service will meet or surpass the expectations that customers have of the business.

42.1 INTRODUCTION

The biggest question in relation to this topic is whether firms try to provide good service to their customers or 'customer service'. In other words, is customer service a label used to describe actions that prevent the customer from inconveniencing the organisation? Or is providing a service a genuine part of the company's attitudes and **culture**?

42.2 HOW IS CUSTOMER SERVICE DELIVERED?

Face to face

The most immediate, most powerful situation in which customer service is seen is in direct, face-to-face dealings with customers. Retailers must focus clearly on how shop staff interact with their customers. This is a situation with which you are likely to be highly familiar, perhaps from both sides. Here, the face of the employee is the face of the company to the customer.

Telephone

Much of customer-service activity now happens in call centres. See Figure 42.1. From finding out the price of a train from Leeds to Plymouth, to making an insurance claim following a car crash, the telephone is a key factor in customer service. Call centres are thought to be cost-efficient, partly because they can be located in Birmingham, Belfast or Bangalore. It is highly questionable, though, as to whether they deliver 'customer service'. Most customers want to talk to an individual, not someone who is reading a script.

Figure 42.1 A call centre

> **A-grade application**
>
> **Customer service at home**
>
> Companies looking for a less controversial alternative to basing call centres in Asia may have found an answer in a concept known as home-shoring. An alternative to 'off-shoring' where customer service is provided from a call centre in another country, 'home-shoring' bases customer service assistants in their own homes. Research evidence seems to suggest that this boosts productivity and increases the level of service provided. The most famous home-shoring success story is US airline JetBlue, where over 1,200 staff work at home. The customer complaint level is, amazingly, only one per 420,000 passengers, while staff turnover is just 3.5 per cent, way below that experienced in a traditional call centre. In June 2010 JetBlue was ranked highest among US airlines for customer satisfaction for the sixth year in a row.

Internet

Many online booking systems have eliminated direct human contact from customer service. Behind the scenes, though, the attitudes within the business remain all-important. You may book a bargain flight online, ticking the box for same-day delivery of the tickets. If the business fails to deliver the tickets on time, however, you will be unable to go on holiday. Will the tickets arrive? The answer to this question is only if the faceless staff do their jobs on time. As customers, we have to trust that an online service will soon fail if it cannot meet its promises.

42.3 METHODS OF MEETING CUSTOMER EXPECTATIONS

To meet customer expectations, a business needs to follow a four-stage process as illustrated in Figure 42.2.

Identify customer expectations

Agree how to meet customer expectations

Train all staff to be able to provide the customer service level the firm is aiming to achieve

↓

Monitor customer service and look for improvements

Figure 42.2 Meeting customer expectations

Market research

In order to find out what customers expect, market research will be used. This is likely to be a mixture of quantitative and qualitative research. The qualitative research is designed to probe selected key customers to find what level of support and service they expect from the firm. Such detailed qualitative research will probably enable the firm to gain a clear understanding of the range of expectations that different customers may have. With these identified, quantitative research can be used to assess how many customers expect certain features of customer service. An example may be using research to identify 'acceptable' queuing times when ringing a call centre.

Decision time

Decisions will need to be made, based on the results of research into customers' expectations, of just what level of service the firm will aim to provide. If money were no object, any firm could provide exquisite customer service. We can only imagine the level of service available from James Bond's Savile Row tailor or Victoria Beckham's Beverly Hills hairstylist. Alternatively, a firm may decide to take a low-cost approach to customer service, perhaps outsourcing enquiries and technical problems to reduce costs. The costs and benefits of spending on customer service will be weighed. For those companies that value their reputation highly, the benefits may outweigh the costs, while for those that rely on low prices to shift their products, they may cut corners on customer service to protect their profit margin.

Training

Staff training can begin once the firm has decided on its customer service policies and practices. Note, however, that firms will have varying levels of commitment to training for staff. Some firms may offer staff just 42 minutes' informal training in customer service. They cannot expect their policies to be implemented as effectively as the firm that sends all new staff to a training centre for a full day's training. In America, McDonald's began a programme of getting staff to work with **zero training**. This was just at the start of the period when the firm's sales and profits collapsed in the period 2002–05. The zero training approach disappeared when new managers decided that McDonald's needed *more* customer training, not less. At McDonald's, and everywhere else, the cost involved in improving the level of customer service must be set against the cost of not doing so.

Quality

As will be discussed in Unit 43, firms looking to ensure the quality of anything that they do, face a choice between quality control and quality assurance.

Quality control methods for customer service involve spotting defective service. The problem here is that poor customer service can be spotted only once it has been delivered, and this means at least one unhappy customer. Anyone who has rung a call centre is likely to have heard an announcement that 'Your call may be recorded for quality control purposes.' Those working in the retail sector are at the mercy of '**mystery shoppers**', who are paid to visit stores and report back on the customer service provided. Other methods of quality control involve planned or unannounced management checks.

Quality assurance is the attempt to introduce systems to ensure that quality errors cannot occur. Therefore quality assuring customer service systems must involve staff training. Given the key role of staff in meeting customer expectations, they will need to be 100 per cent clear on how to deal with any situation they may face. The problem is that staff can start to see themselves, not the customers, as the focal point of the business. Management may keep saying 'the customer is king' or 'the customer is always right', but the staff don't really believe it.

Some of the differences between quality control and quality assurance in relation to customer service are given in Table 42.1.

Table 42.1 Quality control versus quality assurance

Quality control	Quality assurance
'Your call may be recorded for quality purposes'	Thorough, ongoing training in customer service
Mystery shoppers	Customer service is a key feature of company culture
Management checks	Clear systems, set out in writing, about how to deal with each type of customer complaint

Quality standards

Companies can apply for quality standards certification to show the rest of the world that they are serious about the quality of what they do. (See Unit 43.) The basic **ISO 9000** certification series covers customer service in organisations for which the skill is relevant. However, for customer service specialists, there are customer service-specific standards:

- ISO 10002: a customer complaint handling standard
- the BSI runs the CCA Standard: a special quality standard for call centres
- Charter Mark: administered by the government, this is a customer service standard for public- and voluntary-sector organisations, along with firms that provide a public service in the passenger train and bus, water, gas and electricity supply industries.

42.4 MONITORING AND IMPROVING CUSTOMER SERVICE

With a customer service system in place, the final step is to fight complacency. Systems designed to monitor the effectiveness of customer service must be used in order to ensure that standards do not slip and that the quality systems being used for customer service continue to produce the required results. However, in a spirit of continually trying to improve, most firms will monitor their own customer service standards relative to those of their rivals. Innovations in customer service are likely to be copied fairly quickly in most markets. This is why major changes to customer service, such as the use of the internet in the banking industry, tend to become common features of the industry in such a short time.

Benefits of good customer service

There is no doubt that good customer service has positive effects on a business, not just in terms of keeping from jumping to rival firms.

Brand loyalty

Good customer service tends to bring repeat custom. As customers feel positive about the experience they have had with a business, they are most likely to return to that firm for future purchases. Hanging on to existing customers is crucial for any sensible business, since attracting new customers from rivals tends to rely on expensive promotional tools, such as advertising and special offers.

Word-of-mouth promotion

Good customer service can actually generate free promotion, as happy customers tell their friends. Anecdote suggests that word-of-mouth promotion is the most effective promotional tool available to a business. This is because you are more likely to believe your friends than a company's marketing department.

Increased efficiency

Since good customer service is likely to include better advice to customers, firms are less likely to sell inappropriate products or services that fail to meet customer needs. This should mean fewer complaints and therefore a reduced need for 'second phase' customer-service back-up, such as customer complaint lines or product returns.

A-grade application

The best and worst ...

The Institute of Customer Service regularly publishes the results of its survey of customer service in the UK. This provides data on the best- and worst-performing sectors for customer service. It also highlights prime examples of excellent customer service. In the 2010 survey, the top three performers were all retailers: John Lewis, Waitrose and Marks and Spencer (food). Meanwhile, the UK's worst-performing sector for customer service was the utility companies (gas, water, electricity). It is interesting to note that all three of the UK's customer service leaders undoubtedly experience commercial benefits from the reputation their customer service brings.

Source: UK Customer Satisfaction Index, www.ukcsi.com

ISSUES FOR ANALYSIS

- With so much customer service being provided by phone, call centres feature high in the customer service agenda. Churchill Insurance is just one of many companies now stating clearly in its promotional literature that it uses only UK call centres. Why should it use UK call centres when the cost is far higher than for those located in India, and the staff in a UK call centre will be less qualified than their Indian counterparts? Customer service could be argued to be more qualitative than quantitative. Perceptions of customers are probably more important than the service they actually receive; the link between this area of operations management and the marketing department is strong.
- Some companies, notably DIY chain B&Q, believe that some types of people are better at customer service than others. Many major retailers use students and school-leavers as a huge portion of their shop-floor staff. However, B&Q feels that students and school-leavers are naturally less polite than older members of staff. The result is that B&Q actively encourages retired and semi-retired people to apply for positions in its stores, since it believes that these staff can provide the most effective customer service.

42.5 CUSTOMER SERVICE – AN EVALUATION

Good customer service is unlikely to be provided by unmotivated staff. Although systems for ensuring customer service – such as market research, training and quality control systems – do help to improve customer service, it is the staff that will be the vital determinant. The message for businesses is therefore one that stresses the need to look after all staff. Often, a business may pay particular attention to motivating its managers, at the cost of ignoring the needs of staff lower down the organisation's hierarchy. However, in the majority of businesses, the front-line providers of customer service are the staff at the lowest level of the hierarchy. No matter how motivated the store management team, an unmotivated supermarket checkout assistant may well be the main determinant of a customer's shopping experience.

Key Terms

Culture: within a business, this means 'the way we do things round here' (that is, the attitudes and behaviours of staff within an organisation).

ISO 9000: the International Standards Organisation (ISO) has a quality assurance certification system called ISO 9000.

Mystery shoppers: employed to test customer service by visiting a shop or sales outlet unannounced, and therefore have the same experience as customers.

Zero training: the opposite of customer service, in that it implies that staff need neither skills nor positive attitudes to work for the business.

WORKBOOK

A REVISION QUESTIONS

(35 marks; 40 minutes)

1 List three methods of meeting customer expectations. (3)

2 Explain how the use of a mystery shopper can help to maintain standards of customer service. (4)

3 Briefly explain how the following businesses may benefit from providing excellent customer service:
  a) a café
  b) a manufacturer of washing machines
  c) a bank. (9)

4 For a business that you use regularly where you feel customer service could be better, briefly explain:
  a) your own customer expectations
  b) how the business could identify what your expectations are
  c) how the business could try to meet your expectations. (9)

5 Explain why a small local plumber may benefit from offering better customer service than all her local rivals. (4)

6 Explain two benefits that an electricity supplier like npower might find as a result of gaining a customer service quality standard such as the Charter Mark. (6)

B REVISION EXERCISES

B1 DATA RESPONSE

Harry Ramsden's Fish 'n' Chips

In July 2010 Channel 4's 'Undercover Boss' series featured Marija Simovic, chief executive of Harry Ramsden's. She spent a day working as a waitress at the chain's most profitable branch, by Blackpool tower. Within an hour she had a customer complaint. The fish and chips she served were cold. The reason was simple. There was no system for telling waiting staff that their order was ready to serve. Furthermore, poor store layout created a bottleneck very close to where the food was cooked, so it was impossible to hang around waiting for the hot food to be ready.

Despite these problems, Marija was enormously impressed by the friendliness of the customer service. Two waiting staff especially caught her eye. They were warm, friendly and always willing to provide customers with a great experience (for example, 'would you like some extra hot chips, love?'). Marija decided to ask these two staff to get involved in a national training programme on customer service. She also addressed the problem of cold food by investing in a personal buzzer system which would vibrate in the pockets of individual waiting staff when their food was ready to be served.

Overall, the chief executive could see that good service was a combination of staff attitudes and motivation, together with organisational and physical factors such as equipment, store layout and store investment.

Questions

(25 marks; 42 minutes)

1 Explain why customer service is so important to a business like Harry Ramsden's. (6)
2 The problems at the Blackpool store were easily solvable by the chief executive. Why may local managers be unable to solve the day-to-day customer service problems they face? (6)
3 This type of TV programme persuades chief executives to solve the immediate issues they see. Discuss the broader lessons a chief executive such as Marija should learn about how to improve customer service throughout her business. (13)

B2 DATA RESPONSE

Twinkle.com

Twinkle.com is an internet service provider, aiming for the top end of the market in a marketplace that has experienced enormous growth over the past ten years. Twinkle knows the importance of customer service, but has experienced a number of problems over the past year. Its management is disappointed in this because this year it has spent more than ever before on a promotional campaign to recruit new customers. Disappointed with the results produced by its online and telephone customer service teams, Twinkle.com has called in a consultant to improve customer service levels. The consultant has gathered the data shown in Table 42.2.

Table 42.2 Data provided for Twinkle.com

	Quarter 1 (Jan–Mar)	Quarter 2 (Apr–Jun)	Quarter 3 (Jul–Sep)	Quarter 4 (Oct–Dec)
Complaints per month	864	967	932	902
Number of complaints dealt with within 24 hours (in %)	28	24	29	34
Customer service training expenditure (£000s)	12	12	12	10
Overall customer service rating from monthly customer survey (10 = best; 1 = worst)	6	5	5	4
Increase/decrease in total customer numbers (in %)	**+3**	**+2**	**−3**	**−12**

Questions

(30 marks; 35 minutes)

1 Briefly explain how Table 42.2 shows evidence of poor customer service. (3)
2 Identify and explain a possible cause of poor customer service performance suggested by Table 42.2. (4)
3 Analyse two other possible causes of poor customer service within the business. (6)
4 Analyse the reasons why customer service may be especially important for an ISP (internet service provider). (8)
5 To what extent can an external consultant help to improve the customer service levels offered by a firm such as Twinkle.com? (9)

Effective quality management

UNIT 43

Quality management means providing what the customer wants at the right time, with the right level of quality and consistency, and therefore yielding high customer satisfaction.

43.1 WHAT IS QUALITY?

W. Edwards Deming, the American quality guru, said that 'quality is defined by the customer'. The customer may insist on certain specifications, or demand exceptional levels of customer comfort. Another definition of quality is 'fit for use'. Although hard to define, there is no doubt that customers are very aware of quality. Their perception of quality is a key part of the buying decision.

Customers will accept some **trade-off** between price and quality. There is, however, a minimum level of quality that is acceptable. The customer wants the product to work (be fit for use), regardless of the price. If the customers think that the quality is below a minimum level they will not buy the product. Above the minimum level of acceptable quality, customers will expect to get more as they pay more.

The importance of quality is related to the level of **competitiveness** in the market. When competition is fierce, the quality of the product can tip the balance in the customer's decision making. Dell is a hugely successful computer manufacturer, which sells directly to customers through the internet or newspaper advertising. Its mission statement is: 'Customers must have a quality experience and be pleased not just satisfied.'

For all customers, quality is about satisfying their expectations. The customer will take into account the total buying experience. Customer service and after-sales service may be as important as the product itself. The way the product is sold, even *where* it is sold, all contribute to the customer's feelings about the quality of the product.

Quality is a moving target. A quality standard that is acceptable today may not be in the future. Customer expectations of quality are constantly changing. As quality improves, customer demands also increase.

Quality:

- is satisfying (preferably beating) customer expectations
- applies to services as well as products
- involves the whole business process, not just the manufacturing of the product
- is an ever-rising target.

A-grade application

Toyota

Toyota has long had a reputation for superior quality. All this was threatened when some of its cars appeared to suffer from accelerator pedal problems in the United States. Initially Toyota was slow to react but eventually had to recall 2.3 million vehicles across the world. The damaged reputation inevitably led to lower sales.

The president of Toyota Akio Toyoda said the company had identified 2003 as the turning point for its decline in quality. This was when it passed 6 million vehicles and the subsequent growth across the world made it difficult to apply its quality principles for which it was renowned. In June 2010 Toyota announced that all its new cars sold in the UK would come with a five year warranty.

'Our new five-year warranty is tangible evidence of our commitment to quality and to our customers – both those who are loyal to the brand, and those who are considering switching to Toyota for their next car,' said Miguel Fonseca, Toyota GB managing director.

'By taking this major initiative we are giving our customers complete peace of mind. We want to reassure them that, in choosing a Toyota, they are getting the best in quality, reliability and durability.'

43.2 QUALITY DEFINED BY CUSTOMER SPECIFICATIONS

Where the customer is in a powerful position, quality is directly defined by the customer. Many firms lay down minimum standards for their suppliers. Large businesses, such as supermarkets and chain stores, are able to insist on quality standards. They have the buying power to force their suppliers to conform. For many years, Marks & Spencer has worked with suppliers to ensure that standards are met. Other large purchasers, such as government departments and local authorities, are also able to insist on high standards for supplies. As new roads and motorways are built, their surface is checked to ensure its quality. If the surface does not conform to the required standards the contractor will have to re-lay the area.

Other firms, and in particular local and central government agencies, will insist that their suppliers have obtained ISO 9000 (see A-grade application). This ensures that suppliers are operating within a quality framework.

A-grade application

ISO 9000

ISO 9000 is an international standard for quality systems. It is a British standard that is recognised worldwide. Companies that are registered can display the BSI symbol. In order to register, companies have to document their business procedures, prepare a quality manual and assess their quality management systems. They are assessed by an independent assessor. After obtaining the award, businesses are visited at regular intervals to ensure compliance. It is necessary that everyone in the organisation follows the processes outlined in the quality manual. Firms who have registered say that this has provided a range of benefits to the business. These include:

- less waste
- cost savings
- fewer mistakes
- increased efficiency
- improved competitiveness
- increased customer satisfaction
- increased profits.

43.3 WHY IS QUALITY MANAGEMENT IMPORTANT?

Quality is an important competitive issue. Where the consumer has choice, quality is vital. For a new business, effective quality management may mean the difference between success and disaster. If the product or service cannot get a good reputation the business will not last long.

A reputation for good quality brings marketing advantages. A good-quality product will:

- generate a high level of repeat purchase, and therefore a longer product life cycle
- allow brand building and cross-marketing
- allow a price premium (this is often greater than any added costs of quality improvements; in other words, quality adds value, as it generates additional profit)
- make products easier to place (retailers are more likely to stock products with a good reputation).

The consequences of a poor product or poor service for the business are shown in Table 43.1.

Table 43.1 Implications of poor product or service quality

Marketing costs	Business costs
Loss of sales	Scrapping of unsuitable goods
Loss of reputation	Reworking of unsatisfactory goods – costs of labour and materials
May have to price-discount	Lower prices for 'seconds'
May impact on other products in range	Handling complaints/ warranty claims
Retailers may be unwilling to stock goods	Loss of consumer goodwill and repeat purchase

43.4 HOW CAN FIRMS DETECT QUALITY PROBLEMS?

The ideal is to detect quality problems before they reach the customer. This can be done by:

- inspection of finished goods before sale; this has been the traditional method; it may be all goods or only a sample
- self-inspection of work by operatives; this is being used more as businesses recognise that quality needs to be 'everyone's business'
- statistical analysis within the production process; this can be used to ensure that specifications stay within certain limits; for example, Mars may set a target weight for 100g bags of Maltesers of between 96 g to 104 g (see Figure 43.1); only if the weight slips outside this range will an alarm indicator be triggered to warn that the specifications are not being met; staff could then stop the production line and readjust the machine to ensure that the correct weight is being given.

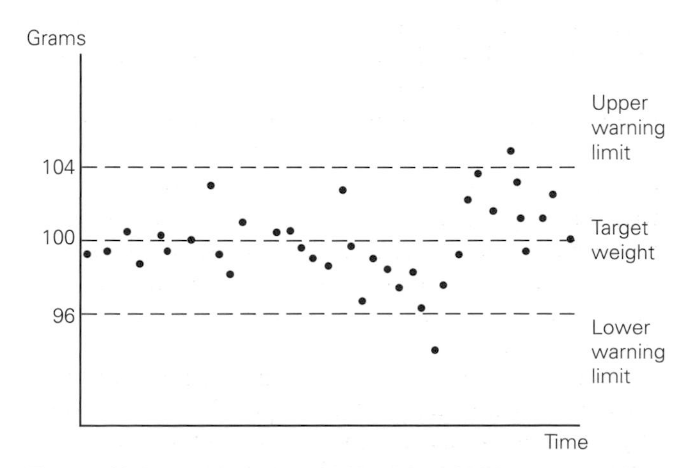

Figure 43.1 Actual weight of 100 g bags of Maltesers coming off the production line

Quality quotes

'Reducing the cost of quality is in fact an opportunity to increase profits without raising sales, buying new equipment, or hiring new people.' *Philip Crosby, American quality guru*

'Quality is remembered long after the price is forgotten.' *Gucci slogan*

'The only job security anybody has in this company comes from quality, productivity and satisfied customers.' *Lee Iacocca, successful boss of Chrysler Motors*

'Good management techniques are enduring. Quality control, for instance, was treated as a fad here, but it's been part of the Japanese business philosophy for decades. That's why they laugh at us.' *Peter Senge, US business author*

'Quality has to be caused, not controlled.' *Philip Crosby*

'Quality is our best assurance of customer allegiance, our strongest defence against foreign competition, and the only path to sustained growth and earnings.' *Jack Welch, General Electric chief*

Source: Stuart Crainer, 1997, *The Ultimate Book of Business Quotations*, Capstone Publishing

43.5 HOW DO BUSINESSES MANAGE QUALITY?

This depends on the size of the business. A small new business will be able to inspect every item and ensure that each customer is satisfied. As the business grows, keeping checks on quality needs to be more systematic. In large manufacturing businesses, quality control has traditionally been the responsibility of the production department. Most quality control processes were concentrated in the factory. These were intended to prevent faults leaving the factory. Today, firms are more likely to see quality as having product and service aspects.

There are four stages to quality management that apply to all businesses. These are prevention, detection, correction and improvement.

Prevention

This tries to avoid problems occurring. It requires thought and care at every stage:

- in the initial product design, to 'build in' quality
- in purchasing raw materials and components (that is, not just trying to buy the cheapest supplies, but caring about quality)
- designing the factory layout to minimise production errors
- ensuring that all staff feel empowered to care about quality; at Toyota car plants, any factory worker with a quality concern can pull an alarm (*jidoka*) chord that stops the whole assembly line; this shows how seriously management takes quality.

Detection

This ensures that quality problems are spotted before they reach the customer. This has been the traditional emphasis of quality control. The use of electronic scanning has given firms better tools to detect faults.

Correction

This is not just about correcting faults. It is also about discovering why there is a problem. Once the problem is identified steps can be taken to ensure it does not recur.

Improvement

Customer expectations of quality are always changing. It is important that businesses seek to improve quality. Therefore, staff need to be encouraged to put forward ways in which their jobs can be done better; the Japanese term *kaizen* (meaning continuous improvement) has become common in British manufacturing.

43.6 PROGRAMMES FOR MANAGING QUALITY

As the importance of quality for both marketing and cost control has been recognised, there has been a growth in initiatives to control and improve quality. Techniques for quality control, such as inspection and statistical control, continue. They have been supplemented by other policies aimed at controlling and improving quality. These include total quality management, quality control and quality assurance. The pros and cons of each of these policies are set out in Table 43.2.

Total quality management

Total quality management (TQM) was introduced by American business guru W. Edwards Deming in the early 1980s. He worked with Japanese firms, and his techniques are said to be one of the reasons for the success of Japanese businesses. TQM is not a management tool: it is a philosophy. It is a way of looking at quality issues. It requires commitment from the whole organisation, not just the quality control department. The business considers quality in every part of the business process – from design right through to sales. TQM is about building-in rather than inspecting-out. It should draw closely on the Japanese experience with *kaizen*, set out below.

Quality control

Quality control (QC) is the traditional way to manage quality, and is based on inspection. Workers get on with the task of producing as many units as possible, and quality control inspectors check that the output meets minimum acceptable standards. This might be done by checking every product; for example, starting up a newly built car and driving it from the production

Table 43.2 Pros and cons of TQM, QC and QA

	TQM	QC	QA
Pros	Should become deeply rooted into the company culture (e.g. product safety at a producer of baby car seats) Once all staff think about quality, it should show through from design to manufacture and after-sales service (e.g. at Lexus or BMW)	Can be used to guarantee that no defective item will leave the factory Requires little staff training, therefore suits a business with unskilled or temporary staff (as ordinary workers needn't worry about quality)	Makes sure the company has a quality system for every stage in the production process Customers like the reassurance provided by a badge such as 'ISO 9000'; they believe they will get a higher-quality service and may therefore be willing to pay more
Cons	Especially at first, staff sceptical of management initiatives may treat TQM as 'hot air'; it lacks the clear, concrete programme of QC or QA To get TQM into the culture of a business may be expensive, as it would require extensive training among all staff (e.g. all British Airways staff flying economy from Heathrow to New York)	Leaving quality for the inspectors to sort out may mean poor quality is built in to the product (e.g. clothes with seams that soon unpick) QC can be trusted when 100 per cent of output is tested, but not when it is based on sampling; Ford used to test just one in seven of its new cars; that led to quality problems	QA does not promise a high-quality product, only a high-quality, reliable process; this process may churn out 'OK' products reliably QA may encourage complacency; it suggests quality has been sorted, whereas rising customer requirements mean quality should keep moving ahead

line to a storage area. Or it might be done by checking every 200th KitKat coming off the end of the factory's production line. If one KitKat is faulty, inspectors will check others from the same batch and – if concerned – may scrap the whole batch. The problem with this system is that faulty products can slip through, and it stops staff from producing the best quality: all they need focus on is 'good enough' to pass the checks. TQM is therefore a superior approach.

Quality assurance

Quality assurance (QA) is a system that assures customers that detailed systems are in place to govern quality at every stage in production. It would start with the quality-checking process for newly arrived raw materials and components. This includes schemes such as ISO 9000. Companies have to have in place a documented quality assurance system. This should be an effective quality system that operates throughout the company, and involves suppliers and subcontractors. The main criticism of QA is that it is a paper-based system and therefore encourages staff to tick boxes rather than care about quality.

43.7 OTHER QUALITY INITIATIVES

Continuous improvement (*kaizen*)

This is a system where the whole organisation is committed to making changes on a continual basis. The Japanese call it *kaizen*. It is an approach to doing business that looks for continual improvement in the quality of products, services, people and processes. In 1991 a book was published in Japan about Toyota, called *40 Years; 20 Million Ideas*. This alerted western business to the amazing ability of the Japanese car companies to get suggestions for improvement from their factory employees.

Six Sigma

A programme developed by America's General Electric Company, which aims to have fewer defective products than 1 per 300,000. To achieve this, staff are trained to become 'Green Belt' or 'Black Belt' quality experts. Although gimmicky, this has been followed widely by other companies.

Quality circles

A quality circle is a group of employees who meet together regularly for the purpose of identifying problems and recommending adjustments to the working processes. This is done to improve the product or process. It is used to address known quality issues such as defective products. It can also be useful for identifying better practices that may improve quality. In addition, it has the advantage of improving staff morale through employee involvement. It takes advantage of the knowledge of operators.

Zero defects

The aim is to produce goods and services with no faults or problems. This is vital in industries such as passenger aircraft production or the manufacture of surgical equipment.

A-grade application

Hewlett-Packard

In March 2010, just as the US government was humiliating Toyota of Japan over its quality problems, 60 Chinese consumers took out a law suit against Hewlett-Packard (HP) of America. The consumers' fury was as much about HP's indifference as the original quality failings.

Although it's the world's biggest computer-maker, HP has struggled in China, caught between Apple and Sony at the top end and Lenovo (of China) at the lower end. So HP seems to have been trying to find a profitable gap in the mid-market, but perhaps with lower-quality products than it sells in the west. Most of the complaints relate to overheating, including one made by a customer who claimed 'it can be used to fry eggs'.

HP admitted there were problems with the motherboard, but if the computer was beyond its guarantee period, it charged $300 to $400 to replace it. Complaining customers found little sympathy from HP's after-sales service centre. It later emerged that this had been 'outsourced': that is, HP was not running its own quality service centre for customers. At the time of writing the outcome of the legal action is unknown.

Benchmarking

Benchmarking is a process of comparing a business with other businesses. Having identified the best, businesses attempt to bring their performance up to the level of the best, by adopting its practices.

Impact of quality initiatives

Most of these initiatives rely on employee involvement. In addition to quality improvements and cost reductions, most businesses find that the initiatives in themselves deliver benefits. These include better working practices, improved employee motivation, increased focus on tasks and the development of team working.

43.8 IS QUALITY EXPENSIVE OR FREE?

The traditional belief was that high quality was costly: in terms of materials, labour, training and checking systems. Therefore, managements should beware of building too much quality into a product (the term given to this was 'over-engineered'). The alternative approach, put forward by the American writer Philip Crosby, is that 'quality is free'. The latter view suggests that getting things **right first time** can save a huge amount of time and money.

- The time required to make it work: quality initiatives take time. Workers may be away from their jobs while attending training or quality groups.
- Short-term versus long-term viewpoints: there may be a conflict between short-term costs and longer-term results. Shareholders may want returns today, but often quality initiatives require a long-term view. The investment will be a current cost. The benefits, however, may take some time to show. They may also be difficult to measure.

If quality control is to be effective it must balance the costs against the advantages; 100 per cent quality is possible, but it may make the product so expensive that it cannot be sold.

ISSUES FOR ANALYSIS

When looking at quality issues in an exam question, the following need to be considered.

- The importance of quality to the business: this will depend on the type of business, the type of product or the service. It will also depend on the market in which the business is operating.
- Whether the firm has adopted the right approach to quality management: perhaps a firm using quality assurance should switch to TQM.
- Quality issues are often closely interwoven with other parts of the business. The role of the employee in quality control is an important issue. Interlinked with this are the changes in management styles and philosophies that come with many of the quality initiatives.

Remember that quality is not just about manufacturing, it is about the whole experience of contact with the business. A poor call centre could just as easily lose a sale as a faulty product.

43.9 EFFECTIVE QUALITY MANAGEMENT – AN EVALUATION

In recent years, there has been a change in the emphasis on quality. The quality business has itself grown. The management section of any bookshop will reveal several titles dedicated to quality management. The growth of initiatives such as TQM and continuous improvement goes on. The number of worldwide registrations for ISO 9000 increases by more than 25 per cent each year. Not all of these are from British businesses; there has been a rapid rise in overseas registrations. With an increase in the international awareness of quality, British businesses will have to ensure that they continue to be competitive.

This growth in emphasis on quality has undoubtedly brought benefits to business. Increased quality brings rewards in the marketplace. Companies have also found that the initiatives, especially where they are people-based, have brought other advantages: changes in working practices have improved motivation and efficiency, and have reduced waste and costs.

This change in emphasis has not been without problems. The shift to a focus on the customer and the role of the employee could result in additional costs. Unless this results in increased profits, shareholders may feel that they are losing out. Some businesses have found that changing cultures is not easy. Resistance from workers and management has often caused problems.

Key Terms

Benchmarking: comparing a firm's performance with best practice in the industry.
Competitiveness: the ability of a firm to beat its competitors (for example, Galaxy is a highly competitive brand in the chocolate market).
Right first time: avoiding mistakes and therefore achieving high quality with no wastage of time or materials.
Trade-off: accepting less of one thing to achieve more of another (for example, slightly lower quality in exchange for cheapness).
Zero defects: eliminating quality defects by getting things right first time.

FURTHER READING

Crainer, Stuart (1997) *The Ultimate Book of Business Quotations*, Capstone Publishing

WORKBOOK

A REVISION QUESTIONS

(35 marks; 45 minutes)

1 State two reasons why quality management is important. (2)
2 How important is quality to the consumer? (3)
3 Suggest two criteria customers may use to judge quality at:
  a) a budget-priced hotel chain (2)
  b) a Tesco supermarket (2)
  c) a McDonald's. (2)
4 Why has there been an increase in awareness of the importance of improving the quality of products? (3)
5 Give two marketing advantages that come from a quality reputation. (2)
6 What costs are involved if the firm has quality problems? (3)
7 What are the four stages of quality management? (4)
8 What is total quality management? (4)
9 Outline two benefits of adopting quality circles to a clothing chain such as Topshop. (4)
10 Outline two additional costs that may be incurred in order to improve quality. (4)

B REVISION EXERCISES

B1 DATA RESPONSE

Trac Parts

Trac Parts is a major manufacturer of parts for farm and construction machinery. It has been operating from a new centralised warehouse for four years. This year the company applied for ISO 9000. It gained accreditation. The main reason for applying was that several large customers had indicated that they would only deal with ISO 9000 companies when negotiating new contracts. The warehouse manager has been pleasantly surprised by the operational performance figures since accreditation:

- orders completed on time up from 75 per cent to 84 per cent
- errors in completing orders reduced by 40 per cent
- average time from order receipt to dispatch reduced by two days.

Questions

(25 marks; 30 minutes)

1 What is ISO 9000? (3)
2 Why may a business want to become ISO 9000 approved? (4)
3 Examine the benefits to Trac Parts of the performance improvements identified in the text. (6)
4 In order to be accepted by ISO 9000, the firm will have had to introduce procedures to ensure that levels of quality are maintained. Using the four stages of quality control (prevention, detection, correction and improvement) examine the actions it might have taken. (12)

B2 CASE STUDY

Manufacturing defects – producer comparisons: PcNow

PcNow is a small computer manufacturer based in the East Midlands. It tailor-makes computers and accessories based on customers' own specifications. Although business grew steadily initially, it is now worried about falling sales. It believes it is losing sales to Japanese and American companies that have set up manufacturing facilities in Europe, as well as to other European and UK-based firms. An industry survey has produced data on industry levels of production defects. It has added its own figures and produced the chart shown in Figure 43.2.

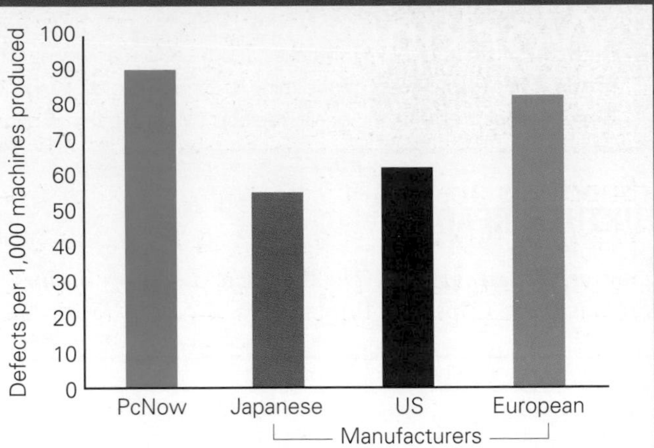

Figure 43.2 **Manufacturing defects: producer comparisons**

The firm realises that survival depends upon addressing the quality problems. It has decided to employ a quality manager, Cara Davenport, to address the issues. Her first suggestion is to get together workers from each department to discuss the problems and issues. Following a survey of the factory she has also suggested that the layout of the production facilities should be changed. This will be an expensive exercise, and management is reluctant to make the changes as they will require production to stop for a week and there will need to be investment in new equipment. The firm's weak cash flow position makes it hard for the owners to accept new capital spending. The other area that Cara has identified is a problem with one particular component. She has suggested that a new supplier should be found, or that she should work with the existing supplier to improve the quality of the component.

Questions

(40 marks; 50 minutes)

1 **a)** What does the chart show? (2)
  b) What further data would help to make the bar chart more useful? (4)
2 From the case study, identify two reasons for the quality problems experienced by PcNow. (2)
3 What are the marketing implications for PcNow of the data in the bar chart? (8)
4 Outline the advantages PcNow may achieve from the discussion group formed to discuss the quality problems. (8)
5 How might Cara convince the firm's management to change the layout of the production facilities? (6)
6 Once these changes have been made, the firm needs to ensure that quality is maintained and improved. Discuss the implications for the firm of implementing a total quality management initiative. (10)

C ESSAY QUESTIONS

(40 marks each)

1 'Quality control is about building quality in, not inspecting it out.' Discuss.
2 Consider whether quality management is solely a matter for the production department.
3 To what extent is quality a major competitive issue in service businesses?

Working with suppliers

UNIT 44

Suppliers are other businesses that provide products or services to a firm. The relationship with suppliers is likely to have a critical impact on a firm. Operational success demands high-quality supplies delivered on time in the right quantities.

44.1 KEY FACTORS TO CONSIDER WHEN CHOOSING SUPPLIERS

Cost

Cheaper supplies mean higher profit margins. The incentive to find a cheap supplier is huge for any firm; therefore, the price charged by a supplier will be a key factor in the relationship between a firm and its suppliers. Large businesses may be able to almost dictate prices to their suppliers. This is because the quantities they purchase may account for the whole output of the supplier, giving a huge amount of power to the buyer. However, for small businesses with limited purchasing power, the supplier may have the upper hand.

As a result of this, small businesses may be advised to shop around, looking for the cheapest supplier they can find. However, this may not always be the most sensible course of action; there are other important factors to consider when choosing suppliers.

Quality

There is frequently a trade-off between the price charged by suppliers and the quality of their offering. The cheapest supplier may be one with a poor reputation for the quality of its products or service. Choosing to use a supplier with quality problems is likely to lead to operational problems. Poor-quality supplies can lead to machinery breakdowns, along with poor-quality output. This can lead to problems with customer complaints, guarantee claims or reputation. Choosing the cheapest supplier may sow the seeds of long-term problems for a business.

Reliability

Supplies at the right price and of a high quality may be of little use if they arrive late. It is important that a supplier can offer reliability to a business. Failure to deliver on time can stop a manufacturing process or leave shop shelves empty. Suppliers' reliability will be easy to assess once a business has started working with them. However, a new business or a business sourcing new supplies may need to rely on word-of-mouth reputation to inform its choice. Larger firms may be able to impose certain penalties on suppliers who prove unreliable but, again, small businesses will be in a weaker position if trying to threaten a supplier.

Frequency

Depending on the type of business and the production system it uses, frequent deliveries may be needed from suppliers. Firms selling fresh produce will need to ensure that they are using suppliers that can supply and deliver frequently – probably as often as a new batch each day. Similarly, a firm that uses a **just-in-time (JIT)** production system will need very frequent deliveries to feed its production system without it having to hold stock (Honda, for example, requires hourly deliveries of parts to its Japanese car factories). For firms such as these, it makes sense to look for a local supplier; they are far more likely to be willing to deliver with a greater level of frequency.

Flexibility

In a similar way to ensuring the right frequency of supplies, many firms will need to find a supplier with the capacity to cope with widely varying orders. Businesses selling products with erratic demand patterns, caused by changes in the weather or fashion, will need to find suppliers that can meet their ever-changing needs. Probably the most common scenario is to ensure that suppliers have the spare capacity available to cope with sudden rush orders. In addition, some firms will need to find suppliers that can supply at the right time; it may be that perhaps night-time deliveries are needed for firms in congested town centres, or in areas where lorries are banned during the day. A key to supplier flexibility is a short **lead time** (that is, there should not be too long a period between placing an order and receiving a delivery).

Payment terms

Most business transactions are on credit, not for cash. If Tesco wants to order 2,000 cases of Heinz Beans, the bill is unlikely to be paid until 30 or more days after the goods have been delivered. This gives time for the goods to be sold, providing the cash to make it easy to pay the bill. Small business start-ups will struggle to get the same terms. A newly opened corner shop will not be given credit by Heinz. The supplier will want to be paid in cash until the new business has shown that it can survive and pay its bills. So a new small firm has to pay up front, placing extra strain on its cash flow. This should not be a problem as long as it has been anticipated (that is, built in to its start-up cash flow forecast).

A-grade application

In the driver's seat

Each spring for the past eight years key suppliers ('Tier 1') to the six major North American car producers have shared with us their experiences of working with Chrysler, Ford, General Motors, Honda, Nissan and Toyota.

This year, the previous pattern of working relationships has changed significantly. For the first time in the study's eight-year history, a US carmaker – Ford – was ranked in the top three, along with, but well behind, Honda and Toyota, who held their respective first and second places. While GM continues in the 'very poor/poor' range, its supplier relations are improving rapidly. For the foreign domestic original-equipment manufacturers (OEMs) the working relations index (WRI) change is a different story. Notwithstanding Nissan's slight improvement last year, Honda, Toyota and Nissan continue their slow four-year downward trend of steadily worsening supplier relations.

The real question behind the annual study and, for that matter, for any company interested in achieving strong supplier relations is – why should they care? The answer is simple. For many years, the study has shown that automakers with the best rankings, specifically Toyota and Honda, receive the greatest benefit from their suppliers in a variety of areas including lower costs, higher quality, increased price reduction concessions, and supplier innovation.

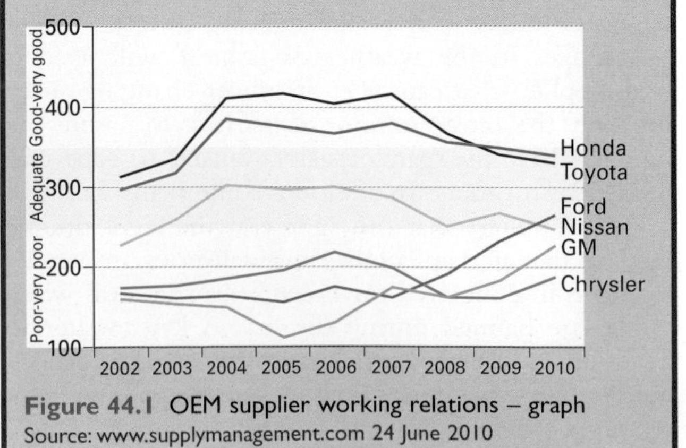

Figure 44.1 OEM supplier working relations – graph
Source: www.supplymanagement.com 24 June 2010

44.2 THE ROLE OF SUPPLIERS IN IMPROVING PERFORMANCE

Some businesses enjoy telling their shareholders how tough they are with their suppliers: after all, the lower the supply cost, the higher the profit. Many firms encourage competition between rival suppliers by threatening to go elsewhere if the terms are not what they want. This approach has been important in building the hugely profitable business of many high-street stores, which find cheap goods by negotiating toughly in Cambodia, China or the Philippines.

An alternative approach was followed in the past by Marks & Spencer, and today by car firms such as Toyota and Honda. These companies build long-term relationships with their suppliers, with the aim of working with, rather than against, them. There are many potential benefits from this approach, as discussed below.

Working together on new product development

Developing new products involves many considerations. One of these will be how the product is to be manufactured, what materials will be used and what properties will be needed. Meanwhile, launching a new product will require careful production planning to ensure that consumers can get hold of the new product that the marketing department has told them about. The result is that suppliers have a major part to play in developing and launching new products. Many firms have recognised the importance of this and work hand in hand with their suppliers from the very earliest stages of developing a new product.

Flexibility

A strong relationship with a supplier should mean it is willing to make special deliveries if a business is running low on stock. A strong relationship may also allow some flexibility on payment. A toy shop may struggle to find cash in the months leading up to Christmas, so a trusting supplier may accept a delay in payment. This could be the lifeline required for the small firm. However, no supplier is likely to be able to sustain this generosity for a long period.

Sharing information to improve the efficiency of the supply chain

Large businesses with sophisticated IT systems have direct links between their cash tills and their suppliers. Cadbury knows at any hour of the day how many Creme Eggs are selling in supermarkets. This enables Cadbury to plan its production levels (for example, pushing up output if sales are proving brighter than expected). The supermarket can even allow Cadbury to make the decisions on how much stock to produce and deliver on the basis of the information it is receiving.

Small grocers use the same laser scanning software at their tills, but it would be rare for a small business to have a direct electronic link with a supplier. This means the shopkeeper has to make the purchasing decisions, or go to a wholesaler to buy the goods, which is much less efficient than the electronic systems of the big companies.

A-grade application

Why do it yourself if suppliers can help?

Wickes is a DIY retailer that has worked hard to develop closer relations with its suppliers. The company invested in improved IT systems to enable better transfer of information between retail outlets and suppliers. Store-level sales and stock data are sent daily to suppliers to allow them to improve their production planning, ensuring the right amount is available to be delivered to each Wickes store. The system has also enhanced the role played by suppliers in the planning and development of new own-brand products for the stores. In the future, the group is hoping to move towards a system where store stock levels are actually monitored and managed by the suppliers themselves.

ISSUES FOR ANALYSIS

- Although firms are likely to try to build a long-term relationship with their suppliers, there will be times when a business will consider changing supplier. This is an issue that has a number of aspects that need consideration, in addition to the standard factors covered earlier. There will be an existing relationship with the current supplier and this may bring advantages that would not be available with a brand new supplier. Meanwhile, the cliché that 'the grass is always greener on the other side' may be a factor in the motive for changing.
- When analysing any choice between suppliers, be sure to consider the consequences of the differences between them. Failure to consider consequences will lose analysis marks. Think through the consequences in your answers with lines of argument such as 'poor-quality materials may lead to poor-quality output, which could lead to customer disappointment, which will hit reputation, probably damaging future sales'.

44.3 WORKING WITH SUPPLIERS – AN EVALUATION

Evaluative themes relating to suppliers will centre on judgements that firms make as to which supplier to choose. This unit has covered a range of factors that need to be considered, but effective evaluation will, as always, come from a willingness to appreciate which factors are most important for the particular business being considered. A retailer that sells high volumes of cheap products at low prices may be right to compromise on quality to use the cheapest suppliers. The reverse would be the case for a firm with a luxury image or targeting socially conscious consumers. Take some time before putting pen to paper to work out which factors will be most important for the firm mentioned in the question.

Another judgement that should improve your answers is to determine who has the most power in the relationship between company and supplier. Larger firms tend to have more power; indeed there are concerns over the way Britain's huge supermarket chains treat small farmers. However, size may not be the only factor to consider. A supplier with a patent on a particular component will need to be dealt with even if it fails to prove 100 per cent reliable. Evaluation will shine through if a candidate judges effectively where power lies in the specific business relationship featured in an exam question.

Key Terms

Just-in-time (JIT): ordering supplies so that they arrive 'just in time' (that is, just when they are needed); this means operating without reserves of materials or components held 'just in case' they are needed.

Lead time: the time the supplier takes between receiving an order and delivering the goods.

WORKBOOK

A REVISION QUESTIONS

(30 marks; 30 minutes)

1 Explain why the cheapest supplier may not be the best choice. (4)

2 Identify two businesses for which daily deliveries may be absolutely crucial. (2)

3 Briefly explain two problems that may arise when a firm uses a supplier with poor levels of quality. (4)

4 Describe why attractive credit terms from a supplier will be particularly useful for a new business. (4)

5 Outline two reasons why a firm may choose to change its supplier of an existing component. (4)

6 Examine one benefit a mobile phone shop may receive by encouraging several suppliers to continually compete with each other for every month's order of components. (4)

7 What benefits could the mobile phone shop miss out on by not building a long-term relationship with its suppliers? (4)

8 Describe how a car manufacturer such as Volkswagen may benefit from including its component suppliers in the development process when designing a new car. (4)

B REVISION EXERCISES
B1 DATA RESPONSE

Doll's Choice

KMH Ltd is a small manufacturer of children's toys. Having developed a brand new child's doll, it is considering which supplier to use for the plastic used in moulding the doll (see Table 44.1). Having started up only 12 months ago, the firm has done well and is eagerly anticipating the Christmas rush that will begin soon. The management hopes that the new doll will be a best-seller this Christmas.

Table 44.1 Potential suppliers for KMH Ltd

Supplier	A	B	C
Price per unit (£s)	3.20	3.50	3.65
Reject rate (per 000 products delivered)	28	18	5
Credit terms (days)	0	60	30
Lead time (days)	7	1	4

Questions

(20 marks; 20 minutes)

1 Which supplier offers the best:
   a) quality
   b) lead time
   c) credit terms? (3)
2 Explain why lead time is important. (5)
3 Which supplier should the firm choose, and why? (12)

B2 DATA RESPONSE

Crêpe Heaven

Carla Turner set up Crêpe Heaven in early 2010. As the only creperie in her local area, she attracted some attention with the launch of her small café which specialised in French pancakes. Business was more brisk than she had expected and she often found herself popping out to the local supermarket to buy extra ingredients halfway through the day. The supermarket was more expensive than her catering suppliers, but Carla found it hard to predict sales in the early months of the business. Her stock of eggs, milk and fruit for fillings had a very limited life and the last thing she wanted to do was buy ingredients she would have to throw away.

After trading successfully for six months, Carla had an encouraging letter from the catering supplier she had been using, telling her that it was now willing to make an afternoon delivery if she needed extra supplies. This lowered her running costs, which was just what was needed as the interest payments on her bank loan were now biting hard into her cash flow. She also realised that she would need a second crêpe-making machine if she was to make sure that waiting times during busy periods were kept to a minimum. She contacted the French supplier of her first machine, to be told that it would be two months before they could deliver and install the model she wanted. Furthermore, she would have to pay cash on delivery and this was something she could ill-afford.

Figure 44.2 Crêpe Heaven

Shopping around on the internet, she found a supplier

in America who could deliver in a week. This was great news, as she knew that some customers took one look at her peak-period queues and headed off to other cafés in the area. She was also grateful that the supplier was willing to accept a small deposit on order, followed by 60 days' interest-free credit. This seemed perfect and she placed her order immediately.

The delivery went smoothly, though she had some trouble installing the new machine as it was rather different to her existing one. Worse was to come some months later, as the new machine started smoking when in use for more than a couple of hours. The American supplier was unhelpful, insisting that the fault must have been due to Carla failing to install the machine properly. The next few months were tough for Carla, as she struggled to get her money back from the US supplier. Fortunately, the shop remained popular and within six months she replaced the second machine with one from her original supplier.

Questions

(30 marks; 35 minutes)

1 Explain why Carla tended to under-order ingredient supplies in the early days of the business. (5)
2 Explain which two factors may have been most important to Carla when originally choosing her ingredient supplier. (6)
3 Analyse the benefits to Carla of choosing the American supplier for her second crêpe machine. (8)
4 To what extent does the case study support the view that building a long-term relationship with a supplier is a better approach than shopping around for 'the best deal'? (11)

Stock control

UNIT 45

Stock control is the management process that makes sure stock is ordered, delivered and handled in the best possible way. An efficient stock control system will balance the need to meet customer demand against the cost of holding stock.

45.1 PURCHASING

Manufacturing businesses rely on stocks being bought in from other firms. These stocks can either be in the form of raw materials or components. They are part of the inputs that manufacturing firms process into outputs.

The purchasing function acts as a service to the rest of the business. Its main objective is to meet the needs of those running the internal operations of the business. In a factory, inefficient purchasing may lead (in the extreme) to a shutdown if key materials or components have not turned up when needed. In a retail store, poor purchasing could mean empty shelves or an over-full stockroom. In order to avoid this, the purchasing function of a business will try to ensure that:

- a sufficient quantity of stocks is available at all times ...
- ... but not so many as to represent a waste of resources
- stocks are of the right quality
- stocks are available where they are needed in the factory
- the price paid for stocks is as competitive as possible
- good relationships are built up with suppliers.

When purchasing stocks, a business must ask a range of questions about potential suppliers. The main thing that the buyer must be convinced of is that the supplier can meet its requirements on quality and on price.

- Quality can be checked through samples and/or a visit to the supplier's factory to inspect methods and conditions. If the supplier has achieved its ISO 9000 certificate this means it has an effective quality assurance system.
- The price may be negotiated, especially if the buyer is purchasing in bulk or is a regular customer. A lower price may be agreed, or longer credit periods established.

In addition, the buyer will have to consider other questions before deciding which supplier to use, such as:

- Will the supplier be consistent, supplying the quantity and quality needed on time, every time?
- Is the financial position of the firm sufficiently safe to guarantee as far as is possible its future survival?
- If the needs of the buyer change, can the supplier change quickly to meet demand?
- Can the supplier expand if the buyer's demand grows?

In the past, firms tended to focus on short-term buying decisions based on the lowest quoted price. Today's supplies might be from XZ Ltd; tomorrow's from PQ & Co. Companies such as Honda and Toyota took a different approach. They aimed to form an effective and lasting partnership with suppliers. In this way both businesses benefit from the relationship. More and more companies are following this lead.

The purchasing department will need to take a strategic decision on how best to operate. Key questions will consider whether the firm:

- should place large orders occasionally, or small orders frequently
- should accept lower-quality stocks at a lower cost
- should rely on one supplier or use several.

45.2 TYPES OF STOCK

Manufacturing firms hold three types of stock. These are:

- *raw materials and components*: these are the stocks the business has purchased from outside suppliers; they will be held by the firm until it is ready to process them into its finished output
- *work in progress*: at any given moment, a manufacturing firm will have some items it has started to process, but that are incomplete; this may be because they are presently moving through the production process; it may be because the firm stores unfinished goods to give it some flexibility to meet consumer demand
- *finished goods:* once a product is complete, the firm may keep possession of it for some time; this could

be because it sells goods in large batches or no buyer has yet come in for the product; for producers of seasonal goods, such as toys, most of the year's production may be building stock in preparation for the pre-Christmas sales rush, a process known as producing for stock, or stockpiling.

The firm's costs increase if it holds more stock. However, this needs to be set against the **opportunity cost** of keeping too little stock, such as not being able to meet customer demand. One theory is that a firm should try to keep as little stock as possible at all times. This system, known as just-in-time, is looked at in Unit 46.

The firm must keep control of all the different types of stock to ensure that it runs at peak efficiency.

45.3 STOCK MANAGEMENT

Stock management is the way a firm controls the stock within the business. If the purchasing function has been efficient, the business will receive the right quantity and quality of stock at the right time. However, once the stocks are inside the firm, they must be handled and used correctly. This is to make sure they are still in peak condition when they are used in the production process.

Stock rotation

Wherever possible, a firm will want to use its oldest stock first. This means that stocks do not deteriorate, go past their sell-by date or become obsolete. Stock can become obsolete if new specifications are used or if the product of which they were a part is no longer manufactured. By using a system of **stock rotation**, the firm will ensure that the risks of stock going out of date are minimised. Supermarkets, for example, should always put new stock at the back of the shelf to encourage shoppers to take the older stock first. The principle behind stock rotation is first-in-first-out (FIFO). This is to avoid a situation in which new stock is used first, leaving older stock to become unusable at the back of a shelf or a warehouse.

Stock wastage

This is the loss of stock in either a production or service process. Any wastage is a cost to the firm, as it has paid for stock it will not use.

In a manufacturing process, the main causes of stock wastage are:

- materials being wasted, such as scraps of cloth being thrown away as offcuts from a dress maker; this can be minimised by careful planning – perhaps helped by computer-aided design (CAD) software
- the reworking of items that were not done correctly first time – good training and a highly motivated staff are the best ways to avoid this
- defective products that cannot be put right, which will often be sold off as seconds or damaged goods.

For a retailer, the main causes of stock wastage will be:

- products becoming damaged due to improper handling or storage
- stealing from the shop, whether by customers or staff
- products such as food passing their sell-by dates.

In all these cases, sound management and administrative techniques could reduce or even eliminate the problem of stock wastage. Any wastage is a cost to the firm, and procedures need to be set up to prevent such losses.

However, it is important that the cost of the processes set up is not more than the money being saved by them. Cost-effective measures are needed to maximise the returns to the firm.

45.4 STOCK CONTROL CHARTS

One way in which a firm analyses its stock situation is by using stock control charts. These line graphs look at the level of stock in the firm over time. Managers will be able to see from these charts how stock levels have changed during the period, and will be able to note any unusual events with which they may need to be concerned.

A typical stock control graph will look like that shown in Figure 45.1. On this chart there are four lines, which represent the levels described below.

- *Stock levels:* this line shows how stock levels have changed over this time period. As the stock is used up, the level of stock gradually falls from left to right. When a delivery is made, however, the stock level leaps upwards in a vertical line. The greater the rise in the vertical line, the more stock has been delivered.
- *Maximum stock level:* this shows the largest amount that the firm is either willing or able to hold in stock. It may show the physical size of the warehouse and be the maximum because no more can be taken in. It may also, however, be set by management on the basis that (a) it is the most that can be used by the production process, (b) it is the most that can be kept to ensure sell-by dates are not missed, or (c) it is sufficient, given the time between deliveries and the rate of usage.
- *Re-order level:* this is a 'trigger' quantity. When stocks fall to this level a new order will be sent in to the supplier. The re-order level is reached some time before the delivery (shown by the vertical part of the stock level line). This is because the supplier will need some 'lead time' to process the order and make the delivery.
- *Minimum stock level:* this is also known as the **buffer stock**. The firm will want to keep a certain minimum level of stock for reasons of safety so that it will have something to fall back on if an order does not arrive on time or if stock is used up particularly quickly, perhaps due to a sudden increase in demand.

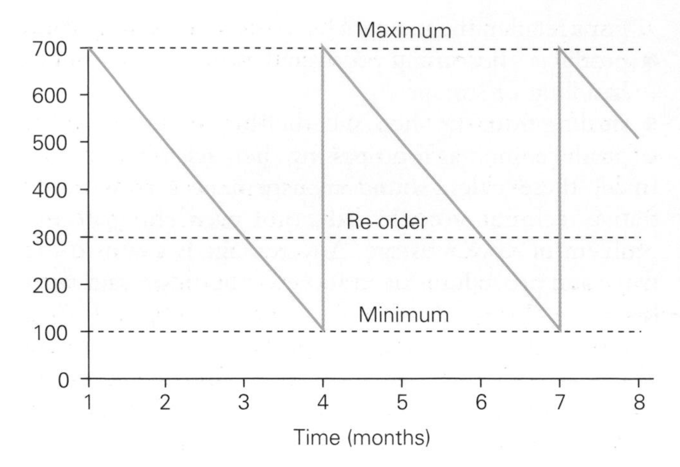

Figure 45.1 Stock control chart

Diagrams such as this, showing a neat and regular pattern to stock holding, will not happen in reality. Orders may arrive late and may not always be of the correct quantity. The rate of usage is unlikely to be constant. The slope of the stock level line may be steeper, showing more stock being used than normal, or shallower, showing a slower use of stock.

However, as a basis for analysing stock levels over time, stock control charts such as these give managers a clear picture of how things have changed, and shows them what questions need to be asked. For example, they may show that stocks are constantly arriving late. Managers would then know to ask if suppliers were taking longer than the agreed lead time, or if orders were not being placed when the re-order level of stock was reached.

Figure 45.2 shows a more realistic stock control graph. It is based on actual sales of Nestlé Lion Bars at a newsagent in south-west London over a three-month period.

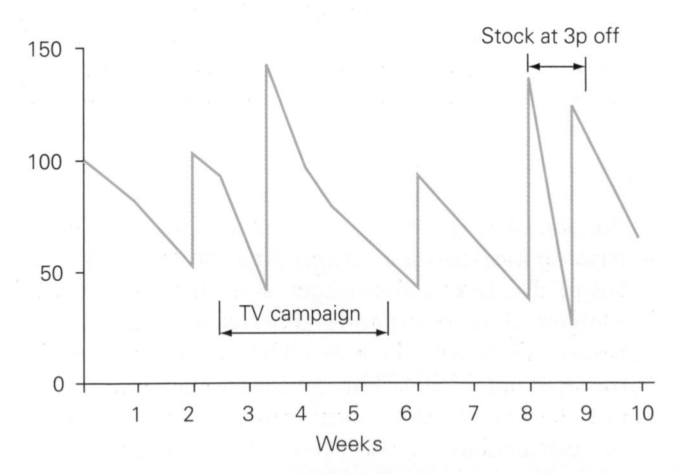

Figure 45.2 Weekly sales of Lion Bars at one newsagent

45.5 THE COSTS OF STOCK

The initial cost of purchasing stock is only one of the costs associated with a firm's stock holding (**stock holding costs**). A firm can hold too much or too little stock. Both cases will add to the costs of the firm.

Too much stock can lead to:

- *opportunity cost*: holding the firm's wealth in the form of stock prevents it using its capital in other ways, such as investing in new machinery or research and development on a new product; by missing out on such opportunities the firm may put itself at a disadvantage when compared with its competitors
- *cash flow problems*: holding the firm's wealth as stock may cause problems if it proves slow moving; there may be insufficient cash to pay suppliers
- *increased storage costs*: as well as the physical space needed to hold the stock, there may be increases in associated costs such as labour within the warehouse, heating and lighting or refrigeration; stocks need to be insured against fire and theft, the cost of which will increase as more stocks are held
- *increased finance costs*: if the capital needs to be borrowed, the cost of that capital (the interest rate) will be a significant added annual overhead
- *increased stock wastage:* the more stock is held, the greater the risk of it going out of date or deteriorating in condition.

This does not, however, mean that the business is free to carry very low stocks. Unless it can confidently run just-in-time systems (see below) the firm may well face increased costs from holding too little stock as well. These could include the following.

- Workers and machines standing idle as there are not enough materials or components to allow the process to operate. This costs the business in lost output and wages being paid even though no work has been done. It could also cost the business at a later date if extra overtime is needed to make up for the production lost.
- Lost orders, as customers needing a specific delivery date that cannot be met will go elsewhere.
- Orders not being fulfilled on time, leading to worsening relations with customers. This could lead to future orders being lost as customers turn to more reliable suppliers. The firm may also have to pay customers financial compensation for missing delivery dates.
- The loss of the firm's reputation and any goodwill it has been able to build up with its customers.

The total cost of stocks to the firm will therefore be a combination of these factors. As the level of stock grows, the costs of holding that stock will increase, but the costs of not holding stock will decrease. The cost of holding stock will therefore look like Figure 45.3.

For a firm, the optimum level of stock to hold will be where the total costs of holding stock are the lowest.

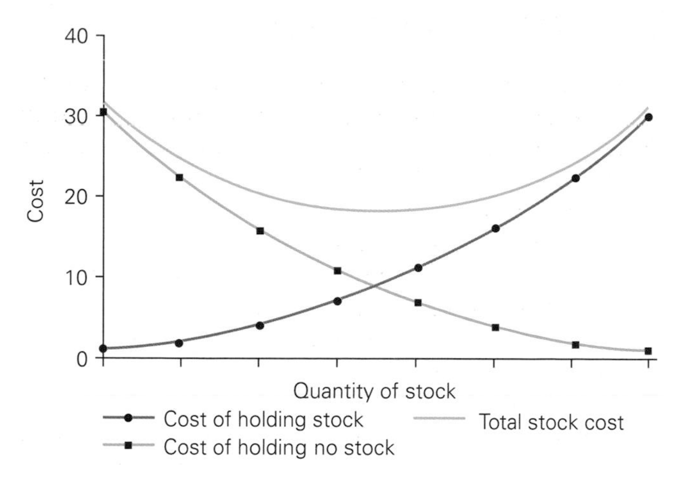

Figure 45.3 The cost of stockholding

A further consideration to the quantity of stocks being held is how much stock to order at any one time. Large orders need only be made a few times to keep sufficient stock levels, while smaller orders will mean that they have to be placed more regularly. The arguments for both of these are shown in Table 45.1.

Table 45.1 Large versus smaller orders

Advantages of many smaller orders	Advantages of a few large orders
Less storage space needed	Economies from buying in bulk
More flexible to changing needs	Avoids chance of running out of stock
Less stock wastage	Prevents machines and workers standing idle

45.6 IT AND STOCK CONTROL

Stock control is all about the efficient handling of information about current and required stocks. Information technology (IT) can handle large quantities of data quickly and easily. Therefore, the use of IT can make the task of stock control both easier and more accurate.

Most businesses will hold records of their stock on large databases. Stock control systems exist that allow these databases to be updated instantaneously as stock leaves the warehouse or goes through the checkout. Traditionally, the systems that achieved this were barcode scanners, which read the details of the stock coming in or going out. Today there is a big switch to RFID (radio frequency identification) systems, which allow the stock to be traced to exactly where it is being held within a warehouse. Either way, the data can be held on the warehouse computer system to keep an accurate, up-to-the-second picture of how much stock is held at any given time. The need to re-order stock can be identified by the system, and the order sent automatically from the warehouse IT system to the supplier's IT system. This largely does away with the need for human involvement in the stock control process.

Stock control systems such as these add to the ability of managers to analyse stock movements. They should make it possible for more accurate decisions to be made on what stock to hold and in what quantities. Supermarkets, for example, make much use of IT as the basis for decisions about stocks. Through electronic data interchange (EDI) links, manufacturers can even see the sales level of their products at supermarket checkouts. This enables them to anticipate the orders the supermarkets will soon be placing. Without such instant information, strategies such as just-in-time would be very difficult.

A-grade application

RFID at Airbus

The world's aircraft industry is dominated by Boeing (US) and Europe's Airbus Industrie. Yet both businesses are as famous for delayed schedules as for great planes. The Airbus A380 (Super-Jumbo) arrived two years late; Boeing's 'Dreamliner' is outdoing it by slipping three years from its original schedule. Part of the problem is that an aeroplane can have more than 1 million components, and managing them is extraordinarily difficult.

So in 2010 Airbus started a new system of RFID tagging of its components. The durable tags, tough enough to handle all kinds of conditions, contain information about where and when the part was built, where and when it was installed and can even contain the parts manual, that is, instructions on maintenance and replacement.

The RFID tags will also provide better, more reliable data about what parts are located where, within every maintenance depot. The current plan is to use RFID tags on all parts in the future. The average cost per tag is estimated at $10 to $30, which comes to a huge total, but may prove a relatively cheap way of making air travel safer in the future.

45.7 JUST-IN-TIME

Just-in-time (JIT) is a system of stock control that has become popular in UK firms over the last couple of decades. The basis of the system is that the costs of holding stock should be unacceptable to a firm, so the level of stock held ought to be as small as possible. In other words, JIT is the attempt to operate with a zero buffer stock. At the same time, a system must be developed so that the costs and risks of running out of stock are avoided by the firm.

A firm adopting the JIT system will attempt to do this by developing a close working relationship with suppliers. By involving suppliers closely with the business, and by demonstrating the benefits to both the supplier and purchaser, it should be possible for both parties to work together for the common good.

The supplier will be required under the JIT system to make frequent deliveries to the purchaser as and when goods are needed. A delivery that arrives too early is as much a cost to the purchaser as a delivery arriving late. The purchaser will have to be certain that the deliveries will be made just in time for the goods to be used.

The advantages and disadvantages of a JIT system are listed in Table 45.2.

Table 45.2 Advantages and disadvantages of using a JIT system

Advantages of using JIT
• Improves the firm's liquidity • The costs of holding stocks are reduced • Storage space can be converted to a more productive use • Stock wastage and stock rotation become lesser issues for management • Response times to changing demands are speeded up as new components can be ordered instantly
Disadvantages of using JIT
• Any break in supply causes immediate problems for the purchaser • The costs of processing orders may be increased • The purchaser's reputation is placed in the hands of the external supplier

Establishing a JIT system is not something that can or should be achieved overnight. The risks of running out of stock are too great. Figure 45.4 shows how a firm might set out to achieve a JIT system in a carefully planned way. The diagram shows five phases, after which the firm would intend to continue with phases 6, 7 and thereafter, until it could get as close as possible to zero buffer stock. The five phases are as follows.

1 The firm orders 20,000 units of stock to arrive every third week.
2 Suppliers are asked to move to weekly deliveries, therefore only one-third of the quantity is ordered.
3 As phase 2 has proved successful, there is no longer any need for such a high buffer stock. Stock levels are allowed to fall to a new, lower level.
4 With phase 3 complete, the firm now moves to receiving deliveries twice a week. Therefore the order level is halved.
5 The suppliers have proved reliable enough to allow the buffer to be cut again ...

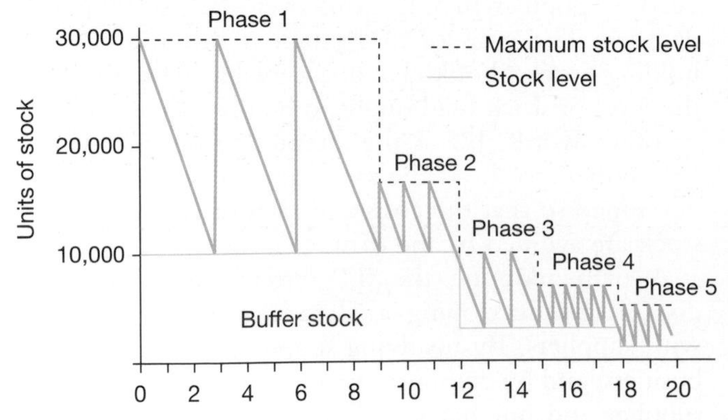

Figure 45.4 Step-by-step progress towards JIT stock control

ISSUES FOR ANALYSIS

- Stock is an important issue for some firms; a vital one for others. Greengrocers with small turnovers cannot survive, because slow-moving stock means poor-quality fruit and vegetables. For many firms, poor stock control leads to increased theft, rising costs and a threat to survival.
- As with many aspects of management, there is no single answer to the question of how best to manage a firm's stock. Different-sized firms in different industries will have widely different stock control needs. JIT may be ideal in one context but inappropriate elsewhere.
- The use of IT as a means of stock control has, until recently, been restricted mainly to large firms needing to control masses of stock in different locations. While the applications are being made available in forms suitable for smaller firms now, it is questionable whether or not such firms are able to use the technology efficiently.
- How will the arrival of internet marketing (home shopping) affect decisions by retailers about stock levels? Will they feel they have to make greater efforts to ensure they have exactly the right size/colour combination for every customer? In other words, should they increase the breadth and depth of their stock levels?

45.8 STOCK CONTROL – AN EVALUATION

Stock control is at the heart of many business operations. For retailers such as Zara, Topshop and Primark, the desire for a constant flow of new, fashion-orientated stock means huge pressure to clear away 'old' stock (which may be only four-weeks-old). Therefore, a JIT approach is ideal, with little or no buffer stock. In some cases it is quite helpful commercially to run out of stock, if it means that, next Saturday, shoppers come earlier to make sure they can get the must-have item. The only thing that will not work is when customers go to a clothes shop and see tired, over-fingered stock that's very outdated.

To make a just-in-time approach work requires close collaboration between purchasers and suppliers. The purchasing firm needs to bring the supplier into discussions on product development. Advice may be needed on components and materials as well as gaining the supplier's commitment to the new project. This Japanese way of doing business has taken off in Britain, making it much easier to provide customers with what they need.

Yet there are still firms that believe mass production plus high stock levels is the only way to be efficient. If that's what Cadbury says about making chocolate – even the highly seasonal Creme Egg – it would be arrogant to argue. So it is always important to keep an open mind about what is right for a specific company. There are few right answers in business – only answers that are right with application to particular circumstances.

Key Terms

Buffer stock: the desired minimum stock level held by a firm just in case something goes wrong.

Opportunity cost: the cost of missing out on the next best alternative when making a decision (or when committing resources).

Stock holding costs: the overheads resulting from the stock levels held by a firm.

Stock rotation: the administrative and physical processes to ensure that older stock is used first.

WORKBOOK

A REVISION QUESTIONS

(35 marks; 35 minutes)

1. Why may it be important to maintain good relationships with suppliers? (3)
2. State the three main categories of stock. (3)
3. What is meant by 'internal customers'? (3)
4. How would stock rotation help a firm to manage its resources better? (4)
5. Sketch a typical stock control chart. (6)
6. State three costs associated with holding too much stock. (3)
7. Give three costs associated with running out of stock. (3)
8. What is meant by just-in-time stock control? (4)
9. Explain the meaning of the sentence in the text 'The purchaser's reputation is placed in the hands of the external supplier.' (3)
10. Why is stock control of particular importance to a greengrocer? (3)

B REVISION EXERCISES
B1 REVISION ACTIVITIES

(35 marks; 40 minutes)

1 A firm sells 40,000 units a month. It receives monthly deliveries. Its maximum stock level is 50,000 and minimum (buffer) stock is 10,000. After two months (eight weeks) it decides to switch to monthly deliveries.
  a) Sketch a 12-week stock control graph to illustrate this situation. Assume the firm starts the first week with 50,000 units of stock. (10)
  b) What short-term problems may the firm face in switching to weekly deliveries? (6)
  c) Consider the long-term benefits that may result from the change. (9)

2 Sketch a graph to show the impact upon stock levels of a downturn in demand for a product for which a company has a non-cancellable fixed order from its suppliers. Fully label the graph to explain *what* happens *when*. (10)

B2 DATA RESPONSE

Ann Brennan established a bakery in Wigan 20 years ago. Although the firm is profitable, Ann is considering the introduction of modern techniques to help the company develop. In particular, she wishes to introduce information technology to improve communications between her five shops and the central bakery, and to help her manage her stock of raw materials more effectively.

Stocks of raw materials at the business are currently purchased in response to usage. For example, the bakery uses on average 500 kg of flour per week. The most Ann wishes to hold at any time is 2,000 kg. She would be worried if the stock fell below 500 kg. An order takes one week to arrive, so Ann always re-orders when her stock falls to 1,000 kg.

Questions

(30 marks; 35 minutes)

1 What is meant by the following terms?
  a) Re-order level
  b) Buffer stock
  c) Lead time. (6)

2 a) Draw a stock control graph for flour at Brennan's Bakery over a six-week period. (6)
   b) Draw a second graph showing the situation if twice the normal amount of flour were used in the fourth week. (6)
3 How might information technology be used to improve communication between Ann's shops and between the bakery and its suppliers? (6)
4 Assess the effect of a 'stock-out' on Brennan's Bakery. (6)

B3 DATA RESPONSE

Is JIT always the best option?

Executives at mattress maker Sealy Corp. learned the hard way in 2005 how much a natural disaster could disrupt a supply chain. That's when hurricanes Katrina and Rita battered the Gulf Coast and caused major damage to petrochemical processing facilities that supply Sealy with a raw material called TDI, which is used to manufacture the foam found in most of Sealy's bedding products.

This was bad news for a company that takes pride in its just-in-time (JIT) operations. In its company statement, Sealy notes that most bedding orders are shipped to warehouses within 72 hours of receipt. With a foam shortage at hand, the company issued a notice in October 2005 acknowledging that production delays were imminent.

Similar stories were reported shortly after the September 11th terrorist attacks in 2001, and doomsday predictions of health epidemics, war and more hurricanes continue to keep many manufacturers aware of potential threats.

But, for the most part, analysts and manufacturers contend the benefits of JIT outweigh the risks. Research published in the *IndustryWeek*/Manufacturing Performance Institute 2006 Census of Manufacturers supports this, with 43.4 per cent of 758 manufacturers responding, saying they use JIT supplier deliveries to manage stock levels.

Preparing for the unpredictable

The typical approach manufacturers take when preparing for the unexpected is to carry some safety stock of the top-selling items. Adding buffer stock may stray somewhat from pure JIT, but it provides manufacturers with some leeway if something goes wrong.

Some manufacturers, like Toyota, don't have to worry too much about delivery problems during crisis situations because their suppliers are nearby. Toyota opened a Tundra plant in San Antonio last autumn in an industrial park that houses 21 of its suppliers.

Understanding demand

Aside from acts of nature and war, manufacturers who want to be successful with JIT need to prepare for demand spikes.* Both Nintendo and Sony Corp. had out-of-stock issues with their popular video game systems after the past holiday season. 'Just-in-time is OK, but if all of a sudden there is a surge in demand, you may not have the flexibility available to meet the demand,' says business analyst Fariborz Ghadar.

* A demand spike is a sudden, unexpected upsurge in demand.

Source: *IndustryWeek*, 1 June 2007.

Questions

(30 marks; 35 minutes)

1 Examine two possible impacts upon Sealy Corp. of its October 2005 warning to customers of production delays. (6)
2 If less than half of US manufacturers were using JIT in 2006, how might the majority have been managing their stock ordering and management? (5)
3 a) Explain the meaning of the term 'buffer stock'. (4)
   b) Explain one benefit to a business from operating JIT with a zero buffer stock level. (5)
4 Discuss whether a JIT approach to stock management is appropriate to a business with demand 'spikes', such as Nintendo. (10)

C ESSAY QUESTIONS

(40 marks each)

1 'The use of information technology makes stock control an automatic function, requiring little input from human beings.' Assess this statement.
2 Evaluate whether a medium-sized retailer such as Next would be wise to move to just-in-time stock control.
3 Assess the view that, with today's information technology, no firm ought to experience stock control problems.

UNIT 46

Lean management

Lean management is a philosophy that aims to produce more using less, by eliminating all forms of waste ('waste' being defined as anything that does not add value to the final product).

46.1 INTRODUCTION

The rise of the Japanese approach to production has been unstoppable in recent years. **Just-in-time** (JIT) and ***kaizen*** have been widely written about, but the underlying philosophy has sometimes been overlooked. The total approach has been termed 'lean production', though its ideas have been spread more generally to include service businesses as well, hence the term lean management (or lean thinking). It is based upon a combined focus by management and workers on minimising the use of the key business resources: materials, manpower, capital, floor space and time. The main components of lean management are:

- just-in-time (JIT)
- total quality management (TQM)
- time-based management.

Toyota and the origins of lean production

In most industries, new ideas and methods tend to emerge during a period of crisis when old ideas no longer seem to work. The motor industry is no different. The inspiration came from Eiji Toyoda's three-month visit to Ford's Rouge plant in Detroit in 1950. Eiji's family had set up the Toyota Motor Company in 1937. Now, in Japan's situation of desperate shortages after the Second World War, he hoped to learn from Ford. On his return, Eiji reported that the mass production system at the Rouge plant was riddled with *muda* (the Japanese term for wasted effort, materials and time). By analysing the weaknesses of mass production, Toyota was the first company to develop lean production.

Toyota realised that mass production could only be fully economic if identical products could be produced continuously. Yet Henry Ford's statement that 'they can have any colour they want ... as long as it's black' was no longer acceptable to customers. Mass production was also very wasteful, as poor-quality production led to a high reject rate at the end of the production line.

Toyota's solution was to design machines that could be used for many different operations – flexible production. Mass producers took a whole day to change a stamping machine from producing one part to making another. Toyota eventually reduced this time to just three minutes, and so simplified the process that factory line workers could do it without any help from engineers! This carried with it the advantage of flexibility. If buying habits changed in the USA, Ford could not react quickly, because each production line was dedicated to producing a particular product in a particular way. Toyota's multi-purpose machines could adapt quickly to a surge of demand for, for example, open-top cars or right-hand-drive models.

By a process of continuous refinement, Toyota developed the approach to:

- maximise the input from staff
- focus attention upon the quality of supplies and production
- minimise wasted resources in stock through just-in-time.

By the 1990s, the company was able to turn the spotlight onto product development – to shorten the time between product conception and product launch.

46.2 THE BENEFITS OF LEAN PRODUCTION

Lean production:

- creates higher levels of labour productivity, therefore it uses less labour
- requires less stock, less factory space and less capital equipment than a mass producer of comparable size; the lean producer therefore has substantial cost advantages over the mass producer
- creates substantial marketing advantages: first, it results in far fewer defects, improving quality and reliability for the customer; second, lean production requires half the engineering hours to develop a new product; this means that the lean producer can develop a vast range of products that a mass producer cannot afford to match.

A-grade application

General Motors fighting back?

In 1998 it took the American car maker General Motors 50 per cent more hours than Toyota to make a car. This poor productivity caused General Motors to make a loss on every car it sold. To survive, General Motors had to close the productivity gap with Toyota.

In 2006 General Motors announced that it had reduced the productivity gap with Toyota to just under 14 per cent. How did it achieve this turnaround? The main change that brought success was to find more reliable suppliers, even if they were slightly more expensive than existing suppliers. General Motors recognised that a failed delivery can lead to stoppages on the production line, which in turn holds back productivity. The improvements proved too little, too late, of course, as General Motors had to be bailed out by the US government in 2009.

46.3 THE COMPONENTS OF LEAN MANAGEMENT

Lean people management

Lean producers reject the waste of human talent involved in narrow, repetitive jobs. They believe in empowerment, team working and job enrichment. Problem solving is not just left to specialist engineers. Employees are trained in preventative maintenance, to spot when a fault is developing and correct it before the production line has to stop. If a problem does emerge on the line, they are trained to solve it without needing an engineer or a supervisor. Teams meet regularly to discuss ways in which their sections could be run more smoothly.

Lean approach to quality

In a mass production system, quality control is a specialised job that takes place at the end of the line. In a lean system, each team is responsible for checking the quality of its own work. If a fault is spotted, every worker has the power to stop the assembly line. This policy prevents errors being passed on, to be corrected only once the fault has been found at the end of the line. The lean approach, therefore, is self-checking at every production stage so that quality failures at the end (or with customers) become extremely rare.

One way to achieve lean quality is **total quality management** (TQM). This attempts to achieve a culture of quality throughout the organisation, so that the primary objective of all employees is to achieve quality the first time around without the need for any reworking. To achieve total quality, managers must 'make quality the number one, non-negotiable priority, and actively seek and listen to the views of employees on how to improve quality' (Roger Trapp, in the *Independent*).

Lean design

As consumers become more demanding and technology advances, car design has become highly complex. This threatens to boost costs and development times. Lean producers combat this by simultaneous engineering. This means integrating the development functions so that separate design and engineering stages are tackled at the same time. This speeds up development times, which cuts costs and reduces the risk of early obsolescence. Whereas US and European car manufacturers take over 60 months (five years!) from conception to launch of a new car model, the Japanese take 40+ months. Crucial to lean design and development is the principle of empowerment. Consequently, team members feel a greater pressure to make the right decision because it is more likely to hold.

Lean component supply

The approach to component supply varies greatly from company to company. Mass producers tend to have rather distant relationships with suppliers, often based on minimising the delivery cost per unit. They may buy from several sources to keep up the competitive pressure. The supplier, in turn, may be secretive about costs and profit margins to prevent the buyer from pressing for still lower prices. Lean producers work in partnership with their suppliers or, more often, with a single supplier. They keep the supplier fully informed of new product developments, encouraging ideas and technical advice. This means that by the time the assembly line starts running, errors have been ironed out so there are very few running changes or failures. Both parties are also likely to share financial and sales information electronically. This encourages an atmosphere of trust and common purpose, and aids planning.

46.4 JUST-IN-TIME

Lean producers run with minimal buffer stocks, relying on daily or hourly deliveries from trusted suppliers. As there is no safety net, a faulty shipment of components could bring an entire factory to a halt. Mass producers rely on stockpiles, **just-in-case**. Lean producers insist on zero defects, whereas mass producers are happy with a quality standard that is 'good enough'.

The just-in-time (JIT) system of manufacturing is perhaps the best-known element of lean production. JIT aims to minimise the costs of holding unnecessary stocks of raw materials, components, work in progress and finished products. The principle that underpins JIT is that production should be 'pulled through' rather than 'pushed through'. This means that production should be for specific customer orders, so that the production cycle starts only once a customer has placed an order with the producer.

Summary of the just-in-time approach

- No buffer stocks of any type are held.
- Production is to order.
- Stock is ordered only when it is needed, just in time.
- Zero defects are essential as no stock safety net exists.
- No 'spare' workers are employed.
- Staff are multi-skilled and capable of filling in for absent colleagues.
- It is used by lean producers.

Summary of the just-in-case approach

- Stocks of raw materials, components, work in progress and finished products are held by the producer.
- Production is frequently stockpiled as manufacturers often seek economies of scale even at a time when sales are falling.
- Stock is ordered less frequently because the average order size tends to be large in order to take advantage of bulk-buying discounts.
- The incentive to achieve zero defects is less strong as stocks at every stage of production are held just in case of mistakes.

Capital and interest waste

Holding stock creates both actual and opportunity costs. The actual costs are the costs of paying for somewhere to keep the stock. The opportunity cost is the interest that could have been received had the capital tied up in stock been available to invest elsewhere.

Defect waste

By holding very little stock, firms no longer have a safety net. Consequently quality must improve, ideally in order to achieve zero defects. Firms must tackle quality problems at source, changing production methods or suppliers where necessary.

Overproduction waste

Mass producers set production levels on the basis of sales forecasts derived from quantitative market research findings. These forecasts may prove wrong. This can lead to heavy price discounting in order to clear surplus stock. By producing to order this wastage is avoidable.

46.5 TIME-BASED MANAGEMENT

Time-based management involves managing time in the same way most companies manage costs, quality or stock. Time-based manufacturers try to shorten rather than lengthen production runs in order to reduce costs and to increase levels of customer satisfaction. To do this, manufacturers invest in flexible capital; that is, machines that can make more than one model. Training must also be seen as a priority because staff have to be multi-skilled. This enables the firm to produce a variety of models without a cost penalty, which is something that mass producers using a high division of labour with inflexible capital thought impossible.

Time-based management creates four benefits.

1. By reducing lead and set-up times, productivity improves, creating a cost advantage.
2. Shortening lead times cuts customer response times, increasing consumer satisfaction as customers receive their orders sooner.
3. Lower stock holding costs: short lead and set-up times make firms more responsive to changes in the market. Consequently there should be less need for long production runs and stockpiles of finished products. If demand does suddenly increase, production can simply be quickly restarted.
4. An ability to offer the consumer a more varied product range without losing cost-reducing economies of scale. Time-based management therefore makes market segmentation a much cheaper strategy to operate.

A-grade application

Time-based management

Zara is a fashion retailing phenomenon built on an understanding of the importance of time. When Christian Dior featured a glamorous embroidered Afghan coat on the catwalk, Zara had its own version in its shops within a fortnight. It was able to design, manufacture and distribute the coat to its shops throughout Europe within 14 days – and sell it for just £95. If a style doesn't succeed within a week, it is withdrawn. No style stays on the shop floor for more than four weeks. The immediate result is obvious. Fashion- and price-conscious women flock to Zara.

Less obviously, Zara benefits from a vital secondary factor. In Spain, Zara's home country, an average high-street clothes store expects its regular customers to visit three times a year. Yet the average is 17 times for Zara! As the stock is constantly changing, the store is constantly worth visiting. Zara's owner started the business with €25 in 1963; today he is one of the world's ten richest men with wealth of over $25 billion. Time well spent.

Figure 46.1 Zara and the Spanish high street

ISSUES FOR ANALYSIS

- Lean thinking seeks to eliminate waste of all forms. By adopting lean techniques, firms should therefore become more efficient. By reducing waste, unit costs will be reduced. This makes it possible for lean producers to offer lower prices without any sacrifice of profit margin, or to offer higher product specifications for the same price as rivals. Consequently, lean production techniques can have an impact on firms' marketing strategies.
- Lean new product development techniques are increasingly decisive in a highly competitive world where product life cycles are becoming shorter. In this environment, reducing design lead times is vital. For a product to be considered innovative it must be launched quickly. If competitors beat you to it, your product will be seen as just another 'me too'.
- The attempt to achieve lean production can be expensive. Some firms have invested heavily in 'flexible' computer-aided manufacturing equipment. True lean production depends upon people rather than machines.

45.6 LEAN PRODUCTION – AN EVALUATION

Some of the arguments put forward above could be criticised for being too black and white (mass production = terrible; lean production = wonderful). The reality of business is often to do with shades of grey, with some lean producers having their own weaknesses. Some trends are unarguable, however. When people first started writing about the Toyota production system, Toyota was a failure compared with the giant US car producers Ford and General Motors. Today Toyota is the world's number one car maker.

However, there is a downside. By definition, lean thinking involves the elimination of waste. This waste could be over-manning. So by switching to a leaner system the consequence could be redundancies. Lean management in this context becomes little more than a 'fig leaf' that a ruthless manager may wish to hide behind when seeking to justify controversial staffing decisions.

Key Terms

Just-in-case: keeping buffer stocks of materials and components just in case something goes wrong.

Just-in-time: producing with minimum stock levels so every process must be completed just in time for the process that follows.

***Kaizen*:** continuous improvement (that is, encouraging all staff to regularly come up with ideas to improve efficiency and quality).

Total quality management: a passion for quality that starts at the top, then spreads throughout the organisation.

WORKBOOK

A REVISION QUESTIONS

(35 marks; 35 minutes)

1. State the three components of lean production. (3)
2. Outline three problems of mass production. (3)
3. Distinguish between just-in-time and just-in-case. (4)
4. What advantages are there in using time-based management? (4)
5. Why is it important to reduce machine set-up times? (3)
6. What are the opportunity costs of holding too much stock? (4)
7. Outline possible sources of waste in any organisation with which you are familiar. (Your school? Your part-time employer?) (4)
8. What is reworking and why does it add to costs? (5)
9. Why could it be important to be first to the market with a new product idea? (5)

B REVISION EXERCISES

B1 DATA RESPONSE

Lean manufacturing in Plymouth

Who wouldn't want to double their revenues in four years? It sounds like any company's dream. But success sets its own challenges, as Kawasaki Precision Machinery (UK) is well aware.

Plymouth-based Kawasaki Precision Machinery (KPM) manufactures and sells hydraulic components – pumps, motors and control valves – for markets in Europe, India, the Middle East, South Africa and Australasia, and it has seen turnover increase from £30 million to nearly £60 million in recent years. Such a dramatic increase in business has inevitably created its own pressures. General Manager Steve Cardew says, 'We've needed to increase the capacity of the plant significantly. Space on the site has also come under pressure, and at present we have to store some goods off-site. But we're now focusing on reducing stocks, which will enable us to free up floor space and make better use of what's available.'

The investment he refers to has been significant and sustained. In fact, the company has bought in new capital equipment at the rate of some £2 million a year. It has also found it necessary to increase the size of its workforce, which now stands at around 300. But this has involved an approach that goes beyond simply raising the headcount. 'There have been difficulties,' comments Cardew, 'given our geographical location. Getting the right skills hasn't been easy, so we've developed a substantial in-house training and upskilling programme. But we've also taken the opportunity to bring in some new people who already have the skills and knowledge we're looking for. In practice, that particularly means people with experience in the automotive industry, who can bring with them an understanding of lean manufacturing.'

It's a policy that can only sustain the impetus of a lean journey that's already well under way. The continuous improvement philosophy is at the heart of KPM's aspirations to become world class. It's necessary, too, to look beyond a company to its sources of supply, and that's a topic that also engages his attention. 'All our processes are only as good as the weakest link in the supply chain, and we have to be conscious of that. A lot of our raw materials are castings and forgings, but many foundries – especially those in the UK – now have a reduced capacity.'

It's clear that there will be no relenting in the quest for improvement. 'We're now in a period of growth,' Cardew concedes, 'but there has to come a time when our currently robust main markets stop growing, and we must be sure that we'll be competitive then. We can't afford to wait around until the demand decreases; we have to be realistic and increase our efficiency now.'

Source: 'Kawasaki precision machinery, living with growth', *The Manufacturer*, February 2008

Questions

(30 marks; 35 minutes)

1 Outline two possible pressures for a lean producer such as KPM of 'a dramatic increase in business'. (6)
2 Outline two elements of lean management being used by KPM. (4)
3 Would you recommend that KPM should move to JIT production and stock control? Justify and explain your reasoning. (8)
4 Discuss whether KPM would be in a strong or weak position if there is a change to a position of 'demand decreases'. (12)

C ESSAY QUESTIONS

(40 marks each)

1 Discuss the difficulties and dilemmas faced by managers who are considering a switch to lean methods of production.
2 In some companies, lean production is viewed as just being another in a long line of management fads. In others it is embraced with enthusiasm by the staff. Why may this be so?
3 Why do some firms seem far better than others in terms of their ability to successfully implement lean production techniques?
4 Discuss the benefits, and the possible disadvantages, of lean production methods being utilised by an aircraft manufacturer. How could the balance between the benefits and the possible disadvantages change in the long term?

UNIT 47

Capacity utilisation

Capacity utilisation is the proportion of maximum possible output that is currently being used. A football stadium is at full capacity when all the seats are filled. A company producing 1,500 units a week when the factory is capable of 2,000 units has a capacity utilisation of 75 per cent.

47.1 OPERATIONAL TARGETS

To run a successful operation such as Primark requires brilliant organisation and clear targets. The role of the targets is to help all staff aim at the same goal. The target at a hotdog stand outside a concert venue is to serve as many people as possible as quickly as possible, before and after the show. To achieve this, the stallholder will plan ahead, cooking the sausages in advance and getting the onions ready. The most efficient stallholder will almost always make more money than the best cook. It is all down to clear targets and clear objectives.

There are three main targets focused on by operations managers:

1. quality targets (for example, to have no more than 1 in 100 customers demand a refund)
2. capacity utilisation targets (such as that the factory should be working at 85 to 95 per cent of its maximum possible capacity)
3. unit costs (for instance, keeping the average cost per unit at below £1.99, in order to keep the selling price below £2.99).

47.2 HOW IS CAPACITY UTILISATION MEASURED?

Capacity utilisation is measured using the formula:

$$\frac{\text{Current output}}{\text{Maximum possible output}} \times 100$$

What does capacity depend upon? The amount a firm can make is determined by the quantity of buildings, machinery and labour it has available. Maximum capacity is achieved when the firm is making full use of all the buildings, machinery and labour available. The firm is said to be working at full capacity, or 100 per cent capacity utilisation.

For a service business the same logic applies, though it is much harder to identify a precise figure. This is because it may take a different time to serve each customer. In a shop or a bank branch, demand may exceed capacity at certain times of the day, in which case queues will form. At other times the staff may have little to do. A service business wishing to stay cost-competitive will measure demand at different times of the day and then schedule the staffing level to match the capacity utilisation.

Many service businesses cope with fluctuating demand by employing temporary or part-time staff. These employees provide a far greater degree of flexibility to employers. Part-time hours can be increased, or extra temporary staff can be employed to increase capacity easily. If demand falls, temporary staff can be laid off without redundancy payments, or part-time staff can have their hours reduced, thus reducing capacity easily and cheaply. Many businesses like this flexibility as it limits wastage on staff costs. However, the situation may not be as appealing for employees, who have fewer rights than their full-time salaried predecessors. Figure 47.1 shows how flexible staffing (C) can reduce the wastage implied by having under-used full-time staff (A).

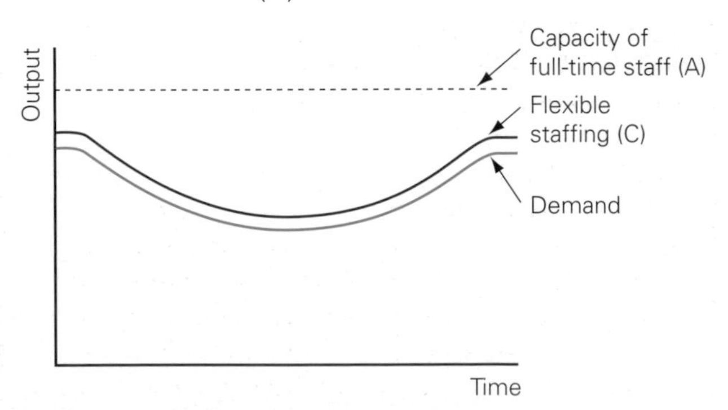

Figure 47.1 How flexible staffing (C) can reduce wastage implied by having under-used full-time staff (A)

47.3 FIXED COSTS AND CAPACITY

It is vital to understand clearly the relationship between fixed costs and capacity utilisation. Fixed costs are fixed in relation to output. This means that whether capacity utilisation is 50 per cent or 100 per cent, fixed costs will not change. The implication of this is clear. If a football club invests in a huge, expensive playing staff (whose salaries are a fixed cost) but matches are played to a half-empty stadium, the fixed costs will become a huge burden. This is because the very fact that fixed costs do not change *in total* as output changes means that they do change *per unit* of output/demand. A half-empty stadium means that the fixed costs per unit are double the level at maximum capacity (see Table 47.1).

Table 47.1 Fixed costs and capacity

	Full stadium	Half-empty stadium
	50,000 fans	25,000 fans
Weekly salary bill (fixed costs)	£250,000	£250,000
Salary fixed cost per fan	£5	£10
	(£250,000/50,000)	(£250,000/25,000)

When the stadium capacity utilisation is at 50 per cent, then, £10 of the ticket price is needed for the players' wages alone. The many other fixed and variable costs of running a football club would be on top of this, of course.

The reason why capacity utilisation is so important is that it has an inverse (opposite) effect upon fixed costs per unit. In other words, when utilisation is high, fixed costs are spread over many units. This cuts the cost per unit, which enables the producer either to cut prices to boost demand further, or to enjoy large profit margins. If utilisation is low, fixed costs per unit become punishingly high. In March 2010 an African newspaper reported that manufacturers in Nigeria were operating at only 27 per cent of capacity, largely due to electricity shortages. This would make fixed costs per unit almost four times higher than necessary, which is an almost impossible situation.

The ideal level of capacity utilisation, therefore, is at or near 100 per cent. This spreads fixed costs as thinly as possible, boosting profit margins. There are two key concerns about operating at maximum capacity for long, however. These are the risks that:

1 if demand rises further, you will have to turn it away, enabling your competitors to benefit
2 you will struggle to service the machinery and train/retrain staff; this may prove costly in the long term, and will increase the chances of production breakdowns in the short term.

The production ideal, therefore, is a capacity utilisation of around 90 per cent.

47.4 HOW TO GET TOWARDS FULL CAPACITY

If a firm's capacity utilisation is an unsatisfactory 45 per cent, how could it be increased to a more acceptable level of around 90 per cent? There are two possible approaches, as discussed below.

Increase demand (in this case, double it!)

Demand for existing products could be boosted by extra promotional spending, price cutting or – more fundamentally – devising a new strategy to reposition the products into growth sectors. If supermarket own-label products are flourishing, perhaps offer to produce

A-grade application

Gordon Ramsay: footballer, chef, TV personality ... and business guru?

In his TV series *Ramsay's Kitchen Nightmares*, the renowned chef spent a lot of time swearing and criticising chefs for the way they cooked. The series placed Gordon at a failing restaurant for a week. His task was to wave a magic wand and turn it into a profitable business. In almost every episode of the series, Ramsay identified each restaurant's failure to use anything near its full capacity. Commonly, he suggested the introduction of a simple lunchtime menu to boost trade during the day, in addition to speeding up service in the evenings to ensure that every table would see at least two sittings in the main evening session. Ramsay's advice, delivered in his own inimitable way, was simply a call to push capacity utilisation higher in order to spread each restaurant's fixed costs over more units of output (customers). The advice usually worked.

A-grade application

Odeon: filling seats with anyone it can

Odeon is acutely aware of the dangers of having capacity empty during quiet times. In an attempt to increase capacity utilisation during the day and on quieter evenings, Odeon has introduced a number of specialised film showings, catering for groups who are more likely to visit the cinema during 'quiet periods':

- Odeon kids: Saturday and Sunday mornings and every day during school holidays
- Senior screen: mid-morning showings of traditional and modern classics for 'mature guests', with free tea and coffee
- Odeon Newbies: for parents with babies, mid-morning showings with volume quieter than usual and lights higher than usual, to try to create a calming environment for babies and parents
- Director's Chair: showing foreign-language, independent and art-house films for serious film buffs, one quiet evening per week.

Even with reduced ticket prices for some of these options, each seat sold is still making a contribution to covering fixed costs as capacity utilisation edges higher for the cinema chain.

2010. Rationalisation programmes must be handled carefully to minimise damage to the morale of the remaining staff and to minimise bad external publicity. Redundancies are never popular, but voluntary redundancy is a more attractive proposition than compulsory redundancy; however, neither is as pain-free as using **natural wastage** to rationalise.

Stock management

The issues already covered show the importance of managing stocks effectively. Stocks of finished goods waiting to be sold may be seen as a buffer against sudden surges in demand. However, keeping too much stock is a dangerously expensive habit. The balancing of stock levels is one of the major issues facing operations managers. Meanwhile, stock of raw materials and components presents similar problems. A lack of production inputs may force production to grind to a halt, while too much stock may lead to wasted materials or space.

Non-standard orders

Sometimes firms will be approached by customers with special orders at a different price to their regular selling price. A customer with special requirements, such as a different design or a very short delivery date, may offer a price above the norm. In other cases customers may try to buy special orders at especially low prices. Retailers such as Lidl and Primark sell cheaply to the public because of their skill at buying cheaply.

High-price special orders

In these cases, the order is likely to look profitable at first glance. However, the special nature of the order is such that it will be more expensive to produce. This will mean that unit costs are going to be higher. Perhaps overtime or subcontracting will be necessary to meet a tight order deadline or to adjust the standard design to meet the customer's needs. In these cases, extra costs must be factored into any calculation of the possible profit from the order.

> **A-grade application**
>
> **The world's biggest private jet**
>
> In 2012 a mystery middle-eastern buyer will take delivery of a customised A380 'double-decker' plane. The giant Airbus plane can take 700 passengers, but this version will have:
>
> - a garage for a Rolls Royce
> - a huge spiral staircase
> - a concert hall
> - a sauna
> - bedrooms for 20 guests.
>
> The plane is believed to have a price tag of £300 million, more than twice the normal price of an A380.

Low-price special orders

There are several reasons why a firm may consider accepting an order at lower than the usual selling price. The key is whether a firm has enough under-used capacity to meet the order and if the order will generate a positive contribution per unit. If the firm is already breaking even, a low-price order that generates a positive contribution per unit will generate extra profit. A further reason to accept the order is the possibility that it could lead to a new customer becoming a regular if they are happy with the quality and delivery of the order.

ISSUES FOR ANALYSIS

- Whenever operational targets are missed, managers will want to know why. In these cases it is vital that you show a clear understanding of cause and effect. There will clearly be links between the three major target variables of unit cost, quality and capacity utilisation. Good analytic arguments will show a clear understanding of which events have caused which consequences. For example, an answer could suggest that unit costs have risen as a result of operating at a lower than anticipated level of capacity. This may have been the result of a fall in demand caused by a poor reputation, created by poor quality levels last month.
- It is useful to experiment by taking each of the three target variables as a starting point, then thinking through the impact on the other two. For example, if capacity utilisation falls, what is the impact on unit costs and what could be the effect on quality? Or, what if quality performance falls?
- Another major analytical theme is likely to be an awareness of the arguments for and against keeping a stable production level month by month, as opposed to attempting to exactly match production with demand. Logically constructed arguments on both sides of this question are likely to lead to effective judgements when asked to evaluate.

48.4 MAKING OPERATIONAL DECISIONS – AN EVALUATION

Operations decisions are at the very heart of any business. Efficiency is king – without it, no firm will last long. Few customers are willing to wait for an unavailable product, while few firms have the financial resources to indefinitely fund inefficient stock-holding. The magical formula for matching production to demand does not exist. Instead, it is important to show an awareness that the forecasting skills and experience of operations managers will need to go hand in hand to ensure that a business is operationally efficient.

Key Terms

Highly price elastic: when customers are so focused on price that a small price change can cause a big switch in customer demand (for example, price up 5 per cent, sales down 20 per cent).
Higher profit margin: a wider gap between price and unit cost; if sales volumes stay the same, this must increase total profit.
Natural wastage: the 'natural' annual fall in staff levels caused by employees retiring, moving away or finding better jobs elsewhere.
Operational targets: the numerical goals set by management at the start of the year (for example, output of 220,000 units with a quality wastage rate of no more than 1 per cent).
Rationalisation: reorganising in order to increase efficiency; this usually leads to redundancies.

48.5 WORKBOOK

A REVISION QUESTIONS

(35 marks; 35 minutes)

1. Briefly explain what is meant by capacity utilisation. (2)
2. Explain why a high level of capacity usage makes cost per unit fall. (3)
3. Calculate the unit cost for a firm that manufactured 23,000 units with total costs of £11,500. (2)
4. Explain why quality targets may suffer if management is concerned only with meeting unit cost targets. (4)
5. Explain what is meant by the term rationalisation. (2)
6. Explain two methods that could be used to improve the level of capacity utilisation in a clothing factory. (4)
7. Explain two possible drawbacks to a farmer of relying on temporary staff when picking strawberries. (4)
8. Explain two benefits to a farmer of using temporary staff to pick strawberries. (4)
9. Explain two reasons why a company may agree to provide a customer with a special order at a selling price lower than its average unit cost. (4)
10. Outline three possible reasons why a cake manufacturer may try to closely match production with demand in order to reduce stock levels to a minimum. (6)

B REVISION EXERCISES
B1 DATA RESPONSE

Hotel Torres is a part of the Hoteles Benitez group of hotels in Spain. For hotels, the main operational target is occupancy rates: the percentage of rooms that are occupied at any time. The chain's head office is assessing last year's performance at each branch and is particularly interested in the data shown in Table 48.2 relating to the Hotel Torres in Barcelona.

Table 48.2 Occupancy rate of Hotel Torres in Barcelona

	Quarter 1	Quarter 2	Quarter 3	Quarter 4
Average occupancy rate (%)	53	66	84	62
Target occupancy rate (%)	55	70	90	75
Group average occupancy rate (%)	58	72	90	75
Cost per guest (euros)	64	58	50	60
Target cost per guest (euros)	62	55	40	

Questions

(25 marks; 25 minutes)

1. Explain what Table 48.2 reveals about Hotel Torres's operational efficiency during the year. (6)
2. Use the data in the table to explain the possible link between room occupancy performance and cost per guest. (6)
3. Analyse the benefits that the hotel could gain by setting targets for occupancy rates and cost per guest. (7)
4. Briefly explain two possible reasons why Hotel Torres failed to meet its targets. (6)

B2 DATA RESPONSE

DWS Ltd is a toy manufacturer, operating in the UK from a factory in the north-east. Having been running for 20 years, DWS is used to the particular problems posed by operating in such a seasonal industry. With 70 per cent of sales being made in November and December, the managers have experience of battling to match production to demand. Their problem is intensified by the short product life cycles involved in manufacturing toys designed to tie in with the latest television and films. Table 48.3 shows units sold, output and maximum capacity month by month for last year.

Table 48.3 Data for DWS Ltd

	Sales (units)	Output (units)	Maximum capacity (units)
January	10,000	5,000	20,000
February	10,000	10,000	20,000
March	15,000	15,000	20,000
April	15,000	15,000	20,000
May	20,000	20,000	20,000
June	20,000	20,000	20,000
July	20,000	20,000	40,000
August	30,000	30,000	40,000
September	60,000	100,000	120,000
October	100,000	280,000	300,000
November	380,000	300,000	300,000
December	320,000	300,000	300,000

The firm uses a range of methods to boost its maximum capacity during busy periods. These include overtime, temporary staff and subcontracting work to another trusted local manufacturer.

DWS has been approached by a major UK greetings card retailer, which is looking for a manufacturer of stuffed toys themed around various holidays, including Valentine's Day, Easter and Halloween. The initial contract would cover a 12-month period and would mean that sales levels would treble in January, March and October. The firm would pay a price equivalent to 5 per cent above the variable cost of each unit of output.

Questions

(35 marks; 40 minutes)

1 a) Draw a graph to show units sold, output and maximum capacity. (6)
  b) Shade the areas on the graph that represent under-use of capacity. (2)
2 Analyse the problems that DWS may experience by maintaining a consistent level of production all year round in order to avoid using overtime, temporary staff and subcontracting. (9)
3 Describe the pros and cons of two possible methods of increasing maximum capacity in the three affected months. (6)
4 Discuss whether DWS should accept this special order. (12)

Using technology in operations

UNIT 49

Technology means the computer hardware and software used to automate systems, and to handle, analyse and communicate business data.

49.1 INTRODUCTION

Information technology (IT) applications in business are various and rapidly changing. Often, though, the changes that occur are to processing speed and business jargon; the essential tasks remain the same. In recent years, the most important business IT innovation has been the emergence of the internet. This will be covered relatively briefly, because the pace of change means that magazine articles will provide a more up-to-date understanding of the internet's business potential than is possible here.

Key applications of technology are:

- automated stock control systems
- computer-aided design (CAD)
- robotics
- information technology, including electronic data interchange (EDI) and the internet
- database management (the organisation behind efficient delivery systems such as Tesco Home Delivery).

49.2 AUTOMATED STOCK CONTROL SYSTEMS

Modern stock control systems are based on laser scanning of bar-coded information. This ensures the computer knows the exact quantity of each product/size/colour that has come into the stockroom. In retail outlets, a laser scanning till is then used to record exactly what has been sold. This allows the store's computer to keep up-to-date records of current stocks of every item. This data can enable a buyer to decide how much extra to order, or an electronic link with the supplier can re-order automatically (see Section 49.6).

All this information will be held in the form of a database. This makes it easy for the firm to carry out an aged stock analysis: the computer provides a printout showing the stock in order of age. Table 49.1 shows a list of stock in a clothes shop, with the oldest first. It enables the manager to make informed decisions about what to do now and in the future. In this case:

- big price reductions seem to be called for on the first five items; they have been around too long
- there should be fewer orders in future for size 8 dresses.

Table 49.1 An example of aged stock analysis

Garment	Received (days ago)	Number received	In stock today
Green *Fabrice* dress, size 8	285	2	1
Blue *Channelle* dress, size 14	241	1	1
Red *Channelle* dress, size 8	241	2	2
Red *Grigio* jacket, size 10	249	4	3
Black *Grigio* dress, size 8	205	3	2
Black *Fabrice* dress, size 12	192	2	1
Blue *Florentine* suit, size 8	179	1	1

49.3 DESIGN TECHNOLOGY

Computer-aided design (CAD) has been around for more than 20 years, but is now affordable and hugely powerful. Before CAD, product designers, engineers and architects drew their designs by hand. A CAD system works digitally, allowing designs to be saved, changed and reworked without starting from scratch. Even better, CAD can show a 3D version of a drawing and rotate to show the back and sides.

For multinationals such as Sony, a product designed in Tokyo can be sent electronically to Sony offices in America and Europe, for local designers to tweak the work to make it better suited to local tastes. And when work is behind schedule, designers in Tokyo can pass a design on to London at the end of the Japanese working day; then the design is sent on to America.

The time differences mean that 24-hour working can be kept up.

A-grade application

A Triumph

The Triumph motorbike business collapsed in 1983, and people said Britain could no longer make bikes. But entrepreneur John Bloor bought the name and rebuilt the company. The first new Triumph hit the streets in 1991 and, incredibly, the business now has 1,400 employees, a turnover of £300 million and a 5 per cent share of the world market for motorbikes.

The success has been built on design. Triumph has the biggest motorcycle design department outside Japan. The designers work on up-to-date CAD systems, to ensure that the bikes have the key combination of looks and performance. Although some of the production takes place in the Far East, all the research, design and engineering jobs are in Britain.

Source: adapted from The *Independent*, 13 May 2010.

Figure 49.1 A Triumph motorbike

The benefits of CAD systems to successful design are that:

- the data generated by a CAD system can be linked to computer-aided manufacturing (CAM) to provide integrated, highly accurate production
- they are hugely beneficial for businesses that are constantly required to provide designs that are unique, yet based on common principles (for example, designing a new bridge, car or office block)
- CAD improves the productivity of designers and also helps them to be more ambitious; the extraordinary buildings of Frank Gehry could not have been produced without CAD (because only computers could calculate whether the unusual structure would fall down in a high wind).

Figure 49.2 A Frank Gehry building

49.4 ROBOTICS

Industrial robots are fundamental to the car industry worldwide, and are becoming increasingly important in the production of electrical goods such as TVs and computers. Nevertheless, it remains a bit of a surprise that robots have not become a more powerful force in industry. Thirty years ago, people assumed that few workers would be left in factories – the robots were coming. In Britain today there are fewer than 50 robots per 10,000 workers. Even in Japan (with more than 40 per cent of the world's robots) the figure is only 490 robots per 10,000 manufacturing workers.

Figure 49.3 shows that worldwide sales of industrial robots were rising until the 2009 recession. The industry expects that there will be a full recovery in sales by 2012/2013.

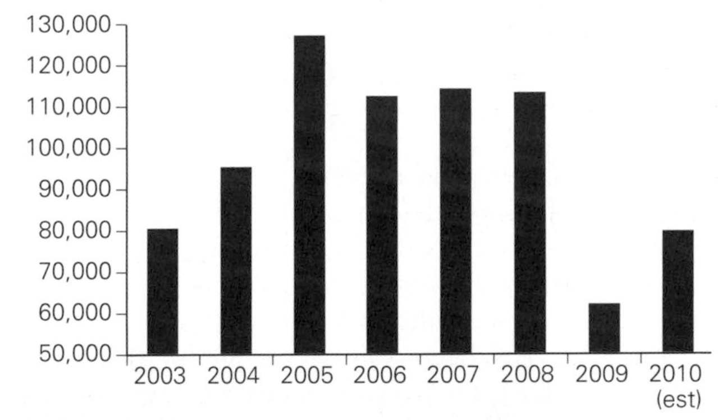

Figure 49.3 Industrial robot sales worldwide 2003–10
Source: World Robotics Report, IFR Statistical Department

Industrial robots have important advantages over human labour. They are programmed to do the same thing over and over again, so repetitive tasks can be completed with 100 per cent consistency. This can be vital, for example, in the production of components for aircraft engines, or in the production of heart pacemakers. Robots are also likely to prove cheaper than people, as long as the business is able to use them effectively (for example, for 20 hours a day).

Yet robots are clearly not a magic solution, or else they would have taken over. They are inflexible, so they cannot easily switch jobs in the way that people can; and they have rarely proved as reliable as they perhaps should be.

A-grade application

Toshiba robots

Three Toshiba robots are used at a pet food factory in Bremen, northern Germany. The company has made substantial investment in factory automation in order to improve productivity. Toshiba Machine robots now package birdseed sticks at a rate of 90 per minute. Where once there were seven people working on the application across three shifts, now three Toshiba Machine TH490 robots achieve the same results. The people have been redeployed across the plant.

The robots are part of a production line that manufactures birdseed sticks that are like a fat-based lollypop, embedded with nuts and seeds. The sticks are fed down three conveyors, each with a ceiling-mounted robot at its end. As this happens, the boxes are fed down another conveyor. A robot gripper then picks up the seed sticks and transfers them into boxes on a moving conveyor. Ceiling-mounted SCARA robots make the best use of the available work area.

49.5 COMMUNICATION WITH CUSTOMERS

There are two main ways firms communicate electronically with their customers. The first is via a website; for example, easyJet receives over 95 per cent of its bookings in this way. The second is through careful database management. A database is a store of information that can be rearranged and sorted in numerous ways. For example, if you had a database of all your friends, classmates and work colleagues, you may like to:

- sort them by birthday, so that you never missed the chance of a party invitation
- sort them by activity, so that you could rustle up a football or hockey team when needed
- sort them by location, to give you a mailing list for organising a school reunion.

For businesses, the ability to store information on thousands, perhaps millions, of customers is invaluable. In order to maximise the speed and flexibility of a database, every type of information needs to be held in a different 'field'. Field 1 may be the surname; field 3 the address; field 7 the age, and so on. This enables the data to be sorted, or picked out, in different ways. If you have a new product aiming at the over-40s, those aged 40 and over can be picked out and a mailing list produced in seconds.

To obtain this data, businesses use various approaches:

- asking customers to fill in their name and address when purchasing goods
- recording the information on product warranty cards
- supplying 'loyalty' cards, such as Tesco's Clubcard
- buying databases from companies that specialise in gathering data.

If building a database, firms are legally required to register it with the Data Protection Registrar. The Data Protection Act 1984 gives people the right to see their personal file; for example, one held by a bank on a customer's creditworthiness.

Marketing and database management

Mailing lists have existed for decades. American Express, *Reader's Digest* and many others have built their business through well-targeted direct mail (sometimes referred to as 'junk mail'). They achieved this through the use of large, expensive mainframe computers. Nowadays even the smallest firm can afford a computer and some database software. Customers can be sorted into regular, light and occasional users, and be sent an appropriate mailshot. Each letter can be personalised (for example, 'Dear Miss Hendrick ...') and is therefore better suited to building a relationship with the customer. Alternatively, telephone sales staff can make direct contact to check on customer satisfaction and enquire whether any extra services are required.

The pursuit of an up-to-date, detailed database has reached its high point with supermarket loyalty cards. A Tesco Clubcard application form requires the customer to state details such as address, number of children, job and income. These details can be related to their lifestyle by recording what they buy and how much they spend. If Tesco then wants to promote wine costing more than £8 per bottle, it can invite to an in-store tasting all those who have spent over £6 on a bottle of wine over the past six months. Having an accurate database minimises the waste, and therefore the cost, of such mailings. This makes them a more attractive proposition when compared to other advertising media.

These are all ways in which technology can cut costs, reduce waste, improve customer service quality and increase productivity.

49.6 COMMUNICATION WITH SUPPLIERS

Electronic data interchange (EDI)

EDI is a permanent link between computers on different sites, enabling specified types of data to be exchanged. By establishing an EDI link, firms can ensure that the latest information is available instantly to other branches of their business, or even to other businesses. For example, Heinz's link with Tesco enables it to see how sales of soups are going this week. If chicken soup sales have pushed ahead by 20 per cent (perhaps because of being featured on a TV programme), production increases can be planned, even before the Tesco head office phones through with a large order. This makes a just-in-time operation far more feasible.

Of course, Tesco does not want Heinz to have access to all its computer files, so the EDI link covers only specified data. Heinz might allow Tesco access to its stock levels and production plans in exchange for Tesco's daily sales data. This cooperation can help to ensure that shelves are rarely empty.

EDI used to be for large companies only. Today, however, the availability of low-cost internet-based EDI means that any small supplier can keep this direct link with a retail customer. Sainsbury's, for example, set up JSnet for its smaller suppliers.

Electronic point of sale (EPOS)

EPOS equipment is at the heart of data collection by retailers. Laser scanning systems gather data from bar codes, which allow the computer to record exactly what has been bought and at what price. This forms the basis of the stock control system and also the recording of sales revenues. As with other aspects of IT, rapid falls in the cost of EPOS systems make them increasingly affordable for small shops.

49.7 USING TECHNOLOGY IN OPERATIONS – AN EVALUATION

Years ago the managers at Guinness thought change management was a technical question. When a change was needed, such as a new distribution system, they hired consultants, whose main focus was to establish effective information and communications technology (ICT) links. Time after time they were disappointed by the results. Improvements began only when they realised that the key variable was not the technology but the people. Not only were results better if staff were consulted fully, but also the new systems were successful only if staff applied them with enthusiasm and confidence.

Technology is only a set of tools. It can form the basis of a major competitive advantage, as with easyJet's initiative with internet bookings. More often, though, the successful application of IT relies on good understanding of customer and staff needs and wants. This suggests that good management of information technology is no different from good management generally.

ISSUES FOR ANALYSIS

Information technology provides a series of tools that can be used to help businesses operate more effectively. This raises many issues for analysis, a couple of which are discussed below.

- Will electronic shopping mean shops are on the way out? The answer is probably no. But internet shopping will put new competitive pressures on high streets and shopping centres. If this book could be ordered in minutes on the internet and arrive in three days' time, would it make sense to go and look for it in a bookshop where it might not be in stock? Retailers are going to have to think very hard about whether they are offering the level of personal service that makes a visit worthwhile.
- Most managers and staff accept that new technology is necessary for businesses to keep up with their competitors. Yes, there are often problems when the time comes to update technology. Staff may worry that suggested 'improvements' are excuses for making people redundant. Managers need to be sensitive to people's fears, and win them over by honesty and openness.

49.8 WORKBOOK

A REVISION QUESTIONS

(35 marks; 35 minutes)

1 A database could be used by an aircraft manufacturer such as Boeing to record the supplier and batch number of every part used on every aircraft. How could this information be used? (3)

2 State two benefits of good database management in achieving efficient stock control. (2)

3 Read the A-grade application on Triumph. Identify one benefit and one drawback of keeping all design work in the UK. (2)

4 Look at Figure 49.3. Explain one possible implication for:

   a) a UK factory owner feeling under pressure from competition from China (3)

   b) a UK worker, with few qualifications or skills, who is thinking of taking a job in a factory. (3)

5 Explain one benefit and one drawback of computer-aided manufacture (CAM). (4)

6 From your reading of the whole unit, outline three ways in which technology can lead to improved quality. (6)

7 How significant could internet retailing become for each of the following types of business?

   a) a music shop specialising in 1960s classic pop and rock (2)

   b) a builders' merchant (selling bricks, cement, etc.) (2)

   c) a mail-order clothing firm. (2)

8 From your reading of the whole unit, explain two ways in which technology can reduce waste within a business. (6)

B REVISION EXERCISES

B1 DATA RESPONSE

Robots

Recently TM Robotics (Europe) Ltd worked with a major UK manufacturer to fit three Toshiba robots as part of an automated system to increase its output of valves.

The managers had to consider: the cost of the robots; the cost of installation and maintenance; the training required for key staff to manage the operation. All of this has to be weighed up against the cost of a manual alternative. One must also bear in mind potential downtime if the automated system is replacing an existing manual one.

The key factors in the success of the automation process were accuracy and flexibility. Accuracy was provided by the ±0.02 mm repeatability of the Toshiba robot, and flexibility allowed the system to cope with 240 different product variants, all consisting of at least five component pieces.

One of the key factors in the installation process was ensuring a quick changeover period between different product variants, in order to minimise downtime. This is where a manual process can be advantageous: the worker simply finishes a batch of one product type and collects the components for another, with no long changeover period required. Careful design ensured that the average changeover time was just 15 minutes, giving an impressive operating efficiency of 90 per cent.

The total cycle time for the three robots to assemble the fitting is just 7.8 seconds, 4.2 seconds faster than the manual method. Furthermore, the automation has the obvious advantage of constant running. It doesn't slow down when it's tired, it doesn't take coffee breaks and never takes long lunches. Faster production time and constant output mean that the robot quickly pays for itself.

Source: adapted from www.tmrobotics.co.uk

Questions

(30 marks; 49 minutes)

1 **a)** Explain in your own words the meaning of 'downtime'. (3)
  b) Why may firms be keen to minimise downtime? (4)

2 Examine the importance to this 'major UK manufacturer' of the accuracy and flexibility of these three robots. (6)

3 **a)** Calculate the percentage increase in production speed now that the robots are producing the goods rather than people. (3)
  b) Analyse two ways in which the manufacturer can benefit from the extra speed. (6)

4 Using the information given in the case study and your own knowledge discuss two ways in which human workers may be more valuable than robots. (8)

B2 DATA RESPONSE

An architect and her iPhone

Patti the Architect, a small architectural firm based in Florida, is turning Apple's iPhone into a productivity-boosting mobile resource for construction-site communications.

With the Apple iPhone, architect Patricia 'Patti' Stough and her staff can now easily access their full library of design and construction documents on the move. The firm designs all its projects in CAD on high-performance Mac hardware, making the files effortlessly portable and displayable on iPhone's high-res widescreen display.

This mobility enables the firm to more easily communicate design intentions to customers on the site, as well as consult more effectively with builders, subcontractors and regulatory inspectors. And even if they had forgotten a document, they can easily retrieve it wirelessly via iPhone's Wi-Fi.

Figure 49.4 Patti the Architect using her iPhone

With a slight tap or pinch of their fingers, users can easily zoom in and out of drawings and 3D high-resolution photos on iPhone, drilling down to the finest of details or panning out for a big picture view via iPhone's revolutionary touchscreen interface. 'The days of hauling scrolls of paper drawings to job sites only to discover I forgot a critical document are over,' says Stough. 'I can now carry even the largest, most complex and detailed CAD models in the palm of my hand. The ability to bring 3D digital drawings on site is a huge advantage, enabling me to better communicate and coordinate with everyone involved in the project.'

Patti the Architect is an award-winning architectural firm that specialises in beachfront townhouses, hotels, churches, schools, offices, retail additions and commercial interior renovations. Stough says that the huge productivity gains of designing in and working with 3D virtual building models are further enhanced through the mobility of iPhone.

Source: adapted from www.architosh.com

Questions

(25 marks; 30 minutes)

1 Outline three benefits of the CAD system to this architectural business. (6)
2 Explain how the iPhone-linked CAD has reduced time wastage for the business. (4)
3 Examine Patti Stough's suggestion that having CAD on the iPhone leads to 'huge productivity gains'. (6)
4 To what extent is the portable CAD system likely to improve Patti's customer service? (9)

C ESSAY QUESTIONS

(40 marks each)

1 Information technology is reducing the need to meet people face to face. Discuss the implications of this for running a successful business.
2 If industrial robots become cheap enough, they may replace almost all unskilled factory workers in the future. Discuss the benefits and costs of this to society.
3 'Internet retailing will mean the death of the high street.' Discuss.

Corporate aims, mission and culture

UNIT 50

Aims are a generalised statement of where you are heading, from which objectives can be set. A mission is a more fervent, passionate way of expressing an aim. Business culture is the ethos of the business; in other words, the ideas and attitudes that prevail among the workforce.

50.1 INTRODUCTION

Some children, as young as 10 or 11 years old, are clear about what they want from life. They are determined to become a doctor or a vet. The clarity of their aim makes them work hard at school, choose science subjects and overcome any setbacks (a weak maths teacher, perhaps). So whereas most GCSE and A-level students drift from one day to the next, these individuals are focused: they have their eyes on their prize. This is the potentially huge benefit that can stem from clear aims.

Indeed, you could say that some of these focused students are driven by a sense of mission. Their aim is not just to get the label of 'doctor' but also to help make the world a better place. The drive shown by these students will be the most impressive of all.

For new small businesses there can also be a powerful sense of mission. A chef may open his or her own restaurant, driven largely by the desire to win a Michelin star (the *Michelin Guide* to restaurants is the world's most prestigious). In Gordon Ramsay style, the approach to achieving this may prove to be ruthless or even fanatical. Such a person is far more likely to achieve this aim than one who opens a restaurant thinking 'It would be nice to get a star; let's see if it happens.'

Figure 50.1 Gordon Ramsay

In marketplaces where competition is fierce, businesses that are passionate and determined are always more likely to succeed than those that are drifting. This has always been one of the secrets to the success of Apple. Its boss and senior managers have always believed in the superiority of Apple design and technology, but were also fanatically hostile to 'the evil empire': Microsoft. This shared view kept Apple going through the dark days before the success of iPod transformed the business.

From the clear sense of mission at Apple has come its workplace culture. This is creative and fun, but also hugely hard-working. At 5.00 pm in many businesses, staff are found streaming towards the exit. This does not happen at Apple, where some work teams may only just be getting warmed up.

To achieve a high grade in Business Studies at A level, full understanding of this unit is critical, because aims, mission and culture are fundamental to business success, and therefore exam success.

50.2 AIMS

Aims are the generalised statement of where the business is heading. Possible examples of aims include:

- 'To become a profitable business with a long-term future' (Zayka Indian restaurant, started in January 2011)
- 'To become a Premier League club' (Southampton FC, currently in football's second tier)
- 'To diversify away from dependence on Britain' (the implicit aim of Tesco in the past ten years).

One of the stated aims of the McDonald's fast food chain is to provide 'friendly service in a relaxed, safe and consistent restaurant environment'. The success of the organisation depends upon turning this aim into practice. In order for this to be achieved, employees must understand and share the aim. When a customer enters a McDonald's restaurant anywhere in the world they know what to expect. The organisation has the ability to reproduce the same 'relaxed, safe and consistent' atmosphere with different staff, in different locations. This has built the company's reputation. This corporate aim is effective because it recognises what lies at the heart of the organisation's success.

But do aims need to be written down? Many businesses do not write down their aims or even spend time trying to define them. This is particularly true of small organisations, where employees know each other and understand their shared purpose. Even when an aim is unstated it may be possible to identify it by looking at the actions taken by a firm over time. Staff in a small firm may work together to achieve a common aim with a level of commitment that may not exist in a large firm that sets out its aims in writing.

Whether stated or unstated, corporate aims act as a basis upon which to form goals or objectives for the organisation. These are the targets that must be achieved if the aims are to be realised. The success or failure of each individual decision within the firm can be judged by the extent to which it meets the business objectives. This allows the delegation of authority within the organisation, while at the same time maintaining coordination.

50.3 MISSION STATEMENTS

A **mission statement** is an attempt to put corporate aims into words that inspire. The mission statement of Walmart, the world's biggest retailer, is 'to give ordinary folk the chance to buy the same thing as rich people'. Shop floor staff are more likely to be motivated by a mission statement of this kind than by the desire to maximise profit.

It is hoped that by summarising clearly the long-term direction of the organisation, a focus is provided that helps to inspire employees to greater effort and ensure the departments work together. Without this common purpose each area of a firm may have different aims and choose to move in conflicting directions.

> **A-grade application**
>
> **Examples of mission statements**
>
> - *Pret A Manger (sandwich chain):* 'Pret creates handmade natural food avoiding the obscure chemical additives and preservatives common to so much of the prepared and "fast" food on the market today'
> - *3M:* 'To solve unsolved problems innovatively'
> - *Body Shop:* 'Tirelessly work to narrow the gap between principle and practice, whilst making fun, passion and care part of our daily lives'
> - *Coca-Cola:* 'To refresh the world – in body, mind and spirit'
> - *Nike:* 'To bring innovation and inspiration to every athlete* in the world' (*If you have a body you are an athlete)

It is also important to note that not every company has a written mission statement. Some companies are clear that they and their staff 'live the mission' and therefore do not need to write it down. Marks & Spencer plc has stopped publicising a mission statement, perhaps because it has learnt that one statement cannot sum up the driving forces behind a whole, complex business.

Elements of a mission statement

For those that do use mission statements, the model shown in Figure 50.2 gives a clear sense of their purpose. To develop a strong mission statement it is necessary to link each of the four elements of the model so that they reinforce one another.

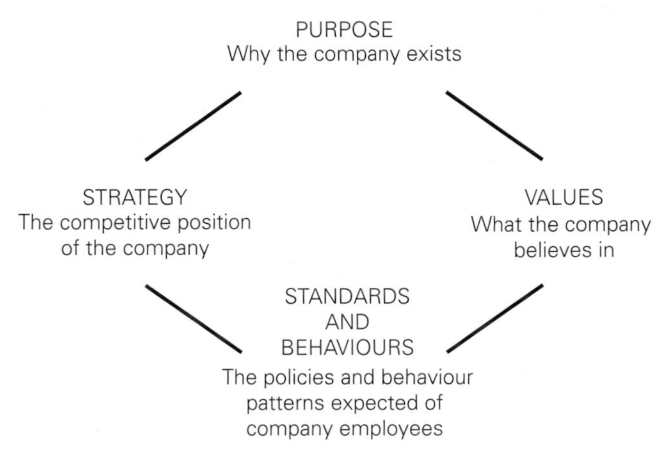

Figure 50.2 The mission model

In turn, each element suggests the following.

Purpose (reason why the company exists)

This is clearly shown by the Nike **mission**, which emphasises the desire to provide innovative products for athletes. In fact a sceptic could point out that Nike builds much of its branding around advertising, imagery and visual design rather than product innovation. Nike's brilliance has been to keep everyone sure that the company cares about supporting athletes, rather than exploiting them.

Values (what the company believes in)

In the case of Pret A Manger, it is not just that it believes in natural, fresh food, but also that the business has always:

- used packaging that is made from recycled materials and can be recycled in future
- taken care to source its products from suppliers that treat staff fairly
- wanted to push customers to try new things, especially from sustainable sources.

The values of the business are a key part of its culture, and should also include the way staff are treated and other ethical considerations.

Standards and behaviours

This refers to the standards set by managers and the behaviour expected from staff. Cambridge graduate Polly Courtney has told the *Observer* newspaper about her experiences as a highly paid banker in the City of London. The work culture meant that people would send emails at 2.00 in the morning to show how late they worked, and Polly found sexism rooted in a 'lads' culture in which nights out ended at the strip club. As the only woman in an office of 21, she was treated like a secretary and bypassed for the more important jobs. Polly wrote a book about her experiences, whereas others have successfully sued merchant banks on grounds of sex discrimination. Clearly the managements are wholly at fault in allowing such a situation to develop.

Strategy

Strategy means the medium- to long-term plans adopted by the business to make the aims and mission achievable. This is dealt with in Unit 51.

How valuable are mission statements?

As an example of the possible downsides of mission statements, it is interesting to look back at what companies used to say. At one time, Coca-Cola's mission statement said: 'Our mission is to get more people to drink Coke than water.' Today that seems quite a shocking idea. Clearly it would mean a dramatic worsening of the obesity problem that affects most of the developed world. The fact that Coca-Cola has dropped this statement in favour of the socially more acceptable 'to refresh the world' raises the question of whether mission statements are little more than public relations exercises.

Even more serious is the possibility that mission statements are a substitute for the real thing. They may be a bureaucratic management's attempt to provide a sense of purpose in a business that has none. If so, this would be the wrong way to approach the problem. If staff lack inspiration, the starting point is to find a real sense of purpose, probably through the staff themselves. For example, British doctors and nurses used to be hugely proud to work for the NHS; now they are more likely to moan about its shortcomings. Writing a mission statement would be treated with derision by the staff. Far more important is to find out from staff what they dislike about the current management and discuss how to restore staff pride in the service.

50.4 CULTURE

Culture can be described as 'the way we do things round here'. In other words, it's the attitudes and behaviours shown within the workplace. This will be built up over many years as a result of:

- the aims or mission of the business: if the aim is to be innovative, this should affect the business culture
- the behaviour of the company directors and other senior staff: if they pay themselves huge bonuses and jump at chances to fly business class to questionable conferences, staff will pick up the idea that 'me, me, me' is at the heart of the business culture
- the attitude of senior management to enterprise and risk: if a failed new product launch leads to the dismissal of the manager leading the project, this will send out a message to all staff to beware of taking on responsibility, which could be very damaging in the long term
- the recruitment and training procedures: research has shown that dynamic companies have a mixture of different types of staff, including some who are very organised, some who are creative but perhaps chaotic, some who are argumentative and so on; some HR departments use psychometric tests to recruit 'our type of person' and screen out potential 'troublemakers'; the culture could become quite passive – safe but dull – if new recruits are always the same type of efficient but uninspired people.

A-grade application

Cultural differences in India

A recent report on takeovers in India cites cultural differences as a high-risk factor in corporate deals. Twenty-nine different languages are spoken by at least 1 million Indian people and customs and working styles differ significantly between regions. Companies in northern India tend to have more assertive, western cultures, while companies in the south are more traditionally Indian; that is, they have a more formal and subtle culture, emphasising protocol, seniority and indirect communication. Western predator companies often fail to understand these differences, seeing 'Indian' in a one-dimensional way. Indian companies have also come unstuck when trying to bring together two conflicting workplace cultures.

The business culture is fundamental to its success

The culture of the business has many aspects that are fundamental to its success or failure. First are the values of the business. An organisation's mission statement provides an opportunity to shape this business culture. The challenge is to develop a set of values that employees can feel proud of. It should also motivate them to work towards the organisation's objectives. This may be difficult to achieve, particularly in large companies where each department of the firm may have its own culture. In this case there may be no dominant corporate culture.

The business culture will show through in many ways, including those described below.

The team versus the individual

Some organisations work in a 'dog-eat-dog' fashion

world is to start a social enterprise (that is, a business with a social rather than financial objective). In the case of One Water, its objective for 2010–11 is 'to build one new Playpump per day'. This would require the business to generate about £2.5 million a year of net profit, which would be an incredible achievement for a business that started only in 2005.

Other businesses may see their task as to improve what people eat, to improve how children learn or to build better houses (Housing Associations are not-for-profit housing 'businesses').

A-grade application

Danone in Bangladesh

After two years of talk and planning, in 2007 a remarkable yoghurt factory opened in Bangladesh. It was remarkable for being small and local, for obtaining all milk supplies from 250 local farmers, and for its sales and distribution method: 300 local women taking the product to local shops. 'Shoktidoi' is also, probably, the world's cheapest yoghurt. It sells in the countryside for about 6p per pot. Yet it's made by the multinational giant Danone. In 2005 Danone and the Grameen social bank decided to set up a project to help cut malnutrition in Bangladesh. After considering, then rejecting, baby food, the final idea was to produce yoghurt. Shoktidoi is a vitamin-fortified yoghurt coming in just two flavours: vanilla and mango. In 2009, 500,000 kg were sold, an increase of more than 200 per cent on 2008. Although Danone has set the business the objective of breaking-even, it hopes to open 20 more local yoghurt factories in Bangladesh by 2020.

51.4 CORPORATE STRATEGY

The managers of a business should develop a medium- to long-term plan about how to achieve the objectives they have established. This is the organisation's corporate strategy (see Figure 51.3). It sets out the actions that will be taken in order to achieve the goals, and the implications for the firm's human, financial and production resources. The key to success when forming a strategy of this kind is relating the firm's strengths to the opportunities that exist in the marketplace.

This analysis can take place at each level of the business, allowing a series of strategies to be formed in order to achieve the goals already established. A hierarchy of strategies can be produced for the whole organisation in a similar manner to the approach adopted when setting objectives.

- Corporate strategy deals with the major issues such as what industry, or industries, the business should compete in, in order to achieve corporate objectives. Managers must identify industries where the long-term profit prospects are likely to be favourable. In 2007, for example, Whitbread decided to pull out of the health club market by selling its David Lloyd Leisure subsidiary. It used the money to pay off some debt and put the remainder behind its fast-growing Costa Coffee chain, in particular, setting up 200 Costa Coffees in China. By 2010 this strategy looked very clever, as Whitbread's shares hit new highs, while David Lloyd Leisure struggled to survive the recession.

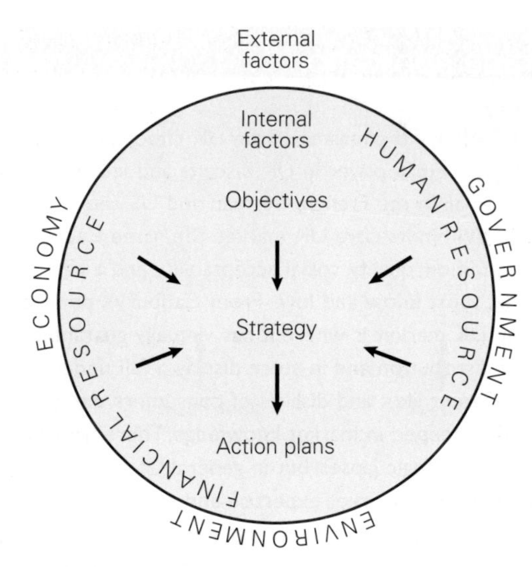

Figure 51.3 Corporate strategy

- Business unit (or divisional) strategy should address the issue of how th
  the industr
  involve se
  distinguish
  of Costa C
  differentiat
- Functional
  order to id
  or targets s

If a strategy is t
the firm's stren
Figure 51.4).
health clubs in
competition w
be better to pu
Costa chain an

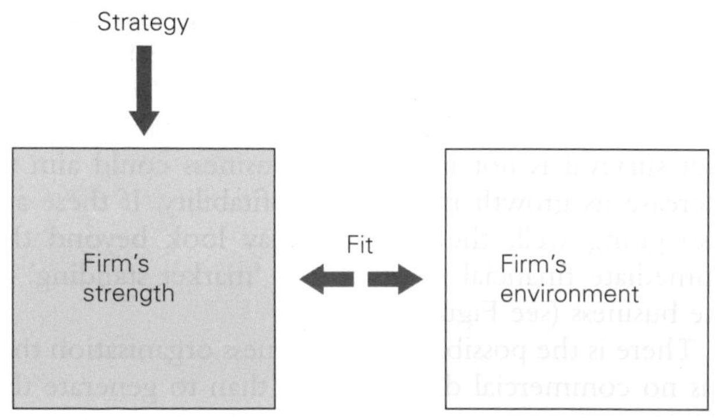

Figure 51.4 If a strategy is to achieve the objectives set, it must match the firm's strengths to its competitive environment

As a company develops over time its employees acquire knowledge and skills. This 'organisational learning' represents what the firm as a whole is good at doing, or its 'core capabilities'. The key products or services produced by the business will reflect these strengths. The 2010 launch of the iPhone 4 represented Apple's innovative abilities as a result of its research and development programme and design expertise.

Core capabilities need not be limited to a particular market. Marks & Spencer's move into financial services was based on a reputation for reliability and quality. This had built up over many years by its operation in the clothing and food markets. Corporate strategy can be shaped by identifying new opportunities to apply the existing strengths of the organisation.

Michael Porter, in his book *Competitive Advantage: Creating and Sustaining Superior Performance*, develops a method by which an organisation can analyse the competitive environment within which it operates in order to create strategic policy. He suggests that firms need to analyse five factors within an industry in order to understand the marketplace (see Figure 51.5). This will help managers to understand how fierce or how favourable the competitive environment is. Each of Porter's '**five forces**' provides information that can be used to help devise an appropriate business strategy.

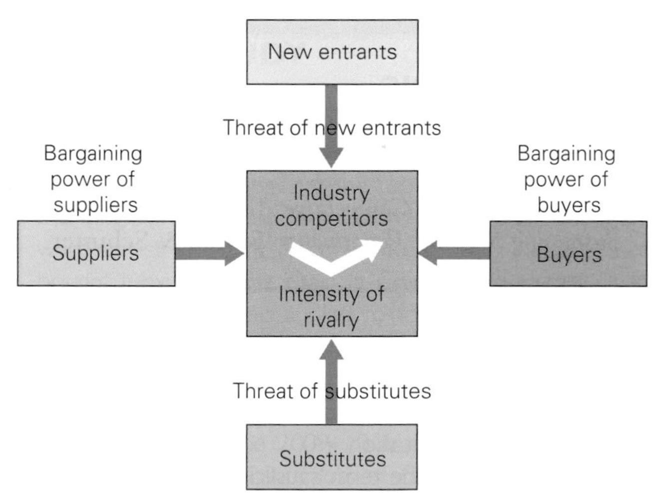

Figure 51.5 Porter's 'five forces' framework

Porter's five forces

Porter believes that the overall strength or weakness of a firm's position depends on the five factors set out below. Understanding these five forces will help you to analyse whether a business is in a strong or weak position overall.

The intensity of rivalry with direct competitors

In the 10-minute south London walk between South Wimbledon tube station and the Merton Park Metro stop there are five men's hairdressers. None stands out, and all charge between £6 and £8 for a haircut. Elsewhere in London the price is more likely to be £15, but the intensity of rivalry here keeps prices down – and makes it impossible for any of the five to make a great living out of their business.

The threat of new entrants

In the case of the hairdressers, there is nothing to prevent someone else opening a sixth shop. The barriers to entry are very low, as all you need is perhaps £10,000 to decorate and equip an existing retail outlet. In other cases, the barrier to entry is huge. For example, who could set up an internet bookshop to rival Amazon today? The millions of pounds needed to build the infrastructure (depots, and so on) would need to be matched by a fortune in advertising to wean people away from the tried and trusted Amazon. So there is very little threat to Amazon, even though it is now a hugely profitable business.

The threat of new substitutes

In the 1870s margarine, which was invented in France, was launched into the American market as a cheap alternative to butter. Sales were poor until it was discovered that adding artificial yellow colourings made consumers far more likely to buy it (margarine is naturally white). Farmers found that sales of milk were hit hard (butter is just churned milk) so they protested against margarine. Today margarine has a large share of the 'butter' market round the world. New substitutes can be bad news for producers.

Bargaining power with suppliers

The buying manager responsible for buying all of Tesco's biscuits has power over the sales of 25 to 30 per cent of all the biscuits made in the UK. Therefore, Tesco has a huge amount of buying power. If a supplier wants to strike a special deal with Sainsbury's, perhaps only selling a new biscuit brand through Sainsbury's stores, Tesco will put a stop to that with one phone call. In contrast, a small corner shop has virtually no buying power (that is, no leverage it can use to try to get a better deal for itself).

Bargaining with customers

When a small firm speaks to a big customer (for example, the NHS, for medicines, or Hertz Rentals, for new cars), the minnow is likely to be very gentle. Only if the supplier is really huge would it be able to talk on level terms with the customer.

Table 52.1 Differing objectives

Type of objective	Example of objectives
• Growth	• To become Britain's number one • To achieve a £1 billion turnover by 2015 • To double the customer base from 1.2 billion to 2.5 billion by 2019 (L'Oréal)
• Profit optimisation	• To achieve profit growth of 10 to 12 per cent a year for the next four years • To return profit margins to the 8 per cent level achieved two years ago
• Profit maximisation	• To drive profit up by at least 50 per cent this year • To become Britain's most profitable window replacement business
• Not-for-profit	• To become Britain's bank of choice for those concerned ethically about how their money is used (Co-op Bank) • To finance and build one water pump a day (One Water)

Profit maximisation

This objective means making as much profit as possible, with the implication that it should be made in as short a time as possible. This is most likely to be the objective for a small to medium-sized business run by individuals with little regard for their customers or for the long-term reputation of their business. 'Cowboy' builders maximise their profit by charging high prices for shoddy work. They do not rely on repeat purchase, but on finding another unsuspecting customer victim. Few large plcs deliberately pursue profit maximisation, though executives with huge share options may take decisions that maximise profit this year at the possible expense of the future.

A not-for-profit motive

The owner of the One Water business, Duncan Goose, has a very unusual business objective. At present his charitable water business funds one new water well in Africa every eight to ten days. His objective is one a day. To achieve this, he needs growth in the sales and in the profits made by selling bottles of One Water in the UK. Other businesses, such as John Lewis Partnership and the Co-op Bank, need profit to survive and to grow, but have not-for-profit objectives.

52.3 FUNCTIONAL OBJECTIVES

Functional objectives are the targets of the individual business departments (functions). They will stem from the corporate objectives and are either set by the chief executive or may be the result of discussion between directors.

Having set the company's objectives, the key is to take care over each department's objectives. They must work separately and together, so that the overall goal can be achieved. For the 2012 London Olympics, the operations function must ensure that the stadium is built, while the marketing department sets ambitious targets for selling millions of tickets to fill it to capacity. If one succeeds while the other fails, the London organisers will be laughed at by the world's media.

Success requires that the leaders within each department/function do the following.

- *Coordinate what they are doing:* what, when and how. Timing will be crucial, such as having the right amount of stock to cope with the demand expected on the launch day. So marketing, operations and personnel must act together, perhaps using **network analysis** software to make sure that the whole project is kept on track.
- *Make sure that all within their own department know the overall objective* as well as the functional one, and that all are motivated towards achieving it. In 2010 British Airways cabin crew staff went on strike repeatedly in the face of the company's attempt to cut costs and restructure the business; the staff refused to believe management's suggestion that BA.'s survival was at stake.
- *Work together to achieve a common goal:* this may seem obvious, but in many organisations managers and even directors jostle for promotions or positions, without really working together. So the marketing director might be happy to see the operations

A-grade application

Starcraft 2

On 27 July 2010, after 12 years in development, the computer game Starcraft 2 was launched worldwide. In London, more than 500 people queued at midnight; in Singapore thousands of people tried to get their hands on the new edition. That evening the first TV advertisements appeared and within 48 hours more than 2 million copies had been sold worldwide. The brilliance of the exercise was in making sure that there was enough stock to cope with the demand, especially as the product was launched with full availability for Apple computers as well as PCs. Software launches tend either to be flops, or big successes followed by stock shortages. Starcraft 2 was the all time biggest-selling software launch. Yet the development, the sales forecasting, the production and the marketing were all coordinated perfectly.

director humiliated. Well-run organisations want to succeed together, not just succeed as individuals.

52.4 FUNCTIONAL STRATEGIES

A strategy is a medium- to long-term plan for meeting objectives. This should be the result of a careful process of thought and discussion throughout the business, though key decisions will almost always be made at the top. To make the right decision about strategy, a useful approach is known as the 'scientific decision-making model' (Figure 52.2). It shows that strategy decisions must:

1 be based on clear objectives
2 be based on firm evidence of the market and the problem/opportunity, including as much factual, quantitative evidence as possible (for example, trends in market size, data on costs, sales forecasts)
3 look for options (that is, alternative theories – hypotheses – as to which would be the best approach); for example, to meet an objective of higher market share we could either launch a new product or put all our energies and cash behind our Rising Star existing product
4 be based on as scientific a test of the alternatives as possible (for example, a test market of the new product in the Bristol area, while doubling advertising spending on the Rising Star in the north-east – then comparing which approach provided the bigger market share gains)
5 control the approach decided upon – the final stage (for example, if it's a new product launch, to manage the quality and timing of every aspect of production, sales, advertising and delivery) – then review, to learn from any mistakes or unexpected successes before (the dotted line on the diagram) starting again with a new objective and a new strategy.

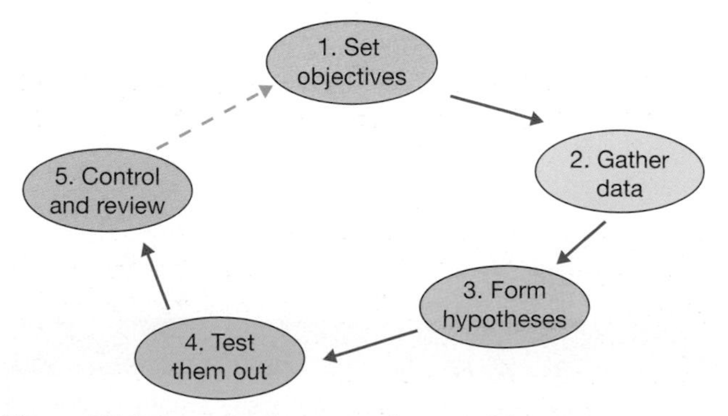

Figure 52.2 Scientific decision-making model

Within this process, the single most important thing is that the business should make sure that the functional strategies are all part of one overall strategy (and match the overall objective). For many years the objective of the Apple Corporation was to succeed by being more customer-friendly than its then only rival, Microsoft. The strategy for achieving this was to be one step ahead in design rather than technology. This strategy focus on design became the beginnings of a goldmine with the 2001 launch of the iPod. Table 52.2 describes what this meant for each functional area.

Table 52.2 Apple iPod strategy

Functional areas	Actual strategy in the early iPod years
Marketing strategy	Quirky poster advertisements emphasising street style rather than the product
Operations strategy	Design a great-looking product with distinctive headphones (the white wires) and a great interface
People strategy	Hire free-thinking people and give them the space and environment to be creative (don't over-manage or over-control them)
Financial strategy	Provide all the finance needed for product development, and don't over-control later decisions (for example, the Nano launched while the original Shuffle model was still in its growth phase)

ISSUES FOR ANALYSIS

Top firms unite behind a single strategy based on clear objectives. Therefore, when analysing case material about any business, it is wise to ask the following questions.

- How clear is the overall company objective? Is it precisely stated, with a timescale, thereby making it easy to measure success or failure? This is often called a **SMART objective** (that is, Specific, Measurable, Achievable, Realistic, Timebound).
- Having considered the overall objective, what are the functional objectives agreed by the directors? Is each one also SMART? Or does HR, for example, have only vague targets because the importance of the human element has been overlooked?
- Then there is the overall strategy, for which each of the functions should be contributing its own crucial part. In July 2010 LG had to admit that its inability to boost production of flat screens was holding back production of Apple's iPad. Between the April launch and July, more than 3.3 million iPads had been sold (more than $1 billion), but supply could not keep up with demand. Apple's superb marketing had been let down by mistakes in its operations (production) supply chain.

As with every aspect of business, success comes from working together towards a common goal.

52.5 FUNCTIONAL OBJECTIVES AND STRATEGIES – AN EVALUATION

Having analysed the business situation, judgements have to be made. If a business hits problems, is one department (function) to blame; for example, has the marketing department let the side down because of

Figure 52.3

a poor advertising campaign? Are there specific staff who lack ability or motivation? Or was the problem more collective, due to poor communications within a department or (much more likely) between the functional areas? A good example of this would be Toyota's quality problems in 2010.

It is sometimes the case that no one deserves blame (or praise for success). After more than ten years of sales and profit growth, Chanel and Gucci both struggled in 2009. The severity of the world recession took both firms (and economists) by surprise. For sales to fall by 7 per cent may be no disgrace just as, years earlier, booming sales in boom times may have deserved little praise.

The key judgement, then, is whether a firm's success is entirely down to its own good management. A better explanation might be that external factors were largely the reason, in which case managers deserve credit for taking advantage of favourable circumstances; but they should beware of jumping to the conclusion that they have the magic touch.

Key Terms

Network analysis: a way of planning that minimises the duration of a project by ensuring that everyone knows the latest completion time for every activity within the project.

SMART objectives: these are more likely to lead to successful outcomes because they are Specific, Measurable, Achievable, Realistic and Timebound.

WORKBOOK

A REVISION QUESTIONS

(25 marks; 25 minutes)

1 What is meant by the term 'functional areas'? (2)
2 Why is it important that objectives should be:
 a) measurable (2)
 b) timebound? (2)
3 Are the following good or bad corporate objectives? Briefly explain your reasoning.
 a) To boost our share of the fruit juice market from its current level of 22.3 per cent. (4)
 b) To become the best pizza restaurant business in Britain. (4)
4 What would be a successful overall objective for each of the following?
 a) the charity Oxfam, which focuses on preventing and relieving famine (2)
 b) a political party. (2)
5 Explain in your own words why it is important that the different business functions should work together to achieve the corporate (overall) objective. (4)
6 Explain the difference between an objective and a strategy. (3)

B REVISION EXERCISES

B1 DATA RESPONSE

In August 2006 Claude and Claire Bosi put their Hibiscus restaurant up for sale. This was a surprise because it had two Michelin stars, making it one of Britain's top ten restaurants. The couple decided that, while still young, they must move from Ludlow in rural Shropshire to the challenges of opening in London. Could Claude Bosi's cooking stand out in London, when in competition with Gordon Ramsay, Jamie Oliver and many Michelin-starred restaurants?

They sold the restaurant for £250,000 and moved to London to look for a good site. Famously, business success in restaurants depends not only on great cooking but also on location, location, location. After several months they found a site in Mayfair that they believed could be turned into a 60-seat restaurant, though the site, the building work and the equipment would cost 'around £1 million'. The finance would come from their own £250,000 plus share capital from a wealthy Ludlow customer and two of his friends.

The objective of the couple was to establish in London a restaurant that was as successful as the one in Ludlow. Clearly, London offers far greater potential, both financially and in terms of personal recognition. To recreate Hibiscus in London, Bosi persuaded most of his staff to move to London and has a menu that is largely made up of the dishes developed in Ludlow. He even buys many of his supplies from farms in Shropshire.

The restaurant opened in London in November 2007 and, as nearly 40 per cent of new restaurants close within three years, its success is confirmed by the fact that it was still successful in November 2010 (and has won back its two Michelin stars). Apart from the quality of cooking, an important issue was pricing. The couple decided to charge the same price for three courses as they charged in Ludlow: £45. This may seem high, but is nothing like as expensive as restaurants such as Gordon Ramsay's, which are twice the price.

Questions

(20 marks; 35 minutes)

1. Explain what you believe to be the business objectives being pursued by Claude and Claire Bosi. (5)
2. From the text, how SMART do the couple's objectives seem to be? (6)
3. Use Google to check on the progress of the business. You will find restaurant reviews and, at www.hibiscusrestaurant.co.uk, the restaurant's latest prices and marketing messages. Then comment on whether the couple seem to be succeeding in achieving their business objectives. (9)

B2 CASE STUDY

L'Oréal: Thinking ahead to 2019

L'Oréal is the world's No 1 cosmetics company. Not many French companies are leaders in their field, so this is remarkable. To stay No 1, L'Oréal has set the objective of doubling its customer base. As almost every woman in the west uses L'Oréal products (whether they know it or not, as brands such as Garnier, Maybelline, Giorgio Armani and Body Shop are actually L'Oréal) growth has to come from developing countries. In 2010 more than 33 per cent of L'Oréal's €16.5 billion of sales came from developing countries. Ten years before, the figure was 16 per cent; ten years before that it had been 8 per cent.

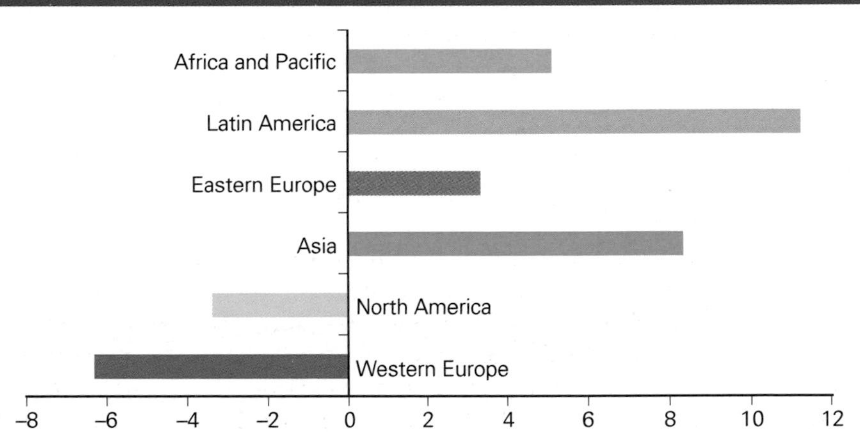

Figure 52.4 L'Oréal sales: percentage change from 2008 to 2009

The strategy for achieving this change is partly based on a refocusing of the marketing efforts. In 2009, for instance, the cover of L'Oréal's annual report did not feature Cheryl Cole, but Freida Pinto: the beautiful young (Indian) star of the hit film *Slumdog Millionaire*. More importantly, though, the decision had been made to invest in Research and Development facilities in China and Brazil. In 2010 the Shanghai R&D centre turned three years of work into a new haircare range. A careful study of Chinese hair, plus market research into local customs and tastes, led to the launch of a range of shampoos and haircare products suited to local hair types and cultural traditions, focusing on fragrance and gloss.

The value of L'Oréal's longstanding focus on developing countries was shown in the 2009 recession (see Figure 52.4).

Questions

(30 marks; 35 minutes)

1. Outline L'Oréal's corporate objective and its strategy for achieving it. (6)
2. Explain why L'Oréal might have chosen this objective and strategy. (8)
3. To what extent does L'Oréal's strategy in relation to its marketing and operations functions seem likely to help it to achieve its corporate objective? (16)

Responsibilities to stakeholders and society

UNIT 53

A stakeholder is an individual or group that has an effect on and is affected by the activities of an organisation. Businesses can also be held to account for their impacts upon society at large.

53.1 INTRODUCTION

All firms come into contact on a daily basis with suppliers, customers, the local community and employees. Each of these groups has an impact on the firm's success and at the same time is likely to be affected by any change in its activities. If, for example, the managers decide to expand the business, this may lead to:

- overtime for employees
- more orders for suppliers
- a wider range of products for consumers
- more traffic for the local community.

Groups such as suppliers, employees and the community are known as the firm's **stakeholder** groups because of their links with the organisation. A stakeholder group both has an effect on and is affected by the decisions of the firm. Each stakeholder group will have its own objectives. The managers of a firm must decide on the extent to which they should change their behaviour to meet these objectives. Some managers believe it is very important to focus on the needs of all the different stakeholder groups. Others believe that an organisation's sole duty is to its investors (that is, that decisions should be made in the best interests of **shareholders** alone).

This is known as the 'shareholder concept'. The logic is clear: the shareholders employ managers to run the company on their behalf and so everything the managers do should be in the direct interests of shareholders. The managers should not take the needs or objectives of any other group into consideration. If the owners want short-run profit, for example, this is what the managers should provide. If the owners want expansion, then this is what the managers should aim for. According to this view, the only consideration managers should have when making any decision is to meet their owners' objectives. Generally, this means maximising **shareholder value** (for example, increasing the share price and the dividends paid to shareholders).

The alternative view places emphasis on the need to meet the objectives of a wider group. This is known as 'the stakeholder concept' as opposed to 'the shareholder concept'. The stakeholder approach suggests that managers should take into account their responsibilities to other groups, not just to the owners, when making decisions. The belief is that a firm can benefit significantly from cooperating with its stakeholder groups and incorporating their needs into the decision-making process. Examples include:

- improving the working life of employees through more challenging work, better pay and greater responsibilities, so that the business benefits from a more motivated and committed workforce
- giving something back to the community to ensure greater cooperation from local inhabitants whenever the business needs their help; for example, when seeking planning permission for expansion
- treating suppliers with respect and involving them in its plans so that the firm builds up a long-term relationship; this should lead to better-quality supplies and a better all-round service; if, for example, your supplier has limited availability of an item, it is more likely you would still get supplied because of the way you have treated the supplier in the past.

The stakeholder approach is, therefore, based on an inclusive view in which the various groups that the firm affects are included in its decision making rather than ignored. This, it is argued, can lead to significant advantages for the firm.

53.2 WHAT ARE THE GAINS OF THE STAKEHOLDING APPROACH?

There are numerous gains that could result from the stakeholding approach. For example, existing employees may be more willing to stay with the firm. It may also attract people to work for the organisation. Employees are increasingly concerned about the ethical behaviour of the organisation they work for. Firms that put the shareholders above all else may deter some people from applying or accepting a job with them. The stakeholder approach is also increasingly popular with investors.

There are a growing number of financial institutions that specifically seek to invest in organisations that follow the stakeholder approach, in the belief that it will lead to long-term rewards. A firm can also gain from better relations with the community, suppliers and distributors, and more favourable media coverage. By working with other groups rather than against them, a firm is also less likely to be targeted by a **pressure group**.

However, while this approach may seem attractive in theory there are a number of problems in practice. First, the owners may insist that the managers serve their interests and no one else's. Many shareholders of public limited companies, for example, demand short-term rewards and may take some convincing that the firm should be paying attention to the needs of other groups. After all, it is their money that is invested in the business. Second, the managers may not be able to meet all their potential responsibilities to these various groups and may have to make some decisions regarding priorities. They may also have to decide between what they regard as their obligations to society and what is commercially viable.

Society's interest in the responsibilities of business seems to grow each year. This means people are expecting firms to take a much broader view of their activities than in the past. In December 2009 the clothes retailer H&M was criticised for allegedly using suppliers that used child labour to make its clothes. Although H&M was not directly employing these children and had clear policies to try to ensure its suppliers did not either, it was still held responsible for the failings of others.

53.3 CORPORATE SOCIAL RESPONSIBILITY (CSR)

In recent years there has been a great deal of interest in corporate social responsibility (CSR). CSR refers to the extent to which a business accepts obligations to society over and above the legal requirements. This obviously refers to how it treats its stakeholder groups. Investors, customers, employees and the media regularly examine the way in which a business is treating various stakeholders. What is it doing to reduce its impact on the environment? To what extent is it protecting its employees and improving the quality of their working lives? How is it helping the local community?

When considering CSR, it is important to be cautious. Is it a reflection of a genuine concern by the business for its customers, staff and society? Or is it part of a public relations campaign to improve the firm's image? In January 2010 Nestlé's KitKat brand started to boast the Fairtrade logo. The company had agreed to source the cocoa beans from better-paid Fairtrade workers. No one would doubt the potential value of this, but why only KitKat? What about all the other Nestlé brands such as Aero, Smarties and Yorkie? The fact that it used Fairtrade with just one brand made it seem that it was using CSR as an arm of marketing, not a meaningful commitment towards a fairer world.

Figure 53.1 Business has an impact on the environment

A-grade application

Sainsbury's and social auditing

A number of companies now undertake a social audit. This means they have an external assessment of the impact of their activities on society. This is to help them understand the effect of their actions so that they can take appropriate steps and can be seen to be concerned about such issues. Supermarket chain Sainsbury's, for example, produces an annual social audit that examines its relationship with the four groups it believes are crucial to its success, namely:

1 customers
2 employees
3 suppliers
4 the community.

According to Sainsbury's, the company plans to make substantial progress on the environment, focused on these commitments (to be measured each year in their Social Responsibility audit report):

- We will reduce our own-brand packaging weight relative to sales by 33 per cent by 2015 against a 2009 baseline
- We will reduce our CO_2 emissions per square metre by 25 per cent by 2012 against a 2005–06 baseline

53.4 ARE THE STAKEHOLDER CONCEPT AND CSR REALLY NEW?

In recent years people have come to expect more from business organisations. In the past they were just expected to provide good-quality goods. Now many consumers want to know exactly how the goods are produced, what the company does for the environment and how it treats its employees. Stories about the exploitation of staff, the sale of goods to a military regime or the pollution of the environment can be very damaging to firms. This has probably resulted in more public companies adopting the stakeholder approach. However, there are a number of companies, such as the John Lewis Partnership, that pioneered this approach long before the term 'stakeholder' was even thought of. Many of the origins of this approach go back to the paternalistic style of companies such as Rowntree and Cadbury in the nineteenth century. These family companies were the major employers in an area, and built a reputation for treating customers, employees and suppliers with great respect.

53.5 CAN A FIRM SATISFY ALL STAKEHOLDER GROUPS?

According to the shareholder concept a firm's responsibilities to other groups directly conflict with its responsibilities to shareholders. If the firm tried to help the local community, for example, this would take funds away from the shareholders. Similarly, more rewards for the owners would mean fewer resources for employees. In the shareholder view, all these different groups are competing for a fixed set of rewards. If one group has a larger slice of the profits it leaves less for others.

Under the stakeholder approach, however, it is believed that all groups can benefit at the same time. By working with its various stakeholder groups the firm can generate more profit. Imagine, for example, that more rewards are given to employees out of profits. In the short run this may reduce rewards for the shareholder, but in the long run it may generate more rewards for everyone. Better-quality work can lead to improved customer loyalty and therefore less marketing expenditure to achieve the same level of sales. Similarly, by building up better relations with suppliers the firm can produce better-quality goods, leading to more orders and more business for both parties. However, at any moment managers are likely to have to decide which group(s) are most important. This will depend on the values of the owners and managers, the interests of different stakeholders and their power to bring about change. If, for example, stakeholders organise themselves into an effective pressure group they may be able to change a firm's behaviour through actions such as demonstrations and boycotts.

A-grade application

Stakeholders: American Apparel

Staff at American Apparel (AA) have long enjoyed some of the best terms and conditions in the US garment industry. Originally, the company put 'sweatshop-free clothing' on every garment, but later changed it to 'vertically integrated'. In other words every part of every garment was made in American Apparel's Los Angeles factories. Even at a time when the US minimum wage was $5.25 an hour, AA workers earned at least $12 an hour. They also enjoyed subsidised lunches and free healthcare benefits (a huge issue in America). In 2008 the same workers received $25 million's worth of shares in the business.

AA's Chief Executive Dov Charney speaks very frankly about why he does these things: 'not for moral reasons, it's just a better business strategy'. Certainly the booming sales of AA products in 2007 and 2008 made it clear that people loved to buy guilt-free, fashionable clothes.

Remarkably, though, Charney's individual dealings with staff have come under great scrutiny. Three women have filed sexual harassment suits against him, all of which have been settled before reaching trial. Then, in 2010, the share price collapsed as the company faced liquidation after admitting to 'material weaknesses' in its financial controls. The share price that had been $15 in 2008 fell to just 75 cents. Shareholders faced losing their shirts.

ISSUES FOR ANALYSIS

When answering a case study or essay question it may be useful to consider the following points.

- An increasing number of firms claim to be adopting the stakeholder approach. They recognise their responsibilities to groups other than the shareholders and are taking their views into account when making decisions. Claims made by firms, though, may largely be for public relations reasons. Companies should be judged on what they do, not what they say.
- Even firms that genuinely mean to change will find many managers stuck in the previous culture of profit/shareholder first. Changing to more of a stakeholder culture will take years.
- The stakeholder approach can lead to many benefits for organisations, such as attracting new customers, attracting and keeping employees, and building a strong long-term corporate image. However, the business may not be able to fulfil the objectives of all groups. Meeting the needs of one group may conflict with the needs of others.
- The stakeholder approach may prove to be a fad. When the profits of firms fall, for example, they sometimes decide that short-term profit is much more important than obligations to other groups. So a sharp recession would be likely to make every business more profit/shareholder focused.

53.6 RESPONSIBILITIES TO STAKEHOLDERS AND SOCIETY – AN EVALUATION

In recent years, there has been much greater interest in the idea that firms should pay attention to their **social responsibilities**. Increasingly, firms are being asked to consider and justify their actions towards a wide range of groups rather than just their shareholders. Managers are expected to take into account the interests and opinions of numerous internal and external groups before they make a decision. This social responsibility often makes good business sense. If you ignore your stakeholder groups you are vulnerable to pressure group action and may well lose employees and investors. If, however, you build your social responsibility into your marketing this can create new customers and save you money through activities such as recycling.

It may not be possible to meet the needs of all interest groups, however. Firms must decide on the extent to which they take stakeholders into account. Given their limited resources and other obligations, managers must decide on their priorities. In difficult times it may well be that the need for short-term profit overcomes the demands of various stakeholder groups. It would be naive to ignore the fact that TV consumer programmes such as the BBC's *Watchdog* keep exposing business malpractice. Even if progress is being made in general, there are still many firms that persist in seeing short-term profit as the sole business objective.

Key Terms

Pressure group: a group of people with a common interest who try to further that interest (for example, Greenpeace).
Shareholder: an owner of a company.
Shareholder value: a term widely used by company chairmen and chairwomen, which means little more than the attempt to maximise the company's share price.
Social responsibilities: duties towards stakeholder groups, which the firm may or may not accept.
Stakeholder: an individual or group that affects and is affected by an organisation.

WORKBOOK

AS LEVEL EXERCISES

A REVISION QUESTIONS

(40 marks; 40 minutes)

1 What is meant by a 'stakeholder'? (2)
2 Distinguish between the 'shareholder concept' and the 'stakeholder concept'. (3)
3 Some people believe that an increasing number of firms are now trying to meet their social responsibilities. Explain why this may be the case. (3)
4 Outline two responsibilities a firm may have to:
   a) its employees (4)
   b) its customers (4)
   c) the local community. (4)
5 Explain how a firm could damage its profits in the pursuit of meeting its shareholder responsibilities. (4)
6 Explain why a firm's profit may fall by meeting its stakeholder responsibilities. (4)
7 Some managers reject the idea of stakeholding. They believe that a company's duty is purely to its shareholders. Outline two points in favour and two points against this opinion. (8)
8 What factors are likely to determine whether a firm accepts its responsibilities to a particular stakeholder group? (4)

B REVISION EXERCISES

B1 DATA RESPONSE

Stakeholders versus shareholders

In a recent poll, 72 per cent of UK business leaders said that shareholders were served best if the company concentrated on customers, suppliers and other stakeholders. Only 17 per cent thought focusing on shareholders was the only way to succeed. This represents a marked change from five years ago, when the stakeholding idea was widely ignored.

However, not everyone agrees with the stakeholder view. According to two UK writers, Shiv Mathur and Alfred Kenyon, the stakeholder view 'mistakes the essential nature of a business. A business is not a moral agent at all. It is an investment project ... Its *raison d'être* is financial.'

Others believe the stakeholder and shareholder views do not necessarily conflict with each other. For example, the US consultant James Knight writes: 'Managing a company for value requires delivering maximum return to the investors while balancing the interests of the other important constituents, including customers and employees. Companies that consistently deliver value for investors have learned this lesson.'

Source: adapted from the *Financial Times*

Questions

(30 marks; 35 minutes)

1 Distinguish between shareholders and stakeholders. (4)
2 Analyse the possible reasons for the growth in popularity of the stakeholder view in recent years. (8)

3 Examine the factors which might influence whether a firm adopts the stakeholder or the shareholder approach. (8)
4 Discuss the view that the interests of shareholders and stakeholders necessarily conflict. (10)

B2 CASE STUDY

BP: shareholder or stakeholder approach?

On 21 April 2010, news emerged of an explosion on a rig on a BP oilfield in the Gulf of Mexico. Eleven people were killed and many others injured. At first BP said there was little chance of an oil spill, but within a few days it was clear that 200,000 gallons of oil were leaking per day. It was being talked about as perhaps the world's biggest ever oil spill. When media criticism began, BP boss Tony Hayward responded by pointing the finger at the oil rig operating company Transocean. This went down badly, as it implied that BP was trying to evade responsibility. It had outsourced the drilling job to Transocean, but was still legally and morally responsible.

Week by week the flow of oil, the disruption to the tourist and fishing industries and the gaffes of Tony Hayward made the situation worse. Worst of all was his crass statement in an interview that he 'wanted his life back'. This did not go down well with the families of the workers who had died in the explosion. The families were even more upset when they heard that problems on the exploration platform had been known about before the accident. It seemed that work had been rushed to save paying additional sums for the hire of the oil rig. Across America the same message seemed clear: BP was putting its shareholders interests above that of its staff.

By 1 May analysts were speculating that the final bill for the accident and clean-up may reach $12 billion, of which BP would have to pay two-thirds. More importantly, though, would be this further reminder to the US motorist that BP is (a) not 'one of us' and (b) not a business to admire. Of course, anyone needing petrol will fill up at the first garage, but there are often competing petrol stations close by, in which case a brand name can matter.

President Barack Obama speaking on 2 May 2010 said: 'Let me make it clear: BP is responsible for this leak. BP will be paying the bill.'

BP's ability to withstand criticism was fatally undermined by its track record in this area. In March 2005, a huge explosion at BP's Texas oil refinery had killed 15 people and injured more than 180. Most were BP's own staff. The year before, two workers had died at this same refinery when scalded by super-heated water that escaped from a high-pressure pipe.

In November 2006, an official US report made it clear that BP managers had known of 'significant safety problems' at the Texas refinery long before the deadly explosion. The US Chemical Safety Board (CSB) found numerous internal BP reports setting out maintenance backlogs and poor, ageing equipment. Late in October 2006 the CSB Chairwoman blamed the explosion on 'ageing infrastructure, overzealous cost-cutting, inadequate design and risk blindness'.

She went on to say that 'BP implemented a 25 per cent cut on fixed costs from 1998 to 2000 that adversely impacted maintenance expenditures at the refinery'. The report stated that 'BP's global management' (that is, British head office) 'was aware of problems with maintenance spending and infrastructure well before March 2005' – yet they did nothing about it. The chairwoman delivered the final critique: 'Every successful corporation must contain its costs. But at an ageing facility like Texas City, it is not responsible to cut budgets related to safety and maintenance without thoroughly examining the impact on the risk of a catastrophic accident.'

BP confirmed that its own internal investigation had findings 'generally consistent with those of the CSB'.

Questions

(30 marks; 40 minutes)

1 Explain two possible reasons why BP was wrong in its attitude to human and environmental safety in its US operations. (6)
2 Discuss whether BP was carrying out a 'shareholder' or a stakeholder' approach to its decision making during the period covered by the text. (12)
3 Is it time for stronger government controls on business activities? Justify your view. (12)

C ESSAY QUESTIONS

(40 marks each)

1 'Meeting the objectives of different stakeholder groups may be desirable but it is rarely profitable.' Discuss.
2 Consider whether the objectives of the different stakeholder groups necessarily conflict.
3 'A manager's responsibility should be to the shareholders alone.' Critically assess this view.

UNIT 54

Financial objectives and constraints

Financial objectives outline what the business wishes to achieve in financial terms during a certain period of time. Constraints are the internal and external factors that affect the firm's ability to achieve these objectives.

54.1 TYPES OF FINANCIAL OBJECTIVE

It is generally assumed that all businesses operate in order to maximise profit. This is of course true to a certain extent. Why would people invest in a business if not to make profit? However, within this there are many other considerations, as outlined below.

Making a profit: other considerations

Ownership versus management

In a small business the management and the owners are often the same people. In large companies such as a public limited company (plc) the management (the directors) and the owners (the shareholders) are usually separate. The shareholders will want to see a healthy and immediate return on their investments but the directors may have other aims: they may be looking for growth or diversification, or may be content to just keep the business ticking along (satisfying). An increasing trend is for the bonuses of company directors to be related to the achievement of the financial objectives. Directors may therefore have an interest in setting targets that are achievable rather than challenging.

Short term versus long term

Some business goals, such as growth or diversification, will need investment. This may mean a reduction in short-term profits with the hope of increasing returns in the future. If a business is in difficulty it will need to focus much more on survival, so increasing profitability will be a definite short-term goal.

Stakeholders versus shareholders

In some businesses the pursuit of profit may cause conflict between the different groups with an interest in the business, as in the following examples.

- The rise of interest in the environment has meant that costs have increased for many firms and therefore profit has been reduced. However, many firms have also discovered that they can make huge savings, such as by limiting waste.
- Some firms, most notably supermarket chains, are accused of driving the prices of their suppliers to the lowest possible level. Low supply costs increase profits. Businesses need to ensure that there is a balance between keeping costs low and maintaining the quality of the supplies. In the food chain, tough bargaining by supermarkets may cause unacceptable welfare conditions for animals such as chickens and piglets; this, in turn, may backfire on the retailer's reputation.

A-grade application

Financial objectives of major businesses

Company	Financial objectives
Valeo (French supplier to the car industry	To achieve a return on capital employed (ROC) of 30% by 2013
Unilever plc (Multinational producer of foods and household brands)	'We will continue to focus on volume growth as the main driver of long-term value creation, whilst delivering steady and sustainable year-on-year improvement in operating margin and cashflow'
Orange (Telecommunications)	'Organic cash flow generation in 2010 and 2011' (i.e. generating enough positive cash flow from day-to-day operations to help repay loans)
WPP Advertising agency	(Objective for 2010): 'A 1% increase in operating profit margins'

- Taxation may be a consideration. Large multinational companies may deliberately reduce profit in one country in order to pay less tax, and increase profit in another where profits are taxed at a lower

level. They are able to do this by charging differential prices between subsidiaries in different countries.
- Public image: a firm may choose to spend money on charitable concerns or sponsorship; this as a cost will reduce profit. However, it may well get a return on its investment through creating a better brand image or good public relations.

Profit is a major objective

Whether it is long or short term it is safe to say that, for most businesses, high and rising profits are a major objective. However, just stating that the firm wants to increase profit is a very general objective. Most companies will be more specific in defining their financial objectives. They may look to increase gross or net profit. They may also use other measures, such as return on capital employed (ROCE). The measurements of profitability are interlinked. Firms that have a high gross profit margin will find it easier to finance high spending on research and development, marketing or investing in assets. Firms that have better control of costs are going to be more profitable than other firms in their sector. Businesses that generate high profits are going to have contented shareholders.

Revenue targets

The directors may set an overall aim, such as to increase revenue by 10 per cent or more. This approach will be especially important for a business in the early stages of a growth market. For example, in the early days of Innocent Drinks, the key thing for the business was to grow rapidly in order to gain market domination before rival PJ Smoothies (owned by the massive PepsiCo) could get fully established.

Figure 54.1

Cash flow targets

All businesses need to keep a healthy **cash flow**. The level of cash flow should be carefully managed. A company that is cash short will have difficulty with the day-to-day management of its liabilities. It may find it difficult to pay **creditors**. It may also miss opportunities to develop the business. A new order may have to be refused if it has insufficient cash available. A business that has cash reserves that are too high will be missing out on opportunities to use that cash to generate additional business. The 'right' level of cash will depend on the nature of the business. The business may set itself a target of keeping cash at a percentage of turnover or as a stated amount.

Cost minimisation

A business may concentrate on minimising costs. Lowering costs will increase profitability. This may be a general overall aim, such as reducing fixed costs by 5 per cent, or it may be more specific such as reduce wastage in the factory and therefore reduce material costs by 4 per cent. A strategy of cost minimisation may be necessary when times are hard (see Table 54.1).

Table 54.1 Cost-cutting strategies

To cut fixed costs	To cut variable costs
• Consider closing loss-making branches or factories • Consider moving the head office or main factory to a lower-cost location • Consider carefully whether a layer of management could be removed to reduce staffing costs	• Renegotiate with existing suppliers to try to agree lower prices • Look for new suppliers, perhaps from a low-cost country such as China • Redesign the goods to make them simpler and therefore quicker and cheaper to produce

Return on capital employed (ROCE)

This is a measure of how well the company is using its assets to create profit. It is calculated by taking net profit or operating profit as a percentage of capital employed (see Unit 57 on Ratio analysis).

Capital employed is all the long-term finance used to operate the business. Although this is a measure of profitability it concentrates on the use the business is making of its assets. Obviously, the business will want the highest possible return. It is important that the business should achieve a ROCE of more than the rate of interest that it is paying on borrowed funds. The ROCE can be improved by reducing capital employed or by increasing net profit.

Shareholder returns

These can be expressed in terms of the dividend payments that will be given to shareholders, or in terms of maintaining or adding value to the share price. Shareholders hope to gain from their investment in the business in two ways.

1. Any increase in the value of their shares will mean that they can sell their shares at a higher price than they were bought at. This is a capital return.
2. Shareholders receive income on their shares through

the payment of dividends by the business. Yearly profit made by the business can either be kept in the business for development (retained profit) or distributed to shareholders as dividends. These dividends are the income that the shareholders receive as a return on their investment. If the company is making insufficient profit to satisfy shareholders then shareholders will sell their shares and invest elsewhere. This is turn will cause the share price to fall.

A business that is seen as a poor investment by shareholders will find it very difficult to attract investment. It is therefore important that the level of profit and the level of dividends are kept at a level that satisfies shareholders. This in turn keeps the value of the share price high. Balancing the retained profit and dividend distribution is a difficult decision. If the business wants to expand or diversify it may wish to retain more profit and therefore risk upsetting shareholders by paying low dividends.

A-grade application

Volcanic ash hits airline profits

Companies, especially travel companies, are used to external factors that affect their profits. But the disruption caused by the volcano in southern Iceland's Eyjafjallajokull glacier was totally unexpected and the severe travel disruption caused by the closure of European airspace during April and May 2010 had a massive impact on airline profits. Ryanair for example announced that the disruption had cost the company £42 million.

Figure 54.2 Volcanic eruption in southern Iceland

54.2 HOW ARE FINANCIAL OBJECTIVES SET?

Financial objectives are determined by taking into account the overall company aims. They express the financial aspects of the overall company plan. They will be decided like any other business objective, by taking into account the internal position of the business and the external business environment. The internal aspects of the business such as what the business is currently doing and what resources it has available, will determine what the business can achieve. This has to be put into the perspective of the external environment. The external environment will affect how easy it is to carry out the plans. An increase in sales is unlikely to be achieved in an economy that is going into recession.

What makes a good financial objective?

As with any other business objective, financial objectives should be SMART:

- *Specific:* they should be clearly defined so that all staff know and understand the aims
- *Measurable:* if the objective can be measured then it is possible to see if the target has been achieved
- *Achievable:* a good objective is challenging but it must be achievable; to set a target that is impossible is demoralising for staff and it could also create poor shareholder and public confidence if objectives are not met
- *Realistic:* any objective should make good business sense
- *Timebound:* financial targets usually relate to the company's financial year; they can also look further into the future.

54.3 INTERNAL AND EXTERNAL INFLUENCES ON FINANCIAL OBJECTIVES

There are many factors that will influence the way a firm sets its financial objectives. These can be categorised as internal and external constraints.

Internal constraints

Financial

Although it may seem strange to talk about internal finance as a constraint on financial objectives, it can play an important part. The pursuit of higher profit might be constrained by lack of cash flow, especially at a time of rising or even booming demand.

Labour force

Any business activity requires the cooperation of the workforce. It is also important that the business has the manpower with the necessary skills.

Type of business

New or young businesses may set themselves financial objectives but because of inexperience or the difficulty in assessing a new market they may set unrealistic targets. Larger, more established businesses will find it easier to set and achieve their objectives because of the experience that they have. Plcs may be more constrained in their objectives, as they will have to satisfy the shareholders as well as the management.

Operational

A firm that is close to **full capacity** may find that it has fewer opportunities for improving the profitability of the business, unless it has the confidence and the resources to increase capacity, perhaps by moving to bigger premises.

External constraints

Competitive environment

The plans of almost every business can be affected by the behaviour and reaction of competitors. A plan to increase profit margins by increasing prices may be destroyed if competitors react by reducing prices or by advertising their lower prices.

Economic environment

The state of the economy plays a vital part in how well businesses can achieve their financial targets. A booming economy will help businesses to improve sales. However, high interest rates would reduce customers' disposable income and therefore spending, so financial targets may not be met. The effect will depend on the business. Supermarket own-brand producers may do better, whereas branded goods may suffer.

Government

A firm may find its financial objectives limited by regulatory or legislative activity. Consumer watchdogs such as the Office of Fair Trading (OFT) have powers to fine businesses that they believe are not acting in the best interests of consumers. Legislation may also be introduced that increases business costs. A recent European Union environmental policy has forced producers of goods such as refrigerators to pay for their disposal when consumers have finished with them.

Building in the constraints

Good business planning involves being aware of the possible constraints. The internal constraints are easier to evaluate. External constraints will always be subject to more uncertainty as they are outside the power of the business. It is therefore important when setting financial objectives that the business includes a series of 'what if' scenarios when setting the objectives.

A-grade application

Zara back in profit

Zara, the High Street Fashion Chain has 1,600 stores in 74 countries. In August 2010 it posted the annual results for the UK branch of its international operation.

This showed that it had made a pre-tax profit of £618,692 for the year to 31 January 2010, compared with a £20 million loss for the previous year. This loss was said by the company to be due to the cost of opening new stores and improving its stores. This investment seems to have paid off, as sales improved by 13 per cent to £310.6 million.

Directors said the main objective for the past year had been to strengthen Zara's profitability by 'focusing on sales growth for the current store portfolio, while keeping operating expenses under tight control'.

Zara said that after a very difficult start to the year with a sharp decline in customer spending, probably resulting from the deepening recession, sales had improved from the summer onwards.

In spite of this improvement Zara warned that rising unemployment and the 'still difficult economic situation' meant consumer spending was expected to remain volatile throughout this year.

ISSUES FOR ANALYSIS

When analysing financial objectives the key issues are as follows.

- How have the objectives been determined? Any consideration of the firm's objectives must be put into the context of the business and its external environment. Think about the type of business and who the objectives are aiming to please.
- You will need to have an understanding of the different measures used to define financial objectives. It is especially important to ask whether a firm is setting the 'right' objectives: is it pursuing revenue growth when a focus on profit would be more appropriate?
- Are the objectives realistic? A challenging objective may look good in the annual report, but is it achievable?
- When looking at why a business has failed to meet or has exceeded its financial objectives you need to consider the part played by both the internal and the external constraints, and the extent to which these are important.

54.4 FINANCIAL OBJECTIVES AND CONSTRAINTS – AN EVALUATION

There are advantages and disadvantages to setting tight financial objectives. Some people consider that objectives are vital to give direction to the business. A good set of objectives will enable plans for each sector of the business to be developed. Each individual within the organisation will then know the role that they are to play. Without objectives, the business may drift aimlessly.

Other people consider that objectives can stifle entrepreneurship and initiative. They feel that managers operate to satisfy the objectives but do not go beyond them. They also feel that they dampen risk-taking, which may prevent a business from taking the kind of leaps forward shown by Apple (iPhone, iPad) and Nintendo (Wii).

Key Terms

Annual report: the annual financial statement showing the financial results for the business; for any limited company this is a statutory requirement.

Cash flow: the flow of cash into and out of the business.

Creditors: people who are owed money by the business.

Full capacity: when the business is fully utilising all its assets.

Public limited company (plc): a company with limited liability and shares that are available to the public. Its shares are quoted on the stock exchange.

WORKBOOK

A REVISION QUESTIONS

(40 marks; 40 minutes)

1 What is meant by financial objectives? (2)
2 Why is improving or maintaining profit likely to be the most important financial objective? (4)
3 Give two examples of how stakeholder interests could affect the setting of business objectives. (6)
4 What is meant by 'retained profit'? (2)
5 List two likely results for shareholders if profits fall. (4)
6 Explain the term 'return on capital employed'. (4)
7 List and explain two possible internal constraints on achieving financial objectives. (6)
8 Discuss two external constraints that should be taken into account when financial objectives are set by one of the following businesses.
   a) Innocent Drinks
   b) Game (software retailer)
   c) Versace clothing. (8)
9 What government activity could act as a constraint on businesses achieving their financial objectives? Give an example. (4)

B REVISION EXERCISES
B1 DATA RESPONSE

What a difference a book makes!

Quercus Publishing plc is an independent publisher based in London. The company was founded by Mark Smith and Wayne Davies in May 2004. Both had previously worked for the Orion Group, one of the United Kingdom's leading publishing companies. In June 2010 they issued the following press statement:

> The Board of Directors at Quercus Publishing Plc, the award-winning independent publisher, are pleased to report on trading for the six months ended 30 June 2010. The Company's interim results are expected to be issued on 27 September 2010.
>
> Sales across all sectors have continued to be well ahead of management forecasts and, as a result, the Company's performance for the year ending 31 December 2010 is now expected to significantly exceed market expectations.
>
> As a result of this strong trading, unaudited management accounts for the six months ended 30 June 2010 show:
>
> Revenue of £15.0 million (compared with revenue of £5.55 million in the same period in 2009).
>
> Group operating profit for the period rising to £3.40 million (against a loss of £0.10 million in the same period in 2009).
>
> Improvement in Group margins, despite the continued decline in the UK book retail market and the wider economic and financial issues.

Mark Smith, Chief Executive of Quercus said: 'Our results continue to be driven by double-digit growth across the business and, most significantly, by the continued success of Stieg Larsson's Millennium Trilogy, for which we own the global English language rights. These books represent the three best selling fiction titles in the UK over the last six months, and Larsson is the first to have sold more than 1 million Kindle e-books through Amazon.

Source: Quercus Publishing Plc.

Questions

(40 marks; 45 minutes)

1 What was the percentage rise in revenue for the six-month period up to June 2010 compared to the same period the previous year? (4)
2 Explain why the rise in pre-tax profits and the rise in revenue are not the same. (8)
3 What is meant by, 'These figures show improvement in Group margins, despite the continued decline in the UK book retail market and the wider economic and financial issues'? (8)
4 What factors would the company have to take into account when setting financial objectives for the next financial year? (8)
5 Discuss whether it is sensible for a business like a publisher to set financial objectives. (12)

B2 CASE STUDY

Paper quality hits De La Rue

De La Rue was founded in 1821 as a printing business. It began printing in 1860 and in 2003 it took over the printing of bank notes for the Bank of England. It now prints bank notes for 150 governments as well as making documents such as passports, driving licences and cheque books. It also prints holograms onto credit cards.

In March 2010 its annual report showed that in the year to 27 March 2010 its revenue was £561.1 million, up by 12 per cent from the previous year, and profit before tax was £96.6 million, up by 13 per cent.

In July 2010 the company announced that it had discovered quality problems at one of its factories that produce specialist paper. Until the problem was revealed the share price had been consistently high, as investors were happy with the performance of the company and its high dividend payout. The shares lost around 20 per cent of their value in the weeks after the problem was announced. The chief executive took personal responsibility for the problem and resigned. The company said that it expected sales in 2010 and 2011 to be 'materially lower' after halting production at the paper factory where the quality problems had been detected.

Questions

(30 marks: 35 minutes)

1 Why would shareholders be happy with a high dividend payout? (4)
2 Explain why the share price fell when the problems that the company faced were announced. (6)
3 Explain how the quality issue is likely to affect the company profits in future years. (8)
4 Examine the financial measures the company may have to take to recover from the quality problem. (12)

C ESSAY QUESTIONS

(40 marks each)

1 Financial objectives are only there to please shareholders. Discuss.
2 Setting financial objectives is a waste of management time. Discuss.
3 Financial objectives are more important for large organisations. Discuss.

Income statements (profit and loss accounts)

UNIT 55

An income statement is an accounting statement showing a firm's sales revenue over a trading period and all the relevant costs generated to earn that revenue. Public limited companies use the term income statements, whereas small firms refer to the profit and loss account (sometimes abbreviated to 'the P&L').

55.1 INTRODUCTION

The function of accounting is to provide information to various stakeholder groups on how a particular business has performed during a given period. The groups include shareholders, managers and creditors. The period in question is usually one year. The key financial documents from which this information can be drawn are balance sheets and income statements. This unit focuses on the income statement; the balance sheet is covered in Unit 56.

The income statement records all a business's costs within a given trading period. Income statements constitute a vital piece of evidence for those with interests in a company. For many stakeholders, profit is a major criterion by which to judge the success of a business:

- shareholders are an obvious example of those assessing profitability
- government agencies such as the tax authorities require data on profits or losses in order to be able to calculate the liability of a business to **corporation tax**
- suppliers to a business also need to know the financial position of the companies they trade with, in order to establish their reliability, stability and creditworthiness
- potential shareholders and bankers will also want to assess the financial position of the company before committing their funds to the business.

For all these groups the income statement provides important information.

Making a profit is one of the most significant objectives for business organisations. It is this profit motive that encourages many people to establish their own business or expand an existing one. Without the potential for making a profit, why should individuals and companies commit time and resources to what may be a risky venture? Even charities must seek to generate revenues to at least match their expenditure, otherwise they cannot survive. Therefore the income statement is as important to a charity as it is to a company.

55.2 THE USES OF INCOME STATEMENTS

The data within an income statement can be used for a number of purposes:

- to measure the success of a business compared with previous years or other businesses
- to assess actual performance compared with expectations
- to help obtain loans from banks or other lending institutions (creditors want proof that the business is capable of repaying any loans)
- to enable owners and managers to plan ahead; for example, for future investment in the company.

55.3 MEASURING PROFIT

Profit is what remains from **revenue** once costs have been deducted. However, the word 'profit' on its own means little to an accountant. Profit is such an important indicator of company performance that it is broken down into different types. This enables more detailed comparisons and analyses to be made.

The main types of profit are described below.

Gross profit

This is the measure of the difference between income (sales revenue) and the cost of manufacturing or purchasing the products that have been sold. It measures the amount of profit made on trading activities alone (that is, the amount of profit made on buying and selling activities).

Gross profit = Revenue − Cost of goods sold

Gross profit is calculated without taking costs, which could be classified as expenses (administration, advertising) or overheads (rent, rates), into account. This is a useful measure as, if a company is making a lower level of gross profit than a competitor, it is clear that the company must look very closely at its trading position.

Key Terms

Corporation tax: a tax levied as a percentage of a company's profits (for example, 25 per cent).
Cost of goods sold: calculation of the direct costs involved in making the goods actually sold in that period.
Gross profit: revenue less cost of goods sold; profit made on trading activities.
Operating profit: gross profit minus expenses.
Private limited company: a business with limited liability whose shares are not available to the public.
Revenue: sales revenue (that is, the value of sales made); also known as income.
Stock exchange: a market for stocks and shares; it supervises the issuing of shares by companies and is also a second-hand market for stocks and shares.

WORKBOOK

A REVISION QUESTIONS

(40 marks; 40 minutes)

1 Give two possible reasons why a firm's bank would want to see its income statement. (2)
2 Outline two ways in which employees may benefit from looking at the income statement of their employer. (4)
3 List the elements necessary to calculate cost of sales. (4)
4 Distinguish between gross and operating profit. (4)
5 Last year Bandex plc made an operating profit of £25 million. £20 million of this came from the sale of its London training centre. The previous year the business made a profit of £15 million. Use the concept of 'profit quality' to decide whether last year was successful or unsuccessful for the business. (6)
6 Explain why even a charity such as Oxfam may want to make a profit. (4)
7 Explain what may be included under the heading 'financing costs'. (4)
8 Give one example each of exceptional and extraordinary items that might appear on the income statement of a business. Briefly explain each one. (4)
9 Look at the Tesco income statement shown in Figure 55.5.
   a) Calculate the percentage increase in (i) its 2010 income and (ii) profit before tax. (4)
   b) Explain one conclusion that can be drawn from those findings. (4)

B REVISION EXERCISES

B1 DATA RESPONSE

Thurton plc

The chairman of Thurton plc has come under some pressure lately. Shareholders have complained about the firm's lacklustre performance. Today, though, he is creating favourable headlines. The *Sunday Press* has announced that 'Thurton drives forward'. In the *Financial Guardian* the chairman is quoted as saying: 'This is a great day for Thurton. Profit before tax is up by more than 50 per cent and we have been able to double our dividends to shareholders. I am confident we will be able to maintain or increase this dividend next year.'

Income statement for Thurton plc

	This year (£m)	Last year (£m)
Revenue	24.5	25.8
Cost of sales	10.0	9.6
Expenses	12.4	11.1
Operating profit	?	?
Extraordinary item	6.4	
Finance income	0.5	0.4
Finance expenses	0.9	0.9
Profit before taxation	?	?
Taxation	2.4	1.4
Profit after taxation for the year	**5.7**	**3.2**

Figure 55.6 Income statement for Thurton plc

Questions

(25 marks; 30 minutes)

1 Calculate Thurton plc's operating profit and profit before taxation for this year and last. (4)
2 Analyse Thurton plc's profit performance this year, by comparing it with last year. Within your answer, consider the quality of the profit made by Thurton this year. (9)
3 Use your analysis to comment on the accuracy of the chairman's statement. (12)

B2 DATA RESPONSE

Reckitt Benckiser plc

Reckitt Benckiser plc is one of the world's leading manufacturers of cleaning products, and a member of the FTSE 100 Index of the largest companies traded on the London **Stock Exchange**. The company was formed by a merger between Britain's Reckitt & Colman and the Dutch company Benckiser NV. Reckitt Benckiser has operations in more than 60 countries and exports to more than 200 countries. The company focuses on high-margin yet steady-selling products such as Cif and Cillit Bang cleaners. It has shown strong growth in profits in recent years.

Source: Reckitt Benckiser Interim Report, 2010

	Six months to 30/06/2010 £m	**Six months to 30/06/2009 £m**
Revenue	4,064	3,783
Cost of sales	?	?
Gross profit	**2,437**	**2,234**
Operating expenses	(1,473)	(1,415)
Operating profit	**964**	**819**
Net finance income	7	(3)
Profit before taxation	**971**	**816**
Taxation	(243)	(203)
Profit after taxation for the year	**728**	**613**

Figure 55.7 Reckitt Benckiser group income statement (summarised)

Questions

(40 marks; 50 minutes)

1 a) Calculate Reckitt Benckiser's cost of sales for both periods. (5)
b) Calculate each figure as a percentage of the company's revenue for the corresponding period. (4)
c) Comment on your findings. (6)
2 a) Calculate the percentage increase Reckitt Benckiser achieved in 2010 compared with 2009 in:
i) revenue (3)
ii) operating profit. (3)
b) Analyse the data to suggest why the increase in operating profit was greater than the increase in turnover. (8)
3 Why may it be risky to judge a firm such as Reckitt Benckiser on its profit performance over a six-month period? (11)

£140,000 of current assets to show net current assets (or working capital) of £100,000.

- Assets employed of £400,000 still balances with the capital employed (total capital).

Capital on the balance sheet

Companies have three main sources of long-term capital: shareholders (share capital), banks (loan capital) and reinvested profits (reserves). Loan capital carries interest charges that must be repaid, as must the loan itself. Share capital and reserves are both owed to the shareholders, but do not have to be repaid. Therefore they are treated separately. Share capital and reserves are known as shareholders' funds.

Assuming Spark Ltd's capital came from £50,000 of share capital, £250,000 of loan capital and £100,000 of accumulated, retained profits, the final version of the vertical balance sheet would look like the one shown in Figure 56.3.

Spark Ltd: Balance sheet for 31 December last year

	£	£
Property	180,000	
Machinery and vehicles	120,000	300,000
Stock	80,000	
Debtors and cash	60,000	
Current liabilities	(40,000)	
Net current assets	100,000	
Total assets less current liabilities		400,000
Loan capital		(250,000)
Net assets		150,000
Share capital	50,000	
Reserves	100,000	
Shareholders' funds		150,000

Figure 56.3 An example of a final version of a vertical balance sheet

The concept of capital as a liability

It is hard to see why money invested by the owners should be treated as a **liability**. This is due to a concept in accounting called 'business entity'. This states that a business and its owners are two separate legal entities. From the point of view of the business, therefore, any money paid to it by the shareholders is a liability because the firm owes it back to them. In reality, capital invested by the owners is likely to be paid back only in the event of the business ceasing to trade.

56.4 MORE DETAIL ON BALANCE SHEET CALCULATIONS

Working capital

Current liabilities need to be repaid in the near future, ideally using current assets. Taking the former away from the latter gives a figure called working capital. This shows an organisation's ability or inability to pay its short-term debts.

If current assets exceed current liabilities the business has enough short-term assets to pay short-term debts. It has positive working capital and should therefore have enough money for its day-to-day needs.

If current assets are less than current liabilities the business does not have enough short-term assets to pay short-term debts. Working capital is negative (for example, current assets are £50,000 but current liabilities are £70,000, so working capital is −£20,000). This may mean a day-to-day struggle to pay the bills. In this case the figure on the balance sheet may be called net current liabilities.

The balance between current assets and liabilities is a very important figure. Suppliers and banks expect to be paid when debts are due. At the very least, the failure to pay on time will mean a worsening in relations. At worst, it may result in court action.

In Figure 56.4, Ted Baker plc has plenty of working capital, because its £32 million of short-term (current) liabilities are easily covered by its £70 million of current assets.

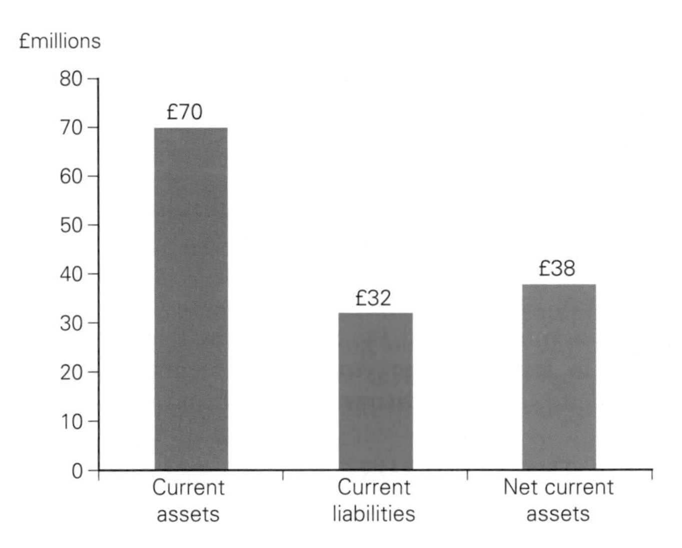

Figure 56.4 Ted Baker working capital

The effect of making a net loss on the balance sheet

In the event that a business makes a net loss rather than a net profit over a financial year, then the layout of the balance sheet remains completely unchanged. The only effect is that the loss reduces the reserves figure and therefore cuts the shareholders' funds. This will be balanced in the accounts by a reduction in the net current assets.

This reflects that if a business has made a loss over the financial period, expenses have exceeded revenues received. Therefore the overall value of the business will have fallen and so must the value of the owners' funds invested.

56.5 THE PUBLISHED ACCOUNTS OF PUBLIC LIMITED COMPANIES

The implementation of International Financial Reporting Standards (IFRS) has required that listed public companies present their balance sheets in a format slightly different from that set out above. There are a number of differences in the terminology used on the IFRS balance sheet, as outlined below.

- Fixed assets are called non-current assets but continue to include tangible and non-tangible assets.
- There are two changes within the current assets section of the balance sheet: stocks are renamed as inventories and debtors are now termed 'trade and other receivables'.
- Under current liabilities creditors are referred to as 'trade and other payables'.
- Long-term liabilities are renamed 'non-current liabilities'.
- Reserves in the final section of the balance sheet are supplemented by 'retained earnings'. Retained earnings are profits that a company has generated that have not been paid out to shareholders.
- Shareholders' funds are termed 'total equity'.

The overall structure of the balance sheet is the same, even though the terminology varies. The two figures that balance are the net assets of the business (simply all its assets less its total liabilities) and the total equity figure (which is share capital invested plus reserves and retained earnings from past trading). The reason for balancing the figures in this way is to enable shareholders to see at a glance what the balance sheet suggests the business is 'worth' – that is, the bottom line of the balance sheet (total equity).

The implications of the changes introduced by IFRS rules are greater than just changes in terminology, but are not within the scope of this book. The main reason is to allow greater comparability between the performances of companies in different countries. It is hoped that this will increase investors' confidence and therefore encourage international investment flows.

A summary of recent balance sheet for the UK pub chain JD Wetherspoon is given in Figure 56.5. This follows the IFRS format for listed companies, though a few minor differences exist between the formats of balance sheets for different public companies. However, it is common for two years to be shown side by side. This is to help financial interpretation of the accounts and the analysis of trends.

Key conclusions to be drawn from JD Wetherspoon's balance sheets over the two years include:

- the company's long-term borrowing (non-current liabilities) has increased significantly between the two years
- current liabilities outweigh current assets, causing net current assets to be strongly negative
- Reserves fell in 2010. This was a reflection of the very difficult trading period for pubs in recessionary Britain.

Balance sheet for JD Wetherspoon as at 25 July 2010

	2010	2009
	£m	£m
Non-current assets	845	797
Inventories	20	18
Receivables & cash	46	41
Total assets	911	856
Current liabilities	(177)	(258)
Non-current liabilities	(572)	(430)
Net assets	162	168
Share capital	145	145
Reserves & retained earnings	17	23
Total shareholders' equity	162	168

Figure 56.5 A summary of a balance sheet for the UK pub chain JD Wetherspoon
Source: adapted from annual accounts for JD Wetherspoon, 2010

Figure 56.6 2010 was a difficult trading period for pubs in Britain

56.6 WINDOW DRESSING ACCOUNTS

Window dressing means presenting company accounts in such a manner as to flatter the financial position of the company.

Window dressing is a form of creative accounting that is concerned with making modest adjustments to sales, debtors and stock items when preparing end-of-year financial reports. There is a fine dividing line between flattery and fraud.

In many cases, window dressing is simply a matter of tidying up the accounts and is not misleading. Two important methods of window dressing are as follows.

1 Massaging profit figures: surprisingly, it is possible to 'adjust' a business's cost and revenue figures. At the end of a poor year, managers may be asked to bring forward as many invoices and deliveries as possible. The intention is to inflate, as much as possible, the revenue earned by the business in the final month of trading.
2 Hiding a deteriorating **liquidity** position: this allows businesses to present balance sheets that look sound to potential investors. A business may execute a sale and leaseback deal just prior to accounts being published. This increases the amount of cash within the business and makes it look a more attractive proposition.

It is important to remember that, although window dressing happens, the overwhelming majority of companies present their accounts as fairly and straightforwardly as possible.

ISSUES FOR ANALYSIS

- The balance sheet is an important statement full of information for anyone with an interest in a business. Analysis of the balance sheet can provide the reader with an insight into the strengths and weaknesses of a business, its potential for growth, its stability and how it is financed.
- The balance sheet gives details as to where and how an organisation has obtained its finance, alongside information about what this finance has been spent on. This allows judgements to be made about the financial performance of the business in question.
- Examining individual balance sheets can be interesting and provides the reader with a great deal of information. However, it must be remembered that a balance sheet is only a 'snapshot' of a business on one day out of 365, and that for a meaningful analysis to take place it must be compared to previous balance sheets, to see what changes or trends can be identified. The primary method of balance sheet analysis is through accounting ratios. These are explained in Unit 57.

56.7 BALANCE SHEETS – AN EVALUATION

Several key areas can be considered with regard to balance sheets. The first is the assumption that just because a company possesses thousands or millions of pounds worth of assets it is doing well. It is how the company has financed these assets that counts. A company could look to be in quite a stable position, but what would be the effect of a rise in interest rates if most of the company is financed by debt?

Similarly, equal importance must be placed on the short-term asset structure of the company. Many profitable companies close down or go into liquidation, not through lack of sales or customers but through poor short-term asset management (that is, management of working capital).

As with all financial data and decisions, it is not sufficient just to consider the numerical information. External considerations such as the state of the market or economy must be taken into account. Comparisons with similar-sized organisations in the same industry must be used. Any worthwhile judgement requires an investigation into the non-financial aspects of the business. A company could have millions of pounds of assets, a healthy bank account, a good profit record and be financed mainly by share capital. However, all this means little if the workforce is about to go on strike for three months or its products are becoming obsolete.

Key Terms

Creditors: those to whom a firm owes money (for example, suppliers or bankers); these may also be called payables.
Fixed assets: items of value the business plans to hold in the medium to long term, such as vehicles or property.
Liability: a debt (that is, a bill that has not been paid or a loan that has not been repaid).
Liquidity: a measurement of a firm's ability to pay its short-term bills.
Working capital: day-to-day finance for running the business (current assets – current liabilities).

WORKBOOK

A REVISION QUESTIONS

(30 marks; 30 minutes)

1 Define the term 'balance sheet'. (2)
2 Distinguish between non-current and current assets. (4)
3 Explain why it is that the two parts of a balance sheet will always balance. (2)
4 What are the main reasons for presenting a balance sheet in vertical format? (3)
5 How would you calculate working capital? (2)
6 Why is it important for a supplier to check on the liquidity of a potential customer? (4)
7 Explain what is meant by the term 'window dressing'. (4)
8 Describe two ways in which a business might window dress its accounts. (4)
9 What is the difference between an intangible and a tangible non-current asset? (3)
10 State two items that may be listed as current liabilities. (2)

B REVISION EXERCISES
B1 DATA RESPONSE

D Parton Ltd: Year ending 31 December 20XX	
	£000
Property	600
Stock	120
Machinery (at cost)*	240
Creditors	100
Cash	170
Reserves	350
less Debtors	280
Tax due	140
Assets employed	(200)
Net current assets	760
Overdraft	200
Share capital	500
Capital employed	760
*Book value: £120,000	

Figure 56.7 Balance sheet for D Parton Ltd

Questions

(20 marks; 25 minutes)

1 **a)** Identify ten mistakes in the balance sheet shown in Figure 56.7. (10)
b) Draw up the balance sheet correctly. (10)

B2 STIMULUS QUESTION

Honda

The balance sheet shown in Figure 56.8 is taken from Honda's 2010 annual report and accounts. Honda is one of the world's best-known and largest manufacturers of cars and motorbikes. In 2010 the company's sales turnover fell to $92 billion, from $102 billion in 2009. In the 2010 financial year the company's operating profit doubled to $3.9 billion.

Honda balance sheet as at 31st March 2010		
	2010	**2009**
	$bn	**$bn**
Intangible non-current assets	7.0	6.5
Tangible non-current assets	68.4	66.8
Inventories	10.1	12.7
Receivables and cash	39.5	34.4
Current liabilities	(36.7)	(43.1)
Net current assets	12.9	4.0
Non-current liabilities	(40.3)	(35.1)
Net assets	**48.0**	**42.2**
Share capital	2.8	2.6
Reserves & retained earnings	45.2	39.6
Total equity	**48.0**	**42.2**

Figure 56.8 Honda balance sheet as at 31 March 2010

Questions

(30 marks; 40 minutes)

1 Explain the meaning of the following terms:
  a) balance sheet
  b) net assets. (4)
2 Describe two external users of financial information, and explain why they may analyse a balance sheet. (6)
3 **a)** Identify three key trends in this data. (3)
  b) Analyse the possible causes and implications of the trends you have identified. (6)
4 Evaluate the usefulness of this data to an investor who is considering purchasing shares in Honda. (11)

B3 CASE STUDY

Imperial Tobacco is the world's fourth-largest international tobacco company; it manufactures, markets and sells a comprehensive range of cigarettes, tobaccos and cigars. The company grew significantly during the 2006–2007 financial year, principally as a result of buying up other companies.

Balance sheet for Imperial Tobacco plc as at 30 September 2009

	2009	2008
	£m	£m
Non-current assets	24,600	22,600
Inventories	2,900	2,800
Trade and other receivables	3,000	2,900
Cash & equivalents	1,300	800
Current liabilities	(11,400)	?
Net current assets/(liabilities)	?	(3,100)
Non-current liabilities	(13,900)	(13,200)
Net assets	6,500	6,300
Total equity	6,500	?

Figure 56.9 Balance sheet for Imperial Tobacco plc

Questions

(40 marks; 50 minutes)

1 Distinguish between net current assets and net current liabilities. (3)
2 **a)** Complete Imperial Tobacco's balance sheet by stating the missing figures. (3)
  b) Explain one way in which Imperial Tobacco plc might have window dressed its accounts to make them look as favourable as possible. (4)
3 Imperial Tobacco is expanding by buying other companies. Analyse whether its balance sheet is strong enough to encourage banks to lend it further capital to finance its plans. (12)
4 To what extent can you judge the performance of Imperial Tobacco plc over the period 2008–2009 from the information included in the company's balance sheet? (18)

C ESSAY QUESTIONS

(40 marks each)

1 'Balance sheets can only measure the financial worth of a business. The real worth depends upon far more.' In relation to any business with which you are familiar, discuss how important a balance sheet is, then, in judging whether a firm is well managed.
2 With reference to any business with which you are familiar, consider whether its balance sheet is more useful than its cash flow forecast, or vice versa.
3 'Balance sheet evaluation is the key to making successful long-term investment decisions.' With reference to any real-world business, consider the extent to which you believe this to be true.

Ratio analysis

UNIT 57

Ratio analysis is an examination of accounting data by relating one figure to another. This approach allows more meaningful interpretation of the data and the identification of trends.

57.1 INTRODUCTION

The function of accounting is to provide information to stakeholders on how a business has performed over a given period. But how is performance to be judged? Is an annual profit of $1 million good or bad? Very good if the firm is a small family business; woeful if the business is KFC and annual sales exceed $10 billion. What is needed is to compare this information to something else. This can provide a way of judging a firm's financial performance in relation to its size and in relation to the performance of its competitors. The technique used to do this is called ratio analysis.

Financial accounts, such as the income statement and the balance sheet, are used for three main purposes:

1 financial control
2 planning
3 accountability.

Ratio analysis can assist in achieving these objectives. It can help the different users of financial information to answer some of the questions they are interested in. It may also raise several new questions, such as:

- Is this company/my job safe?
- Should I stop selling goods to this firm on credit?
- Should I invest in this business?

57.2 INTERPRETING FINAL ACCOUNTS: THE INVESTIGATION PROCESS

To analyse company accounts, a well-ordered and structured process needs to be followed. This should ensure that the analysis is relevant to the question being looked at. The seven-point approach shown in Figure 57.1 is helpful.

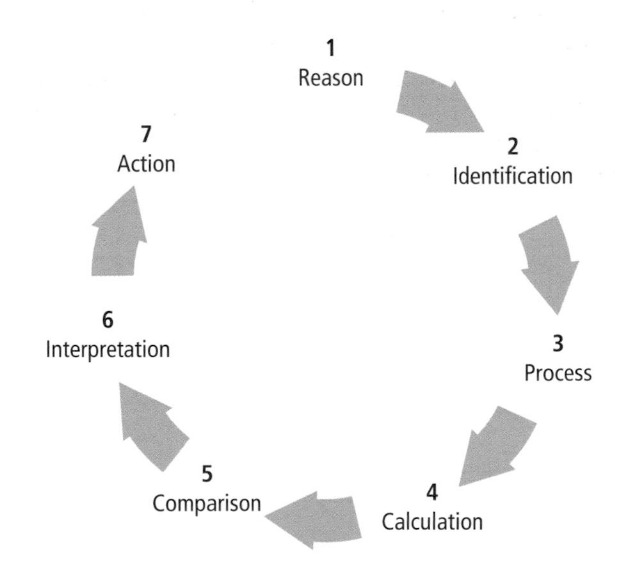

Figure 57.1 Seven-point approach to ratio analysis

57.3 TYPES OF RATIO

The main classifications of ratios are as follows.

- *Profitability ratios:* measure the relationship between gross/net profit and revenue, assets and capital employed. They are sometimes referred to as performance ratios.
- *Activity ratios:* these measure how efficiently an organisation uses its resources, such as inventories or total assets.
- *Liquidity ratios:* these investigate the short-term financial stability of a firm by examining whether there are sufficient short-term assets to meet the short-term liabilities (debts); the 2008–10 credit squeeze showed that even banks can run out of the cash they need to keep operating.
- *Gearing:* examines the extent to which the business is dependent upon borrowed money; it is concerned with the long-term financial position of the company.
- *Shareholder ratios:* this group of ratios is concerned with analysing the returns for shareholders. They

Table 57.1 An explanation of the seven point approach to ratio analysis

The investigation process		
Step 1	Reason	The starting point for interpreting financial accounts is establishing why you are doing so. If you are considering supplying a company with a large order of goods, you want to try to establish its financial stability and ability to pay.
Step 2	Identification	Identify the relevant figures from the financial accounts.
Step 3	Process	Decide what method(s) of analysis will provide you with the most useful and meaningful results.
Step 4	Calculation	Make a comparison between data by calculating one figure as a ratio of another. For example, profit as a percentage of sales revenue or borrowings as a proportion of total capital.
Step 5	Comparison	Compare the figures from this period with the results from the last period, those of your competitors or other companies under investigation.
Step 6	Interpretation	Look at the results obtained and interpret them in relation to values that would be considered poor, average or good.
Step 7	Action	If certain results are worrying, initiate further investigation (maybe into areas which are not covered in the financial accounts), or take corrective action.

examine the relationship between the number of shares issued, dividend paid, value of the shares and company profits.

The following sections look at each classification of ratios in more detail. An explanation of the seven point approach to ratio analysis is given in Table 57.1.

57.4 PROFITABILITY RATIOS

For private businesses, a key objective is to make a profit. But how much profit? Consider the following example.

Example

Companies A and B operate in the same market. At the end of the year they report profits as follows:

	Company A	Company B
Profit	£100,000	£1 million

Which is the more successful company? Company B, surely. However, take into account the following additional information.

	Company A	Company B
Profit	£100,000	£1 million
Capital invested	£200,000	£10 million

This shows that company A has done very well compared with the capital invested in the business. Much better, in fact, than company B. Profitability ratios allow comparisons such as this to be made in detail. The figures can be compared in percentage terms. This makes comparison easier.

	Company A	Company B
Profit	£100,000	£1 million
Divided by	£200,000	£10 million
× 100 (to get a percentage)	50%	10%

Company A's success can now be seen much more clearly.

Unit 55 distinguished between various types of profit. Because of the different types of profit, there are a number of different profit ratios. The net profit margin was looked at as part of Unit 18. There are two other profitability ratios to consider.

Gross profit margin

This ratio examines the relationship between the profit made before allowing for overhead costs (gross profit) and the level of revenue. It is given by the formula:

$$\text{Gross profit margin} = \frac{\text{Gross profit}}{\text{Revenue}} \times 100$$

For example, a furniture shop buys sofas for £200 and sells them for £500 each, making a gross profit of £300 per sofa. In a week it sells ten, so its gross profit is £3,000 and its revenue from sales is £5,000. The gross profit margin is therefore:

$$= \frac{\text{Gross profit}}{\text{Revenue}} = \frac{£3{,}000}{£5{,}000} \times 100 = 60\%$$

Figure 57.2

Note that although this sounds a terrific profit margin, no allowance has yet been made for all the overhead costs of the business, such as rent, rates, staff costs, advertising and much more.

Interpretation

Obviously, the higher the profit margin a business makes the better. However, the level of gross profit margin will vary considerably between different markets. For example, the amount of gross profit percentage on clothes (especially fashion items) is far higher than on food. Any result gained must be looked at in the context of the industry in which the firm operates. It will always be possible to make comparisons with previous years' figures. This will establish whether or not the firm's trading position has become more or less profitable.

Altering the ratio

The gross profit margin can be improved by:

- raising sales revenue while keeping the cost of sales the same, or
- reducing the cost of sales made while maintaining the same level of sales revenue.

Return on capital employed (ROCE)

This is sometimes referred to as being the primary efficiency ratio and is perhaps the most important ratio of all. It measures the efficiency with which the firm generates profit from the funds invested in the business. It answers the key question anyone would ask before investing or saving: 'What annual percentage return will I get on my capital?'

$$\text{ROCE} = \frac{\text{Operating profit}}{\text{Capital employed}} \times 100$$

Operating profit is profit after all operating costs and overheads have been deducted. It is, however, profit before interest and taxation are paid. Capital employed is all the long-term finance of the business (debt plus equity).

Interpretation

The higher the value of this ratio the better. A high and rising ROCE suggests that resources are being used efficiently. ROCE measures profitability and no shareholder will complain at huge returns. The figure needs to be compared with previous years and that of other companies to determine whether this year's result is satisfactory or not.

A firm's ROCE can also be compared with the percentage return offered by interest-bearing accounts at banks and building societies. If bank interest rates are 6 per cent, what is the point of a sole trader investing money in his or her business, working very hard all year and making a return on capital employed of 4 per cent? The sole trader would be better off keeping the money in the bank, taking little risk and staying at home.

So what is the *right* level of ROCE? There is no clear answer, but most companies would regard a 20 per cent ROCE as very satisfactory. The returns achieved by a selection of public companies in 2010 are shown in Table 57.2.

Altering the ratio

The return on capital employed can be improved by:

- increasing the level of profit generated by the same level of capital invested, or
- maintaining the level of profits generated but decreasing the amount of capital it takes to do so.

57.5 FINANCIAL EFFICIENCY RATIOS

These four ratios are concerned with how well an organisation manages its resources. Three of them investigate how well the management controls the current situation of the firm. They consider stock, debtors and creditors. This area of ratios is linked, therefore, with the management of working capital. The fourth ratio looks at the position of the whole business: how well it is generating sales income from the investment it has made in assets. This important ratio is called asset turnover.

Stock (or inventory) turnover

This ratio measures the number of times a year a business sells and replaces its stock; on plc balance sheets stock is termed 'inventories', but for the purpose of this ratio we will use the term stock. For example, if a market stall trader bought stock from wholesalers every morning and sold all the stock by the end of the afternoon, replacing the stock daily would mean a stock turnover of 365 times per year. The formula for stock turnover is:

$$\text{Stock turnover} = \frac{\text{Cost of goods sold}}{\text{Stock}}$$

expressed as times per year.

Table 57.2 The return on capital employed (ROCE) achieved by a selection of public limited companies in 2010

Company	Annual operating profit	Capital employed	ROCE (%)
Apple Inc (electronics)	$17,250,000,000	$49,110,000,000	35.1
Burberry (clothing)	£171,000,000	£638,000,000	26.8
Tesco (retailing)	£3,457,000,000	£30,008,000,000	11.5
Honda Motor	$3,910,000,000	$88,241,000,000	4.4

Interpretation

This ratio can only really be interpreted with knowledge of the industry in which the firm operates. For example, we would expect a greengrocer to turn over stock virtually every day, as the goods have to be fresh. Therefore, we would expect to see a result for stock turnover of approximately 250 to 300 times per year. This allows for closures and holidays and the fact that some produce will last longer than one day. A second-hand car sales business could take an average of a month to sell the cars; therefore the stock turnover would be 12 times.

It is possible to convert this ratio from showing the number of times an organisation turns over stock to showing the average number of days stock is held. It is given by the formula:

$$\text{Stock turnover} = \frac{365}{\text{Number of times}}$$

expressed as days (for example, 'the company holds seven days' worth of stock').

Altering the ratio

The stock turnover ratio can be improved by:

- reducing the average level of stocks held, without losing sales, or
- increasing the rate of sales without raising the level of stocks.

Note that the stock turnover ratio has little meaning for service industries as they do not buy or sell stocks of goods.

Debtor days

This particular ratio is designed to show how long, on average, it takes the company to collect debts owed by customers. Customers who are granted credit are called debtors. On public companies' balance sheets they are called 'trade receivables', but we will use the term debtors for this ratio. The formula for this ratio is:

$$\text{Debtor days} = \frac{\text{Debtors}}{\text{Annual income}} \times 365$$

expressed as days.

The accounts for the fashion clothing business Ted Baker plc make it possible to calculate the following debtor days' position (see Table 57.3).

Interpretation

In other words, the average Ted Baker customer took 49 days to pay in 2009 and 44 days to pay in 2010. By collecting its money faster, Ted Baker would have improved its cash position. Better to have the cash than to be waiting for it.

Table 57.3 Information from the Ted Baker accounts: debtor position

	Annual income (£ million)	Debtors (£ million)	Debtor days (no of days)
Year to 30 January 2009	152.6	20.5	49
Year to 30 January 2010	163.5	19.7	44

Altering the ratio

The debtors' collection period can be improved by reducing the amount of time for which credit is offered (for example, from 60 to 30 days), increasing the efficiency of the credit control department or by offering incentives for clients to pay on time, e.g. cash discounts. A common approach is **aged debtors analysis**; this means sorting debtors into the age of their debts to you – oldest first. This helps to focus upon collecting debts from the slowest payers. It may also encourage a firm to refuse to supply a persistent slow payer in future.

Creditor days

This particular ratio is designed to show how many days, on average, it takes the company to pay its suppliers. Creditors are people and organisations that are owed money by the business. On public companies' balance sheets they are called 'trade payables', but we will use the term creditors for this ratio. The formula for this ratio is:

$$\text{Creditor days} = \frac{\text{Creditors}}{\text{Cost of sales}} \times 365$$

The accounts for the fashion clothing business Ted Baker plc make it possible to calculate the following creditor days' position (Table 57.4).

Table 57.4 Information from the Ted Baker accounts: creditor position

	Cost of sales £ million	Creditors £ million	Creditor days No of days
Year to 30 January 2009	63.3	29.8	172
Year to 30 January 2010	63.6	24.8	142

Interpretation

In other words, the average Ted Baker supplier had to wait 172 days to be paid in 2009 and 142 days to pay in 2010. Ted Baker is getting slightly better, but from a shockingly poor starting point. This would be important to know if your business was considering supplying Ted Baker for the first time (it's a long wait!). From Ted Baker's point of view, though, it's great to be able to hold onto the cash for ages before paying.

Altering the ratio

Creditor days can be reduced by paying bills more promptly. This might actually worsen a business's cash position but could improve its corporate image.

Asset turnover ratio

The asset turnover ratio measures how many pounds' worth of sales a company can generate from its net assets. Net assets are non-current assets plus net current assets less non-current liabilities. In other words, they equal total equity. Company directors often use the phrase 'make the assets sweat'; in other words, make the assets work hard. If there is a period in the year when a factory is quiet, an active company director might want to find a source of extra business. In this way the company could keep generating sales from its existing assets. This would push up the value of the asset turnover ratio.

$$\text{Asset turnover} = \frac{\text{Annual income}}{\text{Assets employed}}$$

expressed as times per year.

The fashion clothing and accessories company, Burberry, had the asset turnover figures in 2009 and 2010 shown in Table 57.5.

Table 57.5 Information from the Burberry accounts: asset turnover figures

Year	Sales revenue £m	Assets employed £m	Asset turnover
2009	1,201.5	578.9	2.08 times
2010	1,279.9	637.8	2.01 times

In 2010, the asset turnover ratio for Burberry fell slightly compared with the previous year. Even so, both figures represented a big increase in the asset turnover figures compared with a few years earlier (it was 1.57 in 2004). A fair conclusion is that a pleasing long-term trend has had a short-term setback, perhaps because of the recession.

Interpretation

Some companies pursue a policy of high profit margins, perhaps at the cost of high sales. An antiques shop in an expensive part of town may be beautifully laid out but never seem to have any customers. Its asset turnover will be low because it generates low sales from its high asset base. Fortunately for the firm, its profit margins may be so high that the occasional sale generates enough profit to keep the business going.

Other companies may follow a low-price, high-sales approach. Tesco used to call this 'pile them high, sell them cheap'. Here profit margins may be low, but the asset turnover is so high that lots and lots of small profits add up to a healthy profit total. Asset turnover, then, should be looked at in relation to (net) profit margins. If net profit margins are multiplied by asset turnover, the result is the company's ROCE. So boosting asset turnover is as helpful to a firm as boosting its profit margins.

Altering the ratio

To increase asset turnover there are two options. Either work at increasing sales from the existing asset base (making the assets 'sweat'). Or sell off under-utilised assets, so that the sales figure is divided by a lower asset total. Either approach would then have the effect of boosting a company's ROCE.

57.6 LIQUIDITY RATIOS

These ratios are concerned with the short-term financial health of a business. They are concerned with the organisation's working capital and whether or not it is being managed effectively. Too little working capital and the company may not be able to pay all its debts. Too much and it may not be making the most efficient use of its financial resources.

Current ratio (also known as the liquidity ratio)

This ratio looks at the relationship between current assets and current liabilities. It examines the **liquidity** position of the firm. It is given by the formula:

$$\text{Current ratio} = \frac{\text{Current assets}}{\text{Current liabilities}}$$

This is expressed as a ratio such as, for example, 2:1 or 3:1.

Example

Bannam Ltd has current assets of £30,000 and current liabilities of £10,000:

Current ratio = Current assets : Current liabilities
= £30,000 : £10,000
= 3 : 1
current ratio = 3

Interpretation

The above worked example shows that Bannam Ltd has three times as many current assets as current liabilities. This means that, for every £1 of short-term debts owed, it has £3 of assets to pay them. This is a comfortable position.

Table 57.6 The current ratios of a selection of public companies in 2010

Company	Balance sheet date	Current assets	Current liabilities	Current ratio
Ted Baker plc	31/01/2010	£67,400,000	£28,600,000	2.37
Burberry plc	31/03/2010	£767,000,000	£501,800,000	1.53
Honda Motor	31/03/2010	$49,600,000,000	$36,700,000,000	1.35
Tesco plc	27/02/2010	£11,765,000,000	£16,015,000,000	0.73
JD Wetherspoon	30/07/2010	£65,719,000	£176,883,000	0.37

Accountants suggest the 'ideal' current ratio should be approximately 1.5:1 (that is, £1.50 of assets for every £1 of debt). Any higher than this and the organisation has too many resources tied up in unproductive assets; these could be invested more profitably (or the cash should be handed back to shareholders). A low current ratio means a business may not be able to pay its debts. It is possible that the result may well be something like 0.8:1. This shows the firm has only 80p of current assets to pay every £1 it owes.

The current ratios of a selection of public companies in 2010 are shown in Table 57.6. As this table shows, it would be wrong to panic about a liquidity ratio of less than 1. Very successful firms such as Tesco have often had spells when their liquidity levels were less than 1.

Altering the ratio

If the ratio is so low that it is becoming hard to pay the bills, the company will have to try to bring more cash into the balance sheet. This could be done by:

- selling under-used fixed assets
- raising more share capital
- increasing long-term borrowings
- postponing planned investments.

Acid test ratio

This ratio is sometimes also called the quick ratio or even the liquid ratio. It examines the business's liquidity position by comparing current assets and liabilities, but it omits stock (or inventories) from the total of current assets. The reason for this is that stock is the most illiquid current asset (that is, it is the hardest to turn into cash without a loss in its value). It can take a long time to convert stock into cash. Furthermore, stock may be old or obsolete and thus unsellable.

By omitting stock, the ratio directly relates cash and near cash (cash, bank and debtors – known as liquid assets) to short-term debts. This provides a tighter measure of a firm's liquidity. It is given by the formula:

$$\text{Acid test ratio} = \frac{(\text{Current assets} - \text{Stock})}{\text{Current liabilities}}$$

Again, it is expressed in the form of a ratio, such as 2:1.

Interpretation

Accountants recommend that an 'ideal' result for this ratio should be approximately 1:1, thus showing that the organisation has £1 of short-term assets for every £1 of short-term debt. A result below this (for example, 0.5:1) indicates that the firm may have difficulties meeting short-term payments. However, some businesses are able to operate with a very low level of liquidity – supermarkets, for example, who have much of their current assets tied up in stock.

The acid test ratios of a selection of public companies in 2010 are shown in Table 57.7.

57.7 GEARING

Gearing is one of the main measures of the financial health of a business. Quite simply, it measures the firm's level of debt. This shines a light onto the long-term financial stability of an organisation.

Gearing measures long-term loans as a proportion of a firm's capital employed. It shows how reliant the firm is upon borrowed money. In turn, that indicates how vulnerable the firm is to financial setbacks. The Americans call gearing 'leverage'. In boom times, banks and investors find leverage (debt) very attractive; but high gearing always means high risk.

Table 57.7 The acid test ratios of a selection of public companies in 2010

Company	Balance sheet date	Current assets – stock (inventories)	Current liabilities	Current ratio
Ted Baker plc	31/01/2010	£33,937,000	£28,600,000	1.19
Burberry plc	31/03/2010	£600,100,000	£501,800,000	1.19
Honda Motor	31/03/2010	$39,533,000,000	$36,700,000,000	1.08
Tesco plc	27/02/2010	£9,036,000,000	£16,015,000,000	0.56
JD Wetherspoon	30/07/2010	£41,065,000	£176,883,000	0.23

Table 57.8 The gearing ratios of a selection of companies in 2010

Company	Balance sheet date	Non-current liabilities (long-term loans)	Capital employed	Gearing (%)
Ted Baker plc	31/01/2010	£1,300,000	£67,500,000	1.9
Burberry plc	31/03/2010	£34,300,000	£637,800,000	5.4
Honda Motor	31/03/2010	$40,343,000,000	$88,241,000,000	45.7
Tesco plc	27/02/2010	£15,327,000,000	£30,008,000,000	51.1
JD Wetherspoon	30/07/2010	£571,700,000	£733,800,000	77.9

Highly geared companies can suffer badly in recessions, because even when times are hard they still have to keep paying high interest payments to the bank.

The formula for gearing is:

$$\text{Gearing} = \frac{\text{Long-term loans}}{\text{Capital employed}} \times 100$$

This is expressed as a percentage.

Interpretation

The gearing ratio shows how risky an investment a company is. If loans represent more than 50 per cent of capital employed, the company is said to be highly geared. Such a company has to pay substantial interest charges on its borrowings before it can pay dividends to shareholders or retain profits for reinvestment. The higher the gearing, the higher the degree of risk. Low-geared companies provide a lower-risk investment; therefore they can negotiate loans more easily and at lower cost than a highly geared company. Banks would be especially reluctant to lend to a firm with poor liquidity and high gearing. It is useful, therefore, to look at the gearing for the same firms whose liquidity was investigated earlier. This is shown in Table 57.8.

> **A-grade application**
>
> **Carlyle Capital Corporation**
>
> During the Credit Crunch a US blogger with the fabulous name of Postman Patel warned that the Carlyle Capital Corporation (an American investment fund) was unable to pay its bills. Within a week it had collapsed, owing over $16 billion. It emerged that Carlyle Capital had a gearing level of 97 per cent. In other words, only 3 per cent of the money it invested was its own money; all the rest was borrowed. When times were good its shares were worth $20 each. Now they were worth nothing. High gearing means high risk. Ridiculously high gearing means ridiculously high risk.

JD Wetherspoon (a chain of low-priced pubs) has a high gearing level. The company could experience difficulties if interest rates rose, or if it encountered a really poor period of trading. However, if its markets have growth potential, the company probably has the resources to benefit from it.

In contrast, Burberry, and especially Ted Baker, have very low gearing levels. This could be a weakness if the economy was expanding rapidly. Their management teams could be judged as timid as the companies are not in a position to benefit from rapid growth. An investment in a firm with a low gearing could be regarded as safe, but dull.

Altering the ratio

The gearing ratio can be altered in several ways, depending on whether the organisation wishes to raise or lower its gearing figure. Ways in which an organisation's gearing figure may be altered are shown in Table 57.9.

Table 57.9 Altering an organisation's gearing ratio

Raising gearing	Reducing gearing
Buy back ordinary shares	Issue more ordinary shares
Issue more preference shares	Buy back debentures (redeeming)
Issue more debentures	Retain more profits
Obtain more loans	Repay loans

57.8 SHAREHOLDER RATIOS

Investing in shares provides two potential sources of financial return. The share price may rise, providing a capital gain. In addition, firms pay annual dividends to shareholders. The size of the dividends depends upon the level of profits made in the year. Shareholder ratios provide a way of judging whether the shares are expensive or inexpensive, and whether the dividends are high enough. They do, however, put some pressure on companies to achieve short-term profits and to pay out high dividends. This may damage the interests of the company's stakeholders in the long term.

Earnings per share (EPS)

This ratio measures the company's **earnings** (profit after tax) divided by the number of ordinary shares it has issued. This can be used to measure a company's

3 The balance sheet for GrowMax Co as at 31 December is shown in Figure 57.3.

	£000
Fixed assets	860
Stock	85
Debtors	180
Cash	15
Current liabilities	200
Loans	360
Share capital	160
Reserves	420

Figure 57.3 Balance sheet for GrowMax Co as at 31 December

a) Calculate the firm's net current assets and capital employed. (4)

b) Last year's revenue was £1,460,000 and operating margin was 10 per cent. Comment on the firm's profitability. (7)

c) GrowMax's main rival offers its customers 30 days' credit.

  i) How does this compare with GrowMax? (4)

  ii) Outline two further questions the GrowMax management should want answered before deciding whether their customer credit policy should be revised. (6)

d) Outline three difficulties with drawing firm conclusions from comparisons between the ratios of two rival companies. (9)

B2 DATA RESPONSE

Phones4 Kids

Since the beginning of the year, Phones4Kids has enjoyed rapid growth as a result of booming exports to America. Financing the increased production has required an extra £80,000 of working capital, and now the production manager has put in an urgent request for £240,000 of new capital investment.

The firm's managing director doubts that he can find the extra capital without giving up control of the business (he currently holds 54 per cent of the shares). The finance director is more optimistic. He suggests that: 'Our balance sheet is in pretty good shape and the mobile phone business is booming. I'm confident we can get and afford a loan.' So it came as a huge blow to hear that Barclays had turned the company down. It wondered what it had done wrong ...

Phones4Kids balance sheet as at 31 December

	£000	£000
Fixed assets[1]	420	420
Inventories	250	
Debtors[2]	140	
Cash	130	520
Current liabilities		(380)
Non-current liabilities		(200)
Net assets		360
Share capital	50	
Reserves	310	
Total equity		360

1 Depreciated straight line over 10 years

2 Including a £15,000 debtors item 12 months overdue

Figure 57.4 Balance sheet for Phones4Kids as at 31 December

Questions

(35 marks; 40 minutes)

1 Analyse why the bank manager might have turned the request down. (10)

2 Recommend how the expansion could be financed, showing the effect of your plan upon key indicators of the firm's financial health. (10)

3 Given your answers to 1 and 2, discuss whether the firm should proceed with its expansion plan. (15)

B3 DATA RESPONSE

The Whitbread Group plc operates a range of brands in the hospitality industry. The company has interests in hotels, restaurants and coffee bars, including Premier Inn and Costa Coffee. Whitbread is listed on the London Stock Exchange and is a part of the FTSE 100 Index. The company was founded as a brewery in 1742 but no longer has any interests in brewing.

Source: adapted from Whitbread plc Interim Report 2010

Whitbread plc: Extract from 2010 Interim (half year) Report and Accounts
Summary Consolidated Income Statement

	2010	2009
	£m	£m
Revenue	805.4	703.3
Gross profit	685.0	598.5
Expenses	(516.6)	(471.4)
Operating profit	168.4	127.1
Finance revenue	2.1	0.2
Finance costs	(19.5)	(21.3)
Profit before tax	151.0	106.0

Balance sheet, 2 September 2010

	2010	2009
	£m	£m
Non-current assets	2,512	2,468
Inventories (stocks)	20	17
Trade & other receivables	98	86
Cash & cash equivalents	35	29
Current liabilities	(340)	(355)
Non-current liabilities	(1,201)	(1,201)
Net assets	1,124	1,044
Share capital	196	192
Reserves	928	852
Total equity	1,124	1,044

Figure 57.5 Summary published accounts for Whitbread plc

Questions

(50 marks; 60 minutes)

1 State Whitbread plc's working capital in 2009 and 2010. (4)

2 Calculate Whitbread plc's:
   a) 2010 cost of sales (2)
   b) 2009 and 2010 gearing. (4)

3 a) Assess the company's profitability in 2010 compared with 2009. (10)
   b) What further information would be needed in order to make a full assessment of the effectiveness of the company's management at generating profit in 2010? (4)

4 a) What are Whitbread plc's current ratios for 2009 and 2010? (4)
   b) Briefly analyse the possible implications of these figures for the managers of the business. (6)

5 A major insurance company is considering buying a large number of shares in Whitbread plc as part of its investment portfolio. Assess the strengths and weaknesses for outsiders of using this company's accounts to decide on such a major decision. (16)

C ESSAY QUESTIONS

(40 marks each)

1 'Ratios are of little to no use to a person intending to make a small investment.' Comment on the accuracy of this statement.

2 'The ability to assess the long- and short-term financial stability of an organisation is vital to every stakeholder.' To what extent do you agree with this statement?

3 With the economy entering a recession, an investor wants to reassess her share portfolio. Examine which ratios she should focus upon, given the economic circumstances.

a key indicator of success. However, it is also worth checking the source of this profit in order to assess the likelihood of such profits continuing into the future. Selling off a piece of machinery at a price above its book value will generate a surplus, but this can only happen once and is, therefore, described as being of low **profit quality**. It is important that a firm's accounts separate 'one-off' low-quality profit from the high-quality profit that results from its normal trading activities.

58.4 MANIPULATING THE PUBLISHED ACCOUNTS

There are a number of reasons why a business may decide to manipulate its accounts in order to flatter its financial position at a particular point in time. Such practices, known as **window dressing** or creative accounting, do not necessarily mean that fraud has been committed, but may nevertheless result in the users of accounts being misled. There are a number of reasons why a firm might window dress its accounts; creating the impression that a business is financially stronger than it actually is can help to secure loans or support the sale of new shares. Common methods of window dressing include the following.

- *Sale and leaseback of fixed assets:* this allows a business to continue to use assets but disguise a poor or deteriorating liquidity position by generating a sudden injection of cash
- *Bringing forward sales:* a sale is recognised (and included in profit calculations) when an order is made, rather than when payment is received. Encouraging customers to place orders earlier than usual will mean that they are included at the end of one financial period rather than at the start of the next, giving an apparent boost to revenue and profit.
- *A change in approach to depreciation:* for example, increasing the expected life of a fixed asset will reduce the annual depreciation charge, increasing the level of reported profit as well as increasing the asset value on the balance sheet. Presenting a more favourable set of accounts may attract more investment or help fight off a hostile takeover bid.
- *Writing off bad debts:* the decision to treat a customer's unpaid bill as a bad debt will mean that the figure has to be charged to the profit and loss account as an expense. This will reduce the firm's net profit figure, reducing the level of corporation tax paid.

The Companies Act 1985 places a legal obligation on companies to provide accounts that are audited and give a true and fair view of their financial position. In addition, the Accounting Standards Board has the responsibility of providing a regulatory framework in order to create greater uniformity in the way company accounts are drawn up. Despite this, the pressure on businesses to not only perform well but to be seen to do so is likely to mean that window dressing practices will persist.

ISSUES FOR ANALYSIS

Opportunities for analysis are likely to focus on the following areas:

- the problems of relying on financial data to analyse a firm's financial position and performance
- the difficulties of trying to get an accurate measure of the value of a business
- the consequences of failing to provide an accurate value of a business
- the reasons why a firm might attempt to window dress its financial position.

58.5 LIMITATIONS OF ACCOUNTS – AN EVALUATION

Accounting information plays a key role in assessing the value and performance of a business. However, using such information alone, and failing to consider other relevant factors, will give an incomplete picture of a firm's current position and future potential. The quality of the workforce, investment in new technology and the state of the market in which it operates may be difficult to quantify but may be more accurate indicators of a firm's long-term success than an impressive set of final accounts.

Key Terms

Bad debts: when a firm decides that amounts outstanding as a result of credit sales are unlikely to be recovered, perhaps because the customer concerned has gone into liquidation.

Going concern: the accounting assumption that, in the absence of any evidence to the contrary, a business will continue to operate for the foreseeable future.

Goodwill: arises when a business is sold and the buyer pays more than its book value in recognition of the good reputation and customer base that is being obtained. This amount is shown as an intangible asset on the firm's balance sheet.

Intangible assets: these are assets that have no physical existence, such as plant and machinery, but contribute to sales and profits. Examples include patents, copyright, brand names and goodwill.

Net realisable value: this is the value given to an asset (usually stock) on the balance sheet if it is expected to be sold for less than its historic cost.

Profit quality: this assesses the likelihood of the source of the profit made by a business continuing in the future. High-quality profit is usually that which is generated by a firm's usual trading activities, whereas low-quality profit comes from a one-off source.

Window dressing: the practice of presenting a firm's accounts in a way that flatters its financial position (for example, selling and leasing back assets in order to generate cash and disguise a poor liquidity position).

WORKBOOK

A REVISION QUESTIONS

(35 marks; 35 minutes)

1 What is meant by the phrase 'a true and fair view' in the context of accounting? (3)
2 Identify three aspects of a business that may increase its value but are unlikely to be included in its accounts. (3)
3 Describe two problems that a firm could experience from understating the value of land or property that it may own. (6)
4 Analyse one reason for and one reason against attempting to include a value for a firm's intangible assets on its balance sheet. (6)
5 Explain the difference between a debtor and a bad debt. (4)
6 What is meant by the term 'window dressing'? (3)
7 Describe two reasons why a firm may window dress its accounts. (4)
8 Outline three ways in which a business could attempt to window dress its accounts. (6)

B REVISION EXERCISES

B1 DATA RESPONSE

Valuing global brands

Diageo is the world's leading producer of alcoholic drinks. Its portfolio includes a number of market-leading brands, including Guinness, Baileys, Smirnoff vodka, Johnnie Walker whisky and Tanqueray gin. Diageo's global sales (net of excise duty) for the year to the end of June 2010 increased from just over £9.3 billion to nearly £9.8 billion. The company's operating profits for the same period amounted to over £2.57 billion, up from nearly £2.42 million in 2009.

Like other breweries, Diageo faced a number of challenges during the year, including continuing recession in many economies and significant increases in the price of wheat and barley. However, according to Diageo's chief executive, Paul Walsh, the global diversity of the business and the strength and range of its brands would allow the company to continue to grow its operating profit. The firm experienced particularly strong growth in Asia, Latin America where it has a large Scotch business, and Africa where brands such as Tusker beer and Guinness are popular. Sales continued to grow in these markets throughout the global downturn and were responsible for around one third of the company's annual earnings. Diageo is also building up a market in China, with brands such as Johnnie Walker. Extracts from Diageo's accounts are shown in Tables 58.2 and 58.3. Diageo's global priority brands are shown in Table 58.4.

Table 58.2 Extracts from Diageo's income statements 2008–10 (for year ended 30 June)

	Year ending 30/06/2010 £ million	Year ending 30/06/2009 £ million	Year ending 30/06/2008 £ million
Net sales	9,780	9,311	8,090
Gross profit	5,681	5,418	4,836
Operating profit	2,574	2,418	2,212

Table 58.3 Extracts from Diageo's balance sheets 2008–10 (for year ended 30 June)

	30/06/2010 £ million	30/06/2009 £ million	30/06/2008 £ million
Non-current assets	12,502	11,951	10,471
Current assets	6,952	6,067	5,521
Current liabilities	3,944	3,986	4,707
Non- current liabilities	10,724	10,158	7,152
Total equity	4,786	3,874	4,133

be paid back. The level of finance available from this source depends on the performance of the business and the rate of dividends expected by the firm's owners. Around 60 per cent of all long-term capital comes from this source (which is also sometimes known as ploughed-back profits).

Sale of assets

Established firms own fixed assets, such as premises and machinery, which have been purchased to be used as part of its operations. Ideally, a firm can use redundant assets to do this (that is, those that are no longer required as part of the production process). It may be possible to raise finance using assets that are still required, via **sale and leaseback**, by paying rent or a fee to the new owner.

Managing working capital more effectively

Established firms may grow complacent when it comes to managing **working capital**. Stocks may begin to build up and outstanding customer invoices may go unnoticed. Squeezing working capital (that is, managing it more effectively) can create more finance for a firm's day-to-day activities, easing pressure on cash-flow. This could involve running down stocks or chasing up debtors. Relationships developed with suppliers over time may also mean that longer credit periods can be negotiated.

> **A-grade application**
>
> **Innocent sells out to Coca-Cola**
>
> Global soft drinks giant, Coca-Cola, acquired a controlling stake of Innocent Drinks in April 2010, after investing an estimated £75 million in the company. The David and Goliath relationship between the two companies began in 2009 when Coca-Cola bought an 18 per cent share of Innocent for £30 million. At the time, Innocent co-founder Richard Reed, refused to confirm or deny whether future funds would be forthcoming, saying 'nothing is definite in the future but of course both sides hope the relationship will prosper'. The 2010 deal resulted largely from the disposal of shares by one of Innocent's original business angel investors. Reed claimed that Coca-Cola would continue to remain a passive investor but support Innocent's objective of further international expansion by helping with issues such as distribution in new markets, including Sweden. According to Reed, 'We remain in full operational control of the business and we should be able to proceed towards our goal of taking Innocent to every country in the world.'
>
> Source: various newspaper reports.

59.3 FINANCE: IS IT ADEQUATE?

Adequate finance means having access to sufficient levels of funding to meet the firm's needs, as and when they occur. Established firms will need to pay workers, suppliers and other expenses on time, regardless of whether enough cash has been generated from sales to cover such expenses. They will also need to replace equipment and machinery when it wears out or becomes obsolete. Few businesses are faced with totally predictable demand. Therefore, adequate resources (including finance) should be available to respond successfully to an unexpected upsurge in orders, as well as allowing a firm to cope with an unexpected fall in sales.

Ensuring access to adequate funding is equally important for those firms looking to expand. Not only will such firms require capital for the purchase of new assets, but also to cover additional working capital requirements in the form of increased materials, wages and fuel. **Overtrading** refers to the situation where a business expands at a rate that cannot be sustained by its capital base. A sudden surge in orders may tempt firms to buy additional stocks on credit. However, a significant gap between having to pay for these stocks and receiving payment from customers could lead to liquidity problems. Inadequate funding is one of the most common reasons why apparently successful businesses with rapidly growing sales end up failing.

59.4 FINANCE: IS IT APPROPRIATE?

Appropriate finance means ensuring that the type of finance matches its intended use. An overdraft may provide a much-needed bridge between having to pay suppliers one month and being paid by customers the next. Yet it would be an expensive method of borrowing to finance asset purchase, unless it could be repaid quickly. Some examples of short- and long-term finance are given in Table 59.1. There are a number of factors that will determine the most appropriate source(s) of finance for established businesses to use in any given situation. These include those set out below.

Factors that determine sources of finance

The type of business

Expanding businesses may decide to become limited companies in order to raise finance more easily and offer owners the protection of limited liability. However, private limited companies may still struggle to find sufficient shareholders, as its shares are not openly available to the general public. Therefore the business may seek a public flotation on the stock market, opening up the possibility of ownership being spread widely among the public, as with a business such as Marks & Spencer plc, which has 250,000 different shareholders.

The level of success enjoyed by the business

It is often said that 'success breeds success', and this is usually the case with finance. Highly profitable firms are able to generate internal finance but are also likely to attract outside investors and creditors. Firms with low or falling profits may struggle to raise the finance needed to improve performance because they are seen as too risky. A well-worn business phrase is that 'banks don't deal with people who need them'.

The use of funds

A business looking to raise finance for working capital would normally use short-term finance (that is, repaid within one year). On the other hand, capital expenditure on an expensive piece of machinery used within the business for a number of years is likely to require long-term finance (that is, that required for much longer periods, usually over five years).

The attitude of the owners /shareholders of the business

There are a number of reasons why the owners of a business may have an influence on the choice of finance. Some may prefer not to use loan finance, because of the risk of not being able to meet repayments on time. Others may avoid bringing in new shareholders or involving venture capitalists, in order to prevent their control of the business from being diluted (watered down). There may also be a conflict of interest between shareholders, who view profit as a source of dividend income, and managers, who would prefer to pay lower dividends in order to retain profits to finance expansion.

The state of the economy

Firms may be reluctant to borrow when economic conditions are deteriorating and sales are predicted to fall. A more buoyant economy may increase business confidence and encourage firms to take greater risks.

Table 59.1 Short-term versus long-term finance: some examples

	Short term	Long term
Internal	Squeezing working capital: • cut stocks (inventories) • cut debtors • delay payments to creditors	Sell underutilised fixed assets Sale (and leaseback) of assets Retained profit
External	Trade credit Debt factoring Overdrafts	Bank loans Share (rights) issue Venture capital

A-grade application

The lack of availability of credit and the tightening of lending terms during the 2008–09 recession has forced UK firms to rethink their attitude to finance, according to the Confederation of British Industry (CBI). In a report entitled 'The Shape of Business – The Next Ten Years', published in November 2009, the CBI claims that the credit crunch will create a new economic landscape where businesses are forced to cut their previous reliance on bank lending and reduce their exposure to risk. The report was based on a survey of business leaders, who together represent a UK workforce of nearly 1 million people with a global turnover of around £1 trillion.

Commenting on the report, the CBI's Director General, Richard Lambert said, 'There are important questions around how businesses are going to finance growth and investment in the future ... closer relationships with customers, suppliers, employees and shareholders look like becoming the norm.' He also suggested that the Government should reduce the cost of raising equity for smaller firms by letting them offset the costs of doing so against tax.

Over half (55 per cent) of the businesses taking part in the survey said that their ability to obtain bank finance had declined during the recession. Nearly 70 per cent felt the situation would not improve in 2010 and would be reshaping their business financing as a result. For example, 50 per cent said that they would use less bank debt and 44 per cent said that they would rely more on equity finance.

More than half of the businesses contacted said that they would now tolerate a lower level of risk in their levels of gearing, with 70 per cent saying that their attitude was unlikely to change despite economic recovery.

Source: based on nebusiness.co.uk

59.5 ALLOCATING CAPITAL EXPENDITURE

Capital expenditure refers to money spent by a firm in order to support its long-term operations. The purchase of fixed assets, such as premises and machinery, is clearly an example of capital expenditure, as they are bought with the intention of using them over a number of years. Funds used to take over other businesses can also be regarded as capital expenditure, even if the assets acquired are subsequently sold off. It could be argued that firms should also regard spending on research and development as an item of capital expenditure, given that it is likely to provide benefits over a lengthy period of time.

The first issue to consider with capital expenditure is the amount needed to maintain a firm's operations in a healthy, efficient state. For example, Network Rail allocates about £2.5 billion a year to maintaining Britain's railway system. This includes replacing ageing trains with new ones, updating tired stations, and so forth. This expenditure can be regarded as essential.

Without it, the business will start to go downhill. To switch examples, in 2010 the average age of British Airways' aircraft was ten years; contrast that with Singapore Airlines, which has an objective of having a fleet with an average age of three years.

Once enough capital is allocated to maintaining a healthy business, the key financial decision is how much to allocate to growth. During the 1990s, McDonald's poured billions of dollars into opening up more stores worldwide. Only in 2004–05, when profits started to sag, did the business switch from quantity to quality. This change of strategy helped in the recent recession. By 2010 McDonalds was enjoying record profits, while rival Burger King was struggling.

Any business, regardless of size, will have more potential uses of funds than the amount of finance available, so the allocation of capital expenditure will depend on corporate objectives and market conditions.

59.6 IMPLEMENTING PROFIT CENTRES IN A BUSINESS

Profit centres are distinct sections within a business that can be regarded as self-contained, and therefore measured for their own profitability. In effect, a profit centre becomes a firm within a firm, which can help to motivate the relatively small number of staff within the section. It is hard to feel important as one person among 450,000 other Tesco staff; but one person among 16 at an individual store can see the impact of their efforts.

The basis for establishing profit centres is very much dependent on the individual circumstances of the firm in question and may be based on:

- a person: individual employees within a business may be responsible for generating revenues and incurring costs
- a product: a multi-product business may be able to distinguish the separate revenues earned and costs incurred by individual product lines
- a department: areas within a business that perform certain functions may generate both costs and revenues
- a location: a business, such as a bank or retailer that is spread geographically, may choose to use each branch or division as a profit centre.

Establishing profit centres can provide valuable information to a business to help it enhance its financial performance, perhaps enabling it to identify unprofitable areas that may need to be closed down. The responsibility delegated to managers of individual profit centres may also inject a degree of motivation. However, there are a number of potential problems in attempting to implement profit centres. For example, it may prove difficult to choose an accurate method of allocating a firm's overheads to each profit centre. It may also lead to a situation where individual profit centres compete against each other, to the detriment of the business as a whole. See Table 59.2.

59.7 COST MINIMISATION

One way that firms can achieve a competitive advantage over their rivals is by pursuing a strategy of cost minimisation. Firms operating in fiercely competitive markets may have little control over the prices they charge but can still make acceptable profits by pushing down unit costs as low as possible. In theory, cost minimisation is straightforward enough. For example, firms may be tempted to switch to the cheapest supplier or cut out staff training in order to offer the lowest prices possible. However, this is likely to lead to a loss of competitiveness in the longer term, as poor-quality and poorly trained employees result in customer dissatisfaction.

The key to implementing this strategy successfully is to charge prices that are close to, but below, the market average, to avoid arousing customer suspicions, and reduce average costs without compromising operations. Lower unit costs can be generated by producing standardised products in large volumes, in order to benefit from economies of scale, and finding ways of keeping overheads as low as possible. Examples of businesses that have been particularly successful at pursuing cost-minimisation strategies include Aldi, Ryanair, AirAsia and Primark. Focusing on price alone can lead to problems, however, if an even lower-cost competitor enters the market.

Table 59.2 Advantages and disadvantages of profit centres

Advantages of profit centres	Disadvantages of profit centres
• The success – or otherwise – of individual areas of the business can be identified more easily • The delegation of control over local operations may increase motivation • Decision making will be localised, making it quicker and better suited to local conditions • When they work well, they are a perfect antidote to big-business bureaucracy that results in diseconomies of scale	• Not all of the costs or revenues of a business can easily be associated with specific areas of operation • Areas of the business may end up competing against each other, damaging overall performance • The good or bad performance of one profit centre may be the result of external changes beyond its control (cutting the link between the performance of the group members and the results of the group activities)

A-grade application

Ryanair: a model of cost minimisation

The establishment of Ryanair as Europe's leading low-fares scheduled passenger airline has been the result of a strategy of cost minimisation adopted in the early 1990s, following the appointment of chief executive Michael O'Leary. By targeting price-conscious leisure and business passengers, the airline has experienced phenomenal growth – from under a quarter of a million passengers in 1990 to over 67 million in the 12 months to April 2010. The company's success has largely been the result of its ability to contain costs and achieve a number of operational efficiencies, without compromising customer service. These have included the following.

Figure 59.1 Ryanair

- *Frequent short-haul flights:* eliminating the need to provide passengers with 'frills' services, such as complimentary meals and drinks, which add to variable costs.
- *Using the internet for flight reservations:* the airline's system was upgraded in 2009 and accounted for over 97 per cent of flight bookings in 2010, helping to keep labour costs down.
- *Favouring secondary routes:* for example, flying to Girona rather than Barcelona in Spain. These less-congested destinations mean faster turnaround times, fewer terminal delays and lower handling costs.
- *Minimising aircraft costs:* initially, this was achieved by the purchase of second-hand aeroplanes of a single type; however, in response to a recent shortage of such aircraft, the company has resorted to purchasing from a single supplier in order to limit training and maintenance costs, as well as the purchase and storage of spare parts.
- *Personnel productivity:* Ryanair controls its labour costs by paying highly competitive salaries to pilots and cabin crew but demanding much higher productivity levels than its competitors.

Source: Ryanair

ISSUES FOR ANALYSIS

Opportunities for analysis are likely to focus on the following areas.

- The benefits and drawbacks of using different forms of finance in different circumstances (for example, seeing that there are costs and risks involved in using an overdraft to finance long-term commitments).
- The need to think about financial strategy in relation to the overall strategy; for example, if the business has a bold, quite risky, marketing strategy (based, perhaps, on new product launches into short product life cycle markets) it is wise to have a cautious financial strategy (for example, low gearing and high liquidity); this is the approach taken by firms such as Nintendo and L'Oréal.
- The advantages and disadvantages of adopting cost minimisation as a financial strategy and seeing its essentially close links with marketing, operational and personnel strategies. This is shown effectively in the A-grade application on Ryanair.

59.8 FINANCIAL STRATEGIES AND ACCOUNTS – AN EVALUATION

Choosing an appropriate financial strategy is crucial to an organisation's continuing success, regardless of its size or its objectives. A business may need to raise finance for a variety of reasons; this finance will need to be both adequate and appropriate to its needs in order to be effective. Financial strategy is also very much concerned with how funds are used to support the development of the business. This involves making choices as to how expenditure is to be allocated between competing capital projects and controlling ongoing costs in order to ensure the firm's long-term financial health.

The most important judgements, though, are about getting the right balance between risk and safety. The 2008 collapse of Lehman Brothers was due to a faulty (foolish, even) financial strategy. Yet if managers are too cautious, they are likely to find their business left behind as rivals sweep past them. Greed is never good, but neither is it right to be too careful. Good chief executives find a way to be bold but sensible.

Key Terms

Capital expenditure: spending on fixed assets (for example, premises and machinery).

External sources of finance: funds generated from sources outside an organisation (for example, bank loans, venture capital).

Factoring: passing a copy of a customer invoice to your bank, which then credits you with 80 per cent of the invoiced sum within 24 hours, then collects the debt for you (for a fee of perhaps 4 per cent).

Internal sources of finance: funds generated from an organisation's own resources (for example, retained profit, sale of assets).

Overtrading: this refers to the liquidity problems experienced by a firm that expands without securing the finance required to support it; for example, to bridge the gap between paying suppliers and receiving payment from customers.

Profit centre: a part of a business for which a separate profit and loss account can be drawn up.

Retained profit: profit left over after all the deductions (and additions) have been made to sales revenue, including cost of sales, overheads, tax and dividends.

Rights issue: giving existing shareholders the right to buy extra shares in the business before allowing outsiders that right to buy; a rights issue usually offers the shares at a discount to the existing market price. It is likely to be cheaper to raise finance by this method than a full public issue.

Sale and leaseback: a method of raising finance by selling an asset but paying to continue to use it.

Working capital: the day-to-day finances needed to run a business – generally seen as the difference between the value of a firm's current assets and its current liabilities.

WORKBOOK

A REVISION QUESTIONS

(45 marks; 45 minutes)

1. State two reasons why an established firm may wish to raise finance. (2)
2. Describe two influences on a firm's choice of finance. (4)
3. Outline two ways in which a firm could raise finance to buy the additional stock needed to meet an unexpected order. (4)
4. Analyse two appropriate sources of finance available to a private limited company that is looking to set up a production facility in Poland. (6)
5. Use numerical examples to explain how a firm's gearing and liquidity position would affect its choice of finance. (6)
6. Explain why a rapidly expanding firm could suffer from overtrading. (4)
7. Using examples, briefly explain the difference between capital expenditure for maintenance and capital expenditure for growth. (4)
8. Explain what is meant by the term 'profit centre'. (3)
9. Analyse one benefit and one drawback for coffee retailer Starbucks from choosing to operate its outlets as individual profit centres. (6)
10. Examine one advantage and one disadvantage for a company such as Ryanair of adopting a strategy of cost minimisation. (6)

B REVISION EXERCISES

B1 DATA RESPONSE

Financing growth at Mulberry

British handbag and leatherware designer and manufacturer, Mulberry, recorded its seventh consecutive year of sales growth in the 12 months to 31 March 2010. Despite trading in conditions that could hardly be described as supportive for luxury brands, Mulberry's revenue increased by 23 per cent to £72.1 million from £58.6 million in 2008–09. The company's pre-tax profits for the period were £5.1 million, up from £4.2 million in the previous year.

Mulberry sells its products worldwide. In 2010, the company had 39 of its own 'full price' shops and department store concessions, as well as selling online via a recently redesigned website. Within the first ten weeks of the financial year beginning April 2010, like for like sales in shops and department stores had risen by 44 per cent, with internet sales up by 99 per cent.

The company's strong organic growth resulted of a significant rise in international sales, as well as increasing demand in the UK. The company's chairman confirmed that, 'A key objective of the management team has been the continued development of our business internationally. In particular, our business in Asia is growing rapidly ... It is clear that our best selling products in our home market have equal appeal internationally.' (See Table 59.3.)

The company intends to continue to finance its expansion

in the UK and across the world from internal sources. According to Mulberry's Chairman, 'These capital projects will absorb a significant amount of cash, as will the increased inventory that will be needed to meet the forecast demand for our products. We expect to be able to fund these investments from our existing cash resources and future cash flows'. (See Table 59.4.)

Table 59.3 Planned new stores for Mulberry: 2010–11

Own stores
• Relocation of New Bond Street store (London) • Relocation of Manchester store to new Spinningfields mall • New flagship store – New York
International partner stores
• Incheon Airport – South Korea • Mall of the Emirates – Dubai • Sydney – Australia • Times Square – Hong Kong • Kuala Lumpur – Malaysia • Qatar

Source: www.mulberry.com

Table 59.4 Summary of Mulberry's results for the year ended 31 March 2010

£000s	2009–10	2008–09
Fixed assets and investments	10,760	11,694
Stock	9,090	14,830
Other working capital	(5,556)	(5,850)
Cash	12,171	3,710
Shareholders' funds	26,465	24,384

Questions

(40 marks; 45 minutes)

1 Calculate the percentage change in Mulberry's profits between 2008–09 and 2009–10. (4)
2 Discuss the suitability of Mulberry's choice of finance for the continued expansion of the company. (18)
3 To what extent do you believe that an effective financial strategy is vital for companies like Mulberry in order to survive and develop in the long term? (18)

B2 DATA RESPONSE

Cost minimisation means success at Aldi

Privately owned German retailer Aldi opened its UK first store in 1990. The opening of the company's store in Exeter in April 2009 took its total number of supermarkets to 467, with a target of 500 by the end of the year. Although its share of the fiercely competitive UK grocery market was just over 3 per cent at the end of 2009, its reputation as a quality discounter has led to a steady growth in popularity, particularly among the country's affluent middle-class. Indeed, this success led to supermarket giant Tesco launching a range of 300 'no frills' products, as well as a March 2008 claim to match Aldi's prices on over 2,000 items.

According to Aldi, its success is down to its 'less is more' approach to retailing, with all decisions aimed at guaranteeing a 'low-cost shop' for its customers. Aldi's operations are designed around the key objective of minimising costs without compromising quality. This objective is achieved in a number of ways, as described below.

- Offering customers a limited range of its most frequently purchased own brand grocery and household products, rather than branded goods, allows the retailer to buy in bulk from suppliers. Only 1,000 products are stocked within its supermarkets, with hardly any duplication of lines, in order to remove the additional costs related to buying, supplying and product development. Many of these suppliers are well-known food manufacturers who are prepared to sell to Aldi at lower prices because of the large volumes involved. (Although Aldi is small in Britain, it is huge in Germany and across Europe with around 7,500 stores.)

- Aldi has a no-frills in-store approach, where products are often sold straight from boxes rather than shelves and staff levels are kept to a minimum; this keeps overheads down. Music is not played in store to avoid the cost of having to purchase music licences. Customers have to pay for carrier bags and the use of a shopping trolley requires a £1 deposit, to encourage its return.
- One of the key reasons for Aldi's growth in popularity is its ability to combine low prices with standards of product quality that match those of leading brands. Despite its low prices, Aldi insists that it does not compromise when it comes to quality. The retailer has received a number of quality related awards in recent years, including 'Which?' 'Best Supermarket', as well as 'The Grocer's Grocer of the Year' and 'Discounter of the Year' in June 2009.

Source: Aldi

Questions

(30 marks; 35 minutes)

1 Analyse the main ways in which Aldi's operations are successful in minimising costs. (10)

2 To what extent do you believe that Aldi's financial strategy of cost minimisation will help it to further increase its share of the UK grocery market? (20)

Investment appraisal

UNIT 60

Investment appraisal is about making investment decisions on the basis of quantitative and qualitative criteria.

60.1 INTRODUCTION

Every day managers make decisions, such as how to deal with a furious customer or whether a cheeky worker needs a disciplinary chat. These can be regarded as tactical **decisions** because they are short-term responses to events. Investment appraisal applies to decisions that concern strategy rather than tactics (that is, the medium- to long-term). As they are significant in the longer term, they are worth taking a bit of time over; ideally, by calculating whether or not the potential profits are high enough to justify the initial outlay (the sum invested). Examples of situations involving tactical and investment appraisal decisions are given in Table 60.1.

To carry out a full investment appraisal might take a manager several weeks, even months. The reason for this is not because the maths is so complex, but in order to find accurate data to analyse. For example, if trying to choose whether to launch new product A or B, a sales forecast will be essential. Carrying out primary market research might take several weeks until the results are received and analysed. Only then could the investment appraisal begin. Yet what is the alternative? Is it to take an important decision without proper evidence and information? Table 60.2 gives an idea of the data required to take effective decisions using investment appraisal.

Quantitative methods of investment appraisal

Having gathered all the necessary facts and figures, a firm can analyse the data to answer two main questions.

1. How long will it take until we get our money back? If we invest £400,000, can we expect to get that money back within the first year, or might it take four years?
2. How profitable will the investment be? What profit will be generated per year by the investment?

To answer these two questions there are three methods that can be used:

Table 60.1 Tactical versus investment appraisal decisions

Tactical, day-to-day decisions	Decisions requiring investment appraisal
Should we open earlier on Saturdays?	Should we launch new product A or B?
We need to appoint one extra cashier	Should we make a takeover bid for L'Oréal?
The production line must stop until we have found out why quality is poor today	Should we relocate our factory from London to Bangkok?
Stocks are high, shall we have a mid-season sale?	Shall we expand capacity by running a night shift?

Table 60.2 The data required to take effective decisions using investment appraisal

Decisions requiring investment appraisal	Information needed to make the decision
Should we launch new product A or B?	Sales forecasts, pricing decisions, and data on fixed, variable and start-up costs
Should we make a takeover bid for L'Oréal?	Forecast of future cash flows into and out of L'Oréal; compare the results with the purchase price
Should we relocate our factory from London to Bangkok?	Estimate of fixed and variable costs there compared with here, plus the initial cost of the move
Shall we expand capacity by running a night shift?	Forecast of the extra costs compared with extra revenues

Table 60.3 Example cash flow table

	Cash in	Cash out	Net cash flow	Cumulative cash total
NOW*	–	£60,000	(£60,000)	(£60,000)
End of Year 1	£30,000	£10,000	£20,000	(£40,000)
End of Year 2	£30,000	£10,000	£20,000	(£20,000)
End of Year 3	£30,000	£10,000	£20,000	–
End of Year 4	£30,000	£10,000	£20,000	£20,000
End of Year 5	£30,000	£10,000	£20,000	£40,000

*NOW = the moment the £60,000 is spent; can also be called the initial outlay or the sum invested.

1 payback period
2 average rate of return
3 discounted cash flows.

Two of these (methods 1 and 2) need to be used together; the third can answer both questions simultaneously. All three methods require the same starting point: a table showing the expected cash flows on the investment over time.

An example would be an investment of £60,000 in a machine that will cost £10,000 per year to run and should generate £30,000 a year of cash. The machine is expected to last for five years. The cash flow table would look like the one shown in Table 60.3.

Exam papers may present this information in the form of a graph. The graph in Figure 60.1 shows the **cumulative cash** total based on the above figures.

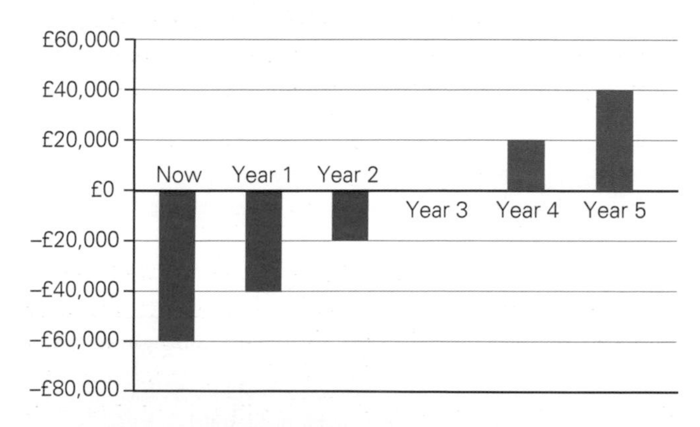

Figure 60.1 Cumulative cash flows on investment of £60,000

These figures will be used to explain the workings of each of the three methods listed above, which we will now look at in more detail.

60.2 PAYBACK PERIOD

Calculation

This method focuses on one issue alone: how long does it take to get your money back? In the above case, the £60,000 investment takes exactly three years to get back, as can be seen in the right-hand column: the cumulative cash total. All the £60,000 is recovered in three years because the business is generating £20,000 of cash per year.

If the annual net cash flows are constant over time, a formula can be used to calculate the payback period:

$$\text{Payback: } \frac{\text{Sum invested}}{\text{Net cash per time period}}$$

$$\text{for example: } \frac{£60{,}000}{£20{,}000 \text{ a year}} = 3 \text{ years}$$

What if the cash flows are not constant over time?

This can make it a little harder to work out a precise answer, though the principles are the same. For example, take the investment of £40,000 shown in Table 60.4.

In this case, payback has not yet occurred by the end of Year 2 (there's still £5,000 outstanding). Yet the end of Year 3 is well beyond the payback period. So payback occurred in two years and x months. To find how many months, the following formula will work:

$$\frac{\text{Outlay outstanding}}{\text{Monthly cash in year of payback}}$$

$$\text{for example: } \frac{£5{,}000}{£12{,}000/12 \text{ months}} = 5 \text{ months}$$

Table 60.4 Finding the payback period

	Cash in	Cash out	Net cash flow	Cumulative cash total
NOW*	–	£40,000	(£40,000)	(£40,000)
Year 1	£20,000	£5,000	£15,000	(£25,000)
Year 2	£30,000	£10,000	£20,000	(£5,000)
Year 3	£36,000	£24,000	£12,000	£7,000

In this case, then, the payback period was two years and five months.

Interpretation of payback period

The word investment suggests spending money now in the hope of making money later. Therefore every investment means putting money at risk while waiting for the profit. The payback period is the length of time the money is at risk. It follows that every business would like an investment to have as short a payback period as possible. Company directors may tell their managers to suggest an investment only if its payback is less than 18 months. This yardstick is known as a **criterion level**.

It is important to bear in mind the risks involved in investment. Even if well-researched sales estimates have led to well-considered cash flow forecasts, things can go wrong. For a new house-building business, an unexpected rise in interest rates may lead cash inflows to dry up, as buyers hesitate. Or a new 'AllFresh' restaurant may find that food wastage levels are much higher than expected, causing cash outflows to be disturbingly high. Getting beyond the payback period is therefore always a crucial phase.

Although managers like a quick payback, it is important to be beware of **short-termism**. If directors demand too short a payback period, it may be impossible for managers to plan effectively for the long-term future of the business. Quick paybacks imply easy decisions, such as for Primark to expand its store chain by opening its fifteenth store in London. A much tougher, longer-term decision would be whether Primark should open up stores in New Delhi. This could prove to be a clever move in the longer term, but the high costs of getting to grips with Indian retailing may lead to a minimum of a three-year payback.

The advantages and disadvantages of payback are set out in Table 60.5.

Table 60.5 The advantages and disadvantages of payback

Advantages of payback	Disadvantages of payback
Easy to calculate and understand	Provides no insight into profitability
May be more accurate than other measures, because it ignores longer-term forecasts (the ones beyond the payback period)	Ignores what happens after the payback period
Takes into account the timing of cash flows	May encourage a short-termist attitude
Especially important for a business with weak cash flow; it may be willing to invest only in projects with a quick payback	Is not very useful on its own (because it ignores profit), therefore is used together with ARR or NPV (see below)

A-grade application

The opposite of short-termism

In 2011 JCB, manufacturer of construction equipment, plans to start boosting its market position in China. It hopes to repeat its amazing success in India, where it is market leader with an astonishing 50 per cent market share. Its achievements in India began 30 years earlier, in 1979, when it opened its first offices. Now it has three huge factories in India, one of which saw a doubling of capacity in 2010.

In its strongest market sector, for the 'backhoe loaders' seen on every construction site, JCB enjoyed a 40 per cent world market share in 2010. Yet in China it has been an also-ran to giant rivals Caterpillar (US) and Komatsu (Japan). Even if it takes 30 years to succeed in China, JCB seems up for the challenge.

Figure 60.2

60.3 AVERAGE RATE OF RETURN

This method compares the average annual profit generated by an investment with the amount of money invested in it. In this way, two or more potential projects can be compared to find out which has the 'best' return for the amount of money being put into it in the first place.

Calculation

Average rate of return (ARR) is calculated by the formula:

$$\frac{\text{Average annual return}}{\text{Initial outlay}} \times 100$$

There are three steps in calculating ARR, as follows.

1 Calculate the total profit over the lifetime of the investment (total net cash flows minus the investment outlay).
2 Divide by the number of years of the investment project, to give the average annual profit.

3 Apply the formula: average annual profit/initial outlay × 100.

For example, BJ Carpets is considering whether to invest £20,000 in a labour-saving wrapping machine. The company policy is to invest in projects only if they deliver a profit of 15+ per cent a year (see Table 60.6).

Table 60.6 Figures for BJ Carpets

Year	Net cash flow	Cumulative cash flow
0	(£20,000)	(£20,000)
1	+£5,000	(£15,000)
2	+£11,000	(£4,000)
3	+£10,000	+£6,000
4	+£10,000	+£16,000

Here, the £20,000 investment generates £36,000 of net cash flows in the four years. That represents a lifetime profit of £16,000 (see bottom right-hand corner of Table 60.6). To apply the three steps, then, proceed as indicated in Table 60.7.

Table 60.7 BJ Carpets: applying the three steps

Step 1	Identify lifetime profit	£16,000
Step 2	Divide by number of years (4)	£4,000
Step 3	Calculate annual profit as a percentage of initial outlay	$\frac{£4,000}{£20,000} \times 100 = 20\%$

BJ Carpets can therefore proceed with this investment, as the ARR of 20 per cent is comfortably above its requirement of a minimum ARR criterion level of 15 per cent.

Interpretation of ARR

The strength of ARR is that it is easy to interpret the result. Clearly, firms want as high a rate of profit as possible, so the higher the ARR the better. This makes it easy to choose between two investment options, as long as profit is the key decision-making factor. (It may not be, because some firms are pursuing objectives such as growth or diversification.)

How do you interpret an ARR result, though, if there is only one investment to consider? For example is 12 per cent a good rate of return? In this case the key is to analyse the **reward for risk**. This compares the ARR result with the only way to achieve a safe rate of return – by keeping your money on deposit at a bank.

Reward for risk

If an ARR result comes out at 12 per cent, ask yourself what the current rate of interest is. If it is 5.75 per cent, for example, a business could receive a 5.75 per cent annual income at zero risk and by doing nothing. So, why invest? Well, in this case, the reward for investing would be the 12 per cent ARR *minus* the 5.75 per cent interest rate, meaning that the investment yields a 6.25 per cent annual reward for taking a business risk. Clearly if the reward for risk was small, or even negative (5 per cent ARR when interest rates are 5.75 per cent), it would seem crazy to invest. Note that an implication here is that the higher the interest rate, the less attractive it becomes to invest. In an exam, the key is to interpret the ARR through the reward for risk, then make a judgement about how risky the investment seems. A 6.25 per cent reward for risk, for example, would seem very low for a brand new restaurant, as 40 per cent of new restaurants fold within three years of starting up.

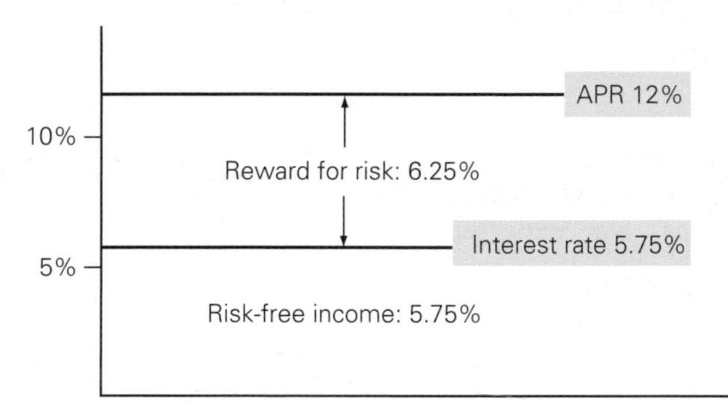

Figure 60.3 Reward for risk

The average rate of return (ARR) method takes account of all the cash flows throughout the life of a project, and focuses on the key decision-making factor: profitability. However, it ignores *when* the cash flows occur, which can have a significant bearing on the risks of a project. Look at the example of the *average* rate of return on two investments, both of £10,000, in Table 60.8.

Table 60.8 Example of the average rate of return on two investments

Year	Investment A net cash flows	Investment B net cash flows
0	(£10,000)	(£10,000)
1	+£10,000	+£3,000
2	+£6,000	+£6,000
3	+£3,000	+£10,000
Average rate of return	30%	30%

Investments A and B come out with the same average profitability. Yet Investment A's quick, one-year payback makes it greatly preferable to Investment B. After all, it is much easier to forecast one year ahead than three years. So Investment B's crucial year 3 may prove to be much worse than expected, which means that the ARR proves much lower in reality than the 30 per cent expected at the start.

Table 60.9 set out the advantages and disadvantages of average rate of return.

Table 60.9 The advantages and disadvantages of average rate of return

Advantages of average rate of return	Disadvantages of average rate of return
Uses all the cash flows over the project's life ...	... but, because later years are included, the results will not prove as accurate as payback
Focuses upon profitability	Ignores the timing of the cash flows
Easy to compare percentage returns on different investments, to help make a decision	Ignores the time value (opportunity cost) of the money invested

A-grade application

Estimating average rate of return

In January 2011 Alan Travis bought a flat in north London for £240,000. His plan was to let it out to tenants for a rental of £1,200 a month (£14,400 a year). Although his mortgage payments would be slightly higher than this, he was sure that the property would enjoy a rise in value over the coming years. His forecasts enabled him to estimate a 7 per cent average rate of return over a five-year period, and a possible 18 per cent ARR if he holds on to the property for ten years. Of course, these figures depend entirely on his forecasts; are they too optimistic, given the weak position of the UK economy?

60.4 DISCOUNTED CASH FLOWS

Useful though payback and ARR can be, they can work effectively only when used together. ARR provides information on average profitability, while payback tells you about the timing of the cash flows. It is better, surely, to have one method that incorporates profits and time. This is the third method of investment appraisal, which is based on 'discounted cash flows'.

Discounted cash flow (DCF) is a method that is rooted in opportunity cost. If a firm invests £10,000 in computer software, it is important not only to ask 'What is the rate of return on my investment of £10,000?', but also 'What opportunities am I having to give up as a result of this investment?' At its simplest, £10,000 tied up in software prevents the firm from enjoying a 5.75 per cent return on its money in the bank (when interest rates are 5.75 per cent).

From the idea of opportunity cost, businesses want to know the implication of the timing of cash flows on different projects. If one investment generates +£40,000 in year 1, while another provides that inflow in year 4, the firm must consider what it is missing out on by waiting four years.

In short, it is always preferable to have money now than the promise of the same quantity of money in the future. This is because money held at the present time has a greater value than the same quantity of money received in the future. In other words, £100 received in a year's time is worth less to a firm than £100 in the bank today. How much less? Well, if interest rates are 10 per cent, £100 in the bank for a year would become £110. So £100 in a year's time is worth 10 per cent less than £100 today.

When considering potential capital investments on the basis of predicted future cash flows, it makes sense to ask, 'What will the money we receive in the future really be worth in today's terms?' These **present values** are calculated using a method called 'discounting'.

To discount a future cash flow, it is necessary to know:

- how many years into the future we are looking, since the greater the length of time involved, the smaller the discounted value of money will be
- what the prevailing rate of interest will be.

Once these have been determined, the relevant discount factor can be found. This can be done by calculation, or looked up in 'discount tables'. An extract from a discount table is given in Table 60.10.

Table 60.10 Extract from a discount table

Table of selected discount factors						
Years ahead	4%	6%	8%	10%	12%	15%
0	1.00	1.00	1.00	1.00	1.00	1.00
1	0.96	0.94	0.93	0.91	0.89	0.87
2	0.92	0.89	0.86	0.83	0.80	0.76
3	0.89	0.84	0.79	0.75	0.71	0.66
4	0.85	0.79	0.74	0.68	0,64	0.57
5	0.82	0.75	0.68	0.62	0.57	0.50

The future cash flows are then multiplied by the appropriate discount factor to find the present value. For example, the present value of £100 received in five years' time, if the expected rate of interest is 10 per cent, would be:

£100 × 0.62 = £62

The higher the rate of interest expected, and the longer the time to wait for the money to come in, the less that money is actually worth in today's terms.

So how does a firm decide which discount factor to choose? There are two main ways.

1 The discount factor can be based on the current rate of interest, or the rate expected over the coming years.
2 A firm may base the factor on its own criteria, such as that it wants every investment to make at least 15

per cent; therefore it expects future returns to be positive even with a 15 per cent discount rate.

This A-level book includes just one technique of discounting future cash flows to find their present value; this is the net present value method.

Net present value (NPV)

Calculation

This method calculates the present values of all the money coming in from the project in the future, then sets these against the money being spent on the project today. The result is known as the net present value (NPV) of the project. It can be compared with other projects to find which has the highest return in real terms, and should therefore be chosen.

The technique can also be used to see if *any* of the projects are worth undertaking. All the investments might have a negative NPV. In other words, the present value of the money being spent is greater than the present value of the money being received. If so, the firm would be better off putting the money in the bank and earning the current rate of interest. Projects are only worth carrying out if the NPV is positive.

For example, a firm is faced with two alternative proposals for investment: Project Z and Project Y (see Table 60.11). Both cost £250,000, but have different patterns of future cash flows over their projected lives. The rate of interest over the period is anticipated to average around 10 per cent. The calculation would be as shown in the table.

Despite the fact that both projects have the same initial cost, and they bring in the same quantity of money over their lives, there is a large difference in their net present values. Project Y, with most of its income coming in the early years, gives a much greater present value than Project Z.

Interpretation

This method of appraising investment opportunities has an in-built advantage over the previous techniques. It pays close attention to the timing of cash flows and their values in relation to the value of money today. It is also relatively simple to use the technique as a form of 'what if?' scenario planning. Different calculations can be made to see what returns will be obtained at different interest rates or with different cash flows to reflect different expectations. The results, however, are not directly comparable between different projects when the initial investments differ.

Table 60.12 sets out the advantages and disadvantages of NPV.

Table 60.12 The advantages and disadvantages of NPV

Advantages of NPV	Disadvantages of NPV
Takes the opportunity cost of money into account	Complex to calculate and communicate
A single measure that takes the amount and timing of cash flows into account	The meaning of the result is often misunderstood
Can consider different scenarios	Only comparable between projects if the initial investment is the same.

60.5 QUALITATIVE FACTORS IN INVESTMENT APPRAISAL

Once the numbers have been calculated there are decisions to be made. On the face of it, the numbers point to the answer, but they are only part of the decision-making process. For example, perhaps a board of directors can afford no more than £2 million for investment and must choose between the two alternatives shown in Table 60.13.

Table 60.13 Investment A versus Investment B

	Investment A	Investment B
Type of investment	New R&D laboratory	Relaunching an existing product with flagging sales
Investment outlay	£2 million	£2 million
Payback period	4.5 years	1 year
Average rate of return (over next five years)	8.2%	14.2%
Net present value	£32,000	£280,000

Table 60.11 Project Z versus Project Y

		Project Z				Project Y	
Year	Cash flow	Discount factor	Present value (£s)		Cash flows	Discount factor	Present value (£s)
0	(£250,000)	1.00	(£250,000)		(£250,000)	1.00	(£250,000)
1	+£50,000	0.91	£45,500		+£200,000	0.91	+£182,000
2	+£100,000	1.83	£83,000		+£100,000	0.83	+£83,000
3	+£200,000	0.75	£150,000		+£50,000	0.75	+£37,500
		NPV =	+£28,500			NPV =	+£52,500

Investment B is clearly superior on all three quantitative methods of appraisal. Yet there may be reasons why the board may reject it. Some of these are outlined below.

- *Company objectives:* if the business is pursuing an objective of long-term growth, the directors might feel that a relaunch of a declining brand is too short-termist; they may prefer an investment that is could keep boosting the business long beyond the next five years.
- *Company strategy:* if the business has been suffering from low-priced imported competition, it may seek higher value-added, differentiated products. Its goal may be to become more innovative and therefore the board may opt for Investment A.
- *Company finances:* if the £2 million investment capital is intended to be borrowed, the company's balance sheet is an important issue. If the business is highly geared, it may be reluctant to proceed with either of these investments, as neither generates an irresistible ARR.
- *Confidence in the data:* the directors will ask questions about how the forecasts were made, who made the forecasts and what was the evidence behind them. If the Investment B data came from the manager in charge of the product with flagging sales, may they be biased? (She or he may have been over-optimistic in interpreting the findings of small-scale market research.) Ideally, data used in investment appraisal should come from an independent source and be based on large enough sample sizes to be statistically valid.
- *Social responsibilities:* investing in recycling or energy-saving schemes may generate very low ARRs, but the firm may still wish to proceed for public relations reasons, to boost morale among staff or just because the directors think it is ethically right.

60.6 INVESTMENT APPRAISAL – AN EVALUATION

Investment appraisal methods will often give conflicting advice to managers, who must be willing to make decisions based on a trade-off between risks and profit. This must be taken alongside the objectives of the business, which could well dictate which of the criteria involved is of most importance to the firm.

The size of the firm will also have an impact. Small firms will often have neither the time nor the resources to undertake a scientific approach to investment appraisal. They will often rely on past experience or the owner's hunches in making decisions such as these. In larger firms, however, the issue of accountability will often lead managers to rely heavily on the projected figures. In this way, should anything go wrong, they can prove they were making the best decision possible at the time, given the information available.

ISSUES FOR ANALYSIS

- Having mastered the mathematics of investment appraisal, the next key factor is to be able to interpret the results effectively. If the business has a payback criterion level of 18 months, is this holding it back in any way? Is there evidence that the firm is *too* focused on the short term? Of course, if the firm's cash flow or liquidity positions are weak, it is understandable if there is a great emphasis on speed of payback. Yet, in some cases, businesses are short-term focused for less acceptable reasons; for example, multi-million-pound short-term profit bonuses for directors may be leading them to ignore the long-term future of the business.
- Always ask yourself about the reliability of the data provided: how were they gathered; who gathered them; what variables were taken into account?
- Decisions should always be based on a mixture of quantitative and qualitative data. Beware of placing too great an emphasis on numbers on the basis that they are somehow more concrete and therefore more reliable. Qualitative factors may be more important, such as considering the environmental impact of a decision. Today's profits can turn into tomorrow's public relations disaster if stakeholders discover unacceptable side-effects of your approach to production.

Key Terms

Criterion level: a yardstick set by directors to enable managers to judge whether investment ideas are worth pursuing (for example, ARR must be 15%+ or payback must be a maximum of 12 months).

Cumulative cash: the build-up of cash over several time periods (for example, if cash flow is +£20,000 for three years in a row, cumulative cash in year 3 is +£60,000).

Present values: the discounting of future cash flows to make them comparable with today's cash. This takes into account the opportunity cost of waiting for the cash to arrive.

Reward for risk: calculating the difference between the forecast ARR and the actual rate of interest, to help decide whether the ARR is high enough given the risks involved in the project.

Short-termism: making decisions on the basis of the immediate future and therefore ignoring the long-term future of the business.

Tactical decisions: those that are day-to-day events and therefore do not require a lengthy decision-making process.

WORKBOOK

A REVISION QUESTIONS

(40 marks; 40 minutes)

1 Distinguish between qualitative and quantitative investment appraisal. (4)
2 Why should forecast cash flow figures be treated with caution? (4)
3 How useful is payback period as the sole method for making an investment decision? (3)
4 Briefly outline the circumstances in which:
  a) payback period might be the most important appraisal method for a firm (4)
  b) average rate of return might be more important than payback for a firm. (4)
5 How are criterion levels applied to investment appraisal? (3)
6 Explain the purpose of discounting cash flows. (4)
7 Using only qualitative analysis, would you prefer £100 now or £105 in one year's time, at an interest rate of 10 per cent? (3)
8 Outline two possible drawbacks to setting a payback criterion level of 12 months. (4)
9 What qualitative issues might a firm take into account when deciding whether to invest in a new fleet of lorries? (4)
10 Why is it important to ask for the source before accepting investment appraisal data? (3)

B1 DATA RESPONSE

Questions

(30 marks; 30 minutes)

1 Net annual cash flows on an investment are forecast to be as shown in Table 60.14.

Table 60.14 Forecast of net annual cash flows on an investment

	£000
NOW	(600)
End of year 1	100
End of year 2	400
End of year 3	400
End of year 4	180

Calculate the payback and the average rate of return. (6)

2 The board of Burford Ltd is meeting to decide whether to invest £500,000 in an automated packing machine or into a new customer service centre. The production manager has estimated the cash flows from the two investments to make the calculations given in Table 60.15.

Table 60.15 Estimated cash flows from two investments

	Packing machine	Service centre
Payback	1.75 years	3.5 years
NPV	+£28,500	+£25,600

a) On purely quantitative grounds, which would you choose and why? (6)
b) Outline three other factors the board should consider before making a final decision. (6)

3 The cash flows on two alternative projects are estimated to be as shown in Table 60.16.

Table 60.16 Estimated cash flows on two alternative projects

	Project A		Project B	
	Cash in	Cash out	Cash in	Cash out
Year 0	–	£50,000	–	£50,000
Year 1	£60,000	£30,000	£10,000	£10,000
Year 2	£80,000	£40,000	£40,000	£20,000
Year 3	£40,000	£24,000	£60,000	£30,000
Year 4	£20,000	£20,000	£84,000	£40,000

Carry out a full investment appraisal to decide which (if either) of the projects should be undertaken. Interest rates are currently 8 per cent. (12)

B2 DATA RESPONSE

Dowton's new finance director has decided that capital investments will be approved only if they meet the criteria shown in Table 60.17.

Table 60.17 Criteria required for approval of capital investments

Payback	30 months
Average rate of return	18%
Net present value	10% of the investment outlay

The assembly department has proposed the purchase of a £600,000 machine that will be more productive and produce to a higher-quality finish. The department estimates that the output gains should yield the cash flow benefits shown in Table 60.18 during the expected four-year life of the machine:

Table 60.18 Yield of cash flow benefits during expected life of the machine

Year	£
0	− 600,000
1	+ 130,000
2	+ 260,000
3	+ 360,000
4	+ 230,000

In addition:

1 the machine should have a resale value of £100,000 at the end of its life
2 the relevant discount factors are: end year 1, 0.91; year 2, 0.83; year 3, 0.75; year 4, 0.68.

Questions

(30 marks; 35 minutes)

1 Conduct a full investment appraisal, then consider whether Dowton's should go ahead with the investment on the basis of the quantitative information provided. (16)
2 Outline any other information it may be useful to obtain before making a final decision. (8)
3 Explain two sources of finance that may be appropriate for an investment such as this. (6)

B3 CASE STUDY

Green Investment?

These days many businesses feel under pressure to show their green credentials. In the hotel business, the desire to become energy-efficient also comes from the finance director. Electricity and gas bills are huge, amounting to more than the cost of the cleaning staff who service the rooms. One London hotel, the Portman Square Radisson, has an annual electricity bill of £500,000.

In February 2011 a Peterborough hotel was offered a £50,000 deal to install a wireless technology system to analyse and control energy consumption throughout the hotel. The supplier made a promise that 'it would pay back within 24 months'. In other words the energy saved would cut the electricity bills sufficiently to provide a 24-month pay-back period.

For the hotel manager, £50,000 is a lot to find in a very tough year for UK hotels, especially those outside London. But Angela loves new technology and loves the idea of being able to boast to guests that hers is one of the first hotels in the country to install the system. Being able to boast an annual saving of 3 tonnes of CO_2 is also a big attraction.

Before signing the deal, she decides to turn the suppliers' figures into an investment appraisal table. She has been told that the system will need replacing every five years.

Table 60.19 Investment appraisal table

	Cash in	Cash out	Net cash	Cumulative cash
NOW		£50,000		
Year 1	£20,000	£2,000		
Year 2	£18,000	£2,000		
Year 3	£18,000	£2,000		
Year 4	£18,000	£2,000		

To help, the supplier company has also provided the data shown in Table 60.20.

Table 60.20 Additional data provided by the energy supplier

	2% discount factors	4% discount factors
Now	1.00	1.00
Year 1	0.98	0.96
Year 2	0.96	0.92
Year 3	0.94	0.89
Year 4	0.92	0.85

Questions

(40 marks; 50 minutes)

1 a) Complete the investment appraisal table, then calculate the payback and average rate of return on the basis of that data. (10)

b) Comment on your results. (6)

2 Calculate the NPV on the investment. Explain which discount factor you are choosing and why. (8)

3 Discuss whether Angela should go ahead, based on quantitative and qualitative factors. (16)

UNIT 61

Understanding marketing objectives

Marketing objectives are the marketing targets that must be achieved in order for the company to achieve its overall goals, such as 'to boost sales from £25 million to £40 million within three years'.

61.1 HOW ARE MARKETING OBJECTIVES SET?

At a very senior level in the company

In most firms, marketing is central to board-level strategic decisions. Not marketing in the sense of price cuts and promotions, but marketing in the sense of analysing growth trends and the competitive struggle within the firm's existing markets, and decisions about which markets the firm wishes to develop in future.

Rooted in the company's vision of its future (its mission)

A **vision** is a company's projection of what it wants to achieve in the future. It should be ambitious, relevant, easy to communicate and capable of motivating staff, or even inspiring them. Bill Gates' 1980s vision for Microsoft was 'a computer on every desk and in every home'. Today, that seems uninspiring, even obvious. In the 1980s it seemed extraordinary.

A firm's marketing objectives need to reflect its long-term aims/mission. The American car company Chrysler's mission statement says: 'Our purpose is to produce cars and trucks that people will want to buy, will enjoy driving, and will want to buy again.' This sets the background for marketing objectives that focus on developing new, probably niche markets, exciting rather than ordinary cars, and promoting them in ways that emphasise fun rather than safety or family.

In his book *Even More Offensive Marketing*, Hugh Davidson suggests that there are six requirements for a successful company vision. These are listed in Table 61.1.

By striking a balance between what is achievable and what is challenging

Objectives work best when they are clear, achievable, challenging and – above all else – when staff believe in them. To fit all these criteria, the firm must root the objectives in market realities. In 2009 Pepsi launched a new, 'all-natural' product, Pepsi Raw, to the UK retail trade. This new product was priced significantly higher than traditional colas, but Pepsi hoped it would establish a new niche in its attempt to dent Coca-Cola's £1,000 million of UK retail sales. By mid-2010 reports suggested that Pepsi Raw sales had not even reached £1 million and within a few months it was withdrawn from sale.

Marketing objectives should not be set until the decision makers have a clear view of current customer

Table 61.1 Vision: six requirements for success

Requirement	Comment
1. Provides future direction	As shown in the above examples of Microsoft and Chrysler
2. Expresses a consumer benefit	e.g. Pret A Manger: 'Our mission is to sell handmade extremely fresh food ...'
3. Realistic	Realistic? Innocent Drinks 2010: 'To be the most talent-rich company in Europe'
4. Motivating	Body Shop: 'Tirelessly work to narrow the gap between principle and practice, whilst making fun, passion and care part of our daily lives'
5. Fully communicated	Easy to achieve if it's as simple as Kwik Fit's: 'To get customers back on the road speedily, achieving 100 per cent customer delight'
6. Consistently followed in practice	A company might claim to be at the leading edge of technology; it will lose all credibility if it reacts to the next recession by cutting spending on research and development

Source: Davidson (1997)

Figure 61.1

behaviour and attitudes. This will probably require a lot of market research into customer usage and attitudes to the different products they buy and don't buy.

Once the marketplace and financial factors have been considered, objectives can be decided that stretch people, but do not make them snap. Cadbury has had a 30 per cent share of the UK chocolate market for decades. Setting a target of 35 per cent for two years' time would be implausible. After all, will Mars or Nestlé just sit and watch? A wise marketing director might accept the challenge of 32 per cent in two years' time, but would warn everyone that it might be very difficult to achieve this. (Note: each 1 per cent of the chocolate market represents over £20 million of sales, so these matters are not trivial.)

A-grade application

Marketing objectives can fail

In early 1997, the business giant Unilever (Walls, Persil, Birds Eye, CK One and much else) set its sights on obtaining one-third of its worldwide sales from Asian markets by 2001. This company objective was based upon observation of the rapid growth rates in economies such as China. It planned to achieve this by launching new products tailored to local tastes and needs. In fact, in 2001 only 22 per cent of its sales came from Asia, which was only just up on the figure for 1997. Even by 2010 the figure of 33 per cent had not been achieved. Its objective was clear, but probably too ambitious. In business there is no magic formula that says objectives + strategy = success.

61.2 TYPES OF MARKETING OBJECTIVE

There are four main types of marketing objective:

1. increasing product differentiation
2. growth
3. continuity
4. innovation.

Increasing product differentiation

Product differentiation is the extent to which consumers see your product as different from the rest. It is the key to ensuring that customers buy from you because they want you, not because you're the cheapest. It is a major influence on the value added and therefore profit margins achieved by the product.

To increase product differentiation requires a fully integrated marketing programme. Objectives must be set that separate your product from its rivals. These include:

- distinctive design and display
- unusual distribution channels – avoiding supermarkets, perhaps
- advertising based on image building, not sales boosting (for example, television and cinema advertising rather than blockbuster sales promotions or competitions)
- an integrated marketing programme focused solely upon the relevant age group or type of person.

Growth

Some firms see growth as their main purpose and their main security blanket. They may reason that once they are number one, no one else will be able to catch them. So they set sales or market share targets that encourage staff to push hard for greater success.

This is understandable, but may prove self-defeating. A school or college pushing hard for rapid growth in student numbers would risk damaging its reputation. Class sizes would rise, hastily recruited new staff may be ineffective, middle management would be overstretched and quality standards would be at risk.

Of course, the pursuit of growth may be essential. When social networking became the hottest property

A-grade application

Market development and the Axe effect

Unilever has a corporate objective of doubling sales volumes within the next five years. Its marketing objectives must match that. Broadly, it must then decide whether to set tough targets for successful new product development, or whether to boost sales of existing products. It has decided to focus on market development, based on such huge worldwide brands as Axe*, which is the world's biggest male deodorant. It plans to achieve its growth targets by the following three aspects of market development:

- more users (increasing market penetration)
- more usage (increasing 'consumption')
- more benefits (getting consumers to buy products with higher value added).

Although it's the number 1 brand, other companies might try to 'milk' the brand to support the launch of new products. Unilever sees more potential in the Axe Effect.

*Axe is marketed as Lynx in the UK.

on the web, Facebook was right to rush to satisfy this demand. If it had not grown rapidly, others, such as Bebo, would have done so. Therefore, the company's objective of rapid growth was very sensible. In this instance 'too slow' would have become 'too late'.

Continuity for the long term

The companies that own major brands, such as Levi's, Bacardi or Cadbury, know that true success comes from taking a very long-term view. Unilever even tells its brand managers that their key role is to hand over a stronger brand to their successor. In other words, they must think ten years, or so, ahead.

Doubtless Bacardi could boost sales and profits this year by running price promotions with the major supermarkets and off-licences. Or it could do so next year, by launching Bacardi iced lollies or bubble gum. But where would the brand's reputation be in a few years' time? Would it still be a classy drink to ask for at a bar?

Large firms think a great deal about their corporate image and the image of the brands they produce. They may try to stretch their brands a little, to attract new customers. Yet Cadbury must always mean chocolate, not just snack products. Levi's must always mean jeans, not just clothes. Only in this way can the brands continue to add value for the long term.

Innovation

In certain major sectors of the economy, a key to long-term competitive success is innovation; in other words, bringing new product or service ideas to the marketplace. Two main categories of business where innovation is likely to be crucial are fashion-related and technology-related, as shown in Table 61.2.

Table 61.2 Businesses where innovation is especially important

Business category	Business sector
Fashion-related	Music business Clothing and footwear Entertainment (e.g. eating out)
Technology-related	Consumer electronics and IT Cars and aircraft Medicines and cosmetics

There are two key elements to innovation: get it right and get in first. Which is the more important? This is not possible to answer, as past cases have given contradictory results. The originator of the filled ice cream cone was Lyons Maid (now Nestlé), with a product called King Cone. Walls came into the market second with Cornetto. In this case, getting it right proved more important than getting in first. In many other cases, though, the firm in first proved dominant for ever. Coca-Cola ('the real thing'); Cadbury's chocolate (in Britain) or Hershey's (in the USA); even the humble Findus Crispy Pancake (with its 80 per cent market share); all have built long-term success on the back of getting in first.

61.3 TURNING OBJECTIVES INTO TARGETS

The purpose of objectives is to set out exactly what the business wants to achieve. To ensure success, it is helpful to set more limited targets – staging posts en route to the destination. For example, a firm pursuing the objective of innovation may want at least 40 per cent of sales to come from products launched within the past five years. If, at present, only 30 per cent of sales come from this source, a jump to 40 per cent will not be easy. The targets listed in Table 61.3 may help, especially if – as below – they are linked with the strategy for achieving them.

Targets such as these:

- ensure that all the marketing staff know what to aim for
- provide a sound basis for cooperation with other departments (such as R&D and operations management)
- provide an early warning of when the strategy is failing to meet the objectives: should it be re-thought? Or backed with more resources?
- help psychologically; just as an end-of-year exam can concentrate the mind of a student, so a target can motivate a manager to give of her best.

These benefits hinge on a key issue: have the targets been communicated effectively to the staff? This is an obvious point, but vital nonetheless. If the entire marketing department is based in one large office, it would be astonishing if anyone was unaware of new objectives. But what if it is a retail business and there are 400 branches around the country? Then a head office initiative can fall down at the local level, when a local manager thinks she or he knows best. Expertly considered **marketing targets** may fail unless they are communicated effectively to all relevant staff.

Table 61.3 Targets and strategies for meeting them

Timescale	Target (percentage of sales from products launched in past five years)	Strategy for meeting target
First year	32	One national new product launch plus another in test market
Second year	35	One national new product launch and two others in test market
Third year	40	Two national new product launches

A-grade application

L'Oréal

Although L'Oréal is brilliant at advertising its products, the heart of its success worldwide comes from innovation. For example, it has recently achieved a breakthrough that allows ammonia (which smells) to be eliminated from hair colourants. This patented technique is one among hundreds that L'Oréal achieves each year. The graph in Figure 61.2 shows that even in a very difficult year for L'Oréal – 2009 – it kept investing in R&D staff and in registering their patents.

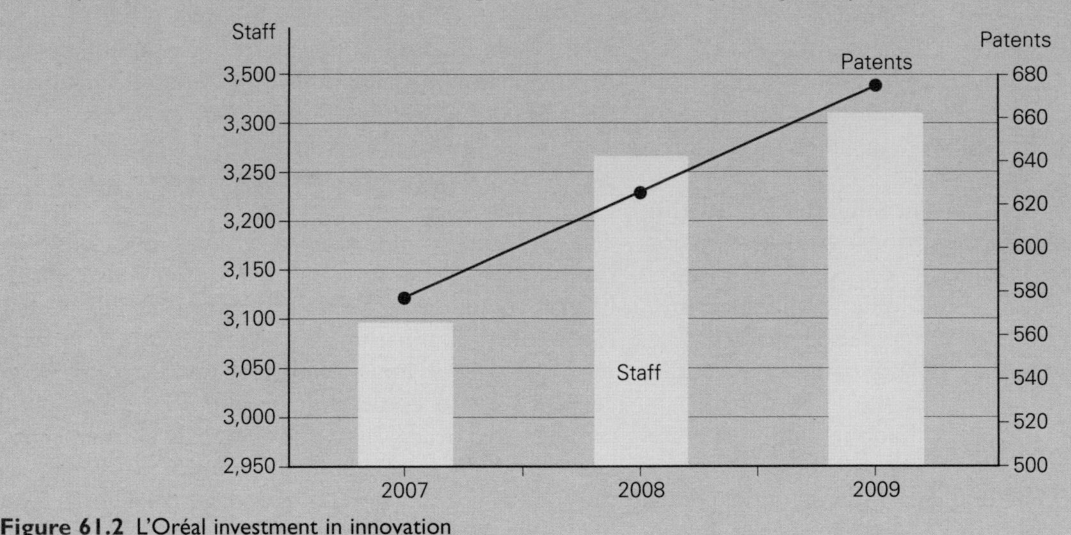

Figure 61.2 L'Oréal investment in innovation

61.4 MARKETING OBJECTIVES AND THE SMALL FIRM

Do small firms set aside time to consider, set and write down objectives and targets? Very rarely. If you interviewed a dozen small business proprietors, you might find none who finds the time and several who would regard such time as wasted.

There are two issues here.

1. In a very small firm, with all business decisions taken by the proprietor, the marketing objectives may be clear in the mind of the boss, even though they are not written down. That may work satisfactorily. When the firm gets 15 or more staff, however, it may have to change.
2. The bosses of small firms often find themselves swamped by day-to-day detail. Customers expect to speak to them personally, staff check every decision and may wait around for their next 'orders'. Only if such bosses learn to delegate will they find the time to think carefully about future objectives and strategy.

61.5 CONSTRAINTS ON MEETING MARKETING OBJECTIVES

However well conceived, objectives do not automatically lead to success. Various factors may occur that restrict the chances of the objectives succeeding. These are known as **constraints**. They may occur within the firm (internal constraints) or may be outside its control (external constraints).

Internal influences

Financial influences

Financial influences affect virtually every aspect of every organisation. Even Manchester United has a budget for players, which the manager must keep within. A marketing objective might be set that is unrealistic given the firm's limited resources. That is an error of judgement. Or the firm may have the finance in place at the start, but setbacks to the firm may cause budget cuts that make the objectives impossible to reach.

Personnel constraints

Personnel constraints may be important. The objective of diversifying may be appealing, but the firm may lack expertise in the new market. A recruitment campaign may fail to find the right person at a salary the business can afford. This may result in the project being delayed, scrapped or – worst of all – carried on by second-rate staff.

Market standing

The marketing objectives may be constrained most severely by the firm's own market position. The big growth sector in food retailing has been in chilled, prepared meals. So why no activity from the food giant Heinz? The answer lies in its success at establishing itself as *the* producer of canned soup, and bottled salad cream and ketchup. The Heinz market image (its key marketing asset) constrains it from competing effectively in chilled foods.

External influences

Competition

Competition is usually the main constraint outside the firm's control. It is the factor that prevents *Emirates* from charging £600 for a flight from London to Dubai. It is also the factor that makes it so hard to plan ahead in business. You may set the objective of gaining an extra 1 per cent of market share, only to be hit by a price war launched by a rival.

Consumer taste

Consumer taste is also important. If fashion moves against you, there may be little or nothing you can do to stop it. A logical approach is to anticipate the problem by never seeking fashionability. When its FCUK logo was trendy, no clothing business was hotter than French Connection. When this joke wore thin, though, sales collapsed as customers steered clear of yesterday's brand.

The economy

The economy can also cause huge problems when setting medium- to long-term objectives. This year's economic boom becomes next year's recession. Sales targets have to be discarded and a move upmarket comes to seem very foolish.

61.6 MARKETING DECISION MAKING: THE MARKETING MODEL

Successful marketing is not just about thinking. It is about decisions and action. Marketing decisions are particularly hard to make, because there are so many uncertainties. The procedure shown in Figure 61.3 is one of the most effective ways of ensuring a decision is well thought through.

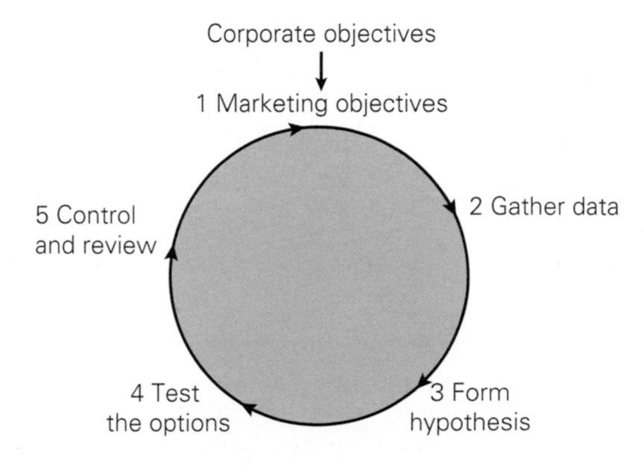

Figure 61.3 Marketing decision making

The intention is to ensure that the strategy decided upon is the most effective at achieving the marketing objectives. In this process, market research is likely to be very important. It is crucial for finding out the background data and again for testing the hypotheses. Test marketing may also be used. This is a way of checking whether the market research results are accurate, before finally committing the firm to an expensive national marketing campaign.

The **marketing model** is the way to decide how to turn a marketing objective into a strategy.

ISSUES FOR ANALYSIS

- Marketing objectives are the basis for all marketing strategy. Therefore they will be central to almost every substantial exam question on marketing. For example, pricing decisions will depend upon the objectives. A firm pursuing growth may price a new product relatively cheaply, to ensure high market share and to discourage competition. Objectives will also affect the advertising approach: aimed at encouraging loyalty from existing users, or developing a new image/customer base.
- To understand objectives fully, it is vital to be able to distinguish them from strategy. It is also important to remember that the setting of objectives cannot be done in isolation. The managers have to bear in mind the market situation, findings from market research, and the financial resources and personnel the firm has available. Warburton's objective of moving into the UK market for crisps foundered when it launched ChippidyDooDaa snacks in 2010. On paper the objective may have looked fine, but in practice it became a classic marketing failure.

61.7 UNDERSTANDING MARKETING OBJECTIVES – AN EVALUATION

What career are you aiming for? If you have a definite answer to that question, you probably have a clear idea of how to achieve it. You are also likely to be very well motivated towards the qualifications you need. Most A-level students have little idea of what they want to do. In other words, they have no objectives. As a result, they have no plan and may struggle to find the motivation to succeed at A-levels.

Marketing objectives are just as important. They allow a clear strategy to be devised, a plan to be set, and give the motivation to succeed. Therefore they are the most important element of marketing.

Key Terms

Constraints: factors that limit a firm's ability to achieve its objectives.

Marketing model: a procedure for making marketing decisions in a scientific manner.

Marketing targets: specific, measurable goals to be achieved within a relatively limited timescale.

Vision: conceiving where the business wants to be in the future; the term implies something ambitious.

FURTHER READING

Davidson, H. (1997) *Even More Offensive Marketing*. Penguin.

61.8 WORKBOOK

A REVISION QUESTIONS

(45 marks; 45 minutes)

1 Explain why it is important for a business to have clear marketing objectives. (3)
2 What do businesses mean by the term 'vision'? (3)
3 Why is it important that marketing objectives should be rooted in thorough market research? (4)
4 a) State the four main types of marketing objective. (4)
   b) Briefly explain which objective is most likely to be important for one of the following.
      a) Coca-Cola
      b) Twitter
      c) Subway. (3)
5 Why may a firm seek to increase the product differentiation of one of its brands? (3)
6 What problems could a firm face if it focuses solely upon short-term objectives? (5)
7 Is it essential that marketing objectives should be written down in detail? Explain your answer. (4)
8 Explain the meaning of the following terms.
   a) internal influences (3)
   b) external influences. (3)
9 Outline two external constraints that could affect car sales over the coming months. (4)
10 Identify and explain two problems that a firm could face if it makes marketing decisions without using a decision-making framework such as the marketing model. (6)

B REVISION EXERCISES
B1 DATA RESPONSE

Beanz meanz roublz?

Figure 61.4 **Heinz markets baked beans in Russia**

In spring 1997 Heinz made its first move into the Russian food market. Although the economy was growing at that time, average wage levels were still very low – typically under £25 per week. Yet Heinz chose to price its Baked Beans at around 50p per can, which was the equivalent of charging £5 in Britain.

Heinz had set its sights on the long-term objective of building a prestigious brand name. When the famous beans first came to Britain in 1901 they were sold by Fortnum & Mason for £1.50 per can. Now Heinz was aiming to repeat the initiative – nearly 100 years later.

Its target sales figure for year 1 was 12 million cans in Russia. This compared with 450 million cans in the UK each year. If the company's strategy was successful, Heinz Beans may become trendy among Russia's growing middle classes. Even before the move by Heinz, its products were available on the black market, gaining it the status accorded to other western products such as Coca-Cola and Levi's.

Soon after launching in Russia, in August 1998, there was a virtual meltdown of the Russian economy that cut living standards sharply. To its credit, Heinz withstood this external constraint and persisted in this new market. In 2010 the Heinz annual report singled out Russia for its 'outstanding' growth. Will beanz mean more and more roublz? That 'remainz' to be seen.

Questions

(30 marks; 35 minutes)

1 Identify Heinz's marketing objective for its beans in Russia. (3)
2 State the target Heinz set as the test of whether its objective was met. (3)
3 a) Explain the strategy Heinz chose to meet its objectives. (4)
   b) Suggest and explain an alternative strategy it might have adopted. (6)
4 a) Outline the external constraints faced by Heinz. (5)
   b) Discuss how a business may react to changed external constraints, if it was determined to achieve its marketing objectives. (9)

B2 CASE STUDY

Hoshil and Sunil's business started in rather dubious circumstances. While students they built up their capital by trading in 'second-hand' mobile phones. Now they were planning to open a nightclub aimed at young Asians. It would have two dance floors, one for Indian music and one for western pop music. One of the bars would be alcohol-free, have pool tables and music soft enough to allow people to chat. It would still be a nightclub, but with some of the benefits of a pub. The vision was clear: to provide a thriving social facility for young Asian men and women.

The investment outlay would be £150,000. Hoshil and Sunil put in £25,000 each and were fortunate that Hoshil's wealthy brother Satyam was able to put in the other £100,000. They would soon be ready to start.

Sunil and Satyam sat down to plan their marketing strategy. The objective was to maximise takings from day one; they needed to pay back their borrowings as soon as possible. After carrying out market research at their local community centre, the boys decided to focus on better-off 16 to 24 year olds. Prices would be kept relatively high, as there was no competition in the area. The location would be in the centre of Croydon, as the Tramlink service would bring people by public transport from a long way away.

Despite the agreement to focus on the better-off, when there was only a week until the opening night, Sunil panicked. Would there be enough people to create a good atmosphere? He printed 2,000 leaflets saying 'Half Price Drinks For All The First Week!' and distributed them through the local newsagents. The opening night went very well and on the following Saturday it was impossible to move. By the second week, though, the numbers were dropping away. When research was carried out it showed that customers thought the drinks were expensive.

It took about six months to establish a really strong reputation as a top club. Large profits were being made and Hoshil's skills as a host were becoming well known. The national paper, the *Daily Jang*, ran a whole feature on him. He was very happy, while Sunil and Satyam were enjoying the large dividends on their investments.

Questions

(50 marks; 60 minutes)

1 Outline the business importance of the following terms.
   a) marketing strategy (5)
   b) market research. (5)

2 How important to the success of the club was the clear vision and objectives? Explain your answer. (10)

3 Examine which of the four types of marketing objective were involved in this business success. (8)

4 How serious a risk did Sunil take by carrying out a marketing campaign that was at odds with the overall strategy? (10)

5 What do you consider to be the most important aspects of marketing for a small business? (12)

Analysing the market

UNIT 62

When businesses refer to the market for their products, they mean the customers: how many there are, whether the number is rising or falling, what their purchasing habits are, and much else. Successful marketing relies on a complete understanding of 'the market'.

62.1 WHAT MARKET ARE WE IN?

This sounds like a daft question, but the marketing guru Theodore Levitt considers it vital. Is Liverpool FC in the football business, the sports business or the leisure business? Long ago, Nintendo was Japan's number one producer of playing cards. It decided that its market was the broader games business and experimented with electronic games in the 1970s. Today it is a fabulously profitable producer of games consoles and software (its 2010 profit of £1.5 billion was much higher than the massive Sony Corporation). Sales of playing cards represent less than 1 per cent of the modern Nintendo.

Figure 62.1

62.2 THE PURPOSE OF MARKET ANALYSIS

Managers tend to get caught up in the day-to-day needs of the business. A photo of Alexa Chan wearing a silk scarf might make sales leap ahead, forcing clothes store managers to focus 100 per cent on how to find extra stocks of scarves. Market analysis should be a cooler, more thoughtful look at the market's longer-term trends. In 2010 Sony decided to focus the whole business on 3D. The company looked ahead at the market opportunity, realising that its strength in films, computer games and TVs put it in a great position to succeed with related technologies and products. It acted sensibly to position the business in the place where the consumer seemed to want to go.

Other clever pieces of market analysis include:

- Tesco spotting the opportunities in Hungary and Poland before other western retailers
- Danone seeing the opportunity for 'functional foods' (that is, foods bought because they are believed to be good for you), such as Activia yoghurt, then putting more money behind its brands than anyone else; it showed huge confidence in its understanding of the market
- Harvey Nichols (classic London posh shop) seeing the opportunity for a branch in Leeds, in an era when there was plenty of money in the north; when it made the move, other retailers doubted whether Leeds would be posh enough – it was and it is.

All these examples have one thing in common: they are the result of careful analysis of trends within a market, backed by an ability to take bold decisions (and get them right).

62.3 CONSUMER USAGE AND ATTITUDES

Market analysis is rooted in a deep understanding of customers. Why do they buy Coca-Cola, not Pepsi? Yet they prefer Tropicana (made by Pepsi) to Minute Maid (made by Coke). And who are the key decision makers? Purchasers (perhaps parents buying a multipack in Tesco) or the users (perhaps young teenage children slumped in front of the television)? Is the brand decision a result of child pester power, or parental belief in the product's superiority? Knowledge of such subtleties is essential. Only then can the firm know whether to focus marketing effort on the parent or the child.

To acquire the necessary knowledge about usage and attitudes, firms adopt several approaches. The starting point is usually qualitative research such as group discussions. Run by psychologists, these informal discussions help to pinpoint consumers' underlying motives and behaviour. For example, it is important to learn whether KitKat buyers enjoy nibbling the chocolate before eating the wafer biscuit; in other words, to discover whether playing with confectionery is an important part of the enjoyment. This type of information can influence future product development.

The major multinational Unilever has appointed a head of knowledge management and development (David Smith), to ensure that insights such as this can be spread around the business. As he says, 'The company's collective knowledge is potentially a great competitive advantage.' By encouraging improved communication and networking, Unilever believes it is benefiting from:

- improved decision making
- fewer mistakes
- reduced duplication
- converting new knowledge more quickly into added value to the business.

Among the other ways to gather information on customer usage and attitudes are quantitative research and obtaining feedback from staff who deal directly with customers. An example of the latter would be bank staff whose task is to sell services such as insurance. Customer doubts about a brochure or a product feature, if fed back to head office, may lead to important improvements.

Quantitative research is also used to monitor customer usage and attitudes. Many firms conduct surveys every month, to track any changes over time in brand awareness or image. This procedure may reveal that a TV commercial has had an unintended side-effect in making the brand image rather too upmarket, or that customers within a market are becoming more concerned about whether the packaging can be recycled.

62.4 CONSUMER PROFILES

Marketing decisions are very hard to make without a clear picture of your customers. Who are they? Young? Outgoing? Affluent? Or not. From product and packaging design, through to pricing, promotion and distribution – all these aspects of marketing hinge on knowing your **target market**.

A consumer profile is a statistical breakdown of the people who buy a particular product or brand (for example, what percentage of consumers are women aged 16 to 25)? The main categories analysed within a consumer profile are customers' age, gender, social class, income level and region. Profile information is used mainly for:

- setting quotas for research surveys
- segmenting a market
- deciding in which media to advertise (*Vogue* or the *Sun*?).

A large consumer goods firm will make sure to obtain a profile of consumers throughout the market as well as for its own brand(s). This may be very revealing. It may show that the age profile of its own customers is becoming older than for the market as a whole. This may force a complete rethink of the marketing strategy. The company may have been trying to give the brand a classier image, but may end up attracting older customers.

62.5 MARKET MAPPING

Having analysed consumer attitudes and consumer profiles, it is possible to create a market map. This is done by selecting the key variables that differentiate the brands within a market, then plotting the position of each one. Usually this is done on a two-dimensional diagram as in Figure 62.2. Here, the image of shoe shops has been plotted against the key criteria of price (premium–budget) and purpose (aspirational–commodity). For example, Bally shoes are expensive and are bought to impress others. Church's are expensive but bought because their buyers believe they are a top-quality product.

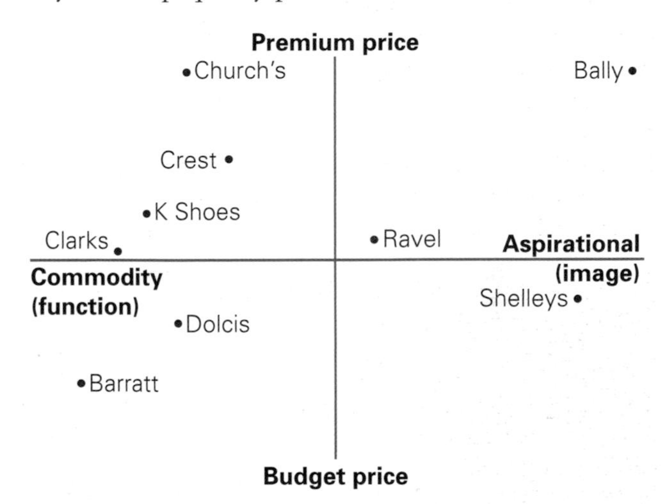

Figure 62.2 Market mapping

Market mapping enables a firm to identify any gaps or niches in the market that are unfilled. They also help to monitor existing brands in a process known as **product positioning**. Is their image becoming too young and trendy? If so, booming sales in the short term might be followed by longer-term disappointment. By monitoring the position of their brands on the market map, firms can see more easily when a repositioning exercise is required. This may involve a relaunch with a slightly different product, a new pack design and a new advertising campaign.

A-grade application

The Jaguar XJ

Launched in 2010, the new Jaguar XJ was deliberately designed to restore the company's position within the luxury car sector. In the days when Jaguar was owned by Ford, the American car producer had pulled Jaguar's model range down towards the mass market. Its XF model, launched in 2009, was successful, but was perhaps too close to the mass market to truly reposition the company. The XJ, with prices from around £60,000, would emphasise that Jaguar should be seen alongside Mercedes and BMW, not Ford or Volkswagen.

ISSUES FOR ANALYSIS

Among the main issues raised by this unit are the following.

- The importance to a firm of constantly measuring and rethinking its position in the market; this is why expenditure on market research needs to be regular and not just related to the latest new project.
- Given the importance of market knowledge, how can new firms break into a market? The answer is: with difficulty. Super-rich Microsoft launched Xbox in Britain in 2002, having to compete with the established Nintendo and Sony consoles. By 2010, despite the higher market share achieved by the Xbox 360, Microsoft was still many billions of dollars down on the Xbox experience.
- If all companies follow similar techniques for market analysis, why don't they all come up with the same answers? Fortunately, there remains huge scope for initiative and intuition. Two different managers reading the same market research report may come up with quite different conclusions. The Apple iPhone was the inspiration of a small group of developers at Apple (plus selected suppliers). The Wii was also a very individual achievement by a select few at Nintendo.

62.6 ANALYSING THE MARKET – AN EVALUATION

Market analysis is at the heart of successful marketing. All the great marketing decisions are rooted in a deep understanding of what customers really want; from the marketing of Lady Gaga through to the sustained success of the (incredibly pricey) Chanel No. 5 perfume. The clever market stall trader acquires this understanding through daily contact with customers. Large companies need the help of market research to provide a comparable feel. Techniques such as market mapping then help clarify the picture.

Having learnt what the customer really wants from a product, perhaps helped by psychological insights from qualitative research, it is relatively easy to put the strategy into practice. If the marketing insight is powerful enough, the practical details of the marketing mix should not matter too much. The Nintendo Wii was a brilliant piece of marketing, but few commentators had anything good to say about the brand's advertising or packaging. The genius came earlier in the process.

Key Terms

Product positioning: deciding on the image and target market you want for your own product or brand.

Target market: the type of customer your product or service is aimed at. For example the target market for KitKat Senses is 15- to 30-year-old women.

WORKBOOK

A REVISION QUESTIONS

(35 marks; 35 minutes)

1 Reread Section 62.1 and ask yourself 'What if Nintendo had not decided to define its market more widely? What would the business be like today?' (3)

2 Explain why Tesco's market analysis in Hungary and Poland can be described as 'clever'. (3)

3 Explain two reasons why it may be important to distinguish 'purchasers' from 'users'. (4)

4 Explain how qualitative research could be used helpfully when analysing a market. (4)

5 When *Look* magazine was launched in 2007 it announced that its target market was '24-year-old women'. Explain two ways it could make use of this very precise consumer profile. (4)

6 Explain how market mapping could be helpful to *two* of the following.
   a) an entrepreneur looking at opening up a new driving school
   b) the brand manager of Werther's Original sweets, worried about falling market share
   c) a private school thinking of opening its first branch in China. (8)

7 Why does market research need to be carried out regularly, not just related to a new product? (3)

8 Explain the importance of market research in achieving effective market analysis. (6)

B REVISION EXERCISES
B1 DATA RESPONSE

What business is Cadbury in? For the first 100 years of the firm's life, the answer would have been chocolate. But in 1989 it bought the Trebor and Bassetts brands, to form a large sugar confectionery unit. With Wrigley enjoying uninterrupted growth in chewing gum, Cadbury then bought Adams – a major US gum producer (for £2.7 billion). It followed this up with purchases of other chewing gum producers in countries that included Turkey.

In 2007, Cadbury launched the Trident gum brand in Britain. This was bold because Wrigley enjoyed a market share of more than 90 per cent in the UK. By March 2008 Cadbury was able to announce that 'an astounding £38 million of extra sales value has been added to the gum category, with 75 per cent of this growth delivered by Trident'. Cadbury's management confidently predicted 5 years of growth for Trident of as much as £20 million of sales per year.

By 2009, though, Trident was in sharp retreat, with sales falling to £19 million. Then Cadbury itself was submerged into the Kraft food business. So is Cadbury in the food business; the chocolate business; or the confectionery business? It's hard to say.

Table 62.1 UK confectionery market 2009

Confectionery	Market value £ million
Chocolate	3,069
Sugar confectionery	1,007
Chewing gum	240
Total market	**4,316**

Questions

(25 marks; 30 minutes)

1 Explain why companies such as Cadbury need to ask themselves, 'What market am I in?' (6)

2 **a)** What is meant by the term 'market share'? (2)

b) Calculate Trident's share of the chewing gum market in 2009. (2)

c) Why might Cadbury have been worried about tackling a business with 'a market share of more than 90 per cent'? (6)

3 Discuss what might have gone wrong with Cadbury's analysis of the chewing gum market. (9)

Measuring and forecasting trends

UNIT 63

Forecasting involves estimating future values.

63.1 INTRODUCTION

It is very important for managers to look ahead. They need to think about what is likely to happen in their industry and prepare accordingly in all areas of the business. One of the most important forecasts that needs to be made is the **sales forecast**. This forms the basis of most of the other plans within the organisation. For example:

- the human resource plan will need to be based on the expected level of sales; a growth in sales may require more staff
- the cash flow forecast will depend on projected sales and the payment period
- the profit and loss forecasts will depend on the level of revenue predicted
- the production scheduling will depend on what output is required
- stock levels will depend on the likely production and demand over a period.

The sales forecast therefore drives many of the other plans within the business and is an essential element of effective management planning.

When a business starts up, it is extremely difficult to interpret its sales data. An ice cream parlour that starts up in April may find that sales double in May, again in June and again in July. Excited by the business success the entrepreneurs may rush to open a second outlet. Yet a wet August may see sales knocked back followed by a sales slump in the autumn. The business may be overstretched and in liquidation by February.

As long as a business can survive the first year or two, managers can start to interpret its sales data. Above all else, managers want to understand the **trend** in product sales and compare it to trends in the market as a whole.

63.2 MOVING AVERAGES

A useful way to show trends is by using a moving average. This is helpful in two main circumstances:

1. where there are strong seasonal influences on sales, such as in the ice cream parlour example
2. when sales are erratic for no obvious reason; wild ups and downs may make it hard to see the underlying situation.

The first column in Table 63.1 shows the 'raw data' for a small supermarket (that is, monthly sales figures). As you can see, they jump around, forming no obvious pattern.

To find the moving average of the data:

- the first step is to calculate a moving total, in this case a three-month total – in other words, the January to March figures are totalled, then the February to April figures, and so on.
- the third column shows the centred average (that is, the January to March total of 156,000 is divided by 3 to make 52,000); this monthly average sales figure

Table 63.1 Example of a moving average

	Raw data (monthly sales) (£)	Three-month total (£)	Centred three-month average (£)
January	48,000		
February	57,000		52,000
March	51,000	156,000	49,000
April	39,000	147,000	47,700
May	53,000	143,000	46,300
June	47,000	138,000	45,300
July	36,000	136,000	44,700
August	51,000	134,000	

for January to March is centred to February, because that is the 'average' of January to March.

Note how well the three-month moving average clarifies the data, revealing the (awful) underlying trend. The graph shown in Figure 63.1 simply plots column 1 and column 3 to show the value of the technique.

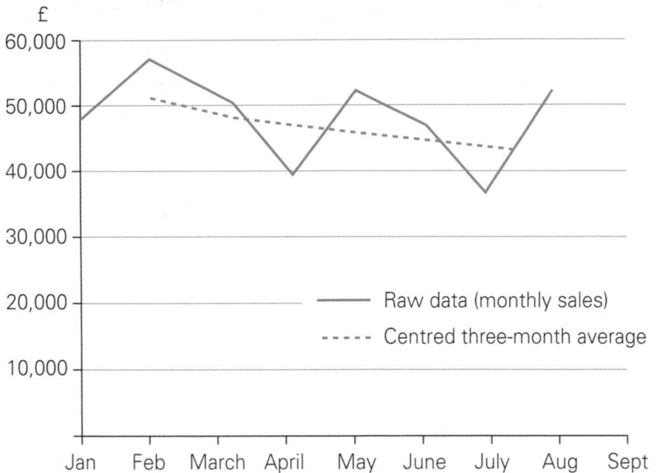

Figure 63.1 How moving averages reveal underlying trends

63.3 FORECASTING SALES USING EXTRAPOLATION

The simplest way of predicting the future is to assume that it will be just like the past. For the immediate future this may be realistic. It is unlikely (though not impossible) that the economy or demand will change dramatically tomorrow; an assumption that the pattern of sales will continue to follow recent trends may therefore be reasonable. If demand for your product has been rising over the past few months, it may not be illogical to assume it will continue in the foreseeable future. The process of predicting based on what has happened before is known as extrapolation. Extrapolation can often be done by drawing a line by eye to extend the trend on a graph (see Figure 63.2).

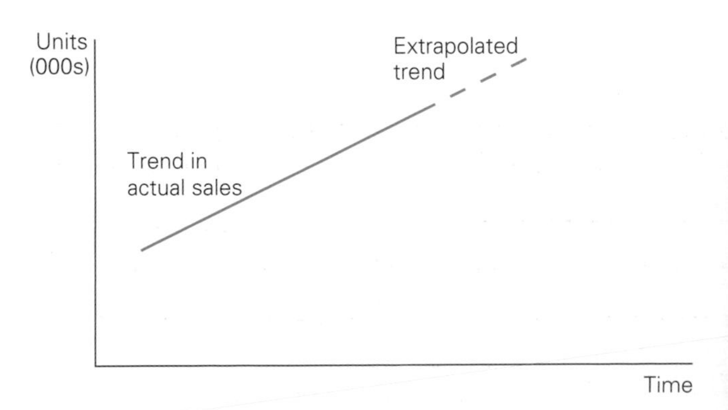

Figure 63.2 An extrapolated sales trend

Here a very steady upward trend over a long period may well continue and be predicted to continue. However, such stability and predictability are rare. The values of data plotted over time, called time-series analysis, can vary because of **seasonal variations**/influences and also because of genuinely random factors, which can never be predicted. For example, another outbreak of foot and mouth disease would lead to a sudden collapse in the sales of meat. Or a revaluation of the Chinese currency could lead to a huge wave of new tourists coming to London. Despite the uncertainties, predicting sales based on extrapolated trends is the most widely used method.

As with every business technique, there is also a need for judgement. Look at Figure 63.3. Based upon the longer-term trend, you might believe that the recent

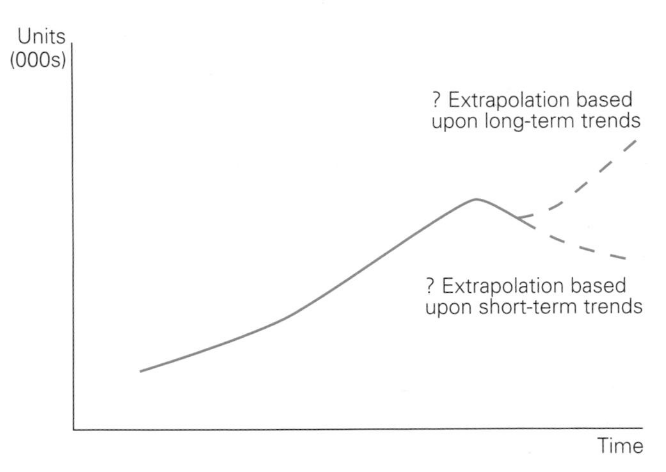

Figure 63.3 Requirement for judgement when extrapolating trends

> **A-grade application**
>
> **Sales Forecasting Manager**
> **Fast-moving consumer goods industry (fmcg)**
> *Merseyside*
> *Salary: £35,000–£40,000*
> We require a Sales Forecasting Manager for a large fmcg business. Reporting to the Supply Chain Manager, you will be responsible for producing sales forecasts, monitoring performance and detecting any deviations from plan to evaluate and make corrective action in order to drive and maintain high performance levels.
>
> *Who we're looking for*
> We require someone with an excellent forecasting background who has the proven ability to monitor actual targets against forecasts and to take action when needed. As Forecasting Manager you will have a proven background and ability to improve accuracy to required standards. You must also possess excellent communication skills, excellent IT skills, be able to work as part of a team and also able to use your own initiative.

downturn is temporary (as with UK house prices, perhaps). Or it may be that you believe that the recent figures have established the likely trend for the future. It is never wise to simply use a calculator, a computer or graph paper without thinking carefully about what makes the most sense.

63.4 CORRELATION

Businesses are always keen to learn about the effect on sales of marketing strategies such as TV advertising, sales promotion or direct mailshots. Often researchers will compare sales volume and advertising expenditure. A good way to do this is on a graph. In Figure 63.4 there is clearly a strong relationship, or correlation, between the two. The correlation is positive: as one increases so does the other. It is important to realise that each point correlating the two variables represents one observation covering a period of time.

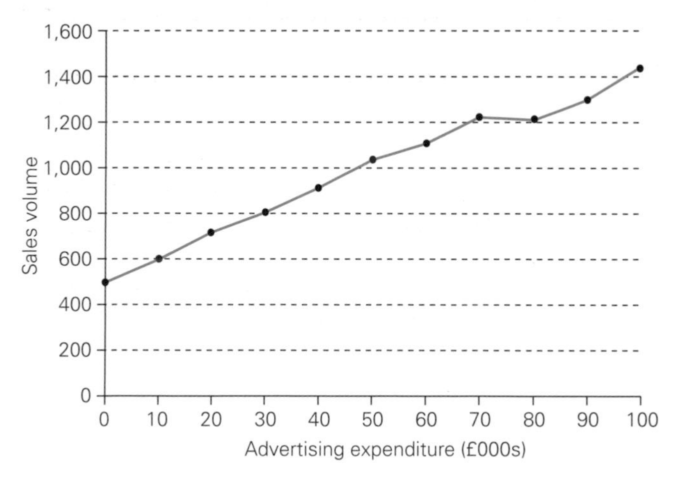

Figure 63.4 Strong positive correlation between advertising expenditure and sales

In Figure 63.5, however, there is not so much linkage, as the diagram is little more than a collection of randomly dispersed points. In this case there is low correlation between advertising and sales, suggesting that the firm should stop wasting its money until it has found a way to make its advertising work more effectively.

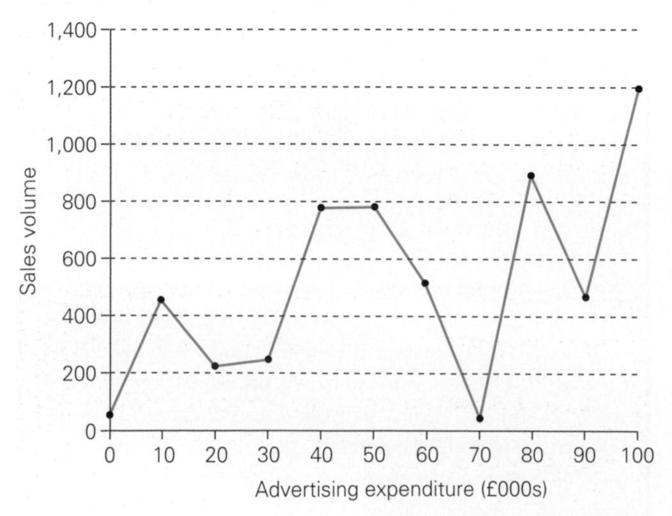

Figure 63.5 Loose correlation: are other variables important?

What the researcher is looking for is cause and effect, namely evidence that the advertising has caused the increase in sales. Now correlation by itself does not indicate cause and effect. The rising of the sun in the morning may be strongly correlated with the delivery time of newspapers to letterboxes, but it does not cause them to be delivered. Strong correlation is evidence that cause and effect *may* be present. Further evidence is needed to know how the variables are affecting each other. Clearly, the purpose of advertising is to generate sales, so it is highly likely that cause and effect may be at work. But managers know there are many variables at work all the time in markets. The sales of a product could rise because of cheaper credit terms, the disappearance of a competitor, or even unusual weather, and not just advertising. In cases like that presented in Figure 63.5, where there is weak correlation, researchers clearly should consider other variables as well as advertising.

> **A-grade application**
>
> **Correlation**
>
> In Britain, the Met Office offers businesses a weather-forecasting service, charging a fee for predicting the sales of products ranging from lemonade to cat food. It uses correlation analysis to predict how demand will vary according to the time of year and the prevailing weather. It has found that lemonade sales rise in the summer, but tail away if the weather is very hot (presumably consumers switch to non-fizzy drinks or to ice lollies). More surprisingly, cat food is weather-affected. Rainy days boost demand (the cats don't go out) while, if it's hot, cats eat less.
>
> The website www.metoffice.gov.uk recently featured a producer of hot ready meals that used the Met Office's correlation software to find out that it lost £70,000 of sales for every 1 degree of temperature increase above 20°C. Needless to say, using a weather forecast could enable the business to forecast sales more accurately, and therefore reduce stock losses on its perishable goods.

63.5 ALTERNATIVE METHODS OF FORECASTING

The moving averages technique of forecasting has some limitations. The points calculated for the trend will always be less than the number of points in the actual raw data. This technique is most appropriate in stable circumstances when elements of the business environment, such as competition, are not expected to change very much. It is less useful in periods of change or instability.

Test markets

If a market or industry is undergoing major change or if you do not have past data to help you forecast sales then you may need to make use of experts' opinions or market research. By testing a product out in a small representative market, for example, you may be able to gather data from which you can estimate sales when you roll out the product on a bigger scale. Alternatively, you could ask experts who know the industry well to help you estimate likely sales.

The Delphi technique

One method of gathering expert opinion is known as the Delphi technique. This involves using experts who are asked for their opinions individually. Their comments are then summarised anonymously and circulated to the contributors, who are then invited to comment again in the light of the previous feedback. Each time the findings are circulated for a given number of times, or until a consensus is reached.

Scenario planning

Some businesses also use scenario planning. This process involves an analysis of particular scenarios in the future. Rather than simply estimating sales, for example, experts try to anticipate what market conditions will be and what will be happening in the market as a whole. For example, a business might try to consider the market in a position of fast growth or steady growth, and the impact of this on a range of business decisions.

The oil giant Shell is known for its use of scenario planning. For example, it will consider what the year 2015 could be like if oil prices rise to $250 per barrel, or fall to $50.

63.6 OTHER VARIABLES TO CONSIDER WHEN FORECASTING

When considering your sales forecast you will want to take into account any internal or external changes that you know are about to happen. External changes could include:

- new entrants into the market
- population changes
- climate changes or changes in weather conditions
- legal changes (for example, limiting particular forms of promotion or increasing taxation)
- internal factors that you know may affect sales; this could include changes in the salesforce, changes in the amount of spending on promotion or the way that the money is being spent, or the launch of a new product.

In most cases the actual sales forecast will not be absolutely accurate. However, this does not make forecasting a waste of time; as long as it can provide an estimate that is approximately correct it will have helped the firm to plan its staffing, funding and production. Better to plan and be approximately right than not plan at all and be unprepared. However, it is always important to review your sales forecasts and compare this with what actually happened; this can help the firm to improve its forecasting techniques and provide better estimates in the future.

A-grade application

Retail sales in China

In 2006, Xu Jian (Vice President, Strategy, Volkswagen China) gave a presentation to analysts and investors. He forecast that the Chinese market for passenger cars would grow to between 4.5 and 5 million by 2010. In actual fact passenger car sales were more than 12 million in 2010! This huge underestimate forced Volkswagen to rush forward plans to boost factory capacity. Luckily for VW, construction projects in China are pushed forward much faster than anywhere else in the world, so the company could make up for its poor forecast.

ISSUES FOR ANALYSIS

- Forecasting is an important element of business planning.
- The sales forecast forms the foundation of many other of the business plans, such as cash flow and workforce planning.
- Sales forecasts are often based on past data, but must also take into account seasonal factors and changes in internal or external factors that are known about.

63.7 MEASURING AND FORECASTING TRENDS – AN EVALUATION

Sales forecasts can be very important to a business because so many other plans rely on them. They can determine how many people to employ, how much to produce and the likely dividends for investors. They may not always be accurate, but they can provide important guidelines for planning.

A badly run business will find itself in a crisis because its precisely forecast future turns out to be surprisingly different in reality. An intelligent manager tries hard to predict with precision, but thinks about the effect of sales being unexpectedly high or low. Nothing demoralises staff more than a sudden lurch by management (hiring one minute, firing the next). So the future needs to be thought through carefully.

Key Terms

Sales forecast: a method of predicting future sales using statistical methods.

Seasonal variation: change in the value of a variable (for example, sales) that is related to the seasons.

Trend: the general path a series of values (for example, sales) follows over time, disregarding variations or random fluctuations.

WORKBOOK

A REVISION QUESTIONS

(35 marks; 35 minutes)

1 What is a sales forecast? (2)

2 Explain how you can show the trend in a series of data. (4)

3 Explain how *two* of the following Heinz managers could be helped by two weeks' warning that sales are forecast to rise by 15 per cent.
   a) the operations manager
   b) the marketing manager, Heinz Beans
   c) the personnel manager
   d) the chief accountant. (8)

4 What do you understanding by the term 'extrapolation'? How is it used to make a sales forecast? (5)

5 Explain how Coca-Cola may be helped by checking for correlations between the following factors.
   a) sales and the daily temperature
   b) staff absence levels and the leadership style of individual supervisors. (6)

6 Explain why it is risky to assume cause and effect when looking at factors that are correlated. (4)

7 What is the Delphi technique? (2)

8 Explain briefly how the 2012 Olympic Committee could make use of scenario planning. (4)

B REVISION EXERCISES

B1 DATA RESPONSE

The US aircraft manufacturer, Boeing, has predicted an increase in demand from airlines for smaller aircraft, but large jumbo jet sales are expected to be lower than expected over the next 20 years. Boeing raised its projected sales of commercial jets by all manufacturers by $200 billion to $2.8 trillion in the next two decades. Regional, single-aisle and twin-aisle jets for non-stop routes would prove more popular than expected, it said. However, it reduced its forecast for jumbos carrying more than 400 people. Boeing now expects that the market will buy 960 of the bigger craft, down from the 990 it set out in last year's forecast.

The 20-year industry forecast is as follows:

- 17,650 single-aisle aeroplanes seating 90–240 passengers
- 6,290 twin-aisle jets seating 200–400 passengers
- 3,700 regional jets with no more than 90 seats, up from 3,450 forecast last year
- 960 jumbo jets seating more than 400 passengers.

According to Boeing, passenger numbers would rise by about 5 per cent a year, while cargo traffic would increase by 6.1 per cent. Emerging markets are crucial for future sales, with about one-third of the demand coming from the Asia-Pacific region.

Boeing believes its success is secure thanks to its relatively small 787 plane. It believes this will take sales from its rival Airbus. Twin-engined but with a long range, it will be able to fly direct to far more of the world's airports. This means that passengers will not need to make a connecting flight first to travel a long distance.

Questions

(30 marks; 35 minutes)

1 Analyse the ways in which Boeing might have produced its industry sales forecasts. (10)

2 Discuss the possible consequences for Boeing of the findings of its research. (20)

'What's the fuss about? It's only a café!'

That summed it up, thought Emma. Her accountant boyfriend Leon simply didn't understand her business. When she bought the Swan Café two years ago, it was so run down that the lease cost just £4,000. And it was now a thriving business. Close to the river in Oxford, it had a great trade from builders between 7.00 a.m. and 9.00 a.m., from students from 9.00 a.m. till 1.00 p.m. and from tourists between 1.00 p.m. and 4.30 p.m. Then students drift back between 4.30 p.m. and 5.30 p.m.

In the first week after opening her café, revenue was just £800. After costs, this left Emma with just £21 for herself. Today, weekly takings are as high as £5,600 and customers often queue to get in. Weekly profits are around £1,500, allowing a healthy cash nest-egg to build up at the bank.

Now Emma wants to buy the shop next door, available for £140,000 freehold. This would allow her to expand the seating area and also extend the size of the kitchen and the range of food offered. Her younger sister (Natalia) has carried out customer research at the café as part of her Business Studies coursework. It shows that customers love Emma's warm personality and the good food, but quite a few want more. The tourists are looking for freshly baked scones and cakes, while the university students would love a roast dinner in the early evening.

Natalia has promised to extrapolate recent monthly sales forward for the next few months, to provide Emma with an idea about how much profit the business should make (the figures from Appendix A form the basis of Figure 63.6).

Emma has asked Natalia to provide a further extrapolation to cover the next four years. She could then use it as a benchmark for judging sales after buying the shop next door. Would the investment of £140,000 be worthwhile? (In fact, the total investment would be £160,000, including the cost of decoration and equipment.)

While Natalia works on the sales figures, Emma is working on the costs. She knows she would need extra

Appendix A: Number of customers per month this year:

Month	Customers
Jan	2,200
Feb	2,300
Mar	2,700
Apr	2,800
May	3,400
June	3,700
Jul	3,400
Aug	3,600
Sep	3,800

Appendix B: Estimated cash flows on the Café extension (Years 1 to 4)

	Cash inflows	Cash outflows
	£000s	£000s
Now		160
Year 1	160	130
Year 2	220	160
Year 3	270	200
Year 4	320	240

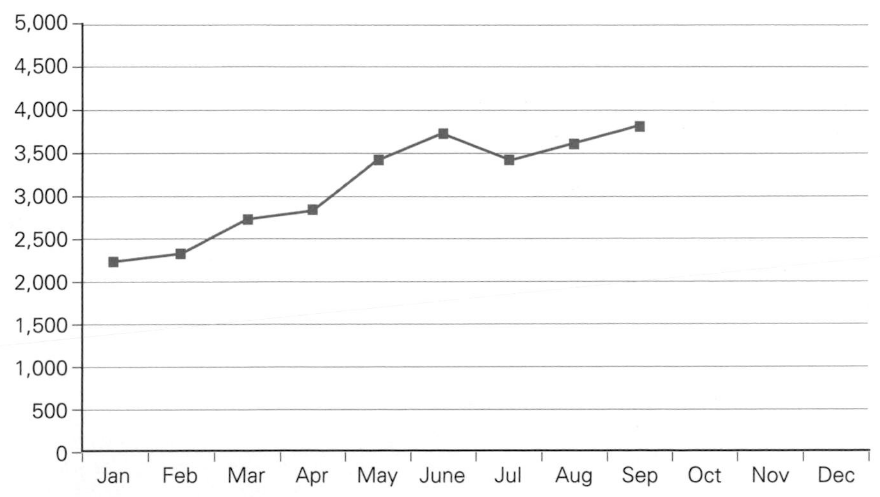

Figure 63.6 Number of customers per month, this year

staff and perhaps some regular spending on advertising. Eventually the sisters are able to put together the data shown in Appendix B. They feel increasingly excited about the project, but Leon remains negative. His view is: 'I'm sorry, love, but I think it's just a small café. If you want to build a better business, open a restaurant. And I certainly wouldn't go ahead unless you can beat the standard industry criterion levels: two-year payback and a 15 per cent ARR. And where's the money coming from? Do you really want such a big loan around your neck?'

Questions
(40 marks; 50 minutes)

1 From the information provided, do there seem good enough underlying reasons for Emma to expand the café? (6)

2 a) Use Appendix A to calculate a 3-month moving average of this year's customer numbers. (7)
  b) Plot your results onto Figure 63.6. (Preferably with a red or blue pen.) (3)
  c) Extrapolate your trend line forward to make an estimate of the number of customers in December. Comment briefly on the result. (4)

3 a) Use the information in Appendix B to calculate the payback and ARR on the café extension. Show your workings. (8)
  b) Taking everything into account, discuss whether Emma should proceed or not with the investment. (12)

C ESSAY QUESTIONS
(40 marks each)

1 'Since we can never know the future, it is pointless trying to forecast it.' Discuss.

2 'Quantitative sales forecasting techniques have only limited use. Qualitative judgements are needed in a constantly changing world.' Evaluate this statement.

UNIT 64

Selecting marketing strategies

Marketing strategies are carefully evaluated plans for future marketing activity that balance company objectives, available resources and market opportunities.

64.1 WHAT ARE THE KEYS TO A SUCCESSFUL MARKETING STRATEGY?

A strategy is a plan of the medium to long-term actions required to achieve the company goals or targets. Selecting the best marketing strategy means finding a fit between the company objectives, customer requirements and the activities of competitors.

The aim of this planning is to shape the company's activities and products to generate the best returns for the business. Marketing strategy is about adding value. It takes advantage of any unique selling points. It helps the business to identify the right mix between design, function, image and service.

Strategy is about the future

The term 'strategy' implies looking to the future. It is important not to look at what is working well now but at what the future prospects are. Toyota recognised that there was a growing interest in environmental issues. It started to invest in the production of hybrid cars. Although requiring significant investment with no sure return, Toyota executives felt that this was the way forward. The move was highly successful, with demand for the Prius surprising everyone by outstripping supply.

Strategy must be achievable

Strategy is concerned with what is possible, not just desirable. It must take into account market potential and company resources. The company needs to recognise its own limitations and potential. It also needs to consider economic and social circumstances. If the world economy is weakening, firms will be much more cautious about entering new export markets. If the home market is stagnating, businesses may well concentrate on lower-priced 'value' products.

Strategy is company specific

Each company will have a different marketing strategy. The strategy selected will reflect the individual circumstances of the business. Different companies within the same industry may be pursuing different goals. The strategies that they select will reflect those different goals. Within the same industry, one company may be aiming to increase market share while another looks for cost reductions in order to compete on price. The tyre industry is a good example of this. The market leaders were faced with increasing price competition from developing countries. They had to develop new marketing strategies. Their responses differed: Goodyear reduced costs; Michelin put its effort into innovation and widened its product range; Pirelli decided to concentrate on the market for luxury and speed.

Marketing strategy is the marketing plan of action that:

- contributes to the achievement of company objectives
- finds the best fit between company objectives, available resources and market possibilities
- looks to the future
- is carefully thought out
- is realistic.

A-grade application

New strategy at Mulberry

Faced with the severe 2009 recession, British leather-goods maker Mulberry needed a new strategy. It-girl Alexa Chung had been seen carrying a classic Mulberry bag. This had created media interest. And Mulberry's creative director Emma Hill had cashed in by launching a wave of new, younger bags. This repositioning of the brand (from middle-aged to young and stylish) was complemented by a redesign of the online store. Sales through the website shot ahead by 80 per cent.

In January 2010 Emma Hill launched an even bolder attempt at young, fashion-conscious consumers: the Alexa bag, an updated version of the classic, but named after Chung herself. A wave of public relations-based articles appeared in publications from *Vogue* to *OK*. The £800 price tag proved no barrier to sales, as the first batch sold out in three weeks.

At the age of 40, Mulberry reinvented itself. Now the question is whether it can translate its UK sales growth into international success. The likely answer is yes. A British luxury brand targeting a younger customer is likely to be received well in America and Asia.

Table 64.1 Strategy versus tactics

Marketing strategies	Marketing tactics
• Keep the main message consistent over time (for example, BMW – 'The ultimate driving machine') • Make sure that every message to the consumer shouts low prices – as Ryanair has done consistently for ten years	• Offer everyone who comes onto the Confused.com website a chance in a £1 million prize draw • Run a midweek special – 'All You Can Eat For a Tenner' during the winter months

64.2 STRATEGY VERSUS TACTICS

Strategy is not the same as tactics (see Table 64.1). Strategy is an overall plan for the medium to long term. Tactics are individual responses to short-term opportunities or threats. The marketing strategy may be to increase sales by developing a new market segment. One of the tactics used may be to undercut a competitor on price in a price-sensitive segment of the market.

64.3 TYPES OF STRATEGY

A useful way to look at marketing strategy is to follow the approach taken by Igor Ansoff, who developed 'Ansoff's matrix'. Before explaining this approach, it is helpful to look at Ansoff's view of 'strategy'. In his 1965 book *Corporate Strategy*, Ansoff described strategy as a decision of medium- to long-term significance that is made in 'conditions of partial ignorance'. This 'ignorance' stems partly from the timescale involved. If you look three years ahead there are huge risks that marketplace changes will make your plans and forecasts look foolish. Such decisions are usually discussed and decided at board level.

Ansoff's matrix (Figure 64.1) is constructed to illustrate the risks involved in strategic decisions. These risks relate to the firm's level of knowledge and certainty about the market, the competition and customer behaviour – both now and in the future. The key issue is that risk becomes ever greater the further a firm strays from its core of existing products/existing customers (that is, the top left-hand corner of the matrix).

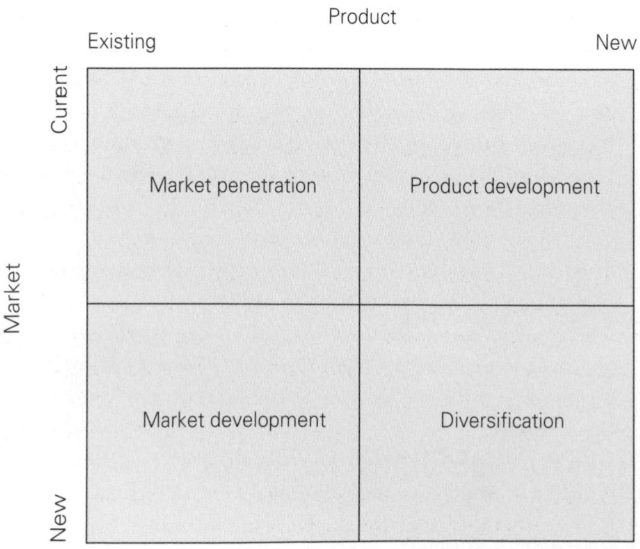

Figure 64.1 Ansoff's matrix

Ansoff identified four types of strategy within his matrix; these are described below.

Market penetration

This is about increasing market share by concentrating on existing products within the existing market. It is the most common and safest strategy because it does not stray from what the company knows best. If Tesco has opened 400 stores in towns all over Britain, and all are profitable, it is a simple matter of market penetration to open store 401 in a good-sized town that has not yet got its first Tesco.

Market penetration opportunities arise by:

- finding new customers, perhaps by widening the product's appeal to attract additional buyers
- taking customers from competitors; this may be achieved by aggressive pricing or by offering additional incentives to the customer
- persuading existing customers to increase usage; many food companies give recipes with their products to suggest additional ways of using the product; shampoo manufacturers introduced a frequent-wash shampoo to boost product usage.

Market development

This is about finding new markets for existing products. It is more risky because the company must step into the unknown. For Cadbury to start selling chocolate in China requires a huge effort to learn to understand the Chinese consumer. Yet that is exactly what Cadbury started to do in 2010.

Market development can be carried out by the following means.

- **Repositioning** the product: this will target a different market segment. This could be done by broadening the product's appeal to a new customer base. Land Rover's traditional market was farming and military use; it has now repositioned the product to appeal to town dwellers.
- Moving into new markets: many British retailers have opened up outlets abroad. Some, such as Tesco and Burberry, have opened up their own outlets. Others have entered into joint ventures or have taken over a similar operation in another country.

Moving Tesco into China was a major market development decision taken in 2004. So far it has proved very successful. Yet the hugely successful sandwich chain Pret A Manger hit problems when opening up in New York and Japan. Even the mighty Gordon Ramsay had an embarrassment when he took a London restaurant concept to Glasgow, and it 'went bust'.

Why the difficulty? Surely market research can reveal whether customers in Glasgow want the same things as those in London? The answer to that question may be, 'up to a point, perhaps'. But the skill with market research is knowing exactly what questions to ask and how to interpret the answers. This requires a degree of market knowledge that cannot always cross county boundaries, let alone national ones. This was why, over 80 years ago, the Ford Motor Company chose to set up a factory and offices in Britain, instead of relying on exporting from America. The rush of US firms that followed (for example, Heinz, Gillette, General Motors/Vauxhall) was followed much later by Japanese companies such as Sony, Hitachi and Honda. All took huge risks at the start, but believed they would only succeed in the long term by getting a deep understanding of local habits and needs. Famously, Sony budgeted for a 15-year payback period when it started up in Britain.

Product development

Product development means launching new products into your existing market (for example, L'Oréal launching a new haircare product). Hard though market development can be, it could be argued that product development is even harder. It is generally accepted that only one in five new products succeeds; and that is a figure derived from the large businesses that launch new products through advertising agencies. In other words, despite their huge resources and expertise, heavy spending on R&D and market research, plus huge launch advertising budgets, companies such as Mars, Walls and L'Oréal suffer four flops for every success.

In highly competitive markets, companies use product development to keep one step ahead of the competition. Strategies may include those listed below.

Changing an existing product

This may be to keep the products attractive. Washing powders and shampoos are good examples of this. The manufacturers are continually repackaging or offering some 'essential' new ingredient.

Developing new products

The iPhone is a fantastic example of a new and successful product development, taking Apple from the computer business into the massive market for 'smartphones'.

Diversification

If it is accepted that market development and product development are both risky, how much more difficult is the ultimate challenge: a new product in a new market, or **diversification** in Ansoff's terminology. This is the ultimate business risk, as it forces a business to operate completely outside its range of knowledge and experience. Virgin flopped totally with cosmetics and clothing, WH Smith had a dreadful experience in the DIY market with Do It All, and Heinz had a failed attempt to market a vinegar-based household cleaning product.

Yet diversification is not only the most risky strategy, it can also lead to the most extraordinary business successes. Nintendo was the Japanese equivalent of John Waddington, producing playing cards, until its new, young chief executive decided in the early 1970s to invest in the unknown idea of electronic games. From being a printer of paper cards, Nintendo became a giant of arcade games, then games consoles such as the Wii.

Even Nintendo's diversification success is dwarfed by that of Nokia, which once made car tyres and toilet rolls. Its transformation into the world's number one mobile phone maker would have been remarkable no matter what, but the fact that it came from tiny Finland makes it an incredible success. Ansoff emphasised the risks of diversification, but never intended to suggest that firms should fight shy of those risks. Risks are well worth taking as long as the potential rewards are high enough.

64.4 MARKETING STRATEGY IN INTERNATIONAL MARKETS

Entering into international markets carries the extra risk identified by Ansoff as market development. Naturally, the extent of the risk will depend on just how different the new market is from the firm's home country. For Green & Black's to start selling chocolate in France may not be too much of a stretch. French tastes are different and the distribution systems are very different from those in Britain, but there are many similarities in climate and affluence. But what about selling organic chocolate to Saudi Arabia? Or China? Or Sierra Leone? Figure 64.2 shows the way Ansoff would indicate the increasing level of risk involved.

It is also possible that the product will need to be modified in order to be successful in the new market. International markets are littered with products and businesses that tried to shift their existing products and business models into overseas markets but failed. Even the best marketing strategies can fail. Some common causes of failure are:

- language/interpretation problems
- misunderstanding the culture
- mistiming; this can be economic or even political.

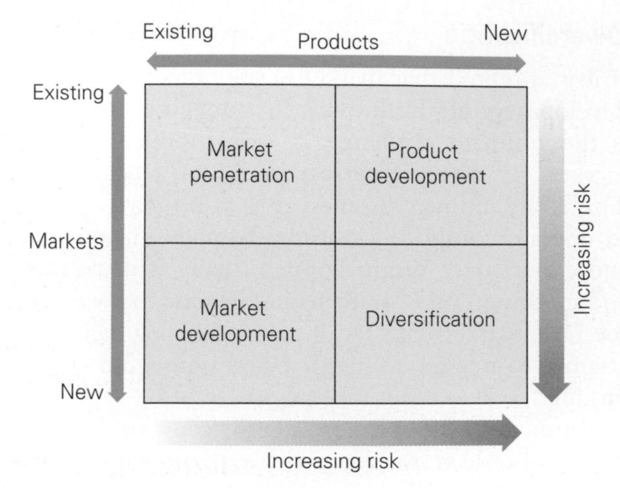

Figure 64.2 Ansoff's matrix and risk

All these can be minimised by careful research to ensure that there is a good understanding of the new market before the company attempts to do business.

Some of the most successful ventures into international markets involve working in cooperation with existing firms in local markets.

64.5 MARKETING STRATEGY: A CONTINUAL PROCESS

Once the strategy has been developed, it needs to be constantly reviewed. An idea that looks good on paper will not necessarily work in reality. There may need to be some testing of strategies, especially if they are risky. Market research and monitoring are necessary to ensure that the actions are producing the desired results. Evaluation of results will feed back into the system and in turn contribute to the development of revised objectives and strategies. This ongoing cycle is known as the strategic cycle (see Figure 64.3).

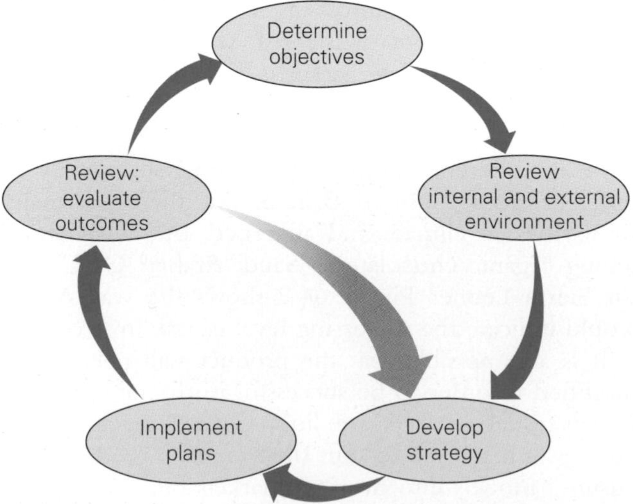

Figure 64.3 The strategic cycle

A company's marketing strategy does not exist in a vacuum. It may provoke responses from competitors. Market opportunities will be changing constantly. If the company is to be successful, it needs to be responsive and to adjust the strategy to cope with any changes in the environment or within the company. For example, the giant Heinz company found that its approach to global marketing was ineffective; it shifted strategy to become more local. Only in Britain were baked beans an important seller, so the baked bean pizza was developed for the UK alone. In Korea, people love to pour ketchup on pizza, so a deal with Pizza Hut put a Heinz bottle on every table.

64.6 ASSESSING THE EFFECTIVENESS OF MARKETING STRATEGIES

An effective marketing strategy achieves the marketing objectives; but is there more to it than that? Could a strategy be too successful? Perhaps yes, if a business is overwhelmed by demand that it is unable to meet. In most cases, though, a marketing campaign that exceeds its targets is something to celebrate (see the A-grade application).

> **A-grade application**
>
> **Meerkats do it for Comparethemarket.com**
>
> The Comparethemarket.com/Comparethemeerkat campaign was a huge commercial success. Since launching the meerkat campaign in January 2009, at a cost estimated to be at least £5 million, Orlov, the star of the films has over 600,000 fans on Facebook and 31,000 twitter followers. Comparethemarket.com has seen a 100 per cent uplift in visits to its website.

More often, the issue will be how to judge a marketing strategy that has under-performed. It may have achieved certain targets, yet failed in the most important: sales. When launching a completely new product, companies know that there are four stages consumers must go through before they purchase (known by the acronym **AIDA**):

- *Awareness:* in 2010 Moneysupermarket.com boasted that its latest advertising campaign had boosted brand awareness from 80 per cent to a record 85 per cent
- *Interest:* 'perhaps I'll have a look at the site'
- *Desire:* this may be conscious such as, for example, 'If I can find that Kate Moss dress in my size I'm buying it', or subconscious (that is, you only realise you wanted that new Malteser chocolate bar when you find you've bought it when buying a magazine)
- *Action:* the actual moment of purchase; though it is important to remember that, for the advertiser, that is only the start; few products survive on single sales; success comes from repeat purchase and brand loyalty.

To assess the effectiveness of the marketing, it is sensible to measure performance at each of these stages. High brand awareness is useless if the brand image is too poor to create interest and then desire (at the time of writing, the Glade Flameless Candle has achieved this doubtful honour in the author's household). The single most important factor, however, is the 'conversion rate' from product trial to product loyalty. If that figure is low, the marketing strategy has failed.

Possible reasons for a marketing strategy that fails to meet its sales objectives are:

- the objectives may have been unrealistic
- the budget (the total amount available to spend on the strategy) may have proved inadequate for the task
- competitors may have reacted unexpectedly fiercely to your launch, making it very difficult to succeed; for example, when Rupert Murdoch launched the free *TheLondonPaper*, the owners of the 50p *Evening Standard* launched the free *London Lite* to stop Murdoch's paper taking a grip on the capital; eventually *TheLondonPaper* was closed down, having lost Murdoch (owner of *The Sun* and Sky TV) more than £50 million. Soon after, *London Lite* was closed as well. It had done its job, maintaining *Evening Standard*'s monopoly in London
- one element of the mix may have proved a disappointment (for example, promised media coverage (PR) never quite happened, or the distribution levels were lower than planned, or the advertising never had the impact that everyone expected).

As is clear, several of these are to do with poor performance by one or more members of the marketing team, but some are out of the company's control.

64.7 SELECTING MARKETING STRATEGIES – AN EVALUATION

It would be nice to think that businesses carefully evaluate the marketing environment and then devise a strategy that fits in with overall company objectives. In reality, the strategy may be imposed by management, shareholders or even circumstances. In some instances, the only business objective may be survival. Strategy may then be reduced to crisis management. The other reality is that the business environment is not always clear and logical, so it may be very difficult to generate realistic and effective strategies.

Key Terms

AIDA: a useful way to remember the stages in getting someone to try a new product – Awareness, Interest, Desire, Action.

Diversification: when a company expands its activities outside its normal range. This may be done to reduce risk or to expand possible markets.

Repositioning: changing the product or its promotion to appeal to a different market segment.

FURTHER READING

Ansoff, I. (1965) *Corporate Strategy*. New York: McGraw-Hill.

ISSUES FOR ANALYSIS

Issues that may need to be considered in response to case study or essay questions are:

- the relative importance of strategic market planning in different types of business: can small firms possibly devote the time, thought and resources to strategy that would be spent by firms such as Heinz?
- the added risk and uncertainty of moving into international markets: firms need to ensure that the market is thoroughly researched; this can be difficult for all firms, but particularly for smaller enterprises
- the extent to which it is possible to develop clear strategies in a constantly changing marketplace
- the influence of individuals may be important: the degree of risk in a firm's strategy may depend partly on the personality of the key decision maker; an entrepreneurial marketing director may achieve breakthroughs (or disasters) that a more cautious person would avoid
- how businesses find a balance between what is desirable and what is achievable: in some firms, the balance is determined at the top (by directors who may not understand fully the market conditions); others adopt a more participative style, in which directors consult junior executives to get a clear idea of what can be achieved.

WORKBOOK

A REVISION QUESTIONS

(40 marks; 40 minutes)

1. What is marketing strategy? (2)
2. What is a unique selling point? Give two examples. (4)
3. What is meant by product differentiation? (3)
4. What are the four steps in developing a marketing strategy? (4)
5. Why is it important for a firm to examine its internal resources before deciding on a strategy? (3)
6. What is the difference between market development and product development? (4)
7. How does marketing strategy relate to the objectives of a business? (4)
8. Why is market research an important part of marketing strategy? (4)
9. Why is market development more risky than market penetration? (4)
10. Apply the AIDA model to the recent launch of any new product or service. Explain how well the business has done at each stage. (8)

B REVISION EXERCISES
B1 DATA RESPONSE

Apple's cash machine

The Apple iPod was launched in 2001, into a market dominated by Sony. For a company based on computers, the move into personal music appeared risky. As the graph in Figure 64.4 shows, sales grew slowly; iTunes was launched in 2002 but only in late 2004 did iPod sales move ahead dramatically. This was partly due to the launch of the iPod Mini, but also coincided with the start of the brilliant 'silhouette' advertising campaign. In fact, Apple has handled iPod's marketing strategy very cleverly.

iPod marketing mix

- *Product:* quick product development, from iPod 2001 to iPod Mini 2003, iPod Photo 2004 to iPod Shuffle 2005, and the iPod Touch in late 2007 and iPod Touch 4g in late 2010. As with all its competitors, the iPod is made (very cheaply) in China, so the key to its success is the stylish design, not high-quality manufacture.
- *Price:* always startlingly high; at launch, the iPod was over £200; even today the iPod Touch 3g is £189, whereas other MP3 players can cost as little as £20. Apple has managed the business dream of achieving market penetration at prices that skim the market.
- *Place:* nothing new here; Apple has distributed the iPod through the normal mixture of department stores, electrical shops and online retailers.
- *Promotion:* brilliant and lavish use of posters and TV, featuring one of the all-time great images, the 'silhouette'.

The key to the strategy has always been to achieve high credibility through brilliant design and a non-corporate image. Consumers have tended not to notice that the iPod is an amazing cash machine. In the year to June 2010, the revenues generated by iPod and iTunes exceeded $12,000 million.

Figure 64.5 iPods

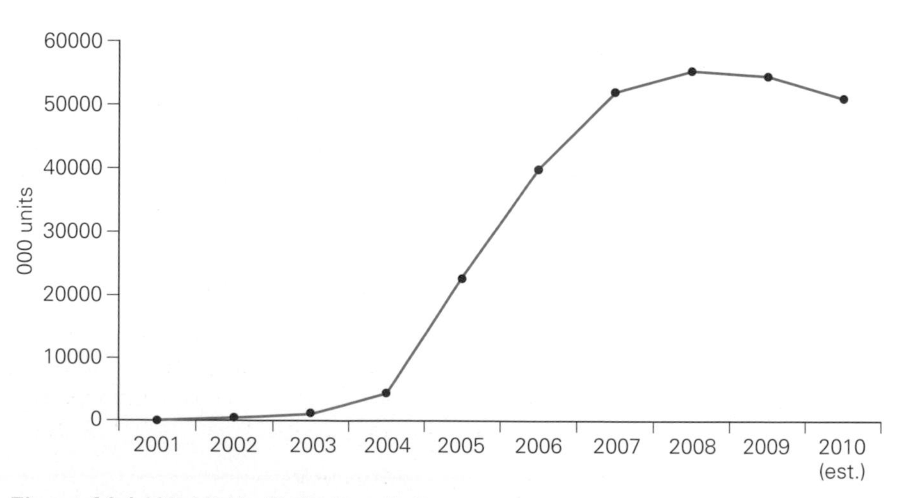

Figure 64.4 Worldwide iPod sales volume

Questions

(40 marks; 50 minutes)

1 a) What is meant by the term 'product life cycle'? (2)
   b) Explain what Figure 64.4 shows about iPod's product life cycle in the period up to the middle of 2010. (5)
2 a) Explain briefly how Ansoff would have interpreted Apple's move into the personal music market. (2)
   b) Explain why Ansoff would have considered this move to be risky. (4)
3 Discuss which of the elements of iPod's marketing mix have been the most important in its sales success. (12)
4 Given the business's success with the iPod, iPhone and iPad, discuss whether Apple should now make a move towards the games console business, competing with Nintendo, Sony and Microsoft. (15)

B2 DATA RESPONSE

Greggs: getting the ingredients right

Kennedy McMeikan, the Chief Executive of Greggs, the High Street Bakers, made the following statement when announcing the half-year results for the company in August 2010.

We are making good progress with our strategy: making Greggs more accessible to more people through our shop opening programme, investing in our bakeries for greater efficiency and capacity for growth and realizing the benefits of a strong, centrally run business.

Our accelerated shop opening and refit programmes are progressing as planned, and delivering encouraging early results.

Results

Total group sales in the 26 weeks ended 3 July 2010 increased by 2.9 per cent to £321 million (2009: £312 million). Like-for-like sales grew by 0.7 per cent, in line with our expectations.

The cost environment in the first half remained in line with our expectations with increases in fuel and wage costs partly mitigated by deflation in energy prices.

Profit before taxation increased by 12.3 per cent to £18.6 million.

Our shops

We opened 26 new shops during the first half and closed eight, giving us a total of 1,437 at the end of the half-year. We are encouraged by the performance of our new shops, almost half of which are in locations such as industrial estates, business parks and transport hubs, improving our accessibility to customers and complementing our established presence on high streets.

We also completed 47 shop refurbishments during the half year. In London, we fitted eight shops based on the concept shop we trialled in 2009, making more space available to our customers to encourage browsing and self-selection in a contemporary shopping environment. These units have shown good sales increases. This reflects our learning from the initial concept shops, and we will refit a further 19 shops in the London area during the second half. If current performance trends are maintained, we will then roll the concept shop format out to other parts of the country as part of our normal store refurbishment programme.

Trading activity

With consumers now having less disposable income than a year ago, we have focused our promotional activity in the first half on ensuring that customers benefit from great value offers throughout the day.

In the first half we have sold more than 2 million meal deals, up 167 per cent versus last year. Our current sandwich meal deal offers a freshly made roll with a choice of fillings, a 500ml soft drink and a packet of crisps. We have also had a good response to our seasonal promotion of two soft drinks for £1.80. We launched our breakfast rolls in February – bacon or sausage in a fresh, Greggs baked roll – and have now sold 4.5 million, helping to grow our sales in the traditionally quieter early morning period.

Our supply chain

Last year we undertook a review of our supply chain and announced plans to invest in our bakeries for significant shop growth and improved efficiencies. We are now beginning the first phase of this investment.

Outlook

The pressure on the trading environment looks likely to increase in the second half and we remain focused on managing costs tightly. We now expect an increase in ingredient cost inflation in the second half of the year, following the recent rise in wheat prices.

Despite the challenging trading environment, I believe that Greggs remains on track to deliver another year of progress.

Source: Extracted from Greggs plc Interim results for the 26 weeks ended 3 July 2010.

Questions

(50 marks 60 minutes)

1 What is meant by 'like-for-like sales'? (2)
2 Why is it an important part of marketing strategy to 'manage costs tightly' especially in a business like Greggs? (8)
3 How may being a strong centrally run business help the marketing strategy? (6)
4 Why is the investment that Greggs is making in their bakeries an important part of the marketing strategy? (6)
5 Using the marketing mix, explain and evaluate Greggs marketing strategy. (16)
6 How important is market research in determining marketing strategy for a firm like Greggs? (12)

C ESSAY QUESTIONS

(40 marks each)

1 How useful is Ansoff's matrix in evaluating the risk involved in new marketing strategies?
2 'Only large companies need and can afford to have a marketing strategy.' Discuss this statement.
3 'Marketing strategy can be successful only if a firm has set the right objectives.' Discuss.
4 'Marketing strategy is the key to business success.' Discuss.

UNIT 65

Developing and implementing marketing plans

A marketing plan is a detailed statement of the company's marketing strategy. It explains how the strategy has been determined and how it will be carried out.

65.1 THE MARKETING PLAN

The marketing plan puts the company's marketing strategy into action. It explains the background to the planned marketing activity. It describes the marketing strategy and explains how it contributes to the overall corporate objectives. The marketing strategy is broken down into action plans. These are the individual activities that put the strategy into practice. In effect, the marketing plan shows how the marketing budget is to be spent.

The purpose of the marketing plan is to ensure that staff understand the actions that will be taken, the reasons behind the actions and the timing of the actions. For example, it is important that the production department knows when an advertising campaign will be run. It can ensure stocks are high enough to cover the boost to demand.

What does a marketing plan look like?

For smaller businesses the **marketing plan** may be an informal document. Larger companies will formalise the plans in report format. Typically it will have the contents shown in Table 65.1.

Table 65.1 Typical contents of a marketing plan

Introduction	Gives an overview of the plan, and the economic and competitive background to it
Corporate and marketing objectives	States the overall business aims and the relevant marketing objectives
Marketing strategy	Outlines the strategy that will be used to achieve the objectives
Action plans	Details the individual marketing activities used to carry out the strategy, including above- and below-the-line activities, plus detailed timings
Detailed budgets	Breakdown of expected revenue and costs by product or department or marketing activity
Control tools	Details of how the budgets and plans will be monitored

Why is marketing planning important?

'If I had eight hours to chop down a tree I'd spend six sharpening my axe.' *(Abraham Lincoln)*

A properly developed marketing plan is important because:

- it helps to ensure that marketing activity is properly focused and integrated
- it enables everyone in the organisation to know exactly what will happen, and when
- it enables the business to take advantage of market opportunities
- it helps to ensure that the business remains healthy by preparing for possible problems
- it puts the business in a better position to react to unexpected events.

65.2 HOW IS THE MARKETING PLAN DETERMINED?

Once the marketing strategy has been agreed it needs to be put into action. The strategy will have been determined taking into account all the internal and external issues that affect the business (see Unit 64). For example, if the strategy is to increase the market share of a product, the competitive situation will help decide whether to cut price or to launch a new product.

The plan must be realistic and take into account the internal situation of the business. It needs to consider, for instance, if there are enough staff with the right skills to carry out the plans.

The most important considerations are those listed below.

- *Finance:* the amount of finance that is available to spend on marketing will obviously be important. A business cannot plan a national advertising campaign if the finance available will only fund a local mail shot. However, even if funding is available, the plan should take into account the return on expenditure. The results of the marketing must be monitored to measure the effectiveness of the expenditure.
- *Operational issues:* the marketing plan should take into account whether the organisation can cope with the increased demand that may result from any marketing campaign. This may be in production

or people terms. Boosting demand that cannot be satisfied by available stocks is a waste of time, effort and money. It may even backfire as ill will is created among retailers and consumers.

- *Competitors' actions:* any marketing effort is likely to promote a response from competitors. This needs to be considered at all stages of the planning process. A price reduction that produces a price war will do nothing except reduce margins for all concerned.

> **A-grade application**
>
> **Nintendo Wii**
>
> In 2007 when Nintendo ran its advertising campaign for its Wii and subsequently ran out of stock, analysts considered it to be a marketing planning failure. However a similar tactic is proving to be successful for Apple. Many analysts are now suggesting that a strategy of deliberately creating shortage was a major part of Apple's marketing plan for its iPad. When it was launched in the USA in 2010 customers seemed happy to queue to buy the product and the launch in Europe was subsequently delayed because of a shortage of the product. That in itself helped to fuel interest and demand. So perhaps the regular shortages of Nintendo products have inspired Apple to make this approach part of its marketing plan.

Once these three issues have been considered, the plans can be developed. The type of marketing activity that is used will be determined in different ways in different businesses. Some businesses will just continue to do what they did in the previous year: 'It seemed to work, so let's carry on.' Others will take a more sophisticated approach. This will involve analysis of what has worked well in the past. Which aspects of the marketing mix are more appropriate? Are there any areas that could be improved? What are the current issues that concern consumers? With the growth of environmental considerations, many businesses are putting green issues at the heart of their marketing approach.

65.3 MARKETING EXPENDITURE

The marketing department will have to work within the constraints of the allocated finance. One of the most difficult questions facing the marketing manager is how to spend the available resources. It is a common error to equate marketing expenditure with the cost of advertising. Many other costs are associated with marketing the product. Among the most important are the design and development of the packaging, thorough and independent market research and the achievement of good distribution.

Factors that determine how the available money is spent

How the available money is spent will depend on many factors. These include those listed below.

The likely return from the expenditure

Any marketing expenditure should produce a return. It should be evaluated in the same way as any investment in the business.

Type of product

Some products are supported by very high levels of spending while others are not. The level of spending may be related to how easy the product is to differentiate in the market. In markets where there is little difference between competing products, businesses will want to use marketing to give their product a competitive edge – to make it seem different. It is only possible to afford high marketing budgets, though, if the value added is high. Cosmetics, cars and washing powder are examples of this. Each is supported by high levels of promotional spending.

Product life cycle

For most products the highest levels of expenditure will be in the launch and growth stages. From time to time the product may need to be supported with additional spending. This will happen when the product is given additional support as part of an extension strategy.

Type of customer

Companies selling consumer goods and services will tend to have higher levels of marketing expenditure than those supplying industrial customers.

65.4 MARKETING BUDGETS

A very important aspect of the marketing plan is the **marketing budget**. Once a plan has been developed it needs to be put into action. It is also important that the plan is monitored so that the business can see if the plan is being achieved and if it is being effective. A marketing budget must be set to both implement and control the firm's marketing expenditure.

In everyday language, a budget is the amount available for spending. In business, a budget is not only an expenditure target but also a target for achievement. The marketing budget is the quantified plan for the marketing department. It shows the marketing objectives in numerical terms, such as market share or distribution targets. It is usually produced as an annual budget, but for the purpose of control will often be broken down into monthly figures.

For example, the marketing objective may be to increase sales by 10 per cent. The budget will give monthly sales targets that will deliver that annual figure. Alongside the sales figures, targets for expenditure will be given. So if the additional sales are to be generated by a new advertising campaign, the budget will include expenditure targets for that advertising.

Measuring performance against budget

If performance is to be measured effectively then it is important that there is a range of data available. The management accounting system will produce some figures, such as sales and costs. It may need to be developed to produce other information to measure marketing effectiveness. Competitive information will be important. Car manufacturers look at market share figures based on new car registrations as a key measure of performance. If Ford's market share figures are slipping behind the targets, the company will step up its marketing effort (including price cutting) to regain its intended levels.

ISSUES FOR ANALYSIS

There are several issues that are likely to be important when looking at marketing plans.

- Consideration should be given to the usefulness or otherwise of the plans. Do they really help the business to manage its marketing effort or does the process constrain real marketing initiatives? Quite often this will depend on other factors in the business, such as management style. Are staff encouraged to stick rigidly to the plan or is initiative rewarded?
- When considering how the plans are developed it is important to put the plans in the context of the business and its competitive environment. Consideration of how well a plan will work for this particular business must take these factors into account.

A key factor for businesses is setting the right level of marketing budget.

A-grade application

Sodastream comeback

In 2010 Sodastream launched a marketing campaign to try to revitalise its product. The machine which was popular in the 1970s and 1980s makes fizzy drinks at home. It is reusing the 'Get busy with the fizzy' tag-line in a series of TV adverts – the first for nearly 20 years – in the hope of enticing a new generation to the product. The product has been redesigned to give it a more modern look and the range of drinks available has been increased to include diet and healthy versions. The whole marketing campaign is costing £3 million.

It will take time to find out if this money has been well spent.

Figure 65.1 Sodastream

65.5 DEVELOPING AND IMPLEMENTING MARKETING PLANS – AN EVALUATION

The two most important aspects of marketing plans are getting the right level of marketing budget, and then finding the right balance between a fixed plan and a flexible one. In a well-run business, the budget will be set after discussion between key managers and set at a level that takes into account the objectives and the difficulty in achieving them. If a new product is being launched into a fiercely competitive market, there should be no halfway house between setting a high budget or scrapping the whole idea. A compromise may be the worst option.

After the budget has been set and decisions have been made about how and when to spend the budget, junior staff can then put the plan into practice. TV commercials can be written and filmed; commercial breaks can be booked. If circumstances change within the year, though, it may be wise to make adjustments. A TV campaign planned for October might be brought forward to September if a rival is bringing out a new product. Every plan needs a degree of flexibility.

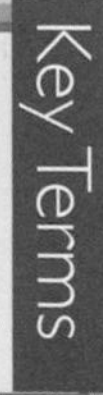

Marketing budget: the sum allowed for spending on marketing a particular product or brand.

Marketing plan: a document detailing how and when the marketing budget will be spent.

WORKBOOK

A REVISION QUESTIONS

(30 marks; 30 minutes)

Read the unit, then answer:

1. What is a marketing plan? (2)
2. List four topics that you would expect to be included in a marketing plan. (4)
3. Outline two reasons why firms prepare marketing plans. (4)
4. Why is company finance an important factor when preparing marketing plans? (5)
5. Why is it important that operational issues are taken into account when determining a marketing plan? (4)
6. How does the competitive environment influence marketing planning? (4)
7. What is a marketing budget? (2)
8. How can a marketing budget help to control marketing expenditure? (5)

B REVISION EXERCISES

B1 DATA RESPONSE

Marketing plans show the shift to internet marketing for business-to-business firms.

A recent survey, undertaken by a business-to-business online magazine, discovered that, in spite of economic problems, businesses were planning to increase their levels of marketing expenditure. The survey also showed that online marketing expenditure would be the main focus of this increase. The survey, which was conducted online, had 250 responses; 60 per cent of the respondents said that their firms planned to increase their marketing budgets, but 80 per cent of them planned to increase their online marketing budgets. This was up from 70 per cent in the previous year's survey. Only 10 per cent of replies indicated that their marketing expenditure would be reduced; 70 per cent of the businesses were planning to launch a new advertising campaign in the coming year and nearly half planned to increase the number of staff employed in marketing.

The main marketing goals identified by the survey were:

- getting new customers – 60 per cent
- increasing brand awareness – 20 per cent
- retaining customers – 15 per cent.

Approximately one-third of marketing budgets would be spent on online marketing. This is a 10 per cent increase over last year's levels. This expenditure would be for:

- website development
- direct email marketing
- search engine marketing
- video webcasting
- sponsorship.

The other main results from the survey were:

- a large rise in the number of businesses planning to use event marketing
- a reduction in the amount of advertising in newspapers and magazines
- continuing growth in the use of direct mailing.

Questions

(35 marks; 40 minutes)

1. What is meant by 'business to business'? (2)
2. Why might the results of this survey not give a true picture of marketing plans for all businesses? (8)
3. Why do you think there could be a trend for businesses to increase their marketing activity online? (5)
4. Why do you think that firms may be considering moving away from newspaper and magazine advertising and towards direct mailing? (8)
5. Discuss whether or not a business such as Marks & Spencer should spend one-third of its marketing budget on online marketing. (12)

B2 CASE STUDY

Ewans Motor Company is a car dealer based in the Midlands. It has two outlets. One has the franchise for a range of small family cars. The other offers larger luxury cars.

Business has been steady over the past few years, but has seen no real growth in total sales or profitability. The business is facing increased local competition from another garage offering a similar range of family cars. There is also the threat of an economic downturn in the area, as one of the largest employers is threatening to cut staff as a result of lower export sales due to the stronger pound.

The owner, Peter Ewans, has brought in a new marketing manager with the hope that the business can cope with these challenges and hopefully increase profitability. The new marketing manager, Sharon Crisp, agreed to join the business providing that the marketing budget was increased from its current 1 per cent of turnover. She feels that in the highly competitive climate of the small car business, the budget needs to be slightly more than doubled. Sharon is sure that she can justify this additional expenditure by raising profitability. She also introduced the concept of a marketing budget that she feels is long overdue. Previously, expenditure has been on a rather ad hoc basis and there have been no targets set for sales or profitability. There has also been little or no monitoring of the results.

After analysing both the market situation and the figures for the business for the last few years, Sharon produced the marketing budget figures shown in Table 65. 2.

Sharon felt that there was going to be a need to use some price discounting on the smaller cars to combat the increased competition in the area. Her plan was to allow the salespeople to discount the price by as much as they felt was necessary to ensure the sale. She allowed an average of £100 for each small car for this. To support the salespeople Sharon planned to double the mail shots. These would inform customers of special offers and also invite them to special family days. These days would be very child orientated, offering family entertainment and gifts for children; all of the slightly increased promotional budget would be spent on this. She also planned to support the family days with additional advertising in the local press. The sponsorship of sporting activities in local schools fitted into the plan, so this would also be continued.

Industry reports suggested that the luxury car business would grow at about 6 per cent in this year, so Sharon decided to do very little except for sending out mail shots to support this sector of the market.

Table 65.2 Marketing budget for Ewans Motor Company

Budget	Last year	This year
Sales: small cars	1,600	2,000
Sales: luxury cars	800	950
Average selling price: small cars	£12,000	£11,900
Average selling price: luxury cars	£25,000	£25,000
Average contribution per small car	£840	£740
Average contribution per luxury car	£3,000	£3,000
Total marketing expenditure	£392,000	£800,000
Breakdown of marketing expenditure:		
Price discounting	0	£200,000
Direct mailing	£100,000	£200,000
Advertising	£150,000	£250,000
Promotional offers	£92,000	£100,000
Sponsorship	£50,000	£50,000

facilitators. They are there to coach and help employees to do their job properly perhaps by ensuring sufficient training is provided and that the employee can develop in his or her career. This approach fits with McGregor's Theory Y style of leadership (see box).

The advantages of a soft approach to HRM are that:

- the organisation is building on the skills and experiences of their employees; this may enable the business to be more creative, more innovative and differentiated from the competition
- the organisation may be able to keep and develop highly skilled employees with expectations of a career with the business
- individuals throughout the business are encouraged to contribute, which may make the organisation more flexible and adaptable to changing market conditions.

The disadvantages of a soft HRM approach may be that:

- time is taken in discussion and consultation rather than 'getting the job' done
- employees may not have the ability or inclination to get involved; they may just want to be told what to do and be rewarded for it; in this case a soft approach to HRM may be inappropriate and ineffective.

Douglas McGregor's Theory X and Theory Y

McGregor's book, *The Human Side of Enterprise* (1960), popularised his view that managers can be grouped into two types: Theory X and Theory Y. McGregor had researched into the attitudes of managers towards their staff. He found that most managers assumed their employees were work-shy and motivated primarily by money; he termed this type of manager Theory X. The alternative view was from managers who thought that underperforming staff were victims of poor management. Theory Y managers think that as long as people are given the opportunity to show initiative and involvement, they will do so.

Which is the right strategy: hard or soft?

The attitude of managers towards their employees can be influenced by many different factors, such as those listed below.

- *Their own experience:* if you have taken an encouraging approach towards staff in the past and been let down then you may be reluctant to try this again.
- *The nature of the employees:* the skills, attitudes and expectations of employees will influence the way in which you manage them. If they are able, engaged and eager to progress then a soft approach is more likely.
- *The nature of the task:* if the task is simple, routine and repetitive then a hard approach is likely to be adopted. If there is little room for creativity or innovation because the task is standardised then the directive approach with clear instructions may well be the most efficient.

However, in general in the UK in recent years there has been a greater expectation by employees that they are involved in decision making and that managers take account of their welfare and skills development. The workforce is, on average, better educated than it was 20 years ago and employees are clearer about their rights. They also have more legal protection than before and expect more in terms of their careers. Most developed countries are 'knowledge economies' requiring innovative thinking, independent decision making and the ability to 'think outside the box' (think of design work, software development, advertising, the music industry). As a result, a soft approach may be more suitable because it encourages individuals' contributions.

ISSUES FOR ANALYSIS

- There are two valuable lines of analysis built into this unit. The first is the question of who is responsible for the key HR decisions. The answer is often *not* the HR department. Most shop-floor workers are trained, managed and appraised by their supervisor. Similarly, most executives deal with their line manager, not their HR manager. In an accountancy department, then, it may be that the manager has little or no skill in people management; yet she or he may make all the most important decisions about the future of junior staff. HR departments can be little more than administration functions; all the key decisions about people are made elsewhere.
- The second issue is 'hard' versus 'soft' HR. This is also important, as it provides a useful analytic comparison. It encourages a view of HR that is questioning rather than flattering. In a world in which large companies worsen the pension rights of their own staff, it is right to be sceptical about whether modern HR methods are truly in the best interests of staff.

66.6 UNDERSTANDING HRM OBJECTIVES AND STRATEGY – AN EVALUATION

Human resource management is one of the functions of a business. The overall approach to HRM (for example, soft versus hard) and specific HRM decisions (for example, to recruit or train) will be linked to the objectives and strategy of the business as a whole. A decision by a business to downsize or to expand abroad, for example, will have major implications for the HRM function. At the same time, the HRM resources of a business will influence the strategies a business adopts.

Key Terms

Hard HRM: when managers treat the human resource in the same way they would treat any other resource (for example, ordering more one week, and less the next); in such a climate, employee relations are likely to be strained and staff may see the need for trade union involvement.

Line managers: staff with responsibility for achieving specific business objectives, and with the resources to get things done.

Soft HRM: when managers treat the workforce as a special strength of the business and therefore make sure that staff welfare and motivation are always top priorities.

Workforce planning: checking on how future workforce needs compare with an audit of staff today, then planning how to turn the skills of today's employees into the skills required from tomorrow's staff.

FURTHER READING

McGregor, D. (1960) *The Human Side of Enterprise*. McGraw-Hill Higher Education.

Price, A. (2004) *Human Resource Management*. Thomson Learning.

WORKBOOK

A REVISION QUESTIONS

(30 marks; 30 minutes)

1 What may be the effects of managing human resources in the same way as all the other resources used by a business? (4)

2 Identify three important features of the job of a human resource manager. (3)

3 Some people think that schools should stop teaching French and instead teach Mandarin (Chinese). If a school decided to do this, outline two implications for its workforce planning. (4)

4 A fast-growing small business might not have a human resources manager. The tasks may be left up to the line managers. Examine two reasons in favour of creating a human resources management post within such a business. (6)

5 Outline two ways in which a human resources manager may be able to help increase productivity at a clothes shop. (4)

6 Briefly discuss whether a Theory Y manager would ever adopt a 'hard HRM' approach. (9)

B REVISION EXERCISES

B1 DATA RESPONSE

Source: Extract from *Human Resource Management* (Price, 2004)

Storey (1989) has distinguished between hard and soft forms of HRM. 'Hard' HRM focuses on the resource side of human resources. It emphasizes costs in the form of 'headcounts' and places control firmly in the hands of management. Their role is to manage numbers effectively, keeping the workforce closely matched with requirements in terms of both bodies and behaviour. 'Soft' HRM, on the other hand, stresses the 'human' aspects of HRM. Its concerns are with communication and motivation. People are led rather than managed. They are involved in determining and realising strategic objectives.

Questions

(25 marks; 30 minutes)

1 The passage explains that hard HRM emphasises 'headcounts' and managing numbers effectively. Outline one strength and one weakness of this type of approach to managing people. (6)

2 Explain what the author means by the phrase 'people are led rather than managed'. (8)

3 Discuss whether staff at a car factory such as Honda's plant in Swindon are likely to want to be 'involved in determining and realising strategic objectives'. (11)

B2 DATA RESPONSE

Transocean

BP was blamed by the public and Barack Obama for the 2010 Gulf Oil explosion and oil spill. But the defective oil rig was owned and operated by the US company Transocean. In September 2010, Britain's independent Health and Safety Executive (HSE) produced a hugely critical account of Transocean's activities in the North Sea. The company was accused of compromising safety by 'bullying, harassment and intimidation' of its staff. This was especially important because a separate HSE report had, in late August, shown that the combined fatality and major injury rate in the North Sea had nearly doubled in 2009–10, compared with the previous year.

In 2009 the HSE visited four North Sea oil rigs operated by Transocean. Inspectors noted a common (and unusual) pattern that staff complained about the attitudes and behaviour of management. The *Guardian* newspaper stated that the (as yet unpublished) HSE report says that:

'The company has not considered the human contribution to safety in a structured and systematic manner', and says the organisational culture is based on blame and intolerance.' (*Guardian*, 6 Sept 2010). The HSE went on to comment that bullying, aggression, harassment, humiliation and intimidation were 'causing some individuals to exhibit symptoms of work-related stress, with potential safety implications'.

A regional organiser for the RMT union's offshore branch in Aberdeen was not surprised by the report, saying that 'I have dealt with three cases where workers were unfairly dismissed by Transocean and in each case I have been able to win compensation for them ... I know ... that other really serious accidents are not being reported because of widespread bullying and intimidation'.

Sometimes people assume that 'soft HRM' is the modern way, with 'hard HRM' a thing of the past. It is important to realise that shocking people management still exists today. It is rare to see it reported.

Source: adapted from an article in the *Guardian*, 5 September 2010.

Questions

(30 marks; 35 minutes)

1 Explain the possible advantages to a company such as Transocean of adopting a 'hard HRM' strategy. (8)
2 Examine the possible advantages and disadvantages of trade union membership to employees on Transocean's North Sea oil rigs. (10)
3 Discuss the possible impact that Transocean's approach to its labour force could have on its workforce plans. (12)

C ESSAY QUESTIONS

(40 marks each)

1 Discuss whether a 'hard HRM' approach is the right way to run a supermarket branch where 50 per cent of the staff are part-time students.
2 In 2010 Sainsbury's announced that it planned to open a supermarket chain in China, the world's fastest-growing major economy. To what extent will Sainsbury's success or failure in China depend upon a successful HR strategy?

Workforce planning

UNIT 67

A workforce plan is developed to ensure a business always has the right number of employees with the right skills to meet the staffing requirements of the organisation.

67.1 INTRODUCTION

Managing a firm's human resources is a key element of business success. This includes ensuring the business always has the number and skills of employees that it requires. The key components of workforce planning are set out below.

1. Audit what you have at the moment; how many staff and what are their skills; ideally, this audit would include aspirations (for example, staff who say 'I'd love to travel' or 'I've always wanted to learn a foreign language').
2. Analyse the corporate plan to turn plans into people. For example, if Sainsbury's corporate plan says '20 new stores to be opened in Britain in the next two years', the workforce plan can be set: 20 new stores, each staffed by 200 people = 8,000 new staff needed.
3. Take into account the changes on the way from here to there. How many will leave to retire, have kids or just to have a career change? Some football teams age together; eleven 29-year-olds may be great, but four years later there will be a problem.
4. Calculate the gaps that need to be filled between now and two years' time. This can be done through the following sum:

Staff needed in 2 years *minus* staff now *plus* staff leaving between now and then = Extra staff required

An example of a workforce plan by UK grocery chain Sainsbury's is given in Table 67.1.

Having completed this process (which should be done carefully, with full consultation with every senior manager), it is time to put it into practice. The process of workforce planning includes recruitment and selection, training and development, and appraisal.

67.2 RECRUITMENT

This topic was covered in Unit 38. The key point to remember is that workforce planning will always emphasise quantity (the right number of people with the right skills), whereas effective recruitment and selection needs to focus on the quality and attitude of staff. Workforce planning provides a structure within which effective recruitment can take place. It will only do so if the character and personalities of the new staff are treated as of equal importance to their skills and aptitudes. The A-grade application below shows the quantitative approach taken by many workforce planners.

Table 67.1 Components of a workforce plan for UK grocery chain Sainsbury's

Component of a workforce plan	Example: UK grocery chain Sainsbury's, starting to investigate opening stores in China and India
1. Audit current staff, to find out their skills	How many current staff speak Mandarin or Hindi, and how many have significant, recent local knowledge?
2. Identify the workforce needs in 2 years' time, based on the corporate plan	How many staff will be needed in the UK in 2 years' time, broken down by skill and seniority and how many will be needed in China and India?
3. Estimate employee loss through natural wastage	Research into HR records to find how many of the 127,000 staff will be retiring; if the labour turnover is 20 per cent, 25,000 people need to be recruited just to maintain the present situation.
4. Calculate the gaps between what exists now and what is needed in 2 years – then plan to fill them	If Sainsbury's plans 20 new store openings in the UK plus 2 in China, it may need 8,000 new staff in addition to the 25,000 needed to replace leavers. These 33,000 must be divided up to plan for how many Hindi speakers, how many butchers, bakers and accountants are needed.

The labour market

The workforce plan is not only influenced by the firm's own strategy. It is affected by the state of the labour market. If there is a skills shortage in the UK, for example, the firm may have to look to recruit from overseas. Alternatively, there may be a large supply of relatively cheap labour available that makes expansion easier or makes it viable to use more labour rather than invest in capital equipment. In 2010 the new UK government decided to cap inward migration – even for those with jobs waiting for them in Britain. This may have an impact on the growth rate of the UK, if those skills cannot be found among the UK workforce.

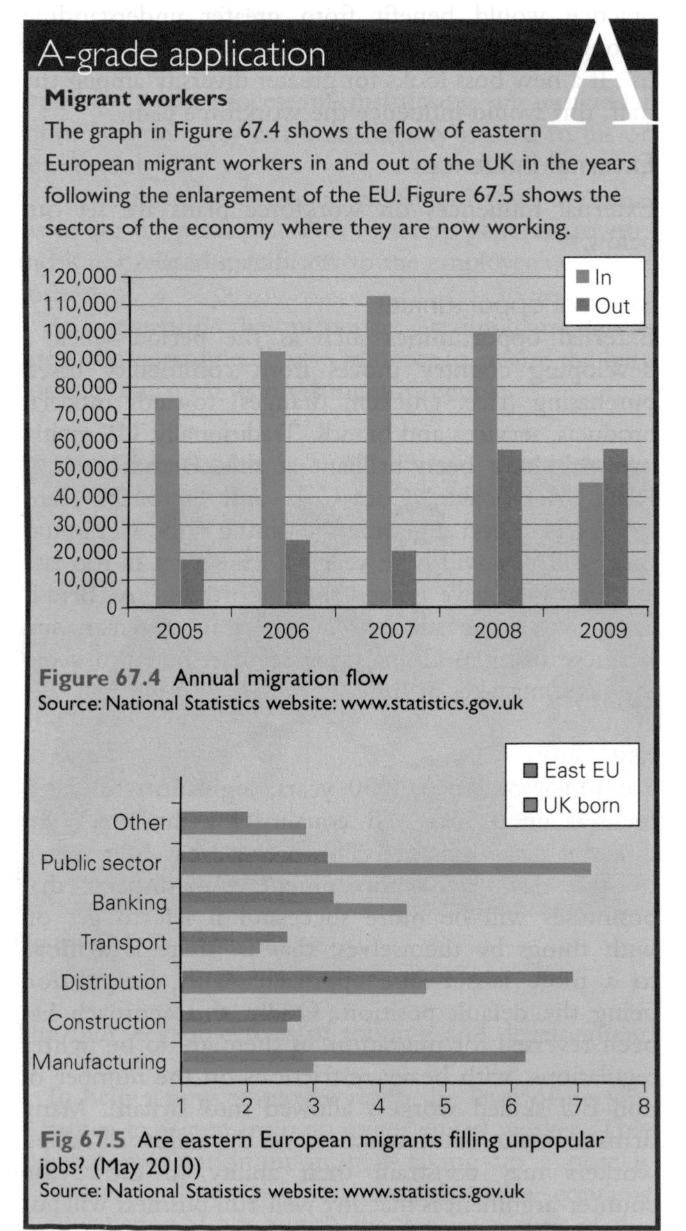

A-grade application

Migrant workers

The graph in Figure 67.4 shows the flow of eastern European migrant workers in and out of the UK in the years following the enlargement of the EU. Figure 67.5 shows the sectors of the economy where they are now working.

Figure 67.4 Annual migration flow
Source: National Statistics website: www.statistics.gov.uk

Fig 67.5 Are eastern European migrants filling unpopular jobs? (May 2010)
Source: National Statistics website: www.statistics.gov.uk

67.6 THE VALUE OF WORKFORCE PLANNING

A well-considered workforce plan is a joy to observe. When Arsenal sold Ashley Cole to Chelsea, the club already had a line of replacements, from Gael Clichy to the even younger Kieran Gibbs. (Arsenal fans may suggest that the goalkeeper succession plan was less successful.) In effect, then, a successful workforce plan is one that you never notice; things simply fit into place. You open your first store in Xian, deepest China, and staff are ready to serve customers efficiently from day one.

The value of workforce planning can simply be defined by the alternative: no workforce planning. In a big organisation, the result would be a dreadful mismatch between what the business needs and what the staff can do. There may be a school with redundant French and German teachers but a huge demand for conversational Mandarin. Or a sandwich chain with a new shop that opens with no one trained to use the coffee machine.

A business cliché can usefully be applied to workforce planning:

'Fail to prepare and you prepare to fail'.

A-grade application

In September 2010, after nearly four years and an incredible £300 million of spending, the super-posh Savoy Hotel reopened in London. When it closed, all but a tiny handful of senior staff lost their jobs, so a brand new HR department was needed to recruit and train hundreds of new employees. Yet, in such an upmarket venue, customer service had to be expert from the opening day. This was accomplished by hiring staff a month before opening day, and giving sustained training throughout the month. Often, staff were training while the builders were still drilling, but opening day proved hugely busy and hugely successful.

Costs associated with workforce planning

When a business enters a tough period, workforce planning may be focused on reducing the wage bill. Because natural wastage ensures that some people are resigning or retiring, the first step in cost-cutting is to plan for redeployment. This means retraining staff so that they can switch from an activity where there are surplus staff to another area where shortages exist. It saves the business having to hire new staff, thereby allowing the overall wage bill to fall.

Unfortunately redeployment may not be enough. There may be a need for further job losses, either through voluntary redundancy (incentivising staff to leave the job) or compulsory redundancy. In the latter case, UK businesses have to pay no less than the legal minimum redundancy pay. This applies only for those who have been employed for more than two years and pays:

- Half a week's pay per year of service for those below 22
- A week's pay per year of service for those between 22 and 40
- A week and a half's pay per year of service for those aged over 40

When you think of the impact of redundancy on family finances, these sums may seem high to employers, but will seem all too low to employees.

Damage to working relationships between employers and employees

Workforce planning can seem a cold, uncaring practice to the staff within a business. Cabin crew who are used to having six staff on a plane may get very upset if that number is to be cut to five; they know they are having to work harder, under greater stress, *and* will have fewer opportunities for overtime. Well-run businesses try to overcome this resistance to change by effective communication of the need for cost-cutting. But if staff read of Directors' pay rising by 15 per cent, they will not take kindly to cutbacks on the shopfloor.

67.7 WORKFORCE PLANNING AND BUSINESS SUCCESS

People play a vital role in the success of most business organisations. The creatives at the Saatchi & Saatchi advertising agency, the programmers at Google, the coaches and players at Manchester United are all essential to the organisation's success. Having the right people, with the right skills, is therefore critical to business planning. Without them you may not be able to expand, you may not be able to deliver the level of service offered and you may not make the profits you expect. Staffing shortages may mean you cannot meet customer orders; skills shortages may mean you lack the flexibility you need to compete effectively. Planning your human resource requirements and reviewing the workforce plan is therefore a major contributor to the overall performance of a business.

67.8 FACTORS THAT CAN UNDERMINE A WORKFORCE PLAN

Every workforce plan is based on predictions of the underlying conditions within a market. The number of staff Tesco will need in China in three years' time is based on estimates of:

- the rate of economic growth in China over the next three years
- the ferocity of competition from multinational rivals Walmart and Carrefour
- the profitability of the UK business and therefore its ability to finance the investment in China.

Needless to say, any of Tesco's underlying assumptions may prove to be incorrect. China may boom next year but suffer a sharp recession the year after; or Walmart may outbid Tesco when dealing with property developers, making Tesco unable to open as many new stores as planned.

As with every other aspect of business, nothing relating to the future can be regarded as certain.

ISSUES FOR ANALYSIS

When analysing a firm's workforce plan be aware of the following aspects.

- Check that the workforce plan is closely linked to the overall corporate plan. Expansion is likely to mean recruitment; relocation may mean transfers or even redundancies. Effective human resource management means planning ahead to identify future workforce requirements. The business should not merely respond to short-term events and allow these to shape human resource policy
- Make sure that there is a contingency plan (a plan B), that is, some thought to what happens if things turn out differently from the plan. Tesco's ambitious plans in China follow on from equally ambitious (but unsuccessful) plans in America. If a business is unsure of long-term success, is it wise to be hiring permanent staff on 'big-money' wages?
- The all-embracing, numerically-driven power of a workforce plan threatens to sideline the ideas on human motivation put forward by Maslow and Herzberg. Recent years have seen a shocking return to the view that financial incentives create the 'right' behaviours in staff. In fact, as with bankers' bonuses, incentives can lead to perverse behaviour. Many a workforce plan ignores the academic work into human psychology – and suffers as a result. Workforce planning is good at getting square pegs into square holes. It is less good at making sure the square pegs find the holes satisfying and rewarding.

67.9 WORKFORCE PLANNING – AN EVALUATION

Managing people effectively is the single most common factor that links successful organisations. This involves planning the human resource requirements very carefully as the business strategy or the external environment changes.

The success of a workforce plan will depend on how well it anticipated the demands for and supply of labour, and how well the corporate and workforce plan is implemented.

The importance of workforce planning has increased as managers have come to see the importance of staff as a provider of **competitive advantage**. Planning itself has become more difficult as the rate of change has increased.

Key Terms

Competitive advantage: factors that enable a business to compete effectively within a marketplace; the business may focus on cost-cutting or on offering a differentiated, value-added service.

Diversity: employing staff from a wide range of social and racial backgrounds. This should give the organisation the ability to understand a wide range of customers.

Investors in People: an organisation that inspects HR practices at a business to see if it deserves the award of Investor in People

Workforce planning: the process of anticipating in advance the human resource requirements of the organisation, both in terms of the number of individuals required and the appropriate skill mix. Recruitment and training policies are devised with a long-term focus, in order to ensure the business is able to operate without being limited by a shortage of appropriate labour.

WORKBOOK

A. REVISION QUESTIONS

(30 marks; 35 minutes)

1 Explain the purpose of a workforce audit when devising a workforce plan. (4)

2 Why is it important that an organisation challenges its existing employment structure each time an opportunity to do so emerges? (4)

3 Look at Figure 67.5 and identify two types of job that are filled particularly by east European migrant workers. (2)

4 Outline the potential value to Google UK of having a three-year workforce plan. (4)

5 What may be the costs of not training the following:

  a) new supermarket checkout operators (4)

  b) crowd stewards at Manchester United? (4)

6 What kinds of non-financial rewards may be offered to employees? (4)

7 Outline two factors that may undermine Primark's workforce plan for the UK over the coming three years. (4)

B REVISION EXERCISES

B1 CASE STUDY

In November 2010 Tesco announced plans to quadruple sales in China over the next five years. The firm aims to build more than 1,000 Chinese hyper- and super-markets by February 2015. It will be focusing upon cities with more than 1 million people, of which there are more in China than in all the 30 countries in Europe. Tesco has started its workforce planning by starting a graduate trainee programme specifically focused on retailing in China. It will need to develop a huge HR division in China to cope with, literally, hundreds of thousands of jobs created by its China plans.

Questions

(30 marks; 35 minutes)

1 Explain the probable value to Tesco from using workforce planning in the lead-up to 2015. (6)

2 Tesco's plans have been stimulated by an external influence: the opportunities in China. Analyse two internal factors that may determine the detailed workforce plan that Tesco now develops for its China operation. (8)

3 To what extent can Tesco management be sure that the use of workforce planning will guarantee an effective and efficient workforce in China? (16)

B REVISION EXERCISES
B2 CASE STUDY

Human resource development at Prest Ltd

Three years ago Prest Ltd, manufacturer of electronic components, closed three factories and concentrated its operations on a single site. At the same time it reorganised the remaining plant to cut costs and improve product quality. Before modernisation, 50 per cent of the machinery being used at the site was over 15 years old. This was replaced by up-to-date equipment. The new production line was designed to run continuously, with operators being expected to take 'first level' decisions at the point of production to keep it functioning. As a result, tasks such as fault finding and machine maintenance became an important part of the job of each worker.

The modernisation of the plant signalled a shift to team working, in order to encourage employee flexibility. Multi-skilled operators were needed with a deeper understanding of the production system. The employees needed to know how the new machinery could best be used to ensure consistently high levels of production quality. These changes had clear implications for the human resource department at Prest. Recruitment would have to focus on a new type of employee, and existing employees would need to be retrained.

The human resource manager conducted a feasibility analysis in order to review the strengths and weaknesses of the company's existing workforce and its ability to handle the new situation. This concluded that both shop-floor supervision and the engineering section needed strengthening. In response, 15 new engineers were recruited and five staff redeployed to improve production supervision.

As an answer to the immediate need for greater skill levels, a comprehensive training programme in quality control was introduced for all staff. Machine operators were encouraged to mix with engineers during this exercise, helping to break down barriers between the two groups. For many individuals, this was the first formal company training they had ever received. The development initiative was successful enough to stimulate requests for further learning opportunities. As a result, Prest created a link with a local technical college to provide more extensive instruction for those who wished to learn more about modern production techniques.

Although the benefits of the training were clear, three problems emerged that Prest had not anticipated. The greater knowledge of the operators made them anxious to put their acquired skills into practice. After nine months the new production line had reached only 80 per cent efficiency. Senior managers believed employees were losing interest when machinery was functioning normally. In addition, some workers felt the extensive training they had received was not reflected in enough increased responsibility. Their expectations of a more interesting job had been raised, but the reality seemed little different than before. Finally, 12 newly trained staff left the company because they could now apply for more highly paid posts at other firms in the area.

Prest also considered the long-term human resource implications of the move to a more sophisticated form of production. The workforce knew little about new production technology, so the firm's training school ran a course on robotics. The decision was also taken to provide a sponsorship scheme to encourage new recruits to study on an engineering degree course at university. The firm wished to ensure it did not face a shortage of talent in the long term.

Questions

(40 marks; 45 minutes)

1 Explain the ways in which Prest Ltd used workforce planning in the period covered by the article. (8)
2 Discuss the human resource issues that could emerge as a result of the feasibility study conducted at Prest Ltd. (12)
3 Analyse the appropriateness of the development programme introduced by Prest Ltd in the light of the problems identified by the feasibility study. (8)
4 Consider whether the difficulties experienced after staff training at Prest Ltd suggest that employees can receive too much training. (12)

C ESSAY QUESTIONS

(40 marks each)

1 Johnson Engineering plc is suffering from a lack of skilled engineers. Consider how its human resource department could set about solving this problem.
2 In order to establish a competitive advantage, a business must make sure its selection, appraisal, development and reward of employees 'fit' together to form a single human resource policy approach. Discuss how this might be achieved and the difficulties that may be encountered.

UNIT 68

Flexibility and insecurity

Flexibility refers to the willingness and ability of a firm to adapt its operations in response to changing circumstances. This will require a workforce that is multi-skilled and a culture that accepts change. It may, however, lead to increased uncertainty and insecurity within the organisation.

68.1 THE NEED FOR A MORE FLEXIBLE APPROACH

The rise and rise of Toyota and its model of lean production has taught many firms many things. Above all else, it showed that mass production systems lack the flexibility needed for today's markets. When oil prices leap from $25 to $100 within a couple of years, whole model ranges have to change. In early 2008, with sales of its Hummer 'beasts on wheels' down by 25 per cent, General Motors needed to switch to smaller, more environmentally friendly cars. It needed a more flexible approach. But if you have forced an employee to work at the same job day in day out for 15 years, it may be very difficult to retrain them.

Today's businesses need a more flexible approach within their operations. The need has arisen for a number of reasons.

- Increasing competition means that the marketplace is subject to frequent and often rapid change. Firms need to be able to anticipate these changes and respond to them quickly in order to maintain a competitive edge.
- Many consumers want more customised goods and services (that is, better tailored to smaller segments of the population); firms have to adapt the production process in order to meet demand, while still operating efficiently and keeping costs down.
- Increasing competition, especially from overseas firms, has forced businesses faced with fluctuating or seasonal demand to introduce greater operational flexibility, in order to eliminate any unnecessary costs.

To succeed in modern markets that are often fragmented into relatively small niches, and where customer tastes are ever-changing, many firms have adopted lean production. This approach implies the use of machinery that can quickly be reprogrammed to carry out a range of tasks, and the creation of a multi-skilled and flexible workforce that can quickly adapt – and be adapted – to meet a firm's changing requirements.

A-grade application

Benefits of flexible working

During the 2008–10 recession, a surprise to many was that unemployment stayed far lower than expected. Only in America did it shoot upwards. In Europe unemployment stayed low because of the willingness of staff to be flexible. In companies such as JCB and Honda UK, employees volunteered in 2009 to have cuts in their hours (and pay), to help their employers survive without needing to slash the workforce. Flexible working proved a benefit for both sides of industry.

68.2 ACHIEVING GREATER FLEXIBILITY WITHIN THE WORKFORCE

There are a number of ways in which firms can attempt to increase the level of workforce flexibility, some of which are described below.

Functional flexibility

This occurs when workers become multi-skilled (that is, they are given the scope and ability to carry out a variety of tasks (functions), rather than specialising in completion of one particular area). This can be encouraged through the use of job rotation, in which workers carry out an increased number of tasks at the same level of difficulty. In a hotel, for instance, the people who are usually on reception could spend time organising wedding receptions, giving them a wider understanding of the business. In Japan this is known as horizontal promotion, as it implies that the company has enough faith in the individual to invest time and money in training him or her for an extra job.

Increasing the level of functional flexibility should, in theory, mean that a firm's human resources can be used more effectively. Keeping workers fully occupied should lead to improved productivity. It should also mean that employees are equipped with the skills needed to cover for staff absences, minimising any

Table 68.1 Creating functional flexibility: benefits and drawbacks

Benefits	Drawbacks
Increases in productivity from greater utilisation of employees	Potential loss of production as workers switch between different tasks
Reduction in disruption to production caused by staff absence	Greater training requirements as individual workers need to acquire a wider range of skills, increasing costs
Greater employee motivation created by more varied and challenging tasks at work	Workers may be reluctant to acquire new skills, especially if there is no corresponding increase in pay

disruption or loss of production that this may otherwise have caused. Individual workers may respond positively to the increased variety and new challenges provided, improving motivation and increasing productivity further. However, firms may be unwilling to bear the costs of additional training unless the benefits of adopting a new approach are obvious and immediate. See Table 68.1.

Numerical flexibility

All firms face the problem of having enough workers to respond to increases in customer demand, without having to bear the cost of employing unnecessary staff should sales decline temporarily. Increasing the level of numerical flexibility involves a firm using alternatives to the traditional approach of employing staff on permanent, full-time contracts. These alternatives include the use of temporary contracts, agency staff, and **subcontracting** or **outsourcing** certain operations to other firms. Flexible temporary staff enable firms to respond to a sudden rise in sales by increasing the workforce quickly – and then reducing its size just as quickly, should the sales increase prove to be temporary. However, while a reliance on temporary staff and external organisations may help to reduce costs and improve reaction to change, productivity may be harmed by a lack of expertise and worker loyalty to the firm.

Time flexibility

Greater flexibility can also be created by moving away from the traditional 9 to 5 working day and 38-hour working week, in order to respond more effectively to customer demands. There are a number of methods used by firms to vary the pattern of working, including the use of part-time work, job sharing, annualised hours contracts and flexitime. For example, banks, insurance companies and mobile phone operators make extensive use of flexitime systems to provide 24-hour employee cover via the telephone and internet, in order to provide customers with greater convenience. Introducing greater time flexibility can also have a number of benefits for employees who may have family or other commitments during normal working hours. Providing staff with more flexible working arrangements can help to improve recruitment, increase motivation and reduce labour turnover, leading to reduced costs and boosts to productivity.

68.3 A MODEL OF THE FLEXIBLE FIRM

The flexible firm is able to change its own structure in response to changing needs. This means creating a structure that allows quick changes to take place. In order to achieve this, firms have tended to identify a 'core', which forms the basis for all its operations, and a

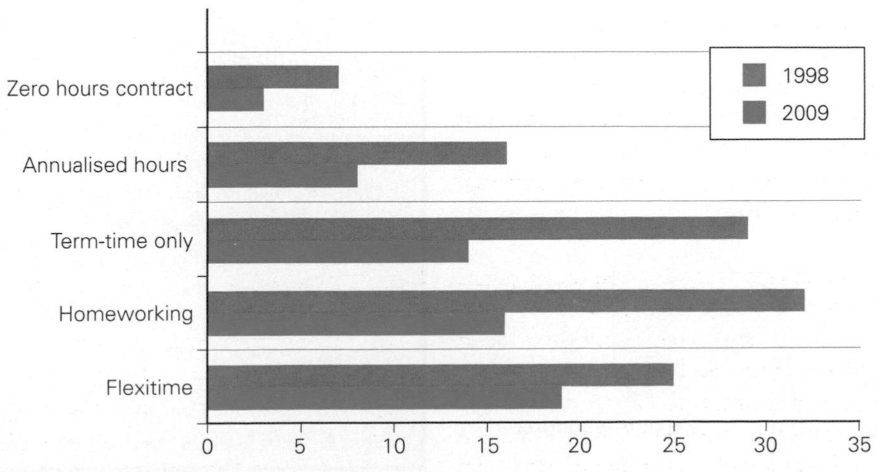

Figure 68.1 Changes in flexible working arrangements in the UK
Source: DTI, CIPD and industry estimates.

'periphery', which consists of all the other tasks needed to run the firm but that are not central to the business.

For a firm producing household goods such as washing machines, **core workers** may comprise designers, the market research team and workers on the production line, among others. The canteen and cleaning staff, and even advertising campaign staff may be seen as being less central to the firm, and so may be employed on a part-time basis, or even brought in at specific times to undertake a specific task; these are known as **peripheral workers** (see Table 68.2).

Table 68.2 Core and peripheral workers

Core workers	Peripheral workers
Full-time employees	Part-time, temporary or self-employed
Do tasks central to the business	Perform less critical, or less permanent, tasks
Secure jobs	Insecure jobs
Committed to the firm's goals	Committed to self-interest

The benefit of being a flexible firm, of course, is that the periphery can be increased quickly when needed to meet a particular change in the marketplace.

In his book *The Age of Unreason*, Professor Charles Handy suggested that instead of firms comprising two elements, the core and periphery, there were actually three parts to modern firms; he called this idea the 'Shamrock Organisation', as illustrated in Figure 68.2. The first leaf of the shamrock represents the professional core, made up of qualified professionals, technicians and managers. The second leaf, called the contractual fringe, is for the work that has been contracted out to someone else because it is not central to the firm. Professor Handy notes that many firms that used to be manufacturers now do little more than assemble parts bought in from suppliers. As much as 80 per cent of a firm's work may be done outside the business itself. The third and final leaf is the flexible labour force, made up of temporary and part-time workers. In effect, Handy has split the periphery into an internal periphery (the flexible labour force) and an external periphery (the contractual fringe).

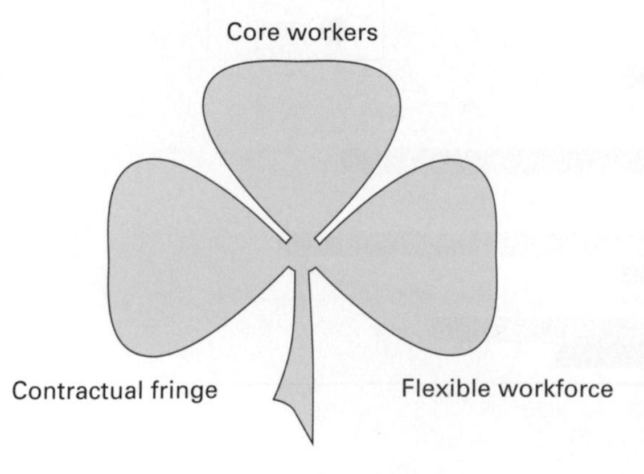

Figure 68.2 Handy's shamrock organisation

A particular type of flexible worker is the homeworker. This is someone who works at home, probably on a laptop connected permanently to the main office. In some cases it can be that a full-time employee does two days a week at home – with fewer distractions from the phone, from meetings and from gossipy staff. In other cases, the business may want as few people as possible at head office, to keep overhead costs down, so they encourage staff to work at home, and perhaps occasionally come in and '**hot-desk**'.

Some really enjoy this arrangement, whereas it makes others feel insecure. Ideally, an employee would have this as an option; it would be much less satisfactory if it were forced upon the worker.

Figure 68.3 Working at home

A-grade application

Homeworking eases stress levels

Working from home reduces stress in office workers, but leads to fears about career progression, according to research. A survey of 749 staff in managerial or professional positions conducted by Durham Business School showed that homeworkers worried about missing out on 'water-cooler networking', where potential opportunities for moving up the ladder are discussed informally in the office.

Despite these concerns, the study also found that working from home generally had a positive effect on an employee's work–life balance, giving them more time with the family, and leading to less stress and less chance of burnout.

Four in ten respondents who worked more than 20 hours per week at home reported feeling a great deal of stress because of their job compared with 65 per cent of employees who worked solely in the office.

Source: *Personnel Today*, 20 March 2008 © Reed Business Information

68.4 FLEXIBLE OPERATIONS AND 'HARD' HRM

Whether or not flexibility was necessary for a firm's success, 'hard HR' managers saw scope for increasing their control over staff. Full-time, permanent staff who were resistant to changes put forward by management may find themselves threatened with being 'outsourced'. Outsourcing is when a firm uses sources outside the business to undertake functions that used to be done internally by a section of the business itself. Tasks such as designing new products or undertaking market research can be bought in by the firm as and when needed. In effect, it turns what used to be a fixed cost (a staff salary) into a variable cost; that is, a cost that need only be incurred when there is demand for it.

Although that may sound logical, it has some serious potential downsides. Outside contractors have no loyalty to the business and no reason to contribute anything that is not being paid for (such as an idea for doing things more efficiently). So firms that shrink their core workforce too much (see Figure 68.4) can find that the organisation is like a Polo – all outside and no heart.

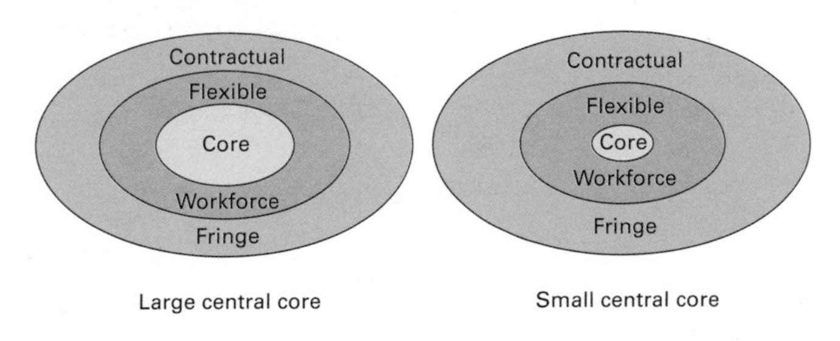

Figure 68.4 The shrinking core

68.5 INSECURITY

The increasing desire for firms to increase their flexibility has generated a number of concerns, in particular, in terms of loss of job security for workers. While those employees in core roles have continued to enjoy a great deal of job security, peripheral workers have experienced a growing sense of insecurity as the use of temporary contracts and the threat of insecurity has increased. An increasing number of workers have also had to overcome an instinctive resistance to change by having to repeatedly retrain in order to carry out new job roles. However, some would argue that demands for increasing flexibility within the workplace have created new opportunities and challenges, including opportunities to learn new skills and diversify into new career paths, rather than ending up 'stuck in a rut'.

ISSUES FOR ANALYSIS

Opportunities for analysis may arise when asking the following questions.

- What is the pressure behind a change in production system from inflexible (mass) to flexible (lean)? If the reasons are positive, it may be easy to convince staff of the benefits. Unfortunately the move to 'lean' can also be a move to 'mean' (that is, increased flexibility may be at the cost of increased insecurity). Always, the question of trust is crucial. Does the workforce trust the management?
- What are the reasons behind a firm's decision to choose a more flexible approach to staffing? Is it to be more helpful to staff, perhaps especially those with small children? Or is it a way of maximising management control over staff, and minimising labour costs?

68.6 FLEXIBILITY AND INSECURITY – AN EVALUATION

The adoption of a more flexible workforce can, in principle, be an attractive prospect for any modern business, offering a number of benefits, including reduced costs and an increased ability to respond to changing customer demands. The separation of employees into a highly valued core and an easily dispensable periphery may allow a business to 'pick and mix' skills and obtain the exact combination required within the market at that particular moment in time.

However, it can also lead to a number of problems in the long term, especially if it creates insecurity among peripheral workers that leads to high levels of staff turnover. The ability to cut labour costs quickly and easily in the face of a downturn in the market has obvious attractions. However, in the long term, the establishment of a multi-skilled and loyal workforce, able to adapt and diversify into new markets, may lead to even greater success.

Key Terms

Core workers: employees who are essential to the operations of a business, supporting whatever makes it distinctive or unique. Such workers are likely to receive attractive salaries and working conditions, and enjoy a high degree of job security.
Flexible approach: an approach to operations that implies a move away from mass production to batch production, the use of machinery that can be quickly reprogrammed to carry out a range of tasks, and the creation of a multi-skilled and flexible workforce that can quickly adapt to meet a firm's changing requirements.
Hot-desk: an approach that provides a temporary desk for homeworkers to use when they come to the main office; they are not allowed to leave any of their own possessions there.
Outsourcing: involves a firm finding an external business to carry out part of the production process, in order to cut costs or achieve a better level of service. For example, it may involve hiring cleaning or catering services from other businesses.
Peripheral workers: those workers who are not seen as being central to a firm's operations. They may carry out necessary tasks, but may be required only on a temporary basis and be easily replaced.
Subcontracting: where another business is used to perform or supply certain aspects of a firm's operations (see '**Outsourcing**').

FURTHER READING

Handy, C. (1989) *The Age of Unreason*. Hutchinson.

WORKBOOK

A REVISION QUESTIONS

(40 marks; 40 minutes)

1 Why could increased market change have an effect on the way people are employed today? (3)
2 Outline two reasons why firms may have chosen to adopt a more flexible approach to workforce arrangements. (4)
3 Briefly explain what is meant by the term lean production. (3)
4 Explain, using examples, what is meant by the term functional flexibility. (4)
5 Outline one advantage and one disadvantage for a small textiles manufacturer of trying to increase the degree of functional flexibility among its workforce. (6)
6 Explain what is meant by numerical flexibility in respect of a firm's workforce. (3)
7 State two ways in which a bank offering telephone and internet services to customers would benefit from introducing greater time flexibility. (4)
8 Explain the idea of the 'Shamrock Organisation'. (3)
9 Outline two reasons why a firm's employees may welcome the decision to move towards increased labour flexibility. (4)
10 Examine two reasons why the move towards greater flexibility might lead to increased insecurity within the workforce. (6)

B REVISION EXERCISES

B1 DATA RESPONSE

Flexible working at First Direct

First Direct is one of the UK's leading commercial banks, providing a wide range of financial services via telephone and the internet to over 1.2 million customers. When First Direct began, high street banks opened only between 9.00 a.m. and 3.00 p.m., Monday to Friday. However, the company set out to create a different business model, based on the customer need for greater convenience. Since its establishment, First Direct's reputation has rested on the fact that it is the bank that never closes and ignores weekends and bank holidays. Operators in the company's call centres handle approximately 235,000 calls each week, more than 13,000 of which each day are outside normal working hours, and with more than 500 coming from overseas.

The company's operations have required it to develop a working culture that is very different from the traditional model. This has included longer shifts, a high proportion of part-time and home-based workers, and reliance on so-called 'mushrooming' – a term used to describe workers employed to work night-time shifts.

According to Jane Hanson, head of human resources at First Direct, 'It's about making life convenient ... We have people phoning us while they're on holiday or in the middle of the night because they wake up worrying that they haven't paid their Visa bill.'

First Direct appears to have succeeded on a number of levels. The quality of its customer service has resulted in high rates of customer retention. Employees also appear to approve of the company's approach to flexible working; the company claims to have very good rates of staff retention, claiming, for example, that 90 per cent of female staff return to their jobs after maternity leave.

Questions

(30 marks; 35 minutes)

1 Identify two examples of flexible working practices used by First Direct. (2)
2 Analyse two possible benefits for a business such as First Direct of creating a more flexible workforce. (10)
3 To what extent is the creation of a more flexible workforce crucial to the continuing success of a company such as First Direct? (18)

B2 DATA RESPONSE

Job insecurity leaves no time for lunch

Research suggests that only one in six workers in the UK take a regular lunch break and that the breaks are getting shorter as a result of increasing job insecurity. A survey carried out by human resources firm Chiumento discovered that only 16 per cent of employees regularly take a 'proper' lunch break, defined as one of around an hour in length, away from their desk or work station at least three times a week. According to Andrew Hill, who helped to conduct the study,

> 'Employees are struggling to keep on top of to-do lists and think the answer is to work harder, eating a sandwich at their desk as opposed to taking a full lunch break, and also not having sufficient breaks during the rest of the day. ... But these breaks are essential for staff to perform at their best and cope with the daily pressures of work. Managers should be encouraging staff to take lunch breaks – their performance, and ultimately the business, may suffer otherwise.'

The UK's average working week is among the highest in Europe, with three quarters of employees regularly working overtime but only one-third being paid or given time off in return. One in six employees in the UK works more than 60 hours a week. Professor Cary Cooper, an occupational psychologist at the University of Lancaster, claims that, despite UK workers being considered the workaholics of Europe, productivity per capita in the UK remains lower than many other European countries. According to Professor Cooper, 'People feel as though they have to get to work early, stay late and not take lunch breaks' because of job insecurity and the desire to show commitment. However, in spite of these concerns, he believes that workers should still take proper lunch breaks two or three times a week because, ultimately, their managers will judge them on their output, not on their 'presenteeism'.

Source: based on BBC News, 11 August 2008

Questions

(30 marks; 35 minutes)

1 Examine two possible causes of increasing job insecurity among UK workers. (10)
2 Discuss the key implications of the findings of the research into UK working practices contained in the case study for businesses. (20)

C ESSAY QUESTIONS

(40 marks each)

1 To what extent do you agree with the view that UK manufacturing firms can survive only by adopting 'hard HRM' methods?
2 Assess the possible impact of adopting more flexible working practices on the international competitiveness of a firm such as Cadbury.

Competitive organisational structure

UNIT 69

A management hierarchy that fits with the current and future needs of the business.

69.1 INTRODUCTION

Organisational structure can be looked at in two ways: as the vertical and horizontal veins that give life to the business; or as a collection of managers and administrators who generate fixed overhead costs that may be so high as to strangle the profitability of the organisation.

For a moment, sticking with the analogy of veins and therefore blood; a successful business will have a free-flowing circulation, bringing oxygen to every part of the organisation. The right communications will reach the right people; the channels going up will be as clear as the channels going down; and there will be little fat to weigh the organisation down. Of course, that's not always the case. Some organisations are so bureaucratic that fresh ideas and innovations are slowed down to a trickle or blocked completely. The veins can get clogged up, threatening an organisational heart attack.

The value of the analogy is to emphasise the link between organisational structure and competitiveness. In most markets, conditions are changing so rapidly that successful organisations have to change at the same time. In 2001 China generated a small proportion of Volkswagen's (VW) sales; in 2010 VW sales in China were twice as high as in the company's second biggest market (Germany). The sudden rise of China forced VW to expand and refocus its organisation. This can lead to new communication problems emerging, though VW managed to avoid these pitfalls.

Despite this important picture of organisational change, it is helpful to remember that some organisations spend decades without threat to their business model. Take Heinz, for example. In the UK, Heinz has enjoyed 50 years of dominant positions in large areas of the market for bottled goods (salad cream; ketchup) and canned goods such as Heinz soup. This probably means that if Heinz needed to change dramatically its management hierarchy would struggle. Its organisational structure will probably resemble that of a government department: slow, cautious and very set in its ways.

And then there's the subject of money, that is, the cost of maintaining the organisational structure. Not that many years ago, a school would have a head, a deputy head and a school secretary. These three salaries were the 'overhead costs' borne by the 'frontline' staff: the teachers, the school meal team and the caretaker. Today a school employing 120 staff may have an organisational structure of 40, leaving just 80 teachers. The cost of the bureaucracy is huge; the benefits yielded may be harder to fathom. People are expensive; managers are even more so. In 2010 the stores of grocery chain Sainsbury's achieved a gross profit of £1,082 million; the administration overhead costs of £399 million absorbed over 35 per cent of that profit.

69.2 FACTORS DETERMINING THE CHOICE OF ORGANISATIONAL STRUCTURE

Scale

When Facebook began, it had two employees: a finance guy and Mark Zuckerberg, the programming brains behind the operation. As it grew, more programmers were employed, but although they were formally answerable to Zuckerberg, the approach was quite laissez-faire. They knew broadly what they were supposed to do (such as design a way to allow users to easily 'poke' each other) and simply got on with it. This was a classic flat hierarchy, allowing close contact between the top and bottom of the organisation, which encourages participation, motivation and creativity.

As the size of an organisation grows, informality becomes more problematic because it's no longer possible for the boss to pop his or her head round every door and say 'What's Up?' Supervisory and then middle-management layers emerge, to enable the business to achieve control and coordination of the employees. In some cases the emergence of more layers of hierarchy encourages the overall boss to **decentralise**. That means delegating power from the centre towards local or more junior staff. In other words a democratic boss may try to keep the workforce engaged by ensuring that local managers and local teams can make significant decisions about how the business works.

Table 69.1 Benefits and drawbacks of decentralisation

Benefits of decentralisation	Drawbacks of decentralisation
• Keeps decision making close to the customer, allowing faster and better decisions to be made	• It can be hard to coordinate the whole organisation when you give decision-making power to branches or local operations
• Bright employees need the opportunity to show their potential; if all decisions are made by 50-year-olds at head office, how are the 25-year-olds to shine? And how can they stay motivated?	• Sometimes, bright young employees can make decisions that prove costly (but, in general, the cost of mistakes can be more than outweighed by the benefits from success, e.g. Kinect)
• Head office should make broad strategic decisions about allocating resources, not meddle in middle-management decisions	• Businesses such as McDonalds pride themselves on consistency (a Big Mac should always taste the same, anywhere in the world), so some centralised decisions are inevitable, even desirable

Table 69.2 Benefits and drawbacks of centralisation

Benefits of centralisation	Drawbacks to centralisation
• Central control may help achieve consistency in every branch and every part of the world	• If every retail outlet has the same stock, the business is failing to match stock to individuals' different requirements
• Central purchasing should reduce variable costs, thereby boosting the firm's gross profit margin	• Centralised processes can become bureaucratic, so the gain in gross margin may be lost in overhead expenses (and therefore the net margin)
• If the industry is one where wage rates are low (such as catering), head office decisions may be better than those of young, perhaps alienated, staff	• The business will never be able to promote senior managers from within if they are never given the opportunity to use their ability

When Microsoft decided that it must find a way to outflank the Nintendo Wii, it set up a secret project team (Project Natal) to work on what became known as Kinect. Although this was a large team with huge financial resources, control was delegated to the project director. By decentralising, Microsoft's Chief Executive was able to get on with running the business as a whole, leaving all key decisions to his Project Natal team. The benefits and drawback of decentralization are given in Table 69.1.

When firms grow even larger, perhaps to the scale of Tesco or Starbucks, decentralised decisions may seem to get in the way of economies of scale. Tesco, in particular, prides itself on its bulk buying. By purchasing centrally for every one of its 2,000 UK stores, it can achieve much lower variable costs than any other supermarket chain. Therefore, Tesco sees benefits in **centralisation**.

If a business is highly centralised, local managers may find it frustratingly hard to feel that their efforts are making much of a difference. Head office may tell them which products to stock, how many to buy, how to display them, how to train the staff and – most commonly – what the budget will be for the coming weeks (for example, must beat a £1 million per week sales target and must stay within a £800,000 expenditure budget). Centralisation may make sense for the business, but it will rarely be liked by the managers who feel trapped by head office policies. The benefits and drawback of centralisation are given in Table 69.2.

So, which is better, centralisation or decentralisation? There is no one answer to this question that may be applied to all situations. It all depends on the type of business, the size of the business and the attitude of management. There is no doubt, though, that bright employees would rather work where their decisions are listened to or acted upon, rather than simply doing what they're told.

A-grade application

A

In October 2010 Sir Phillip Green (owner of Topshop) handed in a report on cost-cutting to the new Conservative-led government. After two months of looking at central government spending he decided that costs could be cut by centralising purchasing. He pointed out that government spending on desktop PCs ranged from £300 to £2,800, implying that if all were purchased centrally, every computer would cost £300 or less. The *Financial Times* was quick to spot the flaw in Green's argument, because government used to have departments that did all government purchasing, such as Her Majesty's Stationery Office (HMSO). These departments were scrapped by a previous Conservative government. Why? The reason was because of the benefits of decentralisation.

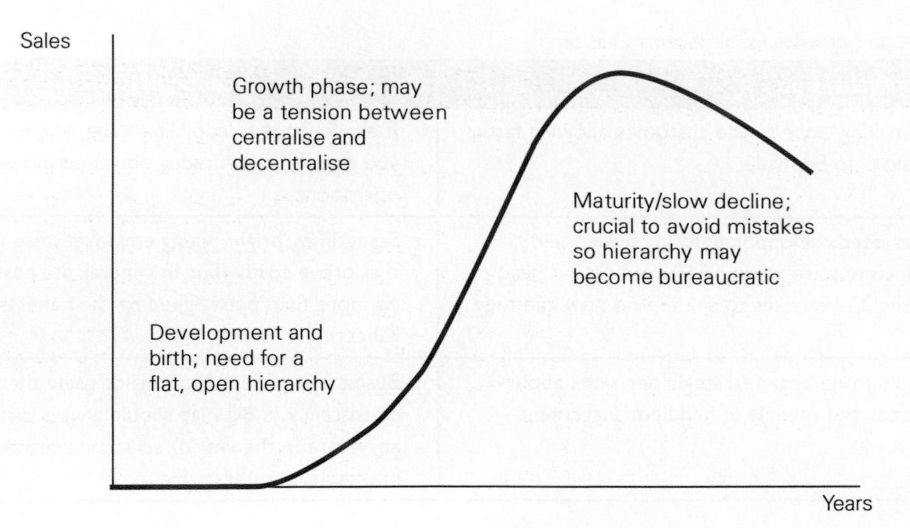

Figure 69.1 Differing structures at different stages of a product or company life cycle.

The length of product life cycle

KitKat has been selling for over 80 years; Cadbury's Dairy Milk for over 100 years. The chocolate market takes its time. Contrast that with the market for mobile phones, where one year is a long time. This is true even when the phones are successful; for example, following its success with the iPhone, Apple brought out the iPhone2 a year later. When markets are this dynamic, creativity and speed of decision making are crucial. Therefore, you can expect Cadbury's organisational structure to be quite hierarchical, because the key thing with cash cows is to avoid making mistakes. Whereas Apple should (and does) have a flatter hierarchy, with extensive delegation to young project teams. Launching the iPad seemed a huge risk at the time, but decentralised businesses accept risks if there is a prospect of a huge reward.

The stage of the life cycle

Although the product life cycle is a valuable marketing concept, many academics are more interested in the life cycle of companies. When Kraft bought Cadbury, a widespread criticism was that Kraft was a mature (perhaps even declining) business buying Cadbury as its own extension strategy. As Figure 69.1 shows, mature companies tend to have tall hierarchies and large bureaucracies. Early stage companies will usually be more entrepreneurial, with a flatter hierarchy.

69.3 ADAPTING ORGANISATIONAL STRUCTURES TO IMPROVE COMPETITIVENESS

In bad times

2009 was one of the scariest years to be running a business. Especially in the first few months of the year, many business sectors witnessed dramatic falls in sales. After several awful months, UK car sales in March 2009 were 30 per cent down on the previous year; a Honda dealership would have struggled even more, with sales down by 40 per cent. Vertu Motors plc (£750 million turnover) responded to the sales collapse by closing down marginal outlets ('to reduce fixed operating costs') then achieved 'payroll savings from headcount reductions' at head office. The latter saved £1.8 million from the salary bill.

When times are tough, businesses have to make a strategic decision. Should they trim staffing by, for example, not replacing those who are leaving by **natural wastage**, or should they restructure in a more fundamental way? If management believes that the good times are over, and the next five years are going to be tough, the answer may be **delayering**. This means cutting out a whole layer of management, restructuring work and responsibilities to cut the salary bill significantly and permanently. In the context of many schools, it may mean eliminating the role of 'faculty head'. Some schools have six of these managers, each earning £50,000. Delayering could remove £300,000 a year from the school's salary bill. As a result, the heads of department would have to take on more decision making responsibility, but that would be better than ending up without maths teachers because leavers are not replaced! The benefits and drawbacks of delayering are given in Table 69.3.

Another feature of managing a competitive organisation in hard times is to manage effectively the **core** and **peripheral workers**. The logic is simple: core workers are critical, partly due to their skills and knowledge, but also because they form the backbone of the business that, in effect, determines its culture. However hard times are, you do not want to cut into your core workforce. It is far better, from the organisation's point of view, to cut peripheral staff, meaning those at the edge of the business. For example, the head chef is at the core (the heart) of a restaurant, but the telephone receptionist (who takes bookings) may not need to be a full-time employee. Perhaps the job could be **outsourced** to a business that provides a telephone booking service to all the restaurants in a town.

Table 69.3 The benefits and drawbacks of delayering

Benefits of delayering	Drawbacks of delayering
• Permanent reduction in the salary bill, often based on senior staff whose salaries are sizeable	• In the short term, making a whole management layer redundant will cause bitterness and disruption; this might be a serious problem when times are tough
• Fewer layers of hierarchy should improve vertical communications, i.e. make them quicker and more effective	• Even when the redundant managers have left there will be short-term disruption as staff get used to their new, greater responsibilities
• Fewer management layers mean that authority for spending and other decisions will have to be distributed to others; this may provide more challenging, interesting jobs to others	• It may be that fewer management layers leads to poorer supervision of key functions; in 2008 the *Societe General* bank lost £4 billion when a single trader racked up amazing trading losses

In good times

When sales are rising and the economy is healthy, businesses may steadily add more staff. In April 2007 Tesco plc employed 380,000 staff. By 2010 the figure was 472,000. This remarkable increase may mean that a rethink is required about the organisational structure. Tesco must look out for signs that the structure is no longer competitive. These may include:

- Signs that vertical communication is weakening or slowing down; Tesco's new boss Philip Clarke started as a Tesco shelf-stacker, so he will know how much business knowledge exists on the shop floor; but do shopfloor ideas reach him? Or are there too many layers of hierarchy? If the ideas do not get to him, Mr Clarke will need to consider whether a delayering or a decentralising strategy would be wise
- Signs that others are moving faster in the market than you; and doing better at keeping up with new trends, fashions or tastes. In November 2010 Marks & Spencer announced an online strategy that should enable the company to catch up, by 2013, to the position where Next and ASOS were in 2010! At the same time it announced a move towards China and India – some five years later than Tesco. Marks & Spencer shows many signs of being behind the market; perhaps its organisational structure is too bureaucratic, thereby undermining the competitiveness of the business.

When times are good, even poorly run businesses can find that sales and profits are rising. The boss may even gain praise or win awards during such times. In November 2010 the collapse of UK housing business Rok plc threatened 4,000 job losses. But just three years earlier its chief executive had won an award as an Outstanding Business Leader. It often takes a recession to separate the well-run companies from the rest.

Often, business leaders ignore warning signs that their organisational structure is no longer fit for purpose. They keep going until a trading downturn forces a serious rethink. In a well-run business this would not be the case. The boss would watch for warning signs, then act quickly if there was clear evidence that the management was getting sloppy or bureaucratic. Delayering when the business is growing would be very controversial, but it may be needed to keep the business sharp, responsive and customer-focused.

ISSUES FOR ANALYSIS

- In the year 2001 it was impossible to see Sony losing its crown as supplier of personal music systems to the world. Yet it was the year that Apple launched the iPod. Today the Sony Walkman is a museum piece. Sony's boss is open about the cause of the problem: the company had grown too big, too fat and too slow. Even if the problem is diagnosed, it may be hard to cure. The organisational structure is not just a hierarchy diagram; it is a grouping of middle managers who may embody the culture of the business. They may have grown up learning to be entrepreneurial in a flat-hierarchy, decentralised business. Or they may have learnt to say no in a bureaucratic culture devoted to avoiding mistakes. And the only way to avoid mistakes in business is to do nothing (though that will eventually prove to be a mistake too).
- Achieving a competitive organisational structure is easier to write about, therefore, than achieve. If the structure and the culture are wrong, it will be extremely difficult to turn them around. The most impressive leaders tackle this issue when it arises, even during good times for the business. More will tackle it only when forced to cut overhead costs during a business downturn. In Sony's case, the failure to tackle the problem has cost the company a fortune, and led – in the long term – to huge numbers of lost jobs in Japan.

69.5 COMPETITIVE ORGANISATIONAL STRUCTURE – AN EVALUATION

TV programmes such as Dragons' Den present business as a simple process of entrepreneurs making individual decisions. If 'Dragon' Peter Jones likes you and your idea, he'll put his money where his mouth is. Big business is not like this. Very rarely have bosses the power to make an individual decision. (And when they have that power, the outcomes can be disastrous, as with Fred Goodwin, the dominant boss who led RBS to effective bankruptcy in the 2007–09 credit crunch.) In large organisations, important decisions are usually made by committees of executives, that is, groups of people, not individuals. This makes the process of decision making slower and more complex than might seem ideal; and makes it subject to the organisational structure and its culture.

When answering exam questions, it is important to be able to reflect on the complexity of this process. This means understanding mistakes or slowness and realistic about the difficulty of getting radical, innovative ideas approved. This makes Apple's achievements since 2001 all the more impressive. Radical innovation shouldn't be expected from big corporations; but Apple shows what's possible.

Key Terms

Centralisation: transferring power over budgets and decision making from local business units to head office.
Core workers: those considered essential to the long-term success of a business.
Decentralise: redistribute power over budgets and decisions from head office to local business units.
Delayering: removing an entire layer of management, redistributing the tasks and responsibilities to others.
Natural wastage: staff leaving their job because of natural, personal reasons such as retirement or the choice of a new career.
Outsourced: transferring a job from your own employees to people employed outside the business.
Peripheral workers: those on the fringe; they may have crucial skills, but they can be bought it when needed.

WORKBOOK

A REVISION QUESTIONS

(30 marks; 30 minutes)

1 How does a bureaucratic organisation stifle innovation? (3)
2 Briefly explain why a multinational car company such as Toyota may want to decentralise. (5)
3 Outline two possible benefits from centralising the purchasing department of a chain of fashion clothing stores. (4)
4 Explain how a business in the decline stage of its life cycle could restructure the organisation to stay competitive. (6)
5 Outline one advantage and one disadvantage to an airline of outsourcing its customer services function to a call centre. (6)
6 Explain why it may be difficult for a business with a flat organisational structure to switch to a tall hierarchy with narrow spans of control. (6)

B REVISION EXERCISES
B1 DATA RESPONSE

This data given in Table 69.4 is produced from unpublished research into the travel industry. Look at the data then answer the questions below.

Table 69.4 Data from unpublished research into the travel industry

	Small business (fewer than 100 employees)	Medium-sized business (100–500 employees)	Large business (500+ employees)
Layers of hierarchy (average)	3	5	11
Span of control (average)	7	4	5
Labour turnover (%)	8	17	14
Employee absence level per day (average) (%)	4.5	7.1	8.7

Questions

(20 marks; 20 minutes)

1 Identify and explain two hypotheses that you can draw from the data table. (8)
2 Discuss the possible ways in which the competitiveness of a travel business may be affected by its number of layers of hierarchy. (12)

B2 CASE STUDY

Following the severe 2009 world recession, Britain was faced with a huge government deficit. Elected in spring 2010, the new coalition government said it would eliminate the budget deficit within four years. The Department of Transport was asked to cope with a budget cutback of £683 million.

The Secretary of State for Transport, Phillip Hammond, had always been critical of bureaucratic government departments. With a business background, he announced in November 2010 that his department would be reorganised, with a new structure to be in place by April 2011. He surprised commentators by announcing that: 'We are massively delayering the management structure from an 11-layer structure down to a 4-layer structure'. He intended this to be a contributor towards cutting the Department's administration budget by a third. He went on to say: 'We're changing the way we work, with more flexible teams coming together for tasks, then dispersing.'

Questions

(30 marks; 35 minutes)

1 Explain briefly why 'delayering' might sound worrying to staff even while sounding attractive to managers. (5)

2 Explain how reducing from 11 to 4 layers of hierarchy may contribute towards cutting a department's administration budget by one-third. (7)

3 Discuss the implications for an organisation of changing from an 11 to a 4-layer hierarchy within 6 months. (18)

Employee participation and team working

UNIT 70

Employee participation refers to the extent to which employees are involved in the decision-making process. Team working means working in a group rather than in isolation, switching tasks as necessary and discussing ways of working more effectively.

70.1 PARTICIPATION IN PRACTICE

As early as 1918, Cadbury pioneered elected works councils in its Bournville factory. Ten years later, Elton Mayo showed that morale and productivity can be boosted if staff feel involved and therefore respected. The main risk is that participation can become a three-monthly chore rather than part of the business culture. Effective participation is part of daily life, not postponed for a meeting. Nearly a century after the Cadbury's initiative, employee participation remains patchy.

Figure 70.1 Working at Cadbury's Bournville factory early in the 20th century

Many managers realise that workers have a tremendous amount to offer in terms of ideas and insight into solving problems. Involving the people who do the work on a daily basis enables managers to learn how the job could be done more effectively. This reveals specific problems faced by the employees in a particular work area.

The importance of managers actually listening to their employees and paying attention to their social needs was highlighted in Mayo's study of the Hawthorne plant (see Unit 34). When employees were asked for their opinions their productivity rose, simply because managers were paying them attention and showing that they were valued. Greater participation has been shown to have tangible results in many companies, such as higher motivation, more innovation and lower labour turnover. This means that developing more effective employee participation can be an important element of business success. It involves using one of your resources more effectively (and the human resource is the only one that can decide to walk out of the door and not return).

There are, of course, problems involved in participation. Involving more people may slow-up decision making, although even this can be a good thing as it forces managers to discuss their ideas and listen to employees' comments. This may help to avoid hasty decisions, which are later regretted. However, there are some situations, such as a crisis, where a quick decision is important and where any delay may prove damaging. In this situation, too much discussion could cause problems.

Participation can also prove frustrating. When people attend a meeting, for example, they often have very different ideas of what they are trying to get out of it. They may well hope to achieve one thing but become irritated when it becomes clear that others are trying to achieve something else. Managers may resent the fact that their ideas are being challenged by workers in meetings and may wish they did not have to discuss things at all. Employees may also be unhappy because they may expect more power than they are actually given. Having become involved in decision making they may well want more information or more control over issues than management is willing to allow.

Simply announcing that employees will be invited to participate more in decision making does not in itself necessarily improve the performance of the business. The process needs to be planned (for example, who is to participate and how), employees need to be consulted so they understand the benefits and do not feel they are being exploited (that is, being asked to give ideas in return for nothing) and the process managed (that is, a regular review of what works and what does not).

> **A-grade application**
>
> **Partnership**
>
> Everyone who works at John Lewis is an owner of the organisation and is called a 'partner'. The fact that partners have a stake in the business means that they have the right to expect managers to explain their decisions to them.
>
> At store level, local managers meet with partners on a regular basis. They provide information on how their part of the business is doing and brief staff on issues concerning the organisation as a whole. Partners have the right to question any decision and receive an explanation. Managers in John Lewis are, therefore, far more accountable to staff than they are in most other organisations.
>
> At the end of each financial year, a percentage of the profits is paid out to each partner. It is often as high as 20 per cent of a partner's annual salary. John Lewis and its sister company, Waitrose, have been successful, growing businesses for many years. This demonstrates that employee participation has the potential to be a successful, profitable approach.

70.2 HOW DO EMPLOYEES PARTICIPATE IN DECISIONS?

There are numerous mechanisms to increase the amount of employee participation within a firm. These occur at different levels within the organisation and deal with different types of issues. They include those described below.

Kaizen groups

Devised in Japan by firms such as Toyota and Nissan, these have become popular throughout the west. *Kaizen* means 'continuous improvement', so the idea is to meet regularly and keep coming up with ways to do things better (or to tackle niggling faults). For example, workers may meet to solve problems of high-wastage levels in one part of the factory. Employees are usually paid for their time in meetings and are expected to present their findings to management.

Works councils

A **works council** is a committee of employer and employee representatives that meets to discuss company-wide issues. Works councils have worked well in some countries, such as Germany, but have not been so popular in the UK. A works council will usually discuss issues such as training, investment and working practices that affect the whole workforce. It will not cover issues such as pay, which are generally dealt with in discussions with trade union representatives.

> **A-grade application**
>
> **Unilever**
>
> In October 2009 Unilever received a complaint from the International Union of Food workers (IUF). A factory closure at Sewri, India, had been poorly handled. Redundant workers had received little warning and no compensation. This, plus other complaints on behalf of Unilever workers in Pakistan and India, made the company hold an international meeting. Representatives of Unilever's 160,000 worldwide workforce met with the IUF and with Unilever management in March 2010. Workers in Europe (including Britain) were represented by Unilever's European Works Council. As a result, the Sewri workers received redundancy compensation and significant changes were made to the terms and conditions of contract workers on Unilever sites. The Works Council forum allowed progress to be made without confrontation or strike action.

Autonomous work groups

An autonomous work group consists of a team of people who are given a high level of responsibility for their own work. These responsibilities may include the scheduling of the work and decisions over the allocation of their tasks (they might choose to use job rotation). To be really effective, such teams should be invited to join recruitment panels for new staff and be given the capital budget necessary to buy new machinery when it is needed.

Employee shareholders

An increasingly common way to develop a common sense of purpose is to give employees shares in the business. For example, employees at Innocent Drinks and at Tesco have the opportunity to buy shares in the company. This should mean they become more interested in the overall performance of the firm, as well their own personal performance. If employees can think of it as 'their' company rather than a company, the job is done.

Other methods

Other methods of encouraging employee participation include suggestion schemes and a more democratic style of management.

When deciding on how to improve participation in the business, managers must therefore consider the options and decide which are most appropriate. The speed and method of introduction must also be considered to ensure that they are accepted and that employees value them as much as managers.

70.3 EUROPEAN DIRECTIVES

In most European countries the works council (which consists of elected representatives) is an integral part of employee participation within the firm. It is consulted whenever management plans to do anything that is likely to affect the majority of employees, such as changing employment terms and conditions or staffing levels. Up until recently, works councils have been very rare in the UK. However, the EU's European Works Council directive is forcing some large UK firms to change their approach to employee participation and introduce works councils.

These works councils will have information and consultation rights in relation to company performance and strategic planning. In effect, there should be consultation and a dialogue on any proposed actions by the employer that could affect employees' jobs.

Consultation is defined in the regulations as 'the exchange of views and establishment of dialogue' between the employer and employees or employee representatives.

70.4 TEAMWORK

Many organisations now expect employees to undertake their work in teams. This is because they believe that **team working** leads to more efficient and effective production. People often respond positively to working with others because this satisfies their social needs (Mayo). The fact that managers are willing to delegate responsibility to teams also meets employees' ego and self-actualisation needs. Teams also allow individuals to gain from the strengths of others. There may be some areas in which you are relatively weak but someone else is strong, and vice versa. Imagine you are trying to solve a crossword, for example. It is usually much quicker and more fun sharing the task with others. Working in teams also allows individuals to change jobs, which can provide some variety at work.

However, some people do not particularly enjoy working in teams. This may be because of their personality or because they think their own performance would be better than that of the other members of the team – they are worried about being dragged down.

Figure 70.2 Working as a team

Teamwork can also bring with it various problems: decision making can be slow and there may be serious disagreements between the members of the group.

70.5 EMPLOYEE PARTICIPATION, TEAM WORKING AND BUSINESS SUCCESS

Employees are an important resource of a business. They provide ideas for new products and new ways of doing things, they solve problems and they move the business forward. Utilising this resource effectively is therefore one of the many challenges of managers. As part of the process of human resource management, managers must decide on the level and method of employee participation. They must weigh up some of the potential problems (such as the time and cost) with the benefits (such as more views and insights into problems).

It is not realistic, or even desirable, for everyone to participate in every decision. This would make for a very unwieldy organisation that is slow to react. So managers must decide who should be involved in various decisions. Teams and committees can help managers to cut across departments, divisions and products to improve communication and the sharing of information. They can provide a diversity of views, which is often essential in a business operating in global markets, and they can share a range of skills and talents. They also build employees' level of commitment and understanding of the firm's values and strategy. All of which makes participation (when done correctly) very important to business success. The benefits of participation can be seen in better decisions, fewer mistakes, higher levels of satisfaction and innovation, and greater effectiveness.

ISSUES FOR ANALYSIS

When analysing employee participation within an organisation you may find it useful to consider the following points.

- Approaches to participation are all rooted in the theories of Mayo, Maslow and Herzberg. Analysis can be enriched by making and explaining the connections between theory and practice.
- Greater participation by employees may provide the business with a competitive advantage. It may provide more ideas, greater motivation, greater efficiency and greater commitment from the workforce. This makes change easier, and – in the service sector – has a direct effect upon customer image.
- There is every reason to suppose that employees today need more opportunities for participation; nowadays employees are generally better educated and have a higher standard of living, and therefore want to be involved to a greater extent.
- Despite this, some researchers argue that many managers have become more authoritarian in recent years. Consequently, participation may have reduced in many organisations. This is especially true in the public sector, where staff in professions such as medicine or teaching find themselves less involved and less often consulted than in the past.

70.6 EMPLOYEE PARTICIPATION AND TEAM WORKING – AN EVALUATION

Managed effectively, employees can provide better-quality and more innovative work at a lower cost and a faster rate. To achieve such improvements in performance employees must be involved. They must have the ability to contribute and feel they are listened to. Greater participation can help a firm to gain a competitive advantage. This is why managers in all kinds of successful organisations claim that their success is due to their people. However, despite the potential gains from participation this does not mean every manager has embraced the idea. After all, the more employees participate in decisions, the more managers have to explain their actions to them. Some managers find this change difficult to cope with.

Participation can also slow up the decision-making process and, if handled incorrectly, can lead to conflict. Greater participation must be part of a general movement involving greater trust and mutual respect between managers and workers. Employees cannot be expected to participate positively if, at the same time, their conditions and rewards are poor. Successful participation is part of an overall approach in which employees are given responsibility and treated fairly.

Managers must also consider the most effective method and the most appropriate degree of participation for their organisation. This will depend on the culture of the organisation, the pace of change, and the attitude and training of both managers and workers. Despite the growth of participation in the UK, employee representation is still relatively low, especially when compared with countries such as Germany, where employees are often represented at a senior level. However, although this system appears to work well in Germany, this does not necessarily mean it will work as effectively in the UK because of the two countries' different traditions and cultures.

Key Terms

Industrial democracy: an industrial democracy occurs when employees have the opportunity to be involved in decision making. In its most extreme form each employee would have a vote. When examining a business you should consider the extent to which employees are involved in decision making.

Teamwork: individuals work in groups rather than being given highly specialised, individual jobs.

Works council: a committee of management and workers that meets to discuss company-wide issues such as training, investment and expansion.

FURTHER READING

Herzberg, F. (1959) *The Motivation to Work*. Wiley International.

Maslow, A. H. (1987) *Motivation and Personality*. HarperCollins (1st edn 1954).

Mayo, E. (1975) *The Social Problems of Industrial Civilisation*. Routledge (1st edn 1949).

WORKBOOK

A REVISION QUESTIONS

(40 marks; 40 minutes)

1 Explain the possible benefits to a firm of greater employee participation. (5)
2 Why do some managers resist greater participation? (4)
3 Why do some workers resist greater participation? (4)
4 Examine two possible problems of involving employees more in decision making in a business such as Tesco plc. (6)
5 Consider the advantages and disadvantages to a Europe-wide business such as Coca-Cola of having a works council covering staff from all its factories across Europe. (6)
6 Outline two benefits of teamwork. (4)
7 How would team working be viewed by a motivational theorist of your choice? (5)
8 Examine the possible impact on a firm's profit of a move towards the use of autonomous work groups in the workplace. (6)

B REVISION EXERCISES

B1 DATA RESPONSE

John Lewis Partnership

John Lewis is one of the world's biggest employee-owned businesses. As all staff are 'partners' with a profit share and voting rights, it should have exceptionally impressive employee participation. In many ways it does. It has employee councils that meet regularly, to provide insights from the shop floor and to involve staff in decision making. And all staff can attend the Annual General Meeting.

As not everyone likes speaking in public, there is also a staff survey, answered by 93 per cent of the 72,000 staff (in most businesses, a 40 per cent response rate would be impressive). In 2009, the survey showed good results on the following four factors: 'be honest', 'show respect', 'recognise others' and 'work together'. Results were less impressive on two other criteria: 'show enterprise' and 'achieve more'. Now the key thing will be how senior managers respond to this information. Only if they can find ways to encourage staff to show more enterprise and gain more of a sense of achievement can the participation be said to be a success.

Questions

(25 marks; 30 minutes)

1 a) Identify two forms of **industrial democracy** used at John Lewis. (2)
   b) Examine how one of the two could affect staff motivation. (4)
2 John Lewis provides the right structures for participation, but may fail to sufficiently encourage day-to-day consultation between managers and staff. Explain why that could undermine the effectiveness of its workplace democracy. (8)
3 Discuss how senior John Lewis managers could set about improving their staff's ability to 'show enterprise' at work. (11)

B2 CASE STUDY

The Old Hen

'I don't know why I bother,' said Nina Burke, the manageress of the Old Hen pub in Oxford. She had just had one of the weekly staff meetings and all she had heard was one complaint after another. 'They want more money, they want shorter working hours, they want free food, they don't like the T-shirts they have to wear, they don't like the shift arrangements. Honestly, I don't know why any of them even turns up to work, the amount they complain. They even seem to resent being asked for their ideas,' said Nina to her husband.

Nina began to wonder whether she was running these meetings effectively. The previous landlord had never really held staff meetings and had certainly not asked employees for their opinions. When she took over, he had said: 'Half of them will be moving on to new jobs anyway within a few weeks or are just doing this as a part-time job, so what's the point? Tell them what to do and then make sure they get on with it.' Nina began to think he may be right, although she had been very enthusiastic when she first had the idea of asking employees for their input.

She had noticed that staff in this pub seemed to leave very frequently and were generally pretty miserable. They seemed much less motivated than at her previous pub (where she was deputy manager). The money was not good but no worse than anywhere else. She decided it must be because they were not involved in decision making at all. In her last job everyone had felt able to give an opinion (even if their ideas were then ignored!) and were often asked what they thought about how the pub was run. It was a good atmosphere and Nina had enjoyed working there. She hoped she could recreate the same feeling here but was losing confidence that it would ever be possible.

Questions

(40 marks; 50 minutes)

1 Consider whether Nina is right to try to introduce greater employee participation at the Old Hen. (10)
2 According to many motivational theorists, employees should respond positively to greater participation. Discuss the possible reasons why Nina's schemes seem ineffective. (15)
3 An increasing number of managers claim to be encouraging employee participation. Consider why greater participation may be regarded as particularly valuable today. (15)

C ESSAY QUESTIONS

(40 marks each)

1 'Greater competitiveness and higher profits in the future will depend upon much more employee participation than in the past.' Critically assess this statement.
2 'Managers are appointed to make decisions. Workers are hired to do the job they are told. Employee participation simply wastes time and money.' Critically assess this view.
3 'Teamwork brings with it more problems than benefits.' Discuss.

Effective employer–employee relations

UNIT 71

Are staff and management able to work together for the good of the business, or is there friction and inefficiency? Motivation can be undermined by poor employer–employee relations.

71.1 INTRODUCTION

The relations between bosses and workers would be effective if communications were good and there was a sensible amount of give-and-take between them. They would be bad if there was a lack of trust, leading to restricted communication ('information is power') and the tendency to make demands rather than conduct conversations. In a perfect world, adults would behave in an adult manner towards each other. But just as no family is perfect, neither is any individual business organisation. The key is not to be perfect, but to be better than most.

There are three main areas to consider within the heading 'effective employer–employee relations':

1 good communications
2 methods of employee representation
3 the causes and solutions to industrial disputes.

A-grade application

ACAS

ACAS (the Advisory Conciliation and Arbitration Service) is Britain's most important, independent voice on the workplace. Over more than 30 years it has developed a view of what it thinks is the 'model workplace'. The ACAS model includes the following six themes:

1 ambitions, goals and plans that employees know about and understand
2 managers who genuinely listen to and consider their employees' views, so everyone is actively involved in making important decisions
3 people to feel valued so they can talk confidently about their work, and learn from both successes and mistakes
4 work organised so that it encourages initiative, innovation and working together
5 a good working relationship between management and employee representatives that in turn helps to build trust throughout the business
6 formal procedures for dealing with disciplinary matters, grievances and disputes that managers and employees know about and use fairly.

Source: www.acas.org.uk

71.2 GOOD COMMUNICATIONS

The importance of effective communication

Effective communication is essential for organisations. Without it, employees do not know what they are supposed to do, why they are supposed to do it, how to do it or when to do it by. Similarly, managers have little idea of how the business is performing, what people are actually doing or what their customers think. Communication links the activities of all the various parts of the organisation. It ensures that everyone is working towards a common goal and enables **feedback** on performance. Imagine studying for an exam if you were not told by the teacher what you were supposed to do and had no idea of your standard. Then you can appreciate how important good communication is. By communicating effectively the management is able to explain the objectives of the organisation and employees can have an input into the decisions that are made.

Effective communication is also vital for successful decision making. To make good decisions, managers need high-quality information. If they do not know

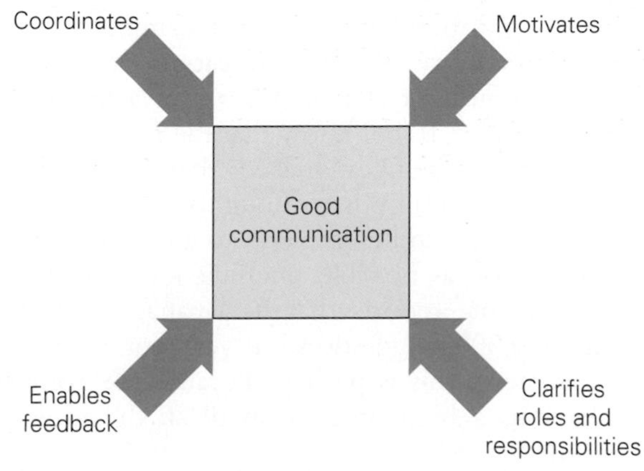

Figure 71.1 Good communication

what is happening in the market, for example, they are less likely to be successful. If, however, their market knowledge is good they are more likely to develop an appropriate marketing plan. Effective communication provides managers with the information they need, in a form they can use, when they need it.

Good-quality information should be:

- easily accessible
- up to date
- cost effective.

Good communication is also extremely important to motivate employees. People need to know how they are getting on, what they are doing right and in which areas they could improve. Working on your own without receiving any kind of feedback at all is extremely difficult. It is much easier if someone is taking an interest and providing support. Interestingly, nearly all staff surveys reveal that employees do not feel that management communicate with them very effectively. So there is clearly a need for managers to improve in this area.

To ensure that communication is motivating, managers need to ensure that employees:

- understand the objectives of the organisation as a whole
- understand why their job is important and how it contributes to the overall success of the firm
- know how the job should be completed
- know how they are performing.

The importance of communication in employee–employer relations

In a well-run organisation with effective delegation and consultation, good communication will flow from the top and to the top. The overall business leader can do many things to help, as outlined below.

- Have a chat with every new member of staff; this may be impossible for the boss of Tesco's 480,000 employees, but is perfectly possible in most cases.
- Take regular initiatives to meet with staff; some retail bosses go out every Friday to two or three different stores to discuss problems with shop-floor staff; this is bound to encourage communication not only then, but also later, if an issue arises that an individual feels very strongly about, such as sex discrimination.
- Treat every piece of communication from staff as being as important as if it were from a friend or a big shareholder. If staff know that their complaints or suggestions are being addressed, they will be happy to keep contributing their thoughts. Most staff want their workplace to be efficient, to allow them to do as good a job as possible; inefficiency is frustrating for all. Toyota reports that its Japanese staff alone make 500,000 suggestions a year for workplace improvement; this is perhaps because the company implements a high proportion of all the ideas put forward.

If the leader can get communications right, there is every chance that staff will do the same. Unfortunately, there are some serious barriers to effective communication. The first is that middle managers may not want staff communicating over their heads to senior staff. If they insist that communications should filter up through the management layers, there is a chance at every stage that the message will be suppressed. Middle managers may not want their bosses to receive grumbles, complaints or suggestions. After all, they could be seen as criticism of the middle layers of management. Bosses have to make a special effort, therefore, to make sure that staff really do feel that they can communicate one to one with the business leader.

If communications are well managed, the impact on employer–employee relations can be huge. The many benefits to the business include those described below.

- Staff that understand the difficulties faced by the organisation, and therefore can seek to help management rather than criticise it. In 2009 the sharp recession meant that Honda UK had to shut its factories down for three months. Keeping staff aware of the problems helped encourage them to cooperate, even when job cuts were called for.
- If **vertical communications** are weak, frustrated staff may look for a trade union to represent their views to management. If the company is reluctant to recognise a union as the representative of staff, employer–employee relations may become very difficult. The Asda supermarket chain and the GMB union recently had a bitter dispute over union recognition for lorry drivers; a planned five-day strike was averted only when Asda backed down, granting recognition to the union.
- Ineffective communication, by comparison, leaves employees frustrated and dissatisfied. Poor communication makes people uncertain about their role or duties. They become unsure of what they are supposed to be doing. It can also lead to rumours going around the firm. This can cause problems if people get worried about things that are not actually true, or resent the fact that they have heard something before being officially told.

Communication and size

As a firm grows it tends to introduce more layers of hierarchy. This makes communication more difficult as vertical communications (from the top to the bottom) have to go through more people. This slows down decision making. It also introduces a greater risk that the message will get distorted. Instead of communicating directly to the person you want to talk to, you have to contact someone else, who then gets in touch with someone else, and so on. In the end your message can become rather confused.

Another problem is that as the number of people involved in an organisation increases, the use of written communication rises even faster. Instead of a quick conversation to sort something out, you can end up passing numerous messages backwards and forwards. This can lead to a tremendous amount of paperwork and is often far less effective than face-to-face communication. When you are actually talking to someone you can get immediate feedback and can see if they do not fully understand something. You can then talk it through until you are happy they have understood what you mean. When you send them a written message, however, you are never quite sure how they will interpret it. What you think you have said and what they think you have said can be very different.

Communication problems can also occur because of different business cultures within the firm. This is usually more of a problem in large firms than in small ones. If there are only a few people working in an office, they tend to share the same approaches to work and the same values about what is and what is not acceptable business behaviour. If anyone new joins the group, they soon learn the way that everyone else works and the newcomer will usually fit in quite quickly. In large organisations, however, it is much more difficult to develop a common approach. People tend to develop their own little groups within the firm so that the mood, attitudes and values of employees can vary tremendously in different parts of the firm. The marketing department, for example, may have a different view from the production department of what the business is trying to achieve and how it wants to conduct its business.

71.3 METHODS OF EMPLOYEE REPRESENTATION

Intelligent bosses realise that success depends on the full participation of as many staff as possible. Football managers typically use the club captain as the representative of the players. Small firms may have an informal group consisting of one person from each department; monthly meetings are used as a way to raise issues and problems, and discuss future plans. In larger firms, more formal methods are used to ensure that there is a structure to allow an element of workplace democracy. These include those described below.

Works council

A works council is a committee of employer and employee representatives that meets to discuss company-wide issues. Although works councils have worked well in Germany they have not been so popular in the UK. However, under European Union legislation larger companies that operate in two or more EU countries must now set up a Europe-wide works council. Works councils will usually discuss issues such as training, investment and working practices. They will not cover issues such as pay, which are generally dealt with in discussions with trade union representatives.

Employee groups, organised by the business but with representatives elected by the staff

These may be little different from a works council, but the fact that they are purely the invention of the business (that is, the management) may mean that they lack real credibility. Staff may know that management frown upon those who raise critical issues. They may be seen as little more than a talking shop that provides a veneer of democratic respectability. In a similar way, some school councils are vibrant and meaningful, while others are largely ignored by the school management.

Employee cooperatives

These range from huge organisations such as the John Lewis Partnership to the 150 staff at Suma (see A-grade application). Because all staff are part-owners of the business, all have a right to have their voices heard at every stage in the decision-making process. Inevitably, the board of directors includes representatives from ordinary shop-floor workers, ensuring that everyone's voice is heard.

A-grade application

Suma

Suma was born in 1975 when Reg Taylor started a wholefoods wholesaling cooperative in Leeds. Its purpose was to allow small independent health food shops to be able to buy together in bulk. Although Reg started it in his back bedroom, within a year a tiny two-storey warehouse had been bought in Leeds. Suma was one of the pioneers of organic foods, and has benefited greatly from the growing consumer interest in chemical-free food. This has caused its own pressures, as the cooperative has had to cope with employee growth from seven members in 1980 to over 150 today. All staff receive the same pay, no matter what their responsibilities may be, and all have an equal say in how the business should be run. The high level of staff motivation and participation has allowed Suma to become the number one organic foods wholesaler in the north of England.

For further information on Suma, go to www.suma.co.uk.

Figure 71.2

71.4 TRADE UNIONS

What is a trade union?

A trade union is an organisation that employees pay to join in order to gain greater power and security at work. The phrase 'unity is strength' is part of the trade union tradition. One individual worker has little or no power when discussing pay or pensions with his or her employer; union membership provides greater influence collectively in relations with employers than workers have as separate individuals.

Some people assume that union membership is only for people in low-status jobs. In fact, although trade unions are in decline in Britain some powerful groups of 'workers' remain committed to membership. For example, the PFA (Professional Footballers' Association) includes almost all Premiership players, and the airline pilots remain loyal to their union BALPA. Two years ago Hollywood script writers went on strike; they thought the film studios were being unfair in not sharing the revenues from sales of DVDs and computer games based on Hollywood films (they won huge concessions from the studios).

Traditionally, unions concerned themselves solely with obtaining satisfactory rates of pay for a fair amount of work in reasonable and safe working conditions. Today the most important aspect of the work of a trade union is protecting workers' rights under the law. Far more time is spent on health and safety, on discrimination and bullying, on unfair dismissal and other legal matters than on pay negotiations. One other important matter today is negotiations over pension rights. Recently, many companies have cut back on the pension benefits available to staff; the unions fight these cutbacks as hard as they can.

Traditionally, the key function of a union was 'collective bargaining'. This means that the union bargains with the employers on behalf of all the workers (for example, that all nurses should get a 4 per cent pay rise). The 2008 industrial dispute between Virgin Atlantic and its cabin crew was a good example of this. Virgin staff wanted a substantial pay rise to match the wages earned by British Airways' staff. They pressed their union to threaten strike action to achieve their objectives.

Union recognition

'Recognition' is fundamental to the legal position of a trade union. In other words, management must recognise a union's right to bargain on behalf of its members. Without management recognition, any actions taken by a union are illegal. This would leave the union open to being sued. Until recently, even if all staff joined a union, the management did not have to recognise it. Why, then, would any company bother to recognise a union?

- Generally it can be helpful for managers to have a small representative group to consult and negotiate with. Collective bargaining removes the need to bargain with every employee individually.
- It may ease cases of possible difficulty, such as relocation or renegotiation of employment conditions and contracts. Trade union officials can be consulted at an early stage about causes, procedure and objectives. This may give the workforce the confidence that management are acting properly and thoughtfully. It also gives the opportunity for the trade union to offer advice or objection at an early stage. It promotes consultation rather than conflict.
- Trade unions provide a channel of upward communication that has not been filtered by middle managers. Senior managers can expect straight talking about worker opinions or grievances.

Today, UK employers with 21-plus staff members must give union recognition if more than 50 per cent of the workforce vote for it in a secret ballot (and at least 40 per cent of the workforce takes part in the vote). This government policy has helped unions to recruit more members at a time when membership is generally falling.

71.5 METHODS OF AVOIDING AND RESOLVING INDUSTRIAL DISPUTES

It is only natural that there will be disagreements between management and staff. Clearly, staff want as high a pay rise as possible, whereas the bosses have a duty to their shareholders to keep costs down (and profits up). Usually, companies and unions are able to resolve their differences by compromising (that is, give and take). Staff may 'demand' 8 per cent, but only be offered 2 per cent. After much wrangling, a compromise of 4 per cent may be agreed. In some cases, though, a build-up of mistrust and hostility over time may mean that compromise is not seen as acceptable. Then an industrial dispute may occur, which may lead to industrial action, such as a strike.

When an industrial dispute occurs, it is up to the management and unions to resolve it. Sometimes, however, there seems to be no compromise that is acceptable to both sides. The result might be a strike; in other words, workers refusing to work and therefore giving up their pay. The inevitable consequence of a strike is that both the company and the employees lose money; therefore there will soon be pressure for a way to resolve the dispute. Often, one or both sides will suggest bringing ACAS in to help. ACAS stands for the Advisory Conciliation and Arbitration Service; it is government-financed, but acts independently of government and politicians.

Founded in 1975, the mission statement of ACAS is:

> to improve the performance and effectiveness of organisations by providing an independent and impartial service to prevent and resolve disputes and to build harmonious relationships at work.

ACAS seeks to:

- prevent and resolve employment disputes
- conciliate in actual or potential complaints to industrial tribunals
- provide information and advice
- promote good practice.

ACAS can be used by employers and employees to help them work together to resolve industrial relations disputes before they develop into confrontation. Where there is a collective dispute between management and workforce, either or both may contact ACAS. Before acting, ACAS will want to see that union officials are involved and that the organisation's disputes procedure has been followed. ACAS can also be used to offer **conciliation** to the parties in a dispute, assuming their own procedures have been exhausted, to avoid damaging industrial action. Such conciliation is entirely voluntary and ACAS has no powers to impose a settlement.

If conciliation is unsuccessful, ACAS can offer **arbitration**, by providing an independent arbitrator who can examine the case for each side and then judge the right outcome to the dispute. If both sides agree in advance, the arbitrator's decision can be legally binding on both sides. Occasionally, ACAS is asked to provide a mediator who can act as an intermediary suggesting the basis for further discussion.

A-grade application

Unite

In summer 2009 the management of the Post Office imposed new working conditions on its staff. In effect, the job of a postman would be casualised. Instead of specific, permanently-employed postmen having 'their round' to look after, workers on short-term contracts would be given different rounds on different days (flexible working). The postmen took unofficial, then official strike action against these changes. Their trade union, Unite, repeatedly offered to take the dispute to ACAS, but Post Office management refused. Eventually, after many days of strikes, management and the union agreed a new deal in April 2010. There would be a minimum of 75 per cent full-time, permanent staff, plus a 6.9 per cent pay rise over the coming three years. Conciliation at ACAS could surely have achieved something similar six months before.

ISSUES FOR ANALYSIS

- When analysing employer–employee relations it is good to start with a clear understanding of the vision and objectives of the business. The vision at Innocent Drinks is 'to create a business we can be proud of'. As long as the company's decisions are in line with that vision, it is easy to see that it could be the basis of close cooperation between employees and their employers.
- Yet Virgin Atlantic boasts that 'our vision is to build a profitable airline where people love to fly and where people love to work'. This did nothing to prevent the 2008 industrial dispute between cabin crew and management. So successful employer–employee relations is about much more than saying the right thing.
- When analysing a business situation, look beyond what managements say and see how they are actually treating their staff. Are they really showing respect by listening to what staff say and acting on their views. That, after all, is how Toyota became the world's number one car maker.

71.6 EFFECTIVE EMPLOYER–EMPLOYEE RELATIONS – AN EVALUATION

Good relations are built on shared goals, on trust and on good communications. Yet they are always fragile. One instance of hypocrisy can ruin years of relationship-building. A boss may claim to be acting for the good of all the staff, yet switch production from Britain to Asia (James Dyson), or cut pension benefits to staff while keeping them intact for directors. In the long term, some firms really stick by the view that 'our people are our greatest asset', while others just pretend they believe that. Staff will learn which is which. Where they find they cannot trust their bosses, joining a trade union becomes a sensible way to get greater protection and greater negotiating power. Union representation will make the employer–employee relationship more formal, and occasionally more fractious. Yet, as Tesco has shown, trade union representation can help to move a business forward. So it would be wrong to jump to the conclusion that unions are 'trouble'. Real trouble comes when employers and employees have no relationship at all.

Key Terms

Arbitration: when an independent person listens to the case put by both sides, then makes a judgement about the correct outcome.

Conciliation: an independent person encourages both sides to a dispute to get together to talk through their differences. The conciliator helps the process but makes no judgements about the right outcome.

Feedback: obtaining a response to a communication, perhaps including an element of judgement (for example, praise for a job well done).

Vertical communications: messages passing freely from the bottom to the top of the organisation, and from the top to the bottom.

WORKBOOK

A REVISION QUESTIONS

(35 marks; 35 minutes)

1. Explain why good communications within a firm are important. (3)
2. Explain why feedback is important for successful communications. (3)
3. State three actions a firm could take in order to improve the effectiveness of communication. (3)
4. Identify three reasons why communications may be poorer in large firms than in small ones. (3)
5. Explain why good communication is an important part of motivating employees. (4)
6. How could a business benefit from a successful works council? (4)
7. Why may an employee cooperative have better employer–employee relations than a public company? (4)
8. Why is it so important to a union to gain recognition from employers? (4)
9. Outline the role of ACAS. (4)
10. Distinguish 'conciliation' from 'arbitration'. (3)

B REVISION EXERCISES

B1 DATA RESPONSE

Employee communication

Faced with intensifying competition and an accelerating pace of change, companies are seeing effective communication with employees as an ever-more important part of organisational efficiency. It is also a constructive way to harness employees' commitment, enthusiasm and ideas. However, companies tend to place considerable emphasis on communicating big but vague messages about change and company performance. It is highly debatable whether such messages are relevant to employees or easily understood by them. Employee-attitude surveys consistently highlight communication as a major source of staff dissatisfaction.

While managers tend to use communication channels that send general messages downwards, employees place more importance on mechanisms that communicate immediate and applicable information. For example, around 40 per cent of staff found one-to-one meetings with their manager very useful while less than 5 per cent gave business television the same rating. Too many businesses try to tell staff too much, leading to communications overload. Successful communication methods involved discussion and feedback, whereas business TV or company newsletters provided purely one-way messages.

Questions

(30 marks; 35 minutes)

1. Outline the possible value to staff of a 'one-to-one meeting with their manager'. (5)
2. Explain why communication is more than just 'the provision of information'. (5)
3. Explain why staff disliked business TV or company newsletters. (4)
4. Examine the importance of good communication within *either* a McDonald's restaurant *or* a supermarket. (7)
5. Discuss the problems that can occur when employees are dissatisfied. (9)

B2 CASE STUDY

Honda China strike could spur broader worker demands

About 100 workers wearing white overalls and blue caps milled about the factory grounds of the Honda Lock plant, a supplier of locks to Honda's car-making operations in China, on Monday after many of the 1,500 workers walked off the job on Wednesday. The standoff was relatively calm, in contrast to last week when hundreds gathered outside the gates and riot police briefly kept workers from leaving.

The strike is the latest in a series to hit factories around southern China's Pearl River Delta and a few other regions by workers demanding a greater piece of China's growing economic pie. Commentator Liu Kaiming explains that:

> We've already seen a growing number of strikes in previous years, especially in 2007 and 2008, when the new labour contract law was introduced, and then there was a gap in 2009, but now we're seeing the trend resume.
>
> The Honda strike is an extension of that ... It also shows that there is a trend that is being driven by a new generation of migrant workers. They are more willing to speak out about their grievances, and are less tolerant of long hours and tough conditions than the older generation.

The strike at Honda Lock was the third to hit a Honda parts supplier in China in the last few weeks. The other two, at suppliers producing transmissions and exhausts, were settled after employees received wage increases.

Management at Honda Lock has offered a pay increase of 100 yuan ($15) in additional wages and another 100 yuan in allowances, but some employees at the plant said that is not enough.

'I'm more optimistic now we'll get more of a wage rise,' said one worker leaving the factory on a bicycle on Monday. 'They urged us to resume work for the next few days and some assembly lines are working again.' Stories of employer intimidation have been balanced by rumours of sabotage of equipment by some employees.

Chang Kai, dean of the school of labour relations at Remin University in Beijing, said in an interview to the Chinese media that employers rarely considered how to link the development of businesses and of employees.

'What many of our businesses think about is how to cut costs, how to lower wages,' he said. 'Collective negotiations are also not mature. There is no appropriate framework for them, nor are there means for applying pressure.'

Source: Adapted from Reuters, 14 June 2010.

Questions

(35 marks; 45 minutes)

1 From the article, explain why the factory workers may benefit from belonging to a trade union. (8)
2 Examine the state of employer–employee relations at this Chinese supplier to Honda. (12)
3 At present, independent trade unions are banned in China. Discuss whether the progress of Chinese industry would be helped or hindered by allowing trade unions to represent workers, when both management and employees are happy to sign an agreement. (15)

C ESSAY QUESTIONS

(40 marks each)

1 Consider the view that effective communications is at the heart of successful operations management.
2 'Good managers welcome trade unions as a way of improving workplace performance.' Discuss.

Understanding operational objectives

UNIT 72

Operational objectives are the specific, detailed production targets set by an organisation to ensure that its overall company goals are achieved.

72.1 INTRODUCTION

All organisations share common operational objectives, regardless of their size and the sector in which they operate. Ensuring that these objectives are met is vital, in order to satisfy customer needs and compete effectively within the marketplace. All firms will attempt to produce goods and services that are 'fit for purpose', delivered quickly and on time. They will also aim to produce the right number of goods as cheaply as possible, bearing in mind the overall strategy.

If, like Ryanair, your target is to be the lowest-cost airline in Europe, every cost will be shaved to the minimum. If your business strategy is to be the highest-rated airline in the world (such as Singapore Airlines), you may accept costs that will seem high to other airlines. The crucial thing is that a firm's operational objectives must be fully in line with its objectives regarding marketing and management of its people.

Finally, there needs to be enough flexibility within operations to allow activities to be varied or adapted quickly, in order to accommodate changes in demand.

72.2 KEY OPERATIONAL OBJECTIVES

The key operational objectives are shown in Figure 72.1 and described below.

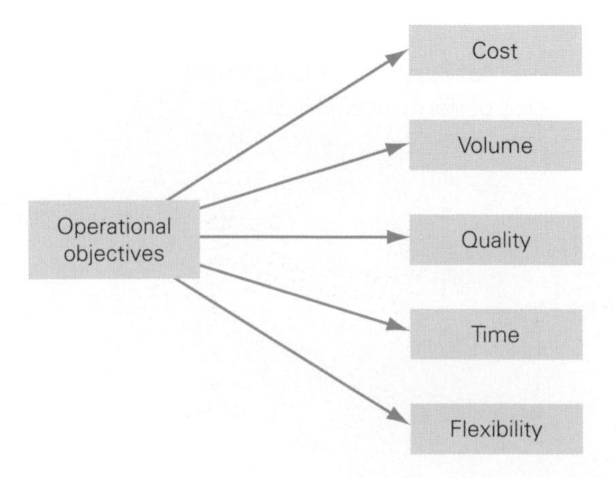

Figure 72.1 The key operational objectives

Cost

All firms are concerned with keeping costs down, particularly those that compete directly on price. Not only do costs determine what is charged to the customer – and, therefore, a firm's ability to compete – but also the profits that can be generated. During a period of economic downturn, a firm's ability to make further cost reductions can mean the difference between survival and failure. Costs are determined by the **efficiency** of a business. This can be measured in a number of ways; for example, wastage rates or the **productivity** of the workforce.

> **A-grade application**
>
> **Cost cutting at Kingfisher pushes profits up**
>
> A programme of tight stock control and direct sourcing from manufacturers helped Kingfisher, the owner of DIY retailer B&Q, to increase its profits for the first half of 2010, despite tough trading conditions and disappointing sales figures. B&Q, which is responsible for 40 per cent of Kingfisher's sales turnover, experienced a fall in like-for-like sales of 3.7 per cent to £2.3 billion in the six months to July 2010. However, retail profit at B&Q increased by 15 per cent to £171 million over the same period. Kingfisher has been sourcing its goods directly from manufacturers for two years. The direct sourcing plan relies on the company's combined group-buying power to source common products that can be sold in its stores across the world.

Volume

Ensuring that goods and services are made available in the right quantities may seem obvious but, in reality, this will require a firm to make decisions and commit resources now based on predictions of future demand. Overestimating the volume required is likely to lead to wasted goods, increased stock-holding costs and price cutting. On the other hand, underestimating the amount of products required will mean missed sales opportunities and customer dissatisfaction.

Quality

The exact meaning of quality for any individual organisation will depend to some extent on the nature of its operations. Put simply, quality is about getting things 'right' by meeting or beating customer expectations over and over again. Quality has a crucial role to play in guaranteeing customer satisfaction. Not only should firms aim to produce goods or services that are 'fit for purpose', they also need to create a sense of dependability by ensuring that products are ready when customers expect them. Failure to do so is likely to create customer dissatisfaction and encourage customers to switch to rival products. A high degree of quality and dependability is also required within the organisation. Managers need to ensure that quality standards are being met. They also need to synchronise production so that products pass smoothly from one stage to the next. This will help to reduce production time and costs, meaning that goods are ready for dispatch to customers sooner.

Time

This factor is important in many ways, both to the consumer and the producer. Many consumers are 'money-rich, time-poor' as they rush from a well-paid job to pick up the kids, eat, then go out. So operations that can save time for the customer can be very successful (for example, Tesco online grocery shopping, pizza delivery). Time-based management is also important to firms in product development. Stung by the success of the Toyota Prius, General Motors was desperate to get the first mass-market electric-only car out by 2010. By developing a successful pollution-free car before anyone else, the company was confident that it could regain its position as the world's number one car producer. At the time of writing, the company's first electric car, the Chevrolet Volt, was expected to be launched in the United States before the end of 2010. This will be followed by the launch of the Vauxhall Ampera, which is based on the same technology as the Colt, in European markets in 2011 and the UK in 2012.

The firm that is first to market is able to charge higher prices than its slower rivals. Speed is also important within the business. The faster items pass through the production process, the lower the costs of warehousing materials and work-in-progress.

Flexibility

Firms need to be able to vary the volume of production relatively easily, in order to respond effectively to unexpected increases or decreases in demand. The ability to adapt or modify a standard product range allows a firm to appear to be offering customised products that meet customer needs more precisely, but still benefit from high-volume production, keeping costs down. This flexible approach to production is a form of **lean production** that has been used successfully by a number of companies, including computer manufacturer Dell.

> **A-grade application**
>
> **Lean production reaches sportswear**
>
> Nike became the first sportswear manufacturer to embrace the concept of lean production when it established a new online design facility. Nike iD allows customers to create their own versions of a range of footwear and clothing. Customers follow a step-by-step customisation process, picking from a choice of colours and materials, and adding logos, names and personalised messages in order to create a 'unique' product. The customised goods are manufactured and delivered within four weeks of an order being placed. A 'teamlocker' version of the service also exists, offering the facility to sports teams and groups. The success of the concept has been followed up with the opening of a number of Nike iD Studios around the world, including London's Oxford Street. Each studio has a team of qualified design consultants on hand to help customers make their choices.
>
> Source: Nike

72.3 THE IMPORTANCE OF INNOVATION

Innovation means more than merely inventing a new product or process; it involves turning a new idea into a commercial success. Innovation within operations is crucial to the long-term survival and growth of a firm, allowing it to keep ahead of the competition. New products will often require new production methods and machinery. New processes for producing existing goods or delivering services can help to reduce costs and improve the quality and speed of production.

In 2003, stung by the success of the European Airbus project, Boeing announced a new 'Dreamliner' plane that would fly 250 passengers longer distances non-stop than ever before. It would also be 20 per cent more

Figure 72.2 Boeing's Dreamliner plane

B2 CASE STUDY

Renault targets the cheap mass market

2009 and 2010 saw a boom in Europe-wide sales of Dacia cars. When Renault bought Dacia in 1999, many commentators thought the French company had made a big mistake. Dacia's productivity was low and profits were non-existent. After a decade of hard work, Renault is enjoying a payback on its investment. Dacia's no-frills Logan saloon has a price tag of the equivalent of around £5,000, while the Logan estate sells for the equivalent of £6,000. Both models are targeted at customers who would normally opt to buy second-hand, rather than a brand new car.

The cars are made at Renault's Dacia plant in Romania. The Logan was originally intended to be sold in Romania only, but proved to be a huge success in both France and Germany, with waiting lists of customers eager to get hold of the car. Annual output at the plant was increased by the company from 200,000 in 2006 to 350,000 in 2008. Although workers at the Dacia plant are highly skilled, the production process is low-tech. However, the main reason behind the car's cheap price is low labour costs; a Romanian car worker gets paid an average of £170 per month, an eighth of the pay of equivalent workers in France.

Source: based on BBC News, 7 March 2007

Questions

(20 marks; 25 minutes)

1 Examine Renault's operational objectives in launching its Logan car range. (8)
2 To what extent do you agree that the other major car manufacturers will be forced to follow Renault and target the low-cost segment of the market? (12)

Economies and diseconomies of scale

UNIT 73

Economies of scale are factors which cause average unit costs to fall as the scale of output increases in the long-run. Diseconomies of scale are factors causing average costs to rise as the scale of output increases in the long run.

73.1 TWO WAYS FIRMS CAN GROW

Internal growth

Internal growth occurs when a firm expands its own sales and output. Firms growing in this manner must invest in new machinery and usually take on extra labour too. Firms that are successful in achieving internal growth have to be competitive. Companies like Ryanair and Nike have grown rapidly by taking market share from their less-efficient competitors.

External growth

External growth is created by takeover and merger activity. In October 2010 John W Henry, owner of the Boston Red Sox baseball team, bought Liverpool FC for just over £300 million. This meant there was a sudden increase in the scale of Henry's business and gave him access to the global market, represented by Premier League football.

There are many reasons why firms may wish to grow by takeover or merger. One of the most significant is that many managers believe growth will create cost savings for their firms. They anticipate benefiting from economies of scale. Unfortunately, this is not always true. Many mergers and takeovers actually reduce efficiency. Many economies of scale prove to be outweighed by diseconomies. Research has shown consistently that, on average, takeovers and mergers fail to improve efficiency.

73.2 ECONOMIES OF SCALE

When a firm grows there are some things it can do more efficiently. The group term given to these factors is 'economies of scale'. When firms experience economies of scale their unit costs fall. For example, a pottery which could produce 100 vases at £5 each may be able to produce 1,000 vases at £4.50 per unit. The total cost rises (from £500 to £4,500) but the cost per unit falls. Assuming the firm sells the vases for £6 each, the profit margin rises from £1 per vase to £1.50. Economies of scale are, in effect, the benefits of being big. Therefore, for small firms, they represent a threat. If a large-scale producer of televisions can sell them for £99 and still make a profit, there may be no chance for the small guy. There are five main economies of scale. These are discussed below.

Bulk-buying economies

As a firm grows larger it will have to order more raw materials and components. This is likely to mean there will be an increase in the average order size the firm places with its suppliers. Large orders are more profitable to the supplier. Both the buyer and the potential suppliers are aware of this. Consequently, firms who can place large orders have significant market power. The larger the order the larger the opportunity cost of losing it. Therefore the supplier has a big incentive to offer a discount. Big multinational manufacturers like Volkswagen have been relentless in demanding larger discounts from their component suppliers. This has helped Volkswagen to reduce its variable costs per car.

Technical economies of scale

When supplying a product or service there is usually more than one production method that can be used. As a firm grows, it will usually have a greater desire and a greater ability to invest in new technology. Using more machinery and less labour will usually generate cost savings. Second, the new machinery may well be less wasteful. Reducing the quantity of raw materials being wasted will cut the firm's variable costs.

These cost savings may not be available to smaller firms. They may lack the financial resources required to purchase the machinery. Even if the firm did have the money it may still not invest. Technology only becomes viable to use if the firm has a long enough production run to spread out the fixed costs of the equipment. For example, a small company may wish to buy a new computer. As the firm is small, it may use it for only two days a week. The total cost of the computer will be the same whether the firm uses it one day or five days per week. So the average cost of each job done will be high, as the small firm is unable to make full use of its

into large-scale production at a viable cost. It is this problem that explains perhaps the major stumbling block to R&D budgets: very few firms are willing to invest when there is not a measurable return. The nature of R&D requires substantial sums to pay for the scientific expertise and equipment needed and, therefore, the only firms willing and able to invest in R&D are likely to be very large firms that also have a management team committed to long-term, rather than short-term, success.

R&D and international competitiveness

Table 74.1 Selected countries' R&D spending as a percentage of GDP, 2007

Rank	Country	R&D as a percentage of GDP
1	Sweden	3.7
2=	Finland	3.5
2=	South Korea	3.5
4	Japan	3.4
5	Iceland	2.8
6	United States	2.7
7=	Denmark	2.6
7=	Germany	2.6
7=	Singapore	2.6
10	Austria	2.5
11	Canada	2.0
12	Belgium	1.9
13	United Kingdom	1.8
14	Slovenia	1.5

Source: The World Bank, World Development Indicators, data source UNESCO Institute for Statistics.

Innovation is a crucial factor in determining the international competitiveness of a country's businesses. A country whose companies invest heavily in R&D is likely to find its economy healthy as its firms find success in export markets and have the innovative products needed to stave off import competition in their home market. It may, therefore, come as something of a worry to UK readers to see the UK in 13th place in the world league of R&D shown in Table 74.1. The implications of this are far reaching and serious for the UK. With higher costs of manufacturing than many countries, allied with a failure to innovate, the UK may struggle to find a genuine competitive advantage in the twenty-first century's global marketplace. This could spell economic stagnation.

ISSUES FOR ANALYSIS

- Invention should not be confused with innovation. The British have a proud record as inventors. Hovercraft, television, penicillin, Viagra and many more products were British inventions. In recent years, however, there has been less success in this country with innovation. The Japanese have been the great innovators in electronics, the Americans in computers and the Swiss in watches. British firms have failed to invest sufficiently to develop ranges of really innovative new products.
- Major innovation can completely change a firm's competitive environment. The market shares of leading companies may change little for years, then an innovation comes along that changes everything. The firm that has not prepared for such change can be swept aside. This has happened to music stores that have not established a major presence on the internet.
- Good management means looking ahead, not only to the next hill but the one after that. Anticipation makes change manageable. It may even ensure that your own firm becomes market leader due to the far-sightedness of your own innovation. In turn, that would ensure high product differentiation and allow relatively high prices to be charged.
- Innovation can happen in management procedures, attitudes and styles. A management that is progressive and adventurous may well find that an empowered workforce is generating the new ideas that seemed lacking before. It would not be wise to assume that invention and innovation is all about scientists and engineering. It is about people.

Figure 74.2 Hovercraft: a British invention

75.5 INNOVATION AND RESEARCH AND DEVELOPMENT – AN EVALUATION

The fundamental theme for evaluating any question involving invention and innovation is long- and short-term thinking. Invention and innovation are long-term activities. Companies whose objective is short-term profit maximisation are unlikely to spend heavily on innovation. However, a firm with objectives directly related to producing innovative products is likely to spend heavily on research. GlaxoSmithKline, Britain's highest spender on R&D (just under £3.7 billion in 2009), is an excellent example.

Most British companies do not have a particularly impressive record in invention and innovation. Table 74.1 shows that a comparison of international R&D spending places Britain outside the top ten. The conclusion could be that short-termism is a particular problem in Britain. An unhealthy focus on success in the short term does not fit in with a commitment to expensive R&D, designed to ensure long-term growth. As a result, British firms have a tendency to please their shareholders with high dividend payments, rather than retaining profits for investment in R&D.

Selling innovative products is not the only way to build a successful business. Many firms carve out a successful segment of their market based on selling copycat products at lower prices and their ability to cut costs to the bone, maintaining a satisfactory profit margin. However, these low-cost firms tend to be based in countries with lower labour costs than the UK. Other costs in the UK, such as property and business services, are also high relative to international rivals and, therefore, this low-cost strategy is unlikely to work for many UK firms trying to compete internationally. As a result, it seems likely that the continued survival of major UK multinationals is dependent on producing innovative products based on successful R&D.

WORKBOOK

A REVISION QUESTIONS

(40 marks; 40 minutes)

1 Distinguish between product and process innovation. (3)
2 Why is it 'vital' to patent an invention? (3)
3 Explain why R&D has an opportunity cost. (2)
4 Briefly explain the role of each of the following departments in the process of successfully bringing a new product to market.
   a) marketing
   b) finance
   c) HR. (12)
5 Why may product-orientated firms produce more inventions than market-orientated ones? (4)
6 How are the concepts of short-termism and innovation linked? (4)
7 What effect would a lack of innovation have on a company's product portfolio? (4)
8 Many businesses are concerned at the fall in the number of students taking science A-levels. How may this affect firms in the long term? (4)
9 Explain how a firm may try to market a brand new type of product developed from successful R&D. (4)

B REVISION EXERCISES
B1 CASE STUDY

Mach 3: at the cutting edge of technology

Gillette's UK research and development facility is located just outside Reading. Men in white coats test revolutionary shaving technologies – all searching for the perfect shaving experience. From its position of UK market dominance (57 per cent market share), which has been based on innovation, including the launch in 1971 of the world's first twin-bladed razor, Gillette is pushing forward the frontiers of shaving technology. The newest model to have been developed by Gillette is the Mach 3. The new product has been described as the 'Porsche of the shaving world', with its sleek design, and its hefty price tag of £4.99 for the handle and two cartridges. The Mach 3 was advertised in America as the 'billion-dollar blade'. However, this was probably an underestimate of the costs incurred during the razor's seven-year development:

- $750 million (£440 million) on building the production system for the razor
- $300 million on the launch marketing
- $200 per year on research and development.

Gillette expects to sell 1.2 billion units of the Mach 3 per year.

The testing regime for Gillette's new products involves a product evaluation group of more than 3,000 men throughout the UK, who are supplied with Gillette products and provide feedback on the level of quality consistency, in addition to testing experimental products. Among these guinea pigs are the mysterious men who turn up at the research facility in Reading every morning – paid for the shaving risks they take there and performing the role of test pilots – sworn to secrecy on the new technology they are using.

The building, an old jam factory, is kitted out with the latest CAD technology. Research focuses on computer models of human skin, a substance that Gillette has found very tough to model accurately. However, its current modelling is the most accurate it has ever used and skin irritation is measured using the same laser technology as that employed in police radar guns. The jam factory was the birthplace of the Mach 3, a birth heralded by success in the long-running attempt to add a third blade without causing blood loss. With sales of the Mach 3 starting off at encouraging levels, the old jam factory appears to have turned out another winning idea.

Questions

(40 marks; 50 minutes)

1 Using examples from the text, suggest what marketing advantages arise from successful innovation. (8)
2 Describe the pre-launch testing methods used by Gillette, and explain why these are so vital to success. (9)
3 Why may the research laboratories for a product as ordinary as a razor be shrouded in secrecy? (6)
4 Using examples from the Gillette story, explain why successful innovation requires input from all departments within a firm, not just the research and development department. (12)
5 Given the information in the text, how long will it take Gillette to recover the research, development and launch costs of the Mach 3, if running costs average out to £2.99 per unit? (5)

B2 CASE STUDY

R&D in pottery

Josiah Wedgwood & Sons Ltd is part of the huge Waterford Wedgwood company formed by the takeover of ceramics firm Wedgwood by the Irish glass manufacturer Waterford Crystal. Despite a history dating back hundreds of years, Wedgwood still needs to carry our R&D to maintain its position in a hugely competitive global market. As is so common for many major British brands, Wedgwood can survive in the global market only by offering top-quality products at reasonable prices. In the push to bring costs down without sacrificing quality of design, Wedgwood has developed a brand new piece of machinery that is able to print intricate designs on non-flat surfaces (that is, cups). Previously, patterns were applied to cups by hand as decals (stickers). New decals took around four weeks to produce, while the application of the decals pushed the lead time for a new design up to 16 weeks. The machine has enabled direct printing onto cups and therefore reduced lead times to just one week for new designs. In addition to making possible far quicker delivery to customers, the machine has significantly reduced material and labour costs while maintaining high-quality products. Wedgwood identified three key factors in the success of the machine's development:

1 management commitment was critical to a potentially high-impact yet risky project in which each machine cost over €0.5 million
2 development engineers with the experience to develop radical new approaches and machinery
3 collaboration between technical, production and engineering departments.

Source: adapted from: www.manufacturingfoundation.org.uk

Questions

(30 marks; 35 minutes)

1 Analyse the financial benefits that Wedgwood will receive as a result of the new machine. (8)
2 Briefly explain how the new machines should provide marketing benefits. (4)
3 Analyse the likely reaction of staff to the development of the new machine. (6)
4 Consider how the case demonstrates the need for collaboration of different departments in successful R&D. (12)

C ESSAY QUESTIONS

(40 marks each)

1 To what extent does an innovative product guarantee success?
2 'Any business has two, and only two, basic functions. Marketing and innovation.' Discuss whether there is value in this statement by Peter Drucker.
3 'Luck is the most important factor in successful innovation.' Discuss the validity of this statement.
4 'Spending on research and development is wasted money since many firms find success through copying other firms' products.' Discuss this statement.

Industrial and international location

UNIT 75

The site(s) where a firm decides to carry out its operations.

75.1 THE LOCATION DECISION

Unit 7 covered 'location factors for a business start-up'. It included an overview of many of the basic issues involved, such as the cost of land and the need for space to expand. This unit looks at the expansion or relocation of a business, including decisions relating to international location.

The choice of location for a business is crucial to its success. Opting for the 'right' location can help to keep costs of production low while generating higher revenue from sales than alternative sites. For instance, costs can be reduced by opting for cheaper premises, closer proximity to suppliers or locating in an area with effective transport links. High-street locations make retailers more visible to customers and are more likely to attract sales.

Once a firm is established, there are two main reasons why managers may be faced with making a location decision.

1. It may be the result, for example, of a decision to expand operations by operating as a multi-site organisation, acquiring additional factories, offices or outlets. This can help to increase capacity and sales, and it may also help the business to recognise and respond to local market conditions more effectively. However, the business may require a new structure in order to continue to perform effectively, and a duplication of certain functions and job roles – especially at management level – can lead to increased overheads.
2. It may also result from a decision to relocate operations to a new site – one that may be in a position to attract more customers, offer better opportunities for modernisation or lead to a reduction in operating costs. Before going ahead, however, the business needs to consider the costs of relocation as well as the benefits. For example, will existing employees accept the move or leave the firm, leading to increased recruitment costs and a loss of expertise?

A-grade application

Relocation packages for BBC staff moving north

Generous relocation packages were offered to BBC employees who were affected by the corporation's decision to move some of its production and broadcasting from London to the north west of England. The incentives included a guaranteed house purchase scheme, payment of solicitors' fees, survey fees and stamp duty, up to £3,000 for new carpets and curtains and £350 per trip to travel to Manchester for house hunting. Five departments – sport, children's, Five Live, learning and parts of future, media and technology – will be based at a new site, known as Media City, in Manchester's Salford Quays, from 2011. Staff who are currently receiving extra 'London weighting' payments would be allowed to keep them, despite no longer living in the capital. The relocation package was made available to over 1,600 of the corporation's staff.

75.2 MAKING THE CHOICE: QUANTITATIVE METHODS

If Boeing wants to set up its first aircraft factory in Europe, it is clear that there are some key issues to do with numbers. It will need a massive site, which may have a cost ranging from £50 to £300 million, depending on where it is. Then there are wages, which might range from £300 to £2,500 per person per month, depending on whether the location is eastern Romania or western Germany.

Given its importance to the success of a business, it is vital that the location decision is based on accurate data. There are a number of quantitative decision-making techniques that can be used, including those discussed below.

Investment appraisal

This refers to a set of techniques that can be used to assess the viability of a project (that is, will the expected returns from the relocation site meet or exceed corporate targets?). Alternatively, they can be used to help choose between two or more sites for expansion or relocation that are under consideration. For example:

Table 75.1 Comparative pay rates between India and the UK

Occupation	Salary in India	Percentage of UK salary
Call centre operator	90p to £1.25 per hour	13–20
Top law graduate	£4,700 per year	11–14
Farm worker	£500 per year	5

Source: various, October 2010.

of higher-value jobs, such as those in research and development (R&D) and financial services. These activities are either carried out in company-owned facilities or outsourced to separate firms based in low-cost countries. Currently, the main offshore bases include India, China, Poland, Russia, South Africa and Brazil. India has proved to be a particularly attractive destination for UK businesses looking to offshore activities, producing over 2 million English-speaking graduates every year. Comparative pay rates between India and the UK are given in Table 75.1.

75.7 POTENTIAL PROBLEMS OF INTERNATIONAL LOCATION

Although expansion or relocation of operations into overseas markets can offer a number of benefits, firms must also be aware of the potential problems that can arise, including those described below.

Language and cultural differences

Given that barriers to communication can exist within firms employing workers that speak the same language, it is not difficult to imagine the potential problems and costs associated with managing an international, multilingual workforce. UK firms have benefited from the fact that English is commonly spoken around the world and remains the language of business. However, there are a number of differences in working practices between countries, including the length of the working week and number of public holidays, which can impact on performance and productivity.

Economic and political instability

The dynamic nature of the business environment means that firms need to be able to adjust to a certain level of change if they are to enjoy long-term success. However, rapid and unforeseen changes can pose serious challenges to survival. Because of this, firms are more likely to opt for international locations with a history of economic and political stability.

Impact on public image

A number of UK companies have attracted media attention over allegations of worker exploitation in low-cost economies, in order to keep costs down and offer cheap prices to consumers. A recent report published by War on Want claimed that workers from Bangladesh were paid less than 5p an hour (less than £80 per month) to produce clothes for UK retailers Tesco, Asda and Primark, despite all three companies being signed up to an initiative designed to provide such workers with an accepted living wage and improved living conditions.

A-grade application

UK taxes force big businesses to consider relocation

A report commissioned by HM Revenue and Customs in 2010 claimed that one in five large businesses operating in the UK were considering relocating abroad for tax reasons. The research also showed that 64 per cent of those surveyed felt that the burden of red tape faced by large companies had also increased. At the time, the chief executives of a number of banks, including HSBC and Barclays, announced that they would seriously consider relocating their head office operations if the UK Government adopted policies that were out of line with other countries.

Source: based on *The Daily Telegraph*, 25 August 2010.

ISSUES FOR ANALYSIS

Opportunities for analysis using this topic are likely to focus on the following areas:

- examining the advantages and disadvantages to a firm of relocating
- comparing quantitative and/or qualitative aspects of different location sites
- calculating and commenting upon the most profitable location for a firm
- analysing the factors that a business would take into account before establishing production facilities overseas.

75.8 INDUSTRIAL AND INTERNATIONAL LOCATION – AN EVALUATION

Location is a key aspect of all business operations. Even in the most footloose of industries, firms cannot afford to ignore the need for sufficient quantities of appropriately skilled workers or effective transport and communications networks. The optimum location is the one that allows a business to keep costs down while maximising revenue opportunities. Once made, incorrect location decisions can be costly to put right, and can lead to customer inconvenience and dissatisfaction. However, in a dynamic and increasingly competitive environment, the pressure on firms' costs is relentless. Therefore, firms need to regularly assess the suitability of their location in order to ensure that their operational strategy continues to be effective.

Key Terms

Business process outsourcing: moving administrative tasks, such as accounting and human resources management, to an external firm.

External economies of scale: cost advantages enjoyed by a firm as a result of the growth of the industry in which it is located (for example, close proximity of a network of suppliers).

Industrial inertia: when firms continue to locate in a particular area or region even after the original advantages of doing so have disappeared.

Investment appraisal: a range of quantitative decision-making techniques used to assess investment projects, including payback, average rate of return and net present value.

Multinational: a business with productive bases – either manufacturing or assembly – in more than one country.

Non-tariff barriers: hidden barriers put in place by governments to restrict international trade without appearing to do so (for example, insisting on technical standards that it is difficult for foreign firms to meet).

Offshoring: the relocation of one or more business processes – either production or services – from one country to another.

Optimal: a decision based on the best available compromise between different objectives or factors.

Outsourcing: moving business functions from internal departments to external firms.

Quota: a trade barrier that places restrictions on the number of foreign goods that can be sold within a market in a given period of time.

Tariff: a tax placed on imports in order to increase their price and therefore discourage demand.

WORKBOOK

A REVISION QUESTIONS

(40 marks; 40 minutes)

1 Outline two reasons why a business may choose to relocate its operations. (4)

2 Identify four factors that could influence a firm's location decision. (4)

3 Examine one advantage and one disadvantage for an estate agent that locates on a town's main high street. (6)

4 Briefly outline two quantitative methods that could be used to help a business decide between two location sites. (4)

5 What is meant by the term industrial inertia? (2)

6 Describe one external economy of scale that may result from the concentration of an industry in a particular area. (3)

7 In September 2006, fashion group Burberry announced its decision to relocate production from its factory in Treorchy, Wales, to a site in Spain, Portugal, Poland or China. Examine two reasons why Burberry may have decided to relocate production overseas. (6)

8 Explain the difference between **outsourcing** and offshoring. (5)

9 Analyse two problems that a bank could experience as a result of relocating some of its business processes to the Philippines. (6)

B REVISION EXERCISES

B1 DATA RESPONSE

Dyson's Asian relocation creates UK jobs

Relocating the production of Dyson vacuums from Wiltshire to Malaysia in 2002 was seen at the time as a serious blow to UK manufacturing. The move, which was followed in 2003 by the transfer of washing machine manufacture to Malaysia by the company, resulted in the loss of 600 workers from Dyson's Malmesbury factory. Inventor and company owner, James Dyson, claimed that lower costs and proximity to both component suppliers and major markets in Japan and the United States were the key reasons for the move. The company had also been refused planning permission to expand the Malmesbury plant. According to Dyson, pre-tax profits per employee tripled within a year of the move. Between 2003 and 2005, Dyson's US sales turnover alone grew from £34 million to £100 million.

By early 2010, Dyson employed around 2,500 staff in 49 countries worldwide. The company's growth has meant that the size of its UK workforce has returned to where it had been before the relocation of production. In April 2010, it announced plans to increase the number of engineers and scientists employed at its Malmesbury headquarters from 350 to 700, taking the total number employed at the site to over 1,600. Dyson believes that investing in design and engineering is key to fighting competition from firms based in low-cost countries, such as China. According to him, '...We can never be cheaper. The only way to win is to keep ahead in terms of innovation.'

Questions

(30 marks; 35 minutes)

1 Examine the key factors that were responsible for Dyson transferring the manufacture of vacuums and washing machines from the UK to Malaysia. (10)

2 To what extent do you agree with the view that all UK manufacturers like Dyson have to locate production abroad in order to remain competitive? (20)

B2 DATA RESPONSE

Made in England – still!

Unlike many other UK textile firms, John Smedley continues to refuse to close down its factories and relocate its production abroad. Despite high costs and a seemingly unstoppable flow of cheap imports, the luxury knitwear manufacturer remains firmly rooted in the Derbyshire location where the business was first established over 225 years ago. According to the company, its heritage is an important part of the 'indefinable quality' of its products. The company's fine-knit wool and cotton sweaters and cardigans have long been popular with royalty and celebrities. Around 70 per cent of its production is exported, mostly to Japan. Annual sales turnover for 2010 was around £17 million.

John Smedley's survival strategy is based on targeting a low-volume niche and competing on the grounds of quality, rather than price. The key ingredients in the manufacturing process are a highly-skilled workforce of around 450 employees, carefully sourced materials and a rigorous system of quality control. According to Dawne Stubbs, the company's creative director, the mineral springs located just behind the mill where production takes place are also responsible for the softness of the knitwear. Each garment produced has been washed in water taken from the springs since the business began in 1704.

Despite the continuing popularity of its products, John Smedley has faced a number of problems in recent years. The company continues to struggle with increasing raw materials and energy costs. A rise in the value of the pound against the yen at one point made the company's products 20 per cent more expensive in Japanese markets. However, it rejected proposals to offshore production to China after discovering that this would result in a price reduction on average of £8 per garment.

Questions

(20 marks; 25 minutes)

1 To what extent do you agree with John Smedley's decision to keep production at its Derbyshire location? (20)

B2 CASE STUDY

Relocating production at Blueberry Fashions Ltd

'It's the decision that no one wanted to face, but we have no choice.' The words of Blueberry Fashions managing director, Susanne Burrell, gradually sank into the other members of the board. Despite 12 months of a high-profile campaign that had included a number of local celebrities, the company had just announced its decision to go ahead with the closure of one of its three factories in the UK in a little over a year's time, resulting in the loss of over 350 jobs. Despite the firm's success in maintaining its reputation as one of the UK's most successful global brands in recent years, there was no escaping the fact that many of its designer items could be made at a higher quality and a significantly lower cost elsewhere in Europe. Sites in a number of locations were under consideration but the board had yet to reach a decision. Comparative figures for sites in Poland, Slovakia and Romania are shown in Table 75.2.

Table 75.2 Comparative figures, 2011

	Poland	Slovakia	Romania
Forecast cost of expansion (€m)	4.2	5.1	3.9
Unemployment rates (%)	12.8	8.6	4.1
Growth rates (%)	6.5	8.8	5.9

Question

(20 marks; 25 minutes)

1 On the basis of the evidence provided, evaluate the relocation options available to Blueberry Fashions. (20)

C ESSAY QUESTIONS

(40 marks each)

1 Lord Sieff, former head of UK retailer Marks & Spencer, is reported to have once said, 'There are three important things in retailing: location, location, location.' To what extent do you agree with this view?

2 Discuss the implications for UK service-sector firms that have offshored IT or administrative functions to low-cost economies, such as India.

Planning operations (including CPA)

UNIT 76

Planning how a project will be carried out to ensure that it is completed quickly, cost-efficiently and on time. A network diagram helps to identify the critical path, which shows the activities that require the most careful management scrutiny.

76.1 OPERATIONAL PLANNING

Operations management involves many considerations, including location, quality, stock control and information technology. Well-run firms will bring all these aspects into a single strategic plan. This should then be turned into a day-by-day plan to show supervisors and workers exactly what they should be doing: what, when and how. This kind of planning and control is fundamental to effective management. A useful model for planning an operational project is network analysis. It provides the basis for monitoring and controlling actual progress compared with the plan.

76.2 NETWORK ANALYSIS

Network analysis is a way of showing how a complex project can be completed in the shortest possible time. It identifies the activities that must be completed on time to avoid delaying the whole project (the 'critical path'). Management effort can be concentrated on ensuring that these key activities are completed on time. This leaves greater flexibility in timing the non-critical items. The objectives are to ensure customer satisfaction through good timekeeping and to minimise the wastage of resources, thereby boosting the profitability of the project.

Have you ever tried to put together some flatpack furniture? Piece of wood A has to be fitted into piece B and then screwed into C. Meanwhile, someone else can be gluing D and E together. Then ABC can be slotted into DE. (And so on until worker/parent A is screaming at worker/parent B.) The manufacturer's instructions follow the exact logic of network analysis. This would work well, were it not that the instructions are usually set out poorly, and the 'workforce' is untrained. In business it is easier to make the technique work effectively.

A **network** shows:

- the order in which each task must be undertaken
- how long each stage should take
- the earliest date at which the later stages can start.

If a house-building firm can predict with confidence that it will be ready to put roof beams in place 80 days after the start of a project, a crane can be hired and the beams delivered for exactly that time. This minimises costs, as the crane need only be hired for the day it is needed, and improves cash flow by delaying the arrival of materials (and invoices) until they are really required.

A network consists of two components.

1 An 'activity' is part of a project that requires time and/or resources. Therefore waiting for delivery of parts is an 'activity', as is production. Activities are shown as arrows running from left to right. Their length has no significance.
2 A 'node' is the start or finish of an activity and is represented by a circle. All network diagrams start and end on a single node.

As an example, the flatpack furniture example given earlier would look like that shown in Figure 76.1.

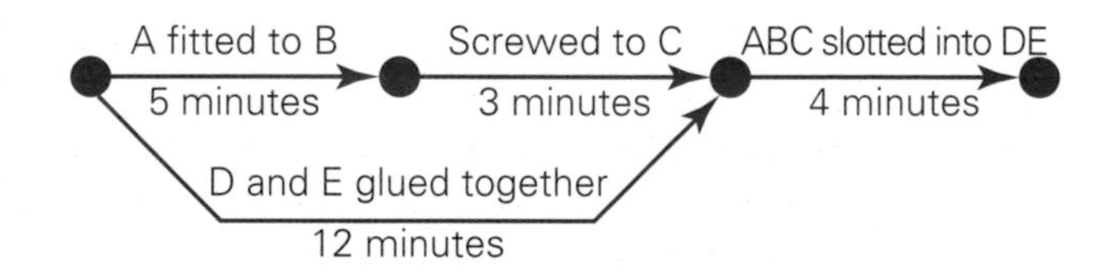

Figure 76.1 Flatpack network

How long should it take to complete this little project? Although A, B and C can be completed in 8 minutes, D and E take 12, so the final 4-minute activity can occur only after the 12th minute. Therefore the project duration is 16 minutes.

76.3 RULES FOR DRAWING NETWORKS

1 The network must start and end on a single node.
2 No lines should cross each other.
3 When drawing an activity, do not add the end node straight away; wait until you have checked which activity follows.
4 There must be no lines that are not activities.
5 Due to the need to write figures in the nodes, it is

helpful to draw networks with large circles and short lines.

> **A-grade application**
>
> **Delays can cost billions**
>
> The first commercial flight of Boeing's 780 'Dreamliner' plane took place in early 2011. This was nearly eight years after the new plane was announced and more than two and a half years after the plane's first test flight. Nippon Airways had been expecting to fly its first Dreamliner in 2008, and was kept waiting for three years!
>
> The problem arose because of difficulties with the new lightweight materials being used in the plane. The most serious was a redesign announced in 2009 to 'reinforce an area within the side-of-body section' of the plane! The direct cost to Boeing has been estimated at more than £4 billion. The indirect effects are no less severe. Before Boeing admitted that its project was behind schedule, its European rival Airbus was struggling to sell its competitor A350 plane. In 2009 Virgin announced it was cancelling its Boeing order to buy Airbus planes. In 2010,* Boeing received net orders for the Dreamliner of *minus* 4 planes, while Airbus enjoyed positive net orders for 58 A350s.
>
> When the design problem became the critical one for Boeing, management failed to find a successful way of coping. In this case, poor critical path analysis cost Boeing billions of pounds.
>
> Note: *Figures correct for January to July 2010.
>
> Source: Airbus and Boeing websites: www.airbus.com and www.boeing.co.uk

76.4 CASE EXAMPLE: THE NEED FOR NETWORKS

A chocolate producer decides to run a '3p off' price promotion next February. Any need for network analysis? Surely not. What could be easier? Yet the risk of upsetting customers is massive with any promotion. What if a huge order from Tesco meant that Sainsbury's could not receive all the supplies it wanted?

Think for a moment about the activities needed to make this promotion work smoothly. It would be necessary to:

- tell the salesforce
- sell the stock into shops
- design the 'flash' packs
- estimate the sales volume for one month at 3p off
- get 'flash' packs printed
- order extra raw materials (for example, a double order of cocoa)
- step up production
- arrange overtime for factory staff
- deliver promotional packs to shops ...
- ... and much, much more.

An efficient manager thinks about all the activities needed, and puts them in the correct time sequence. Then a network can be drawn up (see Figure 76.2).

Once the manager has found how long each activity is likely to take, she or he can work backwards to find out when the work must start. Here, the work must start 70 days before 1 February. This is because the longest path through to the end of the project is 70 (14 + 28 + 21 + 7).

Having drawn a network, the next stage is to identify more precisely the times when particular activities can or must begin and end. To do this, it is helpful to number the nodes that connect the activities. It also makes it easier to follow if there is not too much writing on the activities. Figure 76.3 shows the 3p off example with the activities represented by letters and the nodes numbered.

76.5 EARLIEST START TIMES AND LATEST FINISH TIMES

Space has also been left in the nodes in Figure 76.3 for two more numbers: the earliest start time (EST) and the latest finish time (LFT). The EST shows the earliest time at which following activities can be started. On Figure 76.3, activities C, D and E can begin only after 14 days. Because, although A takes only four days, C, D and E need both A and B to be complete before they can be started. So the EST at node 2 is the longest path through to that node (that is, activity B's 14 days).

Figure 76.4 shows the complete network, including all the ESTs. Note that the start of a project is always

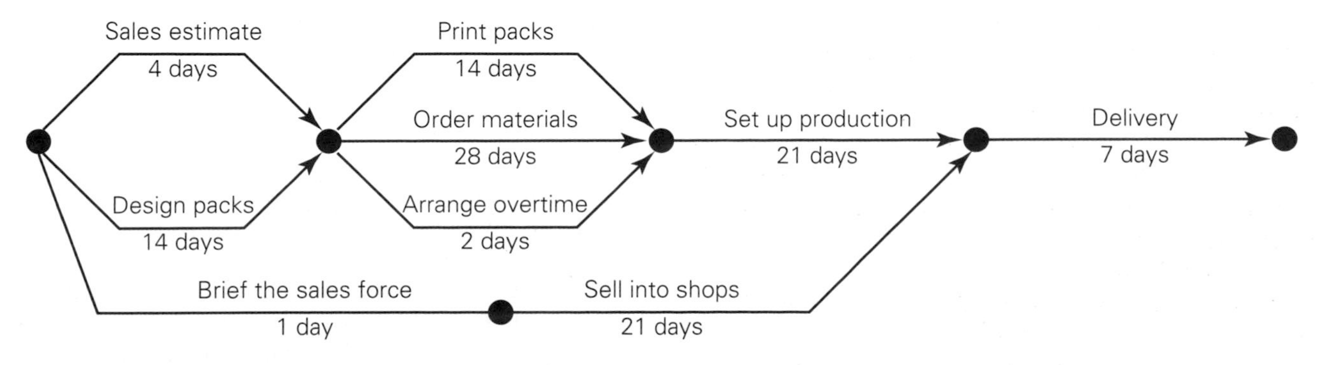

Figure 76.2 '3p off' network (1)

- If the completion of an activity is delayed for some reason, the network diagram is a good starting point for working out the implications and deciding on appropriate courses of action.

Disadvantages

The disadvantages of using network (critical path) analysis are set out below.

- A complex project (such as the construction of the Olympic village) entails so many activities that a drawing becomes unmanageable. Fortunately, computers can zoom in and out of drawings, enabling small parts of the network to be magnified and examined.
- Drawing a diagram does not, in itself, ensure the effective management of a project. Network analysis provides a plan, but can only be as successful as the staff's commitment to it. This suggests that staff should be consulted about the schedule and the likely duration of the activities.
- The value of the network diagram is reduced slightly because the activity lines are not in proportion to the duration of the activities.

ISSUES FOR ANALYSIS

Issues for analysis in relation to networks include the following.

- That critical path analysis (CPA) allows a business to translate strategies into plans of action, enabling each member of staff to know what has to be achieved by when; practical techniques such as this are needed to enable delegation to be effective.
- Drawing networks is a valuable skill, but at least as important is interpreting diagrams that have already been drawn; this can be made easier by asking 'What if?' questions about different scenarios. What if a critical activity is delayed? What if critical activity B can be bought in from an outside supplier who promises to take half the time?
- The need for a technique such as CPA to enable just-in-time to work in practice; care over timing and meticulous organisation are the essentials in both systems.
- Networks are a crucial way to organise resources so that working capital usage is minimised; this is especially important in long-term projects such as construction work or new product development.

76.9 PLANNING OPERATIONS (INCLUDING CPA) – AN EVALUATION

The cliché 'time is money' has been around for years. Only recently, though, have systems such as just-in-time focused clearly on time-based management. Time is vital not only because it affects costs, but also because it can provide a crucial marketing edge. Primark's key advantage over Next is that it is much quicker at getting catwalk fashions into high-street shops. So time can add value. Careful production planning can also help to get a firm's new product to the market before the opposition.

Network analysis is a valuable practical tool for taking time seriously. It involves careful planning and can be used as a way of monitoring progress. If critical activities are falling behind schedule, action can be taken quickly. This serves as a reminder that successful business management is not just about clever strategic thinking. Ultimately, success depends upon what happens at the workplace or at the construction site. Network analysis is a helpful way to ensure that strategies become plans that can be carried through effectively. Nevertheless, they guarantee nothing. Ensuring that the paper network becomes reality will remain in the hands of the managers, supervisors and staff on the job. So effective personnel management and motivation will remain as important as ever.

Key Terms

Critical path: the activities that must be completed on time for the project to finish on time. In other words, they have no float time at all.

Management by exception: the principle that because managers cannot supervise every activity within the organisation, they should focus their energies on the most important issues.

Network: a diagram showing all the activities needed to complete a project, the order in which they must be completed and the critical path.

Network analysis: breaking a project down into its component parts, to identify the sequence of activities involved.

WORKBOOK

A REVISION QUESTIONS

(35 marks; 35 minutes)

1. Explain the business importance of operational planning. (3)
2. Identify two objectives of network analysis. (2)
3. Distinguish between an activity and a project. (3)
4. State three key rules for drawing networks. (3)
5. Explain how to calculate the earliest start time for an activity. (4)
6. Why is it important to calculate the latest finish time on an activity? (4)
7. What is meant by 'the critical path' and how do you identify it? (4)
8. Explain why it would be useful to know which activities have float times available. (3)
9. Analyse the value of network analysis for a small firm in financial difficulties. (4)
10. Explain how the use of critical path analysis could help a firm's time-based management. (5)

B REVISION EXERCISES

B1 DATA RESPONSE

Table 76.1 Data for constructing a network

Activity	Preceded by	Duration (weeks)
A	–	6
B	–	4
C	–	10
D	A & B	5
E	A & B	7
F	D	3

Questions

(40 marks; 40 minutes)

1 a) Construct a network from the information given in Table 76.1. (6)
b) Number the nodes and put in the earliest start times. (4)

2 a) Draw the following network:
Activity A and B start the project. C and D follow A. E follows all other jobs. (6)
b) Work out the earliest start times of the activities and put them in the nodes if, in the above question, A lasts 2 days, B = 9 days, C = 3, D = 4, E = 7. (4)

3 a) Use the information given in Table 76.2 to construct a fully labelled network showing ESTs, LFTs and the critical path. (12)

Table 76.2 Data for constructing a fully labelled network

Activity	Preceded by	Duration
A	–	3
B	–	9
C	–	2
D	A	5
E	C	3
F	B, D, E	5
G	C	9

b) If the firm was offered a £2,000 bonus for completing the project in 12 days, which activity should managers focus upon? Explain why. (8)

Kaizen (continuous improvement)

UNIT 77

Kaizen is a Japanese term meaning continuous improvement. Staff at firms like Toyota generate thousands of new ideas every year, each aimed at improving productivity or quality. Over time, these small steps forward add up to significant improvements in competitiveness.

77.1 INTRODUCTION

'If a man has not been seen for three days his friends should take a good look at him to see what changes have befallen him.'

This ancient Japanese saying seems to sum up *kaizen* quite nicely. Continuous improvement or '*kaizen*' is a philosophy of ongoing improvement based around small changes involving everyone: managers and workers alike. There are two key elements to *kaizen*:

1. Most *kaizen* improvements are based around people and their ideas rather than investment in new technology.
2. Each change on its own may be of little importance. However, if hundreds of small changes are made, the cumulative effects can be substantial.

A-grade application

A *kaizen* improvement at Barclaycard

An example of a *kaizen* improvement is provided by Barclaycard. In processing billions of pounds of credit card transactions per year, a major problem is fraud. An employee suggested a way of analysing bogus calls to the company's authorisation department. This has saved Barclaycard over £100,000 a year. The precise method is secret, but it works by blocking the credit card numbers of callers who are trying to buy goods fraudulently. It can also trace the callers, resulting in the arrest of the fraudsters involved.

In the 1990s, the term '*kaizen*' was virtually unknown outside Japan. Research carried out in Britain in early 2010 showed that over 80 per cent of private sector businesses say they use strategies for continuous improvement.

77.2 THE COMPONENTS OF THE *KAIZEN* PHILOSOPHY

Describing *kaizen* as just 'continuous improvement' is simplistic. To work effectively *kaizen* requires a commitment from management to establish a special, positive culture within the organisation. This culture must be communicated and accepted by all those working at the company. It must permeate the whole organisation. What are the characteristics of this culture or philosophy?

One employee, two jobs

According to the *Kaizen* Institute the goal of any *kaizen* programme should be to convince all employees that they have two jobs to do: doing the job and then looking for ways of improving it. The *kaizen* culture is based on the belief that the production line worker is the real expert. The worker on the assembly line does the job day in day out. This means knowing more about the causes of problems and their solutions than the highly qualified engineer who sits in an office. The *kaizen* philosophy recognises the fact that any company's greatest resource is its staff.

Teamworking

To operate *kaizen* successfully employees cannot be allowed to work as isolated individuals. Teamworking is vital to the process of continuous improvement. These teams are composed of employees who work on the same section of the production line as a self-contained unit. Each team is often referred to as a 'cell'. The members of a cell are responsible for the quality of the work in their section. Over time the cell becomes expert about the processes within its section of the production line. *Kaizen* attempts to tap into this knowledge by organising each cell into a quality circle. The members of each cell meet regularly to discuss problems cropping up within their section. The circle then puts forward solutions and recommendations for the management to consider.

> **A-grade application**
>
> **Tesco: 'Every Little Helps'**
>
> How would you react if Lidl or Aldi announced the intention of becoming Britain's number one, high-quality grocery chain? The better you know these discount stores, the more you would laugh at the thought. Yet that was the position of Tesco when it decided to move upmarket in the early 1980s. It had been famous for being a cheap, low cost, low quality alternative to Sainsbury's. Over the following two decades it had a mountain to climb, yet stumbled upon the slogan 'Every Little Helps'. This not only became the clever advertising line when introducing initiatives such as Clubcard and 'Only One in the Q' (or we'll open another aisle). It also became vital behind the scenes, as staff started to realise that small steps forward were appreciated by management.
>
> Using its 'Every Little Helps' approach has led Tesco to the situation in which, by 2010, its annual profit of £3,400 million dwarfed Sainsbury's £610 million.

Empowerment

Empowerment is essential to any *kaizen* programme. Empowerment involves giving employees the right to make decisions that affect the quality of their working lives. Empowerment enables good shop-floor ideas to be implemented quickly.

Once the necessary *kaizen* apparatus is in place, good ideas and the resulting improvements should continue. The number of suggestions made each month should improve over time once employees see the effects of their own solutions. However, if quality circles and teamworking are to be truly effective, employees must be given real decision-making power. If good ideas are constantly ignored by management they will eventually dry up, as the employees become disillusioned with the whole process.

> **A-grade application**
>
> 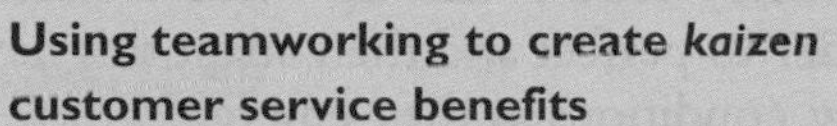
>
> **Using teamworking to create *kaizen* customer service benefits**
>
> Julian Richer is a strong believer in the merits of teamworking and *kaizen*. Richer is the owner of a highly innovative and successful hi-fi retailing chain called Richer Sounds. Apart from offering excellent value for money, Richer has utilised the creative ideas of his staff to create customer service with a difference. For the benefit of every Richer Sounds customer, each outlet is equipped with its own free coffee and mint dispensing machine. Each shop has its own mirror which says 'You are looking at the most important person in this shop' and a bell that customers can ring if they feel that they have received excellent service. Many of these innovations have come from Richer's own style of quality circle. Once a month, staff at each outlet are encouraged to talk to each other about new ideas. To lubricate this process Mr Richer gives each of his staff £5. This is because at Richer Sounds they hold their *kaizen* discussions at the pub!

77.3 POTENTIAL PROBLEMS OF IMPLEMENTING A SUCCESSFUL *KAIZEN* PROGRAMME

Culture

In order for *kaizen* to really work, employees must be proud to contribute their ideas to the company. Japanese companies do not offer financial rewards in return for suggestions. Their attitude is that employees are told that *kaizen* is part of the company policy when they are recruited. For them employee commitment to *kaizen* is gained via genuine staff motivation, rather than by financial bonuses. Creating the right organisational culture is therefore vital for success. Resistance can come from two quarters:

1. Management resistance: managers with autocratic tendencies may be unwilling to pass decision-making power down the hierarchy.
2. Employee resistance: a history of poor industrial relations and a climate of mistrust can create resistance to change among the staff. Employees may see the 'new empowerment programme' as a cynical attempt to get more out of the staff for less. The result? Reluctant cooperation at best, but little in terms of real motivation.

Training costs

Mistakes made by managers in the past can have severe long-term effects. Changing an organisation's culture is difficult as it involves changing attitudes. The training

> **Famous quotes about continuous improvement**
>
> 'Continuous improvement is better than delayed perfection.'
> Mark Twain, famous American writer
>
> 'If there's a way to do it better ... find it.'
> Thomas Edison, inventor
>
> 'If you're not making progress all the time, you're slipping backwards.'
> Sir John Harvey Jones, former chief of ICI
>
> 'I believe that there is hardly a single operation in the making of our car that is the same as when we made our first car of the present model. That is why we make them so cheaply.'
> Henry Ford, legendary car maker
>
> 'Our company has, indeed, stumbled onto some of its new products. But never forget that you can only stumble if you're moving.'
> Richard Carlton, former chief at American giant 3M
>
> 'Be not afraid of going slowly; be only afraid of standing still.'
> Chinese proverb
>
> Source: *The Ultimate Book of Business Quotations*, Stuart Crainer, Capstone Publishing, 1997.

B2 CASE STUDY

Kaizen 2.0: Frugal innovation

Thirty years ago Japan overtook America to become the world's leading car producer. American manufacturers were taken aback – and they were even more shocked when they visited Japan to find out what was going on. They found that the secret of Japan's success did not lie in cheap labour or government subsidies (their preferred explanations) but in what was rapidly dubbed 'lean manufacturing'. Japan had transformed itself from a low-wage economy into a hotbed of employee-led shop-floor innovation. Soon every successful factory around the world was run in a lean way.

Figure 77.1 China's annual growth rate is more than 10 per cent

It is hardly news that the world's centre of economic gravity has shifted towards emerging markets. Buy a mobile phone and it will almost certainly have been made in China. From 2005 to 2010, China's annual growth rate has been more than 10 per cent, and India's more than 8 per cent.

The world is changing even more than these facts suggest. Emerging countries are no longer content to be sources of cheap hands and low-cost brains. Instead they too are concentrating on innovation, making breakthroughs in everything from telecoms to car making to health care. They are redesigning products to reduce costs not just by 10 per cent, but by up to 90 per cent. They are redesigning entire business processes to do things better and faster than their rivals in the West.

Even more striking is the emerging world's growing ability to make products for dramatically lower costs than their competitors: no-frills $3,000 cars and $300 laptops may not make headlines, but they promise to change far more people's lives than iPads will. This sort of advance – known as 'frugal innovation' – is not just a matter of exploiting cheap labour, though cheap labour helps. It is a matter of exploiting the resource of employee ideas to redesign products and processes and cut out unnecessary costs. In India, Tata created the world's cheapest car, the Nano, by combining dozens of cost-saving tricks.

Source: based on a special report in *The Economist*, 15 April 2010.

Questions

(30 marks; 35 minutes)

1. Define the term *kaizen*. (2)
2. Explain two benefits of *kaizen* to companies. (6)
3. Explain how a company such as Tata could set about making *kaizen* improvements. (8)
4. Discuss the possible reasons that could explain why some firms embrace the *kaizen* philosophy, while others reject it. (14)

C ESSAY QUESTIONS

(40 marks each)

1. Two years ago the management team at Lynx Engineering commissioned a benchmarking survey to assess its relative position within the marketplace. To their horror the managers discovered that they were lagging behind their competition in terms of both cost and product quality. In an attempt to rectify the situation a massive £2 million re-engineering programme was announced. Two years later things have still not improved. Assess what could have gone wrong. What should the company do next?
2. How might a firm set about improving its efficiency? What factors are likely to affect the success of any strategy designed to achieve this goal?
3. 'It has been proven time and time again that in order to survive, firms must be willing to initiate change successfully within their own organisations. Firms that are afraid of change will fail because those that are more adventurous will always leave them behind.' To what extent do you agree or disagree with this statement?

Introduction to external influences

UNIT 78

An external influence is a factor beyond a firm's control that can affect its performance. Examples include: changes in consumer tastes, laws and regulations and economic factors such as the level of spending in the economy as a whole.

78.1 THE IMPACT OF EXTERNAL INFLUENCES ON FIRMS

Some external influences have a favourable effect on firms. SAGA holidays specialises in providing holidays targeted at the elderly. A good example of a beneficial external influence for SAGA holidays may be the rising life expectancy. An ageing population will enlarge SAGA's target market, giving the company a good opportunity to increase its revenue and profit. As shown in Figure 78.1, the number of over-65s is set to boom over the coming years.

Other external influences can have adverse effects on firms. In autumn 2010 the UK government's Comprehensive Spending Review announced cutbacks on school-building work amounting to £1,000 million. For private-sector building businesses, this was a direct hit on their revenue, profits and workforce. At the same time, sharp cuts in government spending on the police force may force businesses such as jewellers to spend more on private security guards.

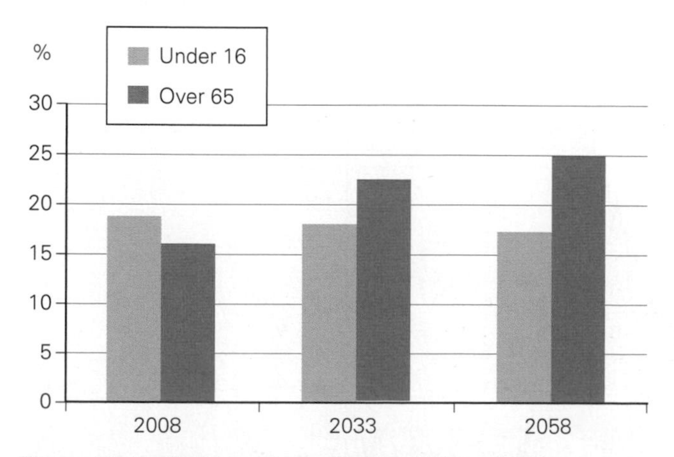

Figure 78.1 Changing age distribution 2008 to 2058
Source: National Statistics website: www.statistics.gov.uk

New laws and regulations

Changes in the law can have a dramatic effect on a business. A good example is the regulation changes made to child car seats, which came into effect in September 2006. They forced all motorists to provide 'seat restraints' for children sitting in the back of a car. For example, every child under the age of 12 must not only wear a seat belt, but must also be sitting on a 'booster seat'. Younger children and babies must have their own special car seat.

Overnight, this regulation created a huge boost for businesses like Britax (car seat manufacturer) and Halfords, the main motor supplies retailer. From a business point of view, this is a marvellous type of external change, because the government announced the change in early 2005, giving the companies involved plenty of time to build production capacity and stock levels.

Demographic factors

Demography refers to changes in the size, growth and age distribution of the population. **Demographic** changes can create opportunities for some firms. However, for other firms the same demographic trend could create a threat.

Opportunities created by changes in demographic factors

In recent times, one of the most important demographic changes to impact upon Britain is immigration. In 2004 the European Union expanded by admitting ten new member states: Poland, Czech Republic, Hungary, Slovakia, Slovenia, Estonia, Lithuania, Cyprus, Malta and Latvia. Britain, along with Sweden and Ireland, granted the citizens of the new EU 10 the immediate right to live and work in Britain. In 2004 wages in eastern Europe were far below those offered to British workers in the UK. Between 2004 and 2008, more than 800,000 eastern Europeans arrived and registered to work in the UK. Since then, job losses in the 2009 recession caused many of them to return home, but firms that have benefited overall from this external influence include:

1 *J D Wetherspoon*. Immigration helps to keep wages in check. Pub chains like J D Wetherspoon have benefited from a plentiful supply of labour provided

Figure 78.2 UK plumbers face competition from migrant workers

by inward migration into the UK. Most migrants from eastern Europe are hard working and have the skills required to work behind a bar. J D Wetherspoon continues to expand, but without immigration the company might have struggled to attract the additional labour required to do so; or it might have had no option other than to pay higher wage rates, which would have affected the company's profitability. Wetherspoon's also siezed the marketing opportunity presented by the increasing numbers of Poles living in the UK by stocking a wide range of Polish bottled beers to help boost the company's profits.

2 *Property developers.* Most east European immigrants to Britain could not afford to buy property, so they rented instead. The increase in the number of potential tenants encouraged property developers to buy property in order to rent out. Britain now has over a million landlords. The boom in buy-to-let property helped house prices to double between 2000 and 2008, creating capital gains for property developers. Without immigration from eastern Europe it is unlikely that this opportunity for property development would have existed.

Threats presented by changes in demographic factors

On the other hand, immigration from eastern Europe has disadvantaged some UK businesses. For example, as a direct consequence of immigration, many UK plumbing firms have been forced into cutting their prices. In the past there was an acute shortage of plumbers in the UK and, given the lack of competition, they could charge customers pretty much whatever they liked. Today the situation is very different. The influx of Polish plumbers into Britain has forced prices down and standards up. This is good news for British homeowners with blocked sinks, but bad news for British plumbers who were able to enjoy high income levels until they faced competition from migrant workers.

Technological factors

Technological change can also create opportunities and threats for firms. Before the advent of digital technology ITV only had two competitors: the BBC and Channel 4. Today the situation is completely different. Technological advances mean that ITV has to compete against the hundreds of channels provided by Sky and cable TV providers such as Virgin. Advances in internet technology have opened up new entertainment possibilities (such as YouTube and Facebook) that compete head on with conventional TV. These technological advances threaten ITV's ability to generate revenue from selling advertising slots. On the other hand, these same technological advances have created opportunities for entrepreneurs with vision, such as Larry Page and Sergey Brin, the founders of Google.

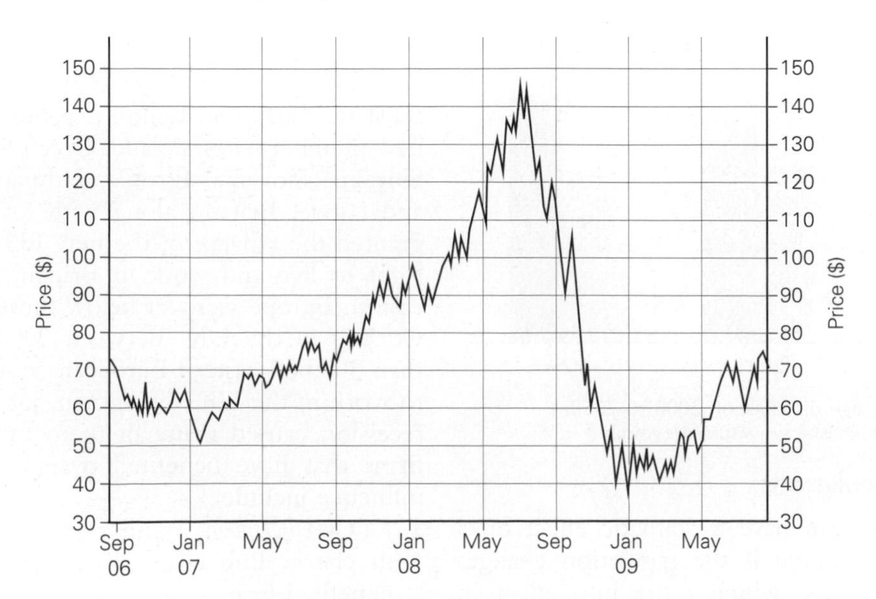

Figure 78.3 Oil prices

Commodity prices

Commodities are internationally traded goods that include oil, copper, wheat and cocoa. Commodities are normally bought by firms as a raw material. For example, as Figure 78.3 shows, the price of oil rose sharply between 2006 and 2008, then fell back in the 2009 recession before recovering again.

The price of oil is an important external influence for most firms. Oil prices affect the cost of transportation because petrol, diesel and kerosene all come from crude oil.

Oil is also a very important raw material. Even companies such as Apple will be affected by rising oil prices because it will cost Apple more to buy in the plastic pellets needed to produce the casings for its laptop computers, iPods, iPads and iPhones. The price of oil is determined by the relative strength of the world supply and the world demand for oil. It is also affected by speculation. In early 2011, protestors took to the streets of Tunisia and Egypt to demand new, honest, democratic governments. Concerns about Middle Eastern oil supplies pushed oil prices up sharply. The world oil price is beyond the control of any single firm; making it an excellent example of an external influence.

A-grade application

Ryanair

Companies such as the airline Ryanair will always suffer when oil prices soar, as fuel is their largest single operating cost. Ryanair operates on slender profit margins, so the 2008 oil price rise forced it to pass most of this cost increase on to customers in higher fares. Unfortunately, most of Ryanair's customers are likely to be quite price-sensitive because most of them travel for leisure, rather than for business reasons. If the price elasticity of demand for Ryanair flights is elastic the airline will lose revenue when fares are raised. Evidence arrived when Ryanair announced that its 2008 profits were 27 per cent down on the year before.

Fortunately, the dramatic fall in the price of oil that occurred in late 2008 enabled Ryanair to cut its operating costs. By March 2010 Ryanair was back in the black, reporting a profit of £289 million for the year.

Economic factors

Individual firms have no influence over economy-wide factors such as the rate of economic growth, the level of unemployment and the rate of inflation. However, these factors will definitely affect firms. Firms will also be affected by government fiscal and monetary policy responses. For more details see Chapter 82.

78.2 WHAT CAN FIRMS DO ABOUT EXTERNAL INFLUENCES?

Make the most of favourable external influences while they last

Luck can play an important role in determining whether a business flourishes or not, especially in the short run. However, over time good and bad luck has a habit of evening out. The key to success then is to make the most of any favourable external influence while it lasts. For example, the debt-fuelled consumer spending boom between 1997 and 2007 greatly assisted companies supplying luxury goods and services.

However, these firms should not have relied on this frothy boom for their success, because it was a factor over which they had no control. They should have made the best of the situation while it lasted, but also asked themselves a series of **'what if' questions**. In this case, 'What if interest rates were suddenly increased?' or 'How would we respond to a sudden drop in demand for our product if the commercial banks withdraw cheap and easy credit?'

Minimise the impact of unfavourable external influences

When faced with adverse external influences, successful firms make compensating internal changes to their business to offset the external constraint. Ryanair can do nothing about rising oil prices; however, it can attempt to cut other costs within the business to compensate for the rising oil price. If Ryanair can improve its internal efficiency the impact of the adverse external influence can be minimised. Successful businesses try as far as it is possible to internalise external constraints.

ISSUES FOR ANALYSIS

- Most firms, most of the time, have their fate in their own hands. Most have built up regular customers who keep coming back and, therefore, have reasonably predictable sales. Poor managers may drive some customers away, but it may take a long time before the cracks start to show. As long as the poor managers are replaced before too long, the business can be brought back on track. This situation has occurred with Marks and Spencer, Sainsbury's, Tottenham Hotspur FC and perhaps every other sports club.
- Just sometimes, though, a company's whole existence can be thrown into question by an external factor. Barratt Homes spent £2.2 billion in 2007 buying out a competitor, and was soon afterwards hit by the credit crunch and property price collapse. Circumstances such as these are a huge test of the management. For other companies, changing technology, new competition or changes in the law may be every bit as significant. The good student spots the big issues and starts to think how to handle them.

78.3 INTRODUCTION TO EXTERNAL INFLUENCES – AN EVALUATION

An important aspect of any evaluation of external factors is to distinguish between external change that is predictable and change that is not. For example, tourist businesses have had five years to plan for the London Olympics in 2012. They can research into previous Olympic events and decide on their strategies. Contrast this with the complete unpredictability of events such as the tsunami wave in 2004, which wiped out the tourist trade in Thailand and Sri Lanka for more than a year, or the flooding that wrecked businesses in Cumbria in November 2009.

Managers that fail to deal with predictable events are exceptionally weak. Those that succeed in unexpected situations are especially impressive.

Key Terms

Demographic: factors relating to the population, such as changes in the number of older people or in the level of immigration.

'What if' questions: these are hypothetical (that is, they are used to test out different possibilities or theories).

WORKBOOK

A REVISION QUESTIONS

(25 marks; 25 minutes)

1 What is an external influence? (2)
2 Explain how a company such as Cadbury may be affected by a decision by Britain to withdraw from the European Union. (6)
3 Give examples of the type of firms that probably benefited from the invasion and military occupation of Iraq. (4)
4 In 2009 Scottish and Newcastle closed its huge brewery in Reading. Give examples of firms in and around Reading that could be adversely affected by this decision. (4)
5 Record companies find it increasingly difficult to generate revenue because of file sharing sites that enable music lovers to illegally download music. What actions should record companies take to minimise this external constraint? (4)
6 British Airways suffered a world-wide humiliation with its 'bag-mountain' at the launch of Terminal 5. Can the management put problems such as this down to bad luck? (5)

B REVISION EXERCISES

B1 CASE STUDY

Britain's monster credit binge

At the beginning of 2008 Britain had not suffered from a recession for well over a decade. During that time interest rates were historically low. These low interest rates led to many consumers in Britain taking on steadily higher levels of debt. So what was the money spent on?

TV property shows such as 'Location, location, location' encouraged many people to borrow huge sums of money to purchase property for investment purposes. Property was seen as a one-way bet. At the time many people believed that 'house prices only ever go up'. The result was a speculative bubble in UK property. Banks also helped to provide the fuel for rampant house price inflation by relaxing lending standards. As house prices rose many households took the opportunity to spend the profit locked up in their homes by re-mortgaging. The equity released was mostly spent on imported luxuries. Britain was living beyond its collective means. Famously, the TV presenter Kirstie Allsopp said she would 'eat my hat' if property prices fall. They did; she didn't.

The banking credit crunch that began in August 2007 saw the beginning of the end. As the availability of credit dried up, house prices began to fall. Consumer confidence nosedived. The boom was over and house prices fell by more than 20 per cent between 2008 and 2009. Although there was then a slight recovery, by autumn 2010 house prices were falling again.

The problem with debt is that it has to be paid back. By April 2008 it was payback time, but by then the total UK personal debt stood at £1,421 billion, more than the entire country's GDP. After lots of effort to repay debts during the recession, the figure was still £1,460 billion in April 2010.

Questions

(35 marks; 40 minutes)

1 What is a recession? (2)
2 Explain how businesses like restaurants and gyms benefited from cheap and easy credit. (5)
3 Explain three examples of firms that benefited from the UK's house price boom. (6)
4 **a)** What is consumer confidence and why is it important to firms? (5)
  b) How could falling UK house prices affect consumer confidence? (5)
5 Discuss the actions that a private school may take in order to prepare for a recession. (12)

B2 CASE STUDY

The UK's smoking ban

In July 2007 the UK government introduced a new law that banned smoking in public places. The ban was argued on public health grounds; each year the NHS has to spend millions of pounds on treating smoking-related health problems. Banning smoking in public places would reduce this expenditure. The quality of life was also expected to rise. The ban applied to all pubs, apart from the bar in the House of Commons.

The smoking ban created an external constraint for the UK pub industry. In the first year of the ban, pub sales fell. Initially, the cause was attributed to an abnormally wet UK summer. However, sales continued to fall and the number of pubs closing down increased. See Figure 78.4. According to research carried out by the British Beer and Pub Association, 98 per cent of landlords blamed the loss of business on the smoking ban. The association argued that the ban had decreased pub sales because it had encouraged more people to drink at home instead, where they were still able to smoke.

By 2010 the pace of UK pub closures had begun to slow down. Landlords realised that the best way of counteracting the ban was to adapt and change their business model. Offering food appears to be the key. The closure rate among drink-led pubs is three times higher than the closure rate among food-led pubs.

The smoking ban is still very unpopular amongst Britain's publicans. Many argue that the legislation has created an unintended consequence: before the smoking ban parents did most of their smoking in the pub. However, due the ban, smoking is now more prevalent in the home, exposing children to the dangers associated with passive smoking.

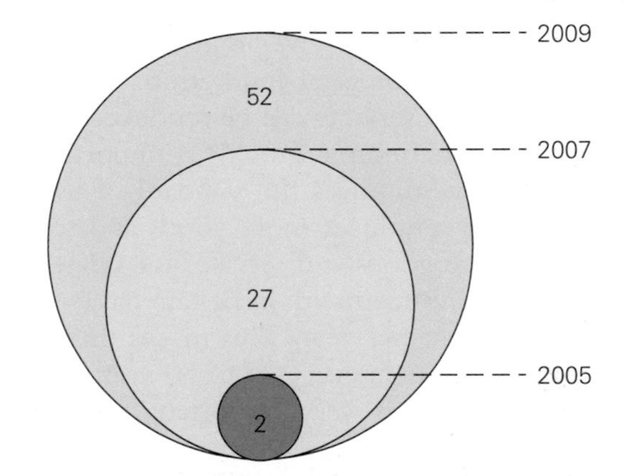

Figure 78.4 Pubs closing per week
Source: British Beer and Pub Association

Questions

(20 marks; 25 minutes)

1 What is an external constraint? (2)
2 Why was the smoking ban an example of an external constraint? (2)
3 Explain two actions that firms typically take to reduce the impact of new laws and regulations. (6)
4 Discuss whether the British Beer and Pub Association were right to attribute pub closures to the smoking ban. (10)

Impact on firms of economic factors

UNIT 79

'Economic factors' can sometimes be described as 'macro-economic factors', that is, affecting the whole economy, such as a change in interest rates.

79.1 ECONOMIC GROWTH AND THE BUSINESS CYCLE

What is economic growth and why does it matter?

Over time the economy tends to grow. This means that the output of goods and services produced by the country increases compared with the year before. Economic growth is caused by productivity advances, perhaps due to technological innovation. This means that more goods and services can be produced with the same population. Economic growth is important to a country because it improves the standard of living. If the UK economy produces more goods and services, there will be more goods and services for UK citizens to consume. Economic growth in Britain has tended to average 2.5 per cent per year. This makes the average level of affluence double every 25 to 30 years.

Economic growth is very important to firms. A growing economy creates more opportunities as consumers' tastes change. It is easier to set up or expand a business in a country that has a rapidly growing economy. New gaps emerge in the market, creating more opportunities for budding entrepreneurs.

The economic growth rate of other countries will also be a concern for British firms. For example, the rapid growth in China has led to rising demand for Rolls Royce cars. To cope with the extra orders Rolls Royce may have to take on extra staff. The company will also have to buy in more components. This will benefit suppliers who will also have to increase output and perhaps employment. The UK is a small country with a domestic market that is also quite small. Ninety per cent of the cars Rolls Royce sell are for export. UK firms like Rolls Royce that want to grow depend, in part, on the economic growth rate in other countries.

The business (economic) cycle

Unfortunately, the economy does not grow at an even rate over time. History shows that the British economy has experienced periods when the economy has grown rapidly. These periods are called booms. Booms are usually followed by recessions; during a recession economic growth grinds to a halt. Technically, a recession is defined as 'two successive quarters of falling output', but even a slowdown can be called a 'growth recession'. If matters do not improve the economy could end up in a slump. A slump is a sustained period of negative economic growth. The Japanese economy experienced this situation during the period 1990 to 2003.

The UK economy has recently suffered from a very severe recession, the deepest since the 1930s. By the

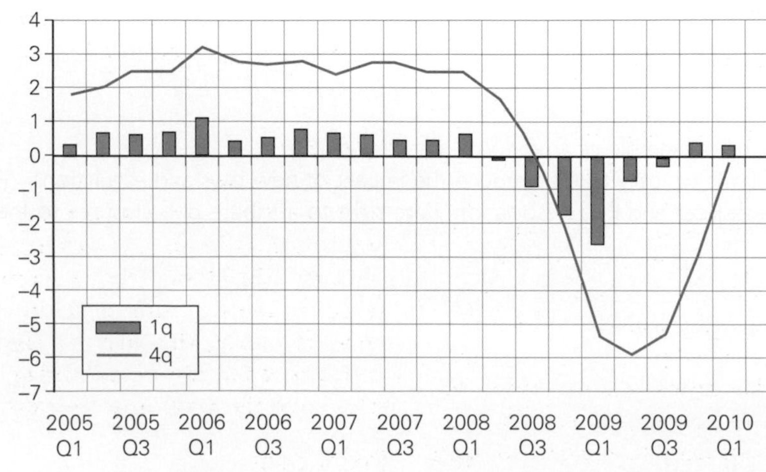

Figure 79.1 UK GDP growth and decline, 2005 to 2010
Source: National Statistics website: www.statistics.gov.uk

Table 79.1 The phases of the trade cycle

	Boom	Recession	Slump	Recovery
Consumer and business confidence	Optimistic	Doubts emerging	Pessimistic	Gradually returning
Consumer spending	High. Low levels of saving. Spending supplemented by credit	Falling. Spending financed by credit starts to fall	Falling. Consumers save to pay off debts built up during the boom	Rising. Debts have now been paid off
Economic growth	Strongly positive	GDP begins to fall	GDP growth might now be strongly negative	Weak, but slowly improving
Unemployment	Close to zero	Low, but starting to rise	High	High, but starting to fall
Inflation	High, and possibly accelerating	Still positive, but falling. Firms now start to think twice about raising prices	Stable prices, or even some deflation (falling prices) is possible	Price stability
Number of firms failing	Low	Low, but rising	High	Falling
Business investment	Firms are optimistic about the future. Investment takes place for both replacement and expansion purposes	Falling. Expansion programmes may be postponed	Close to zero. Even replacement investment may have to be postponed to conserve cash	Slowly rising. Replacement investment projects previously postponed might now get the green light

end of 2009 the recession had caused the output of the British economy to fall by 6 per cent. The recession lasted for a year and a half. The UK economy was helped out of recession during the first half of 2010 by an unorthodox monetary policy measure known as quantitative easing. This added £200 billion of cash to the UK's money supply. By autumn 2010 the new government's policy of sharp cuts in its spending raised the spectre of another economic slowdown. For the UK the only consolation was that this was a world recession, with similar economic problems elsewhere in America and Europe. Only China and India went through this period unscathed.

The impacts of the business cycle

The phases of the trade cycle are given in Table 79.1. The cycle affects firms in different ways according to the type of good or service it sells. In general, luxury goods businesses like Ferrari benefit most from economic booms. On the other hand, firms like Lidl may struggle during economic booms because consumers will probably respond to a boom by 'trading up' to more expensive alternatives such as Waitrose.

Managers must be expert at predicting the future state of the economy. It takes time to plan and introduce changes. Firms that react to economic changes once they have already happened usually struggle to compete.

What actions should a producer of luxury goods take today if it predicts a recession in the near future?

Business objectives

During a recession a producer of luxury goods might need to change its corporate objective from growth or profit maximisation to one of survival. During a recession revenue is bound to fall. The key to survival is to minimise losses, which can be achieved by introducing a package of cost-saving measures. Some of these changes could permanently damage the competitiveness of the business. For example, cutting back on expensive new product development may leave the product with an ageing product range in the future. However, if the firm does not cut costs now the business may not have a future to worry about! In a recession managers usually have to make difficult and unpopular decisions.

Marketing

Some businesses react to a recession by changing their marketing strategy to emphasise value for money in an attempt to hold up revenue at a time when the market may be shrinking. Some companies may consider reacting to a recession by cutting prices to help boost sales. However, this may be risky because a price cut could cheapen the brand's image, resulting in a loss of sales once the economy recovers.

Production

Sales of luxury goods fall during a recession; to prepare

for this, producers of luxury goods should aim to cut production sooner rather than later. Cutting production cannot be achieved overnight. For example, suppliers of raw materials and components will probably have minimum notice periods written into their contracts. If the firm waits until sales start to fall before cutting production the result is likely to be a build-up of stock; this is expensive to store and it also ties up cash. During recessions, expansion plans tend to be shelved because the extra capacity created by expansion will not be needed at a time when sales are expected to fall.

Human resource management

During a recession a manufacturer of luxury goods might not need as many staff because fewer goods are being sold. One way of slimming down a workforce is via compulsory redundancy. Getting rid of staff because they are not needed any more is expensive, may create negative publicity and is bad for staff morale. A better alternative may be to reduce the wage bill via **natural wastage**. This involves suspending recruitment. By not replacing employees who leave or retire, the workforce will fall naturally without the need for redundancies.

Some firms use the job insecurity created by a recession to force through changes in working practices that are designed to reduce costs. During a recession job opportunities elsewhere tend to be scarce. Ruthless managers may use this to their advantage. They would argue that the whole business will be leaner and fitter as a result.

Finance

Firms fail when they run out of cash (creditors with unpaid bills take you to court). During recessions, producers of luxury goods leak cash because of low demand. Logically, the best chance of survival is for those businesses that started the period of recession with healthy balance sheets, low borrowing levels and high liquidity. To conserve cash during an unprofitable period of trading, a business could do the following.

- Carry out a programme of zero budgeting throughout the organisation to trim any waste from departmental budgets.
- Restrict the credit given to customers and chase up debtors who currently owe the firm money.
- Rationalise, that is, sell off any under-utilised fixed assets such as machinery and property. This will bring cash into the business.
- Attempt to re-finance the business by taking on additional loan capital. Unfortunately, during recessions the availability of credit tends to dry up as banks re-assess their attitude towards risk. If a firm can persuade a bank to grant loan capital it will normally only be lent at a penalty rate of interest.

Evaluation

Recessions do not last for ever. Aim to survive so that you can benefit when the economy recovers. Not all firms suffer during a recession. Companies selling essentials may even gain ground. However, during a boom these same companies will probably have to take cost cutting measures in order to survive.

Firms can do nothing about booms or recessions, they are external factors that are beyond the firm's control. However, managers need to make offsetting internal changes to the business, cutting costs for example, to minimise the worst effects of the recession. The challenge for management is to have a long-term strategy that can keep the business healthy in good times and bad.

But what if there is a boom? What should a firm do with the windfall profits it may be able to make? In the UK the threat of takeover may encourage public limited companies to increase their dividend payments to shareholders. Unfortunately, paying increased dividends will do nothing to improve the firm's long-term competitiveness. Managers running companies owned by long-termist shareholders will be able to use the profits made possible by an economic boom to increase their investment in new products and production methods that will make their business more competitive in the long run. Businesses owned or run by more conservative owners may decide to set aside some of the profits made by the boom as a cash reserve that will improve the firm's chances of surviving the next recession, when it arrives.

Most banks react to economic booms by relaxing their lending standards. As a result firms wishing to expand will normally find that it is easier and cheaper to borrow the funds that they need to finance the expansion. Banks also tend to be more willing to lend to customers that want credit. A surge in the availability and the price of consumer credit will obviously help car manufacturers and other firms that produce expensive 'big ticket items' that consumers typically purchase using credit. Spread across the economy, these actions can lead to rising **inflation**.

79.2 THE EFFECTS OF INFLATION ON A FIRM'S FINANCIAL POSITION

Introduction: what is inflation?

Inflation measures the percentage annual rise in the average price level. Inflation reduces the purchasing power of money within an economy. For consumers inflation increases the cost of living. At the same time, inflation usually leads to rising wages, so households are not necessarily any the worse off. Most people's **real wages** may be unchanged in value, so consumer spending in the shops need not be affected.

The impacts of inflation on a firm's finances are mixed.

Advantages of inflation to a business

Real assets become worth more

Inflation makes real assets become worth more. For example, the value of any property or stock that the firm might own will increase if prices are going up. A firm with more valuable assets will have a more impressive balance sheet. As a result the firm may find it easier to raise long-term finance from banks and shareholders because the business now looks more secure.

The real value of money owed is eroded

Firms with large loans also benefit from inflation because inflation erodes the real value of the money owed. Firms with high borrowings find that the fixed repayments on their long-term borrowings become more easily covered by rising income and profits. After, say, five years a £1 million loan may be worth only £0.75 million by the time the borrower repays the loan. In the same way, some householders have trivial mortgage payments because they took out the loan to help buy a house valued then at £40,000 (and perhaps worth £240,000 today).

Drawbacks of inflation

Damage to profitability

Inflation can damage profitability, especially for those firms that have fixed-price contracts that take a long time to complete. For example, a local building company may agree a £5 million price for an extension to a local school, which is expected to take three years to finish. If inflation is higher than expected, profit could be wiped out by the unexpectedly high-cost increases created by the inflation. Even if there were an agreement for the school to pay an inflation allowance on top of the price, the producer would have to fund the unexpectedly high cash outflows.

Damage to cash flow

Inflation can also tend to damage cash flow because inflation will also push up the price of machinery. Consequently, inflation tends to penalise manufacturing companies like Ford, who need to replace their machinery regularly in order to stay internationally competitive.

Damage to industrial relations

Inflation can also damage industrial relations, that is, the relationship between the business and its staff. When making pay claims for the year ahead, staff representatives (perhaps a trade union) will estimate what the inflation rate is likely to be in the future. This estimate may be higher than that expected by management. Differences in inflationary expectations have the potential to cause costly industrial disputes that may damage a firm's reputation.

Evaluation

Inflation will impact upon different firms in different ways according to the type of product they sell, the production methods (and lead times) used and whether the firm has many loans or not. For example inflation might benefit a hairdresser but severely damage a company engaged in heavy manufacturing such as the aeroplane-maker Airbus Industries.

79.3 UNEMPLOYMENT

Unemployment is created when the demand for labour has fallen relative to the available supply of labour. Rising unemployment tends to be associated with recessions. During economic booms unemployment usually falls. In addition to the demand for labour, unemployment can also be affected by factors such as emigration and immigration that affect the supply of labour. Unemployment can be measured as a total or as a rate (the percentage of those of working age who are not in work and who would like a job).

When the recession hit in 2008 some economists expected UK unemployment to rise and reach 3 million. Fortunately, the rise in unemployment was far less dramatic. By June 2010 UK unemployment, as measured by the Labour Force Survey, had only reached 2.51 million. It seems likely that the rise in unemployment was stemmed by a combination of policy interventions, and by a preference on the part of British workers to accept pay cuts, rather than redundancies. The new coalition government elected in May 2010 has decided to try to cut the UK's fiscal deficit sharply. As a result it seems likely that UK unemployment will start to rise again in the near future.

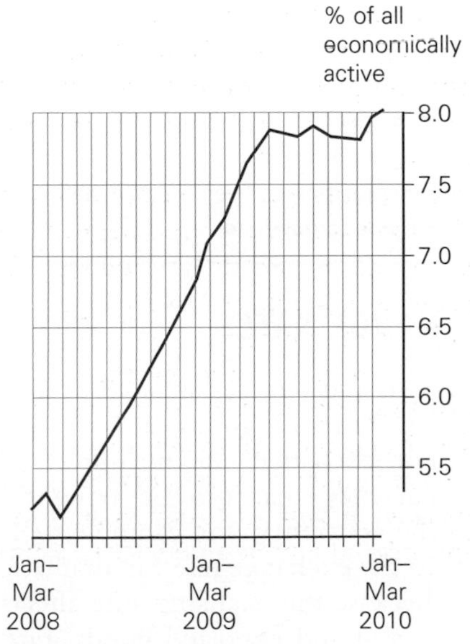

Figure 79.2 UK unemployment rate
Source: National Statistics website: www.statistics.gov.uk

Table 79.2 Unemployment: benefits and costs

Benefits created by unemployment	Costs/problems created by unemployment
• Theory X managers might use the fear created by unemployment and the potential for redundancies to force through cost-saving changes in working practices.	• Unemployment can create insecurity which could sap morale within the business.
• When unemployment is high most employees choose to stay where they are as job vacancies begin to dry up. Labour turnover falls when unemployment is high. Low rates of labour turnover save the firm money on recruitment, selection and training. Over time if the rate of labour turnover falls, productivity could rise as the workforce gains experience.	• Unemployment can affect consumer spending, which in turn can affect a firm's revenue and profit. For example, the credit crunch of 2007–08 caused banks and other financial institutions in the City of London to lay off staff. As a result, local service sector businesses in the area, such as dry cleaners and sandwich shops suffered from a drop off in business.
• Recruitment should become a lot easier. When unemployment is high the firm should receive plenty of applications for any vacant position. The quality of applications should also improve too. For example, during a period of high unemployment it may be possible to hire a graduate for a non-graduate post.	• In areas where unemployment remains high in the long term, firms can be adversely affected by crime and other social problems created by unemployment. Structural unemployment (unemployment caused by a declining industry) can also result in a situation where the unemployed do not possess the 'right' skills.

Figure 79.2 may also be of some interest, as it shows the dramatic increase in unemployment and the recent softening caused by the monetary and fiscal stimulus.

The impacts of unemployment on firms

Unemployment can have both positive and negative impacts on firms, as shown in Table 79.2.

Evaluation: the impacts of unemployment

Theory X managers are unlikely to worry too much about making redundancies at a time when unemployment might already be high. They view employees as tools for making a profit. Theory Y managers are more people-orientated. During recessions they will try their best to avoid redundancies, even if this is at the expense of short-run profit. Japanese companies with a paternalistic culture, such as Mitsubishi, react to structural unemployment by diversifying. They move out of markets that are in decline, such as coal mining and ship building, and invest in markets with better long-term prospects for example, computer software and nuclear power. Then re-train staff to move them from old jobs to new ones.

79.3 EXCHANGE RATES

In Britain goods and services are sold in our currency, the pound. In America goods and services are sold in dollars. The exchange rate measures the quantity of foreign currency that can be bought with one unit of another currency, for example, £1 buys $2. Movements in the exchange rate can dramatically affect profitability because the exchange rate affects both the price of imported and exported goods. Firms cannot influence the exchange rate. For example, the pound's rate of exchange against the US dollar is determined by the supply and demand for the pound on international currency markets. An individual firm is too small to affect the exchange rate; it is a good example of an external constraint that is beyond the control of any one manager. Exchange rates affect firms in different ways.

The impacts of a high exchange rate

On firms with large export markets

UK firms, such as Wedgwood pottery and Morgan cars, that sell a high proportion of their output overseas, will prefer a low exchange rate, that is, a weak pound. Why is this so? The best way of explaining is via a numerical example

America is an important export market for Morgan cars. Morgan charges its UK customers £25,000 for a basic 2 Seater Roadster.

Figure 79.3 Morgan cars

To achieve the same profit margin in America, Morgan will have to charge a price in US dollars that will convert into £25,000. At the end of 2009 the exchange rate against the US dollar was £1: $1.40. To obtain £25,000 per export, Morgan charged its American customers:

£25,000 × $1.40 = $35,000

By November 2010 the exchange rate had gone up to £1: $1.60. To generate the same £25,000 of export revenue per car sold, Morgan now had to charge its American consumers

£25,000 × $1.60 = $40,000

In other words, the rise in the pound sterling meant that Morgan needed to increase the US price of its cars by $5,000 to maintain the current profit per car. If Morgan reacts to a rising pound by putting prices up in the USA, demand for the 2-Seater Roadsters will almost certainly drop, causing Morgan's profitability to fall. On the other hand, if Morgan decides against raising its prices in America, the company will have to accept a lower profit on each car sold; either way Morgan loses out as a result of a higher pound.

Conclusion: exporters hate it when their currency rises in value; they like it to fall, not rise.

On firms that import most of their raw materials or stock

Retailers that import most of their stock prefer a high exchange rate. A high exchange rate reduces the cost of buying goods from abroad. For example, Jack Daniel's whiskey is a popular product with Tesco's British consumers. It has to be imported from the American firm that produces it. If the price of a case of Jack Daniel's is $70 the price paid by Tesco will be as follows:

If the exchange rate is £1: $1.40, the case will cost Tesco $70 / 1.40 = £50.00.

However, if the exchange rate goes up to £1: $1.60 the same case of Jack Daniel's will now cost Tesco £43.75 ($70 / 1.60 = £43.75). A high exchange rate will benefit Tesco because the company can buy imported goods more cheaply. Tesco can then make more profit on each bottle of Jack Daniel's that they sell to UK customers.

The impacts of a low exchange rate

The impacts of a weak exchange rate are the reverse of those from a strong exchange rate. Firms like Morgan that were damaged by a strong currency find life easier when the exchange rate falls. A weak pound makes their exports seem cheaper to foreign consumers, so Morgan should be able to sell more of its cars in America.

A-grade application

One of Europe's most successful manufacturing businesses is Airbus Industrie. Ten years ago the American Boeing was the undisputed leader of aircraft manufacture worldwide. By 2008 Airbus and Boeing were equally successful. Although the world's airlines buy planes priced in US dollars, the Europeans were able to compete. This was until the euro strengthened sharply against the dollar. Between 2005 and early 2008 the euro rose 50 per cent against the dollar. This raised the possibility that Airbus planes would have to be priced far above their Boeing competitors.

The impact on Airbus was awful. It had to price its planes in dollars, but almost all its costs were in euros. This led, in March 2008, to a very unusual announcement: Airbus would insist on paying all its European suppliers in dollars in future. This would pass the exchange rate risks onto those suppliers. Whereas previously a rise in the euro would have made it harder to afford to pay the European suppliers; now, a rise in the euro would be offset slightly by the cheaper prices for supplies. The suppliers (such as Britain's Rolls Royce engines) complained bitterly, but they had little choice but to accept).

Since 2008 the euro has weakened slightly against the dollar, making it easier for Airbus to gain profitable orders. In 2010 Airbus achieved a 54 per cent market share in new orders for 100+ seater aircraft. In 2011 it looks as if Airbus will do even better. This is important as more than 150,000 European jobs rely on Airbus.

Evaluation: What can firms do about the economy and the exchange rate?

- A weak pound may benefit Morgan. However, it would be unwise to rely on a weak pound for its profitability because the exchange rate can change.
- Economic booms will also benefit Morgan because it sells luxury goods that have a positive income elasticity of demand that is well above one. Sales will tend to grow at a faster rate than the general economy. Unfortunately, despite politicians' assurances, economic booms are not permanent. So it would also be unwise for both companies to rely on a favourable external business environment for their profitability.
- No one can reliably forecast economic trends, but successful firms are prepared for any possible circumstances. They will have asked 'What if?' a specific economic trend depresses profitability. Firms can do nothing about the exchange rate and the economy. However, they can make internal changes to their businesses that are designed to minimise the worst effects of a possible economic problem. For example, if Morgan believes that the pound will carry on rising against the American dollar, the company could attempt to cut its costs by automating production. In short, it could aim to internalise external constraints.

On the other hand, firms like Tesco will be damaged by a low exchange rate because it will now cost Tesco more in pounds sterling to buy-in its imported stock. If Tesco reacts to the falling exchange rate by raising its prices the company could lose customers. If Tesco does nothing, it will make less profit on each unit of imported stock sold.

ISSUES FOR ANALYSIS

There are two main ways to consider businesses and economic change.

- The more obvious is how a business should respond, for example, to a rise in interest rates. It may anticipate a rise in customer demand and therefore increase production; it may rethink its marketing strategy.
- The second issue is tougher: what strategies should a firm carry out to protect itself from unknown economic changes in the future. By definition this will be difficult, as how can one anticipate the unknown? Yet, for a housebuilding firm or a bank in early 2007, was it so difficult to anticipate the problems that may arise in the future? The problem, often, is that directors of plcs have such huge financial incentives to achieve profit increases that they ignore actions to protect the business from possible downturns. In a family-run (Ltd) business there is a much greater reason to think about the next ten years, rather than the next ten months.

Key Terms

Inflation: although often defined as the rate of rise in the average price level, inflation is better understood as a fall in the value of money.

Natural wastage: allowing staff levels to fall naturally, by not replacing staff that leave.

Real wages: changes in money wages minus the rate of change in prices (inflation) (for example, if your pay packet is up 6 per cent but prices are up 4 per cent, your real wage has risen by 2 per cent).

79.5 IMPACT ON FIRM OF ECONOMIC FACTORS – AN EVALUATION

Businesses are sometimes badly run, leaving them exposed to potential collapse if interest rates rise or a recession occurs. In other cases bad luck may be a factor, for example, a well-run café has to close because the factory nearby closes down. In an ideal world every business would anticipate every risk facing it, and devised a relevant survival strategy. This may not always be possible.

One of the best judgements a director can make is to ensure that a firm is always equipped financially for any future economic change. If the business keeps its borrowings relatively low and its liquidity relatively high, it will survive almost any problem. The sudden collapse of Bear Stearns and then Lehman Brothers in 2008 showed the level of risk that exists among firms that lack that judgement.

WORKBOOK

A REVISION QUESTIONS

(35 marks; 35 minutes)

1. What is the business cycle? (2)
2. Explain why a business such as Chessington World of Adventures could be affected by a recession in America. (4)
3. Explain two typical features of a recession. (6)
4. Outline an example of a firm that could benefit from a recession in the UK. (2)
5. What is trading down and why does it occur? (5)
6. Why may a firm respond to the threat of a recession by suspending recruitment, even before the recession actually arrives? (4)
7. What are inflationary expectations and why are they important? (5)
8. How could inflation benefit a small one-stop convenience store? (3)
9. Explain two reasons why staff morale can plummet during a recession. (4)

B1 CASE STUDY

Antonia Dyball-Jamieson is worried. She is the founder and managing director of 'Emporium', an up-market chain of clothes shops located in prosperous market towns in Surrey including Reigate and Guildford. Fashion Emporium stocks aspirational high-fashion brands such as Jack Wills and Abercrombie and Fitch that sell at premium prices, for example £70 for a logoed T-shirt. The business serves a target market made up of privately educated teenagers whose expenditure is largely funded by their high-income-earning parents who work, mostly, in financial services in the City of London. The high prices that Antonia is currently able to charge ensure that each of her stores operates with a low break-even point and a healthy safety margin.

Over the last seven years the business has taken advantage of a favourable economic climate and has expanded steadily. On average, Antonia manages to open a new 'Emporium' branch every year and on a like-for-like basis 'Emporium has managed to increase their sales by 7 per cent annually. During the boom years the business has found it relatively easy to raise the additional loan capital required to enlarge the business.'

Over the last couple of months Antonia has become increasingly concerned about the state of the economy. Her favourite economic guru, Evan Davis, the BBC's economics editor, recently predicted that economic growth could grind to a halt next year. Even more alarmingly, Vicky, Antonia's old friend from university, warned that investment banks, such as Goldman Sachs were planning large-scale redundancies. Vicky also complained that she had been told by her boss that her bonus this year would be that she would be keeping her job; last year she received £120,000 in addition to her basic salary of £75,000. 'How will I cope without my bonus?' wailed Vicky.

In the next week Antonia has some big decisions to make. She has found an excellent potential location for her next branch of Emporium in prosperous Godalming, which will cost £5,000 a year to lease. In addition £20,000 will have to be spent fitting out the new site, and five new members of staff will have to be hired and trained. Antonia's Dad, Sebastian, believes that she should not postpone her expansion plans. According to him David Smith, the economics editor of *The Sunday Times*, believes that the economy will continue to grow because interest rates will stay low for the foreseeable future.

Questions

(40 marks; 45 minutes)

1 Explain why businesses such as Emporium are particularly sensitive to movements in the trade cycle. (6)
2 Describe three actions that Antonia could take to help prepare her business for a down-turn in the trade cycle. (9)
3 Should Antonia go ahead with her plans to open a new Emporium store in Godalming? Discuss the arguments for and against. (12)
4 Using the case study as a starting point, discuss whether it is essential that managers, such as Antonia, have a good understanding of economic theory in order to make effective long-run decisions. (13)

B2 CASE STUDY

Table 79.3 British economy statistics

Year	Economic growth rate (%)	Inflation (RPI) (%)	Unemployment rate (based on the claimant count measure of unemployment) (%)
1980	−2.5	17.8	6.0
1981	−1.2	12	9.4
1982	1.6	8.6	10.9
1983	3.3	4.5	10.8
1984	2.6	5.0	11.0
1985	3.8	6.0	10.9
1986	4.3	3.4	11.2

Year	Economic growth rate (%)	Inflation (RPI) (%)	Unemployment rate (based on the claimant count measure of unemployment) (%)
1987	4.8	4.1	10.0
1988	5	4.9	8.1
1989	2.2	7.8	6.3
1990	0.4	9.5	5.9
1991	−2.2	5.9	8.1
1992	−0.5	3.7	9.9
1993	2.5	1.6	10.4
1994	4.3	2.5	9.2
1995	2.8	3.3	7.9
1996	3.4	2.9	7.2
1997	2.7	2.8	5.4
1998	2.7	3.3	4.6
1999	2.7	2.4	4.3
2000	3.0	3.0	3.6
2001	2.4	1.8	3.2
2002	1.8	1.7	3.1
2003	2.5	2.9	3.0
2004	3.2	3.0	2.7
2005	2.1	2.8	2.7
2006	2.6	3.2	3.0
2007	3.1	4.3	3.5
2008	−2.8	4	5.2
2009	−4.8	−0.5	7.2
2010	1.8	4.4	7.8

Note: 2010 figures based on annualised data collected during September of that year

Source: National Statistics website: www.statistics.gov.uk

Questions

(30 marks; 35 minutes)

1 Plot the data shown in the table onto a graph designed to illustrate trends in the UK's economic growth rate, inflation rate and unemployment rate over the period 1980 to 2010. (12)
2 Can you identify any boom or slump years? (4)
3 Compare and contrast the characteristics of a boom with the characteristics of a recession. (8)
4 Outline one key limitation of this data for managers of businesses. (6)

Globalisation and development

UNIT 80

Globalisation: the pressures leading to the world becoming one 'market', with competition between giant firms on a world stage and the risk that national producers (and cultures) may be squeezed out. Development: moving people beyond a life in which feeding the family is a constant struggle and source of uncertainty. 'Underdevelopment' is sometimes measured as having to survive on less than $1 a day.

80.1 INTRODUCTION

Globalisation is by no means a new force. In 1900 a quarter of the world's population lived under a British flag, bringing with it a 'culture' of tea, cricket and – from 1902 – Marmite. In the 1920s, American companies such as Ford and Coca-Cola started their moves to multinational status. By the 1960s Mickey Mouse, US films and British pop music were global forces. Yet the term globalisation only really started to stick in the 1980s. It was in this period that the huge growth of McDonald's, Levi's jeans and Coca-Cola made people start to question whether the world was becoming a suburb of America. The 1990s growth of Microsoft and Starbucks brought the question further into focus. Figure 80.1 gives a sense of the extra-ordinary growth in world trade, but lends little support to any view that globalisation 'arrived in the 1990s'.

The term globalisation encompasses many issues. Some are based on cultural questions, such as whether a language such as French can survive the onslaught of (American) English. Some are based on ethical questions that seem much more stark when a rich western company is getting its supplies from Cambodian labour paid 30p an hour. Others are more focused on the economic question, 'Are global giants wiping out national producers and restricting consumer choice?' Clearly these are all massive questions in a Business Studies A-level course.

80.2 GOVERNMENT EFFORTS TO INCREASE WORLD TRADE

Trade between countries had been growing for centuries until the 1929 Wall Street crash led to increasing **protectionism** worldwide. The political changes in Germany and Japan in the 1930s (which led to the 50 million deaths in the Second World War) were partly due to these two countries' concern at being excluded from export markets. With the lessons learned from this, governments since 1945 have tried hard to make it easier for countries to do business with each other.

Following marathon negotiations lasting from 1986 to 1994, the World Trade Organization (WTO) was established in 1995. Overnight the value of tariff-free imports rose from 20 per cent to 44 per cent of the

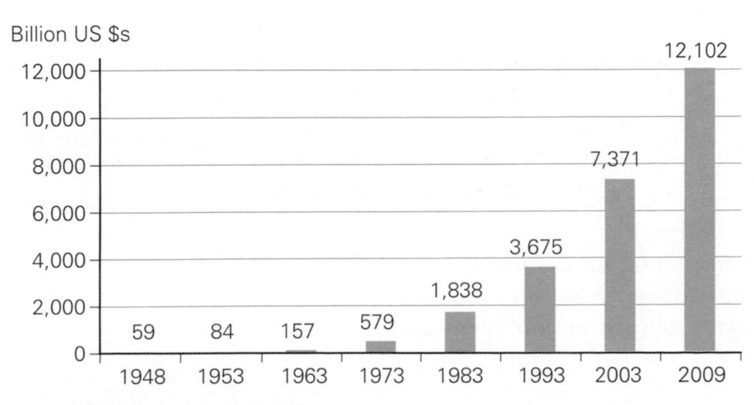

Figure 80.1 Growth in total world exports, 1948 to 2009
Source: World Trade Organization, www.wto.org

worldwide total. Today it is over 50 per cent. In other words, only in a minority of cases are taxes places on imported goods. The development of the WTO was boosted further when China joined in 2001.

The WTO tries to ensure that there is **free trade** between countries, but that the trade is based upon common rules. For example, all WTO member countries should provide legal protection for the **intellectual property** of companies and individuals.

Many people argue that WTO rules favour rich countries against poorer ones. There is a strong case for saying that free trade is the ideal form of trade for countries and companies at a similar stage of development (because it encourages competition). But less developed countries would surely benefit from protection of their **infant industries** until they have developed a scale of production that enables them to compete with multinational giants. In the early days of the motor industry in Japan and China, local car companies were protected by huge tariff barriers (import tax rates of around 40 per cent). In both countries there is no longer any need for import tariffs as the industries are efficient and competitive.

Although the WTO can be criticised for the extent to which policy making is dominated by America and Europe, there is no doubt that the substantial economic growth of the 1998–2008 period spread increased prosperity far and wide around the world.

80.3 THE CASE FOR GLOBALISATION

Joseph Stiglitz, in his book *Globalization and its Discontents* (2002), became the world's most famous critic of globalisation. Yet he identifies many important benefits from increasingly open world trade. To him, the biggest step forward by far is the increase in the number of people in less developed countries whose lives have been improved. He mentions the opening up of the Jamaican milk market (allowing US competition in) as a huge benefit to poor children in Jamaica, even if it hurt the profits of the local farmers. It is also important to bear in mind that, however awful the figures may be for infant deaths before the age of one, they are incomparably better than they were 20, 40 or 50 years ago. Globalisation of healthcare is as important here as the globalisation of the economy.

Among the main advantages of globalisation are:

- increased competition forces local producers to be efficient, thereby cutting prices and increasing standards of living (people's income goes further)
- providing the opportunity for the best ideas to be spread across the globe (for example, AIDS medicines, water irrigation and mobile phones)
- if multinational companies open up within a country, this may provide opportunities for employment and training, and allow local entrepreneurs to learn from the experience of the more established businesses
- providing outlets for exports, which can allow a country to boost its standards of living by reducing dependence on subsistence farming (growing just enough to feed the family)
- it has provided the opportunity for a series of countries (for example, Egypt, Mexico, China and India) to break away from poverty; for example, average living standards in China rose by 1,000 per cent between 1990 and 2010; Table 80.1 shows the impact economic growth can have on infant mortality; sadly the benefits have not shown through in all cases – Nigeria's weak growth keeps the death rate among under-5s shockingly high.

Figure 80.2 Living standards in China have been rising

A-grade application

Bangladesh

In the 20 years until 1990, the annual growth rate in Bangladesh* was an extremely low 0.6 per cent. This left its under-5 mortality rate at 149 per 1,000 in 1990. Each year, more under-5s died in Bangladesh than all the under-5s living in Britain. By 1990 Bangladesh was developing a clothing industry based upon very low-wage labour, targeting western companies. In the period 1990 to 2008 the growth rate rose to 3.3 per cent per person, helping the infant mortality rate to fall from 149 to 54 per 1,000.

Bangladesh has by no means become a wealthy country. Many households have no access to clean water and, by 2008, only 22 per cent of the population had a phone. But economic progress has made an impact, and should continue to do so.

* Bangladesh, with 160 million people, is the world's seventh most populated country.

Table 80.1 Infant mortality (deaths per 000 under-5s)

	1990	2008
Egypt	104	23
Mexico	46	17
China	49	21
India	123	69
Nigeria	230	186
Great Britain (for comparison)	10	6

Source: UNICEF statistics, August 2010.

80.4 THE CASE AGAINST GLOBALISATION

The economic case against

Critics suggest that globalisation has made it harder for local firms to create local opportunities. In 2002 virtually no overseas car producer had a factory in India; but, with the growth of the Indian economy, by 2010 Hyundai, Suzuki, BMW, Toyota, Nissan and Honda were present, with Peugeot and Ford announcing new factories by 2012. Although the local Tata Motors has announced the production of the world's cheapest new car (at £1,250 each), it may be that the middle of the car market will be captured by the big European and Far Eastern car producers.

There is also concern that new production in a country does not necessarily mean new wealth. Some multinational firms establish a factory locally, but use it in a way that could be called exploitation. In India there are many clothing factories that supply companies such as Gap, Primark and Asda. Wage rates are extremely low by western standards, and working conditions are poor. Little of the value created by the sale of a £20 jumper in a London Gap outlet may seep back to India. If the clothing design, the branding and the packaging are all done in the west, all that is left is labour-intensive, low-paid factory work.

The social and cultural case against

In 2002, a French farmer made the headlines worldwide by bulldozing a McDonald's outlet. He was protesting about the Americanisation of France. Remarkably, even the French cosmetics powerhouse L'Oréal is inclined to show English-language television commercials in France. The increasing number of US outlets in French high streets was the farmer's main concern: KFC, McDonald's, Subway, Gap, Starbucks, and so on. Around the world, many agreed that their high streets were starting to look like those in America; they probably discussed it on their Apple phone while also listening to Lady Gaga on their iPod. Globalisation started to be criticised for making our lives less interesting by reducing the differences between countries and cities.

Among the main disadvantages of globalisation are:

- that everywhere starts to look like everywhere else
- that globalisation is built on exploitation – the strong exploiting the rich
- that it may make it hard for local producers to build and grow in a way that is suited to local needs.

A-grade application

Nigeria

There is probably no country in the world that has under-achieved as severely as Nigeria. In the 20 years to 1990 its economy *shrank* by an average of 1.4 per cent a year. Its 1990 child mortality of 230 per 1,000 was among the world's worst. Since then, growth has averaged just 1.3 per cent a year; this is despite the fact that Nigeria is oil rich. Over the past 20 years more than £75 billion of oil has been exported from the country. This has been good for BP and Shell, but the people of Nigeria have little benefit to show for all this wealth. Corruption has been an important problem, but many Nigerians would point to the oil multinationals as well as their own leaders. The benefits of globalisation have passed them by.

80.5 GLOBALISATION AND THE BRITISH ECONOMY

Britain should probably have benefited more from the growth of world trade, given the country's 10 per cent share of world exports in 1950. Since then, though, there has been a process of **deindustrialisation** in Britain, as industries such as textiles, ship building and car production wilted under foreign competition. Figure 80.3 shows Britain's dramatic decline in the years between 1948 and 1973. Since then there has been a further, steady reduction in Britain's share of 'merchandise exports'.

Fortunately for the economy, Britain has kept its strong position in the sales of services to countries around the world. In 2008, Britain was second only to the Unites States in its share of the market for internationally traded services. Whereas the 2008 share of world trade in goods was 3.8 per cent, Britain's share of 'invisible' exports was nearly 10 per cent.

It is also important to remember that the increase in world trade over the past ten years has brought a significant increase in living standards in Britain. On average, those in work are very much better off than ten years ago, with items such as clothes, cars, furniture and household electronics down sharply in price. Cheap imports from China and Cambodia are not only enjoyable, but are also vital in keeping UK inflation low. Low prices help our money to go further, making us all better-off.

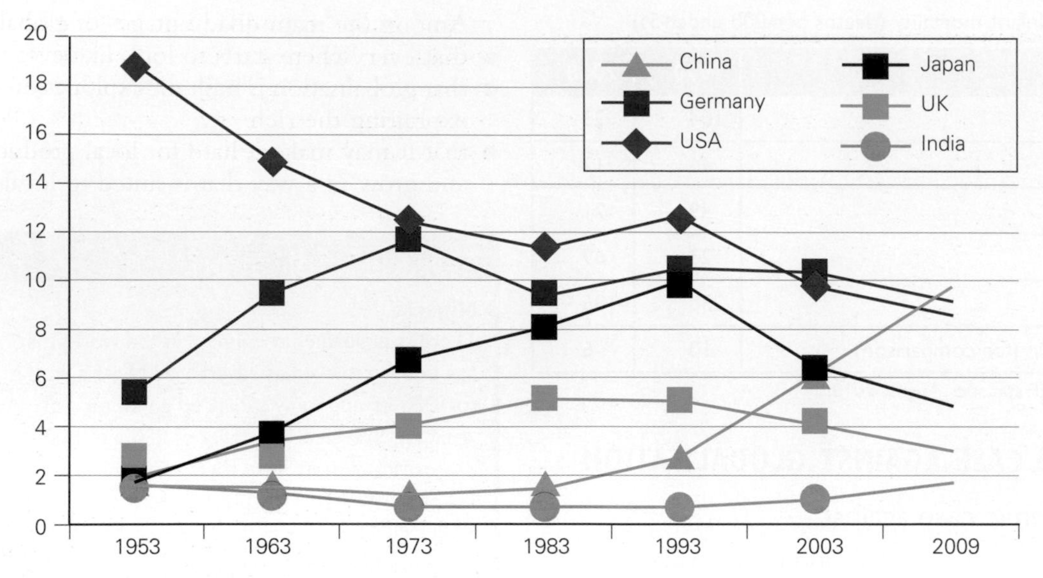

Figure 80.3 World share of exports of goods, 1953 to 2009
Source: World Trade Organization, www.wto.org

80.6 DEVELOPMENT

The most important thing is to realise that development happens. In 1981, 50 per cent of the world's population lived on less than $1.25 a day (about 80p). By 2005 the figure had fallen to 21 per cent (the figures are a true comparison, because changes in prices have been allowed for). By 2015, the World Bank estimates that the figure will have fallen to about 12 per cent. Let's be clear, here, that 12 per cent of a 7 billion world population means that nearly 1,000 million people will still be living on extremely low incomes. That, in itself, is a disgrace in a world where there is so much wealth. But it is wrong to treat the issue of development with a shrug of the shoulders. There are hopeful signs. Table 80.2 shows the economic performance of a selection of less developed countries. Despite the figures in the right-hand column, the two central columns show that improvements are definitely occurring.

In the period since 1981, the big development wins have been achieved in China, in South East Asia more generally, and in South America. Without exception, these gains have come about as a result of economic development. In other words, poverty has not been reduced because rich Chinese have given more to poor Chinese; this has come about because the Chinese economy has been able to produce more wealth for all.

Does economic aid have much to do with this relative success? Not really, as governments and charities rarely do enough to make much impact throughout a country. In China, India and Mexico, for instance, the key factors have been:

- greater willingness to accept inward investment from multinational or other big, wealthy companies from the west or Japan
- greater enterprise on the part of the local business population
- more stable government than before, especially in India and Mexico
- easier access for exports to countries such as Britain, America and the rest of Europe, partly thanks to the World Trade Organization.

Table 80.2 Economic performance of selected countries

	GDP at PPP 2009*	Average annual growth in GDP per head 1970–1990	Average annual growth in GDP per head 1990–2008	Percentage of population below $1.25 a day 1992–2007
Bangladesh	$1,600	0.4	3.3	50
Benin	$1,500	0.3	1.2	47
China	$6,600	6.6	9.0	16
India	$3,100	2.1	4.7	42
Nicaragua	$2,800	−3.7	2.0	16
Nigeria	$2,400	−1.4	1.4	64

Source: *CIA Factbook 2010* and Unicef Statistics, 2010

ISSUES FOR ANALYSIS

Globalisation needs to be seen as a catch-all term that may mean different things to different people. It is assumed to be a very new thing (which is arguable) and is assumed by many to be a bad thing. When analysing issues to do with globalisation it helps to:

- be clear about the definition you are using and the limits you are placing on that definition (for example, 'economic globalisation' but not 'cultural globalisation' – though you may later want to explore whether this separation is artificial)
- be calm, measured and balanced; whatever the strength of your views, push yourself to consider a different perspective; for instance, many people feel strongly about 'sweatshop' work for low pay in Vietnam, for example, but it may be that Vietnamese workers would prefer a factory job to a job in the fields; we cannot jump to conclusions about other people's lives
- avoid slipping into too small-scale a viewpoint; globalisation is at least as much about increasing competition between big western companies as it is between the west and the developing world; unarguably, Volkswagen versus Renault versus Toyota is global rivalry we all benefit from.

80.7 GLOBALISATION AND DEVELOPMENT – AN EVALUATION

The judgements involved in this area need to be especially subtle. Beware of poorly justified judgements that may suggest intolerance towards others, or ignorance of the extreme disparities between incomes in rich and poor countries. The more you read about different countries' successes and failures, the better rooted your judgements will be.

It is also valuable to take a critical look at all the evidence provided, questioning whether the claims made by businesses about their motives is the truth or just public relations. The same sceptical approach should be taken to any other form of evidence, whether from pressure groups such as Greenpeace or from government ministers or officials. Globalisation is a topic in which opinions are often clearer than facts.

Key Terms

Deindustrialisation: the steady decline in manufacturing output and employment that changed Britain from being an industrial powerhouse to a service-sector economy.

Free trade: imports and exports being allowed into different countries without taxation, limits or obstruction. This ensures that companies from different countries compete fairly with each other.

Infant industries: new, young industries in a developing country that may need extra, but temporary, protection until they have grown big and strong enough to compete with global giants (for example, a new Zambian factory producing instant coffee, trying to compete with the global number one – Nestlé/Nescafé).

Intellectual property: legal protection for the rights of the originator of new written, visual or technical material (for example, protected by copyright, trademarks or patents).

Protectionism: government actions to protect home producers from competition from overseas (for example, by setting import taxes – 'tariffs' – or imposing import quotas that place a cap on the number of goods that can enter a country).

FURTHER READING

Stiglitz, J. (2002) *Globalization and its Discontents*. Norton.

WORKBOOK

A REVISION QUESTIONS

(40 marks; 40 minutes)

1 Reread the definition of globalisation at the start of the unit. Outline one advantage and one disadvantage of the world 'becoming one market'. (4)

2 **a)** Use Figure 80.1 to calculate the percentage increases in world exports in the following periods.
   a) 1973–1983
   b) 1983–1993
   c) 1993–2003 (5)
   b How well do these figures support the idea that globalisation 'arrived in the 1990s'? (2)

3 Outline two reasons why consumers may suffer as a result of a government policy of import protectionism. (4)

4 Examine one reason why a new car factory in Nigeria may benefit if the Nigerian government used the infant industries argument to protect it. (4)

5 Outline two other factors that could affect a country's infant mortality, apart from economic development. (4)

6 Use Figure 80.2 to describe three major changes that have happened in the world economy between 1948 and 2008. (6)

7 Should wealthy countries increase the rates of tax on their own populations in order to finance greater help to people living on less than $1.25 a day? (5)

8 Outline three possible reasons that may explain why China's growth rate is so much higher than that of Nigeria or India. (6)

B REVISION EXERCISES

B1 CASE STUDY

Starbucks agrees to Ethiopian coffee branding

CSRwire.com reports that Starbucks and Ethiopia recently signed a distribution, marketing and licensing agreement that should help Ethiopian coffee farmers to reap value from the intellectual property of their distinctive, deluxe coffees:

> 'Eight months ago Oxfam began working to raise awareness of Ethiopians' efforts to gain control over their fine coffee brands. Today, Starbucks has honored its commitments to Ethiopian coffee farmers by becoming one of the first in the industry to join the innovative Ethiopian trademarking initiative.'

We covered this story last winter, looking at how Oxfam threw the weight of its powerful nonprofit brand behind the cause of poor Ethiopian coffee farmers. At stake were the Sidamo, Harrar and Yirgacheffe varietals, thought to be among the best in the world. *Policy Innovations* raises its mug to this multi-stakeholder cooperation.

Source: Fairer Globalization and *Policy Innovations*, 22 December 2007

Questions

(25 marks; 30 minutes)

1 Explain what 'intellectual property' there can be in Ethiopian coffee. (4)
2 Explain how Ethiopian farmers could benefit from this initiative. (6)
3 Discuss the possible reasons why Starbucks may have decided to sign this deal with the Ethiopian coffee producers. (10)
4 Explain what the author means by the phrase 'this multi-stakeholder cooperation'. (5)

B2 CASE STUDY

Channel 4 cleared over Tesco child labour story

A Tesco complaint about a *Channel 4 News* item on child labour has been rejected by media regulator Ofcom. The *Channel 4 News* story alleged that child labour was being used by suppliers in Bangladesh in the production of clothes for Tesco stores.

Tesco complained that the report, which featured a 'little boy who looks no more than eight' and other allegedly underage workers, was unfair. The supermarket company, represented by solicitors Carter-Ruck, said the boy was in fact 12 years old and claimed the 'child' workers featured were aged 18 or over. But Ofcom said the secretly filmed report – made by independent producer Evolve Television for *Channel 4 News* – was 'properly supported' and put in 'fair context'. Ofcom also said Tesco had been given an appropriate amount of time to respond to the allegations.

The media regulator, in its ruling published today, said *Channel 4 News* had not been unfair in its treatment of the supermarket. Ofcom added that the *Channel 4 News* report had 'questioned Tesco's ability to ensure its ethical standards are met throughout the supply chain'.*

'The report did not allege that Tesco was deliberately or knowingly using child labour to produce its clothing,' the regulator said. 'Rather, it showed that companies supplying Tesco were employing workers who were below the legal age limit in Bangladesh (that is, aged under 14) and that some of these workers were producing clothes for Tesco.'

Tesco had claimed the boy who was described as looking 'no more than eight' was in fact 12. The company said he had no connection with the factory and was delivering lunch to his cousin. But *Channel 4 News*, in its response, said Tesco's claim was 'directly at odds' with what its film-makers had seen, 'namely that the boy was sewing creases into denim trousers as part of the production process'.

Channel 4 News editor, Jim Gray, added: '*Channel 4 News*'s reputation is founded upon its track record for delivering high-quality original journalism through thorough, rigorous and accurate investigation. This report possessed all of these qualities and investigative journalism remains at the heart of everything we do.'

Ofcom's Fairness Committee, its most senior decision-making body, made a provisional finding rejecting Tesco's complaint. The supermarket then requested a review of the provisional finding on the grounds that it was flawed. It was also not upheld.

* The supply chain is the network of suppliers that takes a product through all the stages from raw materials through to the retail store.

Source: John Plunkett, *Guardian*, 25 February 2008. Copyright Guardian News & Media Ltd 2008

Questions

(30 marks; 35 minutes)

1 Explain why it would be difficult for Tesco to 'ensure its ethical standards are met throughout the supply chain'. (8)
2 Discuss the probable reasons why Tesco decided to make this public complaint against Channel 4. (10)
3 Discuss whether Tesco should now withdraw all its clothing production from Bangladesh. (12)

B3 CASE STUDY

Globalisation: it isn't easy!

In 1980 it wasn't obvious whether India or Pakistan had the better economic prospects. Yes, India's population was hugely bigger (685 million compared with 85 million for Pakistan) but Pakistan had a higher GDP per capita. Whatever the reasons, Honda opted for Pakistan. By 2005, even though India was the growth story, Honda's 50 per cent share of Pakistan's car market was a big consolation. Honda Pakistan's position was very profitable, and its place was secured by owning Pakistan's only large car factory. For those growing up locally, the Honda Civic and Accord models epitomised luxury driving.

To keep its position strong, Honda embarked in 2005 on heavy investments in capacity expansion. The goal was to be able to produce 50,000 cars a year.

Then it all went wrong. From 2006 the market for passenger cars started to slide. Worse, competition from lower-priced cars from Korea, Malaysia and India chipped away at Honda's market share. In 2007, Honda sales were just 18,709 cars – from a factory capable of producing 50,000. Worse was to come, as sales slid further in the face of world recession and a collapse in security and consumer confidence. Healthy operating profits turned into severe losses.

Naturally enough, Honda's strategy had been to focus on 'the market' – largely companies or government departments buying prestigious cars for managerial staff. Yet from about 2005 the market moved more towards individuals buying cars for themselves. A Honda Civic was priced at about £11,000; a Suzuki Swift would cost half that figure. Honda's marketing strategy was facing the wrong way – looking backwards instead of forwards. In 2010 Honda's market share fell to 23 per cent.

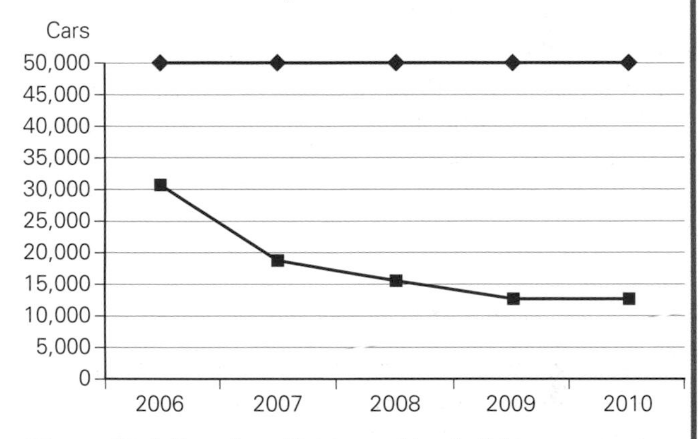

Figure 80.4 Capacity utilisation at Honda, Pakistan

Questions

(30 marks: 35 minutes)

1 Explain why a business might make a mistake when choosing which country to focus on. (6)
2 Honda's international strategy has been hugely successful; but not in this case. Examine why a successful international company such as Honda might fail within one country. (10)
3 Discuss two alternative strategies Honda might choose in the face of its current problems in Pakistan. Explain which you would recommend, and why. (14)

Multinationals

UNIT 81

A multinational is a firm which has its headquarters in one country and branches, manufacturing or assembly plants in others. In other words it is not just an exporter. It has business operations in several countries.

81.1 INTRODUCTION

Some multinationals are giants. Table 81.1 compares the turnover of several large multinationals with the total output of various entire countries. It shows the scope for multinationals such as the oil giants to bully smaller countries like Sri Lanka.

Table 81.1 Comparative size of top five multinational companies and selected national economies.

Country/company	2009 GDP/sales ($ billion)
UK	2,184
Poland	430
1. Walmart	408
Argentina	310
2. Shell	290
South Africa	287
3. Exxon	285
4. BP	246
5. Toyota	204
Nigeria	173
Sri Lanka	41

Source: *Forbes* magazine 2010 and *CIA World Factbook* November 2010.

Traditionally, multinationals had their headquarters in Europe, the USA or Japan. Some of their branches or factories would also be located in highly developed economies, but with others in less-developed nations, especially in South America or Asia. Over coming years, an increasing number of multinationals will be based in India or China. Examples may include the Indian companies Tata (owners of Jaguar Land Rover) and Mittal, plus the Chinese giants Lenovo (owners of IBM computers) and Alibaba.

81.2 ADVANTAGES OF OPERATING IN SEVERAL COUNTRIES

Nearness to local markets

Many multinational expansions are driven by the desire to produce close to the market. Local production facilities will result in lower transport costs and probably more competitive prices. Multinationals may also set up local production facilities in order to avoid import tariffs or taxes. Producing in the country for which the products are required means that no products are being imported. The multinational is able to avoid any import restrictions imposed by the host country. During the 1990s far-sighted car manufacturers such as Volkswagen built factories behind China's high tariff walls. When the boom in China's car market began in 2004, the German multinational was in a great position to become the number 1 overseas brand (as it was in 2009 and 2010).

Some other benefits from local production are as follows.

- It is far easier to tailor products to local customer preferences if senior managers live locally and therefore learn to understand local customs.
- In the long term it may be possible to become thought of as a local company. Many in Britain assume Ford and Vauxhall to be British rather than American, which may make them more inclined to 'buy British'.

Low labour costs

Many multinationals shift production facilities to less economically developed countries where wage rates are low. Mass producers are able to set up production facilities in these countries and employ unskilled or semi-skilled workers to produce their products. If firms can reduce the labour cost per unit, they can either afford to drop prices, or they can keep prices unchanged and accept a higher profit per unit – a pleasant choice to make! This practice is now very common, as any trip to a high street will show.

> **A-grade application**
>
> **Starwood Hotels plans major India expansion**
>
> The American Starwood hotel chain owns luxury brands such as Sheraton and Le Meridien. It has 26 hotels in India but is planning to increase the number by 60 per cent in the three years to 2014. The company's chief executive says that 'We open a hotel with an eye on the next 20 to 30 years. Any hotel in the beginning takes some time to ramp up.'
>
> Starwood sees growth prospects for luxury, western-tourist focused hotels, but also for less expensive hotels targeting Indian business travellers. Starwoods describe the Indian business traveller as 'notoriously value-conscious', so this sector may prove to be a challenge. It is therefore launching its mid-market, younger hotel brand Aloft, opening six hotels in business centres such as Bangalore and Chennai.

Government incentives

Governments of host countries are usually keen to attract multinationals. In order to do this, governments are prepared to offer a range of incentives to encourage multinationals to choose their country rather than any other. Among the methods for attracting this inward investment are reduced or zero tax rates, subsidies and reduced rate loans. These methods helped past British governments to attract foreign investors such as Nissan, Honda and IBM.

Low taxes

This may attract inward investment, as firms seek to find countries where their profits will be taxed at a lower rate than in their home country. This fact is used by many governments as a deliberate incentive to encourage investment by multinationals. The key tax is corporation tax, the percentage tax on company profits. This varies by country, as shown in Figure 81.1. Note that the UK government announced in 2010 that the rate would be cut to 24 per cent by 2014.

The existence of different tax rates in different countries allows multinationals to practise 'transfer pricing'. This is a way to boost profits by taking advantage of different tax levels in their countries of operation. It involves declaring high profits in countries where tax rates are low and minimal profits in countries where tax rates are high. For example, if Tesco UK sold goods cheaply to Tesco Ireland, its profits would rise in Ireland (where profit tax is low), and would fall in Britain. This would reduce Tesco's overall tax bill. The legality of transfer pricing tends to vary from country to country. As a result, it is difficult to clamp down on this practice, which many feel to be unfair.

An even more significant problem, in recent years, has been the increasing use of tax havens such as Bermuda or the Virgin Islands. Multinationals can register their businesses on these islands, where corporation tax may be 0 per cent. By channelling profits to these islands the multinational company can minimise its tax bill.

In 2009 the UK-based drinks multinational Diageo (Smirnoff, Baileys, Guinness) paid a corporation tax rate of 14.3 per cent. Local, probably smaller, British breweries would have had to pay the full 28 per cent tax. It is hard anyway for medium-sized firms to compete with giants. The scope for tax avoidance unfairly favours multinational companies.

81.3 BENEFITS OF MULTINATIONALS TO HOST COUNTRIES

Jobs for local workers

New factories should mean jobs for local workers. Not only directly (that is, jobs in the factory), but also from service jobs such as shopkeeping that stem from the extra cash in the local economy. Also, local suppliers of materials and components will benefit.

New skills

Local workers employed by multinationals are likely to receive training, possibly at a much higher level than is available locally. This will equip them with skills which they may be able to pass on to others or use to start their own business in future.

Improved infrastructure

Particularly in less developed countries, the multinational may be unhappy with existing transport and communication links. They may pay to improve local roads and railway lines to help them to move their

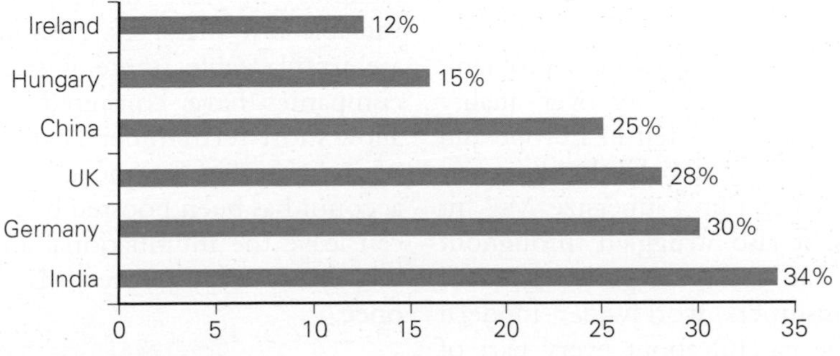

Figure 81.1 Corporation tax in selected countries

goods. Other improvements to the local infrastructure may come in the shape of a hospital for use by the factory staff and local community. At the time of writing the infrastructure of many African countries is being transformed by investment by Chinese multinational companies.

Technology trickle-down

New technology introduced to a country may 'trickle down' to local businesses, enabling them to produce goods and use techniques that were previously unavailable in that country.

Management expertise

Multinationals will usually start new factories using their own managers from elsewhere in the world. However, once the factory is up and running, local staff are likely to be trained for managerial jobs. These local staff may be able to use the knowledge gained in other businesses once they have left the firm. In the last 20 years managers throughout Britain have benefited from the Japanese management techniques introduced by Nissan and Toyota in their Sunderland and Derby factories respectively. Today, American, German or Japanese companies are having the same effect throughout China and India.

81.4 PROBLEMS EXPERIENCED BY MULTINATIONALS

Communication

Communication problems can arise between local workers and foreign managers. Not only may workers be unable to follow instructions due to the language barrier, but also it may be difficult to build the team spirit required for successful motivation.

Geography

Geography can also cause communication difficulties. A multinational with its headquarters in one country and various distant outposts will need to have communication channels in place to enable effective messages to get through to distant countries. Multinational intranets can help, but the richest form of communication is a face-to-face chat. Video conferencing provides that possibility, but users find it rather impersonal.

Multinational structure

A multinational structure can prove to be a problem. When Toyota suffered terrible publicity over quality problems in America in 2010, sales fell in Europe and in China. These days, news is as globalised as business. On a similar basis, when the film 'Supersize Me' hit US sales of McDonalds, it also struggled throughout Europe. This problem can be seen positively, as a potential benefit to consumers worldwide: modern multinationals have to be careful about every part of their operation in every country they operate in. Ask BP.

81.5 PROBLEMS MULTINATIONALS BRING TO HOST COUNTRIES

Safety concerns

Many multinationals that set up production facilities in less economically developed countries are accused of operating sub-standard, outdated safety precautions. Often, safety regulations in these countries are not as tough as those in developed countries. As a result, multinationals can use older equipment and machinery, which is perhaps not so safe as that used in other parts of the world. The result may be higher levels of accidents and injuries.

The world's worst-ever industrial accident, at Bhopal, India, killed 20,000 and injured almost 600,000 people (*Guardian*, 3 December 2009). Poor safety precautions at Union Carbide's chemical plant were to blame when toxic gas escaped from the factory, sending a cloud of poisonous gas onto the nearby town. Despite short-term damage to the firm's reputation and share price, no long-term ill effects were felt by the multinational. It closed the factory and left. Many years later, local residents are still suffering the physical and psychological after-effects.

Adverse effect on local economy

If the multinational is operating in direct competition with local firms, it is possible that the local economy may be adversely affected. Multinationals have tremendous power and may be able to use this to force local competitors out of the market. Rupert Murdoch's TV empire has often been accused of exactly this, by using its huge spending power to buy up the rights to the most important sports or other popular programmes. Local business closures will result in local job losses. This would be especially damaging if the multinational's profits were sent back to its home country, rather than reinvested in the local economy.

Short-term mineral extraction may leave host country poorer

Many multinationals set up production or mining facilities in less developed countries to extract valuable raw materials. Although the resources mined are irreplaceable, there is strong evidence that some companies have conspired with local politicians to allow short-term mineral extraction to be to the benefit of individuals, not the country. Many a Swiss bank account has been boosted by mineral exploitation. This can leave the multinational and the individuals richer, but the country poorer. Minerals can only be mined once.

Traditional, local cultures are weakened

It is said that, after 'OK', the world's best known piece of English is 'Coca-Cola'. This underpins the concern that traditional, local cultures are being weakened by the spread of multinational products. Some suggest that traditions should be preserved, untainted by imported cultures. This whole issue is a difficult one. The Coca-Cola Corporation is not forcing anyone to drink Coke. Multinationals argue that everyone has the freedom to choose.

Lack of commitment to host country

Multinational firms may lack a real commitment to their host country. Therefore, if something happens such as a recession, an overseas plant may be closed down without any serious concern for the local workforce or society. Firms may also prove **footloose**, that is, open a factory one year, but close it and move on to another country where labour costs are even lower.

ISSUES FOR ANALYSIS

- The issue of exploitation is one that is relevant in many questions about multinationals. This is particularly true in a situation where a multinational is operating in a developing country. Local workers may be paid very low wage rates. But are these rates low in comparison to the local standard of living? Early British and American economic growth was associated with very low wages and awful working conditions. If pressure groups are too effective at policing employment practices in countries such as Cambodia, will poor people be put out of work? Can that be a good thing? The balance between fair trade and exploitation is a fine one. Whatever your opinion on any particular situation, you can be sure that there are two sides to the argument – and each needs to be developed.
- Workers in different cultures may be motivated by different things. A study by motivation researcher Don Elizur carried out in various parts of the world discovered that money is the major motivator in some countries while in other countries it was less important. Other factors such as good relations with co-workers and recognition for achievement were much more important than pay. This means that firms may need to use different management techniques in different countries in order to build a motivated workforce. Clearly, this research can be related directly to Maslow's hierachy of needs.

81.6 MULTINATIONALS – AN EVALUATION

When considering the motives behind a host country's decision to encourage multinational investment, it is important to consider the government's objectives. Some governments in developing countries are desperate for foreign currency to repay loans. They may be prepared to accept the damage to the environment and depletion of natural resources which can result from the activities of the multinational. In China and India, though, sophisticated governments have carefully managed the arrival of multinational companies, encouraging inward investment that has helped to boost the country's economic growth rate.

In evaluation of questions on this topic it is important to remember who is in a position of power. Multinationals are huge organisations, as seen earlier in the unit – often larger, in terms of income, than whole countries. The resources available to these companies, both financial and managerial, give them great advantages in any kind of negotiation. For a prospective host seeking inward investment from a multinational, this power can be overwhelming. The incentives offered to multinationals will need to be sufficiently attractive to stop the multinational from choosing to invest elsewhere in the world. Despite all the possible negatives, most countries in the world are keen to experience the benefits brought by multinationals. The critics of multinationals may be overstating their case.

Key Terms

Footloose: a business that feels no commitment to a particular location, and therefore may close down Factory A, reopening in a different part of the world.

Infrastructure: the economic fabric of the country, such as roads, railways, water and energy supplies.

Intranet: an internal internet, in other words, computers which can be linked by telephone anywhere in the world, but only company employees have access.

Less developed nations: countries with low wage levels and standards of living due to their lack of economic development.

Natural resources: raw materials which can be grown, mined, extracted or caught, such as wheat, gold, oil or fish.

Pressure groups: organisations formed to achieve a specific goal by lobbying government or by creating publicity favourable to their cause.

Transfer pricing: a way multinationals can minimise their worldwide tax liabilities by transferring their profits from high-tax to low-tax countries.

WORKBOOK

A REVISION QUESTIONS

(30 marks; 30 minutes)

1 a) State four advantages of operating in several countries. (4)

b) Which of the four would be the most important for each of the following businesses? Explain your reasoning:

i Rolls Royce Motors, if its management decided to open a factory overseas. (3)

ii Cadbury's, if it wanted to open a factory in the Far East. (3)

iii Sports Interactive, the British software firm behind Football Manager and Championship Manager, considering setting up a software development site overseas. (3)

2 State five problems of operating in several countries. (5)

3 What is transfer pricing? (3)

4 How may a multinational seek to overcome language barriers experienced in internal communication? (4)

5 Outline the advantages of producing in the country in which you are selling. (5)

B REVISION EXERCISES

B1 DATA RESPONSE

BMW goes East

2009 was an extremely difficult year for BMW. Its worldwide sales volumes fell 10 per cent in the face of a severe recession. Its only real 'bright spot' was China, where sales not only rose, but rose by 37 per cent.

In 2010 this pattern continued, with newspapers reporting in November that BMW's third quarter profits had risen 11-fold as it continued to benefit from a big increase in sales in China.

Its revenues rose 36 per cent to €15.9 billion, as global quarterly sales of its BMW, Rolls-Royce and Mini cars increased by 13 per cent to 366,190 vehicles. BMW said its Chinese sales were 91 per cent higher than in 2009. By contrast, sales in western Europe rose by 1.8 per cent and in the USA by 9 per cent.

BMW's development in China has been through a joint venture with the Chinese company Brilliance Auto. One of the rules that must be followed in China is that at least 40 per cent of the value of a Chinese-produced car must be purchased locally. Otherwise the car will be subject to the 25 per cent tariff imposed on imported cars. In 2007 BMW decided that the quality of Chinese-produced car parts allowed it to go further than this, announcing that 'Our long-term strategy is to steadily accelerate local purchasing'.

Although BMW did not release a specific figure for India, the German company has been investing heavily since it opened its first BMW factory in India in 2007. As car sales rose by 30 per cent in India in 2010, it is likely that BMW will have benefited. At this stage in its development, though, Indian car buyers are very focused on cheaper, smaller cars. BMW's scope for major growth in India will come later, when middle-class buyers trade up from small family cars to luxury models.

For many years, BMW's main business strategy was to succeed in the USA. Nowadays its brightest young executives look East to build their careers.

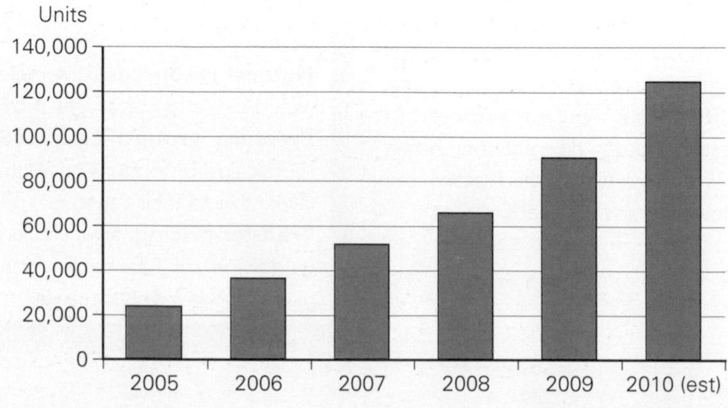

Figure 81.2 BMW sales in China

Questions

(50 marks; 60 minutes)

1 Outline two possible advantages and two possible disadvantages to China of having BMW operating within the country. (12)
2 Discuss whether China would be better off if it scrapped the tariff rules it places on imported cars and car parts. (18)
3 To succeed in India, should BMW develop a range of smaller cars, or wait for consumers to be able to afford the company's range of executive cars? Justify your answer. (20)

B2 CASE STUDY

Bricknell Group

Brickell Group plc manufactures a wide range of electrical goods throughout the world. With production facilities in 18 different countries, it is a true multinational.

One of the firm's products, a food processor, is the current focus of much management attention. The food processor has sold fairly well in its standardised form throughout the developed world. Complex components are manufactured in Indonesia, while the shell and attachments of the processor are made in Hungary. Both plants ship their output to Brickell's new high-tech assembly plant in the Philippines.

The assembly process has been dogged by problems since the plant opened six months ago. Production engineers have tracked the problem to the processor shells they receive, which have been varying too much in size. The high-tech machinery is unable to cope with the inconsistent sizes.

A further issue of concern to the firm's accountants is how to achieve the highest possible profit for the firm from the food processors. Table 81.2 gives certain cost information on the food processors.

Table 81.2 Cost information on food processors

Country	Costs incurred (£)	Local tax rate (in %)
Indonesia	5	25
Hungary	10	30
Philippines	20	10

The firm sells the product for a factory gate price of £45 to distributors in all its markets, where average tax rates are 40 per cent. The accountants at head office are trying to decide how much profit to declare in each location. They have a fair degree of flexibility, as long as the price charged by each plant covers the cost incurred there and the overall prices add up to less than the £45 customer selling price.

Questions

(50 marks; 60 minutes)

1 Explain the business significance of the terms:
 a) plc
 b) standardised. (10)
2 How does the text illustrate the economies and diseconomies of scale experienced by many multinationals? (10)
3 Bearing in mind local tax rates, how would you maximise Brickell's overall post-tax profit per unit on the food processors? (10)
4 a) Outline how and why Brickell uses transfer pricing. (12)
 b) Is transfer pricing ethical? (8)

C ESSAY QUESTIONS

(40 marks each)

1 A Japanese electrical goods manufacturer is considering building a new plant in France to serve the European market. Discuss the factors that may influence this decision.
2 Some industries are dominated by multinational organisations, while others see little or no multinational activity. What could be the reasons for this state of affairs?
3 The major problem associated with multinationals is the difficulty of coordinating the firm's activities. Discuss the steps that may be taken to improve organisational effectiveness for a multinational.

Impact of government economic policy

UNIT 82

Economic policy is the grouping of actions taken by the Chancellor of the Exchequer to try to achieve the government's economic objectives.

82.1 GOVERNMENT ECONOMIC OBJECTIVES

The most important goal of any politician is re-election. Electors make their voting choices partly on the competence of the government at managing the economy. Therefore any government will try hard to achieve its economic objectives, which typically include the following.

Economic growth

Economic growth occurs when the total value of all goods and services produced within the economy in a year increases. If the government can increase the rate of economic growth the material standard of living within the country will grow more rapidly, helping to boost the government's popularity. Economic growth is also beneficial to businesses. If average incomes rise, consumers will have more money to spend, creating larger markets and additional opportunities for UK firms. As the British economy has tended, in the long term, to grow at 2.25 per cent to 2.5 per cent a year, any government would be thrilled to have achieved a higher growth rate. In a recession, governments focus on the need to achieve any positive level of economic growth in order to signal a recovery.

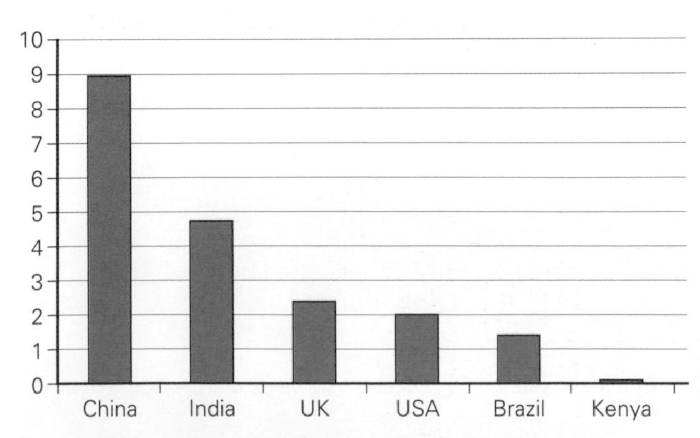

Figure 82.1 Long-run GDP per capita real growth rates, selected economies, 1990–2008
Source: Unicef November 2010.

Low inflation

Inflation is the percentage annual change in the average price level. Price stability will make it easier for UK firms to compete against their foreign rivals, both at home and abroad. The stability created by low inflation also encourages investment, leading to stronger economic growth.

Low unemployment

If the government can reduce the number of people in the country who are without work, the country's output should increase. Spending levels should also increase because those previously unemployed will now have a wage to live off, rather than unemployment benefit. Higher levels of spending will again help firms to expand and grow.

A favourable current account balance

The UK receives income from selling exports abroad. On the other hand, UK citizens also spend money on imported goods and services. The **current account** measures the difference between export income and import expenditure. In general the government would like to avoid a current account deficit, a situation where import expenditure exceeds export income. Current account deficits are financed by a general increase in borrowing, or asset sales, across the economy, leading to a fall in society's collective net worth.

A stable exchange rate

The exchange rate measures the volume or amount of foreign currency that can be bought with one unit of domestic currency (for example, £1: $1.60 means that one pound can buy one dollar sixty cents). A stable exchange rate helps firms to forecast how much profit, or loss, they stand to make from exporting or importing. If firms can forecast the future with greater confidence they will be more likely to go ahead and trade with foreign firms, boosting UK economic activity.

82.2 GOVERNMENT ECONOMIC POLICIES

The government uses economic policies to achieve its economic objectives. As a Business Studies student the key for you is to understand how these policies affect different types of business. The economic policies that you will need to know about are discussed below.

Fiscal policy

Fiscal policy refers to the government's budget. The budget concerns the government's tax and spending plans for the year ahead. The main forecast areas of government expenditure for 2010–11 are as shown in Figure 82.2.

How does government expenditure affect firms?

Government expenditure affects firms in the following ways.

- In general, an increase in government spending will increase the total level of spending within the economy, causing most markets to grow. For example, if the government awards above-inflation pay rises for nurses, this could help businesses such as Asda or Ryanair that target ordinary working people. Nurses are likely to spend the bulk of any pay rise they receive (for example, on a European holiday).
- About 40 per cent of the UK economy revolves around government spending; firms such as construction companies (road and school building), publishers (textbooks) and computer suppliers are all hugely dependent upon government spending (see Figure 82.2). At the time of writing the UK government is planning cutbacks on public spending to get this figure down towards the lower end of the range shown in Figure 82.3.
- Reduced spending on the NHS will cut the turnover of the construction companies that want contracts to build new hospitals. There will be multiplier effects too. For example, firms that supply the construction companies with the concrete, bricks and steel will suffer from government expenditure cutbacks. The same applies to drug manufacturers, and firms that produce medical equipment such as MRI scanners and hospital beds.

The main sources of tax income for 2010–11 are as shown in Figure 82.4.

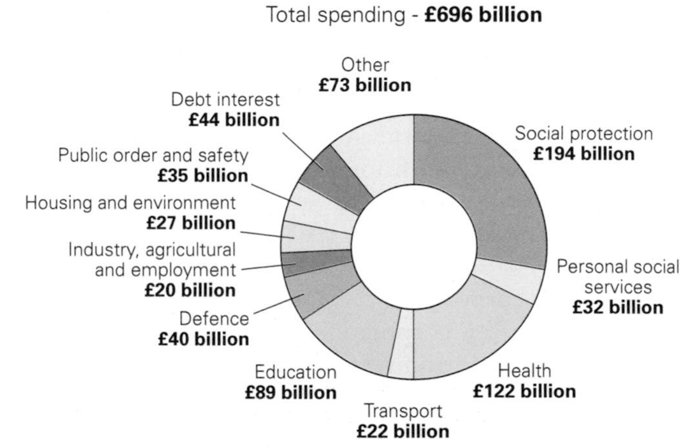

Figure 82.2 Government spending 2010 to 2011
Source: HM Treasury

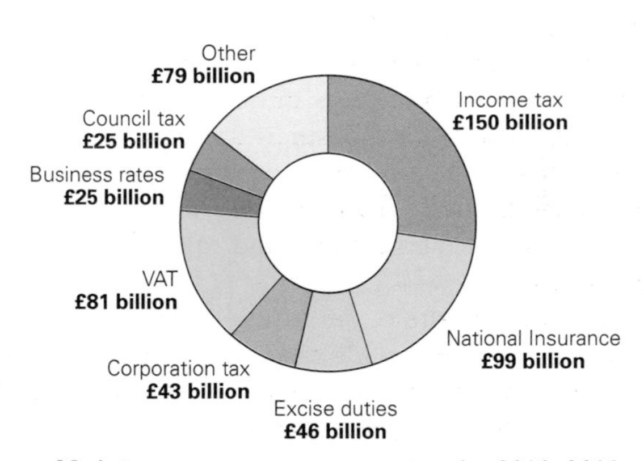

Figure 82.4 Forecast government receipts for 2010–2011
Source: Office for Budget Responsibility

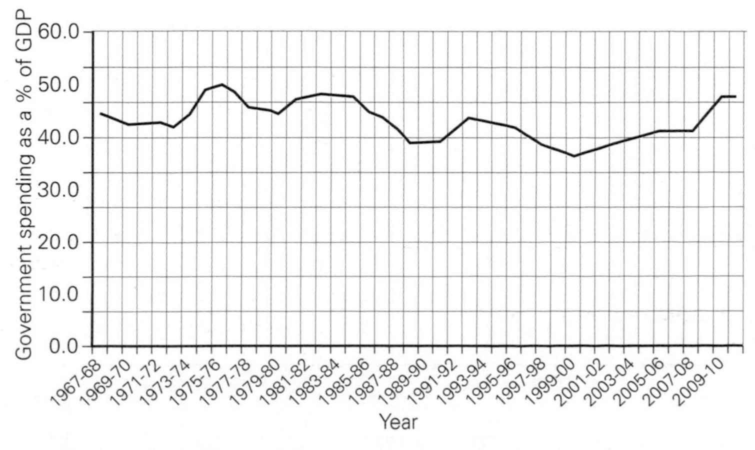

Figure 82.3 Government spending as a percentage of GDP

How does taxation affect firms?

Taxation affects firms in the following ways.

Income tax: the largest component of the UK government's income comes from income tax. Income tax tends to reduce consumer spending because higher income tax rates widen the gap between gross (before tax) and net (after tax) pay. At times the government is forced into collecting more income tax in order to finance increases in public expenditure. This tends not to be a popular policy. Most firms do not benefit. If more money is collected through income tax, demand for products and services may shrink as consumer spending falls. The UK income tax system is mildly 'progressive'. This means that those earning lower incomes pay a smaller percentage of their income in tax than those earning higher salaries. Changes to the income tax system can affect some firms more than others. For example, an increase in the top rate of income tax from 40 per cent to 50 per cent would hit BMW car dealerships but might have no effect on sales of bicycles.

Value added tax (VAT): this is added to the retail price of a product. It is an example of an indirect tax (that is, a tax levied on expenditure, rather than on income). In its first budget since coming to power, the UK's 2010 coalition government announced a target of boosting tax receipts by £8 billion per year by increasing the rate of VAT from 17.5 per cent to 20 per cent. VAT makes goods more expensive. Changes in VAT rules can affect businesses. If the government decided to extend VAT to newspapers the price of newspapers would be forced up, leading to a fall in the volume of newspapers bought and sold.

Excise duties: these are indirect taxes levied, in addition to VAT, on a wide range of products including petrol, cigarettes and alcohol. The impact of excise duties on a market is very much influenced by consumer price sensitivity. For example, petrol retailers such as Shell tend not to be too badly affected by increases in petrol duty because the demand for petrol in the UK tends to be price inelastic. In other words, the price increase created by the increase in fuel duty has a minimal effect on the volume of petrol that Shell sells. Oil companies find it relatively easy to pass on any increase in petrol duty to the motorist by raising petrol prices. Increasing excise duty rates on a price-inelastic product also benefits the government because it will raise more in taxation from this market.

Types of fiscal policy

- *Expansionary fiscal policy:* the government runs an expansionary fiscal policy when planned government spending for the year ahead exceeds planned tax income. Expansionary fiscal policy tends to benefit most firms in the short run because the total level of spending in the economy will rise.
- *Contractionary fiscal policy:* the government runs a contractionary fiscal policy when planned expenditure is less than planned tax income. Contractionary fiscal policy tends to depress the total level of spending within the economy.
- *Neutral fiscal policy:* if planned tax income equals planned government spending the government's budget is said to be 'balanced'.

Corporation tax: this is a tax levied on a company's profits. In 2010 the UK government announced a staged cut in corporation tax from 28 per cent to 24 per cent. A fall in the corporation tax rate will give firms an increased opportunity to invest because, all other

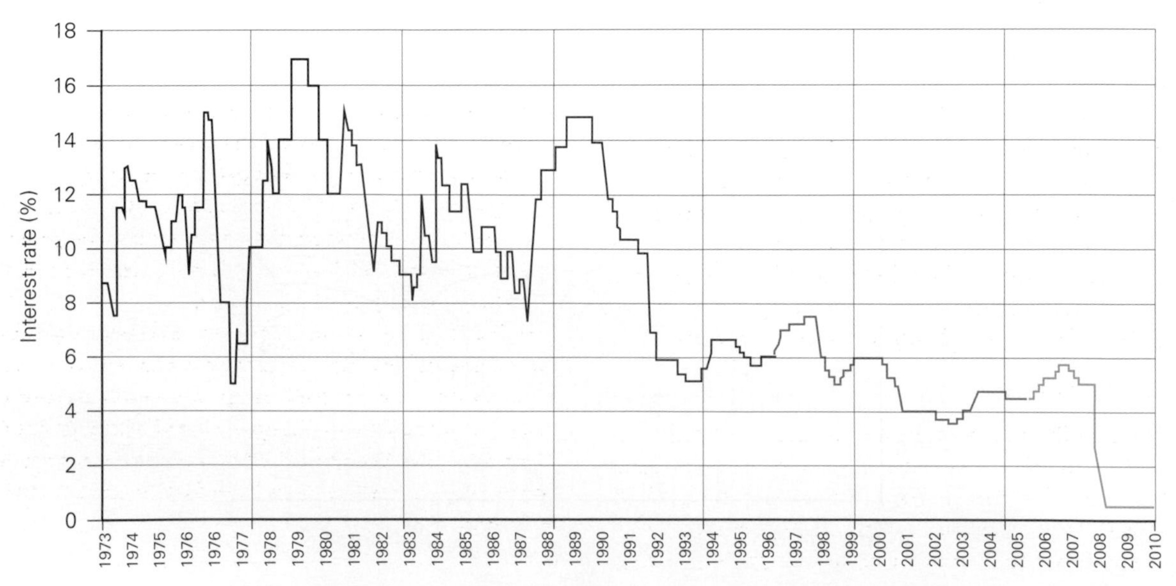

Figure 82.5 The Bank of England's base interest rate (%) since 1973
Source: Bank of England

things being equal, the less paid in corporation tax the greater the level of retained profit.

Monetary policy

Monetary policy concerns the availability and price of credit. In the UK, monetary policy is implemented by the Bank of England. The Bank of England's Monetary Policy Committee (MPC) meets every month to set the interest rate. The interest rate is the price of borrowed money. An increase in interest rates makes borrowing more expensive. On the other hand, saving becomes a more attractive proposition when interest rates rise. Interest rates are a powerful economic policy instrument because they can simultaneously affect a firm's revenue and costs.

Monetary policy can be tightened or slackened according to the economic circumstances. Recessions are caused by a lack of spending. If the economy is in recession the central bank will normally cut the interest rate because lower interest rates encourage people to spend more. Lower interest rates will encourage more borrowing and less saving.

On the other hand, during a boom demand is normally high and this can cause inflation. To reduce this threat the Central Bank normally reacts by 'tightening' monetary policy. This involves increasing interest rates. An increase in interest rates reduces borrowing and increases saving. As a result of the interest rate rise, total spending falls and the threat of inflation reduces.

Figure 82.5 shows the extraordinary variations in interest rates since the mid-1970s.

The impacts of interest rates on firms

The interest rate is a good example of an external constraint; it is a factor that is beyond the firm's control. However, changes in the rate of interest can affect a firm's costs and revenues.

Impacts on cost

Loan capital is an important source of finance for many businesses. The main benefit of a loan is that, unlike retained profit, it can enable a firm to expand rapidly. However, unlike share capital, taking on additional loan capital does not compromise ownership. Highly geared firms, whose share capital is made up mostly of loan capital, can be highly vulnerable to interest rate changes, particularly if they have not borrowed at a fixed rate. A sudden increase in the interest rate will increase their fixed costs, leading to lower profits.

Impacts on revenue

Interest rates influence spending in a variety of different ways. Following the recession of 2009, interest rates had fallen to an all-time low of 0.5 per cent. As the UK comes out of recession and begins to experience inflationary pressures, the Bank of England is likely to begin gradually increasing interest rates. Rising interest rates tend to depress consumer spending because they cut into disposable incomes. Disposable income measures the amount of income a person has to spend once taxes, pensions and other fixed outgoings have been subtracted from gross pay. There are several reasons why an increase in interest rates leads to lower disposable incomes. These are set out below.

Mortgage repayments

Most houses are bought using a mortgage; this is a loan that is secured against the value of the property. If interest rates go up the person owning the mortgage will now have to pay back more to the bank each month in interest, cutting into their disposable income.

Consumer credit

The UK is addicted to credit. According to the pressure group Credit Action, total UK personal debt at the end of July 2010 stood at £1,456 billion. If interest rates go up, those with large personal debts will find their monthly disposable incomes being cut sharply. If interest rates stay high, firms selling products bought on credit, such as cars and furniture, will probably suffer from falling sales.

Impacts on investment

The rate of interest can affect investment decisions. If interest rates rise, the cost of funding an investment project will also increase if the project is financed using borrowed money. For firms with cash in the bank that do not need to borrow, the interest rate can still affect investment decision making because the interest rate also affects the opportunity cost of investing. Interest rates also affect the reward for risk – the difference between an investment's expected profitability (its ARR) and the prevailing interest rate. So the higher the rate of interest the lower the level of investment spending by businesses.

Evaluation

Interest rates changes are mostly likely to affect:

- firms that want to expand quickly, but that lack the retained profit to fund the expansion internally
- highly geared firms that need to borrow heavily to invest in the latest technology in order to remain competitive
- businesses that sell luxury goods or discretionary items that are typically bought on credit.

A sudden rise in interest rates can be a disaster, especially for a company that has just borrowed heavily in order to expand. An increase in the interest rate causes costs to rise and revenues to fall simultaneously. Watch those profits fall! Many firms have been surprised by a sudden unanticipated rise in interest rates and have been forced into liquidation as a result.

B REVISION EXERCISES
B1 DATA RESPONSE

Campaign for better transport slams government plans for 'traffic hell'

The government predicts we will have to contend with 5.7 million more cars on our roads by 2031, a growth of 21 per cent. Simply parking these cars would fill a 52-lane motorway all the way from Edinburgh to London. Worryingly, because we are also driving more, government forecasts show that traffic will increase even more – up 31 per cent by 2025. The result will be 'traffic hell', warns Campaign for Better Transport: more traffic jams, longer journeys, more pollution and more stress. The organisation, formerly known as Transport 2000, is today outlining a better way forward for traffic.

Executive Director Stephen Joseph says, 'We can't go on like this – traffic is destroying our communities, our health and our environment. The Government must stop catering for all this traffic and instead give people and businesses good alternatives to driving. Campaign for Better Transport will continue the organisation's long-standing role of coming up with practical solutions to transport problems.'

Source: press release, Campaign for Better Transport, September 2007.

Questions

(30 marks; 35 minutes)

1 The government predicts that there will be 5.7 million more cars on our roads by 2031. Outline two likely reasons why there may be more cars on our roads in the future. (4)
2 Give two examples of UK businesses that could benefit from greater car ownership. (2)
3 Identify and explain three costs of traffic congestion to a business of your choice. (6)
4 Motoring organisations such as the RAC and AA argue that the government should respond to the threat of growing congestion on the roads by building more roads and motorways. Examine two businesses in the UK that would gain greatly if the UK government decided to increase the amount of money spent on new building roads. (6)
5 Discuss whether UK manufacturers should consider factors such as pollution and stress when making decisions concerning how they should distribute their goods. (12)

B2 DATA RESPONSE

Don't scrap the UK car industry

By early 2009, the UK's economy was nose-diving towards recession and one industry in particular faced disaster head-on. New car sales are always hit hard by economic downturn, since consumers always have a cheaper alternative (buy a used car) or may be easily able to postpone their purchase until they can be more certain of their disposable income. With an estimated 800,000 UK jobs directly affected by the car industry (not just car factories, but suppliers and their suppliers, along with car dealerships), the case for special support for the industry from government was strong. Figure 82.6 shows that UK car sales in the early months of 2009 were 25–30 per cent down on the previous year.

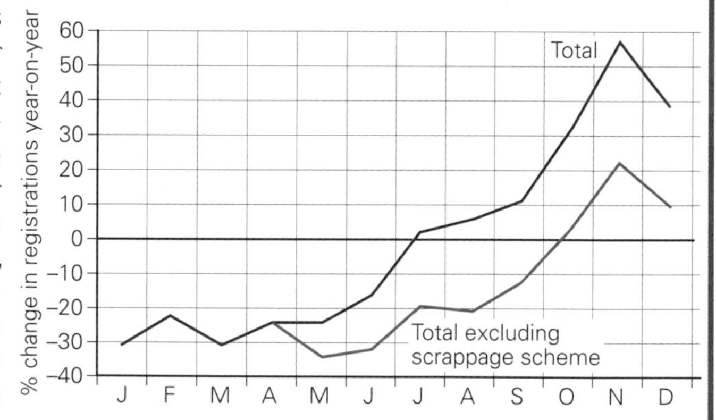

Figure 82.6 Change in monthly new car registrations, 2009

The relief of the car industry is easily seen here in this press release from the car industry pressure group the SMMT (Society of Motor Manufacturers and Traders):

> Government has recognised the strategic national importance of the UK motor industry and taken positive steps to support it with the introduction of the Automotive Assistance Programme and the Scrappage Incentive Scheme. The market has seen some growth, leading to a cut in the rate of decline in production output, but industry remains fragile. It is vital that government continues to sustain and strengthen the economic recovery and build consumer confidence.

The scrappage scheme offered customers £2,000 towards the cost of a brand new car when they traded in a car that was 10 or more years old. Around 330,000 cars were sold under scrappage scheme while government estimates suggested that around 4,000 jobs were saved among manufacturers and suppliers.

The Scrappage scheme finished in early 2010, roughly the same time as VAT went back up from 15 per cent to 17.5 per cent. Other support came in the form of promised government loans totalling around £750 million to help car manufacturers finance the building of new production facilities.

Questions

(40 marks; 50 minutes)

1 To what extent does the graph shown in Figure 82.6 prove that the Scrappage scheme was vital to protecting the long-term future of the UK car industry? (12)
2 Calculate the effect of VAT increase in early 2010 on the price of a car that cost £20,000 before the increase. (4)
3 Analyse how the purchase of a brand new UK car has benefits to companies other than the car's manufacturer. (10)
4 Discuss whether the government was right to single out the car industry for specific support when the whole economy was suffering from a slump. (14)

Government policies affecting business

UNIT 83

The government policies covered in this unit are those that exclude economic policy (about which you have just read a whole unit). These government policies fall into two main categories: government initiatives to pass laws affecting business operations and government foreign policy towards international trade.

83.1 THE EUROPEAN UNION

Britain is a member of the European Union. The European Union is a community of countries that form a single market as a result of laws centred on the free movement of people, goods, services and capital between all member countries.

The EU has undergone a series of expansions since starting with six founder members in the 1950s. At the time of writing there are 27 member countries, creating a market of over 500 million people generating over 30 per cent of the world's economic activity. The map in Figure 83.1 shows the member countries, along with those countries hoping to join the EU at some point in the future.

Figure 83.1 European Union membership

EU expansion

British governments of recent years have tended to be broadly supportive of EU expansion. There are strong economic arguments for the UK to support an expansion of the single European market, based upon two major factors.

Increased size of market for UK exporters

EU enlargement means an increased size of market for UK exporters to other EU countries. Since a UK firm can sell its products in any other EU country without having to worry about paying import taxes or customs duties, membership of the EU provides UK firms with a 'home' market consisting not only of the 60 million or so who live in the UK, but the 500 million EU consumers. This can be contrasted with a similar situation for a US company with a home market of just over 300 million people. This larger 'home' market should give UK firms a competitive advantage over their US rivals.

Source of cheap, often skilled, labour for UK firms

Freedom of movement of people creates a source of cheap, often skilled labour for British firms, especially from newer EU members such as Poland and Romania. The issue of immigration is a controversial one, not just in the UK, but in most other western European countries. Extra workers put downward pressure on wage rates, which helps to prevent wage inflation. It also helps the economy to grow faster than its long-term trend growth rate. Unfortunately, the benefit to business and to shoppers is not shared by British workers, some of whom may have their pay pushed down to minimum wage rates by the competition for jobs.

A-grade application

Immigrants run the UK economy

A recent Bank of England report on the effect of immigrant workers on the UK economy came up with some interesting findings. Relative to UK-born workers, immigrant workers are over-represented in low-paid sectors such as hotels, restaurants and unskilled jobs. Yet they are also over-represented in high-paid occupations (managers and professionals) and high-paid industries (finance, property and business activities). In general, immigrant workers are younger, better educated and work longer hours than those born in the UK. The report suggests that overall productivity within the UK could increase, with those in lower-paid occupations prepared to work harder, with higher skills levels, for less money. Good news for their UK employers!

Source: *Bank of England Quarterly Bulletin*, Winter 2006 ('The economic characteristics of immigrants and their impact on supply').

83.2 A SINGLE EUROPEAN CURRENCY

One political issue on which the UK has failed to join its European partners is that of the single currency, the euro. The UK government has no plans to adopt the euro as the UK's currency. The central benefit is the ability to carry out international transactions without the need to worry about exchange rate fluctuations. At the time of writing (autumn 2010) the pound had risen by around 15 per cent against the euro within the past nine months. This makes exporting harder for UK firms selling to countries using euros, as UK-produced goods seem more expensive.

The UK government's view is that the UK's economy is not currently suited to adopting the euro. The concern is that any country that uses the euro has its monetary policy decided by the European Central Bank. It has to set one interest rate that is correct for all the economies that use the euro. If Germany needs high interest rates at a time when Britain needs low rates, will Britain's needs be taken fully into account? It may be many years before a UK government takes the plunge and starts the process of adopting the single currency, a process that many feel should begin with a referendum of the UK electorate. Table 83.1 lists those EU members who use the single European currency.

Table 83.1 EU members who use the single European currency (the euro)

Austria	Belgium	Cyprus
Estonia	Finland	France
Germany	Greece	Ireland
Italy	Luxembourg	Malta
The Netherlands	Portugal	Slovakia
Slovenia	Spain	

Figure 83.2

83.3 FREE TRADE

The World Trade Organization (WTO) is an international organisation that seeks to promote free trade between nations, by creating agreements governing the way in which global trading is conducted. The ultimate goal of free trade would mean an end to all import taxes (tariffs), and physical limits on the amount of goods that can be imported to any country (quotas).

Though not all countries in the world have signed all the WTO's agreements, all major economies are members or are in the process of securing membership. The WTO also acts as a judge in disputes between countries where one feels another has broken free trade agreements. An example of this role is the WTO's investigation into the aircraft makers Airbus (Europe) and America's Boeing (both private-sector companies). The WTO is looking into whether each business has received illegal government subsidies to help them compete.

Free trade is a noble goal; it provides the chance for the world economy to become truly efficient as those companies that do things best are able to offer their services globally. Unfortunately it is not clear that free trade is always in the best interests of less-developed economies. Japan, South Korea, China and India all began their periods of rapid economic modernisation with quite heavily 'managed' trading, that is, they protected their still-immature companies and jobs until the businesses were big enough to stand on their own feet. Many economists still believe that protecting 'infant industries' can help long-term economic growth.

A government may be keen to protect jobs in its own country, by using trade barriers to discourage foreign competitors from entering the home market. For example, before the European Union, France 'protected' its wine makers from competition from Spain by placing an import tax on Spanish wines. Protectionist measures such as this give home producers a cost advantage. Governments may be keen to provide

C ESSAY QUESTIONS

(40 marks each)

1 'Businesses will continue to infringe the law until the penalties they face are strong enough to hurt the individuals running those businesses.' To what extent is this statement accurate?

2 'Further expansion of the EU represents a great opportunity for large UK companies wishing to become global players.' Discuss why this may or may not be the case.

UNIT 84

How firms respond to potential and actual changes

Potential changes are those that may be needed in future; actual changes are those that have really happened.

84.1 WHAT CHANGES NEED TO BE ADDRESSED?

Operating in a changing environment is an inescapable reality for businesses. Business success depends on how firms respond to both potential and actual changes. The list of changes below suggests the major external causes of changes to which firms will need to find a response. All the changes are covered elsewhere in this book, so the rest of this unit will focus on the following responses to these external changes.

- Economic factors and trends in economic variables – Unit 79 deals with the impact on firms of the major economic variables:
  - the business cycle and economic growth
  - interest rates
  - exchanges rates
  - unemployment
  - inflation.
- Globalisation of markets – covered in Unit 80.
- Emerging markets – the growth of China and India is covered in Unit 90, while other emerging markets are covered in Unit 83 (government policies affecting business).

Responses to change

Responses to change will vary from short-term actions to major changes in the firm's long-term plans. Short-term changes are known as tactical responses, while a long-term change to the firm's overall plans is considered to be a strategic change.

The rest of this unit will consider strategic changes, rather than tactical measures. A summary of common responses to change is given in Table 84.1.

84.2 MARKETING STRATEGY

Product portfolio

Changes to the products made by the firm may represent a sensible response to external change. The basic choice is likely to be between expansion or reduction of the product portfolio. Should the firm launch new products to exploit a newly created opportunity? A firm expecting an economic downturn may consider the option of producing a low-cost version of a best-selling product that is likely to appeal in times when money is tighter. Alternatively, the chance to break into a new market, offered by political change, may result in the need to add a brand new product to the portfolio, specifically designed to cater for the needs of that market. For instance, in early 2011 India still refused to allow large foreign retail companies to operate in the country. Tesco and others would love to have a presence in the world's second most populous country (1,180 million and rising). As yet they cannot. If and when the Indian government changes its mind, there will be a mad rush to be the first supermarket chain into India. The clever ones have already got their plans in place.

Reduction of the product portfolio may also make sense in some cases. External change may make some existing products poor sellers overnight, in which case a firm may decide to drop these immediately.

Image shift

Some external changes may prompt a shift in corporate image. A UK company suffering from increased global competition may find that it can gain a competitive advantage by pushing the 'Britishness' of the brand. Not only could this boost UK sales, but other markets may be keen to buy into a brand that plays on its Britishness, such as Burberry or Aston Martin.

84.3 FINANCIAL STRATEGY

Sources of finance

Responding to changes usually requires cash. Whether launching a new product or laying off staff, some cash outlay will be involved. Therefore financially a firm needs to consider carefully the sources of finance it uses. Increased interest rates make borrowing more expensive and therefore less attractive as a means of raising capital. On the other hand, a booming stock market would mean that expected dividend payments may make share capital more expensive than loan capital. Careful assessment of the gearing ratio in the light of the external change will be the major analysis that needs to be conducted prior to deciding on an appropriate source of finance.

Friedman's view, however, ignores the fact that the interests of the stakeholders may differ. Most people would consider it unethical to make staff redundant if the motive was purely to add to the bonuses earned by directors and dividends paid to shareholders.

85.3 THE DEVELOPING ETHICAL ENVIRONMENT

Every era witnesses a series of ethical crises for companies – individually or collectively. BP disgraced itself in its operations in America in 2005 and 2010. Virtually the entire banking sector has been an ethical no-go area as the pursuit of career progress and huge bonuses led to reckless speculation and a series of products that exploited consumers' naivety about finance.

Yet the picture isn't entirely bleak. In 2009 Cadbury became the world's first major chocolate company to convert all sourcing of a major brand to Fairtrade, when bars of Dairy Milk started to show a new logo. Nestlé soon copied by converting its huge KitKat brand to Fairtrade. This means that both companies promise to pay cocoa and sugar suppliers a generous minimum price to ensure better working conditions for farm workers.

Other companies have tried to operate on ethical principles since their inception. The extract below, taken from Innocent Drink's website, summarises its position.

Our ethics

We sure aren't perfect, but we're trying to do the right thing

---

It might make us sound a bit like a Miss World contestant, but we want to leave things a little bit better than we find them. We strive to do business in a more enlightened way, where we take responsibility for the impact of our business on society and the environment, and move these impacts from negative to neutral, or better still, positive. It's part of our quest to become a truly sustainable business, where we have a net positive effect on the wonderful world around us.

Source: Innocent Drinks website

One of the most significant developments in corporate ethical behaviour in recent years has been the move towards sustainability. Sustainable production means that a business seeks to supply its products in such a way as not to compromise the lives of future generations by, for example, damaging the environment or depleting non-renewable resources. A common feature of this aspect of ethical behaviour is the desire to reduce the company's 'carbon footprint' or even to become a carbon-neutral business. Some businesses find this an easier stance to adopt than others. Nike, the world's biggest sportswear business, has announced that it will become carbon neutral by 2011. Other businesses have found it more difficult to reduce or eliminate their carbon footprints, especially those in the manufacturing sector. However, a wide range of businesses in the UK have recognised the marketing benefits of taking this kind of ethical stance. The Eurostar story in the A-grade application illustrates the importance of sustainability in the transport industry. It also shows how Eurostar can use it as a competitive weapon against rivals such as easyJet and other budget airlines.

A-grade application

Eurostar goes carbon neutral

All Eurostar journeys from the new St Pancras International Station are carbon neutral thanks to offsetting, recycling – and fuller carriages. This makes Eurostar the world's first footprint-free method of mass transport. The impact of rail travel between London and Paris or Brussels had always been at least ten times lighter than the equivalent journey by plane, a traveller generating 11 kilograms of carbon dioxide compared with 122 by his or her counterpart on the plane. It is, the company says, the difference between enough CO_2 to fill a Mini and the amount needed to fill a double-decker bus.

Figure 85.1 Eurostar

But by making a raft of new changes across the business – from installing energy meters on all trains to tightening up on recycling and making 'train capacity efficiencies' (filling every seat, in other words) – the operator is lightening its environmental load. In addition, it has set itself a new target of reducing its carbon dioxide emissions per passenger by a quarter by 2012.

Source: *Daily Telegraph*, 14 November 2007 © Telegraph Media Group Limited 2007

85.4 ETHICAL CODES OF PRACTICE

An example of an ethical code of practice is: 'To meaningfully contribute to local, national and international communities in which we trade, by adopting a code of conduct that ensures care, honesty, fairness and respect.'

As a response to consumer expectations and competitive pressures, businesses have introduced **ethical codes** of practice. These are intended to improve the behaviour and image of a business. The information given below about the Institute of Business Ethics (IBE) highlights the extent to which UK businesses have appreciated the importance of being seen to behave ethically. Furthermore, the very existence of the IBE is evidence of the growing importance of this aspect of business behaviour.

The Institute of Business Ethics (IBE)

The IBE was established to encourage high standards of business behaviour based on ethical values. Its vision: 'To lead the dissemination of knowledge and good practice in business ethics.'

The IBE raises public awareness of the importance of doing business ethically, and collaborates with other UK and international organisations with interests and expertise in business ethics.

It helps businesses to strengthen their ethics culture and encourage high standards of business behaviour based on ethical values. It assists in the development, implementation and embedding of effective and relevant ethics and corporate responsibility policies and programmes. It helps organisations to provide guidance to staff and build relationships of trust with their principal stakeholders.

Source: IBE website

IBE research

IBE research has found that companies with a code of ethics financially outperform those without. Now, most firms (85 of the FTSE100) have codes of ethics and so having a code is no longer a clear sign of being 'more ethical'; it is not sufficient to act as a unique selling point (USP). A commitment to embedding ethical values into business practice through a training programme differentiates companies from those that simply declare a commitment to ethical values.

The results of the IBE's research reveal that companies with a demonstrable ethics programme benefit from the confidence that is instilled in their stakeholders. This helps to build the company's reputation, enhances relations with bankers and investors, assists firms in attracting better employees, increases goodwill, leaves the firms better prepared for external changes, turbulence and crisis, and generally helps the firm run better.

Source: Institute of Business Ethics

An ethical code of practice is a document setting out the way a business believes its employees should respond to situations that challenge their integrity or social responsibility.

The precise focus of the code will depend on the business concerned. Banks may concentrate on honesty, and chemical firms on pollution control. It has proved difficult to produce meaningful, comprehensive codes. The National Westminster Bank, for example, took two years to produce its ten-page document. A typical code may include sections on:

- personal integrity: in dealings with suppliers and in handling the firm's resources
- corporate integrity: such as forbidding collusion with competitors and forbidding predatory pricing
- **environmental responsibility:** highlighting a duty to minimise pollution emissions and maximise recycling
- social responsibility: to provide products of genuine value that are promoted with honesty and dignity.

A common feature of ethical codes of practice is that companies publicise them. This is because they believe that being seen to behave ethically is an important element of the marketing strategy of many businesses.

Critics of ethical codes believe them to be public relations exercises rather than genuine attempts to change business behaviour. What is not in doubt is that the proof of their effectiveness can be measured only by how firms actually behave, not by what they write or say.

85.5 PRESSURE GROUPS AND ETHICS

The activities of **pressure groups** affect all types of businesses and most aspects of their behaviour. Most of the high-profile pressure groups are multi-cause and operate internationally. Greenpeace is one of the best-known pressure groups; it lobbies businesses to restrict behaviour that may adversely affect the environment. Other single-cause pressure groups exist to control the activities of businesses in one particular sphere of operations.

- Action on Smoking and Health (ASH) is an international organisation established to oppose the production and smoking of tobacco. It publicises actions of tobacco companies that may be considered to be unethical. ASH frequently focuses on the long-term effects of tobacco on consumers of the product.
- Compassion in World Farming is a UK-based pressure group campaigning specifically for an end to the factory farming of animals. The group engages in political lobbying and high-profile publicity campaigns in an attempt to end the suffering endured by many farm animals.

A-grade application

Supermarket giant makes huge commitment to chicken welfare

Sainsbury's has made a commitment to improve the lives of 70 million chickens a year by moving away from selling the most intensively farmed chickens in a decision that is heralded as a 'huge step forward' by leading farm animal welfare charity, Compassion in World Farming.

The supermarket giant has announced a move away from stocking poor-welfare factory-farmed chickens across all the chicken it sells and will instead adopt the Freedom Food standard, or equivalent, as the minimum.

Dr Lesley Lambert, Director of Food Policy, welcomed the move, saying, 'This will dramatically improve the lives of 70 million chickens every year and is one of the most significant moves in farm animal welfare in the UK.'

Freedom Food or equivalent standards ensure more space, slower-growing birds with fewer welfare problems, and environmental enrichment such as straw bales, which allow for more natural behaviour.

'By reaching the equivalent of Freedom Food standards, Sainsbury's is leading the way among the big four supermarkets on chicken welfare, joining M&S and Waitrose as pioneers in this area. This is a huge step forward. We urge consumers to support higher welfare for chickens through the power of their purse and preferably choose free range,' continued Dr Lambert.

Source: Compassion in World Farming press release

85.6 THE ETHICAL BALANCE SHEET

Advantages of ethical behaviour

Companies receive many benefits from behaving, or being seen to behave, in an ethical manner. These are discussed below.

Marketing advantages

Many modern consumers expect to purchase goods and services from organisations that operate in ways that they consider morally correct. Some consumers are unwilling to buy products from businesses that behave in any other way. This trend has been accelerated by the rise of consumerism. This has meant that consumers have become increasingly well informed and are prepared to think carefully before spending their money.

Some companies have developed their ethical behaviour into a unique selling point (USP). They base their marketing campaigns on these perceived differences. An example of a high-profile company adopting this strategy is the Body Shop International.

A key point is that not only does the company seek to support relatively poor communities in the less developed world, but it also publicises these actions. By creating a caring image through its marketing the Body Shop hopes to gain increased sales.

Marketing advantages

Companies also gain considerable public relations advantages from ethical behaviour. Once again this can help to enhance the image of the business, with positive implications for sales and profits.

In 2010, the Co-op Bank announced a 21 per cent increase in operating profits to £177 million, while confirming the maintenance of its ethical principles. In the previous year it had enjoyed a 36 per cent increase in current account holders. It put this down to confidence in the bank's security and to its strong ethical stance. The Co-op Bank consistently says it will not lend to any company involved in the arms trade; and the whole Co-op movement is a strong supporter of Fairtrade products.

Positive effects on the workforce

Firms that adopt ethical practices may experience benefits in relation to their workforce. They may be able to recruit staff who are better qualified and motivated, because larger numbers of high-quality staff apply. Innocent Drinks has had an unusually low labour turnover rate since its creation in 1999. This cuts the employment costs associated with recruitment, selection and training. Creating an ethical culture within a business can also improve employee motivation. This may be part of a wider policy towards employee empowerment.

A-grade application

Cafédirect under pressure

Cafédirect plc, the UK's largest and longest-running Fairtrade hot drinks company, suffered in 2009 with a halving of profits and a sales decline of 13 per cent. This was partly because so many rivals now claim to be Fairtrade or backed by the Rainforest Alliance.

Financial returns are only part of Cafédirect's impact, however. The company works directly with 39 grower organisations across 13 developing countries, directly benefiting the lives of 1.4 million people. In the same financial year, the amount paid to coffee, tea and cocoa growers over and above the market price totalled nearly £1 million, bringing the total for the past three years to more than £4 million.

Source: adapted from Cafédirect press release and annual accounts.

Disadvantages of ethical behaviour

Inevitably, a number of disadvantages can result from businesses adopting ethical policies.

Reduced profitability

It is likely that any business adopting an ethical policy will face higher costs. It may also be that the company has to turn down the opportunity to invest in projects offering potentially high returns. Exploiting cheap labour in less-developed countries may be immoral but it can be very profitable. Equally, Cafédirect's commitment to purchasing supplies from sustainable Fairtrade sources means that it incurs higher costs than if it purchased raw materials without regard to the environment.

If a business wants to operate ethically, it must accept that principle has to override profit; this may be much easier to do in a family run business than in a public limited company, with its distant, profit-focused shareholders.

85.7 ETHICAL BEHAVIOUR: FUTURE DEVELOPMENTS

It has been suggested that most of the interest in business ethics and its development has been in universities and colleges. However, there is increasing evidence available to suggest that ethical awareness is becoming more firmly rooted in business practice. A number of arguments can be set out to support the view that ethics will be of increasing importance to businesses throughout the world.

The adoption of ethical practices

By 2007 over 80 per cent of the major businesses in the UK had implemented an ethical code of practice. Over 70 per cent of chief executives see ethical practices and behaviour as their responsibility. Although everyone in a business needs to conform to an ethical code of practice, it is only senior managers who have the power to bring about the necessary changes in corporate culture.

The commercial success of high-profile 'ethical' companies

Companies that are seen to have high ethical standards have enjoyed considerable commercial success over recent years. Innocent Drinks was a stunning financial success until a stumble forced it into the arms of Coca-Cola in 2008–09. Similarly, Toyota has benefited financially from its commitment to sustainable methods of production. The company's environmentally friendly hybrid car, the Prius, has been highly successful in global markets.

With its £177 million of operating profit in 2010, Britain's Co-op Bank shows that ethical principles can be highly attractive to customers. If a business consciously adopts 'ethical marketing' as a strategy – that's business, not ethics. But it's important to remember that 'good businesses' such as the Co-op Bank can make good profits. Principles can prove profitable; but the goal should be principle, not profit.

ISSUES FOR ANALYSIS

- Cynics may well argue that many businesses adopt so-called ethical practices simply to project a good public image. Such organisations would produce an ethical code of practice and derive positive publicity from a small number of 'token' ethical actions, while their underlying **business culture** remained unchanged. Such businesses, it is argued, would not alter the way in which the majority of their employees behaved, and decisions would continue to be taken with profits (rather than morals) in mind.
- This may be a realistic scenario for a number of businesses. But it is also a dangerous strategy in a society where increasing numbers of people have access to information. Certainly the media would be looking to publicise any breaches in a business's ethical code of practice. Being revealed as hypocritical is always a difficult position to defend.
- Among the key issues for analysis are the following.
  - What is the underlying intent? If a decision has been made on the basis of profit, it is not truly ethical. An ethical decision is made on the basis of what is morally correct.
  - What are the circumstances? A profit-focused decision that might be considered questionable in good times might be justifiable when times are hard. For example, a firm threatened with closure would be more justified in spending the minimum possible on pollution controls.
  - What are the trade-offs? In many cases the key ethical question is profit versus morality. In others, though, the trade-offs are more complex. Making a coal mine close to 100 per cent safe for the workers would be so expensive as to make the mine uneconomic, thereby costing the miners their jobs.

85.8 BUSINESS ETHICS – AN EVALUATION

Evaluation involves making some sort of informed judgement. Businesses are required to make a judgement about the benefits of ethical behaviour. Their key question may well be whether ethics are profitable or not.

In this unit, convincing arguments have been put together as to why this might be the case. For example, ethical behaviour can give a clear competitive advantage on which marketing activities can be based. However, disadvantages may lurk behind an ethical approach. The policy can be the cause of conflict and may be expected to reduce profits.

Operating an ethical policy gives a USP if none of your competitors has taken the plunge. Being first may result in gaining market share before others catch up. In these circumstances an ethical code may enhance profitability. It can also be an attractive option in a market where businesses and products are virtually indistinguishable. In these circumstances a USP can be most valuable.

Ethical policies may add to profits if additional costs are relatively small. Thus, for a financial institution to adopt an ethical policy may be less costly than for a chemical manufacturer. Clearly companies need to weigh increased costs against the marketing (and revenue) benefits that may result.

Ethical policies are more likely to be profitable if consumers are informed and concerned about ethical issues. It may be that businesses can develop new niche markets as a result of an ethical stance.

Key Terms

Business culture: the culture of an organisation is the (perhaps unwritten) code that affects the attitudes, decision making and management style of its staff.

Environmental responsibility: this involves businesses choosing to adopt processes and procedures that minimise harmful effects on the environment (for example, placing filters on coal-fired power stations to reduce emissions).

Ethical code: document setting out the way a company believes its employees should respond to situations that challenge their integrity or social responsibility.

Pressure groups: groups of people with common interests who act together to further that interest.

Stakeholder interests: stakeholders are groups such as shareholders and consumers who have a direct interest in a business. These interests frequently cause conflict (for example, shareholders may want higher profits while consumers want environmentally friendly products, which are more costly).

Voluntary codes of practice: methods of working recommended by appropriate committees and approved by the government. They have no legal authority (for example, much advertising is controlled by voluntary codes of practice).

WORKBOOK

A REVISION QUESTIONS

(40 marks; 40 minutes)

1 Define the term 'business ethics'. (2)

2 State two factors that may shape the moral behaviour of businesses. (2)

3 Outline one circumstance in which a company may face an ethical dilemma. (3)

4 Explain the difference between a business behaving legally and a business behaving ethically. (4)

5 Why could decisions made upon the basis of a moral code (ethics) conflict with profit? (4)

6 Look at each of the following business actions and decide whether they were motivated by ethical considerations. Briefly explain your reasoning each time.

a) an advertising agency refusing to accept business from cigarette producers (2)

b) a private hospital refusing to accept an ill elderly person whose only income is the state pension (2)

c) a small baker refusing to accept supplies of genetically modified flour (2)

d) a small baker refusing to deliver to a restaurant known locally as a racist employer. (2)

7 Why could a policy of delegation make it more difficult for a business to behave ethically? (5)

8 Give two reasons why a business may introduce an ethical code of practice. (2)

9 Why might a business agree to abide by a **voluntary code of practice**, when the code has no legal authority? (4)

10 Outline the positive effects the adoption of an ethical policy may have on a business's workforce. (6)

B REVISION EXERCISES

B1 STIMULUS QUESTIONS

Saudi Arabia has agreed to buy 72 Eurofighter Typhoon jets from BAE Systems. The deal is worth about £4,400 million but contracts for maintenance and training are expected to take the bill to £20,000 million. In addition to the price paid for the planes, there is also expected to be a lucrative deal for the munitions that go with them.

BAE Systems is Britain's largest exporter of defence equipment and has publicly adopted a more ethical approach to its operations in recent years. BAE Systems said it welcomed 'this important milestone in its strategy to continue to develop Saudi Arabia as a key home market with substantial employment and investment in future in-Kingdom industrial capability'.

The negotiations had been overshadowed by a UK inquiry into allegations that Saudi Arabia took bribes from BAE under a military-plane deal struck between the two nations two decades ago. Britain's Serious Fraud Office last year investigated BAE Systems' £43 billion Al-Yamamah deal in 1985, which provided Hawk and Tornado jets plus other military equipment to Saudi Arabia. However, the investigation was pulled by the British government in December 2006 in a move supported by then Prime Minister Tony Blair amid statements about the UK's national interests.

Questions

(30 marks; 35 minutes)

1 Explain the phrase 'a more ethical approach'. (3)
2 Explain the ethical dilemma that British Aerospace may face in exporting fighter aircraft to Saudi Arabia. (6)
3 British Aerospace presents itself as a very moral company. Analyse the factors that may shape a moral business culture. (9)
4 Some business analysts have observed that the company's ethical policy will make it less profitable. Discuss whether this is likely to be true. (12)

B2 CASE STUDY

Vivien's bank under fire

Vivien's appointment as chief executive was front-page news. She was the first woman to lead one of Britain's 'big four' banks. Her predecessor, Malcolm Stanton, had been fired due to the bank's poor profit performance. The board made it clear to Vivien that a significant profit improvement was needed within 18 months.

Vivien's approach to management was broadly Theory Y. She trusted that people would give their best as long as the goals were clear. The manager of the bank's overseas section was delighted to be told there would no longer be a monthly review of performance; in future, an annual meeting with Vivien would be sufficient. The target of a 40 per cent profit increase was more of a shock, but after discussion Vivien relaxed it to 33 per cent.

At the half-year stage, Vivien was delighted to see that overseas profits were up by more than 30 per cent. Her delegation programme had worked. The first sign that anything was going wrong came from an article in *Private Eye* magazine. Its headline, 'Vivien's bank under fire!', was followed by an article suggesting that the bank was the main financier of the arms trade in war-torn Central America. Within a fortnight the national papers had dredged up more scandal. The bank was accused of involvement with an environmental disaster in Brazil and a corruption case in the Far East.

Interviewed on BBC Radio 4's *Today* programme, Vivien defended herself by assuring the audience that, 'Neither I nor any board member has any knowledge of any of these cases. I have put in hand a thorough inquiry that will look into every aspect of these rumours. This bank has an ethical code that we take very seriously. I am confident that these stories will prove to be just that. Stories.'

Questions

(50 marks; 60 minutes)

1 Analyse the business benefits Vivien would have been expecting to gain from her policy of delegation. (10)
2 Why might her approach to delegation have created a situation in which unethical practices were adopted by the overseas section of the bank? (12)
3 Consider why the bank's ethical code may have been ineffective in this case. (12)
4 Business ethics are strongly influenced by the culture of the workplace.
   a) What is meant by the term 'culture'? (3)
   b) Discuss the approaches Vivien could take to influence the ethical culture of the bank in future. (13)

C ESSAY QUESTIONS

(40 marks each)

1 'A modern, democratically led company with an empowered workforce would be the type of organisation that would be expected to operate an ethical policy.' To what extent do you agree with this statement?
2 Discuss the view that few businesses take truly moral decisions and that most implement ethical policies to gain a competitive advantage.

World's biggest firms cause $2.2 trillion of environmental damage per year

A report commissioned by the United Nations to be published in late 2010 suggests that the world's 3,000 biggest firms cause $2.2 trillion of environmental damage per year. This is equivalent to roughly one-third of their annual profits. The report seeks to quantify the environmental effects of huge multinational corporations, accounting for damage such as carbon emissions, local air pollution, along with the damage caused by pollution and over-use of water.

'Externalities of this scale and nature pose a major risk to the global economy and markets are not fully aware of these risks, nor do they know how to deal with them' said Richard Mattison, leader of the report team for environmental consultants Trucost.

The final report may come up with an even higher figure, since the $2.2 trillion does not include the effects of household and government consumption of these companies' products.

The debate over whether companies should be held fully financially liable for the environmental costs of their operations will be reignited, leading to further debate on how the world of business should get to grips with environmental change. The issue is already hotly debated, while there are a growing number of examples of businesses that have 'folded' due to the disappearance of the natural resources they need to use – notably the loss of many agricultural businesses in California, caused by water shortages.

Figure 86.4 A wind farm

Source: adapted from the *Guardian,* 18 February 2010.

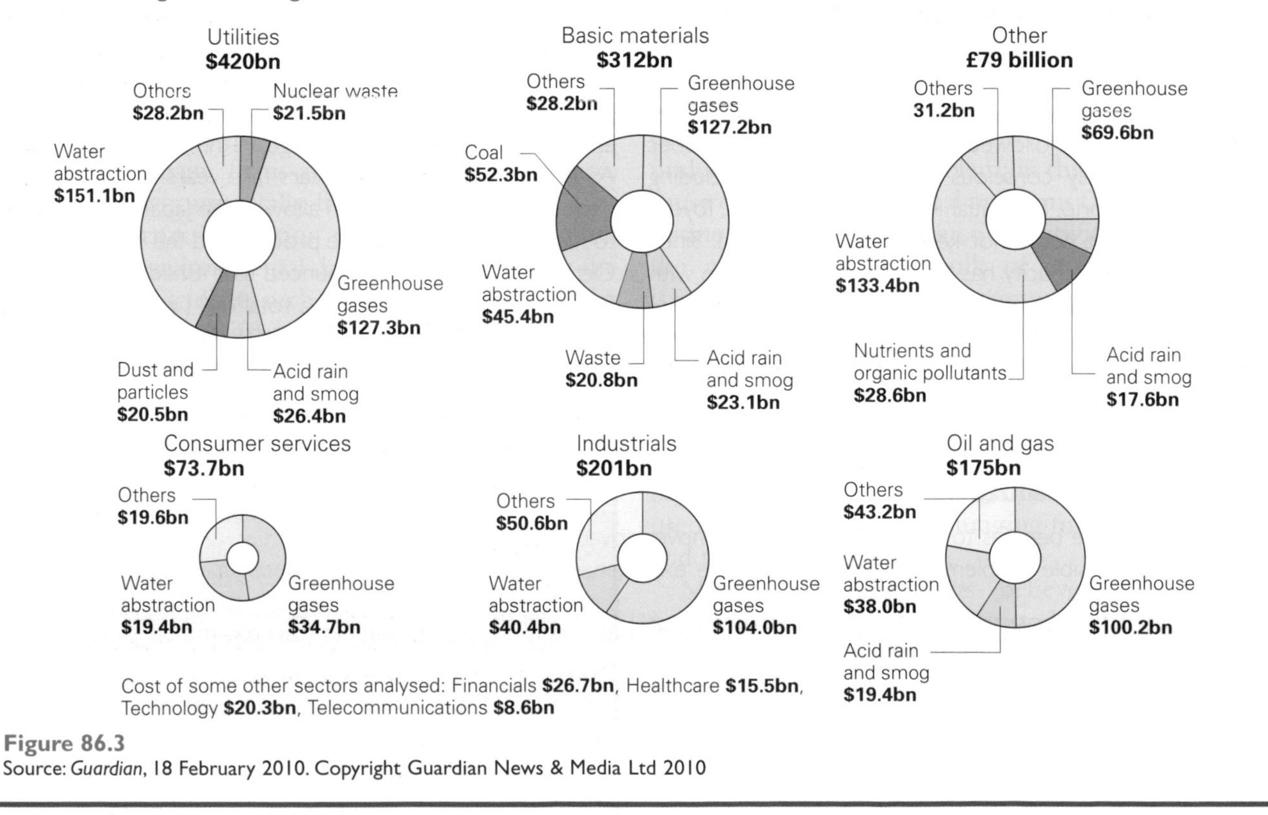

Figure 86.3
Source: *Guardian*, 18 February 2010. Copyright Guardian News & Media Ltd 2010

Questions

(50 marks; 60 minutes)

1 Calculate the average cost to the environment caused by the operation of one of the 300 largest firms. (3)
2 Sectors such as power companies and aluminium producers, along with food and drink manufacturers are said to be the main culprits. Analyse why these companies have such a significant environmental impact. (7)
3 Some argue that businesses should be forced to pay for the full environmental impact of their operating activities, including the environmental damage caused by consumer use after the business has sold the product. To what extent do you agree with this argument? (40)

Business and the technological environment

UNIT 87

The technological environment involves developments both in terms of what is being produced and how it is being made.

87.1 INTRODUCTION

Technology is changing at an extremely fast rate. New products and new processes are being developed all the time. In markets such as computers and mobile phones hundreds of new products are being launched every month. The minute you buy the latest Blu-ray player, MP3, phone or digital camera you know it is about to be outdated. Firms face similar problems. The welding robot bought last month is already less efficient than the model announced for next month, probably at a lower price. Whatever you buy, whatever technology you use, the chances are someone somewhere is working on an improved version.

This rate of change is getting ever faster. Product development times are getting quicker and, consequently, more products are getting to the market in less time. The result is that the typical product life cycle is getting shorter. Naturally this creates serious problems for firms. With more and more products being developed, the chances of any one product succeeding are reduced. For many years, research showed that only one in five new products succeeds in the marketplace. Today the figure is one in seven; in other words, six out of seven fail. Even if a new product succeeds, its life cycle is likely to be relatively short. Given the ever-higher quality demanded by customers, firms are having to spend more on developing products but have less time to recoup their investment.

One of the main reasons for the rapid growth of technology is actually technology itself. The development of **computer-aided design (CAD)** and **computer-aided manufacture (CAM)** has enabled even faster development of new products and processes. Technology feeds off itself and generates even more ideas and innovations. This rapid rate of change creates both threats and opportunities for firms. The threats are clear; firms that do not adopt competitive technology will struggle to:

- keep their unit costs down ...
- ... or provide goods or services of sufficient quality relative to their competitors.

Technology can certainly make life a great deal easier for firms. Just think of how slow it would be to work out all of a large company's accounts by hand instead of using a computer spreadsheet. If one company avoids the latest technology while its rivals adopt it, it is likely to suffer real problems with competitiveness. The rivals may be able to offer lower prices or substantially better or faster service standards.

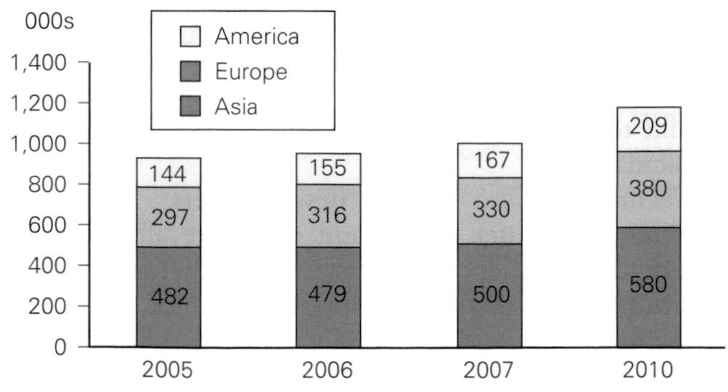

Figure 87.1 The growth in industrial robots

A-grade application

General Motors to take on Toyota

After a slow start, following the introduction of the Toyota Prius to the US market in 2000 the company has been selling over 100,000 of the vehicles a year, taking 50 per cent of the hybrid market. It has taken ten years for General Motors to react to this new technology. They have now launched the Chevy Volt with an eight-year, 100,000-mile warranty on the battery. GM plans to build 10,000 Volts this year and 30,000 in 2011. They claim that their technology is 'far ahead' of the competition. Experts, however, warn that the technology is still very new and until customers start using the car it is difficult to judge how readily the technology will be accepted. Unfortunately for the manufacturers, they need sales to increase production volumes so that they can bring the price of the car down and so attract more buyers.

Source: newspaper reports, 2010

Impact of competitive and market structure

UNIT 88

Competitiveness measures a firm's ability to compete, that is, compares its consumer offer to the offers made by its rivals.

88.1 INTRO: WHAT IS A COMPETITIVE MARKET?

In the past, markets were physical places where buyers and sellers met in person to exchange goods. Street markets are still like that. In modern online markets, such as e-Bay, buyers and sellers are unlikely to meet.

Some markets are more competitive than others. In general, a competitive market could be described as one where there is intense rivalry between producers of a similar good or service. The number of firms operating within a market influences the intensity of competition; the more firms there are, the greater the level of competition. However, the respective size of the firms operating in the market should also be taken into account. A market consisting of 50 firms may not be particularly competitive, if one of the firms holds a 60 per cent market share and the 40 per cent is shared between the other 49. Similarly, a market composed of just four firms could be quite competitive if they are of a similar size.

Consumers enjoy competitive markets. However, the reverse is true for the firms themselves. In competitive markets, prices and profit margins tend to be squeezed. As a result, firms operating in competitive markets try hard to minimise competition, perhaps by creating a unique selling point (**USP**) or using **predatory pricing**.

It could be argued that marketing is vital no matter what the level of competition is. Firms that fail to produce goods and services that satisfy the needs of their target consumers will find it hard to succeed in the long term. Ultimately, consumers will not waste their hard-earned cash on products that fail to meet their needs.

88.2 THE DEGREE OF COMPETITION WITHIN A MARKET

One dominant business

Some markets are dominated by one large business. Economists use the word 'monopoly' to describe a market where there is a single supplier, and therefore no competition. In practice, pure textbook monopolies rarely exist; even Microsoft does not have a 100 per cent share of the office software market (though it does have a 90 per cent share). The UK government's definition of a monopoly is somewhat looser. According to the Competition Commission, a monopoly is a firm that has a market share of 25 per cent and above.

Monopolies are bad for consumers. They restrict choice, and tend to drive prices upwards. For that reason most governments regulate against monopolies and near monopolies that exploit consumers by abusing their dominant market position.

Deciding whether a firm has, or has not, a monopoly is far from being a straightforward task. First of all the market itself has to be accurately defined. For example, Camelot has been granted a monopoly to run the National Lottery. However, it could be argued that Camelot does not have a dominant market position because there are other forms of gambling, such as horse racing and the football pools available to consumers in the UK. Secondly, national market share figures should not be used in isolation, because some firms enjoy local monopolies. A good example of a dominant local market position was the airport operator BAA. The company used to own three out four of London's airports. Acting on complaints made by airlines, the Competition Commission forced BAA to sell off Gatwick airport in December 2009. The commission hopes that additional competition will reduce the fees charged by airports to airlines for use of their facilities, leading to lower fares for passengers.

Firms implement their marketing strategy through the marketing mix. In markets dominated by a single large business firms do not need to spend heavily on promotion because consumers are, to a degree, captive. Prices can be pushed upwards and the product element of the marketing mix is focused on creating innovations that make it harder for new entrants to break into the market. Apple spends millions of dollars on research and development in order to produce cutting-edge products such as the iPad. Apple's ten-year-old iPod is still the market leader in MP3s with a 60+ per cent share of the massive U.S. market. To ensure that Apple maintains its dominant market position new product launches are patented to prevent me-too imitations from being launched by the competition.

Competition among a few giants

The UK supermarket industry is a good example of a market that is dominated by a handful of very large companies. Economists call markets like this **oligopolistic**. The rivalry that exists within such markets can be very intense. Firms know that any gains in market share will be at the expense of their rivals. The actions taken by one firm affect the profits made by the other firms that compete within the same market.

In markets made up of a few giants firms tend to focus on **non-price competition** when designing the marketing mix. Firms in these markets are reluctant to compete by cutting price. They fear that the other firms in the industry will respond by cutting their prices too, creating a costly price war where no firm wins.

The fiercely competitive market

Fiercely competitive markets tend to be fragmented; made up of hundreds of relatively small firms who each compete actively against each other. In some of these markets, competition is amplified by the fact that firms sell near-identical products called commodities; these are products such as flour, sugar or blank DVDs that are hard to differentiate. Rivalry in commodity markets tends to be intense. In such markets firms have to manage their production costs very carefully because the retail price is the most important factor in determining whether the firm's product sells or not. If a firm cannot cut its costs it will not be able to cut its prices without cutting into profit margins. Without price cuts market share is likely to be lost.

In fiercely competitive markets firms will try, where possible, to create product differentiation. For example, the restaurant market in Croydon, Surrey, is extremely competitive. There are over 70 outlets within a two-mile radius of the town centre. To survive without having to compete solely on price, firms in markets like this must find new innovations regularly because points of differentiation are quickly copied.

A-grade application

Market saturation

The pattern of growth shown in Table 88.1 gives an idea of how competition can transform the way businesses operate. In 1970 there would only have been one Indian restaurant in any town or district. By 1990 there would often be two or three. Therefore, to be successful, there had to either be competition on price, or a move to more differentiation of menu and cooking style. Today, in a saturated market, a new Indian restaurant will have to offer something very special to get established.

Table 88.1 Indian restaurants in the UK

Year	No. of restaurants	Market growth rate (in %)
1960	500	
1970	1,200	140
1980	3,000	150
1990	5,100	70
2000	7,940	56
2004	8,750	10
2009	8,750	0

88.3 CHANGES IN COMPETITIVE STRUCTURE

New competitors

The number of firms operating within a market can change over time. If new competitors enter, a market will become more competitive. New entrants are usually attracted into a new market by the high profits or the rapid growth achieved by the existing firms. After the Europe-wide success of airlines such as easyJet and Ryanair, a huge number of imitators came into the airline business, including Air Berlin, Wizz and Spanair. Although most of these have struggled to be profitable, they have unquestionably benefited the traveller, as they have kept prices fairly low.

In markets that are suffering from low or negative profitability firms tend to exit, leaving the market less competitive than it was. A good example is the UK mortgage market. In 2009 many UK lenders reduced the number of home loans available because of falling profitability caused by crashing property prices and an increase in the number of homes being repossessed. As the number of banks operating in the market declined, prices within the market, that is, mortgage interest rates, went up, reflecting a market that had become less competitive.

Cost synergies

Cost savings are often used as a primary argument for corporate integration. It is suggested that **economies of scale** will arise from operating on a larger scale. If two businesses merge, output will increase. As a result, they are more likely to benefit from economies of scale, such as cheaper bulk purchasing of supplies. Synergies are the benefits from two things coming together. In this context, it is that the two firms together will have lower costs (and higher profits) than the two firms separately. In effect, **synergy** means that 2 + 2 = 5.

Diversification

This means entering different markets in order to reduce dependence upon current products and customers. Diversification is a way of reducing the risk faced by a company. Selling a range of different products to different groups of consumers will mean that, if any one product fails, sales of the other products should keep the business healthy. The simplest way to diversify is to merge with or take over another company. This saves time and money spent developing new products for markets in which the firm may have no expertise.

Market power

When two competitors in the same market merge, the combined business will have an increased level of power in the market. It may be possible that this increased power can be used to reduce the overall competitiveness within the market. If prices can be increased a little, then margins will increase and the market will become more profitable.

Table 89.1 Reasons for takeovers, and some examples

Reasons for takeovers	Examples
Growth	• Royal Bank of Scotland beats Barclays to buy ABN Amro (Dutch) bank for £49 billion in October 2007 • Kraft's takeover of Cadbury in 2010
Cost synergies	• The British Airways merger with Iberia is estimated (by the firm itself) to generate some £350 million in cost savings over five years. • Co-op taking over Somerfield (it bid £1.7 billion in 2008)
Diversification	• Tesco buying Dobbies Garden Centres in 2007 • Chip manufacturer Intel's 2010 purchase of computer security software maker McAfee
Market power	• Indian car producer Tata (producers of the world's cheapest new car) buys Jaguar and Land Rover in 2008 • HMV's purchase of 32 Zavvi stores boosted its UK market share in 2009

89.3 TYPES OF BUSINESS INTEGRATION

There are four main types of merger or takeover (see Figure 89.2), as discussed below.

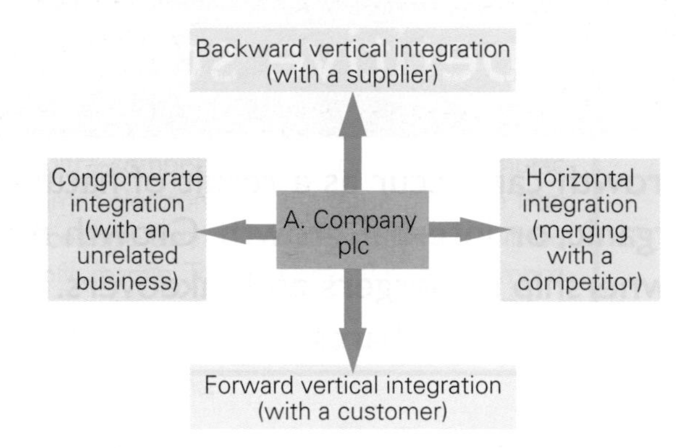

Figure 89.2 Vertical and horizontal integration

Vertical integration

Vertical integration occurs when one firm takes over or merges with another at a different stage in the production process, but within the same industry.

Backward vertical integration occurs when a firm buys out a supplier. In March 2008 Boeing announced the purchase of a key supplier to its 787 aeroplane. Boeing said it hopes this will enable it to overcome production problems that have delayed the delivery of the plane to British Airways and Virgin. The key benefit of a backward vertical takeover is security of supply.

Forward vertical integration means buying out a customer, such as the purchase of retailer Body Shop by cosmetics producer L'Oréal. This shows the major benefit of forward vertical integration, which is that of guaranteed outlets for your products.

The huge reward came in early 2008. In an exact parallel of the earlier video wars, Sony had pitched its Blu-ray HD disk against Toshiba (and Microsoft's) preferred HD DVD. Using its power in Hollywood, Sony persuaded key businesses such as Disney to go for the Blu-ray format. In future, high-definition DVD will mean buying Blu-ray from Sony.

A-grade application

Vertically integrated entertainment

When video recorders were first available, Sony was horrified to find that its high-quality Betamax player was swept aside by the inferior VHS system. Toshiba, the originator of the VHS, had persuaded Hollywood film studios to use the VHS system for the film rental market. Sony decided: never again. The Japanese company chose (in the face of great hostility from America) to buy its way into the Hollywood studios. It bought Columbia Pictures and several other studios. At first it lost billions of dollars, as Sony struggled to manage a Hollywood studio effectively.

Table 89.2 The advantages and disadvantages of backward vertical integration and forward vertical integration

	Backward vertical integration	Forward vertical integration
Advantages to the company	• Closer links with suppliers aid new product development and give more control over the quality and timing of supplies • Absorbing the suppliers' profit margins may cut supply costs	• Control of competition in own retail outlets; prominent display of own brands • Firm put in direct contact with end users/ consumers
Disadvantages to the company	• Supplier division may become complacent if there is no need to compete for customers • Costs might rise, therefore, and delivery and quality become slack	• Consumers may resent the dominance of one firm's products in retail outlets, causing sales to decline • Worries about image may obstruct the outlet, e.g. Levi stores rarely offer discounted prices
Advantages to the workforce	• Secure customer for the suppliers may increase job security • Larger scale of the combined organisation may lead to enhanced benefits such as pension or career opportunities	• Increased control over the market may increase job security • Designers can now influence not only how the products look, but also how they are displayed
Disadvantages to the workforce	• Becoming part of a large firm may affect the sense of team morale built up at the supplier • Job losses may result from attempts to cut out duplication of support roles such as in personnel and accounting	• Staff in retail outlets may find themselves deskilled. Owner may dictate exactly what products to stock and how to display them. This would be demotivating
Advantages to the consumer	• Better coordination between company and supplier may lead to more innovative new product ideas • Ownership of the whole supply process may make the business more conscious of product and service quality	• With luxury products, customer like to see perfect displays and be served by expert staff, e.g. at perfume counters in department stores • Prices may fall if a large retail margin is absorbed by the supplier
Disadvantages to the consumer	• The firm's control over one supplier may in fact reduce the variety of goods available • Supplier complacency may lead to rising costs, passed on to customer as higher prices	• Increased power within the market could lead to price rises • If the outlet only supplies the parent company's products, consumer choice will be hit, as in brewery owned clubs or pubs

Table 89.2 explains the major advantages and disadvantages of backward and forward vertical integration for three important stakeholders: the company (and its shareholders), the workforce and the customers.

Horizontal integration

Horizontal integration occurs when one firm buys out another in the same industry at the same stage of the supply chain; for example, the 2008 purchase of Somerfield by the Co-op. In effect, this means buying a competitor. In the UK, if the market share of the combined companies is greater than 25 per cent, the Competition Commission is likely to investigate before the integration will be allowed.

Of the four types of takeover, the most common by far is horizontal integration with a competitor. Typical examples include:

- Adidas buying Reebok
- China's state oil company CNPC buying a major stake in PetroKazakhstan – the company that controls Kazakhstan's huge oil reserves
- US convenience store leader 7 Eleven's $2 billion bid for main rival Casey's.

For the purchaser, there are three major attractions:

1 huge scope for cost cutting by eliminating duplication of salesforce, distribution and marketing overheads, and by improved capacity utilisation
2 opportunities for major economies of scale
3 a reduction in competition should enable prices to be pushed up.

Of course, no purchaser states publicly that the plan is to push prices up. But if you owned four consecutive motorway service stations covering over 190 km of driving, would you not be tempted to charge a bit more?

As horizontal mergers have particular implications for competition, they are likely to be looked at by the Office of Fair Trading. If there is believed to be a threat to competition, the Competition Commission will be asked to investigate. The Competition Commission has the power to recommend that the Office of Fair Trading refuse to allow the integration, or recommend changes before it can go through. For example, if Unilever (which produces Walls ice cream and much else) made a bid for Mars, the Competition Commission would probably let the takeover through, on the condition that the Mars ice cream business was sold off.

Conglomerate integration

Conglomerate integration occurs when one firm buys out another with no clear connection to its own line of business. An example was the purchase by the household goods giant Procter & Gamble of the Gillette shaving products business. Conglomerate integration is likely to be prompted by the desire to diversify or to achieve rapid growth. It may also be for purely financial motives such as asset stripping (breaking the business up and selling off all its key assets).

Although the achievement of successful diversification helps to spread risk, research shows that conglomerate mergers are the ones least likely to succeed. This is largely because the managers of the purchasing company have, by definition, little knowledge of the marketplace of the company that has been bought.

Retrenchment and demergers

Sometimes firms will decide that they have grown too large to be controlled effectively. This is likely to be the case when diseconomies of scale are causing huge reductions in efficiency. In such cases, directors may pursue a policy of **retrenchment:** that is, deliberately shrinking in size. Reducing overall capacity in order to boost capacity utilisation seems logical. However, in reality retrenchment brings its own problems. Redundancies will lead to an initial hunk of cash outflows, while other effects may linger. Staff who have seen colleagues laid off may well retain a fear for their own jobs; for example, 'will we be laid off in the next round of redundancies?' Maintaining staff morale during and after retrenchment is a great management challenge; retrenchment poses a huge change management challenge.

Meanwhile, there has been growing scepticism about the benefits of mergers and takeovers. Recent research has shown that the majority of takeovers are unsuccessful, as measured by criteria such as profits, market share or the share price. This has resulted in a growing trend in the past few years towards the **demerger**. This occurs when a company is split into two or more parts, either by selling off separate divisions or by floating them separately on the stock exchange. Demergers are often the result of unsuccessful takeovers. Once a firm has seen that the economies of scale it expected are not happening, it will seek to sell off the business it originally bought.

Another common situation leading to demergers is the desire of a company to reduce interest payments in times of economic downturn. Since many takeovers are financed heavily by borrowed capital, selling off recently acquired businesses will generate cash to pay back those loans.

Some firms, however, may simply decide to concentrate on core activities due to a change in their overall strategy. This might be caused by a change in economic circumstances or just because a new chief executive has been appointed. Having identified the core activities they will sell off others, even if they are profitable.

A-grade application

In 1998, Mercedes of Germany bought the US Chrysler car business for $38 billion. What followed was one of the most disastrous takeovers of all time. Not only did Chrysler lose billions of dollers in operating losses, but the German leadership's focus on America led to a downturn at Mercedes. Engineering and quality standards dropped alarmingly in 2003–05, and Mercedes' reputation for quality has only just recovered. In 2007, Mercedes finally accepted its failure and sold Chrysler for $7 billion. By early 2008 the demerger was completed. Some analysts have suggested that the total losses to Mercedes from its ten-year US nightmare may be as high as $100 billion. The 'spun-off' Chrysler was declared bankrupt on 30 April 2009 and later that year, the remnants of the business were bought by Fiat. By 2010, Chrysler sales in the US were up for the first time in five years – perhaps the Italians have handled this takeover better than the Germans?

89.4 PRIVATE EQUITY AND GEARING

Takeovers have always taken place between trading companies; for example, BP buying the US oil giant Amoco. However, a major new force has emerged in takeovers. Half the money spent on takeovers in the UK comes from 'private equity', not from 'ordinary' companies. In 2005 private equity had snapped up Travelex, the Tussauds Group and Kwik-Fit. By 2007 private equity deals for firms as huge as Boots were going through (for £11 billion).

Private equity is a management group backed by sufficient bank finance to make a takeover, which is usually of a public limited company. The financing of these takeovers is typically hugely reliant upon bank loans. The gearing can be as high as 90 per cent. If the business is doing well (perhaps because the economy is in an upturn), the high gearing can boost the profits made by the investors. Unfortunately, if there is an economic downturn, trading losses will quickly eat away the small shareholders' funds within the business, pushing it into liquidation.

Private equity is the latest term for what were once known as leveraged buy-outs (LBOs) in America and **management buy-outs (MBOs)** in Britain. All share a common characteristic: extremely high gearing. This creates a situation of very questionable business ethics

– broadly 'heads I win, tails you lose'. If all goes well, the few private equity shareholders can make fabulous profits. If it goes wrong they can make staff redundant to cut costs and, if things continue to go wrong, pay themselves off before closing the business down. A 2008 report presented to the Davos forum of world leaders showed that private equity businesses cut 7 per cent of staff within two years and have a significantly higher failure rate than ordinary businesses.

Debenhams store group has been a classic example of private equity. Taken private in 2004, the stores were refloated on the stock market in 2006, creating enormous personal profits for the key directors. Since the 2006 flotation, the stores have lost market share and the shares have lost two-thirds of their value.

A serious criticism of a business such as Boots 'going private' is that it no longer has to provide the accounting information demanded from a public company. The people who felt like stakeholders in the old public company (staff, customers and, of course, shareholders) no longer have access to the accounts. Nor can they question the directors personally, as you can at a plc's **annual general meeting**.

89.5 TAKEOVER DECISIONS AND ANSOFF'S MATRIX

A useful way to analyse the risks and rewards from a takeover is to apply Ansoff's matrix (see Unit 64). This considers the extent to which a business is keeping close to its core business (and knowledge/experience) or whether it is moving into new territory. For example, in February 2007 the US retail giant Walmart paid $1 billion to buy a Chinese business with 101 hypermarkets in China. Does Walmart know enough about Chinese grocery shopping to make a success of this takeover? Only time will tell. On Ansoff's matrix, this radical move into a new market would be represented as a major, high-risk move. If Walmart bought a store chain in Canada (or Britain, where it owns Asda), it would be much safer.

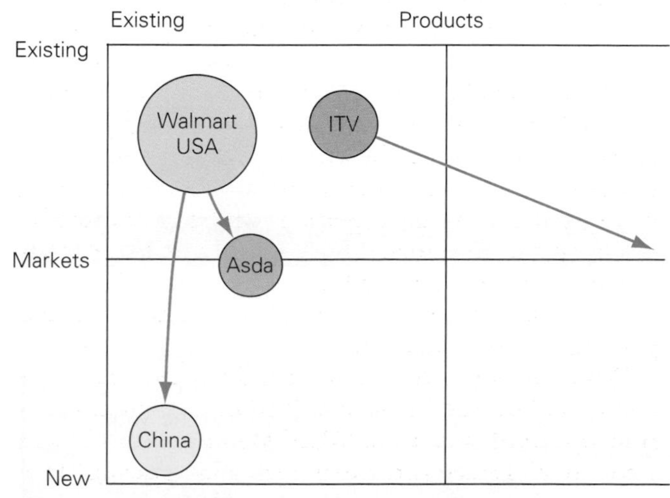

Figure 89.3 Ansoff's matrix applied to takeovers

The same type of analysis could work for considering the risks involved in ITV's 2006 purchase of the social network (for oldies) site, Friends Reunited. What did a television channel understand about running a website? Not a lot, which may explain why this takeover was a flop. It could be debated whether this takeover was an example of product development or diversification. Either way it pushed ITV's management too far away from its area of expertise. It is a tough job running any business; it is often only arrogance that leads business leaders to believe they can run two different businesses at the same time.

ISSUES FOR ANALYSIS

- The key theme for analysis when considering any question on mergers and takeovers is the identification of advantages and disadvantages. These are outlined briefly above, for each type of transaction. It is important to consider which advantages and disadvantages are likely to be relevant in the particular situation being considered. For example, a sugar producer that buys a soft drink manufacturer will not have any significant degree of control over the way its products are sold by retailers. In this case, one of the most significant advantages of forward integration disappears.
- Never forget that a merger or takeover will bring disadvantages as well as advantages. Research in America and Britain has shown consistently that the majority of takeovers fail to improve business performance. This is largely because managers anticipate the economies of scale from integration. However, they overlook the diseconomies from problems such as communication and coordination.
- Another important analytical theme is the differing effects upon different stakeholder groups. Many questions will offer marks for analysing the effects on consumers, or the workforce, rather than simply focusing on the effects on the firm as a whole.

89.6 CHANGES IN OWNERSHIP AND COMPETITIVE STRUCTURE – AN EVALUATION

A key judgement that is required is to see through the public relations 'hype' that surrounds takeover bids. Company leader A makes a bid for Company B, claiming that 'synergies will lead to better service and lower prices to our customers'. Really? Or will it mean factory closures, the elimination of small niche brands and – later – higher prices for all? Similarly, the leader may claim that the reason for a takeover is very businesslike, such as 'creating a world-leading company'. Yet the high failure rate of takeovers must imply that many claimed business benefits are a 'fig leaf'. The real reason for many takeovers is arrogance, and perhaps greed, on the part of the executives concerned.

An explanation for the problems firms may encounter after a merger or takeover is resistance to change. This will be especially true if the business cultures are widely different at the two companies. One may be go-getting and entrepreneurial; the other may be cautious and bureaucratic. Judgement is again required to consider whether a takeover is especially vulnerable to a clash of culture when the firms come together.

The other key issue raised in this unit is that of diversification. Traditionally, diversification was perceived as a good thing. Theorists such as Ansoff, Tom Peters and Bob Waterman have raised serious doubts. The management of the original company may know little about the industry within which the new business operates. This means that those making major strategic decisions may be doing so from a position of ignorance. The advice in recent years has been to 'stick to the knitting' – in other words, concentrate on doing what you do best.

Figure 89.4 Stick to the knitting

Key Terms

Annual general meeting: the once-yearly meeting at which shareholders have the opportunity to question the chairperson and to vote new directors to the board.

Demerger: this occurs when a firm is split into two or more different companies.

Economies of scale: the factors that cause average costs to be lower in large-scale operations than small ones.

Management buy-out (MBO): a specialised form of takeover where the managers of a business buy out the shareholders, thereby buying ownership and control of the firm.

Organic: growth from within the business (for example, getting better sales from existing brands, or launching new ones).

Retrenchment: a deliberate policy of cutbacks, perhaps to lower a firm's break-even point.

Synergy: this occurs when the whole is greater than the sum of the parts (2 + 2 = 5). It is often the reason given for mergers or takeovers occurring.

WORKBOOK

A REVISION QUESTIONS

(30 marks; 30 minutes)

1 What is horizontal integration? (2)
2 For what reasons might a manufacturer take over one of its suppliers? (4)
3 Outline two reasons for each why Nokia might like to make a takeover of:
   a) Motorola (4)
   b) Vodafone. (4)
4 Why may a firm decide to carry out a demerger? (3)
5 Why may takeovers be riskier when financed by 'private equity'? (3)
6 Why may diversification be a bad idea for a growing firm? (3)
7 Explain the meaning of the word 'synergy'. (3)
8 Explain why businesses should consider Ansoff's matrix before making a takeover bid. (4)

B REVISION EXERCISES

B1 DATA RESPONSE

Body Shop: because you're worth it

2006 saw the purchase of the Body Shop by French cosmetics giant L'Oréal. The deal was controversial because Body Shop shareholders and customers were concerned that L'Oréal would fail to maintain Body Shop's unique culture of socially responsible business. However, Body Shop was eventually sold for around £500 million, enabling L'Oréal to add another brand to its portfolio of products including Ambre Solaire, Lancôme, Elvive, Studio Line and Plenitude. L'Oréal's plan was to run Body Shop as a self-contained business, in an attempt to retain the firm's image, its major selling point among a loyal band of customers that undoubtedly makes up a significant niche within the beauty market.

Questions

(35 marks; 40 minutes)

1 Explain the possible motives behind L'Oréal's purchase of Body Shop. (6)
2 Analyse the possible difficulties that L'Oréal may encounter within Body Shop following the takeover. (8)
3 Explain why Body Shop will add to L'Oréal's product portfolio, without cannibalising existing brands. (6)
4 To what extent is L'Oréal's plan to run Body Shop as a separate business a sensible choice? (15)

B2 DATA RESPONSE

The 30%/70% rule

On 15 May 2007, a £9 billion merger was concluded between the publisher Thomson and the news service Reuters. During this period of merger-mania, most corporate bosses hardly bothered to justify the strategic logic behind a bid. Even though research shows that most mergers fail, rising share prices pointed to the love that 2007 stock market investors had for takeovers.

The Thomson–Reuters merger took place in a week when Daimler (Mercedes) sold off the American business Chrysler after suffering losses of more than £20 billion since buying Chrysler in 1998. If Mercedes cannot run a car company, what hope is there for any takeover bidder?

After announcing the merger, senior executives from Reuters and Thomson were interviewed by the *Financial Times*. They acknowledged that academics estimate that 70 per cent of mergers fail, but chief executive Tom Glocer argued that Thomson Reuters should be 'firmly in the 30 per cent camp'. He continued: 'It's important to look at why they fail. A lot comes down to culture. This has been an unusually warm and close transaction.'

The senior executives seem to assume that, because they can work together, all the staff will get along with each other. This remains to be seen. Tom Glocer is right to identify culture as a critical issue, but naive to think it is easy to manage.

When talking about the merger in practice, Glocer outlined the £250 million of cost-saving 'synergies' they hoped to benefit from. He emphasised, though, that staff should not be concerned. Another executive pointed out that: 'The hardest integrations are when you are consolidating. We're not consolidating, we're growing.' (Consolidating means the same as rationalising; that is, usually it amounts to cutbacks in jobs and in the variety of product ranges.)

The big hope is that the merger will boost revenues rather than cut costs. The new chairman said that: 'The strategic fit is about as compelling as can be. Reuters is strong in Europe and Asia and Thomson in North America'.

In 1998 the claims made about Daimler and Chrysler were equally optimistic. The strategy was Mercedes in Europe and Asia, Chrysler in the USA. The failure of that 'merger' was all down to problems in management, notably the inability to create a new common culture. In five years or so it will be clear whether Tom Glocer was right to put Thomson–Reuters 'firmly in the 30 per cent camp'.

Questions

(30 marks; 35 minutes)

1 Explain the meaning of the following terms:
 a) synergies (3)
 b) strategic fit. (3)
2 Discuss whether Tom Glocer is wise to assume that this merger should be 'firmly in the 30 per cent camp'. (12)
3 Examine why it can be hard to motivate middle managers within a newly merged business such as Thomson–Reuters. (12)

B3 CASE STUDY

Intel secures the future

August 2010 saw market leading computer chip manufacturer Intel complete a $7.68 billion takeover of McAfee – a firm that designs and manufactures technology security products, notably anti-virus software. The deal marks a move away from Intel's specialisation in purely making the chips that go into PCs and mobile phones. However, the subtlety of the deal is that it will allow Intel access to the expertise of McAfee's workforce. Security expertise will allow Intel to build security features into their microprocessors used in laptops and mobiles. Industry analysts suggest that as computing becomes increasingly mobile, security for devices such as mobile phones must be stepped up to avoid the myriad internet security problems from hacked bank accounts to computer viruses.

Intel's move also makes sense as it seeks to strengthen a relatively weak position in the mobile market, its core areas of success being desktop and laptop chips.

Details about Intel and McAfee are given in Table 89.3.

Table 89.3 Intel and McAfee

	Intel	McAfee
Founded	1968	1987
2009 Revenue	$35bn	$2bn
2009 Operating profit	$4.4bn	$173m
Number of employees	80,400	6,100

Questions

(50 marks; 60 minutes)

1. Analyse Intel's purchase of McAfee using Ansoff's matrix. (10)
2. Discuss the possible problems that Intel may face in gaining the greatest benefit from their purchase of McAfee. (20)
3. To what extent does the case illustrate the benefits of being a market leader when trying to secure your long-term future? (20)

C ESSAY QUESTIONS

(40 marks each)

1. Discuss the people management problems that may arise within a firm that has been taken over.
2. 'The high level of takeover activity in the UK leads to short-termism'. Explain why this is so and discuss the implications for UK firms.
3. Synergy is often quoted as the reason for mergers and takeovers.
   a) What is synergy?
   b) To what extent is synergy a myth?

UNIT 90 China versus India

90.1 CHINA?

In 2001, investment banks coined the phrase BRICs to sum up the huge growth potential of Brazil, Russia, India and China. In fact the growth in China and India is far, far more significant than in the other two countries. In Brazil a growth rate of 4.5 per cent is applauded; China sees a growth rate of 10 per cent as a disappointment.

In 1997 the streets of every Chinese city were dominated by bicycles. The private car was still quite rare. Fewer than four households in 1,000 owned a car. In 2009 China overtook America to become the world's biggest car market; in just that year, the Chinese car market grew by 40 per cent and in 2010, sales of Rolls-Royce cars rose by 140 per cent. Volkswagen sells more cars in China than in Germany. The boom in China is incredible.

For more than 15 years the Chinese economy has grown at around 10 per cent a year. That is faster than any other major economy in history. Even in Britain's Industrial Revolution the economy only grew at around 2 to 2.5 per cent a year. And, of course, China is not only remarkable for its rate of growth, but also its population size. This is a country with nearly one-quarter of the world's population. If 1,350 million people have economic wealth, even the United States will have to step back. China is set to become the world's superpower. Or is it . . .?

Figure 90.1 Booming car ownership in China

90.2 OR INDIA?

Some argue that India is in an even more powerful position. Although far behind China, its accelerating growth and population may make it the dark horse that eventually wins the prize. India has long been one of the world's poorest countries, yet one of the most populous. At 1,200 million, its position as the world's second-most populated country puts it way ahead of America (in third place with 'only' 310 million).

In the last five years, the growth rate in India has risen to 8 to 9 per cent – a huge increase on the 2 to 3 per cent of ten years ago. Furthermore, its population has two features that China cannot match: it is rising and it is very young. Over the next 20 years there will be far more keen 20-year-olds entering the Indian job market than in China. This is because China has made huge efforts over the past 25 years to curb population growth by pressing its people to have only one child per family. Due to this policy, only 25 per cent of the Chinese population is 18 or under. In India the figure is 37 per cent. Details of the population figures for China and India are given in Table 90.1.

Table 90.1 China and India: population figures

	CHINA	INDIA
Population growth per year (%)	0.6	1.4
Population level 2010 (billion)	1.35	1.20
Population level 2026 (est.) (billion)	1.46	1.45
Population 18 and under (2009) (million)	342	447
Population aged 20 to 30 in 2026 (est.) (million)	190	240

90.3 WHICH HAS BEEN GROWING FASTER?

Here the answer is clear. As shown in Figure 90.2, since 1991 the Chinese economy has completely outstripped that of India and managed to overtake first Britain, then Germany and then Japan. This has largely been due to massive increases in 'fixed capital formation'. In the early 1990s the Chinese government started investing heavily in the economy, and started to encourage western companies to invest as well.

Typically, the western companies invested by building factories (taking advantage of extremely low-cost

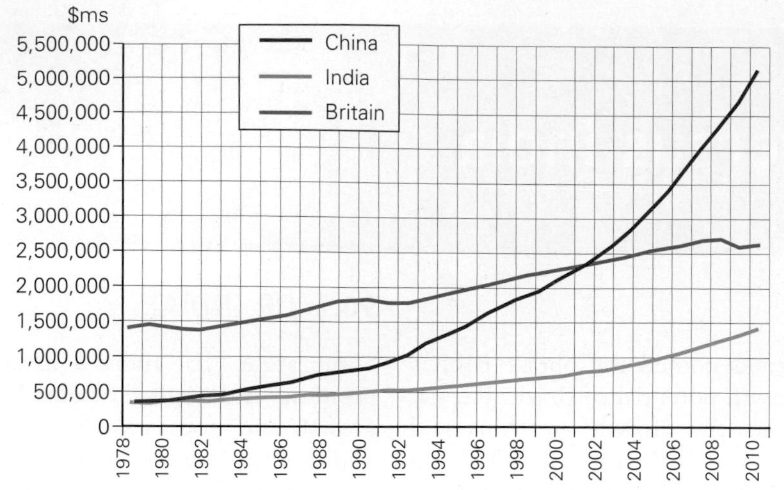

Figure 90.2 Total GDP for China, India and Britain (in US dollars)

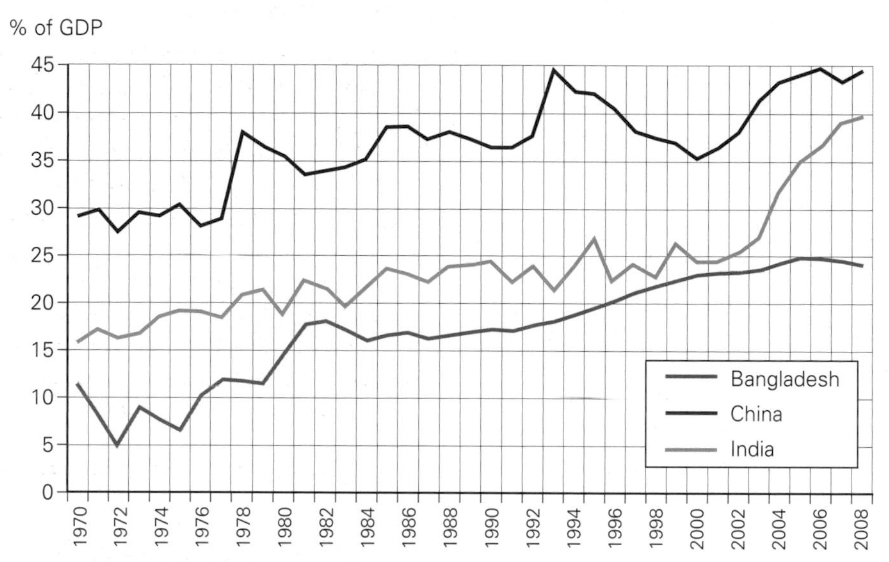

Figure 90.3 Capital formation in China, India and Bangladesh from 1970 to 2008
Source: The World Bank: gross capital formation (% of GDP) dataset: source – WDI and GDF 2010

labour), while the government started building dams (for water and electricity), roads and other forms of **infrastructure**. Today that government investment is going into housing, railways, schools and hospitals. China is gearing up for continuing success. Figure 90.3 shows that China is now spending more than 40 per cent of its annual output on investing in its future (fixed capital formation). For many years India's investment spending was little higher, relatively, than in struggling Bangladesh. But in recent years India has pushed its capital formation rate up towards the level achieved in China; this should help India achieve sustained growth.

China's long-term success has largely been built on export growth. In 2009, China's exports were seven times higher by value than India's. Look, though, at Figure 90.4 and you can see how India's recent performance matches China's. India has important clothing exports and it now also exports steel. At the heart of its commercial success, though, are '**invisible exports**' such as software engineering and running English-speaking call centres. India has two important advantages over China: good English (the global language) and an education system that is excellent at the top end, so it produces many excellent managers and software experts.

The big question now is whether India can sustain its recent success.

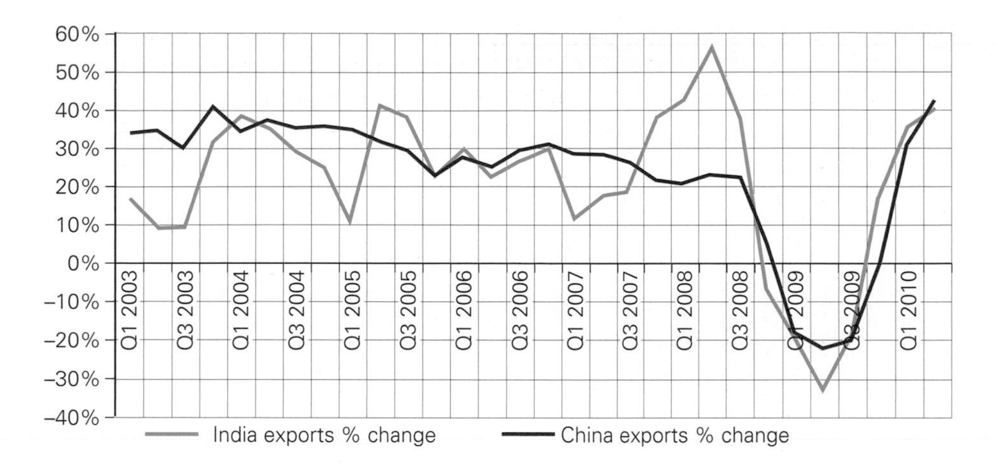

Figure 90.4 Export growth (quarterly change, year-on-year)

90.4 CAN INDIA GROW RAPIDLY AND CONSISTENTLY?

India's key weaknesses

India has three key weaknesses in its attempts to keep up with China.

Its poor infrastructure

Under-investment means that the road system lags behind China's, especially in motorway construction. It is possible that the reason is political. In China the government can dictate to the people that 40 per cent of spending will be on investment. In India, there is a democratically elected government, and it may be that the public is unwilling to cut back too severely on today's spending, in order to invest in the country's future.

The narrow education system

Whereas the literacy level in China is 91 per cent, in India it is only 58 per cent (that is, 42 per cent of the population cannot read or write). Therefore if the growth rate led to job opportunities for a wider range of people, many would be unable to take up the jobs due to illiteracy. The Indian government plans to address this problem in the period 2011–2015.

International trade

Whereas in 2009 China had a current account surplus (more exports than imports) of $297 billion, India had a deficit of $38 billion. The deficit has been growing rapidly as Indian consumers have increased their spending on everything from cars to aircraft. Big deficits would make it hard for India to keep growing without a sharp, inflationary, fall in the value of the rupee.

Inevitable overheating?

This is not an issue of global warming, but of economic performance. In the past, accelerations in industrial production seem to have triggered rises in inflation. This has made the Bank of India respond by pushing up interest rates. Table 90.2 shows the apparent effect of overly rapid growth on India's inflation levels. As the economy enjoyed a rapid recovery after the 2009 recession, inflation in India rose dramatically (at a time when inflation in China and the UK was about 3 per cent) This is a classic sign of overheating. This shows the doubt there must be about India's ability to match China's remarkable growth rates.

Table 90.2 India: growth in industrial production and inflation levels, 2010

	Industrial production (%)	Inflation (CPI) (%)
January	+16.7	16.2
February	+15.1	14.9
March	+13.5	14.9
April	+17.6	13.3
May	+11.3	12.3
June	+7.1	10.6

Source: Indian government statistics, 2010.

A-grade application

Cat versus JCB

Thirty years ago, America's construction equipment giant Caterpillar (Cat) started investing heavily in China. Today its huge strength in China underpins its position as world number one. At much the same time, Britain's JCB chose to invest in India. Today its 50 per cent market share in India is crucial in securing its 12 per cent share of the world market for construction equipment.

Now, both Cat and JCB are following similar strategies: build on strength, while dipping a toe in the weaker market. In 2010 Caterpillar announced expansion plans to increase capacity in China by 400 per cent by 2014. Caterpillar boss Rich Lavin said 'China is a strategically critical market for us'.

At the same time JCB announced factory expansion in India, to consolidate its position. Nevertheless, JCB is investing cautiously in new capacity in China, just as Cat is doing the same in India.

As things stand, it looks as if Caterpillar made the better bet, 30 years ago. Happily for JCB, even if it never breaks into China, its strength in India guarantees it a strong position in the world market for the foreseeable future.

90.5 CAN CHINA OUTSTRIP AMERICA?

Some have expressed doubts about the sustainability of China's growth. They suggest that export growth must flatten out as Chinese wage rates start to rise. At present McDonald's pays its part-time staff in China about 35p per hour, so there is some way to go! In any case, this view assumes that China will remain a producer of low-cost items. In fact, in 2009 China became the world's biggest manufacturer of cars. Within five years China expects to be selling millions of cars in Europe and America. It does not need to rely on tiny wages. Nevertheless, it is true to say that China will lose some low-cost production. For example, at the moment minimum wage rates in India are slightly below £1.20 a day (that is, about 15p per hour). So India can already undercut China.

Others believe that China is an environmental disaster, on the edge of collapse. There is no doubt that pollution is dreadful in industrial towns such as Linfen. Overall, though, China is investing heavily in cleaning up its rivers and air, and the country makes a relatively modest contribution to greenhouse gases (per capita). Table 90.3 shows the major contributors to global CO_2 emissions. Generally, the richer the country, the higher is the total of the CO_2 emissions, though there are some exceptions, such as Russia. For some reason, Russia seems to escape criticism for its environmental record, whereas America is desperate to paint China as the 'bad guy'.

As China grows, its emissions will rise as well. This is why emissions in developed countries will have to be cut if there is to be a chance of stopping the global figure from growing further.

Table 90.3 Global carbon dioxide emissions

	Tonnes of CO_2 per head p.a.	Total CO_2 tonnes (millions)
India	1.4	1,600
China	5.8	7,700
UK	8.4	520
USA	17.4	5,400
Russia	11.3	1,600
World	4.5	30,450

Source: US Energy Information Administration, 2011.

90.6 WHAT OPPORTUNITIES ARE THERE FOR BRITISH BUSINESS?

Every director of every public company knows that she or he must have a strategy for China and India. Tesco has its investment in Chinese superstores and has made clear its desire to get into India (foreign retail chains are not allowed to invest at the moment, for fear that millions of small local shops will be wiped out). Kingfisher owns a successful chain of DIY shops in China.

Yet these are examples of British firms buying their way in to China. What about actually selling to them (that is, competing directly)? Here, Britain has made a very bad start. Today, the value of German exports to China is more than six times the value of Britain's; even France outsells Britain by 2:1. Of all China's imports, Britain supplies less than 1 per cent.

What about India? Britain ran India (as a colony) for 150 years, so there must be trade links remaining. Indeed in 2002 the British share of Indian imports was 4.96 per cent (about in line with Britain's share of world trade). By 2009, however, the British share had fallen to 3.7 per cent. Despite this decline, Britain still has distinct advantages over France, Italy and even Germany. The need is for British businesses to commit themselves to an effective strategy for India.

ISSUES FOR ANALYSIS

- A2 exams are based on corporate (company-wide) objectives and strategy; not, 'Should we put the price up or run a BOGOF promotion?' but 'Should we focus our efforts on India or China?' As few firms can afford to do everything all at once, choices have to be made. Therefore it is vital to have some understanding about the future potential of different countries and their economies. America will remain the richest place to live for years to come, but the growth rate and huge population of China make it inevitable that it will overtake America in the (relatively near) future. Will businesses be ready for this?
- It is interesting to wonder why Britain has done so badly in China. Is it because of a lack of initiative or far-sightedness

by our business leaders? Or is it just a temporary problem at a time when the products China wants are not the ones we produce (for example, cars)? If so, perhaps there will be a future boom period when China starts buying the banking, media, creative and design service skills that generate such a lot of our wealth at the moment.

90.7 CHINA VERSUS INDIA – AN EVALUATION

China has been growing at a rate of 9 to 10 per cent for 15 years and looks capable of doing the same in the future. It may be short of younger people, but it has over 400 million people working on the land, many of whom would be pleased to earn higher wages in a factory. India also has good prospects, though it is less clear that it will be able to deliver high growth year in year out. It needs huge investments in education and infrastructure, but the Indian government is unwilling, or unable, to provide this. In this two-horse race, the one to back is China.

Nevertheless, for an individual business India may be the better bet. For a young British company lacking export experience, it would probably be easier to break into India than China, if only because there are fewer language and cultural barriers. Above all else, India lacks an effective manufacturing sector, so it may be a perfect place for British manufacturing exports or for setting up new factories. As always, each business case is different.

Key Terms

Infrastructure: the name given to the road, rail and air links, sewage and other basic utilities that provide a network that benefits business and the community.

Invisible export: the sale of a service to an overseas customer.

WORKBOOK

A REVISION QUESTIONS

(30 marks; 30 minutes)

1 Outline two reasons why China's growth prospects may be greater than India's. (4)
2 Outline two reasons why India's growth prospects may be greater than China's. (4)
3 Explain the significance of the figures shown for 'capital formation' in Figure 90.2. (6)
4 Explain what is meant by 'overheating', as shown in the text and the data in Table 90.2. (5)
5 Outline two reasons why a British retail firm such as Next may choose to invest in China rather than India. (4)
6 Look at Table 90.3 and answer the following questions.
   a) Why is Russia criticised in the text, given that its total carbon emissions are 'only' 1,600 million tonnes? (2)
   b) America regularly criticises China for its impact on global warming. Analyse this view based on the data provided. (5)

B REVISION EXERCISES

B1 DATA RESPONSE

Table 90.4 Number of grocery outlets in India and China in 2009

	India	China
Hyper/supermarkets	7,500	84,000
Small grocery	9,005,000	420,000
Other grocery	800,000	3,071,000
Specialist food/drink	2,295,000	27,000
(Population)	1,180 million	1,330 million

Source:

Questions

(20 marks; 25 minutes)

1 Outline two key differences between grocery distribution in India and China. (4)
2 Assume you are the boss of Innocent Drinks, trying to decide whether to launch your fresh-fruit 'smoothie' drinks into India or China. On the basis of the data given in Table 90.4, which country would you target first? Justify your answer. (16)

B2 CASE STUDY

Exporting to China

Coventry-based Oleo International is a British company that has built up successful exports to China. In 2004 the Chinese government announced a £100 billion investment in its railways, including the construction of its own, Chinese-built 'bullet' trains. By 2020 China plans on building more new track than in Europe and America combined.

Oleo – a world leader in energy absorption equipment – saw its chance. It makes very advanced shock absorbers for railway carriages. These enable passenger trains to start up and stop with minimal bumping of passengers.

In 2004 Oleo, helped by the government's 'UK Trade & Investment', set up an office in Shanghai and invited Chinese officials to come and visit the Coventry factory. China was building its own track and trains, but still valued the British company's design and engineering expertise.

Oleo managed to obtain over £1 million of sales in 2005, its first trading year in China. Since then things have gone from strength to strength, encouraging the company to open its second sales office on the Chinese mainland. By 2009 Oleo employed 30 sales staff permanently in China. For any engineering business, China is quite simply the biggest opportunity in the world.

Questions

(40 marks; 45 minutes)

1 Outline two entrepreneurial skills shown by Oleo's management in this case. (6)
2 Explain the Oleo story in terms of its aims, objectives and strategy. (10)
3 Is it right that British taxpayers' money should be spent supporting companies such as Oleo to set up in China? Explain your view. (10)
4 One analyst has said that 'any engineering company that ignores China is signing its own death warrant'. To what extent do you agree with this statement? (14)

B3 DATA RESPONSE

Five years ago, no-one would have believed that China would be the world's number one car market by 2010. Yet that is only a small part of the story. The big issue is the market potential. As shown in Table 90.5, only 3.7 per cent of Chinese households own a car. Perhaps by 2020 China's ownership of cars and bicycles will be similar to Brazil's. If so, car sales in China have huge growth prospects. In percentage terms, the growth prospects in India are even more exciting. From an environmental viewpoint, though, the prospects look troubling.

Table 90.5 Comparison of car and bicycle ownership

	Percentage of households with a car* (%)	Percentage of households with a bicycle* (%)	Number of households* (million)	Car market size 2010**	Percentage change since 2008** (%)
China	3.7	73.3	385	16.3	+70
India	2.8	51.1	218	1.8	+50
USA	88.1	44.6	117	11.8	−14
Brazil	35.6	12.8	54	3.5	+21

*Source: © and database right Euromonitor International Ltd (all rights reserved) **Industry estimates October 2010

Questions

(30 marks; 30 minutes)

1 Explain the significance of the data for 'percentage of households with a car'. (8)
2 Explain why 'from an environmental viewpoint, the prospects look troubling'. (8)
3 On the basis of the above information and your wider knowledge, discuss whether China or India has the stronger growth prospects for new car sales over the next ten years. (14)

B4 CASE STUDY

Growth versus inflation in India

It is likely that India's economy will grow almost 9 per cent during this fiscal year, but rising inflation is a cause for concern according to the country's Finance Minister. He said he also worries that some industries are persistently underperforming, despite the buoyancy of the broader economy.

India's economy expanded at a rate of 9.1 per cent in the first half of the fiscal year that ends in March 2007, and the Minister says he expects full-year growth to be almost 9 per cent. That would put India's economic expansion — averaging more than 8 per cent a year during the past three years — close to the rate in China. The record for growth in the Indian economy was 10.5 per cent in the fiscal year ended in March 1990. The economy grew 8.4 per cent last year.

'We look back with considerable satisfaction at what has been achieved in the past year ... [but] the only dark cloud as the year came to a close was rising inflation,' he told business leaders at the annual meeting of the Federation of Indian Chambers of Commerce & Industry. India's inflation climbed to a rate of 5.5 per cent the week ended 23 December, despite falling fuel and raw material prices in recent weeks.

The Finance Minister said the latest upturn in inflation was mostly driven by a rise in prices of some manufactured products. 'Even 4 per cent inflation is unacceptable,' he said, warning that rising inflation could push up interest rates and slow economic growth in coming years. India's central bank has already increased some key rates, and commercial banks have increased their lending and deposit rates by a half to a full percentage point in recent months.

He said he was also concerned over the uneven spread of growth in the manufacturing sector. While overall manufacturing output is growing, several industries showed contraction. Those industries included food processing, paper, leather, chemicals and basic metals. He asked business leaders to look into why production was slackening in these sectors. Some of these industries are labour-intensive and a contraction could fuel unemployment.

Source: Rajesh Mahapatra, Associated Press, 9 January 2007.

Questions

(30 marks; 40 minutes)

1 The Minister seems very gloomy. Outline one reason why he should be very pleased, given the information provided. (5)
2 Explain, in your own words, the Minister's reasons for saying that 'even 4 per cent inflation is unacceptable'. (5)
3 What could be the consequence for Indian firms of the statement that 'India's central bank has already increased some key [interest] rates'? (8)
4 Taking the whole article into account, discuss the extent to which it supports the argument in the chapter that: 'This shows the doubt there must be about India's ability to match China's remarkable growth rates'. (12)

Causes of and planning for change

UNIT 91

Change is a constant feature of business activity. The key issues are whether it has been foreseen by the company – and therefore planned for – and whether it is within the company's control.

91.1 INTERNAL AND EXTERNAL CAUSES OF CHANGE

Change arises as a result of various internal and external causes. The internal ones (such as a change in objectives) should at least be planned for. External causes may be unexpected, which makes them far harder to manage. Table 91.1 sets out some possible internal and external causes of change.

Table 91.1 Examples of internal and external causes of change

Internal causes	External causes
• New growth objectives set by management	• Rising consumer demand/ the product becomes fashionable
• New boss is appointed	• Economic boom benefits a luxury product
• Decision to open up new export markets	• Closure/fire/strike hits competitor, boosting your sales
• A decision to increase the shareholders' dividend makes it difficult to find the capital to invest in the business	• New laws favour your product (e.g. new safety laws boost sales of first aid kits)

Of all the issues relating to change, none is more crucial than when a business has to cope with a period of rapid growth. For example, in the first stage in the rapid growth of Bebo (the social networking site launched in 2005, which sold for $850 million in 2008), the number of employees rose from 1 to 28 within nine months.

91.2 BUSINESS EFFECTS OF FORECAST RAPID GROWTH

In certain circumstances managers can anticipate a period of rapid **organic growth**. This may be temporary (such as the effect of a change in the law) or may seem likely to be permanent (such as the growth in demand for a hot website). The most successful firms will be those that devise a plan that is detailed enough to help in a practical way, but flexible enough to allow for the differences between forecasts and reality.

When rapid growth has been forecast, firms can:

- compare the sales estimate with the available production capacity
- budget for any necessary increases in capacity and staffing
- produce a cash flow forecast to anticipate any short-term financing shortfall
- discuss how to raise any extra capital needed.

Timescales remain important, though. The forecast may cover the next three months; but increasing capacity may involve building a factory extension, which will take eight months, in which case there may be five months of excess demand to cope with (perhaps by subcontracting).

Smooth though all this sounds, there remains a lot of scope for error. The starting point is the increased workload on staff. Extra sales may put pressure on the accounting system, the warehouse manager and the delivery drivers. With everyone being kept busy, things can occasionally start to go wrong. Invoices are sent out

Figure 91.1 Extra sales may put pressure on the warehouse

a little later, unpaid bills are not chased as quickly and stock deliveries are not checked as carefully. Suddenly the cash flow position worsens and costs start to rise. A strong, effective manager could retrieve this, but many are weak and woolly. Once they start to go wrong, plans are hard to sort out.

91.3 MANAGEMENT REORGANISATION DURING GROWTH

Problem of adjustment from boss to leader/manager

The typical creator of a successful new business is lively, energetic, creative, often impatient and always a risk-taker. Such a person will have a strong personality, and quite possibly an autocratic though charismatic leadership style. When the business started, their own speed of decision making, attention to detail and hard work were fundamental to the firm's success.

With success comes a problem. How to cope with the additional workload? At first the boss works ever harder; then she or he takes on more junior staff. Then comes the crunch. Is she or he willing to appoint a senior manager with real decision-making power? Or will a weak manager be appointed who always has to check decisions with the boss?

Staff will always find it hard to accept a new manager because everyone will know that it is really the boss's business. It is said that, ten years after Walt Disney died, managers were still rejecting ideas on the basis that 'Walt wouldn't have done it that way.' How much harder if the founder is still there: James Dyson at Dyson and Larry Page and Sergey Brin at Google.

The boss must make the break, however. No longer should she or he attend every key meeting or demand regular reports on day-to-day matters. Delegation is necessary. In other words, authority should be passed down the hierarchy to middle managers without interference from above. And instead of looking for the next great opportunity, the boss may have to focus on getting the right management structure to ensure a smooth-running business.

Even if the founder of the company *is* able to adjust to managing a large organisation, there remains the problem of motivation. Will the new staff be as 'hungry' as the small team that built the business? Usually the answer is no. The drinks giant Diageo thinks it has a solution, though. It is a business with annual profits of over £2,000 million, based on brands such as Smirnoff, Baileys and Guinness. To keep staff hungry, the chief executive gives managers a 'HAT': a Hairy Audacious Target. In other words, staff are given a bold, challenging goal. Achieving these HATs will give each manager the chance to make huge bonuses. The chief executive believes HATs can stretch 'our people's imaginations to achieve these aggressive targets'.

Change in management structure or hierarchy

As a business grows, the management structure has not only to grow too, but also to change. New layers of management may be needed and completely new departments may be founded, such as personnel or public relations. And all the time, as the business grows, new staff are being recruited, inducted and trained. So there is constant change in personnel and their responsibilities. This can be disconcerting for customers and suppliers. Strong relationships are hard to build, making customer loyalty tough to achieve.

Even more important, though, is the internal effect of these personnel changes. With new staff appearing frequently, and managerial changes occurring regularly, team spirit may be hard to achieve. Junior and middle managers may spend too much of their time looking upwards to the promotion prospects instead of concentrating on their own departments. The potential for inefficiency, or even chaos, is clear. Too many new staff may mean too many mistakes. If customer relations are relatively weak, the result could easily be loss of business.

These unpleasant possibilities can largely be set aside if a good example is set from the top. If the founder of the business continues to be involved – especially on customer service – all may still be well. The leader needs to make sure staff keep sight of the qualities that brought the business its success in the first place. If new management structures threaten to create communications barriers, the leader should set an example by visiting staff, chatting to them and acting on their advice. The leader must fight against being cut off from the grassroots: the staff and the customers.

Risk of loss of direction and control

Each year, Templeton College Oxford produces data on what it calls the Fast Track 100. These are the fastest-growing 100 small companies in Britain. The December 2009 survey showed that, despite the recession, the top ten of these firms enjoyed three-year growth rates of:

- sales turnover +180 per cent per year
- employees +120 per cent per year.

The typical Fast Track 100 firm had gone from 22 staff to 140 staff in the past three years. No wonder, then, that the key challenges faced by these companies were managing the growth in staff and infrastructure (source: www.fasttrack.co.uk).

The **entrepreneurs** who get swamped by the success of the business are those whose firms will fail to sustain their growth. They may become side-tracked by the attractions of expense account living; or – the other extreme – become so excited by their own success that they start opening up several different businesses. They assume that their golden touch will ensure success in whatever they do. Instead, just as their core business becomes harder to handle, they are looking at a different venture altogether. Problems may then hit from several directions at once.

The key message is, therefore: focus on what you are good at.

91.4 PROBLEMS OF TRANSITION IN SIZE

From private to public

At certain points in a firm's life there will be critical decisions to be made regarding growth. Few are more fundamental than the decision to 'go public'. A private limited company is a family business, often dominated by the shareholdings of one person who is probably the founder. Although its accounts must be published, it is still able to maintain a substantial veil over its activities. Its private status minimises the pressures upon the management. A year of poor trading may disappoint the family, but there is no publicly quoted share price to embarrass the firm or to threaten it with a hostile takeover. This protection from outside pressures enables private companies to take a long-term view of what they want to achieve and how.

Switching from private to public company status is not, in itself, a difficult or expensive process. The big change comes when a firm floats its shares on the stock market. Only public companies are allowed to do this. From the protected world of the private company, the firm will enter the glare of public scrutiny. Before floating, the firm must issue a **prospectus** that sets out every detail of the firm's business, its financial record, its expectations and its key personnel. Newspapers and analysts will scrutinise this fully, and carry on writing about the firm when every set of financial results comes out.

The purpose of going public is usually to achieve a substantial increase in share capital. This can enable a highly geared private firm to achieve a more balanced capital structure, as shown in Table 91.2.

Table 91.2 Cutting gearing by going public

Sharps Ltd (before going public) (£ million)		Sharps plc (after raising £4 million on the stock market) (£ million)	
Loan capital	4	Loan capital	4
Share capital	1	Share capital	5
Reserves	3	Reserves	3
Capital employed	**8**	**Capital employed**	**12**
Gearing level:	50%	Gearing level:	33%

In the case of Sharps plc, the addition of 50 per cent more capital (from £8 million to £12 million) will give a huge opportunity for major expansion. Indeed, if the management act slowly, the purchasers of the £4 million extra shares may get restless. So the managers will be inclined to make a big move. Perhaps they will make a takeover bid. Or perhaps a diversification, by launching a new product range. Either way, the risks are substantial. Does this business have the expertise to succeed with either approach? What it needs is the confidence to keep focused upon what the management is good at. But the public pressure to make a big step forward may encourage the management to take a step too far.

Retrenchment

Just as big steps forward can lead to problems, so can steps backward. Yet few firms will keep growing without the occasional sharp setback. Retrenchment

Table 91.3 The benefits and drawbacks of different types of retrenchment

Type of retrenchment	Advantages	Disadvantages
Freeze on recruitment and/or offering voluntary redundancy	• not threatening; should not cause products of job insecurity • viewed by staff as fair	• no chance to reshape the business • good people are always leaving, so they need to be replaced
Delayering (i.e. removing a whole management layer)	• should not affect direct operations (such as staff on the shop floor) • may empower/enrich remaining jobs	• may over-intensify the work of other managers, causing stress • risk of losing a generation of managers • loss of promotion prospects for those who remain
Closure of a division or factory, or a number of loss-making outlets	• sharp reduction in fixed overhead costs will reduce break-even point • capacity utilisation may rise in the firm's other factories	• once closed, the capacity is unlikely to be available for the next economic upturn • loss of many good staff
Targeted cutbacks and redundancies in divisions throughout the business	• can reshape the business to meet future needs (e.g. no cutbacks among IT staff) • by keeping good staff, their average quality level may rise	• huge problems of perceived fairness (unless there is a high degree of trust) • job security may be hit ('Will it be me next?')

means cutting back. This may be achieved through a general reduction in staffing, or perhaps only a halt on recruitment. Most often, though, it will imply a **rationalisation** in which there are significant changes to the organisational structure and/or to the capacity level of the business.

In 2010, there were major worldwide rationalisations by giants such as British Airways, Lloyds Bank and Toyota. In all cases, the key factor is to ensure that retrenchment does not cause lasting damage to morale, relationships and trust. Therefore it is vital to be honest, open, fair and as generous as possible to anyone who is losing a job.

When forced to cut back, firms have many options, as outlined in Table 91.3.

91.5 PLANNING FOR CHANGE

For managers who can foresee significant change, a strategic plan is needed. This should help in managing the change process, ensuring that the business has the personnel and the financial resources to cope. The strategic planning process is undertaken by an organisation's senior managers. The first decision they face is: 'How do we turn this change to our own advantage?'

Having established the strategic direction the organisation will adopt, the senior managers must next set the boundaries within which middle and junior management will take day-to-day decisions. A series of integrated actions must be set out. These will have the purpose of moving the organisation forward in the identified strategic direction. This plan will be introduced over a period of time known as a 'planning horizon'. This will commonly be between one and three years, but may vary depending on how stable the organisation's competitive environment is. The greater the stability, the longer the planning horizon will be.

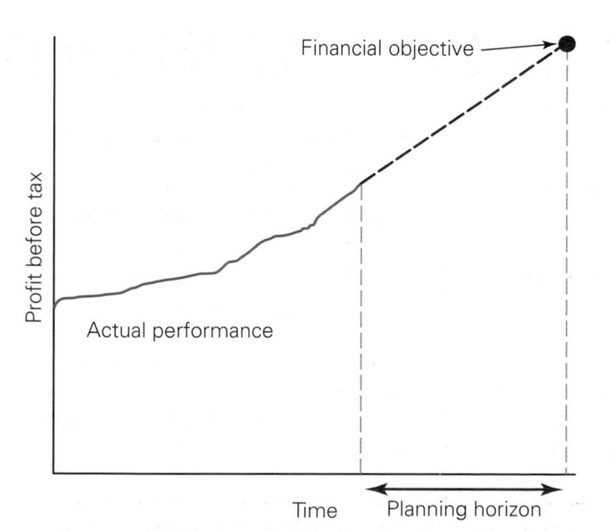

Figure 91.2 Financial objectives

Strategic planning is only necessary because firms operate in a changing environment. If this was not the case then a single strategy, once designed, would bring success to the business on a permanent basis. However, changes in key variables such as technology, consumer tastes and communications make planning strategy increasingly important. The pace of change is intensifying, creating shorter product life cycles and encouraging increased competition. It is change that creates the '**strategic gap**' that must be closed by the second phase of the planning process.

Organisations that seek to achieve objectives such as the maximisation of long-term profits will set themselves financial targets. These will be influenced by shareholders' expectations and the personal and business ambitions of the company directors. These expectations will determine the financial objectives of the organisation over the forthcoming planning period.

The difference between the profit objective and the forecast performance of the business, is known as a strategic gap (see Figure 91.3).

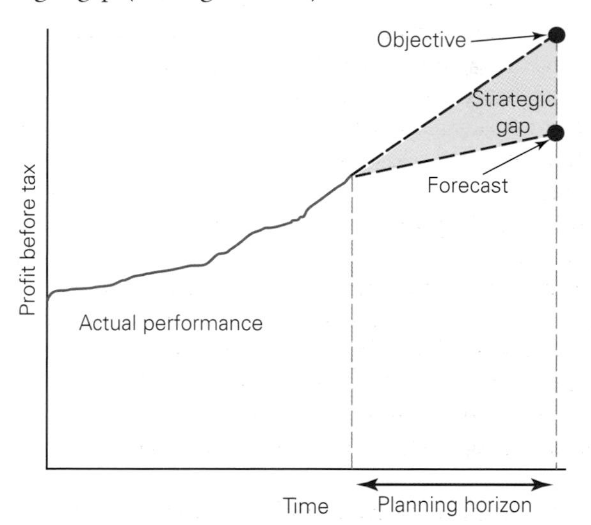

Figure 91.3 A strategic gap

Closing a strategic gap

Once a strategic gap has been identified it is necessary to devise a series of strategies to close it.

It may be possible to achieve this to some extent by performing existing operations more efficiently, in order to reduce costs and boost profit. However, this is unlikely to solve the whole problem. Only careful strategic planning can develop the means by which the organisation can increase its effectiveness in order to meet its financial objective.

The analysis of the strategic gap should reveal how difficult it will be to cope with the change. The future may look bright, such as for an organic farmer in a period of change towards more care and thought over healthy eating. Or it may look bleak, such as for a house-building business in 2008 in the wake of sharp falls in house prices. Whether the gap is upwards or downwards (forcing the business to retrench), a careful planning process should make the transition easier.

Contingency planning

A strategic plan should outline the critical assumptions that have been made about the future competitive environment. If the success of the project depends on these judgements a 'fallback' position, or **contingency plan**, should be developed in case they prove wrong. As part of the planning process, 'What if?' questions should be asked. For example, a manufacturer of bicycles, thrilled about the sales boom in 2006–10 should ask the question: 'What if a slowdown in China forces oil prices back down again?' Lower oil prices would get people back into their cars, forcing demand down for sales of new bicycles. Contingency planning allows the firm to consider what action it will take if particular opportunities or threats emerge as a strategy is implemented.

ISSUES FOR ANALYSIS

When tackling questions about the causes of – and plans for – change, the following lines of analysis are helpful.

- If the business faces rapid growth, is it planned (internal) or unplanned (external)?
- Is the business leader's management style capable of changing as the business develops?
- Does the firm have the financial resources to cope with the need for capital during a time of change?
- How well does the firm cope with growth shocks, such as a stock market flotation? Can the management keep focused upon the strategy and the strengths of the business.
- Would managers who have handled growth well be equally good at handling retrenchment? Only if they have and deserve the trust of the staff.

91.6 CAUSES OF AND PLANNING FOR CHANGE – AN EVALUATION

Change is normal, not abnormal. Therefore firms need to be alert to causes of change and quick to devise a strategic plan for coping. Many successful businesses do not have a formal strategic planning process. This does not mean that the issues raised here are not relevant to these organisations. The same problems must be dealt with when strategy emerges over time as when it is planned more systematically. The advantage of explicitly setting aside time for strategic planning is that managers' minds are concentrated on the key questions facing the firm in the future. Then the actions decided upon can be more closely integrated.

Key Terms

Contingency plan: a Plan B in case Plan A goes wrong.

Entrepreneur: an individual with a flair for business opportunities and risk-taking. The term is often used to describe a person with the entrepreneurial spirit to set up a new business.

Organic growth: growth from within the business (for example, sales growing rapidly because a product is riding a wave of consumer popularity).

Prospectus: a document that companies have to produce when they go public (that is, are quoted on the stock exchange); it gives details about the company's activities and anticipated future profits.

Rationalisation: reorganising to increase efficiency. The term is mainly used when cutbacks in overhead costs are needed in order to reduce an organisation's break-even point.

Strategic gap: the difference between where the business is and where it plans to be.

WORKBOOK

A REVISION QUESTIONS

(50 marks; 50 minutes)

1. Explain why rapid growth can cause problems for a company's:
   a) cash flow (2)
   b) management control. (2)
2. Distinguish between internal and external causes of growth, using examples. (5)
3. Why may there be a problem in adjusting from 'boss' to 'leader/manager'? (4)
4. Identify three problems for a fast-growing firm caused by changes in the management structure. (3)
5. Outline two strengths and two potential weaknesses of stock market flotation for a rapidly growing business. (8)
6. Explain the possible problems (and benefits) to a small computer software firm of changing status from private to public limited company. (4)
7. Explain in your own words the idea of the planning horizon. (4)
8. Explain why it may be hard for young, inexperienced managers of a successful business start-up to cope effectively with an unexpected, dramatic change. (5)
9. **a)** Explain the meaning of the term 'retrenchment'. (3)
   b) Outline two suitable methods of retrenchment for an airline that is losing market share. (4)
10. Explain why it may be hard for a struggling jewellery business to fill the strategic gap. (6)

B REVISION EXERCISES
B1 DATA RESPONSE

Lush profits

In 2010 the cosmetics producer and retailer 'Lush' won an award for being one of Britain's fastest-growing growing international businesses. From its base in the sleepy seaside town of Poole, Lush achieved an overseas sales growth rate of 48 per cent a year between 2007 and 2009. In 2009 70 per cent of the company's sales were made overseas. This helped to support over 4,000 jobs.

When it was founded, in 1990, Body Shop was the store to beat. Now, with 672 stores in 42 countries, Lush's indulgent, attractive – but modestly priced – cosmetics are starting to overshadow Body Shop. Lush also benefits from the enthusiasm of its staff for the company's backing for ethical causes such as banning foxhunting, or demanding legal representation for the Guantanamo Bay detainees Even in the savage 2009 recession, Lush managed to push revenue up from £153 million to £215 million, though profits fell from £19.4 million in 2008 to £13.9 million.

Growing from £0 to £215 million in less than 15 years inevitably involves problems. When it had grown to £50 million of sales the manufacturing staff noticed that products made from essential oils (that can cost £3,000 per kg) were 'behaving' wrongly. After some weeks of panic Lush decided to get a chemist to analyse the oils. It emerged that suppliers had been adulterating the oils with as much as 70 per cent synthetic chemicals. This problem led to the establishment of a professional buying team, together with a quality control manager.

Questions

(30 marks; 35 minutes)

1 a) Explain why Lush is likely to have had a significant increase in the number of layers of hierarchy within its business over recent years. (10)

b) Examine two ways in which an increase in the layers of hierarchy might harm operational performance at Lush. (8)

2 If Lush appointed a new chief executive, discuss the possible difficulties that could arise from a retrenchment plan in order to boost profits. (12)

B2 DATA RESPONSE

From Google to Facebook

Sheryl Sandberg wants to bring to Facebook what she brought to Google: discipline and inventiveness to foster rapid growth. Two weeks into her job as Facebook's chief operating officer (COO), the 38-year-old executive, second in command to 23-year-old CEO Mark Zuckerberg, is rolling out new management and operations procedures. Among these are guidelines for employee-performance reviews, processes for identifying and recruiting new employees, and management-training programmes.

Ms Sandberg's experience in expanding operations and building talent is just what the social networking site may need as it aims for a big expansion. 'Facebook is a different space than Google, with tremendous potential to connect people, but it needs scale, it needs systems and processes to have impact, and I can do that,' she says.

The social networking site, which allows users to create personal profiles to share with friends, had more than 100 million visitors in January 2008, a fourfold increase from the year-earlier period. But it's still burning up more cash than it is generating in revenues, according to people familiar with the company's finances.

At Facebook, which is privately held, Ms Sandberg is in charge of sales, business development, public policy and communications. One immediate focus is on international growth. Until a few months ago, Facebook was for English speakers only. Now it's available in French, German and Spanish, and within the next few months the site will be translated into 21 additional languages.

Meanwhile, Ms Sandberg must rally Facebook's 550 employees, who work at several offices in downtown Palo Alto, to embrace change. Many are recent college graduates who wear flip-flops and jeans to work, and scrawl graffiti on the office walls. At a company meeting two weeks ago, she addressed the concern among some employees that Facebook's close-knit culture will disappear as it grows.

'Scaling up is hard and it's not as much fun not to know everyone you work with,' she told employees. 'But if we get to work on things that affect hundreds of millions of people instead of tens of millions, that's a trade-off worth making.'

Mr Zuckerberg had been looking for a COO who could create a new business model, build a management team, ramp up operations and expand internationally, all of which

Ms Sandberg had done at Google. She joined Google in 2001 without knowing exactly what her job would be. Over the following six years, she built Google's global online sales unit into the company's biggest revenue producer and expanded her staff from four to 4,000.

She developed a reputation for being a charismatic executive. She describes herself as a 'tough-love leader', who aims to 'mentor and demand at the same time, and make it safe to make mistakes,' she says.

Source: Carol Hymowitz, *Wall Street Journal*, 14 April 2008, copyright 2008 Dow Jones & Company

Questions

(30 marks; 35 minutes)

1 Outline two problems that may arise when a 38-year-old is appointed as number two to a 23-year-old. (6)

2 Discuss whether Ms Sandberg's speech to Facebook's employees is likely to have overcome staff concerns about whether 'Facebook's close-knit culture will disappear as it grows'. (10)

3 From the extract as a whole, discuss whether Ms Sandberg's ideas are likely to help or hinder Facebook in the dramatic growth that is forcing huge changes on the business. (14)

C ESSAY QUESTIONS

(40 marks each)

1 Dell Computers has grown at a rate of 50 per cent per year for nearly a decade. Outline the problems this may cause. What may be the most effective way for management to tackle them?

2 Discuss whether corporate plans are an effective way of dealing with unexpected changes such as a sudden collapse in confidence in the housing market.

Leadership and change

UNIT 92

Leadership means taking the initiative to set clear objectives and to motivate or guide staff towards their achievement.

92.1 INTRODUCTION

Christiano Ronaldo has to 'get by' on £200,000 a week, while Britain's best paid boss received £90 million in remuneration in 2009 (£1,800,000 a week). Bart Becht, chief executive of Reckitt Benckiser, has long been Britain's highest paid business leader. He has presided over a hugely successful run since an Anglo-Dutch merger created Reckitt Benckiser (suppliers of Cillit Bang, Air Wick and Dettol) in 1999. Yet the business has had its critics, especially after it was fined £10.2 million in 2010 for anti-competitive tactics relating to its Gaviscon brand. The main criticism of Becht, though, is that he is paid 3,000 times as much as the average Reckitt employee. Is leadership ever worth that much?

In recent years business leadership has become an industry in itself. Typically, business sections in bookshops have a couple of books on motivation, but dozens on leadership. At the same time, leaders have gone from earning 20 times the salary of the lowest paid in an organisation to a figure that is greater than 100 times more. Following behind has been the UK government, setting up special training schools such as the National Leadership College for future head teachers. It is assumed that dynamic success comes from dynamic, charismatic leaders. By implication, therefore, these fabulous people are worth fabulous sums of money.

Sometimes, this is unarguably true. What has Sir Alex Ferguson been 'worth' to Manchester United? And what was Sir Ken Morrison worth, in building his small supermarket business into a national chain between 1967 and 2008? He was worth lots, undeniably lots. Great leaders exist, and they are worth big financial rewards. Unfortunately, there are many examples of ordinary leaders with ordinary achievements also being paid huge sums. Even though the amount paid may be relatively trivial for a big business, the implications are very significant: the media may be over-emphasising the importance of 'the great leader', making it harder for intelligent, but modest, bosses to be given time to succeed.

A-grade application

Fifty British business leaders descended on the European Parliament in November 2010 to lobby against proposals that would give pregnant women 20 weeks' maternity leave at full pay. Current UK rules mean that employers have to pay only six weeks' maternity pay at 90 per cent of the mother's salary. Women then receive a further 33 weeks' statutory maternity pay, funded by the taxpayer, at £124.88 a week.

But the EU proposals, which are due to be voted on by the European Council next week, would cost British businesses £2.5 billion a year, according to the British Chambers of Commerce. The business group said UK companies would bear the brunt of the costs at a time when many were still struggling after the recession.

The previous month, Britain's bosses had been accused of greed and ignoring economic reality after boardroom pay leapt by 55 per cent over the previous year. FTSE 100 directors saw their total earnings soar in the 12 months to June 2010, as a result of sharp rises in bonuses and performance-related pay. The average FTSE 100 chief executive earns £4.9 million a year, or almost 200 times the average wage.

92.2 THE ROLE OF LEADERSHIP IN MANAGING CHANGE

Like families, most organisations get set in their ways. So change is neither welcome nor easy. The job of a leader is to carry out the following.

- Ensure that the pressures for change are understood – first among board members (the parents?) and then throughout the organisation/family.
- Construct a clear vision about what the new future will look like and a narrative that explains the steps in getting from here to there. This should only be done after a process of consultation that clarifies what the staff/family members want. If the vision is contrary to the views of staff, the leader should make sure that everyone understands his or her reasons for change.
- Appoint the right managers to handle each aspect

of the change, ensuring that everyone knows that the leader has delegated full authority to them (and therefore anyone who gets in their way is getting in the way of the boss); then support the managers with necessary resources plus your involvement and backing.
- Keep going, even during the difficult short-term period in which the disruptions caused by change seem to outweigh any possible long-term gains. In this phase, the appointed change managers will need full and public support from the leader.

If that sounds hard, it actually is an understatement of the difficulties. These arise when, in the middle of the change, senior managers realise that their original analysis of the problem was not 100 per cent right, that is, a change is needed to the change! Quite commonly this arises because junior staff or even the customers were not listened to in advance. Then the leader must decide whether to carry on as if nothing has happened ('It'll be better than it was') or to halt the process, rethink, and then change direction midstream.

As explained fully in Unit 36, there are four main styles of leadership: **autocratic, paternalistic, democratic and laissez faire**. When handling change, different leaders are likely to handle the process of change as shown in Table 92.1.

92.3 LEADERS AND MANAGERS

Before examining this topic, it is useful to reflect on a key management issue: the difference between a leader and a manager. Management guru Peter Drucker once said that: 'Managers do things right; leaders do the right thing.'

In other words, an effective manager is someone who can put an idea or policy into action, and get the details right. By contrast the leader is good at identifying the key issues facing the business, setting new objectives, and then deciding what should be done, by when, and by whom. It is also sometimes argued that a leader needs to inspire staff. This is often confused with 'charismatic leadership', that is, when the personal charisma of the leader inspires staff to give something extra or work a bit harder. Although some successful leaders such as Ghandi, Churchill and Mandela had charisma, many others had success despite quite dull personalities. The great British Prime Minister Clement Attlee 'had a lot to be modest about', according to Churchill. Business stars such as Leahy (Tesco) and Bamford (JCB) have also shunned the limelight. If a leader can get the big decisions right, personality becomes irrelevant. Liverpool FC's period as Britain's top club began with the charismatic Bill Shankly; yet the huge haul of trophies came later, under the leadership of the shy, slightly bumbling Bob Paisley.

Table 92.1 Leadership styles and the process of change

	Autocratic	Paternalistic	Democratic	Laissez-faire
Understand the scope of the change needed	Leader hires a management consultant who reports directly to himself or herself	Leader carries out an extensive consultation exercise among staff based on the known issues or problems	Discussion and consultation will be delegated to middle managers, taking care to include shop floor staff	A laissez-faire organisation may have been ahead of the external charge, or may only react very late
Construct a clear vision	The management consultant writes a Vision Statement	This, again, will be done after consultation, though the leader will make the final decision	This should emerge, perhaps from suggestions from the shop floor	A laissez-faire leader may expect staff to grasp the vision as things emerge
Appoint change managers	May, again, be management consultants; any internal appointees are used to doing what the boss wants	These will be appointed from along known 'team players', that is, those who buy into the vision decided by the leader	These will be selected from the brightest and best throughout the organisation	This is unlikely to happen; it will be expected that everyone will change over time
Keep going through short-term problems	Any internal critics may be sidelined or 'made redundant'	When things get tough, the leader will draw upon tough, family love and the need to stick together	If everyone shares the vision and has agreed the strategy, this stage should not be a real problem	Because the change will be less controlled and therefore slower and more organic, this problem may not occur

92.4 ASSESSING INTERNAL AND EXTERNAL FACTORS INFLUENCING LEADERSHIP STYLE

Some businesses are likely to be lead by an autocrat, that is, someone who keeps all the key decisions at the top. This is because of the nature of the business; for example, McDonalds is likely to employ young people for relatively short periods of time, thereby undermining the purpose of delegation. By contrast a business such as Facebook, which needs constantly to be finding new features and services to re-excite users, should naturally be democratic. The leader needs super-bright software geniuses who will stay for as long as they are making an impact. Therefore the boss must make them know that their voices really count for something.

Among the many external factors influencing leadership style are the following.

- The market: is it static and slow-moving or dynamic, with short product life cycles?
- How fierce and competent are the competitors?
- Are major new opportunities opening up internationally; for example, Burberry in China or Sainsbury's in India?

Among the internal factors influencing leadership style are the following.

- The culture and history of the organisation.
- The quality of past recruitment, determining whether the leader can place full trust in the quality and commitment of staff.
- The resources available to the organisation; for example if finances are weak, delayering and then autocratic leadership may be necessary to get things happening.

As with every aspect of business, the key to successful analysis and evaluation is to think long and hard about the individual circumstances of each business in turn. In 2010 in Britain the most admired business was John Lewis, a business led by a managing director that few have heard of – Andy Street. What people admire most about John Lewis is its commercial success despite an ownership structure that gives all power to its staff, not to outside shareholders. Excellent though Andy Street's performance may have been, the key feature of the business was laid down more than 80 years earlier, when the John Lewis cooperative structure was founded.

92.5 ASSESSING THE IMPORTANCE OF LEADERSHIP

Big businesses can have huge impacts on jobs, communities and on people's satisfaction with life. Seeing people queuing for hours for the latest 'Call of Duty' software or Apple iPad is a reminder that some companies help people to enjoy their lives. Yet that can be contrasted with the ghastly 'achievements' of businesses that are responsible for dumping polluted chemical cocktails into the environment. The point is simple: business matters and therefore business leadership matters. From the leader can come:

- the framework of ethics that affects the way staff act and react to pressures and temptations within their working life
- an attitude to business that may be entrepreneurial or may be cautious, even bureaucratic, for example, the spectrum from Apple to Marks & Spencer; the message that comes from the leaders actions and decisions will affect the whole organisation
- the spread of an autocratic or a consultative approach that may affect the management of people throughout the business
- the big strategic decisions that shape the next three to ten years of the business, for example, Kraft deciding to buy Cadbury or if (when?) Facebook decides to start pushing advertising in the way that Google has; leaders are judged on their big decisions.

A-grade application

When new Marks & Spencer boss Marc Bolland was appointed, he wisely announced that he would spend six months on a strategic review. On 8 November 2010 he met the Press to announce his findings. He planned on:

- evolution not revolution
- (another) redesign of the UK stores
- fresh expansion overseas
- reversing the move into stocking branded foods
- building a new website for the food side of the business, though (oddly) not one that could provide a full online service.

The conclusion reached by the Press was that this was cautious, dull and rather negative. Many of the ideas were reversals of those of the previous M&S leader. Staff could not be inspired towards this visionless future.

Key Terms

Autocratic leadership: when the boss keep all key decisions to himself or herself, and gives orders rather than power to subordinates.

Democratic leadership: this implies empowering people; that is, delegating full power over the design and execution of substantial tasks.

Laissez-faire leadership: this means allowing people to get on with things themselves, but without the coordination and control implicit within democratic leadership.

Paternalistic leadership: this means 'fatherly', that is, the boss treats staff as part of the family. Typically, this shows through as consultation, but with decision making remaining at the top ('Dad' decides).

ISSUES FOR ANALYSIS

- Big businesses are like huge ships, sailing straight ahead. Turning them left or right takes a lot of effort and a lot of time. In many cases, the big decisions are made by committees of senior managers – and the result is rubber-stamped by the leader.
- A business such as Toyota employs hundreds of thousands of people in dozens of different countries. How can one person really know so much about everything that she or he can make all the big decisions alone, and make them correctly? And in many cases the organisational culture precedes the new leader and remains unchanged by the time the leader has retired or been sacked. So it is important to analyse the evidence about the actual leader of the actual business in question.

92.6 LEADERSHIP AND CHANGE – AN EVALUATION

The business writer Robert Townsend suggested that many newly appointed leaders 'disappear behind the mahogany curtain', and are rarely seen again by staff. He thought that 'finally getting to the top' made many leaders focus more on corporate luxuries ('Which jet shall we buy?') rather than on hard work. Yet he knew that great leaders can make a huge difference to long-term business performance. He advocated a leadership model based on extensive delegation within tight, agreed budgets. Many follow that model today.

Ultimately, judging a leader takes time. The media may find a new 'darling' – perhaps someone who looks and sounds great on TV. That person's achievements may be praised hugely, and they may win 'Business Leader of the Year' awards. Yet it will be several years before anyone outside the business can appraise the individual's performance. In most businesses it is easy to boost short-term profit: you push prices up here, and make redundancies there. This persuades the media and the shareholders that you are a fine leader. The real question, though, is whether your decisions will push the business forwards or backwards over the coming years. In an exam, therefore, hold back from rushing to praise (or condemn) a boss on the basis of short-term performance. Big business is a long game. Ninety minutes is a long time in football; a week is a long time in politics; five years is a long time in business.

WORKBOOK

A REVISION QUESTIONS

(30 marks; 30 minutes)

1. Why should a business with an ethical culture never engage in 'anti-competitive activities'? (4)
2. How may a paternalistic leader set about generating a clear vision for a business? (4)
3. In your own words, explain what Peter Drucker meant by saying: 'Managers do things right; leaders do the right thing'. (4)
4. Outline two external factors that may be creating pressures for change within:
   a) McDonalds (4)
   b) Toyota. (4)
5. Outline one advantage and one disadvantage to a business of having a leader who has just won an award as 'Business Leader of the Year'. (4)
6. Freedom Foods produces organic, packaged foods such as sweets. A fall in sales has left the business operating at a small loss. It has 140 staff, of which 35 are employed in administrative jobs. Explain how an autocratic leader might attempt to get the business back into profit. (6)

B REVISION EXERCISES
B1 DATA RESPONSE

Curry Karma

Bangalore Balti (BB) started as a small curry house in Leicester. Word of its fresh, fiery food spread rapidly, creating the opportunity for expansion. By 2007 BB had 12 outlets across the Midlands, each run by a member of the owner's family. With plenty of cash in the bank, owner Safiq bought another chain of 16 Indian restaurants and converted them to the Bangalore Balti concept. This pushed the business into needing bank loans, which became a burden during the credit crunch recession of 2008–09.

While Safiq was focusing on the financial pressures, things were slipping operationally. In particular, the managers of the 16 new restaurants showed less respect for the BB menu and seemed much less able to keep costs down and therefore profit margins up. It was also noticeable that labour turnover was higher in the new restaurants than in the original ones.

As the business entered 2011, its profits were below those of four years earlier. See Table 92.2 It was getting hard to pay the interest bills on the loans. Something had to change.

Table 92.2 Data for Bangalore Balti 2007–11

	2007 (%)	2011 (%)
Labour turnover in the previous 12 months	8.4	19.5
Percentage of staff with cooking skills	46.5	28.0
Operating profit margin in the latest 6 months	12.8	4.7
Corporate overheads per £ of sales	8.4	22.3

Questions

(40 marks; 45 minutes)

1 Outline one internal pressure and one external pressure for change at Bangalore Balti. (4)
2 a) Discuss how Rafiq may set about deciding how to change the business in 2011. (16)
b) Analyse the text and the data given in Table 92.2, then recommend to Rafiq the main changes she should make to her Bangalore Balti business. (20)

B2 CASE STUDY

Change at Mulberry

When recession hit in 2008, what were the survival prospects for a 40-year-old producer of not-very-fashionable, expensive handbags; that is, bags costing from £500 to £1,500 each? In the three years prior to 2008, even though sales of luxury products were booming, Mulberry had been 'going nowhere'.

The collapse in consumer confidence in Autumn 2008 caused immediate, dramatic effects. Although Mulberry's Somerset factory is its flagship manufacturing outlet, 70 per cent of its bags (the more labour-intensive, fiddly ones) are made in China, Spain and Turkey. This forces the business to place orders for Autumn/pre-Christmas quite early in the year. Therefore, when demand slumped in the October to December 2008 period, supplies continued to arrive. The company's stocks (inventories) doubled between March 2008 and March 2009. The effect of this on the balance sheet can be seen in Table 92.3.

The bar chart shown in Figure 92.1 gives a clear idea of how the increase in stock stripped the balance sheet of its cash in 2009. For Mulberry, as with every other business, stock management is critical to working capital management – and therefore both to cash flow and to liquidity.

Even though the recession was still in full flow, the period from April to September 2009 saw a remarkable

Table 92.3 Balance sheets for Mulberry as at 31 March 2008 and 31 March 2009

Mulberry balance sheets Correct as at 31 March	2009 £000s	2008 £000s
Non-current (fixed) assets	11,694	10,791
Inventories (stock)	14,830	7,785
Trade receivables (debtors)	6,032	5,548
Cash	**3,710**	**10,237**
Current liabilities	(11,750)	(11,821)
Non-current liabilities	(132)	(21)
Net assets	24,384	22,519
Share capital	9,878	9,878
Reserves	14,506	12,641
Total equity	24,384	22,519

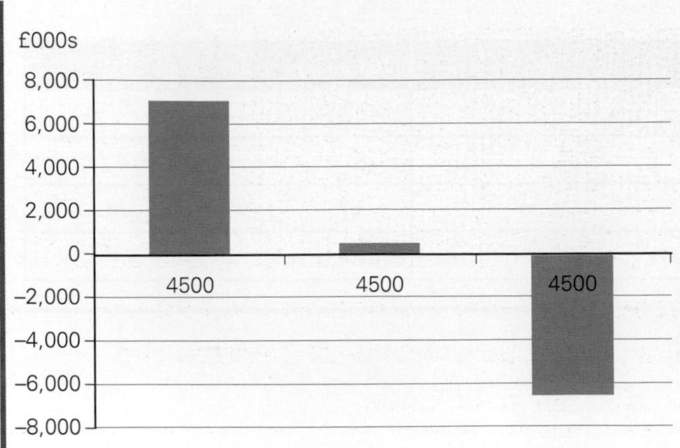

Figure 92.1 Change in current assets at Mulberry, 2009

recovery by Mulberry. At the end of 2009 the company chairman reflected that 'sales for the six months to 30 September 2009 were significantly ahead of our expectations'. Remarkably, UK sales at Mulberry shops were 41 per cent ahead of the previous year. This enabled the excessive stock level to be brought under control.

The explanation was simple. Mulberry had become fashionable. Chief executive Godfrey Davis had seen the changes to the luxury goods market and started to think of the incredible opportunities in China. He hired a creative director (Emma Hill) who saw handbags as fashion items for the younger market, instead of 'classics' for mums and grandmothers. Some middle managers at Mulberry were very critical of a switch from 'tried and tested classics' to the ups and downs of the latest trends. They worried about the ability of their factories to switch production quickly to new designs and doubted their flexibility to increase output to match fashion-related demand spikes. This resistance to change was to prove unnecessary, as customers proved willing to wait to for their latest Mulberry bags.

The repositioning of the brand was complemented by a redesign of the online store. This change was also criticised internally because Mulberry owns some of its own retail outlets. Fortunately, the 80 per cent increase in sales through the website did not seem to dent shop sales.

In January 2010 Emma Hill launched an even bolder attempt at young, fashion-conscious consumers: the Alexa bag, named after style icon Alexa Chung. A wave of public relations-based articles appeared in a range of publications including *Vogue* and *OK*. The £800 price tag proved no barrier to sales, as the first batch sold out in three weeks.

The 2010 annual results showed that Mulberry sales were 23 per cent up on 2009 and operating profit was 49 per cent higher. In the midst of the biggest recession for several generations, Mulberry turned an important corner. In the past the view was that only middle-aged women could afford posh handbags. Now the company believes that young women will find a way to get the bags they want, even if they spend months waiting. In his report to shareholders in June 2010, Godfrey Davis said that the company expected sales to China to rise by more than 100 per cent in the coming year.

All this leaves the shareholders happy, but what about the other stakeholders? The Somerset factory now employs 195 staff, up from 110 four years ago. Chief executive Godfrey Davis admits that some customers complain when they realise that their bag is made in China or Spain, but insists that everything is made with high-quality Italian leather. Therefore the quality is assured and there are no questions about the animal welfare standards, as could be the case with leather from China.

Questions

(40 marks; 50 minutes)

1. Examine the pressures for change that affected Godfrey Davis. (10)
2. Assume that Mr Davis has a paternalistic leadership style. How may he have set about carrying through the process of change at Mulberry? (15)
3. Although Mr Davis is well-rewarded financially, he is not as highly paid as many other chief executives. Discuss how he might have performed if offered a £5 million bonus for boosting the 2010 profits at Mulberry. (15)

Organisational culture

UNIT 93

Organisational culture sums up the spirit, the attitudes, the behaviours and the ethos of 'the organisation'. It is embodied in the people who work within the organisation, often via traditions that have built up over time.

93.1 INTRODUCTION

Unit 51 covered the key elements of business culture, such as:

- entrepreneurial versus **bureaucratic**
- purposeful versus purposeless
- ethical versus profit-driven
- focused on customers versus focused inwards.

In this unit the issues of business culture are developed in three main ways:

1. looking at Professor Charles Handy's famous analysis of types of culture
2. considering how to change an organisation's culture
3. assessing the importance of culture.

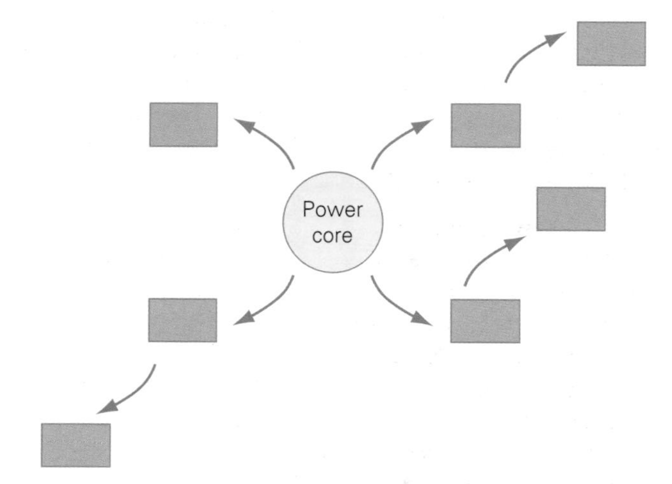

Figure 93.1 In a power culture, a web of power grows from the centre of the organisation

93.2 HANDY'S FOUR TYPES OF CULTURE

In his book *Gods of Management,* Charles Handy developed four ways of classifying business culture. These are discussed below and can be used to analyse business culture in more depth.

Power cultures

Power cultures are found in organisations in which there is one or a small group of power holders. Pleasing the boss can become the driving force behind the daily actions of staff. There are likely to be few rules or procedures and most communication will be by personal contact. This encourages flexibility among employees. Decision making is not limited by any code of practice. This can result in questionable, perhaps unethical, actions being taken in an attempt to please the boss. The leadership style in such a situation is clearly autocratic, and has been displayed in recent times by leaders such as Sir Alex Ferguson of Manchester United and Sir Alan Sugar (boss of Amstrad and notorious as the central character in BBC TV's *The Apprentice*).

Role culture

Role cultures are found in established organisations that have developed a lot of formal rules as they have grown. Power depends on the position an individual holds in the business, rather than the qualities of the person themselves. All employees are expected to conform to rules and procedures, and promotion follows a predictable pattern. This culture is bureaucratic, cautious and focused on the avoidance of mistakes. It may be appropriate when the competitive environment is stable; for example, in industries with long product life cycles. However, if the pace of change becomes more rapid, staff will struggle to adapt to new market conditions. This is the approach taken in businesses such as Microsoft, where the key thing is to preserve its huge share of the software market. The leadership style could be autocratic or paternalistic.

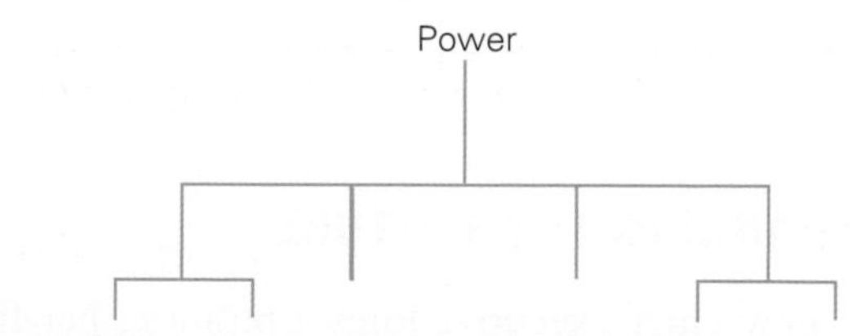

Figure 93.2 In a role culture, power flows down from the top of the organisation

Task cultures

Task cultures have no single power source. Senior managers allocate projects to teams of employees made up of representatives from different functional departments. Each group is formed for the purpose of a single undertaking and is then disbanded. Power within the team lies in the expertise of each individual and is not dependent upon status or role. This culture can be effective in dealing with rapidly changing competitive environments because it is flexible; for example, in markets with short product life cycles. However, project teams may develop their own objectives independently of the firm. The approach to leadership in such organisations is a mixture of paternalistic and democratic.

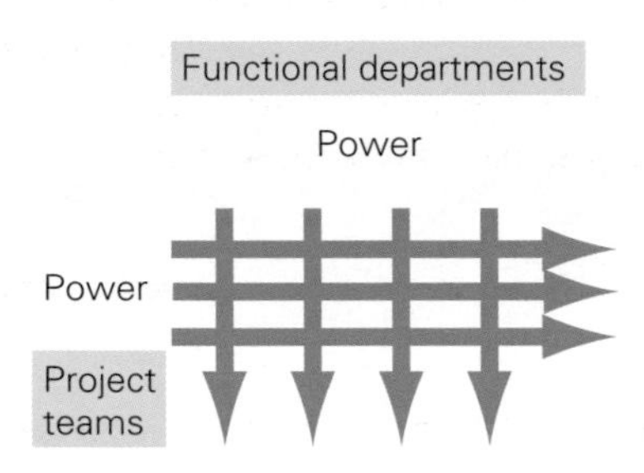

Figure 93.3 In a task culture, power flows down from the functional departments at the top of the matrix, but also lies horizontally within project teams

Person cultures

Person cultures are developed when individuals with similar training and backgrounds form groups to enhance their expertise and share knowledge. This type of culture is most often found within functional departments of large, complex organisations, or among professionals such as lawyers or accountants. It is largely associated with democratic leadership.

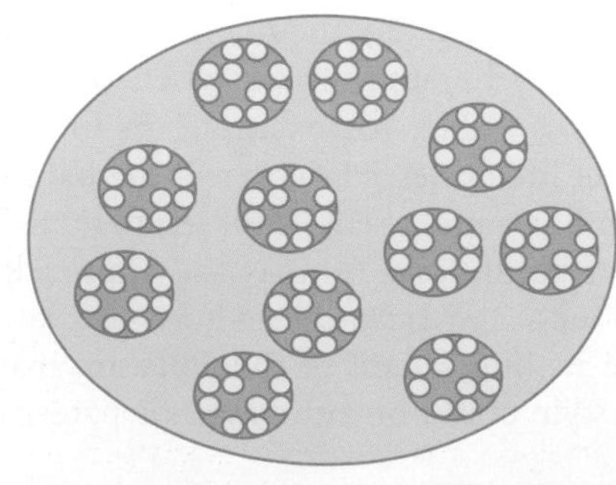

Figure 93.4 In a person culture, power lies within each group of individuals, flowing from their common knowledge and skills

93.3 CHANGING THE CULTURE

When a new chief executive joins a business, her first impressions will be of the culture. Is the customer embraced by the business, or kept at arm's length by voicemail and answerphone messages? Do staff enjoy Monday morning or only Friday afternoon?

If the new chief executive is unhappy about the culture, achieving change is unlikely to come easily. After all, some staff may have been working at the same place for 15 years, and will find it very difficult to change. Even more problematic is that staff collectively have a set of attitudes that may be tough to overcome. A manufacturing business may be dominated by middle-aged engineers who are sure they know best how to make a car or a caramel. Switching to a more market-orientated business may be very difficult.

The key to success in this process will be to ensure that all staff believe that the change is genuinely going to happen (and, preferably, that the change is the right one). There will be middle managers who are crucial to making things happen (for example, human resource managers or the finance staff who supervise the budget-setting process). If these people believe that the change is only skin-deep, they will hold back from supporting it. The engineers are likely to resist the change and perhaps they will prove right. Perhaps the new chief executive will be pushed aside by a board of directors who start to worry about whether a mistake is being made.

The key to cultural change, then, is to have a clear, consistent message. If everyone believes that the change is to be pushed through, they are far more likely to support it.

93.4 ASSESSING THE IMPORTANCE OF CULTURE

In recent years banks turned their backs on tradition and turned themselves into casinos. For centuries, a culture of caution had been at the heart of banking. The successful banker was one who went through a career without making any awful mistakes. Now this approach was considered to be old-fashioned. The focus was no longer on building a career; it was on building a bonus. As that bonus might be from £100,000 to £10,000,000 (a year!), who would look any further ahead than the coming months?

Nor was it difficult to make the profits required to get the bonuses. With plentiful cheap money (low interest rates) the clever thing was to borrow lots and lend it out as fast as possible. Why check on whether 'sub-prime' borrowers were likely to default in a year or two, if this year's bonus could be boosted to £500,000?

The collapse of this house of cards in 2008 and 2009 led to a predictable collapse into huge losses (estimated by the World Bank at $1 trillion). The culture of recklessness and greed had been created by a crazy bonus system that gave people (non-returnable) rewards based on the short term. In the longer term, the shareholders, the bank customers and governments had to pay the bills.

This example shows that culture is at the heart (or *is* the heart) of every organisation. Unusually, the banking example shows that culture can be transformed quite quickly, in certain circumstances. More often, businesses find that 'the way we do things round here' is very resistant to change. In 2007 Newcastle United FC appointed the hugely successful Bolton manager Sam Allardyce to transform its underperforming stars. He brought his own results-orientated approach to St James's Park and soon found himself swamped by the supporters' fury at his boring football. The 'Newcastle way' (the culture) is for bright, attacking, flair football. Big Sam did not last long.

Every organisation has its own culture. One school will have a staff room that is buzzing 40 minutes before the start of the day; another's staff car park will still be almost empty. One clothes shop will have staff who take their time helping customers, while another's staff play and joke with each other. And one charity will be focused entirely on the people it is set up to help, while another will behave as if the charity itself is more important than its 'customers'.

Distinguishing between healthy and unhealthy cultures is not difficult. It can be summed up in the following:

- focus on the customer versus focus on the staff (though senior management should appreciate that only a well-motivated staff will serve customers effectively)
- an attitude of 'can-do' rather than of 'must we?'
- a real feeling for the organisation as 'us', as a long-term commitment
- a conviction among staff that the organisation is a force for good (i.e. not just a money-making machine).

A-grade application

In June 2010 half the top medical staff at Great Ormond Street hospital signed a letter of no confidence in its chief executive, Jane Collins. Consultant Dr Kim Holt told the *Daily Telegraph*: 'Medical staff have growing concerns over patient care. They feel that Great Ormond Street is not really living up to its reputation.' Another consultant said: 'They (management) are completely unwilling to listen. Anyone who complains is treated as a troublemaker and bullied out.'

Dr Holt went on to report other consultants' view of a 'culture of fear and intimidation' within the hospital. In effect, there was a culture clash between the consultants' traditional view of patient care and the chief executive's desire for change.

93.5 IS CHANGE ALWAYS BETTER?

Not all cultural changes prove to be a success. Sometimes new leaders assume that a change in culture is essential, because they do not take the time to understand the strengths of the existing one. The Conservative governments of the 1990s swept away the tradition of NHS hospital wards being run by an all-powerful 'matron'. A failure to clean the ward properly would have meant risking the wrath of matron; cleaners cleaned. The new approach was to award contracts to outside cleaning companies, then check that agreed targets had been met. The matrons were pushed aside in favour of professional, 'can-do' managers. The managers were supportive of the new cleaning businesses; unfortunately, the cleaners were not so committed to cleaning. The later wave of MRSA-bug bacterial problems in hospitals can be put down to a management change based on inadequate understanding.

ISSUES FOR ANALYSIS

- Professor Charles Handy's four types of culture are quite hard to understand, but that can make them especially impressive as a tool to use within an analysis of a firm's culture. The analysis becomes all the more effective if you can relate the types of culture to the leadership style shown within the organisation.
- Yet culture goes far beyond Handy's approach, involving as it does the ethics of the organisation and the staff within it. In 2010, BP was not only humiliated for its huge spill in the Gulf of Mexico, but it was also given a record fine of $52 million for safety breaches at its Texas oil refinery. BP's US operation seemed to have a culture of putting profit before safety. To be able to identify ethical problems as an issue of culture is a vital skill. Analysis requires arguments that can show how one thing relates to another.

93.6 ORGANISATIONAL CULTURE – AN EVALUATION

Business leaders make many claims about the culture among their staff. They enjoy using words such as 'positive', 'can-do' and 'entrepreneurial'. Does the fact that the leader says these things mean that they are true? Clearly not. The leader cannot admit in public that the culture is 'lazy', 'negative' or 'bureaucratic'.

A well-judged answer to a question about culture will look beyond claims and public relations, and look for the evidence. Is there evidence that staff suggestions are welcomed and that they make an important contribution to the business? Is there evidence that mistakes are treated as learning experiences, rather than as reasons to be fired. And, perhaps most important of all, is there evidence that staff love their jobs and look forward to coming to work? All these things are tests of an organisation's culture.

Bureaucratic: an organisation in which initiative is stifled by paperwork and excessive checking and rechecking of decisions and actions.
Person culture: where power comes from groups of people with the professional expertise to dominate and therefore create the culture; for example, a group of professors dominating a university, enabling each, as individuals, to have influence but also independence.
Power culture: where the dominance of the leader (and his or her immediate circle of friends or advisers) overrides systems and conventional hierarchy. (This was the exact culture of Nazi Germany, where relatively junior staff could have power if they had access to Hitler.)
Role culture: where each individual has a tightly defined role that must be stuck to. Such an organisation will be bureaucratic and therefore highly frustrating for an individual with initiative. The culture will be dominated by the avoidance of risks.
Task culture: where groups of employees are delegated the power and resources to tackle tasks and projects, probably in a cross-functional way (so-called 'matrix management'). This is highly motivating, such as for the Nintendo development team that came up with the Wii.

Key Terms

FURTHER READING

Handy, C. (1995) *Gods of Management.* Arrow.

WORKBOOK

A REVISION QUESTIONS

(30 marks; 30 minutes)

1 Explain why it is unlikely that a task culture could exist in a business with an authoritarian leadership. (4)
2 Explain why a role culture would be inappropriate for a new software company seeking to be more innovative than Google. (4)
3 Sir Alex Ferguson has been manager of Manchester United for 25 years. When he retires, the new manager must either fit in with the culture created by Ferguson, or must change it. Examine two problems in changing the culture at an organisation dominated by one person, as at Manchester United. (8)
4 To what extent does the example of the UK banking sector in the lead-up to the credit crunch suggest that an entrepreneurial culture is not always a good thing? (6)
5 Recently a former quantity surveyor told the BBC that he had left the construction industry because he was so disillusioned by the problem of price fixing. Discuss how a new leader of a construction firm may try to change the culture to one of honest dealing. (8)

B REVISION EXERCISES
B1 DATA RESPONSE

The top job advertisement

Company: Topshop/Topman

Post: Area Trainer

Location: Oxford Circus, West London, Middlesex

Salary: circa £21–23K + excellent benefits

Working for Topshop and Topman is not like working for other fashion retailers. The size of the business, the culture of the company, the quality of training and direction of the business all combine to offer exciting and challenging careers. We currently have an exciting opportunity to join us as Area Trainer within our London flagship store, the world's largest fashion store. With over 1,000 employees on site, you will be responsible for the delivery of leading training solutions that directly support the key business objectives.

Source: Myjobsearch.com website.

Questions

(30 marks; 35 minutes)

1 Examine two ways in which the culture of Topshop may be different from that of other clothing retailers. (6)
2 This particular job is at 'the world's largest fashion store' (the Oxford Circus branch of Topshop). Use Handy's four types of culture to discuss how the culture may differ in this Topshop outlet compared with a small Topshop branch employing perhaps 12 people. (12)
3 Discuss whether or not this job as Area Trainer would be one that you would like to get within the next five years. (12)

B2 CASE STUDY

Bakery culture

Gianni Falcone had built his Italian bakery up over a 40-year period in Britain. He came to escape a life dominated in the 1960s by the Sicilian Mafia, and started a bakery in south London. For the first ten years his life had been hard and very poor. Baking only white rolls and white bread, he had to keep his prices low to compete with local supermarkets. He would get up at 1.30 a.m. every day to prepare and then bake the bread, and his working day would end 12 hours later. With a young family of four, he could not get to bed until 8.30 in the evening. Five hours later he would be back at work.

Eventually he started to see ways of adding value to his dough. A half kilogram loaf of bread with 30p of ingredients would sell for 80p, but roll it flat, smear tomato, cheese and herbs on it (cost: 25p) and it became a £3 pizza. A series of value-added initiatives followed, all adding both to the popularity of the shop and to its profitability. By 2000 the queues on a Saturday morning were legendary. Gianni was able to finance houses for all his family and he started to dream of owning a Ferrari.

By 2005 the business employed all the family members plus six extra staff. All worked the Gianni way. All knew the principles behind the business: ingredients should be as natural as possible and of as high a quality as possible. The customer is not always right (rowdy schoolchildren will be thrown out if necessary) but the customer must always be treated with respect. A slightly over-baked loaf will be sold at half price and day-old currant buns are given away to regular customers. Above all else, Gianni wanted to be honest with customers; they knew that all the baked goods were baked freshly on the premises.

Then, in 2007, Gianni was taken ill. The problem was with his lungs; quite simply, 40 years of flour in the bakery air had taken its toll. He had to retire. As none of his family wanted to take on the commitment to the awful working hours, he had to sell up. The only person with the inclination and the money to buy was an experienced baker from Malta, Trevi Malone. He bought the business for £250,000. Gianni was able to retire to the substantial home he had built in Sicily (now relatively Mafia-free).

From the start, Malone's approach was dramatically different. While Gianni had been ill, all the baking had been done by his bakery assistant Carol. She had worked miracles by herself, so that the shelves were full every morning. Now, from the first morning, Malone showed his distaste for her ways of working. Why did she use organic yeast when there were perfectly good, cheaper ones? Why did she 'knead' the dough in batches of 5 kg when it would be better to do it by machine in 20-kg quantities? And when she suggested that it would be good to start making hot cross buns, Malone snapped: 'This crazy place already makes too many different lines; just concentrate on what you're doing.' In the past, Carol's ideas had led to successful new products such as a top-selling apricot doughnut. Now she was to be silenced.

In the shop, Malone's approach was also quite different. Instead of casual clothes, everyone would wear uniforms; customers would be addressed as 'Sir' or 'Madam', and every order must be followed by an 'upselling' suggestion. The person who bought only a loaf of bread should be asked 'Would you like any doughnuts or cakes today?' The sales staff thought this was a daft idea, because – with so many regular customers – people would soon tire of being asked to spend more money. But they had quickly picked up the idea that Malone was not interested in discussion – he knew best.

Over the coming weeks things were changed steadily. The ham used on the meat pizza was changed from 'Italian baked ham' at £10 per kg to a much cheaper Danish one (with 20 per cent added water). As Malone said to Carol, 'Our customers don't see the ingredients label, so who's to know?' Malone noticed that doughnuts took longer to prepare than was justified by their 60p price tag, so he started to buy them in from a wholesale baker. Outsourcing was the sensible approach.

Within two months Carol began to look for a new job. She found it in another bakery, but soon left that as well, and went to college to retrain for a new career. Other staff steadily left, including all of Gianni's family. The newly recruited staff were accepting of Malone's rules, but none seemed particularly keen on the work. Perhaps that was fortunate, because sales started to slip after two months, and then fell at an increasingly rapid pace. Staff who left were not replaced, as they were no longer needed. Even more fortunate was that Gianni was not well enough to travel back to England. He never knew how quickly 40 years of work fell apart.

Questions

(40 marks; 50 minutes)

1. Use the example of Gianni's bakery to discuss whether it is right to say that value added is at the heart of all business activity. (15)
2. Examine why outsourcing the doughnuts may not have been 'a sensible approach' for Malone. (10)
3. Malone paid £250,000 for a business that steadily went downhill. To what extent was the problem due to the change in culture within the workplace? (15)

Making strategic decisions

UNIT 94

A strategic decision is one that is made in a situation of uncertainty and has medium- to long-term significance for the business. Once it has been made, a strategic decision cannot easily be reversed.

94.1 INTRODUCTION

The word 'strategy' means a plan for meeting your objectives. It is therefore subordinate to objectives. Typically, directors set objectives and managers carry out the strategy. Yet the term 'strategic' means a lot more than this. Businesses refer to it in two ways: strategic thinking and strategic decisions.

Strategic thinking involves visualising what you hope to achieve within coming years (given consumer tastes and lifestyles, plus the competition you face), assessing the strengths of your business in relation to those aims, then identifying an approach that can enable you to get there. This process should be carried out with a wide range of senior – and, ideally, some junior – staff, in order to get a wide range of views and a real consensus. After this process of strategic thinking takes place, new objectives can be identified and a new strategic plan put into action.

Strategic decisions, then, are the result of strategic thinking. In 1990 the chairman of car tyre maker Nokia decided to stake the future of the business on a then still trivial business – the mobile phone. In the period 2001–07 the directors of Northern Rock decided to change from being a sleepy building society based in the English north-east to become a major national bank. Both were hugely important **strategic decisions** and these two examples highlight that big decisions are not necessarily correct ones. Table 94.1 shows some examples of strategic decisions, contrasting them with smaller-scale day-to-day **tactical decisions** faced by managers.

94.2 IMPORTANT INFLUENCES ON STRATEGIC DECISION MAKING

Relative power of stakeholders

The 1990s had been very kind to Arsenal FC, as they continued to win trophies and the club rivalled Manchester United as Britain's top football team. The supporters loved the club, the manager and the ground – Highbury – and felt sure the good times would keep on coming. Arsenal's directors were not so sure. Highbury could hold only 38,000 people, while Old Trafford was steadily being expanded to take twice that number. If the Manchester club could generate twice the income, how could Arsenal continue to compete in the long term? So the directors took a £400 million gamble on moving the club to the 60,000-seater Emirates stadium. As the shares in the football club were held by a few wealthy people, this gamble was possible. If the shares had been held by the general public, there would have been much less willingness to such a chance. Directors can take bold strategic decisions only if they are supported by the shareholders. This may be easier in a business that is not a public limited company.

Table 94.1 Examples of strategic and tactical decisions

STRATEGIC DECISIONS	TACTICAL DECISIONS
• Should we relocate our factory from Slough to Sri Lanka?	• Should we replace our CCTV system as our current pictures are too fuzzy?
• Should we close down our out-of-town stores and concentrate more on online sales?	• Should we mark down the prices on this Christmas stock today (23 December), rather than wait until the January sales?
• Should we focus all our investment capital for the next two years on building a sizeable operation in India?	• Our labour turnover has been rising steadily, so should we conduct a staff questionnaire to find out what's wrong?
• Should we move from Anfield to a new, multi-million-pound bigger stadium nearby?	• Should we switch our Sunday opening from 11.00–5.00 to 12.00–6.00?

Available resources

Arsenal's £400 million gamble was very difficult to finance, but it proved possible. In other cases, a business may have a brilliant idea that has huge potential, yet it may be unable to secure the necessary finance. The business may lack the internal finance and find it impossible to persuade outsiders of the attractions of the proposal. In some years banks seem willing to offer finance to very unattractive propositions; in other years they refuse to finance rock-solid ideas.

Top companies try to make sure that they always have enough cash to be able to put strategic decisions into practice. On 26 June 2010, Apple had $46 billion of cash and cash investments on its balance sheet to provide the liquidity to take advantage of any opportunity. Tesco plc also has a hugely strong financial position, allowing it to declare in 2010 a massive store-building programme in China for the three years until 2013.

Ethical position

Some years ago the term business ethics meant little. Today it is a significant part of boardroom discussion in plcs and other businesses. The question remains, however, 'Are the discussions about how to operate ethically, or are they about how to be thought to be operating ethically?' In others words, is it genuine or is it for show? In fact, company directors can be forgiven for being quite cynical about ethics, because consumers are often as hypocritical as companies. People talk about animal welfare, but can't resist two chickens for a fiver; and they talk about global warming as they're driving down to the shops.

There is no doubt, though, that if consumers believe a business is a force for good, there can be financial benefits. Innocent Drinks did relatively little to deserve its reputation as an ethical business. Its high prices hardly implied a social desire to promote healthy living. Yet people accepted its story that it is a pure little company with a big heart. Even after Coca-Cola took a majority stake in the business, the Innocent logo suggested 'healthy' to consumers, whereas the Coke logo shouted 'unhealthy'. Innocent's image adds value to the brand.

94.3 DIFFERENT APPROACHES TO STRATEGIC DECISIONS

There are always two alternative methods to making a decision: evidence-based (scientific) or hunch. It is important to realise that either method may be successful, or unsuccessful. There is no evidence that one is better than the other.

In 2007 senior management at Whitbread plc went through a detailed analysis of the four operating divisions of its business. It decided that it had two rising stars, one dog and one cash cow. It decided that the correct strategy would be to sell the latter two divisions in order to generate more cash to finance the growth of the two stars. Understandably, the 'dog' (the restaurants division, including Beefeater) was difficult to sell, but cash cow David Lloyd Leisure was sold for £925 million. In this case the strategic decision was based on evidence of the financial performance of the different parts of the business. Therefore it was logical – scientific even. Three years later, in 2010, it was clear that the strategic decision had been a brilliant one. Both of the stars (Costa Coffee and Travelodge) were booming.

In 2010, Apple made a significant strategic shift. Partly, perhaps, because of its focus on new product development, it had rather ignored China. Remarkably, in July 2010, the head of the Chinese computer giant Lenovo said: 'We are lucky that Steve Jobs (boss of Apple) doesn't care about China. If Apple were to spend the same effort on the Chinese consumer as we do, we would be in trouble.' That same month Apple opened a huge, modern store in Shanghai. The company announced that it would be the first of 20 new flagship stores throughout China. The reason for Apple's change of strategy was probably because the first half of 2010 saw Apple's sales revenues double in China.

94.4 THE SIGNIFICANCE OF INFORMATION MANAGEMENT

The bosses of most plcs make their decisions on the basis of data, not hunch. Therefore information management is crucial. The first critical issue is to have full knowledge of your own business. This might seem obvious, but in January 2008 a major French bank found that one of its own employees had been gambling with €50 billion of the bank's money. Sorting out the mess cost more than £3,000 million. A huge bank that, one week, was considering plans for its long-term future was – the next week – fighting for its short-term survival.

Few businesses have such problems, but there are others that find out only much too late that sales

A-grade application

Connaught Housing

On 23 June 2010 shares in the housing firm Connaught plc were 323p, valuing the business at £500 million. Then a series of blows came that made the share price crash by 95 per cent within 6 weeks! On 10 August the shares were priced at 15p.

At the heart of the problem was that new management had announced that it was investigating the firm's accounting practices. As the firm had debts of £260 million, operating losses revealed by reworking the firm's income statement showed that the business could not keep up its interest payments.

The line between success and failure can be a fine one.

have been worse than expected. Good companies have good, up-to-date information about themselves. This requires IT systems that show instantly how the business is doing, so that the senior directors can think quickly about whether current strategies are working. If they are not, it may be time for a radical rethink.

ISSUES FOR ANALYSIS

These days chief executives of plcs are paid huge sums (literally, millions of pounds) to run large businesses on behalf of the shareholders. The only reason to pay such high sums is to attract people who can get the key strategic decisions right. Before he stood down as Tesco's boss at the start of 2011, Sir Terry Leahy had successfully steered the company into eastern Europe and the Far East. Yet he made a huge mistake by spending £1,250 million in moving Tesco into America. Although Sir Terry would have gathered as much information about the US grocery market as possible, ultimately the decision was made as much on the basis of hunch (backed by huge experience) as on scientific evidence. But in 14 successful years, Leahy was bound to make one strategic error. Weak leaders postpone decisions until it's too late. Far better to be decisive, even if the occasional decision proves a mistake.

When studying a business situation – perhaps in the exam room – these are the key questions:

- Has the business done all it reasonably can to gather data such as primary research?
- Has the business made effective use of relevant assets (including the expertise within its staff)?
- Does the leadership have the experience, the enthusiasm and the wisdom to make a sound judgement – and then ensure that the new approach is carried through effectively?
- Has the business the financial and human resources to turn the right idea into the right strategy?

94.5 MAKING STRATEGIC DECISIONS – AN EVALUATION

Strategic thinking should be radical, innovative and free from internal constraints such as 'that's not how we do things round here'. The traditions and culture of an organisation should always be taken into account, but cannot be allowed to act as an absolute constraint. Careful discussion with a wide range of staff should help to bring insight to the process and assist in the process of communicating the need for a new approach.

If the strategic thinking is right, the strategic decisions should also be right. Sometimes, though, the pressures upon the decision makers lead to mistaken compromises. Shareholders who are unhappy about short-term profitability may not be willing to back a strategic decision that has a five-year timeframe. Short-term cost-cutting may be the only language the shareholders understand. It is the job of the highly paid chief executives to find the right balance between what is right and what is acceptable.

Key Terms

Strategic decision: one that is made in circumstances of uncertainty and where the outcome will have a major impact on the medium- to long-term future of the organisation.

Tactical decision: deciding what to do in circumstances that are immediate (short term) and where a mistake is unlikely to have a major impact on the business.

WORKBOOK

A REVISION QUESTIONS

(35 marks; 35 minutes)

1 Explain the difference between 'strategy' and 'strategic'. (4)

2 Outline two qualities you would want in a manager who has to take strategic decisions. (4)

3 Look at Table 94.1. Explain why relocation from Slough to Sri Lanka would be regarded as a strategic, not a tactical, decision. (5)

4 Apart from shareholders, explain why two other stakeholder groups may be interested in the strategic decision to 'close down our out-of-town stores and concentrate more on online sales'. (6)

5 Briefly consider how well each of the following businesses may cope with a strategic decision that would require a major capital investment:

a) Business A has a current ratio of 0.95 and a gearing ratio of 55 per cent (5)

b) Business B has an acid test ratio of 1.05 and would need to increase staffing levels by 12 per cent to be able to produce the extra goods required by the strategy. (5)

6 Should business ethics ever be a matter of tactics, or should they always be part of the strategic thinking behind strategic decisions? (6)

B REVISION EXERCISES
B1 DATA RESPONSE

Strategic decisions in the ice cream market

Anglo-Dutch Unilever is the UK ice cream market leader with its Walls ice cream brand. It is looking at whether to expand into China, India, Russia or America. The US ice cream market is mature and is dominated by large, well-regarded, brands. China and India are both under-developed markets; until recently relatively few in the population had any discretionary spending for ice cream. Russians love ice cream, which is locally-made, cheap and very good. Data for ice cream markets is given in Table 94.2.

Table 94.2 Data for ice cream markets

	Spending per capita (US$)	Population (millions)	Market size (US$ millions)	Average market growth p.a. (2007–10) (%)
India	0.33	1,180	389.4	16
China	3.12	1,330	?	18
Russia	14,88	142	?	3
UK	43.66	62	?	0
USA	48.74	308	15,012	0.3
Average market growth p.a. (2007–10)				

Source:

Questions

(25 marks; 30 minutes)

1 **a)** Calculate the ice cream market size for China, Russia and the UK. (3)

b) If the ice cream market grows in 2011 at the average shown in the right-hand column in Table 94.2, what growth (in US dollars) will there be in the Chinese, Indian and US markets? (6)

2 Use all the above information to decide which of the four countries would be the best for Walls to launch into. Justify your answer. (16)

B2 CASE STUDY

Strategic decision for AirAsia

In 2009 and 2010 the award for the World's Best Low Cost Airline went to AirAsia. The company's story began in 2001, when Dr Tony Fernandes and three colleagues bought loss-making AirAsia and turned it into a low-cost carrier. At first they had two ageing Boeing 737 planes, five destinations and 250 staff. By early 2010 they had 90 new planes, 60 destinations and 7,500 staff.

AirAsia's operational strategy largely mimics that of Ryanair and easyJet: no frills, high-aircraft utilisation (rapid turnaround); online booking and a single-aircraft fleet (to minimise staff training and engineering maintenance costs). A significant difference, though, is the desire to offer a friendly, comfortable service (hence the awards).

The biggest strategic difference is that AirAsia has set up a sister company AirAsia X that operates long-haul. From its London–Kuala Lumpur route, 40 per cent of travellers fly onto their local destinations via AirAsia. But this approach has operational risks attached to it, because low-cost flying may be fine for short journeys, but sounds grim for 12- to 14-hour transcontinental flights.

AirAsia X started flying in 2007 and had eight aircraft by the end of 2009. Whereas AirAsia follows easyJet in having a fleet of Airbus A320 planes, AirAsia X flies the much bigger A330. In 2009 the business managed to buy five A330 planes through 'financing raised on its own balance sheet strength, and cashflow' (AirAsia annual accounts 2009).

Now, however, the firm needs to make a big strategic decision. It has been planning to increase its fleet from eight A330 planes to 25 by 2015. But should it switch to the bigger, better, but more expensive A380 plane? Long-haul rivals such as Emirates, Singapore Airways, Qantas and British Airways have all bought the A380 'Superjumbo'. Instead of buying 17 new A330s, some in the boardroom suggest they should buy 15 A380s. As planes are made to order, it usually takes two to three years to receive the finished planes. So AirAsia will have to live with whichever decision is made.

Appendix A: Key features of the two planes

Key feature of the Airbus A380 'Superjumbo' and Airbus A330 are given in Table 94.3.

Table 94.3 Key features of the Airbus A380 and Airbus A330

Feature	Airbus A380 'Superjumbo'	Airbus A330
List price per plane	\$346 million	\$212 million
Maximum passenger capacity	650 (with economy plus 'premium' class) 850 (if all economy class)	340 (with economy plus 'premium' class) 440 (if all economy class)
Special characteristics	Exceptionally quiet for passengers (and residents near airports)	More than 1,000 in service worldwide, so easy to get experienced pilots and engineers
Customer approval	Very high; airlines flying the A380 now (such as Emirates) can get a price premium of 10 to 20 per cent	Nothing special

Appendix B: Selected performance data for AirAsia and AirAsia X

The passenger numbers for AirAsia X are given in Table 94.4. AirAsia passenger numbers are given in Figure 94.1.

Table 94.4 Passenger numbers for AirAsia X

	Passengers
2007	15,000
2008	270,000
2009	1,034,000
2012 (est)	3,000,000
2015 (est)	6,000,000

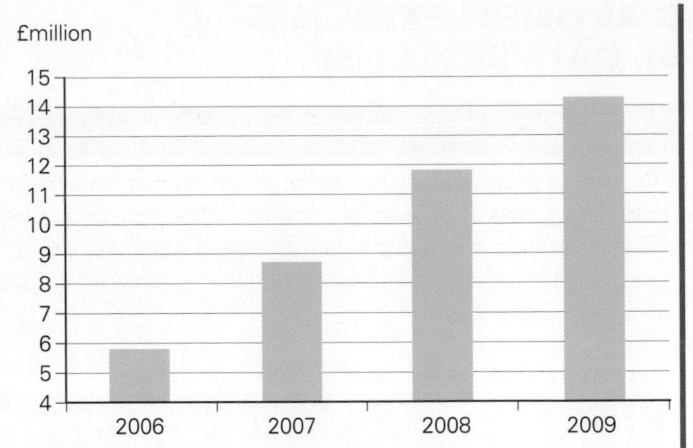

Figure 94.1 AirAsia passenger numbers
Source: AirAsia accounts.

Appendix C: Extracts from company accounts

Table 94.5 shows extracts from AirAsia's balance sheets for 2008 and 2009. Table 94.6 shows extracts from AirAsia's income statements for 2008 and 2009.

Table 94.5 AirAsia: balance sheets for 2008 and 2009

AirAsia balance sheets* As at 31 December	2009 (£millions)	2008 (£millions)
Non-current (fixed) assets	1,835	1,500
Inventories (stock)	4	4
Trade receivables (debtors)	211	206
Cash	230	170
Total current assets	445	380
Current liabilities	(340)	(345)
Net current assets	105	35
Non-current liabilities	(1,415)	(1,215)
Net assets	525	320
Share capital	295	195
Reserves	230	125
Total equity	525	320

*Source AirAsia accounts; all figures converted from Malaysian currency at 5 per £.

Table 94.6 AirAsia: income statements for 2008 and 2009

AirAsia income statements* Year to 31 December	2009 (£millions)	2008 (£millions)
Revenue	627	571
Operating costs	(444)	(641)
Operating profit	183	(70)
Net financing costs	(58)	(104)
Profit before taxation	125	(174)

*Source: AirAsia accounts; all figures converted from Malaysian currency at 5 per £.

Questions

(40 marks; 60 minutes)

1 Based on the evidence available, discuss whether the business is right to buy a significant number of extra planes for its AirAsia X operation. (14)
2 A second strategic decision is whether to acquire 15 A380s or 17 A330s. On the basis of the information provided in the case study, which is the better option? Justify your view. (18)
3 Outline four extra pieces of information it would have been valuable to have had before answering Q2. (8)

Decision trees

UNIT 95

Decision trees are diagrams that set out all the options available when making a decision, plus the outcomes that may result by chance. They help managers to see the best possible outcome, the worst possible outcome, plus an average or composite view of the 'most likely' outcome.

95.1 INTRODUCTION

Decision trees provide a logical process for decision making. The decision problem can be set out in the form of a diagram, like a tree on its side. It can take into account the occasions when a decision can be taken and the occasions when chance will determine the outcome. Chance can be estimated by assigning probability. While the estimate of the probability may only be a guess, at least probability is quantitative and gives the decision process a scientific quality.

The kinds of problems which are suited to decision-tree analysis are those where a sequence of events or options has to be followed in conditions of uncertainty. The decision whether or not to launch a new product, enter a new market, build a new factory, hire or buy machinery, for example, are all cases where decision-tree analysis is appropriate. It would also be possible to use investment appraisal. The advantage of a decision tree is that it allows for uncertainty or chance. This makes it a better model of the reality of an uncertain business world.

95.2 STEP-BY-STEP APPROACH TO DECISION-TREE ANALYSIS

Step 1: the basics

1 The tree is a diagram setting out the key features of a decision-making problem.
2 The tree is shown lying on its side, roots on the left, branches on the right.
3 The decision problem is set out from left to right with events laid out in the sequence in which they occur.
4 The branches consist of:
   a) a decision to be made (see Figure 95.1)
   b) chance events or alternatives beyond the decision maker's control (see Figure 95.2).

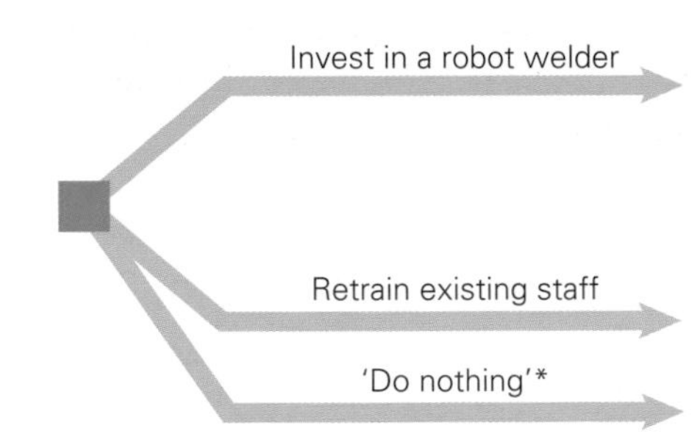

Figure 95.1

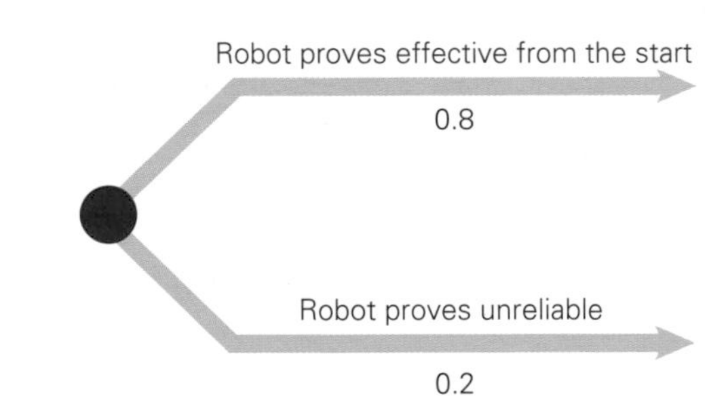

Figure 95.2

Note carefully that a square means a decision and a circle means a chance event, that is, one of two or more events may follow. Therefore:

- there must be a probability attaching to each of the chance events or alternatives
- these probabilities must add up to 1 as one of them must happen.

In Figure 95.2, the decision maker has allowed for an 80 per cent (0.8) chance that the robot will work well and a 20 per cent (0.2) chance that it will prove unreliable. These figures could be arrived at from experience with robots in the past.

At any square, the decision maker has the power to choose which branch to take, but at the circles chance takes over. You can choose whether or not to invest in a robot. But there is a chance that the robot may prove unreliable. The full tree so far is shown in Figure 95.3.

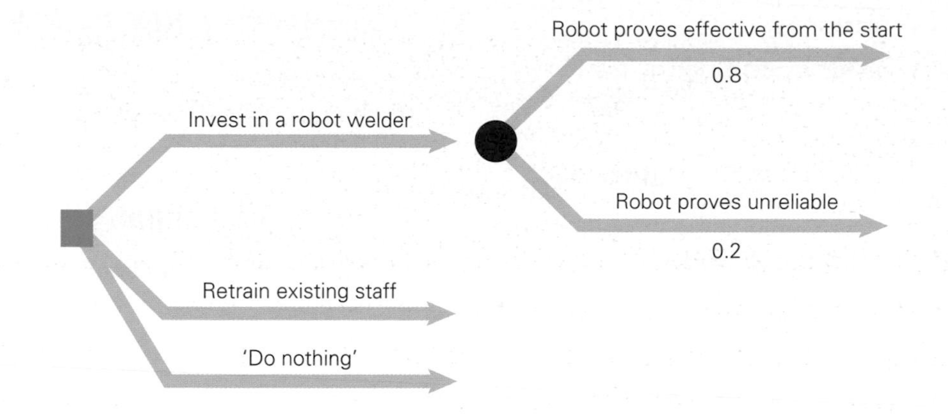

Figure 95.3

The decision maker will choose which branch provides the better or best value.

To consider a different example, if buying costs a net cash outflow of £1,000 per year while hiring costs £800, it is better to hire (see Figure 95.4).

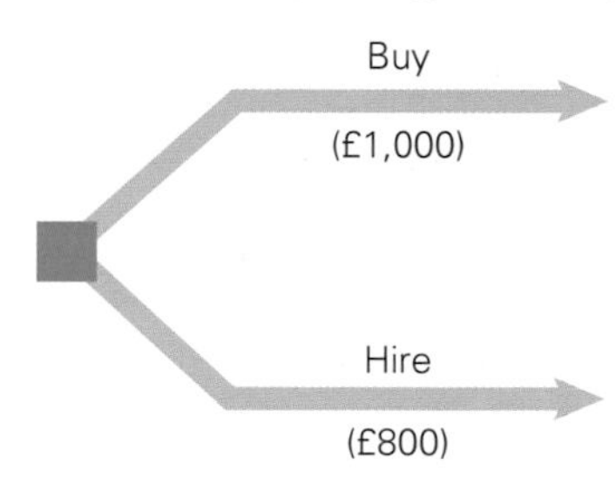

Figure 95.4

Note that the branch not taken is crossed out, as shown in Figure 95.5.

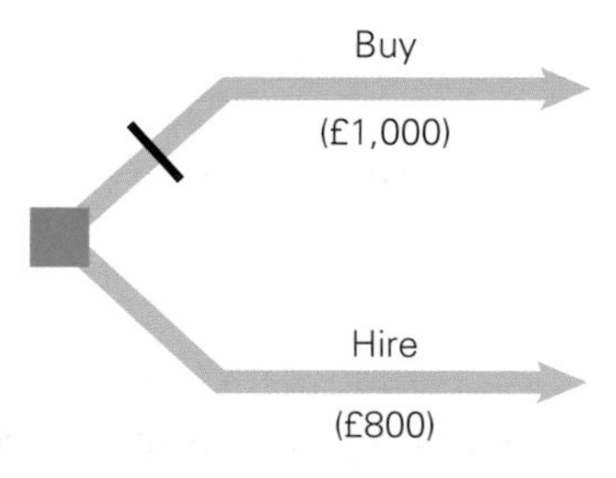

Figure 95.5

Step 2: drawing a decision tree

Bantox plc must decide whether to launch a new product (see Figure 95.6).

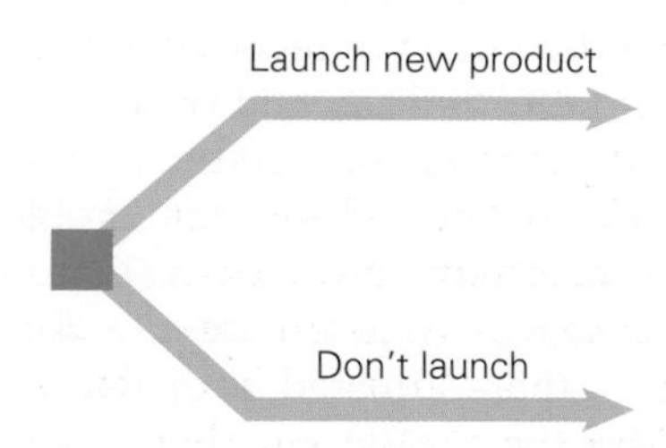

Figure 95.6

Research suggests there will be a 70 per cent chance of success in a new product launch. This would be shown as a probability of 0.7 (see Figure 95.7).

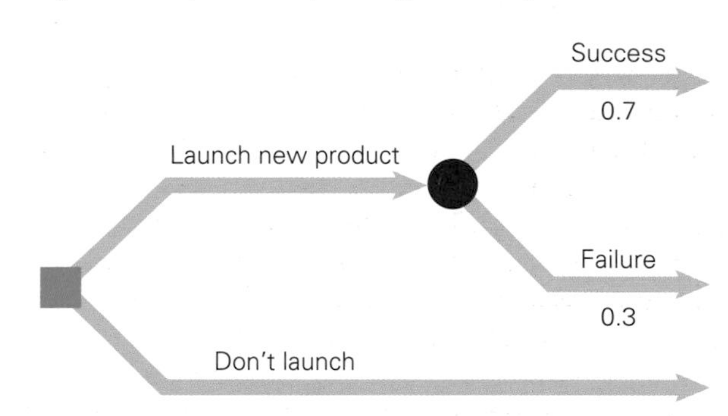

Figure 95.7

Note that, because probabilities must add up to 1, the implied chance of failure is 0.3.

To make a decision based on the above tree, estimates are needed of the financial costs and returns. In this case, let's assume:

- the new product launch will cost £10 million
- a new product success will generate £15 million of positive net cash flows
- a new product failure will generate only £3 million
- no launch means no movements in net cash.

The full decision tree now looks like Figure 95.8.

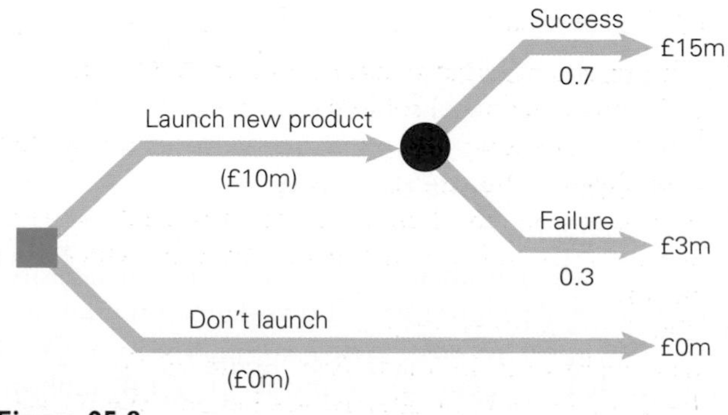

Figure 95.8

Step 3: making calculations

At each probability circle, a calculation is required of the average outcome, given the probabilities involved. If a launch costing £10 million will generate either £15 million or £3 million, what will be the average result, if the same circumstances happened several times over? Sometimes the firm would get £15 million and sometimes £3 million. Usually, to work out an average, you would add the numbers and divide by 2; that is:

£15m + £3m/2 = £9m

That assumes, though, that there is an equal chance of £15 million and £3 million. In fact, the probabilities are not 50/50, they are 70/30. There is a 70 per cent chance of £15 million. So the correct (weighted) average outcome is:

£15m × 0.7	=	£10.5m
£3m × 0.3	=	£0.9m
Total		£11.4m

In decision trees, the expected values at probability circles are always calculated by weighted averages.

Calculations on decision trees are carried out from right to left, that is, working backwards through the tree, making calculations at each probability circle.

In the case of Bantox, only one calculation is needed. If there are several circles, it is helpful to number them, and show your weighted average calculations clearly (see Figure 95.9).

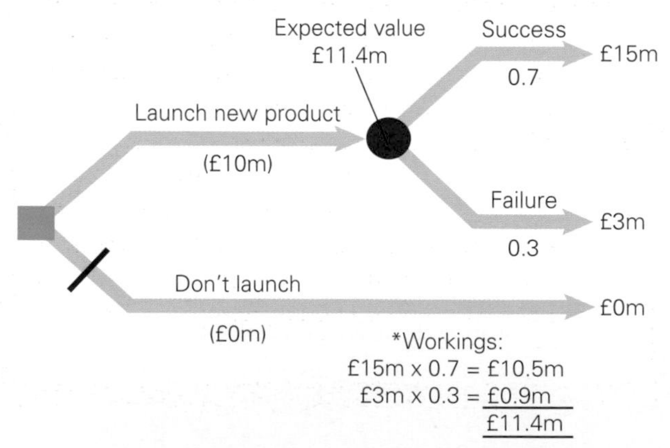

Figure 95.9

Step 4: showing your decisions

Having calculated the expected value (weighted average) at each probability circle, a rational decision can be made. As Figure 95.9 shows, launching the new product will, on average, turn £10 million into £11.4 million, that is, generate a profit of £1.4 million. Therefore it is preferable to launch. The decision to launch is indicated by crossing out the 'don't launch' option.

95.3 SUMMARY OF KEY POINTS

A decision tree is a diagrammatic presentation of a problem involving decisions (squares) and chance events (circles).

1 The problem is laid out from left to right. Decisions are shown as squares, chance events as circles.
2 Each chance event has a probability estimated for it. The probabilities must add up to 1 since one of them must happen.
3 Two money values are shown:
   a) the cost of the decision (shown as a negative number, that is, in brackets)
   b) the benefit or cost of a specific outcome occurring. These are shown at the end of each branch of the tree.
4 Working from right to left, the decision maker calculates the expected value at each circle. These values are calculated by multiplying the money value by the probability, then adding the results.
5 Still working from right to left, the decision maker decides at each square which branches to cross off, leaving only the better or best alternative open.

95.4 ADVANTAGES AND DISADVANTAGES OF DECISION TREES

Advantages of decision trees

The advantages of decisions trees are set out below.

1 Decision trees set out problems clearly and encourage a logical approach. The discipline of setting out the problem in a decision tree requires logical thinking and can also generate new ideas and approaches.
2 Decision trees encourage a quantitative approach and force assessments of the chances and implications of success and failure.
3 Decision trees not only show the average expected values for each decision but also set the probability of a specific outcome occurring.
4 Decision trees are most useful when similar scenarios have occurred before so that good estimates for probabilities and predicted actual values exist.
5 Decision trees are most useful in tactical or routine decisions, rather than strategic decisions.

Disadvantages of decision trees

The disadvantages of decision trees are set out below.

1 It may be difficult to get meaningful data, especially for estimated probabilities and of success or failure.
2 Decision trees are less useful in the case of completely new problems or one-off strategic problems.
3 It can be relatively easy for a manager seeking to prove a case to manipulate the data. A biased approach to the estimated probabilities or values could 'prove' the pre-desired result rather than the logically determined outcome.
4 Decision trees do not take into account the variability of the business environment.

5 Decision trees may divert managers from the need to take account of qualitative as well as quantitative information when making a decision.

ISSUES FOR ANALYSIS

Decision trees raise many issues of value when analysing business problems:

- The importance of allowing for uncertainty. The most common technique for business decision making is investment appraisal. This is based upon a forecast of future cash flows from which the payback period and profitability of the investment can be assessed. The great weakness with this approach is that it is based on a cash flow forecast. In reality, every decision can result in a range of possible outcomes, not just one. By focusing firms on uncertainty, decision trees can help to ensure that managers make more carefully considered decisions.
- The importance of looking at alternatives. Although it is important to be single-minded – to have clear goals – too many managers adopt a strategy without fully considering the alternatives. They perhaps choose the approach that worked last time, or the one adopted by their competitors. Decision trees encourage careful consideration of the alternatives available before a decision is made.
- All quantitative methods can be biased, consciously or unconsciously. Optimism is often a virtue, but it may lead to exaggerated sales figures or excessively high probabilities for success. This does not mean quantitative methods should be rejected. Only that it is sensible to ask who provided the figures and assess whether they had any reason to want a particular outcome. Cynicism about decision trees is out of place; scepticism is wholly valid.

95.5 DECISION TREES – AN EVALUATION

Small firms run by one person benefit from clear, speedy decision making. The entrepreneur knows the customers, the competition and the staff. Therefore he or she can make effective decisions quickly, with no need to justify them to others. Some may prove faulty, but the quick responses of a small firm should ensure that damage is limited. The business will stand or fall on the hunches and judgements of the boss.

In large firms, the same rules do not apply. A successful career path at a company such as Mars or Unilever often depends upon avoiding mistakes. Therefore it is important to be able to justify why a decision was made. Even if it proves to be wrong, that should not matter as long as the method for making the decision was thorough and analytic. After all, if four out of five new products prove to be failures, what would be the reason for firing a manager who has just launched a flop?

It can be a matter for regret that methods such as decision trees are used to 'protect the back' of decision makers. In other words, they may not be valued for themselves, only for their value as a protector. Often, though, the process of trying to protect themselves encourages managers to think hard about their decision-making methods. Those who use decision trees positively may find an improvement in their record of success, and help the big firms to compete with the faster moving small firms.

Key Terms

Actual values: although known as 'actual values' or 'payoffs', these are the forecasts of the net cash flow which result from following a sequence of decisions and chance events through a decision tree. They should always be shown at the ends of the branches of the tree.

Decision tree node: a point in a decision tree. A square is used where a decision is needed; a circle where there are possible paths or chance events that are out of the decision maker's control.

Expected values: these are the forecast actual values adjusted by the probability of their occurrence. Although called 'expected', they are not the actual cash flows which result. Expected equals actual x probability.

Probability: the likelihood of something occurring. This can be expressed as a numerical value, which can be a percentage (for example 50 per cent chance), a fraction (for example ½), or a decimal (for example 0.5). The probability of something certain is 100 per cent or 1. The probability of something impossible is zero. So probabilities range from 1 to zero.

WORKBOOK

A REVISION QUESTIONS

(30 marks; 30 minutes)

1 When drawing a decision tree, what symbol is used to show:
   a) when a decision must be made
   b) when chance takes over? (2)
2 If the probability of the successful launch of a new product is estimated to be 0.72, the probability of a failed launch must be 0.28. Explain why. (3)
3 State whether each of the following is a decision or a chance event:
   a) choosing between three different new product options
   b) a new product succeeding or failing in the marketplace
   c) good weather on the day of the open air concert
   d) whether to advertise or to cut the price. (4)
4 Explain the difference between an expected value and an actual value. (3)
5 State three advantages and three potential pitfalls of using decision trees. (6)
6 Explain the circumstances when decision trees are least useful. (4)
7 If the chance of achieving £200,000 is 0.2 and the chance of £20,000 is 0.8, what is the expected value of a decision? (4)
8 Explain how decision trees may help managers to assess the best decision by 'what if?' analysis. (4)

B REVISION EXERCISES

B1 DATA RESPONSE

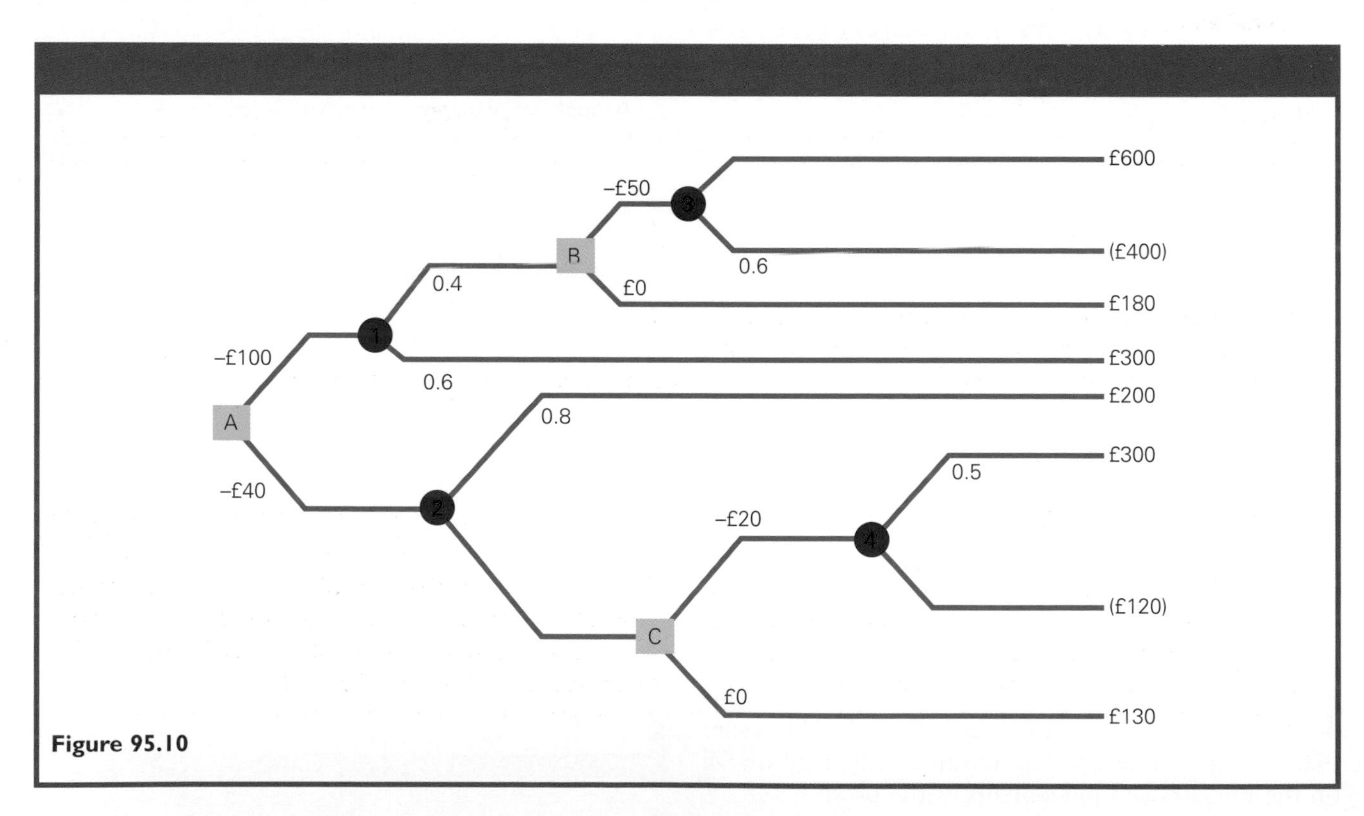

Figure 95.10

Questions

(20 marks; 20 minutes)

1 Look at Figure 95.10. Calculate the expected values at nodes 1–4. (12)
2 State your decisions at decision points A–C. Indicate your decisions on the tree diagram. (8)

B2 DATA RESPONSE

Denham Potteries has a capital spending budget of £100,000. The production manager has put in a bid for £100,000 for a new tunnel kiln. The marketing manager has countered with a proposal to spend £80,000 on launching a new product. This new product is in line with the firm's objective of diversifying, but may be rather risky given the firm's past record of only one success for every five new products.

Ken Coton, the marketing manager, has provided a handy table of figures to summarise the information. This is set out in Table 95.1.

Table 95.1 Denham Potteries

Outcome	Probability (surplus over next 5 years)	Actual value (£)
New product		
Big success	0.1	900,000
Modest success	0.1	500,000
Failure	0.8	30,000
Tunnel kiln		
Success	0.8	200,000
Failure	0.2	60,000

Questions

(25 marks; 25 minutes)

1 Draw a fully labelled decision tree to set out the options. (10)
2 What decision should the firm make on purely numerate grounds? (3)
3 Outline the qualitative factors the board should take into account before making the decision. (12)

B3 DATA RESPONSE

Mansfield Town FC is considering buying a South American centre forward player for its team. The club knows statistics show that only one in four overseas forwards succeeds in the lower divisions. But things are desperate. The player's contract will cost £500,000 and, if successful, could increase home attendances sufficiently to be worth £1.2 million over the three-year contract. Even if the player is unsuccessful, attendances should rise by £200,000.

Questions

(20 marks; 20 minutes)

1 Draw the decision tree and label it carefully. (12)
2 On the basis of the tree, what decision should the club take? (4)
3 Outline two reasons why the club might decide to proceed. (4)

B4 CASE STUDY

The research and development department in Gregson plc has just invented a new higher-quality version of the product sold by a rival business, Winder plc. The product is code named 'Copycat'. At present Gregson lacks the technology to manufacture the product itself. After further research, it decides there are three immediate choices:

1 buy the technology to manufacture the product itself
2 sell all rights to Winder plc
3 sell all rights on a royalty basis to a third company.

The marketing department believes that Copycat, as it stands, has a 50 per cent chance of success, with no further development.

However, the research and development department in Gregson believes it could improve Copycat still further by some design enhancements. However, it only wants to do so if Copycat had already succeeded and if choice 2 above had not been taken. After design enhancement, the chance of a successful launch is estimated to be 60 per cent.

The forecast actual values are shown in Table 95.2.

Table 95.2 Forecast actual values for Gregson (all figures in £000s)

Decision outcome	Manufacture	Sell all rights to Winder	Sell on a royalty basis to a third company
Fails before design enhancement	−262.5	15	7.5
Succeeds after design enhancement	375	–	300
Succeeds but no design enhancement	150	15	82.5
Fails after design enhancement	−412.5	–	−142.5

Questions

(30 marks; 35 minutes)

1 Prepare a decision tree to illustrate this situation, showing branches, probabilities, and actual values. (8)
2 Calculate the expected values. (6)
3 Explain the optimal decision strategy based on these calculations. (8)
4 State and explain two other factors which Gregson may take into account before making the final choice of decision strategy. (8)

Implementing and managing change

UNIT 96

Change management involves controlling the activities required to move an organisation from its current position to a new one.

96.1 IDENTIFYING THE NEED FOR CHANGE

Change is an unavoidable part of life, both for individuals and organisations. Existing markets decline and new products are developed. Experienced workers retire or leave, and are replaced by new employees with fresh ideas. According to recent research published by the Chartered Institute of Personnel Development (CIPD), organisations undergo major change once every three years on average, with smaller changes taking place almost continually.

The need for change can result from influences within and outside the business. Change is an inevitable part of business growth. For a firm that grows organically, this change may be relatively slow and steady, occurring over a prolonged period of time. However, managers will still need to have the skills and expertise required to anticipate and manage this change effectively. Change resulting from merger or takeover will be more sudden, and may be followed by a painful period of adjustment, even if careful planning has taken place beforehand.

Change may be anticipated, such as the introduction of a new marketing strategy, or unanticipated – for example, the collapse of an important supplier or a sudden deterioration in customer satisfaction. Changes may be beyond the control of individual businesses, such as the introduction of a national minimum wage or a ban on advertising during children's television programmes. A successful firm will see change as an opportunity to re-examine its operations and market conditions or, better still, anticipate changes before they occur and develop a competitive advantage over rivals.

Figure 96.1 Causes of organisational change

96.2 ORGANISATIONAL BARRIERS TO SUCCESSFUL CHANGE

No matter how much time and how many resources are put into the planning stage, a number of organisational issues may arise that have a negative impact on the implementation of change within a business. These include the following.

- *A lack of effective leadership and project management:* the failure to coordinate projects effectively can lead to missed deadlines and wasted resources, affecting a firm's performance.
- *A lack of effective training:* a business must ensure that all those involved in implementing change initiatives have the expertise required to do so, including project management and leadership skills.
- *Poor communication:* effective two-way communication must be established between all the individuals and groups affected.

96.3 RESISTANCE TO CHANGE

Resistance to change may be defined as 'an individual or group engaging in acts to block or disrupt an attempt to introduce change' (CIPD). Workers within an organisation may resist change for a number of reasons. For example, people may be concerned about a loss of control or status, feel vulnerable to the threat of redundancy or resent the break-up of social groups within the workplace. Resistance may be directed at the change itself, perhaps because it seems to go against the prevailing culture, such as introducing an extra management layer to a business with an entrepreneurial culture.

Resistance can also come in different forms. Active resistance occurs when opposition is clearly stated, such as when workers decide to take industrial action. Passive resistance may include failing to attend meetings or respond to messages. Although more subtle, passive resistance can be just as (if not more) effective in blocking change, especially as its existence is less likely to be detected.

Dealing with negative responses and resistance to change requires a great deal of skill by managers. Such responses may result from rational and reasonable concerns and therefore need to be handled calmly and sympathetically. Then it should be possible to find a way forward and avoid a situation of stalemate.

> **A-grade application**
>
> In October 2010 London's firemen threatened to go on strike on 5 November, Britain's Firework (Bonfire) night. This night is the busiest of the year for firefighters, so the threat was both serious and extremely unpopular. The firemen were protesting about a change in their shift patterns. For many years they had worked two nine-hour day shifts followed by a 15-hour nightshift, followed by four days off. The employers were demanding a change to 11 hours per dayshift and 13 hours at night. The firefighters say this will leave them with less family time, while leaving London with less night cover. On the face of it, the differences between both sides seem quite small, so it should be easy to negotiate and resolve. The dispute became serious because the firemen disliked the way the management tried to force the change through.

Figure 96.2 Bonfire night

Overcoming resistance to change

To overcome resistance, key factors will be as follows.

- Objectives that are clear to all, and are accepted as necessary or desirable by the great majority of staff.
- Adequate resources for senior management to effect the change efficiently; these include financial resources, human resources, and the right operational and technological back-up.
- An effective training programme: this can be expensive, but not as expensive as the alternative of not training. Unmotivated or sceptical staff can be very critical of what they see as second-rate training. Poorly run training sessions can set the change process back; training must be excellent to be adequate. Therefore it needs to be planned and carried out by an important figure within the change process, such as the **project champion** (see below).

> **A-grade application**
>
> **No product champion for Terminal 5**
>
> In March 2008 the new British Airways Heathrow Terminal 5 opened after 19 years of planning. The new terminal was trumpeted as a customer-service breakthrough, with its high-tech new systems, such as that for baggage handling. Yet its opening proved to be a humiliating fiasco. The key problem was with the baggage-handling systems, leading to chaos as bags piled up.
>
> It later emerged that staff who had been working at Terminals 1, 2 and 3 had received far less training than had been planned on the new technology system. Only 50 of the 400 baggage handlers had received the planned four days of training at Terminal 5. BA Chief Executive Willie Walsh had not delegated effectively to a project champion who could make sure that this big change worked effectively.

96.4 IMPLEMENTING CHANGE SUCCESSFULLY

Despite the individual circumstances and the particular changes faced by any given business, there are a number of key factors that should be considered in order to develop a programme that will incorporate change and overcome any resistance effectively. These factors include those listed below.

Key factors to consider

Ensuring that the objectives and details of any changes are communicated as clearly and as quickly as possible to employees

Leaving staff in the dark can lead to rumours and speculation about the changes that, once established, can be difficult to challenge. It is far better to keep everyone informed of the objective and the plans.

Appointing a project champion

It is easy for new ideas to be stifled by the bureaucracy within middle management; a project champion should have the power and the passion to push the change through and to persuade staff that the new methods will be more successful than the old.

Involving staff rather than imposing change

Unless there is a need for confidentiality, involving staff in the change process can lead to a number of benefits. Consulting staff regularly or setting up **project groups**, taking members from different functional departments, to work on particular areas should help to generate a wider range of ideas, but also help to combat anxieties and increase commitment by creating a sense of ownership.

Ensuring appropriate leadership

No particular leadership style is most effective at dealing with change. The most appropriate style will depend on the circumstances of the particular organisation and the nature of the changes it faces. However, all leaders will need to provide their subordinates with the vision and rationale for change required to make the process a success.

Creating a culture for change

A 'learning organisation' is one where change-orientated thinking has been embodied in all employees, so that change is seen as an opportunity rather than a threat. Such organisations are likely to be more receptive and to adapt more quickly to changes, even those that are unexpected. Over the years the England football team has been very resistant to any change in tactics; this can be contrasted with the huge fluidity of a team such as Manchester United, who accept the manager's decisions without a quibble.

96.5 MANAGING CHANGE

Once the process of change has been implemented, it needs to be managed effectively. This involves two stages.

Control

This involves taking steps to ensure that the final outcome of the change process is as close as possible to the objectives identified at the planning stage. Regular checks will allow the firm to detect problems quickly and deal with them promptly, in order to avoid delays and wasting resources. This will only be possible if the business has set measurable goals (that is, quantifiable targets against which performance can be compared). However, even the SMARTest objectives are subject to influences beyond the control of the organisations that set them. **Contingency planning** encourages firms to attempt to identify what could go wrong and develop strategies to deal with these problems in order to get back on course. For example, training may prove to be inadequate – in which case, new courses need to be made available to remedy the situation quickly.

Review

Once change has been implemented and objectives achieved, the organisation needs to consider the 'What next?' scenario. This may seem strange, given the upheaval created by attempting to adjust to recent changes. However, the nature of business is to keep in touch with its marketplace. Increased competition, changes in technology and customer requirements mean that no business can afford to stand still for long.

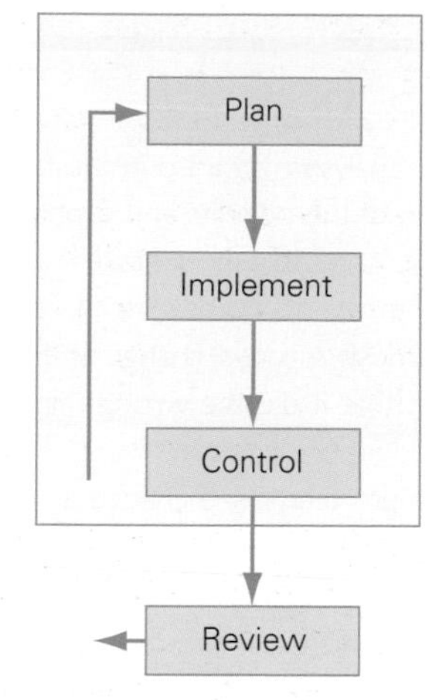

Figure 96.3 The process of managing change

96.6 RADICAL VERSUS CONTINUOUS CHANGE

Business process re-engineering (BPR) is an approach requiring an organisation to totally rethink its approach to its current operations. BPR focuses on the processes undertaken within the organisation, rather than its structure. This requires a clear idea of the specific roles of workers within the organisation and how they relate to customers. Once the aims and objectives have been established, the organisation is completely redesigned from scratch.

A key advantage of BPR is that it considers the efficiency of the organisation as a whole, in terms of meeting customer requirements, rather than simply focusing on individual parts. However, an organisation is unlikely to undergo such radical change unless it is faced with a crisis threatening its very survival, given the upheaval that it is likely to create. In most situations, businesses are more likely to prefer a ***kaizen*** approach (that is, a process of continuous improvement).

Key Terms

Business process re-engineering (BPR): a radical approach to changing an organisation, in which it is completely designed in order to meet the needs of customers more effectively.

Contingency planning: preparing for unlikely and unwanted possibilities, such as the onset of recession, or the collapse of a major supplier or customer.

***Kaizen*:** the Japanese term for continuous improvement.

Project champion: an individual appointed from within an organisation to support the process of change.

Project group: where members of different departments within an organisation are put together (temporarily) to generate ideas, to put the plan into practice and maintain good communications between departments.

ISSUES FOR ANALYSIS

Opportunities for analysis may arise in the following areas.

- A consideration of the benefits and problems of introducing a programme of change; this should take into account the crucial question of whether 'do nothing' is an acceptable alternative. The fiasco of British Airways' change to Heathrow Terminal 5 does not mean that it did the wrong thing; it just did it in the wrong way.
- Many management teams see change as an operational issue. For example, many government departments have wasted billions of pounds in trying to establish new IT systems that proved unusable. They saw the change as a technical, operational issue, driven forward by independent management consultants. Later investigations showed that the mistake was ignoring the importance of staff and the knowledge they have of how the systems really work. There is huge scope for analysing whether the correct way forward is via staff or via operations management (the ideal is an effective combination of the two).
- An analysis of the consequences of resistance to change within an organisation.

96.7 IMPLEMENTING AND MANAGING CHANGE – AN EVALUATION

All organisations need to accept and face up to the need for change and, in the modern business environment, the pace of change appears to show no signs of slowing down. Any business that is unwilling or unable to adapt to the ever-increasing pace of change appears to be doomed to become less and less competitive. Yet there are always exceptions to every rule. In business, every generalisation proves to be a mistake. For every nine businesses that need change to survive, there will be one that thrives on remaining unchanged, from a traditional private school to a producer of handcrafted British sports cars (such as Morgan) or handmade wedding dresses.

It is easy for managers to neglect existing customers or suppliers in an attempt to demonstrate their change management skills, but the resulting damage may cancel out the benefits of change. However, change requires the support of the employees within an organisation; without the support of employees, change is unlikely to succeed. The ability to establish trust between management and workers in the face of change appears to be the way forward in managing the process of change successfully.

WORKBOOK

A REVISION QUESTIONS

(40 marks; 40 minutes)

1. Outline two causes of change that may be generated from within a business. (4)
2. Describe two causes of change that are likely to be outside a firm's control. (4)
3. Examine the main consequences to a fashion clothing business of failing to identify and respond to changes in the external environment. (6)
4. Identify two reasons why a firm could encounter resistance to change from within the workforce. (2)
5. Use examples to explain the difference between active and passive resistance. (4)
6. Examine one way in which a business could attempt to successfully tackle resistance to change. (4)
7. Briefly explain the importance to effective change of a 'project champion'. (4)
8. Analyse one benefit of creating a culture of change within an organisation. (4)
9. Examine one potential benefit and one potential drawback to a business from adopting a programme of business process engineering. (4)
10. Outline the role that human resources managers can play in the change management process. (4)

B REVISION EXERCISES

B1 DATA RESPONSE

Bookstore restructuring leads to success

Foyles is one of the UK's oldest and best known bookstores. However, when Christopher Foyle was appointed chairman of the independent bookseller in 1999, the company was in a mess. Christopher took charge of the business following the death of his aunt, Christina Foyle, who had run the company for 54 years. Under Christina, the store's layout was based on a confusing categorisation of books by publisher, rather than by author or subject. Customers were forced to queue three times to buy books: the first to obtain a handwritten chit, the second to pay and a third to obtain their purchases. Foyle's reputation was such that one rival bookseller used the advertising slogan, 'Foyled again? Try Dillons'. The business suffered from a lack of financial management and the accounts were still being written up manually into ledgers. The market was getting increasingly competitive, with high street chains such as Waterstones and W H Smith, supermarkets and Amazon online selling cheap blockbusters. Sales turnover had fallen to £9.5 million and was falling at 20 per cent a year. Christina refused to issue the staff with contracts and would dismiss them on a whim.

Christopher began a programme of modernisation, installing a new management team, introducing a proper accounting system and investing £4 million on refurbishing the main company's flagship store on the Charing Cross Road in London's west end. Staff were issued with contracts and the store layout was redesigned to be more customer friendly and stock more popular titles. A Foyles website was set up, which now accounts for over 10 per cent of the company's sales, and new stores were opened near the Royal Festival Hall, at St Pancras International station and the Westfield shopping centre in London.

In 2008, Sam Husain was appointed as the company's chief executive. He has a background of accountancy and financial and management consultancy and is only the second non-family member to run the company since it was established in 1903. Christopher remains in the role of company chairman, conducting board meetings by videophone from his home in Monaco.

In September 2010, Foyles reported an impressive increase in operating profits, up from £80,625 in 2009 to £434,588 in the 12 months to June 2010. Sales turnover was up by 1.9 per cent to £25.1 million and like-for-like sales grew by 9.7 per cent in a book market where sales fell by 5.6 per cent. According to chief executive, Husain, the success has come from working hard to provide a 'proper service to book lovers, rather than the heavy discounting used by rivals'. He said, 'We've really concentrated on aspects that make a bookseller a destination, so you look at a service, at quality of staff, at training, and all of these make each of our bookshops a special place to come and visit.'

Source: Adapted from articles in the *Financial Times* and *The Independent.*

Questions

(20 marks; 25 minutes)

1 Examine the key reasons why change was necessary at Foyles. (10)
2 Analyse the possible factors that led to change being implemented successfully at the bookseller. (10)

C ESSAY QUESTIONS

(40 marks each)

1 'The problem of change is people.' Discuss.
2 After 20 years as a full-service Italian restaurant, Luigi Ristorante is to change to a self-service format. Discuss the key aspects of change that Luigi should tackle to ensure that this new plan proves to be a success.

What the examiner wants: understanding assessment objectives

UNIT 97

97.1 INTRODUCTION

A-level examiners love a candidate who understands how to get the marks – it makes their life easier! Getting those marks is, on the face of it, quite simple. All you have to do when answering a question is to:

- define any key terms (show that you know what you're talking about)
- use them to examine the specific business context (the case material you're dealing with)
- analyse the question using theory when necessary, and with reference to the case
- make a judgement when you're asked to do so – and justify it.

The truth is that it is not that easy. Many students are poor at showing these skills in a classroom. Add in the pressure of the exam room and many students' ability to think 'goes out of the window'. It's replaced by one thing alone: the ability to remember. In the exam room, the examiner is trying to tap into the student's brain (have a look around; decide whether it knows enough and is clever enough to be worth an A). But many students are pushing the examiner away ('No, I think you've asked me the wrong question, dear examiner; what you should have asked me is this – look, I prepared it especially for you …').

To the examiner, the pyramid shown in Figure 97.1 is the basis of all exam marking. It forms a pyramid because at the base is the foundation of every good answer: knowledge. If the question is on opportunity cost and you don't know what that is, no amount of waffle will dig you out of the hole. What the pyramid also shows, though, is that no matter how much knowledge you have, you cannot get more than 30 per cent of the marks available, and that is never enough for a pass. Therefore it is essential that you master the other skills too.

At AS-level, the key skills are knowledge and application. Between them they account for 60 per cent of the marks and therefore can enable you to achieve a grade B. At A2, the keys are analysis and evaluation, though it is important to remember that analysis is dependent on knowledge, and evaluation relies on good application. Assessment objectives for all A-level Business Studies specifications from 2008 are given in Table 97.1.

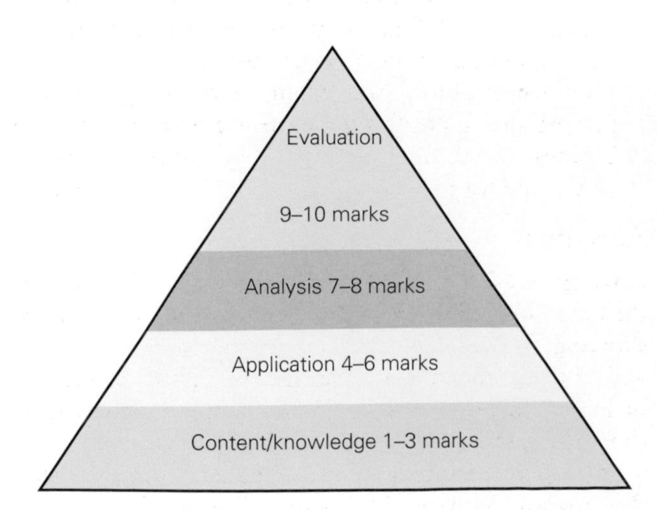

Figure 97.1 Pyramid of marks

Table 97.1 Assessment objectives for all A-level Business Studies specifications from 2008

SKILLS	AS	A2	A-LEVEL
Evaluation	20%	30%	25%
Analysis	20%	30%	25%
Application	30%	20%	25%
Knowledge	30%	20%	25%

98.1 MASTERING EACH OF THE ASSESSMENT OBJECTIVES

Knowledge

Business Studies isn't Chemistry. In Chemistry you either know what happens when iodine is mixed with sulphuric acid or you don't. The same is true in some aspects of business. For example, do you know what happens when a business with cash flow problems turns to factoring? (Yes, it should improve the cash flow position.)

Yet in many other cases it is not obvious that technical knowledge is required. Many questions use words that anyone has access to, whether they have attended lessons or not. Here are a few examples:

1. Discuss how XYZ Ltd should improve the motivation of its workforce.
2. Examine the possible effects on XYZ Ltd of a rise in consumer spending.
3. Explain two ways in which XYZ Ltd could increase its profit.

In each of these three cases, a student with weak knowledge can write plenty and probably come out of the exam feeling great. Their result will be a great disappointment, however. This is because the examiner will see many of this candidate's answers as waffle.

Examiners are actually very generous; they want to give marks. But their great fear is giving a high mark to well-written waffle that, on a second reading, proves to be empty of business knowledge. So help them: start your answer with a precise definition that will convince them that you're a good student who attended lessons, did your homework and bothered to revise.

Your opening sentences in answer to the above three questions may be as follows.

1. Motivation, according to Professor Herzberg, is 'people doing something because they want to, not because they have to'.
2. Rising consumer spending will increase the sales of most products, boost sharply the sales of luxury products (and services), but cut the sales of 'inferior products' such as Tesco Value Beans.
3. Profit is revenue minus costs; therefore it can be increased by boosting revenue or cutting costs (fixed or variable).

Examiner tips on revising knowledge

Examiner tips on revising knowledge are set out below.

1. Four weeks before the exam, make lists of all the key terms within the section of the specification being examined. Use the official exam board specification for this.
2. Write a definition for each of the terms, ideally based either on this book or classroom notes or the *Complete A–Z Business Studies Handbook* (see Further Reading). Beware of Googled definitions, because most will be American and their business terminology is not quite the same as Britain's, and many will be aimed at university, not A-level, students.
3. Keep trying again to write the definitions from your own memory and from your understanding of the topic. For example, the explanation of profit given above is something that you would not memorise, but that you should 'know'.
4. Don't spend time trying to remember lots of advantages and disadvantages of things; this will distract you from the key matter: what is it (that is, the definition).

Application

Application marks are given for your ability to think your way into the specific business situation facing you in the exam. This may be a context you know quite well (the launch of the Nintendo Wii) or could be one you have never heard of before (Tesco's unsuccessful first attempt at operating in America). In fact, it doesn't matter. The text will contain all you need to develop your answers to the questions. Unit 98 gives a very full account of how to get the most out of data when tackling an exam question.

To get 'OK' marks at application, you need to use the material in the text effectively. Not just repeating the company name, but being able to incorporate factors such as Tesco's challenge in building up supply lines in America (that is, making good deals with US suppliers).

To get full marks at application, you need not only to be able to use the context, but also to see its significance; for example, showing that you see the importance of Tesco deciding to halt its US expansion at 50 stores, when it had originally talked of building 200.

Every business is unique. It is also true to say that every year is unique for every business. The more you master the specific issues that relate to the specific company or industry, the better your marks at application.

Examiner tips on revising application

Examiner tips on revising application are set out below.

1. Throughout the course, take every opportunity to read *Business Review* articles, to read business stories in newspapers, to watch business TV (for example, *The Apprentice*, *Dragons' Den*) and take note of relevant news items.
2. Three weeks before the exam, start working on the B1 and B2 exercises within this book. Read the text and write short notes on the key business aspects of that unique business. If possible, do this with a friend, so that you can swap ideas. It is helpful to debate which (of all the points you've identified) is the single most important feature of that business.
3. One week before the exam, start going through past papers. Identify the key features of that unique business and think about how they can be connected to the questions set.

Analysis

Analysis is shown in two main ways. The first is through the build-up of argument, in which you are showing an ever deeper understanding of issues, causes and consequences. This can also be called 'sequences of logic'. In other words, 'if that happens, this will be the consequence'.

It is quite easy to practise sequences of logic using the 'analysis framework' shown in Figure 97.2.

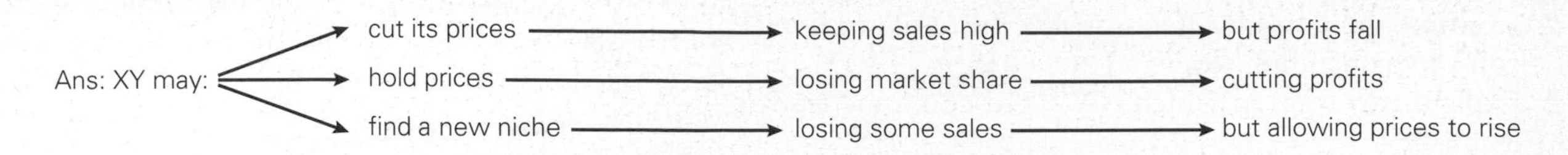

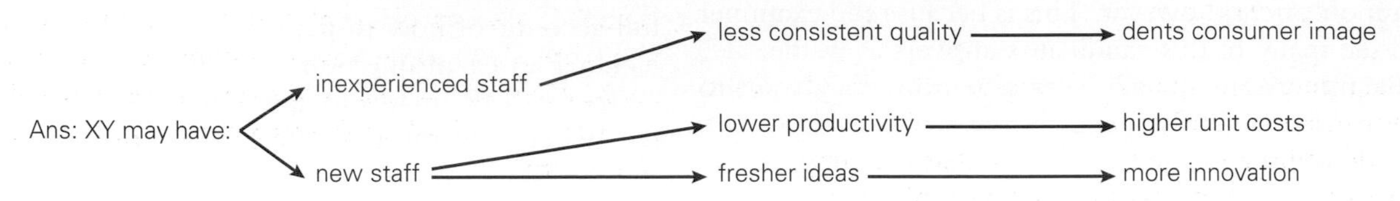

Figure 97.2 Analysis framework

Examiner tips on revising analysis

Examiner tips on revising analysis are set out below.

1 Throughout the course, ask your tutor two questions: 'Why is that the case?' and 'What would be the effect of that?'
2 Two weeks before the exam, use the above model to think through any of the major topics in the specification (the ones on the left-hand side of the document).
3 One week before the exam, go through past papers, using the analysis framework shown in Figure 97.2 on any question that carries more than 8 marks.

Evaluation

Evaluation means judgement. In other words, it's about you making a judgement and giving your reasons (that is, justifying it). Each Friday, Messrs Ferguson and Wenger must make their decisions on team selection. They will talk through their judgements with their closest advisers, explaining their thoughts. The advisers (assistant manager and head coach) may argue or may agree. The managers' decision, of course, is final. In an exam, the ideal answer would give the judgement and explain it (in terms of tactics, the strength of the opposition, which players are on form, which are needed for next Tuesday's game against Barcelona, and so on).

In a business exam, you may be asked to recommend whether the firm should, or should not, launch a new product. You must decide on the basis of the evidence, then explain which aspects of the evidence pushed you towards your decision. You may also reflect on how confident you are of the decision. Is it a 'no-brainer'? Or is it finely balanced?

Other questions are more frustrating because they require you to invent your own evaluation (for example, 'Discuss the advantages to XYZ Ltd of using the Boston Matrix'). This style of question gives you nothing real to evaluate, but needs you to seize any opportunities available to you. For instance, the accompanying text may tell you that XYZ Ltd's sales have been slipping a bit, recently. This may enable you to suggest that, 'The most important benefit to XYZ would be the possibility that using the Boston Matrix will help the business to identify and support one or more Rising Stars. This could enable the company to turn around its poor sales performance.'

Examiner tips on revising evaluation

Examiner tips on revising evaluation are set out below.

1 Practise making judgements. For example, when you see a new restaurant opening up in your high street, do you think it will succeed? Do you think it will fail? Why do you think that? Then keep an eye on it to see how it's going.
2 Two to three weeks before the exam, start going through past exam questions.
3 On the day of the exam, make sure to leave yourself long enough to write a conclusion to any question that starts with trigger words such as 'Discuss', 'Evaluate' or 'To what extent'. Then, before starting to write the conclusion, ask yourself 'What do I really think about the answer to this question in this situation?' Then write your explanation for the judgement you have made.

FURTHER READING

Lines, D., Marcousé, I. and Martin, B. (2009) *The Complete A–Z Business Studies Handbook* (6th edn), Hodder Education.

Tackling data response questions

UNIT 98

98.1 INTRODUCTION

A data response question requires you to do three things simultaneously:

1 understand and use the data (perhaps an article)
2 keep in mind the classroom/textbook theory
3 answer the precise terms of the question set.

It would not be crazy to suggest that most human beings can do only one thing at a time; two at a push. But three? That is why data response papers are harder than they look.

For students who revise at the last minute, the problem is especially acute. Cramming blocks out the other two factors, making the answers one-dimensional. The examiner can see the knowledge, and may admire it, but the marks for application, analysis and evaluation are few and far between.

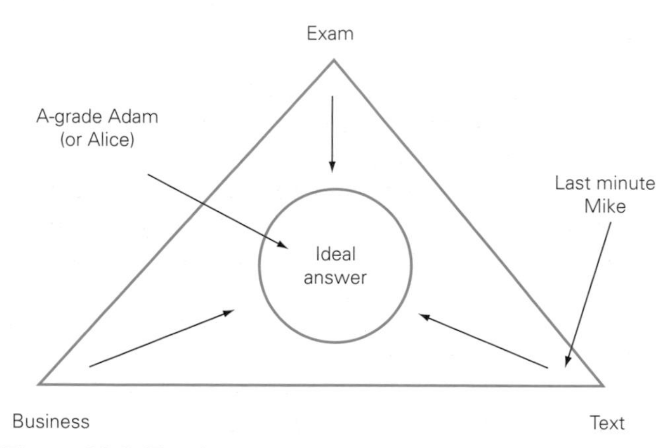

Figure 98.1 The three-way answer

98.2 USING THE DATA

The key is to find a way to get the guts out of the short passage of text; that is, to find the real business bits that matter. Many students use a highlighter pen, but seem to mark-up too much, turning the page from a white to a lurid pink one. That achieves little. It's better to jot down the key points as you go. These amount to:

- key points about the business context: competitors, consumer fashions, and so on
- key points about the business: its products, its image, its efficiency, and so on
- key points about the people running it: their experience, their enthusiasm, their judgement, and so on.

Below is a short piece of text on PD Ltd. Identify at least three key points that you could use to enrich the application within exam answers. Give yourself a few minutes, then look at the suggestions given at the end of the unit.

PD Ltd

Den and girlfriend Pam started PD Ltd with £15,000 borrowed from a friend and £15,000 from HSBC. Both keen surfers, their plan was to open the first surfing school in north-east England, on the coast above Newcastle. They were confident that they could persuade the Geordies to take up surfing, despite the cold weather.

This exercise shows the enormous importance of reading the text with great care. When in the exam room, you can make use of every subtlety built into the text, but some of the more common issues worth looking out for are listed in Table 98.1.

Table 98.1 Some common issues to look out for

Topic or issue	From one extreme ...	... to the other
Seasonal sales	70% of the whole year's sales occur in the three-week run-in to Christmas (e.g. toys, posh perfume)	Sales vary little month by month (e.g. toilet paper)
Degree of competition	Fiercely competitive market in which customers care greatly about price	Few competitors, and they focus on giving high service levels to their own customers
Product life cycle	Very short product life cycles; a brand's sales can be ended by a technological breakthrough by another	Long life cycles protected by the conservatism of consumers (e.g. Heinz Ketchup – people won't try another)
Risk	A sole trader has started a new restaurant using borrowings secured against the family home	Tim started a limited company to run a small education business offering maths tutoring

98.3 USING NUMERICAL DATA

Quite often, data response questions include numerical data such as budget statements or cash flow forecasts. These are very helpful. The reason is that they offer a quick and easy method for getting high marks.

The valuable thing about numbers is that they:

- give you a starting point for building an argument (to get analysis marks) while …
- … forcing the examiner to give you extra marks for application (because if you use the specific numbers given in the exam, your answer is automatically applied to the specific context).

So an answer that uses the numbers effectively is automatically getting double marks. It can also be argued that numbers provide a good student with the opportunity to show both their knowledge of the course and provide a basis for making judgements. In other words, it can generate every one of the assessment objectives.

With numerical data (such as sales figures) it will always be valid to ask yourself certain questions (see Table 98.2).

Table 98.2 Questions to ask yourself about numerical data

Valid questions about data	Example of good data	Example of bad data
Is the data actual or forecast?	Actual data on weekly sales over the last 18 months	A forecast of next year's sales made by a businessman wanting a loan.
Is it based on a valid sample?	Based on a quota sample of 600, carried out by Gallup, an independent research company	Based on research carried out by the sales department
Is there a valid way to make comparisons?	The figures show sales of all our brands compared with the same period last year and the year before	The figures show the huge success of Brand P, which has seen a 70% sales increase in the past two months

98.4 BRINGING IT ALL TOGETHER

The amount of data provided in a data response exam question may be quite substantial. It cannot, therefore, all be used to answer every question. Don't worry: the important thing is *not* to 'know it all'; the key is to have picked out enough key features to show that you're really trying to think for yourself while in the exam room. Examiners are giving you the opportunity to break away from your teacher and show that you're far from just being a puppet, with your teacher pulling the strings.

Having read the text and thought about the numbers, make sure to jot down the key points. If you don't, there's a risk that you'll forget the details by the time you tackle your third question. Every answer requires the context (that is, an effective analysis of the case being looked at).

Application points: PD Ltd

Things to look out for include the following.

- *The 'first' surfing school in north-east England.* This may mean that there is a fortune to be made, but it also suggests high risk (whereas being the 15th surfing school in Newquay, Cornwall, would probably not be a total disaster).
- *'They were confident that …'* The key here is what it does *not* say. It does *not* say: 'They'd done some market research, which gave them confidence that …'. Their confidence may mean nothing. Anyone who watches *The Apprentice* has seen no end of people with confidence but startlingly little ability. The key requirement in this case is evidence not confidence.
- *'£15,000 borrowed from a friend and £15,000 from HSBC'.* No bank would lend unless it has seen the owners invest at least half the start-up capital, so Den and Pam have probably not told the bank that they have borrowed it all. Having such high debts (relatively) must increase the riskiness of the investment.

Other possibilities include: the importance of the Ltd status (protection from unlimited liability); the importance of seasonality (especially in the north-east); the possible significance of the boyfriend/girlfriend relationship – how long have they been together?

How to revise for business exams

UNIT 99

Studies have shown that good revision can add as much as two grades to a student's result at A-level. The aim of this unit is to help you to appreciate what makes up a quality revision programme.

99.1 AIMS AND OBJECTIVES

A good revision programme should be aimed at achieving specific targets that will maximise your chances of success in the exam. How should these targets be set?

The basis for setting revision targets can be found in three places:

1 the specification (syllabus)
2 past papers
3 examiner's reports.

The specification

The content of the course will be outlined in some detail in the specification. Since the questions in the exam will be based closely on this document, you must ensure that you have sufficient knowledge of each area.

The specification will tell you what skills the examiner will be looking for. As well as basic factual recall as appropriate to the case being discussed, there will be a range of other skills you must demonstrate if you are to score highly.

Knowing what skills the examiner is looking for will help you to produce better-quality answers in an exam. However, like all skills these can be developed only through practice. So it is important to start your revision early and not leave it until the end. In fact, you should try to review your work every few weeks to make sure there are no gaps in your notes and that your files are well organised. This way it becomes easier to revise at the end of the course because everything is in place.

Definitions of higher academic skills

Higher academic skills include: analysis, synthesis and evaluation.

Analysis (breaking down). This is:

- identification of cause, effect and interrelationships
- the appropriate use of theory or business cases/practice to investigate the question set
- breaking the material down to show underlying causes or problems
- use of appropriate techniques to analyse data.

Analysis involves a chain of argument linking ideas and concepts, and showing the relationship between them. You may analyse why something happened or the consequence of something occurring.

Look back at previous answers you have written and try to find examples of how you could extend your responses. Were there any occasions when you could have used business theory such as elasticity, motivation or break-even to strengthen your arguments and provided a higher level of analysis?

Synthesis (bringing together). This is:

- building the points/themes within the answer into a connected whole
- logical sequencing of argument
- clarity through summarising an argument.

This skill is particularly important when you have a piece of extended writing such as a report or an essay. In a good essay, for example, each paragraph will have a clear purpose. The arguments will be well organised and lead to a logical conclusion that builds on the earlier analysis. In some exams the synthesis marks may be awarded separately; in others, they will be part of an overall mark for an answer.

Evaluation (judgement). This is:

- judgement shown in weighing up the relative importance of different points or sides of an argument, in order to reach a conclusion
- informed comment on the reliability of evidence
- distinguishing between fact and opinion
- judgement of the wider issues and implications
- conclusions drawn from the evidence presented
- selectivity: identifying the material that is most relevant to the question.

Past papers

Previous exam papers are very important in helping you to prepare for your exam. They will show you exactly what sort of questions you will face and the number of marks available. They will also give you a feel for the type of words used in the question. It goes without saying that exam questions must be read carefully. However, there will be key words used in the questions that tell you how to answer them. There is, for example, a great difference in the answers expected for the following two questions.

1 Analyse the key elements of ABC plc's marketing strategy.

2 Evaluate the key elements of ABC plc's marketing strategy.

Unless you know what is expected from these two questions, you are unlikely to know how much detail is required or how your answer ought to be structured.

Examiner's reports

These are available for each examination and can be found on the relevant exam board's website (e.g. www.aqa.org.uk or www.edexcel.com). They are written by the principal examiner of each exam and provide an insight into what she found worked well or was not so successful. By looking at these reports you will get a good sense of the weak areas of candidates and common issues they had when interpreting questions. This provides another useful input when it comes to revising and knowing where to focus your efforts.

99.2 RESOURCES

The following list contains items that will be of enormous value in preparing for an exam. They should all be familiar to you before you begin revising, and should have played a constant part in your studies throughout the course.

1 Class notes
2 A copy of the specification
3 Past exam papers, mark schemes and examiners' reports
4 A revision plan
5 Newspapers/cuttings files of relevant stories
6 This textbook
7 Access to your teacher
8 Other students.

Class notes

Since these are the product of your work and a record of your activities, they will form a vital part of your understanding of the subject. They should contain past work you have done on exam-style questions and model answers that will help to prepare you for the exam. As you make notes try to make sure these will be legible and useful later on in your revision. Make sure you keep them in the right order as you go; having to sort them out later is much more of a challenge.

A copy of the specification

The specification tells you several important things:

- what knowledge you could be tested on
- what skills the examiner will be looking for
- how the marks will be allocated
- what you will be expected to do in each exam paper you sit.

Past exam papers, mark schemes and examiners' reports

By working from past papers you will develop a feel for the type of question you will be asked and the sorts of responses you will be expected to give. Examiners' reports will give you an insight into what they thought worked well and what surprised them in terms of the responses. This in turn will give you some idea of how and what they want to assess in the future.

A revision plan

As described in the previous section. This will help to keep you on target to achieve everything that you need to cover before the exam.

Newspapers/cuttings files

Since Business Studies is a real-life subject, the ability to bring in relevant examples will boost your answers and grades. By studying what is happening in the business world you will be able to apply your answers much more effectively; this is because you will develop a better understanding of the key issues in different markets and industries. It will also help you to draw comparisons between different types of business, which can lead to good evaluation. Keeping some form of 'business diary', where you track at least one story a week, is a good way of keeping up to date with what is happening. When making notes about your story try to highlight the underlying business issues and relate it to theory rather than just describe it. This will help you to analyse cases and business situations.

A good textbook

In this textbook focus especially on the 'Analysis' and 'Evaluation' sections at the end of each chapter.

Access to your teacher

Asking your teacher for help is vital. She or he is able to give you useful advice and insights, to quell sudden panics and suggest ways to improve your performance. Don't hold back – ask! Whenever you get a piece of work back where the mark is disappointing make sure you know what you need to do differently next time. Read any comments on your work and try to improve in the specific areas mentioned in the next piece of work. Remember, the journey to success is full of small improvements (this is, of course, the philosophy of *kaizen*).

Other students

Talk to other students to help discuss points and clarify ideas. Learning from each other is a very powerful way of revising. Studies often show that you remember something much more when you have to explain it to someone else. Why not agree as a group to revise some topics? Study them individually then get together to test each other's understanding. This works very well. Remember you can all get A*s if you are good enough, so there is no problem helping others to improve their performance (as long as it is all their own work in the exam) and you will almost certainly benefit yourself from working with others.

99.3 LEARNING THE LANGUAGE OF THE SUBJECT

Clear definitions of business terms are essential for exam success. *The Complete A–Z Business Studies Handbook* (see Further Reading), is very helpful for this. They count for much more than the odd 2-mark question here or there. By showing the examiner that you understand what a term means you are reassuring her that your knowledge is sound; this is likely to help your marks for other skills as well. If the examiner is not convinced that you understand what a concept actually means then they are less likely to reward the other skills at a high level. Even on very high-mark questions it is important to define your terms.

For revising business definitions you could use:

- definition cards
- past papers
- crosswords/word games
- brainteasers.

There are many possible sources of good definitions of business terms. In this book, key terms have been highlighted and given clear and concise definitions. Your definitions should be written without using the word in question. ('Market growth is the growth in the market' is not a very good definition, for example!)

It is important, then, that you can produce high-quality definitions in an exam. This can be done only through learning and practice. Possible ways to achieve this are as follows.

Definition cards

Take a pack of index cards or postcards, or similar-sized pieces of thick paper. On each one, write a particular term or phrase that you can find in the specification document. Remember to include things like motivation theories where a clear definition or description can give an excellent overview. It is extremely unlikely that you will be asked to know a precise definition for any term that is not specifically in the specification.

On the back of each card write an appropriate definition. This could come from your class notes, a textbook or a dictionary such as *The Complete A–Z Business Studies Handbook* (see the 'Further reading' section at the end of the unit for details). Make sure that the definition you write:

- is concise
- is clear
- does not use the word being defined in the definition.

Learn them by continual repetition. Put a tick or cross on each card to show whether or not you came up with an acceptable effort. Over time, you should see the number of ticks growing.

Shuffle the cards occasionally so that you are not being given clues to some definitions because of the words or phrases preceding them.

Try doing the exercise 'back to front', by looking at the definitions and then applying the correct word or phrase.

Past papers

By using as many past papers as possible you can find out exactly what type of definition questions are asked. More importantly, you can see how many marks are available for them, which will tell you exactly how much detail you need to go into in your answer.

If possible, get hold of examiners' mark schemes. These will again give you a clear idea of what is being looked for from your answer.

Business crosswords and brainteasers

You will be able to find many examples of word games in magazines such as *Business Review* (see the 'Further reading' section at the end of the unit for details). By completing these you are developing your business vocabulary and linking words with their meanings.

99.4 NUMBERS

All business courses contain aspects of number work, which can be specifically tested in exams. It must be remembered, however, that there are two clear aspects to numbers:

1 calculation
2 interpretation.

The calculation aspects of business courses are one area where practice is by far the best approach. Each numerical element has its own techniques that you will be expected to be able to demonstrate. The techniques can be learnt, and by working through many examples they can become second nature. Even if mathematics is not your strong point, the calculations ought not to cause problems to an A-level student. Something that at first sight appears complex, such as investment appraisal, requires only simple techniques such as multiplying, adding and subtracting. Going through the 'Workbook' sections of this book will provide invaluable practice. Ask your teacher for a photocopy of the answers available in the *Teacher's Guide*.

Once calculated, all business numbers need to be used. It is all very well to calculate the accounting ratios, for example, but if the numbers are then unused the exercise has been wasted. You must attempt to follow each calculation by stating what the numbers are saying and their implications for the business.

99.5 GENERAL TIPS FOR REVISION

1 Start early.
2 Know the purpose of your revision.
3 Work more on weaker areas.
4 Use past papers as far as is possible.
5 Keep a clear perspective.

Finally, do no more revision on the night before the exam; it won't help and can only cause you anxiety. Eat well and get a good night's sleep. That way you will be in good physical shape to perform to the best of your abilities in the exam.

FURTHER READING

Business Review (available from Philip Allan Publishers, see www.philipallan.co.uk).

Lines, D., Marcousé, I. and Martin, B. (2009) *The Complete A–Z Business Studies Handbook* (6th edn), Hodder Education.

How to write an essay

UNIT 100

100.1 INTRODUCTION

Some people believe that essays require a plan. Others favour spider diagrams. In fact, there is no evidence on exam papers that essay plans lead to better essays. Good essays are far more likely to come from practice.

So what are the skills that need practice? The single most important one is the ability to build an argument. Take this essay title question from a past A-level exam:

'A crisis has led to a dramatic loss of confidence among the customers of a medium-sized company. Consider the effects this may have on the organisation and how it may respond.'

Many answers to a title such as this will include six, seven, perhaps twelve points. As a result, each point will be developed through no more than four or five lines of writing. In effect, a point will be made and then given a sentence or two of development. This approach can never develop the depth of analysis required for essay success. A far more successful approach is to tackle only two or three themes (not points), then develop each one into a lengthy (perhaps half page) paragraph. Acquiring the skill of writing developed prose proves equally important in case study work as well.

Having completed your analysis of key themes to answer the question, it is time to write a fully reasoned conclusion. This should be focused upon the question, making judgements on the issues you have analysed. A conclusion is usually worth about one third of the marks for an essay, so it is worth devoting plenty of time to it. Certainly no less than ten minutes.

To help you write a good essay, ten golden rules you should follow are set out below.

100.2 TEN GOLDEN RULES

1 There is no such thing as an essay about a topic

An essay is a response to a specific title. At A-level, the title is usually worded so that it cannot be answered by repeating paragraphs from your notes. Hence there is no such thing as 'the communications essay', because every answer should depend upon the title, not the topic. A past A-level essay question read 'When selling a good, price is the single most important factor. Evaluate this statement.' This popular question was widely misinterpreted and yielded low marks to candidates. The reason was that few students focused upon the words 'single most important'. They chose, instead, to consider price in relation to the remainder of the marketing mix. Therefore they failed to weigh up the market, economic or corporate factors that could lead price to become the single most important factor (or not, as the case may be).

2 There is no such thing as a one-sided essay

If the title asks you to consider that 'Change is inevitable' (as on a past question), do not fall into the trap of assuming that the examiner just wants you to prove it. If there was only one side to an answer, the question would not be worth asking. The only questions A-level examiners set are those which can provoke differing viewpoints. Therefore, after developing a strong argument in one direction, write 'On the other hand, it could be argued that ...' so that you assess the opposite viewpoint.

3 All essays have the same answer

With few exceptions, A-level essay questions can be answered in two words: 'It depends'. Put another way, the cause or solution to a business problem or opportunity usually depends upon a series of factors, such as the company's objectives and the internal and external constraints it faces. Often, then, your main task in planning the essay is to consider what the answer depends upon.

4 Essays need a structure

When marking essays, it is awful to feel you have no idea where the answer is leading. Some structure is needed. If you do not jot down a plan, at least tackle an essay which asks you to 'Discuss the factors...' by stating that 'There are three main factors ...'. A useful trick is to leave the number blank until you have finished the essay – by which time you will have found out how many factors you think there are!

5 Most candidates have forgotten the title by the second page

As set out in points 1 and 2, the key to a good answer is the wording of the title. Discipline yourself to refer back to the question regularly – probably at the end of every paragraph.

6 Every paragraph should answer the question set

A good paragraph is one which answers a specific aspect of the question in enough depth to impress the reader. Read over one or two of your essays and ask yourself whether *every* paragraph is directed at the question set. You will probably find that several are sidetracks or simple repetition of your notes/a textbook. In an exam, such paragraphs gain virtually no marks. The examiner is only interested in material that answers the precise wording of the question.

7 Content

Good marks come from the breadth of your knowledge and the clarity of understanding you have shown. Generally, if you *analyse* the question with care you will pick up most of the content marks in passing. For example, in the essay mentioned in point 2, analysis of the circumstances in which price might not be the most important factor would have led to discussion of distribution, promotion and the product itself. There was no need for a paragraph of description of the marketing mix.

8 Analysis

How well can you apply yourself to the question set? Can you break the material down in a way that helps to reveal the issues involved? Can you think your way into the context outlined by the question? For example, an investment appraisal question set in the context of a stable market such as chocolate should read differently to one set in a frantic market such as for computer games software. Can you use relevant concepts to explore the causes and effects? Analysis means using business concepts to answer the question with precision and depth.

9 Evaluation: the key to high essay marks

Evaluation means judgement. For good marks you need to:

- show the ability to examine arguments critically, and to highlight differing opinions
- distinguish between fact, well-supported argument and opinion
- weigh up the strength of different factors or arguments, in order to show which you believe to be the most important and why
- show how the topic fits into wider business, social, political or economic issues.

10 Play the game

Examiners love to read business concepts and terminology used appropriately. They hate streetwise language ('They're all on the fiddle') and any implication that the issues are simple ('It is obvious that ...'). Keep your work concise, businesslike and relevant, making sure that you leave long enough to write a thoughtful conclusion.

INDEX

Note: page numbers in **bold** refer to keyword definitions.

OPERATIONS ...AGEMENT

We work with leading authors to develop the strongest educational materials in business and management, bringing cutting-edge thinking and best learning practice to a global market.

Under a range of well-known imprints, including Financial Times Prentice Hall, we craft high quality print and electronic publications which help readers to understand and apply their content, whether studying or at work.

To find out more about the complete range of our publishing, please visit us on the World Wide Web at: www.pearsoned.co.uk

Second Edition

OPERATIONS MANAGEMENT

Producing Goods and Services

Donald Waters

An imprint of Pearson Education

Harlow, England • London • New York • Boston • San Francisco • Toronto • Sydney • Singapore • Hong Kong
Tokyo • Seoul • Taipei • New Delhi • Cape Town • Madrid • Mexico City • Amsterdam • Munich • Paris • Milan

To Don and Marjorie

Pearson Education Limited
Edinburgh Gate
Harlow
Essex CM20 2JE
England

and Associated Companies throughout the world

Visit us on the World Wide Web at:
www.pearsoned.co.uk

First published 1996
Second edition published 2002

ISBN 0 201 39849 4

British Library Cataloguing-in-Publication Data
A catalogue record for this book is available from the British Library

10 9 8 7 6 5 4 3 2
07 06 05 04 03

Typeset in 9.5/12.5 pt Stone Serif by 35
Printed and bound by Ashford Colour Press, Gosport

Contents

Preface

The subject

This is a textbook about operations management. Operations are the activities that make an organisation's products. These products can be any mixture of services and goods that satisfy customer demand. In restaurants the operations focus on preparing meals; in factories they make goods; in power stations they generate electricity; in universities they educate. At the heart of every organisation are the operations managers who are responsible for making the products.

As you can see, we take a broad view of operations. We talk about every kind of 'organisation', making any kind of 'product', using any type of 'process'. We make it clear that *everyone* is affected by operations, and should be involved with operations management.

In recent years operations management has become increasingly important. There are many reasons for this, including more intense international competition, rising productivity, more emphasis on product quality, more demanding customers, and so on. The most important point has been the recognition that organisations can only succeed if they supply products that customers want – and they can only do this by managing their operations properly.

The approach of the book

The book gives an introduction to operations management. It can be used by anyone who is meeting the subject for the first time. You might be a student taking a course in business studies or another subject that needs some knowledge of operations management. Or you might read the book to learn more about a central area of management.

The book has a number of features. To be specific, it:

- is an introductory text and assumes no previous knowledge of operations or experience of management;
- can be used by many types of student, or people studying by themselves;
- takes a broad view, covering all types of organisations and operations;
- sets operations management within its strategic context;
- describes a lot of material, concentrating on topics that you will meet in practice;
- develops the contents in a logical order;
- is practical, presenting ideas in a straightforward way, avoiding abstract discussions;
- illustrates principles by examples drawn from international organisations;
- uses different types of material, which includes discussions, practical illustrations, cases studies, projects, worked examples, problems, use of packages, Websites and lists of useful reading;
- is written clearly, presenting ideas in an informative and easy style.

The contents

The book follows a logical path through the decisions made in an organisation. An obvious problem is that topics are all related, and decisions are made simultaneously rather than consecutively. In a book we effectively have to make a linear journey through a complex web of material. To make this easier, we have divided the book into six parts. Part 1 introduces the subject, and defines some terms. Part 2 looks at longer-term strategies, which set the context for all other decisions. Part 3 describes some planning for the product, and Part 4 looks at the process used to make it. Part 5 looks at the hierarchy of planning needed for operations, and Part 6 looks at some aspects of the supply chain. Together, these chapters cover some of the most important decisions made in any organisation.

The format of each chapter

Each of the six parts of the book has an introduction outlining its contents, with a map showing how all the material is related. At the end of each part is a larger 'Integrating case study' which brings together ideas from different areas.

The text is divided into 21 chapters, each of which has a consistent format:

- a list of the chapter contents;
- a list of aims, showing what you should be able to do after reading the chapter;
- the themes covered in the chapter;
- the main material in the chapter, divided into coherent sections;
- review questions at the end of each section, with solutions in the Appendix;
- 'Operations in practice', which show real applications and give a focus for discussions;
- worked examples to illustrate quantitative methods;
- projects to encourage research into specific areas;
- a review at the end of each chapter listing the material that has been covered;
- a list of key terms, pinpointing topics introduced in the chapter;
- a case study to give practice in tackling real problems;
- problems to give practice in quantitative methods;
- discussion questions to stimulate discussion and research into topics;
- references and selected reading, including useful Websites;
- a supplement containing more technical materials that would interrupt the flow of the chapter.

Other material

There is a range of associated material for this book. This includes data, an instructor's manual, additional material and slide masters. This information can be accessed via the publisher's website at *www.booksites.net/waters*. You can contact the author at: *donaldwaters@lineone.net*

If you have any comments, queries, requests or suggestions for the book or associated material, the author and publisher would be very pleased to hear them.

Changes to the second edition

All textbooks evolve to meet changing demands and conditions. This edition contains many changes since the first edition was published in 1996. The whole book has been rewritten to make it even clearer, add new topics, reflect changing importance, and generally update material. Some specific changes include the following:

- rewriting to improve the flow and make parts of the text even clearer;
- general updating, new examples and correction of any errors;
- improved design giving the book a better, clearer, more colourful layout;
- changing the order of materials to give a better flow, and changing chapter contents to bring related material together;
- more features, including integrating case studies, projects, chapter themes, supplements, quotations, etc.;
- the introduction of new material that has become more popular, such as strategic issues, implementing an operations strategy, improving performance, quick response and aspects of supply chain management;
- the removal of some material that has become less relevant, such as some numerical methods;
- more international and strategic examples;
- an assumption that appropriate software is used for all number-crunching, and that the Internet is used as a source for all discussions and exercises;
- more materials for instructors on the author's Website.

Donald Waters
April 2001

Acknowledgements

I would like to thank all of those who helped with the enormous job of completing this book. Three groups of people deserve particular thanks. Firstly, the people who helped provide real examples for case studies and illustrations of operations in practice. I would particularly like to thank Mike Simpson, Jaro Martinec, Andy Moore, Elizabeth Richmond, Geoff Sykes, Jiri Krivski and Tim Henry for writing the integrating case studies. Secondly, the reviewers of earlier drafts of the book who have made a valuable contribution to this edition. At the same time, I would like to thank readers of the previous edition who took the trouble to send me their views and suggestions. Thirdly, all the people in Pearson Education who brought it all together. In particular I would like to thank Alison Kirk, Stuart Hay and Louise Lakey.

In addition the publisher would like to thank Times Newspapers Limited for the use of the 'forecast for the value of the FTSE 100 index' © Times Newspapers Limited, 3 January 1999. Whilst every effort has been made to trace the owners of copyright material, in a few cases this has proved impossible and we take this opportunity to offer our apologies to any copyright holders whose rights we may have unwittingly infringed.

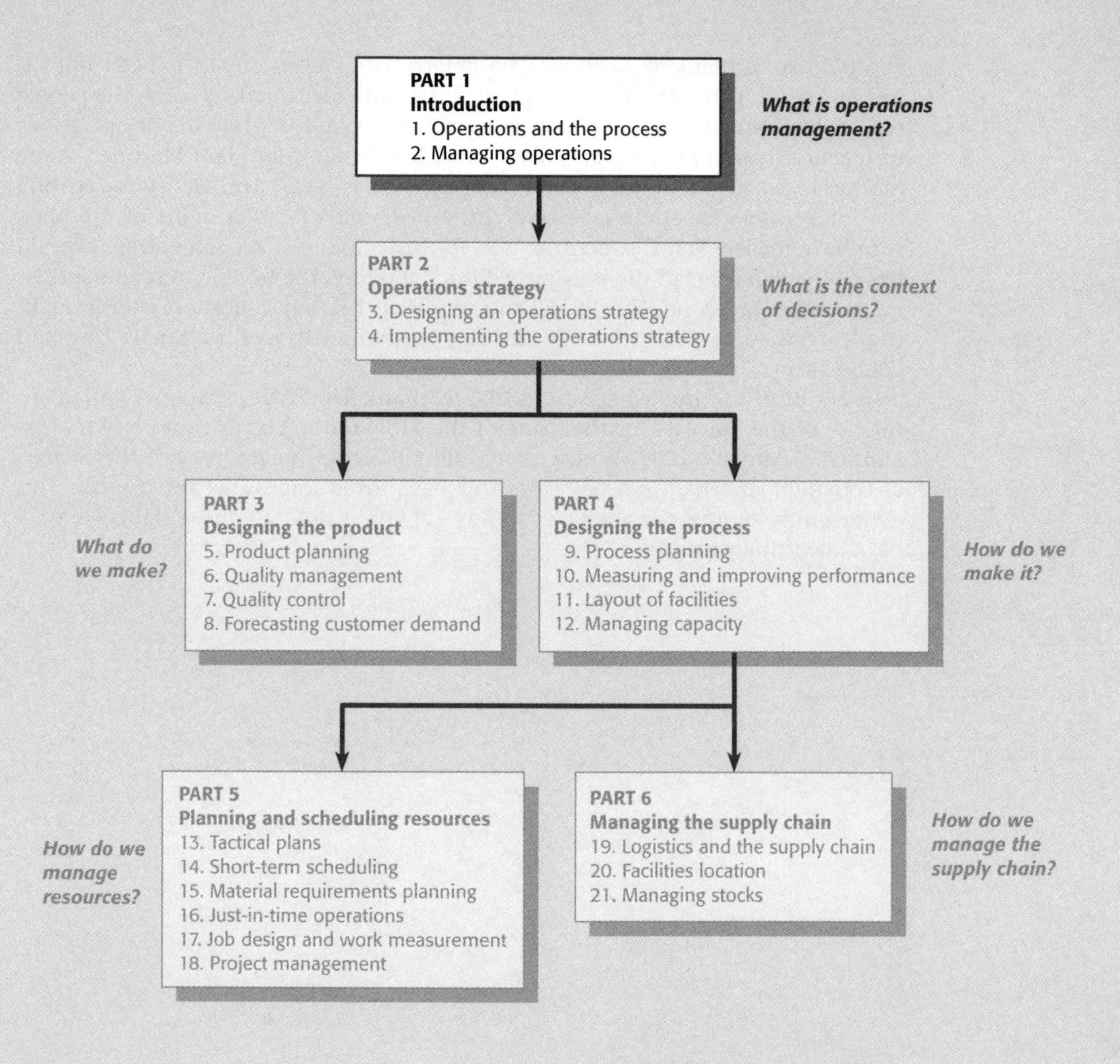
PART 1
Introduction
1. Operations and the process
2. Managing operations
What is operations management?
PART 2
Operations strategy
3. Designing an operations strategy
4. Implementing the operations strategy
What is the context of decisions?
PART 3
Designing the product
5. Product planning
6. Quality management
7. Quality control
8. Forecasting customer demand
What do we make?
PART 4
Designing the process
9. Process planning
10. Measuring and improving performance
11. Layout of facilities
12. Managing capacity
How do we make it?
PART 5
Planning and scheduling resources
13. Tactical plans
14. Short-term scheduling
15. Material requirements planning
16. Just-in-time operations
17. Job design and work measurement
18. Project management
How do we manage resources?
PART 6
Managing the supply chain
19. Logistics and the supply chain
20. Facilities location
21. Managing stocks
How do we manage the supply chain?

Part 1

INTRODUCTION

This book is divided into six parts. Each part describes a different aspect of operations management. This is Part 1, which introduces the subject. There are two chapters in this part. Chapter 1 shows that every organisation makes a product, which is the mixture of goods and services that it supplies to customers. Operations are the activities that make these products. Chapter 2 introduces the role of operations management, which is the function responsible for operations.

Later parts of the book focus on different aspects of operations management. Part 2 shows how the operations strategy sets the context for all other decisions. Part 3 describes the planning of products, while Part 4 discusses the process used to make them. Part 5 looks at the planning and scheduling of resources, while Part 6 describes some aspects of supply chain management.

Operations are at the heart of every organisation – they define what the organisation does, and how it does it. Taken together, these six parts describe the most important decisions made by managers.

Table 1.2 Examples of operations in different types of organisation

Organisation	Inputs	Operations	Outputs
Farm	seeds, fertiliser, fields, animals, machinery	planting, growing, harvesting, milking, shearing	vegetables, cereals, wool, milk, meat
Coal mine	miners, coal seam, tools, explosives, transport	extraction, removing waste, cleaning	coal, waste, by-products
Oil refinery	crude oil, chemicals, energy	refining, processing, distribution	petrol, oils, sulphur, other chemicals
Computer manufacturer	components, materials, designs, energy, robots, people	assembly, finishing, testing, packing	computers, spare parts, wages
House building	land, bricks, woods, cement, people, capital, equipment, plans	bricklaying, plastering, carpentry, plumbing	house, investment, garden
Brewery	hops, water, grain, bottles, experience	preparing, mixing, brewing, bottling	bottles of beer, etc.
Hospital	patients, staff, beds, medicines, equipment	surgical operations, treatment, monitoring	healthy patients, information
Retail shop	goods, customers, premises, servers	selling, displaying, advising, packing	purchases, satisfied customers
Airline	planes, terminals, passengers, agents	booking tickets, flying, entertaining	satisfied passengers, goods moved

hand, some inputs do not change themselves, but bring about transformations, such as the potters and ovens at Wedgwood. These are typically the people employed, equipment and facilities they use. This gives two main types of input as:

- *transformed* – materials that are changed during the operations;
- *transforming* – resources that are needed by the operations, but do not themselves change.

There are also different types of output. Some of these are useful, such as the products and satisfied customers that the organisation is aiming for, but others are scrap and waste that it positively wants to avoid. There is also a range of secondary outputs that are not directly connected to the product, such as wages, profit, cultural identity, corporate citizenship and networks of contacts. Adding these different types of inputs, operations and outputs gives the general view of operations shown in Figure 1.4.

Project 1.1

Find an organisation with which you are reasonably familiar, such as a business, university or club. How would you describe its operations? What are the products, inputs and outputs? Who are the customers? What are the main types of decision in the organisation?

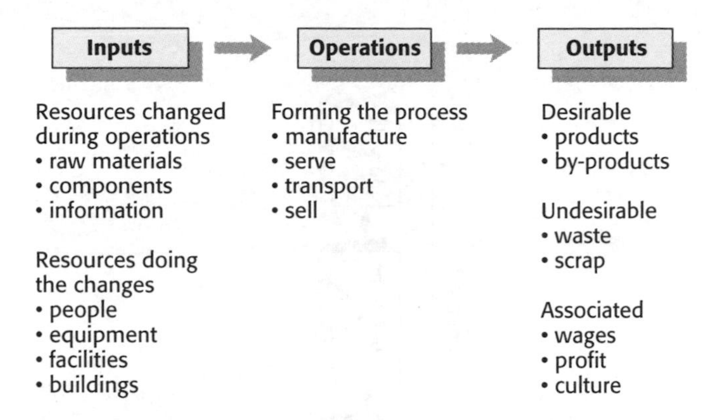

Figure 1.4 Examples of different kinds of inputs, operations and outputs

Combining operations in a process

If you join together all the operations used to make a particular product, you get the **process**. The process starts with the collection of inputs and finishes with the delivery of final products to **customers**. The process for the *Financial Times*, for example, starts with the planning of articles; it continues with sending reporters to collect stories, writing, editing, composing and printing, and finishes when papers are sold to customers. The process at Cadbury starts with picking cocoa beans and includes all the operations needed to deliver bars of chocolate to hungry customers.

The **process** for a product consists of all the operations needed to make it.

The following example shows how the operations for one product join together to form its process.

OPERATIONS IN PRACTICE: The process at Chateau Bel Air

Chateau Bel Air is an *appellation controlée* vineyard in the Haut-Médoc region of France. It uses a traditional process for making wine. Every vineyard uses a similar process, but details vary with the variety of grape, type of wine, region, climate, and so on. The process consists of the following operations:

1. pick the grapes and take them to the vineyard;
2. crush the grapes and remove the stems;
3. press the juice from the skins and seeds (particularly for white wines);
4. treat the must (the juice that turns into wine);
5. ferment the must in vats;
6. do first racking to filter the wine into containers;
7. do second racking to clarify the wine and age it in barrels;
8. blend (sometimes) and bottle;
9. age in bottles;
10. pack bottles in cases and deliver to customers.

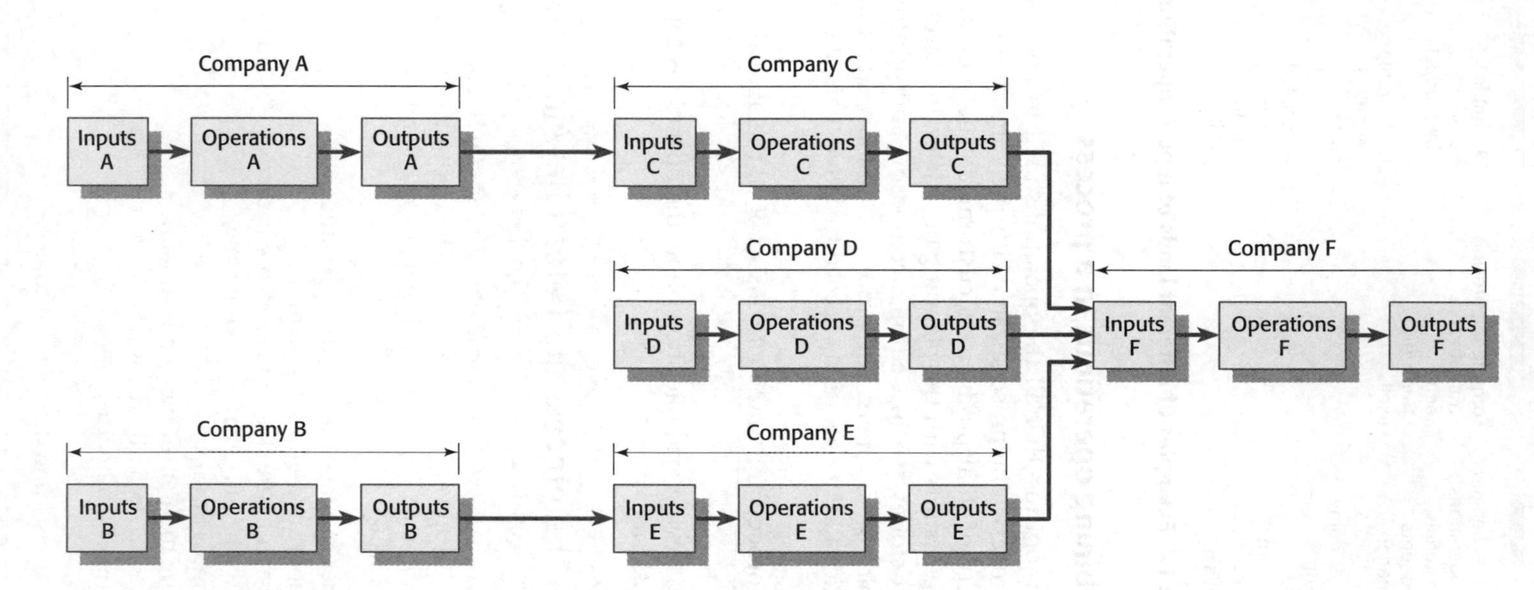

Figure 1.5 Operations in several organisations contributing to the final product

The process at Chateau Bel Air is typical of many organisations: it collects materials, performs a series of operations, and delivers products to customers. It is unusual, though, for the entire process to be within one organisation. Normally, the process consists of a series of distinct parts, with many organisations contributing to the final product. When you buy a computer, for example, Intel might make the processor, Fugitsu the disk drives, Agfa the scanner, Hewlett-Packard the printer, Microsoft the operating system, and so on. Each of these has its own operations, inputs and outputs. Figure 1.5 illustrates a simple arrangement with operations in six organisations contributing to the final product, but only company F dealing with final customers.

Sometimes there are problems connecting the different operations. A customer, for example, might want to buy regular, small numbers of a product, while the supplier wants to deliver infrequent, large orders. To get around these problems, organisations build **buffers** between operations. Typically they keep stocks of raw materials in a warehouse, or have a service department to deal with customers. The purpose of these buffers (illustrated in Figure 1.6) is to insulate operations, and avoid possible disruptions. Stocks of raw materials, for example, allow operations to continue normally when a delivery of materials is delayed. Unfortunately, these buffers can bring their own difficulties, increasing costs, hindering communications, and slowing the movement of products.

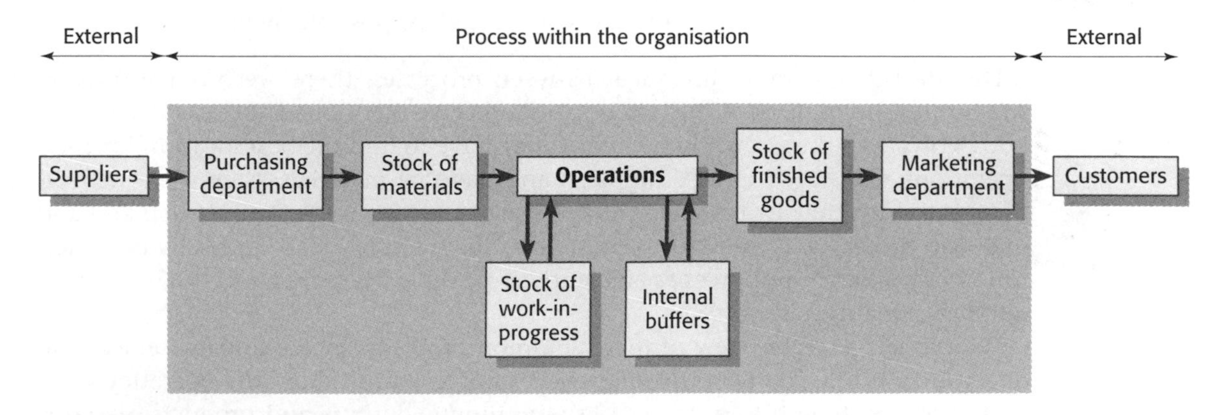

Figure 1.6 Buffering operations to reduce the effect of disruptions

Review questions

1.1 What do you understand by:
(a) goods;
(b) services;
(c) products;
(d) process?

1.2 Why do organisations make products?

1.3 What are operations?

1.4 Table 1.2 lists some of the inputs, operations and outputs for different organisations. What others can you think of?

Operations in practice

Common decisions for operations

At first sight, operations in different organisations do not seem to have much in common. Operations in Volvo, for example, seem completely different from operations in the Crown Inn, Goldsithney. Perhaps the most important differences are:

- *Volume made* – this affects almost every decision from the investment available to the layout of facilities.
- *Variation in demand* – it is much easier to organise a steady process than one with widely varying demand.
- *Continuity* – some organisations have continuous operations (such as generating electricity) while others are discontinuous (such as construction companies building road bridges).
- *Balance between goods and services* – this puts different demands on operations.
- *Variety of products* – it is much easier to make a standard product than a range of different ones.
- *Customer contact* – services typically have much more contact than manufacturing.
- *Objectives* – operations will differ if the organisation is aiming at, say, minimising costs rather than supplying products of the highest possible quality.

Despite the apparent differences between processes, there are often surprising similarities. If you look at the two organisations we mentioned above, managers in both Volvo and the Crown Inn, Goldsithney have to find the best location for their operations; they both choose suppliers and buy raw materials; they use a defined process to turn the raw materials into products; they forecast customer demand and organise the capacity needed to meet this; they employ staff and schedule their time; they organise resources as efficiently as possible; they are concerned with productivity, quality and profit.

We can get a clearer view of these common problems by looking at some actual operations. While you read the following examples, think about the operations and how they combine into a process; list the inputs, outputs and products; describe the customers and what they want; look at the decisions and see what they try to achieve.

WORKED EXAMPLE

The Hans Christian Anderson Café in Copenhagen serves two types of beer: Carlsberg Export (a mass-produced beer) and Fiery Hobgoblin (a specialised beer made at a local micro-brewery). Without going into detail, what do you think are the main differences between the processes used to make these two beers?

Solution

One way of comparing processes uses bars to represent different features, with the position of each process marked on the bars. Figure 1.7 shows one possible comparison of the processes for Carlsberg Export and Fiery Hobgoblin.

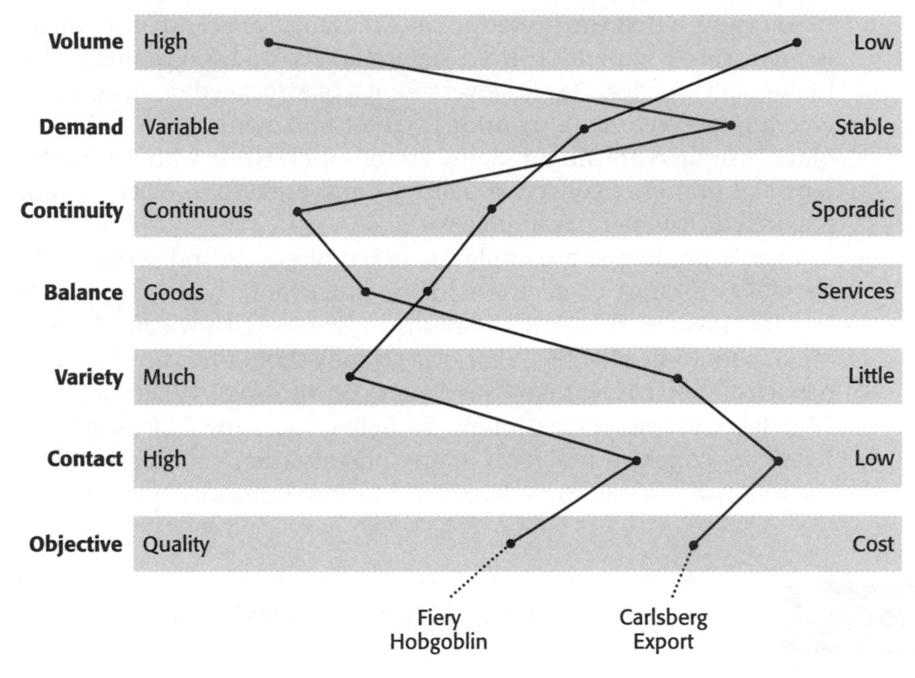

Figure 1.7 Using bar charts to compare processes

OPERATIONS IN PRACTICE

Ace Dairies

Ace Dairies gives a home delivery service for milk, dairy products and a range of related goods. Roger Smitheram has run the dairy for the past 12 years. His product is a combination of goods (the items he delivers) and services (the delivery and associated jobs he does for customers).

At the heart of operations is an information system which contains full details of all Roger's 500 customers, including their regular orders, special orders, where to deliver, how they pay, and so on. Every day the system calculates the likely sales of all products in two days' time. Roger adds some margin of safety, allows for likely variations and passes his order to Unigate Dairy in Totnes. This Unigate depot acts as a wholesaler for milkmen in Wales and the south-west of England. The following evening it delivers to a holding depot in Camborne, and then passes Roger's goods to a cold store in Hayle. At 5.30 the following morning Roger collects the order from his cold store and starts delivering. This normally takes until 1.30 in the afternoon, but on Fridays he spends more time collecting money and can finish after 5.00 pm.

There are several specific problems facing Ace Dairies. There is, for example, some variation in daily demand, so Roger has to carry spare stock. He cannot carry too much, as dairy products have a short life and anything not delivered quickly is thrown away. Roger aims at keeping this waste down to 2 per cent of sales. There are also problems maintaining a service during holidays, or when Unigate has difficulties with its deliveries.

Perhaps Roger's main concern is maintaining his sales over the long term. Demand for doorstep deliveries is declining, as people buy more milk at supermarkets. The number of milkmen in Hayle has declined from 10 in 1987 to three in 2000. Most of Roger's customers have been with him for many years, but he generates new custom by canvassing, delivering leaflets, special offers, carrying a range of other products, and so on.

You can see that the operations at Ace Dairies are centred on milk delivery. There is increasing competition from supermarkets, and Roger meets this by offering a high-quality service. He also gives a range of associated services, including a cheerful greeting to everyone (a traditional job of milkmen), parcel delivery, checking that older customers are alright, doing errands for anyone who is unwell – and repairing taps, lighting fires, collecting pensions and prescriptions, and just about anything else that a customer has trouble with!

Roger's product is a complex package of goods and services. To support this, he makes a range of decisions. How much milk will he sell? Where should he buy it? How can he cover variations in demand? How can he reduce waste? How much should he charge? What other goods should he carry? How can he generate new customers? How many customers can he serve? What facilities does he need? Which routes should he follow on deliveries? How can he measure his success? These are common problems in any organisation, and you can see them again in the following example of a larger, not-for-profit organisation.

OPERATIONS IN PRACTICE

Saint Andrew's Maternity Hospital

Saint Andrew's is the main maternity hospital for a large part of Glasgow. The original hospital was built in 1843, and over the years there have been many changes, which include the following:

- the population of Glasgow has declined, particularly in the city centre;
- other National Health Service hospitals have opened maternity units in or near the city;
- some private hospitals have opened and offer limited services;
- Saint Andrew's has become a regional specialist unit, dealing with all difficult cases;
- the buildings are now small and old fashioned;
- the site is small, congested and noisy with no space for expansion, parking or other facilities.

Because of problems with the site, managers have recently been considering a move to a new location. The current site is commercially valuable and selling it would give enough money for a new hospital at another location, or improved facilities at existing hospitals.

The hospital gives five basic services:

- *Outpatient checks before birth* – women visit the hospital several times during pregnancy to make sure the baby is developing normally and there are no complications.
- *Normal in-patient care* – a short stay in hospital to deliver the baby and to allow recovery: longer stays are sometime needed if the mother or baby has problems.
- *Outpatient checks after birth* – routine checks during a baby's first few months to make sure it is progressing normally.
- *Emergency outpatients* – for problems that need fast, but fairly short treatment.
- *Emergency in-patient care* – for more serious problems.

These services define the operations of the hospital, and managers organise their resources to complete them in the best possible way. Planning starts with long-term forecasts of the expected number of births over the next few years. These forecasts give the overall capacity needed, and this is currently met by the equivalent of 105 beds, 95 medical staff and 115 support staff. If the demand changes, these numbers have to be adjusted, but any expansion is difficult in the existing buildings.

Medium-term plans look at the use of resources over the next few months. These allow managers to make minor changes to resources – typically changing beds from non-emergency to emergency use, arranging staff training and holidays, timing expenditure on equipment, and so on.

Short-term plans include timetables for doctors, nurses, ancillary staff, porters, etc. and schedules for beds, consulting rooms, medical equipment, operating rooms, kitchens, medicines and supplies. These details are based on the number of births expected in the near future. The hospital knows this fairly accurately, as it sees most of the mothers in pre-natal clinics.

As you can imagine, several factors complicate the planning. There is, for example, a variable and unpredictable demand for emergencies. The hospital receives difficult cases from all over the region, and keeps some spare capacity that it can use at short notice. There is also a seasonal variation in the number of births, with more in spring than in autumn, and more on weekdays than at weekends. The hospital must have enough capacity to meet any peak demand, but does not want idle resources at slack times.

The allocation of limited resources is a constant problem in Saint Andrew's. How, for example, can the hospital balance the needs of 100 non-emergency patients and one emergency patient who has the same costs? What happens if it spends its entire grant and then gets new patients? If the hospital put more resources into preventive treatment, it could reduce the cost of emergency care, but where does it find these resources?

As you can see, managers in St Andrew's make decisions about the services they provide, location, likely demand, capacity, schedules for resources and a whole series of related matters. Many of these are similar to the decisions that Roger Smitheram makes at Ace Dairies. Although the circumstances are completely different, managers in both organisations face a range of similar problems. These similarities allow us to develop general rules for operations.

Related operations

We have already seen how the operations in different organisations combine to contribute to an overall process. But we can also divide the operations within a single organisation into smaller parts. In St. Andrew's Hospital the overall operations treat patients, but we can consider the emergency clinic as a distinct operation with its own inputs, outputs, products and customers. In the same way, we can look at operations in the intensive care unit, outpatients department, purchasing department, accounts, fundraising, and so forth. Each of these separate parts performs operations that make its own products, and these pass to other **internal customers**. The products of a purchasing department, for example, are purchased supplies; these pass to internal customers and become inputs for their own operations, as shown in Figure 1.8. At each step, operations contribute to the overall process, and somehow add value for the organisation.

We could continue breaking down the operations into smaller and smaller parts, but would soon get overwhelmed by detail. Instead, we will look at operations at the most appropriate level. Sometimes we will take a broad view of the operations in a whole organisation, and at other times we will concentrate on specific activities.

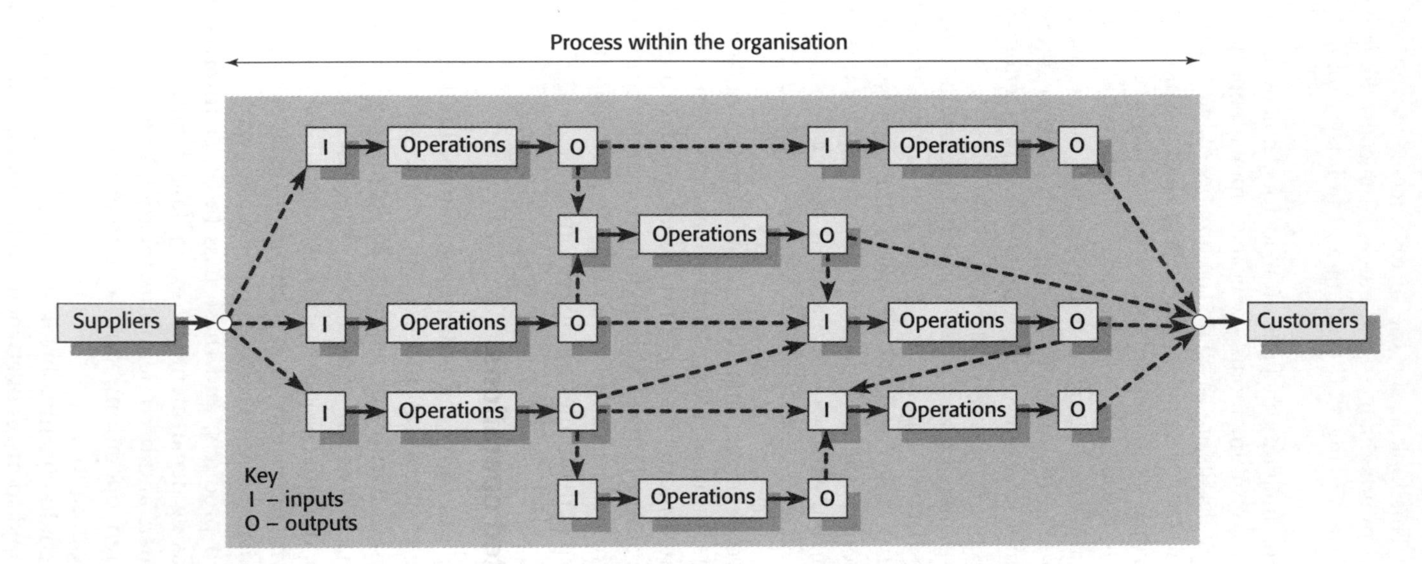

Figure 1.8 Outputs from internal operations giving inputs to internal customers

OPERATIONS IN PRACTICE

Mareco/Gallup International

For almost 50 years, Poland had a centrally planned economy. The government ran most businesses, and there was little need for market research. Then in 1990 the economy was reformed, and newly privatised companies began to look directly at the demands of their customers. The market research industry grew quickly, reaching $50 million a year by 1998.

Mareco was founded in 1993 to run public opinion polls in Poland. In 1994 it joined Gallup International Association and adopted its procedures and standards. Other research companies have appeared, but Mareco is by far the largest with up to 90 per cent of some markets.

Many Polish companies have little interest in market research, which they continue to view as a waste of money. About 80 per cent of Mareco's clients are foreign companies that want to work in Poland, and must learn about local conditions.

Mareco aims to conduct research as quickly and accurately as possible, 'to provide the best insights into our clients' markets'. It organises this from a head office in Warsaw, which has three separate departments.

- *Opinion Polls and Market Research Department.* This works at the start of a project, forming relations with customers, preparing research offers, scheduling work, designing questionnaires, selecting samples, and so on. Then it works on the final part, analysing the results of surveys and writing reports for customers.
- *Field Research Department.* This collects data using a network of 24 co-ordinators and 200 interviewers.
- *Data Processing Department.* This takes the data collected in the field research, analyses it and creates databases.

Mareco's main problem is with its interviewers. Interviewing is not well paid, and it tends to attract students who want temporary jobs. These can do straightforward data collection, but lack the skills needed for in-depth interviews or further analyses. With a staff turnover of 50 per cent a year, Mareco finds it impossible to train interviewers as thoroughly as it would like. This lack of training leads to Mareco's other main concern of ensuring the reliability of replies. Mareco runs checks and controls on the replies it receives, but it can be difficult to guarantee that all replies come from genuine respondents.

You can see that Mareco has several internal operations, each with internal customers, and each contributing to the overall process. The Field Research Department, for example, has its own operations for running surveys. The inputs to these include questionnaires that are designed by the Opinion Polls and Market Research Department – so one department acts as a customer of the other. The outputs from the Field Research Department are the data that are passed to the Data Processing Department, so again one department acts as a customer for the products of another.

You can also see that the operations in Mareco share many features with those in other organisations. The message is clear: all organisations face a range of similar problems, whether it is Microsoft deciding when to launch a new operating system, or your family deciding where to go on holiday. In the rest of this book we look at the most important problems faced in operations, and show how to tackle them.

Review questions

1.5 What is the process for a product?

1.6 How do processes differ from each other?

1.7 Do these differences mean that there are fundamentally different problems in different processes?

Chapter review

- Every organisation makes a product, which is some combination of goods and services.
- Operations are the activities that are directly concerned with making products. They take a range of inputs and transform them into outputs.
- All the operations used to make a product form its process.
- We can look at operations at different levels. Sometimes we take a broad view including many organisations, each of which adds value to the final product. Sometimes we take a narrow view and focus on specific operations within an organisation.
- Organisations vary widely, but people who manage the operations face a range of similar problems.
- The rest of this book shows how to tackle these problems.

Key terms

buffer *p. 9*
customers *p. 4*
goods *p. 3*
inputs *p. 5*
internal customers *p. 13*
outputs *p. 5*
operations *p. 4*
process *p. 7*
product *p. 4*
services *p. 3*

CASE STUDY Nissan Motor Manufacturing (UK) Limited

Nissan was formed in Japan in 1911, and by 1970 was exporting a million cars a year. Its policy of meeting overseas demand by direct exports was becoming less acceptable, and it decided to avoid problems by opening new factories overseas. In 1984 Nissan planned a major facility in the UK. The UK was chosen because of its large domestic market, and its location within the European Union allowed free trade with other major markets. It was also a technologically advanced country with a history of car production, and the necessary skills, education and infrastructure. Nissan considered several sites within the UK, and finally chose one in Sunderland.

In April 1984 Nissan Motor Manufacturing (UK) Limited was established, with the aim of 'building profitably the highest quality vehicles sold in Europe, to achieve the maximum possible customer satisfaction and thus ensure the prosperity of the company and its staff'. It became a European company, using local people and suppliers, but introduced manufacturing methods developed in Japan. These included automated assembly lines, total quality management, just-in-time operations, flexible manufacturing and continuous improvement. We will describe these later in the book, but the important point is that they give a combination of high productivity and high-quality products.

The Sunderland plant is now one of the most productive in the world, and has continued to expand. It has a network of 200 suppliers, several of whom have built dedicated facilities near to the main site. These have reduced lead times for parts from the weeks needed to ship from the Far East to hours or even minutes.

Operations in the Sunderland plant can be summarised as 'making cars'. This process has seven stages:

- *panel pressing*: pressing the panels for car bodies from steel sheets;
- *body assembly*: welding panels together to form the body on an automated assembly line;
- *paint*: painting finished bodies several times in a clean air environment with emissions controlled to surpass all likely regulations;
- *plastics injection and blow moulding*: making parts from plastic, including fuel tanks, bumpers, radiator grills and facia parts;
- *aluminum casting*: making engine parts;
- *engine machining and assembly*: finishing engine parts and assembling them into a range of different models;
- *final assembly*: bringing together all the components to make finished cars.

As you can imagine, co-ordinating these operations is extremely difficult. Collecting the thousands of parts needed to build a car at one place, in the right order and at the right time would be very complicated, but the plant repeats this continually every few minutes. The high-speed operations leave little room for mistakes.

Nissan gives strong support to its workforce. The company clearly states: 'We aim to manufacture the highest quality vehicles sold in Europe. It is the quality of our people that determines the quality of our product . . . we believe that high calibre, well trained and motivated people are the only key to success'.

Questions

- How does Nissan differ from the organisations in the four examples of 'Operations in practice' given in this chapter?
- What are the operations at Nissan?
- What do you think are the main problems that managers face with operations in Nissan? Are these significantly different to problems faced in other organisations?

Discussion questions

1.1 Why are operations important?

1.2 What are the products of Disneyland, the M25 orbital motorway around London, the European Parliament, the Red Cross, a fire service, and Anglia double-glazing? Discuss the operations, inputs and outputs of each.

1.3 Do you think the operations in different types of organisation really are similar? Support your views by discussing the operations in three completely different organisations.

1.4 Outputs from many operations are sent to internal customers, where they form inputs to their operations. How are these internal customers different from external customers?

1.5 Figure 1.6 outlines some buffering of operations. How can you buffer services? Do you think that such buffers are really needed? What are the benefits and problems of buffering?

1.6 Can you list some ways that operations have changed over the past 20 years? What changes might there be over the next 20 years?

1.7 A series of mergers and takeovers (for example, Jaguar–Ford, Daimler–Chrysler, Volvo–Ford and Renault–Nissan) seems to concentrate car assembly in fewer companies. What operational factors do you think encourage these mergers?

Selected reading

Collier D.A. (1987) *Service Management: Operating Decisions*. Englewood Cliffs, NJ: Prentice-Hall.

Dix C. and Baird C. (1998) *Front Office Operations*. Reading, MA: Addison-Wesley.

Flahherty M.T. (1996) *Global Operations Management*. New York: McGraw-Hill.

Heyl J.E., Bushnell J.L. and Stone L.A. (1994) *Cases in Operations Management*. Reading, MA: Addison-Wesley.

Johnson R., Chambers S., Harland C., Harrison A. and Slack N. (1997) *Cases in Operations Management*. 2nd edn. London: Pitman.

Kinni T.B. (1996) *America's Best*. New York: John Wiley.

Ould M.A. (1995) *Business Processes*. Chichester: John Wiley.

CHAPTER 2

Managing operations

If making decisions is so simple and powerful, then why don't more people follow Nike's advice and 'just do it'?
Anthony Robbins
Awaken the Giant Within, Simon & Schuster, New York, 1991

Contents

Aims of the chapter

After reading this chapter you should be able to:

- discuss the role of managers;
- define 'operations management';
- say why operations management is important to every organisation;
- understand the relationship between operations management and other central functions;
- discuss the type of decisions that operations managers make;
- outline some other views of operations management.

Main themes

This chapter will emphasise:

- the role of **managers** in running an organisation;
- **operations management**, which is responsible for all aspects of operations;
- the **types of decision** made by operations managers.

Managers and operations

Managers make decisions

Managers are the people who make decisions in an organisation. They decide what the organisation does, who works there, what they do, when they do it, what resources they have, and everything else about the operations. Although they have many different titles, anyone who makes decisions is acting as a manager.

Managers have a difficult job. They make decisions in complex situations, with rapidly changing conditions, uncertain goals, little information, tight deadlines, external constraints, and uncertain relations with other people and organisations. To be more specific, their jobs include:

- *setting objectives* – giving goals for the organisation to aim at;
- *planning* – showing how to achieve the goals and in what timescale;
- *organising* – setting the best structure for the organisation;
- *staffing* – making sure there are suitable people for all jobs;
- *directing* – coaching and guiding employees;
- *motivating* – empowering and encouraging people to do their jobs well;
- *allocating* – assigning resources to specific jobs;
- *monitoring* – checking progress towards the goals;
- *controlling* – making sure that the organisation keeps moving forward;
- *informing* – telling everyone about progress.

This, of course, is not a complete list and managers can do a range of other work, such as being a figurehead and spokesperson, liaising with other organisations, negotiating, designing systems, handling problems, exercising authority and initiating change.

Operations managers

In the last chapter we described every organisation as making a product. At the heart of the organisation are the operations that actually make this product. Not surprisingly, the people who manage operations are the **operations managers**.

- **Operations management** is the management function that is concerned with all aspects of operations.
- **Operations managers** are responsible for all the activities that make an organisation's products.

It is easy to say that operations managers are the people who manage operations, but what exactly does this mean? We can start to answer this by drawing the schematic view of operations management shown in Figure 2.1. This has managers making the **decisions** that keep an organisation working effectively. Their decisions affect inputs, operations and outputs, and they use feedback on performance and other relevant information to continually update their decisions.

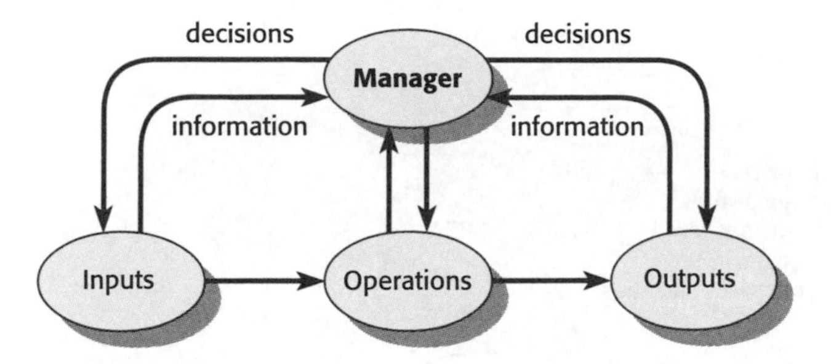

Figure 2.1 Schematic view of operations management

We can add three things to give a more compete view:

1. **customers** who create demand, receive the outputs, give comments and opinions, etc.;
2. an external environment in which the organisation works, including competitors, government, laws, national priorities, society, etc.;
3. the separation of operations into a series of connected operations (as described in Chapter 1).

This gives the overall view of operations management shown in Figure 2.2.

OPERATIONS IN PRACTICE

Gladstone Community School

In the UK, the government has overall control of education, designing the national curriculum, setting attainment targets, monitoring school performance, and so on. Local education authorities have some functions, but since 1988, the 'local management of schools' has made each school largely responsible for its own operations.

Jane Goodall is chairman of the board of governors of Gladstone Community School. This is a primary school in a socially mixed area of Nottingham. The school is considered successful in a number of ways: it encourages links between local industry and pupils; parents actively contribute to the school; it scores well in attainment tests; it encourages understanding of different ethnic traditions; pupils enjoy coming to school; there is low staff turnover; teams are successful in local sports; and the facilities are well maintained.

The board of governors and a management team of teachers are the operations managers in the school. The governors look after major decisions, such as building new classrooms, recruiting staff and buying expensive equipment. The management team consists of the Head, Deputy Head, Head of Infants and Head of Juniors. They make decisions about academic matters and day-to-day running of the school, including the timetable, curriculum, allocation of teaching duties, staff development, maintenance and meals.

To develop their skills and knowledge, the governors and management team attend special training courses. At a recent one they took a broad view and discussed their objectives, their customers, the product they made, and how to measure their success. How do you think their discussions might have developed?

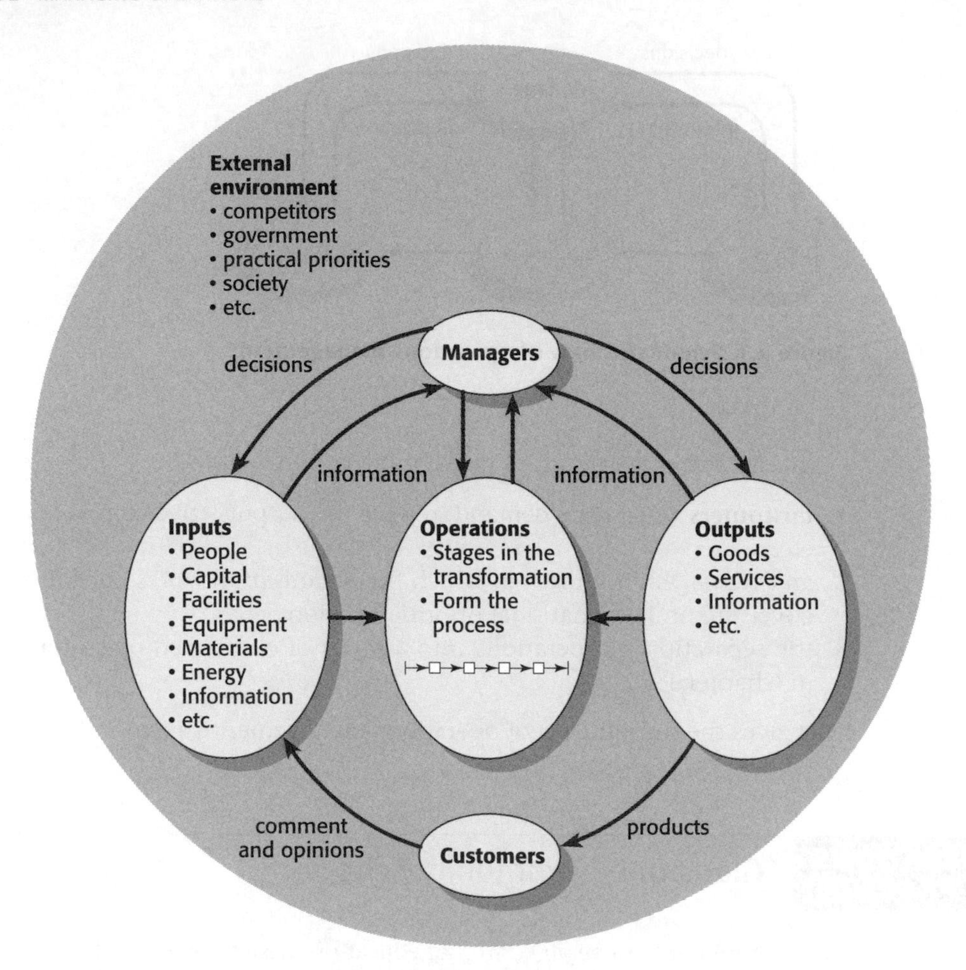

Figure 2.2 More detailed view of operations management

Importance of operations management

To be successful, an organisation must have good operations management. If the operations managers do a good job, the organisation makes products that customers like and it can prosper: if the operations managers do a bad job, customers will not like the product and will not buy it. The next time you are particularly pleased with a product, it will be a sign that operations managers have done a good job. Of course, when you run to catch a train only to find that it has been cancelled, or you cannot connect to your Internet service provider, or find that the colour of a new jumper fades in the wash, or have a water bill that rises at 20 times the rate of inflation, you know that operations managers have done something wrong.

In simple terms, good operations management gives an organisation some kind of competitive advantage. It might:

- make a product that no other organisation can make – like Dyson vacuum cleaners;
- use a process that no other organisation can use – like Eurotunnel;
- improve efficiency to give a cost advantage – like easyJet;

- increase flexibility to customise products – like Thomas Cook holidays;
- respond quickly to changing levels of demand – like 'queuebusters' in Safeway supermarkets;
- reduce development times so that new products can be brought to the market quickly – like Toyota cars;
- schedule operations to give fast delivery – like Federal Express;
- simplify operations and making them easier for customers to use – like Freeserve.com;
- use convenient locations to attract customers – like Heathrow Airport;
- find economies of scale – like Drax power station;
- guarantee high quality – like IBM computers.

To put it briefly, **operations management** is:

- *essential*, because it must be done in every organisation;
- *important*, because it has a real effect on the organisation's performance.

Development of operations management

There have been operations – and operations management – since organisations started to make products. But most of the formal analyses have been done within the last 100 years, and the term 'operations management' has only been used widely since the 1960s.

You can imagine the development of operations management in several waves. The first of these came with the industrial revolution, which laid the foundations for manufacturing and mass production. Then came 'scientific management' early in the twentieth century, with Frederick Taylor[1] suggesting that performance can be improved by using scientific methods to study operations. The next wave emphasised human relations, with studies like Elton Mayo's[2–4] showing that motivation is as important as technical design. In the 1950s the emphasis moved to operational research, which developed models, particularly quantitative ones, to tackle a range of problems. Since the 1960s the dominant theme has been an increasing use of computers and improved communications. Within this overall framework, there have been many related developments that we will discuss later in the book.

Companies in the USA were the first to realise that good operations management could bring them success. They improved their operations and soon dominated many areas of business. By the middle of the twentieth century IBM was the world's largest computer manufacturer; General Motors was the largest car maker; ESSO was the largest oil company; American Express was the leading credit card; and McDonald's was serving billions of hamburgers. Over time, these leading companies seemed to become complacent and did not take advantage of new opportunities. By the 1980s Japanese companies had taken over as leaders in operations management. They concentrated on high quality, customer service and high productivity – and soon took over the lead in many industries including motor cycles, banking, consumer electronics, photocopiers, cameras, machine tools, steel, computer chips, shipping and cars.

Now we cannot say that one country is the clear leader in operations management. There is a continuing trend towards global operations, and all organisations – wherever they work and whatever they do – need efficient and effective operations to remain in business.

Review questions

2.1 What are the main jobs of managers?

2.2 What is operations management?

2.3 Why do you think interest in operations management has increased in recent years?

2.4 What happens if an organisation ignores operations management?

Project 2.1

An 'operations audit' describes the detailed operations in an organisation, including the inputs, outputs, customers, products, problems, decisions, and so on.

In 1987 Peter Blake opened his first ice cream parlour in the Medway Shopping Mall. He served a small selection of snack foods, mainly ice cream, doughnuts, sandwiches and coffee. The main business came from people who wanted a break while shopping in the mall, and those who had a tea break while working in other shops. Peter's shop was comfortable and clean; he left newspapers and magazines around for his customers to read; and he trained his staff to be cheerful and welcoming.

Do an operations audit of Peter's shop or of a similar organisation that you are familiar with.

Central functions in an organisation

Now that we know, in general terms, what operations management is, we can start looking at the details. There are several ways we can approach this. For a start, we can describe it as one of the **central functions** in an organisation.

Operations management as a central function

A traditional view says that every organisation has three central functions (see Figure 2.3).

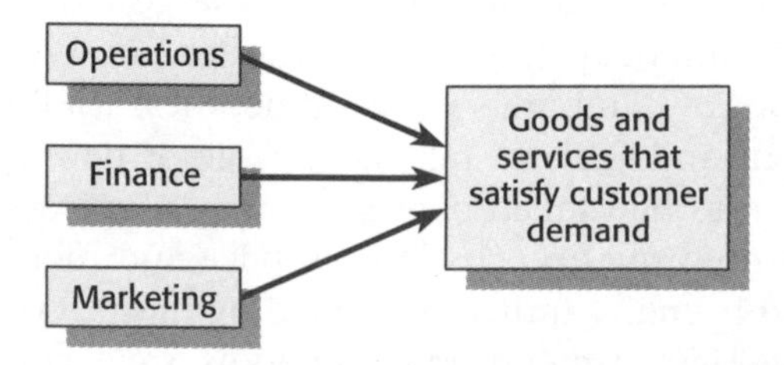

Figure 2.3 Central functions in an organisation

Table 2.1 Examples of central functions in different types of organisation

Organisation	Marketing	Operations	Finance
Brewery	Advertising, marketing, distribution	Brewing, packaging, delivery	Attracting investment, recording costs, analysing profits
Car assembly plant	Advertising, marketing, running dealerships	Assembling cars, making spare parts	Controlling investments, paying suppliers
Hospital	Publicity, improving public relations	Treating patients, doing medical research, training staff	Paying staff, controlling costs, attracting donations
Retail shop	Organising sales, advertising, purchasing, stock	Selling, displaying, advising, stockholding, packing	Recording costs, paying suppliers, collecting cash
Airline	Organising sales, advertising, forming partnerships	Flight operations, ground operations, engineering	Collecting fares, paying expenses, buying planes
University	Attracting students, getting publicity, recruiting staff	Teaching students, research, consulting	Paying staff, collecting fees, contingency planning

- **Marketing** – identifies customer demand, stimulates new demand, analyses customer needs, organises product information, takes orders, delivers products, gives after-sales service, etc.
- **Operations** – are responsible for actually making the products.
- **Finance** – raises capital, invests funds, records financial transactions, arranges transfers of money, collects cost information, maintains accounts, etc.

These central functions are *directly* concerned with the product. You might say that an organisation needs many other functions, such as human resources, research and development, catering, information, and public relations. But these can either be included in one of the central functions, or they are support functions that are not *directly* concerned with the product. Table 2.1 shows some examples of the work done in the central functions of different organisations. As you can see, we are defining each of the functions in a very broad sense.

The three central functions work together to achieve the goals of the organisation. Although they all exist in every organisation, the amount of emphasis given to each will vary. As a manufacturer, Boeing might highlight its operations, but must still market its products and control its finances; Heineken brewery might emphasise its marketing, but still needs efficient operations and control of accounts; Royal and Sun Alliance insurance might focus on its financial performance, but still has to deliver products to customers.

In the 1960s companies tended to emphasise marketing, while the 1980s saw a move towards stronger financial management. More recently there has been a shift towards operations. This is partly a response to major changes in the area, but it also recognises that the operations of a typical organisation employ most of the people, have most of the assets and generate all the income. One view of an organisation has operations generating income, while other functions generate costs.

OPERATIONS IN PRACTICE

Haflinger Electronics

Haflinger Electronics (HE) is a division of a large international conglomerate. It makes a range of domestic electrical equipment, including televisions, CD, DVD, stereo and video equipment. In the first half of 1999 it increased sales by 7 per cent and its profits by 10.5 per cent. This healthy performance came after many years of troubles. These started in 1974 when HE first noticed the affects of Japanese imports, and made a trading loss of DM 20 million. Senior managers felt that the best way to fight the competition was by improved marketing, and in the following year they tripled the advertising budget. Unfortunately, this had little success and HE made a loss of DM 30 million.

The basic problem was that Japanese products were 20 per cent cheaper than equivalent ones from HE. The company started a severe cost-cutting programme, including a reduction of 65 per cent in the research and development budget. Not surprisingly, HE's products soon became outdated and were overtaken by new ideas from competitors. In 1984 HE tried restructuring, closing two plants, selling three others and buying two small manufacturers in South America. In 1992 it lost DM 65 million, and appointed Conrad Staedler as the new chairman.

Staedler immediately saw that despite cosmetic changes, HE had been making the same products and using the same process for 20 years. To meet the new competition, it would have to concentrate on operations – and this meant making better products more efficiently. Staedler started a 'customer focus' campaign, which found out exactly what products customers wanted. Then he invested in research and development to design products that would satisfy these demands. HE needed efficient operations to make the new products, and it built a state-of-the-art manufacturing centre in Munich.

By 1999 sales had doubled and HE was making a profit for the first time in 25 years. Conrad Staedler reviewed his success by saying, 'It was all very easy. We designed products that customers wanted – and then made them using the best operations'.

Source: company records

In practice, the boundaries between the three central functions and the various supporting functions are all blurred. Purchasing, for example, may be an independent support function, or part of logistics within marketing, or part of the process within operations, or a cost centre within finance. The important thing is not to draw boundaries around activities, but to make sure that they all work together to achieve the organisation's goals.

Sometimes this co-operation is surprisingly difficult, especially when different divisions see themselves as working independently rather than as parts of the overall organisation. Some ways of improving co-operation between the functions include:

- designing strategies that are based on co-operation rather than competition (we will talk about this in the next chapter);
- setting common goals for different functions, with explicit co-operation;
- removing internal boundaries within the organisation;

- using a matrix structure and project teams (described in Chapter 18);
- not separating functions in different locations;
- improving information flows around the organisation and sharing ideas;
- rewarding behaviour that encourages co-operation;
- actively bringing people together to make joint decisions;
- transferring people between functions;
- encouraging informal contacts between functions;
- using self-managed work groups.

Review questions

2.5 What are the central functions in an organisation?

2.6 Give some details of the central functions in an organisation that you are familiar with.

2.7 Why is human resource management not considered a central function? What about product design?

Decisions in operations management

Types of decision

We have described operations management as a central function, and can now look at the type of decisions it makes. We know that, in general, managers set objectives, plan, organise, staff, direct and so on. Not surprisingly, operations managers do these jobs for the operations. We can add some details by looking at the decisions in a common operation, such as a supermarket.

OPERATIONS IN PRACTICE

Sainsbury's supermarkets

In 1869 John James and Mary Ann Sainsbury opened a shop to sell butter, milk and eggs in London's Drury Lane. This grew into a major supermarket chain, which went public in 1973. By 2000, the chain had 341 branches, 120,000 full-time and part-time employees, and sales approaching £10 billion.

The basic operations in a supermarket are simple. It gets large deliveries of goods from suppliers, and then sells small amounts to individual customers, but when you walk around a Sainsbury's store you can see the results of many operations management decisions. One store manager described these as follows:

- *Location* – the store must attract large numbers of customers, be convenient, have easy access, be some distance from other stores and be highly visible.
- *Layout* – the store and other facilities must be easy for customers to use and encourage them to buy goods.
- *Capacity* – when building a store, Sainsbury's has to forecast the expected number of customers and the amounts they will buy, and then build a store with enough capacity to meet this demand.

- *Product design* – the product (a package of both goods supplied and supermarket services) must appeal to as many customers as possible.
- *Process design* – this means finding the best way to deliver the product.
- *Performance* – targets are set for all operations, and procedures are established to measure, monitor and improve actual performance.
- *Logistics* – this entails developing relationships with suppliers and transport operators to get a wide range of high-quality goods delivered at the right time and at low costs.
- *Stock control* – there must be enough goods to meet forecast demand, but not so many that they are wasted.
- *Technology used* – supermarkets use a lot of technology, including information exchange in their integrated supply chains, customer-scanning of goods, automated banking, and sales via telephone and the Internet.
- *Staffing* – the workload in a supermarket varies widely over time, so there must be enough staff working at any time, but with no one idle.
- *Pricing* – Sainsbury's sets its prices to be competitive, but prices must still be high enough to make a profit.
- *Vertical integration* – as major buyers of goods, Sainsbury's could increase vertical integration by taking over suppliers.
- *Maintenance* – this requires programmes of maintenance and replacement for all equipment and buildings.
- *Financing* – this means finding the best way of raising money to finance the building and operations in stores.

Source: Annual reports and interviews

The problems faced by operations managers in Sainsbury's supermarkets are similar those faced in every other organisation. When LG Group of South Korea decided to invest £1.7 billion in semiconductor and television plants in Newport, South Wales it looked at a range of similar problems, as did Graham Barnet when he started a painting and decorating business in Derby. Table 2.2 gives a list of the main decisions made by operations managers. This list is not, of course, exhaustive, but it gives an idea of the type of questions they have to answer.

Operations managers make decisions in these, and other, areas with the overall aim of satisfying customers. As Colin Marshall,[5] the former head of British Airways, said, 'The simple principle is that the company exists to serve its customers long into the future'.

Anyone can satisfy customers if he/she has unlimited resources. One of the skills of operations managers is to work with resources that are limited by:

- *internal constraints* – that require efficient use of resources, control costs, meet the wider objectives of the organisation, limit risk, and so forth;
- *external constraints* – of the market, price customers will pay, competition, costs of materials, etc.

This inevitably needs a compromise, giving products that are generally acceptable to customers, while using resources efficiently enough to meet internal requirements (see Figure 2.4). As you will see, such compromise is a standard feature of operations management.

Table 2.2 Some questions commonly answered by operations managers

Objectives	What are our aims? How do we work with other parts of the organisation?
Product	What products do customers want? What products should we make?
Demand	How do we forecast demand? Is there variation in demand?
Capacity	How much capacity do we need? Can we adjust capacity?
Quality	How do we measure quality? How do we maintain high quality?
Process	How do we make our products? What facilities do we need?
Planning	When do we make products and schedule resources?
Performance	How do we measure performance? What targets should we aim for?
Technology	What level of technology should we use?
Layout	How do we arrange the facilities?
Materials	What materials do we need? Where should we get them?
Stocks	What do we keep in stock? How do we minimise the cost?
Logistics	How do we move goods through the supply chain?
Pricing	What prices should we charge customers?
Location	Where is the best place for operations?
Management systems	What type of management systems should we use?
Organisational structure	What is the best structure to support the operations?
People	How many and what type of people do we employ? How do we motivate them?

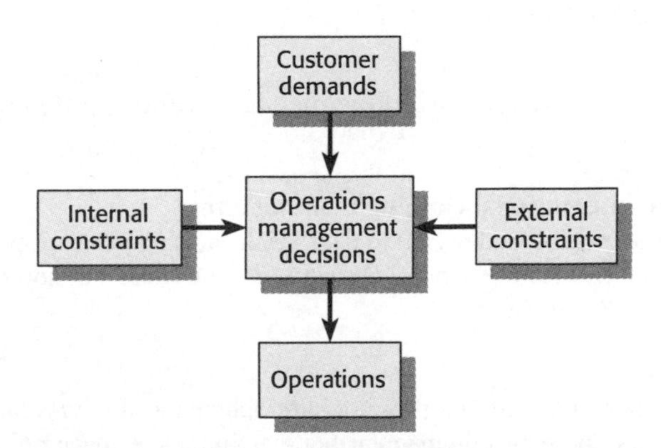

Figure 2.4 Balancing constraints and demands in operations

Review questions

2.8 From an operations point of view, what would you say is the main objective of an organisation?

2.9 What type of decisions do operations managers make?

Other views of operations management

We have already described operations management in several ways: as being responsible for the activities that make products, as a system for transforming inputs into outputs, as a central management function, and by the type of decisions it makes. These are, of course, different ways of looking at the same activities. We could add some other views, perhaps describing operations management as a **profession**, or as a way of tackling management problems.

Operations management as a profession

Manufacturers usually have 'production managers' in charge of their operations. The equivalent jobs in service industries are generally known as 'operations managers'. In recent years, people have recognised that these two jobs are the same, which is why we use the general title **operations manager**. This is, however, not universal and there are many alternatives. Whenever you look at an organisation – whether it is a university, mobile phone company, club, office, airline or any other business – there are people in charge of the operations. These are the operations managers, even if their actual title is production manager, plant manager, site manager, materials controller, shop manager, matron, postmaster, chef, supervisor, headmaster, transport manager, factory superintendent, maintenance manager, production engineer, or any other alternative. You can get a feel for the range of titles from the following examples.

OPERATIONS IN PRACTICE

Job advertisements

The following examples of advertisements for operations managers (under different titles) come from a copy of the *Sunday Times*.

Group Operations Director for an international clothing manufacturer
Sainty Hird & Partners advertised for an experienced person to fill a 'key leadership position' and deliver world class manufacturing performance, customer service, efficiency and business development in a multi-million pound company with 1,700 employees.

Supply Chain Manager for Pepsico
Pepsico invested £11 million in its state-of-the-art European logistics operations, and was looking for people to manage a variety of projects. These include manufacturing performance, inventory management and supply chain planning.

Business Planning Manager for Norwich Union
This major insurance company was looking for someone to work on business planning, performance monitoring, capacity planning, and satisfying customer expectations.

Senior Project Managers at Glaxo-Wellcome
Glaxo-Wellcome was looking for someone to play a vital role within its world class research and development organisation, and 'deliver large-scale, multi-location projects on time, within budget, to exacting quality standards'.

Chief Executive for The Scottish Football Association
The second oldest football association in the world has an objective of fostering the game at all levels across Scotland. The Chief Executive is responsible for efficient administration in all areas, and liaising with a wide range of external organisations – including FIFA and UEFA, sponsors, media and the public at large.

Operations Director for an expanding company
Hoggett Bowers' clients are an expanding company who wanted an experienced operations director to make the most effective use of assets, increase productivity, improve output and quality, and build a motivated team.

GP Practice Manager for Highgate Group Practice
A friendly National Health Service practice with eight general practitioner partners was looking for a practice manager. This person would lead a multi-disciplinary team and provide administrative, financial and management support to the partners.

Programme Managers at PricewaterhouseCoopers
PricewaterhouseCoopers is the world's largest professional services organisation. Business process outsourcing allows clients to concentrate on their core activities, while PricewaterhouseCoopers provides non-core processes. The company wanted people to join its European IT outsourcing team and work with operations management teams.

Supply Chain Project Manager for a retailer
Hoggett Bowers was looking for someone with operational experience to work for a high-profile chain of stores. The person would evaluate the total supply chain, assess business processes, and work with all operations managers to improve performance.

Head of Purchasing for an engineering company
Regent Consulting was recruiting a senior manager to direct the purchasing and materials management operations in a large engineering group.

Sales Quality Manager for Pearl Assurance
Pearl Assurance had been through a period of major change, including simplifying its products for 3.5 million customers. It was looking for someone to review the existing sales quality process, control procedures and create continuing process improvement.

Project 2.2 *Look around and find an organisation that you are reasonably familiar with. Identify the people who manage the operations in this organisation, and list the types of decisions they make. Do they consider any special factors in their decisions?*

Operations management approach to problems

Managers are often problem-solvers, facing a series of **problems** and making the decisions to overcome them. Some problems are very easy and the decisions hardly need thinking about. It is, for example, easy to decide whether or not to pay income tax (assuming that you prefer living at home to living in prison). Most decisions are more complicated, particularly when:

- there are many different alternatives and things happening;
- you have to balance different objectives;
- there are conflicting views of the problem, alternatives, solutions, etc.;
- you have to make decisions quickly;
- the environment is changing quickly;
- many people are affected by the decision;
- there are serious penalties for making a mistake;
- you have to make a lot of assumptions;
- the people who make decisions are not the same people who implement them.

Most of us think that we are good at making decisions. Unfortunately, the reality is that we jump to conclusions, are inconsistent, have preconceived ideas, are prejudiced, use wrong assumptions, ignore available information, lack experience, do not have enough knowledge, and simply make mistakes. To make good decisions, you have to approach them properly – and this means taking a considered view and following some formal procedure. One useful approach has the following seven steps.

1. *Describe the problem properly* – finding the exact problem, its cause, the context, effects, seriousness and variables.
2. *Define your objectives* – showing what you want to achieve, and giving priorities to different objectives.
3. *Collect and analyse data* – getting all the relevant information that you need.
4. *List your alternatives* – finding all your options, including those that are not immediately obvious.
5. *Compare the alternatives and find the best* – examining the consequences of each alternative, and finding the one that best achieves your objectives.
6. *Implement your decision* – doing whatever is needed to carry out the decision.
7. *Monitor progress* – checking what actually happens over time and making any adjustments or new decisions.

You can use this general type of approach to solve many problems. However, this does not mean that problems become easy – or they would not be problems! Perhaps the most common fault is jumping at the easiest or most obvious answer. If a decision is at all important, you should approach it carefully and spend time finding the best solution.

Review questions

2.10 How can you view operations management in four different ways?

2.11 List 10 different titles for 'operations managers'.

2.12 How would you approach an important decision?

Chapter review

- Managers are the people who make decisions in an organisation. They are responsible for everything that the organisation does.
- Operations managers make decisions about the operations. They are responsible for all aspects of the organisation's products and the processes used to make them.

- Operations management is an essential part of every organisation, and the way it is done directly affects performance.
- There are several ways of viewing operations management. The most common sees it as a central function, along with marketing and finance.
- We can also look at the type of decisions made. Operations managers in different types of organisation face a range of similar problems.
- We can also view operations management as a profession, and by its approach to solving problems.

Key terms

central functions *p. 24*
customers *p. 21*
decisions *p. 27*
finance *p. 25*
managers *p. 20*
marketing *p. 25*
operations audit *p. 24*
operations management *p. 20, 23*
operations managers *p. 20, 30*
problems *p. 31*
profession *p. 30*

CASE STUDY British Telecommunications PLC

Since it was privatised in 1984, British Telecommunications PLC (BT) has retained a dominant position in the UK. It has continued to expand and develop in line with its vision of being 'the most successful worldwide communications group'. This growth has been helped by the opening of the European Union to full competition in 1998, liberalisation of other markets, and the growth in global telecommunications to over a trillion dollars a year. By 2000 BT's turnover was approaching £20 billion, with profits of over £3 billion.

To succeed in this highly competitive market, BT is adopting a number of policies for operations.

- It gives customers a high-quality service. This is measured in several ways, including value for money, reliability, response time, clarity of communications, use of technology, and special products and services. It regularly wins UK Quality Awards, and is the largest company to win a European Quality Award prize (1996 and 1997). In the 1998 Annual Report, Bill Cockburn, the Group Managing Director, said: 'Quality . . . is in the bloodstream, part of our everyday working lives. Quality products, services and customer service are crucial in our business.'
- It develops new products, such as Traffic Line for in-car information, Genie for personalised information and various alternatives for e-cash. BT spends £300 million a year on research and development and has 13,000 patents around the world.

- It continually improves its facilities, improving its voice network, building an advanced data network in the UK (including 5 million km of optical fibre) and a pan-European optical fibre network connecting 200 cities.
- It is a major supplier of mobile communications, through BT Cellnet in the UK, SFR in France, Viag Intercom in Germany, Telfort in The Netherlands, Airtel in Spain, LGT in South Korea, and so on.
- It provides Internet service for 1.5 million customers through Lineone, BT Internet, BT ClickFree, Cegetel, Arrakis, etc.
- It is continually expanding the services it offers through the Internet, such as Excite UK, LookSmart, BT Spree, BT Highway, and BT Click.
- It is growing internationally, largely through partnerships. The largest is Concert (a global alliance with AT&T) but there are other alliances including Viag in Germany, Vivendi in France and NS in The Netherlands.
- It provides other services to business, such as Workstyle Consultancy Group which emphasises flexible working, Syncordia Solutions, Syntegra and PULSE (which directs blood supplies to hospitals).
- It supports special initiatives, such as Schools Internet Caller and Future Talk Millennium Project.
- It emphasises community relations, giving at least 0.5 per cent of pre-tax profits to a community partnership programme.

Questions

- What are the products of BT? How would you describe its operations? What would an operations audit look like?
- You can describe the operations in BT at many different levels. How could you start to describe the links between these? What are the differences between external and internal customers?
- What are the main types of operations management decisions within BT?
- Check BT's Website (*www.bt.com*) for details of its latest operations.

Discussion questions

2.1 Why is operations management important?

2.2 'Change is inevitable.' What happens if an organisation does not continually update its operations? Give some examples to support your views.

2.3 What do you think are the most important issues currently facing operations managers?

2.4 Why is it important to approach decisions properly? Give some examples of decisions that have gone wrong, and explain why they went wrong.

2.5 There are three central functions in an organisation. Does this mean the other functions are not needed? What are these other functions?

2.6 How has international trade developed in recent years? What role has operations management played in these changes?

2.7 What do you think are the main operations decisions at Manchester United Football Club? How are these different from the operations at the Channel Tunnel, and at McDonald's?

References

1. Taylor F.W. (1911) *The Principles of Scientific Management*. Norwood, MA: Plimpton Press.
2. Mayo E. (1933) *The Human Problems of an Industrial Civilisation*. London: Macmillan.
3. Fayol H. (1949) *General and Industrial Management*. London: Pitman.
4. Weber M. (1947) *The Theory of Social and Economic Organisation*. New York: Free Press.
5. Marshall C. (1996) Talk at the Marketing Council. London.

Selected reading

Aquilano N.J. and Chase R.B. (1998) *Production and Operations Management*. Homewood, IL: Irwin.
Evans J.R. (1997) *Operations Management*. St Paul: West Publishing.
Galloway L. (1998) *Principles of Operations Management*. London: International Thomson.
Hart A. (1998) *Managing Operations*. London: Butterworth-Heinemann.
Krajewski L.J. and Ritzman L.P. (1998) *Operations Management*. 5th edn. Reading: Addison-Wesley.
Meredith J. and Schafer S. (1998) *Operations Management*. New York: John Wiley.
Slack N., Chambers S., Harland C., Harrison A. and Johnston R. (1998) *Operations Management*. 2nd edn. London: Pitman.
Waller D.L. (1999) *Operations Management*. London: International Thomson.
Wright J.N. (1999) *The Managing of Service Operations*. London: Continuum Publishing.

Some useful Websites

www.iomnet.org.uk – Institute of Operations Management
www.poms.org – Production and Operations Management Society
www.orsoc.org.uk – Operational Research Society
www.ienet.org – Institute of Industrial Engineers

INTEGRATING CASE STUDY

Ciba Speciality Chemicals

by Jaro Martinec of Ciba Speciality Chemicals

For many years Jaro Martinec was responsible for planning and supply chain management at the Pigments Division of Ciba Speciality Chemicals in Basle, Switzerland. He explains how he got interested in operations management.

I was anxious to learn about the process when I realised that we took so much longer than necessary to deliver goods. Typically marketing would ask for a product whose chemical process took 24 hours, but we could not deliver it for three months. It occurred to me that there should be a better way of organising things.

I adopted the aims of reducing the lead-time to an acceptable minimum, reducing the time wasted, reducing the assets used by at least a half, and reducing the amount of idle time. But how could I achieve these goals? To start with, I had to properly understand the process, and its links with other areas of the company, customers, suppliers and finances.

I looked at the way that retailers served their customers, and realised that we could use the same approaches for 80 per cent of our products. So I designed a set of ideal operations. Starting with the customer demands, I looked at the flow of products through the process. Then, working backwards, I systematically found the best way of achieving this flow, and eliminating as much waste as possible. I added a minimum number of decision points, where managers could allocate resources and make decisions about the process, until I got back to the point of ordering materials.

The changes did not occur overnight. It needed people to change their attitudes towards the process and customers. Over time, we made significant improvements to the operations.

Questions

- Why do you think there was such a difference between the times needed to make goods and deliver them? Is this common?
- What kind of operations would there be in Ciba? What are the main problems faced by operations managers?
- How would you set about improving the operations? Could you learn lessons from other organisations?

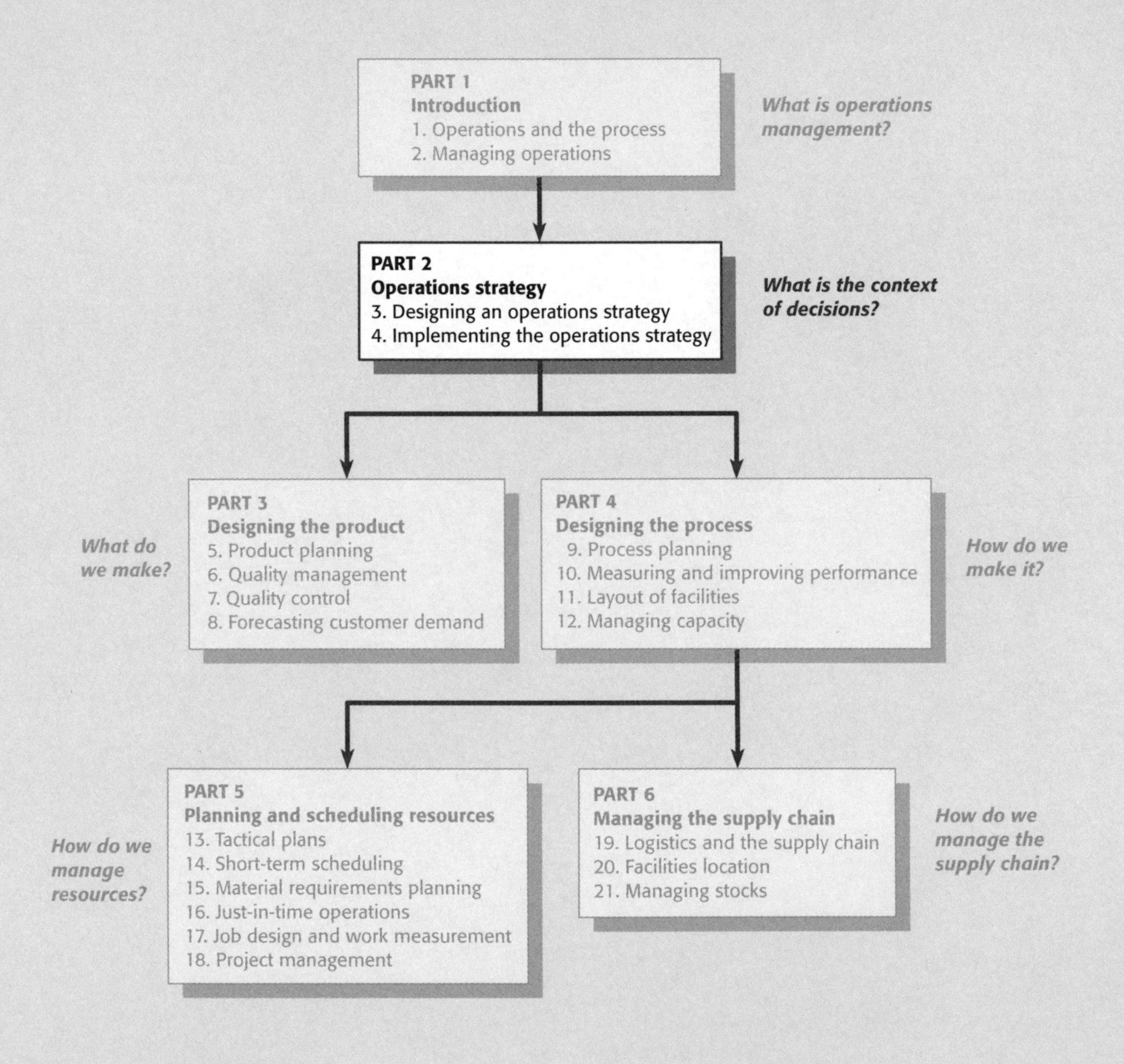

PART 1
Introduction
1. Operations and the process
2. Managing operations
What is operations management?
PART 2
Operations strategy
3. Designing an operations strategy
4. Implementing the operations strategy
What is the context of decisions?
PART 3
Designing the product
5. Product planning
6. Quality management
7. Quality control
8. Forecasting customer demand
What do we make?
PART 4
Designing the process
9. Process planning
10. Measuring and improving performance
11. Layout of facilities
12. Managing capacity
How do we make it?
PART 5
Planning and scheduling resources
13. Tactical plans
14. Short-term scheduling
15. Material requirements planning
16. Just-in-time operations
17. Job design and work measurement
18. Project management
How do we manage resources?
PART 6
Managing the supply chain
19. Logistics and the supply chain
20. Facilities location
21. Managing stocks
How do we manage the supply chain?

Part 2

OPERATIONS STRATEGY

This book is divided into six parts. Each part describes a different aspect of operations management. Part 1 gave an introduction to the subject. This is Part 2, which gives the strategic context for operations.

There are two chapters in this part. Chapter 3 describes different types of strategic decisions and the relationships between them. It emphasises the design and content of an operations strategy. Chapter 4 looks at the implementation of this strategy.

Later parts of the book look in more detail at the decisions made by operations managers. Part 3 describes product planning, and Part 4 discusses the process used to make these products. Part 5 considers the planning of resources to support the process, and Part 6 discusses some aspects of supply chain management.

CHAPTER 3

Designing an operations strategy

A corporation without a strategy is like an airplane weaving through stormy skies, hurled up and down, slammed by the wind, lost in the thunderheads. If lightening or crushing wind don't destroy it, it will simply run out of gas.

Alvin Toffler

The Adaptive Corporation, Gower, 1985

Contents

Aims of the chapter

After reading this chapter you should be able to:

- describe different levels of decisions in an organisation;
- discuss an organisation's mission and aims;
- appreciate the role of corporate, business and functional strategies;
- understand the purpose and contents of an operations strategy;
- approach the design of an operations strategy.

Main themes

This chapter will emphasise:

- the **mission**, which describes the overall aims of an organisation;
- **strategies**, which are the collection of long-term decisions that show how these aims will be achieved;
- **operations strategy**, which includes the long-term plans for operations.

Decisions in an organisation

Levels of decision

Some decisions are very important to an organisation, with consequences felt over many years. Other decisions are less important, with consequences felt over days or even hours. We can use their importance to classify decisions as **strategic**, **tactical** or **operational**.

- **Strategic decisions** are most important; they are long term, use many resources and are made by senior managers.
- **Tactical decisions** are less important; they are medium term, use fewer resources and are made by middle managers.
- **Operational decisions** are least important; they are short term, use few resources and are made by junior managers.

Every organisation makes decisions at these three levels.

- For General Electric, a decision to build a new factory five or 10 years in the future is strategic; a decision to introduce a new product next year is tactical; a decision about the number of units to make next week is operational.
- In Sheffield University, deciding whether to concentrate on post-graduate education in the next few years is strategic; deciding whether to offer a particular post-graduate course next year is tactical; choosing someone to teach a course next week is operational.
- During 1999, Royalty Trust Assurance made a strategic decision to offer single premium pensions, a tactical decision to expand the pension support office over the next year, and operational decisions about the number of staff needed in the office each week.
- First Great Western trains made a strategic decision to continue a passenger service to Penzance, tactical decisions about the fare structures, and operational decisions about crew schedules.

The scale of decisions varies widely between organisations. A strategic decision for National Power considers the number of new power stations it needs over the next 30 years and involves costs of billions of pounds. A strategic decision for Albert Street Newsagent looks a year or two into the future and involves costs of a few thousand pounds. Whatever the scale, the important point is that all organisations make decisions at every level. They must make broad plans for the distant future, and still work out the details of jobs to be done tomorrow. Table 3.1 shows some features of these different levels of decisions.

As you have probably noticed, there is a small problem with names here. Less important decisions are 'operational decisions' and some of these are concerned with the 'operations function'. Then we have to talk about 'operational decisions in operations', which can be confusing, but you should not get the two mixed up.

Table 3.1 Features of different levels of decisions

Decision	Strategic	Tactical	Operational
Level of manager	senior	middle	junior
Importance	high	medium	low
Resources used	many	some	few
Timescale	long	medium	short
Focus	whole organisation	parts of the business	individual activities
Risk	high	medium	low
Uncertainty	high	medium	low
Amount of detail	very general	moderate	very detailed
Data available	limited	some	more
Structure	unstructured	some	structured
Management skills	conceptual	human	technical

Strategic decisions: preliminary considerations

A traditional view is that senior managers make the strategic decisions that set their organisation on its course. These decisions set the context for lower-level decisions; they pass down the organisation to middle management and give the objectives and constraints for their more detailed tactical decisions. These tactical decisions, in turn, pass down the organisation to give the objectives and constraints for the operational decisions made by junior managers. While these decisions are flowing down through the organisation, information about actual performance and other feedback passes upwards. The result is a hierarchy, shown in Figure 3.1.

New styles of management and improved technology have made important changes to this traditional view. In practice, you will rarely see such a rigid hierarchy, and most decisions are discussed, negotiated and agreed rather than simply passed down. There is also a growing recognition that the best person to make a decision is the person most closely involved – and this is often a junior manager. People close to the operations have the necessary information, and can make a quick decision without waiting for information to move up the organisation, followed by decisions moving back down. One effect of these changes is that organisations are becoming 'leaner' by removing layers of management. John Browne, Chief Executive of BP-Amoco explained this trend by saying: 'The

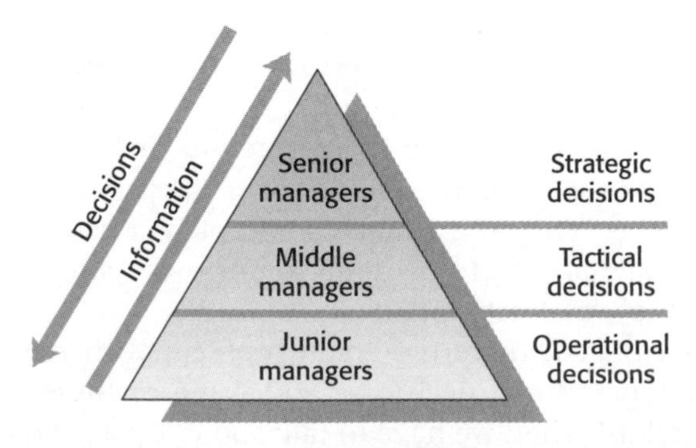

Figure 3.1 Flow of information and decisions in an organisation

organization must be flat, so that the top is connected to the people who actually make the money'.[1]

Review questions

3.1 What are the different levels of decision in an organisation?

3.2 Tactical decisions are most important to an organisation because they concern its day-to-day running. Do you think this is true?

3.3 What level of decision is:
(a) finding the best location for a customer call centre;
(b) deciding how many hours of overtime are needed next week;
(c) deciding whether to start a new air service to South America;
(d) deciding whether to publish a proposed textbook?

3.4 Orders are passed down an organisation from superior to subordinate. Do you think this is true?

OPERATIONS IN PRACTICE

Scottish Mutual Assurance

The Scottish Mutual Assurance Society was founded in Glasgow in 1883. For over 100 years it worked with the belief that the world of finance could – and should – be used for the good of the individual and the community as a whole. By 1990 it employed over a thousand people and looked after £2,300 million of investors' money – mainly in pensions, mortgages, investment and inheritance tax planning.

Senior managers made strategic decisions at their principal office in Glasgow. Details of these decisions were passed to 24 branch offices around the country, which made tactical decisions. Below the branch offices was a network of agents and financial advisers who made operational decisions. A typical decision would have the principal office making a strategic decision to develop single premium pensions. Details of the policies would be settled and passed to branch offices. The branches saw how the new product fitted into their business, and made plans for the medium term – perhaps organising the support needed for the new policy over the next year. The branch offices passed details of the pension policy to agents and advisers who made operational decisions about contacting potential customers, and so on.

The agents and advisers talked to potential customers and collected their views on the new policy. These were summarised and passed back to the branch offices. Each branch office reviewed the reports, summarised them, and passed the regional view back to the principal office. At the principal office, reports from each branch office were reviewed and summarised to find patterns for the whole country

This gave a standard pattern with decisions flowing down the organisation, and information flowing upwards. Then in 1992 everything changed. Senior managers made a strategic decision to de-mutualise and form a proprietary company, Scottish Mutual Assurance PLC, which was sold for £285 million to Abbey National PLC. Scottish Mutual is now part of a finance group with 25,000 employees and assets of £150 billion.

Source: company annual reports and discussions

Strategic decisions

Types of strategic decision

The Institute for Employment Studies says that the boundaries between different management functions are getting blurred, and that diversity is the key feature of senior management jobs.[2] It has also identified functions common to most senior managers, which include:

- setting the organisation's goals and policies;
- managing resources and controlling the business;
- directing their part of the business;
- managing aspects of the environment;
- developing other people in the organisation.

To put it briefly, senior managers set the long-term goals of their organisation, formulate strategies to achieve these goals, and then implement the strategies. This strategic planning is essential in every organisation, or else there is no overall direction. As Laurence Peter said, 'If you don't know where you are going, you will probably end up somewhere else'.[3]

There are several different types of strategic decisions. People use different names for these, but we will consider the:

- **mission** – a statement to give the overall aims of the organisation;
- **corporate strategy** – which shows how a diversified corporation will achieve its mission;
- **business strategy** – which shows how each business within a diversified corporation will contribute to the corporate strategy;
- **functional strategies** – which describe the strategic direction of each function, including operations, marketing and finance.

In practice, the distinction between these decisions is not clear, and organisations classify their strategies in many different ways.

Setting the aims in a mission

Most organisations have an overall statement of their aims. This **mission** or **vision** defines the purpose of the organisation – its reason for existence. The mission of Halifax PLC is 'to become the UK's leading provider of personal financial services'. Marks & Spencer 'aims to become the world's leading volume retailer with a global brand and global recognition'; Tarmac's stated aim is: 'to be an innovative, world-class provider of high-quality products and services, which add value to our customers in the built environment'; SmithKline Beecham says that 'health care prevention, diagnosis, treatment and cure – is our purpose'; Walt Disney aims at 'making people happy'.

The mission is usually a brief statement of purpose, but some organisations go further and include their fundamental beliefs, responsibilities to shareholders and employees, relations with customers and a range of other information. This gives a focus for managers, and makes sure that everyone is working towards the same goals.

OPERATIONS IN PRACTICE Mission statements

The following examples are typical mission statements quoted in annual reports.

The Institute of Management

The mission of the Institute of Management is to promote the art and science of management.

Lunn Poly

Our mission: We will be the UK's leading retailer of overseas holidays in terms of service, profit and volume.

We will achieve this by:

- matching our products and services to the needs of our customers;
- selling significantly more overseas holidays than our competitors;
- continuing to make more profit than our competitors.

Lloyds TSB Group

Maximising shareholder value – by dividend increases and by share price appreciation – remains our governing objective.

- Our aim is to be the best and most successful company in the financial services industry, a leader in our chosen markets.
- We aim to be first choice for our customers by understanding and meeting their needs more effectively than our competitors.
- We aim to reduce day-to-day operating costs through increased efficiency to enable us to invest further in our business.
- Our success is rooted in local communities: they are the source of our staff, our customers, our suppliers, our shareholders.

Source: company annual reports

Project 3.1 *Organisations publish their mission in annual reports, Websites and promotional material, and display them in offices and shops. Have a look around and collect some good examples of mission statements. How do these go beyond the cliché, 'We want to supply the best products, make most money and be world leaders in our field'?*

Corporate and business strategies

The **corporate strategy** shows how a diversified organisation will achieve the goals set out in the mission. It refers to the whole organisation, typically deciding what businesses the organisation should own and describing the relationships between them. The mission at Volvo says that, 'Volvo creates value by providing transportation-related products and service with superior quality, safety and environmental care to demanding customers in selected segments'. In 1999 this led to a corporate strategy of concentrating on commercial vehicles, and it sold its car division to Ford. The corporate strategy at ICI has been to move out of bulk chemicals and into consumer products, so ICI sold the bulk divisions and bought Unilever's

Speciality Chemicals, Acheson Industries, Williams Home Improvement, and National Starch.

Each separate business unit has its own **business strategy**, which shows how it will contribute to the wider corporate strategy. The Kingfisher group, for example, has an overall corporate strategy, and then Woolworth, B & Q, Superdrug, Comet and other businesses within the group each have their own related business strategies. The following list illustrates some typical decisions in each strategic area.

- *Corporate strategy*
  - amount of diversification and integration;
  - which industries to work in;
  - organisational structure, describing the separate businesses and relations between them;
  - businesses to start, acquire, close or sell.
- *Business strategy*
  - type of products to make;
  - relations with customers, suppliers, shareholders and other organisations;
  - geographical locations for operations and markets;
  - competitive position, showing how the businesses stand in relation to their competitors;
  - targets for long-term profitability, productivity and other measures of performance;
  - innovation, describing how the organisation changes over time.

In practice, there may be little distinction between corporate and business strategies, particularly for small organisations. However, if we look at the areas normally included in the business strategy, we can see how these lead to an operations strategy.

Designing a business strategy

There is no standard procedure for designing a business strategy. The usual advice is to look for the best balance between the organisation's internal strengths and the external constraints. Gay Gooderham says:

> *'No one "right" way to develop and implement strategy exists. The key to successful planning is to get the best fit between the chosen tools and techniques, the organisation's current culture capabilities and business environment and the desired outcome.'*[4]

This suggests that managers examine three factors when designing a business strategy. The first is the mission, which sets the overall goals. The second is the environment in which the organisation works. The third is the organisation's distinctive competence that allows it to succeed in this environment (see Figure 3.2).

The **business environment** consists of all the factors that affect an organisation, but which it cannot control. These include customer expectations, market conditions, competition, economic conditions, legal restraints, technology available, shareholder demands, interest groups, social and political conditions. The environment is likely to be similar for all organisations making competing products, so a business can only succeed if it has a **distinctive competence**. This includes the factors that the organisation can control, and which set it apart from its competitors. A company that can design new products very quickly will include innovation as part of its distinctive competence; the Co-operative Bank has a responsible, friendly and personal

Figure 3.2 Factors affecting the business strategy

service as its distinctive competence; Great Ormond Street Hospital specialises in treating children; Rolls-Royce makes cars of unmatched quality; easyJet has low-cost flights, and so on.

A distinctive competence comes from the organisation's assets, which include:

- *customers* – their demands, loyalty, relationships;
- *employees* – skills, expertise, loyalty;
- *finances* – capital, debt, cash flow;
- *organisation* – structure, relationships, flexibility;
- *products* – quality, reputation, innovations;
- *facilities* – capacity, age, reliability;
- *other assets* – knowledge, innovation, patents;
- *processes* – structures, technology used, flexibility;
- *marketing* – experience, reputation;
- *suppliers* – service, flexibility, partnerships.

To a large extent, this distinctive competence depends on operations managers. If, for example, an organisation bases its distinctive competence on innovative products, it relies on the operations managers to provide these. In other words, the business strategy sets the context for operations, and defines their overall requirements. Operations managers then analyse the business strategy and design operations that will achieve it. In practice, of course, such decisions are based on discussion and agreement, and the business strategy needs a substantial input from operations managers to say what they can realistically achieve.

Analyses to help design a business strategy

Several tools can help with analysing circumstances and suggesting the best direction for a business strategy. The most widely used is a **SWOT analysis**, which lists an organisation's:

- *Strengths* – what the organisation does well, features it should build on.
- *Weaknesses* – problems the organisation has, areas it should improve.
- *Opportunities* – openings that can help the organisation.
- *Threats* – hazards that can damage it.

Strengths and weaknesses describe the organisation's internal features, and build on its distinctive competence. Opportunities and threats describe external features and concentrate on the business environment. IBM might start a SWOT analysis by listing its strengths as brand recognition, high reputation and large resources; it weaknesses as slow innovation and high costs; its opportunities as growing demand for computers and new technologies; and the threats it faces as manufacturers copying its products and low-cost competitors. A SWOT analysis by Synergistic Consultants listed its *strengths* as expertise, innovation and local contacts; its *weaknesses* as small size, gaps in experience and local operations; its *opportunities* arose from the increasing use of information technology, new management methods, and growing local economy; *threats* were from larger competitors, high overheads and a possible takeover.

OPERATIONS IN PRACTICE

Objective 1 status for Cornwall

For most people, Cornwall is an attractive place to spend a holiday. Unfortunately, this appeal hides the fact that the county has the lowest average income in Britain. Following a long campaign, the European Union gave Cornwall 'Objective 1' status in 1999. This attracts the highest level of development aid, and it was estimated that the county would get £300 million of aid, with matching funds raising as much as a billion pounds.

To get this money, Cornwall had to prepare a Single Programme Document, which summarised its strategic aims and showed how the development funds would be spent. Six areas were identified as priorities for aid, under the general headings of investment in people, small and medium enterprises, rural and coastal development, community regeneration, the environment and business investment zones.

At this time a SWOT analysis for Cornwall's application had the following comments:

- *Strengths*
  - strong sense of Cornish identity;
  - highly regarded government office handling the application;
  - successful previous programmes of European aid;
  - well-crafted Single Programme Document.
- *Weaknesses*
  - lack of cohesion within the partnership organising the application;
  - inability of partners to act strategically;
  - suspicion of the project and partners;
  - concern over 'driving agendas'.
- *Opportunities*
  - substantial flow of money into a poor area;
  - balanced and sustainable economic development;
  - range of social benefits including health and education;
  - improved environment, infrastructure, transport, communications, etc.
- *Threats*
  - changing European priorities diverting funding to other programmes;
  - competition for Objective 1 funding;
  - difficulties of finding co-finance for projects;
  - problems with efficient administration of funds.

Several similar tools can help design a business strategy. A **PEST analysis**, for example, describes the importance of **p**olitical, **e**conomic, **s**ocial and **t**echnological influences in the environment. **Value chain analysis**[5] emphasises internal strengths and competencies. A **balanced scorecard**[6] concentrates on four perspectives of customer satisfaction, financial performance, internal processes, growth and innovation.

Review questions

3.5 What is an organisation's mission?

3.6 What is a corporate strategy?

3.7 What factors would you consider when designing a business strategy?

Functional strategies

We have just said that operations managers can help to design a business strategy, showing what the operations can achieve and how they might develop a distinctive competence. Operations managers also make strategic decisions within the operations function. These join strategic decisions in the other core functions of marketing and finance, as shown in Figure 3.3.

You might see other types of strategy, relating to the environment, human resource, procurement, information technology, and so on. These can form another layer of strategic decisions below the functional strategies, or they can simply be a part of the functional strategies. The important point is not what you call the strategies, but that they all work together to help the organisation achieve its overall goals.

The functional strategies are not independent, and they should be closely co-ordinated. Sometimes this co-operation is surprisingly difficult. If a company looks for high profits, operations managers might develop a strategy to reduce costs by concentrating on a narrow range of products, while marketing base their strategy

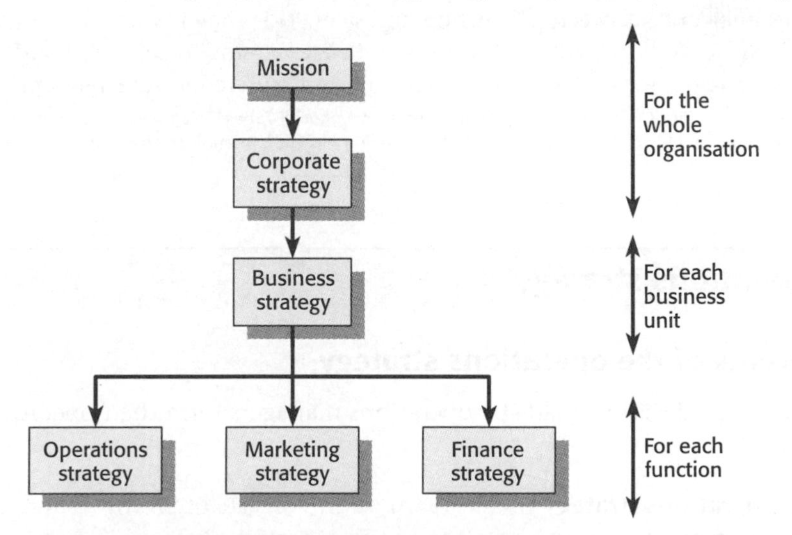

Figure 3.3 Strategic decisions in an organisation

on increasing sales by offering a wide range of products. If Ford designs a longer-lasting exhaust system for its cars, this could give a competitive advantage and increased sales. Of course, the new exhaust might be unpopular with companies that fit replacement systems such as Kwik-Fit. The problem is that Ford bought Kwik-Fit in 1999, and a move that brings benefits to one division of the company can harm another division.

Review questions

3.8 It is important to finalise the business strategy before working on the operations strategy. Do you think this is true?

3.9 How would you describe an operations strategy?

OPERATIONS IN PRACTICE

Kellogg Corporation

Kellogg is the world's best known supplier of breakfast cereals, with assets of US$ 5 billion and sales of US$ 7 billion a year. Its mission says that, 'Kellogg is a global company committed to building long term growth in volume and profit, and to embracing its worldwide leadership position by providing nutritious food products of superior value'.

This mission sets the scene for the corporate strategy, which is based on two divisions: 'ready to eat cereals' and 'convenience foods'. Each of these has a business strategy with, say, the ready to eat cereals division based on large-scale production and distribution of breakfast cereals. There are corresponding strategies for mass marketing and financing the huge global operations.

Unfortunately, in 1983 Kellogg's share of the crucial US cereals market fell to 37 per cent. Sales were falling behind production, so they responded with an aggressive marketing strategy based on a renewed commitment to quality, emphasis on the adult market, and a tripling of the advertising budget to around 20 per cent of sales. By 1987 Kellogg's share of the market had bounced back to 41 per cent.

Times change, and by 1999 Kellogg's share of the US market had fallen to 32 per cent, and there was another imbalance between production and sales. This time it seemed that customers were unwilling to pay for Kellogg's advertising costs and were moving to cheaper brands. Kellogg again adjusted its strategies to emphasise value, and substantially reduced its retail prices.

Sources: Tait, N. 'Kellogg ends difficult year with "disappointing" result' in *Financial Times*, 1 February 1999; Sellers, P. 'How King Kellogg beat the blahs' in *Fortune*, 29 August 1989; You can find more information at *www.kellogg.com.*

Operations strategy

Contents of the operations strategy

The strategic decisions made by operations managers form their operations strategy.

> The **operations strategy** of an organisation consists of all the strategic decisions, policies, plans and culture relating to the operations.

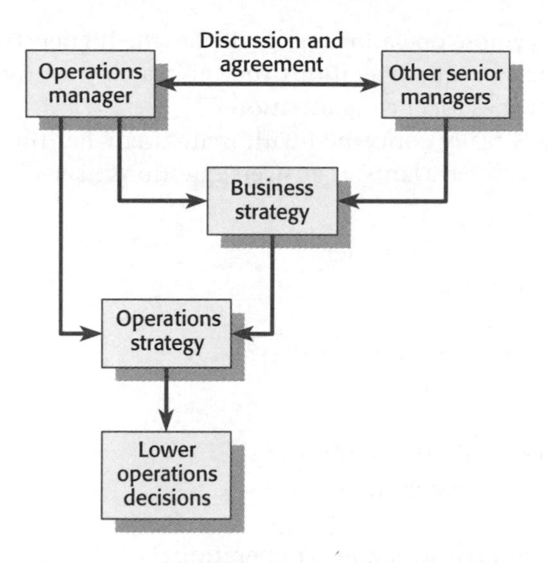

Figure 3.4 Role of operations managers in setting a business strategy

The operations strategy forms a link between the more abstract strategic plans and final products. While the corporate and business strategies describe general aims, the operations strategy concerns the products and processes that can achieve these. EasyJet airlines have a business strategy of competing aggressively on price; the related operations strategy defines a no-frills, low-cost service using secondary airports, with no meals or entertainment, and a simplified booking system. The business strategy of UPS calls for outstanding service to its customers, and this translates into an operations strategy of giving a very fast parcel delivery service to almost any point in the world. In 1997 the Body Shop adjusted its business strategy to regain some of its dramatic growth of the 1980s; the related operations strategy included a new store format, new services, expansion of overseas operations, tailoring products and packaging to tastes in different countries, and tighter control of overheads.

Operations managers do not simply respond to the requirements of higher strategies, but actively contribute to their formulation (Figure 3.4 shows one model for this two-way flow of information and decisions). The size of their contribution can give widely different organisations. At one end of a spectrum (shown in Figure 3.5) are organisations where the operations managers contribute little, and only translate the higher strategies into operations details. Their role is to accept the higher strategies, and design operations to make sure these can be achieved. At the other end of the

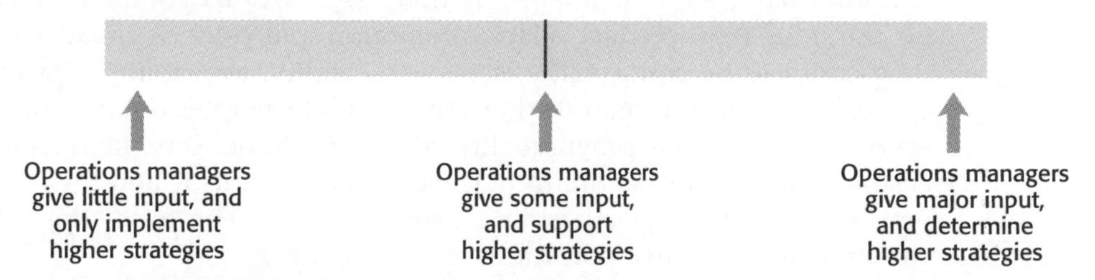

Figure 3.5 Spectrum for the role of operations managers in designing higher strategies

spectrum are organisations whose operations really dictate the higher strategies. Then operations managers design unique operations that give a competitive advantage, which leads to higher strategies for the organisation.

The operations strategy is really concerned with matching what the organisation is good at with what the customer wants. It answers questions like:

- What type of products do we make?
- How wide a range of products do we offer?
- What types of process do we use?
- What level of technology do we use?
- How innovative are our products and processes?
- How do we guarantee high quality?
- How can we plan capacity?
- How do we plan materials and other resources?
- How do we manage the supply chain?
- Where do we locate facilities?
- What is the best organisational structure for operations?

The operations strategy describes the type of products that an organisation makes, and the type of process used to make them. If customers' main priority is low price, the operations strategy should involve low-cost operations; if customers want fast delivery, the operations strategy should emphasise speed. But the strategy only gives general features and not detailed designs. An operations strategy of, say, high quality shows how the organisation will compete, but it does not describe the detailed features of a product. These come later in the planning, as we shall see in Chapter 5.

Focus of an operations strategy

All organisations have competitors, which are other organisations that already supply – or might start supplying – similar products. An organisation can only survive by making products that customers view as somehow 'better' than those from competitors. The operations strategy makes sure that such products are available over the long run. Its essential focus is on products, processes and customer satisfaction.

- Organisations compete by making **products** that **customers** prefer.
- Products depend on the **process** used to make them.
- The features of products and processes are set by the **operations strategy**.

A traditional view of marketing is that organisations compete by concentrating on the 'four Ps' – product, place, promotion and price. A broader view says that they compete by cost, quality, service, reliability, availability, flexibility, delivery speed, location and many other factors. In principle, organisations should do everything well, giving high quality, low cost, fast delivery, high technology, good customer service and so on. In practice, this is unrealistic and they develop a competitive advantage by focusing on specific areas. The following list gives some common areas for their operations strategy focus.

- **Cost**. Most organisations want low costs, but some adopt a positive strategy of minimising costs and supplying products at the lowest possible prices.

- **Quality**. Customers are continually demanding higher quality, so many organisations design strategies to deliver guaranteed high-quality products. It can be difficult to say exactly what customers mean by 'high quality', but we will return to this theme in Chapter 6.
- **Timing**. This strategy delivers a product exactly when customers want it. Often this means short delivery times from stocks of standard items, but it can also mean rapid development of new products, or delivering at the time specified by a customer.
- **Flexibility**. This is the ability of an organisation to meet specific customer requirements. There are two aspects to flexibility. A strategy based on **product flexibility** customises products to individual specifications. A strategy based on **volume flexibility** responds quickly to changing levels of demand.
- **Technology**. Some operations strategies focus on the latest available technology, such as computer manufacturers or mobile communication services.
- **Customer service**. Customers are often more interested in how well they are treated, than the technical details of the product. Organisations with high customer contact can provide an overall experience that sets them apart from competitors.

Table 3.2 outlines some effects of strategies with different focuses. These general strategies are clearly not the only ones. Organisations can also focus on reliability (so that a product is always available and working when needed), environmental protection, location, the process, ethical employment, or a range of other features.

When we say that an organisation focuses on one area, we do not mean that it ignores everything else. Ideally, the organisation would do everything well, but it can be difficult to combine, say, low costs and high quality, or fast delivery and

Table 3.2 Effects of some different focus in operations strategies

Focus	Competitive advantage	Types of operations
Cost	low prices	large-scale production, automation, high productivity, standard products, low overheads
Quality	guaranteed high-quality product	reliable process, total quality management (see Chapter 6), low variability in products and operations, high-quality materials
Timing	delivery of products when customers want them	adequate capacity, responsive operations, efficient scheduling of work, close customer relations
Fast response	no waiting for products	short lead times, spare capacity, dedicated operations
Product flexibility	customised products	versatile and responsive operations, skilled employees, rapid adjustments to the process, customer involvement
Demand flexibility	can meet changing levels of demand	variable capacity, responsive operations, efficient scheduling of work, short lead times
Technology	most advanced products	investment in research and development, continuing stream of new products, exploiting new ideas
Customer service	'pampering' customers	close customer relations, sharing information and views, flexibility, openness to suggestions

customised products. Managers choose the features that an operations strategy will emphasise, and the balance between the different factors. In other words, they **design** the operations strategy.

Project 3.2 *Imagine that you are about to book a summer holiday. List the factors that are important for your choice. Your list might start with expected weather, closeness to beaches, standard of hotel, cost, nightlife, and so on. Are your priorities the same as other people's? How might these priorities lead to different operations strategies?*

Design of an operations strategy

There is no single 'best' operations strategy for an organisation. Instead, managers try to identify the features that they think will give the best results. There are many factors to consider in these decisions (shown in Figure 3.6), particularly:

- *higher strategies* – which gives the aims and context for the operations strategy;
- *other internal constraints and strengths* – including the experience and skills of the organisation, existing products and processes, reputation, location, and so on;
- *customer demand* – including the type of products, quality, timing, price, after-sales support, etc.;
- *competitors* – other organisations trying to meet the same customer demands;
- *other external constraints and features* – including economic conditions, legal requirements, market conditions, etc.

There is no analysis that can find the best balance of these factors, so managers use a mixture of analysis, reasoning, experience and intuition. There are some guidelines they can use, such as Terry Hill's[7] five-step procedure for manufacturing strategy. In this, Step 1 defines the corporate objectives, while Step 2 designs the marketing strategies to achieve these objectives. Then Step 3 looks at the features of products that win orders, and Step 4 designs the best process to supply these. Step 5 provides the infrastructure to support production. This simple approach has been extended and developed in several ways.

A more logical approach to designing an operations strategy has the following steps.

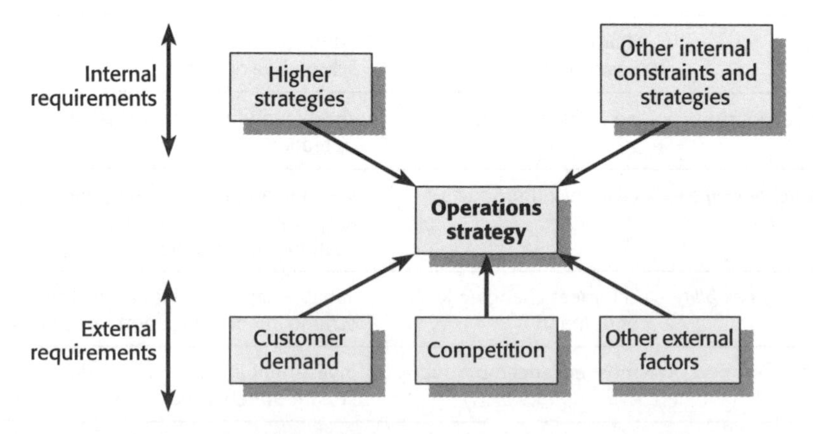

Figure 3.6 Factors in the design of an operations strategy

1. Analyse the business strategy – and other strategies – from an operations viewpoint. This gives the context and overall aims of the operations strategy.
2. Analyse the aims and set goals to show what the operations strategy must achieve.
3. Now look at the existing operations strategy to see how well they achieve these goals, and identify areas that need improving.
4. Understand the environment in which the operations strategy works. This identifies customers, competition, constraints, and so on.
5. Find the factors that will lead to success in this environment, and the importance of each one. This includes the general features that products must have to meet customer expectations.
6. Describe the general features of the process that can best deliver these products. This includes the capacity, technology used, location, and so on.
7. Design the best organisational structure, controls and functions to support the process.
8. Define measures to compare actual performance with planned, optimal and competitors' performances.
9. Implement the plans, setting the aims and conditions for other levels of operations decisions.
10. Monitor actual performance, continually look for improvements, keep the strategies up to date, and give feedback.

These steps may not give a recipe for designing an operations strategy, but they do list the main considerations. We will consider some aspects of implementing the strategy in the next chapter.

Review questions

3.10 What general factors might an operations strategy concentrate on?

3.11 The design of an operations strategy is largely a matter of guessing what customers want in the future. Do you agree with this?

3.12 What, essentially, does the operations strategy describe?

OPERATIONS IN PRACTICE

Sermec Export

Piotr Sermec employs 42 people in his vegetable bottling factory outside Prague. In 2001 he started exporting to the European Union. As Piotr explains, this forced many changes to his operations.

> Our new customers are supermarkets who are far more demanding than our traditional domestic customers. They know exactly what they want, define rigorous standards, and insist on long-term contracts. We used to see what vegetables were available each week and plan our production accordingly; now we need guaranteed supplies years into the future to meet our contracted production.
>
> We aim at continued expansion of the business, and now have an operations strategy that allows us to meet customer demand long into the future. We have installed automated processing lines that give high capacity, and are responding to customer demands by expanding our product range. Our planning and materials handling have been completely updated. By any measure, we are competitive, and productivity continues to rise at over 10 per cent a year.

Chapter review

- Decisions are made at several levels in an organisation. We can classify these as strategic, tactical and operational.
- Strategic decisions are made by senior management and set the overall direction of the organisation. There are several types of strategic decisions.
- The mission describes an organisation's overall aims. The corporate and business strategies show how the organisation will achieve these aims.
- Long-term decisions within each business function form the functional strategies.
- The operations strategy consists of all the long-term decisions within operations. This describes the nature of an organisation's products, its processes and the way resources are organised. The operations strategy sets the context for all other operations decisions.
- An operations strategy identifies the areas on which the organisation will focus. Several factors are important in this decision, including the higher strategies, external conditions and internal constraints.
- There is no 'best' way of designing a strategy, but managers generally approach this in several steps. These start with an analysis of higher strategies and end with implementation and monitoring of results.

Key terms

business environment *p. 46*
business strategy *p. 44*
corporate strategy *p. 44, 45*
design of operations strategy *p. 54*
distinctive competence *p. 46*
flexibility *p. 53*
focus of strategy *p. 52*
functional strategies *p. 44*
mission *p. 44*
operational decision *p. 41*
operations strategy *p. 50*
strategic decision *p. 41*
SWOT analysis *p. 47*
tactical decision *p. 41*
vision *p. 44*

CASE STUDY The University of Rondstat

The Business School is the largest faculty in the University of Rondstat. Within the Business School are nine departments, including the Department of Operations Management.

For some time the University has felt that it lacks direction. While other universities are focusing on specific areas and 'centres of excellence', Rondstat continues in its traditional ways. The University's president wants to adjust the University's operations, and has asked every department to prepare a mission statement and strategic plan. At the same time she has asked for the University's mission and all faculty missions to be updated.

The Department of Operations Management has formed a small committee to consider both its long-term goals, and plans for achieving these goals. As a starting point, this committee looked at the current missions of the University and the Business School.

The mission of the University is rather long and covers several pages. The first paragraph gives the following summary.

The University of Rondstat is a place of education and scholarly enquiry. Its mission is to seek truth and disseminate knowledge, which we achieve by excellence in research and teaching. We contribute to society directly by research, and by preparing students who carry their knowledge on to future generations. We co-operate enthusiastically with other parts of the education system, with government at every level, and with all parts of our community. We pursue this mission for the benefit of all humanity and encourage local, national and international communications.

The Business School's mission is considerably shorter.

The mission of the business school is to be internationally recognised as a leader in management education and research. Our goals are to:

- instill leadership and knowledge of management in our students;
- be a leading contributor to management knowledge through research;
- employ faculty members who achieve excellence in teaching and scholarship;
- maintain outstanding facilities for management education;
- remain close to the practice of management within our community.

Questions

- Does it seem reasonable for the University, Business School and Department of Operations Management all to have their own missions and strategic plans?
- How would you update the mission of the University and Business School?
- Design a suitable mission statement and strategic plan for the Department of Operations Management.

Discussion questions

3.1 Strategic decisions are less structured than tactical and operational ones. What exactly does this mean? How would you describe the important features of different levels of decisions?

3.2 Take a familiar organisation, such as Ford, and outline its corporate and business strategies. How do these translate into operations strategies? How do these lead to tactical and operational decisions?

3.3 Suppose you are about to start a management consultancy. Do a SWOT analysis of your business. What other analyses might be useful? How would these help you design an operations strategy?

3.4 Explain, giving suitable examples, the differences between different types of strategies. Are these real differences or just different names for the same things?

3.5 On what features might an operations strategy focus? How can managers choose the best of these? Why do they not try to be good at everything? What effect does the focus have on other operations?

3.6 Is there any difference between the operations strategies available to services and manufacturers? What happens when a service has a near monopoly, such as health and education?

3.7 There is often inter-departmental rivalry within an organisation. Do you think this should be encouraged or avoided?

3.8 Edwards Deming (whom we shall meet again in chapter 6) discussed 'The Seven Deadly Diseases' of managers:[8]

- *lack constancy of purpose* – as the whole organisation should know where it is heading, and aim at improved performance;
- *emphasis on short-term profits* – when they should take a longer view;
- *evaluation of performance by annual review* – which emphasises short-term performance, and leaves people who do badly feeling bitter, dejected and unfit for work;
- *mobility of top management* – so they are only interested in their own market value, and have no knowledge or interest in the long-term success of a particular organisation;
- *running a company on visible figures alone* – as there are many aspects of performance that cannot be measured but which should not be ignored;
- (The last two of Deming's diseases are only relevant to the USA and are *excessive medical costs* and *excessive costs of lawsuits*.)

How do you think these diseases can be avoided?

References

1. Lorenz A. (1998) 'BP Boss Drives Change through the Pipeline', *Sunday Times*, 26 April.
2. Kettley P. and Strebler M. (1997) 'Changing Roles for Senior Managers', IES Report, no. 327.
3. Peter L. and Hull R. (1969) *The Peter Principle*. New York: Bantam Books.
4. Gooderham G. (1998) 'Debunking the Myths of Strategic Planning'. *CMA Magazine*, May.
5. Porter M.E. (1985) *Competitive Advantage*. New York: Free Press.
6. Kaplan R.S. and Norton D.P. (1996) The balanced scorecard. Cambridge, MA: Harvard Business School Press.
7. Hill T. (1993) *Manufacturing Strategy*. 2nd edn. Basingstoke Hants: Macmillan Press.
8. Deming W.E. (1986) *Out of the Crisis*. Cambridge, MA: MIT Press.

Selected reading

Baden-Fuller C. and Pitt M. (1996) *Strategic Innovation*. London: Routledge.

Brown S., Lamming R., Bessant J. and Jones P. (2000) *Strategic Operations Management*. Oxford: Butterworth-Heinemann.

Harrison M. (1993) *Operations Management Strategy*. London: Prentice-Hall.

Irons K. (1994) *Managing Service Companies*. Wokingham: Addison-Wesley.

Hayes R.H., Pisano G.P. and Upton D.M. (1996) *Strategic Operations*. New York: Free Press.

Johnson G. and Scholes K. (1997) *Exploring Corporate Strategy*. 4th edn. London: Prentice-Hall.

Mintzberg H. and Quinn J. (1995) *The Strategy Process*. 3rd edn. New York: Prentice-Hall.

Vernon-Wortzel H. and Wortzel L. (1997) *Strategic Management in a Global Economy*. NY: John Wiley.

Voss C.A. (1992) *Manufacturing Strategy*. London: Chapman and Hall.

Wheelin T.L. and Hunger J.D. (1998) *Strategic Management and Business Policy*. Reading: Addison-Wesley.

Useful Websites

Useful places to start looking at strategies are:

www.cranfield.ac.uk/public/mn
www.agilityforum.org

Implementing the operations strategy

When you're through changing, you're through. Change is a process, not a goal; a journey, not a destination.

Robert Kriegel and David Brandt

Sacred Cows Make the Best Burgers, Warner, New York, 1996

Contents

Aims of the chapter

After reading this chapter you should be able to:

- see how an operations strategy leads to a range of lower decisions;
- describe the steps needed to implement an operations strategy;
- discuss the focus and links between customers, products and processes;
- recognise the importance of change and its management;
- appreciate the role of human resource management in operations.

Main themes

This chapter will emphasise:

- different **levels of decisions** in operations;
- **implementation** of the operations strategy;
- the **focus** defined by the operations strategy;
- **change** within an organisation;
- the importance of **human resource management**.

Operations management decisions

Tactical and operational decisions

In the last chapter we saw how an operations strategy contains the long-term decisions, policies, plans and culture relating to operations. Like everything else in business, the operations strategy is not static, but continually evolves to meet changing conditions. The changes are usually adjustments rather than radical changes in direction, but operations managers must still see how the new strategies affect their work. Typically, they have to answer questions like the following:

- How will the new strategy affect the design of products?
- What changes will it need to the process?
- Will our approach to planning and scheduling change?
- How can we introduce the changes?
- Do we have, or can we get, the necessary resources?

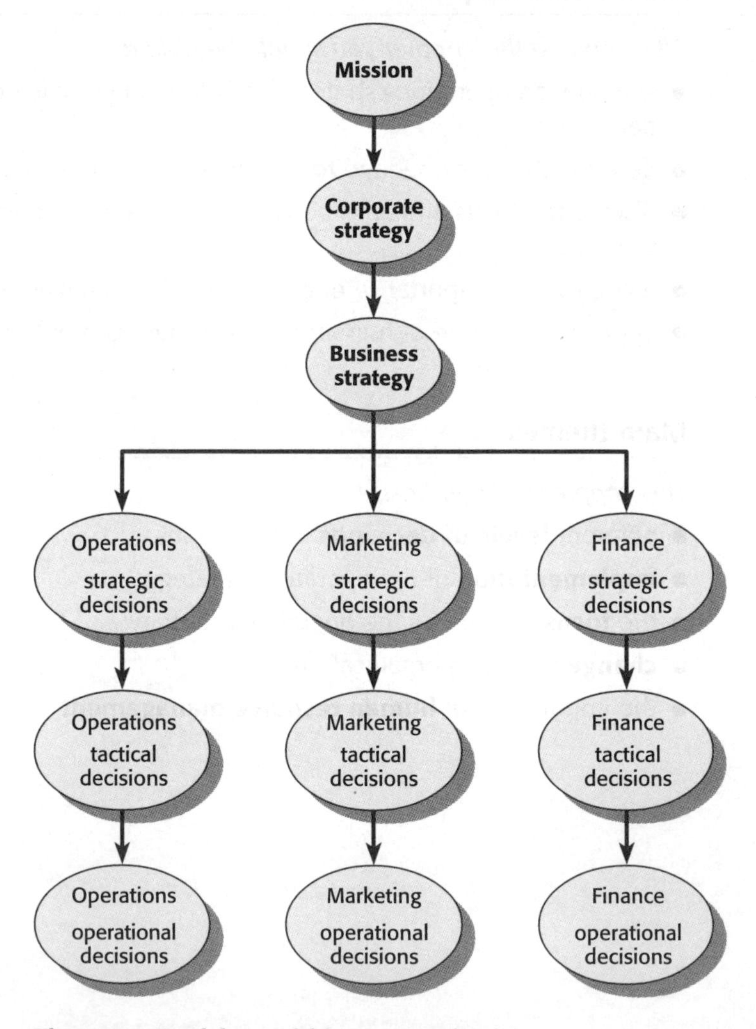

Figure 4.1 Decisions within an organisation

- What timescale are we working to?
- Do we have, or can we train, people with the necessary skills?
- How will the strategy affect present and potential customers?
- What are the impacts on staff, facilities, organisation, technology, and so on?

As you can see, these questions are not strategic, but they look at the shorter term. So the operations strategy sets the overall direction, and then operations managers use it to guide their more detailed tactical and operational decisions. A strategic decision to sell products through a Website, for example, leads to medium-term **tactical decisions** about logistics, investment in stock, capacity planning, recruiting and training, customer service, and so on. These tactical decisions, in turn, lead to short-term **operational decisions** about resource scheduling, inventory control, expediting, vehicle routes, and so forth (shown in Figure 4.1).

Table 4.1 gives some more examples of operations decisions at different levels. Again, we meet this unfortunate problem with terms, where low-level decisions are 'operational decisions', and some of these are in the 'operations function'. We have little choice but to call these 'operational operations decisions', but this is – thankfully – a term that we will not use often.

Table 4.1 Different levels of operations decisions

Decision area	Typical operations decisions
Strategic decisions	
Objectives	Setting the long-term aims and objectives
Business	Deciding the type of business to be in
Organisation structure	Choosing the best way to organise operations
Product	Designing the type of products
Process	Showing how to make the products
Location	Choosing where to make products
Capacity	Setting the size of facilities
Quality management	Setting how good the products are
Vertical integration	Deciding how much of the supply chain to own
Tactical decisions	
Layout	Designing the way operations are arranged
Planning	Deciding when to introduce new products
Quality assurance	Setting checks on product quality
Logistics	Planning the distribution of products
Replacement	Finding the best time to replace equipment
Staffing	Employing people with the right skills
Technology	Choosing the level of technology for the process
Make/buy	Deciding whether to make or buy materials
Performance	Defining measures of performance
Control system	Designing checks for operations
Operational decisions	
Scheduling	Setting the order in which operations are done
Staffing	Designing staff schedules
Inventory control	Deciding how much stock to hold
Reliability	Finding ways to improve equipment reliability
Maintenance	Scheduling maintenance periods
Quality control	Checking that products reach designed quality
Job design	Finding the best way to do an operation
Work measurement	Seeing how long operations take

The distinctions between strategic, tactical and operational decisions are not really as clear as Table 4.1 suggests. Quality, for example, is a strategic issue when a company is planning its competitive strategy, perhaps aiming for very high-quality products. It becomes a tactical issue when the organisation is deciding how to measure quality and set reasonable targets for performance. Then it becomes an operational task when testing production to see if quality targets are being met. Similarly, inventory is a strategic issue when deciding whether to build a warehouse for finished goods or ship directly to customers, a tactical issue when deciding how much to invest in stock, and an operational issue when deciding how much to order this week.

OPERATIONS IN PRACTICE

Sutton Byfleet Council

Two years ago Sutton Byfleet Council introduced a strategic policy of improving efficiency by increasing use of computers. In particular, it planned to reduce paperwork by 60 per cent and increase staff productivity by 50 per cent over the next five years.

In the light of this strategic policy, Operational Services adapted their own plans to include computerisation of all administrative functions. Managers then made a number of tactical decisions about the system, including the type of computer hardware, software design, suppliers, networks, maintenance contracts, staff training, and so on. Then supervisors made a series of operations decisions to use the new system as efficiently as possible. They designed schedules to make sure that everybody was trained for the new systems; they changed the layout of desks in the main office; e-mails and phone calls replaced letters wherever possible; the system automatically recorded workloads and showed productivity changes; a suggestions scheme was started; clerks found new ways of doing jobs.

The new systems encouraged changes in several areas. For example, records became available to show the cost of maintaining the Council's fleet of vehicles. This was so expensive that a private contractor was given the job and reduced costs by 30 per cent. Within two years of their decision to increase computer use, Operational Services had increased productivity by 25 per cent, reduced costs by 15 per cent and reduced the number of complaints from the public by 60 per cent.

Source: Council reports and discussions

Problems with implementation

Even the best operations strategy is no use until it is implemented.

Strategies only become effective when they are **implemented**. Implementation means that all the plans are actually carried out and translated into lower decisions.

It is often difficult to translate abstract higher strategies into more tangible products and processes. A strategy based on very high quality, for example, might be sensible, but implementing this might put considerable strains on operations. An obvious point when designing a strategy is to make sure that it can actually be implemented – and the long-term plans lead to realistic tactical and operational decisions.

OPERATIONS IN PRACTICE

Project Management Group

Management is usually viewed as a continuous process that goes on without a break. Some managers find that their work is not really continuous, but consists of a series of discrete projects. Then they can take advantage of the methods and techniques developed for project management.

The Project Management Group in the University of Southern Alberta was formed to improve the practice of project management. Its mission was to 'be world leaders in research, teaching and practice of project management'. This led to an ambitious operations strategy concentrating on research in four key areas, developing degrees in project management, contributing to a range of university and professional courses, building strong links with the business community, and using their skills on real projects.

Unfortunately, there were only three people in the Project Management Group, and they spent most of their time teaching and doing the related administration. It could be suggested that their operations strategy was not based on concrete realities, which meant that implementing it would be almost impossible.

Implementation is particularly difficult when the organisation has a rigid hierarchy. Then one group of senior managers designs the strategies, while a different group of more junior managers implements them. The two groups have different objectives, goals, information, experience and skills. Even with good communications, senior managers become remote from operations – they see the financial ratios, but have little idea how the operations are really done. On the other hand, people working with the details of day-to-day operations have little time for corporate ideals. Lofty aims such as 'being a global leader' have no relevance for someone who is rushing to finish an overdue job.

Some common problems with strategies are:

- people who design the strategy are not responsible for its implementation;
- strategies are badly designed;
- they are not implemented properly;
- they are not related to actual operations;
- they are not realistic;
- they ignore key factors;
- people only give the appearance of supporting the strategies;
- enthusiasm for the strategies declines over time.

One surprisingly common mistake is to design an operations strategy and then think about implementing it. The obvious way to avoid this is to consider implementation all the way through the design, and always consider the practical effects of any decisions. Managers always have to keep their feet on the ground, and one way of achieving this is to have widespread participation in the design process. In particular, those most closely involved with implementing the strategy should be closely involved in its design. Some other factors that help with implementation include:

- an organisational structure that is flexible and allows innovation;
- formal procedures for translating the strategy into reasonable decisions at lower levels;
- effective information systems to support decisions;
- acceptance that strategies evolve and keep changing operations;
- control systems that monitor progress;
- convincing everyone that the strategy is beneficial, so they conscientiously play their part in implementation;
- developing an organisational culture that supports the strategy.

Review questions

4.1 The operations strategy leads to lower levels of tactical and operational decisions in operations. Do you think this is true?

4.2 What type of decisions do operations managers make?

4.3 After you have designed a strategy you start thinking about its implementation. Do you think this is true?

OPERATIONS IN PRACTICE

Department for Education and Employment

In 1998 the UK Department for Education and Employment (DfEE) published its strategic framework, 'Learning and Working Together for the Future'. This framework, together with the Comprehensive Spending Review and the Public Service Agreement, set the government's long-term targets for education. They described a hierarchy of targets – an overall *aim* led to three main *objectives*, each of which has *key goals* to be achieved by 2000, and *targets* for 2002 and beyond. You can get some flavour for these from the following examples.

The DfEE's aim:
to give everyone the chance, through education, training and work, to realise their full potential, and thus build an inclusive and fair society and a competitive economy.

- *Objective 1:* to ensure that all young people reach 16 with the skills, attitudes and personal qualities that will give them a secure foundation for lifelong learning, work and citizenship in a rapidly changing world.
  - *Key goals for 1999–2000*: to provide a firm foundation for children's education, improve school standards and implement an action plan to create a better led, better rewarded and better trained teaching profession.
  - *Targets for 2002*: an increase in the number of nursery places for three-year-olds from 34 per cent to 66 per cent by 2002, focusing on the most deprived areas of the country.

These give a framework for decisions in education. However, critics point out that the DfEE's job ends with the formulation of strategy – it takes no active role in the implementation and is not concerned with day-to-day operations in schools. Local management of schools means that each of the 25,000 schools in Britain is effectively run as a separate body by its head teacher and governors.

The result is that the DfEE defines policies as directed by the government, but has little contact with operations in schools. The schools receive these policies, which they had virtually no say in formulating, and can interpret them flexibly. This situation can, understandably, lead to conflict.

Sources: DfEE strategic framework, associated publications of the DfEE and its Website at: *www.open.gov.uk/dfeehome*

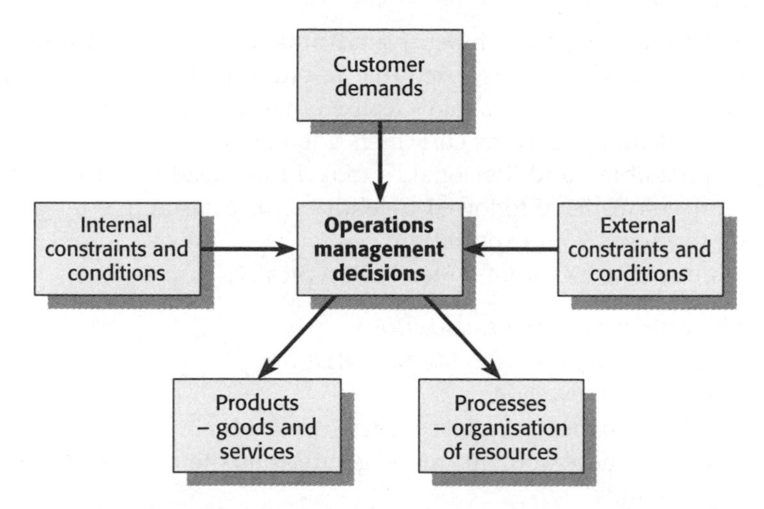

Figure 4.2 Operations management organises products and resources

Translating the strategic focus

The last chapter showed that the operations strategy can give a competitive advantage by focusing on cost, quality, timing, flexibility, technology, customer service or some other factor. When designing an operations strategy, managers balance these, and other, factors to make products that customers want using the most appropriate process (as shown in Figure 4.2).

To put it simply, the **key concerns for operations management** are:

- **customers** who create demand;
- **products** that satisfy this demand;
- **processes** that make the products.

Some people argue that a focus on one aspect of operations suggests that other aspects are ignored – it gives the impression of one dominant focus rather than a more reasonable balance. This is why many organisations describe themselves as focusing on more general themes. In particular, they might focus on one of the three key areas of customer satisfaction, products or processes.

Customer focus

Organisations that emphasise customer satisfaction have a **customer focus**. The justification for this strategy comes from the obvious importance of customers. Without customers an organisation has no sales, no income, no profit, no business – and soon no organisation. As Michael Perry of Unilever says, 'To sustain competitive advantage requires a total commitment to your customer'.[1]

Historically, customer satisfaction came from identifying the minimum standards that customers would accept, and then making products to this standard. Making a product with higher specifications was simply a waste of money. Some organisations realised that they can get a competitive advantage by giving customers more than they expect. When surveys suggested that restaurant customers were happy to wait a few minutes for a meal, McDonald's realised that it could change its operations and serve a meal within seconds. Its customers got a better service than they expected – or imagined possible – and McDonald's took a huge lead over its competitors. This is why organisations have followed Celebrity Cruises' example in saying that they are 'aiming to exceed your expectations'.

Organisations with a customer focus will typically:

- aim for complete customer satisfaction;
- allow customers easy access to the organisation;
- find exactly what they want;
- design products to meet, or exceed, these demands;
- do research and development, making sure that the product range responds to changing demands;
- get a reputation for outstanding quality and value;
- do after-sales checks to make sure the customers remain satisfied;
- look outwards so that they are always in touch with customers, potential customers, competitors, alternative products, etc.

Operations that 'delight' customers have the obvious benefits of bringing them back with repeat business – remembering the rule of thumb that it costs five times as much to attract a new customer as it does to retain an existing one. Delighted customers also attract new business, as they recommend a good product to four or five other people – compared with dissatisfied customers who warn a dozen potential customers about a bad product.

Product or process focus

For many organisations it makes more sense to focus on their products or processes. Often, particularly with services, it is difficult to separate a product from the process used to make it. How, for example, can you separate the product supplied by Singapore Airlines from the process used to deliver it? All organisations both supply a product and use a process, so there may really be no point in trying to separate the two. None the less, some organisations have a strategy of putting more emphasis on either the product or the process.

A house builder has a **product focus**, as it emphasises its products, which are houses; a construction company has a **process focus** as it emphasises its process, which is building. This apparently subtle difference can have important effects on operations. Suppose, for example, the El Misr bottling plant in Cairo notices that demand for its mineral water is falling. The plant has a process focus – concentrating on bottling – and it can simply change to bottling something else, such as fruit juice or beer. On the other hand, the Coca Cola plant in Cairo has a product focus – it makes Coca Cola – and if demand declines, it does not have the flexibility to switch to another product. Similarly, dairy farmers in the European Union have a product focus (producing milk) and are badly hit by quotas that limit the amount they can produce; cereal farmers have a process focus (growing crops) and can switch more easily from one crop to another.

Alternative strategies for products

Organisations with a product focus have some particularly interesting decisions. It is reasonable to suggest that they focus on products that customers want, but there is an obvious problem. Almost every customer wants a different product. Some people value a brand image and buy Calvin Klein jeans; other people look at value for money and buy Eastern Butterfly jeans; others buy Levis because they fit; others buy any jeans they can find in a convenient shop.

Customers look at so many different factors when judging products that it is virtually impossible to make something that is ideal for everyone. The way around this is to give products a range of features that appeals to a large enough group of customers. Few newspapers expect to satisfy perfectly all the needs of all their customers, but they include a range of features that appeals to many different readers.

The best features to include in a product depend on the way that customers make their purchases. When you decide to buy something, you usually approach the purchase in three steps. Firstly, you decide what features you want in the product. Then you look around to see which products can satisfy these needs, forming a shortlist of alternatives. Finally, you look down this shortlist and choose the best product. Terry Hill[2] uses this approach to describe two types of features.

- **Qualifying factors** are the factors that a product must have before a customer will consider it. These are the features needed to get onto the shortlist. Public transport, for example, must be fast, convenient and cheap, or people will not think of using it as an alternative to their own cars.
- **Order-winning factors** determine the best product from the shortlist. These are the factors that make a customer view one product as superior to the others. If several computers all have the qualifying factors, price and reliability might be the order-winning factors that make a customer choose a particular one.

The qualifying factors are more general, while the order-winning factors are more specific. When you open a bank account, the qualifying factors for high street banks might be security, reputation and costs. The order-winning factors might be a branch in a convenient location, and helpful staff. These factors are different for different customers, and they change over time, but an organisation can only compete by having products with all the main qualifying factors and many of the order-winning factors. Michael Porter[3] has suggested two main strategies for achieving this.

- **Cost leadership** makes the same, or comparable, products more cheaply. Organisations lower unit costs by having efficient operations – typically improving the process, simplifying designs, reducing waste, using higher technology, getting economies of scale, locating near to customers, focusing on target products, or reducing the length of the supply chain.
- **Product differentiation** makes products that customers cannot find anywhere else. There are many ways of differentiating products, typically based on quality, performance, technology, reliability, availability, amount of customisation, delivery speed, innovation, reputation, associated services, or location.

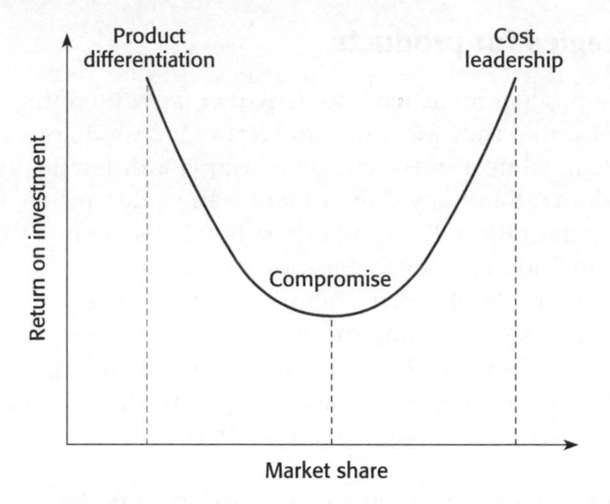

Figure 4.3 Success comes from product differentiation or cost leadership, but not compromise

Lyons Bakeries are cost leaders who make standard cakes so efficiently that their unit costs are low; La Patisserie Française uses product differentiation to make different types of cakes at much higher prices. Skoda and Fiat are cost leaders who make large numbers of inexpensive cars, while Bentley and Lamborghini use product differentiation in their strategy.

You might think that some compromise between cost leadership and product differentiation would appeal to more customers and give better overall results. In practice, this does not seem to work. Companies with 'average' products and 'average' costs usually have worse performance than those which concentrate on either low costs or specialised products (see Figure 4.3). In 2001, for example, analysts suggested one reason for the declining sales of the retailers Marks & Spencer was customers moving away from their mid-price clothes to buy either expensive 'designer' clothes or cheap 'discount' clothes.

Evolution of the operations strategy

We said that managers have to balance a range of internal and external requirements when designing an operations strategy (illustrated in Figure 4.4). An obvious problem is that these requirements are constantly **changing**. The internal requirements of the organisation change as higher strategies are modified, staff change, goals are adjusted, and so on. Perhaps more importantly, the external requirements that the organisation cannot control are also changing. Some continuing trends include more global operations, international competition, deregulation of industry, changing economic systems, increasing technology, improved communications, shorter product life cycles, stronger consumer protection, environmental concerns, and many others.

As circumstances change, the operations strategy has to develop and evolve. Some people suggest that these changes follow a common pattern. Hayes and Wheelwright,[4] for example, suggest that operations strategies develop through four stages.

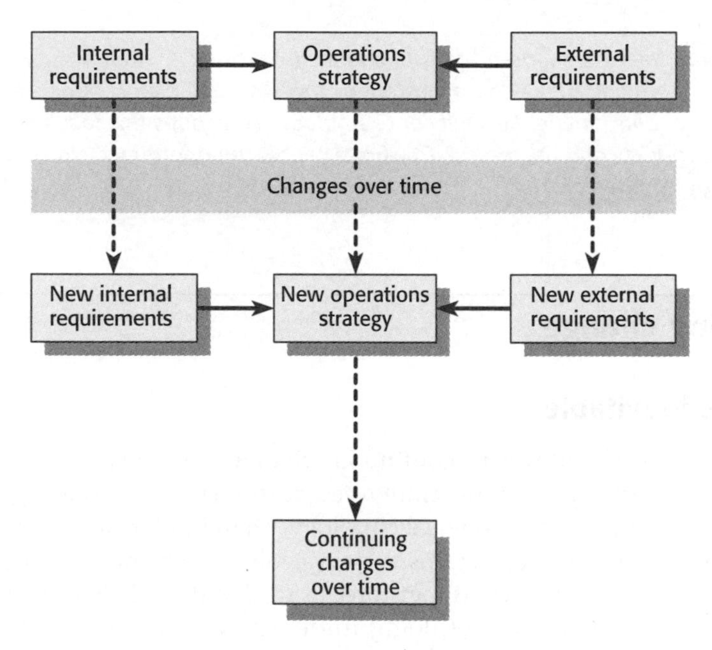

Figure 4.4 Operations strategies continually change over time

1. *Internally neutral* – operations only react to strategies that have already been designed. Here the operations make little positive contribution, only responding to demands put on them, and trying to avoid mistakes.
2. *Externally neutral* – operations look outside the organisation and achieve parity with competitors. Their aim is not to hold the organisation back, but allow it to be competitive.
3. *Internally supportive* – operations are already good, and managers are aiming at further improvement. For this they carefully analyse the business strategy and develop the best operations to support it.
4. *Externally supportive* – operations are more proactive and play a central role in determining the business strategy. Rather than just supporting higher strategies, operations become a major driver in their design.

These four stages give a simplified view, but they emphasise two ways that operations managers contribute to the broader business strategy. Firstly, they implement the business strategy, translating the abstract concepts into products and processes. Secondly, they design good operations that become a strength, which can be exploited in the business strategy.

Review questions

4.4 Why is it so important to focus on customers?

4.5 What is the difference between a product focus and a process focus?

4.6 It is always best to find a compromise between cost and product features. Do you think this is true?

Project 4.1 *Have a look at the operations strategy of a high street bank or similar service organisation. To what extent does this strategy focus on one aspect of operations, such as cost, quality, timing, flexibility or technology? How does this focus affect its customers, products and processes? To what extent is the operations strategy influenced by competitors?*

Managing change

Change is inevitable

Organisations have to deal with continuous change. Products change – as do competitors, costs, markets, locations, employees, customers, the economy, the business environment, company objectives, technology, shareholders and just about everything else. In response, the operations strategy evolves over time. Unfortunately, most of us do not really like changes, as they force us to abandon old and familiar practices, to learn new skills, new ways of doing things, new procedures and to form new relationships. This hesitation towards change can encourage inertia in organisations, with common symptoms including:

- low sales and falling market share, as old products are overtaken by competitors;
- many customer complaints, particularly about product quality and delivery dates;
- reliance on a few customers, especially with long-term, fixed-price contracts;
- old-fashioned processes;
- poor industrial relations, with low employee morale and high staff turnover;
- poor communications;
- too much, inflexible top management;
- inward-looking managers who are out of touch with operations or customers.

Change is a normal part of business and if we do not respond, more flexible competitors will leave us behind. To be more positive, we should welcome change as it creates opportunities, improves work conditions, gives better operations and performance, and more interesting, better-paid and more secure jobs. To quote John F. Kennedy, 'Change is the law of life. And those who look only to the past or the present are certain to miss the future.'[5] It is difficult to develop this constructive attitude as part of an organisational culture, but it can be helped by:

- commitment to change, accepting that continual change is inevitable, necessary and beneficial;
- an experimental approach, encouraging new ideas and practices;
- products and operations based on innovation and new ideas;
- keeping abreast of new developments and likely changes in the industry;
- acceptance that not all new ideas will be successful, and willingness to learn from failures;
- easy communications, so that everyone knows about the changes, why they are needed, and their effects;
- reassurance, guidance and protection of people most affected by changes.

Rate of change

All change has to be managed. One important consideration is the rate of change. Some organisations change very quickly, such as Dell Computers, which works at the frontiers of technology. Others change very slowly and even make a virtue out of stability, such as Morgan sports cars whose basic design originated in the 1930s.

Changes can be disruptive, so most organisations prefer a series of small adjustments to their operations rather than a few major steps. This iterative approach gives **continuous improvements**. Over time these small changes build a momentum that can dramatically improve performance (we will talk about this in Chapter 6). Some people disagree with this approach, and say that small adjustments only tinker with operations and make no real difference. Adjusting a poor order-processing system, for example, still leaves you with a fundamentally poor system. It is often better to have a major redesign, and this is the argument used in **reengineering**, which was described by Michael Hammer and James Champy[6] (we will discuss reengineering in Chapter 10).

The important point about the rate of change – whether it is very slow, continuous improvement, or reengineering – is that it needs a positive decision. It cannot be left to chance, but needs careful planning.

Review questions

4.7 Can you think of any organisations that have not changed for some time?

4.8 What is the main difference between continuous improvement and reengineering?

Project 4.2

Look at some organisations, such as railway operators and Internet service providers, and compare the ways that they have changed over the past fe v years. Describe the types of change, the speed, and whether these have been planned or emerged from external pressures. If the organisations were planning new operations from scratch, do you think they would be different?

Human resource management

We cannot go into the details of **human resource management** (HRM) here, but should emphasise its importance to operations. Without reasonable HRM in an organisation the operations – and just about everything else – cannot work properly.

Most organisations boast that, 'Our most valuable asset is our people', and agree with Tesco that, 'the quality of our people defines the success of the business'.[7] Despite these boasts, the truth is that many organisations treat their employees badly. When it is time to reduce costs, for example, most companies immediately start sacking staff – thereby getting rid of their most valuable assets, while keeping the office furniture, equipment and other peripherals. As John Harvey-Jones says, 'There is practically no area of business where the difference between rhetoric and actuality is greater than in the handling of people'.[8] But if an organisation does not treat its employees properly, why should it expect the employees to work conscientiously in return?

Improving operations with HRM

Taking a simple view, the best operations occur when the aims of an organisation coincide with the aims of its employees. Then everyone pulls in the same direction, working towards the same goals. The problem for operations managers is to make this happen.

When you go into a restaurant 30 minutes before closing time, you are likely to get a different welcome from staff who are paid a reasonable share of the profit they generate, than from staff who are paid a fixed amount to work until closing time. This suggests one obvious way of improving operations, which is to reward people for their performance. There are, of course, many types of reward, not all of which involve money. As a start, we could all be treated with courtesy, respect and consideration. This might involve:

- making sure that people are treated courteously, without favouritism, prejudice, public criticism, malevolent gossip, inconsistent policies or unreasonable behaviour;
- making people feel welcome and comfortable in the organisation, with support and good working conditions;
- avoiding 'macho management' that makes people feel intimidated and insecure;
- giving clear job descriptions so that everyone knows what their job involves, with all necessary training, support and guidance;
- treating people as individuals, with jobs that match their interests and abilities;
- showing the importance of everyone's jobs and rewarding them fairly with money, recognition, and promotion;
- giving people responsibility and allowing them to make as many of their own decisions as possible;
- setting individual goals and making these demanding but achievable;
- measuring everyone's contribution, acknowledging these publicly and having clear links between performance and rewards;
- encouraging teamwork and co-operation, with clear procedures to sort out conflicts;
- having open communications, with no secrets and information flowing freely around the organisation;
- arranging regular meetings to discuss targets, progress, problems, and so forth;
- measuring absenteeism and staff turnover, as these give a clear picture of morale and job satisfaction.

Some of these points reinforce our previous comments, that decisions should made by those most closely affected rather than imposed from a distance. This kind of approach is formalised in **empowerment**.

Empowerment gives people control over – and responsibility for – their work. It allows them to use their own judgement, skills and experience for the benefit of the organisation and its customers.

Empowerment has had a considerable effect on operations by delegating responsibility as far as possible. Then people manage the details of their own jobs, free from the instructions and control of a remote supervisor. This has obvious effects on the way that operations are organised. You can see small examples of this when you go into a shop to exchange a shirt. Marks & Spencer has empowered employees, and the first person you meet will happily refund your money or change the shirt. In Broadbridge & Company, the assistant does not have this authority and posts your request to a supervisor in the head office, who will deal with it when he/she has time.

This delegation of decisions to lower levels brings many benefits, including:

- allows personal development and achievement;
- faster decisions made close to operations;
- better decisions by those with most knowledge and information;
- more time for senior managers to concentrate on strategic issues;
- lower costs, as some layers of management can be removed;
- improved customer service, as people who deal directly with customers can solve their problems;
- employees have more control and responsibility for their jobs;
- employees get more satisfaction, sense of achievement and commitment;
- releases skills, knowledge and creative abilities of employees;
- encourages continuous improvement of processes.

In later chapters we will see many examples of the ways that these, and other developments in HRM, affect operations.

Review questions

4.9 Why is delegating decisions so important?

4.10 What is 'empowerment'?

OPERATIONS IN PRACTICE

McKrindle Transport

This is not a happy tale. It shows what happened when one manager found it difficult to delegate responsibility. The facts are real, but for obvious reasons, we have changed the names.

John McKrindle had always worked for his family's transport company, and took over as managing director when he was 36. John was proud of his hands-on style of managing. He kept a tight control of everything in the company, checked all the operations, and made all the decisions (down to the type of coffee used in the canteen). Nobody else in the company knew the details of operations, nor were they involved in any significant decisions.

It was clear that John was indispensable and the company would not last long when he died of a heart attack at the age of 42. John's widow was now the major shareholder in the company. She ignored the advice of her family, who were the other shareholders, and did not immediately sell the company. Instead she appointed a new management team, headed by three directors who had considerable experience in the industry. They reviewed the operations and introduced a series of changes that had worked in other companies, including delegation of decisions, open communications, employee suggestion schemes, emphasis on customer service, new administration systems, wider use of technology, in-cab information systems and electronic business. These measures helped to double business within two years, triple profits and significantly reduced staff turnover.

Chapter review

- Decisions within an organisation can be classified as strategic, tactical and operational. Implementation of the operations strategy leads to a range of decisions at tactical and operational levels.
- Implementation of an operations strategy can be difficult, and it needs careful planning.
- The operations strategy might suggest a general emphasis, typically giving a customer, product or process focus. Each of these leads to a series of decisions about the nature of products and processes.
- Change is inevitable in an organisation, and it should be managed and welcomed for the benefits it brings.
- The rate of change varies in different organisations. Some change very slowly, others look for incremental improvements, and some use reengineering to give radical transformations.
- Implementation of the operations strategy – and all other aspects of operations – relies on the people involved. HRM approaches, such as empowerment, can make the best use of 'our most valuable asset'.

Key terms

CASE STUDY Markland, Merrit and Anderson

Markland, Merrit and Anderson (MMA) is a well-established company which specialises in arranging marine insurance. Its mission statement is in three parts.

1. Our mission is to be a leader in the international market for marine insurance. We shall achieve this by using the highest professional standards and integrity to provide our customers with the best possible service. We will form long-term, mutually beneficial partnerships with our customers, employees and share holders.
2. To fulfil this mission we must achieve the following objectives:
   - the highest possible level of customer satisfaction
   - efficient and cost effective operations

- high profitability to reward shareholders
- knowledgeable, trained and motivated staff
- long-term commitment to the industry.

3. To achieve these objectives we must adopt the following key values:
   - responsiveness to customers
   - concern for people
   - teamwork and co-operation
   - professionalism and expertise
   - value for money.

The first part of MMA's work is concerned with arranging insurance for clients. These operations start when MMA discusses insurance needs with a client. Then it prepares a policy and agrees the initial details with the client. Based on this policy, insurance cover is arranged either by MMA itself, through another company or directly through Lloyd's of London. When the options are sorted out, MMA finalises the details with its client and does the necessary administration.

The second part of MMA's business looks after claims brought by clients. Here it discusses any claim with the client and agrees the basic information. Then MMA does follow-up work with assessors and any other involved parties. When agreement is reached, it arranges settlement of the claim. Sometimes agreement is impossible and MMA has to take the claim to arbitration or court.

Source: Based on company reports.

Questions

- Do an operations audit of MMA. What aspect of these operations do you think MMA focuses on?
- Given its mission, what kind of things do you think are in MMA's operations strategy?
- What problems do you think MMA has in implementing these strategies? How might it overcome them?

Discussion questions

4.1 Senior managers who make strategic decisions can never be close enough to the operations to understand how they really work. Their strategies are, therefore, based on unrealistic views of the operations and there will always be problems with implementation. To what extent do you think this is true?

4.2 Books on strategic management emphasise the design of policies; in practice managers have more problems with implementing policies than designing them. Why is there this difference in emphases?

4.3 What type of tactical and operational decisions do operations managers make? Give some real examples from organisations that you are familiar with. How are these linked to the operations strategy?

4.4 Customers are only interested in products. If they like your product your company does well; if they do not like your product your company is in trouble. Any talk about strategy, process, human resources and other peripherals is just diverting the organisation from making products that customers like. Do you agree with this?

4.5 An organisation should not focus on one aspect of its operations, like customer service or quality, but it should try to do everything as well as it can. What are the problems with this approach?

4.6 Organisations must constantly change, or competitors will leave them behind, but many people will resist any change. The result is an inevitable conflict within organisations. How can this conflict be resolved?

4.7 Happy workers are productive workers. What does this mean, and to what extent is it true?

4.8 Many people do not like taking responsibility, and prefer to be told what to do. Does this mean that empowerment, or any kind of delegation, is unpopular with employees?

References

1. Perry M. (1996) Talk at The Marketing Council. London.
2. Hill T. (1993) *Manufacturing Strategy*. 2nd edn. Basingstoke, Hants: Macmillan Press.
3. Porter M. (1985) *Competitive Advantage*. New York: Free Press.
4. Hayes R. and Wheelwright S. (1984) *Restoring our Competitive Edge*. New York: Wiley.
5. Kennedy, J.F. (1963) Speech in Frankfurt, West Germany, 25 June.
6. Hammer M. and Champy J. (1993) *Reengineering the Corporation*. New York: Harper Collins.
7. Tesco PLC (1998) *Annual Report*.
8. Harvey-Jones, J. (1994) *All Together Now*. London: Heinemann.

Selected reading

Cummings T. and Worley C. (1997) *Organisational Development and Change*. 6th edn. Cincinnati: South Western.

Harrison R.H. (1993) *Operations Management Strategy*. London: Pitman.

Hendry C., Arthur M.B. and Jones A.M. (1995) *Strategy through People*. London: Thomson International.

Lamarsh J. (1995) *Changing the Way We Change*. Reading: Addison Wesley.

Stacey R.D. (1996) *Strategic Management and Organisational Dynamics*. 2nd edn. London: Pitman.

Ward J. and Griffiths P. (1996) *Strategic Planning for Information Systems*. Chichester: John Wiley.

Worley C.G., Hutchin D.E. and Ross W.L. (1996) *Integrated Strategic Change*. Reading: Addison-Wesley.

Penwith Housing Association

by Andy Moore, Chief Executive of the Penwith Housing Association

Penwith Housing Association (PHA) was formed in 1994 as a registered 'Friendly Society'. It bought the 3,342 houses owned by Penwith District Council – a move that was supported by tenants who had guarantees of rent stability, investment, new building and a greater say in the management of their homes. A board (consisting of eight community members, three Council representatives and four tenant representatives) runs PHA, working through a management team.

PHA has the following mission and core values.

Our mission:
We aim to provide affordable housing and an excellent housing service for tenants and to work in partnership with the wider community.

Our core values:

- To ensure we communicate with all our stakeholders and that our customers are able to fully participate in the development of the Association;
- To provide services which are both cost effective and affordable;
- To promote a partnership approach to development;
- To promote and secure the highest standards of professionalism and integrity in delivering our services;
- To promote quality and equality in the delivery of our services.

PHA manages and maintains its stock of affordable – or social – housing. There are 1,000 local families on a waiting list for new accommodation, suggesting that there is considerable unmet demand. PHA, along with six smaller organisations in the area, is trying to satisfy this demand. It builds an average of 80 units a year, but loses a dozen or so as existing tenants exercise their legal 'right to buy'. The Association employs 58 full-time and 44 part-time staff. These include some technical services, but almost all the actual maintenance, repair and building work is contracted out.

PHA gets its income from three sources – loans for new developments contributing about £4 million a year, rental income on existing houses contributing £9 million, and a variable amount comes from government and private grants for social housing. All of these are tightly controlled, with rents, for example, generally rising by less than 1 per cent above the retail price index. The biggest single cost for PHA is interest on outstanding loans. Finance, and all other operations, can be markedly affected by changing government policies.

Andy Moore, the chief executive of PHA, explains its operations:

We do not make any goods – unless you count new houses that we add to our stock – but we provide a complete housing management service. Our mission is to provide affordable housing for the community, and this determines everything that we do. Our primary job is to manage our existing stock of houses, while keeping rents to affordable levels, doing repairs promptly and to a high standard, improving houses with double glazing, insulation, and so on.

Our forecasts show that there is considerable unmet demand, so we plan to extend our stock. This needs careful financial management to make as much impact as possible with limited resources. We are not a commercial company, so concepts such as profit, share price, dividends and marketing have little meaning to us.

We constantly monitor our operations and look for improvements. At the moment we are developing partnerships with tenants, benchmarking with similar organisations, setting up a consultancy to pass on expertise, monitoring a range of key performance indicators, changing our culture from 'council' to 'business', introducing new technology, working to become an 'investor in people', doing a detailed survey of our stock, and a whole series of other initiatives.

Questions

- How would you describe the operations of PHA? What are its products and inputs?
- What are the overall aims of PHA? What strategies could it adopt to achieve these?
- How would the strategies affect PHA's operations? How could it measure its performance? Where could PHA look for improvements?

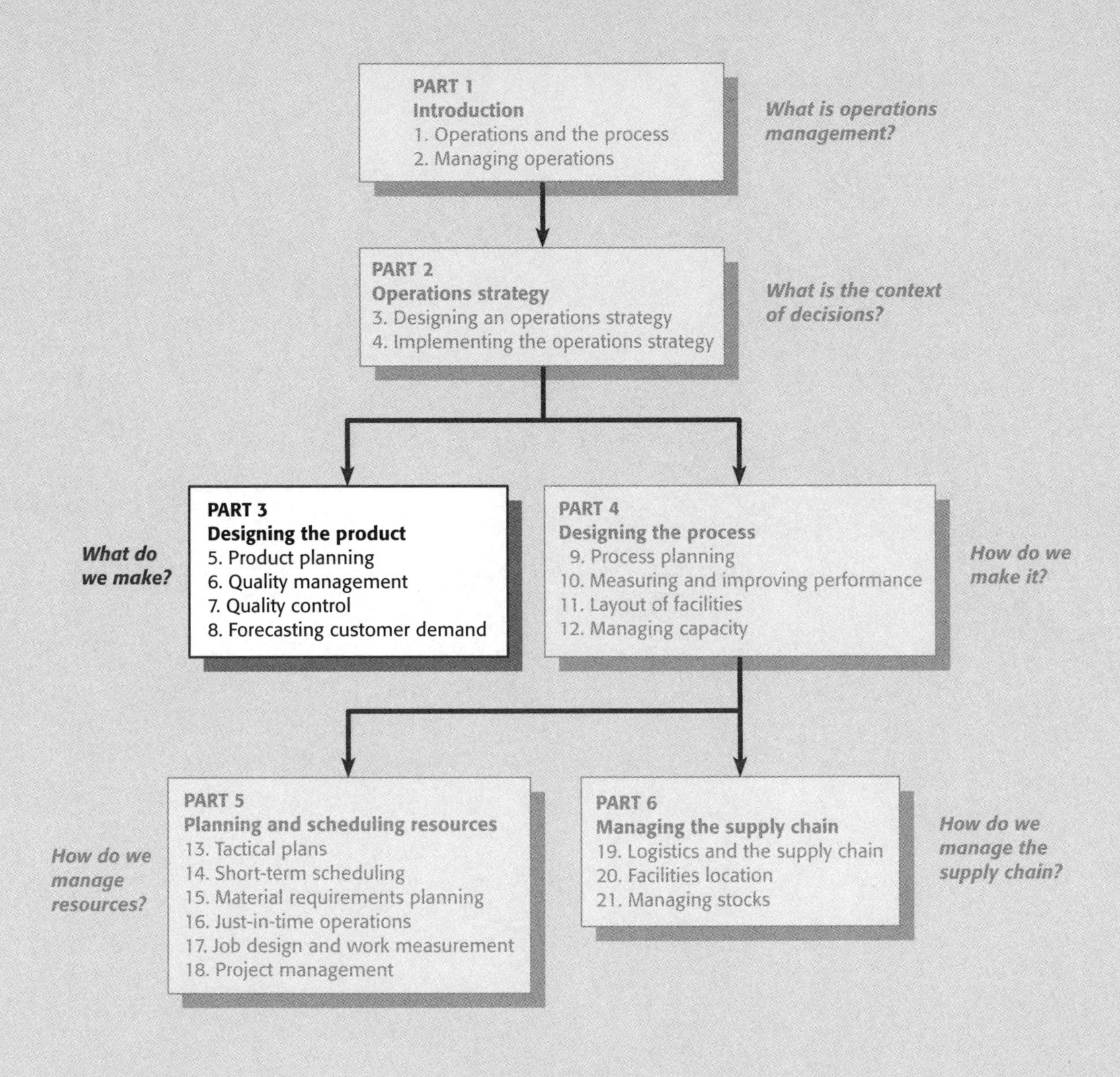

PART 1
Introduction
1. Operations and the process
2. Managing operations
What is operations management?
PART 2
Operations strategy
3. Designing an operations strategy
4. Implementing the operations strategy
What is the context of decisions?
PART 3
Designing the product
5. Product planning
6. Quality management
7. Quality control
8. Forecasting customer demand
What do we make?
PART 4
Designing the process
9. Process planning
10. Measuring and improving performance
11. Layout of facilities
12. Managing capacity
How do we make it?
PART 5
Planning and scheduling resources
13. Tactical plans
14. Short-term scheduling
15. Material requirements planning
16. Just-in-time operations
17. Job design and work measurement
18. Project management
How do we manage resources?
PART 6
Managing the supply chain
19. Logistics and the supply chain
20. Facilities location
21. Managing stocks
How do we manage the supply chain?

Part 3

DESIGNING THE PRODUCT

This book is divided into six parts. Each part describes a different aspect of operations management. Part 1 gave an introduction to the subject. Part 2 talked about strategy, emphasising the design and implementation of an operations strategy.

This is Part 3, which looks at aspects of product design. There are four chapters in this part. Chapter 5 introduces the idea of product planning. A supplement to this chapter describes some ways of comparing products. Chapter 6 discusses quality management, and Chapter 7 continues this theme by looking at quality control. Chapter 8 describes the forecasting of demand.

Later parts of the book look at the way that products are made. Part 4 describes the process used to make a product, Part 5 considers the planning of resources to support the process, and Part 6 discusses some aspects of supply chain management.

Product planning

Our new customer-oriented perspective starts with the market instead of the product. Then the means of production is tailored to give the customer the best possible products.

Jan Carlzon

Moment of Truth, Harper and Rowe, New York, 1989

Contents

Aims of the chapter

After reading this chapter you should be able to:

- appreciate the aims of product planning;
- describe the stages in a product life cycle;
- see how this life cycle affects operations, costs and profits;
- compare different entry and exit strategies;
- discuss the range of products made by an organisation;
- follow a new product through the stages in its development;
- discuss important features in a product's design.

Main themes

This chapter will emphasise:

- **product planning** which shows how an organisation meets changing customer demands;
- **the product life cycle** which shows how the demand varies over time;
- **new product development** to design new products;
- **product design** which defines the features included in a product.

Aim of product planning

In the last two chapters we have seen how an organisation's operations strategy defines the general features of its products. Now we are going to add some details to this general picture, and look more closely at product design. The Imperial Hotel in Dubai has an operations strategy based on 'giving travellers the finest experience in overnight accommodation'. This shows, in general terms, that its product is a very high-quality hotel service. Now we can move from this general picture and look more closely at the details.

Goods, services and products

Every organisation aims at making products that satisfy customer demand. Traditionally these products have been classified as either goods (such as cars, mobile phones, houses and DVDs) or services (such as transport, holidays, Websites and education). In reality, every product is a package that contains both goods and services. A washing machine manufacturer also gives an after-sales service, and a health service also supplies medicines. Organisations have to design every aspect of this package to give a product that customers want. This is the function of **product planning**.

Product planning is concerned with all decisions about the design and introduction of new products, changes to existing products and withdrawal of old products.

A serious problem for product planning is that customer demand changes over time. In winter we want warm clothing, but in summer we want clothes that keep us cool; five years ago it was fashionable to have green cupboards in the kitchen, but this year we want blue ones; now we want portable videophones, but next year we will want some other new electronic gadget.

Organisations respond to these changes by continually checking demand and adjusting their products. This is why Vodafone develops new telephone services, BMW introduces new models of car, Air Canada flies to new destinations, and the BBC replaces a show whose ratings have fallen.

The aim of **product planning** is to make sure that organisations continue to supply products that customers want.

This is clearly an area where operations management and marketing work closely together. They assess customer demands and suggest products that satisfy them. For this, they ask a series of questions.

- Who are our current and potential customers?
- What products do they want?
- What products can we make to satisfy them?
- How should we change existing products?

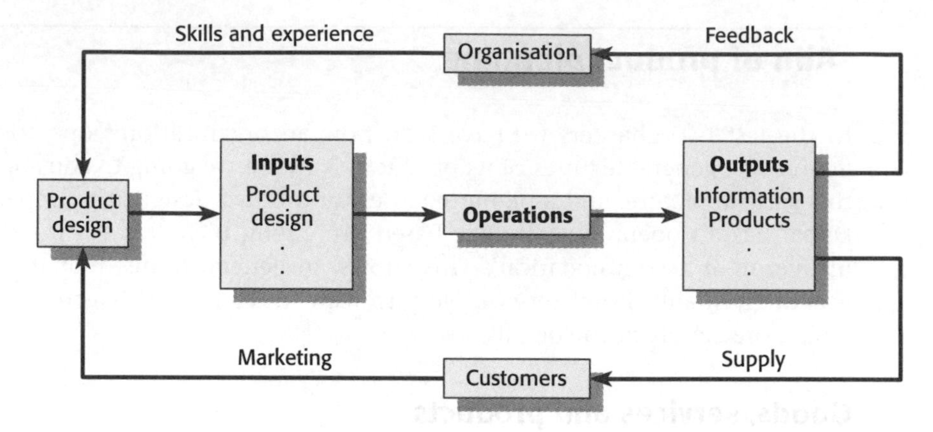

Figure 5.1 Balancing customer demand and organisational strength for product design

- What new products should we introduce and which old ones should we withdraw?
- How should we make these products?
- How do we organise the supply chain?
- How does this affect our operations, marketing and finances?

The answers to these questions define many aspects of the product design. As you can see, managers really have two main concerns. Firstly, they have to design products that customers want. Secondly, they have to design products that they can actually make. These two requirements are not necessarily the same, and managers have to look for the best balance (as suggested in Figure 5.1). We will return to this theme later in the chapter.

Review questions

5.1 What do we mean by a 'product'?

5.2 What is the purpose of product planning?

OPERATIONS IN PRACTICE

Data storage for PCs

Early PCs did not have any secondary storage. Commodore introduced tape cassettes in the 1970s, but these were very slow and had limited capacity. Other formats were tested, and the 5¹/4 inch floppy disk, holding about 64 Kb, eventually became standard. In the 1980s, this was replaced by the 3¹/2 inch 1.44 Mb floppy, which is still used on most PCs. Four billion of these disks were sold in 1999, but this was 20 per cent less than in 1998 and demand is continuing to fall.

Many users now find 1.44 Mb is too limiting. Standard software, high-quality graphics and downloads from the Internet can quickly fill dozens of disks. At first, it seemed that the answer was to increase the capacity of the disk to create a 'superfloppy' – such as the lomega Zip (100 Mb), Imation SuperDisc (120 Mb), Samsung Pro-FD (123 Mb), Caleb UHD144 (144 Mb) and Sony HiFD (200 Mb). Superfloppies continued to expand, but they had variable success. Perhaps the main problem was the lack of an agreed standard format.

The more common alternative at present is to use CDs holding about 650 Mb. Sales of CD-RW drives are growing, but the computer industry is always moving on and it is replacing CDs by DVDs – digital versatile disks. Initially, 2.6 Gb and 5.2 Gb DVDs were introduced in 1998, and these continue to grow. Other alternatives are being developed with, for example, Norsam using a gallium ion beam to etch 165 Gb of data onto a nickel disk.

Sources: Anon. (1999) 'New 144 Mb Floppy Drive', *PC Plus*, January, p. 20; Anon. (1999) 'Floppy Wars', *PC Plus*, March p. 21.

Project 5.1 *Find a product that has clearly evolved over time – perhaps a mobile phone or package holiday – and describe the main changes. What has caused these changes? What would have happened if the products did not change? What were the competitors doing? What are the effects on operations?*

Product life cycle

Stages in the life cycle

Demand for a product changes over time. It usually follows a standard **life cycle**, which has the five stages shown in Figure 5.2.

1. **Introduction**. The product is new, and demand is low while people learn about it, try it and see if they like it. Current examples include WAP telephones, e-mail ordering from supermarkets, and electric cars.
2. **Growth**. New customers buy the product, it becomes more popular and demand rises quickly. For example, telephone banking, clothes shopping via the Internet and adventure holidays.
3. **Maturity**. Demand stabilises as most potential customers know about the product, and they buy it in steady numbers. For example, television sets, insurance, newspapers and postal services.
4. **Decline**. The product is now getting old, and sales fall as customers start buying new alternatives. For example, tobacco, full-cream milk, porters in hotels and suntan lotion.
5. **Withdrawal**. Demand declines to the point where it is no longer worth making the product. For example, black and white television sets, asbestos, telegrams and vinyl records.

This life cycle occurs in general types of products – such as beer, microwave ovens and running shoes – as well as specific brands – such as Castlemain XXXX beer, Toshiba ERX-8820C microwave ovens, and Asics 2060 running shoes. These two types of life cycle are not synchronised, so that an individual product might be in a decline, even though the overall market is rising (and vice versa).

The most important feature of a life cycle is its length. Each edition of a newspapers goes through its life cycle in a few hours; clothing fashions have life cycles of months or even weeks; consumer durables like washing machines have life

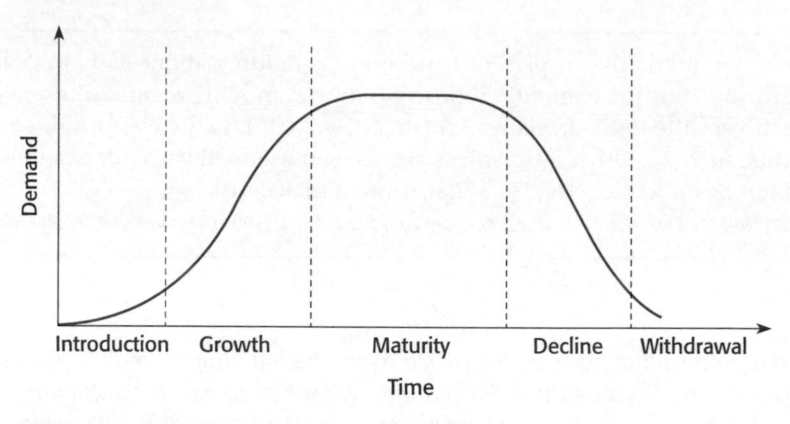

Figure 5.2 A standard product life cycle

cycles of five or 10 years; some basic commodities like soap and coffee remain in the mature stage for decades. Unfortunately, there is no way of forecasting the length of a life cycle. Some products have an unexpectedly short life, and they are quickly withdrawn; others stay at the mature stage for a surprisingly long time. Some products, like full-cream milk and beer stayed at the mature stage for a very long time and are now in a decline. Some products appear to decline and then grow again; cinema attendance in the UK, for example, fell from 1,640 million in 1946 to 54 million in 1984, before rising again to 140 million in 1997.

Operations and the life cycle

The product life cycle has four important consequences for operations.

1. Organisations focus on different aspects of operations at each stage of the cycle.
2. Costs, revenues and profits vary considerably.
3. Organisations with different expertise start (and later stop) making products at different points in the cycle.
4. Organisations make a range of products to smooth overall production.

1. Focus of operations during the life cycle

We can see how operations change during a life cycle by following a typical product. Before the beginning of the cycle, organisations do a lot of work on research, development, design and testing. This gives a product that is ready to sell to customers, and move to the introduction stage. Initial demand is low, and can be met by small-scale operations – perhaps making units for specific orders. The initial design of the product is adjusted as customers give their reactions, so the operations must be flexible enough to deal with changing specifications and customisation. This early stage sets the image of the product, so operations must gain a good reputation by meeting quality targets and delivery dates.

If customers like the new product, it moves into the growth stage and the scale of operations increases. It is difficult to get accurate forecasts of demand, but these are needed to organise the resources for rapidly growing operations, develop the supply chain, and to make sure that there is enough capacity. If this is done well, the operations can give a combination of high quality and low costs that discourages competition.

As a product moves through its life cycle, its design becomes more fixed. Increasing standardisation means that products are no longer made for specific orders, but demand is met from a stock of finished goods.

At some point demand stabilises and the product moves into its mature stage. Forecasting and production planning become much easier. Some early competitors have probably moved on, leaving the market to a few larger companies which are competing on price. This forces managers to look for efficient operations and improved productivity, typically by using automation to make a standard product in long production runs. At this point, innovation is more likely in the process design than in the product.

Eventually demand falls, and organisations are left with spare capacity. More competitors drop out of the market, some adjust operations to reduce capacity, and others change the product design to extend its life. When these adjustments are no longer worthwhile, they design termination procedures and stop production.

This is obviously a simplified view, but it shows how the operations might evolve during a life cycle. At the start they emphasise research, development and design; then they may move on to forecasting, capacity planning, scheduling and developing the supply chain; then on to cost reduction, automation and improving the process; then on to reducing capacity and extending the life. You can see that most changes to the product come near the beginning of the cycle, and it is standardised in later stages. The process, however, evolves more steadily, perhaps with more changes in the later stages.

2. Costs, revenues and profits during the life cycle

At the beginning of the life cycle, an organisation can spend a lot of money on research, development, design, planning, testing, setting up new facilities, and so on. Boeing spent $8 billion in developing the B777; in 1996 McDonnell Douglas cancelled plans for a new MD-11 as it could not afford development costs (it merged with Boeing the following year); Intel spent more than $4 billion developing the Pentium III. Even apparently simple products can have high development costs – Cadbury spent £6 million on new production equipment for its Fuse bar in 1997, and Gillette spent $600 million before launching its Mach 3 razor in 1998.

These high development costs mean that it is usually cheaper to extend the life of an existing product than to introduce a new one. There are several ways of doing this, including:

- increasing advertising and market support;
- finding new uses for the product and hence new markets;
- modifying the product to make it appear new or different;
- changing the packaging with new sizes, different emphasis, and so on;
- selling the product in new geographical areas.

Unfortunately, these adjustments are generally short term and only give cover until a new product is available.

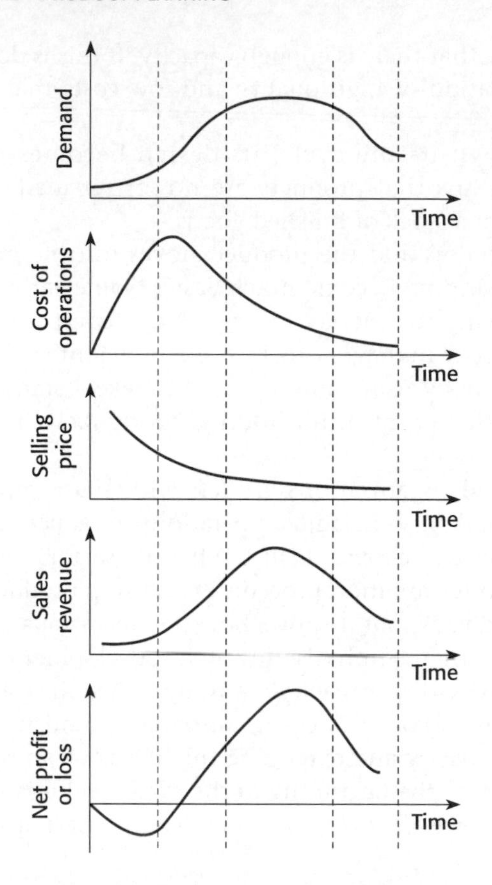

Figure 5.3 Revenue, cost and profit during a typical life cycle

In the early stages of the life cycle, small numbers are made. Low-volume processes are usually more expensive, so unit costs are high. Organisations may also recover some of the development costs by assigning them to early sales. At this stage the profit on each unit is also high, as customers are willing to pay a premium for a new or novel product.

Initially total revenue is limited by small sales, but begins to rise when the product moves into the growth stage. At this point, sales are rising and the profit per unit remains fairly high (as customers are still willing to pay a premium, operations are becoming more efficient and there is limited competition). The development costs are recovered as the product starts to make a profit (as shown in Figure 5.3).

Revenue peaks somewhere in the mature stage. At this point efficient operations can reduce unit costs, but competition constrains the selling price. Beyond this, the product is in a decline and profit inevitably falls.

WORKED EXAMPLE

KMP Cleansing recorded the following revenues and costs for its carpet repair service (values are in thousands of pounds). Where do you think the product is in its life cycle and what plans would you expect KMP to be making for the service?

Month	1	2	3	4	5	6	7	8	9	10
Revenue	12.8	13.0	13.3	13.0	12.6	12.0	10.8	9.2	8.0	6.9
Cost	4.8	4.4	3.9	3.4	3.0	2.7	2.4	2.1	1.8	1.7

Solution

The following spreadsheet subtracts the cost from the revenue to give the profit, and draws a graph of the results. Although we do not know the demand, the revenue and profit have started to go down. This suggests the product has moved from maturity to decline. As the decline is quite fast, the product is clearly approaching the withdrawal stage. KMP should have already introduced a replacement product or have one very close to introduction.

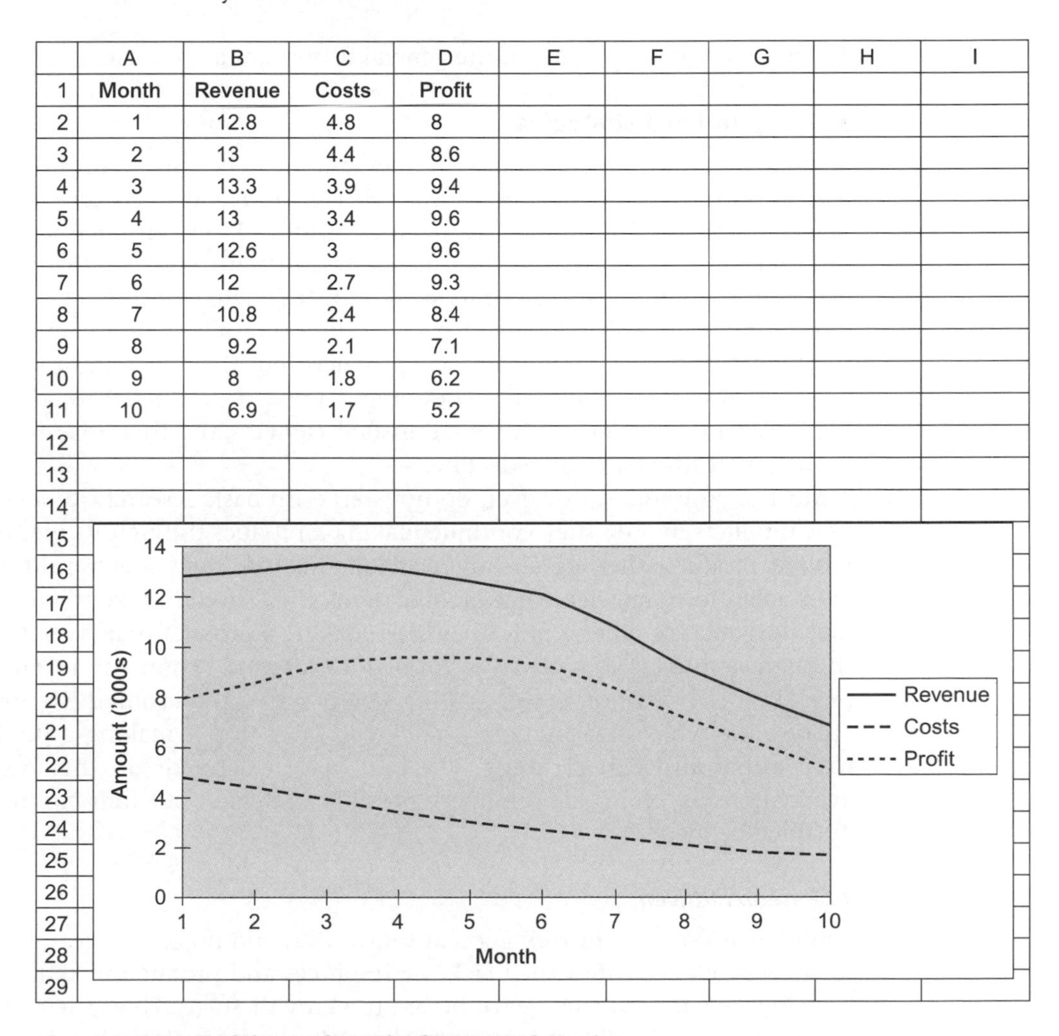

	A	B	C	D	E	F	G	H	I
1	Month	Revenue	Costs	Profit					
2	1	12.8	4.8	8					
3	2	13	4.4	8.6					
4	3	13.3	3.9	9.4					
5	4	13	3.4	9.6					
6	5	12.6	3	9.6					
7	6	12	2.7	9.3					
8	7	10.8	2.4	8.4					
9	8	9.2	2.1	7.1					
10	9	8	1.8	6.2					
11	10	6.9	1.7	5.2					
12									
13									
14									

Figure 5.4 Spreadsheet of results for KMP Cleansing

Table 5.1 Features of the product life cycle

Stage	Introduction	Growth	Maturity	Decline
Demand	low	rising	steady	falling
Product design	changing	some change	standard	adjustments
Process	small scale	larger scale	mass production	adjustments
Selling price	high	fairly high	lower	low
Total revenue	low	rising	peaks	falls
Unit costs	high	falling	lower	variable
Profit	low	rising	peaks	falls
Number of competitors	few	rising	stable	falling
Focus of operations	flexibility, reliability	scheduling, capacity	cost reduction, productivity	cost control, new products

Table 5.1 summarises some of the general features of a life cycle.

3. Entry and exit strategies

Some organisations spend a lot of money on research. This might be **pure research** that looks for new discoveries, or **applied research** that looks for solutions to particular problems. The aim of this research is to find new products, in the way that pharmaceutical companies do research to find entirely new drugs. SmithKline Beecham spends 21 per cent of its sales on R & D, while both Roche and Ciba both have annual research budgets of over a billion pounds. These companies look for the high profits that come from new products, but they have to bear the high cost of research and development. They might make a product throughout its entire life. Polaroid, for example, invented instant cameras and then made them through growth, maturity and into a decline.

Most organisations, however, do not start with basic research to develop entirely new products, nor do they continue making a product through its life. Instead, they look at products that are already available, identify ones that would fit into their own operations, and see what modifications they should make to create their own 'new' product. In other words, they start making a product that is already some way through its life cycle. Janusz Pac formed a tour guide company in Prague, but his product was a variation on an existing service rather than something entirely new.

The time when organisations start – and later stop – making a product defines their **entry and exit strategy**. The best option depends on their expertise and available resources. There are many possible strategies, but four common ones are outlined below.

1. Research driven

Some organisations are very good at innovation and do basic research to find ideas for new products. Often they lack the resources and production skills to manage a growing demand, so they leave before the growth stage. Then their main product is the ideas and intellectual property that other organisations can develop for their own products.

2. New product exploiters

Other organisations look for research that has commercial potential and exploit it during the growth stage. They aim for the high prices available during growth, and exit when profit margins begin to fall. These organisations are good at identifying concepts with commercial potential, marketing new ideas, organising for a growing demand, and developing processes through an increasing output.

3. Cost reducers

Some organisations can design very efficient operations, so they enter the market at the mature stage and produce large quantities with low enough costs to compete with existing suppliers. Then they exit when demand starts to decline. These organisations are very good at high volume, low cost production.

4. Life extenders

When a product is clearly declining, there is often spare production capacity. Some organisations buy this cheaply, and with a combination of marketing, efficient operations and adjusted design, they can extend the product's life. This approach can give short-term profits before a continued decline, but there are many examples of products recovering and returning to a strong position.

OPERATIONS IN PRACTICE

Arm Holdings

In 1990 Acorn, Apple, VLSI and a number of other companies formed a joint venture in Cambridge called Advanced Risc Machines. This company employed 12 people to design faster, cheaper and more efficient Risc (reduced instruction set computing) processors. Renamed Arm Holdings, the company went public at the beginning of 1998, with a value of £264 million. During the next year staff increased to 360, sales increased by 60 per cent, profit more than doubled and the value of the company rose to a billion pounds.

Most mobile telephones use Arm's technology and its products are becoming more widely used in cars and other equipment. Over 90 per cent of Arm's sales are in America, Japan and South Korea. But Arm does not manufacture any of its own products. Its expertise is in research, design and development; it designs products and then licenses the use of its intellectual property to other companies. It has licenses with 130 partners, including IBM, Texas Instruments, NEC and LG Semicom, to insulate itself against the widely variable demand in semiconductor markets.

Robin Saxby, the chairman, says: 'We set a new trend in the industry. We invented the IP (intellectual property) model so we design rather than produce chips.'

Sources: Taylor, P. (1998) 'ARM Price Tag Set at £264 m', *Financial Times*, 18 April; Oldfield, C. (1999) 'Cambridge Chip Maker Rivals Silicon Valley', *Sunday Times*, 21 February.

4. Range of products offered

Ideally, organisations would like to supply a single product, as this makes their operations very simple and efficient. Unfortunately, customers all have slightly different needs. We all buy clothes, for example, but we want different sizes, styles and colours. The overall demand for a product is made up of a large number of individual demands, each of which is slightly different. Organisations allow for these differences by supplying variations of a basic product. Universities offer different courses; construction companies build different types of houses; bakers make different kinds of cake; and banks give different types of account. In other words, most organisations supply a **range** of similar or related products.

There are obvious reasons for an organisation to concentrate on one kind of product. A company that builds ships has the knowledge, skills and experience to build a new type of ship, but it does not have the expertise to start making perfume. So Ford concentrates on making cars; Axa offers different types of insurance; Sega makes new computer games; and Haagen-Dazs makes new flavours of ice cream. When planning a product range, organisations look for new products that are similar to those they already make, but are different enough to create new demands. (There are, of course, conglomerates that make ranges of completely different products, but these are usually organised as independent business units.)

The obvious question is: How wide a range should we make? The answer comes from a compromise between the demands of customers and operations. Customers want as wide a range as possible, so they can choose a product that closely fits their needs. Operations want a narrow range so they can get the advantages of:

- long production runs that reduce equipment set-up times;
- using specialised equipment that has high productivity;
- making operations routine and well practised;
- increasing employee experience and expertise with the product;
- encouraging long-term improvements to the product and process;
- reducing staff training time;
- lower stocks of parts and materials.

If we make the range too narrow, we can use standard operations – but lose customers who want something different. If we make the range too wide, we can satisfy varied customer demands – but lose the efficiency that comes from standardisation. The best decision depends on many factors, including general market conditions. When there are a few producers working with a near monopoly, they have most power and offer a narrow range of products; in a more competitive market, customers have more power and there is more variety.

An important benefit from a range of products is that each can be at a different point in its life cycle. This can stabilise production, with new products being phased in to replace older ones that are declining and being withdrawn (as shown in Figure 5.5).

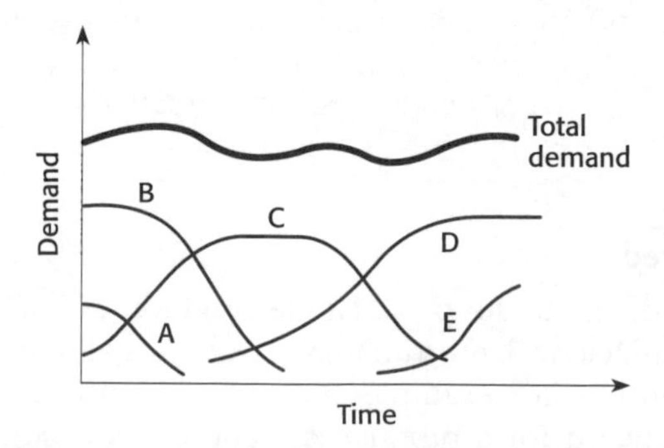

Figure 5.5 Introduction and withdrawal of products (A–E) to give stable demand

Review questions

5.3 What are the usual stages in a product life cycle?

5.4 What are typical lengths for the life cycle of:
(a) a model of personal computer;
(b) a model of car;
(c) a particular insurance policy;
(d) a copy of a newspaper?

5.5 How do costs and profits vary over a product's life?

5.6 How could you classify organisations based on their entry and exit strategies?

5.7 Why do organisations supply a range of products?

Project 5.2

Find a series of related products that are at different stages of their life cycle – perhaps computer printers, pharmaceuticals or videos. Describe the demand for each product and say how these have changed over time. How wide is the product range – why? How do the stages in the life cycle affect the operations? What are the effects on costs, profits, process, operations, etc.?

Developing new products

Stages in product development

As the demand for old products declines, organisations replace them by new ones. They obviously want a continuing stream of new products, and this needs careful planning. This planning typically has six stages, with the first generating ideas and the next five refining these into viable products.

1. Generation of ideas

Ideas for new products can come from a variety of sources, including:

- work in research and development departments;
- marketing departments reporting opportunities or changes in customer demand;
- operations department suggesting changes to an existing product, perhaps to make the process more efficient;
- other internal sources, ranging from suggestion boxes to 'think-tanks';
- customers suggesting new products;
- focus groups organised to collect ideas;
- competitors' products that can be adapted;
- government regulations that create demand for new products;
- other external sources.

People often say that if you build a better mousetrap, the world will beat a path to your door. Unfortunately, the inventors of thousands of better mousetraps know that this is not true. New ideas are easy to find; the difficulty is looking at these ideas, choosing the best and turning them into viable products that customers will buy.

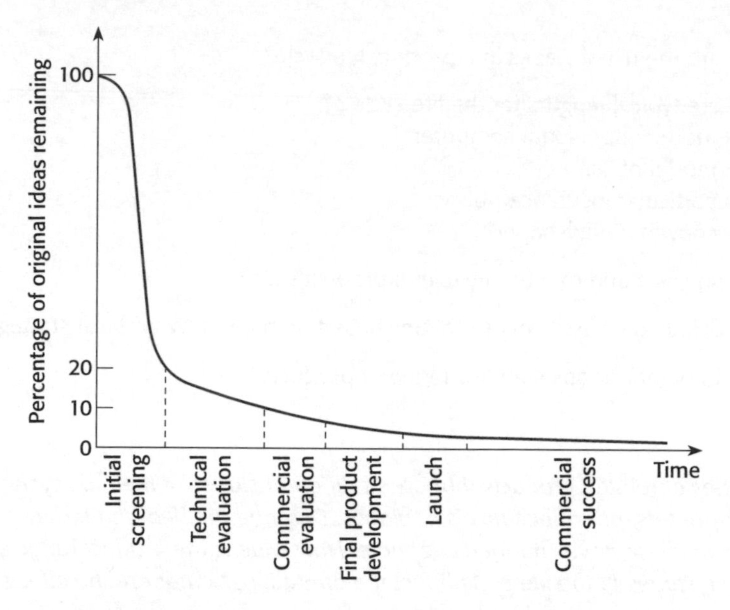

Figure 5.6 Proportion of ideas surviving each stage of development

2. Initial screening of ideas

An initial screening can quickly reject ideas that have obvious flaws, such as products that:

- are impossible to make, or are technically too difficult;
- have been tried before and were unsuccessful;
- duplicate an existing product;
- use expertise or skills that the organisation does not have;
- do not fit into current operations;
- would obviously not sell;
- would obviously not make a profit;
- are too risky.

This screening might remove 80 per cent of the original ideas (as shown in Figure 5.6).

3. Technical evaluation – initial design, development and testing

At this point the idea seems feasible, so details are added to take it from a general concept through to initial designs. This stage gives a technical evaluation of ideas, and makes sure that the organisation can actually make the product. For this it asks two types of questions.

- General questions about the concept. Is the idea based on sound principles? Is it safe and legal? Is it a new idea or a variation on an old one? If it is an old idea, why has the organisation not made it before? Are there problems with patents? Are other developments likely to overtake the product?
- Specific questions about the proposed design. Is it technically feasible? Can it be made with available technology? Does it fit into current operations? Does the organisation have the necessary skills and experience? Is there enough capacity?

At this stage, prototypes and trials help develop the best technical designs.

4. Commercial evaluation – market and financial analysis

The technical evaluation makes sure that the organisation can make the product, while the commercial evaluation sees if it will make a profit. This stage removes products that:

- customers will not buy;
- are too similar to existing products;
- are so different from existing products that customers will not accept them;
- are in a rapidly declining market;
- do not fit into existing strategies;
- will not make enough profit, or have margins that are too small;
- need too much capital or have poor returns on investment;
- have too high production or operating costs.

This stage builds a commercial case for continuing development. If this case is sound, the product moves forward to full development. Unfortunately, the commercial evaluation rejects many ideas that are technically sound. People sometimes find it difficult to accept that a good idea that is technically feasible will not necessarily generate enough sales to make a profit.

The technical evaluation and commercial analysis together form the **feasibility study**.

5. Final product development

Products that pass the feasibility study move on to final design and testing, giving the product that customers actually see. These final designs are not just drawings of the product. They describe the whole product package, including goods, services, environment, and associated items (which we discuss in the next section). The designs also give a description of how the product is made, including details of the process, quality measures, materials used, supply chain, and everything else that might affect the final product. At this stage the organisation has complete specifications for the product and can start production.

6. Launch of product

Now the organisation can start production, launch the new product and test customer reaction. This is the first chance to see if the planning has worked and the product is actually a success. Many products are not successful and are quickly withdrawn. Some have been spectacular failures. The Ford Edsel lost $350 million in the late 1950s; Joseph Schlitz produced 'the beer that made Milwaukee famous', but sales plummeted in the 1970s when the company introduced 'accelerated batch fermentation' which customers did not like; IBM's PC junior lost $100 million by 1985; in the 1980s Coca-Cola changed its recipe, but customers forced a return of the original 'classic' range; in 1994 Lever Brothers launched Persil Power – but quickly withdrew it when they found that it weakened fabric and faded colours.

Very few of the initial ideas reach the point where they are launched on the market, and even fewer become commercial successes. One rule of thumb suggests that 250 ideas lead to one product, and 25 products lead to one success. The pharmaceutical industry study 10,000 chemicals to find one that they can market – which partly explains the cost of $1 billion to develop a new drug.

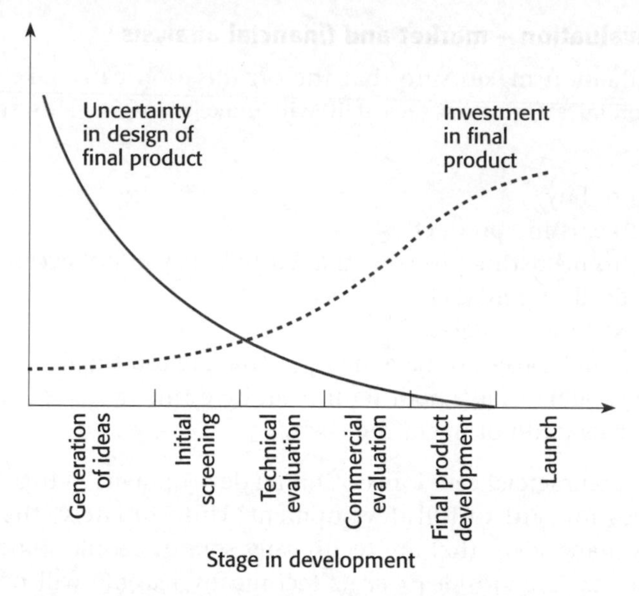

Figure 5.7 Uncertainty in final product design

Time taken by development

As a product goes through these stages, the design becomes more firmly defined, investment increases, and the flexibility to make changes declines (as shown in Figure 5.7).

This assumes that the development is straightforward and moves easily through the stages. Suppose, though, that the results of the commercial evaluation are unclear. The organisation might not drop the project and waste its investment, but can adjust the designs and return to get a new technical and commercial evaluation. Most product development has a lot of cycling and repetition of this kind, which explains the long times needed. Peugeot, for example, takes five or six years to develop a new model; Cadbury took five years to develop its Fuse bar; and a new insurance policy needs several years for the details to be finalised.

There are obvious benefits of speeding up the development. Getting a new product to the market before competitors allows a price premium, gains a dominant position and sets standards for later entrants. A shorter development time also frees up cash and resources, and speeds the generation of income needed to recover development costs.

One obvious way of reducing the development time is **concurrent development**. Rather than wait until each stage is completed before moving on to the next, concurrent development starts each stage as soon as possible. The initial screening of ideas, for example, need not wait until all ideas have been generated, but can quickly remove non-starters while other ideas are still being considered. Similarly, the commercial evaluation can run in parallel with the technical evaluation. The more overlap between stages the shorter the overall development time, and companies have reported reductions of up to 70 per cent.

Review questions

5.8 What are typical stages in the introduction of a new product?

5.9 What criteria are used to judge a new product?

5.10 The most difficult part of launching a new product is getting new ideas from the research team. Do you think this is true?

5.11 What is concurrent development?

OPERATIONS IN PRACTICE

Gillette Mach 3

Almost 100 years ago, men stopped shaving with cut-throat razors and started using safety razors. Gillette became the world's largest supplier of these razors and their big, disposable blades.

In the 1970s Gillette's standard product was in a decline, as competitors offered cheaper alternatives and electric shavers had become more popular. Gillette looked for new products, and began work on multi-blade systems. In 1976, its R & D laboratories in Reading started trials with two narrow blades on springs, which would follow the contours of the face and be easier to rinse. In 1989, Gillette launched this as the Sensor, with a £12 million advertising campaign. Sensor was a clear success, and was soon used by over half the men who shaved in Britain. It had worldwide sales of 400 million razors and 8 billion blades and, as Gillette was able to charge a premium for a technologically advanced product, it generated more than $6 billion in sales.

Gillette continued its development of multi-bladed razors, and, in the early 1990s, developed a razor with three spring-loaded blades. It argued that this would give an even closer shave, with fewer problems for men who have never learnt to shave properly (in other words, the majority). The Mach 3 was introduced as 'the Stealth Bomber of shaving' and included 35 patented features, such as 'microfins' to stretch the skin taut, a diamond-like coating on the three narrow blades, and a lubricating strip that changes colour when the blade needs changing.

The Mach 3 was launched in 1998 following a $120 million marketing campaign and a total of $600 million in development costs. To pay for this, the price of the razor was 35 per cent higher than that of its predecessor.

Source: Wavell S. (1998) *'Billion Dollar Shave'*, *Sunday Times*, 19 April, p. 19

Product design

Product package

An operations strategy sets the general features of a product, and then product development takes the general concept and adds the details to give a viable product. This development is concerned with all aspects of the product, including the process used to make it, materials, the supply chain, and so on. Now we can look at those parts of product development which specifically set the features of the product.

Product design is the specific part of product development that defines the features included in the product.

Even taking this narrow view, designers have to do far more than mull over the appearance of finished goods. Designers at Burger King are not only interested in how the Whopper looks, but also how it tastes, how customers like it, the design of the restaurant and its decor, how food is served, facilities offered, staff uniforms, and all other parts of the **product package**. This might include:

- goods that customers buy;
- associated goods that support the main product;
- services that are part of the product specifications;
- associated services that support the product;
- surroundings in which customers receive the product;
- items changed, typically when products are repaired or modified.

With a car-exhaust service, the goods are new car exhausts, associated goods include materials and information that comes with the exhaust, services are fitting the exhaust, associated services include a guarantee and coffee in the waiting room, the surroundings are the customer waiting area, and the item changed is the car. In a restaurant, the goods are the food, associated goods include the cutlery and crockery, service is preparation, cooking and serving, associated services include advice and entertainment, the surroundings are the dining area, and there are not really any items changed (except customer hunger and mood).

It can be difficult to design any product package, and you can see many examples that go wrong. Some houses have poor layouts; VCRs are too complicated to use; kitchen gadgets break when you use them; trains do not keep to schedules; chairs are uncomfortable; food containers are too difficult to open. To avoid these problems, it would be useful to have a set of rules for getting good designs. Sadly this is not possible. There is such a wide range of products, and so many different factors to consider, that we cannot really develop any universal principles. The best we can do is to mention some general requirements.

Customer requirements

We know that customers have different priorities to suppliers. Customers want products that are inexpensive, high quality, reliable, attractive, readily available, and so on. Suppliers want products that are easy to make, use standard parts, fit into the current range, use common materials, allow automation, and so on. Product designers have to satisfy both of these, and a useful starting point suggests that products should be functional, attractive and easy to make.

1. Functional

Being functional means that a product can do the job it is designed for. Consumer protection laws often state that a product must be 'of satisfactory quality and fit for the purpose intended'. This seems obvious, but you can see many products – ranging from investment services through to bottle openers – that simply do not work.

The best way to get a functional design is to ask customers exactly what they want the product to do, get a team of designers to create a product to do this, and then test the product to make sure that it actually works. Prototypes and test marketing are invaluable for such trials. Another useful tool is **quality function deployment**

Product design	Processor	RAM	Hard drive	Operating system	DVD/CD, etc	Type of battery	Type of keyboard	Type of screen	Case material
Customer demands									
Small size	2		1		3	2	1	1	
Light weight						2			2
Compatible with desktop	1			3	2				
Fast	3	1			1				
Large memory		3	3		1				
Durable							2	2	3
Comfortable keyboard							3		
Long time between charges			1		1	3			
Readable screen								3	

3 – strong relationship
2 – medium relationship
1 – some relationship

Figure 5.8 QFD matrix for a portable computer

(QFD). In its basic form, this has a matrix with the customer demands listed down one side, the proposed design features listed across the top, and an indication of how these two are related in the body.

Figure 5.8 shows a simple QFD matrix for a laptop computer. Here the customer demand for a fast computer depends strongly on the processor used; the demand for small size depends to some extent on the type of battery, and so on. We can also use this type of matrix to see how closely a particular design meets specific customer requirements. We could, for example, note that our laptop design includes a very fast processor, and this completely satisfies customer requirements for high speed. Then we could identify areas that are not being met, and adjust the designs accordingly.

2. Attractive designs for customers

An organisation has to design products with features that customers want. As usual, though, there is the problem that different customers judge products in different ways – one man's meat is another man's poison. There are also trends, and many customers now consider, for example, environmental features and insist that products be recyclable, use recycled and less harmful materials, and need less energy to make and operate. This might be analysed in 'full life costing', which includes not only the cost of making a product, but also the cost of disposal at the end of its life.

As we saw in Chapter 4, customers approach a purchase in three steps.[1] In the first step they decide what features they want in a product. In the second step they look around to see which products have the qualifying factors to satisfy these needs, giving a shortlist of possible products. In the third they use the order-winning factors to choose the best alternative from the shortlist. To be successful, a product needs qualifying factors to get on most shortlists, and enough order-winning factors to give a broad appeal. These features might include:

- **Style**. The product is aesthetically pleasing, pleasant to look at and use.
- **Price**. If similar products are competing, the one with the lowest price is usually most successful. This is not always true and there are many examples ranging from perfumes to luxury cars where it seems better to charge higher prices.
- **Availability**. The most obvious aspect of availability is fast delivery. More people will buy a washing machine or use a bus if it is available immediately, than if they have to wait.
- **Designed quality**. This shows how good a product is meant to be. A silk shirt has a higher designed quality than a polyester one; the Dorchester Hotel in London has a higher designed quality than Sunnyview Bed and Breakfast.
- **Achieved quality**. This sees how the quality actually achieved compares with designs. If Connex schedules a train journey to take an hour, and it actually takes two hours, the achieved quality is considerably lower than designed quality.
- **Reliability**. This shows how often a product is available for use when it is needed. If an Internet service is not available when you want to use it, you will not be impressed by its reliability.
- **Customisation**. A flexible organisation can adapt products to meet individual customer specifications.
- **Durability**. We generally, but not inevitably, want products to last a long time. It is no good buying a nice teddy bear if it falls to pieces when a child starts to play with it.
- **Service**. This includes many aspects of the service given before, during and after sales.

In practice, it is often difficult to design features that appeal to customers. We can collect and analyse customer opinions, but there are several opportunities for misunderstanding (shown in Figure 5.9). To start with, customers' actual demand

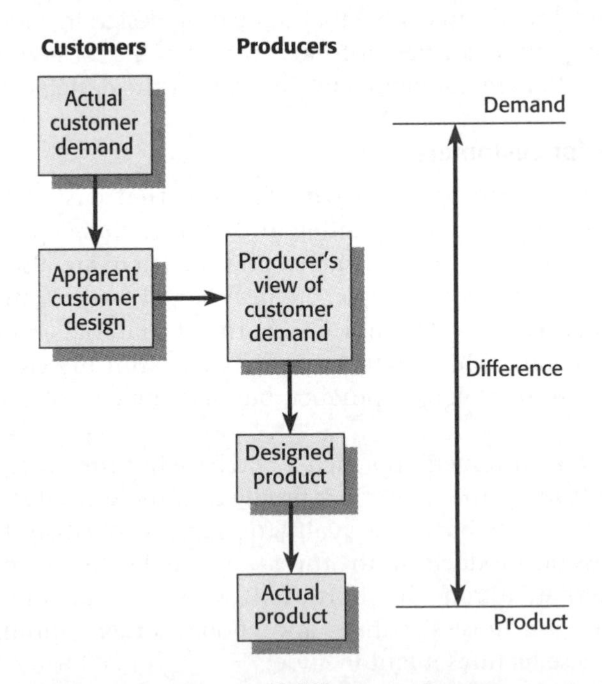

Figure 5.9 Sources of differences between customer demand and products

might be different from their apparent demands. Most people, for example, apparently want better services from government departments, but they do not want these improvements if it means paying higher taxes.

Organisations may also make mistakes translating their customer demands into products. In the 1980s Lymeswold was designed to meet the clear demand for a soft British cheese. Unfortunately, it never really caught on with customers, and was soon withdrawn. Even if the design is right, there can be mistakes in making the products, giving differences between designed and achieved quality. The result is that organisations can make a series of apparently sensible decisions, and still end up with a product that customers do not like.

OPERATIONS IN PRACTICE

Le Café des Artistes, Marseille

In the 1960s Le Café des Artistes attracted customers who considered themselves part of the intellectual *avant garde*. Times change and the café's 1,000 customers a week are now largely middle-class locals. There have also been changes in people's attitudes towards smoking. In one month, the café got 87 complaints from people who did not want to sit in smoke-filled rooms. The owners responded by introducing a non-smoking area. French culture is not so critical of smoking in restaurants, and many people simply ignored the no-smoking signs. The next month, the number of complaints rose to 118. Some people complained because it was still too smoky, others complained that the no-smoking signs were being ignored, and others complained that they could no longer smoke where they wanted to.

The café manager decided to take drastic action and banned smoking completely. This brought 53 complaints from people who wanted to smoke. At this point, the manager realised that it was impossible to design a product that left all his customers happy, or even reduced the number of complaints to a reasonable level.

3. Easy to make

From an operations point of view, the best products are fast, cheap and easy to make. This means that operations managers do *not* like designs that have:

- a lot of work in a long or complicated process;
- steps that must be done manually;
- non-standard procedures, parts or components;
- too many, or too expensive materials;
- designed quality that is too high;
- operations that inevitably give low or variable achieved quality;
- many variations or different products;
- interference with the production of other items.

To avoid these, operations managers look for designs that simplify and standardise. **Simplifying** means reducing the number of parts and removing unnecessary features so that a product is easier to make. This might mean, for example, using moulded plastic parts that snap together rather than metal ones that need welding, or using a limited menu in a hamburger restaurant. **Standardising** uses common parts and materials in a range of different products. This gives easier purchasing of materials, discounts for larger orders, smaller stocks of parts, and longer production runs for components. Standardisation does not necessarily reduce the choice of products, as the same parts can be used in a variety of ways, which is why a pizzeria can serve a standard pizza in a hundred different disguises.

Many organisations go further and use **design for operations**. This focuses on the way that a product is made, so that it is specifically designed to ease operations. Typically, it involves a minimum number of parts, modular designs, common parts across the product range, off-the-shelf components, easily assembled components and any other features that can ease operations.

Another useful tool is **value analysis**, which asks whether customers see a product as giving good value. Essentially, it compares the cost of production (and hence the price) with the perceived benefits to customers (and hence the amount they are willing to pay). Then a team of people looks for improvements in the designs, which will reduce production costs and give better value for money.

OPERATIONS IN PRACTICE

Go airlines

Air travel in Europe is dominated by the major airlines, which have traditionally given a high-quality, high-cost service. De-regulation of the airline industry has allowed smaller companies to develop niche markets. Fairlines International, for example, offers a luxury service between Paris, Milan and Nice. A more significant development is the growth of cut-price operators.

By 1998, there were three cut-price operators in the UK: Debonair, easyJet and Ryanair. These airlines cut costs to a minimum, by offering a basic, no-frills service. They use slightly older aircraft, secondary airports, less popular times, have a simplified booking system with no reservations, give no food or free drinks and have fast turnarounds to increase the actual flying time of the aeroplanes. The low-cost operations allow substantial reductions in fares, which are typically £100 for a journey that would cost £400 with one of the major airlines. This appeals to leisure travellers, who are willing to put up with some inconvenience in exchange for cheap flights. The services are not widely used by business travellers, who are more interested in convenient schedules, reliability, connections to other services and central airports.

Forecasts suggest that the no-frills market will grow very quickly, but it is still risky as the major airlines fight any competition. Between 1993 and 1996, 80 new airlines were formed in the European Union, and 60 of these soon went out of business.

In May 1998, British Airways formed ‘Go’ as its own cut-price company. The first flights were from Stansted to Rome, Milan and Copenhagen, at a cost of £100 – 20 per cent less than the three existing low-cost operators, and up to £400 less than the major airlines. In addition, the aeroplanes were newer Boeing 737s, and the flights were at peak times. When Go announced its new services, the existing cut-price operators complained to the European Commission that BA was using its dominant position to drive them out of business. KLM, Lufthansa, SAS, SwissAir and Iberia all responded by cutting their prices.

Sources: Hewson D. (1999) Tactic that’s Really Taking Off, *Sunday Times*, 23 May, p. 10; *www.go-fly.co.uk*

Comparing products

Suppose that an organisation has several new concepts that it might turn into products, and it wants to choose one in preference to the others. There are several ways it can make such comparisons, including scoring models, break-even points, net present value and internal rate of return. These are described in the supplement at the end of this chapter.

Review questions

5.12 The aim of product design is to make goods that are aesthetically pleasing. Do you think this is true?

5.13 What are the main features of a good design?

5.14 The operations strategy describes the products to be made. Is this true?

Chapter review

- An organisation can only be successful if it makes products that customers want. Product planning is concerned with all decisions about a product. It aims at giving a continuous supply of suitable products.
- Customer demand varies over time, giving products a characteristic life cycle. This has five stages of introduction, growth, maturity, decline and withdrawal. Each stage has different emphasis of operations, costs, revenue and profit.
- Most organisations supply a range of related products to meet varied customer demands. This range must be continually updated, with new products introduced and old ones discarded.
- Most organisations do not develop entirely new products, but adapt existing ones. The organisation's strengths and objectives determine the best entry and exit strategies.
- The introduction of a new product has six stages between the initial idea and its launch onto the market. Only a small percentage of ideas pass though all of these stages and become successful products.
- All aspects of the product package have to be designed. The features of the product must both appeal to customers and fit into existing operations. Such designs should be functional, attractive to customers and easy to make.

Key terms

concurrent development *p. 96*
design for operations *p. 102*
entry and exit strategies *p. 90*
feasibility study *p. 95*
focus of operations *p. 86*
life cycle *p. 85*
new product development *p. 93*
product design *p. 97*
product planning *p. 83*
quality function deployment *p. 98*
range of products *p. 91*
simplifying *p. 101*
standardising *p. 101*
value analysis *p. 102*

CASE STUDY Escential Fragrances

Escential Fragrances is a wholly owned subsidiary of a major French fashion house. It makes a number of well-known perfumes, which are transferred to the parent company to sell under its own name. Some of the production is 'exclusive' brands, but most problems come from the less expensive 'mass' brands. These have a limited life cycle which usually lasts around three years.

All marketing is done by the parent company. This allows Escential to concentrate on production, but it also separates the subsidiary from its final customers. As its income is fixed by the internal transfer prices set by the parent company, Escential's main aim is to use its facilities to full capacity. The capacity is 5,300 bottles of perfume a day, of which 500 are bottles of exclusive brands. There is some flexibility, and the capacity can be varied in the short term by changing working hours.

The design of a new perfume is fairly straightforward. Escential keeps 500 basic ingredients, and a 'designer' mixes a selection of these to give a new perfume. The designer can make a new brand in a very short time, but before production starts Escential runs a series of market surveys and must convince the parent company that the new brand fits into current needs. Suitable bottles and artwork are designed and manufactured, and the parent company runs a marketing campaign to launch the new brand. This increases the time needed to introduce a brand to about nine months.

A meeting was recently held to discuss medium-term production plans. The following records show average daily sales of the nine current mass perfumes.

Month	Perfume code number								
	LP4098	LP6032	LP6275	LT3127	LT4092	MA985	LP1075	MA247	LT2240
1	120	1,170	–	1,030	680	–	320	724	403
2	150	1,180	–	1,040	660	–	286	693	519
3	190	1,170	–	1,050	610	–	307	751	622
4	250	1,170	–	1,050	560	–	310	660	540
5	310	1,150	–	1,060	500	60	324	703	490
6	450	1,130	–	1,070	410	100	301	691	603
7	600	1,080	–	1,080	320	150	279	673	397
8	770	1,050	–	1,090	240	310	292	711	501
9	940	970	50	1,200	150	370	314	741	488
10	1,000	940	50	1,210	110	390	288	687	561
11	1,050	930	50	1,190	90	380	292	729	473
12	1,100	890	60	1,200	80	380	301	700	502
13	1,150	850	70	1,210	70	390	314	691	450
14	1,180	840	80	1,200	60	370	306	673	423
15	1,210	780	90	1,210	60	380	285	659	607
16	1,230	730	100	1,210	60	370	299	712	555
17	1,240	670	120	1,090	50	360	305	736	487
18	1,250	560	160	1,000	50	320	289	705	491
19	1,250	450	210	860	40	280	310	603	497

Guy Mignard, the marketing director, suggested that to remain competitive Escential needed to appeal to different type of people and that it should expand its range as soon as possible. He suggested rushing an additional perfume on to the market in six months and adding another three brands within a year.

Marcel Gagnon, the operations director, took the opposite view and said that production was already stretched beyond capacity and should be reduced. He said that large batches were more efficient, and thus that they should remove the four brands with lowest sales and concentrate on the remaining five.

Jean Pouliot, the company secretary, took a middle view. He said that recent production levels had certainly been too high and should be cut back. No extra brands should be considered immediately, but sales of three brands were clearly falling and the company should plan their replacement. He had talked to the parent company who suggested three new brands, with forecasts of quarterly costs and revenues summarised in the following table.

Quarter	Code Number					
	LP6587		LP7045		LT4950	
	Costs	Revenue	Costs	Revenue	Costs	Revenue
1	3,000	200	3,500	1,500	1,500	100
2	1,000	400	2,000	2,000	1,500	100
3	–	600	1,000	2,500	1,000	100
4	–	800	600	3,000	1,000	200
5	1,000	1,000	1,500	3,000	500	300
6	–	1,000	1,000	2,500	500	500
7	–	1,000	600	2,000	500	800
8	–	1,000	–	1,500	500	1,200
9	1,000	1,000	1,000	1,100	100	1,600
10	–	1,000	600	700	100	2,000
11	–	1,000	–	300	100	2,200
12	–	1,000	–	–	100	2,200

Note: these figures are in thousands of francs, without discounting, and are based on an average transfer price of 50 francs a bottle.

Questions

- At what stages in their life cycles are the nine mass perfumes? What are likely future sales?
- What should Escential do about withdrawing, replacing or extending its current brands? Which of the new products gives the best returns?
- What would you do if you were in these circumstances? How would you justify your decisions?

Problem

The following table shows the revenue and costs of supplying a product over the past 11 months (values are in thousands of pounds). Where is the product in its life cycle and what plans would you expect the supplier to be making?

Month	1	2	3	4	5	6	7	8	9	10	11
Income	3.5	4.8	7.0	8.9	10.2	11.9	12.7	13.4	13.7	13.7	13.5
Cost	7.5	8.7	10.2	10.5	9.8	8.8	7.7	6.8	5.2	3.8	3.0

Discussion questions

5.1 How does an organisation decide the number and variety of products to make? Give some examples of product ranges in different organisations, explaining why they have chosen this structure for their range.

5.2 Describe a product you would like to market and discuss the steps needed to launch it. How would you set about designing your product package? What time-scale and budget would you need?

5.3 Some people suggest that ideas for new products only really come from changes – which might be in the economy, society or demography, technology, political or legal constraints or other market conditions. Do you think that this is true? How can organisations make sure they have enough ideas to give a continuing stream of new products?

5.4 Describe in detail the changes in a specific product as it moved through its life cycle. You might consider a particular type of computer, fast food, a fashion accessory or any other product you are familiar with.

5.5 Demand for few products actually follows the precise life cycle described in this chapter. Do you think this is true? Give evidence to support your views.

5.6 Describe the entry and exit strategies of a number of national companies. Why have they adopted these strategies? How does their choice affect operations?

5.7 The Amantti Foundation is a privately funded think-tank, which considers the effects of technological developments on society. A recent study looked at some products that are ready to be marketed and could have a widespread impact. These include advanced virtual offices, smart money to replace coins and notes, hybrid biodiesel/electric cars, mobile information systems, genetic engineering to grow organs for human transplants, and so on. What stage do you think these products are at in their development? What products would you add to this list?

Reference

1. Hill T. (1993) *Manufacturing Strategy*. 2nd edn. Basingstoke Hants: Macmillan Press.

Selected reading

Baxter M. (1995) *Product Design*. London: Chapman and Hall.
Boothroyd G., Dewhurst P. and Knight P. (1994) *Product Design for Manufacturing*. New York: Marcel Dekker.
Crawford C.M. (1997) *New Products Management*. 5th edn. Chicago: Irwin.
Hollins B. and Pugh S. (1990) *Successful Product Design*. London: Butterworths.
Kuczmarski T.D. (1992) *Managing New Products*. 2nd edn. Englewood Cliffs, NJ: Prentice-Hall.
Ulrich K.T. and Eppinger S.D. (1995) *Product Design and Development*. New York: McGraw-Hill.
Urban G. and Hauser J.R. (1993) *Design and Marketing of New Products*. 2nd edn. Englewood Cliffs, NJ: Prentice-Hall.
Wheelwright S.C. and Clark K.B. (1992) *Revolutionising Product Development*. New York: Free Press.

Useful Websites

Some interesting examples are given in: *www.baddesign.com*

SUPPLEMENT TO CHAPTER 5

Comparing products

Contents

Scoring models

This supplement describes some ways of comparing products. Perhaps the simplest is to use checklists. Here the important factors are listed, and managers decide whether a product gives a satisfactory performance in each. All things being equal, better products give satisfactory performance for more factors.

WORKED EXAMPLE

Clawson Preserves lists 10 factors that are important for jam. It is considering four new flavours, but only wants to develop one of them. After lengthy discussions, managers have agreed some aspects of performance, with a tick in the following table showing that a flavour has reached a reasonable standard. Which flavour do you think the company should develop?

	Flavour			
	A	B	C	D
Time to develop	✓			✓
Expected life				✓
Cost of developing	✓	✓	✓	
Fit with other products	✓			
Equipment needed	✓		✓	
Initial demand		✓		✓
Stability of demand	✓	✓		
Marketing required		✓		✓
Competition	✓		✓	
Expected profit	✓		✓	✓

Solution

Flavour A gives satisfactory performance for more of the criteria and should be considered further. Obviously, managers have to include many more factors before they make any final decision.

A weakness of these simple checklists is that they treat each factor as equally important. **Scoring models** allocate points to each product, with the maximum number of points for each factor showing its relative importance. Expected sales might be twice as important as the equipment needed, so its maximum score is twice as high. We can summarise the procedure for a scoring model in the following list.

1. Decide the most important factors in a decision.
2. Assign a maximum possible score to each factor, showing its relative importance.
3. Consider each product in turn and give a score for each factor up to the maximum.
4. Add the total scores for each product.
5. Find the best product as the one with the highest total score.
6. Discuss the result, look at other factors, and make a final decision.

WORKED EXAMPLE

When Sit Yuen Software compared four systems, it found the results in the following table. What is the relative importance of the factors? Which system would you recommend?

Factor	Maximum	System			
		A	B	C	D
Technical	20	11	15	18	15
Finance	30	28	16	26	12
Market	15	9	13	12	8
Production	25	18	19	20	19
Competition	10	9	7	6	9

Solution

The most important factor is finance, which has the highest maximum score. Production is slightly less important (25/30 times as important), then technical (20/30 times as important), market and competition. Adding the scores for each product gives totals of:

$$A = 75 \qquad B = 70 \qquad C = 82 \qquad D = 63$$

On this evidence, product C is clearly the best.

Break-even point

The profit from selling a product is:

Profit = income − total costs

The total costs come from a number of sources and can be classified as:

- **fixed costs**, which are constant regardless of the number of units made;
- **variable costs**, which depend on the number of units made.

Research and development costs, for example, are fixed regardless of the number of units made. Other fixed costs come from marketing, administration, lighting, heating, rent, debt repayments and a range of overheads. On the other hand, the cost of raw materials, direct labour, maintenance and some other costs are directly affected by output – a doubling of output will double these costs.

Then:

$$\text{Total costs} = \text{fixed cost} + \text{variable cost}$$
$$= \text{fixed cost} + \text{number of units made} \times \text{cost per unit}$$
$$= F + nV$$

Where:

n = number of units made
F = fixed cost
V = variable cost per unit

The income is simply:

$$\text{Income} = \text{number of units sold} \times \text{price charged per unit}$$
$$= nP$$

Where: P = price charged per unit.

The income and total costs both rise linearly with the number of units made, as shown in Figure 5s.1. The **break-even point** is the number of units that must be sold to cover all costs and start making a profit. This is the point when the income equals the total costs, and is the point where the lines cross each other in Figure 5s.1.

Suppose a new product has \$200,000 spent on research, development and overheads before production. During normal production each unit has a variable cost of \$300 and sells for \$400. The product only starts to make a profit when the original \$200,000 has been recovered. The point when this occurs is the break-even point. Each unit sold contributes \$400 – 300 = \$100, so 200,000/100 = 2,000 units must be sold to cover the fixed cost. Then:

- the break-even point is 2,000 units;
- if less than 2,000 units are sold, the product makes a loss;
- if more than 2,000 units are sold the product makes a profit.

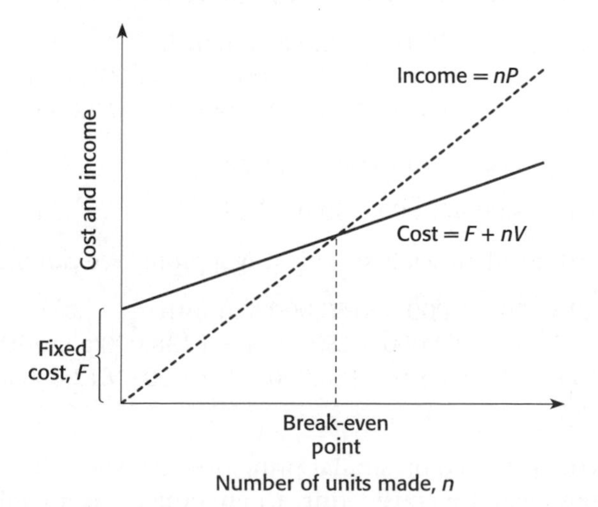

Figure 5s.1 Defining the break-even point

At the break-even point:

$$\text{Income} = \text{total cost}$$
$$nP = F + nV$$
$$\text{or} \quad n = F/(P - V)$$

This also shows one reason why organisations can get economies of scale. With higher production the fixed costs are spread over more units, so the average unit cost falls.

WORKED EXAMPLE

Glenrock Adventure Holidays sells an average of 100 holidays a month. The income generated has to cover fixed costs of £63,000 a month. Each holiday sold has travel, accommodation and other variable costs of £500.

(a) Does Glenrock make a profit if it charges £1,200 for each holiday?
(b) If the price of a holiday is reduced to £1,000 and sales increase to 150 a month, does Glenrock make a profit?

Solution

(a) We know that:

Fixed cost, F = 63,000
Cost per unit, V = 500
Selling price per unit, P = 1,200
Number of units sold = 100

The break-even point is:

$$n = F/(P - V) = 63{,}000/(1{,}200 - 500) = 90$$

Glenrock is actually selling 100 a month. This is more than the break-even point, so it makes a profit. We can find the profit from:

Income = nP = 100 × 1,200 = £120,000 a month
Total costs = $F + nV$ = 63,000 + 100 × 500 = £113,000 a month
Profit = income – total costs = 120,000 – 113,000 = £7,000 a month

(b) Reducing the price gives a new break-even point:

$$n = F/(P - V) = 63{,}000/(1{,}000 - 500) = 126$$

Actual sales are 150, so Glenrock is still making a profit. We can find this from:

Income = nP = 150 × 1,000 = £150,000 a month
Total costs = $F + nV$ = 63,000 + 150 × 500 = £138,000 a month
Profit = income × total costs = 150,000 – 138,000 = £12,000 a month

---

Cost-benefit analyses are based on similar principles, but they give a much more general picture. Suppose you are considering a new project. You could list all the benefits from doing the project, including those which are intangible. Then you could assign a notional value to each of these, and add them to find the total notional benefit of doing the project. Similarly, you could get a figure for the total notional costs. Comparing these two gives some idea of whether you should continue with the project, or not.

Net present value

Suppose you put an amount of money A_P into a bank account and leave it untouched for a year earning interest at a rate I (expressed as a decimal fraction). At the end of the year you will get interest and the amount will have grown to $A_P (1 + I)$.

If you leave the money untouched for a second year, it will earn interest not only on the initial amount, but also on the interest earned in the first year. The amount will then grow to:

$$[A_P (1 + I)] \times (1 + I) \quad \text{or} \quad A_P (1 + I)^2$$

The amount of money will grow in this compound way, so that n years in the future the account will contain an amount, A_F, where:

$$A_F = A_P (1 + I)^n$$

Turning this equation around, we can say that an amount, A_F, n periods in the future has a present value, A_P, of:

$$A_P = A_F/(1 + I)^n$$

Calculating the present value of a specified future amount is called **discounting to present value**. This gives a way of comparing amounts of money that are available at different times in the future.

WORKED EXAMPLE

A company is comparing two possible new products. Although the revenues are phased over many years, they can be summarised as:

- product 1 gives a revenue of £300,000 in 5 years' time;
- product 2 gives a revenue of £500,000 in 10 years' time.

Which product is better if the company uses a discounting rate of 20 per cent a year?

Solution

The discounting rate is 20 per cent, meaning that $I = 0.2$, and we can use this to find the present value of all amounts.

- **Product 1**: Revenue is £300,000 in 5 years' time. Then:

$$\text{Present value} = 300{,}000/(1 + 0.2)^5 = 300{,}000/2.488 = £120{,}563$$

- **Product 2**: Revenue is £500,000 in 10 years' time. Then:

$$\text{Present value} = 500{,}000/(1 + 0.2)^{10} = 500{,}000/6.192 = £80{,}753$$

Product 1 is better as it gives a higher present value.

As well as discounting incomes to their present values, we can also discount costs. Then subtracting the present value of all costs from the present value of all incomes gives a **net present value**.

Net present value = sum of discounted incomes – sum of discounted costs

WORKED EXAMPLE

Judy Blom has found the initial development costs and projected net incomes for three potential products shown below (values are in thousands of kroner).

Product	Initial cost	Income generated in each year				
		1	2	3	4	5
A	2,000	1,000	800	600	400	200
B	1,400	100	200	500	600	700
C	800	100	200	300	200	0

If Judy uses a discounting rate of 10 per cent a year to compare the products, which will she recommend?

Solution

Figure 5s.2 shows a spreadsheet where all the amounts have been discounted to their present value. Subtracting the present value of costs (in this case the single initial project cost) from the present value of income gives the net present value.

	A	B	C	D	E	F	G	H
1	Year	Discounting factor	Product A		Product B		Product C	
2			Income	Present value	Income	Present value	Income	Present value
3								
4	1	1.1	1000	909	100	91	100	91
5	2	1.21	800	661	200	165	200	165
6	3	1.331	600	451	500	376	300	225
7	4	1.4641	400	273	600	410	200	137
8	5	1.61051	200	124	700	435	0	0
9								
10	Totals	Income	3000	2418	2100	1476	800	618
11		Cost		2000		1400		800
12								
13	Net present value			418		76		–182

Figure 5s.2 Spreadsheet calculation of net present value

Product A has the highest net present value and is, all other things being equal, the one Judy should recommend. Product C has a negative net present value and should be avoided.

Internal rate of return

An obvious problem with present values is finding a reasonable discounting rate that takes into account interest rates, inflation, taxes, opportunity costs, exchange rates and everything else. An alternative approach is to find the discounting rate that leads to a specified net present value. The usual target is a net present value of zero, and the discounting rate that gives this is the **internal rate of return**. Then we can compare products by finding the internal rate of return for each, and the product with the highest value is the best. There is no easy formula for calculating the internal rate of return, but the calculations are done automatically with a spreadsheet or other software.

WORKED EXAMPLE

What is the internal rate of return for a product that gives the following net cash flow?

Year	0	1	2	3	4	5	6	7	8
Net cash flow	–2,000	–500	–200	800	1,800	1,600	1,500	200	100

Solution

Figure 5s.3 shows a spreadsheet where the internal rate of return is calculated as 20 per cent, with checks to show that this gives a net present value of zero (allowing for rounding).

	A	B	C	D
1	Year	Net cash flow	Discounting factor	Discounted value
2				
3	0	–2000	1.0000	–2000
4	1	–500	1.2000	–417
5	2	–200	1.4400	–139
6	3	800	1.7280	463
7	4	1800	2.0736	868
8	5	1600	2.4883	643
9	6	1500	2.9860	502
10	7	200	3.5832	56
11	8	100	4.2998	23
12				
13	Totals	3300		0
14				
15	Internal rate of return		20%	

Figure 5s.3 Spreadsheet calculations with the internal rate of return

Problems

1 Four products are judged by 10 criteria, with points given to each as shown below. What is the relative importance of the criteria? Which product would you recommend?

Factor	Maximum	Product			
		A	B	C	D
Resources	10	8	10	8	7
Finance	30	28	27	24	17
Market	35	17	33	22	18
Production	25	18	19	20	19
Competition	20	12	11	16	19
Technical	15	10	9	5	12
Skills	10	9	4	3	9
Compatibility	5	3	3	1	5
Location	10	6	10	7	6
Experience	15	8	6	4	12

2 Every week a company makes 100 units of a product that it sells for $100 each. Unit variable costs are $50 and fixed costs amount to $150,000 a year. What is the break-even point for the product, and what profit is the company making? What is the average cost per unit? How much would production have to rise to reduce the average unit cost by 25 per cent?

3 AirBC is considering a new service between Paris and Vancouver. Its existing aeroplanes, each of which has a capacity of 240 passengers, can be used for one flight a week with fixed costs of C$30,000 and variable costs amounting to 50 per cent of the ticket price. If the airline plans to sell tickets at C$200 each, how many passengers will it need to break even? Does this seem a reasonable number?

4 How much will an initial investment of £1,000 earning interest of 8 per cent a year be worth at the end of 20 years?

5 Several years ago Jaydeep Kumar invested in an endowment insurance policy that is about to mature. He has the option of receiving £10,000 now or £20,000 in 10 years' time. He could invest the money with a real interest rate expected to remain at 10 per cent a year for the foreseeable future. Which option should he take?

6 A product has projected costs and revenues (in thousands of pounds) as follows:

Year	1	2	3	4	5	6
Costs	100	–	–	50	–	–
Incomes	100	20	50	80	60	40

What is its net present value? What is the internal rate of return?

7 The costs and incomes for three products are shown below (in thousands of pounds). Which do you think is the best?

Year	Product A		Product B		Product C	
	Income	Costs	Income	Costs	Income	Costs
1	10	70	80	30	120	40
2	20	60	90	20	110	40
3	50	45	90	10	100	50
4	100	40	100	20	100	60
5	150	40	100	20	90	60
6	170	40	110	30	90	70
7	180	40	110	30	80	80

Quality management

Everybody in the organisation has to believe their livelihood is based on the quality of the product they deliver.

Lee Iacocca

Talking Straight, Bantam, New York, 1988

Contents

Aims of the chapter

After reading this chapter you should be able to:

- discuss different views of quality;
- appreciate the importance of product quality;
- define the costs of quality management;
- describe the features of total quality management (TQM);
- see how to introduce TQM to an organisation;
- discuss quality management in services.

Main themes

This chapter will emphasise:

- different views of **product quality**;
- **customer satisfaction** as the most important measure of quality;
- **quality management** which is concerned with all aspects of quality;
- **total quality management** where the whole organisation works towards perfect quality.

Defining quality

Customer satisfaction

Organisations pay a lot of attention to the quality of their products. Ford uses the slogan of 'Quality is Job 1'; IBM says: 'We will deliver defect-free competitive products and services on time to our customers'; Vauxhall says that 'Quality is a right, not a privilege'; many companies aim at making 'products of the highest quality', and thousands of companies advertise that they are 'ISO 9000 registered'. But what exactly do they mean by quality – and how can they guarantee to supply high-quality products?

We have to start by saying that 'quality' is very difficult to define. Occasionally there are agreed measures, such as industry standards for concrete, but these are very specific and only refer to one aspect of quality. In practice, it is difficult to give a clear view of the quality of almost any product. If someone asks you to judge the quality of a novel, you can say whether you enjoyed reading it, but would find it difficult to describe its quality. Similarly, you could describe the various policies of a government, but could not give a convincing description of their overall quality. You see this problem clearly when sports commentators try to say how good a football match was, or wine tasters compare different vineyards, or enthusiasts discuss a new computer game.

As a starting point, we can look at our own experiences of product quality. When we use a ballpoint pen, we are happy with its quality if it writes easily and clearly; an airline gives a high-quality service if we get to our destination on time and without too much hassle; an electricity supplier gives high quality if we never have to worry about supplies or costs. In other words, we think that products have high quality if they do the jobs they were designed for. This fairly obvious statement gives one view of quality, which is based on a product's ability to meet customer expectations.

In its broadest sense, **quality** is the ability of a product to meet – and preferably exceed – customer expectations.

Unfortunately, this definition is still rather vague, especially as different customers have different expectations. Perhaps we can look at some specific products and see why they are generally considered to have high quality. A Rolls-Royce is probably the highest quality car available; a Wedgwood dinner service is much higher quality than a plastic equivalent; Hamlet is higher-quality drama than a television soap opera, but if we try to explain these judgements, we run into problems. If the purpose of a car is to provide transport between two points, then a cheap car will do this just as well as a Rolls-Royce; if the purpose of a dinner service is to give a surface to rest food on while we eat, a cheap plastic one works just as well as an expensive china one; audience figures show that far more people watch a television soap opera than go to see Hamlet.

Faced with the problems of explaining what they mean by 'quality', many people give up and simply say, 'We don't know how to define quality but we recognise it when we see it'. Others make vague statements about inherent values, such as, 'Quality measures innate excellence'. Others look at the product's design and say, 'Quality measures the degree to which a product conforms to designed specifications'. Some typical definitions of quality include the following.

- innate excellence;
- fitness for intended use;
- performance;
- reliability;
- durability;
- specific features, perhaps for safety or convenience;
- level of technology;
- conformance to design specifications;
- uniformity, with small variability;
- perception of high quality by customers;
- convenience of use;
- designed with attractive appearance and style;
- value, or the ratio of performance to cost;
- customer service before and during sales;
- on-time deliveries;
- after sales service.

The problem is that operations managers have to take these vague ideas about quality and turn them into products that get customer approval.

Different views of quality

In reality, we rarely judge quality by one criterion, but consider a number of different ones. Consider, for example, a television set. We might judge its quality by how expensive it is, how attractive the cabinet is, how big it is, how easy it is to use, how clear the picture is, how accurate the colours are, how often it needs repairing, how long it will last, how many channels it can pick up, how good the sound is, what additional features it has, and so on. Any reasonable view of quality must take into account many such factors, and it is foolish to judge a product by some factors and ignore others. We cannot, for example, judge doctors' quality by the number of patients they treat, without considering how good and effective their treatment is.

Some factors of quality can be measured – such as weight, number of breakdowns, delivery time and guaranteed life. It is fairly easy to design specifications for these factors, and then test the products to make sure they actually achieve the designed standards. Other factors cannot be measured but rely on judgement – such as appearance, taste, comfort and courtesy of staff. It can be very difficult to get a coherent view of these subjective factors, especially when they depend on the perspective of the person giving them. A school with large classes might be considered high quality by a government which judges efficiency, but low quality by parents who look at educational achievements.

So far, we have emphasised the customer's view of quality, but there are really two opinions:

- An **internal** view of the producer, who measures a product's quality by how closely it comes to its designed specifications. A bar of chocolate, for example, is high quality if it is close to the specified weight, contains the right amount of cocoa, and so on.
- An **external** view of the customer, who judges quality by how well a product does the job it was bought for. A bar of chocolate is high quality if it tastes good, satisfies hunger, etc.

We have already discussed this balance needed between internal and external views with product design in the last chapter. In the past, organisations tended to emphasise the internal view, suggesting that a product that meets the standards of the producer should be acceptable to customers Now they take more notice of customer opinions. Unfortunately, this is not universal, and you can still find many companies that apparently have little regard for their customers. Elizabeth Richmond had a disagreement with Tiny Computers in 2000 and was surprised when the customer service department effectively said: 'We have considered your complaint, feel that we have done nothing wrong, and there is no point in discussing the matter further'.

One important point is that customers do not always demand products with the highest technical quality. We want some balance of features that gives an acceptable overall picture. A Rolls-Royce car has the highest possible quality of engineering, but most people include price in their judgement and buy a cheaper make. Hand-made shirts may have the highest quality, but most of us buy clothes from local stores. We can use this distinction to consider another two views of quality:

- **designed quality** – sets the quality that a product is designed to have;
- **achieved quality** – shows how closely the product conforms to its designed quality.

An airline that aims at having 98 per cent of its flights arrive on time has a high designed quality. If only 30 per cent of flights are actually on time, its achieved quality is much lower. This distinction suggests a general approach to quality. Organisations should design products with the designed quality that customers demand, and then check that achieved quality actually meets these specifications.

Review questions

6.1 If the price is right, people will buy a product regardless of its quality. Do you think this is true?

6.2 Why is it so difficult to define 'quality'?

6.3 Which do you think is more important, the external view of quality or the internal view?

Quality management

In an organisation, all decisions about quality are joined together under the general title of **quality management**.

Quality management is the management function that is responsible for all aspects of a product's quality.

In recent years there have been so many developments in quality management that some people refer to a 'quality revolution'. This happened for four main reasons:

1. improved processes can make products with guaranteed high quality;
2. high quality gives producers a competitive advantage;
3. consumers have become used to high-quality products, and will not accept anything less;
4. high quality reduces costs.

These show why organisations *must* make high-quality products. If you make poor products, customers will simply move to a competitor who is better at meeting their expectations. If you buy a pair of shoes that get a hole the first time you wear them, you will not buy another pair, no matter how cheap they are. (This explains Gucci's motto: 'Quality is remembered long after the price is forgotten'.) So, high quality will not guarantee a product's success, but low quality will certainly guarantee its failure.

Another important benefit of high quality is that it reduces costs. At first this seems to go against the traditional view that higher quality can only be bought at higher cost. Surely, a higher quality product uses more time, more careful operations, a more skilful workforce, better materials, and so on? But if you look at the wider costs, you see that some actually go down with increasing quality. Imagine that you buy a washing machine that is faulty. You complain, and the manufacturer arranges for the machine to be repaired. The manufacturer could have saved money by finding the fault before the machine left the factory – and it could have saved even more by making a machine that did not have a fault in the first place. We will discuss these costs in the following section, but there is a clear message that higher quality can give benefits to both the organisation and its customers (see Figure 6.1).

Review questions

6.4 What is 'quality management'?

6.5 Why is quality management important to an organisation?

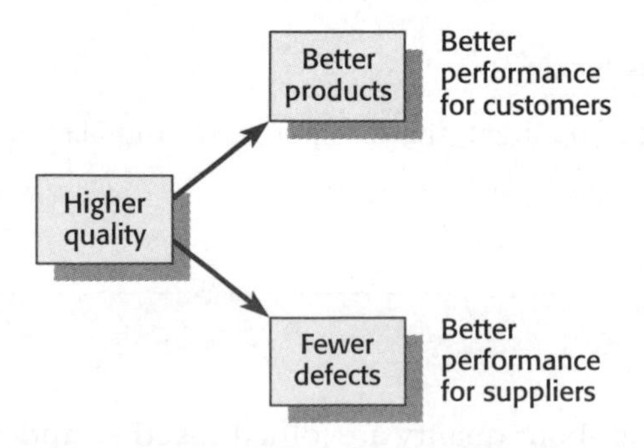

Figure 6.1 Higher quality benefits both customers and producers

OPERATIONS IN PRACTICE

Federal Express

Gill Seymour had sent an important legal document from New York to Turin. It was Friday and she had expected a phone call from Turin to acknowledge receipt of the document. This had not come, so she phoned Federal Express to see if it had delivered the document, bearing in mind its stated policy of 'Absolutely, Positively, Overnight'. Using Federal Express's free enquiry line, she talked to Fran in customer liaison, who could tell her exactly what had happened to the document.

Our Super Tracker computer system shows a complete log of your document's journey. Our service man, Jim Baxter, picked it up from Martin Pearce in your New York office at 4.30 pm on Wednesday; it was routed through our Superhub in Memphis, Tennessee and was put on our overnight flight to Paris and then Rome. It arrived in Rome by 1 pm on Thursday, and our delivery van took it to your Turin office at 4.00 pm. Unfortunately, there was a local holiday and your office was closed. This office had previously agreed that packages which couldn't be delivered should be returned first thing the following day. We delivered the package again at 9.00 o'clock this morning, where it was signed for by Paulo Carerra. We pointed out the note asking him to phone you and confirm delivery.

The product supplied by Federal Express is a very efficient parcel delivery service. The company uses high technology and efficient operations to give a consistently high-quality service.

You can find more information at *www.fedex.com*.

Project 6.1 *Find a service that you have been unhappy with (unfortunately, this should be quite easy). Say exactly why the service was poor. What had you expected, and how had this compared with what you actually got? How could the service be improved?*

Costs of quality management

Types of cost

Suppose that a manufacturer sells products with such poor quality that 5 per cent of the output is defective. When customers report these defects, the manufacturer replaces them under its warranty. This is clearly inefficient. To start with, the manufacturer has to increase production by 5 per cent to cover the defects. It also has to maintain a system for dealing with customer complaints, and associated systems for collecting defective units, inspecting, repairing or replacing them, and returning them to customers. If the defects are eliminated, productivity rises, unit costs fall, there are no customer complaints so the cost of dealing with them is eliminated, and the whole system for correcting faults becomes unnecessary.

You can see from this, that the benefits of high quality include (see Figure 6.2):

- less waste and increased productivity;
- lower unit costs and improved profitability;
- reduced warranty costs;
- elimination of procedures for correcting defects;

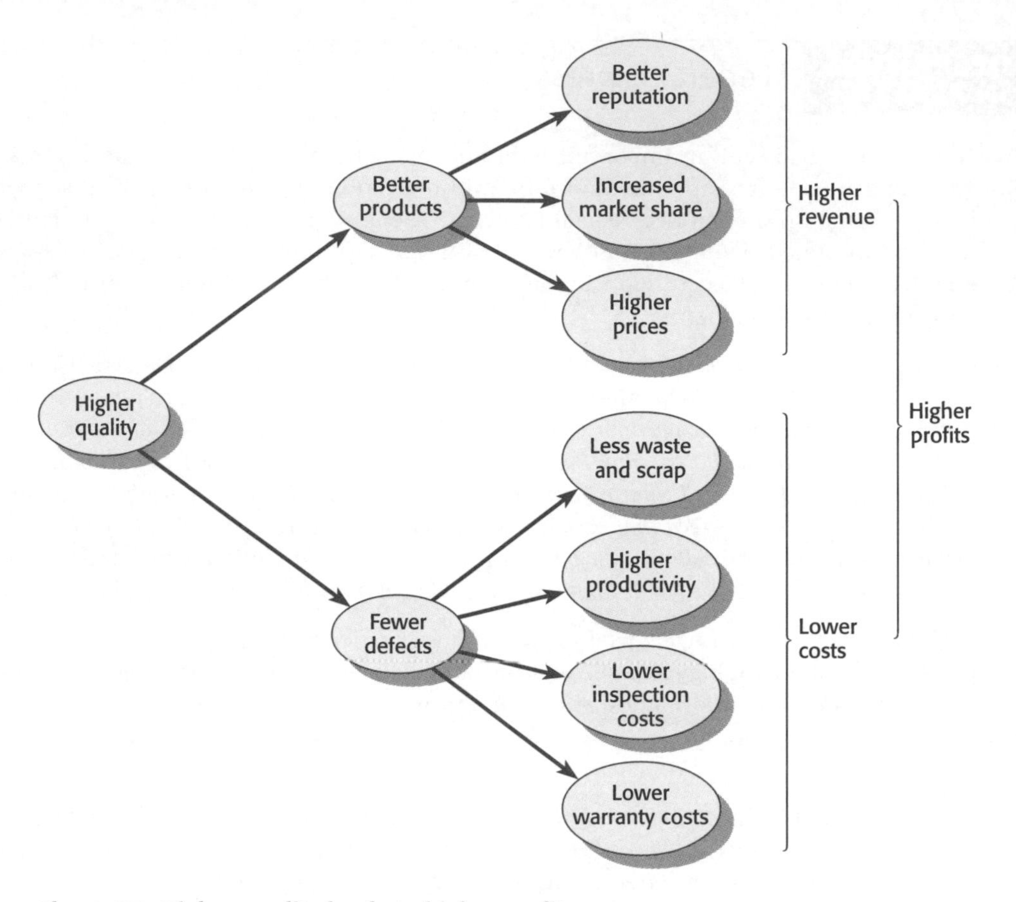

Figure 6.2 Higher quality leads to higher profits

- reduced administration costs for dealing with customer complaints;
- reduced liability for defects;
- competitive advantage coming from an enhanced reputation;
- larger market share with less effort in marketing;
- enhanced motivation and morale of employees;
- removal of hassle and irritants for managers.

Some costs fall with higher quality, but common sense says that there will be some costs that rise. Unfortunately, it is quite difficult to identify the costs of quality, largely because accounting systems do not separate them from other costs. There is, however, a general feeling that quality costs are somewhere around 15–25 per cent f sales. We can separate this total cost into four components.

ntion costs

costs incurred to prevent defects happening. The quality of a product is
gn stage, so the best way to guaranteeing high quality is by designing
ct in the first place. Prevention costs cover all aspects of quality that are
a product, together with costs incurred to ease production and reduce
making a defect. They include direct costs for the product itself, such

the use of better materials, inclusion of features to ensure good quality, and extra time to make the product. They also include indirect costs of employee training, pilot runs, testing prototypes, designing and maintaining control systems, improvement projects, etc. All things being equal, prevention costs rise with the quality of the product.

2. Appraisal costs

These are the costs of making sure the designed quality is actually achieved. As units move through their process, they are inspected to make sure they actually reach the quality specified in the design. Related costs include sampling, inspecting, testing and all the other elements of quality control (which we discuss in Chapter 7). The appraisal costs also cover administrations and audits for quality programmes. Generally, the more effort that is put into quality control, the higher is the final quality of the product and the higher are the costs needed to achieve this.

3. Internal failure costs

As a product goes through the various operations in its production, it may be inspected several times. Any units that do not meet the specified quality are scrapped, returned to an earlier point in the process, or repaired. These options all involve extra work. The cost of this forms part of the internal failure cost, which is the total cost of making defective products that are detected somewhere within the process.

Part of the internal failure costs come directly from the loss of material, wasted labour, wasted machine time in making the defective item, extra testing, duplicated effort, and so on. Another part comes from the indirect costs of higher stock levels, longer lead times, extra capacity needed to allow for scrap and rejections, loss of confidence, etc.

The further a product goes through the process, the more money is spent on it and the more expensive it is to scrap or rework. Ideally, then, defects should be found as early in the process as possible. If a defective unit is allowed to continue in the process, more money is wasted on a unit that is already known to be faulty.

4. External failure costs

Producers normally give a guarantee with their products, and are responsible for correcting any faults. If a unit goes through the entire production process, is delivered to a customer, and is then found to be faulty, the producer must bring it back from the customer and replace, rework or repair it as necessary. The cost of this work is part of the external failure cost, which is the total cost of making defective units that are not detected within the process, but are recognised as faulty by customers.

External failure faults are often the highest costs of quality management and are the ones that should be avoided. In a typical year, car manufacturers in the USA spend billions of dollars recalling 10 million vehicles with production faults. The cost of failures can be even higher if, say, faulty parts in an aeroplane cause it to crash; an oil tanker spills its cargo; or a drug gives severe side-effects. There are some spectacular examples of failures, such as Chernobyl, Three Mile Island, Exxon Valdese and the Challenger Space Shuttle.

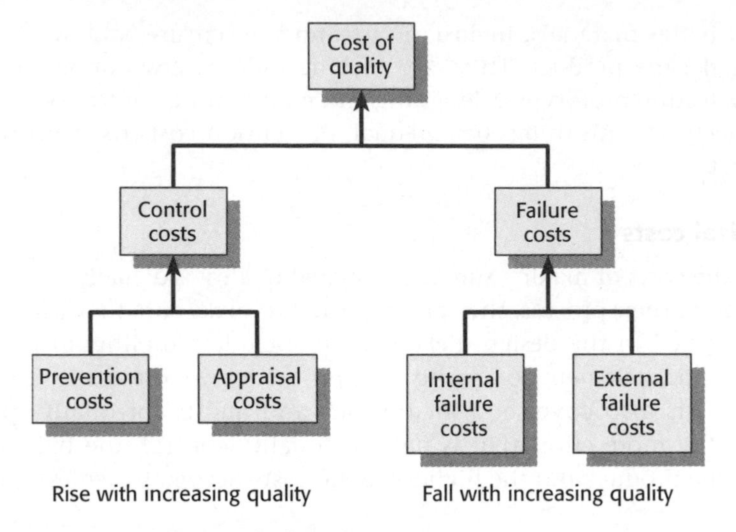

Figure 6.3 The costs of quality

External failure costs, like internal failure costs, generally decline with higher quality (see Figure 6.3).

Minimising the total cost of quality

We can find the total cost of quality by adding the four separate components. The result is often surprisingly high. The failure costs, in particular, are so high that organisations should try to avoid them. As the failure costs fall with increasing quality (shown in Figure 6.4), the best way of avoiding them is to make products without defects, in other words, to make products of 'perfect quality', where every unit is guaranteed to be fault free. This is the idea of **total quality management**.

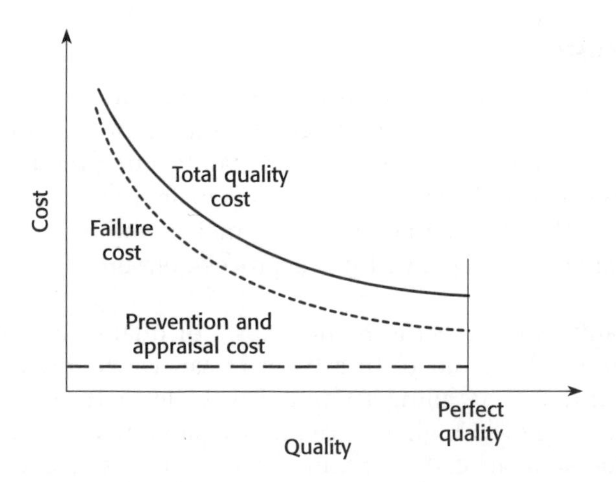

Figure 6.4 Minimum cost comes with perfect quality

WORKED EXAMPLE

Benjamin Naylor recorded his company's costs (in thousands of pounds a year) during a period when they introduced a major new quality management programme. How effective do you think the new programme has been?

Year		−3	−2	−1	0	1	2	3
Sales value		1,225	1,247	1,186	1,150	1,456	1,775	1,865
Costs (£000s)	Prevention	7.3	8.1	9.1	26.8	30.6	32.9	35.2
	Appraisal	27.6	16.9	20.1	47.4	59.7	59.6	65.5
	Internal failure	72.8	71.9	75.0	40.3	24.0	20.0	19.4
	External failure	66.5	59.9	65.8	27.3	18.8	15.6	12.5

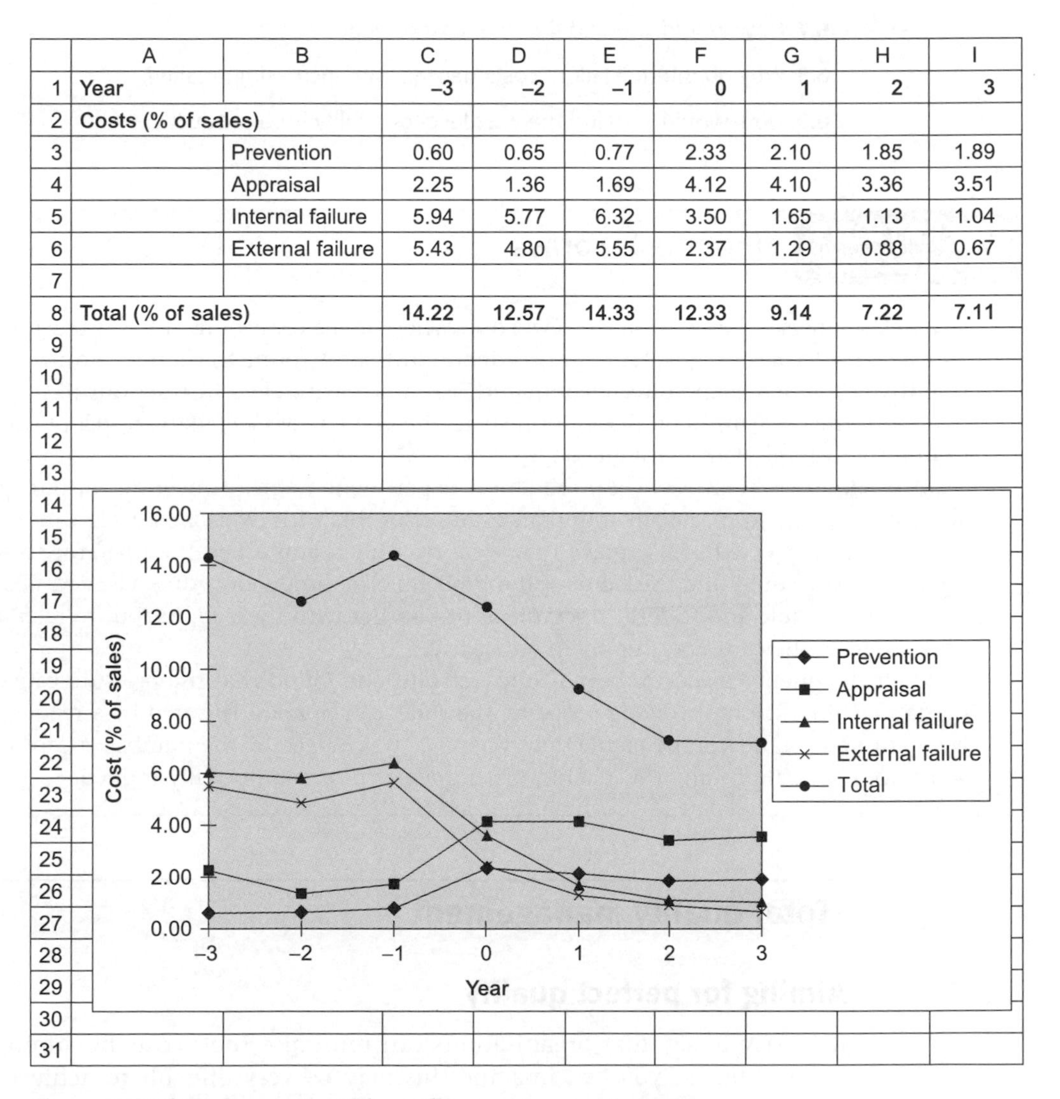

	A	B	C	D	E	F	G	H	I
1	Year		−3	−2	−1	0	1	2	3
2	Costs (% of sales)								
3		Prevention	0.60	0.65	0.77	2.33	2.10	1.85	1.89
4		Appraisal	2.25	1.36	1.69	4.12	4.10	3.36	3.51
5		Internal failure	5.94	5.77	6.32	3.50	1.65	1.13	1.04
6		External failure	5.43	4.80	5.55	2.37	1.29	0.88	0.67
7									
8	Total (% of sales)		14.22	12.57	14.33	12.33	9.14	7.22	7.11
9									
10									
11									
12									
13									
14									
15									
16									
17									
18									
19									
20									
21									
22									
23									
24									
25									
26									
27									
28									
29									
30									
31									

Figure 6.5 Changing costs with quality management programme

Solution

The easiest way of judging the quality management programme is to calculate the total cost of quality as a percentage of sales. The results for this are shown in the spreadsheet in Figure 6.5.

The quality management programme was introduced in year zero. This put more emphasis on prevention and appraisal, where costs have risen. Product quality has risen, giving lower failure costs. Customers have apparently noticed the improvement, with sales no longer falling but rising sharply. Overall, quality costs have fallen and sales have risen, so we must judge the programme a success.

Review questions

6.6 Higher quality inevitably comes at a higher cost. Do you think this is true?

6.7 How would you find the total cost of quality?

6.8 Why do internal failure costs decline with increasing quality?

6.9 How would you find the best level of quality for a product?

OPERATIONS IN PRACTICE

Pinefresh Sprays

Pinefresh Sprays is based around New York, where it makes a range of scented products in spray cans. These include hair sprays, deodorants and room fresheners. John Kantz was recently appointed as the director of quality assurance, with clear instructions to improve the quality of the company's products. John spent the first few weeks talking to people and trying to find the real problems with quality.

An obvious problem was the production department's aim of meeting output quotas at almost any price. John quickly found an example of this with over-pressurised cans. A quality inspector had rejected some sprays that were over-filled and asked the operator to set them aside until she could find the cause of the problem. The production supervisor was concerned about his schedule and told the operator not to bother with these faults, but to release a little pressure from the cans and ship them out as usual.

When the quality inspector began to investigate, she found that the pressure gauge on the filling machine was not working properly, the spray can nozzles delivered by a regular supplier were not up to standard, the production supervisor was judged by the number of cans produced – but not the quality – and the machine operator was new and not fully trained.

Total quality management

Aiming for perfect quality

It is easy to say that organisations can minimise their costs by aiming for perfect quality, but as you can imagine this may be very difficult to achieve in practice. Perhaps an obvious starting point is to use more rigorous inspections to detect faults. For many years this was the main tool for controlling quality. Then some organisations realised that, 'you can't inspect quality into a product' and they found a better alternative. This is based on the simple observation that the best way to improve quality is not to inspect production and discard defective units, but to make sure that no defects are made in the first place.

Then **quality management** becomes the broad function that is responsible for ensuring quality, while **quality control** is a more limited function that does statistical sampling and testing. Quality control is still important, but its purpose has changed from inspecting units to find the defects that are known to be there, to confirming that there really are no defects being made (we will discuss this in the next chapter).

The important point about quality management is that it is not organised as a separate function, but is an integral part of all operations. Suppose you go to a tailor and order a suit. You will only be satisfied if the suit is well designed, if it is well made, if there are no faults in the material used, if the price is reasonable, if the salesperson is helpful, if the shop is pleasant, and so on. This means that everyone in the tailor – from the person who designs the suit to the person who sells it, and from the person who owns the organisation to the person who keeps it clean – is directly involved in the quality of their product. This is the view taken by **total quality management** (TQM).

Total quality management has the whole organisation working together to guarantee, and systematically improve, quality. The aim of TQM is to satisfy customers by making products with **zero defects**.

Proctor and Gamble summarise this by saying: 'Total quality (management) is the unyielding and continually improving effort by everyone in the organisation to understand, meet and exceed the expectations of customers'.[1]

Japanese manufacturers developed many of the ideas behind TQM. In the 1940s they had been disrupted by wars, plant and equipment were out of date, productivity was low and their domestic markets had been destroyed. To start rebuilding its industry, Japan made cheap, low-quality imitations of products from other countries. Over time, living standards rose and operating costs became higher. It became increasingly difficult to make cheap products, so Japanese manufacturers began to concentrate on more expensive ones with high added-value. They were obviously successful and by the 1970s dominated world markets in motor cycles, consumer electronics, cars, machine tools, steel, computer equipment, shipbuilding, banking, etc.

Japan's success came from making products that were not only competitively priced, but were clearly of better quality. Studies in the early 1980s found that air conditioners made in the United States had 70 times as many defects on the assembly line as those made in Japan, and had 17 times as many breakdowns in the first year of operation. A US manufacturer of television sets had 150 defects per 100 completed sets, and was trying to compete with Japanese companies that averaged 0.5 defects. US manufacturers of car components had warranty costs 10 times higher than their Japanese counterparts. In 1977 Hertz reported that its fleet of Chevrolets needed 425 repairs per 100 vehicles in the first 12,000 miles of operation, while its Toyotas needed 55 repairs.

Organising for TQM

The first step in TQM is to realise that processes can be designed to guarantee high quality, so there are no excuses for poor quality. Then achieving perfect quality is a strategic issue, which involves the whole organisation.

As everyone is involved with TQM, the functions of quality management move back to the people who actually do the work. Quality management stops being a separate function and becomes an integral part of the process, with production departments taking responsibility for their own quality. This moves the emphasis away from inspections at the end of the process to focus on:

- operations during the process itself, to make sure that no defects are being produced; and
- planning stages before production, to make sure that designs allow high quality.

With more effort concentrated at the beginning of the process, organisations avoid the high costs of failures nearer the end, as shown in Figure 6.6.

If production departments are responsible for their own quality, you might ask what the quality management people to do. The answer is that they spend less time on routine inspections and more on facilitating. They work with customers, operations, marketing, engineers, and anyone else, to look for ways of improving products and processes.

Transferring quality management from a separate department to become an integral part of the process does not mean that different people simply do the same inspections. It is part of a fundamental change in an organisation's attitude towards quality. You can imagine the effects on people working on a process. Each person becomes responsible for only passing on units that are of perfect quality. This is **quality at source**. It involves **job enlargement** for each person who is now responsible for both his/her previous job and an inherent quality management function. If anyone finds a fault, it means that something has gone wrong. With quality at source, everyone has the authority to stop the process and investigate. They find the

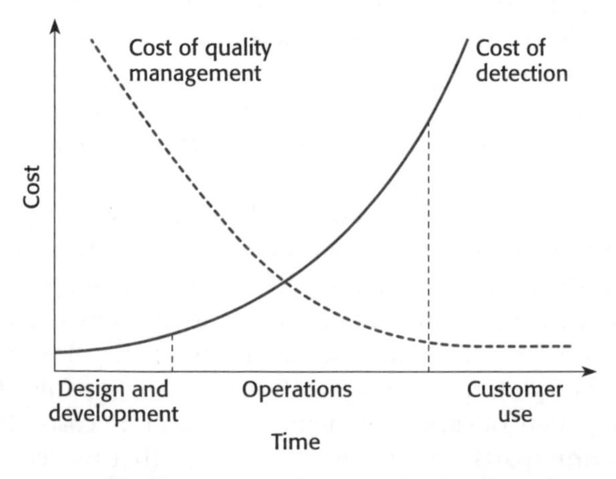

Figure 6.6 Moving quality management to the start of the process avoids the high cost of later failures

Table 6.1 Different attitudes introduced by TQM

Criteria	Traditional attitude	New attitude with TQM
Importance	quality is a technical issue	quality is a strategic issue
Cost	high quality costs money	high quality saves money
Responsibility	quality assurance department	everyone in the organisation
Attitude	inspect quality in	build quality in
Emphasis	detecting defects	preventing defects
Target	meet specifications	continuous improvement
Defect level	acceptable levels	zero defects
Defined by	organisation	customers

cause of the fault and suggest ways of avoiding it in the future. This is in marked contrast to traditional operations that only stop the process as a last resort, and the cause of the fault then goes unnoticed until the problem becomes severe. Some other changes in attitude with TQM are shown in Table 6.1, while Figure 6.7 summarises some of the results.

People and TQM

People working with TQM need a variety of new skills. They must, for example understand some statistics so that performance analyses can be displayed and everyone knows how well each operation is working. They must also be able to notice, analyse and solve any problems as quickly as possible. Moving this kind of responsibility down to those working directly on the operations means that fewer supervisors are needed and the organisation becomes flatter (reinforcing the trend that we have already mentioned).

TQM also affects the way people are paid. Traditionally people have been paid for the number of units they made, often regardless of quality. TQM says that they should also be rewarded for quality, encouraging them to do good work. People might also be rewarded for making suggestions for improvement. These might be collected through suggestion boxes or informal progress meetings. Other suggestions might be collected in **quality circles**. These are informal, voluntary groups of about 10 people who meet regularly to discuss ways of improving their process and raising product quality. A typical quality circle meets for an hour once or twice a month, and they might discuss a problem that is affecting quality, discuss alternatives for improvements, examine comments put into a suggestion box, suggest modifications to designs, and so on.

Developments such as quality circles can give considerable benefits, but they rely on the people involved. In particular, they need:

- a well-educated workforce capable of recognising, analysing and solving problems;
- people who are able and willing to exchange ideas;
- people who see themselves as working for the good of the organisation;
- managers who are willing to share information about operations and costs;
- devolved management that can implement suggested improvements.

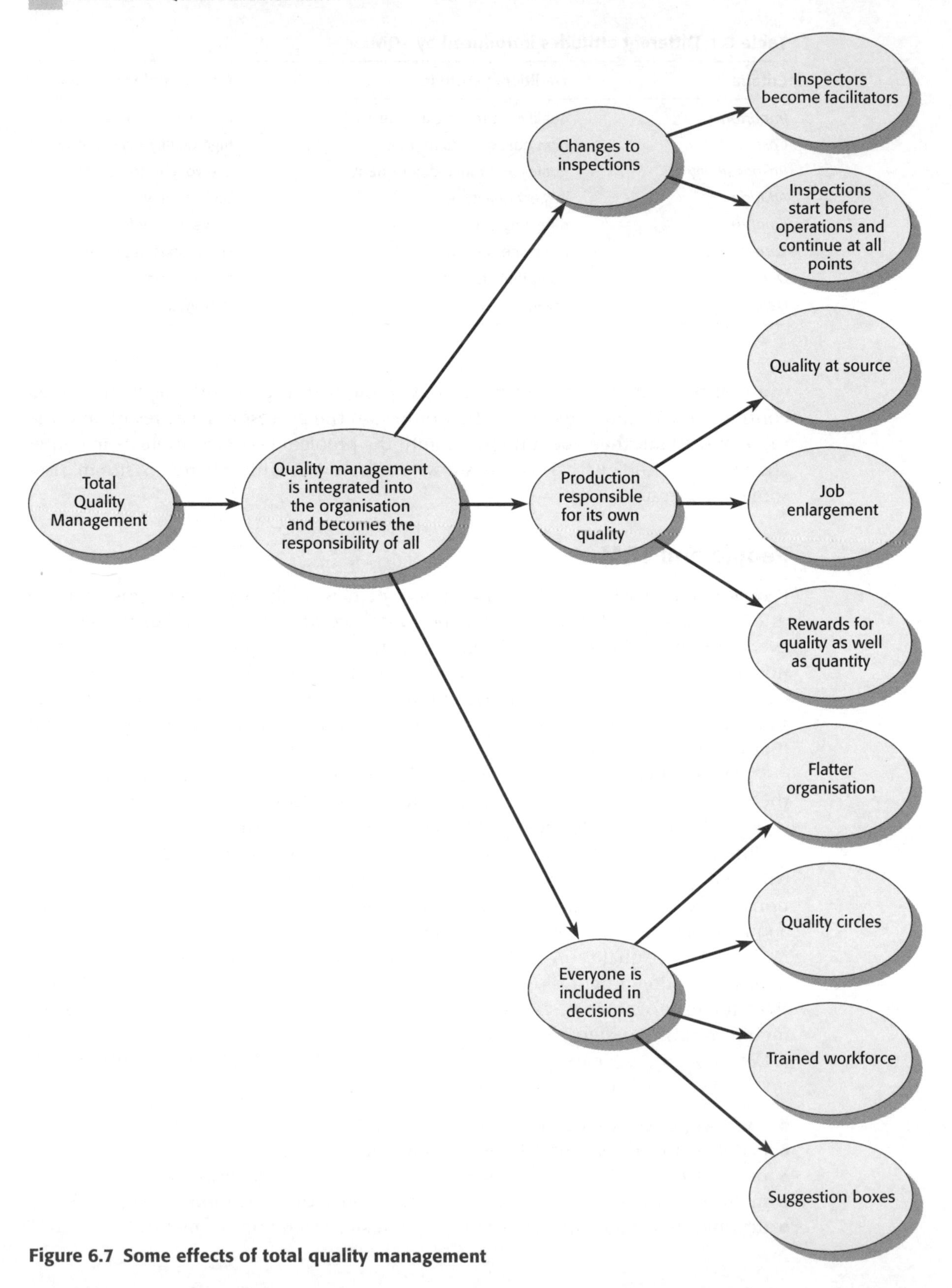

Figure 6.7 Some effects of total quality management

OPERATIONS IN PRACTICE

Total quality management

There are many stories about the benefits gained by the first companies to introduce TQM. Most of these are anecdotal, as shown in the following examples.

- Japan Steel Work Hiroshima Plant began work on TQM in 1977. Between 1978 and 1981 production rose 50 per cent; the number of employees fell from 2,400 to 1,900; the accident rate fell from 15.7 per million man-hours to 2.3; the cost of defects fell from 1.57 per cent of sales to 0.4 per cent; and the number of suggestions per employee rose from 5.6 a year to 17.6.
- In 1984 Ford of America had been running its 'Quality is job 1' programme for five years. During this period the number of warranty repairs dropped 45 per cent; faults reported by new owners fell 50 per cent; its share of the US market rose to 19.2 per cent; sales rose 700,000 units in a year to 5.7 million units; pre-tax profits rose to $4.3 billion; annual operating costs fell by $4.5 billion.
- Within one year Hewlett-Packard's Computer Systems Division increased direct labour productivity by 40 per cent; faults with integrated circuits fell from 1,950 parts per million to 210; faults with soldering fell from 5,200 parts per million to 100; and faults in the final assembly fell from 145 parts per million to 10.

'Quality gurus'

Edwards Deming was an American who visited Japan in the late 1940s to promote his ideas on productivity improvement and quality management. He found a receptive audience in Japan, but was largely ignored everywhere else. In 1979 he gave a seminar on quality management in the USA, which attracted an audience of 15. By 1984 the movement towards quality had started and Deming's seminar attracted 1,700 people, with 3,800 the following year.

Many other people encouraged the development of quality management, and a group of them have become known as the 'quality gurus'. Different people claim to be in this group, but the main members are:

- *Edwards Deming,*[2] who emphasised the role of management in setting quality and the importance of reducing variability in the process.
- *Armand Fiegenbaum,*[3] who looked at failure costs and developed the idea of 'total quality' involving everyone in the organisation.
- *Joseph Juran,*[4] who emphasised the role of senior management and the definition of good quality as satisfying customer demand.
- *Philip Crosby,*[5] who analysed the total costs of quality and described straightforward methods for implementing quality management.
- *Genichi Taguchi,*[6] who showed the importance of product designs that allow high quality, with suitable control of the process.
- *Kaoru Ishikawa,*[7] who emphasised the contribution of 'workers' to quality and introduced the idea of quality circles.

Review questions

6.10 What is the difference between quality control and quality management?

6.11 TQM means that quality is totally controlled by production departments. Do you agree with this?

6.12 What is meant by 'quality at source'?

6.13 What are the benefits of TQM?

OPERATIONS IN PRACTICE

Standard Aero

Standard Aero is an engine repair company. Bob Hamaberg became its president in 1996 and soon realised that the company was inefficient and heavily dependent on US government contracts. If it was to survive, Standard Aero had to change the way it worked.

Hamaberg knew that Standard Aero did not currently give a high-quality service, so he decided to introduce TQM. He formed a team of nine members from various departments, who decided that TQM should be gradually phased into the organisation, starting with the T56 Allison turboprop engine line.

The team's first job was to find out what customers really wanted. The team spent two months and $100,000, and to its surprise found that customers' main concerns were not cost and workmanship, but lead times and ease of doing business.

Standard Aero decided that it wanted to be twice as good as the next best company, so it set a target of overhauling a T56 in 15 days compared to the industry average of 75 days and the industry best of 35 days. The team studied, analysed, simplified and improved the engine overhaul process, and reduced the process from 213 steps to 51, cutting 93 per cent of non-chargeable steps and 80 per cent of the distance travelled.

When the company bid for a $10 million contract to overhaul gearboxes for the US military, the company was 50 per cent below the competition with a much shorter delivery date. The Pentagon would not believe the bid, so it sent a team of 13 senior officers to inspect the company. The officers liked what they saw and Standard Aero was awarded the contract. Hamaberg firmly believes they only won because of TQM.

You can find more information at *www.standardaero.com.*

Project 6.2

Find a product that you have been particularly pleased with. Describe the aspects of its quality that you like. How many of these can you measure? How many people – from initial designers through to the person who delivered it – were involved in supplying this high-quality product? How could you make the product even better?

Implementing total quality management

Deming's 14 principles of quality management

TQM needs major changes to an organisation. We have already mentioned some of these, including a reorganised quality management function, involved workforce, quality at source, devolved decisions, quality circles, and so on. Actually achieving these changes can be very difficult. Deming spent 40 years developing his ideas of TQM and compiled a list of 14 'principles', which give some guidelines for implementation.

Deming's 14 principles

1. Create constancy of purpose towards product quality.
2. Refuse to accept customary levels of mistakes, delays, defects and errors.
3. Stop depending on mass inspection, but build quality into the product in the first place.
4. Stop awarding business on the basis of price only – reduce the number of suppliers and insist on meaningful measures of quality.
5. Develop programmes for continuous improvement of costs, quality, productivity and service.
6. Institute training for all employees.
7. Focus supervision on helping employees to do a better job.
8. Drive out fear by encouraging two-way communication.
9. Break down barriers between departments and encourage problem solving through teamwork.
10. Eliminate numerical goals, posters and slogans that demand improvements without saying how these should be achieved.
11. Eliminate arbitrary quotas that interfere with quality.
12. Remove barriers that stop people having pride in their work.
13. Institute vigorous programmes of life-long education, training and self-improvement.
14. Put everyone to work on implementing these 14 points.

These 14 principles show the direction in which organisations should move. They emphasise the fact that managers are in charge of the organisation, and are responsible for quality. People used to assume that poor products were caused by poor workpeople. But this is like blaming drivers when your bus is late – it may be their fault, but it is more likely to be caused by traffic, road works, a breakdown, poor schedules, or some problem in the system that is outside their control. You can think of a process in two parts:

- the *system* over which managers have control, and which contributes 85 per cent of the variation in quality;
- the *workers* who are under their own control, and who contribute 15 per cent of the variation in quality.

Major improvements in quality come from managers improving the system rather than workers improving their own performance. A person working conscientiously to get high quality in a poor system will get worse results than a careless person working in a better system.

Another of Deming's principles is that everybody should be properly trained for their jobs. This seems obvious, but how often have you bought something in a shop and found that cashiers do not know anything about the products, how to serve customers, or even how to use the till properly. This is not their fault, but simply a sign that managers have not done the training properly.

In contrast, many organisations put a lot of effort into training, and become 'investors in people'. When Ford of America introduced TQM, it sent more than 6,000 people on training courses in two years. Ford also realised that it could only make good products if it had good suppliers, so it arranged training for 1,000 of them.

Steps in implementation

Deming gives some general principles for implementing TQM, but we have to translate these into positive actions. There are many ways of approaching this, but a useful one has the following seven steps.

1. *Get top management commitment*, which is usually the key factor. Managers control the organisation, and they must realise that TQM is not another management fad that will disappear in a few months, but is a way of thinking that improves long-term performance. They might formalise these ideas in a 'quality strategy', which sets product quality in the context of other strategic decisions.
2. *Find out what customers want.* We have said that high quality means meeting or exceeding customers' demands, but we can only achieve this if we know exactly what they want. This goes beyond simply asking for opinions and gets customers involved in the process, perhaps discussing designs in focus groups.
3. *Design products with quality in mind.* Products must have the features demanded by customers, and they must also satisfy the internal requirements. There is always some variation between units, and the product designs must be robust enough to allow for these variations and still meet all specifications.
4. *Design the process with quality in mind.* The quality of the final product depends on the process used to make it. The process must work efficiently, giving consistent products with minimal variation and guaranteed perfect quality. One approach to process design includes **poka yoke**. This designs operations that can only be done in the correct way, and it becomes impossible to do things wrongly.
5. *Build teams of empowered employees.* Quality depends on everyone in the organisation. The only way of ensuring high-quality products is to recognise that employees really are an organisation's most valuable asset – and make sure they are trained, motivated, able and willing to make high-quality products.
6. *Keep track of results.* An important point in TQM is that organisations do not stand still, but look for continuous improvement. This is *kaizen*, which we mentioned in the last chapter. Its adjustments to products and processes can have a dramatic effect over time. To monitor these, we need to track various aspects of performance.
7. *Extend these ideas to suppliers and distributors.* Organisations do not work in isolation, but are part of a supply chain. The quality of the final product depends on every link of this chain, so it is important that every related organisation is committed to high quality.

Introducing TQM fully needs a lot of effort over many years. Not surprisingly, many organisations cannot maintain this effort and fail somewhere on the road. There are many reasons for these failures. Perhaps suppliers cannot guarantee the quality of materials; or managers only give lip service to TQM without really becoming committed; or everyone assumes that someone else is dealing with quality; or administration and bureaucracy get out of hand; or the process cannot reduce the variability enough; or people resist the necessary changes.

Many organisations have gained considerable benefits from TQM, but few say that it is easy to introduce. Some go further and say that the benefits are not worth the effort. They argue that they can give high quality by traditional means, and without all the complex procedures of TQM. They even say that TQM puts so much emphasis on the process, that it actually diverts attention away from the quality of the product. Perhaps the most consistent criticism of TQM is that it raises unrealistic expectations; perfect quality is impossible to achieve in practice, so TQM sets targets that can never actually be reached. It is important to discuss all issues of this kind before leaping into the major effort of implementing TQM.

Continuous improvement

You can see from step 6 above, that TQM is not installed in one go and then left alone. **Kaizen** means that it continually evolves, with a series of improvements that can be absorbed without major disruption. Over time these small improvements build a momentum that can give dramatic results.

The iterative improvements come from many sources, such as the quality circles and suggestion boxes that we have already mentioned. Sometimes there is a more formal arrangement, such as the plan-do-check-act cycle, or 'Deming wheel' (shown in Figure 6.8).

This uses a team of people who go through an organisation to find improvements using the cycle of:

- **plan** – looking at the existing operations, collecting information, discussing alternatives, and suggesting a plan for improving operations;
- **do** – where the plan is implemented, and data is collected on performance;
- **check** – which analyses the performance data to see if the expected improvements actually appeared:
- **act** – if there are real improvements the new operations are made permanent, but if there are no improvements, lessons are learnt and the new operations are not adopted.

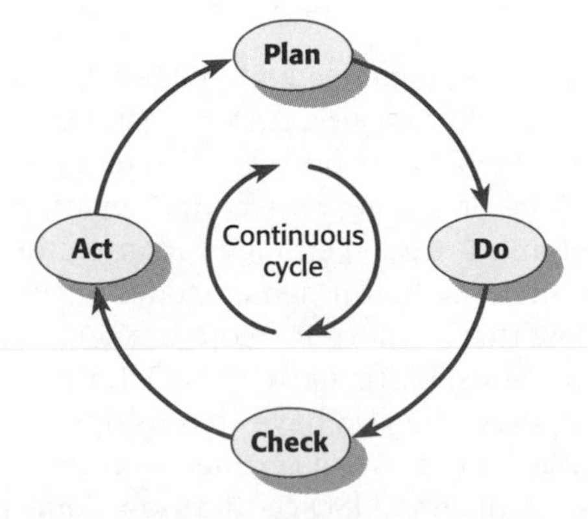

Figure 6.8 Plan-do-check-act cycle

The team is continuously looking for improvements, and at this point the team returns to the beginning of the cycle and starts looking for more improvements.

ISO 9000 standards

When Ford of America introduced TQM, it gave a clear statement that it would only consider suppliers whose feelings towards quality matched its own. Ford is a very large company, and can exert a lot of pressure on suppliers. Other organisations cannot do this, but they still need a way of ensuring suppliers' commitment to quality. This is the purpose of the International Standards Organisation's (ISO) 9000 family of standards. If an organisation can achieve certain quality standards, it can apply for ISO 9000 certification. There are actually five separate standards.

- ISO 9000 defines quality, discusses quality standards that an organisation might aim for, and gives guidelines for their use.
- ISO 9001 is used by organisations that design and make products. It is the most comprehensive of the standards and deals with the whole range of TQM, from initial product design and development, through to standards for inspecting and testing final products.
- ISO 9002 is used by organisations that make standard products and have less involvement in the design – it concentrates on the actual process, and how to document quality.
- ISO 9003 deals with final product inspection and testing procedures.
- ISO 9004 is a guide to overall quality management and related systems, and says how operations can develop and maintain quality.

ISO 9000 and 9004 are guides for organisations starting quality management programmes. ISO 9001, 9002 and 9003 describe what a quality management system must achieve to be certified.

The standards are designed for almost any organisation. Certification is administered by independent third parties who check that an organisation:

- says what it is going to do to ensure high quality, describing its procedures, operations and inspections;
- actually does the work in the ways described;
- proves that the work has been done properly by doing audits and keeping records.

Many people think that the ISO standards guarantee high quality. Unfortunately, this is not true, as they only guarantee *consistent* quality. A manufacturer of plastic pipes, for example, might specify the acceptable limits on the diameter of a pipe. ISO certification means that the pipe is more or less guaranteed to be within these limits, but it does not judge whether the limits are good enough for any intended use.

The main benefits of ISO certification are that it demonstrates organisations' commitment to quality, and shows how they achieve it. More importantly in the long term, a growing number of organisations, particularly those who have certification themselves, will only deal with suppliers who also have certification. It must become increasingly difficult for an organisation that is not certified to compete.

Unfortunately, there are also disadvantages to ISO certification. Some organisations complain about the cost and effort involved in getting certification. Others say that the maintenance of the systems needs too much administration and time. Other complaints are that the standards give too little advice on the best measures of quality, and use terms that are only familiar to manufacturers. In response to such complaints (and in the spirit of *kaizen*), these standards are regularly updated, with new versions published in 2000.

Review questions

6.14 To implement TQM, you have to follow Deming's 14 principles. Is this true?

6.15 Who is responsible for the quality of products?

6.16 How does ISO certification guarantee high-quality products?

6.17 What is the most important factor for implementing TQM?

6.18 What is *kaizen*?

Quality in services

It is often easier to imagine the quality of tangible goods, rather than intangible services. These have features that we can measure, such as the weight of a sack of potatoes or the volume of detergent in a bottle. Then it is relatively easy to check that each unit satisfies some measure of quality. But even with goods there are other intangible factors – such as how the potatoes taste or how the detergent smells – and the overall quality includes subjective judgements.

The problem with services is that there are fewer tangible properties to measure, and more intangible opinions. Ray Kroc, the founder of McDonald's, said that his restaurants should combine 'Quality, Service, Cleanliness, and Value'. Even the most intangible service has some features you can measure – such as the percentage of letters that arrive on time, the space between aeroplane seats, and the number of mistakes in accounts. But these measures are dominated by judgements about:

- reliability and reputation;
- availability;
- responsiveness to customers' needs;
- competence of staff;
- courtesy and helpfulness of staff;
- understanding of customers' needs;
- credibility and standing;
- security;
- comfort of surroundings for customers;
- communication between participants; and
- associated goods provided with the service.

Although we cannot measure many of these features, this does not mean that we cannot tell a good one from a bad one. We may not be able to measure the quality of a haircut, but most of us know when we get a bad one. To give a more specific example, we can look at reports of the UK's rail watchdog (the Central Rail Users' Consultative Committee). In the first full year of privatisation, it reported 260,000

Explicit services – benefits that are readily observable and define the essential features of the service. G & T believes that its staff are the most important part of the service package, and their working hours are scheduled so that no customer has a long wait, even at busy times. All staff have on-the-job training, weekly meetings to discuss products, concerns and plans, and they are encouraged to study product development, sales techniques, etc. G & T aims for a consistent service across its shops, and job training includes the details of services that staff must give to customers.

Implicit services – benefits that are not readily observable but which enhance the customers' experience. G & T attracts the best employees by offering competitive wages, benefits, opportunities for promotion and an attractive workplace. Because of these good conditions, the staff are friendly to customers, proud of their company and enthusiastic about their job. Surveys have found a very high level of customer satisfaction with the staff and shops in general.

You can find more information at *www.grandandtoy.com.*

Chapter review

- It is difficult to give a general definition of quality. A common view suggests that it is the ability to meet – and preferably exceed – customer expectations.
- Quality management is the broad function responsible for all aspects of product quality. It designs products that satisfy customers and other requirements, and then it ensures that products actually meet these specifications.
- There are four components of the cost of quality: prevention, appraisal, internal failure and external failure costs. The failure costs can be particularly high, but fall with increasing quality.
- Organisations can reduce their overall costs by making products with perfect quality. This brings benefits to both customers and the organisation.
- Total quality management focuses the effort of everyone in the organisation on quality. It encourages features like quality at source, quality circles and ISO certification.
- TQM is not a programme with a fixed duration, but needs wider change in the organisational culture. An important part of this is continuous improvement.
- Assuring the quality of services can be particularly difficult, as it relies more on the subjective opinions of customers.

Key terms

achieved quality *p. 119*
appraisal cost *p. 123*
continuous improvement *p. 135*
design costs *p. 122*
designed quality *p. 119*
external and internal failure cost *p. 123*
ISO 9000 *p. 136*
job enlargement *p. 128*
kaizen *p. 135*
prevention cost *p. 122*
quality at source *p. 128*
quality circles *p. 129*
quality control *p. 127*
quality management *p. 119*
total quality management (TQM) *p. 127*
zero defects *p. 127*

CASE STUDY The Great Bake Cake Company

The Great Bake Cake Company is a large supplier of cakes to supermarkets, restaurants and company canteens in eastern Australia. The company makes a range of products that taste reasonably good for their low price.

Two years ago the company narrowly avoided prosecution by a local consumer protection department, when a customer reported a rusty nail in one of Great Bake's cakes. The company was not prosecuted because of its good record and rigorous quality-control procedures.

Quality is checked by the quality control department, which does a series of inspections and tests. Ingredients are brought from national suppliers and cause almost no concern. None the less, they are given a visual inspection before being mixed into batches. There are further tests on each batch after mixing, before baking, after baking, after finishing and after packing. Most of these tests concern taste and appearance, and make sure the products are consistent and meet design specifications.

Recently the company has been having some difficulties. In particular, the number of customer complaints has risen by 15 per cent over the past two years, and there are now around 80 complaints per million sales. Most of these complain about taste, but occasionally there are foreign bodies or other serious faults. The company has responded by increasing the quality control budget by 20 per cent, employing more inspectors and making the inspections more rigorous. It is a joke with the baking staff that they now have an inspector looking over each shoulder.

As an experiment, managers of the company deliberately introduced faults into 20 cakes as they passed through the process. Quality control inspectors only found 12 of these before they were due to leave the bakery.

Questions

- How can the Great Bake Cake Company assess the quality of its products?
- How do you think the company can start looking for improvements?

Problem

A company had the following costs (in thousands of pounds) over the past six years. Describe what has been happening.

Year		1	2	3	4	5	6
Sales value		623	625	626	635	677	810
Costs	Design	6	8	18	24	37	43
	Appraisal	15	17	22	37	45	64
	Internal failure	91	77	32	36	17	10
	External failure	105	101	83	51	27	16

Discussion questions

6.1 What are the consequences of poor quality products? How could you find the costs involved? How accurate are these costs likely to be?

6.2 Who is the best person to define the quality of a product, and what criteria might he/she use? Who else might be involved?

6.3 Do you think it is reasonable for organisations to aim for perfect quality? Would the costs of achieving this be too high?

6.4 Explain, giving suitable examples, the difference between designed and achieved quality. Why are they different, and which is more important?

6.5 Is Deming's the only view of quality management? Do the 'quality gurus' say the same things in different ways?

6.6 There are now more concerns with the quality of services rather than the quality of goods. Why do you think this is? How can service quality be improved?

6.7 Describe the development of quality in a specific product you are familiar with, such as computers, education, health, cars, houses, etc.

6.8 What incentive is there for a monopoly to improve the quality of its product?

6.9 Honda believes that it cannot make exceptional products by using the same manufacturing processes as other companies, so it designs and builds its own manufacturing systems. These manufacturing systems are designed for two groups of customers:

- external customers who buy Honda products;
- internal customers who use the systems to make these products.

Do these two groups have different aims and views about quality? Could there be conflicts between the two? Do other organisations have to balance the needs of different customers?

References

1. Proctor and Gamble (2000) *Annual Report.*
2. Deming W.E. (1986) *Out of the Crisis*. Cambridge, MA: MIT Press.
3. Fiegenbaum A. (1983) *Total Quality Control*. New York: McGraw-Hill.
4. Juran J.M. (1988) *Juran on Planning for Quality*. New York: Free Press.
5. Crosby P.B. (1979) *Quality is Free*. New York: McGraw-Hill.
6. Taguchi G. (1986) *Introduction to Quality Engineering*. Tokyo: Asian Productivity Association.
7. Ishikawa K. (1985) *What is Total Quality Control?* Englewood Cliffs, NJ: Prentice-Hall.
8. Yuille M. (1998) '103% Increase in Rail Complaints', *The Express*, 27 August.
9. Anon. (1998) 'Level of Complaints Rise, So Office Cuts Hours', *The Cornishman*, 19 November.

Selected reading

Evans J.R. and Lindsay W.M. (1996) *The Management and Control of Quality*. 3rd edn. St Paul, Minneapolis: West Publishing.

Ghobadian A., Gallearr D., Woo H. and Liu J. (1998) *Total Quality Management*. London: Chartered Institute of Management Accountants.

Heaphy M. and Gruska G. (1995) *The Malcolm Baldridge National Quality Awards*, Reading, MA: Addison-Wesley Longman.
Ho S. (1999) *Operations and Quality Management*. London: International Thomson Business Press.
Kehoe D.F. (1996) *The Fundamentals of Quality Management*. London: Chapman and Hall.
Oakland J.S. (1992) *Total Quality Management*. 2nd edn. London: Heinemann.
Ramaswamy R. (1996) *Design and Management of Service Processes*. Harlow: Addison-Wesley Longman.
Rust R.T. and Oliver R.L. (eds) (1994) *Service Quality*. London: Sage Publications.
Thomas K. (1996) *How to Keep ISO 9000*. London: Kogan Page.
Whitford B. and Bird R. (1996) *The Pursuit of Quality*. London: Prentice-Hall.

Useful Websites

www.asq.org – the American Society for Quality
www.iso.org – International Standards organisation
www.qualitydigest.com – a useful magazine

CHAPTER 7

Quality control

If you turn out a superior product, it will be patronised by the public. Our policy is not simply to turn out a product because there is a demand, but to turn out a superior product and create demand.

Siochiro Honda

Journal of Commerce, 6 November 1965, p. 23

Contents

Aims of the chapter

After reading this chapter you should be able to:

- see how quality control forms part of the broader function of quality management;
- appreciate the variation in a process;
- understand the role of inspections and quality control;
- use sampling distributions and design sampling plans;
- organise acceptance sampling;
- use control charts for process control.

Main themes

This chapter will emphasise:

- **quality control**, which does the independent tests that make sure designed quality is actually being achieved;
- **samples**, which are used to test quality;
- **acceptance sampling** to check the quality of a batch of products;
- **process control** to make sure that a process continues to work properly.

Controlling quality

The last chapter showed how total quality management (TQM) has the whole organisation focused on making products with perfect quality. Then quality becomes a strategic issue, and top management set the overall goals and policies. Middle managers translate this strategy into medium-term tactics and implement the policies. Then junior managers make the short-term decisions to monitor and control quality. This gives a general structure for quality management shown in Figure 7.1.

Product variability

No matter how good the operations are, there will always be some variation in the products. Differences in materials, weather, tools, employees, moods, time, stress and a whole range of other things combine to give these, apparently random, variations. The variations may be small, but they are always present. This is why marathon runners never finish a series of races in exactly the same times, and products never finish their process with exactly the same performance.

The design of products and processes must be robust enough to allow for such variations, and still give perfect quality. The traditional way of arranging this is to give a tolerance in the specifications. Provided that a unit's performance is within a specified range, it is considered acceptable. A 250 g bar of chocolate might weigh between 249.9 g and 250.1 g and still be considered the right weight. A unit is only considered faulty if its performance is outside this tolerance, as shown in Figure 7.2.

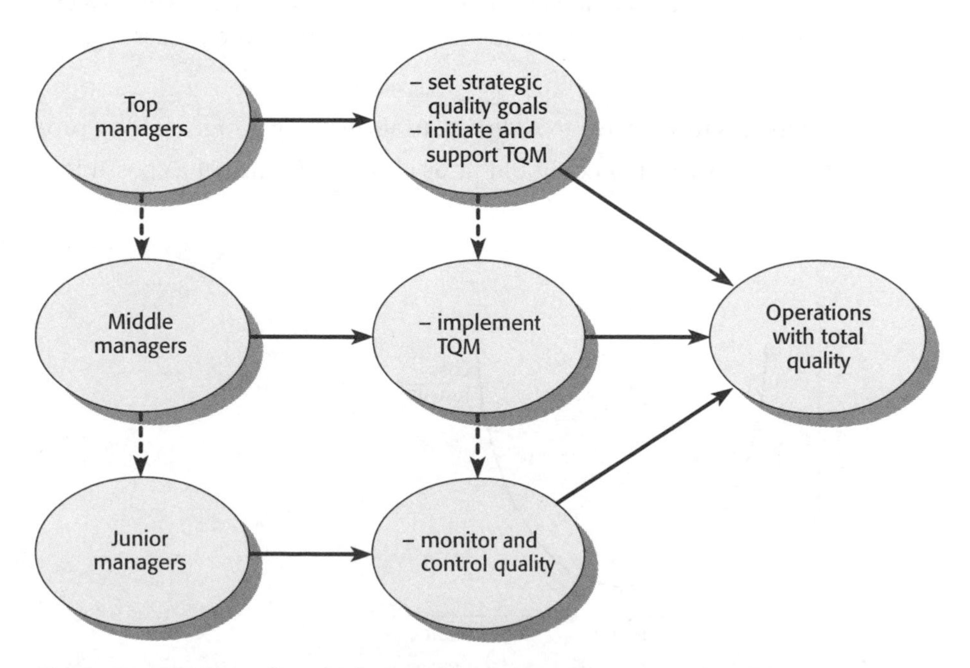

Figure 7.1 TQM has the whole organisation working towards perfect quality

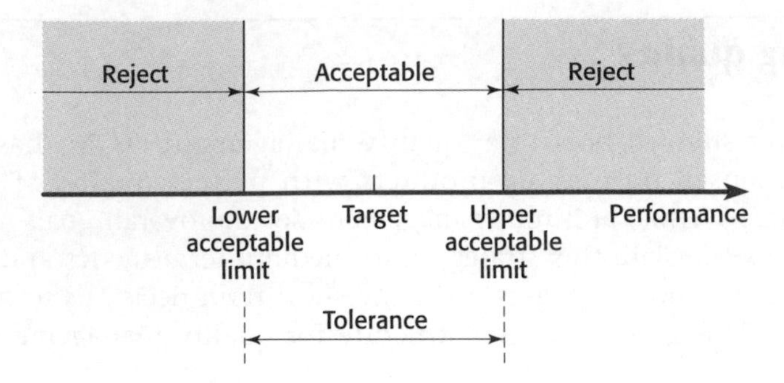

Figure 7.2 Traditional view of acceptable performance

Unfortunately, Genichi Taguchi[1] pointed out that this approach has an inherent weakness. Suppose a bank sets the acceptable time to open a new account as between 20 and 30 minutes. If the time taken is 20, 25 or 30 minutes, the traditional view says that these are equally acceptable – the process is achieving its target so there is no need for improvement. But customers would probably not agree that taking 30 minutes is as good as taking 20 minutes. On the other hand, there might be little real difference between taking 30 minutes (which is acceptable) and 31 minutes (which is unacceptable). The answer, of course, is that there is not such a clear cut-off. If you are aiming for a target, then the further you are away from the target, the worse your performance is. We can describe this effect in a **loss function**, which gives a notional cost of missing the target (see Figure 7.3).

Organisations should clearly aim at minimising the cost in this loss function, and this means getting the actual performance as close to the target as possible. To achieve this, they have to reduce the variability in the process.

- Organisations have to **reduce variability** to get high-quality products.
- Actual performance should be as **close to the target** as possible.

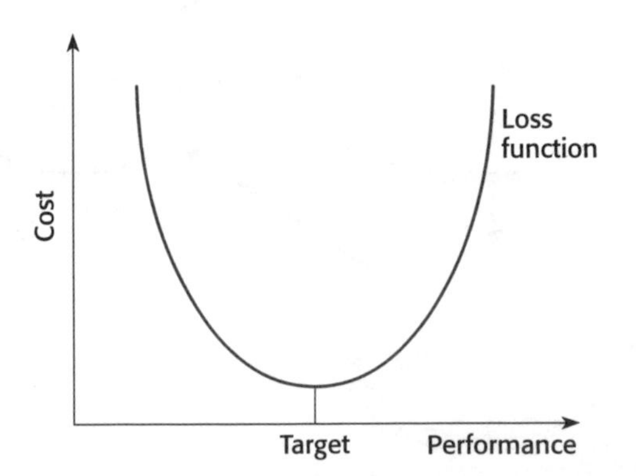

Figure 7.3 Loss function gives the cost of not achieving the specified target

An organisation can only check the amount of variation by monitoring performance over time. It has to inspect units, test them, make sure that everything is working properly and check that the variation between units is small. This is the purpose of **quality control**.

Quality control uses a series of independent inspections and tests to make sure that designed quality is actually being achieved.

With quality at source, no defective units should be made. So, the purpose of quality control is not to find faults, but to give independent evidence that the process is working properly and that there really are no defects.

OPERATIONS IN PRACTICE

Health insurance and Unisys

Unisys Corporation was founded in 1986 when Sperry and Burroughs merged. It now has a revenue of over $7 billion and works in 100 countries. For over 40 years the companies in Unisys have supplied computers and computer services to government departments in the USA. They have contracts with all 50 state governments and over 900 local governments. They deliver public assistance benefits in eight of the 10 largest states, and process 250 million tax returns a year. Unisys companies clearly have immense experience of running computer services for governments.

Government employees in Florida have a health insurance programme that pays their medical costs. Unisys had been processing the claims for this programme for many years. Then in 1996 it won a contract to provide systems for more of the business, organising doctors and hospitals.

Competitors appealed against the decisions to award the contract to Unisys, and although the appeal was lost, it reduced the amount of time available for development. Then, when the system was introduced, there were clearly problems. To start with, there seemed too many cases where Unisys and its subcontractors gave conflicting information to customers. There were also problems with the security of customer information. Then there were too many insurance claims with mistakes in the processing (the industry standard allows errors in 3.5 per cent of claims, but an audit found that Unisys made errors in 8.5 per cent). There were also problems with timing. The contract with Unisys specified that at most 5 per cent of claims should take longer than 30 days to process. A sample of one month's claims showed that 13 per cent of claims took Unisys more than 30 days.

Florida's Department of Manpower Services looked at the performance of the system and found that Unisys was not meeting agreed performance standards.

Source: Bernstein, N. 'Giant companies entering race to run state welfare programs' in *New York Times*, 15 September 1996; You can find more information at *www.unisys.com*.

Cause of faults

If everything is working properly, quality control inspections should not find any faults. If they do find a defective unit, it means that something has gone wrong with the process. Then we should find the cause of the problem and correct it before any more defects are made. Typical causes of faults are:

- human errors of various kinds;
- machine faults, perhaps caused by poor maintenance;
- poor materials;
- faults in operations, such as speed or temperature changes;
- changes in the environment, such as humidity, dust or temperature;
- errors in monitoring equipment, such as errors in measuring tools.

It is often surprisingly difficult to find the cause of a fault. Sometimes you can repeatedly ask questions until the cause becomes clearer. A session of this kind might run as follows.

Question: What is the problem?
Answer: A customer complained because we couldn't serve her.
Question: Why?
Answer: Because we had run out stock.
Question: Why?
Answer: Because our suppliers were late in delivering.
Question: Why?
Answer: Because our order was sent in late.
Question: Why?
Answer: Because the purchasing department got behind with all its orders.
Question: Why?
Answer: Because it used new staff who were not properly trained.

By this point it is clear that something has gone wrong in the purchasing department, and with more questions you could pinpoint the cause of the problem more accurately. For obvious reasons, this approach is called the 'five whys' method. Other ways of finding the cause of problems use simple diagrams, such as **cause-and-effect diagrams** and **Pareto charts**.

A cause-and-effect-diagram (sometimes called an ishikawa diagram) shows the possible causes of a problem in a **fish bone diagram**. Suppose a customer complains at a hamburger restaurant. The problem may be caused by the raw materials, the cooking, the staff or the facilities. Problems with the raw materials may, in turn, be caused by suppliers, storage or costs. A cause-and-effect diagram draws these relationships as coming from spines, like fish bones, as shown in Figure 7.4.

Cause-and-effect diagrams are usually drawn by a team of people – typically the members of a quality circle – who are familiar with the problem. Laying out the possible causes of faults in this form allows the team to analyse the problem and find ways of overcoming it.

Pareto charts use the observation that 80 per cent of problems come from 20 per cent of causes. So Woolworth's might find that 80 per cent of customer complaints come from 20 per cent of its products. A Pareto chart lists the possible causes of problems, counts the number of faults that come from each, and shows the results on a bar chart. Then managers can concentrate on those areas that need special attention.

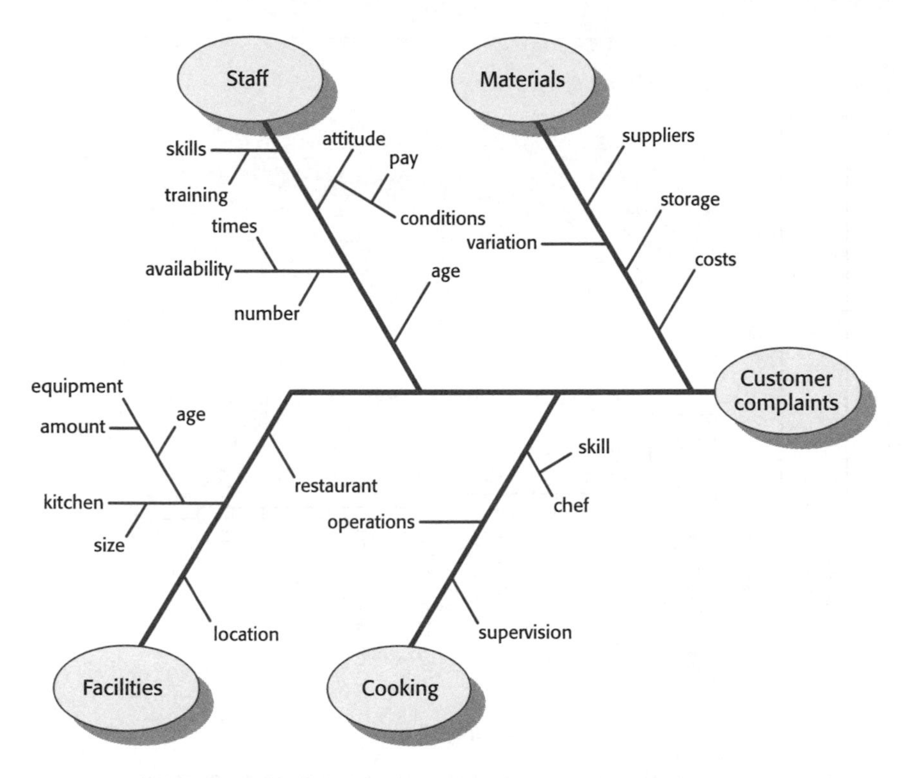

Figure 7.4 Cause-and-effect diagram for a complaint at a hamburger restaurant

OPERATIONS IN PRACTICE Freemantle Restaurant

The Freemantle Restaurant is a well-established business near the centre of Manchester. It serves business lunches, and there is a healthy demand for its high-quality, expensive dinners. Paul Samson is the owner of Freemantle, and looks after all the administration personally. There are few complaints from customers, but Paul always keeps a record of them. Over the past three years he has collected the following figures.

Cause	Number of complaints	Percentage of complaints
Faults in the bill	80	51
Slow service	31	20
Smokers too near non-smokers	19	12
Comfort of the chairs	11	7
Wine	5	3
Temperature of the restaurant	5	3
Wait for a table	2	1
Too limited a menu	2	1
Food: ingredients	2	1
Food: cooking	1	1

From this data, Paul drew the Pareto chart in Figure 7.5.

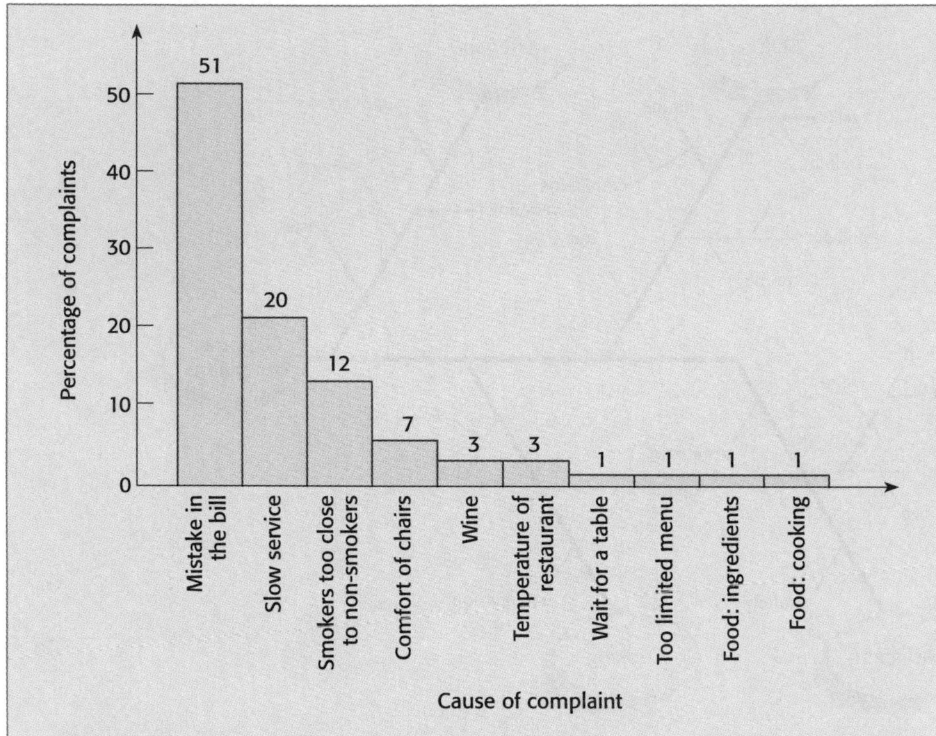

Figure 7.5 Pareto chart for the cause of complaints at Freemantle Restaurant

This highlights the main areas for concern. There were almost no complaints about the food, so customers were clearly pleased with what they were eating. Over half of the complaints came from faults in the bill. Paul reduced these by installing a new computerised cash register. Sometimes the service was slow, particularly at busy times or when one of the staff was away. Paul contacted an agency that could provide waiters at very short notice. These two measures alone dealt with almost three-quarters of complaints. When the restaurant needs refurbishing, Paul could get some more comfortable chairs and increase the size of the non-smoking area. This would deal with another 19 per cent of complaints. By these simple procedures, Paul had dealt with 90 per cent of complaints.

Review questions

7.1 The best way to get high-quality products is to have a lot of inspections to find faults. Do you think this is true?

7.2 What is the difference between quality control and quality management?

7.3 What is a loss function?

7.4 What is the purpose of quality control?

Project 7.1

Find a product that clearly has a fault – perhaps congestion at an Internet service provider (ISP), a cancelled train, or poor response in some other service. See if you can find the real – rather than the apparent – cause of this fault. What are the alternatives for correcting the fault? Which of these seems best?

Timing of inspections

Traditionally, most effort was put into quality control in the later stages of the process, often just before finished products were delivered to customers. At first, this might sound sensible, as all faults can be found in one big **inspection**. However, as we saw in the last chapter, the longer a unit is in a process, the more time and money is spent on it. This means that faults should be found as early as possible, before any more money is wasted on a defective unit. It is, for example, cheaper for a baker to detect bad eggs when they arrive, rather than use the eggs in cakes – and then scrap these when they fail a later inspection. The main effort in quality control should be at the beginning of the process. Organisations should test materials as they arrive from suppliers, and there is also a strong case for inspections to start within suppliers' own operations (see Figure 7.6).

After this early start, there should be a series of inspections all the way through the process, right up to the delivery of final products to customers. If the main effort is started early enough, there should be very few defects in the later stages. Certainly by the time the product gets to the customer it should be as nearly free from errors as possible.

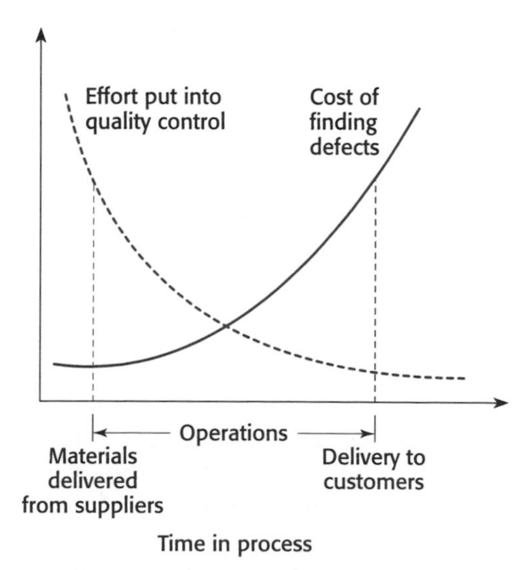

Figure 7.6 Quality control should start early when the cost of finding defects is low

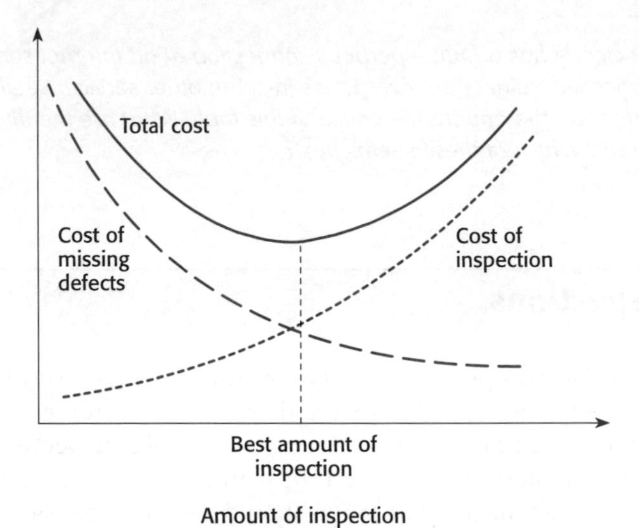

Figure 7.7 Finding the best amount of inspection

There are some specific points in a process where inspections are most useful, including:

- *for raw materials*
  - during material suppliers' operations;
  - on arrival at the organisation;
- *during the process*
  - at regular intervals during the process;
  - before high-cost operations;
  - before irreversible operations, such as firing pottery;
  - before operations that might hide defects, such as painting;
- *for finished products*
  - when production is complete;
  - before shipping to customers.

Inspections are an essential part of quality management, but it is possible to have too many. Each inspection raises costs, and there comes a point where the benefit is less than the costs involved. Ideally, we could analyse costs to find an optimal number of inspections, as shown in Figure 7.7.

WORKED EXAMPLE

Svenson Electrics make light fittings on an assembly line. When the electric wiring is fitted, faults are introduced to 4 per cent of units. An inspection at this point would find 95 per cent of these faults, with costs of £1 for the inspection and £1.50 to correct a fault. Any fault not found continues down the line and is detected and corrected later at a cost of £10.

Without the inspection after wiring, later tests cost an extra £0.60 a unit and each fault corrected costs £20. Is it worth inspecting light fittings when the wiring is fitted?

Solution

We can answer this by comparing the expected cost per unit of doing the inspection and not doing it.

1. With an inspection after wiring the expected costs per unit are:
   - Cost of inspection = £1.00
   - Cost of faults detected and corrected after wiring
     = proportion of faults detected × cost of repairing each
     = 0.04 × 0.95 × 1.5 = £0.057
   - Cost of faults not found until later
     = proportion not detected × cost of later repair
     = 0.04 × (1 – 0.95) × 10 = £0.02

   This gives a total of 1.00 + 0.057 + 0.02 = £1.077 a unit.

2. Without an inspection after wiring the costs per unit are:
   - Additional cost of later inspection = £0.60
   - Faults detected and corrected
     = proportion with faults × cost of repair
     = 0.04 × 20 = £0.80

   This gives a total of 0.60 + 0.80 = £1.40 a unit.

It is clearly cheaper to do an inspection when the wiring is fitted and correct faults as soon as they are found.

Review questions

7.5 When should checks for quality be started in a process?

7.6 Inspections find faults, so the more the better. Do you agree with this?

Sampling

Why take samples?

Inspections often test every unit that passes through a process. Walls, for example, automatically weigh every packet of sausages they produce. Such complete testing is often impossible. Car manufacturers have to test the strength of their cars during impacts, but they obviously cannot test every car or they would have none left to sell. In these cases, quality control relies on a sample of units. If this sample performs well, it is assumed that every unit made is also acceptable: if the sample performs badly, something has gone wrong and the organisation has to check its operations.

Reasons for testing samples rather than the whole output include:

- *Destructive testing*. If you want to find the average life of light bulbs, you could test all production, but would have none left to sell.
- *Expense*. Each test may be expensive, and if the number of defects is small, the cost is not worthwhile.
- *Time needed*. Some tests are so long or complicated that they could not be fitted into normal operations.
- *Reliability*. Testing all the units does not necessarily give better results than a sample. No inspection is completely reliable as there are random variations; inspectors become tired; people make mistakes; automatic tests develop faults; and so on.
- *Feasibility*. In some cases there is an infinite number of tests that could be done. To completely test the effectiveness of a medicine, it must be given to everybody who might take it, in all possible circumstances. This would give an almost infinite number of possible combinations.

There are clearly good reasons for using a sample, but we have to use some formal procedure. A general approach has the following steps:

1. Set the features that you are going to measure.
2. Define the acceptable quality – or tolerance – for each measure.
3. Set a sample size and number of units that must reach the acceptable quality.
4. Take a sample – usually random – of units.
5. Measure the features for each unit in the sample and see how many reach the acceptable quality.
6. Say that the product is satisfactory if more than the specified number of units reach the acceptable quality.
7. Say that the product is unsatisfactory if fewer than the specified number of units reach the acceptable standard.

There are many variations on this general approach, but no sampling can ever be completely accurate. An inspection might reject good products because the sample has an unexpectedly large number of defects, and it might accept bad products because the sample has an unexpectedly small number of defects. Suppose, for example, materials arrive in batches of 100 units, and each batch has an average of 10 defects. If you inspect samples of 10 units from each batch, you would expect about one defect in each sample. But there will be random variations, and in the extremes you could take a sample with either 10 defects or none. On the whole, the sample should give a reasonable view of a batch, but it can never be completely accurate.

The way to get more accurate samples is to make them bigger: essentially the larger the sample the more reliable the results. Unfortunately, bigger samples are more expensive, and we have to look for a compromise. We want a sample that is big enough to be accurate and representative of all units, but small enough to be reasonable and cost effective. We will see how to do this in the following section.

OPERATIONS IN PRACTICE

Stroh Brewery Company

Until 1999 when it sold its brands, the Stroh Brewery Company was the third largest producer of beer in the USA. One of its plants was the Winston-Salem brewery, which occupied over 100,000 square metres and made 200 million gallons of beer a year.

Quality control of beer was rigorous, with the brewery checking everything from taste to the quantity in each can. For this it employed 38 people in three separate laboratories for microbiology, brewing and packaging. These people did 1,100 separate tests on each batch of beer. If they found problems, the quality control department stopped production and investigated.

A typical test in the brewing laboratory took a small sample during fermentation, diluted it, and counted the yeast cells. (Beer must have a standard 16 million yeast cells (± 2 million) per millilitre of beer.)

A typical test in the packaging laboratory checked the amount of air in a beer can. Because air can affect the taste, the company allowed a maximum of 1 cc of air in a can. This was checked by testing three cans from the production line, five times a shift. If a sample was found with more than 1 cc of air, the entire batch was put into 'quarantine' and systematically tested to find the point where the canning went wrong. As each line filled 1,600 cans a minute, this was potentially a lot of testing.

Sampling distributions

One of the key decisions in sampling sets the sample size and number of units that must have an acceptable quality. To find these, we have to use some statistics. In statistical terms, all the units made form the **population** of units. We take representative samples from this population. Because of random variations, there will always be some variation between the samples.

Imagine that you have a warehouse full of boxes of apples that claim an average weight of 25 kg. You could pick a random sample of five boxes, weigh them, and you would not be surprised if the average weight was 25.2 kg. You could repeat this, and find that following samples had average weights of 24.8 kg, 25.1 kg and 25.0 kg. If you took more samples, the mean weight would follow a distribution. This is called the **sampling distribution of the mean**.

The sampling distribution of the mean has three useful properties:

- If the population is normally distributed, or if a sample of more than about 30 is used, the sampling distribution of the mean is normally distributed.
- The mean of the sampling distribution of the mean equals the mean of the population, μ.
- The standard deviation of the sampling distribution of the mean is $\sigma/\sqrt{n}$, where σ is the standard deviation of the population and n is the sample size.

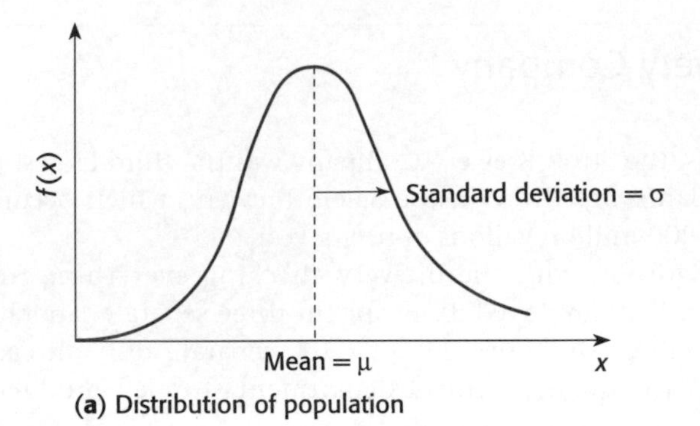

(a) Distribution of population

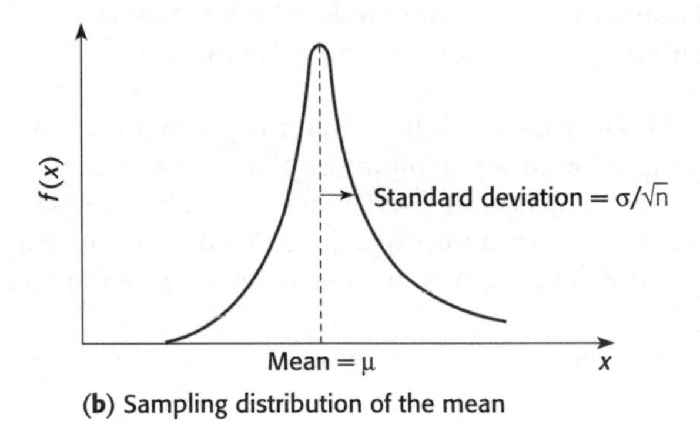

(b) Sampling distribution of the mean

Figure 7.8 Comparison of the population distribution and the sampling distribution of the mean

This third property confirms our view that larger samples give more reliable results (see Figure 7.8).

WORKED EXAMPLE

Midland Steel makes pipes with a mean length of 100 cm and a standard deviation of 1 cm. What is the probability that a random sample of 35 pipes has a mean length of less than 99.6 cm?

Solution

With a sample size of 35 the sampling distribution of the mean is normally distributed with a mean of 100 cm and a standard deviation of $\sigma/\sqrt{n} = 1/\sqrt{35} = 0.169$ cm. So, the sampling distribution of the mean is normally distributed with mean 100 cm and standard deviation 0.169 cm.

The number of standard deviations 99.6 cm is from the mean is:

$$Z = (100 - 99.6)/0.169 = 2.37$$

This corresponds to a probability of 0.0089, as shown in Figure 7.9. So, 0.89 per cent of samples will have a mean length of less than 99.6 cm.

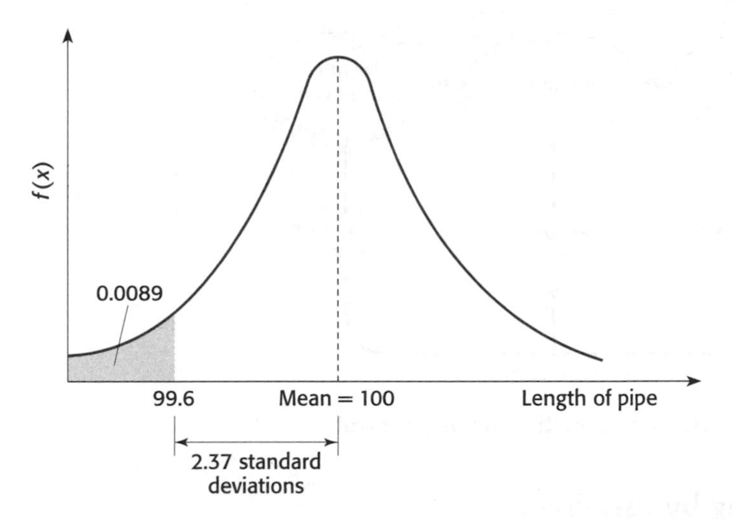

Figure 7.9 Sampling distribution of the mean for worked example

Review questions

7.7 Why are samples used?

7.8 Are the results from statistical sampling completely accurate?

7.9 What is the sampling distribution of the mean?

Project 7.2

Find a product with some feature that you can measure, such as the time to serve customers in a shop. How can you measure the variation in the population? Take samples from the population and find the sampling distribution of the mean. Do these follow the patterns you expected?

Acceptance sampling

Sampling distributions are used for two types of **statistical quality control**.

- **Acceptance sampling** tests the quality of a batch of products. It takes a sample of units from a batch, and tests to see whether the whole batch should be accepted or rejected.
- **Process control** tests the performance of the process. It takes a sample to see if the process is working within acceptable limits or if it needs adjusting.

Acceptance sampling looks for faulty units and checks the actual quality of products; process control looks for problems with the process, and is more concerned with the prevention of faults. We will start by looking at acceptance sampling, and move on to process control in the next section.

Acceptance sampling checks the quality of a batch of products. It tests a sample of units to see if the batch is likely to reach designed quality.

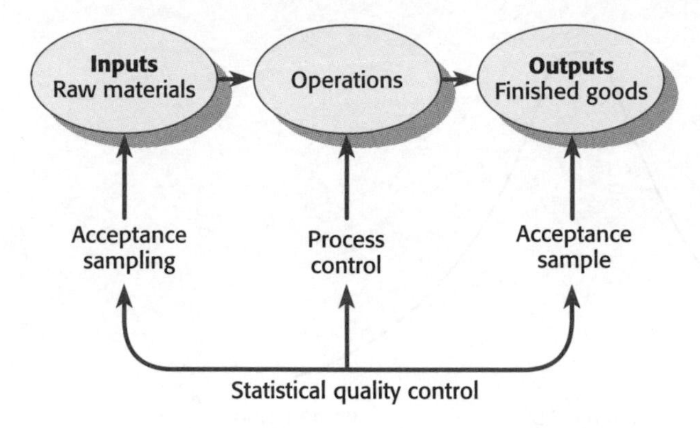

Figure 7.10 Types of statistical quality control

Sampling by variables

Suppose we are interested in some continuous property, such as the weight, length, time or strength. We can take a sample and find the average performance of this property. Then we can use the sampling distribution of the mean to see if this sample is likely to come from a good batch, or whether the batch should be rejected. This is called **sampling by variables**.

WORKED EXAMPLE

Batches of raw materials arrive at a factory with a specified average weight of 25 kg a unit and standard deviation of 1 kg. A sample of 20 units is taken to test each delivery. Within what range should 95 per cent of the sample means lie?

Solution

We can use the standard results given above for a variable:

	Population	Sampling distribution of the mean
Mean	μ	μ
Standard deviation	σ	$\sigma/\sqrt{n}$

The mean weight of samples is normally distributed with mean, $\mu = 25$ kg and standard deviation $= \sigma/\sqrt{n} = 1/\sqrt{20} = 0.224$ kg.

95 per cent of samples will be within 1.96 standard deviations of the mean, giving a range of:

$$25 + 1.96 \times 0.224 = 25.44 \text{ kg} \quad \text{to} \quad 25 - 1.96 \times 0.224 = 24.56 \text{ kg}$$

Sampling by attributes

The alternative to sampling by variables is called **sampling by attributes**. This needs some criterion of quality that allows us to describe a unit as either 'acceptable' or 'defective'. Sometimes this criterion is obvious. A light bulb either works or it does not; boxes either contain at least 1 kg of soap powder or they do not; a train either arrives on time or it does not. Sometimes the criterion relies less on measurement and more on judgement. A piece of furniture, for example, may be rejected because its polished finish does not look good enough to an experienced inspector.

A standard result shows that if the proportion of defective units in a population is p, the proportion of defects in samples of size n is:

- normally distributed;
- with mean = p; and
- Standard deviation = $\sqrt{\frac{p(1-p)}{n}}$

WORKED EXAMPLE

Imperial Motor Insurance uses outside contractors to check details of its policies. It insists that the contractors make errors in less than 4 per cent of policies. One day Imperial receives a large shipment of policies from the contractors. It taks a sample of 200 policies and checks them. What criterion should Imperial use to reject a batch if it wants to be 97.5 per cent sure of not making a mistake?

Solution

If the proportion of errors is 4 per cent, $p = 0.04$. In samples of size n, the proportion of defective units is normally distributed with:

- Mean $p = 0.04$;

and

- Standard deviation = $\sqrt{p(1-p)/n} = \sqrt{(0.04 \times 0.96/200)} = 0.014$.

95 per cent of sample proportions are within 1.96 standard deviations of the mean, so 95 per cent of samples have proportions of defects between:

$$0.04 + 1.96 \times 0.014 = 0.067 \quad \text{and} \quad 0.04 - 1.96 \times 0.014 = 0.013$$

With a sample of 200, 95 per cent of batches will have a number of defects between:

$$200 \times 0.067 = 13.4 \quad \text{and} \quad 200 \times 0.013 = 2.6$$

Only 2.5 per cent of batches will have more than 13.4 defects by chance. If the company rejects batches with more than this, it can be 97.5 per cent sure of making the right decision.

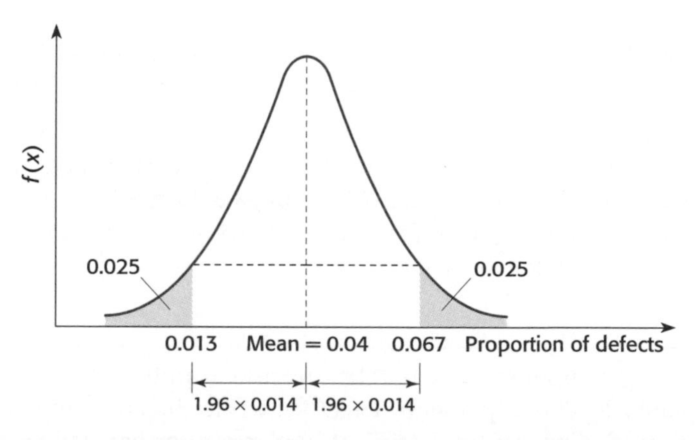

Figure 7.11 Range for accepting a batch in worked example

Designing an acceptance sampling plan

Now we have looked at the probabilities behind acceptance sampling, and we can start designing a **sampling plan**. For the simplest form of sampling plan outlined above, key decisions are the sample size, n, and the maximum allowed number of defects in the sample, c. To a large extent, the values for c and n are a matter of policy, relying on managers' judgements about acceptable levels of quality.

Of course, you might ask why *any* defects are allowed when we are aiming for perfect quality. The usual answer is that the producer specifies higher quality levels than the customer. Then the producer can still classify units as 'bad', even though customers would happily accept them.

We want batches with few defects to have a high probability of acceptance, and batches with more defects to have a high probability of rejection. The subjectivity comes with setting exactly what we mean by a 'high probability' and 'few defects'. In practice, we can set these with four related measures.

- **Acceptable quality level** (AQL). This is the poorest level of quality that we will accept – or the maximum proportion of defects that allows us to describe a batch as 'good'. We should accept any batch with fewer defects than AQL. Figures of around 1 per cent are often quoted here.
- **Lot tolerance per cent defective** (LTPD). This is the quality that is unacceptable – or the highest proportion of defects that customers are willing to accept in a batch. We should reject any batches with more defects than LTPD.

We want to accept any batch with a proportion of defects lower than AQL. There is always uncertainty in the sampling, so we really aim at a low probability of rejecting a good batch with fewer defects than AQL. We can formalise this statement by defining:

- **Producer's risk** (α). This is the highest acceptable probability of rejecting a good batch, with fewer defects than the AQL. This is typically set around 5 per cent.

Similarly, we want to reject any batch with a proportion of defects higher than LTPD. Again, the uncertainty means that we really aim at a low probability of accepting a bad batch with more defects than the LTPD. We can formalise this statement by defining:

- **Consumer's risk** (β). This is the highest acceptable probability of accepting a bad batch, with more defects than LTPD. This is typically set around 10 per cent.

Using these four measures we can use standard analyses to find values for n, the sample size, and c, the maximum number of allowed defects. A huge amount of work has been done on quality control statistics, and we do not have to duplicate this. The easiest way of finding values for n and c is to use a standard quality control package, many of which are available.

WORKED EXAMPLE

A company buys components in batches from a supplier. The supplier uses an acceptable quality level of 2 per cent defective, while the company accepts batches with a maximum of 6 per cent defective. What are appropriate values of n and c?

Solution

From the values given, we can assume that $AQL = 0.02$ and $LTPD = 0.06$. A standard program finds the values for n (165) and c (6) as shown in Figure 7.12.

Title: **Design of Quality Control Sampling Plan**

For: Attribute sampling

Data entered:	AQL =	0.02		acceptable quality level
	LTPD =	0.06		lot tolerance percent defective
	α =	0.05		producers' risk
	β =	0.10		consumers' risk
Critical values:	LTPD/AQL =		3.00	
	Inferred c =		6	maximum number of defects
	n × AQL =		3.29	
	Inferred n =		165	sample size

Sampling plan: Take a samples of 165 units from a batch.
If 6 or less units are defective accept the batch.
If more than 6 units are defective reject the batch.

1.	n = 165	c = 6	α = 0.050	β = 0.100

Sensitivity and alternative plans:

2.	n = 165	c = 6	α = 0.051	β = 0.137
3.	n = 176	c = 6	α = 0.067	β = 0.099
4.	n = 200	c = 7	α = 0.051	β = 0.090
5.	n = 197	c = 7	α = 0.048	β = 0.098

Figure 7.12 Printout for the design of a sampling plan

Operating characteristics

The aim of a sampling plan is to accept good batches and reject bad ones. Unfortunately, the variation in samples means that this separation cannot be perfect. The **operating characteristic** (OC) curve shows how well a sampling plan actually separates good and bad batches.

An OC curve shows the probability that a sampling plan accepts batches with different proportions of defects. Each combination of n and c has a distinct curve with the general shape shown in Figure 7.13. The shape of this curve is set by two points, one defined by AQL and α, and the second defined by LTPD and β.

We would like a clear distinction between good and bad batches, so the OC curve should be as steep as possible. Ideally it would be vertical, differentiating perfectly between a good batch (with a probability of acceptance of one) and a bad batch (with a probability of acceptance of zero). The way to get a steep curve is to take large samples. Even if the proportion of defects remains the same, taking a larger sample will give more reliable results, as shown in Figure 7.14.

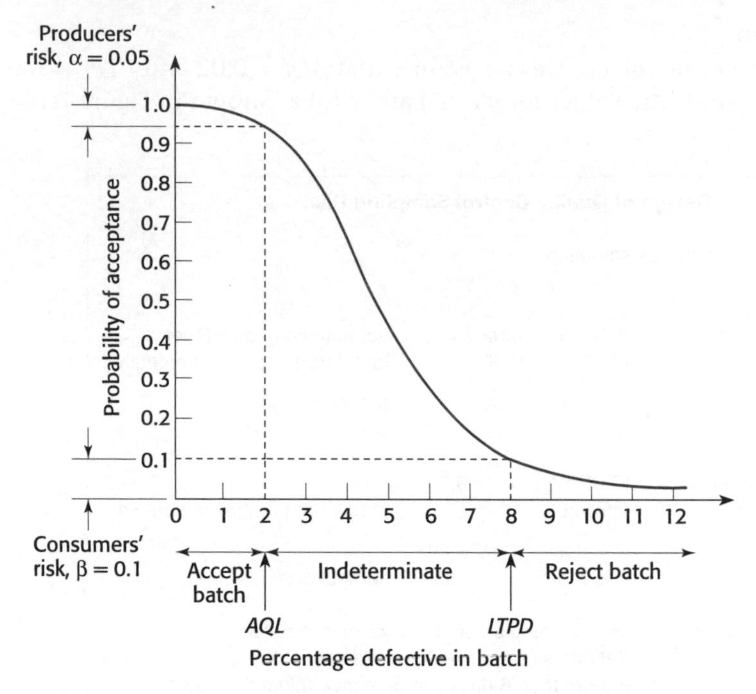

Figure 7.13 Typical operating characteristic curve

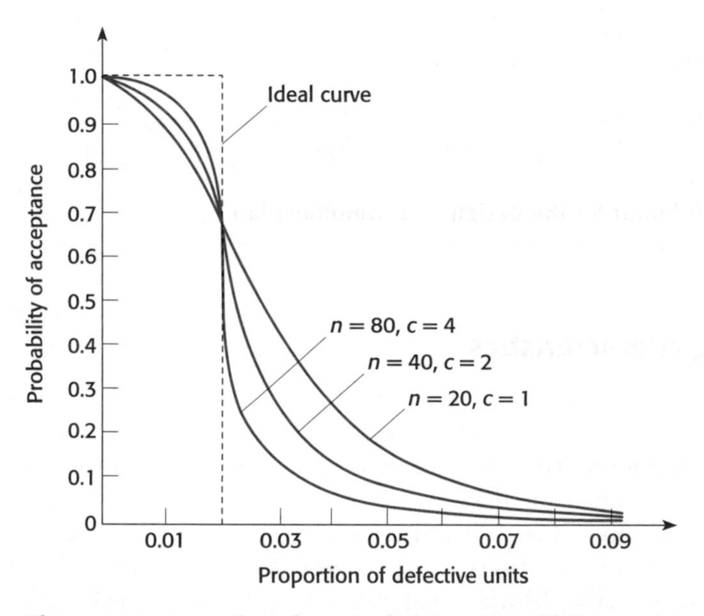

Figure 7.14 Operating characteristic curves with increasing sample size

The operating characteristic curve shows how poor batches are more likely to be rejected than good ones. By selectively rejecting low-quality batches we improve the overall quality of the output. This raises the obvious question: How good is the quality of the remaining output? The answer is defined as the **average outgoing quality** (AOQ).

The **average outgoing quality** is the expected proportion of defects that passes through a sampling plan.

When the proportion of defects in the population, *p*, is small, most batches are accepted and AOQ is low (remembering that AOQ refers to the expected proportion of **defects**). As *p* increases, the AOQ also rises, but most batches are still better than the AQL, and the sampling plan continues to accept them. As *p* rises further, more batches are rejected, particularly those with a lot of defects, and the AOQ begins to fall. With high values of *p*, most batches are rejected and the AOQ is again low. This pattern is shown in Figure 7.15.

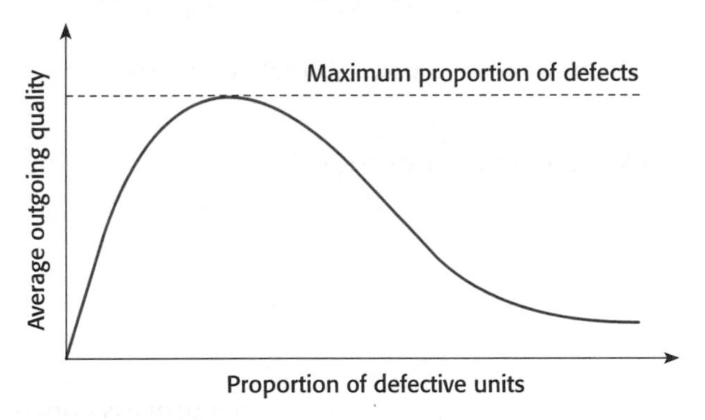

Figure 7.15 Variation in AOQ with proportion of defective units

Review questions

7.10 What is the difference between acceptance sampling and process control?

7.11 What is the difference between sampling by attribute and sampling by variable?

7.12 What are α and β and why are they used?

7.13 Why is an ideal operating characteristic curve vertical?

7.14 Average outgoing quality must increase as average product quality increases. Do you think this is true?

OPERATIONS IN PRACTICE

Summerview Stoneground Mill

Summerview Stoneground Mill produces wheat and corn flour. Most of its production is put into 25 kg bags and is sold to commercial customers, such as bakeries, hotels and restaurants.

One week the operations manager, Paula Lam, received a couple of complaints from customers. One of the complaints said a recent delivery of bags did not seem very full. The second was more specific, and said that a delivery of 10 bags weighed only 246 kg. Both of these batches came from the same day's production.

Paula immediately checked the procedures for testing the weight of bags. Tim Price, the quality manager, explained:

At the beginning of a run we weigh a few bags, and adjust the machines until they are filling properly. Then the process is largely automatic, so we don't weigh any more samples. We do a visual inspection of all bags to check the seams and stitching. This would also find any bags that look a bit light. If the operator thinks the machines are not filling properly, he'll take some samples and weigh them.

Many organisations use an informal approach to quality control, but this rarely gives good results.

Process control

Process control is the second type of statistical quality control.

Process control checks samples of units to make sure that the process continues to work as planned.

Process control makes sure that the random variation in a process stays within acceptable limits. It does this by taking samples over time to see if there are any noticeable trends. If there is a clear trend, or poor individual results, the process needs adjusting. The easiest way of showing the results is in a **process control chart**.

Control charts for attributes

We will start looking at control charts for attributes, where outcomes are either 'good' or 'bad'. For this we take a series of samples over time and plot the proportion of defective units in each. This gives a **p-chart**.

The proportion of defective units in a sample is usually close to the proportion of defective units in the population. Provided that it does not vary far from this value, the process is working normally. If there is a sudden jump in the proportion of defects, or a trend away from the mean, the process is out of control and needs adjusting. To see when this happens, we need two limits: an **upper control limit** (UCL) and a **lower control limit** (LCL). If the proportion of defects stays between these two limits, the process is under control; if it moves outside the limits, it is out of control (as shown in Figure 7.16).

For sampling by attributes, we can use the standard result we met earlier; if the proportion of defects in a population is p, the proportion of defects in a sample of size n is normally distributed with mean, p, and standard deviation of $\sqrt{(p(1-p)/n)}$. If the process is working properly, 95 per cent of samples have a value of p within 1.96 standard deviations of the mean. Only 5 per cent of samples are outside this range, so finding one means that there is a good chance that something is wrong with the process. We can use this result to define the control limits.

- Upper control limit = $UCL = \mu + 1.96 \times$ standard deviation
- Lower control limit = $LCL = \mu - 1.96 \times$ standard deviation

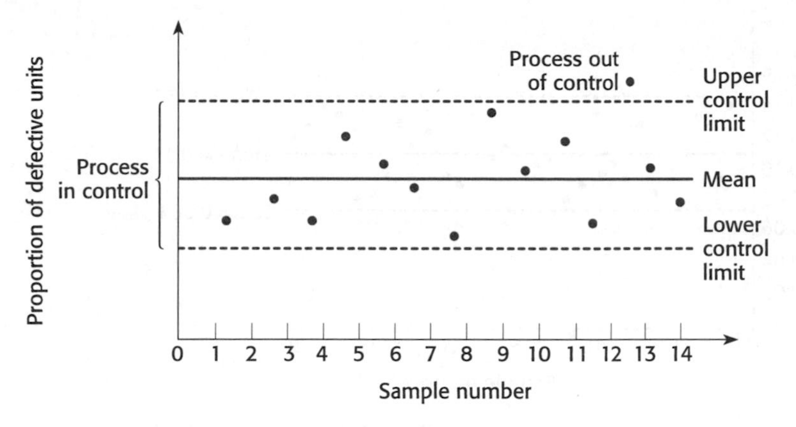

Figure 7.16 A typical process control chart

WORKED EXAMPLE

June Springwell collected a random sample of 500 units from a process for each of 30 working days when it was known to be working normally. She tested these samples and recorded the number of defective units as follows.

Day	Number of defects	Day	Number of defects	Day	Number of defects
1	70	11	45	21	61
2	48	12	40	22	57
3	66	13	53	23	65
4	55	14	51	24	48
5	50	15	60	25	42
6	42	16	57	26	40
7	64	17	55	27	67
8	47	18	62	28	70
9	51	19	45	29	63
10	68	20	48	30	60

Draw a control chart with 95 per cent confidence limits.

Solution

The average proportion of defects is:

$$p = \frac{\text{total number of defects}}{\text{number of observations}} - \frac{1{,}650}{30 \times 500} = 0.11$$

$$\text{Standard deviation} = \sqrt{p(1 - p)/n} = \sqrt{(0.11 \times 0.89/500)} = 0.014$$

Then the control limits are:

- $UCL = p + 1.96 \times$ standard deviation $= 0.11 + 1.96 \times 0.014 = 0.137$
- $LCL = p - 1.96 \times$ standard deviation $= 0.11 - 1.96 \times 0.014 = 0.083$

The process is working normally while the proportion of defects stays between 0.083 and 0.137. If it goes outside this range, the process has gone out of control and needs adjusting (see Figure 7.17).

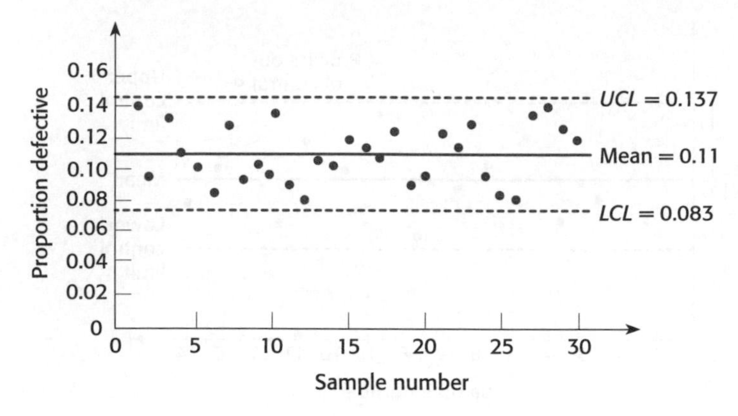

Figure 7.17 Control chart for proportion of defects in worked example

Some observations will lie outside the control limits purely by chance. So when a sample gives an unexpected result, we have to check whether the process is really out of control, or whether it is an unusual result from a process that is still working normally. Apart from a single reading that is outside the control limits, some other results that need investigating include:

- a clear trend;
- several consecutive readings near to a control limit;
- several consecutive readings on the same side of the mean;
- a sudden change in readings;
- very erratic observations.

Control charts for variables

We can also use process control charts for sampling by variables. We again define upper and lower control limits that are a number of standard deviations from the mean, but now we find the standard deviation using the sampling distribution of the mean.

WORKED EXAMPLE

Karen Henrisch makes packaged food with a mean weight of 1 kg and standard deviation of 0.05 kg. She takes periodic samples of 10 units to make sure the process is still in control. Find the control limits that include 99 per cent of sample means.

Solution

Using standard results, we know that the sampling distribution of the mean is normally distributed with:

Mean = 1 kg and Standard deviation = $\sigma/\sqrt{n} = 0.05/\sqrt{10}$

99 per cent of samples are within 2.58 standard deviations of the mean, so:

- $LCL = \mu - 2.58 \times \sigma/\sqrt{n} = 1 - 2.58 \times 0.05/\sqrt{10} = 0.959$
- $UCL = \mu + 2.58 \times \sigma/\sqrt{n} = 1 + 2.58 \times 0.05/\sqrt{10} = 1.041$

If the mean of samples stays within this range, the process is in control. If the mean moves outside the range, it is out of control and needs checking.

An obvious problem in the last example is that we used the mean and standard deviation of the population, which is all of the output. With samples, however, we do not check all the output, so are unlikely to know these values. The usual way around this is to approximate the population mean and standard deviation by the sample mean and standard deviation. Then to give another check, we add a second control chart to record the ranges of samples (the range is simply the difference between the biggest observation and the smallest). Then we have two charts and can plot:

- the series of sample means on an *X* chart;
- the series of sample ranges on an *R* chart.

As always, these calculations are best done using any statistical package, as shown in the following example.

WORKED EXAMPLE

Samples of 10 units were taken from a process in each of the past 20 days. Each unit in the sample was weighed, and the means and ranges found. The data were put into a standard package, with the results shown in Figure 7.18.

Title: Process Control Chart

For: Variable sampling

Data entered:

Sample	Mean	Range	Sample	Mean	Range
1	12.2	4.2	11	12.5	3.3
2	13.1	4.6	12	12.3	4.0
3	12.5	3.0	13	12.5	2.9
4	13.3	5.1	14	12.6	2.7
5	12.7	2.9	15	12.8	3.9
6	12.6	3.1	16	12.1	4.2
7	12.5	3.2	17	13.2	4.8
8	13.0	4.6	18	13.0	4.6
9	12.2	4.3	19	13.2	5.0
10	12.0	5.0	20	12.6	3.8

Totals: for means = 252.9 for ranges = 79.2

Sample size: 10

Means: for means = 12.65 = M for ranges = 3.96 = R

Factors for control limits: A = 0.31 D1 = 0.22 D2 = 1.78

For X chart of means:

- LCL = M − A × R = 11.42
- UCL = M + A × R = 13.88

For R chart of ranges:

- LCL = D1 × R = 0.87
- UCL = D2 × R = 7.05

Figure 7.18 Computer printout of control limits for worked example

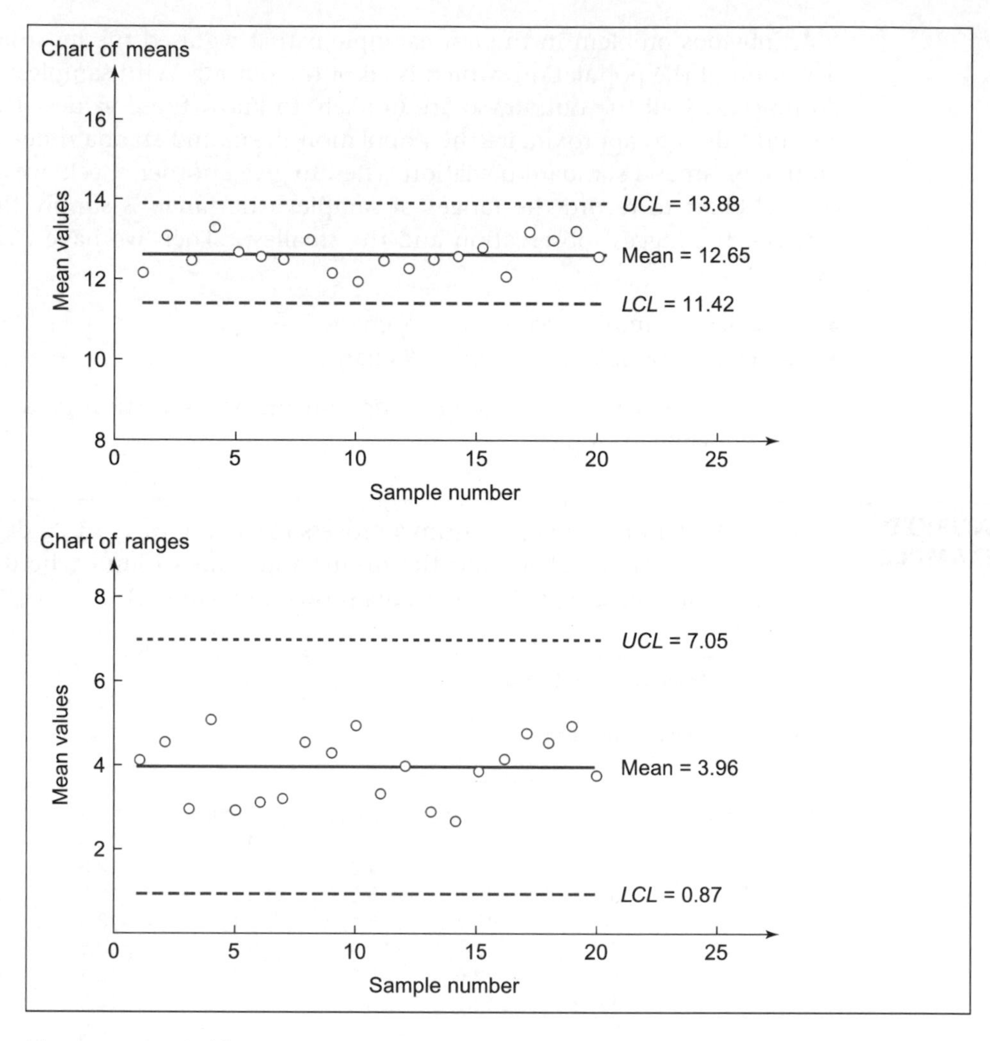

Figure 7.18 cont'd

Solution

The program automatically calculates the upper and lower control limits for the means and ranges. Provided that future samples keep within these ranges, the process is in control, but if they move outside these ranges, the process is out of control.

Review questions

7.15 What does it mean if an observation is outside the control limits in a process control chart?

7.16 What patterns should you investigate in a control chart?

7.17 Why would you use an *R* chart?

OPERATIONS IN ACTION

Running times

Today's Runner published a reader's method for checking if your times for running a given distance were changing. This had the following seven steps:

1. Keep a record of your times to run the distance.
2. Take the first eight to 15 times.
3. Find the average of these times, μ.
4. Calculate the differences between each pair of consecutive times.
5. Find the average of these differences, d.
6. Calculate an upper control limit as: $\mu + 2.66 \times d$
7. Calculate a lower control limit as: $\mu - 2.66 \times d$

If your time is below the lower limit, you are getting faster: if it is above the upper limit, you are getting slower.

Source: Day M. (1999) 'Teacher's Pet', *Today's Runner*, March.

Project 7.3 *There is a lot of commercial software for statistical quality control. Look at a selection of this and see what analyses the programs do. Record the actual output from some real process. Now use the software to see how easy it is to use, how useful it is, and how well it explains the results.*

Chapter review

- Quality management aims for perfect quality, but even the best processes have some variation. High quality only comes by reducing the amount of variation and keeping actual performance close to the target.
- Quality control is an important part of quality management. It is responsible for the sampling, inspecting and testing needed to ensure that planned quality is actually being achieved.
- Inspections and tests are done throughout the process, with the main emphasis at the start where errors are less expensive to correct.
- Quality control is usually based on random samples from the population of units. These are tested to check either the quality of a batch of products or the performance of the process.
- Acceptance sampling checks that a batch of products reaches the designed quality standards. Typically, this takes a single random sample from a batch and checks that the number of defects is below a maximum permitted number.
- Sampling is also used to check that a process continues to work normally. Process control draws charts to plot the performance of a series of samples over time.

Key terms

CASE STUDY
West Midland Electronic Car Component Company

David Brown is the Quality Control Manager of West Midland Electronic Car Component Company. On Tuesday morning he got to work at 7.30 and was immediately summoned by the General Manager. As David approached, the General Manager threw him a letter that had obviously come in the morning mail. David saw that the General Manager had circled two sections of the letter in red ink.

> We have looked at recent figures for the quality of one of the components you supply, AM74021-74222. As you will recall, we have an agreement that requires 99.5 per cent of delivered units of this product to be within 5 per cent of target output ratings. While your recent supplies have been achieving this, we are concerned that there has been some inconsistency. We had hoped for more positive signs of quality improvement.
>
> We put considerable emphasis on the quality of our materials, and would like to discuss a joint initiative to raise the quality of your components. By working together we can share ideas and get mutual benefits.

The General Manager waited for a few minutes and said:

> *I find it incredible that we are sending poor quality goods to one of our biggest customers. We have a major complaint about our quality. Complete strangers clearly think that we can't do our job properly, so they'll come and show us how to do it. This is your problem, and if you don't come up with some quick suggestions we should start looking for someone who can.*

The General Manager's tone made David rather defensive and his reply was less constructive than normal.

> *There is absolutely nothing wrong with our products. We agreed measures for quality and are consistently achieving these. We haven't improved quality because we didn't agree to improve it, and any improvement would increase our own costs. We are making 995 units in a thousand at higher quality than they requested, and the remaining 0.5 per cent are only just below it. To me, this seems a level of quality that almost anyone would be proud of.*

The process for making AM74021–74222 is in five stages, each of which is followed by an inspection. The units then have a final inspection before being sent to customers. David now considered more 100 per cent inspections, but each manual inspection costs about £0.60 and the selling price of the unit is only £24.75. There is also the problem that manual inspections are only 80 per cent accurate. Automatic inspections cost £0.30 and are almost completely reliable, but they cannot cover all aspects of quality and at least three inspections have to remain manual.

Dave produced a weekly summary of figures to show that things were really going well.

Week	**Inspection**											
	A		**B**		**C**		**D**		**E**		**F**	
	Inspect	**Reject**	**Inspect**	**Reject**	**Inspect**	**Reject**	**Inspect**	**Reject**	**Inspect**	**Reject**	**Inspect**	**Reject**
1	4,125	125	350	56	287	0	101	53	3,910	46	286	0
2	4,086	136	361	0	309	0	180	0	3,854	26	258	0
3	4,833	92	459	60	320	0	194	0	4,651	33	264	0
4	3,297	43	208	0	186	0	201	0	3,243	59	246	0
5	4,501	83	378	0	359	64	224	65	4,321	56	291	0
6	4,772	157	455	124	401	0	250	72	4,410	42	289	0
7	4,309	152	420	87	422	0	266	123	3,998	27	287	64
8	4,654	101	461	0	432	0	278	45	4,505	57	310	0
9	4,901	92	486	0	457	0	287	0	4,822	73	294	0
10	5,122	80	512	0	488	0	301	0	5,019	85	332	0
11	5,143	167	524	132	465	48	290	61	4,659	65	287	0
12	5,119	191	518	0	435	0	256	54	4,879	54	329	0
13	4,990	203	522	83	450	0	264	112	4,610	55	297	0
14	5,231	164	535	63	475	0	276	0	5,002	32	267	0
15	3,900	90	425	56	288	0	198	0	3,820	37	290	58
16	4,277	86	485	109	320	0	229	0	4,109	38	328	0
17	4,433	113	435	0	331	0	265	67	4,259	29	313	0
18	5,009	112	496	0	387	0	198	62	4,821	52	269	0
19	5,266	135	501	65	410	0	299	58	5,007	51	275	64
20	5,197	142	488	0	420	72	301	73	4,912	48	267	0
21	4,932	95	461	0	413	0	266	0	4,856	45	286	0
22	5,557	94	510	0	456	0	160	64	5,400	39	298	61
23	5,106	101	488	74	488	0	204	131	4,795	36	326	0
24	5,220	122	472	0	532	0	277	125	4,989	29	340	56
25	5,191	111	465	0	420	0	245	185	4,927	42	321	0
26	5,620	87	512	45	375	0	223	134	5,357	48	332	0

Notes on inspections

For sampling inspections, all production is considered in notional batches of one hour's output. Random samples are taken from each batch and if the quality is too low, the whole batch is rejected, checked and reworked as necessary.

A – automatic inspection of all units: rejects all defects.
B – manual inspection of 10 per cent of output: rejects batch if more than 1 per cent of batch is defective.
C – manual inspection of 10 per cent of output: rejects batch if more than 1 per cent of batch is defective.
D – manual inspection of 5 per cent of output: rejects batch if more than 2 per cent of batch is defective.
E – automatic inspection of all units: rejects all defects.
F – manual inspection of 5 per cent of output: rejects batch if more than 1 per cent of batch is defective.

Questions

- Do you think the General Manager's view is reasonable? What about David Brown's reaction?
- How effective is the quality control at West Midland?
- Do you think the product quality needs to be improved? How would you do this?

Problems

7.1 A part is made on an assembly line. At one point an average of 2 per cent of units are defective. It costs £0.50 to inspect each unit at this point, and the inspection would only find 70 per cent of faults. If the faults are left, all parts will be found and corrected further down the line at a cost of £4. Is it worthwhile inspecting all units at this point?

7.2 A machine produces parts that have a standard deviation in weight of 1 g. A sample of 100 parts had a mean weight of 2 kg. What is the 95 per cent confidence interval for the true weight of the parts?

7.3 On-line Phoneback answers customer enquiries with calls having a standard deviation in duration of two minutes. A sample of 40 calls is taken and found to have a mean duration of 14.9 minutes. What are the 95 per cent and 99 per cent confidence intervals for the true length of calls?

7.4 Soft drinks are put into cans that hold a nominal 200 ml, but the filling machines introduce a standard deviation of 10 ml. The cans are put into cartons of 25 and exported to a market that demands the mean weight of cartons is at least the quantity specified by the manufacturer. To make sure this happens, the canner set the machines to fill cans to 205 ml. What is the probability that a carton chosen at random will not pass the quantity test?

7.5 Feltham Catering says that its suppliers should send at most 2 per cent of units that do not meet its 'outstanding' standard of quality. It receives a large shipment and takes a sample of 100 units. The company wants to be 95 per cent sure that a rejected batch is really unsatisfactory. What criteria should it use to reject a batch?

7.6 A component is made in batches and transferred from one part of a plant to another. When it is made an acceptance quality level of 1 per cent defective is used, but transferred batches are allowed a maximum of 4 per cent defective. The company accepts a 5 per cent risk of rejecting good batches, and a 10 per cent risk of accepting bad batches. Design a suitable sampling plan for the component.

7.7 Elliot and Hang Quality Consultants take 24 samples of 200 units from a process that was known to be working properly. The numbers of unsatisfactory recordings were as follows.

Day	Number of defects	Day	Number of defects	Day	Number of defects
1	21	9	15	17	20
2	32	10	13	18	19
3	22	11	16	19	25
4	17	12	17	20	16
5	16	13	20	21	15
6	14	14	19	22	13
7	21	15	17	23	24
8	17	16	22	24	25

Draw control charts with 95 per cent and 99 per cent confidence limits on the process.

7.8 A particular operation takes a mean time of 75.42 minutes with a standard deviation of 2.01 minutes. If samples of eight are taken, find the control limits that will include 99 per cent of sample means if the process is working normally.

7.9 Thirty samples of size 15 have been taken from a process. The average sample range for the 30 samples is 1.025 kg and the average mean is 19.872 kg. Draw X and R control charts for the process.

Discussion questions

7.1 What are the differences between quality management and quality control?

7.2 Now that TQM has become so widespread, there is no need for traditional quality control. Do you think that this is true? How has the function of quality control changed in recent years?

7.3 What are the advantages and problems of using samples rather than complete inspections? Describe some examples of each that you are familiar with.

7.4 Is it true that quality control guarantees the quality of products? What is meant by producers' and consumers' risks? Describe exactly how an OC curve works.

7.5 Most quality control tests allow a certain proportion of units to be defective. How does this fit in with the ideas of total quality management?

7.6 Why are there variations in a process? How can these be reduced? What is the purpose of control charts? Are there other ways of getting equivalent results?

7.7 OFSTED (the Office for Standards in Education) is often criticised for its approach to testing schools' performance. How does it organise its testing? What does it measure?

7.8 How does acceptance sampling differ from process control? If the process is under control, batches of units should always be acceptable. So why do we use different tests?

7.9 Most local councils have a well-established procedure for taking samples of milk at points on the journey from cows to final customers. In practice, most of the tests are done at dairies, where there is almost never any problem. Last year the Consumer

Protection Department in East Yorkshire took six tests per thousand population. The population of the area is 2 million, so this meant about 50 samples a working day. Only 26 of the milk samples had any problems and the Council received another 15 complaints from the public. What are the tests on milk meant to achieve? How can the Council set a reasonable number of samples? As it finds so few problems, is the money spent on testing milk being wasted?

Reference

1. Taguchi G. (1986) *Introduction to Quality Engineering*. Tokyo: Asian Productivity Association.

Selected reading

Dale B.G. (1994) *Managing Quality*. 2nd edn. Englewood Cliffs, NJ: Prentice-Hall.

Duncan A.J. (1986) *Quality Control and Industrial Statistics*. Homewood, IL: Irwin.

Evans J.R. and Lindsay W.M. (1996) *The Management and Control of Quality*. 3rd edn. St Paul, MN: West Publishing.

Gitlow H.S., Gitlow S., Oppenheim A. and Oppenheim R. (1989) *Tools and Methods for the Improvement of Quality*. Homewood, IL: (1989) Irwin.

Kehoe D.F. (1996) *The Fundamentals of Quality Management*. London: Chapman and Hall.

Montgomery D. (1996) *Introduction to Statistical Quality Control*. 3rd edn. New York: John Wiley.

Oakland J.S. and Followell R.F. (1996) *Statistical Process Control*. Oxford: Butterworth-Heinemann.

Roberts H.V. (1998) *Total Quality Management and Statistics*. Oxford: Blackwell.

Useful Websites

www.qualitydigest.com
www.deming.eng.clemson.edu

Forecasting customer demand

The future is not 'knowable' in the sense of exact predictions. Life is filled with surrealistic surprise. Even the seemingly 'hardest' models and data are frequently based on 'soft' assumptions.

A. Toffler

Powershift, Bantam, New York, 1990

Contents

Aims of the chapter

After reading this chapter you should be able to:

- appreciate the importance and context of forecasting;
- describe different approaches to forecasting;
- use a variety of judgemental forecasting methods;
- define 'time series' and appreciate their importance;
- understand the approach of causal forecasts;
- use linear regression;
- understand the approach of projective forecasting;
- use a variety of projective forecasting methods;
- use a good overall approach to forecasting.

Main themes

This chapter will emphasise:

- **forecasts**, which predict aspects of the future;
- **judgemental forecasts**, which are based on opinion;
- **causal forecasts**, which use relationships between variables to forecast;
- **projective forecasts**, which project past patterns into the future.

OPERATIONS IN PRACTICE

Midway Construction

Jim Brown, owner of Midway Construction, was in a bad mood. Business had been slack for the past few months and he now had too many workers on his construction sites. He had just fired 25 people. Unless things picked up, he would have to fire another 30 before the end of the month. Jim thought:

> *This is crazy! This is the fifth time in two years that I've laid off good, reliable workers. What usually happens next is that business picks up, and I desperately look for people to hire. Our workload varies enormously, and there is so much uncertainty in the industry. If I could forecast the amount of work some time in advance, I could smooth it out and not have to go through these peaks and troughs.*

Nobody at Midway liked the current 'hire-and-fire' arrangement. Unfortunately, none of the managers knew of any alternatives, and they did not have the time to investigate.

Introduction to forecasting

Importance of forecasts

All management decisions become effective at some point in the future. So these decisions should not be based on present circumstances, but on prevailing conditions when they take effect. When British Aerospace plans production, it does not make enough aeroplanes to meet current demand, but enough to meet future demand when the planes are ready.

Unfortunately, we never know exactly what conditions will be like in the future, so the best we can do is use forecasts. These forecasts will not be perfect, but they give the best information available.

All **decisions** need information about **future circumstances**.

- The best we can do is to **forecast** these circumstances.

Now you can see why forecasting is so important. If forecasts are accurate, our plans are based on the right information and can be successful. On the other hand, if the forecasts are wrong, our plans are based on faulty assumptions and we will inevitably get poor results.

Use of forecasts

When you think about forecasts, you might imagine a group of specialists working away in a distant office doing lots of analyses and eventually producing a forecast. Rather like the Treasury, which has departments of people making economic forecasts, but we only see the occasional representative when they present their latest ideas.

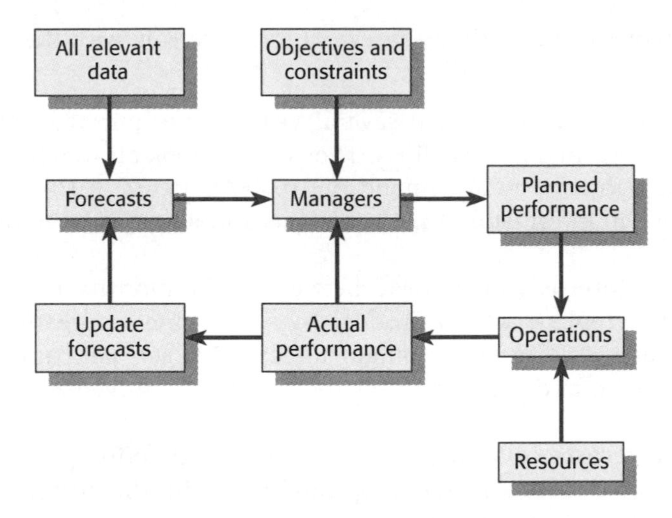

Figure 8.1 Role of forecasting in decision making

This view of isolated experts working in the background is totally misleading. Forecasts are used throughout an organisation, and they should be integrated into the decision making. They should certainly not be prepared by an isolated group of specialists. Neither is forecasting a job that is done once and is then finished. It is continuous, and as time moves on actual circumstances are compared with forecasts, original forecasts are updated, plans are modified, decisions are revised, and so on. This process is shown in Figure 8.1.

In this chapter we generally talk about forecasting 'demand'. Remember that this is just for convenience and almost everything is forecast somewhere – whether it is the price of oil, the number of passengers using a bus service, or the winner of a horse race. You can think of 'demand' as a general term for anything that you want to forecast.

Ways of forecasting

There are many different ways of forecasting. It would be useful to say: 'A lot of work has been done on forecasting and the best method is . . .' Unfortunately, we cannot do this. There are so many different things to forecast, and so many different circumstances, that no single method is always the best. The best we can do is look at a variety of methods and see when each can be used. In general, the choice of forecasting method depends on factors like:

- the time covered in the future;
- availability of historical data;
- relevance of historical data to the future;
- type of product, particularly the balance between goods and services;
- variability of demand;
- accuracy needed and cost of errors;
- benefits expected from the forecasts;
- amount of money and time available for the forecast.

We can classify forecasting methods in several ways, starting with the time covered in the future.

1. **Long-term forecasts** look ahead several years – the time needed to build a new factory or organise new facilities. They usually look at overall demand, so a hospital might forecast total demand of 10,000 patients in three years' time. This gives enough information to plan budgets and major facilities over the next few years.
2. **Medium-term forecasts** look ahead between three months and a year – the time needed to replace an old product by a new one or organise resources. The hospital above, for example, might forecast 200 surgical patients a month for the next years, and use this to set the number of surgeons and associated facilities.
3. **Short-term forecasts** cover the next few weeks – describing the continuing demand for a product or scheduling operations. Again, the hospital might forecast 10 surgical treatments a day for the next month, and use this to schedule operating theatres, staff and so on.

There is a clear link between the time covered by the forecast and the levels of decision described in Chapter 3. Generally, long-term forecasts are for strategic decisions; medium-term forecasts are for tactical decisions; and short-term forecasts are for operational decisions. Not surprisingly, the further into the future you look, the less reliable your forecast is likely to be.

Another classification of forecasting methods shows the difference between qualitative and quantitative approaches (shown in Figure 8.2).

If an organisation is already making a product, it has records of past demand and knows the factors that affect this. Then it can use a quantitative method to forecast future demand. There are two ways of doing this:

1. **Projective methods** look at the pattern of past demand and extend this into the future. If demand in the last four weeks has been 10, 20, 30 and 40 units,

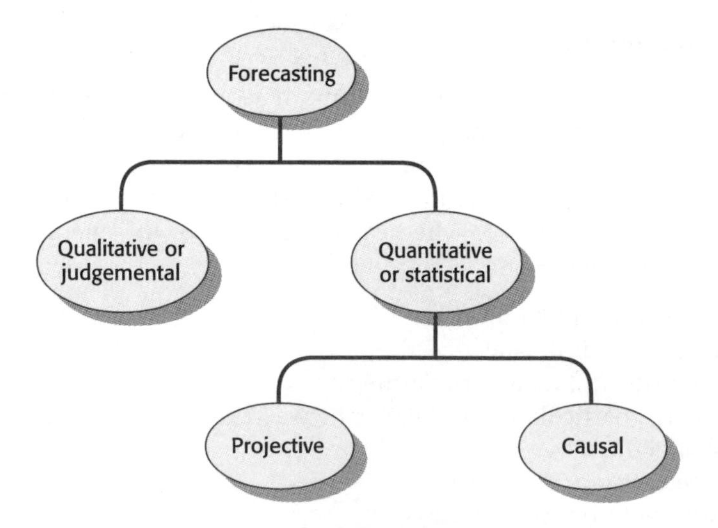

Figure 8.2 Quantitative and qualitative forecasts

we can project this pattern and suggest that next week's demand will be around 50 units.

2. **Causal methods** look at the factors that affect demand and use these to forecast. The amount of money borrowed from a bank depends on the prevailing interest rate. It is more reliable to use the planned interest rate to forecast borrowings than to project figures from the past few months.

Both of these approaches rely on accurate, numerical data. Suppose, though, that an organisation is introducing an entirely new product. There are obviously no past demand figures to project into the future, and the organisation does not yet know what factors affect demand. As there are no data for a quantitative method, the only alternative is a qualitative one. These are generally called **judgemental**, and they rely on subjective views and opinions.

Whichever method we use, we want the best information for our decisions. To be specific, we want a good forecast that is:

- *accurate* – with small errors;
- *unbiased* – so it does not always under or over estimate demand;
- *responsive* to changes in demand;
- *not affected* by the odd unusual figure;
- *in time* for its purpose;
- *cost effective*;
- *easy to understand*.

We do not have to limit ourselves to one method, but can compare and combine the results from several different methods. Managers should consider all available information before making their decisions. At the very least, they should give forecasts a subjective review before using them (as illustrated in Figure 8.3). This allows for information that cannot be fitted into a standard forecasting method – such as competition, economic conditions, exchange rates, political climate, demographic trends and government regulations.

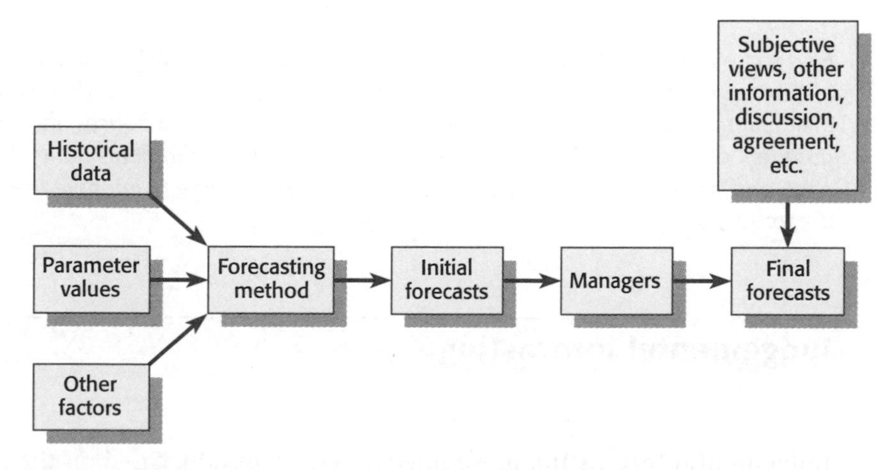

Figure 8.3 Use of managers' views to update forecasts

Review questions

8.1 Why is forecasting used in operations management?

8.2 Forecasting is a specialised function that uses mathematical techniques to project historical data. Do you think this is true?

8.3 List three different approaches to forecasting.

OPERATIONS IN PRACTICE

Rain and floods

The Meteorological Office uses the latest technology, enormous resources and huge amounts of money to make the best weather forecasts available. Despite widespread opinions to the contrary, its short-term forecasts are usually good, but there can still be problems.

Easter weekend of 1998 saw the worst floods in eastern England for 150 years. Many parts of the country were covered in snow three weeks after the official end of winter, and exceptional rainfall caused damage estimated at £1.5 billion. This bad weather raised some interesting points.

- The severe rain came as a surprise. Weather forecasts did not predict either the amount of rain or the time it would arrive. As a result, nobody could take precautions, and there was severe flooding and damage to property.
- The National Rivers Authority manages the flow of water down rivers. It was not given warnings of the heavy rains and could not implement plans for dispersing large amounts of water. Many rivers burst their banks, and there were suggestions that sluice gates were opened to deliberately flood some areas and leave other areas less badly affected.
- Water UK said that 95 per cent of the water was wasted, and that areas under water at Easter could face water shortages and droughts in the next summer.

There are two important lessons here. Firstly, even if you put a lot of effort into forecasts, they can still be wrong. Secondly, forecasts are not an end in themselves, but are an important part of planning.

Project 8.1

Find some forecasts that have been wrong. You might, for example, look at forecasts of the cost of the Channel Tunnel, the number of visitors to Disneyland Paris or the Millennium Dome in London, the value of the euro, the price of houses, the winning numbers in the national lottery or the results of football tournaments. Why did the errors arise and what were the effects? What could have been done to improve the quality of the forecasts?

Judgemental forecasting

Judgemental forecasting uses subjective views, usually based on the opinions of experts. It is sometimes called **qualitative forecasting** or **subjective forecasting**.

Imagine that AstraZeneca is about to market an entirely new product, or a medical team in Papworth Hospital is considering a new organ transplant, or the European Union is looking at the effects of adding new members. They clearly have no relevant historical data for a quantitative forecast. Sometimes there simply are no data, and at other times the available data are unreliable or irrelevant to the future. Without relevant historical data, we have to use a judgemental method. Five widely used methods are personal insight, panel consensus, market surveys, historical analogy and the Delphi method.

1. Personal insight

This has a single person who is familiar with the situation making a forecast based on his or her own judgement. This is the most widely used forecasting method, and has the benefits of being fast, cheap and convenient. Unfortunately, it relies entirely on one person's judgement – as well as that person's opinions, prejudices, ignorance and mood. It can give good forecasts, but often gives very bad ones. This unreliability is its major weakness and the reason why you should avoid it. Studies consistently show that someone who is familiar with a situation, using experience and subjective opinions, produces *worse* forecasts than someone who knows nothing about the situation but uses a more formal method.

2. Panel consensus

One person can easily make a mistake, but collecting together a group of people should give a consensus that is more reliable. This is the principle of 'focus groups'. If there is no secrecy and the panel members talk freely and openly, a genuine consensus can emerge. On the other hand, it is difficult to combine the views of different people when they cannot reach a consensus.

Although it is more reliable than one person's insight, panel consensus still has the major weakness that everybody – even experts – can make mistakes. There are also problems of group working, where 'those who shout loudest get their way', everyone tries to please the boss, some people do not speak well in groups, and so on. Overall, panel consensus is an improvement on personal insight, but you should be cautious about the results from either method.

3. Market surveys

Rather than asking the opinion of experts, it is sometimes better to go straight to potential customers. This is the usual way of getting information for, say, the launch of a new product. Market surveys collect data from a sample of people, analyse their views and make inferences about the population at large. This tends to be time consuming and expensive but surveys can give useful information. On the other hand, there are many examples of misleading results. In the 1990s Coca Cola reputedly interviewed over 300,000 people before changing its recipe – and still got it wrong. To get reasonable results, market surveys need:

- a sample of customers that accurately represents the population;
- carefully worded, useful, unbiased questions;
- fair and honest answers;
- reliable analyses of the answers;
- valid conclusions drawn from the analyses.

4. Historical analogy

Chapter 5 described a typical product life cycle. If an organisation is introducing a new product, it might have a similar product that was launched recently, and can assume that demand for the new product will follow the same pattern. A publisher introducing a new book assumes that its demand will be the same as demand for a similar book that it published recently.

The problem, of course, is that historical analogy can only be used if a similar product has been introduced fairly recently.

5. Delphi method

This is the most formal of the judgemental methods and has a well-defined procedure. A number of experts are posted a questionnaire to complete. The replies from these questionnaires are analysed and summaries are passed back to the experts. A questionnaire avoids the pressures of face-to-face meetings or group discussions, and each reply is anonymous to avoid the influences of status, etc.

Now each expert is asked to reconsider his/her original reply in the light of the summarised replies from others. They may be convinced by some of the arguments, and adjust their answers for a second round of opinions. This process of modifying responses in the light of replies made by the rest of the group is repeated several times – usually between three and six. By this time, the range of opinions should be narrow enough to help with decisions.

The main problems with the Delphi method are designing appropriate questionnaires, finding a suitable mix of experts, the time involved and keeping the same group involved over this time. The experts are also likely to give answers that depend on their own responsibilities and aims rather than objective analyses. A lot of anecdotal evidence suggests that these surveys give disappointing results.

OPERATIONS IN PRACTICE

RJD Systems

RJD Systems is a high-technology development company. It does research on innovative ideas that may lead to actual products in the long term, and its products are patented knowledge that it licenses to other companies.

RJD recently finished a forecasting exercise to see when 3D-video conferencing might reasonably be developed. The aim is to hold 'cyber meetings' to replace actual meetings or 2D-video conferencing.

For this study, RJD contacted a total of 20 experts to start a Delphi process. These experts come from various backgrounds, including software designers, hardware manufacturers, optical physicists, technical staff from communications companies and physiologists. The overall problem was explained, and each of the experts was sent a questionnaire about 3D-conferencing. The initial returns gave a wide range of dates for a realistic system, ranging from 2006 to 2060. These results were summarised and sent back to the experts, who were asked if they would like to modify their previous answer in the light of the other replies. This was repeated four times, by which time 16 of the experts gave a date between 2020 and 2025. This is close enough to help RJD with its planning.

Source: Stockholm, (2001) *RJD Technical Report Series.*

Table 8.1 Comparison of judgemental forecasting methods

Method	Accuracy in term			Cost
	Short	Medium	Long	
Personal insight	Poor	Poor	Very poor	Very low
Panel consensus	Poor to fair	Poor to fair	Poor	Low
Market survey	Very good	Good	Fair	High
Historical analogy	Poor	Fair to good	Fair to good	Medium
Delphi method	Fair to very good	Fair to good	Fair to good	High

Comparison of methods

Each of the judgemental methods works best in different circumstances. If you want a quick response, personal insight is fastest and cheapest. If you need reliable forecasts, it may be worth organising a market survey or Delphi method. Table 8.1 shows a general comparison of methods.

Review questions

8.4 What are judgemental forecasts?

8.5 List five types of judgemental forecast.

8.6 What are the main problems with judgemental forecasts?

OPERATIONS IN PRACTICE

The solar eclipse of 1999

At 9.35 a.m. on Wednesday August 11 1999 the moon moved between the earth and the sun to give a total eclipse of the sun. This was the first total eclipse visible on the British mainland since 1927, and the next is due in 2091. The 'line of totality' crossed the south-west of England near to Penzance.

Tourism is an important industry in the south-west, and the eclipse gave a unique opportunity to attract new visitors. Careful planning was needed, and this started with a forecast of the likely number of visitors. There was no real precedence for the eclipse, but expert advice a year in advance gave an initial forecast of three million.

This forecast had many effects. Uninformed commentators started rumours that all accommodation was full; roads would be blocked by traffic; food would run out as delivery lorries failed to get through; electricity, gas and water suppliers could not meet demand; health and sewage services could not cope; troops would have to help police deal with 'public order issues'. The local council banned a series of festivals that would attract more people; access to open areas was blocked to stop illegal camping; small holiday cottages were advertised with rents up to £25,000 for the week. Some people lost all sense of reality. Apparently forgetting that the eclipse only gave two minutes and six seconds of darkness, they suggested that cliffs be fenced-off to stop cars from driving over the edge; that alcohol be banned; and that outside lighting be set up to stop animals from becoming confused.

Not surprisingly, many people read these reports and decided not to go. Six months before the eclipse, the forecast number of tourists was reduced to one million. Three months before the eclipse, a survey of Tourist Board members found that holiday bookings were generally about normal, but with many reporting lower bookings than previous years. An advertising campaign to encourage visitors was largely unsuccessful, and in the end the eclipse attracted virtually no additional visitors.

Time series

Quantitative forecasts often consider **time series**. These are series of observations taken at regular intervals, such as daily cost figures, weekly sales, monthly production or annual rainfall.

If you have a time series, a simple analysis draws a graph to show any underlying patterns. Figure 8.4 shows the three most common patterns:

- **constant series**, where values stay more or less the same over time, such as annual rainfall;
- **trends**, which either rise or fall steadily, such as the gross national product, price of petrol, and beer consumption;
- **seasonal series**, which have cycles, such as sales of soft drinks, electricity consumption and cough medicine.

If demand followed such simple patterns, we would have no problems with forecasting. Unfortunately, there are always differences between actual demand and the underlying pattern. These differences form a random **noise** that is superimposed on the underlying pattern. Then:

200 205 194 195 208 203 200 193 201 198

is a constant series of 200 with superimposed noise.

Actual value = underlying pattern + random noise

The noise is a completely random effect that is caused by many factors, such as varying customer demand, hours worked, speed of working, weather, rejections at inspections, time of year, wider economic influences, and so on. It is the noise that

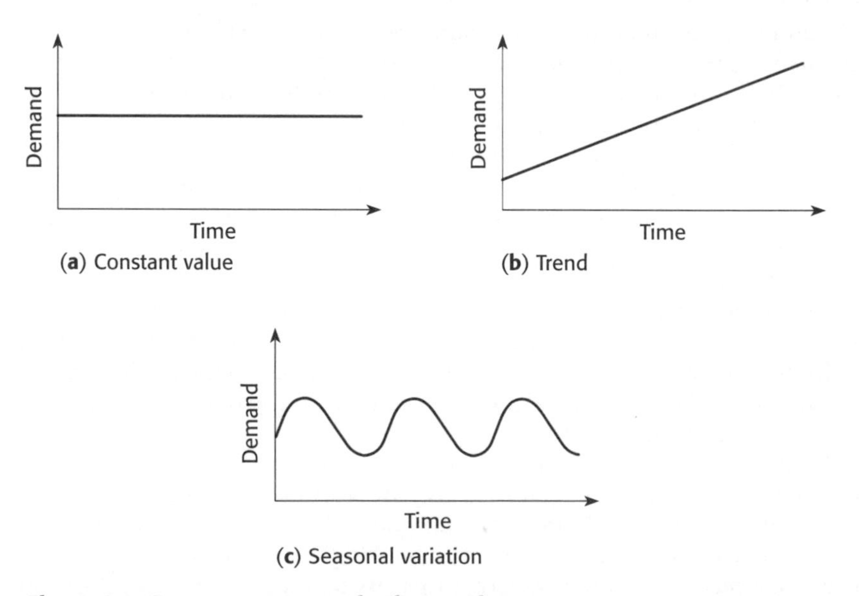

Figure 8.4 Common patterns in time series

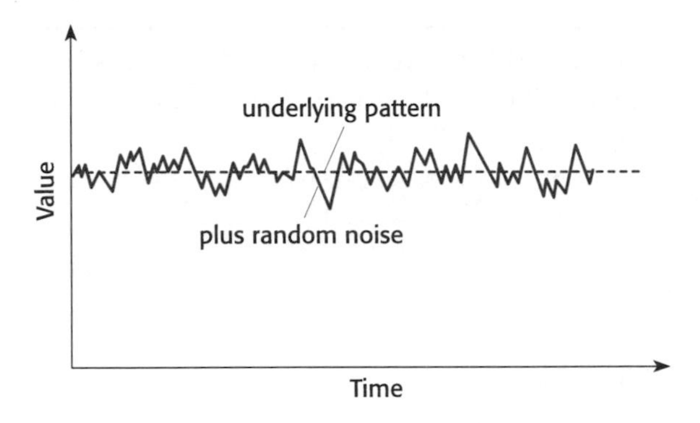

Figure 8.5 Random noise superimposed on an underlying pattern

makes forecasting difficult. If the noise is relatively small, actual demand is close to the underlying pattern and we can get good forecasts: if there is a lot of noise, it hides the underlying pattern and forecasting is more difficult.

Because of the noise, our forecasts are almost always wrong. In other words, there is a difference between the forecast and the actual values. If we forecast next week's demand for a product as 100 units, we would not be surprised if actual demand turns out to be 105 units. Then our forecast has an **error** of:

Error = actual demand – forecast = 105 – 100 = 5 units

With a good forecast this error should be relatively small. If we continue making a forecast every period, we can see how it performs over time. We could, for example, find the error every period and use this to calculate the longer-term average error. Unfortunately, we meet a problem here, as positive and negative errors cancel each other. Then very poor forecasts can have zero mean error, as you can see in the following table.

Period	Demand	Forecast	Error
1	100	0	100
2	200	0	200
3	300	0	300
4	400	1,000	–600
Total	**1,000**	**1,000**	**0**
Mean	**250**	**250**	**0**

The mean error does not really show how accurate forecasts are, but it measures bias. If the mean error has a positive value, the forecast is consistently too low; if it has a negative value, the forecast is consistently too high.

We clearly need some other measure of error, and the simplest is to take the absolute values of the errors and calculate a **mean absolute deviation**. This shows how far, on average, a forecast is away from the actual value. We can also square the errors in each forecast and calculate a **mean squared error**. This value does not have such a clear meaning, but it is useful for other analyses and we shall meet it again in the next section on linear regression.

WORKED EXAMPLE

The Bayview Hotel has compared the actual demand for rooms booked each week with its short-term forecasts. What are the errors? What do these errors show?

Week	1	2	3	4	5	6	7
Demand	20	34	39	35	22	15	11
Forecast	19	31	43	37	25	16	12

Solution

The error for the first week is:

Error = demand − forecast = 20 − 19 = 1

Repeating this calculation for the other weeks gives:

Week	1	2	3	4	5	6	7
Demand	20	34	39	35	22	15	11
Forecast	19	31	43	37	25	16	12
Error	1	3	−4	−2	−3	−1	−1

Then the mean errors are:

- Mean error = (1 + 3 − 4 − 2 − 3 − 1 − 1)/7 = −1
- Mean absolute deviation = (1 + 3 + 4 + 2 + 3 + 1 + 1)/7 = 2.14
- Mean squared error = (1 + 9 + 16 + 4 + 9 + 1 + 1)/7 = 5.86

The mean error of −1 shows that the hotel's forecast is an average of one room too high. This is reasonably close, but it shows some bias, and if the bias becomes too large, the hotel would be planning for more guests than it actually gets. The mean absolute deviation shows that the forecast is an average of 2.14 away from the actual demand. The mean squared error does not have such a clear meaning, but is useful for other analyses.

Review questions

8.7 Why are forecasts usually wrong?

8.8 What is the mean error of a forecast and why is it of limited use?

8.9 How would you compare different forecasting methods?

OPERATIONS IN PRACTICE

Errors in FTSE forecasts

At the beginning of 1999 there were signs that the UK economy was weakening, and the Bank of England's monetary policy committee lowered interest rates in an attempt to avoid an economic recession. City strategists were looking for further cuts, which they hoped would raise the sluggish stock market.

The *Sunday Times* collected some expert forecasts for the value of the FTSE 100 index at the end of the year. Most analysts predicted that 1999 would be a subdued year, and their forecast values were:

Forecaster	Forecast of FTSE 100 value at year end
HSBC	6,800
Lehman Brothers	6,400
BT Alex brown	6,350
Credit Lyonnais	6,300
Barclays	6,300
Morgan Stanley	6,250
Salomon Smith Barney	6,000
Chase Manhattan	6,000
Panmure Gordon	5,800
JP Morgan	5,700
River and Mercantile	5,600

The FTSE 100 is a basic measure of economic performance, so it is surprising that expert forecasts ranged over 1,200 points. At the close of the last day of trading in 1999, the FTSE 100 actually stood at 6,930, but this was a peak and it quickly fell back.

Source: Smith D. and Waples J. (1999) 'Bank Will Freeze Base Rate as Shoppers Rush for the Sales', *Sunday Times*, 3 January

Causal forecasting

Linear regression

You can often see relationships between two variables. The sales of a product, for example, depend on its price. If we can find a relationship between the price and sales, we can use a proposed price to forecast expected sales.

Causal forecasting looks for a cause or relationship that can be used to forecast.

You can find similar relationships between the speed of a machine and its output, bonus payments and productivity, interest rates and amount of money borrowed, amount of fertiliser used and crop size, etc. These are true relationships where changes in the first, **independent variable** actually cause changes in the second, **dependent variable**. In other relationships there is no apparent cause and effect, but we can still use them for forecasting.

We will illustrate causal forecasting by **linear regression**. This assumes that the dependent variable is linearly related to the independent one, as shown in Figure 8.6.

Linear regression looks for a relationship of the form:

$$\text{Dependent variable} = a + b \times \text{independent variable}$$

Or: $y = a + bx$

where: x = value of the independent variable
y = value of the dependent variable
a = intercept, where the line crosses the y axis
b = gradient of the line

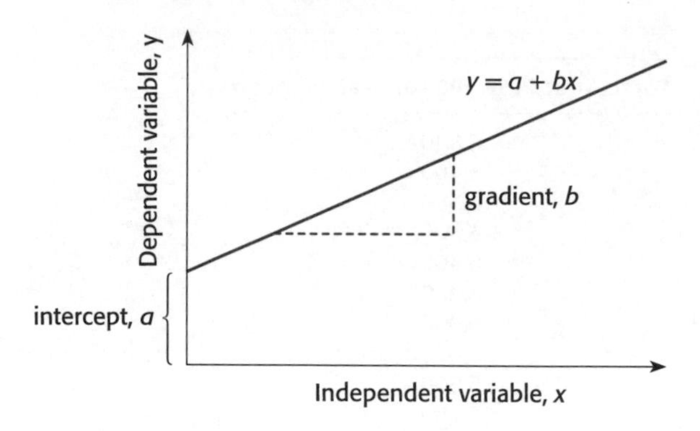

Figure 8.6 A linear relationship between variables

To find the relationship, we need a series of values for the independent variable and related ones for the dependent variable. Then we find the best line through these. So we are looking for the best values for the constants *a* and *b*. The random noise means that even the best line will not be a perfect fit to the data. There is an error in each observation, and we want the line that minimises the overall error. In practice, the most useful line is the one that minimises the mean squared error. The arithmetic for this is described in the supplement to this chapter. In practice, the calculations are always done by computer.

WORKED EXAMPLE

Clients in Nadine Kubat's sports clinic complained when they had to wait for treatment. Nadine could employ more staff to reduce waiting times. As an experiment, she adjusted the number of staff working and counted the number of complaints. The following table shows her initial findings.

Staff	0	1	2	3	4	5	6	7	8	9	10
Complaints	92	86	81	72	67	59	53	43	32	24	12

If Nadine employed six staff, how many complaints would she expect? What is the effect of employing 20 staff?

Solution

The independent variable, *x*, is the number of staff employed; the dependent variable, *y*, is the corresponding number of complaints. We are looking for the best values (those that minimise the mean squared error) of *a* and *b* for the equation:

$$\text{Number of complaints} = a + b \times \text{number of staff}$$

Figure 8.7 shows a spreadsheet of the results, with the calculated results as:

- *a*, the intercept = 95.9
- *b*, the gradient, labelled '*X* Variable 1' = −7.9

Giving:

$$\text{Number of complaints} = 95.9 - 7.9 \times \text{number of staff.}$$

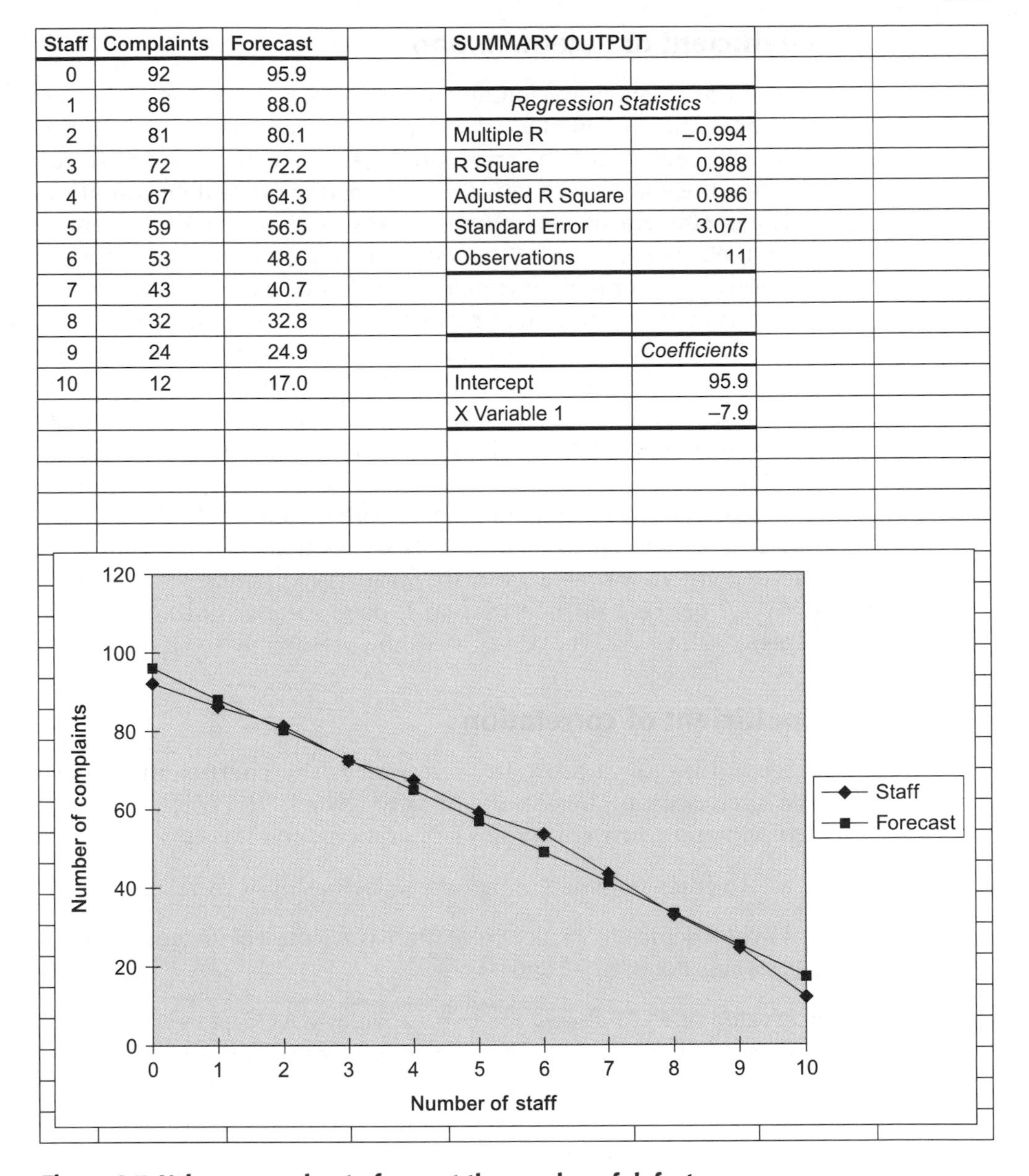

Staff	Complaints	Forecast
0	92	95.9
1	86	88.0
2	81	80.1
3	72	72.2
4	67	64.3
5	59	56.5
6	53	48.6
7	43	40.7
8	32	32.8
9	24	24.9
10	12	17.0

SUMMARY OUTPUT

Regression Statistics	
Multiple R	–0.994
R Square	0.988
Adjusted R Square	0.986
Standard Error	3.077
Observations	11

	Coefficients
Intercept	95.9
X Variable 1	–7.9

Figure 8.7 Using regression to forecast the number of defects

The forecasts show that with six staff Nadine should expect 48.6 complaints. This figure comes from substitution:

$$\text{Number of complaints} = 95.9 - 7.9 \times 6 = 48.6$$

With 20 staff Nadine has to be a bit more careful as substitution gives:

$$\text{Number of complaints} = 95.9 - 7.9 \times 20 = -61.8$$

She obviously cannot have a negative number of complaints, so should forecast zero.

Coefficient of determination

In the last example we found the line of best fit through a set of data. But how well does this line fit the observations? If the errors are small, the line is a good fit to the data, but if the errors are large, even the best line is not very good. To measure the goodness of fit we use the **coefficient of determination**.

The coefficient of determination sees how far the dependent values are away from their mean. Some of the variation from the mean is explained by the linear relationship – some is unexplained and is due to random noise. The coefficient of determination gives the proportion of the total error that is explained by the linear relationship. It has a value between zero and one. If it is near to one, most of the variation is explained by the regression; there is little noise and the straight line is a good fit to the data. If the value is near to zero, most of the variation is unexplained; there is a lot of random noise; and the line is not a good fit.

The coefficient of determination is often called 'r^2'. The printout in Figure 8.7 has an entry 'R Square 0.988'. This shows that 98.8 per cent of the variation of the dependent variable from its mean is explained by the linear relationship. Only 1.2 per cent of the variation is due to noise, so the errors are very small. In general, values of r^2 above, say, 0.5 show reasonably small errors.

Coefficient of correlation

A second useful measure in regression is the **coefficient of correlation** which asks the question: Are x and y linearly related? The coefficients of correlation and determination answer very similar questions, and it is easy to show that:

$$\text{Coefficient of determination} = (\text{coefficient of correlation})^2$$

As the coefficient of determination is r^2, the coefficient of correlation is r, and has a value between +1 and –1.

- a value of $r = 1$ shows the two variables have a perfect linear relationship with no noise at all, and as one increases so does the other;
- a low positive value of r shows a weak linear relationship;
- a value of $r = 0$ shows there is no correlation at all between the two variables and no linear relationship;
- a low negative value of r shows a weak linear relationship;
- a value of $r = -1$ shows the two variables have a perfect linear relationship, and as one increases the other decreases.

A correlation coefficient near to +1 or –1 shows a strong linear relationship. However, when r is between 0.7 and –0.7 the coefficient of determination is less than 0.49 and less than half the variation is explained by the regression. As a rule of thumb, linear regression is not very reliable when the coefficient of correlation is between about 0.7 and –0.7.

In Figure 8.7, you can see an entry 'Multiple R –0.994'. This is the label for the coefficient of correlation, which again confirms a very good fit, with the number of complaints falling as the number of staff rises.

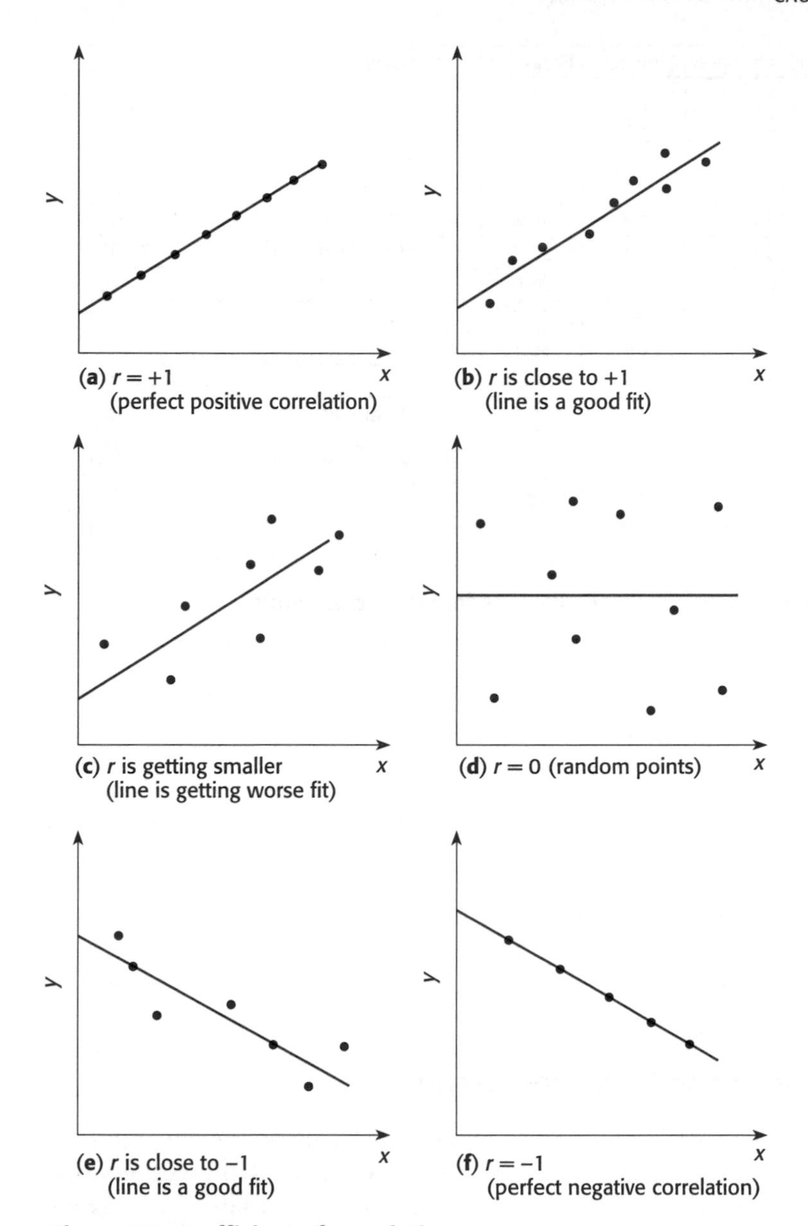

Figure 8.8 Coefficient of correlation

WORKED EXAMPLE

The amount of time lost in a process seems to be related to the number of product changes. Find the coefficients of correlation and determination for the following data, and see if this is true.

Product changes	4	17	3	21	10	8	4	9	13	12	2	6	15	8	19
Time lost	13	47	24	41	29	33	28	38	46	32	14	22	26	21	50

Solution

Figure 8.9 shows the result from a spreadsheet. As you can see the:

Product changes	Time lost	Forecast
4	13	21.6
17	47	41.6
3	24	20.0
21	41	47.8
10	29	30.8
8	33	27.7
4	28	21.6
9	38	29.3
13	46	35.5
12	32	33.9
2	14	18.5
6	22	24.6
15	26	38.6
8	21	27.7
19	50	44.7

SUMMARY OUTPUT	
Regression Statistics	
Multiple R	0.797
R Square	0.635
Adjusted R Square	0.607
Standard Error	7.261
Observations	15
	Coefficients
Intercept	15.38
X Variable 1	1.55

Figure 8.9 Regression calculations for worked example

- Line of best fit is: time lost = 15.38 + 1.55 × product changes
- Coefficient of correlation is 0.797
- Coefficient of determination is 0.635

The line is clearly a good fit, as 80 per cent of the variation is explained by the regression, and only 20 per cent is due to random noise.

Sometimes, especially with small numbers of observations, the coefficient of determination is a bit optimistic. Then a small correction finds the 'Adjusted R Square' shown in the printout.

Extensions to linear regression

There are several extensions to the basic linear regression model. One considers multiple linear regression (invariably called **multiple regression**), which looks for a linear relationship between a dependent variable and several independent ones.

$$y = a + b_1 \times \text{variable } 1 + b_2 \times \text{variable } 2 + b_3 \times \text{variable } 3 + b_4 \times \text{variable } 4 \ldots$$

The sales of a product, for example, might depend on its price, the advertising budget, number of suppliers, local unemployment rate, and so on.

Another extension looks at non-linear regression, where a more complicated line is fitted to data. A population might, for example, grow exponentially, with:

$$\text{Population, } y = a \times b^{\text{period}}$$

where a and b are constants. Spreadsheets and other packages have a range of standard procedures for dealing with more complicated regressions of this type.

Review questions

8.10 How does causal forecasting work?

8.11 What is 'linear regression'?

8.12 What is measured by the coefficient of determination?

8.13 The coefficient of correlation sees if changes in the independent variable cause changes in the dependent variable. Is this true?

OPERATIONS IN PRACTICE

Elsom Service Corporation

Elsom Service Corporation provides a range of commercial services. Conrad van Hoeffer runs a catering department that delivers sandwiches and other snacks to office blocks around the centre of Brisbane, Queensland. Conrad tried to improve performance by looking at the relationships between 'production' and other variables, such as the number of shifts worked, bonus rates paid to employees, average hours of overtime, staff turnover and morale. Figure 8.10 shows the results of one quick analysis.

Production	Shifts	Bonus	Overtime	Turnover	Morale
5330	7	14	7	4	5
4120	3	20	9	3	6
5600	2	3	21	6	5
6520	4	4	31	3	2
3710	1	7	10	5	8
5690	2	12	22	1	10
6920	3	16	21	3	5
4730	7	8	5	1	7
4350	1	14	14	3	5
5880	8	6	18	2	3

SUMMARY OUTPUT	
Regression Statistics	
Multiple R	0.9257
R Square	0.8570
Adjusted R Square	0.6781
Standard Error	593.1412
Observations	10.0000
	Coefficients
Intercept	–460.581
X Variable 1	335.476
X Variable 2	71.686
X Variable 3	153.309
X Variable 4	192.031
X Variable 5	126.366486

Figure 8.10 Sample figures for Elsom Service Corporation

This shows that the line of best fit is:

$$\text{production} = -460.6 + 335.5 \times \text{shifts} + 71.7 \times \text{bonus} + 153.3 \times \text{overtime} + 192.0 \times \text{turnover} + 126.4 \times \text{morale}$$

This line fitted the data well, and the coefficient of correlation of 0.857 shows that the model explains 92.6 per cent of variation in production. This result was, however, only an initial trial and more work was needed on, for example, the measure of 'morale', and other variables that might be included.

Source: van Hoeffler C. (2000) 'Explaining Performance', Presentation to the Operations Forum, Brisbane, June.

Project 8.2 *Look for an example of a true relationship, where changes in the independent variable cause changes in the dependent variable. Collect some data for this relationship. Analyse the data and draw the line of best fit. What can you learn from the analysis?*

Projective forecasting

Projective forecasting examines historical values for demand and projects these forward to forecast the future.

We will describe the four most widely used methods, based on simple average, moving averages, exponential smoothing and a model for seasonality and trend.

Simple average

Suppose you are organising an annual trade show at the National Exhibition Centre and want to know the number of people who will attend. The easiest way of finding this is to look up records for previous years and take an average. The average numbers attending over, say, the past five years should give a reasonable figure for next year's attendance. This is an example of forecasting using a simple average.

WORKED EXAMPLE

Use simple averages to forecast demand for period six of the following two time series. How accurate are the forecasts? What are the forecasts for period 24?

Period	1	2	3	4	5
Series 1	98	100	98	104	100
Series 2	140	66	152	58	84

Solution

- **For series 1**

$$\text{Forecast} = \text{the average demand} = (98 + 100 + 98 + 104 + 100)/5 = 500/5 = 100$$

- **For series 2**

$$\text{Forecast} = (140 + 66 + 152 + 58 + 84)/5 = 500/5 = 100$$

Although the forecasts are the same, there is clearly less noise in the first series than the second, so you would be more confident in this result.

Simple averages assume the demand is constant, so the forecasts for period 24 are the same as the forecasts for period six (that is 100).

Forecasting using a simple average is easy and can work well for stable demands. However, it does not work so well if the demand pattern changes. Older data tends to swamp the latest figures and the forecast does not respond to the change. Suppose demand for an item has been constant at 100 units a week for the past two years. A simple average clearly forecasts demand of 100 for week 105. If the actual demand in week 105 suddenly rises to 200 units, the simple average gives a forecast for week 106 of:

Forecast = (104 × 100 + 200)/105 = 100.95

A rise in demand of 100 gives an increase of 0.95 in the forecast. If demand continues at 200 units a week, the following forecasts are 101.89, 102.80, 103.70 and so on. The forecasts are rising but the response is very slow.

Very few time series are stable over long periods, so the restriction that a simple average only works for constant series makes it of limited use.

Moving averages

Demand usually varies over time, so only a certain amount of historical data is relevant to the future. This means that we can ignore all observations older than some specified age. A **moving average** uses this approach by taking the average demand over a fixed number of previous periods. It might, for example, use the sales over the past six weeks as a forecast, and ignore any data that is older than this.

WORKED EXAMPLE

The demand for a product over the past eight months is as follows:

Month	1	2	3	4	5	6	7	8
Demand	150	130	125	135	115	80	105	100

The market for this item is unstable, and any data over three months old are unreliable. Use a moving average to forecast demand for the item.

Solution

Only data from the last three months are relevant, so we can use a three-period moving average to forecast. If you look at the situation at the end of month 3, the forecast for month 4 is:

- Forecast = (150 + 130 + 125)/3 = 135

At the end of month 4, when actual demand is known to be 135, we can update this forecast to give the forecast for month 5:

- Forecast = (130 + 125 + 135)/3 = 130

Repeating this calculation gives the result in the following table.

Month	1	2	3	4	5	6	7	8	9
Demand	150	130	125	135	115	80	105	100	–
Forecast	–	–	–	135	130	125	110	100	95

You can see in the last example how the forecast is responding to changes, with a high demand moving the forecast upwards, and a low demand moving it downwards. The **sensitivity** of a forecast shows how quickly it responds to changes.

We can adjust the sensitivity of moving averages by altering the number of periods we average. Taking the average of a small number of observations gives a responsive forecast that quickly follows changes in demand – but it may be too sensitive and follow atypical values and random fluctuations. Taking the average of more observations gives a less sensitive forecast that smoothes out random variations, but it may not follow genuine changes in demand. We need a compromise that gives reasonable results, and a typical value is around six periods.

WORKED EXAMPLE

The following table shows monthly demand for a product over the past year. Use moving averages with n = 3, n = 6 and n = 9 to give one month ahead forecasts.

Month	1	2	3	4	5	6	7	8	9	10	11	12
Demand	16	14	12	15	18	21	23	24	25	26	37	38

		Moving averages		
Month	Demand	3-period	6-period	9-period
1	16			
2	14			
3	12			
4	15	14.0		
5	18	13.7		
6	21	15.0		
7	23	18.0	16.0	
8	24	20.7	17.2	
9	25	22.7	18.8	
10	26	24.0	21.0	18.7
11	37	25.0	22.8	19.8
12	38	29.3	26.0	22.3
13		33.7	28.8	25.2

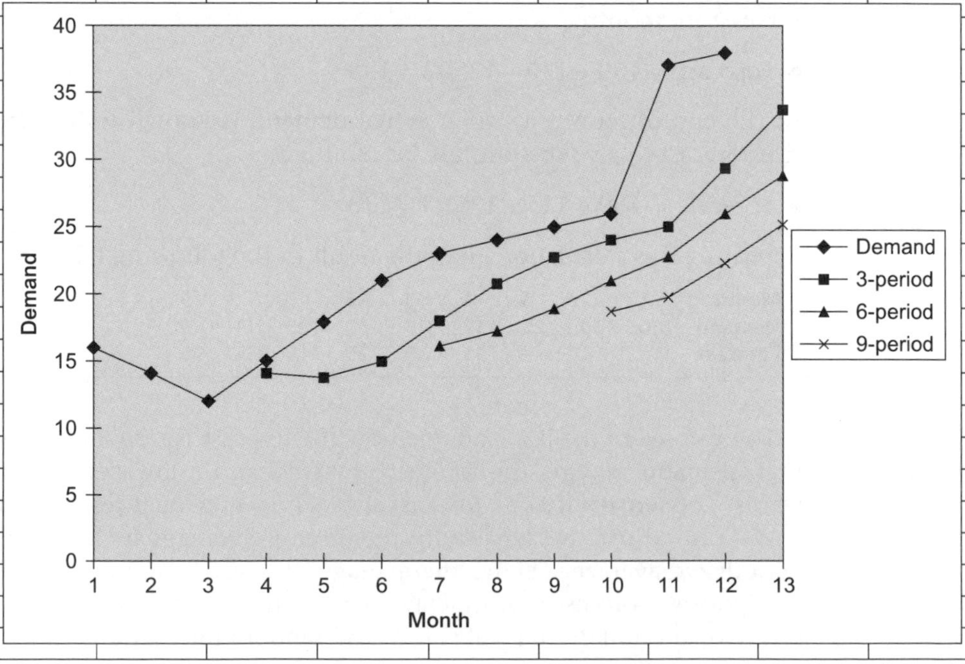

Figure 8.11 Moving averages with different periods

Solution
Figure 8.11 shows the result from a spreadsheet. As you can see, the three-month moving average is clearly most sensitive to change, while the nine-month moving average is least sensitive.

Moving averages have two major defects:

- all historical values are given the same weight;
- the method only works well with relatively constant demand.

Both of these problems are avoided by **exponential smoothing**.

Exponential smoothing

Exponential smoothing is the most widely used method of projective forecasting. It is based on the idea that as data gets older it becomes less relevant and should be given less weight. In particular, exponential smoothing gives a declining weight to older data, as shown in Figure 8.12.

In practice, we can get this declining weight using only the latest demand and the previous forecast. To be precise, we find the new forecast by adding together a proportion, α, of the latest demand and a proportion, $1 - \alpha$, of the previous forecast.

For exponential smoothing:

New forecast = $\alpha \times$ latest demand + $(1 - \alpha) \times$ last forecast

In this equation, α is the **smoothing constant**, which usually takes a value between 0.1 and 0.2.

You can see how exponential smoothing adapts to changes in demand with a simple example. Suppose a forecast was optimistic and suggested a value of 200 for a demand that actually turns out to be 180. Taking a value of $\alpha = 0.2$, the forecast for the next period is:

New forecast = $\alpha \times$ latest demand + $(1 - \alpha) \times$ last forecast
$= 0.2 \times 180 + (1 - 0.2) \times 200 = 196$

The lower demand has clearly reduced the forecast for the next period.

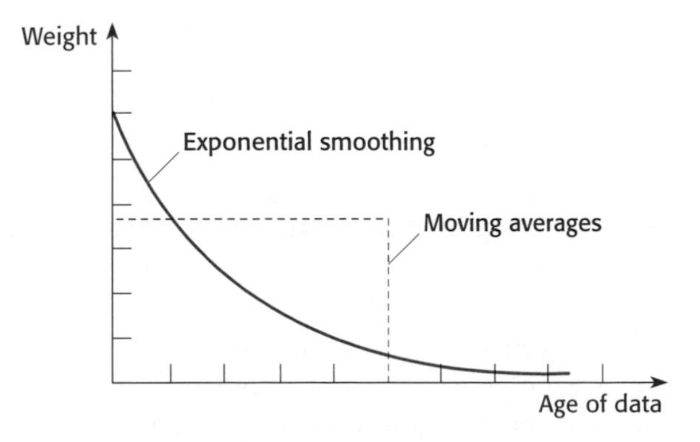

Figure 8.12 Weight given to past data

WORKED EXAMPLE

Use exponential smoothing with $\alpha = 0.2$ and an initial forecast of 170 to give one period ahead forecasts for the following time series.

Month	1	2	3	4	5
Demand	178	180	156	150	162

Solution

Imagine yourself at the end of period 1. The last forecast was 170, the actual demand was 178, and we are using a smoothing constant of 0.2. So the forecast for period 2 is:

- New forecast $= \alpha \times$ latest demand $+ (1 - \alpha) \times$ last forecast
  $= 0.2 \times 178 + 0.8 \times 170$
  $= 171.6$

At the end of period 2, we know that the actual demand was 180, so the forecast for period 3 is:

- New forecast $= 0.2 \times 180 + 0.8 \times 171.6 = 173.3$

Repeating these calculations gives the following results.

Month	1	2	3	4	5	6
Demand	178.0	180.0	156.0	150.0	162.0	–
Forecast	170.0	171.6	173.3	169.8	165.9	165.1

The value given to the smoothing constant sets the sensitivity of the forecast. A high value of α (say 0.3 to 0.35) puts more weight on the latest demand and gives a more responsive forecast: a lower value (say 0.1 to 0.15) puts more weight on the old forecast and gives a less responsive forecast. Again, we need to compromise between a responsive forecast that might follow random fluctuations, and an unresponsive one that might not follow real patterns.

WORKED EXAMPLE

The *Newhaven Review*, a magazine describing the literary scene of New England, reduced its cover price and had a sudden surge in sales. The following table shows the effectively monthly sales (in hundreds). What forecasts would you get over this period with exponential smoothing?

Period	1	2	3	4	5	6	7	8	9	10	11
Demand	480	500	1,500	1,450	1,550	1,500	1,480	1,520	1,500	1,490	1,500

Solution

No projective forecasting method can deal with this kind of sudden surge in demand. However, we can see how exponential smoothing copes by taking a range of values for α. The spreadsheet in Figure 8.13 shows results for $\alpha = 0.1$, 0.2, 0.3 and 0.4.

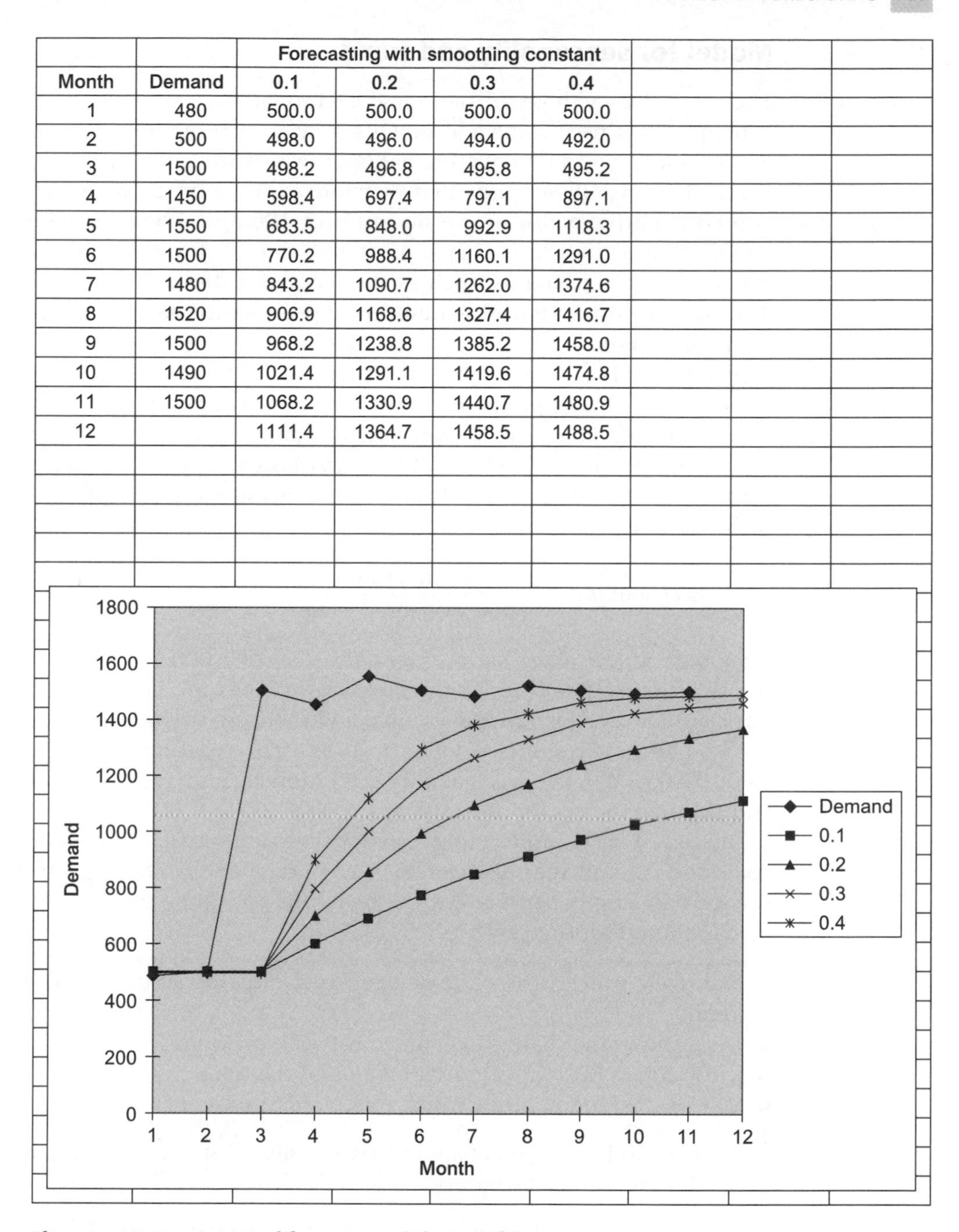

		Forecasting with smoothing constant			
Month	Demand	0.1	0.2	0.3	0.4
1	480	500.0	500.0	500.0	500.0
2	500	498.0	496.0	494.0	492.0
3	1500	498.2	496.8	495.8	495.2
4	1450	598.4	697.4	797.1	897.1
5	1550	683.5	848.0	992.9	1118.3
6	1500	770.2	988.4	1160.1	1291.0
7	1480	843.2	1090.7	1262.0	1374.6
8	1520	906.9	1168.6	1327.4	1416.7
9	1500	968.2	1238.8	1385.2	1458.0
10	1490	1021.4	1291.1	1419.6	1474.8
11	1500	1068.2	1330.9	1440.7	1480.9
12		1111.4	1364.7	1458.5	1488.5

Figure 8.13 Forecasts with exponential smoothing

You can see that all the forecasts are following the demand upwards, but higher values of α give more responsive forecasts that make this adjustment more quickly.

Source: company annual accounts

Model for seasonality and trend

The projective methods we have described so far are really only useful for constant demand. They need some adjustments to deal with other patterns. In this section we develop a model for data that has both seasonality and trend.

Trend shows the amount that demand grows between consecutive periods. If two consecutive periods have demands of 100 and 120, the trend is 20: if two consecutive periods have demands of 100 and 80, the trend is –20. You can see many examples of trends, such as the long-term decline in beer sales, increasing disposable income, increasing numbers of people with degrees, increasing traffic on roads, and so on.

Seasonality is a regular cyclical pattern, such as the average daily temperature, sales of daily newspapers, amount of money in your bank account, or sales of ice cream. Each cycle repeats the same general pattern, so that sales of newspapers are always highest at the weekend, it is always hottest around midday, etc. Each cycle contains a number of 'seasons', and we can measure the variation in demand using seasonal indices.

$$\text{Seasonal index} = \frac{\text{seaonal value}}{\text{deseasonalised value}}$$

Suppose a newspaper has average daily sales of 1,000 copies in a particular area, but this rises to 2,000 copies on Saturday and falls to 500 copies on Monday and Tuesday. The cycle is seven days long, and there are seven seasons in this repeating cycle. The deseasonalised value is 1,000; the seasonal index for Saturday is 2,000/1,000 = 2.0; the seasonal indices for Monday and Tuesday are 500/1,000 = 0.5; and seasonal indices for other days are 1,000/1,000 = 1.0.

The easiest way of forecasting complex time series is to split demand into separate components, and then forecast each component separately. Then we recombine the separate components to get the final forecast. To be specific, we shall split the demand into four components:

- *Underlying value* is the basic demand that must be adjusted for seasonality and trend.
- *Trend* shows the change in demand between periods.
- *Seasonality* is the cyclical variation around the trend.
- *Noise* is the random noise whose effects we cannot explain.

Then demand is made up of an underlying value, with added trend, multiplied by a seasonal index, and added noise.

$$\text{Demand} = (\text{underlying value} + \text{trend}) \times \text{seasonal index} + \text{noise}$$

In practice, forecasting is easier if we combine the underlying value and trend into a single figure for the underlying trend. There is nothing we can do about the noise, so our forecast becomes:

$$\text{Forecast} = \text{underlying trend} \times \text{seasonal index}$$

Now we can get forecasts using the following seven steps.

- **Step 1**. Take the time series of historical data.
- **Step 2**. Use linear regression to find the underlying trend. This gives a deseasonalised value for each period.
- **Step 3**. We now have the original seasonal data for each period, and corresponding deseasonalised values from regression. Dividing the first of these by the second gives a seasonal index for each period.
- **Step 4**. Look at the data to see how many seasons there are in each cycle.
- **Step 5**. Find the average seasonal index for each season of the cycle, i.e. the average index for the first season, second season, etc.
- **Step 6**. Find deseasonalised values for the future – usually by projecting the regression line.
- **Step 7**. Get the final forecast by multiplying these values by the relevant seasonal indices.

The following example illustrates these steps, and the Supplement to the chapter expands the related calculations.

WORKED EXAMPLE

Forecast demand for the next four quarters of the following time series.

Quarter	1	2	3	4	5	6	7	8
Demand	986	1,245	902	704	812	1,048	706	514

Solution

Figure 8.14 shows the calculations in a spreadsheet. The historical data is given for quarters 1 to 8 and the forecasts are calculated for quarters 9 to 12.

- **Step 1**. We already have a time series of historical data.
- **Step 2**. Linear regression finds the best line through the eight quarters of demand data as:

  $$\text{Demand} = 1156.75 - 64.92 \times \text{quarter}$$

  This equation is used to calculate the deseasonalised values.
- **Step 3**. Dividing the actual demand by the deseasonalised value gives a seasonal index for each of the first eight quarters.
- **Step 4**. The data has two cycles with four quarters in each.
- **Step 5**. The first quarters in the first two cycles are quarters 1 and 5; the average seasonal index for these two quarters is (0.90 + 0.98)/2 = 0.94. Average seasonal indices for the other three quarters are found in the same way, as 1.29, 0.97 and 0.90.
- **Step 6**. The regression line is projected to give deseasonalised values for quarters 9 to 12.
- **Step 7**. Now we find the forecasts by multiply these deseasonalised values by the appropriate seasonal index found in step 5. In period 9, for example, the deseasonalised value is 572.2, the seasonal index for the first quarter is 0.94, and multiplying these together gives a forecast of 538.

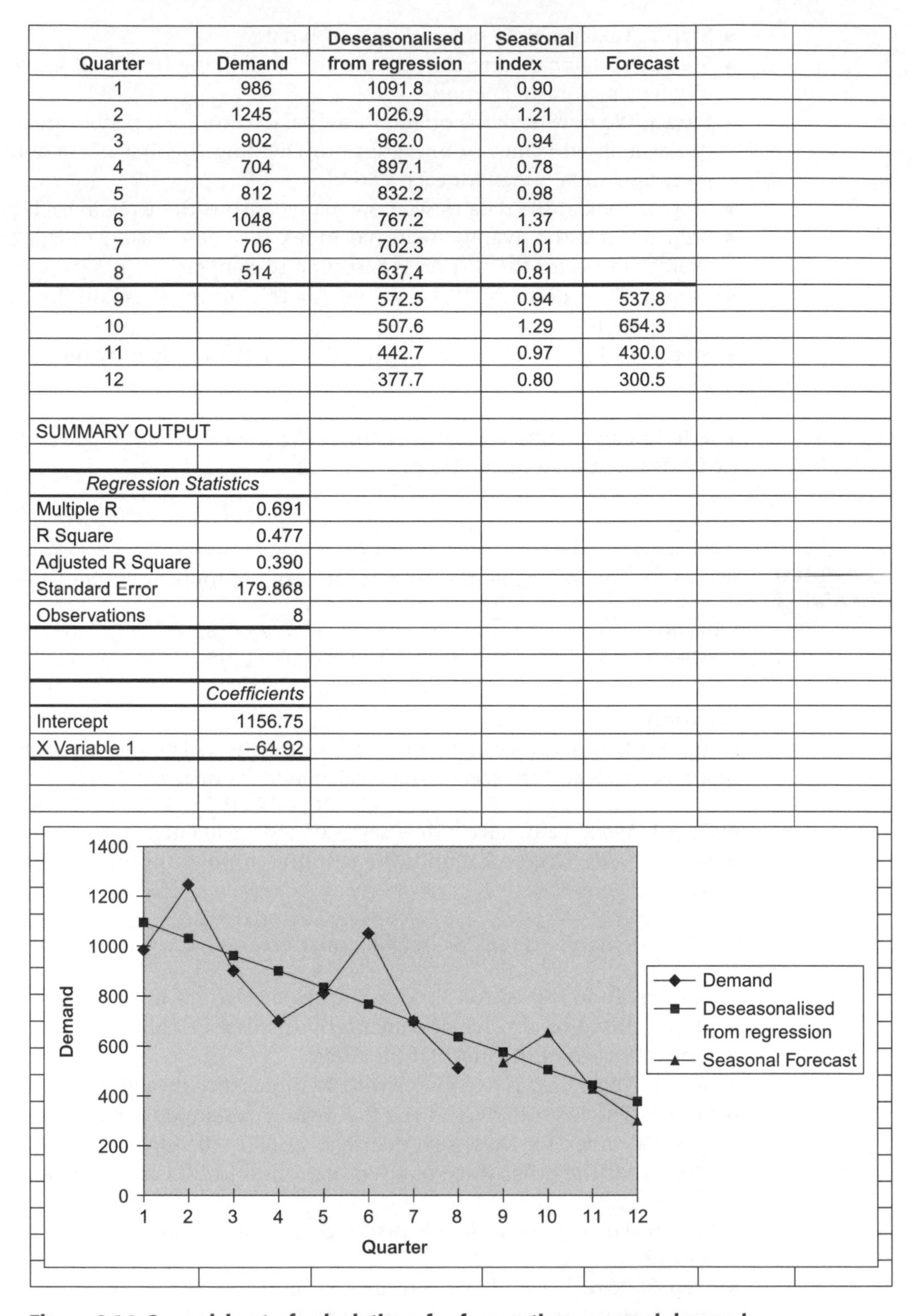

Quarter	Demand	Deseasonalised from regression	Seasonal index	Forecast
1	986	1091.8	0.90	
2	1245	1026.9	1.21	
3	902	962.0	0.94	
4	704	897.1	0.78	
5	812	832.2	0.98	
6	1048	767.2	1.37	
7	706	702.3	1.01	
8	514	637.4	0.81	
9		572.5	0.94	537.8
10		507.6	1.29	654.3
11		442.7	0.97	430.0
12		377.7	0.80	300.5

SUMMARY OUTPUT

Regression Statistics	
Multiple R	0.691
R Square	0.477
Adjusted R Square	0.390
Standard Error	179.868
Observations	8

	Coefficients
Intercept	1156.75
X Variable 1	−64.92

Figure 8.14 Spreadsheet of calculations for forecasting seasonal demand

Review questions

8.14 Why are simple averages of limited use for forecasting?

8.15 How can you make moving average forecasts more responsive?

8.16 Why is the forecasting method called 'exponential smoothing'?

8.17 How can you make exponential smoothing forecasts more sensitive?

8.18 What is a seasonal index?

8.19 There is only one method of forecasting demand with both seasonality and trend. Do you think this is true?

Project 8.3

Look at the way that share prices have varied over recent months. You might also look at the sales of commodities, travel, production of different types of food or some other time series. See if you can use the patterns to forecast future values. What problems and successes do you have?

OPERATIONS IN PRACTICE

Generating electricity

The principles of forecasting are relatively simple, but the practice can become very complicated. You can see this when people try to forecast the winner of a horse race, lottery numbers, the price of oil, interest rates and the weather.

One of the most difficult problems of forecasting is the demand for electricity. Electricity cannot be stored – except in very small quantities using batteries – so all demand must be exactly matched by the supply from power stations. Any shortages in electricity generation give power cuts, which customers would not accept, while excess capacity wastes expensive resources.

The long-term demand for electricity is rising steadily, so enough power stations must be built to meet this increase. Planning and building a power station takes many years, so decisions are based on forecast demand 20 or more years in the future.

In the shorter term, demand for electricity follows an annual cycle, with demand generally higher in winter when more heating systems are switched on. There are also short, irregular periods of especially high demand during cold spells. There are cycles during the week, with lower demand at the weekends when industry is not working so intensely. On top of this are cycles during the day, with lighter demand during the night when most of us are asleep. Finally, there are irregular peaks during the day, perhaps corresponding to breaks in television programmes when people turn on electric kettles.

Power stations need 'warming-up' before they start supplying electricity, so a stable demand would make operations much easier. In practice, though, they have to forecast demands with long-term trend, annual cycle, short-term peaks, weekly cycles, daily cycles and short-term variations.

Guidelines for forecasting

Many things can go wrong with forecasts, so it is worth giving some guidance on how to avoid the most common mistakes. Many of these points are obvious, but you can see from the wealth of poor forecasts that they are often forgotten.

1. Start by clearly defining the purpose of the forecast. What are you trying to forecast, why, how will you use the results, and when will you need them? Avoid the temptation to look at some available data and 'do a bit of forecasting'.
2. Aggregate forecasts are more accurate than specific ones. A brewer, for example, can get more accurate forecasts for the total sales of beer, than for sales of each individual brand.
3. Decide what time horizon the forecast must cover. Short-term forecasts are more accurate than long-term ones.
4. Involve other people in the forecasting, particularly those who have most knowledge of the operations, and those who will use the results.
5. Recognise different people's needs. Sales people, for example, tend to prefer optimistic forecasts, while finance people tend to prefer pessimistic ones. People who are paid a bonus for exceeding their forecast performance will always look for very low forecasts.
6. Choose a suitable forecasting method. If there are historical data, quantitative methods are more reliable. The final choice of method depends on many factors, including the time covered, variability of demand, accuracy needed, the amount of time and money available, etc.
7. Consider the balance between costs and benefits. It is no use spending a lot of time and money on an unimportant forecast. On the other hand, some forecasts are very important and you should do enough work to get the best possible results.
8. Test the method over a typical historical period to make sure that it gives good results. Do not assume that using a good method automatically gives good results. Collect any additional data needed and test different parameter values.
9. Do not give too many details in your results. It is easy to do every possible test and analysis, but no one is interested in these and they serve no useful purpose.
10. Do not let people develop too high expectations of a forecast. Try to estimate the likely errors, and warn people that the results will not be perfect.
11. Be careful when implementing new forecasting methods. Run new methods and old ones in parallel for some time and make sure that the new methods really are an improvement.
12. Monitor the performance of new forecasting methods. Keep looking for improvements and better parameter values.
13. Do not let the forecasts become an end in themselves. A forecast is not just a set of numbers, but is done for a purpose, which is to give information that managers can use to make informed decisions.

Review questions

8.20 The most important thing for successful forecasting is choosing the right method. Do you think this is true?

Chapter review

- Managers do not base their decisions on present circumstances, but on prevailing circumstances when the decisions become effective. We do not know what will happen in the future, so the best we can do is use forecasts.

- Forecasting is an important function in every organisation. Despite this, there has been limited progress in many areas.
- There are many different methods of forecasting, each of which is best in different circumstances. Three basic approaches are judgemental, causal and projective.
- When there are no relevant quantitative data, judgemental or qualitative methods must be used. These collect opinions from groups of experts – and range from personal insight to the more formal Delphi method.
- Most quantitative forecasts are concerned with time series, where demand is measured at regular intervals of time. Demand usually has an underlying pattern with superimposed noise. This random noise is the reason why forecasts usually contain errors.
- Causal forecasts looks for relationships between variables. Linear regression draws the line of best fit through a set of data and uses the known value of an independent variable to forecast the value of a dependent variable.
- Projective forecasts look at the patterns in historical data and project these into the future. There are many ways of doing this, and we considered the simple average, moving averages, exponential smoothing and a model for seasonality and trend.
- Real forecasting can be difficult, but there are many useful guidelines.

Key terms

causal forecast *p. 179*
coefficient of correlation *p. 190*
coefficient of determination *p. 190*
Delphi method *p. 182*
dependent variable *p. 187*
exponential smoothing *p. 197*
independent variable *p. 187*
judgemental forecast *p. 180*
linear regression *p. 187*
market survey *p. 181*
mean squared error *p. 185*
moving average *p. 195*
noise *p. 184*
panel consensus *p. 181*
personal insight *p. 181*
projective forecast *p. 178*
seasonal index *p. 200*
sensitivity *p. 195*
simple average *p. 194*
smoothing constant *p. 197*
trend *p. 184*
time series *p. 184*

CASE STUDY Workload planning

Mary James worked in the purchasing department of a medium-sized construction company. One morning she walked into the office and said:

The problem with this office is lack of planning. It seems to me that forecasting is the key to an efficient business. We have never done any forecasting in this department, but simply rely on experience to guess our future workload. I think we should start using a more formal method, and I like the look of exponential smoothing.

Mary thought that they could use forecasts to predict likely bottlenecks and adjust their schedules to use resources more efficiently. As she was in charge of the office, other people happily agreed with her. Unfortunately, they were going through a busy period and nobody had time to work on Mary's 'Workload Forecasting Project'. A month later nothing had actually happened.

Mary was not pleased by the lack of progress, and felt sure that the current high workload was a symptom of poor planning and poor forecasting. To make some progress on her project, she seconded John Barnes, a management trainee, to work on some figures.

John examined the work of the department and divided it into seven main categories, of searching for business, preparing estimates, submitting tenders, finding suppliers, etc. For each of these categories, he found the number of distinct jobs that the office had completed each quarter of the past three years. These figures are summarised in the following table.

Quarter	Work category						
	1	2	3	4	5	6	7
1, 1	129	74	1,000	755	1,210	204	24
2, 1	138	68	1,230	455	1,520	110	53
3, 1	110	99	890	810	1,390	105	42
4, 1	118	119	700	475	1,170	185	21
1, 2	121	75	790	785	1,640	154	67
2, 2	137	93	1,040	460	1,900	127	83
3, 2	121	123	710	805	1,860	187	80
4, 2	131	182	490	475	1,620	133	59
1, 3	115	103	610	775	2,010	166	105
2, 3	126	147	840	500	2,340	140	128
3, 3	131	141	520	810	2,210	179	126
4, 3	131	112	290	450	1,990	197	101

John decided to use these figures to forecast the number of jobs in each category for the next two years. He was not sure that exponential smoothing was the best approach, but he could do some experiments.

Mary was more interested in finding the overall workload and using this for planning. So John looked for a way to combine the different categories of work. For this he defined a 'standard work unit', and found the average number of work units needed to complete a job in each category.

Work category	1	2	3	4	5	6	7
Work units	2.0	1.5	1.0	0.7	0.4	3.0	2.5

Questions

- How can John approach the forecasting of workload in the purchasing department?
- What results would he get and how reliable are they?
- How could the forecasts be used in planning decisions?

Problems

8.1 Carnwath amateur dramatic society is staging a play and wants to know how much to spend on advertising. Its aim is to attract as many people as possible, up to the hall's capacity of 300. For the past 11 productions the spending on advertising (in hundreds of pounds) and resulting audience is shown in the following table. How much would you spend on advertising?

Spending	3	5	1	7	2	4	4	2	6	6	4
Audience	200	250	75	425	125	300	225	200	300	400	275

8.2 The number of accident-free shifts worked in a company over the past 10 months is shown below. Use linear regression to forecast the number of accident-free shifts for the next six months. How reliable are these figures?

Month	1	2	3	4	5	6	7	8	9	10
Shifts	6	21	41	75	98	132	153	189	211	243

8.3 Jerry Chan collected the following data relating to sales. What information can he get from this?

Sales	420	520	860	740	510	630	650	760	590	680
Month	1	2	3	4	5	6	7	8	9	10
Market	3	7	9	3	1	6	2	9	6	6
Personnel	23	15	64	52	13	40	36	20	19	24
Competition	109	121	160	155	175	90	132	145	97	107

8.4 Find the 2, 3 and 4 period moving average for the following time series, and say which gives the best results.

Period	1	2	3	4	5	6	7	8
Demand	280	240	360	340	300	220	200	360

8.5 Use exponential smoothing with smoothing constant equal to 0.1, 0.2, 0.3 and 0.4 to produce one period ahead forecasts for the following time series. Use an initial value of 208 and say which value of α is best.

Week	1	2	3	4	5	6	7	8
Sales	212	216	424	486	212	208	208	204

8.6 The following figures show the number of road accidents per quarter in a Nielands Haven. Deseasonalise the data and find the underlying trend.

Quarter	1	2	3	4	5	6	7	8	9	10
Number of accidents	75	30	52	88	32	53	90	30	56	96

8.7 In the past two years Sunter Egland had the following demands for a product. Forecast demand for the following year.

Month	Jan	Feb	Mar	Apr	May	June	July	Aug	Sept	Oct	Nov	Dec
Year 1	100	87	86	75	92	107	115	131	120	118	120	142
Year 2	123	101	105	93	121	136	130	155	158	142	147	181

Discussion questions

8.1 Is forecasting really essential for all decisions? Can you give examples of decisions that do not depend on forecasts?

8.2 How might poor forecasts affect an organisation's performance? Give some real examples to support your views.

8.3 What factors should managers consider when choosing a forecasting method?

8.4 How can organisations integrate forecasting with other operations?

8.5 Many forecasting methods depend on a detailed knowledge of statistics. General managers do not have this specialised knowledge. How can they be involved in – or understand – these specialised methods?

8.6 What are the assumptions of linear regression? Are these generally realistic? How can the method be extended to deal with more complicated situations?

8.7 How could you judge the best level of sensitivity for a forecast?

8.8 Projective forecasting cannot deal with sudden, unexpected changes. In July of 1993, for example, Rupert Murdoch's News International decided to boost sales of *The Times* and cut the price from 45p a day to 30p. The resulting average daily sales (thousands of copies) of quality newspapers between June 1993 and April 1994 are as shown below.

	June	July	Aug	Sept	Oct	Nov	Dec	Jan	Feb	Mar	Apr
Daily Telegraph	1,012	1,017	1,028	1,008	1,011	1,032	1,008	1,033	1,015	1,001	999
Financial Times	283	288	275	287	288	294	294	284	300	304	299
Guardian	407	403	392	404	403	402	389	406	405	403	397
Independent	339	335	326	332	329	314	302	291	292	277	271
The Times	362	360	354	442	445	445	439	456	468	471	478

Source: Audit Bureau of Circulations

How do you think newspapers forecast their demands? Could they have forecast the effects of a sudden drop in price of *The Times*?

Selected reading

Armstrong J.S. (1995) *Long Range Forecasting*. New York: John Wiley.

Bomhoff E. (1994) *Financial Forecasting for Business and Economics*. London: International Thomson Business.

De Lurgio S.A. (1998) *Forecasting Principles and Applications*. New York: Irwin–McGraw-Hill.

Diebold F. (1998) *Elements of Forecasting*. Cincinnati: South Western.

Gaynor P. And Kirkpatric R. (1994) *An Introduction to Time Series Modelling and Forecasting for Business and Economics*. London: McGraw-Hill.

Hanke J.E. and Reitsch A.G. (1997) *Business Forecasting*. 5th edn. Englewood Cliffs, NJ: Prentice-Hall.

Jarrett J. (1991) *Business Forecasting Methods*. Oxford: Blackwell.

Pecar B. (1994) *Business Forecasting for Management*. London: McGraw-Hill.

Wheelwright S.C., Makridakis S. and Hyndman R. (1998) *Forecasting Models for Management*. 7th edn. New York: John Wiley.

Useful Websites

www.autobox.com
www.wharton.upenn.edu/forecast

SUPPLEMENT TO CHAPTER 8

Forecasting

Contents

Calculations for linear regression

Linear regression looks for the line of best fit through a set of data. It finds the best values for the intercept, a, and gradient, b, in the equation:

Dependent variable, $y = a + b \times$ independent variable, x

It is fairly easy to calculate the mean squared error, and show that the values which minimise this are:

$$b = \frac{n\Sigma xy - \Sigma x \Sigma y}{n\Sigma x^2 - (\Sigma x)^2}$$

$$a = \frac{\Sigma y}{n} - b\frac{\Sigma x}{n}$$

Where n is the number of observations. The coefficient of correlation, r, has the equally messy equation:

$$\text{Coefficient of correlation} = \frac{n\Sigma xy - \Sigma x \Sigma y}{\sqrt{[n\Sigma x^2 - (\Sigma x)^2] \times [n\Sigma y^2 - (\Sigma y)^2]}}$$

Then we find the coefficient of determination, r^2, by squaring this value.

WORKED EXAMPLE

A factory keeps records of the number of shifts worked each month and the output. If the factory needs 400 units next month, how many shifts should it work?

Month	1	2	3	4	5	6	7	8	9
Shifts worked	50	70	25	55	20	60	40	25	35
Output	352	555	207	508	48	498	310	153	264

Solution

'Shifts worked' gives the independent variable, with 'output' as the dependent variable. We can add the values to get:

$n = 9$ $\Sigma x = 380$ $\Sigma y = 2{,}896$

$\Sigma xy = 145{,}870$ $\Sigma x^2 = 18{,}500$ $\Sigma y^2 = 1{,}172{,}355$

Substituting these gives:

- Gradient, $b = [n\Sigma xy - \Sigma x\Sigma y]/[n\Sigma x^2 - (\Sigma x)^2]$
  $= [9 \times 145{,}870 - 380 \times 2{,}895]/[9 \times 18{,}500 - 380^2] = 9.63$
- Intercept, $a = \Sigma y/n - b\Sigma x/n = 2{,}895/9 - 9.63 \times 380/9 = -84.76$
- Coefficient of correlation, $r = [n\Sigma xy - \Sigma x\Sigma y]/[n\Sigma x^2 - (\Sigma x)^2] \times [n\Sigma y^2 - (\Sigma y)^2]$
  $= [9 \times 145{,}870 - 380 \times 2{,}895]/[9 \times 18{,}500 - 380^2] \times [9 \times 1{,}172{,}355 - 2{,}895^2] = 0.97$
- Coefficient of determination, $r^2 = 0.972^2 = 0.94$

The coefficient of determination is high, showing a close linear relationship. We want to find the value of x (the number of shifts) that will give a value of y (the output) of 400. Substituting the known values gives:

$y = a + bx$
So: $400 = -84.76 + 9.63x$
Or: $x = 50.3$

The factory needs to work about 50 shifts next month.

Calculations for projective forecasting with seasonality and trend

We can go through an example of forecasting with seasonality and trend to show the arithmetic. As you can see, it is easy to get bogged down in the details of this arithmetic and lose sight of the overall method.

WORKED EXAMPLE

The demand for a product over the past 12 periods is:

Period	1	2	3	4	5	6	7	8	9	10	11	12
Demand	291	320	142	198	389	412	271	305	492	518	363	388

Forecast demand for periods 13 to 17.

Solution

We will follow the seven-step procedure described in the main chapter.

- **Step 1**. We already have the time series and are ready to start the analysis.
- **Step 2**. Use linear regression to find the underlying trend. This gives a deseasonalised value for each period.
  With the values given:

  $n = 12 \quad \Sigma x = 78 \quad \Sigma y = 4{,}089 \quad \Sigma x^2 = 650 \quad \Sigma xy = 29{,}160$

  Substituting these in the standard linear regression equations gives:

$$b = \frac{n\Sigma xy - \Sigma x\Sigma y}{n\Sigma x^2 - (\Sigma x)^2} = \frac{12 \times 29{,}160 - 78 \times 4{,}089}{12 \times 650 - 78 \times 78} = 18.05$$

$$a = \Sigma y/n - b\Sigma x/n = 4{,}089/12 - 18.05 \times 78/12 = 223.41$$

The line of best fit gives the trend as:

Demand = 223.41 + 18.05 × period

The deseasonalised underlying trend for period 1 is 223.41 + 1 × 18.05 = 241.46; for period 2 it is 223.41 + 2 × 18.05 = 259.51, and so on. These deseasonalised values are shown in the following table.

- **Step 3**. We now have the original seasonal data for each period, and corresponding deseasonalised values from regression. Dividing the first of these by the second gives a seasonal index for each period. Taking a single period, say 4, we have an actual demand of 198. The deseasonalised value from linear regression is 295.61, so the seasonal index 198/295.61 = 0.67. Repeating this calculation for other periods gives the following results.

Period	Actual demand	Deseasonalised trend value	Seasonal index
1	291	241.46	1.21
2	320	259.51	1.23
3	142	277.56	0.51
4	198	295.61	0.67
5	389	313.66	1.24
6	412	331.71	1.24
7	271	349.76	0.77
8	305	367.81	0.83
9	492	385.86	1.28
10	518	403.91	1.28
11	363	421.96	0.86
12	388	440.01	0.88

- **Step 4**. If you look at the data there is an obvious pattern with four seasons in each cycle.
- **Step 5**. Now we find the average seasonal index for each season of the cycle. We have calculated a seasonal index for each season, so we can take averages to find more accurate values. There are four seasons in a cycle, so we have to calculate four seasonal indices.

  Taking periods 1, 5 and 9 as the first seasons in consecutive cycles gives an average seasonal index for the first season as:

  - First season in the cycle (1.21 + 1.24 + 1.28)/3 = 1.24

  Similarly, the average indices for other seasons are:

  - Second season in the cycle (1.23 + 1.24 + 1.28)/3 = 1.25
  - Third season in the cycle (0.51 + 0.77 + 0.86)/3 = 0.71
  - Fourth season in the cycle (0.67 + 0.83 + 0.88)/3 = 0.79

- **Step 6**. Find deseasonalised values for the future by projecting the regression line. We found the trend line as:

  Demand = 223.41 + 18.05 × period

  Now we can substitute 13 to 17 for the period and find the deseasonalised trend for these periods. In period 13, for example, the deseasonalised value is 223.41 + 18.05 × 13 = 458.06. These results are shown in the table below.

- **Step 7**. Now we can make our forecasts. Starting with period 13, the deseasonalised forecast is 458.06. This is the first season in a cycle, so the seasonal index found in step 5 is 1.24. Multiplying these together gives the forecast of 568. The other values are shown in the following table.

Period	Deseasonalised value	Seasonal index	Forecast
13	458.06	1.24	568
14	476.11	1.25	595
15	494.16	0.71	351
16	512.21	0.79	405
17	530.26	1.24	658

INTEGRATING CASE STUDY

Customer service

by Mike Simpson of Sheffield University Management School, and
Elizabeth Richmond of St Mary's Primary School

Organisations put a lot of effort into making products with the design and quality that customers want, but things still go wrong. Customer service departments deal with a wide range of problems. The following extracts illustrate the approach of two companies to customer complaints.

1. Company 'H' Foods Group

Extract from a letter to Company 'H' Foods Group

Recently I purchased two cartons of your brand of Soya Milk from my local supermarket. On opening the cartons my husband discovered that the milk had curdled in both cartons and was very unpleasant looking. I have enclosed the batch numbers from the cartons and hope that this will be useful to you.

Reply from Company 'H' Foods Group

Thank you for your letter regarding our Soya Milk. We sincerely apologise for the inconvenience caused to you. On investigation we have identified the problem to be of an isolated nature.

Tetra pack cartons are made up of various laminates, sometimes there can be interruptions in the laminates, resulting in a negative effect in the barrier properties of the cartons which may allow air to enter causing curdling of the product.

Carton integrity is checked regularly during production, at intervals dictated by the nature of the product, etc. The sampling interval on the batch in question was 15/20 minutes. As a standard procedure, if a failure is detected on a sample, then all product packed prior to detection and up to the previous sampling point is rejected. All laboratory and QC testing results on the batch you bought were satisfactory and no anomaly was evident.

In view of your complaint, the sampling frequency of 15/20 minutes is being reviewed with the intention of taking samples more frequently.

I hope you will accept the enclosed postal order to cover the cost of your purchase. In the meantime if we can be of any further assistance, please do not hesitate to contact us.

2. Tiny Computers

Extract from a letter to Tiny Computers

You can see our main problem with our purchase in the following sequence of events.

1. Early in 2000 the Department for Education and Employment (DfEE) announced a Computers for Teachers Initiative. This gave eligible teachers half the value of a new computer up to £500.
2. My wife is a teacher, and was persuaded by this offer to buy a computer.

3. Tiny sold systems approved by the DfEE. At the beginning of February we went to your office in Truro and chose a system costing £1,099.15, which was eligible for the £500 DfEE grant.
4. We asked about administration, and your shop told us to complete the DfEE forms and return them to the shop, and they would check them and send them off.
5. My wife completed the forms, and we returned them to your Truro shop.
6. In September, other teachers were getting cheques from the DfEE, so we contacted them to ask when we could expect ours. They searched their records, and found that they had never received our application. Tiny had clearly not passed on the forms as promised.
7. We contacted the Tiny shop in Truro several times, and they eventually decided that they did not recall the details of their conversation with us, and if we had any problems we should contact customer service.
8. We sent in a duplicate application to the DfEE. They returned this saying that the scheme had ended and they could not consider my wife's application.
9. My wife made several phone calls to discuss things with your Truro shop, customer relations and BECTA office. There were differences in detail, but they gave the essential message that our business with Tiny was complete.
10. In November your BECTA office assured me that there was nothing that Tiny could or would do about our purchase, they would never change this position, and that our phone calls served no useful purpose.

We have now talked to a number of people in Tiny, and their reactions have ranged from concern to amusement. I am not happy with the treatment we have had from Tiny. I do not admire the attitude of your customer service department, who assure me that they will do nothing and have no interest in our problem.

Reply from Tiny Computers

After receiving this letter, the customer service department of Tiny Computers telephoned the customer to repeat their position that there was nothing they could do, and further discussion was pointless.

Questions

- Do you think the replies from the two companies are reasonable? What could they have done differently? Which of the two companies handled their customer relations better?
- Despite the efforts that organisations put into product design and quality, things still go wrong. Why? What can be done to avoid such problems?
- How well do organisations generally handle their customer relations?

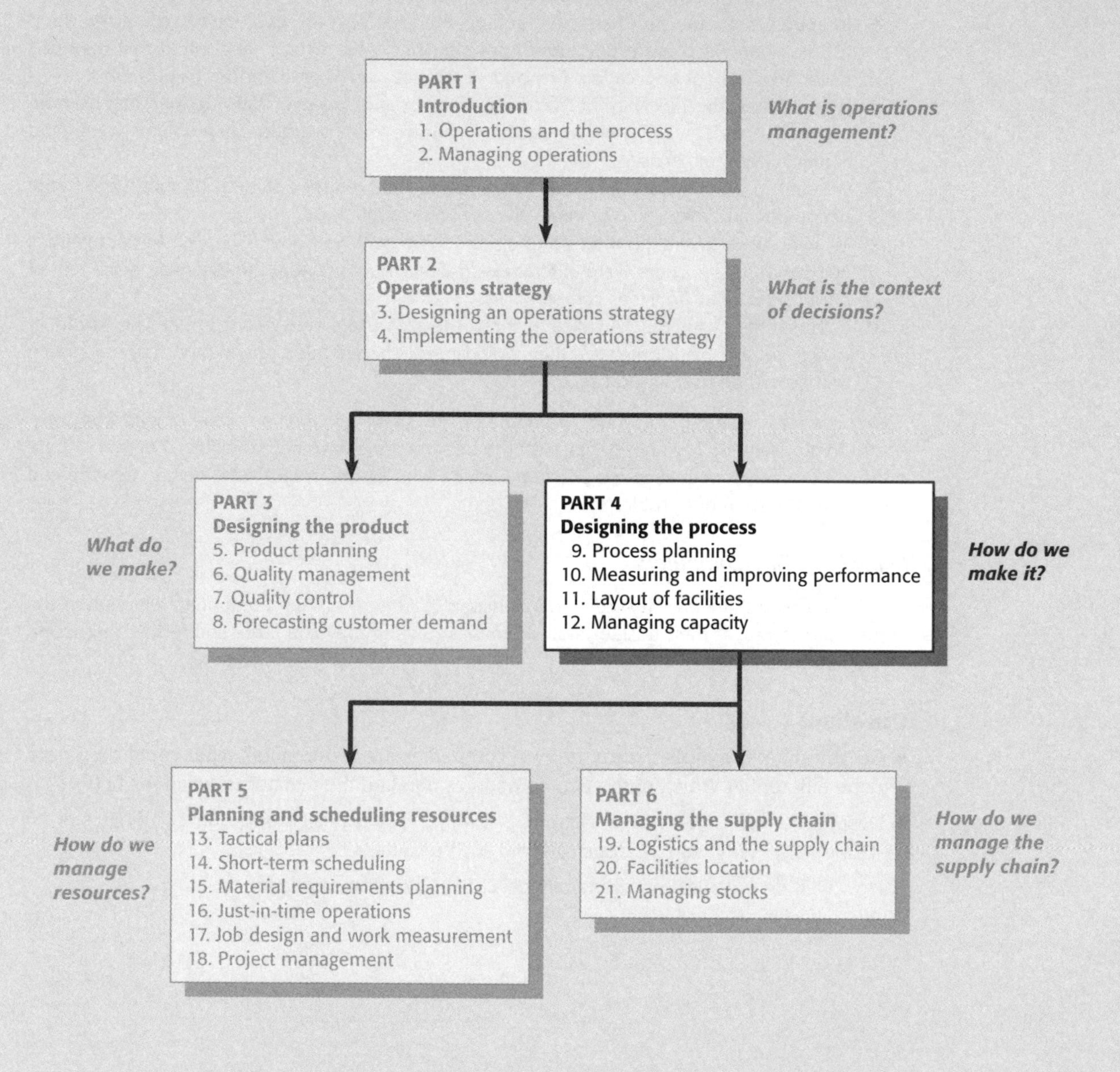
PART 1
Introduction
1. Operations and the process
2. Managing operations
What is operations management?
PART 2
Operations strategy
3. Designing an operations strategy
4. Implementing the operations strategy
What is the context of decisions?
PART 3
Designing the product
5. Product planning
6. Quality management
7. Quality control
8. Forecasting customer demand
What do we make?
PART 4
Designing the process
9. Process planning
10. Measuring and improving performance
11. Layout of facilities
12. Managing capacity
How do we make it?
PART 5
Planning and scheduling resources
13. Tactical plans
14. Short-term scheduling
15. Material requirements planning
16. Just-in-time operations
17. Job design and work measurement
18. Project management
How do we manage resources?
PART 6
Managing the supply chain
19. Logistics and the supply chain
20. Facilities location
21. Managing stocks
How do we manage the supply chain?

Part 4

DESIGNING THE PROCESS

This book is divided into six parts. Each part describes a different aspect of operations management. Part 1 gave an introduction to the subject. Part 2 talked about strategy, emphasising the design and implementation of an operations strategy. Part 3 focused on the design of the product.

This is Part 4 which looks at the design and planning of the process. There are four chapters in this part. Chapter 9 introduces the idea of process design. It describes different types of process, the circumstances in which each is used, and the technology available. Organisations must constantly improve their processes, and some ways of measuring and improving performance are described in Chapter 10. Chapter 11 looks at the layout of facilities. Chapter 12 discusses aspects of capacity management.

Capacity management leads to the planning of resources, which is covered in Part 5 of the book. Part 6 discusses some aspects of supply chain management.

Process planning

The time of process has come. No longer can processes be. . . . toiling away without recognition, attention and respect. They now must occupy centre stage in our organisations. . . . They must influence structure and systems. They must shape how people think and the attitudes they have.

Michael Hammer

Beyond Reengineering, Harper Collins, New York, 1996

Contents

Aims of the chapter

After reading this chapter you should be able to:

- appreciate the relationship between a product and its process;
- understand the role of process planning;
- describe different types of process;
- see how different factors affect the choice of process;
- understand the use of different levels of automation;
- discuss the types of automation used in different organisations;
- appreciate the factors that are important when choosing technology.

Main themes

This chapter will emphasise:

- the **process**, which describes the operations needed to make a product;
- **process planning**, which designs the best process to make a particular product;
- **process technology**, which describes the level of technology used in a process.

Processes make products

Defining the process

The last few chapters have looked at various aspects of product planning – what product to make, how to get high quality, how many to make, etc. In this chapter we are going to look more directly at how to make the product. In other words, we are looking at the **process**.

> The **process** consists of all the operations used to make a product.

A product is a package that contains both goods and services, so the process includes all the related activities that make this package. In different circumstances, this might include:

- *manufacturing* – to change physical form;
- *chemical processing* – such as refining crude oil;
- *information processing* – supporting operations;
- *supply* – to change ownership;
- *transport* – to change location;
- *warehousing* – storing goods until they are needed;
- *other service* – both personal and for business.

Process planning

Most products can be made in many different ways. A wooden table can be hand-built by craftsmen; it can be assembled from bought-in parts; it can be made automatically by machines on an assembly line. If your product is information, you can distribute it in a newspaper, by letter, via e-mail, through a Website, over the telephone, on television or a host of alternatives. In other words, we can use many different processes to make a product.

The design of the process obviously affects features of the product, so organisations have to match the features designed into the product with the best process for making it. If you want to make large numbers of cheap, woollen jumpers, you would not use a process with people knitting them by hand, but would have automated knitting machines. **Process planning** finds the best process for a particular product.

> **Process planning** is responsible for all decisions about a process.
>
> - It describes the details of the operations needed to make a product.
> - Its aim is to design the best process for a particular product.

Process planning is needed whenever there are significant changes to operations, including:

- introduction of an entirely new product;
- changes to an old product;
- changes in demand or the market;
- changes to the cost of inputs or operations;
- competitors with new products;
- unsatisfactory current performance;
- new objectives.

OPERATIONS IN PRACTICE

van Heugen Fabricators

In The Netherlands van Heugen Fabricators run several workshops. They take customers' designs and can make almost any product in metal from ornamental paper clips through to pre-formed industrial buildings. Most of their products use one of five processes:

- *casting* – where liquid metal is poured into a mould;
- *hot forming* – where metal is heated until it can be shaped under pressure;
- *cold forming* – where high pressure is used to shape metal without heating;
- *machining* – where machines remove metal by drilling, boring, turning, milling, shaping, planing or grinding;
- *assembly* – where components are joined together.

When customers submit a design, a production planning team meets to consider the best process to make it. The team often suggests changes to improve the quality or reduce the cost of the finished product.

Process-centred organisations

In principle, customers are more interested in the products they buy than the process used to make them, but we cannot really separate the two, as the product inevitably depends on the process. With services, in particular, it is difficult to draw a line between the products offered by, say, HSBC bank, the Globe Theatre or a taxi service, and the processes used to deliver them. This close connection shows why organisations have to plan their processes carefully:

- all organisations aim at making a product that satisfies customer demand;
- the product must, in some way, be better than competitors' products;
- the process makes the product and determines its features;
- to make better products, an organisation needs a better process.

Some organisations place so much emphasis on the process that they are **process-centred**. They argue that even the best product currently available will soon be overtaken by improved technology, competitors' designs or changing demands. So they should not concentrate on the short term and current product designs, but on the longer term and the process that can deliver a stream of products for the future. Pfizer makes the hugely popular drug Viagra. A process-centred organisation would argue that Viagra will inevitably be overtaken by other products, and Pfizer should not concentrate on the product, but on the process used to develop this and similar drugs in the future. (This, of course, is why Pfizer spends so much on research and development.)

A process-centred organisation looks at the whole, integrated process of satisfying customer demand. This is the reverse of specialisation, which divides the process into a number of tasks, each of which is largely self-contained. When an order comes to a traditional organisation, everyone does a separate part of the process: manufacturing makes the goods; warehousing adjusts the stocks; transport delivers the goods; accounting sends out the invoices. Each of these parts essentially works in isolation: the job of a sales department is finished when it collects an order; the job of a manufacturing department ends when it passes products to the stock of finished goods; the job of the purchasing department is finished when it buys materials. The problem is that no one looks after the whole process, or integrates the different operations, or even makes sure that customers actually get their products.

With a process-centred organisation everyone works as a team, with:

- the single purpose of satisfying customer demand;
- concentration on the whole process of delivering products that customers want;
- expansion of jobs beyond traditional functions, with employees making decisions and dealing with all types of customer issues;
- access to all types of information throughout the organisation;
- a matrix or cross-functional management structure.

OPERATIONS IN PRACTICE

Opticians as retailers

There are about 3,000 opticians' shops in Britain which supply prescription glasses. Their service has traditionally been broken into a series of distinct tasks. One group of people organises eye tests and gives information; another group tests eyes and prescribes lenses; another group makes the lenses; another designs frames; another sells frames to customers; and another group treats eye disease.

But the industry has been affected by major changes.

- The major chains of opticians are taking a larger share of the market, led by Dolland and Aitchison, Specsaver, Boots Opticians and Vision Express.
- Sales are continuing to rise – due to an ageing population, eyewear as a fashion accessory, more regular and rigorous eye tests, developments in contact lenses, and non-essential uses like driving.
- Deregulation of the sale of spectacles in 1986 has encouraged non-traditional suppliers – led by Asda and Tesco supermarkets.
- There is more sophisticated equipment for the automatic testing and monitoring of eyes.

In the early 1990s these changes left too many companies competing for business and the number of optician shops started to decline. The biggest chain, Dolland and Aitchison, fell from 500 shops in 1992 to 427 in 1998. Increased competition encouraged opticians to become more process centred, and look at the overall process of satisfying customer needs. This led to many changes, with opticians moving away from their professional roots and emphasising their work as retailers. They stopped looking at the industry as a series of distinct operations and concentrated on the overall process of supplying glasses to customers, paying more attention to customer service, stocking more frames in the shops, making lenses in the shop to cut down delivery times, introducing new testing equipment, using computer simulations to show the effects of different frames, and so on.

The complete process for even a simple product can be surprisingly complicated. The process in Levi Strauss, for example, includes all the operations that collect materials from suppliers, make clothing and pass this on to final customers. For this discussion, we have to simplify things and concentrate on key parts of the process. We can do this by looking at the way they actually make jeans (concentrating on manufacture), or the way they deliver clothes (concentrating on logistics), or the way they control materials (concentrating on information processing). We know that the process is best viewed as a set of integrated activities that do everything needed to make a product, but we must simplify the discussions by focusing on specific areas.

Review questions

9.1 What is a process?

9.2 What is process planning and when is it used?

9.3 What is a 'process-centred' organisation?

Project 9.1

Look at a familiar product, such as a piece of computer software, and describe the total product package. Can you describe the process used to make all of the elements in this package? Are there any alternative processes? What are the key parts of the process?

Types of process

Two key factors for process planning are the total volume produced and the amount of variation in the product. These are clearly related, and higher volumes usually mean that there is less room for variation in the product. When dairies make cartons of milk, they make very large numbers of a standard product; on the other hand, dentists see a relatively small number of customers, and give each one a distinct, personalised service.

Different types of process are best at dealing with different combinations of volume and variation. There are basically three types of process: those that make a single unit, such as satellite manufacturers; those that make products in batches, such as bakers; and those whose products come in continuous flows, such as oil refineries. Most organisations work with batches, so these processes are usually divided into three types, effectively corresponding to small, medium and large batches. This gives a spectrum of the following five types of process. Although some of the terms seem to refer to manufacturing, remember that they apply equally well to services.

1. **Project**. This is at one end of our spectrum and makes a single unit, usually tailored to customer specifications, such as building a Formula 1 racing car, writing a management consultant's report or building the Channel Tunnel.

The product from each project is essentially unique, so there is a lot of variety with little standardisation. Projects typically take a relatively long time, involve a lot of work, are expensive and include uncertain and changing conditions. The process needs a lot of flexibility to deal with new situations and problems. This needs a skilled and well-trained workforce using general-purpose equipment. Resources are often organised specially for each project, and may remain with the projects for some time before being dispersed. Organisations generally tender for each project, so there can be a lot of variation in workload. The process is controlled by project management methods, which we look at in Chapter 17.

This is generally the type of process that people like to work with. There is more variety, and people get satisfaction from making a significant contribution to an identifiable end result. Examples are shipbuilding, satellite assembly, building an office block, writing a book, making a film, developing software for a new computer system, and preparing for a major sporting event.

2. **Jobbing process**. This is next in our spectrum and makes small numbers of a wide variety of products. It is used in small engineering works, and if you want a set of pistons for a vintage car, they will be made in a job shop (which is obviously where the process gets its name). Jobbing processes usually make products for specific customer orders, so there are no stocks of finished goods. The overall workload varies, depending on the organisation's success at winning orders.

Jobbing processes make a narrower range of products than projects, but there is still a lot of variety. Each product goes through a different sequence of operations, so the process must be flexible, with skilled people working on general-purpose equipment. As each product uses a different mix of resources, there can be short-term mismatches between workload and capacity. Figure 9.1 shows two jobs going through their operations, and you can see that there is a bottleneck at operation 5, while operation 1 is left idle. More time is lost in setting up equipment between products, so the utilisation of resources is low, typically around 25 per cent and often a lot lower. As a result, jobbing processes have relatively low capital costs, but high unit

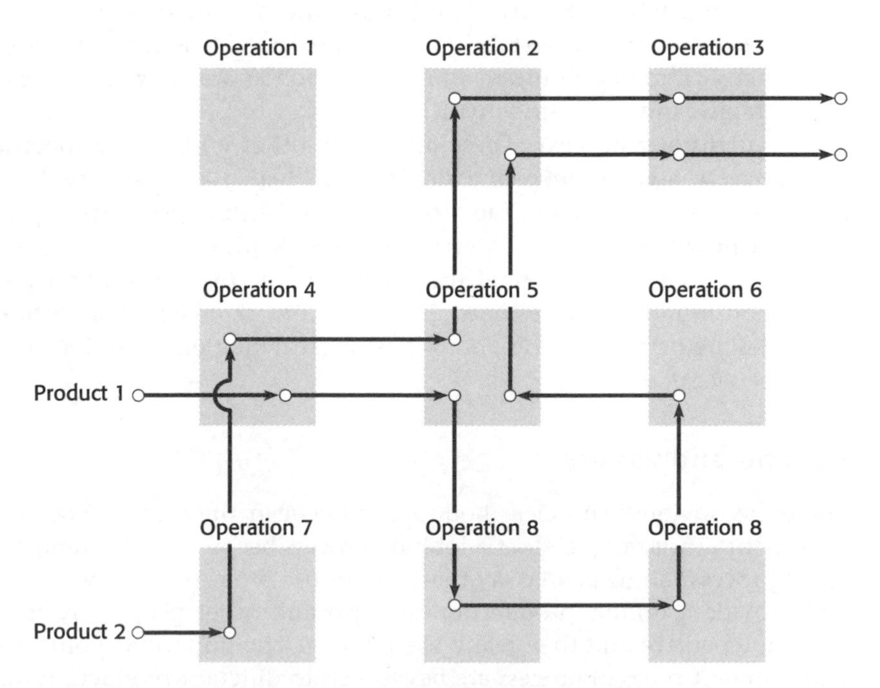

Figure 9.1 Scheduling different jobs through operations

costs. The mix of different products makes scheduling and keeping track of work difficult. Examples are makers of specialised vehicles, printers, customised furniture makers, restaurants with limited menus, and travel agents arranging holidays.

3. **Batch process.** This is the middle of our spectrum, with larger batches of similar products made on the same equipment. With a jobbing process, every time a new customer order is started there are delays and costs for adjusting and setting up equipment. Batch processes reduce these by making more units in each run, with any units not needed for current orders put into a stock of finished goods. The savings from longer production runs more than cover the cost of storing finished goods.

Batch processes are used for medium volumes of products, so there is room for some specialised equipment and skilled people. Products have less variety, so they use almost the same equipment. This makes one product for a certain time, then switches to another product, giving much higher utilisations. Examples are book printers, pharmaceutical and clothing manufacturers, bottling plants, university courses, and insurance companies processing different types of policy.

4. **Mass process.** This is typical of an assembly or production line that makes large numbers of a standard product. Computers, washing machines and cars are made by mass processes. There is little variety in the product, except small changes to the basic model introduced in the finishing. This allows specialised equipment with units moving down a line from one operation to the next. The capital cost is generally high, but unit costs are low.

As the product does not change, there are no disruptions to the process and few problems with control. There is, for example, no need to schedule individual pieces of equipment, or check the progress of individual units through the process. Once the process is set up, it needs a small workforce to keep it going and in extreme cases may be completely automated. This is fortunate, as people do not generally like the repetitive and monotonous work on mass processes. Examples are cars, computers, consumer electronics, domestic appliances such as washing machines, developing photographs, and processing invoices.

5. **Continuous process.** These are at the other end of our spectrum, and are used for very high volumes of a single product such as electricity, bulk chemicals, insurance cover and paper. The process works continuously with a product emerging as a flow without any interruptions. Such processes use highly specialised equipment that can be capital intensive. But the high utilisation gives low unit costs. Continuous processes need a very small workforce and are often automated. Examples are petrol refineries, breweries, sugar refineries, television broadcasts, and police services.

Volume and variety

There are obviously no clear boundaries between these fives types of process. At what point, for example, does a jobbing process become stable enough to become a batch process? Some people say that doctors use projects, as they organise resources and provide a unique product for each patient; other people say that their work is more repetitive and they really use jobbing. The important point is to recognise that different types of process are best suited to different production quantities and variety (as shown in Figure 9.2).

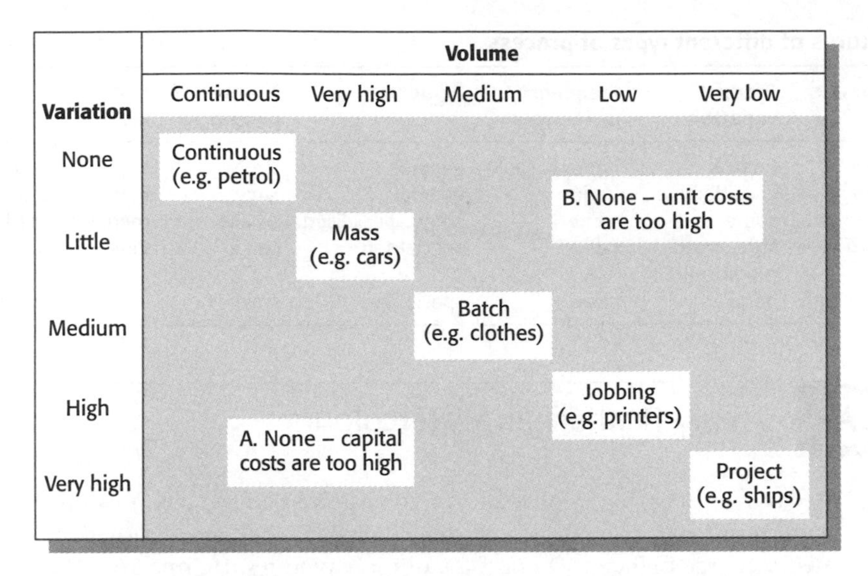

Figure 9.2 Types of process and the variation in products and volumes

As you can see, the processes form a diagonal across the graph. The traditional view is that processes away from this diagonal are not really successful. If you find yourself in area A, making high volumes of a highly variable product, you should move towards the diagonal and reduce the variation or reduce the volume. If you find yourself in area B, making small numbers of the same product, you should increase the volume of a standard product, or allow more customisation. If you already work on the diagonal, it might be better to move along it, so that a low-volume restaurant, serving a wide variety of meals, might move towards higher volumes and less variety. A language school might concentrate on its more profitable clients, and offer a smaller range of more specialised courses.

This traditional view has changed somewhat, as increasing technology and improved operations allow more flexibility. Many organisations have found that they can combine – at least to some extent – both high volumes and product variation. Dell computers, for example, use this **mass customisation** to tailor products to individual customer specifications.

Other descriptions

Project, jobbing and batch processes are sometimes called **intermittent**, as they make a variety of different products and keep changing between them. Mass and continuous processes always make the same basic products.

Another important difference is that projects and jobbing processes are **make-to-order**, which wait for a customer order before starting work. Batch, mass and continuous processes are **make-to-stock** systems, which make the product according to plans and then keep it in stock until needed. These differences are summarised in Table 9.1.

Table 9.1 Features of different types of process

Process type	Volume	Product variation	Frequency of changes	Equipment	Number of people	Skill level	Capital cost	Unit cost
Project	one	one-off	not applicable	general	large	high	low	high
Jobbing	low	considerable	frequent	general	large	high	low	high
Batch	medium	some	some	some specialised	smaller	medium	medium	medium
Mass	high	little (minor modifications)	rare	specialised	small	low	high	low
Continuous	very high	none	none	specialised	small	low	very high	low

OPERATIONS IN PRACTICE

Henry Penhaligan Watercolours

Henry Penhaligan lives in St. Ives, Cornwall. For 20 years he painted commissions for tourists, but always found it difficult to make a comfortable living. He had two alternatives for increasing his income: to charge higher prices or to paint more pictures. He ruled out the first option because tourists would not pay much more than his current prices. So he decided to paint more pictures.

Henry realised that the best way to increase his output was to change the process. His initial process was essentially a project, where each picture was a unique product. He decided to aim for larger sales of mass-produced pictures. He designed some standard views of the coast with cliffs and a beach, and then organised different people to work quickly on each painting. One person painted the sky and cloud formations, a second person added the cliffs, a third painted the sea, a fourth added the beach in the foreground, and so forth. In terms of his process, he had moved along the diagonal in Figure 9.2 towards jobbing.

Over time Henry refined his operations so that paintings now move past a series of artists each of whom adds a small part to the picture. Using this method, which clearly moves towards a mass process, he can get a finished painting in under an hour. The product is very different from his original paintings, but his output and profits have risen dramatically.

Processes for services

Every product is a combination of goods and services, but some parts of a process clearly manufacture while other parts give services. It is often easier to imagine the processes we have described in terms of manufacturing – you have probably seen films of car assembly lines, but are not so sure about the operations in a life assurance office. But remember that the ideas we are discussing apply equally to manufacturing and services. When we talk about a mass process, it can refer to the services provided by the Post Office, tax office, American Express or any other provider of mass services.

Some people argue that the names for different types of process are too closely associated with manufacturing, and we should use other terms for services. There is some disagreement about the best terms, but common ones are:

- *Professional service*. A highly customised personal service such as those offered by doctors, solicitors, consultants and architects (equivalent to project or jobbing).

- *Service shop*. A higher-volume service that still has a lot of personal contact, but less customisation. Examples include hospitals, Hertz car rentals or specialised restaurants (equivalent to a batch process).
- *Mass service*. Giving higher volumes of a more general service with less customer involvement, such as a Booker wholesalers, Pickfords removals or Manchester United Football Club (equivalent to a batch or mass process).
- *Service factory*. Has little customer involvement, and offers large volumes of a standard service, such as National Coaches, the Post Office, a fire service or Visa International (generally equivalent to a mass or continuous process).

Review questions

9.4 Name five different types of process.

9.5 Which type of process would be best for making:
- (a) washing machines;
- (b) liquid fertiliser;
- (c) 'home baked' cakes;
- (d) specialised limousines;
- (e) printed T-shirts;
- (f) aeroplanes?

9.6 What types of processes can be used for services?

9.7 What types of process have highest productivity and why?

Choosing the best type of process

Decisions about the process can have long-term effects on profits, production, costs, flexibility, and most measures of performance. When BMW builds an assembly line, it costs hundreds of millions of pounds. If the company makes a mistake with its process, it is very expensive to put things right.

Sometimes the best overall features for the process seem clear, but not necessarily. For example, the best process for mass-producing cars is clearly an assembly line. But in 1990 Volvo questioned this view, and built a plant at Uddevalla in Sweden that had small groups of people assembling separate cars in workshops.[1] This was popular with the workers, but high costs forced it to close in 1993, and it was re-opened in 1996 using a conventional assembly line.

Even when the overall features of a process seem clear, there are many variations in the detail. The design of the process has to consider many factors. So far we have emphasised two of these – the overall demand and variability in the product – but the following list gives some others.

- **Overall demand**. We have seen how the total volume produced affects the best type of process. Portraits, for example, can either be painted or photographed – painters use a project or jobbing process to produce small numbers, while film processors use mass production to make very large numbers. If demand is high enough, an organisation can use high-volume processes that reduce unit costs.

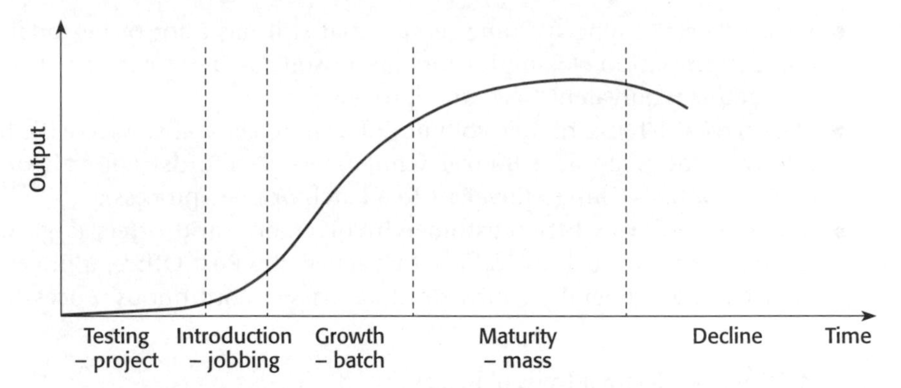

Figure 9.3 Relating the type of process to the life cycle

- **Variability in design**. Customers are often happy with identical, or nearly identical, products. With newspapers or milk, for example, we are generally content with standard products. Then organisations can get low unit costs that come with mass production. They only need to use a more flexible – and more expensive – process when customers demand more variety.
- **Point in the product life cycle**. There is often a link between the stage in a product's life cycle and the process used to make it. We can illustrate this with a simplified example.

During the planning, prototypes of the product are made as projects. Then during the introduction stage, demand is small and several variations are used to test market reaction. These are made by a jobbing process. As the product moves through introduction and into its growth stage, the variety of the product is reduced by removing versions that customers do not like. The volume of remaining versions increases and batch processing is most effective. As the product moves to maturity, demand is stable, product variation is reduced even more and competition increases. Higher efficiency is needed to produce higher volumes at lower costs, so the process moves toward mass production.

This is obviously a simplified view (illustrated in Figure 9.3) and many products never reach the volumes needed for a batch process let alone mass production. None the less, it does show that organisations have to adjust both the product and the process as they move through the life cycle. In general, the main effort of product planning is near the beginning of the life cycle, as organisations develop and refine a product that customers want. The main effort in process planning comes later in the life cycle, with improvements leading to continually better use of resources. Figure 9.4 shows the pattern of innovation in a typical life cycle.

- **Product design**. The product's design often sets the best type of process. If a bespoke tailor makes a high-quality suit to specifications given by a customer, the process is fixed as a hand-made project rather than a mass process. The design of many products explicitly includes details of the process. The design of Princess Caribbean Cruises, for example, includes full details of the process for delivering holidays to customers.

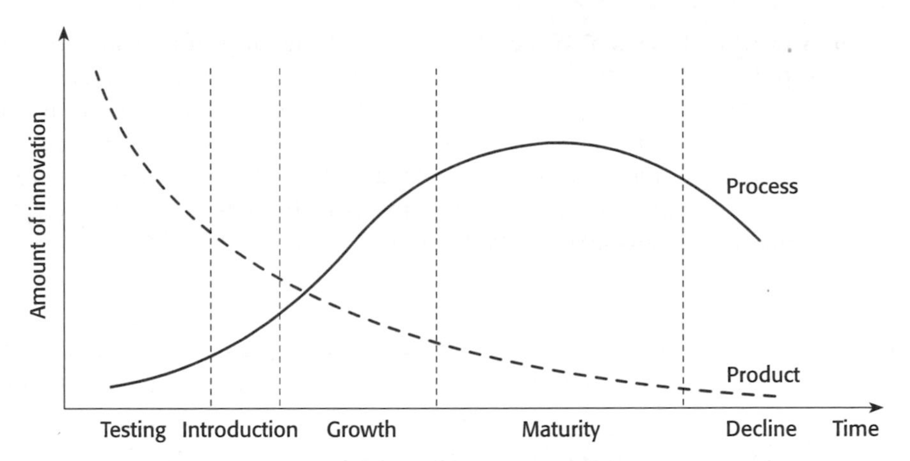

Figure 9.4 Pattern of innovation during a product life cycle

- **Changes in demand**. As well as the total volume, the amount of variation in demand can affect the choice of process. If production changes to meet a highly seasonal demand, it must use a flexible process that can meet peak demands and still work efficiently during slacker times. Hotels, for example, must cater for large numbers of guests in holiday seasons, but still work efficiently with smaller numbers out of season.
- **Product flexibility**. This basically describes the speed a process has to stop making one product and start making another. If customer demand changes quickly, a more flexible process is needed.
- **Human resources**. Different processes need different qualities in the workforce. A flexible process, for example, relies on people who are skilled enough to do a variety of different jobs. The choice of process can depend on the skills and experiences available in the workforce, and the training needed.
- **Automation**. The traditional view is that automation can only be used for high-volume processes. It needs expensive, specialised equipment that gives little flexibility. On the other hand, low-volume processes use cheaper, more flexible, general-purpose equipment. This view is still largely correct, but there have been changes and we will talk about some aspects of flexible automation later in the chapter.
- **Customer involvement**. Customers are not usually involved in manufacturing, but they can play an active part in services. Petrol stations, supermarkets, buffets in restaurants and automated banking machines use customers as active participants in the process. Such customer involvement can give a personal service, but the process must take account of their skills and needs.
- **Product quality**. The traditional means of getting high quality was to use highly skilled craftsmen making small numbers of a product. These craft processes are still best for some products, but automation is better at guaranteeing high quality in a wide range of other products. The most reliable computers, for example, are not hand-made but come from automated assembly lines.
- **Finances**. Different processes have widely different costs. The choice of process can be affected by the capital available and installation cost. Then the process affects the operating costs, return on investment, purchase price of the product, and so on.

- **Amount of vertical integration**. Vertical integration refers to the amount of the supply chain that is owned by one organisation. A manufacturer that buys all components from suppliers and sells finished products to wholesalers has little vertical integration. Another manufacturer that makes all its own components and sells to customers through its own distributors has a lot of vertical integration. Vertical integration makes more sense with higher-volume processes, as organisations can safeguard their investment in production facilities.

WORKED EXAMPLE

Nancy Chu runs a customer helpline for her software business. The choice of best process is complicated, but one aspect of costs is summarised as follows.

Type of Process	Annual fixed cost	Variable cost per transaction
jobbing	£100,000	£50
batch	£250,000	£40
mass	£1,000,000	£15

What do these costs show? What other factors should Nancy consider for the process design?

Solution

The costs show break-even points for different types of process.

- The jobbing process has lowest costs for demand from zero until the point when batch process becomes cheaper: At this point the demand, D, is:

$$100{,}000 + 50D = 250{,}000 + 40D \quad \text{or} \quad D = 15{,}000$$

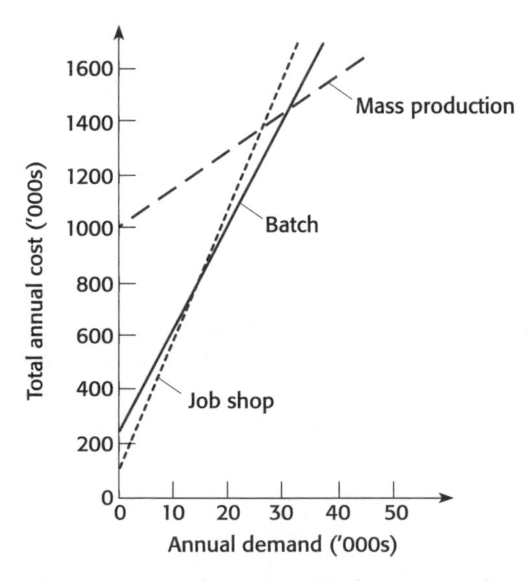

Figure 9.5 Break-even point for Nancy Chu

- The batch process has lowest costs for demand from 15,000 until:

$$250{,}000 + 40D = 1{,}000{,}000 + 15D \quad \text{or} \quad D = 30{,}000$$

- After this the mass process gives lowest costs.

The figures show one aspect of costs. There are many other factors that Nancy should consider in her choice of process, including those in the list above. She must design the process that best matches her product to customer demand, and this probably means a more flexible, personal service.

Review questions

9.8 What factors are important in process design?

9.9 How is the choice of process related to the product life cycle?

Different levels of technology

One of the obvious features of a process is the level of technology that it uses. We can describe this as manual, mechanised or automated.

Manual processes

People have full control over operations that need their constant attention. An operator might load a piece of equipment, work with it and then unload it. Driving a bus is an example of a manual process.

Manual systems have the benefits of flexibility, low capital costs and low risk. Their disadvantages are high unit cost, the need for a skilled workforce, variable quality and low output. If an organisation wants to increase production with a manual processes, it employs more people and equipment. There comes a point, however, when it is cheaper to invest in a mechanised process.

Mechanised processes

A typical mechanised process has an operator loading a piece of equipment, which can work without further intervention until the task is finished, when the operator unloads it. Using a VCR is an example of a mechanised process.

Mechanised processes have the advantages of producing high volumes of uniform products at low unit cost, but the disadvantages of high capital cost and inflexibility. They still need operators to do some of the operations and deal with problems. Unfortunately, humans slow down a process, add variability to the quality and increase unit costs. These problems can be overcome by automation.

Automated processes

This is a broad category, in which equipment performs a series of operations without any operator involvement. A telephone exchange is an example of an automated process. We will talk about some different types of automation in the next section.

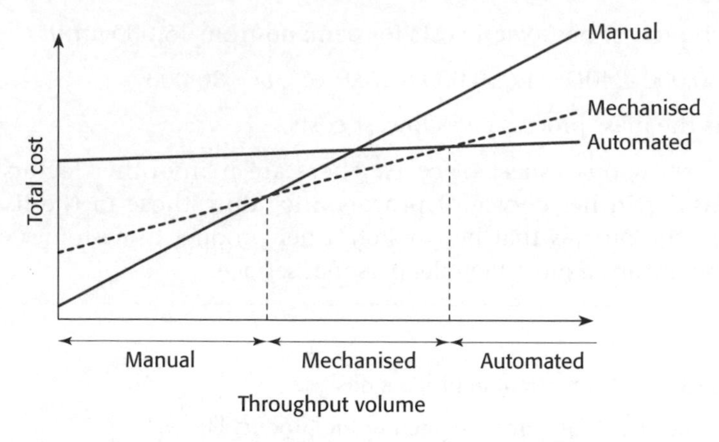

Figure 9.6 Costs with different types of automation

Examples

It may be easiest to imagine these different levels of technology with some examples:

- A manual system for paying accounts has someone sitting at a desk writing cheques by hand; a mechanised system has someone using a word processor; an automated system prints cheques automatically or arranges the electronic transfer of funds.
- A manual lathe needs an operator to load it and then control the operations; a mechanised lathe is loaded manually but then works by itself; an automated lathe works without an operator.
- A manual system for sorting letters in a post office needs people to put letters into appropriate bags; a mechanised system has operators directing equipment to route letters; an automated system scans the post code and automatically moves letters.

In general, higher volumes of output use higher levels of automation. Thus, low-volume processes are usually manual; medium-volume processes are mechanised; and high volumes use automation, as shown in Figure 9.6. You might imagine:

- manual processes for projects and jobbing;
- mechanised processes for batches;
- automation for mass and continuous processes.

Review question

9.10 How can you describe the different levels of automation found in processes?

Automation in manufacturing

Some types of **automation** are clearly used more in manufacturing than services; industrial robots, for example, are widely used in factories, but you could not find many in services. In this section we look at automation for manufacturing goods, and in the next section we will give some examples of automation in services.

Computer-aided manufacturing

Many people imagine automation in terms of assembly lines making cars. This is an example of **fixed** or **hard automation**, where highly specialised equipment is dedicated to making a single product. The process typically has a conveyor moving units along a fixed path between single-purpose machines. As the conveyor moves a unit down the line, each machine takes a turn at working on it. The result is a highly specialised, efficient operation, but with little flexibility. This kind of automation is capital intensive and few organisations can justify its use.

Ideally, organisations want to combine the efficiency and low costs of automation with the flexibility of lower volume processes. There has been a lot of progress in this direction, and the result is **flexible** or **programmable automation**. This is at the heart of 'mass customisation'.

Flexible automation for intermittent processes really started in the 1950s with **numerically controlled** (NC) machines. These were general-purpose machines that could do a series of tasks without any intervention by an operator. Paper tapes or cards controlled the machines and they were quickly reprogrammed by replacing the tape. Such machines have the advantages of giving consistently high quality with low unit cost, and they only needed a human operator for loading and changing programs.

NC machines grew more complicated, and modern versions can follow a long series of programmed instructions, typically drilling, planing, milling, boring and turning products of many different shapes and sizes. Magnetic tapes replaced paper tapes for control, and these, in turn, were replaced by microcomputers, where each **computerised numerically controlled** (CNC) machine is controlled by a dedicated microcomputer. Readily available programs allow even small numbers of units to be made reliably and at low cost. These 'workhorses' have become the most widely used form of automation in manufacturing.

Systems where computers help in the actual manufacturing processes are called **computer-aided manufacturing** (CAM). Automation moved forward in the 1960s with **industrial robots**. These are stationary machines that have programmable arms or manipulators to move materials through a variety of tasks. They were first used in car assembly lines, where they could spot weld, spray paint, test, inspect and do limited assembly. Robots are particularly useful in reaching places that are difficult for humans to get at or for handling dangerous substances, such as explosives, hot steel ingots or radioactive materials.

The next stage in automated production is **flexible manufacturing systems** (FMS). These combine the computers that control each piece of equipment (CNC or robot) so that a number of separate machines are under the control of a central computer. This computer co-ordinates the operations and finds the best timetables for doing work. It also controls the flow of materials, typically using wire-guided vehicles to move products, components, materials and tools between machines. Then automatic loading and unloading stations transfer the materials between the transport system and manufacturing equipment. So the four essential parts of FMS are:

1. a central computer to schedule, route, load, and control operations;
2. a number of machines automatically working under the control of the central computer;
3. an automatic transport system for moving materials between the machines;
4. automatic loading and unloading equipment.

Once an FMS is programmed, the system can work with very little human intervention. This brings a number of advantages.

- It works continuously allowing high output.
- Its work is consistent, giving products of guaranteed high quality.
- It does many jobs at once, including those that are difficult or dangerous.
- It is fast and can change quickly between different products.
- The computer takes over the difficult jobs of scheduling and routing.
- It also controls inventories, reducing stocks of raw materials and work-in-progress.
- Utilisation of resources is very high, helping to give low operating costs.

Despite these benefits, there are some disadvantages of FMS.

- The equipment is expensive to buy and set up.
- The technology is not yet fully developed and there can be teething troubles.
- Systems can be programmed to make many different products, but there are limits and they lack the flexibility of some other processes.
- Systems are designed to match current production, so major product changes in the future might cause problems.
- FMS works best with families of similar products that need small changes, rather than radically different products.

Computer-aided design

As well as being directly involved in production, automation is also used in associated functions, like product design. Designers use appropriate software to build up designs, enhance drawings, show different views, allow very quick changes to plans, and so on. They can cut the time for product design by storing electronic libraries of designs and modifying them as necessary. Computers also check for faults, do related engineering and cost calculations, and generate lists of parts and materials. The results are printed and transmitted to distant sites. This whole approach is **computer-aided design** (CAD).

Now we have computers designing the products (with CAD) and controlling production (with CAM), so it makes sense to join these two parts into a single CAD/CAM system. This takes the designs from the CAD part and automatically transfers them to the CAM part, which generates programmes to control machines and actually makes the products.

This approach is sometimes called **computer-integrated manufacturing** (CIM). Terms in this area are used rather vaguely, but most people view CIM as a further extension of FMS. Then FMS consists of the actual production machines, while CIM includes related functions, such as product design, process control, procurement, costing, and logistics.

If we can get all the related systems working together, we can move on to the next step of an **automated factory**. This would take the design for a product, and then have a completely automated process for making and delivering the final product. Computers would plan and control the operations, order materials, deliver final products, update bank accounts, and do all the related work without any

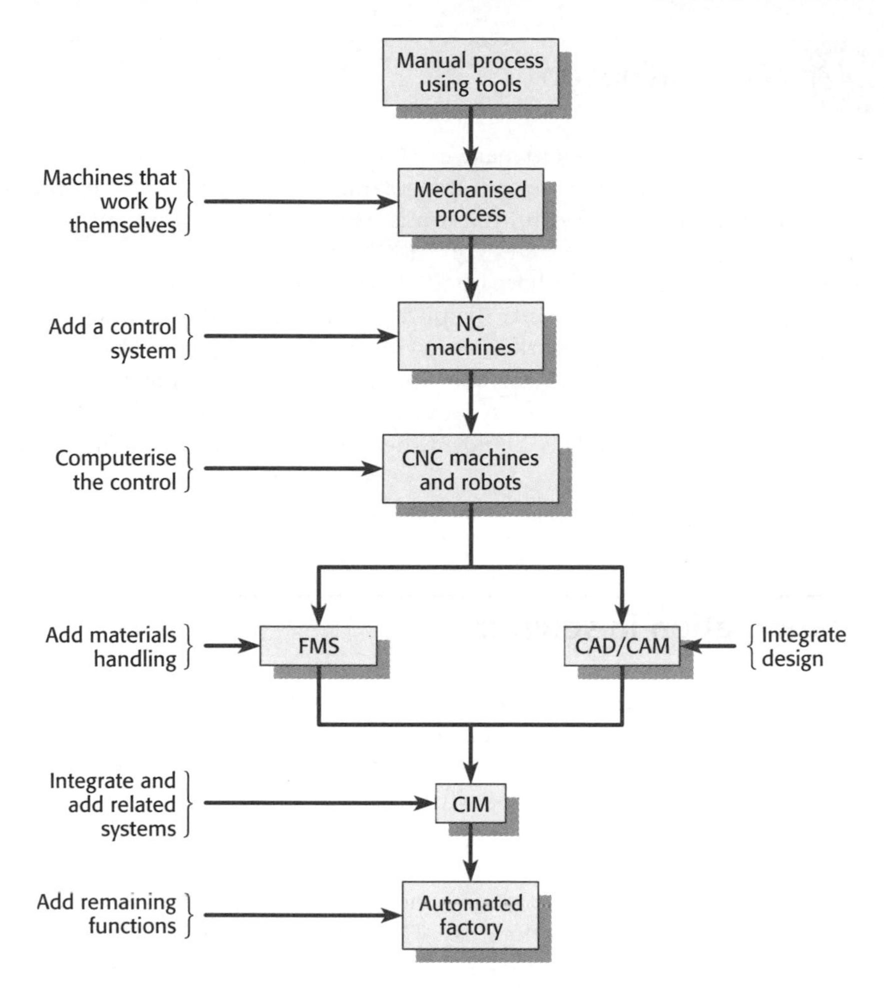

Figure 9.7 Levels of technology in manufacturing

human intervention (see Figure 9.7). There are not really any automated factories working at the moment, but the principles are established and the reality is not far away.

Review questions

9.11 What do the following abbreviations stand for:

(a) NC;
(b) CNC;
(c) CAM;
(d) CAD;
(e) FMS;
(f) CIM?

9.12 Rank the following in terms of increasing levels of automation: CIM NC FMS CAM CNC.

OPERATIONS IN PRACTICE

Paula Minuetto

Paula Minuetto employs 15 craftsmen to make musical instruments. She specialises in different kinds of brass instruments, particularly the trumpet family. The output is small, but quality is very high. Most customers are successful musicians who want an instrument customised to their needs.

For many years, Japanese companies have been selling mass-produced instruments, and Paula has decided to move towards this market. She plans to make an additional range of standard quality instruments for a broader market. She will not make large numbers, so the extra production will use equipment in the assembly area more fully and allow the automation of some standard operations. She will hire a few extra people, but existing staff will do most of the work on the new products. Paula is confident they can fit this new work into slack periods of their traditional work.

Automation in services

Services have traditionally been labour intensive and expensive, but service organisations realise that they can get the same benefits from automation as manufacturers. If they reduce the variability of their service, they can design very efficient automated processes, as you can see with products as diverse as automated banking and 'Superloos'. In different circumstances, organisations automatically process customers themselves (like ChampionChips which record runners' progress in a marathon), customers' materials (like baggage-handling equipment in an airport) or information (like Shell customer reward cards). There are clear trends in services towards less personal services, but ones that are a lot cheaper. Of course, there are many services – such as dentists, lawyers, doctors and hairdressers – which are highly customised and are not suited to automation. Like jobbing processes in manufacturing, these will inevitably remain expensive.

Services are so diverse that it is difficult to describe automation in the same general terms we used for manufacturing. The service offered by a lawyer, for example, has little in common with a postal service. Perhaps we can best illustrate the principles by some specific examples.

- **Offices**. Offices prepare, store, analyse, copy and distribute information. Until fairly recently, all of these were done manually, with an electric typewriter as the most sophisticated technology available. Clerical jobs have now been transformed, and most have been computerised. Many clerical jobs are no longer needed as we apparently move towards paperless offices.
- **Cash**. In the past you could either pay a bill by cash or by writing a cheque. Banks introduced credit cards as a way of reducing costs, so they pay a bill and you repay them at the end of the month. They saved even more money with debit cards, which transfer money directly from your account to a payee. Technology opens many new ways of paying bills, including intelligent switch cards, telephone transactions, e-commerce, etc. At some point, all coins and notes will presumably be replaced by machine-readable formats.

- **Supermarkets**. Customers used to be served in food shops, with someone to fetch the goods, weigh and wrap them, and present a bill. Supermarkets give a mechanised system, where customers do most of the work themselves, and checkout operators calculate and present the bill. Increasing automation has self-scanning of goods, computer-readable shopping lists, telephone shopping, virtual shopping via the Internet, and connections to home computers that automatically transmit an order when something is used from the pantry.
- **Mail**. This used to mean letters, which were posted, sorted by hand and delivered. Then postcodes and high-speed scanners sorted letters automatically. For many purposes, the need to send letters has declined, to be replaced by voice mail, fax messages and e-mail; 1993 was the first year when the number of letters posted in the UK declined.
- **Warehousing**. Traditionally, warehouses had people moving goods to and from shelves, with stock movement recorded on cards. More efficient mechanised warehouses have people using equipment such as forklift trucks. Automated warehouses have computers in control, running equipment for moving goods and doing all the administration.

You can see many examples of service organisations using automated processes to improve their performance. As the productivity of service industries is relatively low, this is an area with considerable potential.

OPERATIONS IN PRACTICE Automatic banking machines

Banks encourage customers to get cash from their simple dispensing machines. More advanced machines allow customers to pay bills, transfer funds, update account information, and do most of their usual banking tasks.

People often prefer some personal service, so the next generation of machines allows contact with bank staff. All major banks have experimented with video links to 'branches', which can be little more than kiosks in supermarkets. Customer reaction to these is not wholly positive, but they are probably better than having no branch at all. On-line banking can include video links to PCs, giving virtual face-to-face contact. Smartcards, which use an embedded chip to store a range of personal information, can automate even more bank transactions.

Security is a common problem with these automated services that rely on machine-readable cards. A simple PIN number or signature can easily be duplicated. Many machines use a pinhole camera to photograph the person using the card. Experiments to link this picture with a stored photograph of the person authorised to use the card have met with limited success. A more reliable alternative of 'iris identification' was tested in 1998 by the Nationwide Building Society. This uses a machine to scan the user's iris and compare this with a recorded version.

As computers use increasingly sophisticated ways of identifying a customer, there is really no need for the smartcard and a customer can stand in front of a machine, be recognised, and do any transactions automatically. At present, cards cannot deal profitably with a transaction of less than about £25. Most purchases are less than this, so we still have to carry cash. Automatic identification will allow even small electronic transactions and should eventually do away with the need for cash.

Sources: Gardner N. (1998) 'Future of Finance is Real Eye Opener', *Sunday Times*, 26 April; Fleet M. (1998) 'Cash Machine Will Pay in Twinkling of an Eye', *Daily Telegraph*, 24 April.

Information technology

Information technology has obviously had a dramatic effect on operations – improving the efficiency of some, and allowing new operations that were previously impossible. We cannot go into details about IT here, but should mention some developments that have most effect on operations.

- **Distributed processing**. Data used to be stored in big, mainframe computers, and anyone wanting information had to use this machine. Distributed processing allowed information to be stored in machines near to its source and use. People most closely involved with the data could now maintain it and access it quickly. An important requirement, however, is that remote users should also be able to access the data. This became possible when standard protocols were developed for communications between remote machines.
- **Local area networks**. A local area network (LAN) is a communications system that connects a series of computers in a specific area – typically within a building, site or organisation. All computers connected to a LAN can share common databases, peripherals and other facilities. Now the inventory system, for example, can be linked to the procurement system, so that removing an item from stores triggers a message to buy a replacement.
- **Electronic data interchange**. The benefits of LANs are so obvious that organisations have moved to the next stage, and linked their computers to other organisations. Instead of linking the inventory system to a purchasing system, they can send a message directly to the supplier, who automatically sends a replacement. (We will return to this theme in chapter 19.) This is the basis of electronic data interchange (EDI), which allows documents and information to move directly between different organisations.
- **The Internet**. There are obvious benefits of moving information between, say, customers and suppliers. But there may also be benefits from moving information between organisations that are not so closely connected. Research departments in universities, for example, do not necessarily have close links, but it is useful to see what problems each is working on. This became possible with the Internet, which gave a standard format for communicating between LANs. By linking separate networks, it became possible to communicate with other systems around the world.
- **World Wide Web**. By the 1990s the Web gave a standard way of organising data for the Internet. This opened a variety of new services, such as virtual shopping (with Amazon stocking far more books than any conventional shop), home banking (with banks such as Egg opening with no conventional branches), access to music and video (though there are still copyright problems here) and many other virtual organisations.
- **Management information systems**. Managers need information to make their decisions, and much of this comes from within the organisations. Technology can support this with almost limitless amounts of information from anywhere in the world. Management information systems are needed to organise this flow of information. They collect, analyse, summarise, distribute and present relevant information to managers in the most appropriate forms.

- **Decision support system.** A management information system essentially presents information, while a decision support system plays a more positive role in decisions. Imagine a group of managers that is making a decision about investing in new equipment. A management information system will give them the information they need; a decision support system will also analyse the consequences of various decisions, do a series of 'what-if' calculations, suggest new alternatives, and recommend the best options.
- **Expert systems.** These go one step further than decision support systems and take part in the actual decision. An expert system records the skills of experts in a knowledge base. Then when it faces a decision, it uses an 'inference engine' to select and use these rules to duplicate the decision making of the human expert.
- **Artificial intelligence.** This attempts to give computers the ability to understand language, to reason, make assumptions, learn and solve problems. In other words, to create computers that can make reasoned decisions in the same way as humans. Practical progress in this area is still fairly limited.

Information technology is changing many aspects of operations, but there has been so much hype and over-selling that the reality does not often live up to expectations. Introducing new IT does not automatically improve an organisation's performance or give it a sustained competitive advantage. By itself, IT does not give better products or even a better process. Many organisations have failed to realise this, and been caught in the 'IT productivity paradox'. This happens when an organisation spends large amounts to improve IT, but gets no apparent improvement in overall performance.

Review questions

9.13 How could you classify the types of process used in services?

9.14 Services are expensive because the need for personal service means that each job is really a project. Do you think that this is true?

9.15 Better information technology gives better processes. Can you explain why this is true?

OPERATIONS IN PRACTICE

Multimedia education

Schools have traditionally used a batch process, where a class of children are all taught the same things at the same time. Most educators want to move towards a project process, where each child is taught as an individual. At the moment this is too expensive, as pupils would need a lot of teachers' individual attention, but multimedia computers and access to the Web can revolutionise the way children learn. They give pupils access to vast amounts of information, which can be presented in the most interesting formats. Most importantly, they allow interaction so that pupils can control the pace, depth and direction of their learning.

The British government has launched many initiatives to increase the use of computers in schools. Surveys suggest that 80 per cent of parents think they are a good way of enhancing learning. While traditional teaching methods can appear uninteresting, the market for 'edutainment' or 'infotainment' is likely to continue its expansion.

Project 9.2 *Find a long-established service, such as a postal service, shop, library or taxi service. What product does this service provide? How and why has the process changed over recent years? How might it change in the future?*

Choosing the level of technology

Some people assume that higher levels of technology inevitably give better processes. They certainly have the advantages of:

- working continuously without tiring;
- doing operations consistently and always conforming to specifications;
- giving higher quality;
- being very fast and powerful;
- working efficiently and giving higher productivity;
- doing boring, difficult and dangerous jobs;
- storing large amounts of information and analysing it quickly;
- allowing tighter control with short lead times and lower stocks;
- reducing labour costs.

But these do not necessarily give better processes. Each level of technology is best suited to certain types of operations, and it is just as bad to use too much technology as to use too little. When Nokayama filling stations installed new pumps that work automatically, show videos, serve coffee, and offer e-mail services, they were not popular with customers who only wanted a fast service. This is also why offices found that replacing paper memos with e-mail increased their workload, as they were swamped with duplicated messages and junk mail.

Organisations have to consider many factors in their choice of technology, the most obvious of which is the capital cost. Unless large numbers are made, the capital costs of high technology processes are spread over too few units and the unit cost becomes prohibitive.

WORKED EXAMPLE

Anton uses a manual process with fixed costs of $150,000 a year and variable costs of $40 a unit. He is considering a new automated process that has fixed costs, including capital repayment, of $450,000 a year and variable costs of $20 a unit. At what production level is this new system cheaper?

Solution

Based on the very limited information on costs, the new process is cheaper when:

$$450{,}000 + 20P < 150{,}000 + 40P \quad \text{or} \quad P > 15{,}000$$

Where P is the annual production. If Anton makes less than 15,000 units a year, his present process is cheaper.

Higher levels of automation can bring other problems, apart from high costs. We have already seen that they tend to reduce flexibility and variability of a process. Another problem is that customers may not like the technology, which is why we walk past information machines in tourist offices and talk to someone behind the counter. Perhaps the major criticism of automated systems is that they ignore the skills that people can bring to a process, including:

- giving a personal service;
- drawing upon varied experiences;
- using all available information intelligently;
- being creative and adapting to new and unusual circumstances;
- using subjectivity and judgement;
- generating entirely new solutions;
- being flexible and finding acceptable compromises.

People and machines are better at different jobs, and because automation is better in some circumstances you should not assume that it is better for everything.

Review questions

9.16 In the long run, it is always better to replace a process by a 'high-tech' alternative. Do you think this is true?

9.17 Automated processes can work faster and are more reliable than people. What can people do that automated processes cannot?

OPERATIONS IN PRACTICE

Electronic dealing at the Liffe

The London International Financial Futures Exchange (Liffe) was formed in 1982 so that companies could protect themselves against sharp fluctuations in currencies. It had an open dealing floor where 2,000 traders, wearing multi-coloured jackets, worked in trading pits. They made deals using a combination of shouting and hand signals. This apparently chaotic system was one of the most successful markets in the City of London, with contracts of £160 billion traded every day.

By 1998 the 'open-outcry' system was showing signs of strain, and some of the big banks were pressing for change. Lloyds TSB pulled out of trading on the floor; Nikko reduced its presence; and SBC Warburg stopped trading German government bonds.

The alternative to open trading is computer-based dealing, with operators sitting at terminals. This system was used in Frankfurt, which was rapidly taking over from London as the European centre for financial futures. Screen trading has been used by the London Stock Exchange for years, and this has the advantage of being cheaper to run and more efficient. The screen system for futures in Frankfurt, for example, cost 30 per cent less than the open system in London. On the other hand, the screen system could be inflexible, poor at dealing with unusual deals, and favouring big traders over the locals (individuals who deal for their own account and make up about 30 per cent of Liffe business).

In May 1998 the Liffe voted to move most business to screen dealing. The decision to change was needed quickly, as the Liffe was due to move from Cannon Street to a proposed new £300 million headquarters in Spitalfields, which included a 10,000 square metre trading floor. The change to screen trading made this floor unnecessary.

Electronic trading was phased in from November 1999; the Liffe did not move; and in August 2000 trades reached £215 billion a day.

Sources: Hamilton K. (1998) 'Liffe cries out for electronic future', *Sunday Times*, 15 March; Guarente M. (1999) 'It's Liffe, but not as we know it', *Business Life*, November.

Project 9.3

In 2000 the London Stock Exchange had a difficult time, with several rumours of mergers and takeovers. Many people said that it was late in adopting new technology, and allowed other stock exchanges to gain a competitive edge. Do you think the London Stock Exchange, or any other organisations that you are familiar with, has suffered because of the availability of high technology processes?

Chapter review

- The process consists of all the operations needed to make a product. Process planning designs the best process for any particular product.
- We can describe processes with different features as project, jobbing, batch, mass or continuous.
- The best type of process depends on a number of factors, including demand, variation in demand, variation in products, stage in the product life cycle, product mix, capital available, workforce skills, and so on.
- We can classify different levels of automation as manual, mechanised or automated. Higher levels of technology generally have higher productivity.
- Manufacturers can use several levels of automation, ranging from numerically controlled machines to automated factories.
- Some services give a personal service that needs a project or jobbing process. Many, however, can reduce the variation in their product and make higher volumes. This encourages the use of higher levels of technology.
- Organisations should choose the level of technology that best fits their process, and not the highest level that is available.

Key terms

automation *p. 232*
batch process *p. 224*
computer-aided design (CAD) *p. 234*
computer-aided manufacturing (CAM) *p. 233*
computer-integrated manufacturing (CIM) *p. 234*
computerised numerically controlled (CNC) *p. 233*
continuous process *p. 224*
flexible manufacturing (FMS) *p. 233*
information technology *p. 238*
jobbing process *p. 223*
mass process *p. 224*
numerically controlled (NC) *p. 233*
process *p. 219*
process centred *p. 220*
process planning *p. 219*
project *p. 222*
technology *p. 231*

CASE STUDY Syncrude

Most of the oil we use comes from wells, either on land or in relatively shallow water of the continental shelf. Crude oil is pumped to the surface, giving a varying mixture of hydrocarbons that has to be refined before use. Oil refineries distil the crude oil into separate products, ranging from light gasses through to heavy bitumen. The products are used as fuel, lubricants, industrial gasses and raw materials for the huge petrochemical industry.

We are all vaguely familiar with this process that starts with crude oil being pumped from a well. It is continuous, uses high levels of technology, and deals with huge volumes. In reality, up to half the world's known oil reserves are not at the bottom of wells, but in the oil sands spread over 60,000 square km around Athabasca in northern Canada. Syncrude is the world's largest producer of oil from sands, and is owned by a consortium of 10 oil companies.

Syncrude started work in 1973, when 10,000 construction workers moved 450,000 tonnes of materials and equipment up to the remote site in Alberta. After an initial investment of $5 billion, the site settled down to employ 4,500 people producing 235,000 barrels of oil a day – or a total of over a billion barrels since production started in 1978. Reserves are estimated at almost 2 trillion barrels of bitumen, 300 billion barrels of which are recoverable.

The oil sands are a mixture of bitumen and sand covered by more than 50 m of earth and muskeg. The process for recovering oil from the sands is in four steps.

1. The sands are mined. About 100 million cubic m of overburden are removed every year by electric shovels and 150-tonne trucks. Then the exposed oil sand is excavated by draglines and piled along the sides of the pit. Reclaimers move 25,000 tonnes of this sand an hour along conveyor belts to the extraction plant.
2. The bitumen – which is the raw oil and looks rather like heavy molasses – is separated from the sand. Hot water, steam and caustic soda are mixed with the tar sands, and they form a froth that contains the bitumen. This froth is removed, diluted with naphtha and sent to centrifuges and settlers to remove the solids and water. Then the naphtha is removed by distillation to leave pure bitumen. The sand, clay and other materials left are removed to tailing ponds.
3. The bitumen is upgraded to give synthetic crude, using the process shown in Figure 9.8.
4. Finally, the synthetic crude is sent by pipeline to refineries in Edmonton.

Syncrude produces about 26 per cent of Canada's oil, and as experience and investment have grown, the cost of production has fallen to about $12 a barrel.

Source: reports prepared by Syncrude Canada Limited.

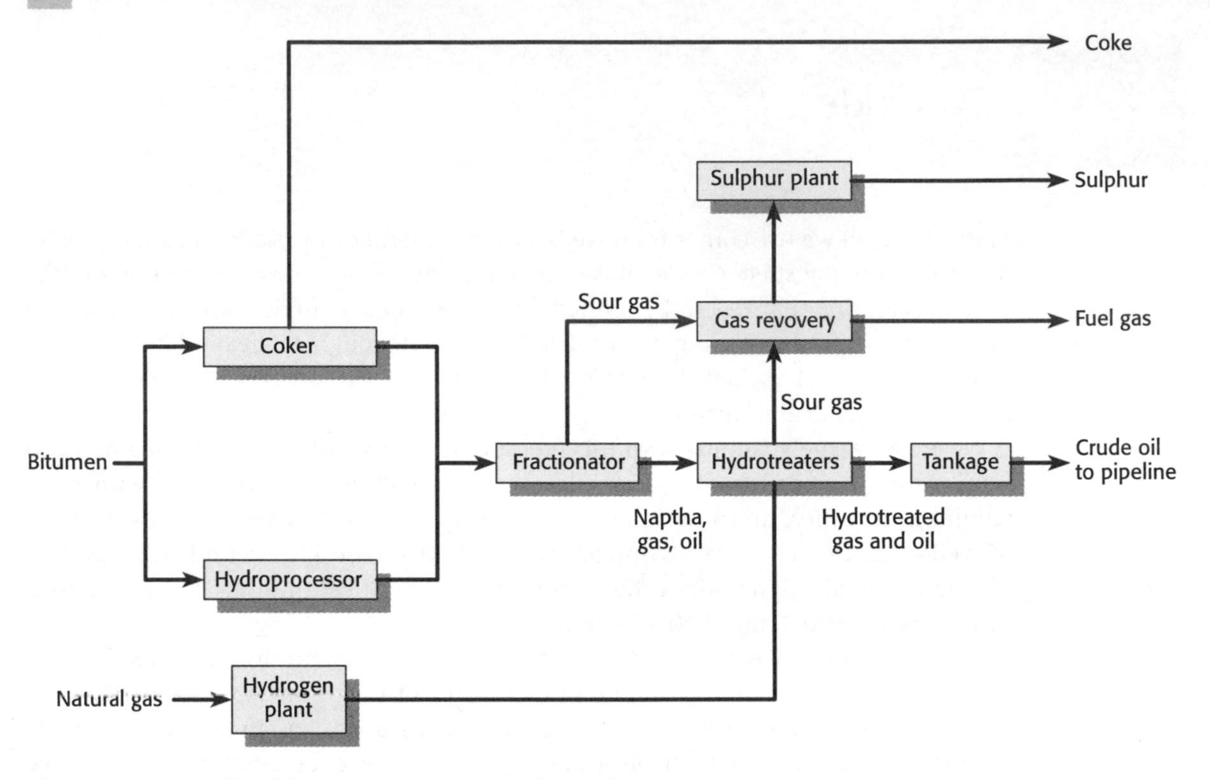

Figure 9.8 Upgrading bitumen to give synthetic crude oil

Questions

- How does the process at Syncrude compare with the usual process for producing oil? What particular problems do you think Syncrude has with its process?
- What are the main factors that affect the design of this process?

Problems

9.1 Alamantic pty is considering a new product for its 'service factory'. It can use several types of process, and experience suggests that the costs will be as follows:

	Annual fixed cost	Variable cost
Project	100,000	2,000
Jobbing	150,000	250
Batch	450,000	150
Mass production	1,500,000	100

Within what ranges of production will each process have lowest costs?

9.2 J. Kerrigan (Fabrications) PLC works two eight-hour shifts a day, five days a week for 50 weeks a year. Welders have the unpleasant job of getting into an awkward, enclosed space to spot weld two parts. For this, they are paid £7 an hour directly with a further

£3 an hour in other costs. The operations manager has suggested that a robot for this job would cost £150,000. This would work virtually non-stop for an expected life of seven to 10 years, and with operating costs of £2 an hour. Do you think this is a reasonable investment?

9.3 A communications company staffs a transmission centre for three eight-hour shifts a day, five days a week. It could save £20 an hour in labour costs by using an automated system that costs £250,000. If the company pays 15 per cent interest on a debt with the bank, and the equipment has a life expectancy of seven years, is this a good investment?

9.4 You know that a new machine will generate the following incomes and costs over the next five years. Use a discounting rate of 12 per cent to see if the machine is a good investment.

Year	Income	Costs
0	–	36,000
1	5,000	–
2	27,000	12,000
3	36,000	–
4	12,000	4,000
5	2,000	–

Discussion questions

9.1 What technological developments do you think have had the most effect on operations over the past decade or so? What developments will affect future operations?

9.2 It isn't the process that matters but the final product. Do you agree with this? To what extent is the design of the process separate from the design of the product?

9.3 There are continual improvements to technology, so organisations can only plan for the medium term. To what extent is the use of technology in an organisation a strategic rather than a tactical issue?

9.4 Some people suggest that operations can only be automated at the expense of the people working in them. Do you think this is true? Do you think that increasing automation reduces the skills people develop?

9.5 Our prosperity depends on increasing productivity. Automation increases productivity. The inevitable conclusion is that automation should be introduced as widely as possible. Do you agree with this?

9.6 When people think about automation they often imagine car assembly lines. Most people work in services. Describe some specific areas where automation has effected services. What do you think will happen in the future?

Reference

1. Volvo advertising campaign (for example: *Financial Times* (1990) 22 March).

Selected reading

Anupindi R. (ed.) (1999) *Managing Business Process Flows*. Englewood Cliffs, NJ: Prentice-Hall.
Benders J., DeHaan J. and Bennett D. (eds) (1995) *The Symbiosis of Work and Technology*. London: Taylor and Francis.
Cohen M.A. and Apte U.M. (1997) *Manufacturing Automation*. Chicago: Irwin.
Collier D.A. (1985) *Service Management: the Automation of Services*. Reston: Reston Publishing.
Davenport T.H. (1993) *Process Innovation*. Cambridge, MA: Harvard Business School Press.
Ramaswamy R. (1996) *Design and Management of Service Process*. Harlow: Addison-Wesley Longman.
Wu B. (1994) *Manufacturing Systems Design and Analysis*. 2nd edn. New York: Chapman and Hall.

Useful Websites

www.ame.org – Association for Manufacturing Excellence
www.brint.com – Business Research in Information and Technology
www.agilityforum.org – a useful discussion site

CHAPTER
10

Measuring and improving performance

Change is the law of life. And those who look only to the past or the present are certain to miss the future.

John F. Kennedy, Speech in Frankfurt, Germany, 25 June 1963

Contents

Aims of the chapter

After reading this chapter you should be able to:

- recognise the importance of measuring performance;
- describe different measures of performance for operations;
- measure different measures of productivity;
- discuss the best measures and their use;
- use benchmarking;
- understand the need for change and how to manage it;
- discuss different approaches to improving a process;
- analyse a process using different charts.

Main themes

This chapter will emphasise:

- **measures of performance**, which show how good a process is;
- **productivity**, which shows the output of a process for each unit of input;
- **process improvement**, changing operations to improve performance;
- **process charts**, to describe the details of a process.

Measuring performance

Measures for operations

Every organisation has to measure performance. If managers do not take measures, they have no idea how good the operations are, whether they are improving, whether they meet targets, or how they compare with competitors. An old maxim says, 'what you can't measure, you can't manage'. The problem, of course, is finding what to measure and how to measure it.

There are many possible measures of performance: gross profit, profitability, return on investment, return on assets, share price, price to earnings ratio, productivity, sales, market share, stock turnover, output per employee, etc. Many of these relate to finance. These financial measures can give a broad view of the organisation, and allow direct comparisons for judging management skills. They also sound convincing and are easy to measure. On the negative side, they concentrate on past rather than current performance, are slow to respond to changes, rely on accounting conventions, and do not record important aspects of operations.

Financial measures might reflect the performance of an organisation, but they do not show how to improve things. This is like doctors taking your temperature – a fever shows that you are unwell, but does not show how to get better. In the same way, poor financial performance is only a symptom of something wrong in the organisation. The way to improve performance is to do better operations. Improving profitability, for example, does not mean juggling the finances, but improving operations and making them more profitable. So now we need some direct measure to see how well we are doing the operations.

Capacity and related measures

A basic measure of operations performance is the **capacity**.

> The **capacity** of a process sets the maximum output from an operation in a specified time.

We talk about managing capacity in Chapter 12, but essentially we have to create enough capacity to meet the forecast demand. Figure 10.1 shows a simplified view of this planning. In practice, the planning is not done in this strict sequence, and designing the product and designing the process, for example, are done concurrently rather than consecutively.

At first, it might seem strange to describe capacity as a measure of performance, rather than a fixed value or constraint on the output. There are two reactions to this. Firstly, we can say that the capacity of a process depends on the way that resources are organised. So two organisations can use identical resources in different ways, and get different capacities. Then the capacity gives a direct measure of their relative performance. It was, for example, always claimed that the Ford plant in Cologne had a higher capacity than the virtually identical plant in Dagenham.

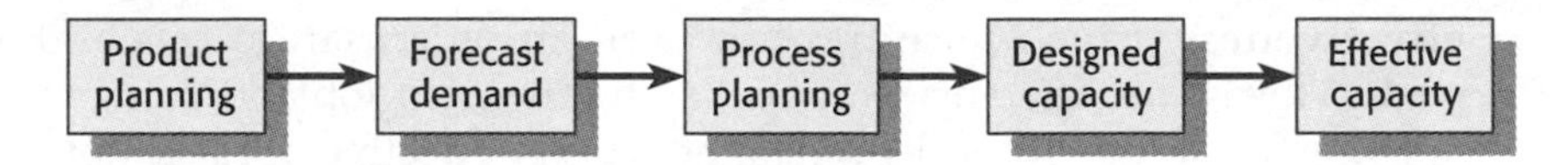

Figure 10.1 Simplified view of capacity planning

Secondly, we can point out that the capacity is not fixed. Imagine a team of people who are employed to shovel sand. At eight o'clock in the morning they are fresh and working hard; by six o'clock in the evening they are tired and their work rate is much lower. Although the process remains unchanged, its capacity has declined over time.

To allow for these effects, we can define difference types of capacity. **Designed capacity** is the maximum possible output from a process in ideal conditions; **effective capacity** is what we can actually achieve over the long term. The designed capacity of DGH's double-glazing plant is 1,000 windows a week. They might achieve this for a short period, but after taking into account product changes, workable schedules, staff holidays, defects, and other factors the effective capacity is 850 windows a week. Last year they actually produced 710 windows a week.

When we have measured the capacity of an operation, the **utilisation** shows how much of this is actually used.

Utilisation measures the proportion of designed capacity that is actually used.

Suppose you have a process with a designed capacity of 100 units a week, but only make 60 units in a week.

$$\text{Utilisation} = \frac{\text{amount of capacity used}}{\text{designed capacity}} = \frac{60}{100} = 0.6 \quad \text{or} \quad 60 \text{ per cent.}$$

Perhaps the most widely used measure of operations is **productivity** (we discuss this in more detail below).

Productivity measures the amount of output achieved for each unit of resource used.

If a process uses 25 hours of machine time to make 50 units, then the productivity is two units per machine-hour.

A problem with these measures is that people often use the terms very loosely. The **production** is the total output from a process, but some people confuse this with **productivity**, which is the output achieved for each unit of resource. Then production might be 100 units while the productivity is 10 units per machine-day. Another term that causes confusion is **efficiency**. Efficiency describes the percentage of possible output that is actually achieved – usually taken as the ratio of output over effective capacity. If people working in an office can process five forms in an hour, but someone has just spent an hour processing four forms, their efficiency is 4/5 = 0.8 or 80 per cent. Sometimes efficiency is confused with

effectiveness, which measures how well an organisation sets and achieves its goals. This is the difference between 'doing the right job and doing the job right' – opening a walnut with a sledgehammer is very effective but it is not very efficient; building a wall without cement is very efficient (as the work is done very quickly) but it is not very effective.

To summarise these measures:

- **Capacity** is the maximum amount of a product that can be made in a given time.
- **Utilisation** measures the proportion of designed capacity that is actually used.
- **Production** is the total amount of a product that is made.
- **Productivity** is the amount produced for each unit of resources used.
- **Efficiency** is the ratio of actual output to possible output.
- **Effectiveness** shows how well an organisation sets and achieves its goals.

WORKED EXAMPLE

Two machines are designed to make 100 units each in a nine-hour shift. During one shift, the machines actually worked for eight hours, and made a total of 140 units. What measures of performance can you give?

Solution

- *Capacity* is the maximum amount that can be made in a given time, which is:

  Number of machines × maximum output per shift
  $= 2 \times 100 = 200$ units a shift, or 22.2 units an hour

- *Utilisation* is the proportion of available capacity actually used, which is:

  Actual output/designed capacity $= 140/200 = 0.7$ or 70 per cent

- *Production* is the amount actually made, which is 140 units.
- *Productivity* is the amount produced for each unit of resources used, so a reasonable measure is:

  Number of units made/machine time used
  $= 140/(2 \times 8) = 8.75$ units a machine hour

- *Efficiency* is the ratio of actual output to possible output, which is:

  Actual output/possible output in the time used
  $= 140/(8 \times 22.2) = 0.788$ or 78.8 per cent

Review questions

10.1 What direct measures can you use for operations?

10.2 What is the difference between capacity, utilisation, productivity and efficiency?

10.3 Is it possible for the utilisation of an operation to rise while the productivity declines?

OPERATIONS IN PRACTICE

The Johnson-Mead Company

In July 2000, The Johnson-Mead Company had 10 people organising 1,000 specialised life insurance policies for high-risk travellers. In theory they could process 1,250 policies a month but breaks, interruptions, holidays, schedules and other factors limited this to about 1,150. The direct costs of this operation were £115,000.

There was growing demand for the service, and in September the company did a small reorganisation. After this it employed 11 people, who could deal with a maximum of 1,600 policies a month, but with a more realistic limit of 1,300. The company was a little disappointed to find that in the following month they had only processed 1,200 policies, with direct costs of £156,000. Some measures of this performance are given in the following table.

	Before reorganisation	After reorganisation
Number of policies processed per person	1000/10 = 100	1200/11 = 109
Direct costs per policy	115,000/1000 = £115	156,000/1200 = £130
Designed capacity	1250	1600
Effective capacity	1150	1300
Utilisation	1000/1250 = 80%	1200/1600 = 75%
Efficiency	1000/1150 = 87%	1200/1300 = 92%

Even these simple measures have to be interpreted with some care. Johnson-Mead's reorganisation increased the number of policies processed per person, but it also increased the direct costs per policy. The capacity has risen along with efficiency, but the utilisation has declined. Whether performance has improved or not depends on the objectives of the company.

Productivity

Different definitions

Productivity is the most widely used measure of operations. Unfortunately, people often confuse its meaning, typically assuming that it is the amount produced per person. As we saw above, productivity shows the amount produced for each unit of resources used. Most managers agree that increasing productivity is good, as it shows how well resources are being used, but really we need to look at our definition more closely to see if this gives a true picture.

There are several kinds of productivity. The broadest picture of operations comes from **total productivity**, which relates production to *all* the resources used.

$$\text{Total productivity} = \frac{\text{total output}}{\text{total input}}$$

Unfortunately, this definition has a number of drawbacks. The input and output must use consistent units, so they are normally translated into units of currency. This depends on the accounting conventions used and we no longer have an objective measure. Another problem is finding *all* the inputs and outputs. Some inputs are difficult to value, such as sunlight and reliability – as are some outputs, such as pollution and reputation. We could say that we are only interested in the important factors, but then someone has to decide which these are, and we have again lost our objectivity.

Because of these practical difficulties, most organisations use **partial productivity**, which relates the output to a single type of input.

$$\text{Partial productivity} = \frac{\text{total output}}{\text{units of a single resource used}}$$

In practice, we are primarily concerned with the output of products, so we ignore secondary outputs, such as waste, by-products and intangibles. Then partial productivity gives the volume of products made for each unit of chosen resource. The four main types of partial productivity are:

- *equipment productivity* – such as the number of units made per machine hour, miles flown per aeroplane, or customers served per petrol pump;
- *labour productivity* – such as the number of units made per person, tonnes produced per shift, and orders shipped per hour worked;
- *capital productivity* – such as the number of units made for each pound of investment, sales per unit of capital, or production per dollar invested in equipment;
- *energy productivity* – such as the number of units made per kilowatt-hour of electricity, units made for each pound spent on energy, and value of output per barrel of oil used.

WORKED EXAMPLE

The following data was collected for a process over two consecutive years.

	1999	**2000**
Number of units made	1,000	1,200
Selling price	£100	£100
Raw materials used	5,100 kg	5,800 kg
Cost of raw materials	£20,500	£25,500
Hours worked	4,300	4,500
Direct labour costs	£52,000	£58,000
Energy used	10,000 kWh	14,000 kWh
Energy cost	£1,000	£1,500
Other costs	£10,000	£10,000

How can you describe the productivity?

Solution

We can use several measures of productivity.

- Total productivity in 1999 is:

$$\frac{\text{total output}}{\text{total input}} = \frac{100 \times 1{,}000}{20{,}500 + 52{,}000 + 1{,}000 + 10{,}000} = 1.2$$

By 2000 this had risen to 120,000/95,000 = 1.26, which is a rise of 5 per cent.

- Units of output per kg of raw material in 1999 was 1,000/5,100 = 0.196. In 2000 it was 1,200/5,800 = 0.207 which is a rise of 5 per cent.
- Some other measures are:

	1999	2000	Percentage increase
Total productivity	1.20	1.26	5
Units/kg of raw material	0.196	0.207	5.6
Units/£ of raw material	0.049	0.047	−4.1
Units/hour	0.233	0.267	14.6
Units/£ of labour	0.019	0.021	10.5
Units/kWh	0.100	0.086	−14.0
Units/£ of energy	1.000	0.800	−20

In general, labour productivity has risen, raw materials productivity has stayed about the same, and energy productivity has fallen.

Balancing different views

The last example shows how different measures of productivity can give conflicting views, simply because they are measuring different things. It is quite usual for some measures of performance to rise while others fall. When you drive a car faster than usual, your miles per hour go up, but your miles per litre of fuel go down; when a shop is refurbished, its sales per square metre go up, but its sales per pound invested go down; increasing the amount of automation gives higher labour productivity but lower capital productivity.

You can also see why it is not always a good idea to raise productivity. We might improve one type of productivity that has little relevance to overall performance, and actually damage the wider organisation. When Pradesh Gupta replaced old knitting machines in his factory by sophisticated new ones, his labour productivity rose, but his income did not cover the increased debt charges and he soon went bankrupt.

To get a broader view, we should balance several different productivity measures that look at different aspects of operations. Sometimes this is rather difficult. If you look at the productivity of a school, for example, it is easy to calculate the ratio of pupils to staff, but it is almost impossible to get equivalent measures for the academic standards, learning skills, teaching quality, and so on. Then people are tempted to concentrate on the easier measures, and forget the other factors that may really be more important. It is, for example, wrong to measure police performance by counting the number of crimes they solve per employee, when a better target is to stop crime and have none to solve.

Review questions

10.4 What is the difference between total and partial productivity?

10.5 Is it possible for some measures of productivity to rise while others fall?

10.6 Labour productivity is the best measure of an organisation's performance. Do you think this is true?

OPERATIONS IN PRACTICE British Coal

At the beginning of the twentieth century the British coal industry employed over a million miners. In 1947 most of the fragmented industry was nationalised to form the National Coal Board, which was later reorganised as British Coal. In 1980 British Coal employed 250,000 miners, and over the next 12 years productivity rose by a factor of three (as shown in Figure 10.2).

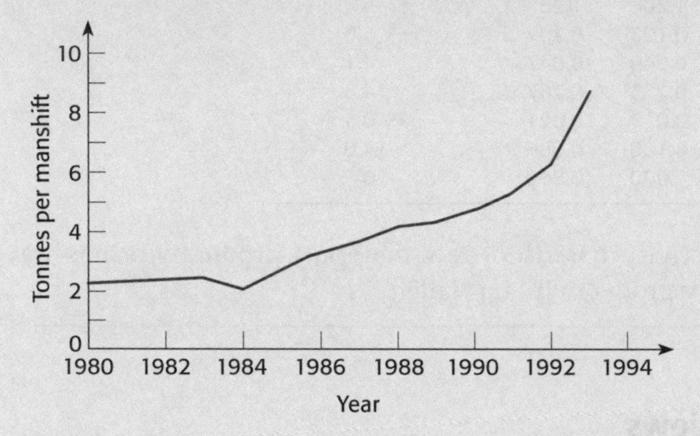

Figure 10.2 Productivity reported by British Coal

Superficially, these productivity figures show an industry that has made considerable progress. Certainly British deep-mine coal was among the cheapest in the world, and the industry was recognised as among the most efficient, but the figures hid the fact that British Coal could not compete with cheap imported coal from open-cast mines. By 1994 the government had closed most of the British mines and was selling the remainder. Employment and production were falling, as shown in Figure 10.3.

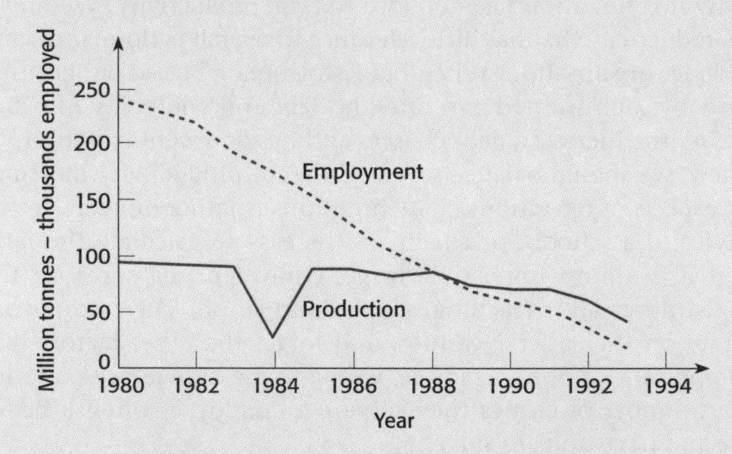

Figure 10.3 Production and employment in British Coal

Historically it had been important for British Coal to aim for high output. Mining was labour intensive, so the industry measured productivity by the number of tonnes of coal produced per shift. This gives a very limited view of operations that were increasingly automated.

Comparing performance

Using the right measure

We have mentioned the most common measures of operations performance, but there are many others, including production rate, stock turnover, amount of scrap, lead time, number of customer complaints, innovation, absenteeism, production time, and a whole host of others. Some of these are difficult to quantify – such as morale and innovation – but they can still be important. Organisations run extensive surveys to measure things like 'customer satisfaction', 'staff morale' and 'management leadership', but you should remember that they are trying to give numerical values to essentially non-quantifiable factors, and you should treat the results with caution. It is better to use quantitative measures whenever possible.

Measuring performance is not an end in itself, but gives basic information for managers to use in their decisions. This is why you hear: 'what gets measured, gets done'. Managers have to use the right measures, or else they base decisions on faulty information. By the 'right measures' we mean those that show how well the operations are achieving their goals. Unfortunately, managers often ignore the 'right measures', and use ones that are easiest to find, have always been used in the past, or show themselves in the best light. Some consequences of this are warehouses full of unsold goods because production is judged by output and not sales, rushed service because servers are judged by the number of clients they speak to and not the quality of their service, and double booked seats because airlines are judged by seat occupancy. The following list gives some more examples of using the wrong measure.

- Chandros Discount Stores measured the sales per square metre of retail floor space. A few managers realised that they could improve this performance by converting some retail space into storage space. Their sales per square metre improved, despite falling sales, income, profit and return on investment.
- In the UK, hospital trusts are judged by the number of patients on their waiting lists for treatment. These can be reduced by giving priority to people with minor problems, who are treated quickly and removed from the system. Anyone needing more complicated treatment has to wait. This reverses usual healthcare practice.
- Firefighters in Illinois were given a bonus related to the number of fires they attended. Not long after this system was introduced, one of the firefighters was charged with multiple acts of arson.
- Bus drivers in Brazil found that they could keep to their schedules better if they did not stop to pick up passengers.
- Texas Steak Restaurants left customer comment forms in all its branches. One branch regularly won prizes for having virtually no complaints – largely because the manager 'forgot' to put the forms on display.

There are several reasons why measures may not serve their intended purpose. Some are simply irrelevant or misleading; others only look at a single aspect of performance and avoid an overall view; others do not relate to real objectives; others come too late to be useful (like student evaluations at the end of a course). To give a reasonable view of operations, a measure must:

- relate to the objectives of the operations;
- focus on significant factors;
- be measurable;
- be reasonably objective;
- allow comparisons over time and between operations;
- be understood by people working on the operations;
- be agreed by everyone concerned;
- be linked to the reward and recognition system of employees;
- be difficult to manipulate to give false values.

OPERATIONS IN PRACTICE

The performance of banks

The high street banks are constantly criticised for their poor customer service.[1] There are many cases where banks overcharge customers, make mistakes, are negligent or simply do not give a reasonable level of service. Newspaper articles brought a huge response from readers who had complaints about their banks, and the *Sunday Times* concluded that the big banks were so absorbed with making profits that they were 'probably the least popular private institutions in the country'.[2]

Some banks clearly worked against customers' interests. One threatened to punish staff who told customers about accounts that paid higher rates of interest than their existing deposits. One threatened to close the accounts of customers who complained. Several banks offered accounts that paid high interest for a short time, and then locked in the money for long periods at much lower rates. Supposedly high-interest-rate accounts were a gimmick that actually paid lower rates than normal accounts. Banks charged customers for no apparent reason, such as overdraft charges on accounts that had never been overdrawn. They also stopped co-operating with agents who tried to help customers get the lowest possible bank charges.

The *Sunday Times* suggested some measures for minimum standards of service. These proposed that banks:

- tell customers of any changes in their interest rates at the time the changes are made;
- give comparisons between existing account rates and alternative, suitable accounts;
- publish all charges clearly, including fees;
- tell customers if instant-access accounts pay higher interest rates than 30-, 60- or 90-day notice accounts;
- give customers the right to negotiate through agents.

Standards for comparison

When managers use appropriate measures, they can use the results to

- see how well objectives are being achieved;
- compare the current performance of the organisation with its performance in the past;

- make comparisons with other organisations that have similar operations;
- compare the performance of different parts of the organisation;
- make decisions about investments and proposed changes to the process;
- measure the effects of changes to operations;
- help with other internal functions, such as wage negotiations;
- highlight areas that need improvement.

As you can see, many of these uses involve comparisons. This is because absolute measures often have little real meaning. If you know that a shop has annual sales of $1,200 per square metre, you cannot say whether this is good or bad until you know the sales in comparable shops. Performance is generally compared with four types of standard:

1. *Absolute standards* – these give the best performance that can ever be achieved. This is an ideal performance that operations might aspire to, such as the target of zero defects in TQM.
2. *Target performance* – this is a more realistic target that is agreed by managers who want to set tough, but attainable, goals. The absolute standard for the number of customer complaints received each week is zero, but a more realistic agreed target might be four.
3. *Historical standards* – these look at performance that was actually achieved in the past. As organisations are looking for continuous improvement, we can regard this as the worst performance that might be accepted.
4. *Competitors' standards* – these look at the performance actually being achieved by competitors. This is the lowest level of performance that an organisation must achieve to remain competitive. Federal Express delivers packages 'absolutely, positively overnight', so other delivery services must achieve this standard to compete.

These comparisons can be organised in many ways. When pub managers visit other pubs, they get ideas for improving their own operations, as do football managers when they watch other teams. Often it is better to use a more formal approach, and this is done by **benchmarking**.

Benchmarking

With benchmarking, an organisation compares its performance with a competitor. There is no point in comparing performance with some random competitor, so benchmarking actually compares an organisation's performance with the best operations in the industry.

There are several steps in benchmarking. These start with an organisation recognising the need to improve a process. Then it has to define the most appropriate measures of performance, identify the leading competitor in the industry, and examine their operations to see how they achieve this superior performance (see Figure 10.4).

To be blunt, organisations use benchmarking to find ideas for operations that they can copy or adapt. You may think that competitors would be reluctant to

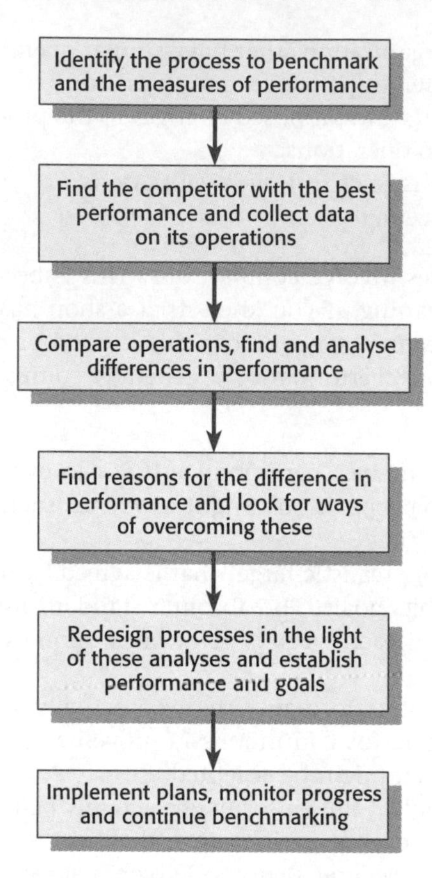

Figure 10.4 Steps in benchmarking

give out details of their operations to competitors. In practice, it can be fairly easy to get this information, and fears that it will be exploited are largely groundless. Everyone knows how to generate electricity, assemble cars, run buses, make ice cream and deliver parcels – but organisations work very successfully in these industries, despite the fact that everyone knows all about their operations. Organisations in the same industry are often willing to share information, as they can all benefit from the results. Even the best performers can learn things that make them even better.

Sometimes it is difficult to find a direct competitor for benchmarking. Then it is useful to look at organisations that are not in the same industry. BP is not a direct competitor of Tate & Lyle, but they both run fleets of tankers and may learn from each other's transport operations. Sometimes it is possible to learn from completely different types of organisation. Train operators, for example, might find improvements from bus operators, airlines or other companies that are not involved in transport but which give high customer service, such as supermarkets. The easiest benchmarking to organise is internal, with one division of an organisation comparing its operations with another division.

The clear message is to take a broad view, and look for possible improvements anywhere you get the chance.

OPERATIONS IN PRACTICE

Charles Friderikson Car Rentals

When Charles Friderikson Car Rentals (CFCR) started business in Copenhagen, there were already many competitors in the market. In general, the major international companies tended to compete by service, including Hertz ('Call the world's No. 1'), Avis ('We try harder'), Eurodollar ('Rent from the best'), Europcar ('All around – a better service'), Ford ('A big name in rental'), Thrifty ('World class service at your doorstep'). The smaller, more local companies tended to compete on price, such as Economy ('The lowest prices around'), Capital ('Competitive rates, best value') and Harald ('Lowest rates in town').

CFCR decided to compete by giving a good, personal service at a reasonable price. CFCR obviously could not give the scale of service offered by the international companies, but learnt a lot from their operations. For example, CFCR have automated their administration, so that after his/her first visit, a customer can pass a plastic card through a reader and pick up a car immediately.

At the same time, CFCR recognised that private customers were more interested in price, so they looked at the operations of the smaller companies to see how they could reduce operating costs. For example, they do not use expensive locations like airport arrival lounges, keep their cars for rather longer than normal, and have more flexible pricing.

CFCR effectively benchmarked their operations against international companies when looking at the quality of service, and local companies when looking for low costs.

Source: company annual reports

Review questions

10.7 Why do organisations use measures of performance in comparisons?

10.8 Benchmarking looks for useful ideas from the best available operations. Do you think this is true?

Improving the process

Benefits of better performance

In Chapter 3 we saw how organisations work with continual change. Products, competitors, costs, markets, locations, employees, customers, the economy, the business environment, company objectives, technology, shareholders, etc. change over time. If organisations do not respond to these changes, they get left behind by more flexible competitors. The argument is that competitors are always trying to get an advantage by improving their own operations, so every organisation has to keep improving just to stay in the same place. Then the main benefits of better performance include:

- long-term survival;
- lower costs;
- less waste of resources;
- increased profits, wages, real income, etc.;
- realistic targets for improving performance;

- monitoring improving performance;
- allow comparisons between operations;
- measures management competence.

So how do we make sure that our organisation is continuing to change and improve? As we saw in Chapter 3, the best answer is to develop an organisational commitment to change, accepting that continual change is inevitable, necessary and beneficial. But how can we translate this into practical changes? We look at this question in the next sections.

Problems and improvement

Perhaps the best place to start looking for improvements is to see what goes wrong. According to Robert Townsend, 'All organisations are at least 50 per cent waste – waste people, waste effort, waste space and waste time'.[3] The following list is based on Toyota's view of the most common problems in a process.[4]

- **Quality** – that is too poor to satisfy customers (who may be either external or internal).
- **Production level** – making products or having capacity that is not currently needed.
- **Processing** – having unnecessary, too complicated or time-consuming operations.
- **Waiting** – for operations to start or finish, for materials, repairs, etc.
- **Movement** – with products making unnecessary, long or inconvenient movements during operations.
- **Stock** – too much stock that needs storing and raises costs.

There are countless suggestions for dealing with these, most of which develop around general themes, such as:

- quality management;
- increasing levels of technology;
- emphasising human resources;
- timely operations, such as just-in-time;
- control of inventories and other waste;
- alliances, partnerships and other types of integration.

We have already talked about quality management in Chapters 6 and 7, and will meet the other ideas at various points. One clear point, however, is that the old-fashioned idea of 'getting people to work harder' has very little to do with performance. A hard-working person with a spade is far less productive than a lazy person with a bulldozer. About 85 per cent of performance is set by the system that is designed by management; only 15 per cent is under the control of the individual worker. If things are going well, it is largely because the managers are doing a good job: if things are going badly, it is probably the managers who are to blame.

Finding improvements

The best people to ask about improvement are those most closely involved. They may already have a string of suggestions: Why is my computer at an angle rather than straight in front of me? Why is the receptionist so rude to customers? Why do we not use contract caterers? Why do we not export to Canada? Why do we keep buying these machines when there are better alternatives?

Sometimes, people working on a process are reluctant to suggest improvements. They may be so closely involved with the details that they simply do not notice better options. If they do find improvements, there is the unpleasant suggestion that they have been doing things badly in the past. A more pressing problem is that people who know how to make improvements do not have the authority to make the changes themselves, and are never asked for their opinion by those who could change things. They have no incentive to push forward their views, as unsolicited advice is not usually welcomed, and if their suggestion reduces the amount of work, they may be putting themselves out of a job.

One way of avoiding such problems is to have a more formal approach to change, probably with a team whose job is to go around and positively search for improvements. This is the approach we met in Chapter 6 with the plan-do-check-act cycle. But suppose the suggestion boxes, comments, improvement teams and all other sources of improvement produce several thousand suggestions a year. No organisation will have the resources to implement all possible ideas, and will want to avoid too much disruption. Priority then will have to be given to certain types of change. One way of setting priorities is to look at the effects of changes, and give the highest priority to those which give most benefit. Another approach looks at the reason for change in terms of, say, customer satisfaction. If competitors are already getting higher customer satisfaction, then the organisation must change as a matter of urgency simply to remain competitive (as shown in Figure 10.5). If the change would give an advantage over competitors, there is less urgency but the change should still be considered seriously. If the organisation already has considerably higher customer satisfaction than competitors, the change might be delayed.

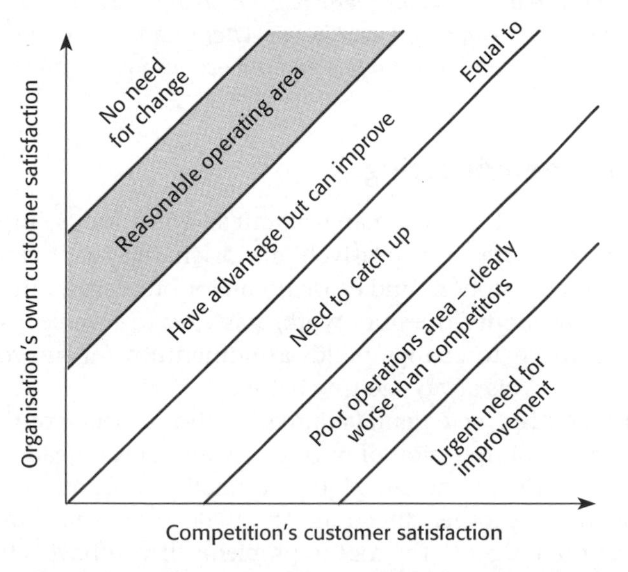

Figure 10.5 Illustrating the urgency of improvements

Another common problem is that organisations do not implement the improvements carefully enough. Changes cannot just be announced, but they need careful preparation. A reasonable approach has the following steps:

1. Make everyone aware that changes are needed, describing the reasons, alternatives and likely effects.
2. Examine the current operations, using benchmarking and other comparisons to identify areas that need improvement.
3. Design better operations using the knowledge, skills and experience of everyone concerned.
4. Discuss the plans widely and get people committed to the new methods.
5. Design a detailed plan for introducing the improvements, anticipating likely problems rather than waiting for them to happen.
6. Make any necessary changes to the organisation.
7. Give appropriate training to everyone involved.
8. Set challenging but realistic goals for everyone, and make it clear how these can be achieved.
9. Have a specific event to start the new methods.
10. Establish milestones and monitor progress to make sure they are achieved.
11. Give support and encouragement to everyone concerned.
12. Have continuing discussions about progress, problems, adjustments, etc.
13. Monitor progress, remaining committed to the new methods while they are giving improvements, and updating them as necessary.
14. Accept that the new methods are only temporary, and continually look for further improvements.

Project 10.1 *Take a critical look around you and see how many improvements you can make to everyday operations. You might find, for example, that a library opens at the wrong times, you have to spend too long in a queue, some operations are poorly laid out, a water company is not dealing properly with a complaint, and so on. What could you do to improve these operations? Why do you think that no one has made these obvious improvements?*

Business process reengineering

One of the features of total quality management is continuous improvement or *kaizen*. This emphasises a stream of relatively minor changes that can be absorbed by the process, give few disruptions and cause no major problems. There is little risk, as if one of the 'improvements' does not work, it is easy to reverse a small change. This incremental approach to change builds a momentum for improvement, and makes sure that the process is always getting better.

But there are critics of this incremental approach, who say that continually tinkering with a process gives an impression of uncertainty and lack of leadership. It might also move the process in the wrong direction, as a small change might block the way for much bigger gains in another direction. The major criticism, however, is that incremental changes do not get to the root of problems. If you have a fundamentally bad process, then making small adjustments will still leave you with a bad process.

These critics say that organisations should not tinker with the existing process, but they should start from scratch and design a completely new one. This gives the opportunity to create a dramatically improved – and the best possible – process. The best known approach of this kind is **business process reengineering** (BPR).

> **Business process reengineering** is the fundamental rethinking and radical redesign of business processes to achieve dramatic improvements in critical, contemporary measures of performance, such as cost, quality, service and speed.[5]

The idea behind reengineering is that you do not look for improvements in your current operations, but you start with a blank sheet of paper and design a new process from scratch. This is rather like running an old car. You can tinker with it to keep it going a bit longer, but the reengineering solution is to buy a new car. If you have a poor purchasing system, you should not waste time tinkering to find small improvements, but should throw away the whole system and design a new one from scratch (see Figure 10.6).

OPERATIONS IN PRACTICE

Procurement at Ford

Hammer and Champy[5] describe a classic example of reengineering. In the 1980s Ford's North American accounts payable department employed 500 people. They used the following standard system for buying materials.

1. The purchasing department sent a purchase order to a supplier and sent a copy to the accounts payable department.
2. The supplier shipped the goods and sent an invoice to accounts payable.
3. When the goods arrived at Ford, they were checked and sent to stores. A description of the goods arriving was sent to accounts payable.
4. Accounts payable now had three descriptions of the goods – from the purchasing department, supplier and arrivals – and if everything matched, it paid the invoice.
5. Sometimes the paperwork did not match, and problems had to be sorted out. This took a lot of effort, often lasting several weeks.

Ford could have improved this system, but it chose a more radical solution. The new reengineered system is based around its database, so that:

1. The purchasing department sends a purchase order to a supplier and updates the database.
2. The supplier ships the goods.
3. When the goods arrive at Ford, they are checked against outstanding orders on the database.
4. If the details match, the goods are accepted, the database is updated to show they have arrived, and the supplier is paid.
5. If the details do not match, the goods are not accepted and are sent back to the supplier.

Suppliers soon learnt that the new system would not allow any mistakes in deliveries, so these were quickly eliminated. The streamlined system reduced Ford's accounts payable department to 125 people, giving a 400 per cent increase in labour productivity.

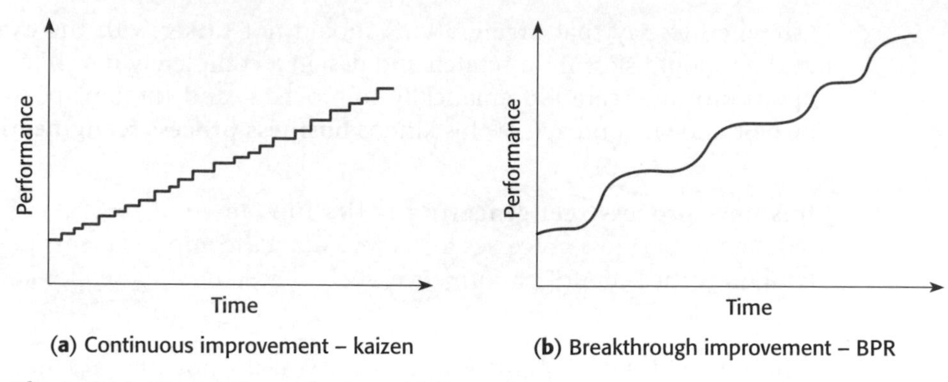

Figure 10.6 Comparison of rates of improvement

BPR does not give new methods, but it consolidates several related ideas. Some of its main principles are:

- A process should be designed across functions and allow work to flow naturally through the process, concentrating on the whole process rather than the separate parts.
- Managers should strive for dramatic improvements in performance by radically rethinking and redesigning the process.
- Improved information technology is fundamental to reengineering as it allows radical new solutions.
- All jobs that do not add value should be eliminated.
- Work should be done where it makes most sense – information processing, for example, becomes a part of the process rather than a separate function.
- Decisions should be made where the work is done, and by those doing the work.
- You do not have to be an expert to help redesign a process, and being an outsider without preconceived ideas often helps.
- Always see things from the customer's point of view.

One important point is that BPR does not replace continuous improvement. It is possible to have a series of radical improvements, and still introduce smaller continuous improvements (as shown in Figure 10.7).

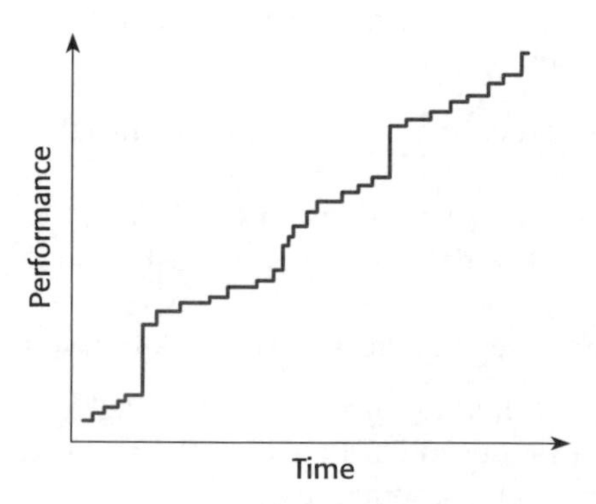

Figure 10.7 Rate of improvement combining BPR and *kaizen*

BPR is a general approach to change rather than a formal procedure, so we cannot say, 'this is how to reengineer a process'. Perhaps because of this, organisations have mixed experiences with its use. Some have reported outstanding results – like the early work in the IBM Credit Corporation which increased output by a factor of 100. But around three-quarters of organisations fail to get the improvements they hoped for.[6] There are many reasons for this, including:

- trying to adjust a process rather than fundamentally redesigning it;
- settling for minor improvements;
- stopping before all the work is done;
- pulling back when there is resistance to change;
- not putting enough resources into the BPR;
- not getting senior management support;
- appointing a leader of the exercise who is not interested;
- setting-up a separate and remote working group;
- burying BPR in other initiatives.

These may be valid reasons, but many people feel that BPR has fundamental faults. Introducing major changes is always risky, and having a policy based on this must be questioned. Other criticisms include:

- Realistically, it is very difficult to get the dramatic improvements promised.
- Sudden changes to the process can be very disruptive, expensive and risky.
- Dramatic changes might use new technology beyond the experience and skills of the organisation.
- A new process takes a long time to settle down before starting to work properly.
- BPR is seen as the latest management fad and is not taken seriously.
- It always uses a radical approach, even when minor adjustments would be best.
- It can put short-term cost reduction ahead of longer-term interests.
- BPR emphasises staff reductions, and becomes an excuse for getting rid of employees.
- Downsizing can lose valuable skills and experience from the organisation.
- Reengineered organisations can be inflexible and vulnerable to changes in the environment.

Review questions

10.9 Why is change necessary within an organisation?

10.10 What are the most common faults in operations?

10.11 What is BPR?

10.12 It is better to use BPR instead of continuous improvement. Do you think this is true?

Project 10.2

Look at the process for collecting individuals' income tax – or another process that you think needs radical improvement. Now start from scratch and design a new process. How is this better than the existing one?

OPERATIONS IN PRACTICE

SW Kobi Electricity

SW Kobi Electricity (SWK) supplies electricity to around 400,000 domestic users. Every three months it sends a meter reader around to all its customers. The meter readings are passed to an accounts department which calculates the bill. This basic process has remained the same for many years. Originally the whole process was manual, but now the meter readers carry a hand-held terminal on which they enter the current reading, and at the end of the day this is plugged into the accounts department computer which automatically prints the bills.

The process of reading meters is labour intensive and SWK was looking for ways of reducing costs, perhaps by improving the hand-held terminals, sending out estimated bills every other period, or combining with other utility companies to have joint meter readers.

SWK then decided to reengineer the process. It could install 'intelligent' meters at customers' premises, which connect to telephone lines or mobile systems. Central computers could automatically interrogate these meters at regular intervals, and links to bank accounts could automatically deduct the amount owing. This would eliminate almost all the meter readers and the accounts department.

Unfortunately, progress on this system hit some problems. Many customers were not happy with the idea of automatic billing, and were even less happy about automatic withdrawals from their bank accounts. The banks realised that electricity bills cause many complaints, so they were reluctant to use a system that would be certain to involve them in disagreements.

Analysing a process

Process charts

Whether we look for improvements in the existing process, or reengineer a completely new one, we need some way of describing its details. In other words, we have to list the individual operations and show the relationship between them. The easiest way of doing this is with a **process chart**.

A **process chart** shows the detailed relationships between the operations that form a process.

There are several types of process chart, but they all start by breaking down the entire process into separate operations. Suppose, for example, we look at the process of visiting a doctor's surgery. We can describe the separate operations as:

- enter and talk to the receptionist;
- sit down and wait until you are called;
- when called, go to the examination room;
- discuss your problems with the doctor;
- when you have finished, leave the examination room;
- talk to the receptionist and leave.

We can draw this as the informal process chart shown in Figure 10.8.

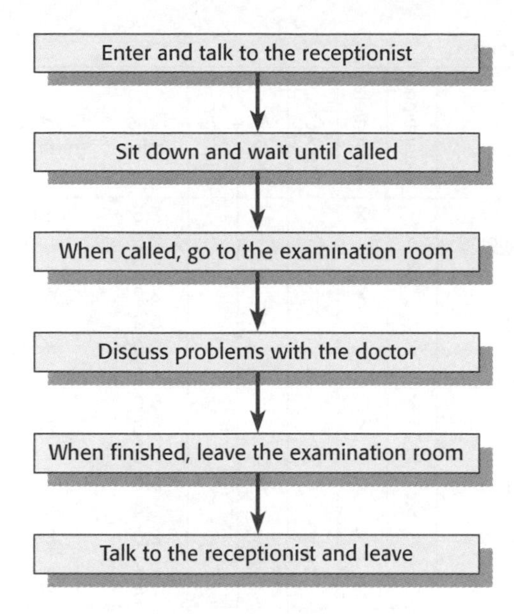

Figure 10.8 Informal process chart

This informal chart gives a general view of the process, but it does not give many details. A better approach starts by dividing activities into:

- *operation* – where something is actually done;
- *movement* – where products are moved;
- *storage* – where products are put away until they are needed;
- *delay* – where products wait for something to happen;
- *inspection* – to test the quality.

Now we can follow the operations in a process, describe what happens, and look for improvements. For this, we use the following six steps.

- Step 1. Look at the process and list all the operations in their proper sequence from the start through to the finish.
- Step 2. Classify each step according to operation, movement, inspection, delay and storage. Find the time taken and distance moved in each step.
- Step 3. Summarise the process by adding the number of operations, total times, rate of doing each operation, and any other relevant information.
- Step 4. Critically analyse each operation, asking questions like: Why is it done this way? Can we eliminate this activity? How can we improve this operation? Can we combine operations?
- Step 5. Now revise the process, to give fewer operations, shorter times, less distance travelled, and so on. Make sure that each operation can still give the output needed by the process. If there are bottlenecks or equipment being used inefficiently, adjust the process to give improvements.
- Step 6. Check the new process, prepare the organisation for changes, train staff, etc. and implement the changes.

Process chart: Part 421/302									
Step number	Description	Operation	Movement	Inspection	Delay	Storage	Time (min)	Distance (metres)	Comment
1	Fetch components		X				2.5	50	
2	Put components on machine	X					2.0		
3	Start machine	X					1.2		
4	Fetch sub-assembly		X				3.0	40	
5	Wait for machine to stop				X		5.2		
6	Unload machine	X					2.0		
7	Inspect result			X			1.5		
8	Join sub-assembly	X					5.0		
9	Move unit to machine		X				2.5	25	
10	Load machine and start	X					2.0		
11	Wait for machine to stop				X		5.0		
12	Unload machine	X					1.4		
13	Carry unit to inspection area		X				2.0	25	
14	Inspect and test			X			5.2		
15	Carry unit to finish area		X				1.4	20	
16	Finish unit	X					5.5		
17	Final inspection			X			3.5		
18	Carry unit to store		X				5.3	45	

Summary		No.	Time		
	Operations	7	19.1	Time:	56.2 min
	Movements	6	16.7	Distance:	205 metres
	Inspections	3	10.2		
	Delays	2	10.2		
	Storage	0	0		
		18	56.2		

Figure 10.9 Example of a process chart

The first three steps give a detailed description of a process, and an example of the resulting chart is shown in Figure 10.9. Steps 1 and 2 are usually done by observation, while step 3 is a calculation.

The last three steps look for improvements to the process. We can start this by finding the maximum output from the process. Operation 1 takes 2.5 minutes, so the maximum output is 60/2.5 = 24 an hour. Operation 2 takes two minutes, so the maximum output is 30 an hour, etc. The overall output is limited by the longest operation. Finishing takes 5.5 minutes, so the product cannot be made faster than 60/5.5 = 10.9 units an hour. If forecast demand is higher than this, we have to change the process, perhaps adding more finishers, or changing the way the finishing is done.

You can also see that in operations 5 and 11 the operator has to wait a total of 10.2 minutes for the machine to stop. Now we can start looking for ways to reduce this. The chart also shows the distance moved, and you can see that operations 1, 4, 9, 13, 15 and 18 need a total of 205 metres, taking 16.7 minutes. We might redesign the layout to reduce this.

WORKED EXAMPLE

Draw a chart of the process involved when a person goes to a bank and asks for a personal loan.

Solution

Details of the process, and particularly the time, will vary considerably. Figure 10.10 shows an example of a chart from one branch of a high street bank.

Process chart – Personal bank loan									
Step number	Description	Operation	Movement	Inspection	Delay	Storage	Time (min)	Distance (metres)	Comment
1	Customer selects bank and visits		X						
2	Initial screening	X					5		
3	Move to loans office		X				2	15	
4	Wait				X		10		
5	Discuss with loans officer	X					15		
6	Complete application forms	X					15		
7	Carry forms to verifier		X				2	10	
8	Forms are checked			X			2		
9	Wait as credit analysis and verification is done				X		25		
10	Supply further information	X					5		
11	Move back to loans office		X				2	15	
12	Wait				X		20		
13	Forms are checked			X			5		
14	Complete arrangements	X					15		
15	Leave		X						

Summary		No.	Time		
	Operations	5	55	Time:	123 min
	Movements	5	6	Distance:	40 metres
	Inspections	3	7		
	Delays	3	55		
	Storage	0	0		
		15	123		

Figure 10.10 Process chart for worked example

Precedence diagrams

We can also describe a process using a **precedence diagram**, which uses a network of circles and arrows. Suppose a very simple process has two operations A and B, and A must finish before B can start. We can represent the operations by two circles and the relationship by an arrow, as shown in Figure 10.11.

We can extend this method to more complex processes, as shown in the following examples.

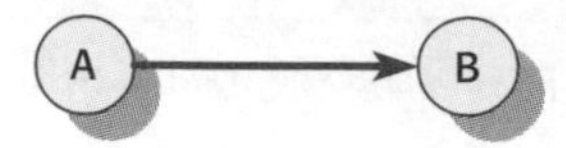

Figure 10.11 Relationship between two operations

WORKED EXAMPLE

The process in a bottling hall consists of five operations:

1. clean and inspect the bottle;
2. fill the bottle;
3. put a cap on the bottle;
4. stick a printed label on the bottle;
5. put the bottle in a box and move it away.

Draw a precedence diagram of this process.

Solution

Some operations must clearly be done before others – the bottle must be filled before the cap is put on, etc. So we start by defining all these relationships in a precedence table. Operation 1 (cleaning and inspecting the bottle) can be done right at the beginning. Operations 2 (filling) and 4 (labelling) can both be done immediately after operation 1. Operation 3 (capping) can be done after operation 2, while operation 5 (putting the bottle in a box) must wait until both operations 3 and 4 are finished. This gives the following precedence table.

Operation	Must be done after
1	–
2	1
3	2
4	1
5	3, 4

We can draw these relationships in a precedence diagram. This starts with the earliest operations and moves systematically through the process. Operation 1 is at the left, and then we can add operations 2 and 4. Operation 3 comes after operation 2, and finally we put operation 5 after both operations 3 and 4. The complete precedence diagram is shown in Figure 10.12.

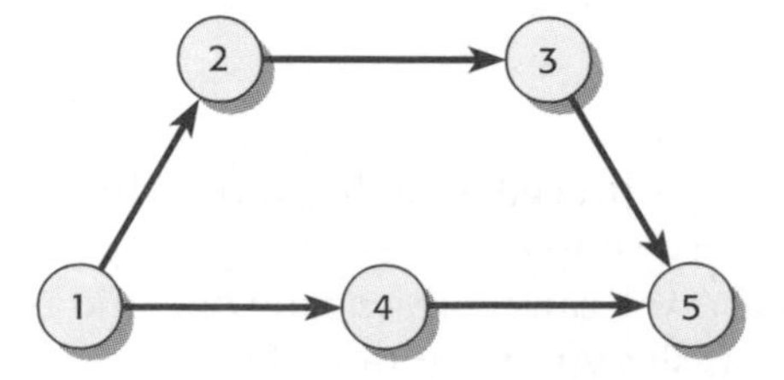

Figure 10.12 Precedence diagram for bottling hall

WORKED EXAMPLE

A process has eleven operations with the precedence shown in the following table. Draw a precedence diagram of the process.

Operation	Must be done after
1	–
2	1
3	1
4	2, 3
5	4
6	4
7	4
8	5
9	6, 7
10	8, 9
11	10

Solution

Operation 1 can be done right at the start. When this is finished both operations 2 and 3 can start. Operation 4 can be done after both operations 2 and 3, and so on. Continuing with this logic gives the diagram shown in Figure 10.13.

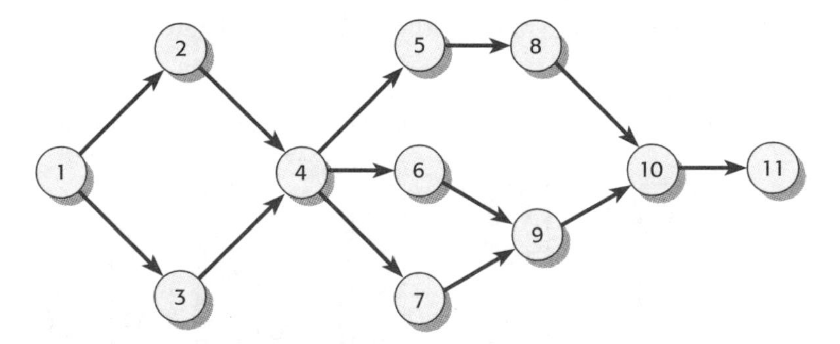

Figure 10.13 Precedence diagram for worked example

Multiple activity charts

It is often useful to see what each person, or other participant in the process, is doing at any time. We can do this kind of analysis with a **multiple activity chart**. This has a time scale down the side of the diagram, with all the participants listed across the top. The time each participant works on the process is blocked off (as shown in Figure 10.14).

This chart is for two people working in a small warehouse. When they get an order they go around and put the goods in a trolley, then they take them to a packing machine. The participants in the process are two people, two trolleys and the packing machine. The chart shows that each person works on a series of orders, each of which takes 15 minutes to collect and five minutes to pack. We can see exactly what each participant is doing at any time, and we can look at the pattern of work to identify bottlenecks and idle periods.

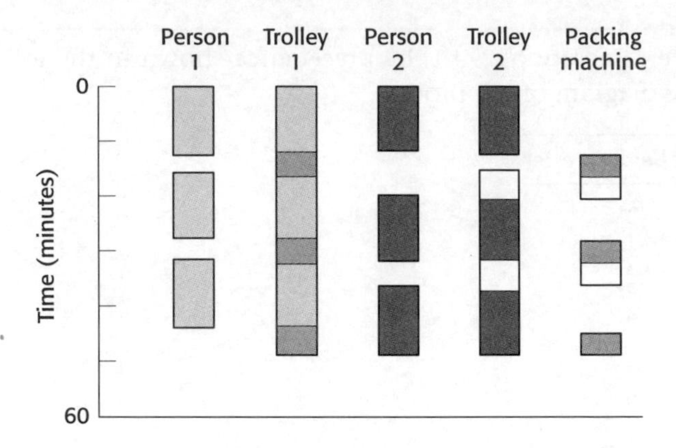

Figure 10.14 Multiple activity chart for warehouse

WORKED EXAMPLE

One operator is currently assigned to each of three machines. The machines work a cycle with six minutes for loading, six minutes of operating and four minutes for unloading. An operator is needed for the loading and unloading, but the machines can work without any supervision. The operations manager plans to make savings by using two people to operate the three machines. Draw a multiple activity chart to see if this can be done.

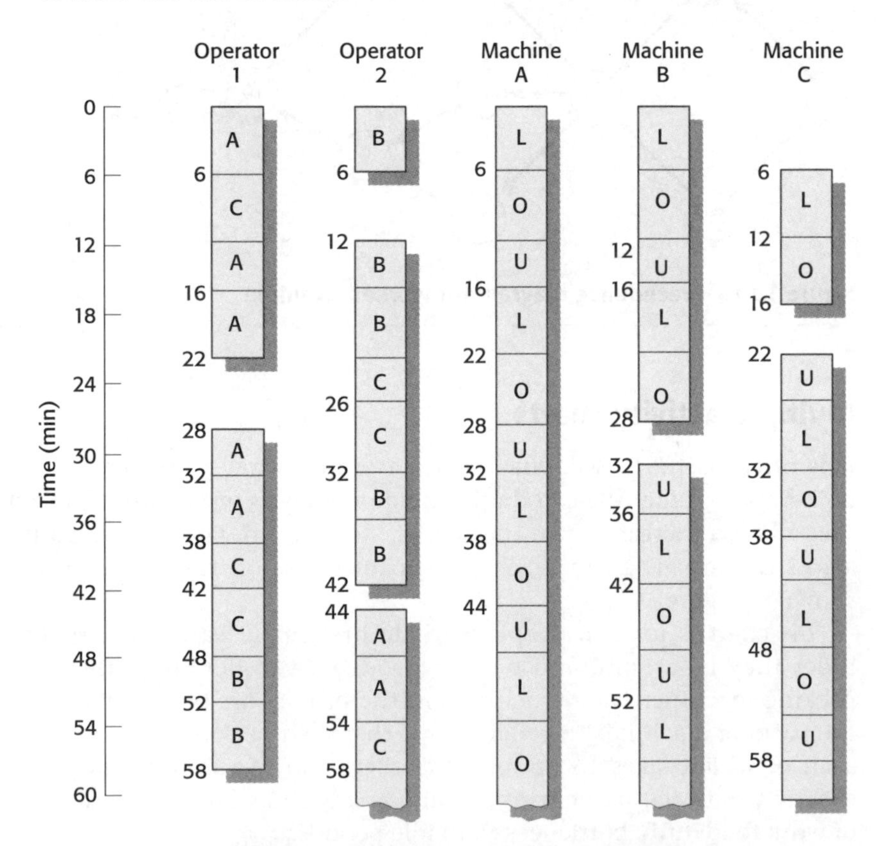

Figure 10.15 Multiple activity chart for worked example

Solution

Figure 10.15 shows a multiple activity chart for three machines and two operators, assuming all people and machines are idle at the start, and we follow the process for the first hour.

The process starts with operators 1 and 2 loading machines A and B respectively. These machines start working, while operator 1 loads machine C. The operators unload machines A and B as soon as they are finished, and then they reload the machines. Machine C has to wait to be unloaded until an operator is free. The chart follows this process for the first hour, at which point both operators have been idle for eight minutes, and the three machines have been idle for zero, four and 10 minutes. Some of this idle time was needed to get things going at the start of the day, so it does look as if the new arrangement will work.

Review questions

10.13 What is the purpose of process charts?

10.14 What are precedence diagrams and when are they used?

10.15 When would you use a multiple activity chart?

Chapter review

- Every organisation has to measure its performance. Financial measures are most common, but it is important to have some direct measures of operations.
- There are many possible measures, but the most common are capacity, efficiency, utilisation, and productivity.
- There are several types of productivity. Most organisations use a balanced view of different types of partial productivity.
- Measures help managers make decisions. For this, they are often used for comparisons against standards. Benchmarking is a formal method of comparing operations with the best in the industry.
- Organisations must continuously improve their operations to remain competitive. Improving a process involves change. Two approaches to change have small continuous improvement, or radical change such as reengineering.
- Process charts describe the details of an existing process and highlight areas that need improvement. There are many useful charts, including process charts, precedence diagrams and multiple activity charts.

Key terms

benchmarking *p. 257*
business process reengineering (BPR) *p. 262*
capacity *p. 248*
effectiveness *p. 250*
efficiency *p. 249*
multiple activity chart *p. 271*
partial productivity *p. 252*
precedence diagram *p. 269*
process chart *p. 266*
productivity *p. 249*
reengineering *p. 263*
total productivity *p. 251*
utilisation *p. 249*

CASE STUDY Registration at the IMA Conference

The autumn 1999 conference of the International Management Association in Frankfurt had 2,100 delegates. All of these had to register at the conference, using a procedure that had been used for several years. This started with delegates queueing to pick up registration documents at an information booth. They filled out the forms and walked 30 m to the hotel reception, where they formed another queue at the front desk. Here a receptionist checked the delegates' details, confirmed their hotel booking and gave them information about the hotel and their room.

After the hotel, delegates went up two floors, walked 120 m to the conference administrators, and joined a queue to have their registration forms checked, see what sessions and functions they planned to attend, and what special arrangements they needed. Then they walked 50 m to the conference registrar's office, where a clerk calculated any fees they had to pay, and handed over tickets and information abut the various functions. Then the delegates walked 30 m to a cashier's window to pay their fees and get a receipt.

If delegates wanted car parking at the hotel, they had to go to the parking desk, which was 150 m from the cashier. Anyone who wanted special arrangements had to visit other areas.

The wait at each window was about 10 minutes and the actual processing time was two minutes. The registration usually took over an hour and delegates had to walk 400 m. Sometimes the system was busy and people took a lot longer.

One delegate was so annoyed by the system that he suggested a streamlined process in which they would walk 30 m and take an average of 10 minutes.

Questions

- Draw a process chart for delegate registration for the conference.
- Calculate the average time a delegate needs to go through the whole process.
- What improvements can you suggest to the process?

Problems

10.1 Machines in a canteen are designed to serve up to 2,000 cups of coffee in a two-hour meal break. During a typical break they were used for 90 minutes and served 1,000 cups. How can you measure their performance?

10.2 A family doctor sees patients for an average of 10 minutes each. There is an additional five minutes of paperwork for each visit, so appointments are made at 15-minute intervals. Each surgery lasts for five hours a day, but during one surgery the doctor was called away for an emergency that lasted an hour. Four patients who had appointments during this time were told to come back later. How could the doctor's performance in the surgery be measured?

10.3 In two consecutive years a process had the following characteristics:

	Year 1	Year 2
Number of units made	5,000	6,500
Raw materials used	15,000 kg	17,500 kg
Cost of raw materials	£40,000	£50,500
Hours worked	1,200	1,500
Direct labour costs	£2,000	£18,000
Energy used	20,000 kWh	24,000 kWh
Energy cost	£2,000	£3,000

What can you say about the productivity?

10.4 Draw two alternative charts to describe the process of getting a mortgage from a building society.

10.5 A product goes through eight operations with the precedence table shown below. Draw a precedence diagram of the process.

Operation	Must be done after
1	–
2	1
3	2
4	1
5	4
6	3, 5
7	3, 6
8	5, 6

10.6 Inspectors at James Pettigrew and company take random samples of products. An inspection involves three separate tests, each of which uses a different type of machine. There are two machines of each type. Each test takes three minutes for assessment, followed by two minutes for fine adjustment. There are three inspectors working in the area. Draw a process chart for the inspection area. How many units can be inspected each hour?

Discussion questions

10.1 What you can't measure you can't manage. To what extent do you think this is true?

10.2 Managers can be tempted to use the easiest measures of performance, or those that show themselves in the best light. What are the consequences of this? Can you give examples of problems this creates?

10.3 Performance measures can give conflicting views. Changes that improve some measures, are likely to make others worse. How can you decide whether the overall effect is beneficial or not?

10.4 The general manager of Asiatic Pine adjusted the way that annual overheads were divided between production and customer service. The following table shows the results (in thousands of pounds).

	Before change		After change	
Production	Overheads	50	Overheads	30
	Direct costs	120	Direct costs	120
	Total	**170**	**Total**	**150**
Customer service	Overheads	20	Overheads	40
	Direct costs	30	Direct costs	30
	Total	**50**	**Total**	**70**

The company made no changes at all to operations, but got the double benefit of reducing production costs and increasing customer service. What do you think about this – and similar – changes?

10.5 Employees in a company say that productivity rose by 20 per cent, so they deserve a pay rise. Employers say that the amount of overtime worked has risen by 20 per cent, raising the wage bill by 30 per cent, so employees should take a pay cut. Senior executives say that their sound management has raised profits by 30 per cent, so they deserve a substantial performance bonus. What do you think of such arguments? Can you find other examples?

10.6 Some people say that productivity can mean whatever you want it to mean. Are they right? What happens when you do not define your terms carefully enough?

10.7 One of the problems with benchmarking is getting enough reliable data. Competitors are unlikely to give information so that you can copy their best ideas. How can you get around this problem?

10.8 Do you really think that change is inevitable in an organisation? Can you think of organisations that have not changed over time but still seem to be working successfully?

10.9 Continuous improvement is not really useful as it just tinkers with existing operations and does not look for significant gains. To what extent do you think this is true?

10.10 Is reengineering a new idea, or is it just a new term for a collection of old ideas? What do you think it contributes to operations management?

References

1. Norris D. (1998) 'Paying a High Price', *Daily Mail*, 17 August.
2. Ham P. (1998) 'It's Time for the Banks to Clean up their Act', *Sunday Times*, 19 April.
3. Townsend R. (1970) *Up the Organisation.* London: Coronet Books.
4. Monden Y. (1983) *Toyota Production System*. Atlanta, GA: Industrial Engineering and Management Press.
5. Hammer M. and Champy J. (1993) *Reengineering the Corporation*. New York: Harper Collins.
6. Hammer M. (1996) *Beyond Reengineering.* New York: Harper Collins.

Selected reading

Armistead C. and Roland P. (1996) *Managing Business Processes: BPR and Beyond.* Chichester: John Wiley.

Berry L.G. (1995) *Great Service.* New York: Free Press.

Edelson N.M. and Bennett C.L. (1998) *Process Discipline.* White Plains, NY: Quality Resources.
Gilgeous V. (1997) *Operations and the Management of Change.* London: Pitman.
Gouillant F. and Kelly J. (1995) *Transforming the organisation.* New York: McGraw-Hill.
LaMarsh J. (1995) *Changing the Way we Change.* Reading, MA: Addison-Wesley.
Leibfried K.H.J. and McNair C.J. (1992) *Benchmarking: a Tool for Continuous Improvement.* New York: Harper Collins.
Ramaswamy R. (1996) *Design and Management of Service Processes.* Harlow: Addison-Wesley Longman.
Robbins H. and Finley M. (1997) *Why Change Doesn't Work.* London: Orion Business Books.
Tenner A.R. (1996) *Process Redesign.* Reading, MA: Addison-Wesley.
Watson G.H. (1993) *Strategic Benchmarking.* New York: John Wiley.
Wu B. (1994) *Manufacturing Systems Design and Analysis*. 2nd edn. New York: Chapman and Hall.

Useful Websites

www.ame.org – Association for Manufacturing Excellence
www.pmbn.org – Process Management Benchmarking Network
www.worksimp.com – Ben Graham Corporation

CHAPTER 11

Layout of facilities

Layout decisions are important for three basic reasons: (1) they require substantial investments of both money and effort, (2) they involve long-term commitments . . . , (3) they have significant impact on the cost and efficiency of short term operations.

William J. Stevenson

Production/Operations Management. 4th edn. Irwin, Homewood, IL, 1993

Contents

Aims of the chapter

After reading this chapter you should be able to:

- understand the importance of facility layout;
- describe different types of layout;
- discuss the features of process layouts;
- design process layouts that minimise movement between areas;
- discuss the features of product layouts;
- design product layouts that give a balanced flow;
- describe different types of hybrid layouts;
- discuss some other types of layout including fixed position, warehouses, offices and shops.

Main themes

This chapter will emphasise:

- **layout**, the physical arrangement of facilities in a process;
- **layout planning**, to find the best type of layout for a process;
- **layout design**, which adds the details to a layout plan.

OPERATIONS IN PRACTICE

Hart House Restaurant

'It is very simple', said Joe Mellors, owner of the Hart House Restaurant:

We have a popular bar, and behind this is a restaurant. Last year people would come for a meal in the restaurant. They would walk through the main door into the bar, see the crowds, assume the restaurant was also full, and go somewhere else to eat. Often the restaurant was almost empty, but people were leaving to eat next door.

To solve this problem I changed the layout. I moved the main entrance closer to the restaurant and added a reception area. Now people come through the main door and turn left to go into the bar. To the right a receptionist meets those who want the restaurant, and takes them through to the tables. They never need to go into the bar, and they know straight away that there is room in the restaurant. It may seem simple, but changing the layout increased the restaurant's income by 180 per cent.

Planning a layout

Definitions

Chapter 9 described the different types of process that an organisation can use to make its products. In this chapter we look in more detail at the way the resources in these processes are physically arranged or laid out.

Facility layout is the physical arrangement of equipment, offices, rooms, etc. within an organisation.

- It describes the location of resources and their relationship to each other.

When you go into a Sainsbury's supermarket you see that goods are arranged in parallel aisles. A lot of thought and experiment has gone into this layout. It is especially designed to encourage customers to buy more goods. Every other organisation has to consider the layout of its operations, whether it is a shop, manufacturer, warehouse, office or government debating chamber.

Facilities that are laid out well are efficient and allow a smooth and easy flow through the process: poorly laid out facilities disrupt operations and reduce the efficiency. You can see this in, say, libraries – one library is convenient and easy to use, while another is confusing and poorly arranged. In the same way, some airports handle large numbers of people very efficiently, while others have queues, crowds milling around and people wandering around looking lost. The aim of **layout planning** is to design the best layout for facilities.

Layout planning finds the physical arrangement of facilities and resources that makes operations run as efficiently as possible.

Layout planning looks at a series of related questions, about how much space to give to each operation, how to arrange this space, what types of equipment to use, what services to put in each area, how to organise information flows, how to minimise movements, and so on. The following list gives some examples of layout decisions.

- Shop managers choose the best type of displays, how to arrange them, how much space to give each product, and where to put products on the displays. Their aim is to encourage customers to buy goods.
- Librarians arrange books on shelves, assign space to categories of books, and decide where these categories should be put. Their aim is to make books easy to find.
- Bus station managers find the best arrangements for their bus stops and facilities. Their aim is to give a smooth flow of passengers onto and away from the buses.
- Hotel managers design reception areas so that guests can easily check-in, find information and do all the other things that they want.
- University lecture theatres give a suitable environment for classes, have related classes that are close together, corridors and common spaces that can handle sudden surges of people, facilities such as coffee bars are nearby, etc.

Project 11.1 *Have a look at your local town centre or other facility that you think has a particularly poor layout. What are the problems with the layout? What would be a better arrangement? What benefits would your improvements bring? Why do you think nobody has already improved the existing layout?*

Types of layout

The most important factor in layout planning is the type of process. You would not expect Thompson's Micro-brewery, which makes one small batch of beer a day, to arrange its facilities in the same way as the Guinness brewery in Dublin. The type of process sets the overall features of the layout, but there are many variations in detail that depend on the objectives and constraints. This suggests the approach to layout design shown in Figure 11.1.

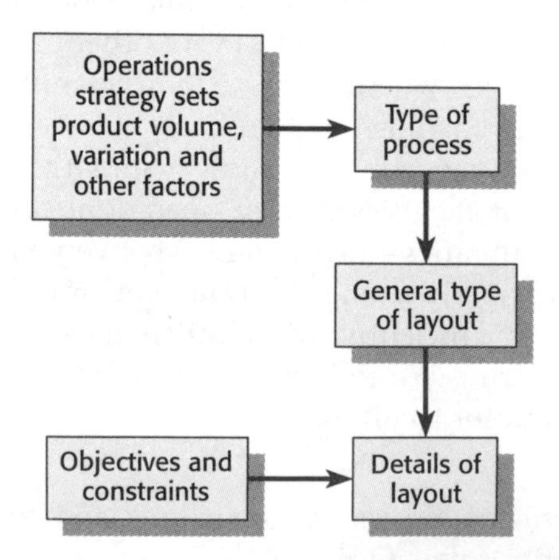

Figure 11.1 Approach to layout planning

Table 11.1 Relating processes and layouts

Type of process	Usual type of layout	Example
Project	Fixed position	Road resurfacing
Jobbing	Process	Hospital kitchens
Batch	Hybrid	Airport terminals
Mass	Product	Assembly line
Continuous	Product	Oil refinery

There are five general types of layout:

- *process layout*, which puts similar resources together, such as hospitals, kitchens and job shops;
- *product layout*, which puts resources for a particular product together, such as assembly lines, bottling plants and production lines;
- *hybrid layout*, which is a mixture of these two, such as fast food restaurants and airport terminals;
- *fixed position layout*, where everything is done in the same place, such as road laying, bridge building and ship repair;
- a series of *specialised layouts*, such as retail shops, offices and warehouses.

As a rule of thumb, you are most likely to find process layouts for jobbing processes, and product layouts for mass and continuous processes. Hybrid layouts come in the middle of these, and are often used for batch processes. Fixed position layouts are most common for projects. These links are shown in Table 11.1.

Once we have chosen the general type of layout, we can add some details. These depend on the objectives and constraints. Some of the overall objectives are set by the operations strategy. If, for example, an organisation has a customer focus, the layout must allow customers to play their part in the process; if the strategy emphasises speed, the layout must allow rapid throughput. Two other common objectives are to use the minimum amount of resources to get planned output, and arrange available facilities to get the maximum output from them.

More specific objectives of layout design are to make sure that there is enough space for all operations, that materials can move efficiently through the process, that available space is used efficiently, costs are low, all unnecessary movements between areas are eliminated, necessary movements are as easy as possible, all health, safety and comfort requirements are met, that the facilities are aesthetically pleasing, and any special requirements are met. The layout design has to achieve these objectives in the face of many types of constraint, including:

- the product design, and whether this calls for a specific layout;
- planned capacity;
- total space available;
- building used and the arrangement of spaces;
- other site constraints, such as access;
- material handling and difficulty of movement;
- capital available;

- service areas, for both employees and customers;
- information flows needed by the process;
- safety needs;
- quality of the work environment;
- flexibility, setting how quickly the layout can be changed.

OPERATIONS IN PRACTICE

West Marshes Post Office

The purpose-built post office in West Marshes was opened in the 1920s. Seventy years later, changing government policies transferred the counter service away from the publicly owned post office to a privately owned newsagent. A post office counter was opened at the back of the newsagent, with the layout shown in Figure 11.2.

This layout did not work well. People did not know where to queue in front of the counters, it was not clear if there was one queue or several, queues got in the way of people wanting to look at the shelves in the shop, people waiting for the post office noticed that others waiting for the newsagent got served faster, there was nowhere to fill in forms, people looking at magazines got in the way of those wanting to get to the post office, and so on.

The newsagent changed the details of layout of the shop over the next three years, adding barriers to form a single queue, adding a counter to fill in forms, closing the end of aisles so that newsagent customers were kept more separate from post office customers. Despite these changes, there was a general feeling that the service had declined since the purpose-built post office was closed.

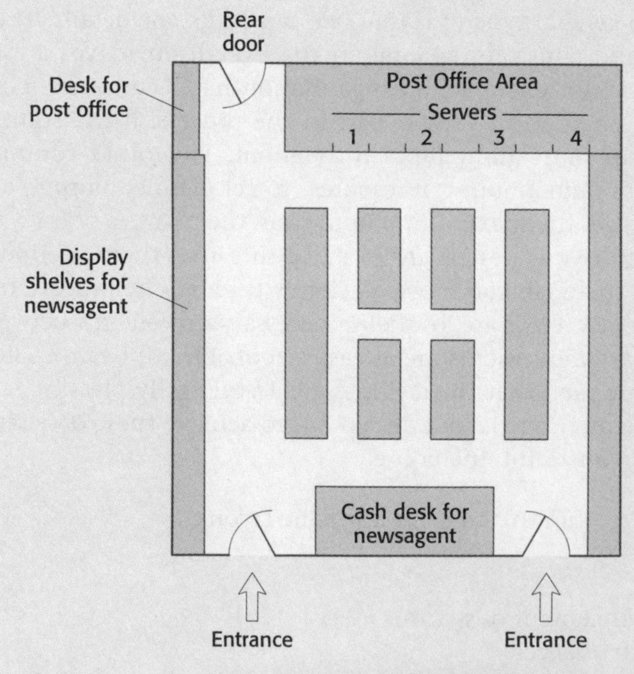

Figure 11.2 West Marshes Post Office/newsagent

Review questions

11.1 What is meant by 'layout' and why is it important?

11.2 What are the objectives of layout design?

11.3 What different types of layout are there?

Process layouts

In a **process layout** all similar pieces of equipment and facilities are grouped together. Hospitals use a process layout when they put all equipment for emergencies in one ward, surgical patients in another, paediatrics in another, and so on. A job shop has all drilling machines in one area, grinders in another area, sanding machines in a third area, and milling machines in a fourth. This layout works best when different products use the same resources, and every product follows a different route through them. Figure 11.3 shows some resulting routes when each product uses the facilities in a different order. As you can imagine, it is difficult scheduling operations in a process layout, and then keeping track of the movement of jobs. Some other advantages and disadvantages are listed below.

- Advantages of process layout:
  - A variety of products can be made on the same facilities.
  - Equipment is general purpose and less expensive than specialised equipment used in product layouts.
  - Operations continue if some equipment cannot be used because of breakdown or planned maintenance.
  - It is suitable for low volumes and variable demand.

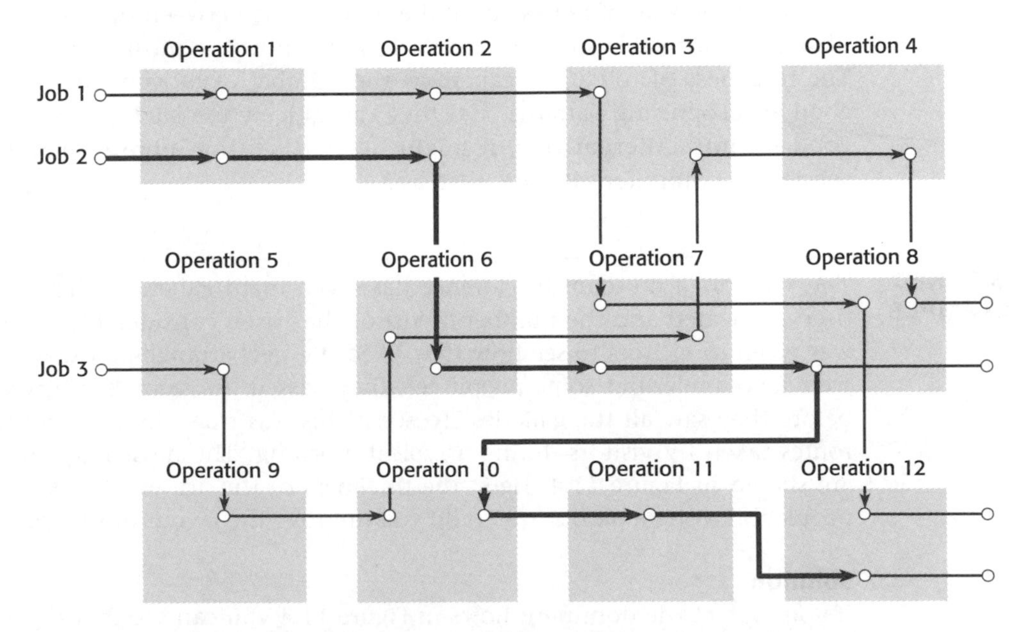

Figure 11.3 Process layout with similar facilities grouped together

  - Products can be made for specific orders.
  - People work in cohesive groups and generally enjoy the environment.
  - Training and professional development is easier.

- Disadvantages of process layout:
  - Small batches give low utilisation of equipment.
  - Unit costs are high.
  - There is a lot of handling of products and materials.
  - The physical movement of jobs between operations is complicated.
  - Scheduling jobs and equipment is difficult.
  - There are high stocks of work-in-progress.
  - Employees need more skills.
  - Controlling the flow of work is difficult.

One feature of process layouts is that people work in groups according to their skills. Offices, for example, often have accountants working in one area, lawyers in another, planners in a third, and so on. These can form cohesive groups that work together well, giving both high morale and productivity, but it is difficult to make changes because the groups do not want to split up.

Movements between operations

In process layouts every unit must physically move between operations. This leads to a common objective of designing the layouts to minimise the total distance travelled. There are several ways of approaching this, but the most common use simple rules of thumb. Suppose a process has a lot of movement between two operations, say, packing and mailing. It makes sense to put these operations as close together as possible. Other areas with no movement between them can be further apart.

One simple way of representing the movements between operations is to draw a plan of the available space and add arrows to show the most frequent movements. The thickness of the arrow can show the number of movements. People are very good at recognising patterns, and they can quickly use such plans to get ideas for good layouts. Alternatively, it might be worth using more formal analyses and specialised computer software, such as XCELL+.

WORKED EXAMPLE

The Via Longa museum in Florence has seven main galleries. These have recently been renovated and the number of visitors has risen considerably. A questionnaire was given to visitors to see how they liked the new arrangements. Most comments were favourable, but some people felt they passed the same exhibits several times before they saw all the galleries. To see if this was true, the museum recorded the routes taken by visitors during a typical morning. The most frequent movements are shown in Figure 11.4. Here, the thickness of the arrows shows the number of people following a path. How could you improve the layout of the galleries?

Solution

If you look at the dominant flows in Figure 11.4 you can see that the visitors' criticisms are justified. We can suggest some improvements to the layout as follows:

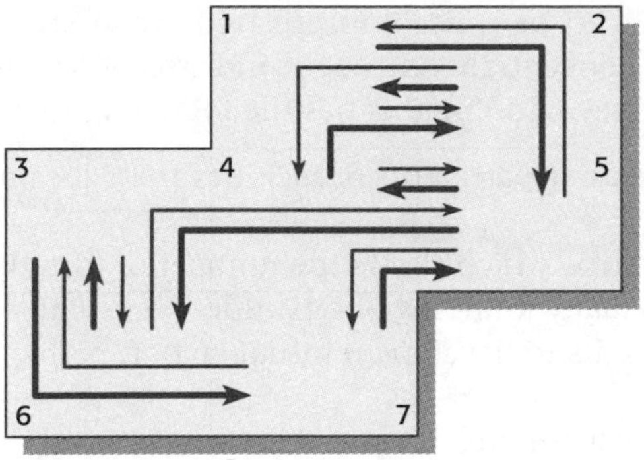

Figure 11.4 Original layout of seven galleries in Via Longa museum

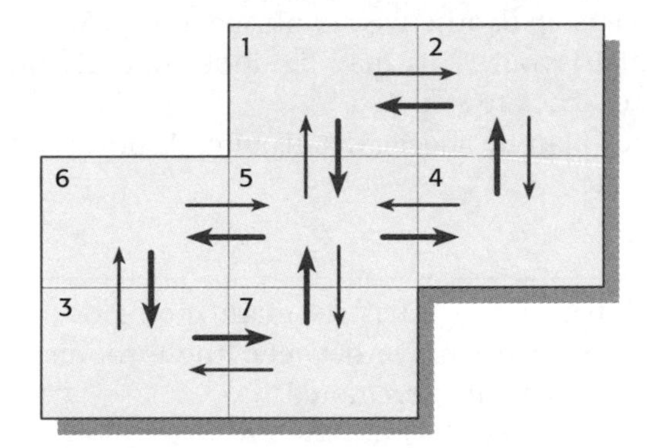

Figure 11.5 Improved layout that reduces movement

- Most people walk through gallery 4 as they move from gallery 5 to gallery 6. On the other hand, gallery 5 is visited twice (after both galleries 1 and 7) but it does not have a central position. An obvious improvement is to exchange galleries 4 and 5.
- Most people walk through gallery 3 to get to gallery 6 and then return to gallery 3. These two could also be exchanged.

These simple adjustments give the improved movements shown in Figure 11.5.

Designing process layouts

Informal approaches to layout design work well with small problems, but we need a more formal approach for larger problems. One widely used procedure has the following three steps.

1. Collect relevant information about:
   - the space needed for each area;
   - the amount of movement between facilities;
   - constraints on the shape of areas, etc.;
   - desirability of have facilities close together.
2. Build a general block plan and try to minimise the total movement.
3. Talk to architects, engineers, consultants and other experts to add details to the block plan and give a final layout.

In practice, this procedure can be quite complicated. Each step has potential difficulties, but here we will concentrate on the second step of actually designing a general block plan. The best way of doing this has the following steps:

- Step 1. List the separate areas, departments or facilities to be located and find the space needed by each one.
- Step 2. Build a 'from-to' matrix, which shows the number of trips directly between each pair of areas, and is usually found by observation over some typical period.
- Step 3. Use sensible arguments to develop an initial layout, perhaps based on the current layout.
- Step 4. Find a notional cost for this layout. This might be the total distance moved, time spent travelling, total weight-distance moved (equal to the number of movements × distance × weight), or some other convenient measure. If this solution is acceptable, go to step 6, otherwise continue to step 5.
- Step 5. Improve the initial layout. This may be done by trial and error, some algorithm or experience. Go back to step 4.
- Step 6. Complete the block plan by adding details of cost, other constraints, preferred features, problems, etc.

WORKED EXAMPLE

The seminar block in Meescham College has six main rooms of equal size fitted into a rectangular building. Students move between these rooms, and during a typical period the following movements were noted.

		To					
		a	b	c	d	e	f
	a	–	30	10	0	12	0
	b	0	–	10	40	5	0
From	c	0	5	–	60	0	20
	d	0	10	15	–	0	10
	e	60	20	0	0	–	10
	f	0	0	30	5	10	–

Draw a block diagram of a good layout for the building.

Solution

Following the procedure described above:

- Step 1 has already been done with six rooms, a to f, each needing the same amount of space.
- Step 2 builds a from-to matrix. Assuming that a journey from a to b is effectively the same as a journey from b to a, we can combine to top and bottom halves of this matrix to give a revised from-to matrix.

		To					
		a	b	c	d	e	f
	a	–	30	10	0	72	0
	b		–	15	50	25	0
From	c			–	75	0	50
	d				–	0	15
	e					–	20
	f						–

- Step 3 uses sensible arguments to develop an initial layout. One approach is to rank the links according to the amount of movement. The busiest link is c–d with a value of 75, next comes a–e with a value of 72, and so on.

Rank	Link	Value
1	c–d	75
2	a–e	72
3	b–d	50
4	c–f	50
5	a–b	30
6	b–e	25
7	e–f	20
8	b–c	15
9	d–f	15
10	a–c	10
11	a–d, a–f, b–f, c–e, d–e	0

Common sense suggests that rooms c and d should be close together as they have most movements. Concentrating on rooms that should be close together, and moving down the ranking above, we can draw the layout shown in Figure 11.6.

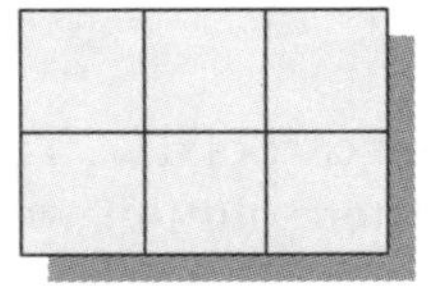

(a) rectangular building with six rooms

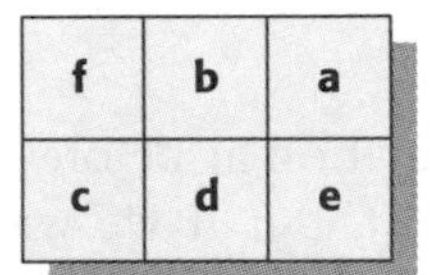

(b) initial solution

Figure 11.6 Layout of seminar block in Meescham College

- Step 4 finds a cost for this layout. We can find a notional cost by multiplying the movements in the from-to matrix by the distance on each journey. To make things easier, we can assume the rooms are squares with sides one unit long and use rectilinear distances, which are simply the sum of horizontal and vertical distances moved. Then f is 1 unit from c, 2 units from d and 3 units from e, and so on. These distances are given in the following table. We only want to compare different layouts, so the actual units are not important, as long as they give consistent values.

		To					
		a	**b**	**c**	**d**	**e**	**f**
	a	–	1	3	2	1	2
	b		–	2	1	2	1
From	**c**			–	1	2	1
	d				–	1	2
	e					–	3
	f						–

Multiplying the number of movements by the distance gives the following costs:

		To a	b	c	d	e	f
	a	–	30	30	0	72	0
	b		–	30	50	50	0
From	c			–	75	0	50
	d				–	0	30
	e					–	60
	f						–

The total cost for this layout is the sum of these individual costs, which is 477.

- Step 5 looks for improvements to the layout. One weakness is the distance between e and f, which contributes 60 to the total cost. We can reduce this by rearranging the rooms as shown in Figure 11.7.

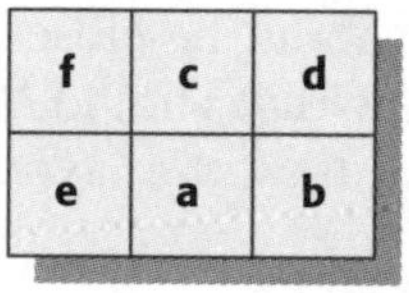

f	c	d
e	a	b

Figure 11.7 Improved layout for Meescham College

Using the same calculation as before gives a total cost of 417. This is much lower than the original cost, but if we wanted a better solution we could continue looking for improvements.

		To a	b	c	d	e	f
	a	–	30	10	0	72	0
	b		–	30	50	50	0
From	c			–	75	0	50
	d				–	0	30
	e					–	20
	f						–

- Step 6 adds details to this block plan. These details might include the exact size and shape of each room, as well as layout of corridors, stairs, offices and other general-purpose areas. Later we can add individual pieces of equipment, furniture, partitions and all the other details to give the final designs.

An obvious problem with this procedure comes in step 5, where we look for improvements. Common sense works well for small problems, but it is difficult for larger ones. There are many more formal methods, such as CRAFT,[1] which iteratively looks for improvements by exchanging the positions of two or three areas.

WORKED EXAMPLE

Figure 11.8 shows a printout from a typical package for layout planning. This starts by summarising the data. There are nine departments, and areas that cannot be used are described as a tenth Department A that occupies a fixed space. The next tables show the current layout and the movements between departments. The computer then iteratively checks for improvements to the layout and prints the best results.

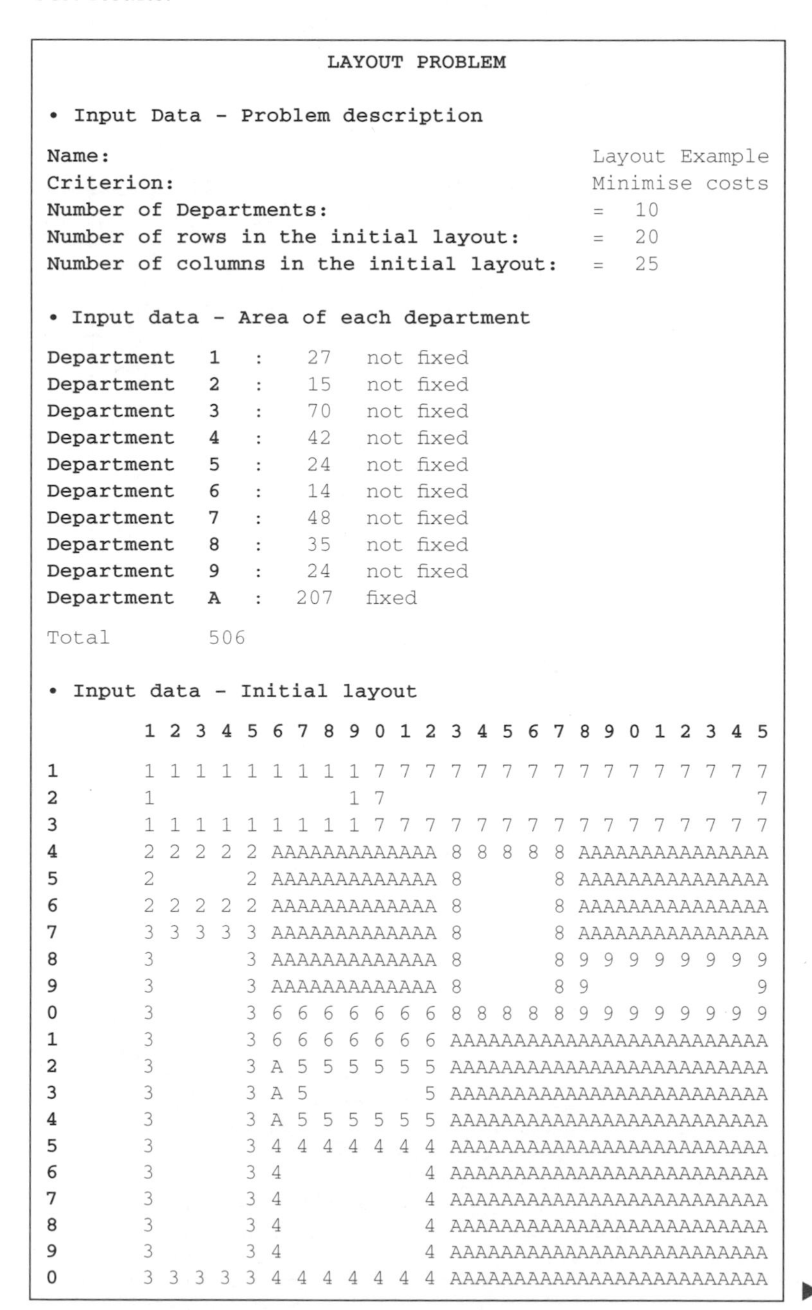

```
                         LAYOUT PROBLEM

• Input Data - Problem description

Name:                                        Layout Example
Criterion:                                   Minimise costs
Number of Departments:                       =  10
Number of rows in the initial layout:        =  20
Number of columns in the initial layout:     =  25

• Input data - Area of each department

Department  1  :   27   not fixed
Department  2  :   15   not fixed
Department  3  :   70   not fixed
Department  4  :   42   not fixed
Department  5  :   24   not fixed
Department  6  :   14   not fixed
Department  7  :   48   not fixed
Department  8  :   35   not fixed
Department  9  :   24   not fixed
Department  A  :  207   fixed

Total          506

• Input data - Initial layout

       1 2 3 4 5 6 7 8 9 0 1 2 3 4 5 6 7 8 9 0 1 2 3 4 5

1      1 1 1 1 1 1 1 1 1 7 7 7 7 7 7 7 7 7 7 7 7 7 7 7 7
2      1               1 7                             7
3      1 1 1 1 1 1 1 1 1 7 7 7 7 7 7 7 7 7 7 7 7 7 7 7 7
4      2 2 2 2 2 AAAAAAAAAAAAA 8 8 8 8 8 AAAAAAAAAAAAAA
5      2       2 AAAAAAAAAAAAA 8       8 AAAAAAAAAAAAAA
6      2 2 2 2 2 AAAAAAAAAAAAA 8       8 AAAAAAAAAAAAAA
7      3 3 3 3 3 AAAAAAAAAAAAA 8       8 AAAAAAAAAAAAAA
8      3       3 AAAAAAAAAAAAA 8       8 9 9 9 9 9 9 9 9
9      3       3 AAAAAAAAAAAAA 8       8 9             9
0      3       3 6 6 6 6 6 6 6 8 8 8 8 8 9 9 9 9 9 9 9 9
1      3       3 6 6 6 6 6 6 6 AAAAAAAAAAAAAAAAAAAAAAAAA
2      3       3 A 5 5 5 5 5 5 AAAAAAAAAAAAAAAAAAAAAAAAA
3      3       3 A 5         5 AAAAAAAAAAAAAAAAAAAAAAAAA
4      3       3 A 5 5 5 5 5 5 AAAAAAAAAAAAAAAAAAAAAAAAA
5      3       3 4 4 4 4 4 4 4 AAAAAAAAAAAAAAAAAAAAAAAAA
6      3       3 4           4 AAAAAAAAAAAAAAAAAAAAAAAAA
7      3       3 4           4 AAAAAAAAAAAAAAAAAAAAAAAAA
8      3       3 4           4 AAAAAAAAAAAAAAAAAAAAAAAAA
9      3       3 4           4 AAAAAAAAAAAAAAAAAAAAAAAAA
0      3 3 3 3 3 4 4 4 4 4 4 4 AAAAAAAAAAAAAAAAAAAAAAAAA
```

Figure 11.8 Typical printout for process layout software

```
• Input data - Inter-departmental movement

From : To:

1       1:  20     2:  0      3:  0      4:  35     5:  70
        6:  0      7:  0      8:  45     9:  0      A:  0

2       1:  30     2:  0      3:  50     4:  0      5:  20
        6:  0      7:  0      8:  0      9:  10     A:  0

3       1:  10     2:  10     3:  0      4:  0      5:  35
        6:  40     7:  0      8:  0      9:  70     A:  0

4       1:  0      2:  0      3:  0      4:  0      5:  10
        6:  50     7:  40     8:  80     9:  0      A:  0

5       1:  10     2:  0      3:  10     4:  0      5:  0
        6:  0      7:  25     8:  25     9:  50     A:  0

6       1:  25     2:  0      3:  30     4:  45     5:  70
        6:  25     7:  50     8:  20     9:  15     A:  0

7       1:  0      2:  0      3:  0      4:  70     5:  0
        6:  60     7:  0      8:  80     9:  0      A:  0

8       1:  0      2:  0      3:  0      4:  0      5:  0
        6:  120    7:  0      8:  0      9:  0      A:  0

9       1:  0      2:  25     3:  0      4:  35     5:  0
        6:  15     7:  0      8:  10     9:  0      A:  0

• Optimising procedure - run - solution found

• Output data - Optimal solution

Iterations = 4
Costs = 15564.53

• Output data - Optimal layout

        1 2 3 4 5 6 7 8 9 0 1 2 3 4 5 6 7 8 9 0 1 2 3 4 5

1       7 7 7 7 7 7 7 7 7 8 8 8 8 8 8 8 8 8 7 7 7 7 7 7 7
2       7               7 8               8 7           7
3       7 7 7 7 7 7 7 7 7 8 8 8 8       8 8 7 7 7 7 7 7 7
4       2 2 2 2 2 AAAAAAAAAAAAA 8 8 8 8 8 AAAAAAAAAAAAAAA
5       2       2 AAAAAAAAAAAAA 8 5 5 5 5 AAAAAAAAAAAAAAA
6       2 2 2 2 2 AAAAAAAAAAAAA 8 5     5 AAAAAAAAAAAAAAA
7       3 3 3 3 3 AAAAAAAAAAAAA 8 5     5 AAAAAAAAAAAAAAA
8       3       3 AAAAAAAAAAAAA 5 5     5 1 1 1 1 1 1 1 1
9       3       3 AAAAAAAAAAAAA 5 5 5 5 5 1             1
0       3       3 6 6 6 6 6 6 6 5 5 1 1 1 1 1 1 1 1 1 1 1
1       3       3 6 6 6 6 6 6 6 AAAAAAAAAAAAAAAAAAAAAAAAA
2       3       3 A 4 4 4 4 4 4 AAAAAAAAAAAAAAAAAAAAAAAAA
3       3       3 A 4         4 AAAAAAAAAAAAAAAAAAAAAAAAA
4       3       3 A 4         4 AAAAAAAAAAAAAAAAAAAAAAAAA
5       3       3 4 4 4 4 4 4 4 AAAAAAAAAAAAAAAAAAAAAAAAA
6       3       3 4 4 4 9 9 9 9 AAAAAAAAAAAAAAAAAAAAAAAAA
7       3       3 4 4 9 9     9 AAAAAAAAAAAAAAAAAAAAAAAAA
8       3       3 4 4 9       9 AAAAAAAAAAAAAAAAAAAAAAAAA
9       3       3 4 4 9       9 AAAAAAAAAAAAAAAAAAAAAAAAA
0       3 3 3 3 3 4 4 9 9 9 9 9 AAAAAAAAAAAAAAAAAAAAAAAAA
```

Figure 11.8 cont'd

Systematic layout planning

Sometimes we may not want to base layouts on the number of movements between areas. We might, for example, be designing the layout for a completely new process and not have any movements to count, or collecting the data may be particularly difficult, or the amount of movement may not be the best measure for layout. Whatever the reason, we need some other approach. The most common is **systematic layout planning**. This replaces the from-to matrix by subjective views of how close areas should be together. Suppose, for example, a large office block has a security group. There may not be many movements between this group and the main reception area, but the group should be put nearby so it can control access to the building. On the other hand, a noisy piece of machinery should be put far away from quiet offices. We can formalise these subjective views of the importance that departments are close together by defining six categories.

Importance that two areas are close together:

A – Absolutely essential
E – Especially important
I – Important
O – Ordinary importance
U – Unimportant
X – Undesirable

We can also add a note giving the reason for the decision. The most usual reasons for decisions are:

1. sharing the same facilities;
2. sharing the same staff;
3. ease of supervision;
4. ease of communications;
5. sequence of operations in a process;
6. customer contact;
7. safety;

or

8. unpleasant conditions.

Then A/5 means it is absolutely essential that two operations be close together because of the sequence of operations. We can put these codes into a matrix, as shown in the following example. This shows that areas b and d must be close together because they share the same facilities, while c and e must not be close together because of unpleasant conditions, and so on.

		Area				
		a	**b**	**c**	**d**	**e**
	a	–	U/–	O/3	O/3	X/8
Area	**b**		–	A/5	E/1	U/–
	c			–	U/–	X/8
	d				–	I/2
	e					–

The most common way of using this information is an informal method that starts by taking the links in the order of importance: X, A, E, I, O and U. It finds all the Xs and put them as far apart as possible, then finds all the As and put them as close together as possible, then puts the Es close together, and so on.

WORKED EXAMPLE

A new office is about to be opened, with six equally sized areas as shown in Figure 11.9(a). The importance that areas are close together is described by the following matrix.

	Area a	b	c	d	e	f
a	–	E/2	U/3	U/2	A/1	I/2
Area b		–	X/8	O/3	U/–	U/–
c			–	X/8	I/8	U/–
d				–	O/5	E/2
e					–	E/1
f						–

Suggest a layout for the office.

Solution

We can start by putting the two X links (b–c and c–d) as far apart as possible. Then we can add the A link (a–e) close together. One trial layout for this is shown in Figure 11.9(b).

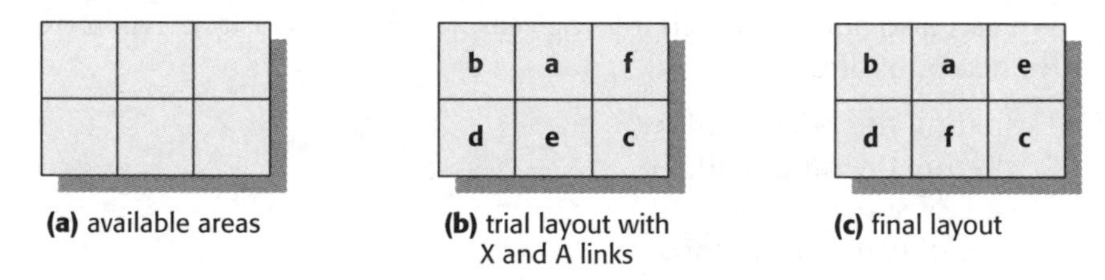

(a) available areas **(b)** trial layout with X and A links **(c)** final layout

Figure 11.9 Example of systematic layout planning

When we look at the E links (a–b, d–f and e–f), this trial layout only satisfies one of these. An obvious improvement is to exchange e and f, as shown in Figure 11.9(c). This still satisfies all the X and A links, but also satisfies two of the E links. This solution seems reasonable, but if we are not happy we can continue looking for improvements.

Review questions

11.4 Product layouts are usually used for intermittent processes like job shops. Do you think this is true?

11.5 Good process layouts can often be found by looking at the pattern of movements. Do you agree with this?

11.6 Why might the number of movements between areas not be a reasonable way of judging a layout?

Product layouts

Production lines

A **product layout** groups together all the facilities and equipment used to make a particular product. A common form of product layout lines up equipment in the order it is needed for a process, and passes each unit of the product straight down the line. In manufacturing this is the basis of production lines, as shown in Figure 11.10.

Product layouts use dedicated equipment that is arranged so the units can move in a steady flow. This is obviously related to mass processes, so it works best with stable, high demand for a standard product, with established supplies of raw materials, and so on. Then we can summarise the advantages and disadvantages of product layouts as follows.

- Advantages of product layout:
  - It can achieve a high rate of output.
  - High equipment utilisation gives low unit costs.
  - Few operators are needed with increased automation.
  - Material handling is easy.
  - Scheduling and controlling operations are easy.
  - There are smaller stocks of work-in-progress.
- Disadvantages of product layout:
  - Operations are inflexible and it is difficult to change the output rate, product or process.
  - Equipment failure and routine maintenance can disrupt the whole process.
  - Equipment may be specialised and expensive.
  - It cannot deal with variable demand.
  - People do not like working in process layouts because the repetitive work is boring.

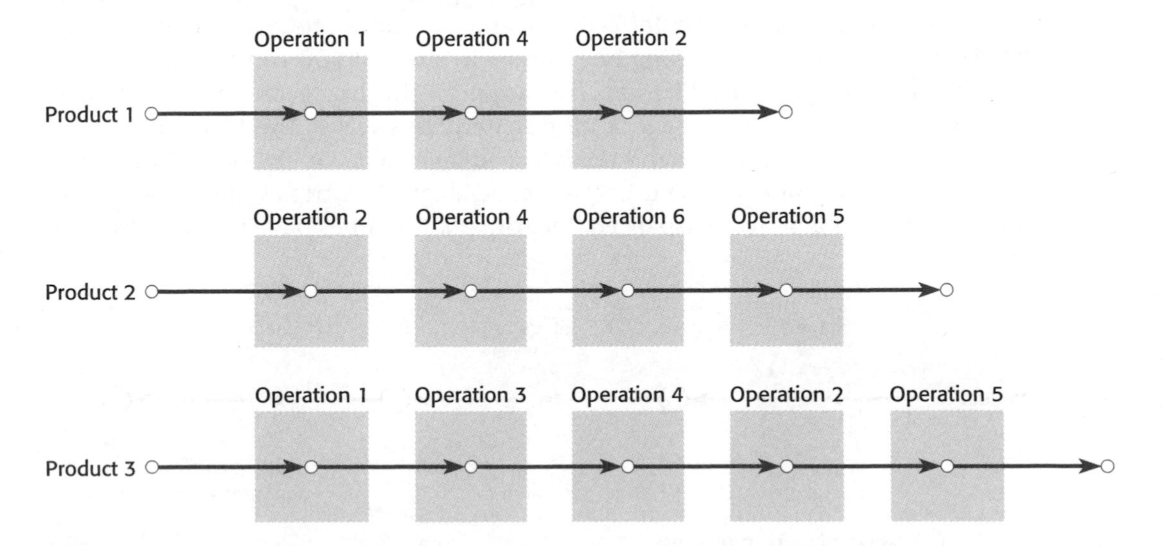

Figure 11.10 Product layouts are like assembly lines

Designing process layouts

In principle, it is easy to plan a product layout, as it consists of a series of facilities through which the product moves, but getting a smooth flow of units may be more difficult than it seems. Any bottleneck, for example, will limit the output, disrupt the smooth flow and leave other resources under-used.

Facilities in a product layout are usually divided into a number of distinct stages. In manufacturing these are called **workstations**, but we use the general 'stages in the process'. A number of operations are done at each stage. You can imagine this with a washing machine moving down an assembly line. It arrives at one stage and has the drum and mechanical parts fitted; then it moves to the next stage and has all the electrical components fitted; then it moves to another stage where the seals and pipes are fitted, and so on through the process. Then an assembly line consists of a series of discrete stages, each of which does a number of operations, and products are passed from one stage to the next. A typical product layout is shown in Figure 11.11.

The stocks of work-in-progress between each stage 'decouple' adjacent stages, so that the rest of the line can continue working normally if one stage develops short-time problems. There are disadvantages of these stocks of work-in-progress, the main ones being the cost, the need for storage space near to operations, and the delays in moving each unit through the process. It is much better to reduce these stocks and have units moving quickly down the line.

The main aim in product layout design is to have a smooth flow of products down the line, with high utilisation of all resources. Typically this uses automation. Having people work on the line generally slows down the operations, but productivity may be increased by giving them very specialised jobs. Then everyone repeatedly does a small job, and they become very efficient at doing it. Unfortunately, this specialisation also reduces the skills needed, variety of work, opportunity to show initiative – and people get bored. This leads to dissatisfaction, lower morale, absenteeism, high employee turnover and low productivity. We will discuss this again in Chapter 17.

A smooth flow means the amount of time spent in each stage must be about the same. The line is then **balanced**. Imagine a simple product layout that has two stages with operations taking one minute in the first and three minutes in the second, as shown in Figure 11.12(a). The output of this line is one unit every three minutes, set by the second stage. Unfortunately, this leaves the first stage with a utilisation of only 33 per cent and the line is unbalanced. An obvious solution here is to put three sets of equipment in the second stage. This triples output, and gives full utilisation of a perfectly balanced line. Unbalanced lines have bottlenecks, high

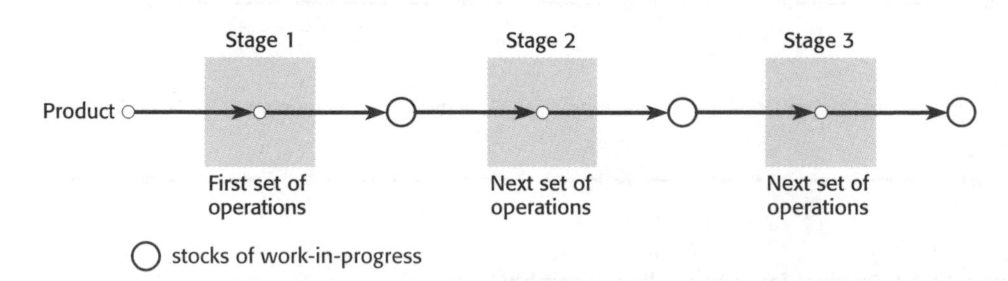

Figure 11.11 Dividing a product layout into discrete stages

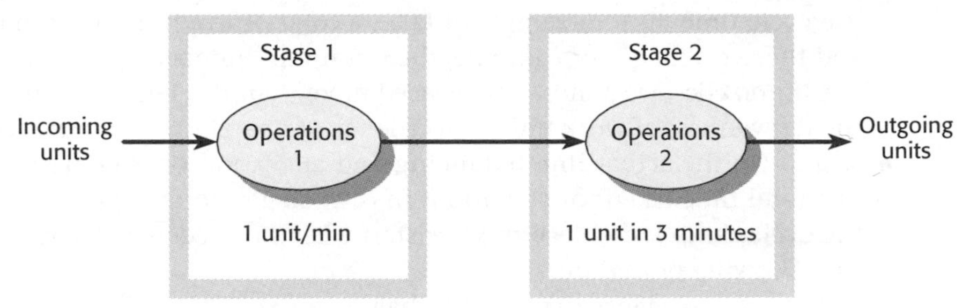

(**a**) Product layout making one unit in 3 minutes

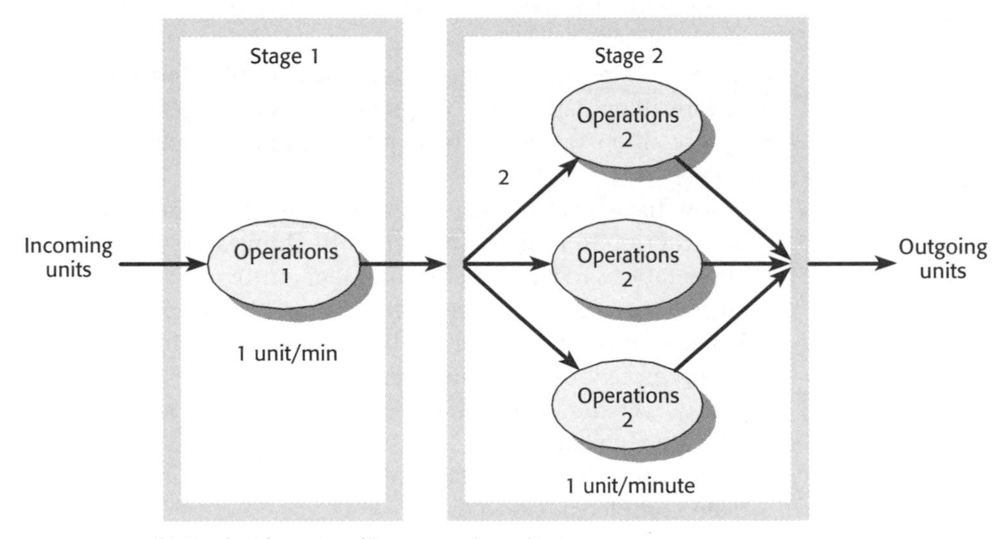

(**b**) Product layout making one unit a minute

Figure 11.12 Unbalanced and balanced lines

stocks of work-in-progress in front of slow stages, and low utilisation of faster stages. To avoid this, we use **line balancing**.

> **Line balancing** assigns operations to each stage so that the line is balanced.
>
> - This gives a steady flow of materials through the process and high utilisation of facilities.

Line balancing

The procedure for line balancing has three steps.

- *Step 1.* Find the **cycle time**, which is the maximum time any stage can work on a unit. We can find this by dividing the planned output by the time available. If, for example, planned production is 60 units an hour, then each operation in the line can last at most one minute. If the operations at any stage take longer than this, there is a bottleneck and we cannot reach the planned output.
- *Step 2.* Calculate the **theoretical minimum number of stages** needed for the entire process. We find this by dividing the total time needed to make a unit by

the cycle time. If, for example, it takes a total of five minutes to make a product and the cycle time is one minute, the minimum number of stages along the line is five. In practice, we almost always need more than this because of fractional values, the unevenness of work times, precedence of operations and other constraints.

- *Step 3.* Do the actual **line balancing** and allocation of operations to each stage. The total time taken for operations in each stage should be as close as possible to the cycle time. To achieve this, we start with a precedence diagram. Then we use the following procedure:
  1. Draw a precedence diagram for the process.
  2. Take the next unassigned operation and assign it to a new stage.
  3. Starting with the earliest operations (which are normally at the left-hand side of the diagram):
     - ignore all operations that have already been assigned to stages;
     - ignore all operations whose predecessors have not yet been finished;
     - ignore all operations for which there is not enough time left on the current stage.
  4. We now have a set of operations that we could add to the current stage. Use some criterion to rank these, such as the longest operations first.
  5. Add operations in this order to the stage until:
     - either, there are no more operations in the list identified in 4. If there are still operations that have not been allocated, go back to 2;
     - or, no more jobs in the list identified in 4 can be added to the stage without going over the cycle time. If there are still operations that have not been allocated, go back to 2;
     - or, all operations have been allocated, in which case the initial design has been completed. Go to 6.
  6. Calculate the utilisation of each stage and make small adjustments to improve the line.

This may seem a complicated procedure, but is actually straightforward, as you can see from the following example.

WORKED EXAMPLE

The operations in a product layout are shown in the following precedence table.

Operation	Time (minutes)	Operation must follow
A	5	–
B	10	A
C	4	B
D	6	B
E	4	C, D
F	2	E
G	4	F
H	5	G
I	3	H
J	2	G
K	5	J
L	8	G
M	4	L
N	2	I, K, M
O	6	N
P	1	O
Q	5	P

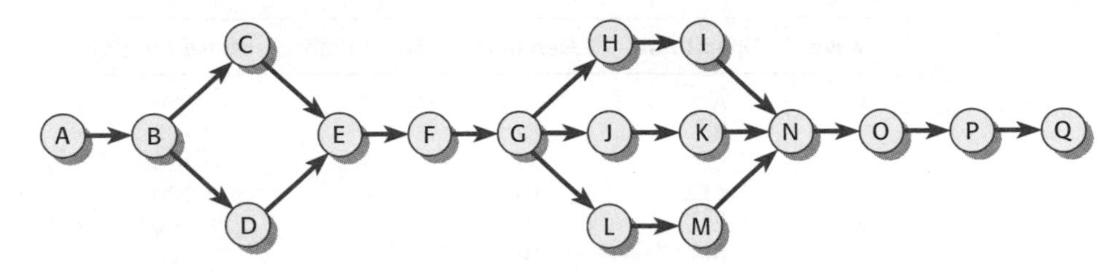

Figure 11.13 Precedence diagram for worked example

The line works an eight-hour day, during which the planned output is 48 units. Design a balanced layout for the process.

Solution

We can tackle this using the three steps described above.

- Step 1. Calculate the cycle time.

$$\text{Cycle time} = \frac{\text{time available}}{\text{number of units to be made}} = \frac{480}{48} = 10 \text{ minutes}$$

  If any stage spends more than 10 minutes on a unit, the target output of 48 units a day cannot be reached.
- Step 2. Calculate the theoretical minimum number of stages. This is the total time to make one unit of the product divided by the cycle time. Adding the time for all operations shows that it takes 76 minutes to make a unit, so:

$$\text{Theoretical minimum number of stages} = \frac{\text{total time for a unit}}{\text{cycle time}} = \frac{76}{10} = 7.6$$

  This theoretical minimum number of stages is the ideal, where each stage is fully occupied all the time. As we cannot have a fraction of a stage, we need at least eight.
- Step 3. Use the procedure described for assigning operations to stages.
  1. Draw the precedence diagram, which is shown in Figure 11.13.
  2. Assign operation A to stage 1.
  3. Ignore all activities except B, as their preceding activities have not yet been finished, but we cannot add B to stage 1 because the time needed (5 + 10 minutes) is longer than the cycle time.
  4. There are no operations that can be added to the current stage.
  5. Go back to 2.

  2. Starts stage 2 with operation B.
  3. Ignore all operations except C and D because their preceding operations have not yet been finished, but we cannot add either of these to stage 2 as they give times longer than the cycle time.
  4. There are no operations that can be added to the current stage.
  5. Go back to 2.

  Returning to 2, the procedure assigns operation C to stage 3. Then it considers D and E for adding, and arbitrarily chooses D as the longer. We can continue this procedure to give the following results:

Stage	Operations	Used time	Spare time	Utilisation (%)
1	A	5	5	50
2	B	10	–	100
3	C,D	10	–	100
4	E,F,G	10	–	100
5	L,J	10	–	100
6	H,K	10	–	100
7	M,I,N	9	1	90
8	O,P	7	3	70
9	Q	5	5	50

6. Calculate the overall utilisation of the process as:

$$\text{Utilisation} = \frac{\text{time used in a day}}{\text{number of stages} \times \text{time on each}} = \frac{76 \times 48}{9 \times 480}$$

$$= 84.4 \text{ per cent}$$

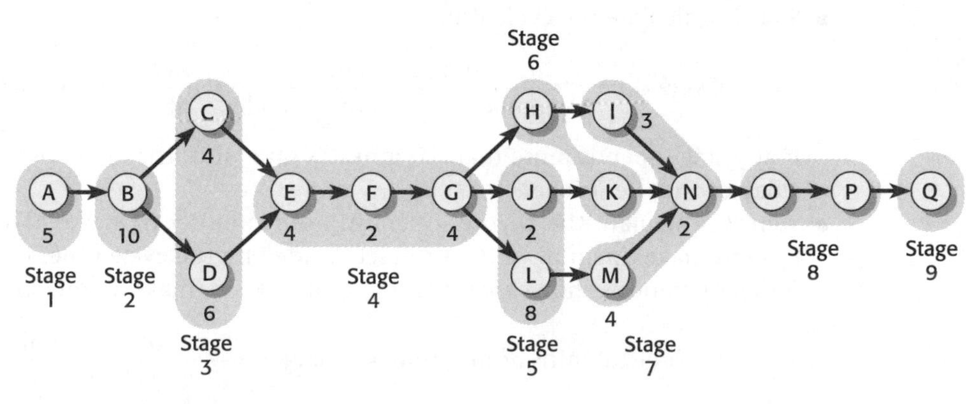

Figure 11.14 Assigning operations to stages

Review questions

11.7 Product layouts are generally more capital intensive than process layouts, but give lower unit costs. Do you think this is true?

11.8 What is the purpose of stocks of work-in-progress?

11.9 What sets the maximum output from a product layout?

11.10 What is the aim of line balancing?

Hybrid layouts

Often the best layout is neither a pure process layout nor a pure product layout, but is some combination of the two. Most of an airport terminal is designed with a process layout, so there are different areas for checking-in, eating, shopping, and so forth – but there are parts that have a product layout, such as passport control and

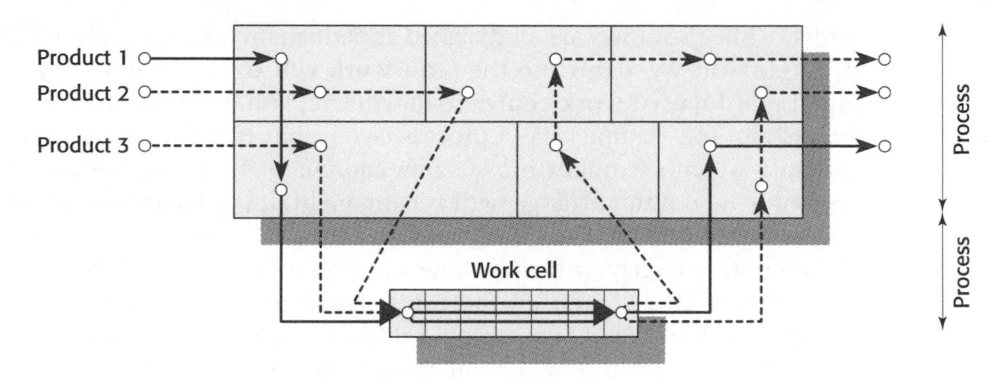

Figure 11.15 An example of a work cell

customs clearance. In the same way, a final product might be assembled from two components, one of which is made in a job shop with a process layout, while the other is made on a production line with a product layout. Arrangements of this kind are called **hybrid layouts**.

One common hybrid arrangement is a **work cell**. This is an arrangement with a dominant process layout, but with some operations set aside in a product layout. You can imagine this in a factory where most machines have a process layout, but a certain sequence of operations is repeated so often that a special area, or work cell, is set aside to deal with them on an assembly line. These work cells form islands of product layout in a sea of process layout, as shown in Figure 11.15.

Product layouts can give high utilisation and low unit costs. Even when demand is not high enough to justify a complete product layout, work cells can give these advantages in a predominantly process environment. These arrangements are sometimes called 'plant-within-a-plant', which are variations of the 'shop-within-a-shop' that you can see in large department stores.

In manufacturing, work cells are often combined with **group technology**. This combines families of products that share some common characteristic, so they can be processed in larger batches. For example, several different products might each need a 5 cm hole drilled. These products can be combined into bigger batches for the drilling. If these batches are big enough, it makes sense to do the common operations using a product layout, even though most other operations use a process layout.

You can see many examples of work cells, such as a fast-food restaurant that has a dominant process layout in the kitchen, but a special line laid out to make hamburgers. Other examples of work cells are:

- Littlewood stores have a process layout for shelves, with similar products in the same areas, but a product layout at 'customer service' where you pay.
- Treliske Hospital has a process layout for wards that treat different types of illness, but the patient admissions area has a product layout.
- Semple Avionics got an order to make a large number of struts for the construction of the Millennium Dome. They kept their overall process layout, but set aside a separate work cell as an assembly line to meet the order.

Some people suggest that there is an important difference between the last of these examples and the others. The arrangement in Semple is temporary to meet a specific order, while the others are all designed as permanent arrangements. If this distinction is important, we might use the term **work cell** to describe a temporary arrangement and **focused work centre** to describe a permanent arrangement. A car repair workshop, for example, has a process layout, but if it does a lot of work replacing exhaust systems it might move some equipment to a separate area and build an assembly line. If this arrangement is permanent, it is a focused work centre.

The borderline between work cells and focused work centres is unclear and the distinction is largely artificial. None the less, we can extend the idea of a focused work centre to get **focused factories**. These move the focused operations into another building, perhaps run by a different company. Then an efficient factory uses a product layout to make components for another facility.

Review questions

11.11 What are hybrid layouts?

11.12 What are work cells and why are they used?

OPERATIONS IN PRACTICE

Dalmuir Knitwear

Dalmuir Knitwear makes fairly small numbers of fashion garments. It weaves, knits, sews and finishes a range of knitwear, mainly for women but with some sportswear for men. Because of the fairly small production quantities, Dalmuir uses a process layout, with a weaving room, knitting room, finishing room, and so on.

Two years ago it won a large contract to supply garments to Marks & Spencer. This was a major success for the company, which was pleased that it could meet the very high standards demanded by Marks & Spencer. Because these standards were higher than their usual operations, Dalmuir set aside a specific area of the factory solely to make the order. This area was completely refurbished and the latest machines were moved in. Everything was arranged in a product layout, so that the Marks & Spencer products moved in a straight line through the factory.

The plant manager at Dalmuir created a production line to meet this one contract. Any spare capacity on the line was used to make a new range of high-quality garments for other customers.

Fixed position and specialised layouts

Many organisations need layouts for very specialised purposes, such as airports, theatres, shopping malls and cruise ships. These need considerable knowledge of the operations and skills in design. We can illustrate some aspects of these specialised layouts by four common examples: fixed layouts, warehouses, offices and retail shops.

Fixed position layout

In fixed position layouts the product stays still and operations are all done on the same site. This usually happens when a product is too big or heavy to move around. Common examples are house painting, shipbuilding, aeroplane assembly and construction sites. Fixed layouts are also useful to give special environments, such as dust-free rooms.

Fixed layouts have many disadvantages, including:

- all materials and components must move to the site;
- all people involved with operations have to travel to the site;
- there is often limited space;
- scheduling operations is difficult;
- disruptions to the schedule cause delays in completion;
- the intensity of work varies;
- external factors, such as weather conditions, can affect operations.

Because of these disadvantages, fixed position layouts are only used when moving the product is impossible or very difficult. One way to partially avoid the disadvantages is to do as much of the work as possible off-site. Small road bridges, for example, can be pre-fabricated and assembled off-site, and then moved to the site for erection.

Warehouses

The purpose of a warehouse is to store goods at some point on their journey between suppliers and customers. The essential elements in a warehouse (illustrated in Figure 11.16) are:

- an arrival bay, where goods coming from suppliers are delivered, checked and sorted;
- a storage area, where the goods are kept as stock;
- a departure bay, where customers' orders are assembled and sent out;
- a material handling system, for moving goods around;
- an information system, which records the location of all goods, arrivals from suppliers, departures to customers and other relevant information.

The detailed layout of a warehouse depends, to a large extent, on the type of goods being stored and the handling equipment used. If the goods are small and light, such as boxes of pills, they can be moved by hand. Then the warehouse

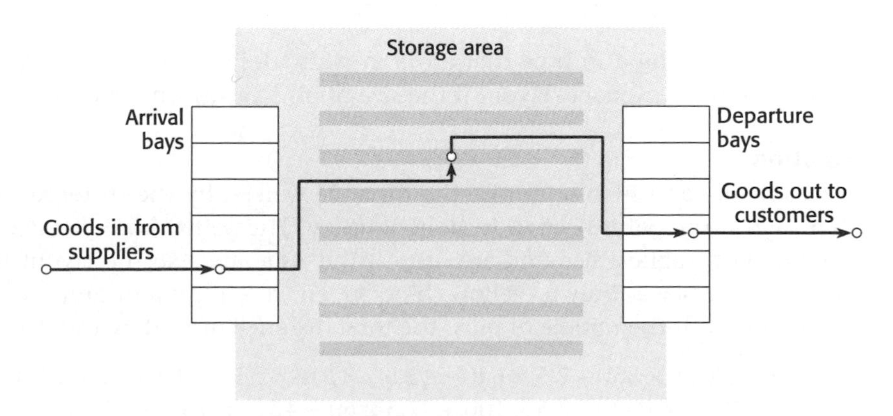

Figure 11.16 Layout of a typical warehouse

must have goods stored within easy reach, and be small enough to walk round. If the goods are large and heavy, such as engines, they need heavier handling equipment such as forklift trucks. Then the warehouse must be big enough for these to manoeuvre. These two examples show manual and mechanised layouts, which we mentioned in Chapter 9. The third level of technology is automated, where all materials handling is managed by a central computer. These three levels of technology give warehouses with completely different characteristics.

- **Manual**. Warehouses are small and store light items that are easy to lift. Storage is in shelves that are close together, but no higher than about 2 m. The warehouse must be heated, lit and allow people to work comfortably.
- **Mechanised**. Warehouses are much bigger and store heavier goods that are moved using forklift trucks, conveyors and tow lines. This equipment often needs wide aisles to manoeuvre, but shelves can be higher – typically up to 12 m with a forklift truck and higher with conveyors.
- **Automated.** These can be very big and use guided vehicles, robots and automated material handlers to move goods to and from storage areas. They use narrow aisles that can be very high, allowing computer-controlled cranes to reach all items very quickly. No people work in the storage areas, so there is no need for heat and light.

Many costs of running a warehouse are fixed, such as rent, local taxes, utilities and depreciation. Some of these fixed costs are set by management policy, such as the total investment in stock. The main variable cost comes from the details of the layout, and depends on the time needed to locate items and either add them to stock or remove them. When there are thousands of items in store, a small difference in the way they are arranged can give markedly different service and costs.

WORKED EXAMPLE

A small store has a rack with nine colours of paint in five-litre tins. At one end of the rack is an issue area where the storekeeper works. Weekly demand for the paint is as follows.

Colour	Red	Blue	White	Black	Brown	Green	Yellow	Grey	Pink
Tins	100	140	860	640	320	120	240	40	60

If all paint is stored in bins that are 5 m wide, design a reasonable layout for the rack. Design a reasonable layout if the size of bins varies with the weekly demand.

Solution

A reasonable aim is to minimise the distance walked by the storekeeper, assuming that each tin of paint needs a separate journey. The paint should be laid out so that colours with highest demand are nearest the issue area, so the layout has paint in order white, black, brown, yellow, blue, green, red, pink and grey. Assuming that tins come from the middle of bins, the total distance moved by the storekeeper is:

$$= 2 \times (2.5 \times 860 + 7.5 \times 640 + 12.5 \times 320 + 17.5 \times 240 + 22.5 \times 140 + 27.5 \times 120 + 32.5 \times 100 + 37.5 \times 60 + 42.5 \times 40)$$
$$= 57{,}600 \text{ m}$$

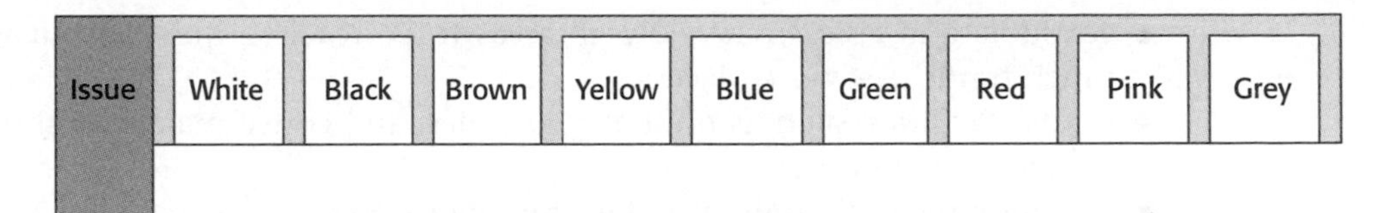

Figure 11.17 The best layout for paint rack

If the size of bin is proportional to the weekly demand, and assuming that paint is taken from the middle of the bins, the paint can be stored equally well in any order.

Offices

Offices are mainly concerned with the movement of information. This can be done:

- individually, face-to-face;
- in meetings or groups;
- by telephone, intercom or conference links;
- on paper;
- by some kind of electronic mail.

If all communications were indirect using e-mail, fax, telephones or other equipment, the amount of movement in offices would be small, as you can see in customer call centres. In practice, the best communications are done face-to-face, and this needs more planning. Those areas with most personal contacts should clearly be put near to each other. Another important consideration is the amount of customer contact. 'Front offices' are those which customers visit; 'back offices' are those which have no customer contact. If you want to arrange insurance, for example, you might visit a broker to discuss details in the front office, while all the following administration is done in the back office. When you catch a bus, you are effectively visiting the front office, while all the planning and administration has been done at the back office.

People working in offices must have conditions that are comfortable and allow them to work properly. Some jobs are best done in private offices, while other jobs are best in open areas or areas with moveable partitions. The choice of layout depends on the type of work, and factors such as:

- amount of face-to-face contact, and the total amount of movement;
- type of work;
- status and special requirements of the occupant;
- areas that are visited by customers;
- special facilities, such as conference or committee rooms, lecture theatres and board rooms;
- areas for lounges, rest rooms, cloak rooms, storage areas, cleaning equipment, and so on;

- corridors and aisles that allow all areas to be reached quickly, but without too much traffic past work places;
- shared facilities, such as photocopiers, files, and coffee machines should be convenient for everyone;
- 'hot desking' or 'hotelling' assigns temporary space to people who are away from their desks for long periods.

Retail shops

In principle, retail shops are similar to warehouses, as they both get deliveries of goods, store them and then remove the goods and pass them on to customers. In practice, however, there is a fundamental difference. A good warehouse design minimises the total distance travelled to collect goods, so those with highest demands are kept near the issue area. In a shop, the longer we walk around the more we buy, so a good layout maximises the distance travelled between purchases. You can see this clearly in supermarkets which spread high-demand items of basic food, like bread and milk, around the shop, forcing customers to pass lots of other goods before finding them all.

Many guidelines have been suggested for shop layouts, including:

- disperse basic goods around the shop, preferably around the outside aisles, so people have to walk past lots of other items;
- have long aisles without crossovers so that customers have to walk the full length of each aisle;
- put related items close together, such as tea and sugar, so that buying one may encourage people to buy the other;
- use the busy first and last aisles for high-impulse items that have high profit margins;
- set the image for the store near the door – if customers see a lot of special offers here, they will assume all prices are low;
- put magazines and chocolates near the checkouts to encourage spontaneous purchases;
- use the ends of aisles for special promotions;
- put goods that are attractive to children within their reach.

Review questions

11.13 Fixed layouts keep all equipment in fixed locations and move products through these in a specified sequence. Do you think this is true?

11.14 What are the disadvantages of fixed layouts?

11.15 What determines the best level of automation in a warehouse?

11.16 The layout of supermarkets should allow customers to collect their goods as quickly as possible. Do you think this is true?

Project 11.2

Some buildings win prizes for architectural merit. The buildings often do not work well, so the prizes seem to put more emphasis on appearance than function. Do you think that this is a reasonable view? Find some examples to support your views.

OPERATIONS IN PRACTICE

Swindon Truck Stop

Swindon Truck Stop is a service area for long-distance lorry drivers. They can park there, take legally required breaks from driving, rest, have meals, take showers, sleep, check vehicles, fill them with fuel, and so forth.

The original layout of the Truck Stop caused some problems. The main area is a fenced enclosure with controlled access, but lorries trying to leave this enclosure at busy times were held up by other vehicles filling up with fuel. In some cases there were delays of 10 or 15 minutes. Obviously, this kind of delay was not popular with drivers.

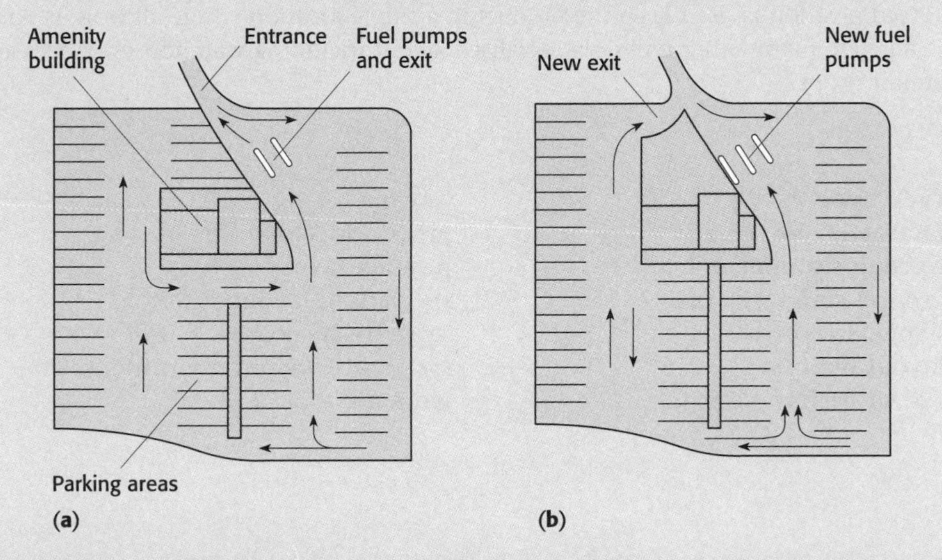

Figure 11.18 (a) Original layout of Swindon Truck Stop; (b) Modified layout of Swindon Truck Stop

Truck Stop solved the problem by redesigning the layout. In particular, it built an extra exit, added more fuel pumps and adjusted the road layout. These changes, shown in Figure 11.18, may seem fairly obvious, but you can see many other facilities that have not made obvious improvements.

Source: company promotional material

Chapter review

- Layout is concerned with the physical arrangement of facilities in a process.
- Layout planning finds the best overall arrangement for operations in a process. The layout must help achieve the aims of the operations strategy. A good layout will make sure operations run smoothly, while a poor layout will cause disruption, delays, congestion and other problems.
- An approach to layout planning uses the operations strategy and other requirements to find the general type of layout, and then adds details to this design.

- There are many types of layout, which we classified as process, product, hybrid, fixed and specialised layouts.
- Process layouts group together similar types of facilities. A common problem is to minimise the amount of movement between areas.
- Product layouts group together the facilities needed to make a product, typically in some form of production line. The main problem in product layouts is to get a balanced flow of products down the line.
- Hybrid layouts use a mixture of product and process layouts. Work cells are common examples, with some product layout in an area with an overall process layout.
- Fixed position layouts keep the product in a single location where all work is done. There are many other types of specialised layout including warehouses, offices and retail shops.

Key terms

cycle time *p. 295*
facility layout *p. 279*
fixed position layout *p. 300*
group technology *p. 299*
hybrid layout *p. 298*
layout planning *p. 279*
layout design *p. 285*
line balancing *p. 295*
process layout *p. 283*
product layout *p. 293*
specialised layout *p. 300*
stage in the process *p. 294*
systematic layout planning *p. 291*
work cell *p. 299*

CASE STUDY Bartholemews Mail Order

James Bartholomew opened a clothes shop near the centre of Leeds in 1947. His advertisements in local newspapers encouraged people living in remote areas to write for items, and he would return these by post. James realised that this side of the business had less competition than the shop and could be organised more efficiently. Over the next few years he developed the postal service and eventually formed the mail order business as a separate company. In 1968 a major national supplier bought the business.

Bartholemews now sells almost everything from plants to porcelain figures by a combination of catalogues, direct mailings and e-commerce. Its Website has a virtual shop that accounts for a relatively small, but rapidly growing part of their business.

The company is about to move to a new logistics centre on the Hinde Leys Trading Estate. This centre has a large warehouse with adjacent offices, and the company now has to design the interior layout. The warehouse can be sorted out fairly easily, but the offices are more sensitive. A 'relocation team' is arranging the 16 main departments, and started by asking how much space each department wanted (in square metres), and how much they had at present.

Department	Requested space	Current space	Staff
1	300	220	21
2	350	220	17
3	500	640	44
4	1,350	950	60
5	1,000	220	10
6	300	400	15
7	1,000	800	40
8	600	220	8
9	300	200	37
10	180	40	7
11	1,000	400	18
12	200	250	23
13	400	220	21
14	100	100	17
15	400	400	24
16	150	100	9

The space currently used includes corridors and facilities such as photocopiers and coffee machines. Most people work in open areas, so the space of each department should generally be related to the number of people who work there. There are, however, variations as some departments have more equipment or a higher workload. Most departments also have a manager and one or two others with individual offices.

The new office block is six storeys tall. It is essentially a rectangle with sides 40 m and 30 m and at the centre is a 10 m by 10 m block of stairs, lifts, washrooms and so on. At the moment the rest of the building is completely empty.

The relocation team looked at the number of movements within departments and between departments. During a typical period they recorded the following movements.

	1	2	3	4	5	6	7	8	9	10	11	12	13	14	15	16
1	457	22	47	15	19	125	256	632	87	19	44	86	188	14	223	321
2		31	91	88	28	263	472	103	37	25	137	42	501	23	145	90
3			603	99	421	682	721	284	871	23	656	92	643	57	465	653
4				72	41	132	61	72	12	52	76	65	56	17	87	20
5					128	87	23	68	234	76	451	47	71	19	67	17
6						455	14	35	26	19	109	23	56	22	121	45
7							128	12	32	10	64	61	23	17	209	331
8								78	16	21	69	30	79	32	44	36
9									864	93	237	35	566	60	77	24
10										21	56	31	72	50	69	57
11											683	43	66	23	63	23
12												92	77	20	189	49
13													440	11	445	67
14														67	623	17
15															834	77
16																125

Questions

- If you were a member of the relocation team, how would you set about designing a layout for the new building? What factors would you consider important?
- Draw an initial design for the new building. What are the strengths and weaknesses of your design? What still needs to be done to finish the design?

Problems

11.1 A process layout has five identically sized areas in a line. During a normal period, the number of movements between areas was as follows:

		To a	b	c	d	e
	a	0	17	12	42	2
	b	12	0	1	22	6
From	**c**	0	22	0	17	7
	d	47	11	3	0	12
	e	53	5	6	25	0

Suggest a good layout for the areas.

11.2 One floor of the Mendip Gallerie has six office areas, which are all the same size. The current layout is shown in Figure 11.19.

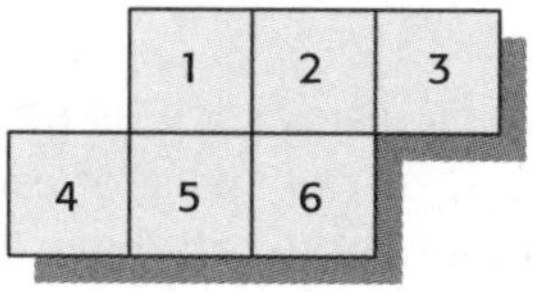

Figure 11.19 Office layout

During a typical period, the number of movements shown in the following table were recorded. Can you improve the layout?

		To 1	2	3	4	5	6
	1	–	–	100	–	35	–
	2	120	–	10	20	15	10
	3	–	15	–	80	–	75
From	**4**	–	55	–	–	75	–
	5	–	10	–	125	–	–
	6	80	20	–	–	–	–

11.3 Some equipment uses a product layout. The process consists of a sequence of 15 operations with the following times:

Operation	1	2	3	4	5	6	7	8	9	10	11	12	13	14	15
Time in minutes	2	6	8	4	10	2	1	15	11	8	2	4	10	7	5

Find the best allocation of operations to stages for different levels of production.

11.4 Han Schuman's bottling plant has seven activities, with times and precedence shown below.

Activity	Description	Time (seconds)	Activity must follow
A	Clean bottle	20	–
B	Inspect bottle	5	A
C	Fill bottle with liquid	20	B
D	Put top on filled bottle	5	C
E	Put label on bottle	5	B
F	Put bottles into boxes	10	D,E
G	Seal boxes and move	5	F

The forecast demand for bottles is 120 an hour. Find the cycle time and minimum number of stages needed. Balance the line by assigning operations to stages.

11.5 If each operation described in Figure 11.20 takes four minutes, design a line that will process six units an hour.

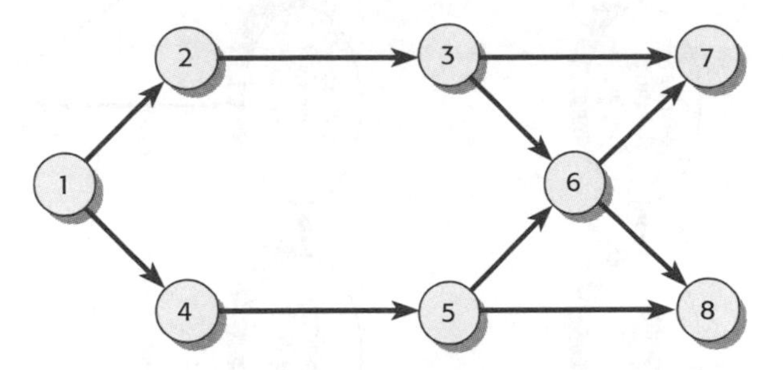

Figure 11.20 Precedence diagram

11.6 A warehouse has a single aisle with 12 bins as shown in Figure 11.21. It stores six products with the following features. Design a reasonable layout for the warehouse.

Product	Withdrawals	Bins needed
1	150	1
2	700	3
3	50	1
4	900	3
5	450	2
6	300	2

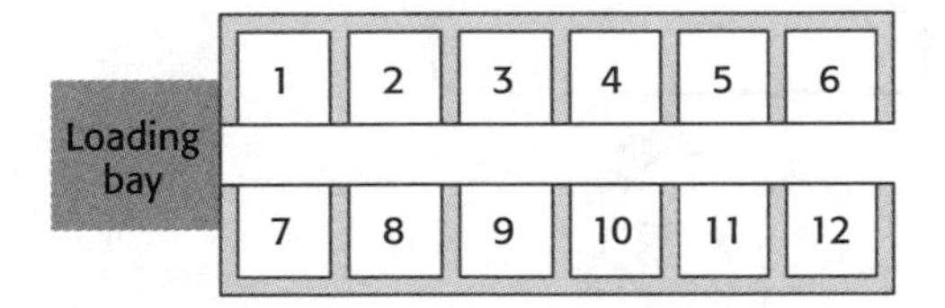

Figure 11.21

If the layout were for a supermarket, would the design be different?

Discussion questions

11.1 Do you think that layout design is a strategic issue for an organisation? Can it be a tactical or an operational issue? Give examples to support your views.

11.2 Describe some successful layouts that you have seen. What makes these successful? Compare them with other unsuccessful layouts for similar operations.

11.3 Layout design should be left to architects and planners. Do you think this would give good results?

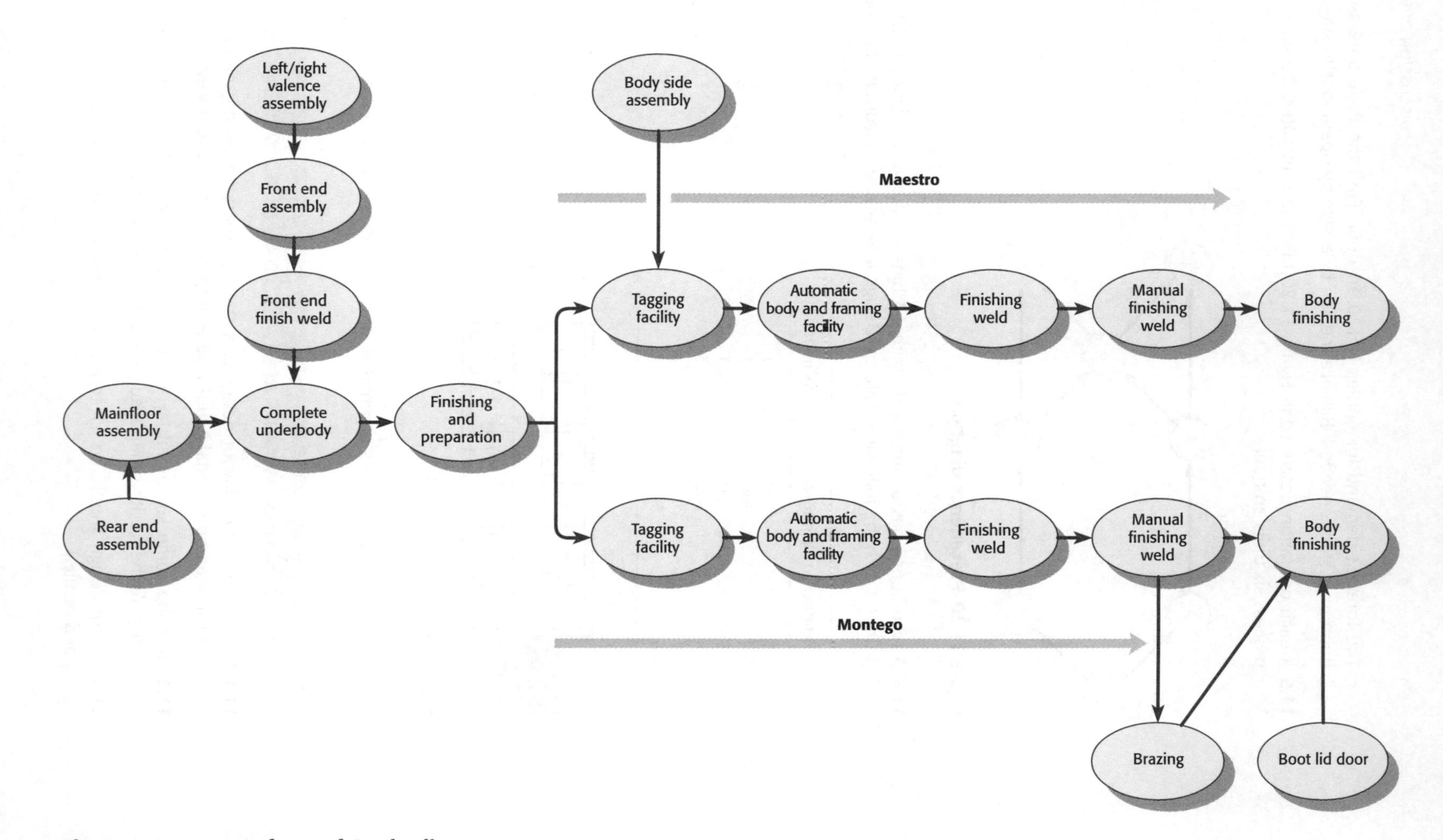

Figure 11.22 Layout of part of Cowley line

11.4 Have a look at the software that is available for layout design. What does this aim to do, and how good are the results? Some programs look for optimal layouts. Do you think there is such a thing as an optimal layout?

11.5 The sales of Allison's FK Sporting Dinghy have risen sharply in recent years. The company started making each boat with a fixed position layout, but now uses a process layout. To improve performance with the higher volumes, the company is considering moving to a product layout. What changes will this bring? What are the likely benefits and problems?

11.6 People do not like working on production lines. Describe the features you would expect to see on a production line and explain why they are unpopular. How can things be improved?

11.7 The layout of a supermarket has to balance the convenience of customers with the desire of managers to keep them in the shop as long as possible. How do they achieve this balance? Can you think of other services that face similar problems?

11.8 Banks and similar organisations often have luxurious front offices, but back offices that are small, cramped and less attractive. Why should front offices that customers visit briefly be more luxurious than back offices where people work all day?

11.9 In the 1980s Austin-Rover (since reorganised and renamed several times) built Maestros and Montegos on its production lines at Cowley. The layout for the underbody and side panel assembly is shown in Figure 11.22. As you can see, parts for both models come down the first part of the line together, but are then separated for the second part. Each model goes down its own production line for almost identical operations.

What problems do you think there were with this layout? By 1986 Montego sales were twice as high as those for the Maestro. Do you think this is important?

Reference

1. Armour G.C. and Buffa E.S. (1963) 'A Heuristic Algorithm and Simulation Approach to the Relative Location of Facilities', *Management Science*, vol 9(1), pp. 294–309.

Selected reading

Black J.T. (1991) *The Design of the Factory with a Future*. New York: McGraw-Hill.

Eley J. and Marmo A. (1995) *Understanding Offices*. Harmondsworth: Penguin.

Francis R.L., McGinnis L.F. and White J.A. (1992) *Facility Layout and Location: an Analytical Approach*. 2nd edn. Englewood Cliffs, NJ: Prentice-Hall.

Heragu S. (1997) *Facilities Design*. Boston, MA: PWS Publishing.

Luggen W. (1991) *Flexible Manufacturing Cells and Systems*. Englewood, Cliffs, NJ: Prentice-Hall.

Wu B. (1994) *Manufacturing Systems Design and Analysis*. 2nd edn. London: Chapman and Hall.

Useful Websites

www.manufacturing.net/magazine/mmh – gives various plans

CHAPTER 12

Managing capacity

Had our great palace the capacity to camp this host, we all would sup together.

William Shakespeare, *Anthony and Cleopatra*

Contents

Aims of the chapter

After reading this chapter you should be able to:

- define capacity and discuss its measurement;
- appreciate the aims of capacity planning;
- use a general approach to capacity planning;
- see how capacity planning occurs at different levels;
- discuss some of the difficulties met in capacity planning;
- see how capacity changes over time;
- develop policies for maintenance and replacement of equipment;
- calculate the reliability of equipment.

Main themes

This chapter will emphasise:

- **capacity**, the maximum output that can be achieved in a given time;
- **capacity planning**, to match available capacity to product demand;
- **other levels of planning**, which follow from the capacity plans;
- **changing capacity**, why it varies over time.

Measuring capacity

Definitions

In Chapter 10 we described capacity as one of the basic measures of performance.

The **capacity** of a process sets the maximum amount of a product that can be made in a given time.

All operations have some limit on their capacity: a factory has a maximum number of units it can make a week; a university has a maximum intake of students; an aeroplane has a maximum number of seats; a hotel has a maximum number of rooms; and a lorry has a maximum weight it can carry. Sometimes the stated capacity has an explicit reference to time, such as a maximum number of customers that can be served in a day. Even when it is not mentioned explicitly, every measure of capacity refers to time. The number of seats on an aeroplane sets the capacity as a maximum number of passengers on a particular flight; the number of rooms in a hotel sets the maximum number of guests who can stay each day; the maximum weight of a lorry sets the most it can carry on a single journey. Capacity is a constraint on the rate of output, and should always refer to a relevant time period.

Sometimes the capacity of an operation seems obvious, such as the number of seats in a theatre, beds in a hospital or tables in a restaurant. At other times the capacity is not so clear. How, for example, can you find the capacity of a supermarket, university, music festival or bank? The usual answer has a surrogate measure, such as the number of customers per square metre of floor space in night clubs and ice rinks. Such measures are the result of discussion of relevant factors and agreement rather than any physical limit. The maximum size of classes in schools, for example, is limited by government policy rather than the physical limits of buildings.

OPERATIONS IN PRACTICE

Security at Queen Elizabeth Hospital

Queen Elizabeth Hospital has a security force of 26 people, who are responsible for security in four hospital buildings and the seven-hectare site. There are very few serious problems, but a few months ago three unrelated incidents raised concerns. When local newspapers published details of these incidents, people demanded more security. Hospital managers passed the demands on to the facility operations manager (FOC).

The FOC increased the number of patrols and put more security people in places where they were clearly visible. He also improved the camera surveillance system and experimented with better identity cards for staff and patients. There were no further incidents, but the security people were now working an average of 14 hours a week overtime. The FOC knew that they could not keep working at this level, so he put in a request for five more permanent staff, plus an additional six part-time staff to get over the current demand.

Hospital managers were trying to cut overheads, and were reluctant to divert money away from direct medical care. They thought the problem was temporary and would solve itself if they waited a little longer.

Designed and effective capacity

The capacity of a process is its maximum output. However, most operations do not work at their full capacity, as this tends to strain the resources and put stress on the people. Instead they work at a lower level that they can sustain over time. We can allow for these effects by defining several types of capacity.

If you imagine a process that is working in ideal conditions with no disruptions or problems of any kind, then the maximum output is the **designed capacity**. In reality, operations do not work in such ideal conditions, and a more realistic measure is the **effective capacity**. This is the maximum output that can be sustained under normal conditions, and allows for set-up times, breakdowns, stoppages, maintenance periods, and so on. The designed capacity of a ski lift might be 600 people an hour – but some seats are not filled; people arrive in groups; people have problems getting on and off; and there are various other disruptions – so the effective capacity might be nearer 400 people an hour. This gives three measures.

- **Designed capacity** is the maximum possible output in ideal conditions.
- **Effective capacity** is the maximum realistic output in normal conditions.
- Actual **output** is normally lower than effective capacity.

In Chapter 10 we saw how these were related to measures of performance. Utilisation, for example, measures the ratio of output to designed capacity, while efficiency measures the ratio of output to effective capacity.

WORKED EXAMPLE

A machine is designed to work for one eight-hour shift a day, five days a week. The machine can produce 100 units an hour, but 10 per cent of its time is taken by maintenance and set-ups. In one week the machine made 3,000 units. What measures can you use to describe its performance?

Solution

- The designed capacity of the machine is the maximum output it can achieve in ideal circumstances.

  Designed capacity = production per hour × number of hours available
  $= 100 \times 8 \times 5 = 4{,}000$ units a week

- The effective capacity is the maximum output that can be expected under normal conditions. This takes into account the time needed for maintenance and set-ups.

  Effective capacity = production per hour × number of hours that can be used
  $= 100 \times 8 \times 5 \times 0.9 = 3{,}600$ units a week

- The actual output was 3,000 units a week.
- Utilisation is the ratio of actual output to designed capacity.

  Utilisation $= 3{,}000/4{,}000 = 0.75$ or 75 per cent

- Efficiency is the ratio of actual output to effective capacity.

  Efficiency $= 3{,}000/3{,}600 = 0.833$ or 83.3 per cent

Bottlenecks

A common reason for actual output to fall below effective capacity is the problem of scheduling products that use different amounts of resources. One product might use all the available supply of one resource – perhaps all the time on a machine – and this forms a bottleneck. This single machine might be working at full capacity, but all the other resources have spare capacity. Operations that form the bottlenecks limit the capacity of the overall process. The kitchens in Jameson Restaurant, for example, can cook 300 meals in an evening, but the restaurant can only seat 150 customers, so seating is the bottleneck that limits capacity. Wendy Jones Associates can make 30 gold brooches a week, but can only afford to buy enough gold for 20, so the capacity is set by the supply of gold.

The only way of increasing overall capacity is to increase the capacity of the bottleneck. Jameson Restaurant can only increase capacity by adding more seats, but improving the kitchen will have no effect at all. This seems obvious, but you can see many examples of organisations that do not identify the actual bottlenecks. Companies recruit more managers to give leadership, when they are actually short of workers to do the jobs; services increase the size of customer waiting areas, when they should increase the serving areas; manufacturers recruit more salespeople, when production cannot meet existing demand; airlines use bigger aeroplanes, when passenger terminals are already over-crowded.

WORKED EXAMPLE

Trivistor Soft Drinks has a bottling hall with three distinct parts:

- two bottling machines each with a maximum throughput of 100 litres a minute and average maintenance of one hour a day;
- three labelling machines each with a maximum throughput of 3,000 bottles an hour and planned stoppages averaging 30 minutes a day;
- a packing area with a maximum throughput of 10,000 cases a day.

The hall works 12 hours a day filling litre bottles and putting them in cases of 12 bottles.

What can you say about the capacity of the hall? If the bottling hall works at its effective capacity, what is the utilisation of each part? If the line develops a fault that reduces output to 70,000 bottles, what is the efficiency of each part?

Solution

Figure 12.1 gives an outline of the bottling hall. We must work in consistent units, and 'litre bottles a day' seems the most convenient. Then the designed capacities of each stage are:

- bottling: Designed capacity = 100 litres/minute on 2 machines
  $= 2 \times 100 \times 12 \times 60$ bottles a day = 144,000 bottles a day
- labelling: Designed capacity = 3,000 bottles/hour on 3 machines
  $= 3{,}000 \times 3 \times 12$ bottles a day = 108,000 bottles a day
- packing: Designed capacity = 10,000 cases/day
  $= 10{,}000 \times 12$ bottles a day = 120,000 bottles a day

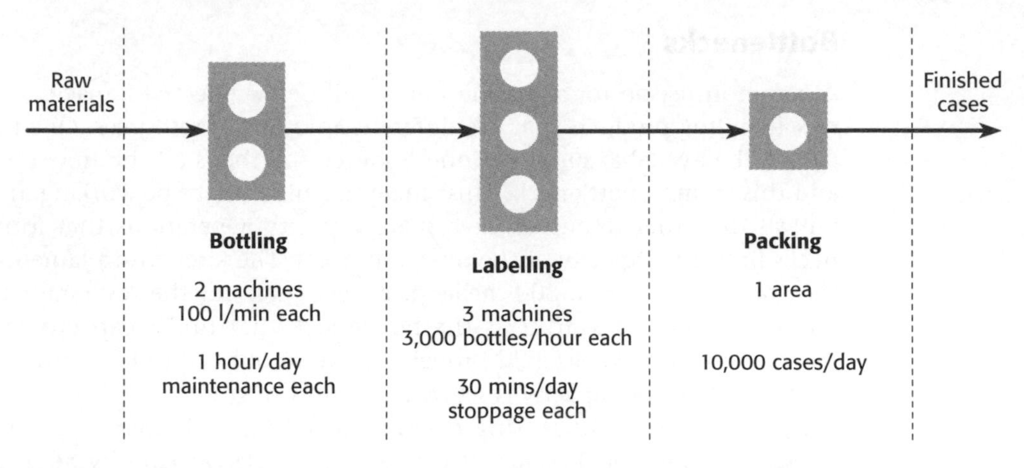

Figure 12.1 The bottling hall at Trivistor Soft Drinks

The designed capacity of the whole process is set by the smallest capacity of any operation, and this is clearly labelling. The maximum throughput of the bottling hall is 108,000 bottles a day, and this is its designed capacity.

The effective capacity of each stage takes into account planned stoppages, so this gives:

- bottling: 144,000 × 11/12 = 132,000 bottles a day
- labelling: 108,000 × 11.5/12 = 103,500 bottles a day
- packing: = 120,000 bottles a day

The limiting capacity is still the labelling operation, and effective capacity is 103,500 bottles a day.

If the output of the hall is 103,500 bottles a day, the utilisation of each part of the line is:

- bottling: 103,500/144,000 = 0.72 or 72 per cent
- labelling: 103,500/108,000 = 0.96 or 96 per cent
- packing: 103,500/120,000 = 0.86 or 86 per cent

With an actual output of 70,000 bottles the efficiency of each operation is:

- bottling: 70,000/132,000 = 0.53 or 53 per cent
- labelling: 70,000/103,500 = 0.68 or 68 per cent
- packing: 70,000/120,000 = 0.58 or 58 per cent

Review questions

12.1 Why is the capacity always related to a specific period of time?

12.2 What is the difference between designed capacity and effective capacity?

12.3 What units could you use to measure the capacity of:
(a) a train;
(b) a cinema;

(c) an oil well;
(d) a squash club;
(e) a social work department;
(f) an arable farm?

12.4 Which is largest: actual output, designed capacity or effective capacity?

OPERATIONS IN PRACTICE

Texas Instruments

The Consortium for Advanced Manufacturing – International (CAM-I)[1] has developed a model of manufacturing capacity. This divides the designed capacity into three parts:

Designed capacity = productive capacity + non-productive capacity + idle capacity

- *Designed, or rated, capacity* is the total amount of capacity that is available in any period.
- *Productive capacity* is the capacity that is used to actually make good products.
- *Non-productive capacity* does not make products, but includes set-ups, maintenance, time spent on scrapped units, waste and standby.
- *Idle capacity* is not used, because there is no demand, or there are other legal, contractual or management reasons why it cannot be used.

Texas Instruments is one of the companies represented at CAM-I. It uses their capacity model, and assigns colours to the different types of capacity: productive capacity is green; non-productive is red; and idle is yellow. Operations teams are responsible for reducing the red capacity and turning it into yellow, hence the company call to 'get the red out'. Management teams are responsible for turning the yellow capacity into sales, giving additional green capacity.

Project 12.1 *Look at a local supermarket, or any other service operations that you find interesting. How would you describe its capacity? What are the bottlenecks that set this capacity? What other measures of performance would be useful?*

Capacity planning

Approach to planning

Organisations have to plan their capacity carefully.

The aim of **capacity planning** is to make the useable capacity match the demand for products over the long, medium and short term.

Any mismatch between capacity and demand is expensive. If capacity is less than demand, the organisation cannot meet all the demand and it loses potential customers. If capacity is greater than demand, the organisation meets all the demand but it has spare capacity and under-used resources. You can see these effects in shops. When you go into some shops there are not enough people serving and you have to wait. The capacity of the shop is less than demand, and you probably go to a competitor where the queues are shorter. In other shops there are lots of people waiting to serve – there are no queues, but the cost of paying these under-used people is added to your bill.

There is a standard approach to capacity planning that we can illustrate by a simple example.

WORKED EXAMPLE

Anne Jenkins has a contract to supply 1,000 leather purses a week. The purses are made on a machine that has a designed capacity of 10 units an hour, but its expected efficiency is 80 per cent. Her company works a single eight-hour shift five days a week, but could move to double shifts or work at weekends. How many machines does she need?

Solution

Listing the things that are fixed:

- forecast demand, $F = 1{,}000$ units
- time to make a unit, $T = 0.1$ hours
- hours worked a shift, $H = 8$
- efficiency, $E = 0.8$.

Now defining the things we can vary as:

- N = number of machines
- S = number of shifts worked a day
- D = days worked a week.

Each week the total time available on N machines is $NHSD$. Lower efficiency adjusts this to an effective time of $HNSDE$. As it takes T to make each purse, we have:

$$\text{Effective capacity} = NHSDE/T \text{ units a week}$$

We want this to be at least equal to the forecast demand, F, so:

$$NHSDE/T \geq F$$

Putting in the fixed values that we know:

$$N \times 8 \times SD \times 0.8/0.1 \geq 1{,}000$$

Or: $N \geq 15.6/SD$

Now we can look at different ways of meeting the demand.

- Working a single shift on weekdays has $S = 1$ and $D = 5$ to give:

$$N \geq 15.6/5 \geq 3.1$$

As machines come in discrete quantities, this number must be rounded up to 4. The utilisation of these would be:

$$\text{Utilisation} = FT/NHSD = 100/(4 \times 8 \times 1 \times 5) = 0.63 \text{ or } 63 \text{ per cent}$$

This low utilisation comes from having to buy four machines when only 3.1 are really needed. Anne could increase utilisation by buying three machines and making short-term adjustments to make up the difference.

- If the company moved to a double shift, $S = 2$ and $D = 5$ to give:

  $$N \geq 15.6/10 \geq 1.6$$

  The company would need two machines, but again utilisation is only 63 per cent.

- If the company stayed with a single shift but worked at weekends, $S = 1$ and $D = 7$ to give:

  $$N \geq 15.6/7 \geq 2.2$$

  The company would need three machines and utilisation is:

  $$\text{Utilisation} = 100/168 = 0.60 \text{ or } 60 \text{ per cent}$$

Anne now needs to complete her capacity planning by comparing these alternatives and implementing the best. One major consideration is that the first alternative keeps a normal working week, while the others need people to work at weekends or on shifts, neither of which is popular.

This last example shows how we can set about capacity planning. Essentially, we see what resources we need, compare these with the resources we have available, and then develop plans for overcoming any differences. To be more specific, we:

1. examine forecast demand and translate this into a capacity requirement;
2. calculate the available capacity of present facilities;
3. identify mismatches between capacity needed and that available;
4. suggest alternative plans for overcoming any mismatch;
5. compare these plans and find the best;
6. implement the best.

This is a standard approach to all kinds of planning, which we will meet again in later chapters. It is sometimes called **resource requirement planning**.

Unfortunately, taking the steps in this straightforward sequence does not usually work. In most circumstances, there are a huge number of possible plans, and it is impossible to look at all of them in detail. It is also difficult to compare the alternatives, as there can be many competing objectives and non-quantifiable factors. A more realistic view replaces the single procedure with an iterative one. This designs a plan and sees how close it gets to achieving its objectives; if it performs badly, the plan is modified to find improvements. In effect, steps 4 and 5 are repeated until they give a reasonable solution.

This iterative procedure recognises that it is rarely possible to find the single 'best' plan, and we are really looking for one that is generally accepted. Plans that appeal to the marketing department may be very inefficient for operations; the best plans for operations may not suit personnel; the best plans for personnel may be too expensive for finance. We usually have to make a compromise between a variety of conflicting objectives and views. This compromise must consider many factors, including:

- *demand* – forecast sales, sales already made, back orders, variation in demand;
- *operations* – machine capacity and utilisation, aim of stable production, plans for new equipment, use of subcontractors, productivity targets;
- *materials* – availability of raw materials, inventory policies, current stock levels, constraints on storage;
- *finance* – costs, cash flows, financing arrangements, exchange rates, general economic climate;
- *human resources* – staff levels, skill levels, productivity targets, unemployment rates, hiring and training policies;
- *marketing* – reliability of forecasts, competition, plans for new products, product substitution.

Finding a reasonable balance between these factors is difficult, and the iterative planning procedure may be repeated many times before a plan is finally accepted.

Discrete capacity

The last worked example shows one of the problems with matching capacity and demand. While demand comes in small quantities and can take almost any value, capacity often comes in large discrete amounts. Typically, capacity can be increased by using another machine, opening another shop, employing another person, using another vehicle, building another factory, and so on.

Suppose that demand for a product rises steadily over time. Capacity should be increased at some point, but the increase will come as a discrete step. There is no way of exactly matching the discrete capacity to a continuous demand, so we have to use one of three basic strategies (as shown in Figure 12.2):

(a) capacity is more or less matched to demand, so that sometimes there is excess capacity and sometimes a shortage;
(b) capacity is made at least equal to demand at all times, which needs more investment in facilities and gives lower utilisation;
(c) capacity is only added when the additional facilities would be fully used, which needs lower investment and gives high utilisation, but restricts output.

Each of these strategies is best suited to different circumstances. Factors that encourage an early increase in capacity, as shown in Figure 12.2(b) are:

- uneven or variable demand;
- high profits, perhaps for a new product;
- high cost of unmet demand, possibly with lost future sales;
- continuously changing product mix;
- uncertainty in capacity;
- variable efficiency;
- capacity increases that are relatively small;
- low cost of spare capacity, which might be used for other work.

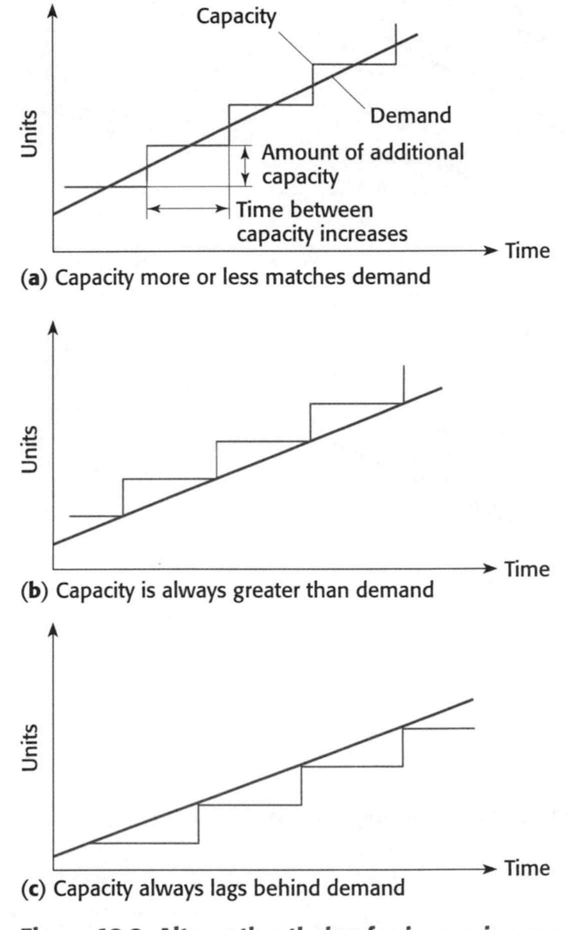

Figure 12.2 Alternative timing for increasing capacity

On the other hand, the main factor that encourages organisations to wait as long as possible before increasing capacity (as shown in Figure 12.2(c) is the capital cost. Under-used resources can be very expensive, and it may be difficult to argue that spare capacity will be needed for higher demand at some point in the future.

If you think of a large furniture shop, like MFI, its capacity to serve customers is largely set by the number of sales people. Because of the nature of the product and its demand, the shop is likely to increase capacity early and make sure there are always enough staff to serve customers. On the other hand, new motorways are expensive and controversial, so expansions are delayed for as long as possible, and the road is crowded immediately it opens.

Size of expansion

A related question about changes to capacity is how big the changes should be. If you want to hire four new people over the next few months, should you

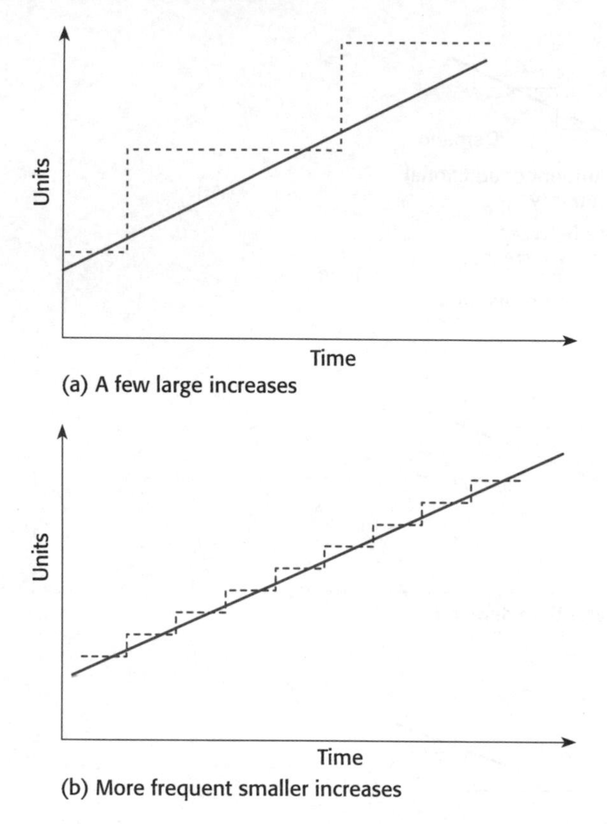

Figure 12.3 Alternative sizes for increasing capacity

recruit them all in one big campaign, or would it be better to add them in smaller steps? Any change in capacity is likely to disrupt operations, so it might be better to have a few large increases rather than more smaller ones (as shown in Figure 12.3).

The benefits of large increases include the following:

- capacity stays ahead of demand for longer;
- one is more likely to meet all demand;
- the expansion might give economies of scale;
- advantages might be gained over competitors;
- there are less frequent disruptions;
- one gets better value, so reducing the cost per unit of expansion.

On the other hand, there are disadvantages:

- capacity does not match demand so closely;
- disruptions may be more serious;
- there are high capital costs;
- utilisation will be low, at least for some time;
- there is high risk if demand changes.

WORKED EXAMPLE

One of Excelsior Boat's most profitable products is a set of sails for racing yachts. Excelsior is looking at its plans for these sails over the next three years. The demand this year is 100 units, and this is rising by 50 units a year. To meet this demand the company can expand capacity now, or at the beginning of next year. Each expansion includes a set of equipment whose capacity only comes in discrete steps of 50 units. Each unit of spare capacity has notional costs of £400 a year (mainly interest charges), while each unit of shortage has costs of £1,000 a year (for lost custom and goodwill). Which expansion plan has lowest costs over the three years? What other factors should Excelsior consider?

Solution

Excelsior has five alternatives.

- *Alternative 1.* Do not increase capacity, but keep making 100 units a year, to give:

Year	Demand	Sales	Spare capacity	Shortage
0	100	100	0	0
1	150	100	0	50
2	200	100	0	100
Total	**450**	**300**	**0**	**150**

This has total costs of 0 × 400 for spare capacity plus 150 × 1,000 for shortages, totalling £150,000 over the three years.

- *Alternatives 2 and 3.* Increase capacity by either 50 or 100 units now, giving:

		50 increase to 150			100 increase to 200		
Year	**Demand**	**Sales**	**Spare**	**Shortage**	**Sales**	**Spare**	**Shortage**
0	100	100	50	0	100	100	0
1	150	150	0	0	150	50	0
2	200	150	0	50	200	0	0
Totals	**450**	**400**	**50**	**50**	**450**	**150**	**0**

  – Increasing capacity by 50 now has total costs of 50 × 400 + 50 × 1,000 = £70,000
  – Increasing capacity by 100 now has costs of 150 × 400 + 0 × 1,000 = £60,000

- *Alternatives 4 and 5.* Increase capacity by 50 units or 100 units next year, giving:

		50 increase to 150			100 increase to 200		
Year	**Demand**	**Sales**	**Spare**	**Shortage**	**Sales**	**Spare**	**Shortage**
0	100	100	0	0	100	0	0
1	150	150	0	0	150	50	0
2	200	150	0	50	200	0	0
Totals	**450**	**400**	**0**	**50**	**450**	**50**	**0**

  – Increasing capacity by 50 next year has total costs of 0 × 400 + 50 × 1,000 = £50,000.
  – Increasing capacity by 100 next year has costs of 50 × 400 + 0 × 1,000 = £20,000.

The policy with the lowest costs is to increase capacity by 100 units next year.

Many other factors might be important in this decision, such as future plans, longer-term forecast demand, changes to the process or technology used, economies of scale, finance available, competitors' plans, other alternatives for expansion, etc. The most obvious factor not included in the calculation is the additional profit generated by the extra capacity. As the proposed plan meets all the demand and leaves Excelsior with spare capacity, this seems to be a reasonable solution.

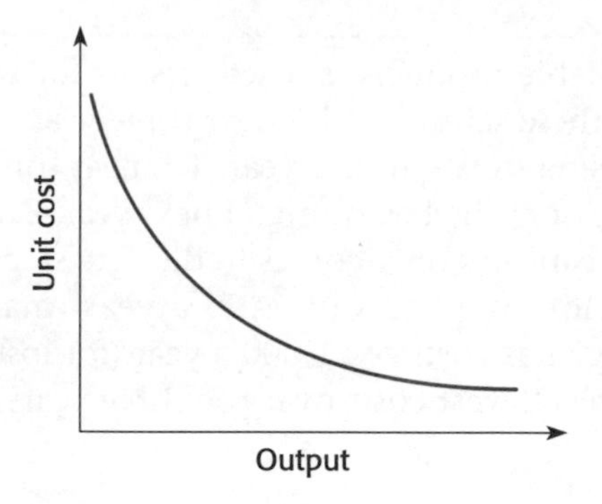

Figure 12.4 Economies of scale giving lower unit cost

Economies of scale

Large increases in capacity can give economies of scale. We mentioned these in Chapter 8, where we said that bigger operations give lower unit costs than smaller ones. This is why supermarkets charge less than corner shops, and colour supplements to newspapers are cheaper than limited edition prints.

There are three main reasons for getting economies of scale:

- fixed costs are spread over a larger number of units;
- more efficient processes can be used, with larger batches and more automation;
- more experience with the product raises efficiency.

You often hear that companies are merging to get economies of scale. In the pharmaceutical industry it typically costs US$1 billion to bring a new drug to market, but bigger companies can get economies of scale in their research laboratories. This is why SmithKline Beckman merged with the Beecham Group in 1989 to form SmithKline Beecham. Then Glaxo and Welcome merged in 1995 to form Glaxo Wellcome, and in 2000 these two companies merged to form Glaxo SmithKline, with annual sales of more than £16 billion.

The problem is that economies of scale are not inevitable, and it is possible for increasing size to give 'diseconomies of scale'. The communications, management and organisation structure needed to support large operations get too complex and become less efficient. Some people suggest, for example, that centralised government is inherently inefficient, as such huge organisations have to struggle with very complex interactions between large numbers of departments.

WORKED EXAMPLE

Karen Thorburn runs a tax advisory clinic. She offers help to self-employed people and small companies filing their annual tax returns. Karen employs a number of full-time and part-time staff, who are a mixture of accountants and 'accounting assistants'. Not surprisingly, the number of clients she can help in any period depends on the number of staff she employs. Figures for the past three years show:

Staff	1	2	3	4	5	6	7
Clients	25	60	110	150	180	205	220

Staff	Total clients	Additional clients per staff member	Average clients per staff member	Variable cost	Variable cost per client	Total cost	Total cost per client
1	25	25	25.00	25.00	1.00	75.00	3.00
2	60	35	30.00	50.00	0.83	100.00	1.67
3	110	50	36.67	75.00	0.68	125.00	1.14
4	150	40	37.50	100.00	0.67	150.00	1.00
5	180	30	36.00	125.00	0.69	175.00	0.97
6	205	25	34.17	150.00	0.73	200.00	0.98
7	220	15	31.43	175.00	0.80	225.00	1.02

Figure 12.5 Spreadsheet of calculations for Karen Thorburn

The fixed costs of Karen's operation are £50,000, and each staff member costs an average of £25,000. What do these figures show?

Solution

The spreadsheet in Figure 12.5 shows a table of costs with values in thousands of pounds.

The number of clients seen per staff member is rising for the first four, suggesting economies of scale. After this it declines, suggesting diseconomies. Four staff give the highest average output per person. They also give the lowest variable cost per client. The total cost per client, which we find by adding the variable and fixed costs and dividing by the number of clients, is lowest with five staff.

Of course, this only gives one view, and the staff and type of work may vary. The figures do, however, give a useful starting point for further analysis and discussion.

Review questions

12.5 What are the basic steps in capacity planning?

12.6 Why is capacity planning usually iterative?

12.7 Why do discrete increases in capacity cause problems?

12.8 Why would you use a few large increases in capacity rather than more smaller ones?

12.9 Give three reasons for declining unit cost with increasing output.

OPERATIONS IN PRACTICE

Telephone capacity and customer relations

Private Patient Plan (PPP) offers a range of private medical care. It used to rely on written information to attract new customers. PPP would place advertisements in newspapers and magazines, and the advertisements included an enquiry form which people could cut out and post back to PPP. When PPP received the form, it would post back details of its services.

▶

In the late 1980s PPP started a free 0800 telephone line. It had no previous experience with this type of operation and did not know how many enquiries to expect. PPP severely underestimated the popularity of the service, and was immediately swamped with enquiries. PPP's telephone operations had nowhere near enough capacity to deal with the demand, and the numbers were immediately increased. The success of this service was an important factor in a rapid doubling of PPP's business.

PPP is not alone in misjudging the capacity needed by its service. In 1998 Prudential set up 'Egg' for its direct banking operations. This gave a low-cost service based on telephone banking and the Internet. The initial £15 million advertising campaign led to 150,000 enquiries, which overwhelmed its call centre. Egg had to stop taking enquiries until it could catch up with demand. Within a year Egg had taken £6 billion in deposits and had 500,000 customers, and 1,500 employees in its national centre in Derby.

Many people have problems with Internet service providers (ISPs) that do not have enough capacity to deal with peak demands. In 1999 Screaming.com was the first to introduce a completely free service, including the telephone call. It immediately had 34,000 new subscribers, but many people reported that their automatic diallers would call over 100 times and still not get through. This, and problems of transferring customers' telephone service from BT to LocalTel, caused some concerns about the quality of the service.

Source: BBC Radio 4 (1999) *Today Programme*, January

Different levels of capacity plans

Capacity planning is largely a strategic function. Organisations can increase the overall capacity of a process by opening a factory, designing a new process, opening new offices, or moving to a new location. They can reduce excess capacity by closing offices, shutting down a plant, or transferring facilities to other products. These are strategic decisions with long-term consequences. They lay the foundations for the next levels of planning, which include a range of tactical and operational plans (as shown in Figure 12.6).

An organisation might change its capacity by leasing extra space, working overtime, employing temporary staff, or subcontracting parts of the work. These are clearly tactical and operational decisions. So capacity planning has to include decisions at all levels, with strategic plans giving the overall picture, which is modified by shorter-term adjustments.

The aim of **capacity planning** is to match available capacity to forecast demand over the long, medium and short terms.

Short-term adjustments to capacity

We have concentrated on changing capacity to meet demand, but there are really two types of short-term adjustments:

- adjusting demand to match available capacity;
- adjusting capacity to match demand.

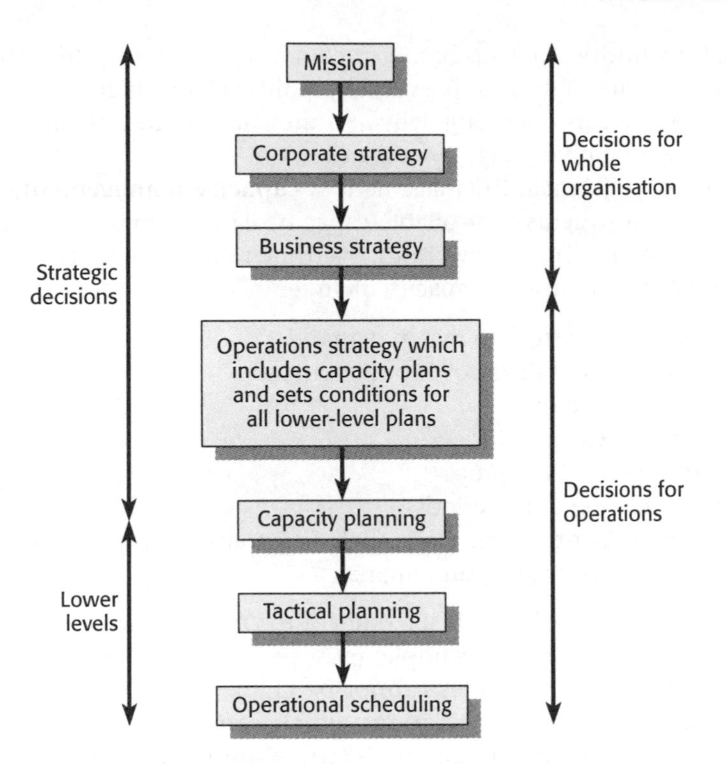

Figure 12.6 Hierarchy of planning within an organisation

Imagine a wholesaler that runs a 12,000 square metre warehouse. This sets the normal capacity. If there is a temporary increase in business because of orders from a nearby construction site, the wholesaler can rent extra space for the duration of the construction project. This gives a short-term adjustment of capacity to meet higher demand. Alternatively, there may be some reason why the wholesaler does not want to increase capacity, so it can increase prices and reduce demand to match the existing capacity.

The obvious way of adjusting demand is to change the price – but there are limits, and prices must be high enough to cover costs, low enough to be competitive, and not change too many times to confuse customers. Reasonable ways of adjusting demand include:

- *limiting the customers served*, by demanding specific 'qualifications';
- *varying the price;*
- *changing the marketing effort;*
- *offering incentives*, such as free samples of products with spare capacity, or discounts, such as off-peak telephone calls or travel;
- *changing related products*, to encourage substitution of, say, holiday destinations;
- *varying the lead time;*
- *using a reservation or appointment system;*
- *using stocks to cushion demand.*

One result of this **demand management** is that business can be actively discouraged at times of high demand. You may think this is strange, but it is really quite common.

Professional institutions put up barriers against new entrants; popular restaurants routinely have queues outside at busy times; airlines charge high rates for 'executive' facilities; expensive cars offer long delivery times; artists produce limited editions of prints; perfumes sell at very high prices; and so on.

The alternative to demand management is **capacity management**, which looks for short-term adjustments to available capacity. The obvious way of doing this is to change the working time, by working overtime to increase capacity or undertime to reduce it. Ways of adjusting capacity include:

- changing the work pattern to match demand;
- employing part-time staff to cover peak demands;
- using outside contractors;
- renting or leasing extra facilities;
- adjusting the speed of the process;
- rescheduling maintenance periods;
- making the customer do some work, such as automatic cash dispensing machines, or packing their own bags in supermarkets.

These adjustments cannot be made too often or too severely, as they affect employees, operations and customers. For example, most people have their own arrangements to make, so their work schedules cannot be changed every few days. There are, however, some very flexible operations which can adjust very quickly, such as 'queuebusters' in Safeway supermarkets: these are people who always work on operations that are currently busiest. If they are stacking shelves and see that customers are waiting at checkouts, they immediately change jobs to work on the cash register.

Review questions

12.10 Capacity planning is largely a strategic function that sets the scene for lower-level planning decisions. Do you think this is true?

12.11 What are the two alternatives for dealing with short-term mismatches in demand and capacity?

OPERATIONS IN PRACTICE

Capacity of Heathrow Airport

BAA runs seven airports in the UK, including the three London airports at Heathrow, Gatwick and Stansted. In the year to April 2000, BAA handled 118 million passengers, an increase of 4.7 per cent over the previous year. Passenger demand is particularly strong in the south-east of England, where the number of passengers is forecast to double over the next 15 years. To meet this rising demand, BAA has a continuing programme of airport expansion.

London Heathrow is the world's biggest international airport, and in the year to 2000 handled over 62 million passengers. This rise of 2 per cent a year is modest compared with other airports around London. Stansted handled 10 million passengers, a rise of 33 per cent, Gatwick grew at 3 per cent to 30 million passengers, Luton airport is doubling its capacity to 10 million passengers a year, and the smaller London City Airport is growing by 9 per cent a year to 2 million passengers.

The reason for Heathrow's relatively slow growth is that the runways and – more obviously – the four terminals are already working at full capacity. A fifth terminal, due to increase passenger capacity to 85 million a year, has been delayed by a public inquiry lasting four years – the longest-ever hearing for a development project in the UK. The government makes its next decision in 2001, making 2006 the earliest possible opening date. There are continuing improvements to facilities to give smaller increases in capacity, including an express rail link to Paddington, a second express rail link to St Pancras, improved access roads, extension to the London Underground Piccadilly Line, and £1 million a day spent on upgrading the existing four terminals. Discussions are also starting to reduce the gap between aeroplanes, and so allow more take-offs and landings.

Realistically, the congestion at Heathrow is likely to continue for the foreseeable future. This has forced growth at other airports. British Airways switched its African services to Gatwick in 1996, and its South American services in 1997. By 1998, Gatwick was serving 276 destinations – more than any other European gateway, including Heathrow. It spent £500 million to increase its capacity from 27 million to 30 million passengers, and is currently expanding to a capacity of 40 million. Stansted is expanding from 8 million to 15 million passengers a year. Luton has spent £170 million on new facilities to become London's fourth airport.

Sources: Ellson C. (1998) 'London's Airports Set for Expansion', *The Times*, 30 April; Skapinker M. (1999) 'BAA Plans to Expand Capacity at Gatwick', *Financial Times*, 31 May

Changing capacity over time

So far we have assumed that capacity is constant over time. In practice, the effective capacity of a process can change quite markedly. Even if there are no changes to the process, there are short-term variations due to staff illness, interruptions, breakdowns, weather, enthusiasm of employees, and so on. We have already mentioned the example of people shovelling sand. At the end of an eight-hour shift they will be tired and their effective capacity will be far lower than at the beginning of the shift, even though there has been no change in their situation. We can illustrate some of the more systematic changes by learning curves and the effects of maintenance.

Learning curves

The more often you repeat something, the easier it becomes. This is why musicians and sportsmen spend a long time practising, so they become more skilful and find it easier to perform at a given level. This effect appears in almost all operations, and it means that the time needed to complete a specific job declines as the number of repetitions increases. Figure 12.7 shows this effect in a graph, which is called a **learning curve**.

A common shape for learning curves has the time taken to do an operation falling by a fixed proportion – typically about 10 per cent – every time the number of repetitions is doubled. If someone takes 10 minutes to do a job for the first time,

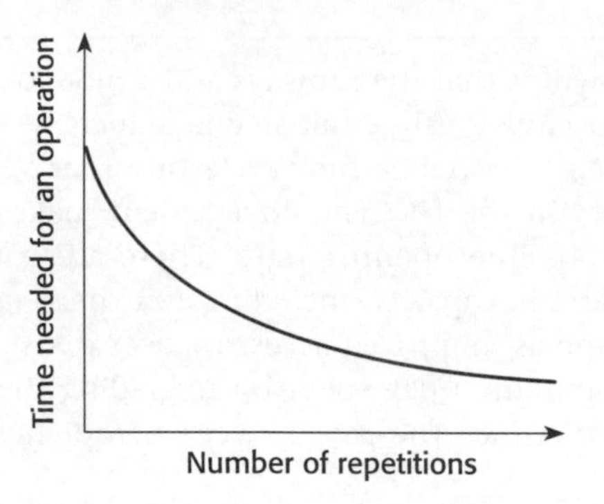

Figure 12.7 A typical learning curve

the second time takes only 90 per cent of this or nine minutes; the fourth time takes 90 per cent of the time for the second repetition or 8.1 minutes; the eighth time takes 90 per cent of the time for the fourth repetition or 7.29 minutes; the sixteenth time takes 90 per cent of the time for the eighth repetition or 6.561 minutes, and so on. A more detailed analysis of this is given in the Supplement at the end of this chapter.

The learning curve increases the effective capacity of a process and the level of skill. If you organise a party with a few dozen people, it is surprisingly difficult to get a venue, food, music, drinks and everything else, but the Glastonbury Festival organises a giant party for hundreds of thousands of people, and everything works (relatively) smoothly. The difference is that the Festival has decades of experience and has moved a good way down the learning curve.

Maintenance of equipment

As equipment gets older, it breaks down more often, develops more faults, gives lower quality, slows down and generally wears out. This reduces the effective capacity. Sometimes the changes are slow – like the fuel consumption of a car, which rises steadily with age. Sometimes the change is very fast, like a bolt, which suddenly breaks.

In the past, the performance of equipment was often described by a 'bath-tub curve'. Figure 12.8 shows a typical example, where the probability that equipment fails is plotted against its age. There are three main areas in this graph.

- During an initial running-in period all the faults in the equipment are found, people learn how to use it, and there are general teething problems.
- As the teething problems decline, the equipment has a period of relative stability, which lasts through its normal working life.
- At some point, the equipment begins to wear out, and problems become more frequent as it reaches the end of its planned life.

This view of performance is now less acceptable. Quality management suggests that few organisations would be happy with new equipment that did not work perfectly. Even complicated equipment is expected to work perfectly as soon as it is delivered, and Swissair would certainly not be impressed if it received a new Boeing 757 and then had to sort out the teething troubles.

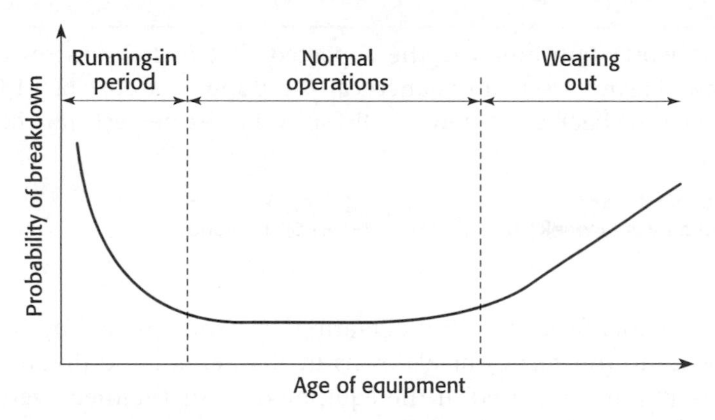

Figure 12.8 Bath-tub curve showing performance during equipment life

At the other end of equipment life is the assumption that performance must start to deteriorate. There are many products that need not deteriorate in this way, ranging from mobile telephones to tea services. Even if performance does decline, we can reduce the effects by doing **preventive maintenance** and having rational **replacement policies**.

With preventive maintenance, equipment is inspected and vulnerable parts are replaced at regular intervals or after a certain period of use. This happens when cars have a regular 5,000 km service. By replacing bits that are worn – or are most likely to wear – the equipment is restored to give continuing, satisfactory performance. But how often should we do this maintenance? If it is done too often, the equipment will run efficiently but the maintenance costs will be too high; if it is not done often enough, the maintenance cost will be low but the equipment will still break down. To find the best compromise, we add together the costs of maintenance and expected failure. If this total cost is plotted against the frequency of maintenance, we get a U-shaped curve that has a minimum. This minimum cost shows the best time between maintenance periods (as shown in Figure 12.9).

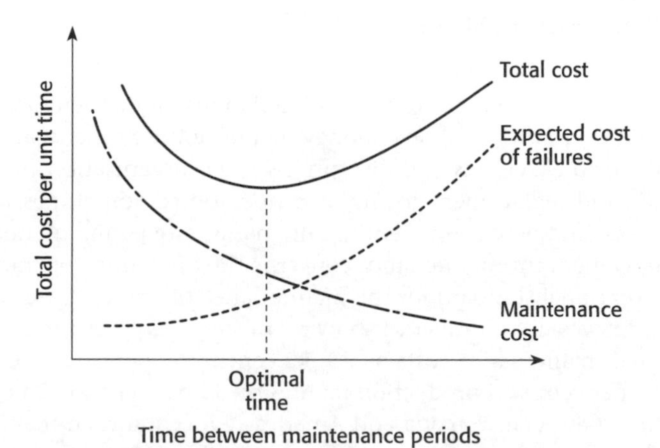

Figure 12.9 Finding the best timing of maintenance periods

WORKED EXAMPLE

If a machine works continuously the expected cost of failure rises each week as shown below. Preventive maintenance can be done at a cost of £1,000 and this brings the machine back up to new condition. What is the best time between maintenance periods?

Weeks since maintenance	0	1	2	3	4	5
Cost of breakdowns in week	0	50	150	200	1,600	3,000

Solution

We can find the total weekly cost of operating over some period by adding the cost of maintenance to the cost of breakdowns in the period, and dividing this by the number of weeks in the period. If the equipment is maintained every week, there is no cost for expected breakdowns; if maintenance is done every two weeks, the expected cost of breakdowns is £0 in the first week plus £50 in the second week; if maintenance is done every three weeks, the expected cost of breakdowns is £0 in the first week, plus £50 in the second week, plus £150 in the third week, and so on. Then adding the routine maintenance cost of £1,000 and dividing the costs by the number of weeks gives the following results:

Weeks between maintenance	Maintenance cost	Cost of breakdowns in week	Cumulative cost of breakdowns	Total cost	Average cost per week
1	1,000	0	0	1,000	1,000
2	1,000	50	50	1,050	525
3	1,000	150	200	1,200	400
4	1,000	200	400	1,400	350
5	1,000	1,600	2,000	3,000	600
6	1,000	3,000	5,000	6,000	1,000

The cheapest alternative is clearly to do maintenance every four weeks. As usual, there may be other factors to consider in the final decision.

OPERATIONS IN PRACTICE

Maintenance of cranes

Maintenance of equipment can have a major effect on its reliability and, therefore, on the cost of operations. An organisation that tries to save money by not doing proper maintenance can find itself with high bills for breakdowns and disruptions. Each organisation has to find the best level of maintenance and replacement for its own operations. Sometimes there are agreed maintenance procedures – and new equipment usually has approved maintenance procedures. One international agreement for maintenance concerns the operations of cranes.

ISO TC 96/SC 5[2] is the international standard for the maintenance of cranes. Case studies at paper mills in Canada, Finland, Sweden and America show that using the procedures described in this standard reduced annual maintenance costs by 33 per cent to 64 per cent, the number of defects by 46 per cent to 60 per cent and production failures by 33 per cent to 97 per cent.

Similar studies in steel mills in Sweden, Canada and America reduced annual maintenance costs by 28 per cent to 56 per cent, the number of defects declined by 50 per cent to 83 per cent and the number of production failures by 63 per cent to 95 per cent.

The improved performance given by the maintenance programmes include benefits to:

- *operators* who have safer working conditions;
- *owners* who save money with fewer repairs, production failures, injuries, insurance, etc.;
- *manufacturers* who get higher quality.

Once introduced, these standards for maintenance can be used for ISO 9000 certification.

Replacement of equipment

Routine maintenance keeps equipment working efficiently, but there comes a point when maintenance and repairs become too expensive and it is cheaper to buy a replacement. These replacement decisions can be expensive. There are, for example, many nuclear power stations being phased out and replaced. Nobody is really sure of the costs involved because there are still no satisfactory means of dealing with nuclear waste. Other examples of expensive replacement decisions include office blocks, hotels, steel mills, ships and aeroplanes.

Figure 12.10 shows two approaches to the timing of replacements. In the first, equipment is replaced when its performance falls so low that it is no longer acceptable – the output may be too low, quality too poor, breakdowns too frequent, and so on. The drawback with this approach is that its response is too late; it comes when the equipment is already unsatisfactory. The second approach shows a better alternative, which analyses performance and keeps the equipment working for the

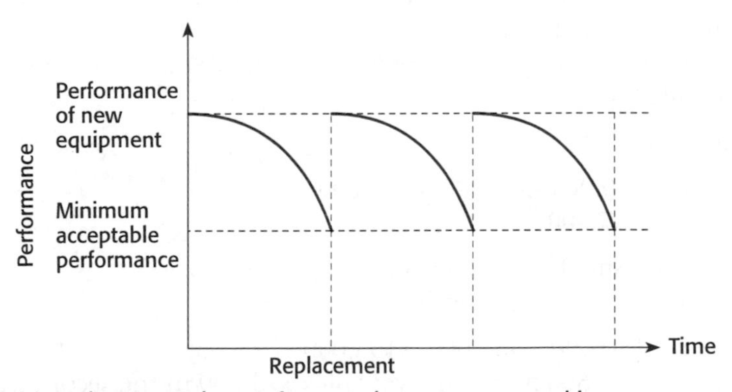

(a) Replacement when performance becomes unacceptable

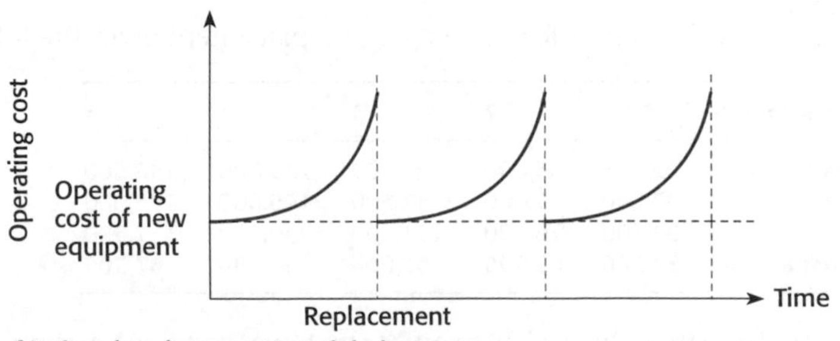

(b) Timed replacement to minimise costs

Figure 12.10 Two approaches to replacement

time that minimises total costs. This leads to a policy of replacing delivery vans every five years, say, or replacing computer systems every three years.

One drawback with this planned replacement is that all equipment is routinely replaced when it appears to be working well. This is why you often hear people asking: Why are they throwing away perfectly good light bulbs (computers, telephone, cars, tyres, refrigerators, desks, etc.)? It is often difficult to persuade people that this really is better than waiting until the equipment is obviously not working.

A useful way of finding the best age of replacement is to add the cost of operating equipment over a number of years and dividing this by the age to give an average annual cost.

WORKED EXAMPLE

Every year Alex Ho reviews the performance of his company's production machines so that replacements can be delivered before the end of the financial year. The cost of replacing each machine is $150,000. Expected resale values at the end of each year, average annual operating costs and maintenance costs are given in the following table. What is the best age to replace the machines?

Age of machine	1	2	3	4	5
Resale value	75,000	45,000	22,500	15,000	7,500
Running cost in previous year	7,500	13,500	22,500	61,500	90,000

Solution

When Alex sells a machine, the total cost of using it during its lifetime is in two parts:

- a capital cost equal to the difference between the price of a new machine and the resale value of the old one;
- a running cost that is the cumulative cost of maintenance and operation over the machine's life.

If a machine is sold after one year:

- capital cost is 150,000 – 75,000 = $75,000
- running cost is $7,500

The total cost of using the machine for one year is $82,500.

If the machine is sold after two years:

- capital cost is 150,000 – 45,000 = $105,000
- running cost is $7,500 in the first year plus $13,500 in the second year.

The total cost of using the machine for two years is $126,000, which is an average of $63,000 a year.

Repeating these calculations for other ages of replacement gives the following values:

Age of replacement	**1**	**2**	**3**	**4**	**5**
Capital cost	75,000	105,000	127,500	135,000	142,500
Running cost	7,500	21,000	43,500	105,000	195,000
Total cost	82,500	126,000	171,000	240,000	337,500
Average cost a year	**82,500**	**63,000**	**57,000**	**60,000**	**67,500**

Replacement after three years clearly gives the lowest average annual cost.

OPERATIONS IN PRACTICE

Trident submarines

For many years the UK had a fleet of nuclear submarines which carried Polaris missiles. By the 1980s these were getting old and the government decided to replace them with larger submarines that carried Trident missiles. These were introduced throughout the 1990s.

An important question was how many of the new submarines should be bought. Each new submarine had considerably more power than the older ones, so the navy would need fewer of them. At the same time, the ending of the 'cold war' reduced the perceived need for massive defence expenditure and most countries were significantly reducing their arms budgets.

The solution adopted by the government was to have a base of four Trident submarines. But at any time only one of these would be on active duty; a second would be getting ready to go on active duty; a third would be in dock for a refit (equivalent to a minor service); the fourth would be in dock for an overhaul (equivalent to a major service).

Reliability of equipment

Preventive maintenance and planned replacement affect the reliability of equipment, and its effective capacity. But most of the reliability is set by the initial design. If equipment is poorly designed no amount of maintenance will make it work better; if it is designed with reliability in mind, it can have a long and trouble-free life.

We can define the **reliability** of something as the probability that it continues to work throughout an entire period. A stage light with a reliability of 90 per cent has a probability of 0.9 of continuing to work normally during a performance; a tennis racquet with a reliability of 95 per cent has a probability of 0.95 of continuing to work all through a tournament.

We can use this reliability to analyse overall performance. To simplify things, we will talk about 'equipment' made up of 'components', but remember that this is just for convenience and we can use the same analyses for many types of problem. The overall reliability of equipment depends on both the reliability of each component and the way they are arranged.

If a single component has a known reliability, putting two identical components in parallel will increase the overall reliability. The assumption is that the second component will only start to work when the first one fails, and that the equipment can work with only one of the components operating. This is the basis of **redundancy** where back-up systems are kept to start working whenever there is a breakdown in the main system. If each component has a reliability of 0.9, putting three components in parallel will increase overall reliability to 0.999.

On the other hand, if components are added in series, the reliability of equipment is reduced. This is because equipment with components in series only works if all separate components are working. If each component has a reliability of 0.9, putting three components in series reduces overall reliability to 0.729.

The lesson is that back-up equipment increases reliability, but equipment in series reduces reliability (as shown in Figure 12.11). You can find the more detailed calculations for this in the Supplement at the end of this chapter.

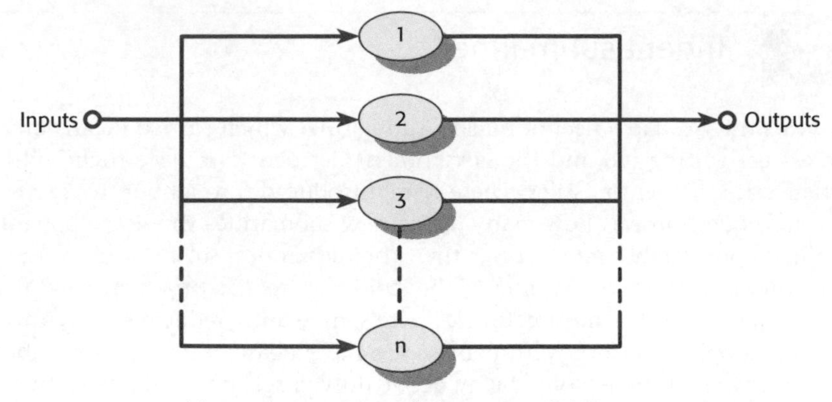

(**a**) Components in parallel increase reliability

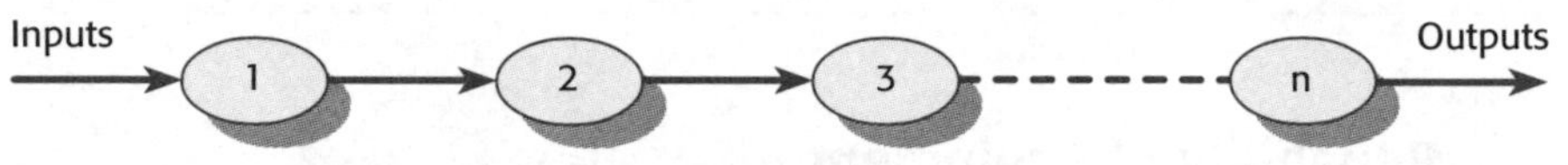

(**b**) Components in series reduce reliability

Figure 12.11 Arrangement of components affects the overall reliability

Review questions

12.12 What is meant by an 80 per cent learning curve?

12.13 Why does the time taken to do an operation decline over time?

12.14 What is the purpose of preventive maintenance?

12.15 Do you think it likely that maintenance costs for a machine will decline over time?

12.16 When do you think a machine should be replaced?

12.17 What is meant by 'reliability'?

Chapter review

- Every process has a capacity, which is the maximum output in a specified time. This is sometimes obvious, but it usually needs calculating or agreement.
- Designed capacity is the maximum output of a facility in ideal conditions. Effective capacity is the sustainable output under normal circumstances.
- The aim of capacity planning is to match available capacity to forecast demand. There is a standard approach to this, sometimes called capacity resource planning.
- Practical difficulties mean that capacity planning is usually iterative, looking for a generally 'acceptable' solution rather than an optimal one. These solutions have to balance many competing factors.
- Capacity planning is essentially a strategic function, but it includes both tactical and operational elements. Shorter-term mismatches between capacity and demand can be overcome by either demand management or capacity management.

- Specific complications with capacity planning are the discrete nature of capacity, timing of changes and economies of scale. Capacity also changes over time because of effects like learning curves, preventive maintenance and replacement policies.
- The reliability – and effective capacity – of equipment is primarily set by its design.

Key terms

capacity *p. 313*
capacity management *p. 328*
capacity planning *p. 317*
demand management *p. 327*
designed capacity *p. 314*
economies of scale *p. 324*
effective capacity *p. 314*
learning curve *p. 329*
maintenance *p. 330*
preventive maintenance *p. 331*
reliability *p. 335*
replacement policies *p. 333*

CASE STUDY Ravenstone Hotel

The Ravenstone Hotel was built 10 years ago on the seafront at Scarborough. It has 105 rooms and attracts people staying both for business and on holiday. During the peak months of June and July it is fully booked and has to turn away potential guests. During quieter months there are empty rooms and the hotel tries to encourage business.

The hotel has a wide range of rates, depending on the season, the days, length of stay, number of people sharing a room, whether they use group bookings, conference rates, senior citizens' discounts, weekend specials, and so on. The average number of people in a room is 1.5, and the total income from room bookings in 1999 was £1,290,000. About 60 per cent of this was spent in direct operating costs.

The other main source of income for the hotel is its restaurant. This is open for breakfast, morning coffee, lunch, afternoon tea and dinner. These meals are designed as a service to guests and just cover costs, with the exception of the evening dinner, which is very popular and runs at a profit. A small survey suggested that about half the people who stay in the hotel plan to eat dinner in the restaurant. It is often difficult to get a table at a convenient time and guests change their plans, so only about 40 per cent of guests actually eat dinner there. Throughout the year 30 per cent of people eating in the restaurant are guests, and the remaining 70 per cent are visitors. There is a limit to the number of people who can eat dinner in an evening, and this is currently about 160, depending on the composition of parties.

Again, it is difficult to suggest a typical meal cost, but in 2000 the total income from the restaurant was £800,000 from food and £530,000 from the bar service.

Roughly 40 per cent of the average bill for food is spent directly on buying and preparing the food, 25 per cent of the average bar bill is spent on buying and preparing drinks, and about 10 per cent of both bills are needed to cover miscellaneous operating costs.

The management of the hotel is now considering expansion, and has collected the following figures:

Year	1995	1996	1997	1998	1999	2000
Number of guest nights	10,200	13,100	18,800	24,900	28,800	33,300

Month	Average rooms booked per night		
	1998	1999	2000
January	31	36	42
February	12	17	25
March	23	29	36
April	41	48	61
May	76	85	92
June	105	105	105
July	98	104	105
August	52	78	103
September	43	59	70
October	12	17	24
November	10	14	23
December	39	39	40

Some figures were also collected for a small sample of days to see how many enquiries they had to turn away. There is no way of saying if these figures are typical.

	Number turned away per day	
Month	Hotel	Restaurant
January	1	6
May	3	12
July	30	36
August	24	41
November	2	8

Three alternative expansions are possible, each of which is largely independent of the others.

- When the hotel was built, the top floor was never completed. This can now be finished, making 30 more rooms, with a capital cost of £375,000, and additional fixed costs of £65,000. Operating costs would rise by about £55,000 a year.
- An additional wing can be added to the hotel, adding 60 more rooms, with a capital cost of £850,000, and additional fixed costs of £150,000. Operating costs would rise by about £100,000 a year.

- The restaurant can be extended. This can either be a major extension to add 160 diners a night, or a smaller extension to add 80 diners a night. The larger expansion has total capital costs of £600,000 and additional operating costs of £250,000 a year. The smaller expansion has total capital costs of £450,000 and additional operating costs of £150,000 a year.

Questions

- What are the capacities of the hotel and dining room? How fully are these being used?
- What suggestions would you make for matching capacity and demand more closely?
- Do you think the hotel should expand? Which expansion plan seems best?

Problems

12.1 A ski lift at Mount Rainier has pairs of chairs pulled on a continuous wire from the bottom of a ski run to the top. Ordinarily, one pair of chairs arrives at the bottom of the slope every five seconds. If the lift works 10 hours a day for 100 days a year, what is its designed capacity? On a typical day 10 per cent of users need help getting on the lift, and they cause average delays of 10 seconds. A further 25 per cent of people using the lift are alone, and only one chair of the pair is used. How can you describe the performance of the lift?

12.2 Harald Eng asa. analyses blood samples collected from patients. It tries to deal with 100 samples a day. Each person in Harald Eng can analyse three samples an hour, but has to do associated paperwork which takes an average of 40 minutes a sample. Employees also lose about 20 per cent of their time doing other things. The standard working day in Harald Eng is from 09.00 to 16.00 five days a week, with an hour off for lunch. How many employees do you think Harald Eng should have, and what is their utilisation? In one week Harald Eng only dealt with 90 samples. What were the resulting efficiency and utilisation?

12.3 The fixed cost of a process is £110,000, and the capacity can be increased by using more machines at a cost of £55,000 each. The total output of the operation, measured in some consistent units, is:

Machines	1	2	3	4	5	6	7	8
Output	55	125	230	310	375	435	460	470

How would you get the lowest unit cost?

12.4 Conrad Black estimates that his periodic plant maintenance costs £50,000. If he does not close the plant and do this maintenance, his breakdown costs rise as shown below. How often should he maintain the plant?

Time since last maintenance (years)	0	1	2	3	4	5
Annual cost of breakdowns ($000)	0	10	40	80	150	240

12.5 New cars cost a company £12,000 each, with resale values and maintenance costs shown below. What is the best age to replace the cars?

Age of car (years)	1	2	3	4	5	6
Resale value	8,000	5,000	3,000	2,000	1,200	600
Annual maintenance	1,000	1,200	1,500	2,000	3,000	8,750

Discussion questions

12.1 Do you think that capacity is really a measure of performance, or is it a fixed constraint?

12.2 Why do you think organisations are so keen to have quantitative measures of performance? How reliable are these? Does this reduce the emphasis that is put on qualitative factors in performance?

12.3 You often see notices at the entrance to pubs, clubs, halls and other buildings saying: 'The capacity of this facility is 200 people'. What does this really mean? What sets the capacity?

12.4 Is it always possible to find the capacity of a process? How, for example, could you find the capacity of a holiday beach, a national park or a shipping lane? Can you give examples where it is difficult to find a capacity, and say how these difficulties are overcome?

12.5 Capacity plans depend on forecasts which contain errors. The output of a process varies over time. Such factors make capacity planning very difficult. Say, giving examples, whether you think this is true. Why do organisations not simply get enough capacity to cover all possible demand?

12.6 Nobody would seriously consider limiting demand for a product, when capacity could be increased to make it. To what extent do you think that this is true?

12.7 How can routine maintenance and replacement programmes help to increase the effective capacity of an organisation? Do these methods work equally well in services and manufacturing?

12.8 Many of the calculations for maintenance and replacement decisions can be done using spreadsheets. Design a spreadsheet to help with such decisions.

12.9 The Clear Path Club is a group of walkers which meets regularly to clear public footpaths through the countryside. These paths often get overgrown or blocked, and the Clear Path Club volunteers to keep long sections of footpaths open. How do you think the Club could measure its capacity and performance?

References

1. Stratton A. (1996) 'Capacity Management', *Canadian Management Accountants Magazine*, February.
2. Website of the International Standards Organisation: *www.iso.org*

Selected reading

Comel J.G. and Edson N.W. (1995) *Gaining Control: Capacity Management and Scheduling*. New York: John Wiley.

Condra L.W. (1993) *Reliability Improvement with Design of Experiments*. New York: Marcel Dekker.

Klammer T.P. and Klammer T. (1996) *Capacity Management and Improvement*. Homewood, IL: Irwin.

Menasse D. (1993) *Capacity Planning: a Practical Approach*. Englewood Cliffs, NJ: Prentice-Hall.

Vollman T.E., Berry W.L. and Whybark D.C. (1996) *Manufacturing Planning and Control Systems*. 4th edn. Homewood, IL: Irwin.

Useful Websites

www.apqc.org – American Productivity and Quality Centre
www.sre.org – Society for Reliability
www.smrp.org – Society for Maintenance and Reliability Professionals

Learning and reliability

Contents

Learning curve

A learning curve describes the effect where repeating a task reduces the time it takes. As we saw in Chapter 12, a common pattern has the time needed reducing by a fixed proportion – typically around 10 per cent – for every doubling in the number of repetitions. If a task takes 10 minutes the first time it is done, the second repetition takes 90 per cent of this or nine minutes; the fourth repetition takes 90 per cent of this second repetition or 8.1 minutes; the eighth repetition takes 90 per cent of the fourth repetition or 7.29 minutes; the sixteenth repetition takes 90 per cent of the eighth repetition or 6.561 minutes, and so on.

The following table shows how the time needed for various repetitions declines with 90 per cent, 80 per cent and 70 per cent learning curves.

Repetition	90% learning curve	80% learning curve	70% learning curve
1	1	1	1
2	0.9	0.8	0.7
4	0.81	0.64	0.49
8	0.729	0.512	0.343
16	0.656	0.410	0.240
32	0.590	0.328	0.168
64	0.531	0.262	0.118
168	0.478	0.210	0.082
256	0.430	0.168	0.058

We do not have to use such tables, as it is fairly easy to find the equation for a learning curve.

For a **learning rate** of ***R***, the equation of a learning curve is:

$$Y = TN^b$$

Where: Y = time taken for the Nth repetition

N = number of repetitions

T = time taken for the first repetition

$b = \log R/\log 2$

R = learning rate

You can see that the value of b is fixed for any particular learning rate.

- For a 90 per cent learning curve, $R = 0.9$

  So: $b = \log 0.9/\log 2 = -0.046/0.301 = -0.152$

- For an 80 per cent learning curve, $R = 0.8$

  So: $b = \log 0.8/\log 2 = -0.097/0.301 = -0.322$

- For a 70 per cent learning curve, $R = 0.7$

  So: $b = \log 0.7/\log 2 = -0.155/0.301 = -0.515$

WORKED EXAMPLE

It takes one hour to produce the first unit of a product. How long will it take to make each of the first eight units with a learning rate of 0.8?

Solution

For an 80 per cent learning curve $b = -0.322$, and we know that T is 60 in minutes, so:

$$Y = TN^b = 60\ N^{-0.322}$$

Substituting:

- $N = 1$ gives $Y = 60 \times 1^{-0.322} = 60.0$
- $N = 2$ gives $Y = 60 \times 2^{-0.322} = 48.0$
- $N = 3$ gives $Y = 60 \times 3^{-0.322} = 42.1$

and so on, giving the following results:

Unit number	1	2	3	4	5	6	7	8
Time to make unit	60	48.0	42.1	38.4	35.7	33.7	32.1	30.7

Adding these eight times gives the total time to make the first eight units, which is 320.7 minutes. The average time for each of the eight units is 320.7/8 = 40.1 minutes.

Reliability

The overall reliability of equipment depends on both the reliability of each component and the way they are arranged. If a single component has a reliability of R, putting two identical components in parallel will increase the overall reliability (assuming that the second component will only start to work when the first one fails, and that the equipment can work with only one of the components operating).

Consider two identical components in parallel with the reliability of each component R, as shown in Figure 12s.1.

The probability that a component continues to work normally is R, so the probability that it will stop working is $1 - R$. The probability that both components fail is $(1 - R)^2$. The reliability of the equipment is the probability that at least one of the components is operating which is $1 - (1 - R)^2$. Similarly, the probability that n identical components in parallel will all fail is $(1 - R)^n$, and the reliability of the

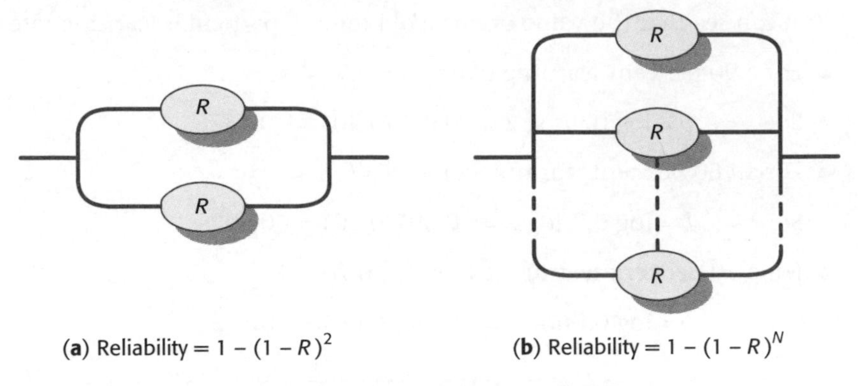

Figure 12s.1 Components in parallel increase reliability

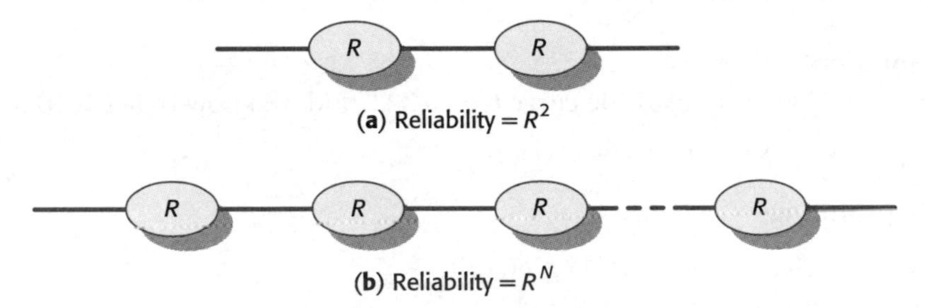

Figure 12s.2 Components in series reduce reliability

equipment is $1 - (1 - R)^n$. So, putting components in parallel makes the equipment more reliable.

If components are added in series, the reliability of equipment is reduced. This is because the equipment will only continue to work if all the separate components are working. Consider two components in series. If the reliability of each is R, the reliability of the two is the probability that both are working, which is R^2. If there are n components in series, their reliability is R^n (as shown in Figure 12s.2).

You can find the reliability of complex systems of components by reducing them to simpler forms, as illustrated in the following worked example.

WORKED EXAMPLE

Four pieces of equipment on an assembly line can be viewed as the components shown in Figure 12s.3. What is the overall reliability of the line?

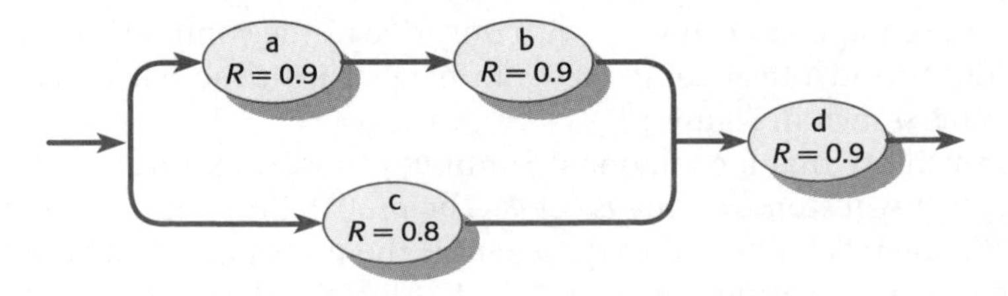

Figure 12s.3 Equipment reliability for worked example

Solution

We can simplify the components in steps, as shown in Figure 12s.4.

1. Take the top two components, a and b, which are in series and have a combined reliability of $0.9 \times 0.9 = 0.81$. We can put this as a single component, *e*, in parallel with component *c*.
2. The probability of both *e* and *c* failing is $(1 - 0.81) \times (1 - 0.8) = 0.038$. So the reliability of these two is $1 - 0.038 = 0.962$. We can put this as the single component *f*.
3. We now have two components, *f* and *d*, which are in series. The reliability of these is $0.962 \times 0.9 = 0.866$.
4. We now have a single component, *g*, giving the overall reliability as 0.966.

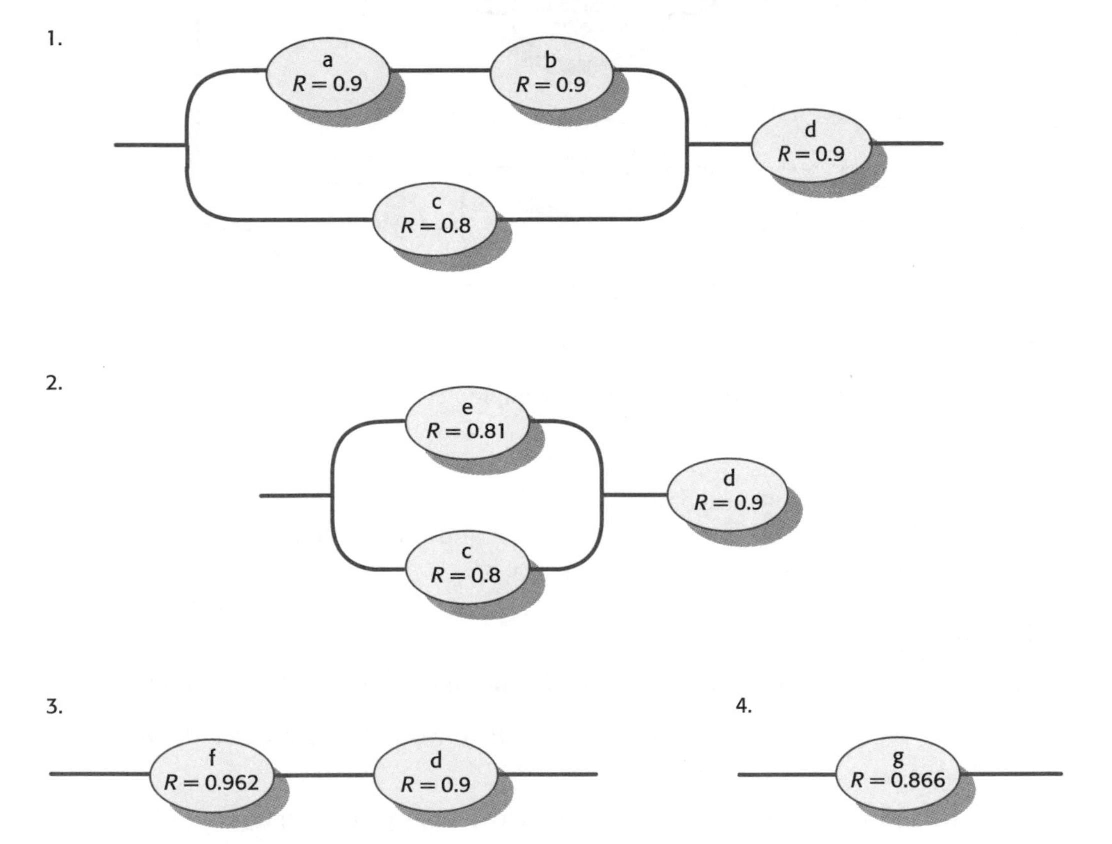

Figure 12s.4 Stages in simplifying the assembly line

WORKED EXAMPLE

Figure 12s.5 shows the layout of a shop floor in Kaiser Winter Garments. This consists of three parallel production lines A, B and C, whose outputs are 10,000, 12,000 and 20,000 units a week respectively. The diagram shows the reliability of each machine and if a line fails during the week all its production during the week is lost.

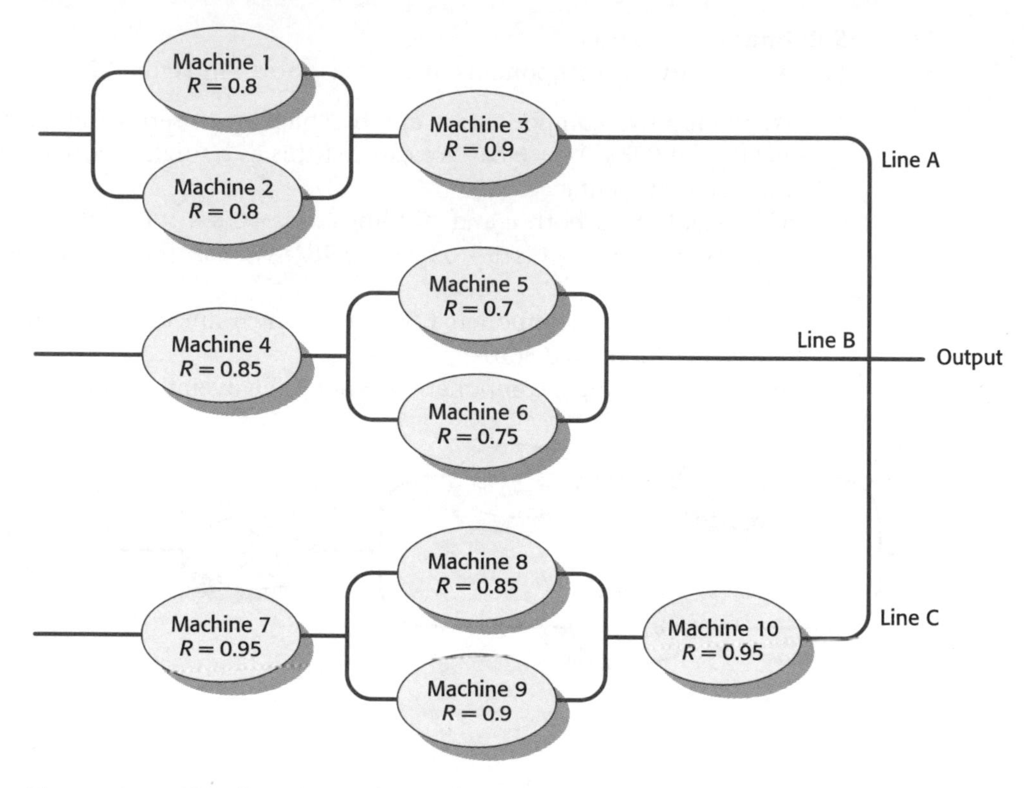

Figure 12s.5 Shopfloor layout for worked example

(a) Find the reliability of each line.
(b) Find the possible outputs from the process and the probability of each.
(c) What is the expected output of the process?

Solution

(a) The first step is to simplify the diagram and find the reliability of each line.

If R_i is the probability that machine i continues to work during a week, the reliability of line A is:

$$R_A = [1 - (1 - R_1) \times (1 - R_2)] \times R_3 = [1 - (0.2 \times 0.2)] \times 0.9 = 0.864$$

The reliability of line B is:

$$R_B = R_4 \times [1 - (1 - R_5) \times (1 - R_6)] = 0.85 \times [1 - (0.3 \times 0.25)] = 0.786$$

The reliability of line C is:

$$R_C = R_7 \times [1 - (1 - R_8) \times (1 - R_9)] \times R_{10} = 0.95 \times [1 - (0.15 \times 0.1)] \times 0.95 = 0.889$$

(b) We can find the total output by taking various combinations of lines failing. If lines A and B fail while line C continues, the output is 20,000. This has a probability of $(1 - R_A) \times (1 - R_B) \times R_C = 0.136 \times 0.214 \times 0.889 = 0.026$. The other possible outputs are shown in the following table.

Output	Probability	
0	$(1 - R_A) \times (1 - R_B) \times (1 - R_C)$	= 0.003
10,000	$R_A \times (1 - R_B) \times (1 - R_C)$	= 0.021
12,000	$(1 - R_A) \times R_B \times (1 - R_C)$	= 0.012
20,000	$(1 - R_A) \times (1 - R_B) \times R_C$	= 0.026
22,000	$R_A \times R_B \times (1 - R_C)$	= 0.075
30,000	$R_A \times (1 - R_B) \times R_C$	= 0.164
32,000	$(1 - R_A) \times R_B \times R_C$	= 0.095
42,000	$R_A \times R_B \times R_C$	= 0.604

(c) The expected output is the sum of (probability × output), so:

$$\text{Expected output} = (0 \times 0.003) + (10{,}000 \times 0.021) + (12{,}000 \times 0.012) + \ldots$$
$$= 35{,}852$$

Problems

12s.1 It takes 25 minutes to make the first unit of a product. How long will it take to make each of the next nine units with a learning rate of 0.9?

12s.2 What is the reliability of each of the sets of components shown in Figure 12s.6?

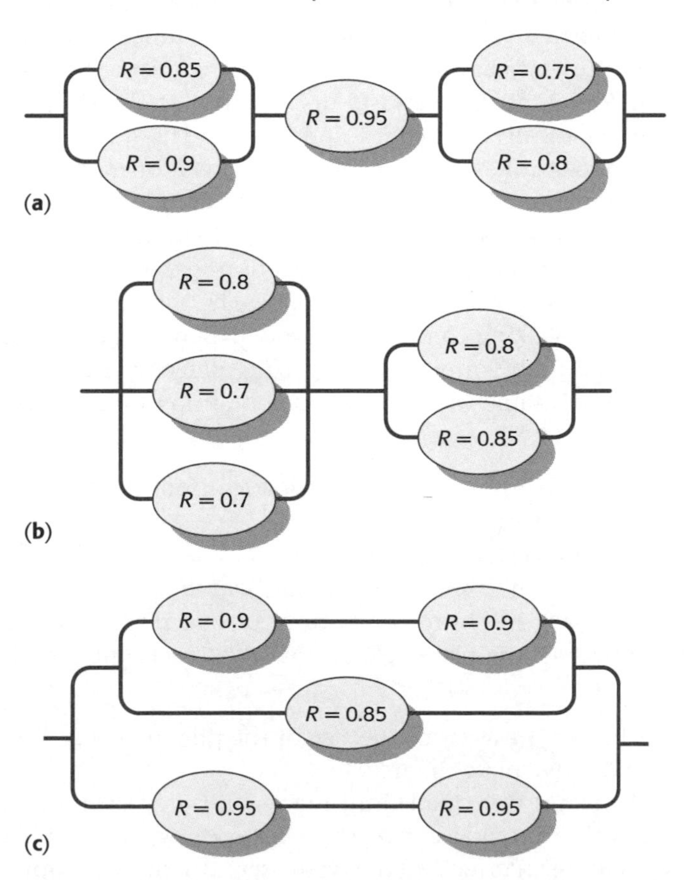

Figure 12s.6 Layout of components for Problem 12s.2

INTEGRATING CASE STUDY

The Bulldog Pottery

By Mike Simpson and Geoff Sykes of the Sheffield University Management School

It was a beautiful summer day for two consultants to visit Stoke-on-Trent and look around a pottery making ceramic tableware (plates, saucers, mugs, cups, teapots, etc.) for the hotel and catering market. The company was well known in the industry and had a healthy profit of £1.6 million on a turnover of £18 million. Its current stocks of finished goods were about £4 million, with £2 million of work-in-progress.

The personnel manager showed the two consultants around the factory. They saw the manufacturing process from start to finish. At each point they observed the operations, made notes, chatted with people and took photographs.

At one point the company's trademark and name were printed on the bottom of previously fired but unglazed plates. To do this the plates travelled along a special conveyor and a patterned stamp was applied to the underside of the plate. This marked the plate with water-based ink. All along the conveyor hot-air blowers were trained on the underside of the plates to dry the ink. At the end of the conveyor the plates were automatically stacked into piles of 20. The stacked plates were then removed, loaded on to a trolley, and wheeled to the next operation.

This next operation applied a thin layer of glazing compound before firing in the kiln. The glazing solution was sprayed on the plate, which was spun to remove excess solution, and dried. The operator at this workstation loaded each plate individually into the glazing machine. As he loaded the plates, he inspected their 'quality' and looked for defects. The glazing compound is very expensive and he had to prevent wasted material and time by unnecessarily glazing defective items. This operator's work area consisted of a table with four areas containing piles of plates. The areas were:

1. incoming unglazed plates in piles of 20 unloaded from the trolley from the previous ink stamping process;
2. good plates coated in the glazing compound;
3. plates where the material or shape of the plate was defective;
4. plates where the black ink from the bottom of one plate had been transferred to the upper surface of the plate below, leaving a black smudge, thus making it useless.

The pile of plates in area 4 was twice the size of the pile in area 2, and 10 times the size of the pile of defective plates in area 3.

After glazing, the plates were loaded into racks and fired over a 24-hour cycle in a tunnel furnace with a moving conveyor. After cooling, the plates were sent for inspection and grading. 'Perfect' plates were sent to the warehouse, and some defective ones were sold as 'seconds' in the factory shop. Others were identified for rework, grinding off any raised areas of glaze on the edges or underside of the plates. After this treatment they were automatically regarded as 'seconds'. Other plates were rejected, broken up in a skip and taken away to a landfill site. These reject plates had to be broken up because in the past thieves had raided the factory at night and over holiday periods, stolen plates from the skips and sold them as seconds at local markets and car boot sales. Sometimes, when the factory shop had sold out a particular line but expected more customers, perfect items were transferred from the warehouse and sold as seconds at the reduced price.

The tour of the factory was satisfactorily concluded and the consultants went for lunch in the management canteen. Over lunch the personnel manager explained the piece rate payment scheme, bonuses and the various rates for different types of work. The higher paid jobs were those requiring delicate work such as the application of transfers to plates and dishes. Hand-painting of decorative lines around the tops of cups and mugs was particularly difficult and attracted the highest rates of pay. This hand-painting was gradually being phased out, with the skilled craftsmen replaced by machines, but the personnel manager stressed that traditional skills were highly valued within the company. He also mentioned that most of the members of the senior management team had worked their way through the business and understood the industry and manufacturing process very well.

After lunch the consultants met the senior management team, which included the managing director, quality manager, works manager, production director, assistant quality manager, production supervisor, training manager and . . . the works cat! The consultants proceeded with their presentation.

Questions

- Do an operations audit for The Bulldog Pottery. What type of operations does it emphasise?
- What problems, if any, do you think the company has? Justify your answer.
- What do you think caused the consultants most concern? What would you say at the presentation?

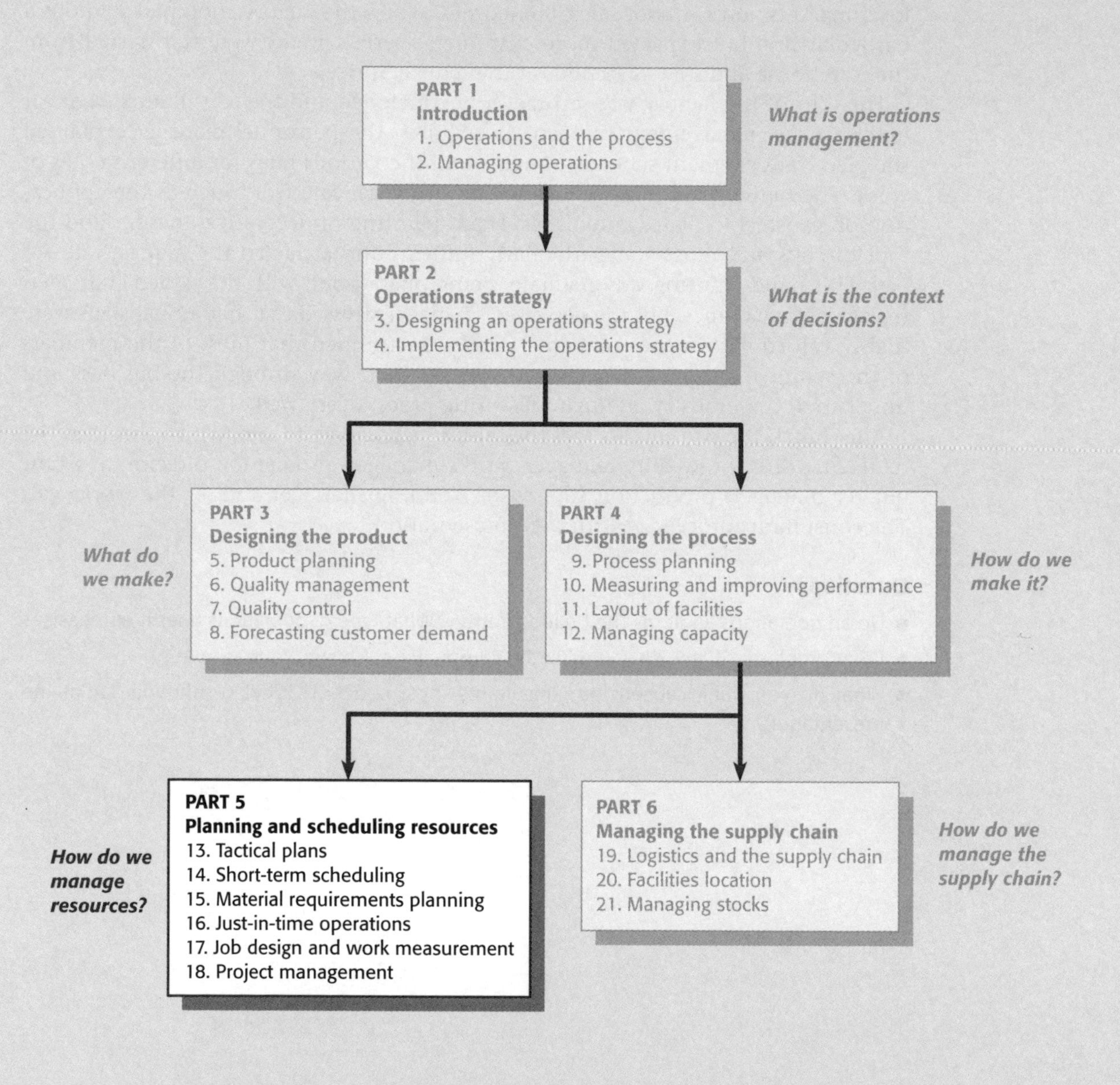

PART 1
Introduction
1. Operations and the process
2. Managing operations
What is operations management?
PART 2
Operations strategy
3. Designing an operations strategy
4. Implementing the operations strategy
What is the context of decisions?
PART 3
Designing the product
5. Product planning
6. Quality management
7. Quality control
8. Forecasting customer demand
What do we make?
PART 4
Designing the process
9. Process planning
10. Measuring and improving performance
11. Layout of facilities
12. Managing capacity
How do we make it?
PART 5
Planning and scheduling resources
13. Tactical plans
14. Short-term scheduling
15. Material requirements planning
16. Just-in-time operations
17. Job design and work measurement
18. Project management
How do we manage resources?
PART 6
Managing the supply chain
19. Logistics and the supply chain
20. Facilities location
21. Managing stocks
How do we manage the supply chain?

Part 5

PLANNING AND SCHEDULING RESOURCES

This book is divided into six parts. Each part describes a different aspect of operations management. Part 1 gave an introduction to the subject. Part 2 talked about strategy, emphasising the design and implementation of an operations strategy. Part 3 looked at the design and planning of a product. Part 4 described the design and planning of the process.

This is Part 5, which looks in more detail at the planning and scheduling of resources. Here we show how tactical and operational decisions support the strategic choices made earlier. There are six chapters in this part. Chapter 13 shows how strategic capacity plans are translated into medium-term tactical plans. Chapter 14 moves to the next level of detail and describes short-term scheduling. Chapter 15 looks at the supply of materials, emphasising materials requirement planning. Chapter 16 continues this theme by describing just-in-time systems. Chapter 17 moves to the most detailed level of planning with job design and work measurement. Finally, Chapter 18 describes some methods used in the important area of project planning.

Part 6 of the book will discuss some aspects of supply chain management.

CHAPTER

13

Tactical plans

The main purpose of the aggregate plan is to specify the combination of production rate, the work-force level, and inventory on hand.

Richard Chase and Nicholas Aquilano

Production and Operations Management, Irwin, Homewood IL, 1996

Contents

Aims of the chapter

After reading this chapter you should be able to:

- understand the relationships between different levels of planning;
- describe the factors that make planning difficult;
- use a general approach to planning;
- appreciate the purpose and aims of aggregate planning;
- use a number of methods for aggregate planning;
- appreciate the purpose and aims of master schedules;
- design a master schedule.

Main themes

This chapter will emphasise:

- **planning**, which organises the resources needed by operations;
- **aggregate plans**, which are plans for making families of products;
- **master schedules**, which show the timetables for making individual products.

Overall approach to planning

In the last chapter we saw how capacity planning fitted in with other planning. The mission, corporate and business strategies give the long-term direction of the whole organisation. These lead to strategic decisions within the central functions – including an operations strategy. This operations strategy includes capacity plans, which make sure there is enough capacity to meet the long-term demand (see Figure 13.1).

Now we are going to look at the next stages of planning, which move down to tactical and operational levels. These lower plans give timetables for operations, and organise the resources needed to support these. To put it simply, we are going to start planning production. You might think that only manufacturers do production planning, but this is not true. All organisations, including services, have to plan their production. If they do not plan for the future, they are working day-to-day, without any continuity, and in constant danger of meeting unexpected circumstances that they cannot cope with. Planning lets us all face the future with some confidence, rather than descending into inevitable chaos.

You can see how planning works in Capital Trains. Their strategies and product planning lead to a description of their products, which are public train services around Washington. Capital forecasts the overall demands for their services, and plans capacity to make sure they can meet this. In other words, they buy enough

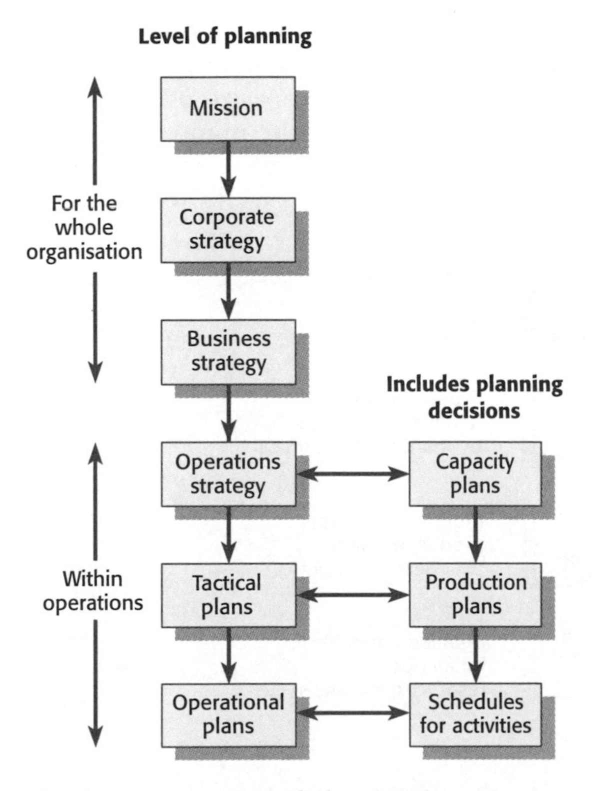

Figure 13.1 Summary of planning process

trains and hire enough staff to meet their forecast demands. Then they move on to more detailed plans, which give their timetable of services, saying which routes they will serve and when the trains will arrive. Capital Trains then expand these timetables into detailed schedules for individual trains and drivers, inspectors, materials and any other resources they need.

Capital Trains move down from strategic capacity plans, through medium-term schedules of operations, and on to detailed timetables for all of their resources. This planning process is essentially the same for all organisations. Unfortunately, there is some disagreement about the terms used for different levels of planning. We will use the fairly standard terms:

- **Capacity plans**, which we have already discussed in Chapter 12, make sure that there is enough capacity to meet long-term demand.
- **Aggregate plans** show the overall production for families of products, typically by month at each location.
- **Master schedules** show a detailed timetable for making individual products, typically by week.
- **Short-term schedules** show detailed timetables for jobs and resources, typically by day.

Using these terms, we can summarise the overall planning process as follows. An organisation's strategic decisions lead to strategic decisions about what products to make, where to make them, the process to use, and so on. These decisions, together with long-term forecasts, lead to capacity plans which match available capacity to forecast demand. The capacity plans set overall production levels in each facility over the next few years. The capacity plans are expanded to give medium-term aggregate plans, which show the numbers of each family of products to make each month for the next year or so. Then the aggregate plans are

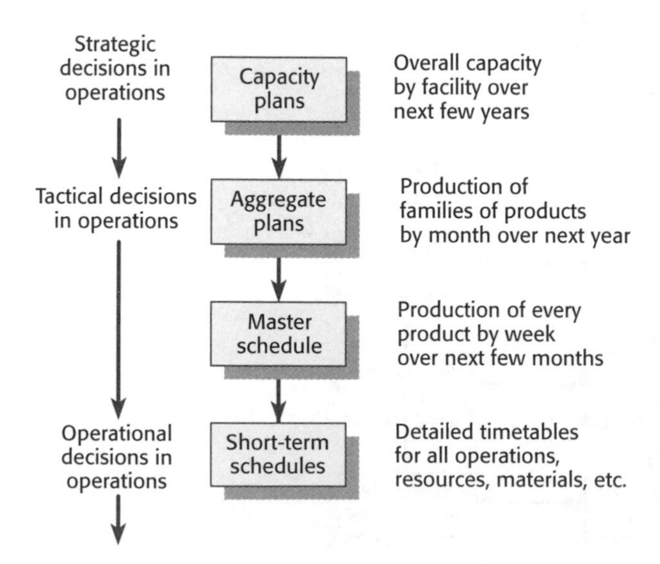

Figure 13.2 Capacity plans lead to other planning decisions in operations

expanded to give the master schedule, which shows a timetable for the production of individual products, typically by week. The weekly master schedule is expanded to give short-term schedules, which show daily timetables of machines, operators and other equipment.

OPERATIONS IN PRACTICE

Allenby Tools

Allenby Tools make a variety of garden tools in three factories. The following summary outlines their planning process for the financial year 2000/2001.

- **Strategic plans** – making the fundamental decisions.
  The board of directors, with George Allenby as its chairman, decides to continue making garden tools of high quality and using appropriate processes. They will continue operations in three factories at Gateshead, Bradford and Exeter.
- **Capacity plans** – examine long-term forecasts of demand and make adjustments to match capacity to these.
  Jane Lucas, the operations director, looks at their long-term forecasts. These show demands of 50,000 garden tools a year, which means there is a shortage in capacity of 10,000 tools a year. Jane, along with her senior management team, makes a decision to overcome this shortage by increasing the staff in Exeter and working two shifts at Bradford. Then forecast demand can be met by having capacities of:
  - 10,000 tools a year at Gateshead;
  - 20,000 tools a year at Bradford;
  - 20,000 tools a year at Exeter.
- **Aggregate plan** – breaks down the capacity plans into monthly plans for each location.
  The three plant managers get together, look at the capacity plans, and design aggregate plans to meet these:
  - Gateshead makes 1,000 tools in January (this needs a staff of 10 and gives 90 per cent utilisation of equipment);
  - Bradford makes 2,500 tools in January (this needs 20 staff and gives 85 per cent utilisation of equipment);
  - Etc.
- **Master schedule** – breaks down aggregate plans into weekly plans for individual products.
  George Thirkettle, the plant manager at Gateshead, passes the aggregate plan to Mary Wilson who produces the master schedules:
  - Gateshead:

Week 1 of January	100 spades
	50 forks
	100 rakes
Week 2 of January	50 spades
	250 rakes
Week 3 of January	100 spades
	100 rakes
	etc.

- **Short-term schedules** – break down the master schedule into daily timetables for individual batches of tools and equipment.

Mary Wilson passes the master schedules to her assistants, who design detailed daily timetables.

- Gateshead:

Week 1 of January

Monday morning shift	10 spades on machines 1 to 4
	10 rakes on machines 5 to 8
	10 forks on machines 1 to 8
Monday afternoon shift	20 forks on machines 1 to 8
Tuesday morning shift	10 spades on machines 1 to 4
	10 forks on machines 5 to 8
	10 rakes on machines 1 to 8
	Etc.

Allenby Tools make a series of plans, starting with their mission and ending with detailed operational schedules. But this only describes one part of their planning process. The next stage is to implement the plans, control them to make sure they work properly, and then continually revise them to give a series of plans into the future.

Sources: company reports and planning documents

Review questions

13.1 What is the usual sequence of planning decisions?

13.2 Which types of plan are likely to refer to:
(a) overall production at different locations;
(b) individual products;
(c) individual pieces of equipment;
(d) equipment operators?

13.3 Most organisations go through their planning process once every year. Do you think this is true?

Procedure for planning

Overall procedure

In the last chapter we described a general procedure for capacity planning. This had six steps:

- Step 1 – translate the forecast demand into a capacity needed.
- Step 2 – calculate the capacity available in present facilities.
- Step 3 – identify mismatches between the capacity needed and that available.
- Step 4 – suggest alternative plans for overcoming any mismatches.
- Step 5 – compare alternative plans and choose the best.
- Step 6 – implement the best.

We can use this same approach (sometimes called **resource requirement planning**) for all other types of planning. Its general approach is shown in Figure 13.3.

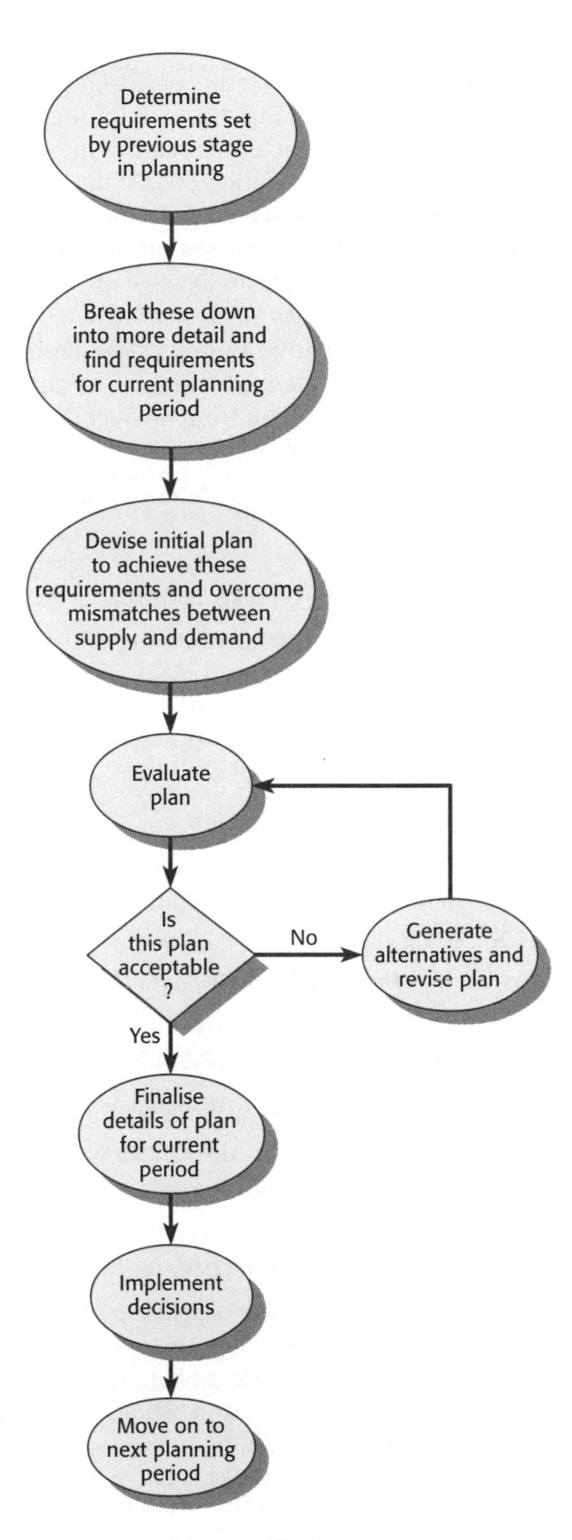

Figure 13.3 Iterative planning procedure

WORKED EXAMPLE

A & B Coaches of Blackpool plan their capacity in terms of 'coach-days'. They classify their business as either 'full day', which are long-distance journeys, or 'half day', which are shorter runs. Forecasts show expected annual demands for the next two years to average 400,000 full-day passengers and 750,000 half-day passengers.

A & B have 61 coaches, each with an effective capacity of 40 passengers a day for 300 days a year. Breakdowns and other unexpected problems reduce efficiency to 90 per cent. They employ 86 drivers who work an average of 220 days a year, but illness and other absences reduce their efficiency to 85 per cent.

If there is a shortage of coaches, the company can buy extra ones for £110,000 or hire them for £100 a day. If there is a shortage of drivers, the company can recruit extra ones at a cost of £20,000 a year, or hire them from an agency for £110 a day.

How should the company approach its planning?

Solution

Following the steps listed above:

- *Step 1 – translate the forecast demand into the capacity needed.*

400,000 full-day passengers are equivalent to 400,000/40 = 10,000 coach days a year, or 10,000/300 = 33.33 coaches. 750,000 half-day passengers are equivalent to 750,000/(40 × 300 × 2) = 31.25 coaches. Adding these two gives the total demand as 64.58 coaches. Each coach needs 300/220 drivers, so the company needs a total of 88.06 drivers.

- *Step 2 – calculate the capacity available in present facilities.*

The company has 61 coaches, but the efficiency of 90 per cent gives an availability of 61 × 0.9 = 54.9 coaches. There are 86 drivers, but an efficiency of 85 per cent reduces this to 86 × 0.85 = 73.1 drivers.

- *Step 3 – identify mismatches between the capacity needed and that available.*

Without details of the timing, we can only take overall figures. There is a total shortage of 64.58 – 54.9 = 9.68 coaches and 88.06 – 73.1 = 14.96 drivers.

- *Step 4 – suggest alternative plans for overcoming any mismatches*

In this case the alternatives are either to buy or hire coaches, and employ drivers or hire them from an agency. The only information we have about these alternatives are some costs.

- *Step 5 – compare alternative plans and implement the best.*

To buy 10 coaches would cost £1,100,000. To hire coaches to make up the shortage would cost 9.68 × 300 × 100 = £290,400 a year. There is, of course, the alternative of buying some coaches and hiring others. We do not have enough information to make the final decisions, but a reasonable solution would go along the line of buying eight coaches and making up any shortages by hiring.

Similarly, to hire 15 drivers would cost £300,000 a year, while using temporary drivers from an agency would cost 14.96 × 220 × 110 = £362,032 a year. There is also the option of hiring some drivers, say 13, and making up shortages from an agency.

This gives an overall picture of plans for coaches and drivers. Now A & B can start looking at the more detailed schedules.

Practical difficulties

This last worked example illustrates the general approach of planning but, as you can imagine, there are many practical difficulties. Perhaps the most important is the way that alternative plans are generated and compared. There are usually so many possible plans that it is impossible to list them all, let alone compare their merits. There are also so many competing objectives and non-quantifiable factors that it can be difficult to find any plan that satisfies everyone, let alone identify the 'best'.

A more realistic view is the one we described for capacity planning, which replaces the single run with an iterative procedure that keeps modifying plans until it finds a satisfactory result. In other words, steps 4 and 5 are repeated until the plans are generally accepted by everyone concerned. This inevitably needs a compromise that takes into account a large number of factors, including patterns of demand, type of operations, materials used, costs, people working on the process, marketing position, and so on. Finding this reasonable balance is difficult, and the iterative procedure may be repeated many times until a plan is finally accepted.

Planning over many periods

We have looked at planning for a single period, but it is really a continuous job that never ends. As plans for one period are finalised and implemented, planning moves on to the next period. The usual way of organising this is to work on plans for several periods at the same time; plans for the near future are fixed, while those for the more distant future are still tentative. Planning is then done in cycles. In one cycle an organisation might finalise plans for the next period and make tentative plans for the following period, and outline plans for the period after that. This gives the pattern of planning shown in Figure 13.4. It is difficult to generalise, but strategic plans might cover the next five years and be updated annually; aggregate plans might cover the next year and be updated every quarter; master schedules might cover the next three months and be updated monthly.

This pattern of repeated cycles actually makes planning a lot easier. Most operations are relatively stable, so the plans for one period can be used as the basis for plans in following periods. We adjust previous plans to take account of changing circumstances, and get plans for following periods. We can see how this works by looking at a stock of goods.

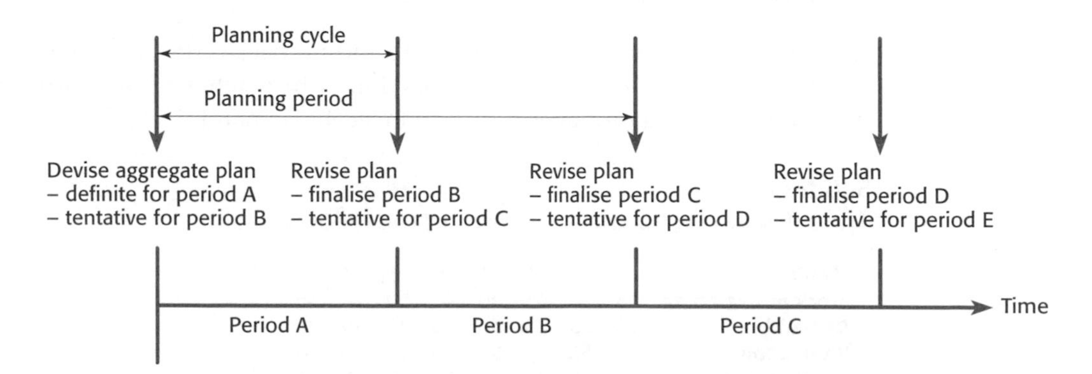

Figure 13.4 Continual updating of plans in cycles

Stocks can be important in planning as they give a buffer between supply and demand. They mean that production during a period need not exactly match demand in the period, as demand can be met from:

- stocks already held at the beginning of the period;
- production during the period;
- future production with late delivery.

The best mix of these is the one that minimises costs, maximises profit, or meets some other measure of performance.

We can find the amount of stock at the end of a period from the following argument:

Stock at end of this period = stock at end of last period + production during this period – demand in this period

This assumes there are no back-orders, where demand in one period is met by production from the following period. If we add this we have:

Stock at end of this period = stock at end of last period + production during this period – demand for this period – stock that is used to meet demand from earlier periods + demand this period that will not be met until later periods

We can use a similar approach to other resources, such as manpower planning:

Number employed this month = number employed last month – dismissals and resignations at end of last month + new hires at beginning of this month

Developing this idea of repetitive updating can lay the foundations for further schedules.

WORKED EXAMPLE

Demand for a product over the next eight months has been forecast as follows.

Month	1	2	3	4	5	6	7	8
Demand	15	25	25	30	40	40	25	20

A minimum of 10 units is kept in stock, and no back-orders are allowed. There are currently 35 units in stock and production is in batches of 50, with a very short lead time. Design a production plan to meet the demand.

Solution

The calculations for this are shown in the following table.

Month	1	2	3	4	5	6	7	8	9
Stock at beginning	35	20	45	20	40	50	10	35	15
Demand	15	25	25	30	40	40	25	20	
Production	0	50	0	50	50	0	50	0	
Stock at end	20	45	20	40	50	10	35	15	

At the beginning of the first month there are 35 units in stock and demand during the month is 15. No production is needed and the stock at the end of the month is 35 – 15 = 20. This stock of 20 is available at the beginning of the second month.

Demand in the second month is 25, so we need to schedule some production. We have to schedule a batch of 50 units, to give stock at the end of the second month of 20 + 50 – 25 = 45.

As there must be at least 10 units left in stock, we schedule a batch of 50 units in any month when the stock at the beginning of the month minus demand in the month is less than 10. This leads to a production schedule with batches of 50 units in months 2, 4, 5 and 7. This plan is only one alternative, and others should be examined before a plan is finalised.

Review questions

13.4 Where do the initial requirements for a planning period come from?

13.5 A planning process starts of with general plans, and adds more details at each stage of planning. Do you think this is true?

13.6 Why are updating procedures useful?

OPERATIONS IN PRACTICE

Kawasaki Heavy Industries

Kawasaki Heavy Industries is probably best known for its motorcycles, which are made in several plants around the world. Production planning at these plants has inputs from several sources, including forecasts of local demand and requirements of the main plant in Akashi, Japan. Kawasaki's current planning procedure is outlined below, but it looks for continuous improvements and frequently changes this.

- The process starts with a **sales forecast**, which gives the monthly demand for each model of motorcycle for the next year. This is updated every three months.
- The forecasts are consolidated into a **sales plan**, which shows the number of each model that must be available for sale each month for the next year. The plan is updated every three months, with the final three months considered firm.
- The sales plan is one input to the **production plan** at plants. This production plan looks up to 18 months ahead and is used for capacity planning and budgeting. The production plan is updated every three months, with the last three months fixed to agree with the sales plan. Scheduled deliveries of parts allow no changes in the last six weeks.
- The production plan is expanded into a **daily production schedule**, which is the master schedule and shows the daily assembly programme. Details of this are added four or five months in advance, and plans are updated every three months to fit into the cycles of the sales and production plans. The last six weeks of this plan are fixed by the production plan, but minor adjustments are made every week.
- The daily production schedule is expanded to give **fabrication schedules**, which show the timetable for making components needed for final assembly.
- The fabrication and schedules are expanded to find the **purchase orders** needed to get parts and materials from suppliers.

Aggregate plans

Definitions

Aggregate plans and master schedules bridge the gap between strategic capacity plans and operational details. In this section we look at aggregate plans, and move on to master schedules in the next section.

Aggregate planning takes the forecast demand and capacity, and uses them to design production plans for each family of products for, typically, each of the next few months. Aggregate plans only look at families of products and are not concerned with individual products. A knitwear manufacturer, for example, produces different styles, colours and sizes of jumpers and skirts. The aggregate plan only shows the total production of jumpers and the total production of skirts – it does not look in any more detail at the production of a particular style, colour or size. Aggregate plans look at the total number of barrels of beer to be produced or books to be printed, but not the number of barrels of each type of beer or the number of copies of each title.

Aggregate planning makes the tactical decisions that translate forecast demand and planned capacity into production schedules for families of products.

Aggregate planners try to meet forecast demand, while using capacity as efficiently as possible. They typically aim at minimum production costs, high customer service, stable operations, full utilisation of resources or some other objective.

The aim of **aggregate planning** is to design medium-term schedules for making families of products that:

- meet all forecast demand;
- keep within the constraints of the capacity plan;
- keep production relatively stable;
- use available resources efficiently;
- meet any other specific objectives and constraints.

To achieve this, the planners have a number of variables they can control. They may, for example, be able to change the product mix, or the number of people employed, the hours worked, the amounts of stock, the amount subcontracted, demand, and so on. Essentially, aggregate planners are looking for answers to a series of questions, such as:

- Should we keep production at a constant level, or change it to meet varying demand?
- Should we adjust the product mix by putting more resources into products with heavier demand?
- Should we use stocks to meet changing demand – producing for stock during periods of low demand and using the accumulated stocks during periods of high demand?
- Should we vary the size of the workforce with demand, hiring or laying-off people?

- Can we change work patterns to meet changing demand by changing shifts or the amounts of overtime and undertime?
- Should we use subcontractors or other outside organisations to cover peak demands?
- Can we have shortages, perhaps with late delivery?
- Can we smooth the demand (using demand management that we mentioned in the last chapter)?

The answers to these questions lead to a set of aggregate plans. These follow one of three alternative policies: produce at constant rate, chase demand, or a mixture of these two.

1. **Produce at a constant rate** – production is constant at the average demand for the planning period. Since the production rate is constant and demand is variable, the differences are met by building or using stocks. This always gives inventory costs and maybe some shortage costs, and it makes the policy difficult to apply in services. None the less, it has some real advantages. Planning is much easier; there is a smooth flow of products through the process; there are no problems with changes; employees work regular schedules; there is no need to 'hire and fire' or use subcontractors; people become experienced with the operations, etc.

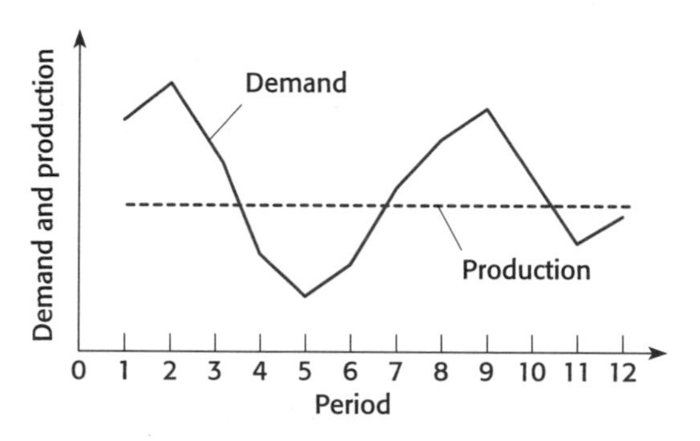

Figure 13.5 Policy of constant production

2. **Chase demand** – production exactly matches demand. This gives no stocks, but we have to change production every period. This can be very difficult to organise, as well as expensive. None the less, it is often the best policy, particularly with services that cannot be kept in stock. McDonalds, for example, uses a chase policy when it adjusts the number of hamburgers it makes throughout the day to match varying customer demand.

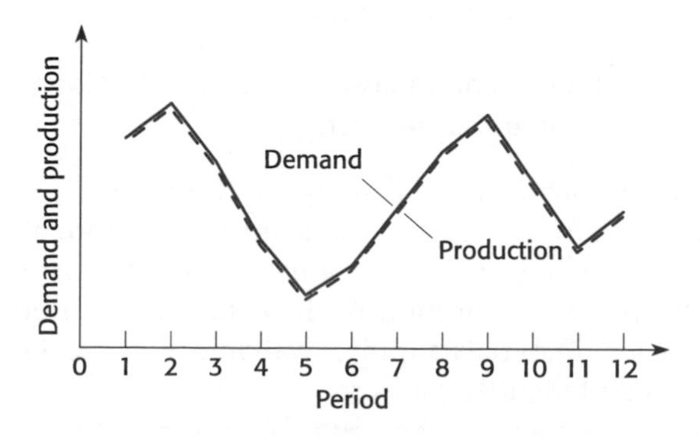

Figure 13.6 Chase demand, where production exactly matches demand

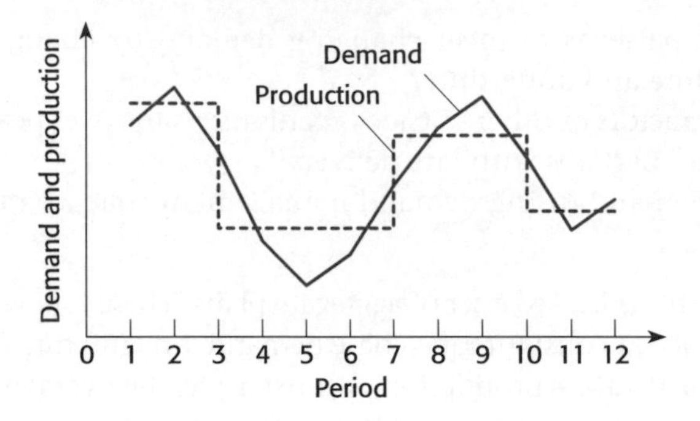

Figure 13.7 A mixed production strategy

3. **Mixed Policy** – is a combination of the first two policies. Here there are some changes in production rate, but not enough to follow demand exactly. The policy finds a compromise that gives fairly stable production, but with some changes. In practice, this is the most commonly used plan.

WORKED EXAMPLE

Fenmore Enterprises have forecast the following aggregate, monthly demand for a family of products. If this is the only information you have, what production plan would you suggest?

Month	Jan	Feb	March	April	May	June	July
Aggregate demand	80	70	60	120	180	150	110

Solution

You might suggest that monthly production exactly matches demand. But demand varies quite widely and most organisations prefer more stable production.

You could also suggest a steady production equal to the average demand of 110. During the first three months the demand will be less than supply, so stocks will rise, but these will be used during the following months:

Month	Jan	Feb	March	April	May	June	July
Demand	80	70	60	120	180	150	110
Production	110	110	110	110	110	110	110
Stock at month end	30	70	120	110	40	0	0

The stock at the end of each month is found from:

Stock at month end = stock at end of last month + production in month – demand in month

The high stock levels are an obvious disadvantage of this plan.

These two policies are a chase policy and constant production. We can design a number of mixed policies, such as making 70 a month for the first three months, and then 140 a month for the next four months. If we had more information about costs, stock holding policies, materials supply, availability of workforce, etc., we could compare these plans and identify the best.

Generating plans

In the last example, we suggested a mixed policy, and gave one plan that was based on common sense. But how can we get a more reliable way of designing these plans? In practice, there are many ways ranging from simple intuition through to sophisticated mathematical models. We will outline some of these in the following sections. The most appropriate depends on a number of factors, ranging from skills available within the organisation to the cost of production. If you run a large oil company, production costs are very high and it is worth putting a lot of effort into sophisticated mathematical programming models that get very good results. On the other hand, a small business is unlikely to have the resources for this, and the effort involved would be far more expensive than the extra cost of using slightly lower quality plans.

1. **Negotiations**. Planning is so complicated, with many subjective factors and people affected, that the best approach is often to negotiate a solution. This may not give the best technical answer, but it has the support of everyone concerned.
2. **Adjust previous plans.** We have already seen that operations can be fairly stable, and work in cycles. A useful approach to planning has an experienced planner reviewing present circumstances and updating previous plans to allow for any changes. This has the benefit of being relatively easy and causing little disruption. It also uses a well-understood procedure and experts can give results that are trusted by the organisation. Unfortunately, the results can also be of variable and uncertain quality, the plans may take a long time to design, and they rely solely on the skills of a planner.
3. **Other intuitive methods**. These include a range of methods that use the skills, knowledge and experience of planners, who will typically use a series of heuristic rules that have been successful in the past.
4. **Graphical methods**. Planners often find it easier to work with graphs or diagrams. The most popular format uses a graph of cumulative demand over some time period, and the corresponding line of cumulative supply. The aim is to get the cumulative supply line nearly straight – giving constant production – and as close as possible to the cumulative demand line. The difference between the two lines shows the mismatch:

- if the cumulative demand line is below the cumulative supply line, production is too high and the excess is accumulated as stock;
- if the cumulative demand line is above the cumulative supply line, production has been too low and demand is not being met.

WORKED EXAMPLE

McGrath Holdings have forecast monthly demand for a family of products, as shown below. At the end of each month they assign a notional holding cost of £10 to every unit held in stock. Any shortages are satisfied by back-orders, but each unit of shortage is assigned a notional cost of £100 for lost profit, goodwill and future sales. Each time the production rate changes it costs £10,000. The designed capacity for the products is 400 units a month, but maximum utilisation is generally around 75 per cent of this. McGrath Holdings want to spend less than £1,900 a month on these activities. Design an aggregate plan for the products.

Month	1	2	3	4	5	6	7	8	9
Aggregate demand	280	320	260	160	120	100	60	100	130

Solution

The designed capacity is 400 units a month, but utilisation is generally around 75 per cent, so we can assume a maximum production of 400 × 0.75 = 300 a month. McGrath Holdings want stable production as changes are very expensive. A starting point is to suggest constant production at the average demand of 170 a month. The cumulative demand and supply for this are shown in Figure 13.8.

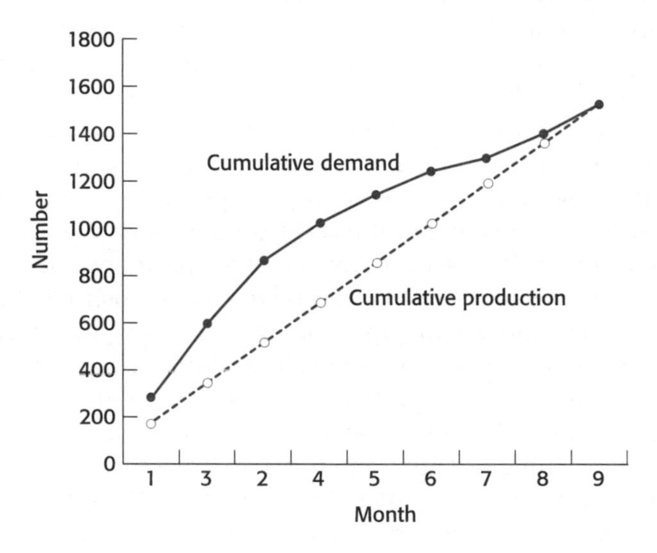

Figure 13.8 Initial aggregate plan with constant production

The cumulative demand line is always above the cumulative supply, showing continuous shortages. The spreadsheet in Figure 13.9 show the total cost of these shortages.

This plan has no storage costs, but the high costs of shortages gives a result which is considerably above the company target of £1,900 a month.

Changing the production rate is expensive, but it might be worthwhile to reduce the shortages in the initial plan. As demand is heavy in the first three months, we might try increasing supply by running the process at its maximum output of 300 units a month. The total demand to be met from production in the remaining six months is (1530 − 3 × 300) = 630, averaging 105 a month. Then a reasonable production plan is 300 for the first three months and 105 for the next six months. There is clearly a better match between the graphs of cumulative supply and demand shown in Figure 13.10, and Figure 13.11 confirms the lower costs.

This revised plan is much better, but it still does not meet the company target and we must try some more adjustments. Shortages still give high costs, so we can try maintaining production at 300 units for another month. Then the average production in the remaining five months is (1530 − 4 × 300)/5 = 66.

You can see from Figures 13.12 and 13.13 that the total cost is now £1,800 a month. This is within the company target and we can leave this as our final

	A	B	C	D	E	F	G
1	Month	Aggregate	Cumulative	Production	Cumulative	Shortage	Stock at
2		Demand	Demand		Production	in Month	End of Month
3							
4	1	280	280	170	170	110	0
5	2	320	600	170	340	260	0
6	3	260	860	170	510	350	0
7	4	160	1020	170	680	340	0
8	5	120	1140	170	850	290	0
9	6	100	1240	170	1020	220	0
10	7	60	1300	170	1190	110	0
11	8	100	1400	170	1360	40	0
12	9	130	1530	170	1530	0	0
13							
14	Totals					1720	0
15							
16	Costs		Production changes			0	0
17			Shortages			1720	172000
18			Storage			0	0
19			Total				172000
20			Monthly				19111

Figure 13.9 Spreadsheet calculations for constant production

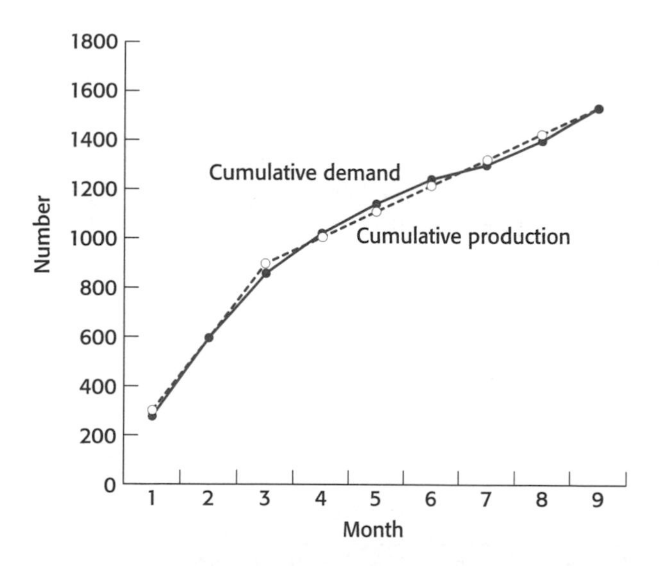

Figure 13.10 Modified aggregate plan for worked example

aggregate plan. The match between supply and demand is obviously not as good as the previous plan, but the balance between shortage and storage costs makes it cheaper. If necessary, we can make some more adjustments and keep looking for a better solution.

	A	B	C	D	E	F	G
1	Month	Aggregate	Cumulative	Production	Cumulative	Shortage	Stock at
2		Demand	Demand		Production	in Month	End of Month
3							
4	1	280	280	300	300	0	20
5	2	320	600	300	600	0	0
6	3	260	860	300	900	0	40
7	4	160	1020	105	1005	15	0
8	5	120	1140	105	1110	30	0
9	6	100	1240	105	1215	25	0
10	7	60	1300	105	1320	0	20
11	8	100	1400	105	1425	0	25
12	9	130	1530	105	1530	0	0
13							
14	Totals					70	105
15							
16	Costs		Production changes			1	10000
17			Shortages			70	7000
18			Storage			105	1050
19			Total				18050
20			Monthly				2006

Figure 13.11 Calculations for modified plan

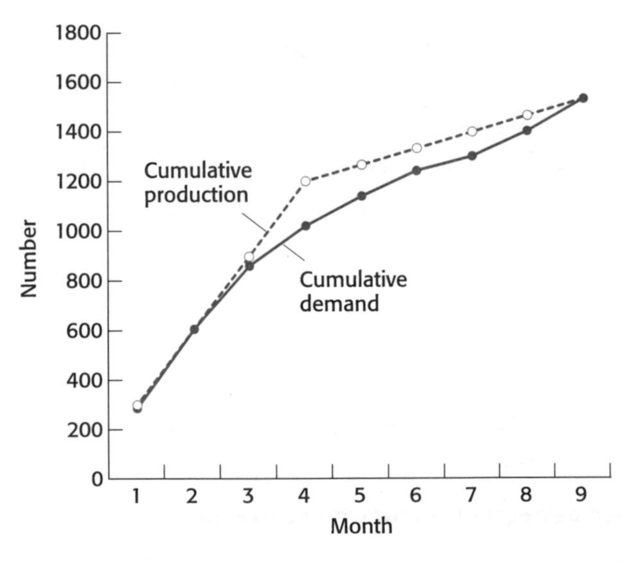

Figure 13.12 Final aggregate plan for worked example

	A	B	C	D	E	F	G
1	Month	Aggregate	Cumulative	Production	Cumulative	Shortage	Stock at
2		Demand	Demand		Production	in Month	End of Month
3							
4	1	280	280	300	300	0	20
5	2	320	600	300	600	0	0
6	3	260	860	300	900	0	40
7	4	160	1020	300	1200	0	180
8	5	120	1140	66	1266	0	126
9	6	100	1240	66	1332	0	92
10	7	60	1300	66	1398	0	98
11	8	100	1400	66	1464	0	64
12	9	130	1530	66	1530	0	0
13							
14	Totals					0	620
15							
16	Costs		Production changes			1	10000
17			Shortages			0	0
18			Storage			620	6200
19			Total				16200
20			Monthly				1800

Figure 13.13 Calculations for final plan

Graphical approaches have the advantages that they are easy to use and understand. But they are really only one step better than an intuitive method. They do not guarantee optimal solutions, sometimes give very poor results, may take a long time, and still rely on the skills of a planner.

5. **Other spreadsheet calculations**. In the last method, we concentrated on the graphs, and used a spreadsheet to do related calculations. Concentrating on the graphs might show the overall patterns, but it might lose some of the details. An alternative is to concentrate on the spreadsheet calculations and look at the patterns in the numbers.

A common format used in spreadsheets lists the resources down the left-hand side and the time periods across the top. The available capacity for each resource is shown down the right-hand side of the spreadsheet, and the demand is shown across the bottom. The body of the spreadsheet contains two values – the cost of using resources, and amount of resources used in a period. An example of this is shown in Figure 13.14.

There is a simple method of tackling such problems, or at least finding good initial solutions. This has the following steps.

1. Take the next time period.
2. Find the lowest cost in this column.
3. Assign as much production as possible to the cell with lowest cost, without exceeding either the supply of resources or demand for products.

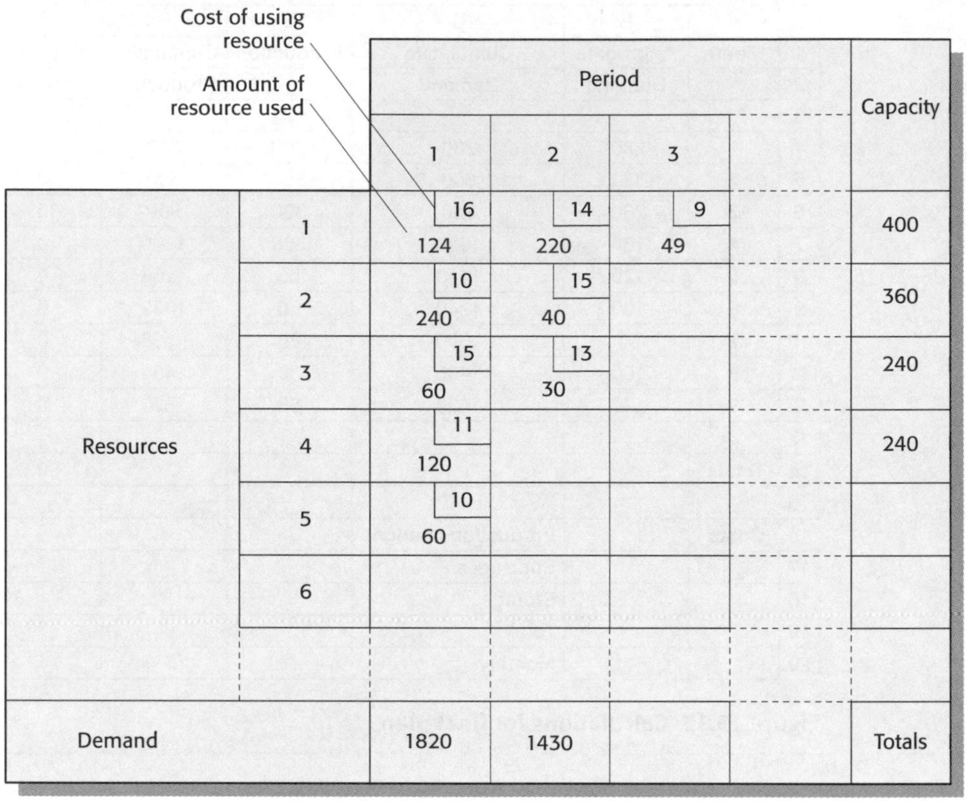

Cost of using resource
Amount of resource used

		Period				Capacity
		1	2	3		
Resources	1	16 124	14 220	9 49		400
	2	10 240	15 40			360
	3	15 60	13 30			240
	4	11 120				240
	5	10 60				
	6					
Demand		1820	1430			Totals

Figure 13.14 Typical matrix format for aggregate planning

4. Subtract the amount assigned from the total capacity to give the spare capacity, and calculate the unmet demand.
5. If there is unmet demand, go to step 2; if all demand has been met, move on to the next period in step 1.

WORKED EXAMPLE

Jim Cooper is the operations manager for a small manufacturing company. He forecasts the demand for a family of products for the next four months as 130, 80, 180 and 140. Normal capacity of the company is 100 units a month, overtime has a capacity of 20 a month and subcontractors have a capacity of 60 units a month. The unit costs are £10 for normal capacity, £12 for overtime and £15 from subcontractors. It costs £1 to stock a unit for a month, and no back-orders or shortages are allowed. How might Jim use a spreadsheet to design aggregate plans?

Solution

Our first step is to build a spreadsheet with costs, capacities and demand, as shown in Figure 13.15.

The demands and capacities are given in the problem. The costs in each cell are a combination of production and stock holding cost. It costs £10 to make a unit in normal work, but if this is used in a later period holding costs are added and

			Period				Capacity
			1	2	3	4	
Period 1	**Normal**	**Cost**	10	11	12	12	
		Hours					**100**
	Overtime	**Cost**	12	13	14	15	
		Hours					**20**
	Subcontract	**Cost**	15	16	17	18	
		Hours					**60**
Period 2	**Normal**	**Cost**		10	11	12	
		Hours					**100**
	Overtime	**Cost**		12	13	14	
		Hours					**20**
	Subcontract	**Cost**		15	16	17	
		Hours					**60**
Period 3	**Normal**	**Cost**			10	11	
		Hours					**100**
	Overtime	**Cost**			12	13	
		Hours					**20**
	Subcontract	**Cost**			15	16	
		Hours					**60**
Period 4	**Normal**	**Cost**				10	
		Hours					**100**
	Overtime	**Cost**				12	
		Hours					**20**
	Subcontract	**Cost**				15	
		Hours					**60**
Demand			130	80	180	140	

Figure 13.15 Initial matrix for worked example

the cost rises to £11 in the following period, £12 in the next period, and so on. No back-orders are allowed, so the cells for producing in period 2 for demand in period 1, etc. are crossed out.

Using the procedure described above, the first step is to look down column 1 and find the lowest cost for the first period. This is £10 for normal work done in period 1. We make as much there as possible, which is the normal capacity of 100 units, leaving a shortage of 30 units. The next lowest cost is £12 for overtime, which has a capacity of 20 units. Using all of this still leaves a shortage of 10 units, which must be made by subcontracting. These amounts are subtracted from capacities.

Moving to period 2, the lowest cost is the £10 for normal work done in period 2, which can meet all demand.

Moving to period 3, the lowest cost is the £10 for normal work done in period 3. This can meet 100 of the demand. The next lowest cost is £11 for normal work done in period 2. There is still capacity of 20 units here, so this leaves a shortage of

			Period				Capacity
			1	2	3	4	
Period 1	Normal	Cost	10	11	12	12	
		Hours	100				0
	Overtime	Cost	12	13	14	15	
		Hours	20				0
	Subcontract	Cost	15	16	17	18	
		Hours	10				50
Period 2	Normal	Cost		10	11	12	
		Hours		80	20		0
	Overtime	Cost		12	13	14	
		Hours			20		0
	Subcontract	Cost		15	16	17	
		Hours					60
Period 3	Normal	Cost			10	11	
		Hours			100		0
	Overtime	Cost			12	13	
		Hours			20		0
	Subcontract	Cost			15	16	
		Hours			20		40
Period 4	Normal	Cost				10	
		Hours				100	0
	Overtime	Cost				12	
		Hours				20	0
	Subcontract	Cost				15	
		Hours				20	40
Demand			130	80	180	140	

Figure 13.16 Final solution for worked example

60 units. The next lowest cost with spare capacity is £12 for overtime in period 3. This meets 20 units of demand, but there is still a shortage of 40 units. The next lowest cost is £13 for overtime in period 2. This meets 20 units of demand, but there is still a shortage of 20 units, which can best be met from subcontracting in period 3.

This process is repeated for period 4, to give the results shown in Figure 13.16.

---

6. **Simulation**. Simulation is one of the most flexible approaches to solving problems. It gives a dynamic view by imitating real operations over a typical period. Suppose that you want some information about a clerical process. You could stand and watch the process for some time, and see what was happening. This might give a good idea of the normal operations, but it would take a long time to get results and people may not work normally while there is someone watching.

An alternative is to simulate the process. Then you use a computer to generate some typical units, and follow their progress through the process. Rather than watching and timing a customer being served, for example, a computer generates a typical service time – and any other features that you want. The computer can repeat this for a large number of customers, and analyse the results to show how well the process performs.

Simulation for aggregate planning starts with an appropriate model of the process. Then you can fit alternative plans into this, and compare the performance. It can take some time to build and test the simulation model, but the results give useful insights into the working of a process.

OPERATIONS IN PRACTICE

Ed's Drive Through Bottle Shop

Ed's Drive Through Bottle Shop sells alcoholic drinks in Brisbane, Australia. The prices are low and the 'drive through' shop is busy. Customers accept some delays to get cheap drinks, but at busy periods the manager (who took over from Ed many years ago) saw that he was losing customers.

The basic plan of the shop has a single line of cars driving past a service window (customers can park and visit the shop as normal, but relatively few do this). The obvious way of reducing the delays is to have more service windows working in parallel, but the site is rather long and narrow, so this is impossible.

	A	B	C	D	E	F	G	H	I	J
1	Customer	A			B			C		
2		Join queue	Start service	Leave	Join queue	Start service	Leave	Join queue	Start service	Leave
3										
4	1	8.45	8.47	8.51	8.52	8.55	8.60	8.61	8.62	8.64
5	2	8.45	8.51	8.53	8.53	8.60	9.01	9.02	9.04	9.07
6	3	8.58	8.58	9.01	9.02	9.07	9.09	9.10	9.10	9.13
7	4	9.00	9.01	9.04	9.05	9.09	9.10	9.11	9.13	9.16
8	5	9.05	9.05	9.06	9.06	9.10	9.13	9.13	9.16	9.18
9	6	9.20	9.20	9.21	9.21	9.21	9.23	9.23	9.23	9.25
10	7	9.20	9.21	9.24	9.25	9.25	9.28	9.29	9.29	9.33
11	8	9.22	9.24	9.26	9.27	9.28	9.30	9.30	9.33	9.35
12	9	9.25	9.26	9.29	9.30	9.30	9.34	9.35	9.35	9.38
13	10	9.25	9.29	9.32	9.33	9.35	9.38	9.39	9.39	9.44
14										
15	Analysis									
16	Number of customers			10						
17	Time in queue A			2.10		Service time A			2.50	
18	Time in queue B			2.30		Service time B			2.10	
19	Time in queue C			1.20		Service time C			2.40	
20										
21	Time in queues			6.00		Time being served			7.40	
22						Time in system			15.20	

Figure 13.17 Part of a simulation for Ed's Drive Through Bottle Shop

The manager decided to try a number of improvements, such as dividing the service into several parts. He found the distributions of times for various operations, and then used a spreadsheet to simulate a number of options.

Figure 13.17 gives an idea of his approach. For this he put three servers in series. The first server, A, took the customer's order, the second, B, looked after the bill and payment, and the third, C, delivered the goods. The spreadsheet follows 10 customers through the process. It generates times for each activity (randomly generated to follow actual distributions), and shows how the process performs during a typical short period. By following longer periods and more variations, the manager can look at different aspects of operations and see which configuration gives the best performance.

7. **Expert systems**. These specialised programs try to make computers duplicate the thinking of a skilled scheduler. The basic skills, expertise, decisions and rules used by experts are collected in a knowledge base. A user of the system passes a specific problem to an inference engine, which is the control mechanism. This looks at the problem, relates this to the knowledge base and decides which rules to use for a solution.

Expert systems have been developing for many years, and some organisations report useful results, particularly for straightforward applications. In general, it is fair to say that the results are disappointing. They can be difficult to design and need a lot of expertise before they work properly.

8. **Mathematical models**. Most of the approaches we have described so far rely, at least to some extent, on the skills of a planner. More formal mathematical approaches give optimal – or near optimal – solutions without any human intervention. In practice, aggregate plans include so many subjective and non-quantifiable factors that optimal solutions in the mathematical sense may not give the best answers for the organisation.

The most common mathematical approach uses linear **programming**. These methods are rather complicated, so they are generally limited to small problems. If, however, you work in a chemical plant that produces millions of litres a month, a small change in the aggregate plans may make a significant difference in costs, and it is certainly worth looking at mathematical approaches. The supplement to this chapter gives a linear programming formulation of a very simple scheduling problem. From this, you can see the amount of effort needed to solve a real problem.

Review questions

13.7 What is the main output of aggregate planning?

13.8 What period would a typical aggregate plan cover?

13.9 Aggregate plans show detailed production by individual product. Do you think this is true?

13.10 What are the benefits of intuitive aggregate planning?

13.11 How can you recognise a good aggregate plan from a graph?

13.12 What are the benefits of using spreadsheets for aggregate planning?

OPERATIONS IN PRACTICE

Sigismund Major Products

Marisia Paliwoda is the operations manager of Sigismund Major Products in Warsaw, Poland. Every month she designs – or updates – the aggregate plan to cover the next six months. At the beginning of 2001 she had the following information:

Month	January	February	March	April	May	June
Forecast	80	100	125	130	150	75

The dominant market for these products is the European Union, so the company uses internal costs based on 'notional euros'. The main costs are:

- stock holding = €10 a unit held at the month end;
- shortage/back-order cost = €100 a unit a month;
- cost of moving an employee to this product from other jobs = €400 per employee;
- cost of moving an employee from this product to other jobs = €300 per employee.

At the beginning of the period, 16 people were employed, each of whom can make five units a month, and there were no stocks.

Marisia has a simple spreadsheet to help with aggregate planning. She looks at the existing plans, and then makes adjustments to allow for changing circumstances. The spreadsheet does the associated calculation, but little else. The following tables show how she developed her initial ideas.

Chase demand

No.	Period	1	2	3	4	5	6	Total
1	Forecast demand	80	100	125	130	150	75	660
2	Cumulative forecast demand	80	180	305	435	585	660	660
3	Production rate	80	100	125	130	150	75	660
4	Cumulative production	80	180	305	435	585	660	660
5	Ending inventory	0	0	0	0	0	0	0
6	Stockout/back-order	0	0	0	0	0	0	
7	Inventory carrying cost (Line 5 × €10)	0	0	0	0	0	0	0
8	Stockout cost (Line 6 × €100)	0	0	0	0	0	0	0
9	Number of employees	16	20	25	26	30	15	
10	Cost of moving employees	0	1,600	2,000	400	1,600	4,500	10,100
11	Total cost (Line 7 + Line 8 + Line 10)	0	1,600	2,000	400	1,600	4,500	10,100

Constant production rate

No.	Description	1	2	3	4	5	6	Total
1	Forecast demand	80	100	125	130	150	75	660
2	Cumulative forecast demand	80	180	305	435	585	660	660
3	Production rate	110	110	110	110	110	110	660
4	Cumulative production	110	220	330	440	550	660	660
5	Ending inventory	30	40	25	5	0	0	100
6	Stockout/back-order	0	0	0	0	35	0	35
7	Inventory carrying cost (Line 5 × €10)	300	400	250	50	0	0	1,000
8	Stockout cost (Line 6 × €100)	0	0	0	0	3,500	0	3,500
9	Number of employees	22	22	22	22	22	22	
10	Cost of moving employees	2,400	0	0	0	0	0	2,400
11	Total cost (Line 7 + Line 8 + Line 10)	2,700	400	250	50	3,500	0	6,900

▶

Mixed policy – initial plan

No.		1	2	3	4	5	6	Total
1	Forecast demand	80	100	125	130	150	75	660
2	Cumulative forecast demand	80	180	305	435	585	660	660
3	Production rate	90	90	130	130	130	90	660
4	Cumulative production	90	180	310	440	570	660	660
5	Ending inventory	10	0	5	5	0	0	20
6	Stockout/back-order	0	0	0	0	15	0	15
7	Inventory carrying cost (line 5 × €10)	100	0	50	50	0	0	200
8	Stockout costs (line 6 × €100)	0	0	0	0	1,500	0	1,500
9	Number of employees	18	18	26	26	26	18	
10	Cost of moving employees	800	0	3,200	0	0	2,400	6,400
11	Total cost	900	0	3,250	50	1,500	2,400	8,100

Project 13.1 *It is probably easiest to imagine aggregate planning in terms of goods made by a manufacturer. But the same types of planning are needed in services. Look at the products provided by British Airways – or another service company that you find interesting – and see how it approaches aggregate planning. What does it call the different levels of planning?*

Master schedule

We can expand the aggregate plan to give more details, which are shown in a **master schedule**. This master schedule 'disaggregates' the aggregate plan and shows the number of individual products to be made in, typically, each week. This detailed timetable of planned production shows the due dates or completion times of individual products. An aggregate plan of Thermaprod Inc. might show 3,000 radiators being made next month. Then the master schedule gives details for each product with, say, 150 1 m 'Superads' and 200 1.5 m 'Standrads' in week 1; 100 1.5 m 'Superads' and 225 2 m 'Stanrads' in week 2; and so on.

The **master schedule** gives a detailed timetable for making individual products.

- This schedule achieves the production specified in the aggregate plan as efficiently as possible.

The master schedule is derived from the aggregate plan, so the total production given in the master schedule must equal the production specified in the aggregate plan. There may be some differences to allow for short-term variations, incorrect forecasts, capacity constraints and so on, but these should be small.

Figure 13.18 shows a simple master schedule. Lines 2 and 3 show the monthly and quarterly production targets from the aggregate plan. Lines 6, 7 and 8 show the master schedule (for three products Alpha, Beta and Gamma) for meeting

1		Jan				Feb				Mar
2	Month	1680				1470				1520
3	Quarter	4670								
4										
5	Week	1	2	3	4	1	2	3	4	1
6	Alpha	300	250	0	100	0	300	0	150	0
7	Beta	0	400	200	200	200	120	140	200	200
8	Gamma	80	0	100	50	120	160	80	0	120
9	Totals	380	650	300	350	320	580	220	350	320
10	Planned	1680				1470				1520
11										
12	Alpha	650				450				500
13	Orders	200	80	70	50	20	10	10		
14	Committed	80	60	50	20	10				
15	Planned				40	80	60	40		
16	Forecast						30	80	110	200
17	Total	280	140	120	110	110	100	130	110	200

Figure 13.18 Part of a master schedule

these targets. Lines 9 and 10 confirm that the master schedule matches the aggregate plan.

Master schedules are designed close to the start of production, so some orders may already have been received. Then we can find the demand from:

- production specified by the aggregate plan;
- updated figures from more recent forecasts;
- actual customer orders booked for the period.

If forecasts were completely accurate, these would all give the same results. But we know that forecasts are never perfect, so this is the first chance to compare actual customer orders with forecast demand.

The bottom part of Figure 13.18 looks at demand for Alpha. Line 12 shows the planned monthly production, and line 13 shows the orders already received. Lines 14 and 15 show other intermediate stages where production is 'committed' (perhaps for orders that are expected but still being negotiated) and 'planned' (perhaps for tentative orders or other management reasons). The remaining demand is still 'forecast', as shown in line 16. There are no obvious problems here, as the master schedule for Alpha meets all the weekly targets. This table can be extended downwards to show the master schedules for Beta and Gamma, and to the right to cover more time in the future.

Project 13.2 *Have a look at the master schedule shown in Figure 13.18 and make sure that the figures are reasonable. Design a spreadsheet that can help with this kind of planning. Add some costs and design schedules for making Alpha, Beta and Gamma. What other features would be useful?*

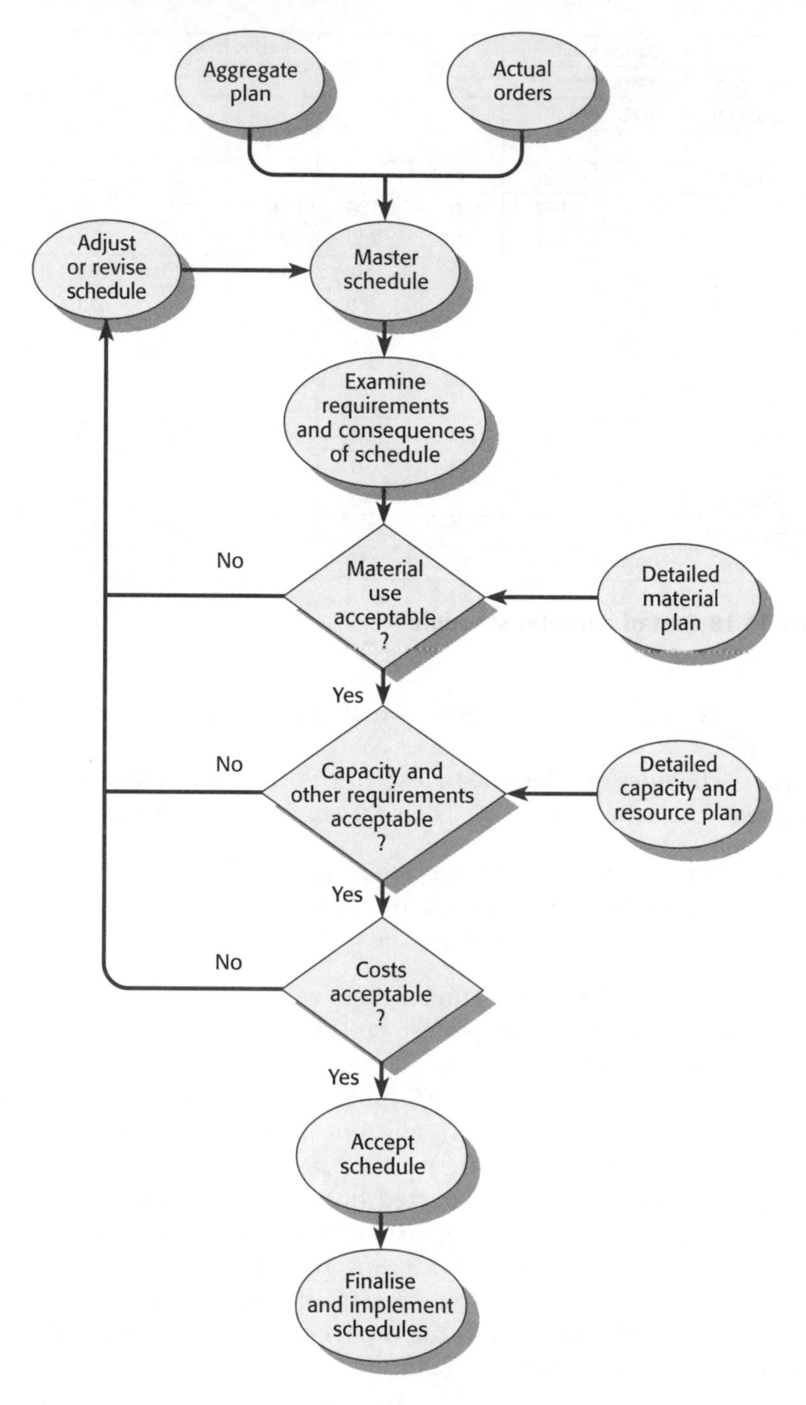

Figure 13.19 An approach to designing master schedules

Designing master schedules

In principle, designing the master schedule is similar to designing an aggregate plan, so methods again range from discussion through to mathematical models. As we are looking at lower levels and more details, plans become increasingly complicated and messy. They can involve a lot of subjective views, so master schedules are more likely to be designed by skilled schedulers using some intuitive approach. Then a general, iterative approach to designing master schedules is shown in Figure 13.19.

The iterative adjustment of master schedules can be done up to some time – say three weeks – before production, but after that it must be finalised. This is because the master schedule is used for more detailed planning of materials, people and other resources. It must, therefore, be fixed some time before production starts to allow this short-term scheduling. We will talk about these lower levels of planning in the following chapters.

WORKED EXAMPLE

Comark Bicycles produce two basic bicycles: a women's and a men's. The aggregate plan has 8,000 bicycles made next month, and 6,400 the month after. Current stocks are 500 men's and 300 women's, and the factory has a capacity of 2,200 bicycles a week. Men's bicycles usually account for 60 per cent of sales, and actual orders have been received for the following deliveries:

Week	1	2	3	4	5	6
Men's	1,400	1,200	1,000	700	300	–
Women's	2,000	800	400	100	–	–

Design a master schedule for the next eight weeks.

Solution

There are unexpectedly high sales of women's bicycles in the first week. There are 300 in stock, so Comark Bicycles have to make 1,700 more. Even using the full capacity of 2,200 bicycles a week, this leaves only enough capacity for 500 men's bicycles. These, together with current stocks of 500, still leave a shortage of 400 men's bicycles which must be met by back-orders.

In the second week the back-orders for 400 men's bicycles can be cleared together with the 1,200 actually ordered. This leaves only capacity for 600 women's bicycles, so 200 must be back-ordered to meet the 800 orders.

The aggregate plan calls for 8,000 bicycles the first month. 4,400 were made in the first two weeks, so another 1,800 should be made in each of the last two weeks. In week 3 the back-orders for 200 women's can be cleared, plus the 1,400 ordered (both men's and women's), and an additional 200 for stock (say 100 men's and 100 women's). In week 4 dividing the 1,800 into 1,080 men's and 720 women's (to match the expected 60:40 ratio) covers all orders and adds spare units to stock.

In weeks 5 to 8 the planned production of 6,400 can be divided into weekly production of 1,600 (960 men's and 640 women's). So far there are only orders for 300 units in this period, and the rest are added to stock.

This reasoning gives the following master schedule. You can see that there is an apparent build-up of stock in later weeks, as this production has not been allocated to customers yet (so this would be the stock level if no more orders were received).

Week	1	2	3	4	5	6	7	8
Men's								
Actual orders	1,400	1,200	1,000	700	300	–	–	–
Opening stock	500	−400	0	100	480	1,140	2,100	3,060
Production	500	1,600	1,100	1,080	960	960	960	960
Women's								
Actual orders	2,000	800	400	100	–	–	–	–
Opening stock	300	0	−200	100	720	1,360	2,000	2,640
Production	1,700	600	700	720	640	640	640	640
Total production	2,200	2,200	1,800	1,800	1,600	1,600	1,600	1,600
Aggregate plan	←——— 8,000 ———→				←——— 6,400 ———→			

This is, of course, only one of many feasible schedules. It has the advantages of meeting the aggregate plan and keeping production at a stable level, but we could now start looking for improvements.

This last example suggests some of the skills that schedulers need, including the ability to:

- identify all known demands – forecasts, actual sales, internal transfers, etc.;
- evaluate the conditions set by the aggregate plan and other constraints;
- make sure that existing customer orders are met;
- balance the needs of production, marketing, finance and other functions;
- design alternative plans and evaluate them;
- find improvements to plans and test them;
- identify problems and resolve them;
- communicate well with all functions.

Review questions

13.13 What is the main purpose of the master schedule?

13.14 What are the main constraints on the master schedule?

OPERATIONS IN PRACTICE

Amunsen Classical Furniture

Amunsen Classical Furniture makes a range of reproduction antique furniture in its factory outside Stockholm. It has three product lines: tables, chairs and other items. An outline of their planning is shown below.

1. The mission is an agreed statement of the directors, which states the overall aim of the company.
2. The business strategy is prepared by the directors, and shows what the company plans to do over the next five to 10 years.
3. The managing director designs a business plan for the next year. This business plan is based on projected sales and available capacity, and gives an overall view of the company's operations. Target figures are set for each month, with the following table illustrating typical values.

Summarised business plan (with values in thousand kronor)

	January	February	March	April	...	...	...	December
Sales	15,000	12,500	11,000	...	...	...	...	
Cost of sales	5,500	5,000	4,000	...	...	...		
Other costs	9,000	6,500	6,500	...	...			
Profit	500	1,000	1,500	...				
Assets employed	...	...	...	...				

4. The production manager designs aggregate plans to cover the next 12 months. The inputs to the aggregate plan include the business plan, machine capacities, workforce size, and so on. These plans are updated monthly, with the following table showing typical values.

Summarised aggregate plan (in units)

Product line	January	February	March	April	...	...	December
1. Tables	100	110	180	...	...		
2. Chairs	690	750	400	...			
3. Others	850	850	600	...			

5. The deputy production manager designs the master schedule to give production of each type of furniture over the next three months. The inputs to the master plan include the aggregate plans, actual production, customer orders, and available machine capacities. This is updated weekly, with the following table showing typical values.

Summarised master schedule (in units)

Product	Week 1	Week 2	Week 3	Week 4	5	6	7	8	9	10
Table A10	25									
Table B20		30	30							
Table C30				15						
Chair K11	250									
Chair L22		1,000	1,000							
Chair M33				2,400						
Quilt stand X19		250								
Magazine rack Y29			400							
Book case Z39	200									

Chapter review

- The operations strategy includes long-term capacity plans, which make sure that there is enough capacity to meet forecast demand. This leads to a series of lower-level tactical and operations plans.
- Resource requirement planning gives a general approach to this planning. It starts by finding the requirement for resources set by higher levels of plans, and compares these with the resources available. Then it designs alternative plans to overcome any mismatch, compares these alternatives and implements the best.

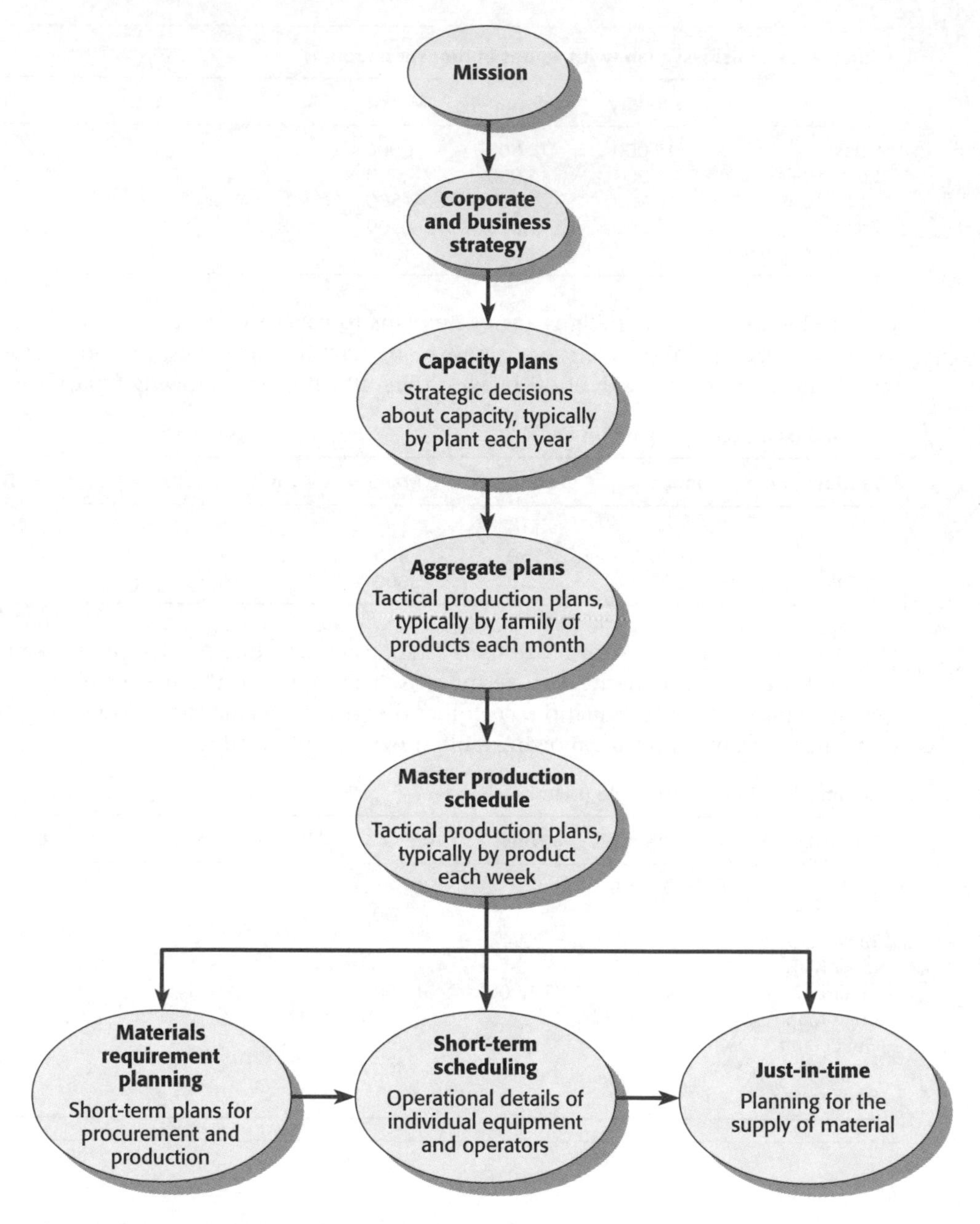

Figure 13.20 Summary of the planning process

- In practice, planning is difficult, and usually has an iterative approach to get generally acceptable results.
- Tactical plans include aggregate plans and master schedules.
- Aggregate plans give schedules for making families of products, typically for each of the next few months. The aim of aggregate planning is to meet demand, while keeping within capacity and other constraints.

- There are many ways of designing aggregate plans, ranging from negotiation, through spreadsheets, and on to mathematical models. Subjective factors and other complications mean that experienced planners usually have a significant input.
- Details are added to aggregate plans to give master schedules. These give timetables for making individual products, typically each week. Designing a master schedule is similar in principle to designing an aggregate plan, and similar methods can be used. The subjective decisions needed mean that schedulers are likely to use heuristic rules to design master schedules.
- The master schedule is used for short-term scheduling. Then the whole planning procedure is summarised in Figure 13.20.

Key terms

aggregate planning *p. 362*
capacity planning *p. 353*
hierarchy of plans *p. 354*
intuitive planning *p. 365*
master schedule *p. 376*
planning *p. 353*
planning cycle *p. 359*
programming *p. 374*
resource requirements planning *p. 356*
scheduling *p. 379*
short-term schedule *p. 354*
simulation *p. 372*
spreadsheets *p. 369*
tactical plans *p. 353*
updating procedure *p. 360*

CASE STUDY Natural Home Brewers

In 1932 James Galloway founded Natural Home Brewers outside Dundee on the eastern coast of Scotland. At the time, all the local pubs were owned by three national brewers, but a small number of independent clubs sold speciality beer, mainly imported from Scandinavia and Germany. James founded Natural Home Brewers to sell his locally brewed beer to these clubs.

The local government encouraged new industries in the area and gave him a grant. He used this, together with a personal loan from the bank, to start his company. He did most of the work himself, with help from his brother and wife.

There was a clear demand for their beers, but James was more interested in traditional brewing for the local market than making large profits. By 1945 the company was brewing 1,500 gallons a week and employed six people. Then there was a sudden surge in demand as new clubs opened in the area, and a number of pubs began selling Natural Home Brew as a special attraction. By 1955 Natural Home Brewers company was employing 120 people. At this point a national brewery made a generous offer and bought the company.

The new owners were keen to maintain the image of Natural Home Brewers and kept the name and brands. They started selling the products in their own pubs, as well as maintaining the original markets. By 1990 Natural Home Brewers employed 1,500 people. During various expansions the brewing had been largely automated and although customers thought they were buying from a local brewery, they were actually buying a fairly standard product.

The brewery is now having trouble with its planning. Several of its most experienced production planners retired in the same year, and the current planning often seems haphazard. In particular, there are times when the brewery has trouble meeting demand. Management feels that it is time to change their planning procedures, and find some way of guaranteeing reasonable schedules. Getting descriptions of the current procedures is the first step in computerising the whole planning process.

A sample of data was collected over eight months, and agreement was reached about a range of variables. Forecast demand for this period was found, in barrels, as follows:

Month	Demand	Month	Demand
January	9,000	May	6,000
February	8,000	June	8,000
March	6,000	July	10,000
April	4,000	August	10,000

Costs and manpower requirement were agreed. Although these are not necessarily exact figures they can be used for comparing plans. These include:

- production cost of £200 a barrel;
- storage cost of 1.5 per cent of production cost a month;
- shortage cost of £10 a barrel a month;
- five man-hours to produce a barrel;
- direct labour force of 225;
- standard wage rate of £8 an hour;
- overtime wage rate of 1.5 times standard rate;
- a standard working week of five days;
- hiring and training cost of £400 a person;
- lay-off cost of £500 a person;
- subcontractors can be used at an additional cost of £5 a barrel;
- opening stock is 2,000 barrels;
- a reserve stock is kept of 25 per cent of forecast monthly demand;
- all shortages are back-ordered;
- the three main products are lager, bitter and mild which generally account for 50 per cent, 40 per cent and 10 per cent of sales respectively.

Question

The management of Natural Home Brewers now wants your ideas about the plans. In particular, it wants you to design a set of alternative aggregate plans for the eight-month period, compare the costs for these plans and recommend the best. Then the management wants a master schedule for the period. For the longer term it wants a more formal procedure for designing reliable aggregate plans and master schedules.

Problems

13.1 A machine makes two different products A and B. The machine works for 250 days a year, with two eight-hour shifts a day and a utilisation of 95 per cent. Other information is as follows.

	A	B
Forecast annual demand (units)	2,100	5,600
Time to make one unit (hours)	2.0	1.5
Batch size	50	100
Set-up time per batch (hours)	5	6

If the company has three identical machines, how can it start capacity planning?

13.2 Hazelbank Fibres has monthly demand (in tonnes) for a family of products as shown below. Use intuitive reasoning to suggest an aggregate production schedule for the products.

Month	1	2	3	4	5	6	7
Aggregate demand	90	120	100	120	180	270	225

13.3 George Martyn forecasts monthly demand for a family of products as shown below. At the end of each month he assigns a notional holding cost of £20 to every unit held in stock. If there are shortages, 20 per cent of orders are lost with a cost of £200 a unit, and the rest are met by back-orders, with a cost of £50 a unit. Each time the production rate is changed it costs £15,000. Designed capacity of the process is 400 units a month, but utilisation seldom reaches 80 per cent. Use a graphical method to design an aggregate plan for the products.

Month	1	2	3	4	5	6	7	8
Aggregate demand	310	280	260	300	360	250	160	100

13.4 The aggregate demand for a family of products for the next five months is 190, 120, 270, 200 and 140 units. Normal capacity is 150 units a month, overtime has a capacity of 10 units a month and subcontractors can handle any amount of production. The unit cost is \$100 for normal capacity, \$125 for overtime and \$140 from subcontractors. It costs \$15 to stock a unit for a month, while back-orders have a penalty cost of \$100 a month. Use a spreadsheet to design an aggregate plan for the products.

13.5 The aggregate plan of DHR Tubing has 12,000, 10,000 and 10,000 metres of pipework made in the next three months. The management wants a master schedule for two products, A and B. Current stocks are 700 metres of A and 500 metres of B, and the factory has a capacity of 3,000 metres a week. Sales of A are usually twice as large as sales of B, and actual orders have been received for deliveries of:

Week	1	2	3	4	5	6	7
A	2,100	1,800	1,600	1,100	800	200	–
B	3,000	1,400	700	400	100	–	–

Design a master schedule for the next 12 weeks.

Discussion questions

13.1 Planning is only done by manufacturers who can keep stocks of their goods. Services do not need this planning, as they are forced to match their production to customer demand. Do you think this is true?

13.2 What kind of planning would you expect to see in a firm of management consultants? Where would the planning start? What results would they want? Would you expect to see the same types of planning in every other organisation?

13.3 All lower levels of planning are derived from the long-term forecasts and capacity plans. But these are notoriously inaccurate. Does this mean that all planning in an organisation is based on little more than informed guesswork?

13.4 Why do people say that planning is difficult? Plans simply give a timetable for the production of products – surely this cannot be so complicated?

13.5 What do you think are the advantages of level operations? If these are significant, why do some organisations clearly have a 'hire and fire' policy for staff? How can contractors, who have major variations in their workload, do any planning?

13.6 What advantages do human schedulers have over computers? What are the benefits of automated scheduling? Why not get the benefits of both in expert systems?

13.7 Spreadsheets are widely used in planning. Why? Design a spreadsheet that can be used for planning. How does this compare with commercial packages?

13.8 For their aggregate plans, most organisations assume that their employees are willing – at least to some extent – to work the hours dictated by the organisation. What are the consequences of this in terms of fatigue, stress, staff turnover, etc.? Are there any particular problems when the employees are doctors, nurses, pilots, truck drivers, etc.?

Selected reading

Brandimarte P. and Villa A. (eds) (1999) *Modelling Manufacturing Systems*. Berlin: Springer Verlag.

Browne J., Harhen J. and Shivnan J. (1996) *Production Management Systems*. 2nd edn. Reading, MA: Addison-Wesley.

Dauzere-Peres S. and Lasserve J.B. (1994) *An Integrated Approach to Production Planning and Scheduling*. Berlin: Springer Verlag.

Fogarty D.W., Blackstone J.H. and Hoffman T.R. (1991) *Production and Inventory Management*. 2nd edn. Cincinnati, OH: South-Western.

Hess R. (1997) *Managerial Spreadsheet Modelling and Analysis*. Chicago: Irwin.

Lindbeck J.R. and Wygant R.M. (1994) *Product Design and Manufacture*. Englewood Cliffs, NJ: Prentice-Hall.

Proud J.F. (1999) *Master Scheduling*. 3rd edn. New York: John Wiley.

Vollman T.E., Berry W.L. and Whybark D.C. (1996) *Manufacturing Planning and Control Systems*. 4th edn. New York: McGraw-Hill.

Useful Websites

Some personal views are given in:
www.hometown.aol.com/williamfla.html
www.mscmqa.ms.ic.ac.uk/jeb/or/masprod.html

SUPPLEMENT TO CHAPTER 13

Planning with linear programming

Linear programming gives a way of finding optimal solutions, at least in the technical sense, to many different scheduling problems. The following worked example illustrates the approach to one problem.

WORKED EXAMPLE

A company is designing an aggregate plan. Some important factors are inventory levels, changes in production rate and availability of workers. There are costs for:

- supplying a unit of product;
- holding stocks;
- every unit of unmet demand;
- amount of overtime used;
- amount of undertime used (that is normal working time which is not used);
- increase in production rate;
- decrease in production rate.

The immediate objective is to minimise total costs. How would you formulate this as a linear programme?

Solution

We can start by defining the costs as:

C_V = variable cost of supplying a unit
C_H = cost of holding a unit of stock for a unit time
C_S = shortage cost per unit of unmet demand
C_O = additional cost per unit made with overtime
C_U = cost per unit of undertime
C_I = cost of increasing the production rate
C_R = cost of reducing the production rate

There are two other constants:

D_t = demand in period t
N_t = normal capacity in period t

Now we can define the variables:

P_t = production in period t
H_t = stock held at the end of period t
S_t = shortage, or unmet demand in period t
O_t = units produced on overtime in period t
U_t = units of undertime in period t
I_t = increase in production rate during period t
R_t = reduction in production rate during period t

With these values we can define the objective function as minimising the total cost:

$$\text{Minimise } \{C_V P_t + C_H H_t + C_S S_t + C_O O_t + C_U U_t + C_I I_t + C_R R_t\}$$

There are constraints that hold for every period:

- supply and demand must be balanced:

$$H_t = H_{t-1} + P_t - D_t + U_t$$

- Total production must equal normal production plus overtime minus undertime:

$$P_t = N_t + O_t - U_t$$

- Changes in production rates are consistent with production in each period:

$$P_t - P_{t-1} = I_t - R_t$$

This example is a very simple version of a real problem, but for a 12-month period it still needs accurate values for seven costs, 24 constants, 84 variables and 36 constraints. Problems of any real size and complexity soon become unwieldy. So linear programming has the disadvantage of being complicated and needing a lot of effort, skills and experience. It is also difficult to understand, time-consuming, expensive, needs a lot of reliable data, and the model still may not be a good description of the real situation. On the other hand, it has the advantage of guaranteeing an 'optimal' solution.

If you are thinking of using linear programming for an aggregate plan, you must balance the costs against the benefits. In operations like oil companies, small variations from optimal plans give much higher costs, so linear programming is always used for aggregate planning. In most other organisations small variations from optimal plans add relatively little extra cost. Then aggregate planning usually relies on intuition, graphical methods, spreadsheets or some other simple approach.

CHAPTER 14

Short-term scheduling

Those who make the worst use of their time are the first to complain of its brevity.

Jean de la Bruyère

Characters, 1688

Contents

Aims of the chapter

After reading this chapter you should be able to:

- see how short-term schedules fit in with other planning;
- appreciate the aims of short-term scheduling;
- use a variety of simple scheduling rules;
- see how to extend these rules to more complicated problems;
- solve some specific problems of scheduling services and people;
- appreciate the use and importance of control systems.

Main themes

This chapter will emphasise:

- **short-term schedules**, which give timetables for all the resources used in a process;
- **scheduling rules**, which give reasonable solutions to a range of problems;
- **control of schedules**, to make sure the operations are done as scheduled.

OPERATIONS IN PRACTICE

Ceska Language School

Radka Kubat is the co-ordinator of programmes in the Ceska Language School in Prague. This school gives training in several languages, but most of their work helps Czech executives improve their English. The school employs a varying number of teachers to work with small groups of managers. The school has some central facilities, but each programme is specially tailored and teachers normally travel to company offices.

At the start of every month Radka has a familiar problem.

It should be easy. I know how many clients have booked lessons next month, and I know roughly how many more will sign-up during the month. All clients have conditions about the languages and levels they want, when and where they want lessons, how long they want, and who they want to give the lessons. I have five full-time and up to 40 part-time teachers. All teachers have different language skills, conditions about when they want to work, the hours they have available, where they will travel to, who they will teach, and so on. All I want to do is match the teachers to the clients and make everyone happy. I also have to schedule four classrooms, six cars, a small language laboratory, laptop computers and associated software to help with teaching.

Why does it take me so long to schedule everything? And why are there always last-minute problems and disagreements?

Purpose of scheduling

Definitions

The last two chapters have shown how organisations start with strategic plans and move down to tactical aggregate plans and master schedules. At this stage they have timetables for making individual products. But this is not the end to planning, as we now have to organise resources for making the products. In other words, we have to design timetables for jobs, equipment, people, materials, facilities and all other resources that are needed by the production plans. This is the purpose of short-term scheduling.

Short-term schedules give detailed timetables for jobs, people, materials, equipment and any other resources used in the process.

Short-term schedules show the sequence of jobs done in the process, and the times when they are done. They also show timetables for the use of resources used to support the operations. 'Sam the Fridge's' repair service, for example, has a schedule of customers to visit (giving the order and time of jobs) and the resources needed (the repair people, tools, spare parts, vans, and so on needed for the jobs).

You can imagine short-term scheduling in a football club. At the beginning of a season the club gets a master schedule to show all the matches it will play during the season. Then it has to arrange the resources for these matches, such as trainers, grass cutters, line painters, people to work on the gates, physiotherapists, catering,

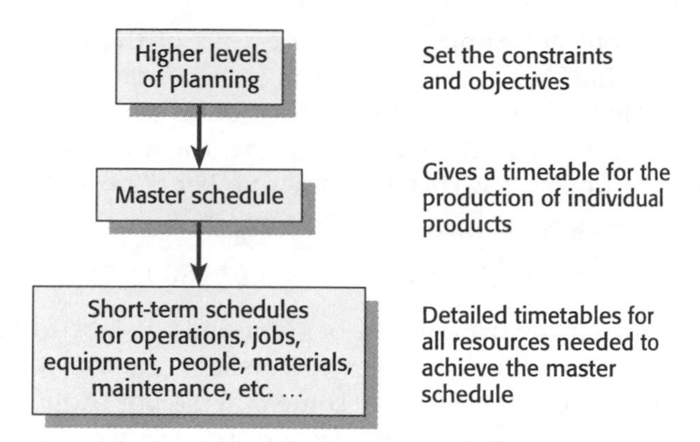

Figure 14.1 The role of short-term schedules

transport to away games, and so on. In other words, the club has to design timetables – or short-term schedules – for these resources.

Some other examples of schedules are:

- University of Sheffield's schedules for classes, rooms, instructors and students;
- Cathay Pacific's schedules for aeroplanes, pilots, flight attendants and food;
- *Guardian* newspaper's schedules for reporters, editors, compositors and presses;
- Leicester Royal Infirmary's schedules for patients, nurses, beds and operating theatres;
- Allen Marsh Furniture's schedules for customer orders, employees, machines, material purchases and shipping of completed orders.

Designing these operational schedules is one of the most common problems in any organisation (see Figure 14.1). Every resource needs some kind of schedule, or else the operations – and the overall process – would be disorganised and chaotic.

The aim of short-term scheduling is generally phrased in terms of achieving the master production schedule, while using resources efficiently.

The **aim** of short-term scheduling is to design timetables for the operations and resources needed to achieve the production specified in the master schedule.

- The schedules should use resources efficiently to give low costs and high utilisations.

As well as these general aims, short-term scheduling can have many other goals, such as minimising the time customers wait for a product, minimising the processing time, meeting promised delivery dates, keeping stock levels low, minimising costs, giving preferred working patterns, and so forth.

Difficulty of scheduling

You might think that short-term scheduling seems rather easy. The master schedule tells you what to make, so you just add some details and allocate available resources to operations. In practice, it is notoriously difficult. To start with there are many possible schedules to consider. Suppose you write a list of the jobs that you must finish today, and find that there are ten of them. In how many different ways can you arrange the 10 jobs? You can choose the first job as any one of the 10; then the second job can be any one of the remaining nine, the third job can be any one of the remaining eight, and so on. This gives the number of possible schedules you have to consider as:

$$10 \times 9 \times 8 \times 7 \times 6 \times 5 \times 4 \times 3 \times 2 \times 1 = 10! = 3{,}628{,}800$$

If you have a real problem with hundreds or thousands of jobs to schedule, you have a huge number of possible schedules to consider. Each of these schedules has different features, and performs well by some criteria, but badly by others. You have to balance these factors, and take into account the many complicating factors that appear in real problems, such as:

- the patterns of job arrivals;
- amount and type of equipment needed;
- number and skills of people assigned to jobs;
- materials needed for operations;
- patterns of work flow through equipment;
- different priority of jobs;
- disruptions caused by customer changes, breakdowns, etc.;
- methods of evaluating schedules;
- objectives of the schedulers.

OPERATIONS IN PRACTICE

Scheduling at Sentinel Taxis

Sentinel Taxis have a fleet of 120 cars working around Madrid. They employ 150 full-time drivers, each of whom works an average of 40 hours a week. Sentinel also employ a varying number of part-time drivers. Usually there are around 100 of these, but at busy times there can be up to 200. Their aim is to keep the taxis in use for almost 24 hours a day.

The taxis are maintained in Sentinel's garage. This has four bays, six full-time mechanics, two part-time mechanics and four apprentices.

Sentinel also employ 12 controllers. These take telephone calls from customers, schedule the work, and pass instructions on to taxis. The controllers keep a continuous check on the location and work of each taxi.

You can already see that Sentinel have to do a range of scheduling. They start by scheduling the hours worked by cars, so that there are always enough taxis on the road to meet demand from customers. Then they schedule the drivers to make sure that there are enough drivers for the cars. The controllers design routes for each cab, starting with customers who make advance bookings and a list of regular customers who have block bookings. These routes are continually modified as customers telephone in with new jobs (which are assigned to the nearest car with enough free time) or the cars pick up passengers who hail them on the streets.

As well as scheduling the cars, drivers and routes, the controllers design schedules for the maintenance and repair of cars, other internal work in the garage, work for external customers of the garage, hours worked by all other staff, purchase of parts and materials, cleaning and maintaining the building, staff training and all other operations of the business.

The result is that apparently simple scheduling jobs are very difficult to solve in practice. Sam Eilon noted that this type of problem 'has become famous for its ease of statement and great difficulty of solution'.[1]

Notice that we have started talking in terms of 'jobs' being scheduled on equipment. This is just for convenience, as scheduling occurs almost everywhere. We all schedule our own time; buses and trains work to schedules; delivery vehicles use drop-lists that show when to visit customers; classes are scheduled into rooms; newspapers have print schedules; doctors have appointment books; television channels have schedules of programmes; and so on. When describing 'jobs' on equipment we are using one type of process to illustrate an approach to a very widely occurring problem.

Review questions

14.1 What are short-term schedules?

14.2 What are the main aims of short-term scheduling?

14.3 What factors should you consider when designing short-term schedules?

Approaches to scheduling

Typical scheduling problem

In Chapter 9 we looked at jobbing processes. These have different types of equipment, and each batch of units – or **job** – goes through different equipment in a different order (as shown in Figure 14.2). As you can imagine, with a large number

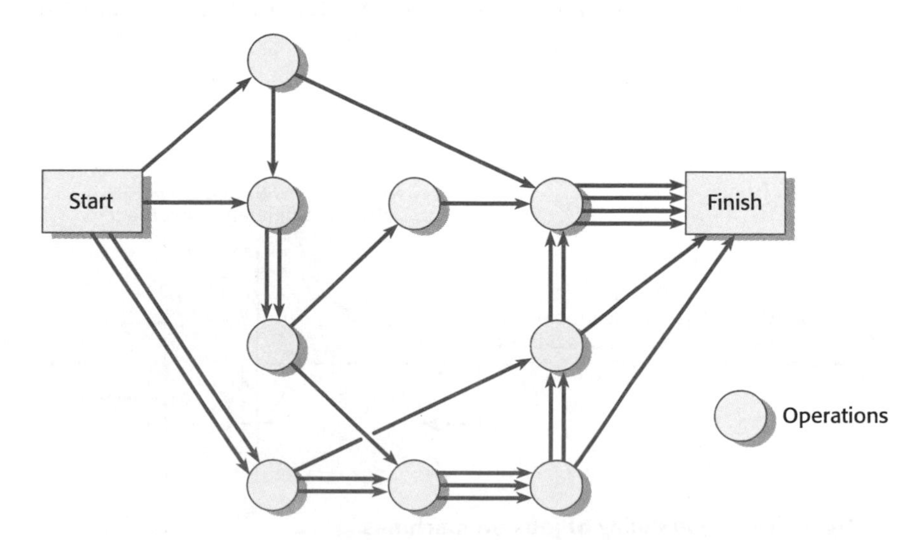

Figure 14.2 Complex flow of work in a jobbing process

of jobs and pieces of equipment, there is a huge number of ways of arranging the jobs. Each of these schedules performs differently; some give higher utilisations of equipment, some give fast delivery, some give fewer set-ups, and so on. Schedulers have to look at the possible schedules, and find one that achieves their specific objectives.

This example of a jobbing process illustrates a standard scheduling problem. You have a set of jobs waiting to use a set of equipment, and you want to organise the jobs to achieve some objective, such as high utilisation of resources. But remember that we are just using the terms 'jobs' and 'equipment' for convenience, and they actually refer to a wide range of circumstances.

In practice, schedulers can have many objectives, including high utilisation of equipment, minimum waiting time, minimum total processing time, reducing the maximum lateness, giving low stocks of work in progress, minimising costs, reducing changes to machines or some other objective. Usually, the most relevant comes from the operations strategy. If the organisation is competing by speed of delivery, the schedules try to move units through as quickly as possible; if the operations strategy focuses on low costs, the schedules support this by looking for high utilisation. Then the problem is to find the sequence of jobs that comes closest to achieving the objectives – or at least achieves some satisfactory level of performance.

Forward and backward scheduling

Consider a basic scheduling problem (shown in Figure 14.3) where we have a queue of jobs waiting to be processed on various equipment.

We know from the master schedule when the jobs have to be finished, and they may have to be ready for a specific customer order. So schedules must take into account the due date of products. There are two ways of doing this.

- **Forward scheduling**: schedulers know the start date for the first operation, then they can work through all operations needed for a job and find the date when it will be finished.

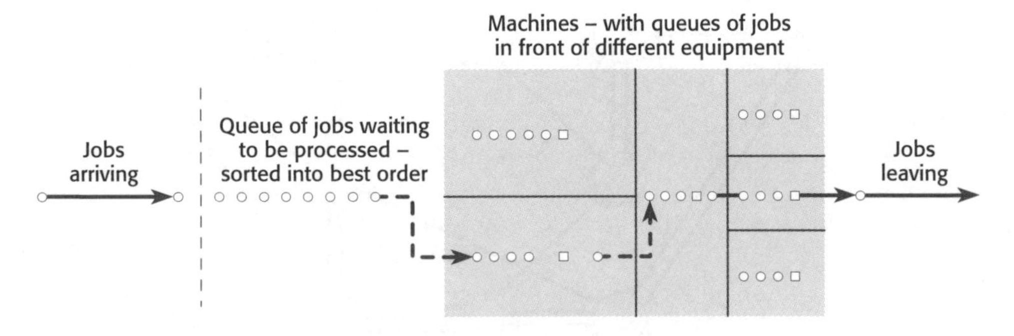

Figure 14.3 Scheduling of jobs on machines

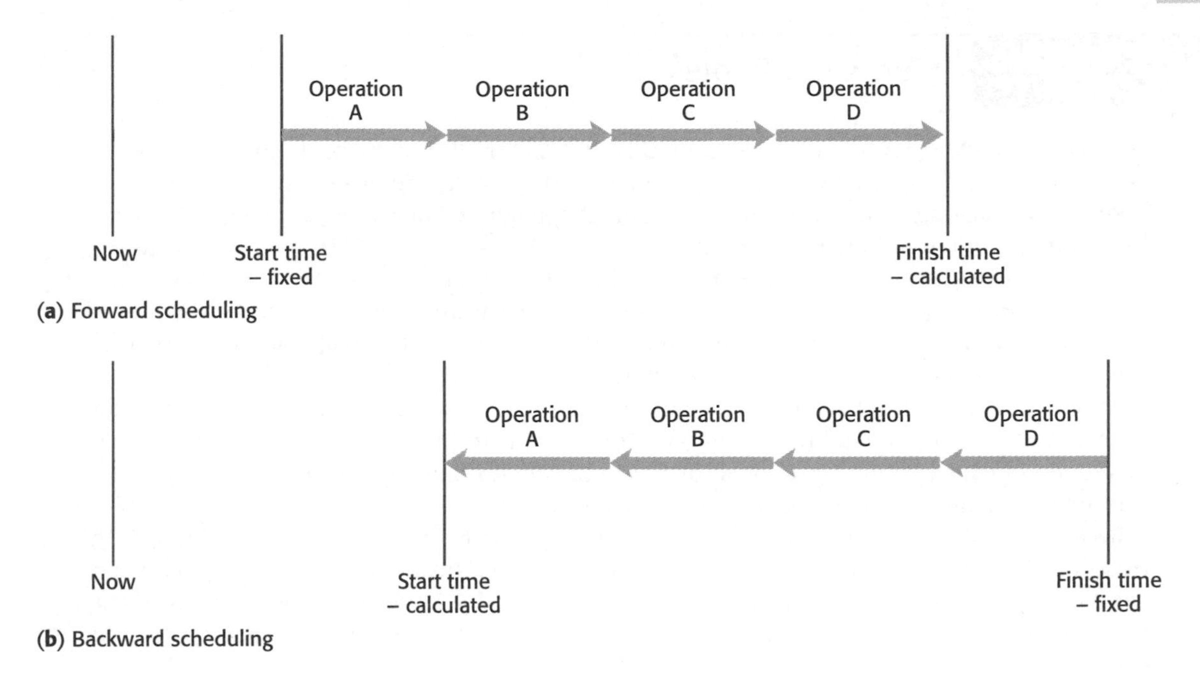

Figure 14.4 Setting times for schedules

- **Backward scheduling**: the customer gives a due date. This due date is the finish date for the last operation, so the schedulers must work back through the operations to find the date when the job must be started.

Suppose you are giving a talk in three weeks' time and want some photographs to illustrate this. It will take one week to prepare the photographs. With forward scheduling, you prepare the photographs as early as possible – starting now and finishing next week. With backward scheduling you know that the photographs must be ready in three weeks, so you can prepare them in two weeks' time.

The main benefit of forward scheduling is that work is done early, and any problems are noticed in time to solve them. There may also be advantages in giving customers their products early – before their due dates – and getting earlier payment. Backward scheduling has the benefits of reducing the effects of last-minute changes to specifications, and lowering some costs (such as materials which are bought nearer the delivery date).

Rather than make a choice between forward and backward scheduling, organisations are often forced into one or the other. If there is strong competition in a buyer's market, or if speed of delivery is an important way to compete, organisations have to specify a delivery time and then arrange operations to achieve this. External conditions force organisations into backward scheduling. If there is less competition in a seller's market, or competition is not based on delivery speed, organisations have more flexibility to set their own delivery dates. Internal conditions control the choice of delivery date through forward scheduling.

OPERATIONS IN PRACTICE

Marc's Car Bodies

For many years Marc West worked for a local Ford dealer in Birmingham. He specialised in car body repairs, and was well known for his high-quality work. When he started his own car body shop, Marc knew that it would be difficult. Although he knew a lot about repairing cars, he had no experience of managing a business.

One problem that surprised Marc was the difficulty of planning his work. He knew that scheduling was very important, because customers always want their cars back quickly and at the promised time. But this was more difficult than it seemed. The main problem was that every job seemed to take a different – and often unpredictable – time.

At 8:00 a.m. one Monday morning, a customer brought in a car for repairs. It needed a lot of work on the body, including welding, finishing and painting. Marc thought that it would take one hour for welding, two hours for finishing and 1.5 hours for painting. The customer wanted to pick up the car at 5:00 p.m. on the same day.

Because of the emphasis on delivery times, Marc generally used backward scheduling. On this occasion he did some experiments to compare different approaches, and to see what would happen if a second car arrived at 9:00 a.m. needing 1.5 hours of work in each of the three areas, followed by a third car arriving at 12.00 a.m. for one hour of emergency work in each area.

For the single car he designed the following two schedules:

Forward scheduling		*Backward scheduling*	
08.00	Start welding	12.30	Start welding
09.00	Start finishing	13.30	Start finishing
11.00	Start painting	15.30	Start painting
12.30	Car is finished	17.00	Car is finished

With a second car arriving, Marc used common sense to get the following forward schedule:

08.00	Start welding car 1
09.00	Start welding car 2
10.30	Start finishing car 2
12.00	Start painting car 2
13.30	Car 2 finished; start finishing car 1
15.30	Start painting car 1
17.00	Car 1 is finished

If a third car arrived, it would not fit into the working day. Marc would have to assign some priority to decide which car would not be finished until 20.00 at the earliest.

Source: Marc West (2001) 'Scheduling for Customer Satisfaction', Talk to the Western Management Circle, 14 March

Scheduling rules

People have tried many methods to get optimal solutions to scheduling problems. In the last chapter we mentioned methods like linear programming, simulation and expert systems to get good solutions. Unfortunately, these are so complicated that they are difficult to use for real problems, and they always involve a lot of effort. For many organisations this effort is simply not worthwhile, so the most effective way of scheduling is to use simple rules that give reasonable results. You meet one of these rules in banks, which schedule customer service at their teller windows in the order of first-come first-served. We can develop many other rules for different circumstances. If, for example, you have a number of reports to write, it makes sense to use a rule such as 'most important first'.

If you have a number of 'jobs' waiting to use a single piece of equipment, then the total processing time is fixed regardless of the order in which the jobs are scheduled (provided that the set-up time for each job is constant, regardless of the job that was done previously). But the order of taking jobs does change other measures of performance. You can see this in the following four standard scheduling rules.

1. *First-come first-served.* This is the most obvious scheduling rule and simply takes jobs in the order they arrive. It assumes no priority, no urgency, or any other measure of relative importance. The drawback with this rule is that urgent or important jobs may be delayed while less urgent or important ones are being processed. The benefits are simplicity, ease of use and a clear fairness. Most queues are based on this system, and when you are standing in a long line it is reassuring to know that everyone is being treated in the same way.

2. *Most urgent job first.* This rule assigns an importance, or urgency, to each job and they are processed in order of decreasing urgency. Emergency departments in hospitals, for example, treat those who are most seriously in need first. A manufacturer can check when current stocks of parts will run out – then the most urgent jobs are those that replenish parts that will run out soonest. The benefit of this rule is that more important jobs have higher priority. Unfortunately, jobs that have low priority may be stuck at the end of a queue for a very long time. (Having part-finished jobs waiting a long time for processing is generally a sign of poor planning.)

3. *Shortest job first.* A useful objective is to minimise the average time spent in the system, where:

Time in the system = processing time + waiting time

If a job needs one day of processing but it waits in the queue for four days, its time in the system is five days. (Again, having a job wait so long is generally a sign of poor planning.)

Taking the jobs in order of increasing duration minimises the average time spent in the system. It allows those jobs that can be done quickly to move on through the system, while longer jobs are left until later. The disadvantage is that long jobs can spend a long time waiting.

4. *Earliest due date first.* This sorts jobs into order of delivery date, and those which are due earliest are processed first. This has the benefit of minimising the maximum lateness of jobs, but again some jobs may wait a long time.

Each of these rules is useful in particular circumstances. Students doing coursework, for example, often use such rules implicitly, without necessarily thinking about their methods. Some students do work in the order it is set, using a first-come first-served basis; a more common approach is to do coursework in the order it is due (most urgent first, which in this case is the same as earliest due date first). If students develop a backlog of coursework, they may do the shortest first. This clears their desks quickly, but minimising the time coursework is in the system may be a questionable objective.

WORKED EXAMPLE

You have the following six jobs to schedule on a piece of equipment. Each job fully occupies the equipment for the duration specified.

Job	A	B	C	D	E	F
Duration in days	6	4	2	8	1	5

Assume that you are now at some notional starting point of zero:

(a) How long would it take to finish all jobs if you scheduled them in order of arrival?
(b) What schedule would minimise average time in the system?
(c) Suppose each job makes a batch of products that is put into stock. If the demand for these products and current stock levels are as follows, what schedule would you suggest?

Job	A	B	C	D	E	F
Demand	10	15	40	2	5	80
Current stock	260	195	880	20	75	1,280

(d) Returning to the basic problem, suppose each job has been promised to customers by the following dates. What schedule would minimise the maximum lateness?

Job	A	B	C	D	E	F
Due date	6	20	22	24	2	10

Solution

(a) Using the rule first-come first-served gives the schedule:

Job	Duration	Start	Finish
A	6	0	6
B	4	6	10
C	2	10	12
D	8	12	20
E	1	20	21
F	5	21	26

The jobs are finished by day 26. Every sequence is going to give this same completion time, but they will perform differently when judged by other measures (see Figure 14.5).

(b) We can minimise the average time in the system by taking jobs in the order of 'shortest first'. This gives the schedule:

Job	Duration	Start	Finish
E	1	0	1
C	2	1	3
B	4	3	7
F	5	7	12
A	6	12	18
D	8	18	26

The average time in the system, which is the same as the average finish time, is 67/6 = 11.2 days (compared with 95/6 = 15.8 days for 'first-come first-served'). By day 18 this schedule has finished five jobs, while the previous schedule had only finished three.

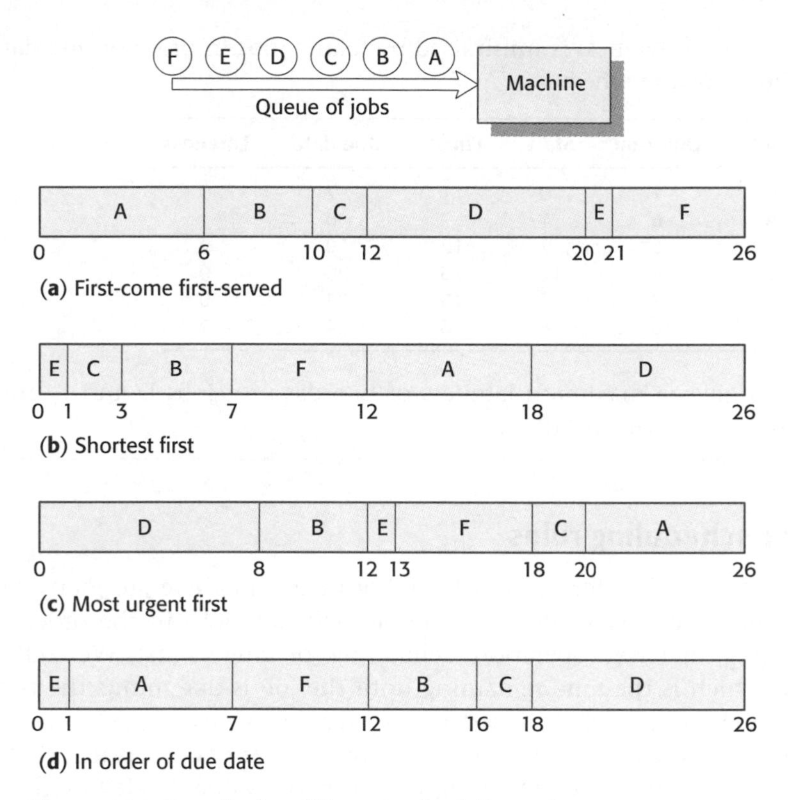

Figure 14.5 Results for different scheduling rules

(c) It would be sensible to schedule the jobs in order of urgency, where urgency is measured by the number of days of remaining stock. We can find this from the current stock divided by the demand.

Job	A	B	C	D	E	F
Stock remaining	260	195	880	20	75	1,280
Demand	10	15	40	2	5	80
Day's stock remaining	26	13	22	10	15	16
Order of urgency	6	2	5	1	3	4

This gives the schedule:

Job	Days' stock remaining	Duration	Start	Finish
D	10	8	0	8
B	13	4	8	12
E	15	1	12	13
F	16	5	13	18
C	22	2	18	20
A	26	6	20	26

All jobs are finished before the products are due to run out, except F where stocks run out two days before the job is finished.

(d) Maximum lateness is minimised by taking jobs in order of due date. This gives the following schedule:

Job	Duration	Start	Finish	Due date	Lateness
E	1	0	1	2	0
A	6	1	7	6	1
F	5	7	12	10	2
B	4	12	16	20	0
C	2	16	18	22	0
D	8	18	26	24	2

This gives a maximum lateness of two days for jobs D and F, and an average lateness of 5/6 = 0.8 days.

Other scheduling rules

We have only described four scheduling rules, but there are many others for different purposes. We could, for example, schedule jobs in the order of least work remaining, or fewest operations remaining, or longest first. We could look at the **slack** (which is the time remaining until the job is due minus the time needed to complete it) and schedule in order of smallest slack first.

One commonly used rule schedules jobs in order of decreasing **critical ratio**. The critical ratio is the time remaining until the job is due divided by the time needed to complete it.

$$\text{Critical ratio} = \frac{\text{due date} - \text{today's date}}{\text{time needed for the job}}$$

If this ratio is low, the time to complete the job is short compared with the time available and the job becomes urgent. If the ratio is high, there is plenty of time left and the job is less urgent. In particular, if the critical ratio is:

- less than zero, the job is already late;
- between zero and one, the job is behind schedule, but not yet late;
- equal to one, the job is exactly on schedule;
- greater than one, the job is ahead of schedule.

The critical ratio changes as jobs move through the process, so priorities also change.

Review questions

14.4 Why do organisations rarely use optimal short-term schedules?

14.5 What is a scheduling rule?

14.6 Which scheduling rules might you use for:
(a) hospital admission;
(b) selling fresh cream cakes;
(c) telephone calls;
(d) writing reports for consulting clients?

14.7 Are the scheduling rules described the only ones worth considering?

OPERATIONS IN PRACTICE

Wrightson Duplication

Wrightson Duplication reproduces any kind of document. Most of its customers are businesses which deliver documents during the working day and want copies within 24 hours. These jobs might need typesetting, formatting, scanning, graphics work, printing, photocopying, collating, stapling, binding, folding, putting in envelopes or a range of other operations.

Wrightson has about 50 paper-handling machines that are organised as a job shop. When a job arrives, a receptionist puts it in a standard box, together with a form describing the work to be done, and the route through the various machines. The box is put into a queue in front of the first machine it needs and waits for the machine to become free. When the job is finished on one machine, the operator checks it, and passes it to the queue in front of the next machine it needs. This is repeated until the job is sent to a finishing area, where it is checked, costed and left for the customer to collect.

When Wrightson first opened, the boxes were taken in the order of first-come first-served. This led to complaints from some customers, especially those with short, urgent jobs that had to wait behind longer, less urgent ones. Wrightson quickly added an order code, based on length and urgency, to each job description. Taking the jobs in order of this code reduced complaints, but the flow of work was sometimes erratic and some jobs were left waiting for several days.

Eventually Wrightson bought a computerised scheduling system from a local consultant. This scans the job description form for all new jobs and finds the requirements, length, urgency, customer and any other relevant information. Then it compares the new job with existing schedules and automatically revises the schedules, adding the new job in the best positions. It does this using a hierarchy of scheduling rules that were originally developed in a local factory. Whenever a job leaves one of the machines, an operator updates the computer, which then signals the next job to be done.

This scheduling system virtually eliminated all customer complaints. It also gives a variety of data to managers who feel it is largely responsible for an increase of 200 per cent in workload over the past three years. The computer system cost £40,000 to install and it paid for itself within six months.

Project 14.1 *Have a look at the timetables for a local railway company – or any other organisation that you find particularly interesting. What factors had to be taken into account when designing these schedules? How do you think they did the scheduling? Can you see any way that they could be improved?*

More complicated schedules

Johnson's Rule

We can extend the simple scheduling rules by designing more complicated versions. A parcel delivery service, for example, could design routes for its delivery vans using scheduling rules based on guaranteed delivery times, distance travelled, journey time, importance of each parcel, order in which they are put into the vans, ease of delivery, and so on. Unfortunately, as the rules get more complicated, they become more specific and deal with a narrower range of circumstances.

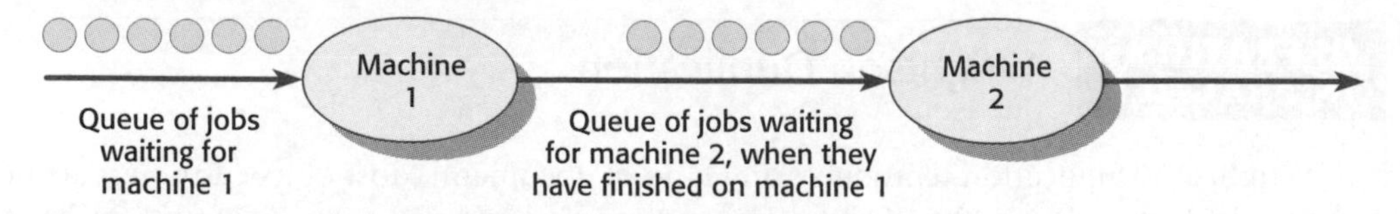

Figure 14.6 A two-machine scheduling problem

One rule that is a bit more general looks at a problem where there are only two machines, and every job is processed on machine 1 followed by machine 2 (as shown in Figure 14.6). This may seem a fairly limited problem, but we can extend the approach to deal with other circumstances.

For this we can use Johnson's Rule.[2] This gives the minimum **makespan**, which is the time between starting the first job and finishing the last job. There are four steps in Johnson's Rule.

- *Step 1.* List the jobs and their processing time on each machine.
- *Step 2.* Find the job with the next shortest processing time on either machine.
- *Step 3.* If this processing time is on machine 1, schedule the job as early as possible without moving jobs already scheduled; if the processing time is on machine 2, schedule the job as late as possible without moving any jobs already scheduled.
- *Step 4.* Repeat steps 2 and 3, at each stage ignoring all jobs that have already been scheduled, and working inwards from the ends of the sequences. Stop when all jobs have been scheduled.

WORKED EXAMPLE

A series of four jobs has to be processed on machine 1 followed by machine 2. The hours needed on each machine are as follows. Design a schedule that minimises the makespan.

Job	A	B	C	D
Time on machine 1	30	20	60	80
Time on machine 2	50	40	10	70

Solution

- *Step 1* of Johnson's rule has been done, and we now have a list of jobs and their processing times.
- *Step 2* finds the shortest processing time as job C on machine 2.
- *Step 3* recognises that this is on machine 2, so the job is scheduled as late as possible. This gives a sequence which is currently:

  . . . C.

- *Step 4* now ignores job C and returns to step 2.
- *Step 2* finds the shortest remaining processing time (from jobs A, B and D) as job B on machine 1.
- *Step 3* recognises this is on machine 1, so the job is scheduled as early as possible to give the sequence:

  B . . . C.

Now we continue cycling around steps 2, 3 and 4 until we schedule all the jobs.

- Ignoring jobs already scheduled, the shortest remaining processing time (for jobs A and D) is job A on machine 1. This is scheduled as early as possible to give the sequence:

  B A . . . C.

- Now ignoring job A as well, the shortest remaining processing time is job D on machine 2. This is scheduled as late as possible to give the final sequence of:

  B A D C

Then the finished schedule, assuming a notional starting time of 0, is:

	Machine 1			Machine 2		
Job	**Duration**	**Start**	**Finish**	**Duration**	**Start**	**Finish**
B	2	0	2	4	2	6
A	3	2	5	5	6	11
D	8	5	13	7	13	20
C	6	13	19	1	20	21

You can see from the table that jobs can only start on machine 2 when they have finished on machine 1 and when the previous job on machine 2 has finished. So job B has to wait until job A is finished before it can start, while job D is only held up by the time it takes on machine 1.

The makespan with this solution is 21 days, which compares with a makespan of 26 days for 'first-come first-served' (shown in Figure 14.7).

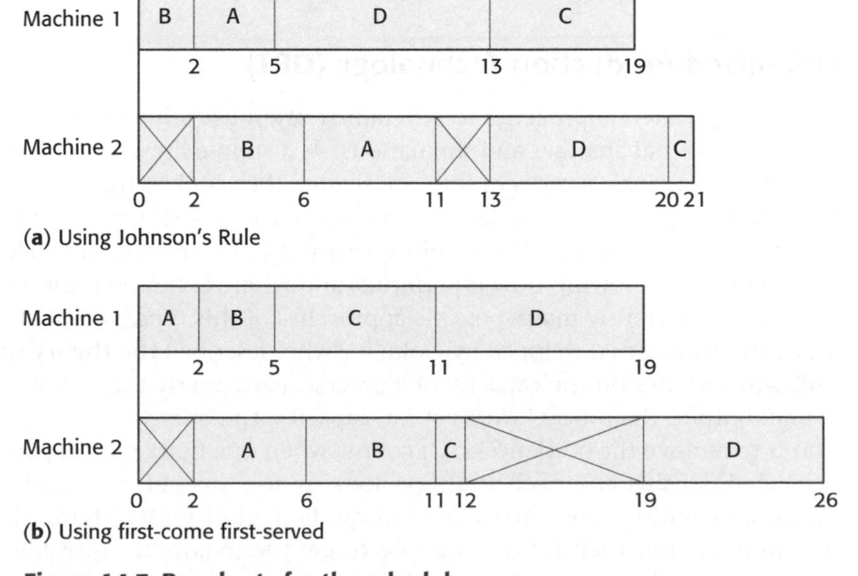

Figure 14.7 Bar charts for the schedule

	Machine 1			Machine 2		
Job	**Duration**	**Start**	**Finish**	**Duration**	**Start**	**Finish**
A	2	0	2	4	2	6
B	3	2	5	5	6	11
C	6	5	11	1	11	12
D	8	11	19	7	19	26

OPERATIONS IN PRACTICE

Satellite communications

Long-distance television, radio, telephone and data communications are transmitted through satellite networks. Each satellite, such as INTELSAT and EUTELSAT, is shared by dozens of earth stations. The signals to and from each of these must be kept separate to avoid interference.

Each earth station digitises the incoming data and stores them in buffers. These buffers are emptied in bursts of high-speed transmission to the satellite. Each burst of transmission lasts about 2 milliseconds, and transmissions are made in cycles to give Time Division Multiple Access.

A communication satellite consists of transmit and receive antennae which cover fixed geographical spots, and a set of repeaters which connect these. The satellite receives a burst of signal from an earth station, routes it through a repeater and transmits the burst to the appropriate area on earth, where it is picked up by a receiving station.

Satellite operators face a standard scheduling problem. They have a limited resource: the capacity of the satellite. There are many jobs to be processed, i.e. the messages from earth stations. These jobs must be scheduled so the satellite can handle as much work as possible. A number of algorithms have been developed for this. Even when there are hundreds of millions of pounds' worth of equipment to consider, the most useful algorithms use fairly simple procedures that aim for good solutions with a reasonable amount of computing.

Optimised Production Technology (OPT)

More complicated approaches to scheduling often use a hierarchy of rules, together with more formal analyses and simulations. As a simple illustration, schedulers might start by putting jobs in order of the critical ratio; then look at the jobs with similar critical ratios and move the shortest to the front of the queue; then adjust the schedules to smooth the workload. This might give an initial solution, with relevant analysis and simulation showing how it performs, and where it can be improved.

There are obviously many possible approaches of this type. One that has received a lot of attention was developed by Goldratt[3] who described the **theory of constraints**. This concentrates on the capacity of a process, particularly the bottlenecks that limit overall output. If a process works at full capacity, the only way of increasing production is to remove the bottlenecks. Of course, when one bottleneck is removed, another is created, so this approach is always looking for ways of overcoming the current limiting operation. The theory of constraints works by identifying the bottlenecks in a process, and then scheduling jobs to get the maximum possible flow through these bottlenecks.

The theory of constraints does not describe any fundamentally new approach to scheduling, but it brings together a series of related ideas. These are used in **Optimised Production Technology (OPT)**,[4] which is a well-known software package that is based on the theory of constraints. Like similar packages, OPT is a proprietary product and its details are not published. It is, however, based on a series of nine well-known principles:

1. Schedules should balance the flow through the process rather than the capacity. They should give a smooth flow of products through the process, and this need not keep all resources fully occupied.
2. There are two types of resources: bottleneck and non-bottleneck. The capacity of the process is set by the bottlenecks. The utilisation of non-bottleneck resources is not set by its own capacity, but by some other operation.
3. Activating a resource (which means doing work that is really needed) is not the same as using the resource (which might include work that is not really needed at the particular time).
4. An hour lost at a bottleneck cannot be recovered, and gives an hour lost for the entire process.
5. Saving an hour at an operation that is not a bottleneck gives no benefits.
6. Bottlenecks control both the throughput of the process and the stocks of work-in-progress. A bottleneck will slow down throughput, and cause an increase in work-in-progress.
7. The size of a transfer batch (the number of units moved together between operations) need not equal the size of the process batch (the total number of units made in a production run).
8. The size of the process batch should vary to meet circumstances and not be fixed.
9. Schedules should be designed by looking at all constraints simultaneously and not sequentially.

Review questions

14.8 When would you use Johnson's Rule?

14.9 What exactly is OPT?

Scheduling services

There is no basic difference between scheduling services and scheduling manufacturing. They both have jobs to do, and want the best timetables to achieve certain objectives. But services do have some features that give specific problems. For example, customers are more directly involved in services; they often form queues to wait for a service, and this makes the lead time before delivery particularly important. At the same time, services cannot be held in stock, so they must be scheduled to arrive exactly when customers want them. This causes particular problems as the demand for services often varies widely. These three factors – customer involvement, no stocks and variable demand – can make scheduling difficult. There are several ways of easing the problems.

1. *Appointment systems*. These are widely used by doctors, lawyers, hairdressers, and many other personal and professional services. They increase the utilisation of resources by ensuring a smooth flow of customers through a process, but they have the drawback of making customers wait for a fixed – and often long – time. They also reduce the effective capacity when customers miss an appointment, or cancel too late to get a replacement.
2. *Fixed-schedule system*, where a schedule of operations is published and known by customers some time in advance. This is used when a service is given to many customers at the same time, such as bus services, theatres and football matches.
3. *Delayed delivery*, where organisations do not deliver the service immediately a customer wants it, but delay it until they can fit it into their schedules. This is used when customers are willing to wait, such as a television repair shop or a roof repair service. This gives the organisation a much better chance to smooth its workload and use its resources more efficiently.
4. *Queues*. This is the most common way of levelling demand for services. Customers are simply dealt with in the order they arrive, or some other appropriate order.

OPERATIONS IN PRACTICE

Port of Piraeus

Piraeus in Athens is by far the largest port in Greece. In 1996 it had 12 million passengers, 10 million tonnes of non-containerised cargo, and 585,000 TEUs (20-foot equivalent units: the size of a standard container). The income of $120 million a year comes from cargo handling, port dues, storage and charges for any other services given by the port.

Shipping lines work a 'hub-and-spoke' system, with large ships stopping at the hubs, and smaller feeder vessels connecting to local ports. The Mediterranean has a main trunk route from the Suez Canal to Gibraltar, and there are several ports along this route competing for the hub traffic – including Piraeus, Malta, Algeciras in Spain, Damietta in Egypt and Gioia Tauro in Italy.

In 1996 Piraeus was surprised by a fall of 3 per cent in container traffic, at a time when it was expanding and building new facilities. Now the port had to make sure that it could generate enough new traffic to justify the expansion. To get fast results, it concentrated on the transhipment trade – where shipping lines use the port to move containers between large ships. Then a number of significant changes were made:

- with its increased capacity, the port could guarantee ships arriving immediate access to berths and cranes;
- transhipment tariffs were too high to be competitive, so these were reduced and simplified;
- berths had been scheduled on a first-come first-served basis (the port changed this to give a clearly fair allocation of resources to different types of customers);
- the port developed a booking system, where shipping lines could book a time slot and services in advance and get guaranteed service;
- the port improved the allocation of cranes and shifts of workers to each ship berthing;
- arrangements in the stacking areas were improved; these are areas where containers are continually rearranged as they are consolidated for movement to and from ships.

With these changes the container traffic rose by 16 per cent to 600,000 TEU in 1997 and another 32 per cent to 900,000 TEU in 1998.

Source: Psaraftis H.N. (1998) 'When a Port Calls', *OR/MS Today*, April, pp. 38–41

Review questions

14.10 How does scheduling in services differ from scheduling in manufacturing?

14.11 It is better to level demand by an appointment system rather than have people queueing. Do you agree with this?

Scheduling people

Assigning people to equipment

We have been using the ideas of 'jobs' scheduled on 'equipment' to illustrate some ideas of scheduling. But real problems come in many forms, and one of the most common designs people's work schedules. If the same people are always assigned to the same equipment, such as a lorry driver always working on the same vehicle, the equipment schedule effectively fixes the staff schedule. But usually this does not happen, and the staff schedules are designed separately.

As you might expect, there are many ways of designing staff schedules, but the most common use simple rules. Suppose that you have sets of jobs waiting at various equipment. You have operators standing by, and want to know which equipment they should work on. You might start by assigning them to the equipment that:

- has the most jobs waiting to be processed;
- has the job with the earliest due date;
- has the job which has been waiting longest.

There are many simple rules of this kind. Sometimes, however, it is worth using a more formal approach. One of these describes an **assignment problem**, where we have a number of pieces of equipment, and want to assign opera ors so that the total cost is minimised. This problem is quite easy to solve, but it is so common that standard programs do the calculations automatically. The following example shows a typical result when the problem is phrased in terms of assigning sales people to territories.

WORKED EXAMPLE

A sales manager has to assign six salesmen to different territories. The salesmen have different contacts and techniques, so their expected monthly sales (in thousands of pounds) are shown in the following table. What assignment would maximise the monthly income?

		Territory					
		1	2	3	4	5	6
Salesman	1	17	24	41	19	33	28
	2	22	22	31	14	27	26
	3	9	33	25	26	30	31
	4	29	43	45	8	22	20
	5	39	19	17	30	32	30
	6	31	37	27	23	37	10

Solution

This is a standard assignment problem, and Figure 14.8 shows a typical printout for the calculations. The first matrix shows the data as it is given. The method usually looks for schedules that minimise costs rather than maximise income, so we have

ASSIGNMENT PROBLEM SOLUTION

PROBLEM: Sales Manager

ORIGINAL PROBLEM DATA

	Territory1	Territory2	Territory3	Territory4	Territory5	Territory6	:	Totals
Salesm1:	17.00	24.00	41.00	19.00	33.00	28.00	:	1
Salesm2:	22.00	22.00	31.00	14.00	27.00	26.00	:	1
Salesm3:	9.00	33.00	25.00	26.00	30.00	31.00	:	1
Salesm4:	29.00	43.00	45.00	8.00	22.00	20.00	:	1
Salesm5:	39.00	19.00	17.00	30.00	32.00	30.00	:	1
Salesm6:	31.00	37.00	27.00	23.00	37.00	10.00	:	1
Totals:	1	1	1	1	1	1	:	6

REVISED COST DATA

	Territory1	Territory2	Territory3	Territory4	Territory5	Territory6	:	Totals
Salesm1:	28.00	21.00	4.00	26.00	12.00	17.00	:	1
Salesm2:	23.00	23.00	14.00	31.00	18.00	19.00	:	1
Salesm3:	36.00	12.00	20.00	19.00	15.00	14.00	:	1
Salesm4:	16.00	2.00	0.00	37.00	23.00	25.00	:	1
Salesm5:	6.00	26.00	28.00	15.00	13.00	15.00	:	1
Salesm6:	14.00	8.00	18.00	22.00	8.00	35.00	:	1
Totals:	1	1	1	1	1	1	:	6

REDUCED MATRIX

	Territory1	Territory2	Territory3	Territory4	Territory5	Territory6	:	Totals
Salesm1:	24.00	17.00	0.00	15.00	8.00	11.00	:	1
Salesm2:	9.00	9.00	0.00	10.00	4.00	3.00	:	1
Salesm3:	24.00	0.00	8.00	0.00	3.00	0.00	:	1
Salesm4:	16.00	2.00	0.00	30.00	23.00	23.00	:	1
Salesm5:	0.00	20.00	22.00	2.00	7.00	7.00	:	1
Salesm6:	6.00	0.00	10.00	7.00	0.00	25.00	:	1
Totals:	1	1	1	1	1	1	:	6

Figure 14.8 Printout for the assignment problem in worked example

OPTIMAL SOLUTION

	Territory1	Territory2	Territory3	Territory4	Territory5	Territory6	:	Totals
Salesm1:	0.00	0.00	1.00	0.00	0.00	0.00	:	1
Salesm2:	0.00	0.00	0.00	0.00	0.00	1.00	:	1
Salesm3:	0.00	0.00	0.00	1.00	0.00	0.00	:	1
Salesm4:	0.00	1.00	0.00	0.00	0.00	0.00	:	1
Salesm5:	1.00	0.00	0.00	0.00	0.00	0.00	:	1
Salesm6:	0.00	0.00	0.00	0.00	1.00	0.00	:	1
Totals:	1	1	1	1	1	1	:	6

Assign	To
Salesm1	Territory3
Salesm2	Territory6
Salesm3	Territory4
Salesm4	Territory2
Salesm5	Territory1
Salesm6	Territory5

Maximum profit is = 212

Figure 14.8 cont'd

to make a small adjustment. The second matrix shows 'revised costs' which you can find by subtracting each gain in the original matrix from the highest overall gain, which is 45. This gives values that we want to minimise. The third matrix shows a 'reduced cost matrix', which contains at least one zero in each row and column. These zeros identify the initial solution, and the computer now iteratively improves this until it reaches the optimal assignment. The final matrix shows the best assignment, which it identifies by the '1's.

Scheduling days off

Another common problem designs staff timetables that give each person a particular work pattern. We might, for example, want to give everyone two consecutive days off a week. A simple method for this has the following five steps:

- *Step 1*. Find the minimum number of operators needed each day of the week.
- *Step 2*. Identify the two adjacent days with smallest needs. For this we find the day with smallest needs, then the day with next smallest, then the next smallest, and so on until we have identified two adjacent days.
- *Step 3*. Give the next operator these two days off (perhaps giving priority to weekends).
- *Step 4*. Reduce the staff needed on the five days when this operator works by one. If the numbers go negative, it means that there are spare people.
- *Step 5*. If there are still more operators needed, go to step 2, otherwise we have found a schedule.

WORKED EXAMPLE

Jane Schultz wants to design schedules for the people working full-time in her shop. She estimates the number of people needed each day as follows:

Day	Monday	Tuesday	Wednesday	Thursday	Friday	Saturday	Sunday
People	2	0	2	3	4	4	2

Each person has two consecutive days off. What would be a reasonable schedule?

Solution

We can find a reasonable schedule by using the five-step procedure described above.

- Step 1 is already done with the figures given.
- Step 2 finds the two adjacent days with smallest numbers of people. This is Monday and Tuesday.
- Step 3 gives the first person these two days off.
- Step 4 reduces the needs for Wednesday to Sunday by one, and we return to step 2.

Day	Monday	Tuesday	Wednesday	Thursday	Friday	Saturday	Sunday
Still needed	2	0	1	1	1	1	1

- The next cycle finds Tuesday and Wednesday as the adjacent days with lowest demand, so the second person works Thursday to Monday. Repeating this another three times gives the following results (where days off are underlined).

Day	Mon	Tues	Wed	Thurs	Fri	Sat	Sun
Cycle 1	2	0	2	3	4	4	2
Cycle 2	2	0	1	2	3	3	1
Cycle 3	1	0	1	1	2	2	0
Cycle 4	1	0	0	0	1	1	−1
Cycle 5	0	0	0	−1	0	0	−2

This completes the schedule, with all demand met by four operators.

Day	Mon	Tues	Wed	Thurs	Fri	Sat	Sun
Operators needed	2	0	2	3	4	4	2
Operators available	2	0	2	4	4	4	4
Operators off	2	4	2	0	0	0	0
Spare operators	0	0	0	1	0	0	2

Review questions

14.12 When does scheduling people to equipment become a problem?

14.13 Most schedules for employees are designed using simple scheduling rules. Do you think this is true?

Project 14.2 *Some people start their day (or some other period) with a 'to-do list'. Make a list of the jobs that you have to finish in some convenient period. How can you schedule these? How will varying this schedule change the things that you achieve?*

Control of schedules

Short-term schedules show what each job, piece of equipment, person and every other resource should be doing at any time, but there is a difference between designing timetables and having them actually happen. Qantas may schedule a flight to leave Brisbane for Singapore at 12:30, but if the aeroplane develops a fault on its previous flight from Perth, it cannot meet the schedule.

Plans and schedules show what an organisation intends to do, but there may be unforeseen factors which prevent the plans actually happening:

- equipment may develop a fault or breakdown;
- people may be ill and not available for work;
- suppliers may not send the right materials or they may be late;
- new customers may send additional orders to be added to schedules;
- customers may change the specifications or cancel existing orders;
- other problems within the organisation may disrupt the process;
- external factors that the organisation cannot control may affect operations.

To keep a check on such problems and to find ways of overcoming them, organisations use a **control system** for their schedules.

A **control system** for schedules monitors what actually happens.

- It reports performance of the operations.
- It also identifies any divergence from plans, and makes necessary adjustments.

Control systems have two main parts. The first part checks the progress of jobs and gives information back to managers. This is the part that is always working, monitoring operations and making sure that things are working smoothly. It checks the details of jobs' progress, reports the actual times of operations, records measures of performance (such as efficiency, productivity and utilisation) and reports any problems.

The second part of the control system starts working when circumstances change, or something goes wrong. Then the plans have to be revised, and the control system either warns about the changes needed, or it may actually adjust the schedules.

To be more specific, the purpose of a control system is to:

- monitor operations and report on their performance;
- make sure jobs are scheduled according to plans;
- warn of problems with resources, delivery dates, etc.;
- check progress as jobs move through the process;
- make small adjustments as necessary to plans;
- allow rescheduling if there is a major disruption to plans;
- give information on current activities.

At the heart of most control systems is some kind of **dispatch list**. This shows the schedules as an ordered list of the jobs to be done, the exact times they should be done, how long each will take, their importance, and any other relevant information.

Assembly Operation 14			Manual assembly	Week 17	Day 4	Operator 2	Tolerance ,,10
Week	**11**	**12**	**13**	**14**	**15**	**16**	**17**
Inputs							
Planned	240	240	200	200	200	240	240
Actual	215	210	200	180	165	200	210
Difference	–25	–30	0	–20	–35	–40	–30
Cumulative Difference	–25	–55	–55	–75	–110	–150	–180
Outputs							
Planned	220	220	220	200	200	200	220
Actual	205	200	195	195	180	190	190
Difference	–15	–20	–25	–5	–20	–10	–30
Cumulative Difference	–15	–35	–60	–65	–85	–95	–125

Figure 14.9 A section from an input–output report

This dispatch list shows exactly what should be done at any particular time. The control system keeps a check of this list, and checks that everything is done at the planned times. If a job is not finished on time, then the second part of the control system starts working, reports the problem and starts looking for solutions.

Other inputs to the control system might include stock levels, bills of materials (which list the materials needed for a product), routes of products through equipment, late orders, constraints on operations, and so on. The main outputs from a control system are performance reports, current status and exception reports, and adjustments to schedules – which together show what is happening, what should be happening and how to overcome any differences.

Some organisations link the control system to an 'input–output report', which keeps a check on the units entering an operation and those leaving. Obviously these should match or work is accumulating somewhere. Figure 14.9 shows a section from an input–output report, and you can see that actual output is well below plans. As the inputs are also below plans, this suggests that there must be a hold-up in some previous operation. The inputs do not exactly match the outputs, so the operation probably has a varying stock of work-in-progress.

In principle, planning is done before operations, and then control takes over while the operations are actually being performed. But if there are discrepancies between plans and actual performance, the control system might get involved in rescheduling. Then there would be no clear separation between planning and control. The two functions would tend to merge, as shown in the summary of the scheduling process in Figure 14.10.

In Figure 14.10, we expand the master schedule to give the best sequence and times for jobs – these are the basic short-term schedules. Then we look at the details of all the resources used and assign these to jobs. This gives detailed timetables for all resources. A convenient way of presenting these schedules is in a dispatch list. When operations are actually done, there are differences between plans and actual performance, caused by new orders, disruptions and other effects. The control system monitors these differences and makes adjustments to the schedules.

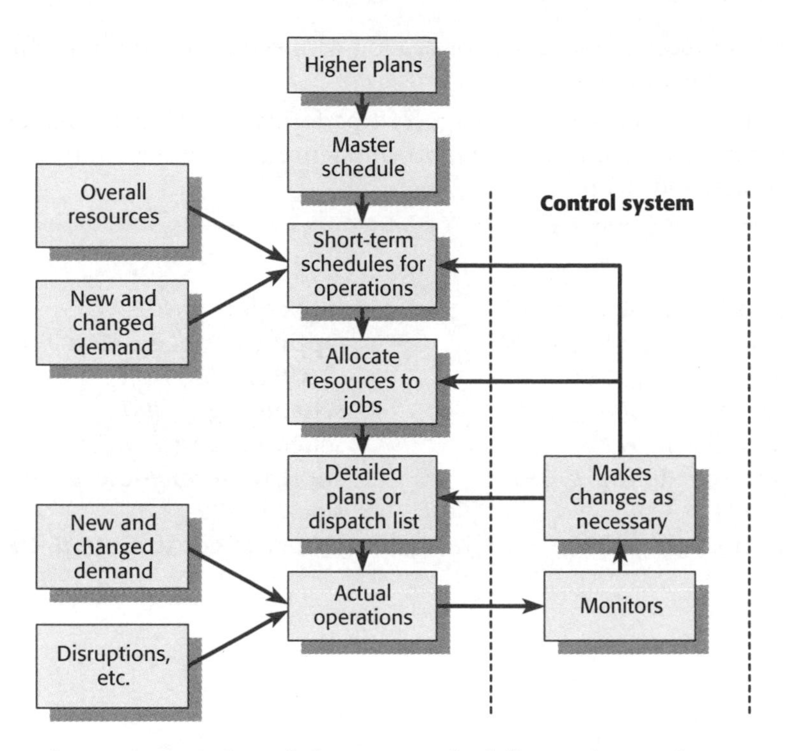

Figure 14.10 A view of short-term scheduling and control

Review questions

14.14 What is the purpose of a control system for schedules?

14.15 The control of schedules is only important when something goes wrong. Do you think this is true?

Chapter review

- Master schedules show the plans for making individual products. These are expanded to give short-term schedules for operations – including jobs, people, materials, equipment and all other resources needed by the process.
- Designing short-term schedules is one of the most common jobs of managers, but it is deceptively difficult. This is largely because there are so many factors to consider, and a huge number of options are available.
- There are many ways of designing schedules, but the most common uses simple rules that give consistently good results. There are many rules for achieving different objectives.
- Sometimes it is worth using more complicated approaches to scheduling. This might use linear programming, for example, some other model, or more complicated heuristics like OPT.
- Most scheduling problems share common features, and there is no fundamental difference between scheduling services, manufacturing or anything else.

- There are special procedures for dealing with certain common problems, such as the assignment problem.
- A control system is needed to record performance, compare actual production with planned performance, report differences, make necessary adjustments to schedules, and so on.

Key terms

assignment problem *p. 407*
backward scheduling *p. 395*
control system *p. 411*
critical ratio *p. 400*
dispatch list *p. 411*
forward scheduling *p. 394*
job *p. 393*
Johnson's Rule *p. 401*
makespan *p. 402*
Optimised Production Technology (OPT) *p. 404*
scheduling *p. 390*
scheduling rule *p. 396*
short-term schedule *p. 390*
slack *p. 400*
theory of constraints *p. 404*

CASE STUDY Bangor Production Consultants

Bangor Production Consultants is a partnership of 34 people. They produce computer software for a range of general management problems. At the moment, their best-selling packages prepare payrolls in small companies, control stocks in warehouses, organise vehicle fleet maintenance, and forecast sales. Their usual approach is to prepare a general package, and then tailor this to meet individual customers' needs.

Several local companies have approached them with different kinds of scheduling problems. As a result, Bangor are planning a new set of packages for planning and scheduling. As usual they plan to design a general package, and then tailor this to the specific needs of customers.

This will not be their first step in this direction. For some time they have had a spreadsheet program that helps with aggregate planning. This connects to a program for generating master production schedules, and there is a separate program for planning material purchases. The new step for Bangor is to design a broad program for various aspects of short-term scheduling, and – more importantly – to integrate their various programs into a comprehensive planning and scheduling system.

Questions

- What features do you think Bangor should include in their package?
- Could they use standard spreadsheets to help with their package?
- Who do you think will be their major customers?

Problems

14.1 Eight jobs are to be processed on a single machine, with processing times as follows:

Job	A	B	C	D	E	F	G	H
Processing time	2	5	3	8	4	7	2	3

Use a number of different scheduling rules, and compare the results.

14.2 What order should the jobs in the last problem be scheduled if they have the following due dates?

Job	A	B	C	D	E	F	G	H
Due date	13	7	8	30	14	20	2	36

14.3 Compucash Services has to prepare the payrolls of eight factories at the end of each week. This needs the following times for computing and printing. What schedules would you recommend?

Factory	1	2	3	4	5	6	7	8
Computing time	10	20	20	35	10	15	40	30
Printing time	20	15	40	50	15	30	55	35

14.4 The WellerKraft Museum needs the following numbers of guides:

Day	Mon	Tues	Wed	Thurs	Fri	Sat	Sun
Guides	4	6	8	8	10	14	12

Design a schedule that gives each guide two consecutive days off.

14.5 The South Shore Club is looking at the number of part-time bar staff it employs. It has recorded the demand over the past three weeks, and found the following figures. These show the average number of customers per hour wanting service at the bar.

Week	Mon	Tues	Wed	Thurs	Fri	Sat	Sun
1	32	31	37	61	115	142	23
2	42	38	26	59	132	151	25
3	27	46	45	68	154	138	27

Each of the bar staff can serve about 20 customers an hour. Standard work conditions specify that each person should work a minimum of two nights a week and a maximum of three nights, and that any nights worked are consecutive. How would you start scheduling the staff?

Discussion questions

14.1 What is short-term scheduling and when is it used? How does short-term scheduling fit in with other planning decisions? How does the operations strategy affect the aims of short-term scheduling?

14.2 Scheduling rules are little more than guesses. The best way of scheduling is to use mathematical analyses that guarantee optimal solutions. Do you agree with this? What kind of methods could you use? What might be the difficulties?

14.3 Why is scheduling so difficult? What factors cause particular problems? Are there any problems with scheduling people? Give real examples to support your views.

14.4 How would you set about scheduling the operations in a hamburger restaurant? Would you use a different approach in a doctor's surgery? What other examples can you give where different approaches are used?

14.5 Spreadsheets are widely used for different aspects of planning. How can they help with short-term scheduling? Design a spreadsheet that would help with scheduling problems.

14.6 You can find the effects of different scheduling rules by using simulation. What does this statement mean? How can simulation help in scheduling?

14.7 What do control systems do? What features would you expect to see in a control system? Could expert systems do anything useful for control systems?

References

1. Eilon S., Watson-Gandy C.D.T. and Christofides N. (1971) *Distribution Management.* London: Charles Griffen.
2. Johnson S.M. (1954) 'Optimal Two Stage and Three Stage Production Schedules with Setup Times Included', *Naval Logistics Quarterly*, vol. 1 (1), pp. 61–68.
3. Goldratt E. and Cox J. (1984) *The Goal.* New York: North River Press.
4. COI (1979) *OPT Management System.* Milford, CT: Creative Output Inc.

Selected reading

Baker K.R. (1995) *Elements of Sequencing and Scheduling.* Hanover, NH: Baker Press.

Browne J., Harhen J. and Shivnan J. (1996) *Production Management Systems.* 2nd edn. Reading, MA: Addison-Wesley.

Fitzsimmons J.A. and Fitzsimmons M.J. (1994) *Service Management for Competitive Advantage.* New York: McGraw-Hill.

Fogarty D.W., Blackstone J.H. and Hoffman T.R. (1991) *Production and Inventory Management.* 2nd edn. Cincinnati, OH: South-Western.

Morton T.E. and Penticto D.W. (1993) *Heuristic Scheduling Systems.* New York: John Wiley.

Vollman T.E., Berry W.L. and Whybark D.C. (1992) *Manufacturing Planning and Control Systems.* 3rd edn. Homewood, IL: Irwin.

CHAPTER 15

Material requirements planning

The use of MRP systems is so widespread in the US that many managers have come to think of them as a necessary part of manufacturing, along with buildings, machines, and workers.

Michel Baudin

Manufacturing Systems Analysis, Prentice-Hall, 1990

Contents

Aims of the chapter

After reading this chapter you should be able to:

- describe dependent demand systems for managing materials;
- use material requirements planning (MRP) to timetable orders and operations;
- describe the information needed by MRP;
- appreciate the benefits and problems with MRP;
- use batching rules and consider other adjustments to MRP schedules;
- see how to extend the MRP approach.

Main themes

This chapter will emphasise:

- **dependent demand systems**, where the demand for materials is found from production plans;
- **material requirements planning**, which explodes a master schedule to give a timetable for supplying materials.

Background to material requirements planning (MRP)

Chapter 13 showed how tactical plans add the details to longer-term strategic plans. They lead to the master schedule which typically shows the amount of each product planned in each week. In Chapter 14 we saw how short-term schedules organise the resources needed by the master schedule. When the master schedule of Vermont Analysis includes 80 blood tests a day, the short-term schedules make sure that the laboratories have all the facilities they need.

In this chapter we are going to describe a different approach to scheduling. This is the widely used method of **material requirements planning.**

Essentially, MRP gives a detailed timetable for the delivery of materials. Here we are using 'materials' to mean a range of resources that are needed to support the master schedule. These can either be bought-in or made internally, so the main results of MRP are:

- timetables to show when all materials are needed;
- timetables to show when these materials should be ordered or made.

The characteristic of MRP is that it finds these timetables by 'exploding' the master schedule.

Material requirements planning uses the master schedule, and related information, to plan the supply of materials.

- It expands the master schedule to give **timetables** which make sure that materials arrive when they are needed.

Dependent and independent demand

The conventional approach to planning is based on forecasts of demand. This assumes that overall demand for a product is made up of individual demands from many separate customers. We assume that these demands are independent of each other, so that the demand from one customer is not related to the demand from another customer. If you are selling Nike shoes, the overall demand comes from hundreds of separate customers, all independently asking for a pair of shoes. This gives an **independent demand**.

But there are many situations where demands are not independent. One demand for a product is not independent of a second demand for the product; or demand for one product is not independent of demand for a second product. When a manufacturer uses a number of components to make a product, the demands for all components are clearly related, since they all depend on the production plan for the final product. This gives **dependent demand**, which we can use for another approach to planning the supply of materials.

Traditionally, organisations assume that demands for materials are independent, forecast demand, and then use these forecasts in their short-term scheduling. MRP assumes that demand for materials is dependent, and uses the master schedule to design timetables to get all materials delivered exactly when they are needed. This

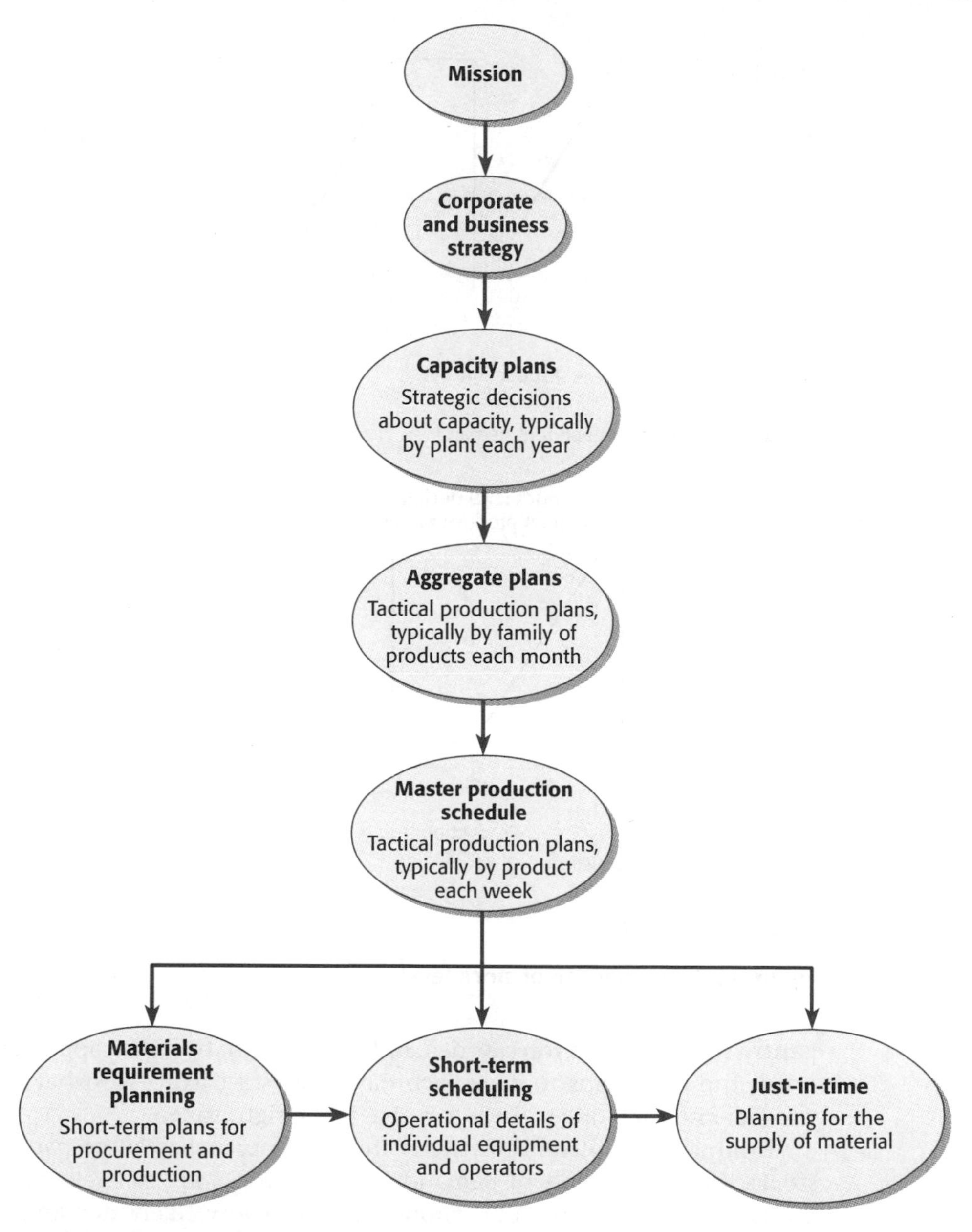

Figure 15.1 Summary of the planning process

gives the hierarchy of plans shown in Figure 15.1. As you can see, this mentions a third approach to planning materials, called just-in-time planning, which we shall meet in the next chapter.

You can see the differences between the traditional approach and MRP in the way a restaurant chef plans the ingredients for a week's meals. An independent demand system sees what ingredients were used in previous weeks, uses these past demands to forecast future demands, and then makes sure there is enough in the

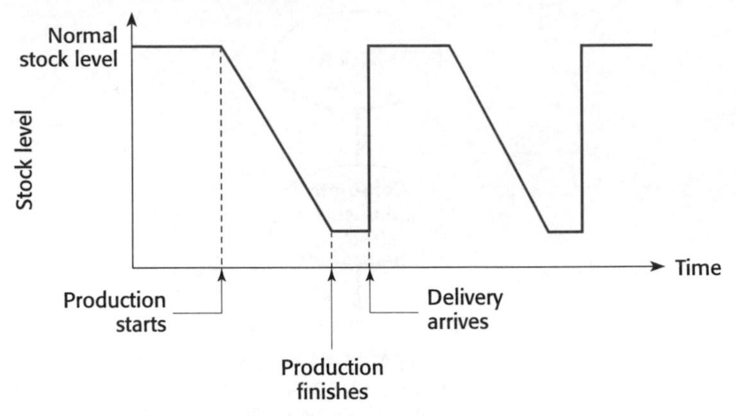

(a) Stock level with independent demand

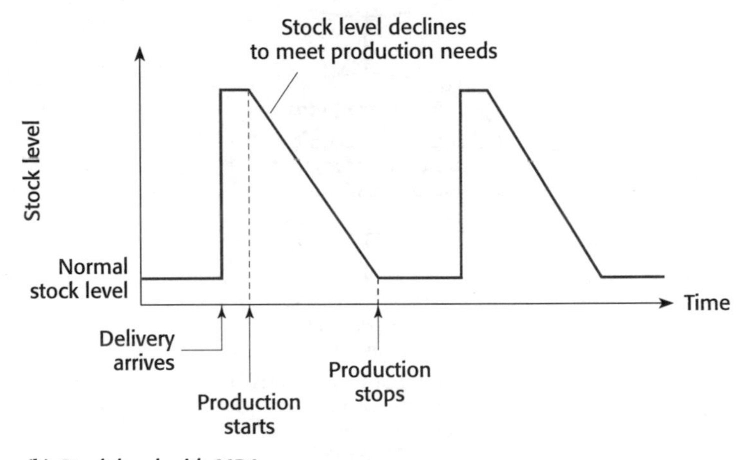

(b) Stock level with MRA

Figure 15.2 Comparison of stock levels

pantry to cover these forecast demands. The alternative MRP approach looks at the meals the chef plans to cook each day, analyses this to see what ingredients are needed, and then orders them to arrive at the right time.

An important difference between the two approaches is the pattern of material stocks. With independent demand systems, stocks are not related to production plans so they must be high enough to cover any likely demand. These stocks decline during operations, but are replenished as soon as possible to give the pattern shown in Figure 15.2(a). With MRP, stocks are generally low but rise as orders are delivered just before operaions starts. The stock is then used during production and declines to its normal, low level. This pattern is shown in Figure 15.2(b).

As a rule of thumb, independent demand systems are most useful for stocks of finished goods; dependent demand systems are most useful for stocks of raw materials. When Raleigh makes bicycles, the numbers of pedals, saddles and wheels it needs are directly related to the number of bicycles it makes. If it is going to make 1,000 bicycles next week, it will need 2,000 pedals, 1,000 saddles, 2,000 wheels, and so on. The demands for these parts clearly depend on the production of bicycles – so it is better to use known production schedules than projections of historical demands. On the other hand, supermarkets do not have a detailed master schedule, so they are more likely to use forecasts in traditional independent demand systems.

Material requirements planning was originally designed for manufacturing industries. It is still used most widely in mass production, but has been adopted by many other organisations. Universities, airlines, dentists, consultants and many other services know in advance which customers they will serve. They can then use these known schedules to plan the facilities they need. When we talk about materials being delivered for products, remember that, as always, our products are a combination of goods and services. The product might be education, banking or health, and the materials might be information, knowledge and skills.

Review questions

15.1 What is MRP?

15.2 What are the important differences between dependent demand systems and independent demand systems?

The MRP approach

Information needed

Material requirements planning needs a lot of information about schedules, products and materials. It analyses this information using a huge amount of simple arithmetic, so it is always computerised. The main inputs come from three sources (shown in Figure 15.3):

- master schedule;
- bill of materials;
- inventory records.

We start the MRP procedure with the master schedule. This gives the number of every product to be made in every period. Then MRP 'explodes' this master schedule using a **bill of materials** to give details of the materials needed.

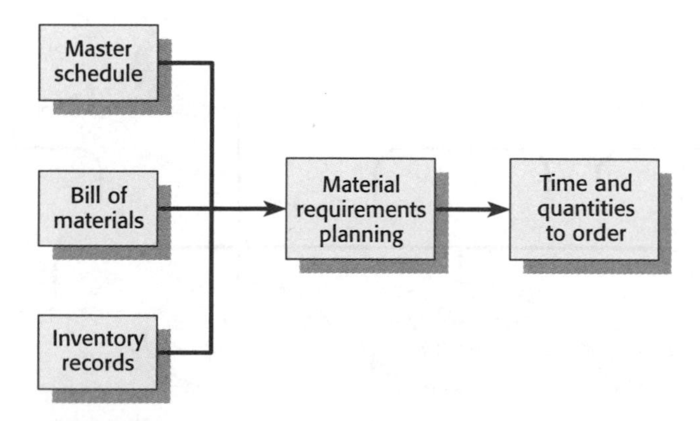

Figure 15.3 Outline of the MRP approach

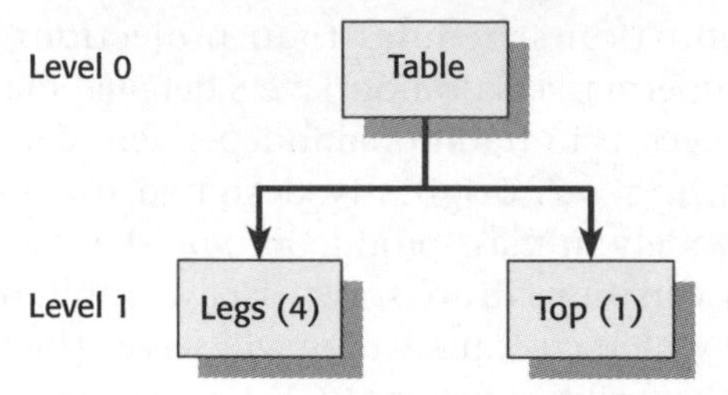

Figure 15.4 Simple bill of materials for a table

A bill of materials is an ordered list of all parts that are needed to make a particular product. It shows the materials, parts and components needed, and the order in which they are used. Suppose a company makes tables from a top and four legs. This is shown as the simple bill of materials in Figure 15.4. You can see that every item has a 'level' number that shows where it fits into the process, and figures in brackets show the numbers needed to make each unit. The finished product is level 0; level 1 items are used directly to make the level 0 item.

If we look at the bill of materials in more detail, we might see that each top is made from a wood kit and hardware, and that the wood kit has four oak planks which are 2 m long and 30 cm wide, and so on. Part of this more detailed bill of materials is shown in Figure 15.5. This gives more levels, with level 2 items used to make the level

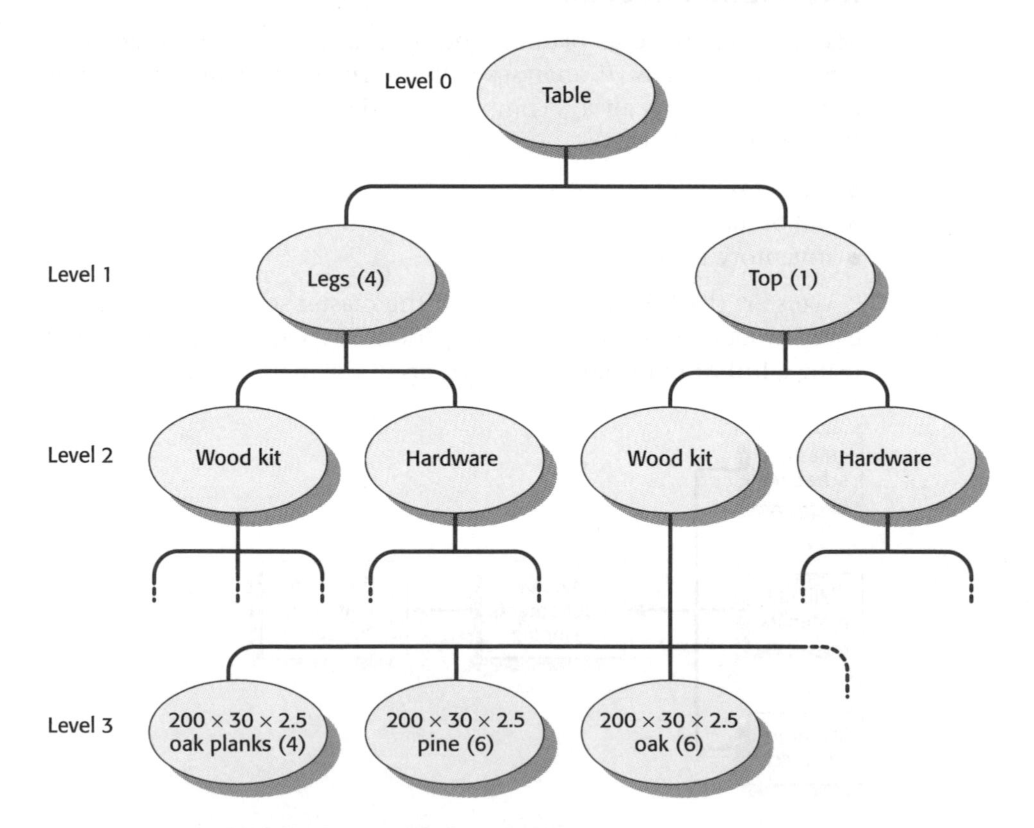

Figure 15.5 Partial bill of materials for a table

1 items, and so on. The full bill of materials keeps going down through different levels until it reaches materials that the organisation always buys in from suppliers. By this time, there might be hundreds or even thousands of different materials.

Every product has a bill of materials that is prepared at the design stage. You remember from Chapter 5 that the design of a product does not only show how it looks, but covers the complete package including associated services, materials, quality measures, process used, and so on. Part of this design gives the complete bill of materials.

Project 15.1 *Take a fairly simple product that you can study, such as a desk or restaurant meal. Find the materials that are needed for this product. What would the bill of materials look like? How would you begin to design the bill of materials for something complicated like a car or film set?*

Calculations for MRP

We can continue with our example of a table to show the MRP approach. Suppose the master schedule shows that 10 tables are planned for February. We obviously need 10 tops and 40 legs ready for assembly at the beginning of February. In practice these are the **gross requirements**. We may not have to order them all, as we may already have some in stock, or have outstanding orders that are due to arrive shortly. If we subtract these from the gross requirements, we get the **net requirements** for materials. We need 40 table legs by the beginning of February, but if we already have eight in stock and an order of 15 that is due to arrive in January, our net requirement is for 40 – 8 – 15 = 17.

Net requirements = gross requirements – current stock – stock on order

Now we know the quantities to order, and when these orders should arrive. The next step is to find the time to place the orders. For this we need the lead times – and we place orders this lead time before the materials are actually needed. If we buy the table tops and legs from suppliers who give a lead time of four weeks, we need to place orders at the beginning of January. These orders will arrive by the end of January just before assembly is due to start. This is called **time shifting**.

Finally, we have to consider any other relevant information, such as minimum order sizes, discounts, minimum stock levels, variation in lead time, and so on. When we take all of this into account we can get a detailed timetable for orders. This procedure is shown in Figure 15.6.

We can summarise this procedure in the formal description of MRP given by the following steps.

- *Step 1.* Use the master schedule to find the gross requirements of level 0 items.
- *Step 2.* Subtract any stock on hand and orders arriving to give the net requirements for level 0 items. Then schedule production, with starting times to meet these net requirements.

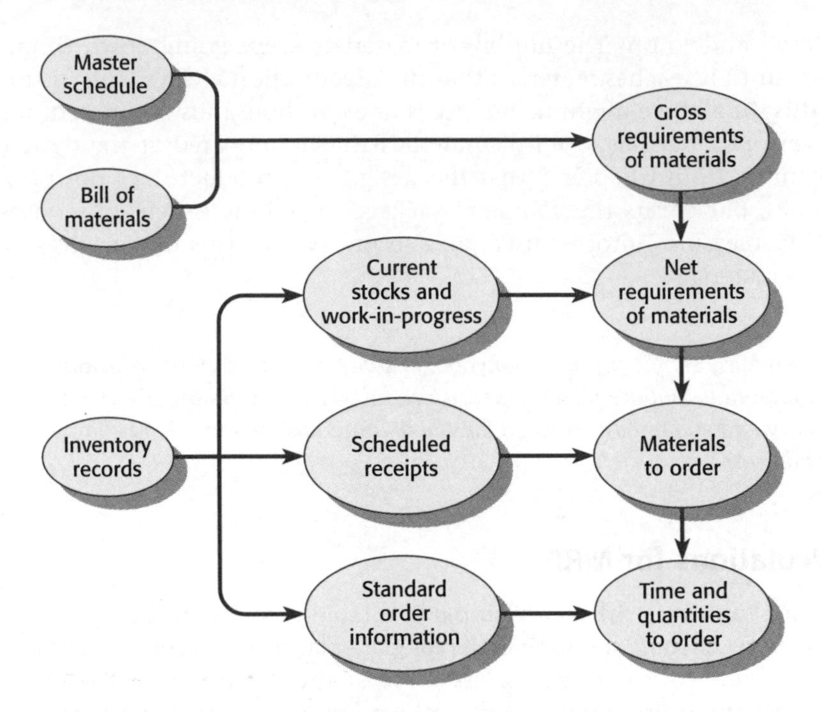

Figure 15.6 The MRP calculations

- *Step 3.* If there are more levels of materials, use the bill of materials to translate the net requirements from the last level into gross requirements for this level. If there are no more levels, go to step 5.
- *Step 4.* Take each material in turn and:
  - subtract the stock on hand and scheduled deliveries to find the net requirements, which are the amounts to order;
  - use the lead time and any other relevant information to give the timing of these orders;
  - go back to step 3.
- *Step 5.* Finalise the timetable, adding any specific adjustments.

WORKED EXAMPLE

Johnson's Furniture assembles dining room tables using bought-in parts of four legs and a top. These have lead times of two and three weeks respectively, and assembly takes a week. The company receive orders for 20 tables to be delivered in week 5 of a planning period and 40 tables in week 7. It has current stocks of two complete tables, 40 legs and 22 tops. When should it order parts?

Solution

The orders give Johnson's production schedule as shown below. This gives the gross requirements for level 0 items, which are finished tables. Subtracting the stock of finished tables gives the net requirements. Then allowing a week for assembly gives the start times shown in the following assembly plan.

Level 0 – dining room tables

Week	1	2	3	4	5	6	7
Gross requirements					20		40
Opening stock	2	2	2	2	2		
Net requirements					18		40
Scheduled receipts					18		40
Start assembly				18		40	

The 'Scheduled receipts' show the number of units that become available in a week, which is the number started the lead time earlier.

We have already met the bill of materials for this example in Figure 15.4. We can use this, together with the assembly plans, to find gross requirements for level 1 items, which are legs and tops. In week 4 there is a net requirement of 18 tables, which translates into a gross requirement of $18 \times 4 = 72$ legs and $18 \times 1 = 18$ tops. Similarly, we can find the other gross requirements as:

- legs: $18 \times 4 = 72$ in week 4, and $40 \times 4 = 160$ in week 6;
- tops: 18 in week 4, and 40 in week 6.

Subtracting the stock on hand from these gross requirements gives the net requirements. To make sure the parts arrive on time, they must be ordered the lead time in advance, which is two weeks for legs and three weeks for tops.

Level 1 – legs

Week	1	2	3	4	5	6	7
Gross requirements				72		160	
Opening stock	40	40	40	40			
Net requirements				32		160	
Scheduled receipts				32		160	
Place order		32		160			

Level 1 – tops

Week	1	2	3	4	5	6	7
Gross requirements				18		40	
Opening stock	22	22	22	22	4	4	
Net requirements						36	
Scheduled receipts						36	
Place order				36			

There are no more levels of materials, so we can finalise the timetable of events:

- week 2: order 32 legs;
- week 3: order 36 tops;
- week 4: order 160 legs and assemble 18 tables;
- week 6: assemble 40 tables.

WORKED EXAMPLE

Lorengren (Assembly) has a production schedule that needs 45 units of a product in week 9 of a cycle, 60 units in week 10 and 40 units in week 13. It currently has 10 units of the product in stock, but the company always keeps five units in reserve to cover emergency orders. Each unit of the product takes two weeks to assemble from two units of part B and three units of part C. Each unit of part B is made in one week from one unit of material D and three units of material E. Part C is assembled in two weeks from two units of component F. Lead times for D, E and F are one, two and three weeks respectively. Current stocks are 50 units of B, 100 of C, 40 of D, 360 of E and 100 of F. Lorengren keeps minimum stocks of 20 units of D, 100 of E and 50 of F. The minimum order size for E is 300 units, while F can only be ordered in discrete batches of 100 units. Outstanding orders for 10 units of D will arrive in week 6; 300 units of E will arrive in week 7; 200 units of F will arrive in week 6; and 20 units of C will arrive in week 8. Design a timetable of activities for the company.

Solution

As you can see, even a simple MRP problem needs a lot of calculation and gets very complicated. In practice, a computer is always used, and Figure 15.7 shows the printout from a simple program.

Material Requirements Planning

Number of Time Periods : 13
Bill of Materials

```
                         End Item Product A
                                 |
     ----------------------------------------------
     |                                            |
     X      Part B                                X      Part C
     |      2 units                               |      3 units
     |                                            |
     -----------------------                      ----------------
     |                     |                      |
     X      Material D     X      Material E      X      Component F
     |      1 unit         |      3 units         |      2 units
     |                     |                      |
```

Analysis

Level 0 - End Item

Item Number: Part-0
Description: Product A

Beginning Inventory: 10
Lead Time: 2
Safety Stock: 5
Lot Size: 1

	Week 6	Week 7	Week 8	Week 9	Week 10	Week 11	Week 12	Week 13
Gross Requirements :	0	0	0	45	60	0	0	40
Available :	10	10	10	10	5	5	5	5
Net Requirements :	0	0	0	40	60	0	0	40
Receipts :	0	0	0	40	60	0	0	40
Requests :	0	40	60	0	0	40	0	0

Level 1 - Comp 1

Item Number: Part-1
Description: Part B
Bill of Materials: 2

Beginning Inventory: 50
Lead Time: 1
Safety Stock: 0
Lot Size: 1

Figure 15.7 Computer printout for worked example

	Week 6	Week 7	Week 8	Week 9	Week 10	Week 11	Week 12	Week 13
Gross Requirements :	0	80	120	0	0	80	0	0
Available :	50	50	0	0	0	0	0	0
Net Requirements :	0	30	120	0	0	80	0	0
Receipts :	0	30	120	0	0	80	0	0
Requests :	30	120	0	0	80	0	0	0

Level 2 - Comp 1-1

Item Number: Part-2 | Beginning Inventory: 40
Description: Material D | Lead Time: 1
Bill of Materials: 1 | Safety Stock: 20
Lot Size: 1

	Week 6	Week 7	Week 8	Week 9	Week 10	Week 11	Week 12	Week 13
Gross Requirements :	30	120	0	0	80	0	0	0
Available :	40	20	20	20	20	20	20	20
Net Requirements :	10	120	0	0	80	0	0	0
Receipts :	10	120	0	0	80	0	0	0
Requests :	120	0	0	80	0	0	0	0

Level 2 - Comp 1-2

Item Number: Part-3 | Beginning Inventory: 360
Description: Material E | Lead Time: 2
Bill of Materials: 3 | Safety Stock: 100
Lot Size: 300

	Week 6	Week 7	Week 8	Week 9	Week 10	Week 11	Week 12	Week 13
Gross Requirements :	90	360	0	0	240	0	0	0
Available :	360	270	210	210	210	270	270	270
Net Requirements :	0	190	0	0	130	0	0	0
Receipts :	0	300	0	0	300	0	0	0
Requests :	0	0	300	0	0	0	0	0

Level 1 - Comp 2

Item Number: Part-4 | Beginning Inventory: 100
Description: Part C | Lead Time: 2
Bill of Materials: 3 | Safety Stock: 0
Lot Size: 1

	Week 6	Week 7	Week 8	Week 9	Week 10	Week 11	Week 12	Week 13
Gross Requirements :	0	120	180	0	0	120	0	0
Available :	100	100	0	0	0	0	0	0
Net Requirements :	0	20	180	0	0	120	0	0
Receipts :	0	20	180	0	0	120	0	0
Requests :	180	0	0	120	0	0	0	0

Level 2 - Comp 2-1

Item Number: Part-5 | Beginning Inventory: 100
Description: Component F | Lead Time: 3
Bill of Materials: 2 | Safety Stock: 50
Lot Size: 100

	Week 6	Week 7	Week 8	Week 9	Week 10	Week 11	Week 12	Week 13
Gross Requirements :	360	0	0	240	0	0	0	0
Available :	100	140	140	140	100	100	100	100
Net Requirements :	310	0	0	150	0	0	0	0
Receipts :	400	0	0	200	0	0	0	0
Requests :	200	0	0	0	0	0	0	0

Figure 15.7 cont'd

The program starts at level 0, with production of the final product, A. Lorengren keeps a minimum stock of 5 units of A, and this reserve stock must be set aside when calculating the net requirements.

Then the program moves on to level 1 materials and expands the assembly plan for A into gross requirements for components B and C. The 40 units of A assembled in week 7 is expanded into gross requirements of 80 units of part B and 120 units of part C. The 60 units of A assembled in week 8 is expanded into gross requirements of 120 units of B and 180 units of C, and so on.

Gross requirements for B and C can be partly met from opening stocks, with the shortfall shown as net requirements. We also have to remember the planned delivery of 20 units of part C in week 7. This schedule for level 1 parts can now be expanded to give the timetable for level 2 items.

The gross requirements for materials D and E come from the assembly plans for part B. 30 units of B are started in week 6 and this expands into gross requirements for 30 units of D and 90 units of E, and so on. One complication here is the minimum order size of 300 units of E. In week 7 there is a gross requirement of 360 for material E, 170 of which can be met from free stock (keeping the reserve stock of 100). The net requirement is 190, but 300 have to be ordered with the spare 110 added to stock.

Finally, the gross requirements for component F can be found from the assembly plan for part C. 180 units of C are started in week 6 so this expands into a gross requirement of 360 units of F, and so on. Orders must be in discrete batches of 100 units, so they are rounded to the nearest hundred above net requirements.

The timetable of activities now becomes:

- Week 6 Start making 30 of B and 180 of C
  Place orders for 120 units of D and 200 units of F
  Orders arrive for 10 units of D and 400 units of F
- Week 7 Start making 40 of A and 120 of B
  Finish 30 units of B
  Orders arrive for 20 units of C, 120 units of D and 300 units of E
- Week 8 Start making 60 of A
  Finish 120 units of B and 180 units of C
  Place order for 300 units of E
- Week 9 Finish making 40 units of A
  Start making 120 of C
  Place order for 80 units of D
  Order arrives for 200 units of F
- Week 10 Finish 60 units of A
  Start making 80 units of B
  Orders arrive for 80 units of D and 300 units of E
- Week 11 Start making 40 units of A
  Finish 80 units of B and 120 units of C
- Week 13 Finish 40 units of A

Project 15.2 *Look at the results in the last worked example, and make sure that you understand what is happening. Check all the calculations to make sure that they are right. Design a spreadsheet to help you.*

Outputs from MRP

You can see that the main inputs to MRP are the master schedule, bill of materials, inventory records and any other relevant information. The main output is a timetable for material orders. But with all of this data, a system can generate different kinds of output including:

- *timetables of operations* needed to achieve the master schedule, particularly production times to start making materials;
- *a list of planned orders* for materials from external suppliers;
- *changes to previous orders* – whenever the master schedule is revised, or any other changes are made, the MRP schedules have to be updated. The system will list changes to order quantities, cancelled or changed orders, changes of due dates, and so on;
- *exceptions* – the system cannot deal automatically with unusual circumstances, and will report these as needing management action. These include problems with schedules, late orders, overloaded capacity, excessive scrap, requests for non-existent parts, shortage, and so on;
- *performance reports* – which show how well the system is working, including measures for investment in stocks, inventory turnover, costs and number of shortages;
- *planning reports* – which give information for longer-term planning decisions;
- *records of inventory transactions* – keeping accurate records of current stocks and allowing checks on progress.

These give the overall view of an MRP system summarised in Figure 15.8.

As you can see, MRP systems can generate a huge quantity of reports (some people say that MRP stands for 'More Reams of Paper'). MRP is typically run every week, and it can swamp managers with unimportant details. The implication is that the MRP reports have to be carefully designed so that each manager is only given relevant and appropriate information.

Review questions

15.3 MRP is only used by manufacturers. Do you think this is true?

15.4 What information is needed for MRP?

15.5 How do you find the net requirement for materials in MRP?

15.6 What outputs would you expect from an MRP system?

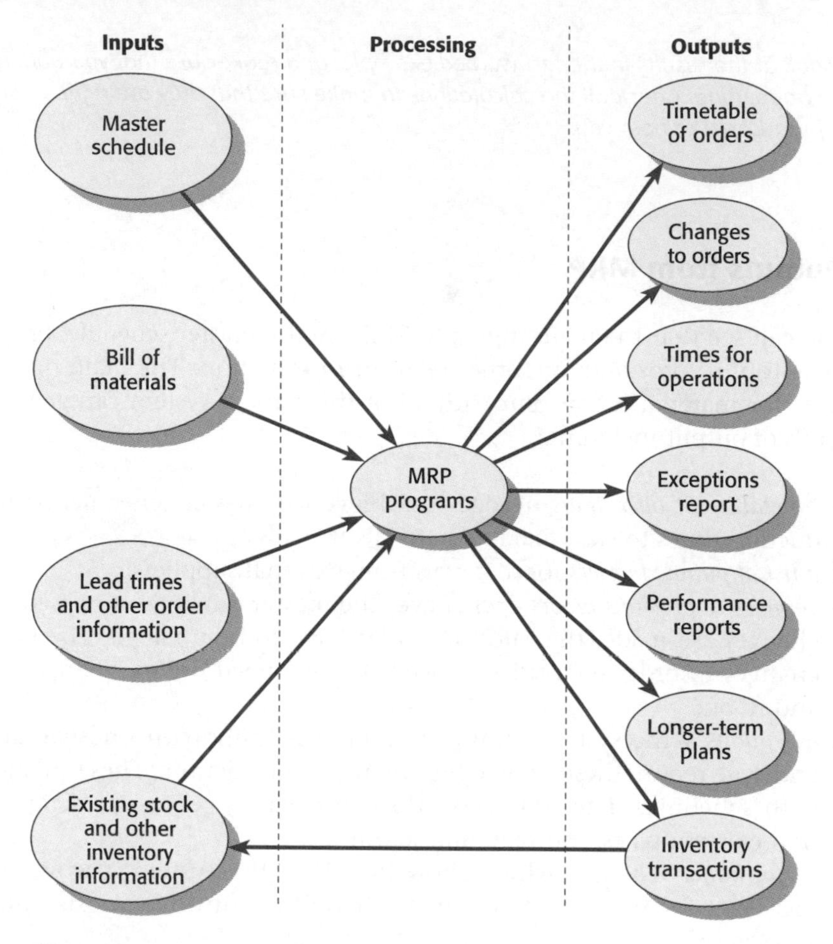

Figure 15.8 Summary of an MRP system

Benefits and problems with MRP

Benefits

Traditional, independent demand systems forecast likely demand for materials, and then hold stocks that are high enough to meet these. Unfortunately, we know that forecasts are usually wrong. To allow for these errors, organisations hold more stocks than they really need. These extra stocks give a measure of safety, but they also increase the inventory costs. MRP avoids these costs by relating the supply of materials directly to demand. The result is much lower stocks and related costs. Benefits that come from this direct link between the demand for products and the supply of materials include:

- materials supply is linked directly to known demand;
- lower stock levels, with savings in capital, space, warehousing, etc.;
- higher stock turnover;

- better customer service – with no delays caused by shortages of materials;
- more reliable and faster delivery times;
- higher utilisation of facilities – as materials are always available when needed;
- less time spent on expediting and emergency orders;
- MRP schedules can be used for short-term planning;
- assigns priorities for jobs supplying materials;
- encourages better planning.

This last benefit is particularly interesting. MRP effectively links several aspects of planning, including tactical master schedules and operational scheduling of resources. This puts pressure of organisations to design good plans and then to stick to them. The result is better planning. MRP can also give early warning of potential problems and shortages. If necessary, expediting can be used to speed up deliveries, or production plans can be changed. In this way MRP improves the wider performance of the organisation, measured in terms of equipment utilisation, productivity, customer service, response to market conditions, and so on.

Another broad benefit of MRP comes from its detailed analyses that highlight problems which have previously been hidden. For example, an organisation might not notice an unreliable supplier if it keeps enough stock to avoid problems. This effectively hides the problem, but increases costs. With MRP, stock levels are much lower and the organisation will notice the supplier's unreliability. Then they can take steps to improve things, either by changing the supplier or discussing ways of improving their performance.

Problems with MRP

In contrast to these advantages, there are also some problems with MRP. The most obvious is the amount of information and calculation that it needs. MRP starts with a detailed master schedule, so it cannot be used if:

- there is no master schedule;
- the master schedule is not designed far enough in advance;
- the master schedule is inaccurate, not showing what actually happens;
- plans are changed frequently.

Other requirements of MRP include a bill of materials, information about current stocks, orders outstanding, lead times, and other information about suppliers. Many organisations simply do not record this information. Others find that their information does not include enough detail or that it is in the wrong format for MRP.

Even when an organisation seems to have all the information, there can be problems with accuracy. Inventory files, for example, are updated with every transaction, but large numbers of small transactions easily introduce errors. Ordinarily such small errors are not important, as stocks are high enough to cover problems until the errors are detected. MRP, however, does not have these high stocks, so production depends on accurate records. Stocks are only available for the specified master schedule, and if there are errors in stock records, this schedule cannot be completed. Then even small errors become important.

People often suggest that inflexibility is a problem with MRP. The only materials available are those needed for the specified master schedule, so an organisation cannot rapidly adjust this schedule to allow for changing circumstances. There are simply no materials available to make any revised schedule.

Some general disadvantages of MRP include:

- reduced flexibility to deal with changes;
- needs a lot of detailed and reliable information;
- involves a lot of data manipulation;
- systems can become very complex;
- assumes that lead times are constant and independent of the quantities ordered;
- in practice, materials are made in a different order to that specified in the bill of materials;
- using MRP to schedule the production of parts can give poor results;
- the lot sizes suggested by MRP can be inefficient;
- MRP may not recognise capacity and other constraints;
- can be expensive and time consuming to implement.

Review questions

15.7 What is the main advantage of MRP?

15.8 What is the main problem with using MRP?

OPERATIONS IN PRACTICE

Alco Office Supplies

Alco Office Supplies make a range of desks, filing cabinets and other office furniture. In 1989 they introduced MRP for the manufacture of standard filing cabinets. The manufacturing process was simple, and with the help of a consultant, a new system was working in slightly less than a year at a cost of £95,000. By the end of the second year the system was judged a success and was extended to other products.

Alco's move to MRP illustrates the amount of information needed. Although they had integrated computer systems, these had to be thoroughly checked and overhauled before they were reliable enough for MRP. The biggest single job was getting data in a suitable form. Some of the old systems updated data records overnight. These had to be replaced with real-time systems, with all data files consolidated into a company-wide database.

Alco's experience also shows the complexity of real MRP systems. Their standard four-drawer filing cabinet is assembled from 218 different parts. Many of these are small and duplicated, but exploding the master schedule needed a lot of calculation. They make 38 variations on this basic filing cabinet, and a total of 3,500 different products. Each of these needs a separate MRP run, and then common parts are combined into larger orders.

On their first trial run of the MRP system, the weekly report was over 8,000 pages long. Needless to say, when the system became operational this was trimmed to 200 pages. You can get a feel for this report from the simplified printout in Figure 15.9.

******* ALCO OFFICE SUPPLIES - MRP SYSTEM *******

TITLE : DEMONSTRATION
DATE : Sunday 18-07-1999
TIME : 10:36 PM

ANALYSIS REQUESTED - DEMONSTRATION

Product (488 available)	- DR-45672 - Four Drawer Filing Cabinet
Product Options (24 available)	- vertical, sizes, green, locks, fittings.
Components (162 available)	- first 4 level 1, first 4 level 2
Weeks (104 available)	- first 5
Continuity	- no
Report Formats (34 available)	- 1, 2, 3
Details (62 pages available)	- Summary 2 pages
Options	- off

Report 1 - Bill of Materials

```
Level 0       DR-45672
               |----------------------------------------- + others
               |             |             |             |
               |             |             |             |
Level 1       DR-46831      FN-53762      FN-62534      FN-26374
               |
               |---------------------------------------------------- + others
               |             |             |             |
Level 2       FN-63541      PR-3645       PR-7495       PR-1135
```

Report 2 - Inventory

NAME	# OF SUBCOMP	# PER PARENT	INVENTORY ON HAND	LEAD TIME	LOT SIZE
DR-45672	4	-	125	1	50
DR-46831	8	4	487	2	1250
FN-53762	16	4	257	2	1200
FN-62534	16	4	1253	2	2000
FN-26374	16	4	566	3	2000
FN-63541	8	4	124	4	1000
PR-3645	4	2	255	1	1500
PR-7495	4	2	458	1	1500
PR-1135	4	2	1087	1	2500

Figure 15.9 Example of a simplified MRP printout for Alco Office Supplies

Report 3 - Master Production Schedule

```
---------------------------------------
|   The Master Production Schedule    |
|-------------------------------------|
| PRODUCT NAME             : DR-45672 |
| NUMBER OF SUBCOMPONENTS  : 4        |
| ON HAND INVENTORY        : 125      |
| LEAD TIME (WEEKS)        : 1        |
|=====================================|
| WEEK              REQUIRED QUANTITY |
|    1                            175 |
|    2                            250 |
|    3                            250 |
|    4                            175 |
|    5                            175 |
-------------------------------------|

------------------------------------------------------------------
| Item: DR-45672                                Level: 0       |
| Parent: NONE                                  Lead Time: 1   |
|----------------------------------------------------------------|
|      | Gross      On hand     Net         Planned    Planned   |
| Week | Required   Inventory   Required    Receipts   Releases  |
|----------------------------------------------------------------|
|    1 |      175         125          50         50        250  |
|    2 |      250         ---         250        250        250  |
|    3 |      250         ---         250        250        175  |
|    4 |      175         ---         175        175        175  |
|    5 |      175         ---         175        175        ---  |
------------------------------------------------------------------

------------------------------------------------------------------
| Item: DR-46831                                Level: 1       |
| Parent: DR-45673                              Lead Time: 2   |
|----------------------------------------------------------------|
|      | Gross      On hand     Net         Planned    Planned   |
| Week | Required   Inventory   Required    Receipts   Releases  |
|----------------------------------------------------------------|
|    1 |     1000         487         513       1250       ----  |
|    2 |     1000         737         263       1250       ----  |
|    3 |      700         987         ---       ----       1250  |
|    4 |      700         287         413       1250       1250  |
|    5 |     ----         837         ---       ----       ----  |
-----------------------------------------------------------------

------------------------------------------------------------------
| Item:  FN-53762                             Level: 1         |
| Parent:DR-45672                             Lead Time: 2     |
|----------------------------------------------------------------|
|      | Gross      On hand     Net         Planned    Planned   |
| Week | Required   Inventory   Required    Receipts   Releases  |
|----------------------------------------------------------------|
|    1 |     1000         257         743       1200       ----  |
|    2 |     1000         457         543       1200       ----  |
|    3 |      700         657          43       1200       1200  |
|    4 |      700        1157         ---       ----       1200  |
|    5 |     ----         257         ---       ----       1200  |
------------------------------------------------------------------

-------------------------------------------------------------------------
```

Figure 15.9 cont'd

Project 15.3 *MRP needs specialised software. Some of this only does the basic calculations, and you can even get useful results from a spreadsheet; on the other hand, there are some huge systems designed for complicated manufacturing processes. See what programs you can find for MRP and compare their features.*

Adjusting the MRP schedules

So far we have described the basic approach of MRP, but there are some adjustments that can improve the results. For example, we have only considered a single product taken in isolation. Several different products might use the same materials, so MRP should link these products and combine orders before sending them to suppliers. Really, we should always think about combining small orders into larger ones.

Batching MRP orders

MRP is typically run every week, so the basic system might suggest a series of small orders placed every week or so. These frequent orders can be inconvenient and have high administration and delivery costs. It is more convenient and cheaper to combine several of these small orders into fewer, larger ones. This is called **batching** or **lot sizing**.

There are four common approaches to lot sizing.

1. **Lot-for-lot** – you order exactly the net requirement suggested by MRP for each period. This is the method we have used so far. It minimises the amount of stock, but can give high ordering, set-up and administration costs.
2. **Fixed order quantity** – you find an order size that is convenient, and always order this same amount. This might, for example, be a truckload, a container load, an economic order quantity (which we describe in Chapter 21) or some other convenient size.
3. **Periodic orders** – you combine the net requirements over some fixed number of periods, and place regular orders for different quantities. An organisation might, for example, place an order every month. Working to such a regular timetable can give the benefits of simplicity and making operations routine.
4. **Batching rules** – these use some specific procedure to calculate the best pattern of orders. Typically they look for the combination of orders that gives the minimum overall cost. In practice, this can be quite a difficult scheduling problem, so organisations generally use simple rules that give reasonable results. There are many available batching rules, and the supplement to this chapter describes a useful approach.

Closed-loop MRP

We have already suggested that MRP systems should link different products that use the same materials, and generate combined orders. We have also said that it should combine small orders into larger ones. But this can give problems with sporadic demand. The demands generated by MRP follow the master schedule, and this might create widely varying demands for materials, especially when small orders are combined into larger ones. Suppliers might have limited capacity and not be able to meet this demand pattern. It is obviously best to anticipate such bottlenecks during the planning stage, so that schedules or capacity can be adjusted before the plans are finalised. In other words, we introduce feedback between capacity planning and MRP.

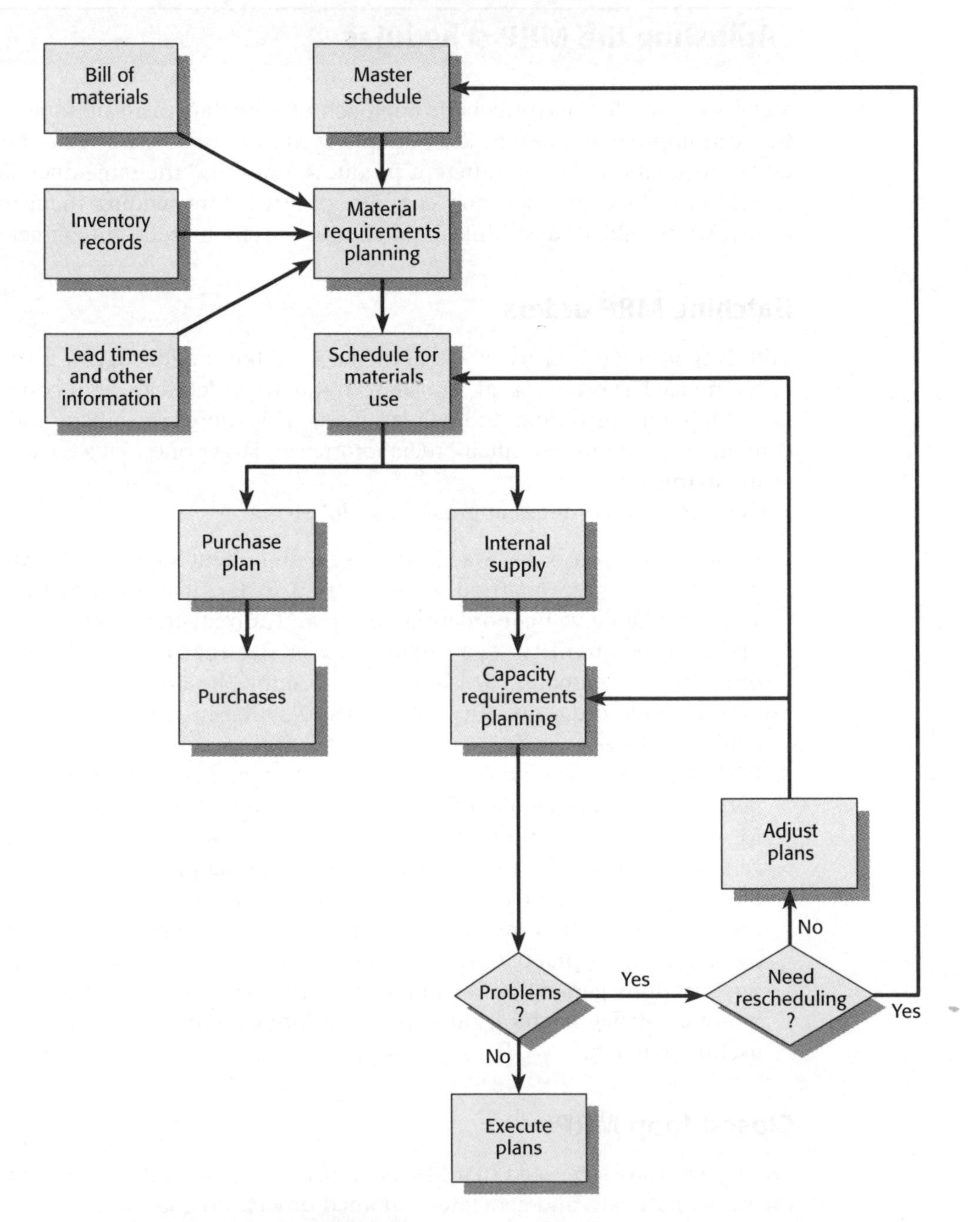

Figure 15.10 Closed-loop MRP system

Two important aspects of feedback occur when:

- proposed plans would break some capacity constraint; then the MRP system detects the overload and initiates early rescheduling. In this way, the MRP system takes an active part in capacity planning;
- operations are interrupted; the control system detects this and updates the master schedule. But it must work with the MRP system to see what production is feasible with the materials available. Now MRP forms part of the control system.

Systems with this kind of feedback are called **closed-loop MRP**. You can imagine a typical operation with feedback. The initial MRP run gives schedules for the supply of materials, and these are translated into required capacities. If available capacity is less than demand the system makes changes by adjusting capacity to meet the higher demand, rescheduling to make demand fit into the available capacity, or some compromise between these two. In practice, this third option is the most common. The system generally uses an iterative approach, of the kind that we have already met with resource requirements planning. These iterations are continued until it finds a reasonable solution. This approach of linking capacity planning to MRP is sometimes called **capacity requirements planning**, and is summarised in Figure 15.10.

Closed-loop MRP can overcome problems with capacity, but it can be much more flexible than this. Capacity requirements planning is really a way of extending the MRP approach further into the organisation. We started by using MRP to schedule orders for materials, and are now using it in capacity planning. We might continue and use MRP for more functions, which we will discuss in the next section.

Review questions

15.9 Why might several small orders be combined into a single larger one?

15.10 What is a batching rule?

15.11 What is the key element of closed-loop MRP?

OPERATIONS IN PRACTICE

Mokkelbost Maintenance Division

Mokkelbost Maintenance Division (MMD) is a medium-sized company with offices in Copenhagen. Its main business there is the maintenance of industrial heating systems. On a regular basis, MMD inspects, tests, repairs and maintains the heating systems in commercial buildings. It currently has contracts with 800 companies occupying 3,500 buildings.

In recent months MMD has had a disappointing number of problems. MMD has been late visiting companies and overtime costs are rising. On several occasions, it started work on a system, scheduled overtime so it could close the system down at a convenient time for the customer, and then found that it did not have the materials to finish the job. Even with 50 million kroner of inventories, MMD frequently had shortages of parts. The following memo started to change things.

▶

Memorandum

To: Helena Maestriani, Manager Service Planning and Inventory Control
From: Per Svensen, VP Operations

Our customer service level, measured as on-time services of customer equipment, has been showing a steady downward trend. Our objective is 95 per cent, but, for the last six months, we have been averaging 85 per cent.

I have talked to the president about your suggestion that we consider an MRP system to solve our planning and materials problems. He likes the idea but would like some more details.

Please prepare a brief report about MRP, explain what it is, what it will do for us and how you would go about implementing it. I will take up your report in the next management committee.

Helena wrote a convincing report about the long-term benefits of MRP. Within 18 months MMD had an initial system working. At the end of the first year, customer complaints had fallen back to a reasonable level, stock levels were lower and the company was thinking of extending its MRP system to look at related activities.

Sources: Svensen P. (2000) 'Introducing MRP', Presentation to the Western Operations Forum, June; and internal company reports.

Extensions to MRP

Initial ideas

The idea of MRP is not particularly new. Some organisations used basic manual methods for many years. Practical MRP needs a lot of computing and integration of several related systems, and this only became possible in the 1970s. At this time Joseph Orlicky[1] laid some foundations for reasonable systems, and Oliver Wight[2] extended these ideas. Manufacturing companies were the first to develop large MRP systems. Other types of organisation followed, and MRP is now widely used. It can be more difficult to apply in services, largely because they do not always have a detailed master schedule to define production. None the less, many services have successfully adopted MRP.

- In a university, the finished product is graduating students. The master schedule shows the number of students who will graduate from each programme in each semester. The bill of materials shows the courses each student takes in each semester. Then we can use MRP to find the timetable for materials needed, which are the instructors, classrooms, laboratories, and so on.
- Hospitals use MRP to schedule surgical operations and make sure that supplies and equipment are ready when needed. The master schedule gives the planned surgical operations in any period. The bill of material contains information about the facilities, equipment and resources needed for each type of surgery. The inventory file contains information about theatres, staff, surgical instruments, disposable materials, reusable instruments, and so on.
- Restaurants use MRP to schedule their food and equipment. The master schedule gives the meals the restaurant plans to prepare each mealtime. The recipes for each meal give the bill of material.

You can imagine the movement of MRP from its roots in manufacturing into a wider range of organisations as the first extension to basic MRP. We have also talked about the second type of extension which added extra facilities, such as batching rules to combine small orders, combining orders for common materials used in several products, and including feedback in capacity resource planning. Other extensions improved procedures for dealing with variable supply, supplier reliability, wastage, defective quality, variable demand and variable lead times. Often these problems are dealt with by simple rules. If, for example, an organisation finds that the timing of deliveries is unreliable, it can order materials some specified time in advance of actual needs; if quality is a problem, it can add some safety stock to replace materials that do not meet quality standards; if materials are cheap, it can use some minimum order size. Simple rules of this kind have been developed to deal with many different problems. Often they raise costs, but this price is worth paying to ensure uninterrupted operations. Now we can look at a further extension into MRP II.

Moving to MRP II

So far we have emphasised MRP's role in scheduling materials: it basically designs timetables for ordering materials. Closed-loop MRP took this one step further and made sure that there was enough capacity in operations to actually supply these materials. But materials are only one resource, and organisations have to schedule several others, including people, equipment, facilities, finances, logistics, and any other resources. Surely we can use the same MRP approach to consider these other resources. This thinking has led to a major extension of MRP into **manufacturing resource planning**, or **MRP II**.

Suppose we use MRP to get timetables for making some materials within the organisation. MRP shows us when to start making the materials, so it effectively schedules the related operations. Now we have used MRP not only to schedule the arrival of materials, but also to schedule the jobs needed to make these materials. But when we know the timetables for these jobs, we can use them to schedule the equipment needed. And when we have timetables for the equipment, we can use them to schedule the people needed to work them. And when we have timetables for people, we can use them to schedule other facilities, such as catering and transport. We can go even further than this. If we know when we are getting deliveries, we can schedule transport operations; looking at the finished goods, we can plan distribution. Continuing in this way, we could eventually build an integrated system that would 'explode' the master schedule to give timetables for all the jobs, equipment, operators, machines, facilities, and so on needed to achieve it.

In principle, there is no reason why we should stop at using MRP to schedule operations. Why not, for example, continue and look at the associated finance, marketing, human resource management, etc.? Eventually we would have a completely integrated system that would use the master schedule as the basis for planning all the resources in an organisation. This is the aim of MRP II.

MRP II (manufacturing resource planning) gives an integrated system for synchronising all functions within an organisation.

- It connects schedules for all functions back to the master schedule.

Linking all activities to the master schedule can give very efficient operations. No unnecessary jobs are done, there are no delays because of late deliveries or shortages, no stocks of work in progress accumulate, and products move smoothly through the whole process. These benefits have encouraged many organisations to extend their MRP systems towards MRP II.

Although the idea of MRP II seems fairly straightforward, there are considerable practical difficulties. At a simple level, it is difficult to get schedules that everyone accepts as being good and workable. In common with most planning, MRP II does not stop at a single run to find the 'best' solution, but uses an iterative approach to find a reasonable solution that everyone will accept. It is clearly difficult to get agreement from so many people with different interests and aims, and the series of 'what-if' tests that look for improvements can become daunting. Jones and Towill describe these as 'monster systems'.[3]

Perhaps the most serious problem with MRP II is the difficulty of getting complete integration of all functions and systems. Many organisations have asked if the effort needed to get such close integration is actually worth the rewards. We have already said that MRP systems tend to be inflexible and unable to respond quickly to changes, so a whole organisation run in this way might become cumbersome and unwieldy. Rather than give an efficient process, MRP II might leave it vulnerable to changing conditions. It is certainly fair to say that very few organisations work with full MRP II. Most are happier to implement parts of the system, often using different names, such as **distribution resource planning** to schedule all logistics activities.

Working with other organisations

MRP II is not the end of the story. The systems we have described so far are all used within an organisation, but there is a clear trend towards integration of the supply chain (which we discuss in Chapter 19). This means that organisations along the supply chain improve their overall performance by co-operating, exchanging information, and co-ordinating their operations. Now you can see the next extension to MRP, which is to co-ordinate operations of different organisations within the supply chain. This is the basis of **enterprise resource planning** (ERP).

ERP emphasises the whole supply chain, extending the MRP approach to include suppliers, and other organisations (as shown in Figure 15.11). Suppose, for example, that a manufacturer ran its own MRP and found that it needed 1,000 units of some materials at the beginning of June. If its MRP system is linked to the supplier's system, it can now start scheduling activities to make sure these materials are ready in time. Similarly, the supplier could link its system to its own suppliers, and so move backwards through the supply chain, creating an integrated planning system.

ERP obviously relies on complete trust between organisations, and a free flow of information. In principle, this is relatively easy to organise, using the Internet and other aspects of e-commerce. However, you can imagine the complexity of systems needed, and the practical problems that arise. At the moment it is fair to say that ERP is still being developed and is not widely used.

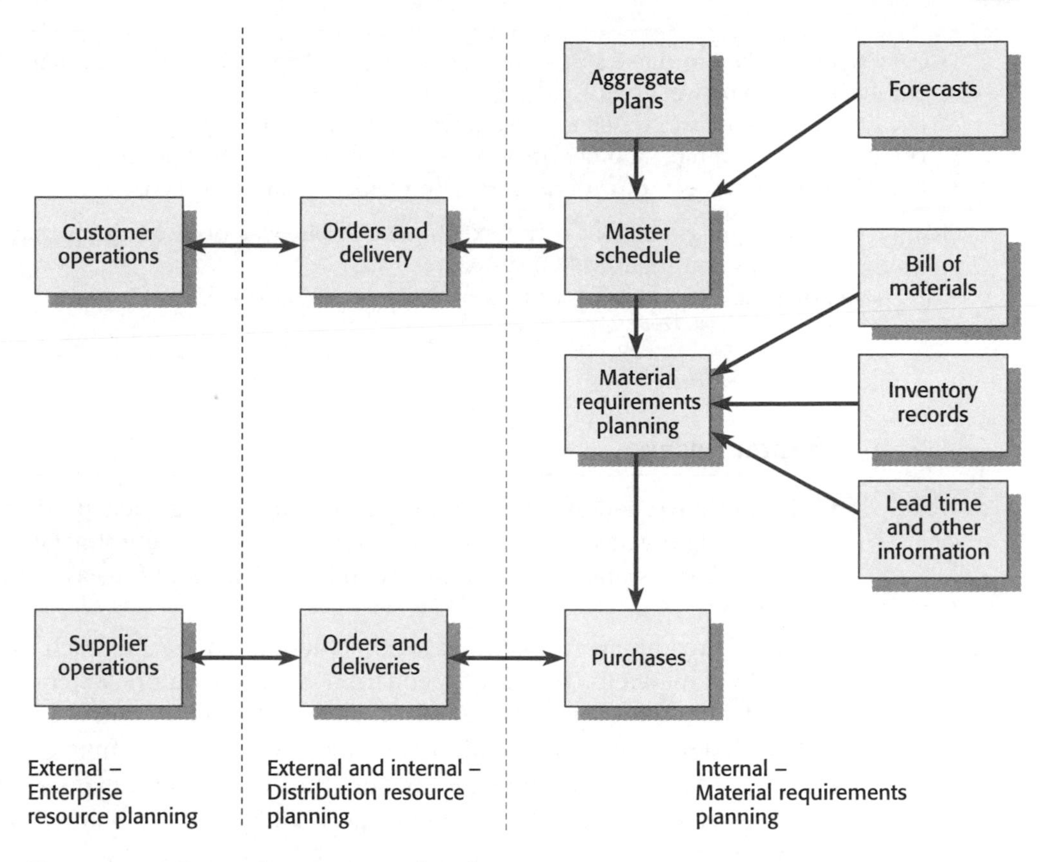

Figure 15.11 Enterprise resource planning

Review questions

15.12 How could you extend the approach of MRP?

15.13 What exactly is MRP II?

15.14 Distribution resource planning relies on integrated computer systems. Do you think this is true?

OPERATIONS IN PRACTICE

Publishers Equipment Corporation

Publishers Equipment Corporation (PEC) was one of the early companies to move beyond MRP and aim for an integrated MRP II system. It did this for two reasons:

- to improve customer service;
- to organise its manufacturing more efficiently.

You can think of MRP as an information system that collects data from various parts of the organisation, analyses it, and uses the results for planning. PEC wanted a very sophisticated MRP II system, but this would be too big a change to introduce in one step. Instead PEC implemented its plans in several phases. The first phase checked the MRP and extended it to include accounting and purchasing systems. In turn, PEC introduced this first phase in four steps.

1. Data were checked to make sure that they were complete and accurate enough. Then the links were tested between MRP and other systems.
2. The MRP II software was tested to make sure that it was working properly and had no errors.
3. The master scheduling and order entry systems were linked to the MRP II system and tested.
4. The whole system was run, with the results implemented and checked.

This gave a successful extension to the existing MRP, but was only one step that PEC was planning towards its ambitious MRP II system.

Source: Ormsby J.G., Ormsby S.Y. and Ruthstrom C.R. (1990) 'MRP II Implementation: a Case Study', *Production and Inventory Management Journal*, 31(4), pp. 77–81

Chapter review

- The master schedule contains timetables for making each product. Short-term scheduling organises the resources needed to achieve these timetables. Traditional approaches assume that demands are independent, and forecast requirements for resources.
- Material requirements planning (MRP) is an alternative approach to planning the supply of materials. This is a dependent demand inventory system which assumes that demands for materials are related, and can be found from the master schedule. It 'explodes' the master schedule to find the quantities and timing of material orders.
- MRP needs a lot of accurate information. It can use this for many related purposes, such as generating timetables of operations and purchases, status reports, changes, performance information, exception reports, and so on.
- The main benefits of MRP come from the close match between material supply and demand, and include low stocks and associated costs. But there are problems with MRP, including its limited use and the very complicated systems.
- Basic MRP schedules can be improved in several ways, such as batching small orders into larger ones, smoothing demand and iteratively improving schedules.
- There are several extensions to MRP, including closed-loop MRP which leads to capacity resource planning. Manufacturing resource planning (MRP II) extends the idea of MRP to other functions. Enterprise resource planning (ERP) extends the approach to other organisations in the supply chain.

Key terms

batching *p. 435*
bill of materials *p. 421*
capacity requirements planning *p. 437*
dependent demand *p. 418*
distribution resource planning *p. 440*
enterprise resource planning (ERP) *p. 440*
gross requirement *p. 423*
independent demand *p. 418*
lot sizing *p. 435*
manufacturing resource planning (MRP II) *p. 439*
material requirements planning (MRP) *p. 418*
net requirement *p. 423*
time shifting *p. 423*

CASE STUDY Schmidt Machine Works

Sityuen Feng and Helmut Bayer worked for Schmidt Machine Works. This is a leading manufacturer of parts for knitting and sewing machines, based in Basel, but with manufacturing facilities in Austria and Germany.

For several weeks Sityuen and Helmut had been talking about MRP. At last, they decided to do an experiment to see if it was worth considering this in more detail. To help in this decision, they talked to Pieter Keller from the Production Section, who said:

The principles of MRP are very easy, but are difficult to implement. I suggest we pick a couple of products at random and see if MRP would give any savings. We currently make around 2,500 different products so this experiment would simply lay the foundations for a more detailed study. I have chosen two products, and as I couldn't get all the information about these I just made up some typical figures. The real process is so complicated that I made a number of simplifications.

Pieter also explained the present inventory system. This has stock levels reviewed at the end of each fortnight, with orders placed to bring stocks up to target levels. This level is set by a formula where each item is classified as A, B or C. Then the target stock levels are:

- A – 1.2 times expected demand in lead time plus two weeks;
- B – 1.4 times expected demand in lead time plus three weeks;
- C – 1.6 times expected demand in lead time plus four weeks.

The figures suggested by Pieter related to two products with codes AP4072 and FL7341. The expected production of AP4072 will remain steady at around 100 units a week for the next two years. FL7341 varies a little more, and monthly production is estimated as follows:

Year 1		Year 2	
Month	**Production**	**Month**	**Production**
1	24	1	60
2	20	2	56
3	18	3	45
4	25	4	65
5	31	5	93
6	45	6	110
7	56	7	132
8	50	8	124
9	46	9	117
10	40	10	110
11	38	11	98
12	56	12	136

Stock holding costs are 0.2 per cent of unit cost a week with shortage costs of 10 per cent of unit cost a week. If stocks of an item are about to run out, it is possible to request urgent deliveries, which cost about twice as much as normal deliveries. Much of Schmidt's production is sold to Germany, so it is common to quote prices in Deutschmarks. Times are quoted in weeks and other details are given in the following table:

Product code	Unit cost	Reorder cost	Category	Current stock	Lead time	Assembly time	Made from code (units)
AP4072	–	–	–	6	–	2	LF3281 (4) LF3282 (1)
LF3281	–	–	–	10	–	1	SF3822 (25) TG4071 (5)
SF3822	4	80	A	200	2	–	–
TG4071	20	120	B	75	3	–	–
LF3282	–	–	–	16	–	2	AX0012 (50) AX1012 (50) LX6734 (4)
AX0012	10	50	A	1,000	2	–	–
AX1012	20	50	A	625	2	–	–
LX6734	–	–	–	104	–	1	LK0039 (10) LK0040 (10)
LK0039	5	120	A	240	3	–	–
LK0040	6	180	A	360	2	–	–
FL7341	–	–	–	14	–	3	CD4055 (2) CD5988 (4) CE0993 (1)
CD4055	–	–	–	83	–	2	ML8001 (1) MK0126 (2) MK0288 (4)
CD5988	–	–	–	122	–	3	LY4021 (10) LY4022 (20) LY4023 (10)
CE0993	–	–	–	96	–	2	NY0032 (6) NX9774 (3) NX0312 (12)
ML8001	–	–	–	50	–	1	ML0082 (20) ML0083 (10)
MK0126	–	–	–	122	–	2	FY0017 (6) NP4021 (24) LF7031 (12)
MK0288	–	–	–	124	–	1	ML0082 (40) ML0094 (10)
ML0082	–	–	–	250	–	1	BP0174 (4) BR3051 (1)
ML0083	–	–	–	220	–	1	BQ7441 (4) BQ7442 (8)
FY0017	4	80	B	86	4	–	–
NP4021	2	160	A	450	2	–	–
LF7031	6	120	B	265	3	–	–
ML0094	–	–	–	150	–	1	PX1570 (5) PX1571 (5) PX1572 (1)

Product code	Unit cost	Reorder cost	Category	Current stock	Lead time	Assembly time	Made from code (units)
LY4021	–	–	–	200	–	3	ML0083 (6) BQ6399 (2)
LY4022	–	–	–	122	–	4	ML0094 (12) LF7031 (12) LF7032 (2) LF7033 (1) LF7034 (12)
LY4023	–	–	–	60	–	1	LF7033 (1) LF7939 (60)
NY0032	–	–	–	24	–	1	ML0083 (10) ML8001 (1)
NX9774	–	–	–	36	–	1	LF7032 (2) LF7034 (12) BQ7742 (8)
NX0312	–	–	–	240	–	1	ML0094 (12) LF7031 (12) AP7031 (1)
BQ6399	43	220	B	33	3	–	–
LF7033	86	380	C	40	1	–	–
LF7939	75	420	A	120	2	–	–
ML8001	118	420	B	22	2	–	–
LF7032	66	120	B	145	4	–	–
LF7034	–	–	–	850	–	2	PX4971 (12) PX3055 (2)
BP0174	8	40	A	85	2	–	–
BR3051	6	80	A	155	2	–	–
BQ7441	–	–	–	360	–	1	FY0017 (6) FZ0149 (1)
BQ7442	24	40	B	86	3	–	–
LF7031	6	120	A	780	4	–	–
AP7031	–	–	–	66	–	2	PX1571 (10) PX1420 (2) PX3055 (1)
FZ0149	120	420	C	260	5	–	–
PX1420	69	120	B	857	3	–	–
PX1570	12	40	A	1,250	2	–	–
PX1571	8	40	A	2,450	3	–	–
PX1572	86	80	B	475	2	–	–
PX3055	57	80	B	125	1	–	–
PX4971	15	80	A	750	2	–	–

Questions

- Would a trial, like the one suggested, give any useful information?
- For the products chosen, how well do you think the present inventory control system works?
- Would MRP bring any benefits for these products?
- What would be the next step for introducing MRP in Schmidt Machine Works?

Problems

15.1 An agency for temporary office staff has urgent orders for 40 people in week 16 of a planning cycle, 60 people in week 13 and 50 people in week 12. There is no shortage of people applying to work for them, but each is given a 'personal pack' and two 'business packs' containing information about the work they do, and what is expected by the client. The packs are prepared by specialist suppliers, who quote lead times of three and two weeks respectively. It takes two weeks to become familiar with material in these packs. The agency has five people on its books who are already familiar with the packs and are ready to work, and they have 10 personal packs and 20 business packs in stock, and a delivery of 40 business packs is expected in week 7. What does it have to do to get ready for its clients?

15.2 Each unit of product AF43 is made from 12 units of BL19, 10 units of CX23 and 20 units of DY33. Each unit of BL19 is made from two units of EM08, two units of FF87 and two units of GO95. Each unit of both EM08 and DY33 is made from six units of HX22. A master schedule needs 60 units of AF43 to be ready by week 8 of a planning cycle and 50 units by week 10. There are minimum order sizes of 2,000 units for HX22, and 500 units of both FF87 and GO95. Information about stocks and lead times in weeks (either for assembly or orders) is as follows:

	Current stocks	Minimum stocks	Lead time (weeks)
AF43	20	10	2
BL19	230	50	3
CX23	340	100	1
DY33	410	100	3
EM08	360	200	2
FF87	620	200	2
GO95	830	200	2
HX22	1,200	200	4

Design an order schedule for the materials.

15.3 Product A is assembled from two units of B and one unit of C. Component C is assembled from one unit of D and two units of E. Part D also needs one unit of E. Product F is assembled from one unit of C and two units of D.

A master schedule makes 80 units of product A in April and 120 units in July. It makes 150 units of product F in June. Design separate material schedules for the two product A and F. How can you combine these two into a single schedule?

Discussion questions

15.1 In what type of companies do you think MRP is most widely used? When is it most effective? Some people say that MRP only really works when there are more than, say, six levels in the bill of materials and large lot sizes. Why do you think this is?

15.2 MRP was developed by manufacturers, so how can it be used in services? Give some specific examples to support your views. Are there any specific problems using MRP in services?

15.3 MRP links operations to the master schedule, but many operations are done more efficiently in a different order and with different batch sizes to those given by MRP. How do you think such problems can be overcome?

15.4 Closed-loop MRP gives feedback for capacity planning. How exactly does this work – does the schedule for operations set the capacity needed, or does the capacity available limit the possible schedules? What about distribution resource planning?

15.5 What features would you expect to see in a commercial MRP package? Describe some examples to illustrate your views.

15.6 MRP has evolved from a simple method of calculating order times, to a huge system for controlling all functions along the supply chain. What are the most important steps in this evolution? What are the next steps?

15.7 MRP is complicated – and if you start linking other operations, systems, functions, and organisations, the result becomes hugely complicated. The ideas of MRP II and ERP seem good in principle, but the systems become so unwieldy that they can never work properly. Even if they did work, operations would be too inflexible and burdensome to cope with more agile competitors. Do you think that this is true? Explain your views.

References

1. Orlicky J. (1975) *Material Requirements Planning*. New York: McGraw-Hill.
2. Wight O.W. (1984) *Manufacturing Resource Planning: MRP II*. Essex Junction, VT: Oliver Wight Publications.
3. Jones D. and Towill D. (1998) 'New Directions in Logistics Research', *Control*, March, pp. 15–19.

Selected reading

Baudin M. (1990) *Manufacturing Systems Analysis*. Englewood Cliffs, NJ: Prentice-Hall.

Browne J., Harhen J. and Shivnan J. (1996) *Production Management Systems*. Reading, MA: Addison-Wesley.

Hill T. (1995) *Manufacturing Strategy*. Basingstoke: Macmillan.

Landvater D.V. and Gray C.D. (1989) *MRP II Standard System*. Essex Junction, VT: Oliver Wight Publications.

Luscombe M (1993) *MRP II: Integrating the Business*. London: Butterworth-Heineman.

Turbide D.A. (1993) *MRP+*. New York: Industrial Press.

Vollman T.E., Berry W.L. and Whybark D.C. (1996) *Manufacturing Planning and Control Systems*, 4th edn. New York: McGraw Hill.

Waters C.D.J. (1992) *Inventory Control and Management*. Chichester: John Wiley.

Useful Websites

www.SAP.com – a major supplier of MRP software

www.grms.com – views from another supplier

www.apics.org – American Production and Inventory Control Society

SUPPLEMENT TO CHAPTER 15

A batching rule for MRP

Contents

Batching rules

The basic calculations of MRP suggest the quantity and timing for orders of materials. MRP is typically run every week, and this can give a series of small, weekly orders. This can be inconvenient and give high administration costs, so it is often better to combine several small orders into larger, less frequent ones. The most common way of organising this uses a **batching rule**, which is a simple rule that gives a reasonable pattern of orders. There are several possible rules, but the following procedure usually gives a good result.

Procedure

This rule finds the best number of periods' demand to combine into a single batch. If orders are placed more frequently than this, the administration and delivery charges rise and give higher costs; if orders are placed less frequently, stock levels rise and again give higher costs. In other words, we are working with a cost curve with a distinct minimum, as shown in Figure 15s.1.

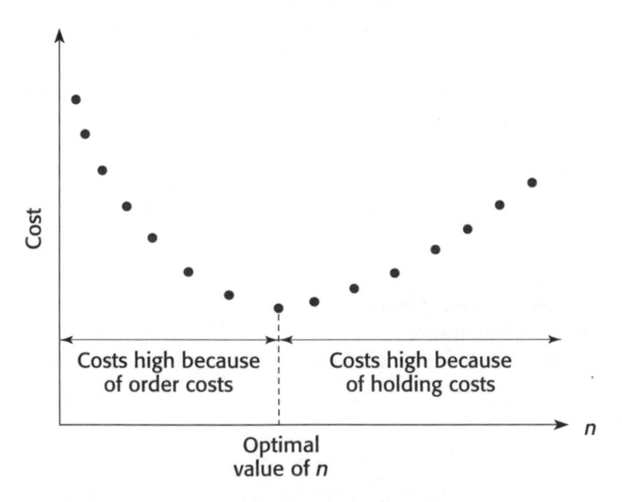

Figure 15s.1 Variation in cost with the number of periods combined into a single order

We can add all the costs of placing and receiving an order into the single figure R, the reorder cost. In the same way, we can add all the costs of holding a unit of stock for a unit of time to give the single figure H, the holding cost. It might, for example, cost £25 to place an order for office chairs (so $R = 25$), and then cost £20 a year to keep each chair in stock until it is needed (so $H = 20$).

When we buy enough stock to cover all orders for the next n periods, we can calculate the total cost per unit time based on H and C. Our aim is to find the value of n that minimises this cost. The easiest way of doing this is to start by taking small values of n, so that we are at the left-hand side of graph in Figure 15s.1. Then we slowly increase n, following the graph downward until the point where the cost starts to rise. At this point we have found the lowest cost and the corresponding optimal value of n. The details of this procedure are as follows:

- First calculate the cost of buying for a single period and compare this with the cost of buying for two periods. If it is cheaper to buy for two periods than for one, we are going down the left-hand side of the graph in Figure 15s.1 and costs are falling as n increases.
- Next compare the cost of buying for two periods with the cost of buying for three periods. If it is cheaper to buy for three periods, we are still going down the left-hand side of the graph and have not yet reached the bottom.
- Continue this procedure, comparing the cost of buying for three periods with the cost of buying for four periods, and so on. Keep on comparing the cost of buying for the next n periods with the cost of buying for the next $n + 1$ periods.
- At some point the cost of buying for $n + 1$ periods becomes greater than the cost of buying for n periods. At this point we have reached the bottom of the graph and found the minimal cost. Any further increases in n increase costs as we climb up the right-hand side of the graph.

Fortunately, there is a short cut to the arithmetic that removes most of the work. We will not bother with the derivation of this, but the result is:

$$n(n + 1)D_{n+1} \geq 2R/H$$

Where: R = cost of placing an order
H = cost of holding a unit in stock for a period
D_{n+1} = demand in the $(n + 1)^{th}$ period

If this inequality is **not true**, it is cheaper to order for $n + 1$ periods than for n, so we are on the left-hand side of the graph of costs in Figure 15s.1. If we increase n until the inequality becomes **true**, it is cheaper to order for n periods than $n + 1$, and we are on the right-hand side of the cost graph. This suggests a procedure where we set n to 1 and check the inequality. If it is not true, we increase n to 2 and check the inequality again. Then we keep on increasing n, until eventually the inequality becomes true. At this point we are at the bottom of the cost curve and have found an optimal value for n. The procedure then stops. Figure 15s.2 shows a flow chart for this procedure.

This batching rule usually gives good results, but it does not guarantee optimal ones – because of the assumptions of fixed and known costs, fixed demand, an optimal solution that occurs as soon as costs begin to rise, and so on.

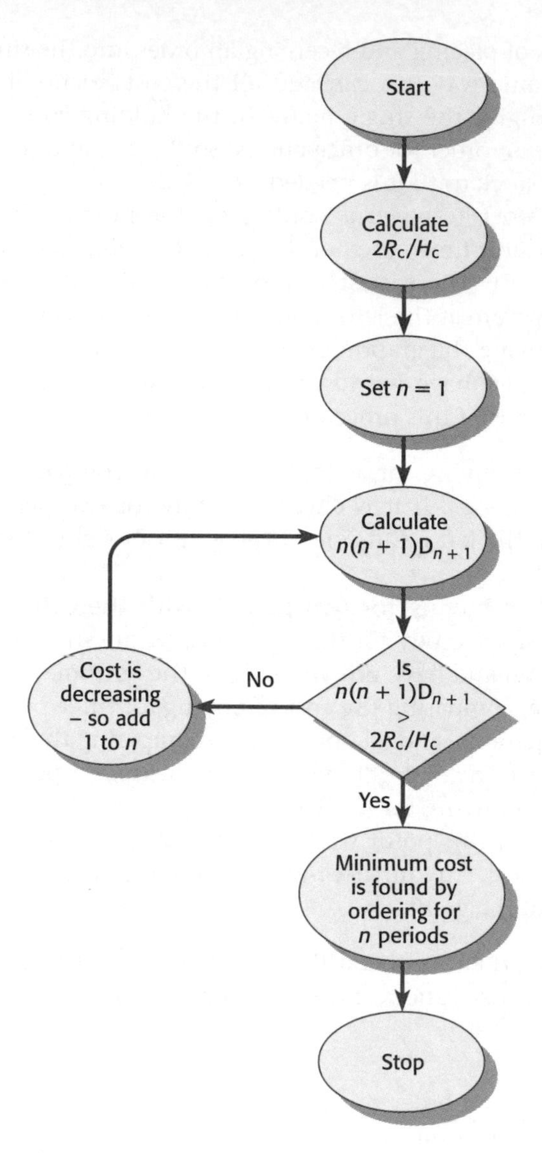

Figure 15s.2 Procedure for lot sizing

WORKED EXAMPLE

The procurement manager of Associated Services knows that the total cost of placing an order and having it delivered is £90. The holding cost of an item is £4 a month. If MRP shows the following demand for the item, find an ordering policy that gives reasonable costs.

Month	1	2	3	4	5	6	7	8	9	10	11	12
Demand	1	3	5	8	8	5	2	1	1	5	7	9

Solution

Following the procedure shown in Figure 15s.2, with $R = 90$ and $H = 4$:

$$2R/H = 2 \times 90/4 = 45$$

- Starting with $n = 1$, $n + 1 = 2$ and $D_2 = 3$ we calculate:

$$n(n + 1)D_{n+1} = 1 \times 2 \times 3 = 6$$

As this is less than 45, the inequality is not true and we have not reached the minimum.

- Next taking $n = 2$, $n + 1 = 3$ and $D_3 = 5$ we calculate:

$$n(n + 1)D_{n+1} = 2 \times 3 \times 5 = 30$$

This is less than 45, so the inequality is still not true and we have not reached the minimum.

- Next taking $n = 3$, $n + 1 = 4$ and $D_4 = 8$ we calculate:

$$n(n + 1)D_{n+1} = 3 \times 4 \times 8 = 96$$

This is more than 45, so the inequality is true and we have found the minimum cost with $n = 3$.

This means we order enough at the beginning of month 1 to last for the first three months (i.e. 1 + 3 + 5 = 9) and schedule this to arrive before the beginning of month 1.

It is easier to do these calculations in a table, as shown below.

Month, *i*	1	2	3	4
Demand, D_i	1	3	5	8
n	1	2	3	
$n(n+1)D_{n+1}$	6	30	96	
Delivery	9			

Now we can continue the analysis for the next months. The only thing to remember is that every time we start a new cycle, the value of n returns to 1.

Month, *i*	1	2	3	4	5	6	7	8	9	10	11	12
Demand, D_i	1	3	5	8	8	5	2	1	1	5	7	9
n	1	2	3	1	2	3	4	5	6	1	2	1
$n(n+1)D_{n+1}$	6	30	96	16	30	24	20	30	210	14	54	
Delivery	9			25						12		

A good ordering policy makes sure that nine units arrive by month 1, 25 by month 4 and 12 by month 10.

Problems

15s.1 It costs £0.125 to store a unit of an item for one month. The total cost of placing an order for the item, including delivery, is £100. An MRP analysis finds the following demands for the item:

Month	1	2	3	4	5	6	7	8	9	10	11	12	13
Demand	100	50	60	60	100	100	80	60	40	70	80	100	140

Find a good ordering policy for the item.

15s.2 It costs $1 to hold one unit of an item in stock for one month, and each order costs a total of $60. There are currently no stocks of the item. MRP has suggested the following demands. Find a good ordering policy.

Month	1	2	3	4	5	6	7	8	9	10	11	12
Demand	40	39	60	81	238	722	998	1,096	921	161	0	40

Do you think this is the best possible ordering policy? Explain your reasoning.

CHAPTER 16

Just-in-time operations

Just-in-time purchasing at Xerox reduced the number of suppliers from 5,000 to 400, cut stocks of copier parts by $240 million, and automated its warehouses.

Jacobson G. and Hillkirk J.

Xerox: American Samurai, Macmillan, New York, 1986

Contents

Aims of the chapter

After reading this chapter you should be able to:

- appreciate the principles of just-in-time (JIT) operations;
- describe the main features of JIT and its effects on operations;
- know when JIT can be used;
- understand the changes that JIT brings to business relationships;
- design kanban systems for controlling JIT;
- list the benefits and disadvantages of JIT.

Main themes

This chapter will emphasise:

- **just-in-time**, when operations are done just as they are needed;
- **pull systems**, which pull materials through a process;
- **'kanbans'**, for controlling JIT operations.

Principles of just-in-time

Definitions

In essence, **just-in-time** or **JIT** organises all operations so they occur at exactly the time they are needed. They are not done too early (which would leave products and materials hanging around until they were actually needed) and they are not done too late (which would give poor customer service). You can see this effect when you order a taxi to collect you at 08:00. If the taxi arrives at 07:30, you are not ready and it wastes time sitting and waiting; if it arrives at 08:30, you are not pleased and will not use the service again. When the taxi arrives at 08:00 – just-in-time for your trip – it does not waste time waiting, and you are pleased that the service arrives exactly when you wanted it (see Figure 16.1).

With **just-in-time** operations, everything is arranged to occur at exactly the time it is needed.

It seems an obvious idea to have everything occurring at exactly the right time. Is this really just being punctual? In practice, it is much more than this, and we shall see how it has major effects on an organisation.

OPERATIONS IN PRACTICE

Ed's Diner, Melbourne

Tom Adams likes steak and eggs for breakfast. Every working day for the past 23 years he has arrived at Ed's Diner at 6 a.m. for breakfast – always 6 a.m. and always steak and eggs.

At 5.40 Ed starts preparing Tom's breakfast. At 5.59 he is finishing the cooking and pouring the coffee. At 6.00 he puts it on to a tray, and Tom arrives. At 6.30 Tom finishes breakfast, puts his newspaper away and heads out to open his shop down the road. Ed clears away the dishes and tidies up.

This ritual is repeated every working day. The surprising thing is that neither Ed nor Tom is ever late or early – and nothing ever goes wrong. Tom says that he enjoys Ed's steak and eggs before opening his own shop at 6.45. This means that he must leave Ed's by 6.30 and, therefore, must arrive at 6.00. Their timing is perfectly synchronised, and neither has to think about what they do. In recent years, they have started talking about their 'just-in-time meal'.

As you can imagine from the example of Ed and Tom, operations can become very efficient if they are organised to occur at just the time they are needed. You can see one effect of this with stocks of materials. The traditional approach buys materials early and keeps them in stock until they are needed by operations. This is expensive and a more efficient – just-in-time – approach co-ordinates materials so that they are delivered directly to operations as they are needed. In this way, stocks of materials are virtually eliminated. This approach is known by various names, including stockless production, zero inventory, lean production, Toyota system, Japanese manufacturing, world-class manufacturing and continuous flow manufacturing.

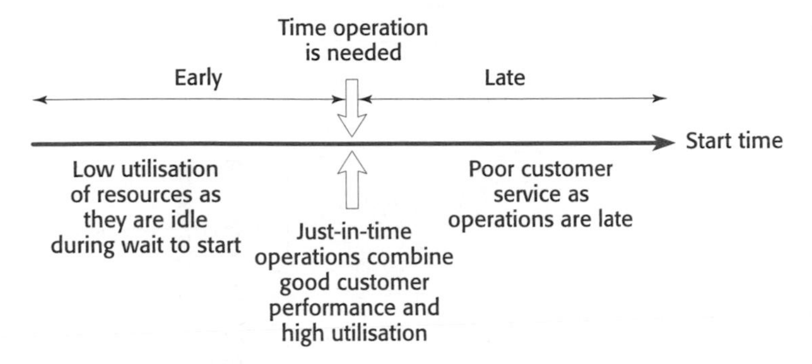

Figure 16.1 Just-in-time operations

In Chapter 15 we saw how MRP also aims to eliminate stocks by matching supply to demand. However, it can only be used in certain circumstances and has other problems, such as the amount of computing. Just-in-time suggests an alternative approach, which was largely developed by Japanese manufacturers. Companies such as Toyota spent years developing JIT methods through the 1970s, and their ideas have been widely adopted by other organisations. By the early 1990s half of European manufacturers used some form of JIT, and this continues to grow as organisations see the obvious benefits. Now, it is fair to say that all major organisations use some elements of JIT.

But JIT is not a new idea. In the 1920s iron ore arriving at Ford's plant in Detroit was turned into steel within a day and into finished cars shortly afterwards; McDonald's has made billions of hamburgers using elements of just-in-time; television news services collect reports just-in-time for their transmissions. The difference is that Toyota, and others, showed how JIT principles can ·e extended to all operations. One story says that the idea originated when executives from Honda were visiting California, and they saw how a system for restocking supermarket shelves could be extended to their own operations.

JIT and stocks

We can start describing JIT by looking at its effect on stocks, but remember that this is only one aspect of just-in-time operations.

The main purpose of stock is to give a buffer between operations. Then if some equipment breaks down, the process can still work normally for a time by using the stocks of work-in-progress. This leads to the traditional view that organisations can only guarantee smooth operations by holding stocks. Managers know that these stocks are expensive, but they are the only way of allowing for short-term mismatches between supply and demand. As you can see in Figure 16.2, stocks of raw materials form buffers between suppliers and operations, stocks of work-in-progress form buffers between the separate operations, and stocks of finished goods form buffers between the operations and customers.

Traditional inventory control systems (which we shall describe in Chapter 21) avoid problems by keeping stocks that are high enough to cover any likely circumstances. Sometimes, particularly with widely varying demand, this traditional

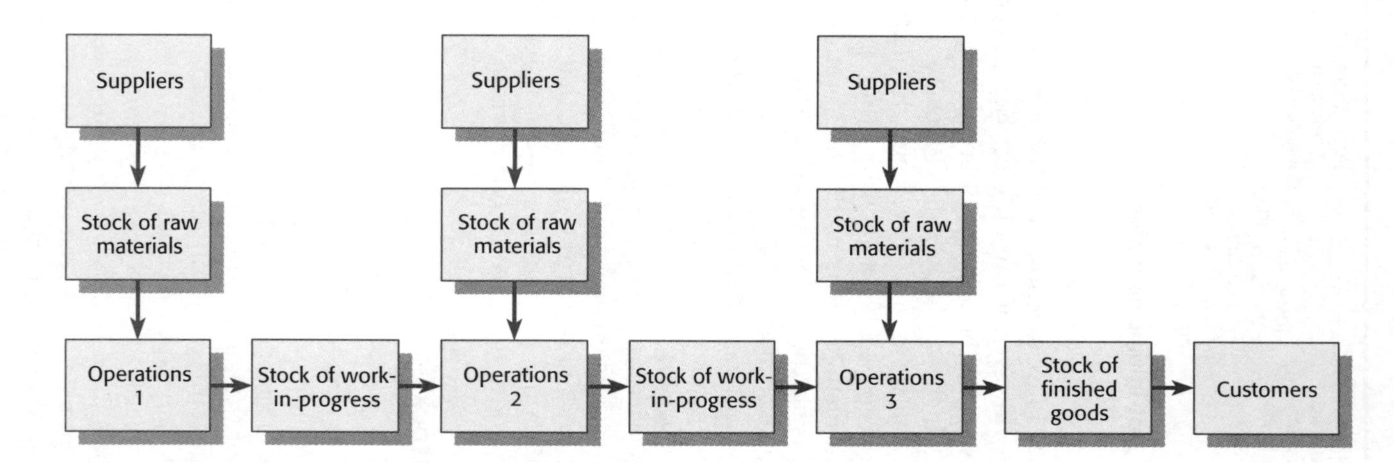

Figure 16.2 Stocks as buffers between operations

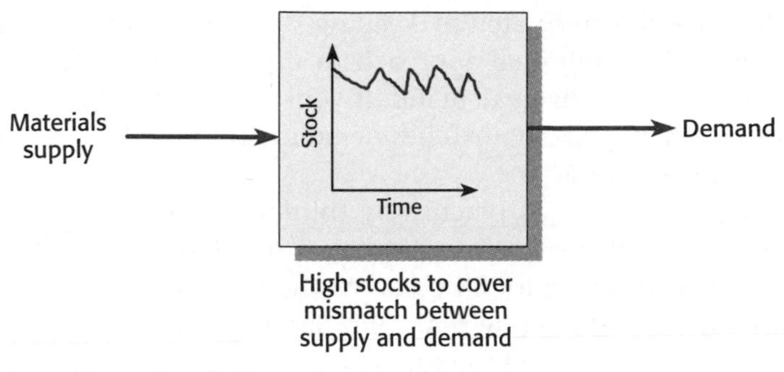

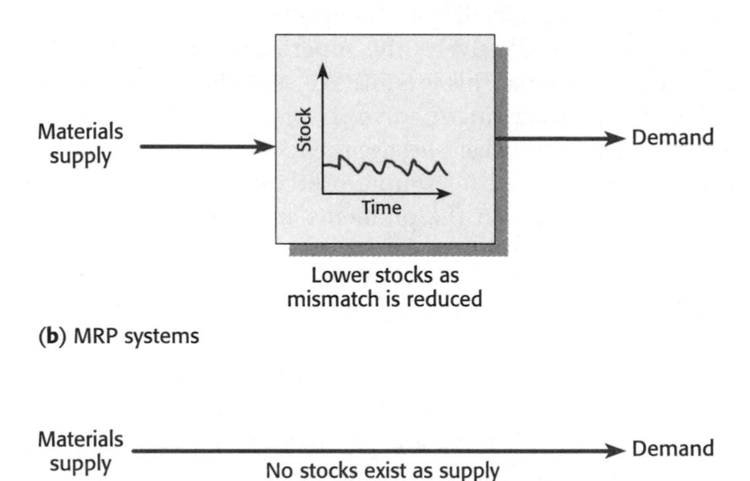

Materials supply → Demand

No stocks exist as supply exactly matches demand

(c) JIT approach

Figure 16.3 Stock levels with different approaches to planning materials

approach can give very high stocks. MRP reduces the amount of stock by using the master schedule to match the supply of materials more closely to demand. In practice, however, MRP systems still work with uncertainty and keep smaller stocks to allow for problems with operations or deliveries. The more closely we can match supply to demand, the less stock we need to cover any differences. If we can completely eliminate any mismatch, we need no stocks at all. This is the basis of just-in-time systems (see Figure 16.3).

> **Just-in-time** systems organise materials to arrive just as they are needed.
>
> - By co-ordinating supply and demand, they can eliminate stocks of raw materials and work-in-progress.

You can see an example of just-in-time operations when you buy fuel for a lawnmower. If your lawnmower has a petrol engine, there is a mismatch between the fuel supply which you buy from a garage, and demand when you actually mow the lawn. You allow for this mismatch by keeping stocks of fuel in the petrol tank and spare can. This is the traditional approach to inventory control, where stocks are high enough to cover any likely demand. If your lawnmower has an electric motor, the supply of electricity exactly matches demand and you do not need any stocks. This is a just-in-time system.

Now you can imagine JIT in practice by thinking of a car assembly line. Just as the chassis moves down the line to one stage, an engine arrives at the same point and is fitted. This is repeated for all parts. As the car body arrives at another stage, four doors also arrive and are fitted. All the way down the line materials arrive just at the time they are needed, and the car is assembled in one smooth process.

So what happens when there really is a mismatch between supply and demand? What does a supermarket do when it sells loaves of bread one at a time, but gets them delivered by the truckload? The traditional answer is to hold enough stock to cover the mismatch – effectively, the supermarket must store bread until it is sold or goes stale. JIT says that this is a mistake, and the alternative is to remove the mismatch. The supermarket might solve its problem by having smaller delivery vehicles, or opening a small bakery on the premises.

As you can see, JIT is based on simple principles. Instead of holding stocks to allow for problems, you look at the problems and solve them. We can summarise its argument about stock as follows.

- Stocks are held in an organisation to cover short-term variation and uncertainty in supply and demand.
- These stocks serve no useful purpose: they only exist because poor co-ordination does not match the supply of materials to the demand.
- As long as stocks are held, there are no obvious problems and no incentive for managers to improve the flow of materials.
- Then operations continue to be poorly managed, with problems hidden by stocks.
- The real answer is to improve operations, find the reasons for differences between supply and demand, and then take whatever action is needed to overcome the differences.

Wider effects of JIT

So far we have concentrated on JIT as a way of reducing stock levels, but it is much more than this: it involves a change in the way an organisation looks at all its operations. Its supporters describe JIT as 'a way of eliminating waste', or, 'a way of enforced problem solving'. Starting from its aim of organising operations to occur at exactly the right time, JIT becomes a way of removing all waste from an organisation.

In this wider sense, JIT sees an organisation as having a series of problems that hinder efficient operations. These problems include long equipment set-up times, unbalanced operations, constrained capacity, machine breakdowns, defective materials, interrupted operations, unreliable suppliers, poor quality, too much paperwork and too many changes. Managers try to overcome the effects of these problems by holding large stocks, buying extra capacity, keeping back-up equipment, employing 'trouble-shooters', and so on. But these methods do not solve the problems, they only cover them up. A much more constructive approach is to identify the real problems and solve them. This approach leads to a number of changes in viewpoint.

- *Stocks*. As we have seen, organisations hold stocks to cover short-term differences between supply and demand. JIT assumes these stocks are actually used to hide problems. Organisations should find the reasons for differences between supply and demand, and then take whatever action is needed to remove them.
- *Quality*. Historically, organisations have defined some arbitrary level of acceptable quality for their products, such as, '1 defective unit in 100 means the quality is acceptable'. JIT recognises that all defects have costs and prevent smooth operations. It is better to find the cause, and make sure that no defects are produced. This reinforces the principles of total quality management that we met in Chapter 6.
- *Suppliers*. Many people feel that suppliers and customers are in some sort of conflict, where one can only benefit at the expense of the other. JIT systems rely totally on their suppliers, so they cannot allow this kind of friction. Instead they show that customers and suppliers are partners with a common objective. They should work closely together and preferably form long-term partnerships and alliances.
- *Batch size*. Operations are often more efficient with large batch sizes, as they reduce set-up costs and disruptions. But if demand is smaller, the big batches are held in stock for a long time. JIT looks for ways of reducing the batch size so that it more closely matches demand.
- *Lead times*. Lead times are often fixed by suppliers, and can be quite long. Long lead times reduce flexibility and encourage high stocks to cover uncertainty before another order can arrive. JIT looks for ways of avoiding this by moving to small, frequent deliveries with short lead times.
- *Reliability*. When equipment breaks down, most organisations transfer operations to another process or start making another product. JIT is based on continuous, uninterrupted production, so it does not allow this kind of flexibility. Managers are forced to recognise the problem with reliability, they find the reason for the breakdown, and take actions to make sure it does not happen again.
- *Employees*. Some organisations still have a friction between 'managers' and 'workers'. JIT argues that this is a meaningless distinction. The welfare of everyone depends on the success of the organisation, so all employees should be treated fairly and equitably.

By now, you can see that JIT is not just a way of minimising stocks, but is a whole way of viewing operations. Its overall aim is to minimise waste by identifying and solving problems.

Review questions

16.1 What is the main feature of JIT?

16.2 How does JIT's approach to problems differ from traditional approaches?

16.3 How does JIT view stocks?

16.4 The main benefit of JIT is that it reduces stocks of work-in-progress. Do you think this is true?

OPERATIONS IN PRACTICE

Just-in-time at Guy La Rochelle International

Guy La Rochelle International is one of Europe's leading manufacturers of cosmetics and toiletries. It has a major production plant near Lyons that employs more than 700 people.

One of the problems with La Rochelle's market is the speed that customers' tastes change, with consequent changes in demand. To maintain its market share and meet these changing demands, La Rochelle has to be flexible. It has improved its response to customers and reduced costs, by introducing just-in-time manufacturing. This includes small batch sizes, short production runs, low stocks, fast changeover between products, reliable delivery from suppliers, efficient shipment of goods to customers and fast response to changing customers' tastes. Now customers are guaranteed products that have been made within the past few days and have not spent weeks sitting on a warehouse shelf.

Holding stock is expensive, so when La Rochelle reduced its stock of lipstick by $1 million, it saved $250,000 a year. Its Baby Soft bath oil has changed from a production run of 60,000 units every 30 days, to 10,000 units every five days; the run of 200,000 units of lipstick every 65 days has changed to 60,000 units every 20 days.

The conversion to JIT is well supported and liked by La Rochelle's employees. Every worker now has a variety of skills, and they work in teams rather than as individuals.

Project 16.1 *Have a look around and find a local warehouse – perhaps run by a wholesaler or do-it-yourself store. See what stock it holds. Why are these stocks held? How much do they cost? Can you suggest ways of reducing – or eliminating – these stocks?*

Features of just-in-time operations

Simplicity of JIT operations

JIT aims at eliminating waste from an organisation by doing operations at exactly the time they are needed. An important point is that administration is seen as an overhead that is largely wasted. So JIT looks for ways of simplifying operations, and minimising the effort needed for administration and control. In particular, it uses manual systems, with little paperwork, and most decisions made on the shopfloor. This is in marked contrast to MRP systems, which are computerised, expensive to control and have decisions made by planners who are remote from the operations.

This aim of simplicity means that JIT methods are straightforward and based on common sense. For example, the layout of facilities is simplified to reduce the amount of movement, routine maintenance of equipment avoids breakdowns; everyone is trained in quality management to reduce the number of defects; designs are simplified to reduce processing times; equipment set-ups are improved to save time; reorder costs are reduced to allow smaller deliveries; suppliers are encouraged to make more frequent deliveries; and so on.

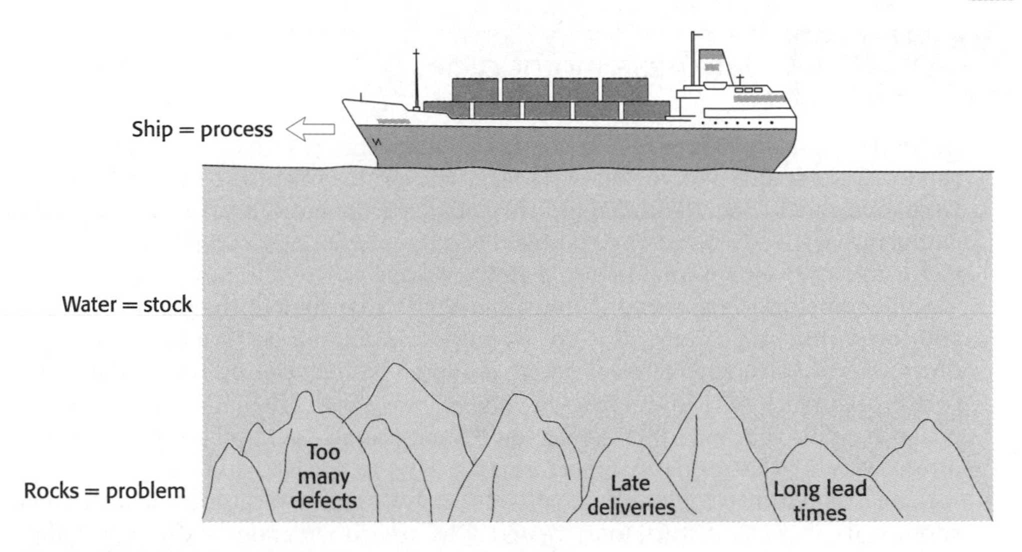

Figure 16.4 Stocks are like the water under a ship

These changes may seem fairly obvious, but they have major effects on operations. It is easy to say, for example that suppliers are encouraged to make more frequent deliveries, but this can be very difficult to organise in practice. The changes cannot be introduced in one step, but evolve with small continuous improvements over a long period. Toyota is said to have made continuous improvements in its operations for 25 years before it had a reasonable JIT system.[1–3] This is the kind of continuous improvement that we met with *kaizen* in total quality management.

There is a common analogy to illustrate the approach of JIT. Imagine a ship sailing over rocks (see Figure 16.4). The rocks represent problems, the ship represents operations, and the water represents stock. The ship is going smoothly because of the cushion of water protecting it from the rocks. JIT wants to lower the water level – removing stock – but when it does this the ship begins to hit problems. At this point the traditional approach is to put back more water, thus raising the ship; the JIT approach is to identify the cause of the problem and solve it, thus lowering the rocks. When one problem is solved, the water level is again reduced, solving each problem in turn, until it reaches a minimum.

There has been a lot of enthusiasm for JIT, but you can see why there has also been a lot of misunderstanding. Many organisations claim to use JIT when they obviously have little idea of its meaning. JIT is based on deceptively simple ideas, but unfortunately these can be very difficult to implement.

Key elements in JIT

One problem with JIT is that it only works well in certain types of organisation. The most successful users of JIT are currently car assembly plants, which make large numbers of similar products in a continuous process. You can see why this is, from the following arguments.

OPERATIONS IN PRACTICE

Japanese motor cycles

In the 1960s many countries had domestic manufacturers of motorcycles which met most of the local demand. These included Harley-Davidson in America, BSA in Britain and BMW in Germany. But in the 1970s the industry changed dramatically, and many well-established companies went bankrupt. Their problem was the sudden new competition from the Japanese companies of Honda, Yamaha, Suzuki and Kawasaki.

These four companies could supply motorcycles anywhere in the world with higher quality and lower cost than competitors. In 1978 Harley-Davidson in America tried – but failed – to prove that the Japanese companies were dumping motorcycles on the market at less than the cost of manufacture. During these hearings it was shown that the Japanese companies had operating costs that were 30 per cent lower than Harley-Davidson's. One of the main reasons for this was their use of JIT manufacturing.

Harley-Davidson recognised that it could only compete by using the same methods, and adopted JIT in 1982. It stuck to its 'materials as needed' programme through initial difficulties and once again succeeded in a very competitive market. In a five-year period, Harley-Davidson reduced machine set-up times by 75 per cent, warranty and scrap costs by 60 per cent, and work-in-progress stocks by $22 million. During the same period, productivity rose by 30 per cent.

Sources: company reports; *www.HarleyDavidson.com*

- Every time there are changes to a process, or it switches from making one product to making another, there are delays, disruptions and costs. JIT says that these changes waste resources and should be eliminated. In other words, JIT needs a stable environment where a process makes large numbers of a standard product, at a fixed rate, for a long time.
- This stable environment can reduce costs by using specialised automation. Then JIT works best with high-volume mass production.
- The level of production must allow a smooth and continuous flow of products through the process. Each part of the process should be fully utilised, so the process is likely to be a well-balanced assembly line.
- Deliveries of materials are made directly to the assembly line at just the time they are needed. Suppliers must be able to adapt to this kind of operation. It would be impractical to bring each individual unit from suppliers, so the next best thing is to use very small batches.
- If small batches are used, reorder costs must be reduced as much as possible or the frequent deliveries will be too expensive.
- Lead times must be short or the delay in answering a request for materials becomes too long. This means working closely with suppliers, and even having them build facilities that are physically close.
- As there are no stocks to give safety cover, any defects in materials would disrupt production. Suppliers must, therefore, be totally reliable and provide materials that are free from defects.
- If something goes wrong, people working on the process must be able to find the cause, take the action needed to correct the fault, and make sure that it does not happen again. This needs a skilled and flexible workforce that is committed to the success of the organisation.

We can continue arguing in this way and arrive at a list of the key elements in JIT operations. These include:

- a stable environment;
- standard products with few variations;
- continuous production at fixed levels;
- automated, high-volume operations;
- a balanced process that uses resources fully;
- reliable production equipment;
- minimum stocks;
- small batches of materials;
- short lead times for materials;
- low set-up and delivery costs;
- efficient materials handling;
- reliable suppliers;
- consistently high quality of materials;
- flexible workforce;
- fair treatment and rewards for employees;
- ability to solve any problems;
- an efficient method of control.

Several of these are obviously different aspects of the same issue, as we can see in Figure 16.5.

Figure 16.5 Example of related benefits of JIT

JIT changes almost everything within an organisation, from the way that goods are ordered to the role of people working on the shop floor. Introducing JIT is a major step that needs commitment from the workforce at all levels. The usual way of introducing it has an initial programme to set up basic procedures (which we describe in the next section) followed by continuous improvements over many years.

Review questions

16.5 What type of process is JIT most suited to?

16.6 JIT principles cannot be used for small service operations. Do you think this is true?

Relationships between parties

JIT inevitably changes the relationships between parties. Here we will outline its view of suppliers and employees.

Relations with suppliers

Traditionally there has been some friction between organisations and their suppliers. Organisations pay money to suppliers, and many people think that one can only benefit at the expense of the other. If an organisation gets a good deal, it automatically means that the supplier is losing out; if the supplier makes a good profit, it means that the organisation pays too much. This friction means that there is little loyalty or co-operation between the two. Suppliers set rigid conditions, and as they have no guarantee of repeat business, they try to make as much profit from each sale as possible. At the same time, organisations shop around to make sure they get the best deal, and remind suppliers of the competition. Each is concerned only with their own objectives and will, when convenient to them, change specifications and conditions at short notice. The result is uncertainty about orders, constant changes in an organisation's suppliers and customers, changing products, varying order sizes, different times between orders, uncertainty about repeat orders, changes in the costs, and so on.

JIT recognises that organisations and their suppliers really have the same objective: they both want a mutually beneficial trading arrangement. If they can agree conditions that satisfy both the organisation and the supplier – with both feeling that they get the best possible deal – this is far better than continuing with unnecessary friction. The implication is that organisations should identify the single best supplier for a product, and always order from them. This is called **single sourcing**.

When such a relationship is formed, it is in both their interests to continue it for as long as possible. Then suppliers know that they have repeat business for a long period, and they can develop their products and operations; the organisation knows that it has guaranteed – and continually improving – supplies. These long-term relationships are often formalised in some form of 'preferred supplier' status, **strategic alliances** or **partnerships**. At one point, before General Motors Corporation introduced JIT, it was using 4,000 major suppliers; Toyota had already introduced JIT and had long-term relationships with its 250 suppliers.

The stability of a long-term agreement encourages suppliers to specialise in one type of product, and they might reduce their product range and number of customers. Many suppliers to JIT organisations build focused factories (which we described in Chapter 9) with a small plant concentrating almost entirely on one product, but making this very efficiently. They can share information, without the threat that this will be used to get some form of trading advantage, and they can share ideas about products and designs. Long-term agreements also reduce the threat that a dominant organisation will look for vertical integration and either buy out a supplier or start making materials itself.

Often this close co-operation encourages suppliers to use JIT in their own operations. Ideally, then, suppliers become a part of an extended JIT system (as suggested in Figure 16.6). If this does not happen, it can become difficult for suppliers to co-ordinate their deliveries with demands, and they often respond by increasing their stock of finished goods to ensure the required pattern of delivery. In effect, the stocks have moved from an organisation's raw materials store to the suppliers' finished goods store. This does not really reduce any costs in the supply chain, and might even increase them. This is certainly not the aim of JIT, which tries to eliminate stock rather than simply move it to another location.

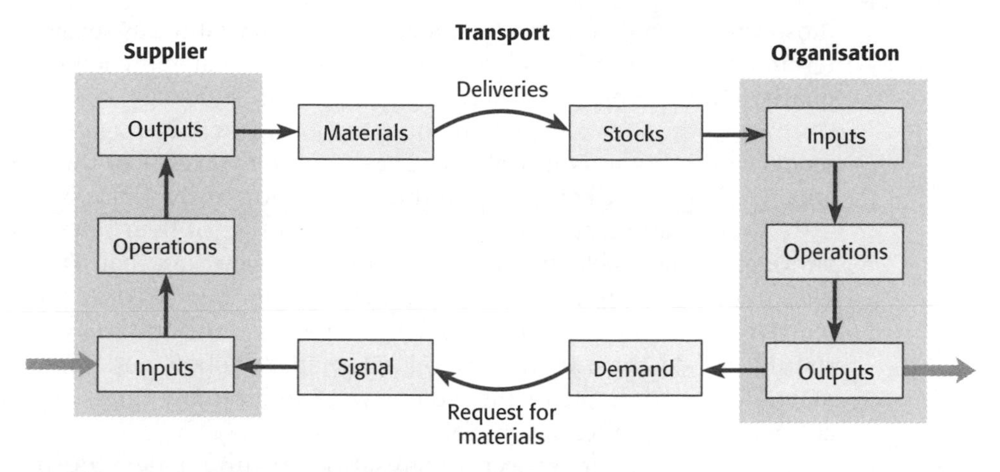

Figure 16.6 Integrating a supplier into the JIT system

Close relationships between an organisation and its suppliers can bring benefits, but they can also bring problems. JIT can be very demanding of suppliers, insisting on perfect quality, small orders, frequent deliveries, short lead times, shared information, simple control systems, little paperwork, nearby locations, low costs, continuing improvement in performance, extension of JIT to suppliers, continuing improvements to products and processes, and so on. These conditions would be difficult even for a supplier with only one customer, but most suppliers have to consider many different customers with different needs. In reality, there has to be some compromise on both sides to give continuing benefits.

Respect for employees

Japanese companies have traditionally offered their employees a job for life. In return, employees are expected to stay with the same organisation for their entire working lives. This pattern is undoubtedly changing, but it is still the dominant feature of organisations that see employees as the most important part of their operations. Many companies outside Japan also claim that their employees are their most valuable asset, but in reality they still treat their employees very badly. When companies hit any financial problems, you will see them reacting quickly to announce staff reductions, and you might ask why they are so willingly to give up their most valuable assets.

Respect for employees is a central part of JIT. Here 'employees' are not just the 'workers' but everyone employed within an organisation. There has traditionally been some friction between 'managers' and 'workers' in an organisation. This is largely caused by their different aims. Managers are seen as employers who are judged by the performance of the organisation, and are rewarded for high profits. On the other hand, workers are seen as employees whose wages are a drain on profits. JIT says that all employees should be concerned with the success of their organisation – and they should all be treated equally and fairly. For example, all employees, regardless of their position, contribute to their organisation's performance, and they should be rewarded with a share of the profits.

If all employees are rewarded for the organisation's performance, they are more likely to actively look for improvements. The best people to suggest improvements are those who actually work on the process. So JIT inevitably has suggestion boxes, with rewards for people offering good ideas. A more formal approach uses some form of **quality circles** (which we met in Chapter 6). This democratic approach gives a sharp contrast to the situation in many organisations, where managers look for improvements while they work in isolation away from the process – or they employ consultants who have little knowledge of the organisation, its products or the process.

JIT's use of automation can also be seen as a sign of their respect for employees, although some people disagree about this. One view says that JIT encourages automation because it is more reliable and cheaper for high-volume processes. Another view is that some jobs are so boring, repetitive and unsatisfying that humans should not do them if there is any alternative. Robots and computer-controlled machines can do most of the tedious work in assembly lines, and this should be automated as a matter of principle.

In return for their respect, organisations using JIT demand more from their employees. For example, with JIT, people working on a process have the authority to stop work and investigate any problems. This means that they must have the skills to identify a problem, look for the cause, find a solution and implement it. JIT also needs people who are flexible enough to do a variety of jobs. They must adopt new practices, possess relevant skills and knowledge, participate actively in the running of the organisation, be interested in its success, and so on.

Decision making and responsibility are always devolved to the lowest possible level. This can bring a problem that is only recently getting attention, which is increased stress in the workforce. There is some evidence that employees who work on JIT assembly lines have higher levels of stress than those who work on traditional lines. More work is needed in this area, but even a suggestion of dissatisfaction in the workforce goes against JIT principles.

Review questions

16.7 What is JIT's view of the relationship between an organisation and its suppliers?

16.8 What are the benefits of single sourcing?

16.9 Because JIT relies on automated processes, it puts less emphasis on people. Do you think this is true?

OPERATIONS IN PRACTICE

Hungry Harry's Burger Bar

Juan Ridellos runs a chain of fast-food restaurants around the Mediterranean coast. He is a leading member of the local Institute of Management. Last summer he went to one of the Institute's talks, where a manufacturer of electric fans was describing its new just-in-time system.

At the end of this talk, Juan was not impressed. 'I do that all the time', he said to a colleague. 'My hamburger restaurants buy bread from the local baker, we get meat from the local butcher and vegetables from the local market. We can get any supplies within a few minutes. Then we cook exactly what the customer wants and deliver it a few minutes later. We have been using just-in-time for years, but nobody congratulates us on our new management methods. Do the same thing with electric fans and you're a hero!'

Achieving just-in-time operations

Push and pull systems

So far we have said that JIT organises operations to occur just as they are needed, and thus aims at eliminating all waste from an organisation. Now we have to ask how it can arrange its operations so effectively. The answer comes from the distinctive approach of JIT, which 'pulls' materials through the process.

In a traditional process, each operation has a timetable of work that must be finished in a given time. Finished items are then 'pushed' through to form a stock of work in progress in front of the next operation. Unfortunately, this ignores what the next operation is actually doing – it might be working on something completely different, or be waiting for a different item to arrive. At best, the second operation must finish its current job before it can start working on the new material just passed to it. The result is delays and increased stock of work-in-progress.

You can see this effect when you visit a large office. Your first call is at the reception desk, where you are pushed through to the next person you have to see. This completely ignores what the next person is doing when you arrive. If that person is already busy, you have to wait in a queue, forming a 'stock of work-in-progress'.

JIT uses another approach to 'pull' work through the process. When one operation finishes work on a unit, it passes a message back to the preceding operation to say that it needs another unit to work on. The preceding operation only passes materials forward when it gets this request. As you can see, this kind of process does not have earlier operations **pushing** work through, but has later operations **pulling** it through. You can see the difference in a take-away sandwich bar. With the traditional push system, someone makes a batch of sandwiches and delivers them to the counter where they sit until someone buys them. With a JIT pull system, a customer asks for a particular type of sandwich, and this is specially made and delivered. As you can see, this eliminates the stocks of work-in-progress. You can also see that there is inevitably some lead time between an operation requesting material and having it arrive. In real JIT systems, messages are passed backwards this lead time before they are actually needed. Materials are also delivered in small batches rather than continuous amounts. This means that JIT still has some stocks of work-in-progress, but these are much smaller than for equivalent 'push' systems. It is, though, fairer to say that JIT minimises stocks rather than eliminates them.

An obvious problem with pull systems is that operations must be perfectly balanced, with the output from each stage in the process exactly matching the demands from following stages. If there is an imbalance, some equipment remains idle until it gets a message to start producing, and the utilisation of this equipment declines. This problem occurs in all operations and is by no means unique to JIT. The distinctive feature of JIT is that it considers any imbalance to be a waste and finds ways of eliminating it. If the imbalance cannot be eliminated, JIT says that it is better to have some equipment under-used than to keep it busy doing work that is not really needed.

OPERATIONS IN PRACTICE

Bavarian Health Products

Bavarian Health Products (BHP) sell a range of 210 products to customers in northern Europe. They deliver products by post, with orders received by e-mail, telephone, fax and post. Their main products are vitamin pills, mineral supplements, oil capsules, herb extracts and a range of other natural products that foster good health.

Operations in BHP centre on four sections:

- At the beginning of each day the Receipt Section looks at all new orders, checks the details and sends orders down to the warehouse.
- The Warehouse Section looks at each order, collects the products requested in a box and passes this to the Finishing Section.
- The Finishing Section checks the contents of each box against the order, checks the bill, adds some promotional material and seals the box.
- The Transport Section consolidates and wraps the boxes, and at 4 o'clock each afternoon takes the day's orders to a national parcel delivery service, which guarantees delivery by the following morning.

This process should work smoothly, but the people in the Finishing Section always complained that they had to work late, and orders often missed the post. Eventually, Kurt Brandt, one of the managers, decided to see what was going wrong. It did not take long to identify the problem as the trolleys that were used to move boxes between the warehouse and finishing. These trolleys carried over 100 boxes. People in the Warehouse Section loaded up a trolley, and when it was full they used a forklift truck to push it through to the Finishing Section.

On most days the Finishing Section would get a surge of work at the end of the day as the Warehouse Section cleared its orders before going home, and pushed through two or three trolleys just before the four-o'clock deadline. The people in Finishing could not deal with these in time, but worked on, some doing overtime at the end of their working day, and left the remainder until the next morning.

Kurt Brandt found a simple solution to the problem. He reduced the working day of the people in the Finishing Section so that they arrived 15 minutes later than those in the warehouse. In return, rather than wait for the trolleys to be delivered, people in the Finishing Section went to collect them when they had run out of work. The big trolleys were replaced with small ones that only carried five boxes and which could be pushed by hand. People in the Warehouse Section made sure that there were always three or four of the new trolleys filled and waiting for the Finishing Section to collect.

Kanbans

JIT needs some way of organising the flow of materials that are pulled through the process. The simplest possible system for this moves materials between two stages in containers. When a second stage needs some materials, it simply passes the empty container back to the previous stage as a signal to fill it (see Figure 16.7).

This approach is not reliable enough for most operations, so the usual alternative uses **kanbans**. *Kanban* is Japanese for a card, or some form of visible record.

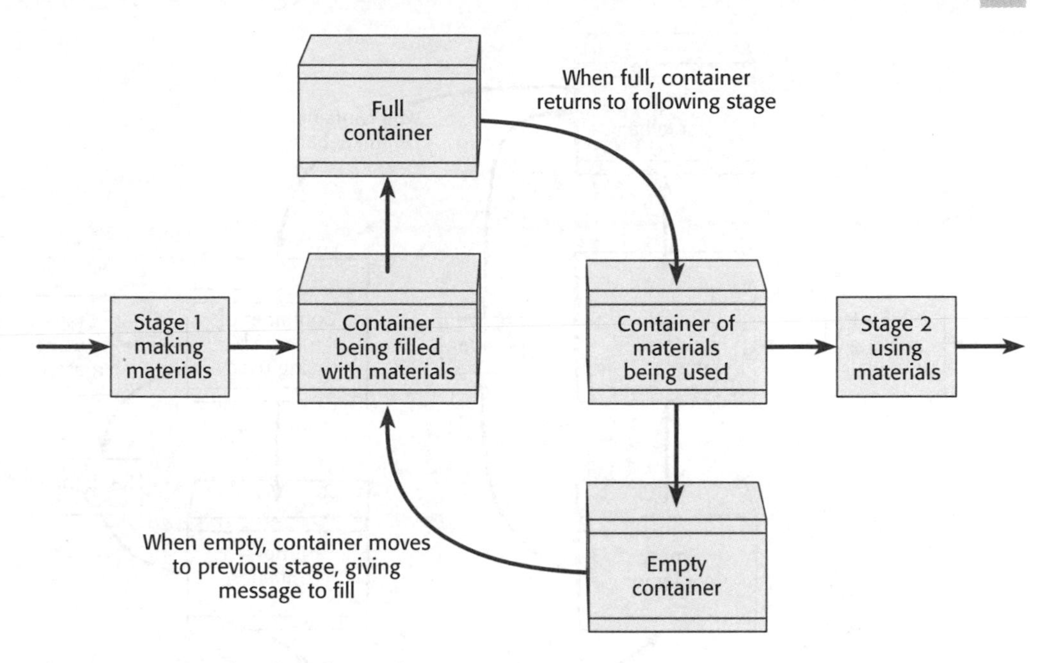

Figure 16.7 The simplest form of message in JIT

Kanbans are cards that control the flow of materials through JIT operations.

- They arrange the 'pull' of materials through a process.

There are several ways of using kanbans. The simplest method (shown in Figure 16.8) is as follows:

- all material is stored and moved in standard containers, with different containers for each material;
- a container can only be moved when it has a kanban attached to it;
- when one stage needs more materials, i.e. when its stock of materials falls to a reorder level, a kanban is attached to an empty container and this is taken back to the preceding stage. The kanban is then attached to a full container, which is moved on to the operation;
- the empty container is a signal for the preceding operation to start work on this material, and it produces just enough to refill the container.

The main features of this single kanban system can be summarised as follows:

- A message is passed **backwards** to the preceding workstation to start production, and it only makes enough to fill a container.
- Standard containers are used which hold a specific amount. This amount is usually quite small, and is typically 10 per cent of a day's needs.
- The size of each container is the smallest reasonable batch that can be made, and there are usually only one or two full containers at any point.
- A specific number of containers and kanbans is used.

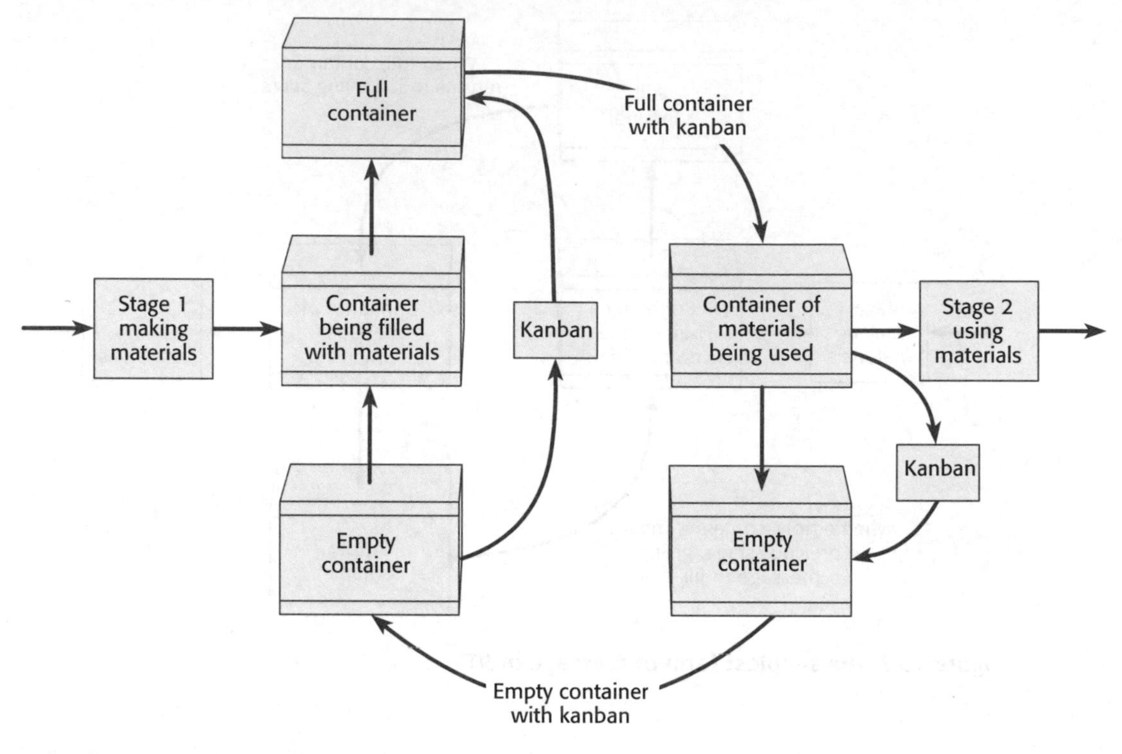

Figure 16.8 A simple kanban system

- The stock of work-in-progress is controlled by limiting the size of containers and the number of kanbans.
- Materials can only be moved in containers, and containers can only be moved when they have a kanban attached. This gives a rigid means of controlling the amount of materials produced and time they are moved.
- While it is simple to administer, this system makes sure that stocks of work-in-progress cannot accumulate.

The most common kanban system

A more usual kanban system (shown in Figure 16.9) is slightly more complicated. This uses two distinct types of card, a **production kanban** and a **movement kanban**.

- When one stage needs more materials, a movement kanban is put on an empty container. This gives permission to take the container to a small stock of work-in-progress.
- A full container is then found, which has a production kanban attached.
- The production kanban is removed and put on a post. This gives a signal for the preceding workstation to make enough to replace the container of materials.
- A movement kanban is put on the full container, giving permission to take it back to the operation.

Although this system has a stock of work-in-progress, this stock is small. When a full container is removed, it is usually the only container in stock, and the parts are

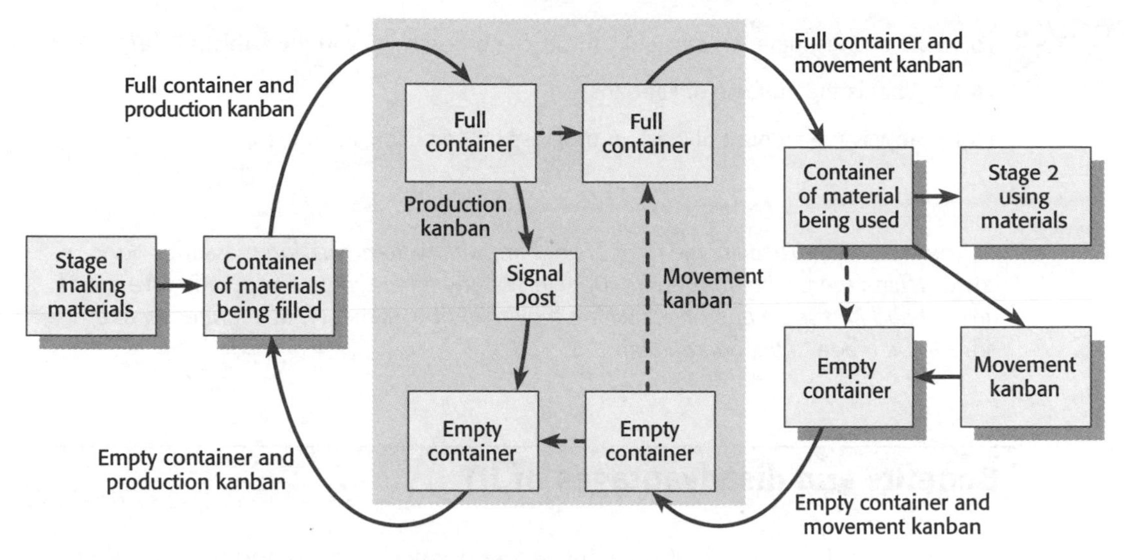

Figure 16.9 A common two-card kanban system

not replaced until the previous workstation makes them. JIT almost always uses a product layout, such as an assembly line, so this stock of work-in-progress is really a small amount that is kept in the line, and there is no actual movement.

Each full container in the store has a production kanban attached to it, so the number of kanbans effectively fixes the amount of work-in-progress. If there is only one production kanban, it means that the stock of work-in-progress is limited to at most one container of items. If there are two production kanbans, this doubles the stock of work-in-progress, and more kanbans would give even higher stocks. The aim of JIT is to work with minimum stocks and, therefore, a minimum feasible number of kanbans. When an organisation introduces JIT, it might initially keep some flexibility by having a fairly large number of kanbans, but reduces these over time.

There are many different ways of using kanbans. Some systems use different kanbans for emergency requests, high-priority needs, materials requested from suppliers, signals for batch processes to start, and so on. The amount of information given on each kanban can vary from almost nothing to detailed instructions for production. Many organisations use electronic kanbans, coloured balls, bar codes and optical character readers. John Bicheno says: 'There are many types of kanbans . . . "kanbans for all seasons"'.[4] Whatever the differences in detail, each system is based on a signal passed backwards from one stage in a process to the previous stage, to show when it is time to start operations.

Andon

Another aspect of the control of JIT comes into play when things go wrong. JIT often uses a system called '**andon**'. This has three signals – often coloured lights – above each operation. A green signal shows that the station is working as planned; an amber signal shows the work station is falling a bit behind; a red signal shows a serious problem. Everyone can see where problems are growing, and can look for ways of solving them.

Review questions

16.10 JIT pushes materials efficiently through a process. Do you think this is true?

16.11 What is the purpose of kanbans?

16.12 How is the amount of work-in-progress limited using kanbans?

Project 16.2 *Restaurants often use a simple form of kanban, with waiters passing messages back to cooks, telling them what to prepare. Do you see any other types of kanban? Have a look around and find some operations where they might be useful. What changes would have to be made to the operations?*

Benefits and disadvantages of JIT

We introduced JIT as a way of reducing stocks of raw materials and work-in-progress. Some organisations have reduced these by 90 per cent.[5] This gives a number of related benefits, such as reduced space needed (up to 40 per cent less), lower procurement costs (up to 15 per cent), less investment in stocks, and so on. Other benefits of JIT come from the reorganisation needed to get a working system. We have already mentioned several of these, including:

- lower stocks of raw materials and work-in-progress;
- shorter lead times;
- shorter time needed to make a product;
- higher productivity;
- higher equipment capacity and utilisation;
- simplified planning and scheduling;
- less paperwork;
- improved quality of materials and products;
- less scrap and wastage;
- better morale and participation of the workforce;
- better relations with suppliers;
- emphasis on solving problems in the process.

Unfortunately, some of these benefits can only be bought at a high price. Making high-quality products with few interruptions by breakdowns, for example, can mean buying better quality, more expensive equipment. Reduced set-up times usually need more sophisticated equipment. Small batches can increases production costs. Higher skills in the workforce increase training costs and the subsequent wage bill. Equipment must respond quickly to changing demands, so there must be more capacity. Many organisations, particularly small ones, are unable to take on these costs, even when there are potential overall benefits.

Another disadvantage of JIT is that it is notoriously difficult to introduce, and might take many years before the process is working efficiently. Its inflexibility is another weakness. JIT essentially sets up a whole system for making a product, so it is difficult to change product design, mix or demand levels. This means that JIT does not work well with irregular demand, small production numbers or specially ordered material. Seasonality also causes problems, which can be overcome in four ways. Firstly, stocks of finished goods can be used to buffer demand, but this option of adding stock is contrary to basic JIT principles. Secondly, production can be changed to match demand, but again these changes are contrary to JIT principles. Thirdly, demand can be smoothed by pricing policies. Fourthly, the delivery time promised to customers can be adjusted. None of these options really satisfies JIT principles, so you can see that real systems need a deal of flexibility.

Some of the benefits of JIT may also be seen as disadvantages. Having frequent set-ups and small batches, for example, is essential for JIT. When they have done the reorganisation necessary to achieve these, most organisations find that they become an advantage, but some find that they give much higher costs. Similarly, JIT devolves decisions and responsibilities down to people working on the process. This kind of devolved decision making can be an advantage or a disadvantage depending on your viewpoint.

Some specific problems listed by JIT users include:

- high risks of introducing completely new systems and approaches;
- initial investment and cost of implementation;
- the long time needed to get significant improvements;
- reliance on perfect quality of materials from suppliers;
- the inability of suppliers to adapt to JIT methods;
- the need for stable production when demand is highly variable or seasonal;
- reduced flexibility to meet specific or changing customer demands;
- the difficulty of reducing set-up times and associated costs;
- the lack of commitment within the organisation;
- the lack of co-operation and trust between employees;
- problems linking JIT to other information systems, such as accounts;
- the need to change layout of facilities;
- increased stress in the workforce;
- inability of some people to accept devolved responsibilities.

Perhaps one disadvantage of JIT is its deceptive simplicity. This has led many organisations to try JIT without understanding its underlying principles. Some companies try to introduce elements of JIT into an existing operation. Sometimes they assume that JIT involves nothing more than reducing lead times. In an extreme case one manager circulated a note simply stating that, 'The company is adopting JIT principles by eliminating stocks of work-in-progress over the next two months. Please change your practices accordingly.' In reality, JIT is an approach that needs a complete change of attitudes and operations within an organisation. It is likely to take several years of careful planning and controlled implementation to get it working successfully.

Comparisons with MRP

There are obvious similarities between JIT and MRP. For example, they both try to reduce stocks by matching the supply of materials to demand. There are, however, some fundamental differences.

- JIT is a manual system, while MRP relies on computers.
- JIT 'pulls' materials through a process, while MRP 'pushes' them with pre-defined schedules.
- JIT emphasises the control of operations, while MRP is more concerned with planning.
- JIT emphasises physical operations, while MRP is largely an information system.
- JIT puts control of the process on the shopfloor, while MRP gives control to more distant planners.
- JIT works with a minimum amount of data, while MRP tries to collect all possible data.
- JIT reduces the amount of clerical effort, while MRP increases it.
- JIT needs a constant rate of production, while MRP can work with varying production.
- JIT has reducing set-up cost as a priority, while MRP considers this to be fixed.
- JIT can be easily understood by everyone using it, while MRP is more difficult to understand.
- JIT reduces batch sizes to a minimum, while MRP uses batching rules.
- JIT typically carries hours' stock of material, while MRP carries days'.

Despite these differences, you should not imagine that JIT and MRP are completely separate methods. There are certainly differences, but they both aim at an efficient means of planning and controlling operations, particularly the flow of materials. A single organisation might have some operations that work better with MRP (perhaps the lower-volume batch processes), while others work better with JIT (perhaps the higher-volume mass processes).

Some people suggest that MRP is more a planning system, while JIT is more a control system. This allows organisations to work successfully with a combination of both systems. Then MRP does the overall planning, making sure that in the longer term there are enough materials arriving to support the process, while JIT controls the flow of materials within the process. You might imagine MRP controlling the external flow of materials into the organisation, with JIT taking over the internal flow within the organisation (see Figure 16.10).

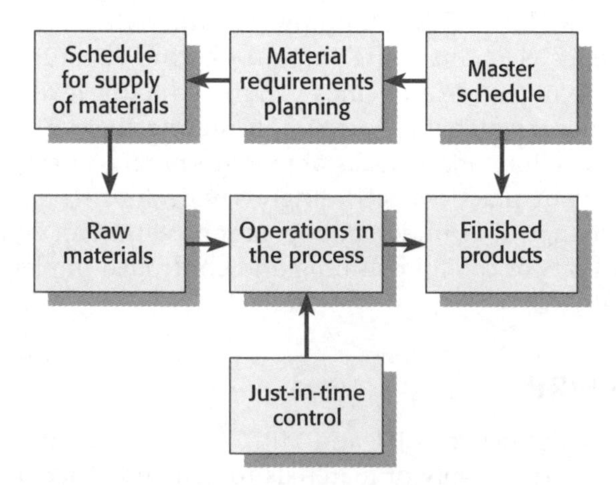

Figure 16.10 A combination of MRP and JIT

In general, organisations making lower volumes of more varied products might do best using MRP; those making higher volumes of similar products might do best using JIT; and those in between might use some combination of the two.[6]

Review questions

16.13 JIT is a system for controlling stocks. Do you think this is true?

16.14 What do you think are the three main advantages of JIT?

16.15 Would it be a good idea to introduce JIT in part of a process to see how it works?

Chapter review

- Just-in-time systems aim at eliminating waste from an organisation. They do this by organising operations to occur just as they are needed. This needs a new way of thinking, which solves problems rather than hides them.
- JIT can only be used in certain types of organisation. It needs a stable environment, small batches, short lead times, total quality, and so on.
- JIT is not installed and left to work, but it looks for continuous improvements.
- An important part of JIT is its emphasis on good relations with suppliers and employees. JIT realises that co-operation is more productive than conflict.
- JIT matches the supply of materials to the demand by 'pulling' materials through the process, rather than traditional approaches that 'push' them through. This can virtually eliminate stocks of work-in-progress and give very efficient operations.
- JIT needs a simple, practical method of controlling the flow of materials. This is given by kanbans, which are cards that pass messages back to previous operations.
- JIT can bring substantial benefits to organisations, but it is difficult to introduce and can bring disadvantages.
- Although there are fundamental differences in approach, JIT can provide a control system for the plans provided by MRP.

Key terms

andon *p. 471*
JIT *p. 454*
just-in-time *p. 454*
kanbans *p. 468*
movement kanban *p. 470*
partnerships *p. 464*
production kanban *p. 470*
pull system *p. 467*
push system *p. 467*
single sourcing *p. 464*
strategic alliance *p. 464*
total quality management *p. 459*

CASE STUDY JIT at Pentagon Plastics

Pentagon Plastics make small injection moulded parts for a number of manufacturers. A few years ago, they were faced by a new problem. One of their best selling parts was used by an instrument maker, and eventually was put into Ford cars. When Ford expanded its quality management programme, all its suppliers – including those that were several steps down the supply chain – had to change their habits. In particular, they had to introduce total quality management and just-in-time operations.

Jaydeep Julami was the production manager at Pentagon, and he was wondering how to meet the new demands on his operations. There were 30 main products and 120 minor ones, and the plant worked a single shift of five days a week. Their current production planning was based on a regular six-week cycle. The first 15 days of this cycle were spent making the main products, and the next 15 days making the minor products. This schedule gave little disruption from batch set-ups. These usually took less than an hour, but could take up to four hours if things went wrong.

A dashboard instrument panel was typical of Pentagon's main products. This was made in batches of 25,000 and sent to a store of finished goods. When customers ordered the panel there was a minimum order quantity of 4,000. Most orders were met from stock, but if Pentagon did not have enough stock to meet an order, they would reschedule production. This might give a week's delay, as well as upsetting the schedules of other products.

Transport was arranged with a local company. They picked the parts up from Pentagon and delivered them directly to customers, usually within two weeks.

Jaydeep was reading an article about Hewlett-Packard's introduction of JIT. This said that they introduced JIT in seven stages:

1. design an efficient mass production process;
2. implement total quality management;
3. stabilise production quantities;
4. introduce kanbans;
5. work with suppliers;
6. continually reduce stocks;
7. improve product designs.

Jaydeep thought about how he could use Hewlett-Packard's experience in his own plant. He knew roughly what was involved, but still was not confident they could make JIT work.

Questions

- Describe in detail the steps that Hewlett-Packard used to introduce JIT.
- Do you think that JIT could work in Pentagon Plastics? How could they set about introducing it?
- What benefits do you think Pentagon could get from JIT?

Discussion questions

16.1 If you were in hospital and needing a blood transfusion, would you rather the transfusion service used a traditional system of holding stocks of blood, or a just-in-time system? What does your answer tell you about JIT in other organisations?

16.2 JIT aims for simple operations; MRP designs huge, complicated systems. What are the main differences and similarities between these two approaches? Are they so different that they can never work together?

16.3 Some people say that JIT only transfers some common practices of services into manufacturing. Do you think that this is true? Where is JIT most widely used now? How do you think this will change in the future?

16.4 What happens if an organisation wants to introduce JIT, but finds that its suppliers cannot cope with the small batches and frequent deliveries?

16.5 JIT reduces waste in an organisation. What is meant by waste in this sense, and how can it occur? If a manufacturer only has enough demand to work for seven hours in an eight-hour shift, would it be more wasteful to leave all operations idle for an hour, or to make extra units and put them into stock?

16.6 What factors are important for the successful implementation of JIT? Who is affected most, those working directly on a process, or those managing it?

16.7 JIT eliminates paperwork for many operations. Does this have any consequences for information flows around the organisation? What about, for example, accounting data, or the 'paper trail' needed for ISO certification?

References

1. Womack J.P., Jones D.T. and Roos D. (1990) *The Machine that Changed the World*. New York: Rawson.
2. Monden Y. (1994) *Toyota Production System*. 2nd edn. London: Chapman and Hall.
3. Shingo S. (1981) *Study of Toyota Production System from an Industrial Engineering Viewpoint*. Tokyo: Japanese Management Association.
4. Bicheno J. (1999) 'Kanban: the Old and the New', *Control*, September, pp. 22–26.
5. Hay E.J. (1988) *The Just-in-Time Breakthrough*. New York: John Wiley.
6. Voss C.A. and Harrison A. (1987) 'Strategies for implementing JIT', in Voss C.A. (ed.) *Just-in-Time Manufacture*. Berlin: IFS/Springer-Verlag.

Selected reading

Ansari A. and Madarress B. (1990) *Just in Time Purchasing*. New York: Free Press.
Cheng T.C.E. and Podolsky S. (1996) *Just in Time Manufacturing*. 2nd edn. London: Chapman and Hall.
Fucini J. and Fucini S. (1990) *Working for the Japanese*. New York: Free Press.
Hutchins D. (1999) *Just in Time*. 2nd edn. London: Gower.
Louis R.S. (1997) *Integrating Kanban with MRP II*. Cambridge, MA: Productivity Press.
Sandras W.A. (1995) *Just in Time*. Essex Junction, VT: Oliver Wight Publications.
Schniederjans M.J. (1993) *Topics in Just in Time Management*. Boston: Allyn and Bacon.

Schniederjans M.J. and Olson J.R. (1999) *Advanced Topics in Just in Time Management.* New York: Quorum Books.

Waters C.D.J. (1992) *Inventory Control and Management.* Chichester: John Wiley.

Womak J. and Jones D. (1996) *Lean thinking*. New York: Simon and Schuster.

Useful Websites

You can get some useful information from the Websites of consultants, such as:
www.kanbanexperts.co.uk
www.theacagroup.com

CHAPTER 17

Job design and work measurement

Our product is steel, but our strength is people.
Motto of Dofasco, a Canadian steel producer

Contents

Aims of the chapter

After reading this chapter you should be able to:

- understand how job design and work measurement form the most detailed level of planning;
- see how different structures for an organisation affect the work;
- appreciate the aims of job design;
- discuss ways of motivating and rewarding employees;
- understand the important factors in a job;
- break down a job into microelements and look for improvements;
- discuss the aims of work measurement;
- calculate standard times for jobs.

Main themes

This chapter will emphasise:

- **motivation**, which encourages people to be more productive;
- **job design**, which looks for the best way of doing a job;
- **work measurement**, which sees how long a job will take.

1. Teams

Teams are groups of people with complementary skills who work together towards a specified goal. The main features of these teams are:

- agreed and common goals;
- all members of the team working together to achieve these goals;
- the aims of the team transcending individual aims;
- more democratic management, making joint decisions rather than being controlled by a superior;
- authority to make decisions, implement them and take responsibility for the outcomes;
- performance of the team judged by its joint results rather than by individual efforts;
- active involvement of all team members, with clear roles for each;
- mutual trust, open communications and co-operation between all members;
- acceptance of members' differences, with constructive resolution of difference.

As you can see, a team is a cohesive group that works together, and is not just a collection of people who have similar jobs. If you look at any sport, you can clearly see the difference between teams working closely together, and groups of individuals who simply put on the same colour of shirt.

2. Process-centred organisations

In Chapter 3, we mentioned that some organisations put so much emphasis on the process that they become 'processed centred'. Then the whole organisation concentrates on the process of supplying products that satisfy customer demand, and everyone is seen as contributing to this process. Such organisations typically have:

- all work directly related to the process;
- people working in teams;
- the work of each team directly contributing to the process;
- no separation of teams into departments;
- operations driven by customer demands;
- a flat and responsive organisation.

3. Matrix organisations

Matrix organisations are a compromise between traditional departmental structures and teams. A departmental structure has people working for a department; teams have people working together to achieve a specified goal. With a matrix structure, people are notionally in a department, but they are assigned to work on specific projects, or seconded into teams. An accountant, for example, might be based in the accounting department, but is assigned to a team to develop a new product. This structure aims at the advantages of both departmental and team structures and is widely used in projects (as we shall see in Chapter 18).

Review questions

17.1 How can the structure of an organisation improve its productivity?

17.2 Happy people are productive people. Do you believe this statement?

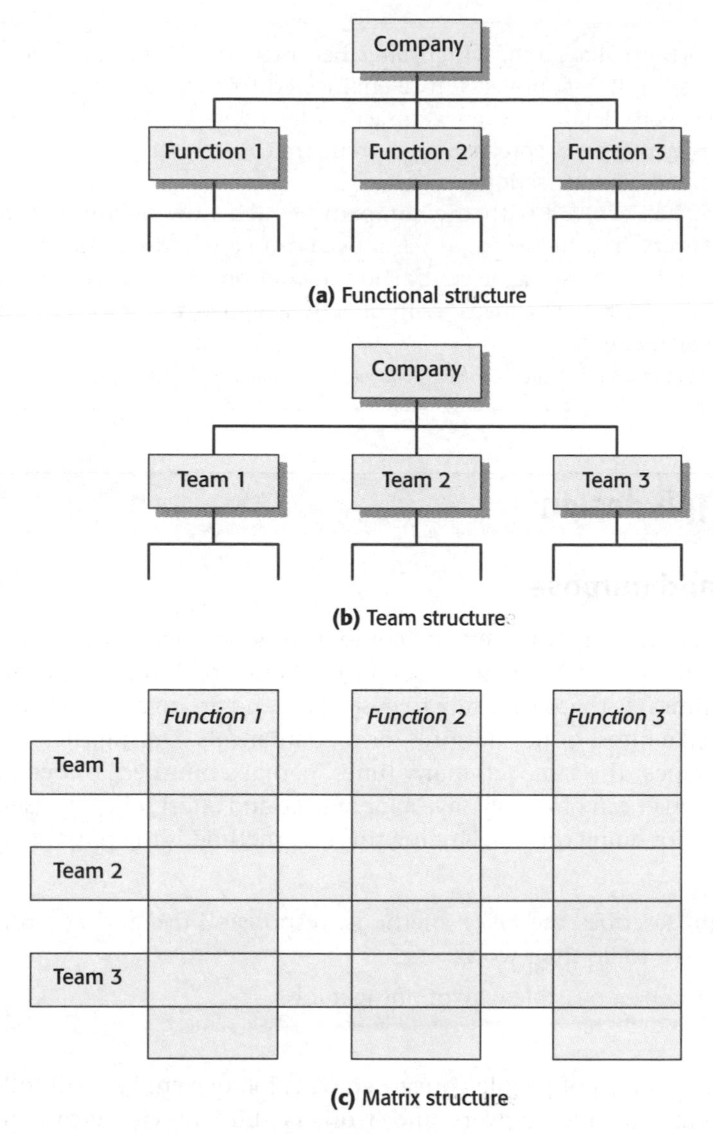

Figure 17.3 Some alternative structures for organisations

OPERATIONS IN PRACTICE Research and development at Nortel

Expenses in an organisation are traditionally collected and reported by departments. Then R & D costs are collected by functional departments, and then assigned to separate projects. This can be confusing to project managers, who cannot see how the costs originated, how they are allocated, or how they can be controlled. This confusion can cause problems in a company the size of Nortel, whose R & D work costs US$2 billion a year, employs 20,000 people, and has 5,000 active projects.

In the 1990s Bell Northern Research, which later became Nortel, started to look for an improved method of costing R & D projects. It re-engineered its costing systems to give project managers direct access to details of every transaction for their project, wherever it occurs in the world. This was based on a spreadsheet system that assigns a project number and regional code to every financial transaction.

The financial system has evolved with the company, which now organises R & D programmes into business units. In other words, it has moved from a functional structure towards a team structure. This removes most of the central administration of R & D, and devolves the work closer to customers. All R & D expenses are directly assigned to a project, rather than through functional departments.

Source: C. Dorey (1998) 'The ABCs of R & D at Nortel', *Certified Management Accountants Magazine*, March

Aim of job design

Context and purpose

The organisational structure sets the context for job design. In this context, a **job** is the basic set of tasks that a person does for his/her work. Most people repeat the same jobs many times. Perhaps they talk to customers and arrange insurance, or they drive trains, or make films, or put out fires, or prepare meals. During their working day, a person can repeat the same job many times, perhaps hundreds or even thousands of times. The worker can obviously save a lot of time and effort if he/she uses the best possible method for doing the job. Finding this best method is the purpose of **job design**.

Job design describes the tasks, methods, responsibilities and environment used by individuals to do their work.

- It finds the best possible way of doing a job.

There are two groups of people concerned with job design. We will follow the usual habit of calling them 'employers' and 'workers', but we will be careful not to draw firm boundaries between these. Many people both own a part of, and work in, a company. In the same way, managers are often seen as an employer's representatives, even though they are also employees.

Taking a simple view of the two groups, job design must satisfy both of their needs. The problem is that they seem to want completely different things. Employers want the workers to be productive so they meet output, quality, service and other targets at low costs. These are largely economic and technical aims, and their main concern is that the value added by the workers is greater than the wages paid to them. On the other hand, the needs of workers are social and psychological. People want to interact with other people, to be recognised, appreciated and properly rewarded, so we have two main objectives in job design:

- to meet the productivity, quality and other goals of the organisation;
- to make the job safe, satisfying and rewarding for the individual.

Investing in people

Until quite recently the first objective – satisfying the economic needs of the organisation – was given far more attention than the second. Traditionally, employers viewed any investment in their workers' welfare as an extra cost that had few returns. Over recent years, we have learnt that this view is mistaken. It is a simplification to say that a happy worker is a productive worker, but there is certainly some justification in it. People are clearly more productive when their work is rewarding, so money spent on designing a job properly and training people to do it well becomes an investment rather than a cost.

You can see evidence for this change in assembly lines. At the beginning of the last century Henry Ford got high productivity by organising people in an assembly line. Each person on the line did a simple, specialised job – often to the point where he or she might only tighten two screws in a door assembly. The person repeated this job many times – perhaps thousands of times – a day, and the pace of work was set by the assembly line so that high output could be almost guaranteed.

These assembly lines had several advantages for the organisation, which could:

- employ unskilled or low skilled people;
- train them quickly to do the simple jobs;
- pay low wages;
- get high output;
- reduce non-productive time, such as reaching for tools;
- control the flow of work;
- introduce automation for simple jobs.

Unfortunately, this **division of labour** has disadvantages. It tends to be less flexible and needs more supervision, but the main problem is that people find the work boring, tiring and unsatisfying. They have no chance of showing initiative, getting promotion, communicating with colleagues or having control over their work. The result is a workforce that has no motivation and low morale. This in turn leads to low productivity, absenteeism, grievances and high staff turnover – and the high productivity that these lines were supposed to guarantee often has not been achieved. This is why manual production lines are far less common now, as they have usually been automated or redesigned.

Review questions

17.3 What is the purpose of job design?

17.4 Who are the main people concerned with job design?

17.5 How do the needs of employers and workers differ?

Motivation

Job design aims to satisfy both employers and workers. We have already described productivity, efficiency and other aspects of performance that concern employers, and should now mention some factors that are important to workers. This is not the place to give a long description of human resource management, but we can mention some specific topics, starting with **motivation**.

Theories of motivation

It is easy to list things that make us unhappy with our work, but it is more difficult to find factors that we find rewarding and that make us more productive. Some people only work to get high pay; others like challenges; others like the opportunity to socialise; others like to contribute to human welfare; others like to be left alone. As you can imagine, there have been thousands of studies that try to analyse the needs of people and see what makes us more productive. The following theories introduce some core ideas.

Taylor's scientific management[3]

Frederick Taylor suggested that there is one best way to do a job, and managers can find this best way by observation, analysis and use of scientific methods. He was the first person to analyse work and use rational methods for improving performance. To a large extent *Taylorism* is now unpopular, as it is characterised by rigidity, too much management control and a general lack of humanity.

The Gilbreths and work study[4]

Frank and Lillian Gilbreth reduced a job to its basic movements. Then they removed unnecessary elements of the work, and organised the remaining parts as efficiently as possible. This kind of 'work study' could make jobs very efficient, but their approach is, like Taylor's, often criticised for concentrating on small details rather than taking a broader view. In one famous example, Frank showed why it is more efficient to button a waistcoat from the bottom upwards, than from the top downwards (when buttoning from the bottom, your hands finish near your tie which you can then straighten).

Maslow's hierarchy of needs[5]

Abraham Maslow suggested that people have a **hierarchy of needs** to fulfil. This hierarchy starts with physiological or survival needs, which include food, shelter and clothing. Once these survival needs are met, there is another level of needs for security. When security needs are met, there is another level of social needs, etc. This hierarchy is shown in Figure 17.4. The implication is that good performance comes from designing jobs that satisfy these needs.

Hertzberg's two-factor theory[6]

Frederick Hertzberg studied over 200 engineers and accountants and found two types of factors important for motivation:

- **Hygiene factors** – without which employees are unhappy. Examples are wages, job security, working conditions, relationship with supervisor, company policies, etc.
- **Motivators** – which motivate employees to work. Examples are recognition, promotion, responsibility, sense of achievement, pleasure in the work itself, etc.

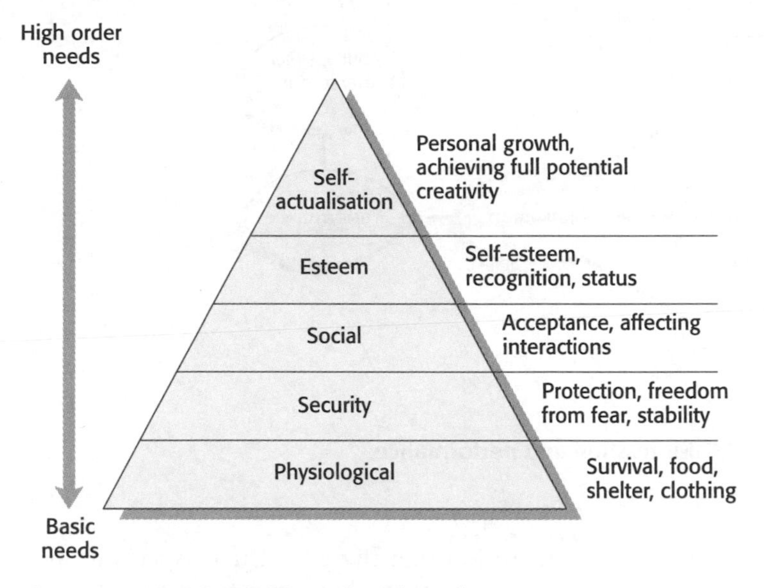

Figure 17.4 Maslow's hierarchy of needs

McGregor's theory *X* and theory *Y*[7]

Douglas McGregor asked the simple question: Why do people work? He suggested two answers for this, which he called Theory *X* and Theory *Y*.

- **Theory *X*** assumes that people are essentially lazy, dislike work, lack ambition and avoid responsibility. They will only work because they have to. The implication is that organisations can only get people to work by using close supervision, threats, punishments, incentives, etc.
- **Theory *Y*** assumes that people work because they like to, meaning that work is as natural as rest or play. The implication here is that organisations only have to supply the right conditions and people will work as effectively as they can.

Generally

These few examples can only suggest the directions in which pioneers of work methods and motivation were moving. It does, however, begin to suggest the wide range of opinion. No one knows the best way of getting motivated workers, but there is no shortage of ideas, and an enormous amount of research has been done in the area. One point where there is widespread agreement is that we respond better to motivation than harsh discipline: the carrot works better than the stick. This accounts for the trend in job design away from rigid controls and over-specialisation that forces people into simple but unrewarding jobs, and towards motivational concerns that give conditions that encourage people to work hard.

> **Motivation** is difficult to define, but we generally say that a person is motivated if he/she keeps working hard to achieve an appropriate goal.

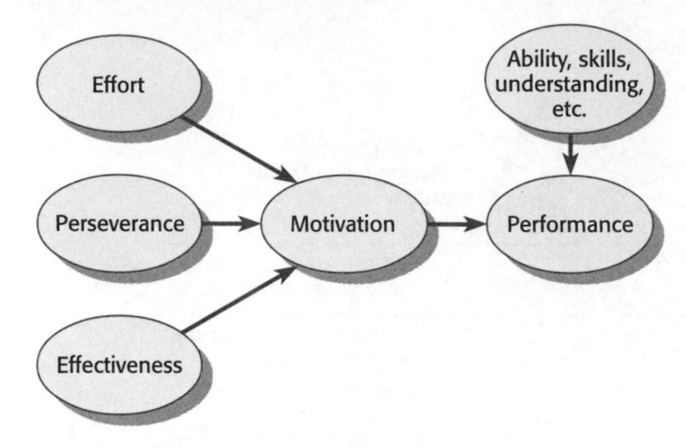

Figure 17.5 Motivation and performance

You can see from this definition that there are three aspects to motivation (shown in Figure 17.5). The first is the effort that a person puts into a job: a motivated person works hard. The second is the perseverance of the effort: a motivated person continues the effort for as long as needed. The third is effectiveness: a motivated person works towards an appropriate goal.

Designing jobs that motivate

Every organisation wants a motivated workforce. The way to get this is for managers to design jobs that motivate their workers. They can do this in several ways. We have already mentioned the benefits that can come from organising people to work in coherent teams. We can extend this to **self-directed work teams** or **self-managed teams**, which have day-to-day responsibility for managing themselves and the process they work with. Instead of being instructed by supervisors, self-directed work teams take the work to be done in a period, and organise themselves to achieve this. This approach needs a variety of skills within the team, but many organisations have used it to both increase productivity and reduce costs.

Some other methods of improving motivation include the following:

- *Job rotation* – the job each person does is rotated, perhaps daily, so that people do not get into a rut of doing the same specialised job all the time. On the positive side, this can give people more varied work and a broader range of skills. On the other hand, some organisations have found that it only gives a temporary improvement as people soon feel they are being switched around a series of equally boring jobs.
- *Job enlargement* – this combines several simple jobs into a larger one. You can view this as a horizontal expansion, where a range of similar jobs of the same type are combined. On the positive side, this gives broader jobs with more variety and interest. On the negative side, some organisations again find that this gives only a temporary improvement as it replaces a short boring job by a longer boring job.

- *Job enrichment* – this adds more responsibility to the job, and makes it inherently more interesting. You can view this as a vertical expansion, which adds more responsibility, perhaps for planning, scheduling and design. We have touched on this approach with total quality management, where everyone adds responsibility for quality to their previous work.
- *Empowerment* – this delegates responsibility and control to people working on the process. It is based on the idea that those most closely involved with operations are in the best position to make decisions about them. By delegating responsibility as far as possible, people can use their own knowledge and abilities to manage the details of their own jobs, free from the instructions and control of a remote supervisor.

There are many other options for improving motivation. We cannot discuss all of these, but the following list gives some ideas that can be developed for a motivated, productive workforce.

- Do not treat people as part of the machinery, but as the most important part of the organisation.
- Treat people with courtesy and respect, without favouritism, prejudice, public criticism, malevolent gossip, inconsistent policies or unreasonable behaviour.
- Do not use 'macho' management to make people feel intimidated and insecure.
- Make people feel welcome and comfortable in the organisation with support and good working conditions.
- Give clear job descriptions so that everyone knows exactly what their job involves.
- Give people training, support and guidance so that they can do their job properly.
- Give people broad training for multi-skilled jobs.
- Treat people as individuals, designing jobs to match their interests and abilities.
- Show the importance of everyone's job and reward them fairly with money, recognition, promotion and other incentives.
- Give people responsibility and allow them to make as many of their own decisions as possible.
- Set individual goals and make these demanding but achievable.
- Measure everyone's contribution, acknowledge these publicly and reward them, making a clear link between performance and rewards.
- Form worker councils and other means of participating in management.
- Arrange regular meetings to discuss targets, progress, problems, etc.
- Encourage teamwork and co-operation, and bring people together to sort out conflicts.
- Remove artificial barriers between functions, departments, trades, levels, etc.
- Have direct and open communications, with information flowing freely around all levels of the organisation – do not keep secrets from people.
- Have well-developed career paths.
- Automate dull or dangerous jobs.
- Measure absenteeism and staff turnover as these give a clear picture of morale and job satisfaction.

Such suggestions do, of course, have their critics. Job enrichment, for example, might give higher capital costs, higher wages for more skilled employees, and higher training costs. Some people do not want job enlargement with its extra responsibilities, but prefer to stick with smaller, simple jobs. Empowerment means extra responsibility for some people – and correspondingly less responsibility for others, who might be reluctant to give it up. Sometimes the available technology or process design does not allow jobs to change. Sometimes jobs can change, but at a cost of less flexibility, lower production or more accidents.

Motivation is an area with huge amounts of uncertainty. One organisation will do everything right, and still have an unmotivated workforce; another will do everything wrong and get high motivation. Others pay lip service to all the latest ideas, but in reality continue in their own way. Perhaps the only certainty is that motivation and productivity are sensitive areas that we have to approach with caution.

Payment schemes

Many people suggest that pay is a key element in motivation. It is certainly important to treat all employees fairly and reasonably, but motivation does not depend on the amount of pay. There are many organisations where pay is low, but a well-motivated workforce give very good performance. You can see this, for example, in charities and non-profit organisations such as health and education. On the other hand, there are many organisations where pay is high, but the workforce is not motivated and gives poor performance. Unfortunately, you can see many examples of this in governments and industry. None the less, successful organisations usually give good conditions of employment – including pay, employee discounts, profit sharing and share ownership schemes.

There are two ways of setting wages:

- **Time-based systems**. Employees are paid for the amount of time they spend working. This includes all hourly-paid and most salaried employees. It has the advantage of being simple to use and control, but the disadvantage of not rewarding effort or results.
- **Output-based systems** or incentive plans. Employees are paid for the amount they actually produce. There are many types of incentive plans, including:
  - *piece rate or commission* – where an organisation pays an agreed amount for each unit of output;
  - *basic pay plus bonus* – which pays a basic wage for a basic amount of work, but anyone producing more than this is paid a bonus for each additional unit;
  - *standard-hour plans* – where an organisation sets a standard time to do a job and the worker is paid for this regardless of how long it actually takes. The standard time for a job might be one hour, and if employees produces nine units in a day they are paid for nine hours of work, regardless of how long they actually took;
  - *group incentive systems* – share any gains among all employees. In many operations no single person can set the output, so any bonus should be shared between everyone involved. There are many types of group plans, including 'Scanlon plans', which share profits from any productivity gains between the workers and the organisation.

Individual incentive plans have several disadvantages. They do not encourage co-operation and team work among employees; some people try to make extra money by working faster but ignoring quality; different people work at different paces so it is difficult to balance work flows; and so on. Group incentive schemes go some way to overcome these problems.

If we add factors such as rewards and satisfaction to Figure 17.5, we get the fuller picture of motivation shown in Figure 17.6.

OPERATIONS IN PRACTICE

The Magna Employee's Charter

Magna International Inc. is a global supplier of high-technology systems, assemblies and components. Frank Stronach, the chairman of Magna, believes in fairness and concern for his employees. He has created *The Magna Employee's Charter*, which has the following points:

- *Job Security*. Being competitive by making a better product for a better price is the best way to enhance job security. Magna is committed to working together with you to help protect your job. To assist you Magna will provide: job counselling, training and employee assistance programs.
- *A Safe and Healthful Workplace*. Magna strives to provide you with a working environment which is safe and healthful.
- *Fair Treatment*. Magna offers equal employment opportunities based on an individual's qualifications and performance, free from discrimination or favouritism.
- *Competitive Wages and Benefits*. Magna will provide you with information which will enable you to compare your wages and benefits with those earned by employees of your competitors, as well as with other plants in your community. If your total compensation is found not to be competitive, then your wages will be adjusted.
- *Employee Equity and Profit Participation*. Magna believes that every employee should own a portion of the company.
- *Communication and Information*. Through regular monthly meetings between management and employees and through publications, Magna will provide you with information so that you will know what is going on in your company and within the industry.

Magna has a hotline to register any complaint if an employee feels that these principles are not being met. It also has an Employee Relations Advisory Board to monitor, advise and make sure that Magna operates within the spirit of the Employee's Charter. In addition, Magna's Corporate Constitution allocates 10 per cent of pre-tax profit to employees.

Review questions

17.6 People will work hard if they know they can be fired at any time. Do you think this is true?

17.7 What exactly is motivation?

Project 17.1

Think of any task that you have done recently with enthusiasm. Why were you enthusiastic? How could an organisation add these features to a job? On the other hand, what features would you not like to see in a job?

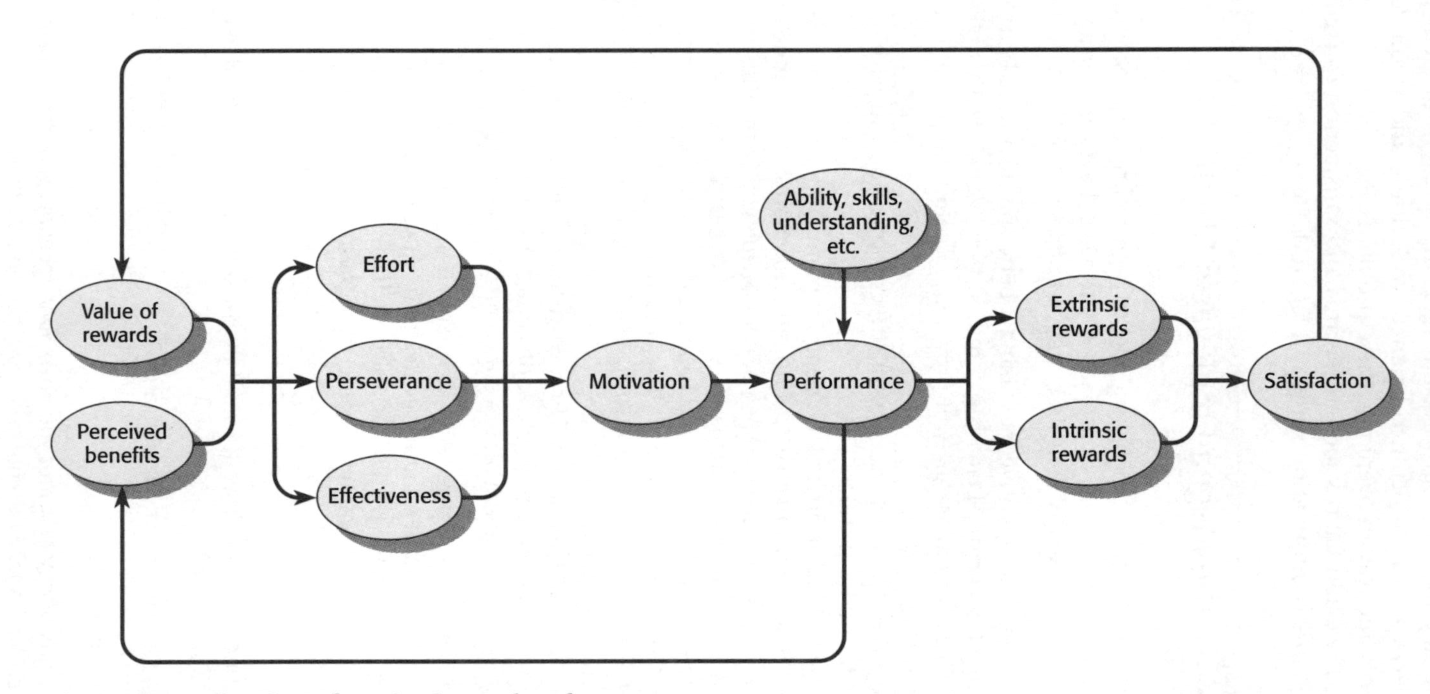

Figure 17.6 Fuller view of motivation and performance

Elements of job design

We have outlined some of the needs of organisations and employees, and can now look in more detail at the design of jobs that satisfy both of these. For this we need to look at three main elements:

- *physical environment,* where the job is done;
- *social environment,* which affects the worker's psychological condition;
- *work methods,* which describe how the job is done.

Physical environment

This describes the place where the job is done, its layout, the tools used, equipment available, and so on. If these are badly organised the environment can be distracting, put heavy burdens on a worker, and even be dangerous. Work on the physical environment is part of **ergonomics**, which designs tools, machines, workplaces, layouts, etc. to take into account the physical capabilities of people. You can see one specialised example of this in any infant school, where all the furniture is small and easy to handle. The same principles apply at work, such as a person repeatedly leaning forward to adjust a lever. We know from data banks of body measurements that 75 per cent of people can remain sitting and reach forward a distance of 53 cm or more. Of course, this leaves 25 per cent of people who cannot reach this far, so job design has to ask who will be doing the job, whether they will be sitting, how much they have to move, if there is anything in the way, how much time is available for the adjustment, could the lever be moved, and is the adjustment necessary?

Most early work in ergonomics looked at operators of manufacturing machines. Nowadays, it emphasises office work, so designers consider the layout of an office, the height of chairs and tables, the position and size of keyboards, the size of computer screens, and so on. Such designs go beyond the basics, and Egg's customer service office won an award in 2000 for including an internal lawn for thinking and recreation.

Other aspects of the work environment concern:

- *Light* – in general, jobs that need higher speed and accuracy need more light. The type of light can also be important, so we have to consider the colour, contrast and direction.
- *Temperature and humidity* – most people work at their best in temperatures around 18 to 22 degrees.
- *Noise and vibrations* – noise can be annoying, but it can also damage hearing. There are limits on the time people can work with loud noise.
- *Air pollution* – pollution or fumes can be irritating and dangerous. This pollution need not be exotic chemicals, but can include dust, petrol fumes or cigarette smoke.
- *Safety* – people must always have safe working conditions and protection from possible dangers.

Social environment

The social environment concerns the psychological well-being of employees. As a start, organisations must prepare employees to do the job. They must give adequate job training, appropriate supervision and help, knowledge of the organisation's policies and rules, a clear statement of what is expected from them, and credit for good work.

While working, the organisation must provide opportunities for employees to meet their social needs. This might mean something simple such as a coffee lounge, or as complicated as redesigning the process to allow more interaction. Perhaps jobs should be changed to make sure they have:

- *task significance* – so that employees feel the job has a substantial impact on the organisation or the world;
- *task identity* – so that employees can see the job as a whole, single piece of work from start to finish;
- *task variety* – to give jobs that contain a variety of different tasks;
- *skill variety* – so that employees can use a variety of skills and talents;
- *autonomy* – so that employees have a level of independence and personal control over their work;
- *feedback* – to give everyone clear, timely information about their performance.

Work methods

Work methods look at the details of how a job is actually done, and how it should be done. It usually starts by looking at the way a job is done at present, and breaks it down into small parts. A men's hairdresser, for example, spends a lot of time cutting hair. This involves a series of standard tasks such as washing hair, giving an initial cut with scissors, tidying loose ends, trimming with shears, drying hair, and so on. Each of these tasks can be broken down into **microelements**, such as reaching out, picking up a hair drier, moving the hair dryer back to the customer's head, switching it on, etc.

The whole job can be broken down into a series of microelements. Analysing these and showing the relationships between them gives a starting point for finding improvements. We can use several types of diagram for these analyses. In Chapter 10 we looked at process charts, and now we can adjust these to describe the details of the microelements. We can, for example, use multiple activity charts to describe what an operator's left and right hand are doing at any time (see Figure 17.7). Slow motion videos and computer analysis of movements are widely used to pinpoint inefficient operations.

Now we have a detailed description of the job we can look for improvements, and find the most efficient way of doing it. The hairdresser, for example, might spend too long reaching for various objects, so the job could be improved by moving them nearer the customer. For these analyses we ask a series of questions: Why is this done? How is it done? Why is it done this way? Could the step be missed out? Could it be done at another time? Could it be done automatically? How could the layout of the workplace be improved? Would different tools help? The answers to these questions lead to better ways of doing the job.

Operation: assembly
Standard Time: 30 seconds
Equipment: punch, die, press, holder

Left Hand	Right Hand
Reach for casing	Put last assembly into bin
Pick up casing	
Put casing into holder	Put casing into holder
Reach for washers	Reach for insert
Pick up washers	Pick up insert
	Fit insert to casing
Add washers to insert	Hold casing
Hold casing	Reach for punch
	Pick up punch
Adjust punch and press	Adjust punch and press
	Operate press
Remove assembly	Remove assembly

Figure 17.7 Example of an activity chart for two hands

Review questions

17.8 Why is job design important?

17.9 What are the main elements in job design?

17.10 From a social point of view, what factors will improve the design of a job?

OPERATIONS IN PRACTICE

Moorhead Stamping Works

Moorhead Stamping Works is a medium-sized company that supplies stamped parts for consumer appliance industries. Moorhead's process starts with coils of sheet metal. These coils are cut into smaller strips using shearing machines. The strips are passed to stamping presses that form the products. Other processes used at the works include welding, painting, plating and assembly.

The working conditions in the plant are generally unpleasant. It is noisy, cluttered and congested, and there is poor heating and ventilation. Production is badly planned, so customer orders are continually being expedited, and it is common to rush jobs to try and meet impossible deadlines. This puts a lot of pressure of workers. Sometimes the machines are operated in unsafe conditions and often by poorly trained workers. Government safety and welfare offices are aware of working conditions, and have often sent inspectors.

There is poor communication between managers and the workers. Mike Peterson has worked for Moorhead for many years, but he cannot remember a single occasion when a manager has shown any appreciation of the job done by a worker. On the other hand, he hears continual complaints from managers about the amount of overtime worked, increased costs and low profits. Mike is not surprised that the company is noted for high employee turnover, low pay, poor quality, and low productivity.

Work measurement

Purpose of work measurement

Job design looks for the best way of doing the tasks. Now we can use these designs to help in broader planning, provided we know exactly how long each job will take. This is the function of **work measurement**.

Work measurement finds the time needed for a job.

- It forms the link between job design and wider planning.

Work measurement tells us how long a job should take, that is, its **standard time**. When we know this standard time, we can use it to plan the requirements for equipment, people and other resources. We can also use it for a range of other functions, such as wage incentive schemes, monitoring worker performance, and allocating costs.

It might seem easy to find how long a job will take. In practice, however, there are many complications, which is why a garage might take four hours to repair a car, when they estimated that it would only take two hours. You know from experience that different people take different times to do a job. You also know that if the same person does a job several times, each repetition will take a different time (we discussed one reason for this with the learning curve in Chapter 12). These variations simply show that humans have different abilities, and each individual has some inconsistency.

Work measurement starts by finding the basic amount of work in a job. This basic work content gives the minimum time theoretically needed to complete it. This is the time needed if the design of the product is perfect, the ideal process is used, no time is lost, materials are delivered on time, and everything works smoothly. The actual time needed for a job is greater than this basic time. When actually working, we have to allow for real circumstances, including:

- *work added by poor design of the product* – the product design may not allow the best process to be used, it may need additional or complex tasks, there may not be enough standardisation, quality standards may not be set properly, it may use too many materials, etc.;
- *work added by inefficient operations* – using the wrong type or size of equipment, not doing operations properly, having a poor layout, using methods that give extra work, poor management adding work, too many design changes, poor delivery of materials, poor maintenance of plant and equipment, poor working conditions, morale, etc.;
- *ineffective time within the control of the worker – such as* absenteeism, lateness, idling, careless workmanship or unsafe behaviour causing accidents.

Allowing for these practicalities, the job will actually take longer than the basic time. To see how much longer, we use **rating**.

Standard times

The International Labour Organisation gives the following definition of work measurement:

> **Work measurement** is the application of techniques designed to establish the time for a qualified operator to carry out a specific job at a defined level of performance.

As you can see, this definition is based on a *qualified operator*, which assumes that he/she is properly prepared and qualified, properly trained and experienced, and physically and mentally capable of doing the job. Then it refers to a *specific job*, which includes defining the job, the method to be used, and the conditions in which the job is done. Finally, the definition specifies a *defined level of performance*, and this is related to a standard rate of working.

> The **standard rate** of work is the average rate that qualified workers will naturally achieve without overdue exertion over their working day, provided that they know and adhere to the specified method and are motivated to apply themselves to the work.

Now we have the idea of a qualified operator, doing a specified job, at a standard rate of work. Combining these should allow us to find a standard time for a job. In principle, we can simply watch someone working in these conditions, and time that worker.

The problem, of course, is finding the standard conditions. The person we watch may be particularly good at the job, or in a hurry, or he/she may have problems, or something unexpected may happen, or the person may not do the job in the standard way. We can then find the actual time taken to do the job, but this is certainly not a standard time.

The way around this is to compare the person's actual work rate with a standard rate. This comparison is called **rating**. In practice, rating relies on judgement and experience. The person measuring the rate of work must know what a standard rate is, and then compare the worker's actual performance to this standard. This probably seems difficult, but we do it informally all the time. When you see people walking down the street, you can easily tell if they are hurrying or strolling casually; when you see people working in a shop you can tell if they are working hard or having an easy time. With experience, you can do the same rating for a range of other operations.

Now we can use the work rating to develop four different times for a job: basic, actual, normal and standard times.

- **Basic time**: this is the theoretical time needed to complete the basic work content of a job under ideal conditions.
- **Actual time**: this is the time actually taken by someone to finish the essential parts of a job. These essential parts exclude avoidable delays that should not

- be sure the correct methods are used for the job;
- set the number of repetitions and choose the people to study;
- break the whole job into a series of tasks that have distinct beginnings and ends and can easily be timed;
- time each task and rate the operator's performance over the number of repetitions;
- find the actual time for the whole job, usually from the average of repetitions;
- adjust the actual time by the rating to give the normal time;
- find the allowances and calculate the standard time.

2. **Internal standard data**. Results from stopwatch studies can be saved, and eventually the organisation will have a database of times for various jobs. This can give times for similar jobs, perhaps using regression to find relationships between types of jobs and time needed.

3. **Pre-determined motion-time standards**. These are similar to internal standard data, except the times for tasks are not found from the organisation's experience, but from other organisations. Experience over many years has led to standard times for certain basic movements, such as reaching, grasping, turning, and releasing. Computers can analyse video recordings of jobs, find the times for each microelement, and combine these to give an overall time for the job.

4. **Work sampling**. Many jobs, such as cooking meals, answering telephones and interviewing customers are too variable for standard times. None the less, we still want some analysis of activities, and one alternative is **work sampling**. This has random visits, and records what is happening at each one. Over many visits we can build a general picture of how the people spend their time – typically finding the proportion of time a person spends doing particular activities, or the utilisation of equipment.

Review questions

17.11 What is the purpose of work measurement?

17.12 What is the difference between actual, normal and standard times?

17.13 How could you find the normal time for a job?

17.14 What time would you use to schedule resources?

OPERATIONS IN PRACTICE

Saving money on telephone dialling

A company was recently thinking of upgrading its telephone system. The IT department was keen on this upgrade because it would help consolidate its internal data network. The finance department was less keen, as it was only two years since its last major upgrade.

The supplier did a study to justify the new system, and part of this looked at the expected costs and savings. When the people in the finance department looked at this, they found a large figure for 'reduced delays in dialling internal calls'. When asked for an explanation, the supplier said that the upgraded system reduced the pause between finishing dialling an internal number and the first ring of the phone by almost a second. There were 1,000 people using the internal telephone network, and if each of them made 30 internal calls a day this would save 30,000 seconds or almost 10 hours a day. With an average cost of £40 an hour, this would give annual savings of over £100,000 a year.

Project 17.2 *Find a reasonably complicated task that either you, or someone you can see, do repeatedly. You might consider a particular journey, or making hamburgers in a restaurant. Time this task over a number of repetitions. How does the time vary? Why? What is the standard time for the task?*

Chapter review

- The way that jobs are done can depend on organisational structure. This affects job design and work measurement, which look in detail at how jobs are actually done. They can be viewed as the most detailed level of planning.
- The aim of job design is to find the best way of doing tasks. This has to consider both the economic targets of 'employers' and the social and psychological needs of 'workers'.
- It is in everyone's interest to have a motivated workforce. This means that managers have to design jobs that motivate their workers. A huge amount of work has been done in this area, and there are many suggestions for motivating employees. Often there is little agreement, in an area that has to be approached very carefully.
- Job design looks for the best way of doing a job. It usually breaks jobs into small elements, analyses these, and sees how the tasks can be done more efficiently.
- Three important parts of job design are the physical environment, social environment and work methods.
- Work measurement finds the time needed to do a job. There are really four times: theoretical basic time, actual time, normal time and standard time. The standard time is the total time needed for a job under ordinary working conditions and is used in all related decisions.
- Times can be estimated from historical data, estimation or time studies.

Key terms

CASE STUDY Moncton Welding and Fabrication

Workers in the welding department at Moncton Welding and Fabrication are worried. They heard from their supervisor, Karim Ahmed, that the new production manager is about to implement time standards in the department. There is a general feeling that this is really a way of reducing pay and making working conditions less pleasant.

Moncton recently hired Cedric Paxton as the production manager. The senior managers at Moncton gave him clear instructions to reduce the company's costs and make it more profitable. Cedric has a long record of successfully doing this with his previous employer.

Moncton makes a standard range of heat exchangers for the chemical industry. There are five different models of heat exchangers, each of which needs a lot of welding. The welding department has seven experienced welders and a supervisor. The quality of their work is very good, but Cedric is concerned that each welder uses his or her own method of working. He feels that better results would come by using standard methods.

One morning, to the surprise of Karim and the welders, Cedric showed up in the welding department with a stopwatch. He started to time a welder working on the tubes of a model XL1-50 heat exchanger. Cedric had taken seven readings when he was called away for an important meeting.

Later in the day, Cedric mentioned to Karim the results of his stopwatch study and asked for his opinion. Cedric had set the standard time of 10.5 minutes for welding the tubes in the XL1-50 heat exchanger. He had calculated this from five good readings he had taken earlier in the day. Karim knew from experience that it was an unrealistic standard, and the welders would not accept it.

Questions

- What do you think of Cedric's stopwatch study? What did he do wrong?
- What should Karim tell Cedric?
- What do you think Cedric should do next?

Problem

An analyst times 10 people doing a job. The times they take, in minutes, for the essential elements are:

14.3 12.8 13.9 16.2 14.8 15.2 13.6 15.8 14.4 14.0

What is the normal time for the job and the rating of each worker who was timed? What is the standard time if allowances of 20 per cent are given?

Discussion questions

17.1 Do you really believe that happy workers are productive workers? Is a motivated workforce really more productive? What about people who are motivated – but to do the wrong things?

17.2 Experience shows that the hierarchical structure of organisations is the only one with enough stability to last through the long term. Do you think this is true? What alternative structures are possible? What are the benefits and disadvantages of each?

17.3 It is said that the morale of schoolteachers is at an all-time low. How would you set about improving it? Do different methods work best in different types of organisation?

17.4 What factors do you think are most important in designing a job? Who are the best people to design jobs?

17.5 What special needs do knowledge workers have in their jobs and workplaces?

17.6 Organisations seem to be more 'human' in their approach to employees. Can you find any evidence to support this? If it is true, why has it happened? What are the effects of these changes?

17.7 How would you set about designing a fair scheme for paying employees?

17.8 What is the purpose of work measurement? How realistic are the times? If they are based on approximations, are they really useful for planning and measuring performance? Is work measurement is becoming less relevant with increasing automation?

References

1. Porter M.E. (1985) *Competitive Advantage*. New York: Free Press.
2. Harvey-Jones J. (1993) *Managing to Survive*. London: Heinemann.
3. Taylor F.W. (1911) *Principles of Scientific Management*. New York: Harper and Brothers.
4. Gilbreth F.B. and Gilbreth L.M. (1979) *Fatigue Study*. New York: Macmillan.
5. Maslow A.H. (1970) *Motivation and Personality*. 2nd edn. New York: Harper and Row.
6. Herzberg F., Mausner B. and Snyderman B.B. (1965) *The Motivation to Work*. New York: John Wiley.
7. McGregor D. (1960) *The Human Side of Enterprise*. New York: McGraw-Hill.

Selected reading

Armstrong M. (1999) *A Handbook of Human Resource Management Practice*. London: Kogan Page.

Beardwell I. (2000) *Human Resource Management*. Harlow: Financial Times/Prentice-Hall.

Brattan J. and Gold J. (1999) *Human Resource Management*. London: Palgrave.

Fisher K.K. (1993) *Leading Self-Directed Work Teams*. New York: McGraw-Hill.

Graham H.T. (1992) *Human Resources Management*. London: Pitman.

Grensing L. (1991) *Motivating Today's Workforce*. North Vancouver: Self-Counsel Press.

McKenna E. and Beech N. (1995) *Essence of Human Resource Management*. Englewood Cliffs, NJ: Prentice-Hall.

Niebel R. W. (1993) *Motion and Time Study*. 9th edn. Homewood, IL: Irwin.

Osborne D.J. (1995) *Ergonomics at Work*. 3rd edn. Chichester: John Wiley.
Smithers R.D. (1994) *The Psychology of Work and Performance*. 2nd edn. Reading, MA: Addison-Wesley.

Useful Websites

www.osha.gov – Occupational Safety and Health Administration
www.mtm.org – Time Measurement Association

CHAPTER 18

Project management

The true definition of a project, according to the modern acceptation, is, as said before, a vast undertaking, too big to be managed, and therefore likely enough to come to nothing.

Daniel Defoe

Essays upon Projects, 1697

Contents

Aims of the chapter

After reading this chapter you should be able to:

- appreciate the need to plan complex projects and the aims of project management;
- discuss the stages in a project and the key stakeholders;
- draw networks of activities to represent projects;
- analyse the timing of projects, finding the critical activities and overall duration;
- draw Gantt charts;
- change the timing of activities to achieve different objectives;
- make adjustments to minimise the total cost of a project;
- schedule the resources needed by a project and adjust activities to smooth these.

Main themes

This chapter will emphasise:

- **projects**, which are self-contained jobs that create a unique product;
- **project management**, which deals with every aspect of managing a project;
- **project networks**, which describe the activities in a project.

Projects and their management

Definitions

The last few chapters have looked at various aspects of planning and scheduling. We have assumed, at least to some extent, that operations are continuous and we are planning resources over some long period. But we saw in Chapter 9 that some operations are projects, and make a one-off product. These operations do not continue, but stop when the project is finished.

A **project** is a unique job that makes a one-off product.

- It has a distinct start and finish, and all operations must be co-ordinated within this timeframe.

With this broad definition, you can see that each of us does a number of small projects every day, such as preparing a meal, writing a report, building a fence or organising a party. These small projects do not need much formal planning, and a little thought is enough to make sure they run smoothly, but some projects are very big and expensive. Building a power station, organising the Olympic Games, digging the Channel tunnel, building the Three Gorges dam on the Yangtze River and developing the Hibernia oil field off Newfoundland are examples of large projects. These can have budgets of billions of pounds and take years to complete. Some projects involve hundreds or even thousands of organisations working together and co-ordinating their activities. Such projects need a lot of planning, and this is provided by **project management**.

Project management deals with all aspects of planning, organising, staffing and controlling a project.

- The operations manager in this case is a **project manager**.

Although each project is unique, they share a number of common features:

- a well-defined objective, usually making a unique product;
- a series of related activities needed to make this product;
- fixed start and finish dates within which all the activities must be completed;
- a budget for the completion of the project;
- customers who want the final product and provide the funds;
- a project manager and team who work on the project.

Each project is unique, so there may be little chance to learn from experience with similar projects. This is why there is considerable uncertainty in projects, with high risks of going over budget and schedule. When this happens, particularly with large projects, the costs can be very high. The size and impact of these large projects mean that a lot of people – the **stakeholders** – are concerned with the results.

You can probably imagine a project most easily with some type of construction, such as building the London Millennium Dome. In practice, however, you can find projects in almost every kind of organisation. Ford runs projects to design new cars; NASA runs projects to launch each shuttle; Rail Track runs projects to upgrade lengths of rail lines; Pfizer runs projects to develop new pharmaceuticals; Lotus runs projects to develop new software.

In recent years more managers have realised that their work is not continuous, but actually consists of a series of projects. Management consultants, for example, work on a series of projects for different clients, a doctor will do a series of projects with different patients, a chef can view each meal as a project, and a marketing team can view each new campaign as a project. The benefit of this is that they can use methods developed for project management to plan their daily operations. These methods are included in the **project management body of knowledge**.[1]

Approach to project management

All projects have two main phases:

- a *planning phase* – during which the project's purpose is defined, its feasibility tested, goals are set, detailed design work done, resources allocated, times agreed, management and work organised, etc.;
- an *execution phase* – during which materials are purchased and delivered, the work is done, finished products are handed over to customers, initial operations are tested, etc.

You can imagine these phases with building a house. In the planning phase an architect draws plans, a site is found, local authorities give planning approval, a building company is chosen, and all arrangements are finalised. In the execution phase, the site is prepared, foundations are dug, walls are built, electrical and plumbing work is done, and the house is actually built. As you can see from this example, projects bring together people with a range of knowledge and skills. Most of these work on the project for some time, and then move on to other jobs.

The planning for major projects can be very complicated, so it is divided into more than these two basic phases. One common approach for construction projects has engineering, procurement and construction, which is why you hear about 'EPC companies'. There are many different views about the number of phases in a project life cycle, and what they are called. One common approach has the following five phases (see Figure 18.1).

1. *Concept phase*. The starting point for a project is the identification of a need. When, for example, Macy's department store recognises that it must plan its Christmas sales campaign, this is best organised as a project. Then the concept phase gets to the point of describing, in general terms, the aims of the project and how these will be achieved. When Powergen looks at alternative sources of energy, one project might consider a barrier across the River Severn. The concept phase for this would not show any details, but present an outline of the aims, work, costs, results, resources and time. At this point the potential customers can look at the desirability and feasibility of the project and decide whether they want to move ahead.

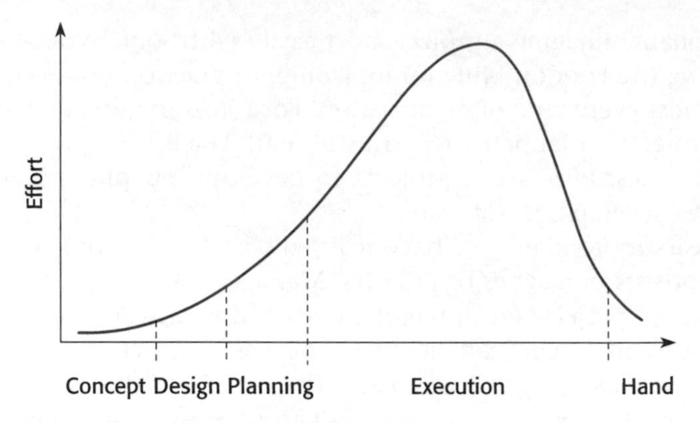

Figure 18.1 Intensity of effort during a project life cycle

2. *Design phase*. The general concept seems reasonable, so some details are added in the design phase. This describes the objectives of the project, the end results, measures to show if these results are achieved, more detailed costs, timings and resources. The design phase includes a **project scope** or **statement of work**, which describes all the work to be done. At the end of this phase customers effectively commit themselves to the project.

3. *Planning phase*. By this time we know the work to be done for the project – from the scope – the time and resources available. So we can start planning the resources to make sure that the project is done as efficiently as possible. These plans consider:

- A **work breakdown structure**. Projects can be very complicated, so the work has to be broken down into manageable bits (illustrated in Figure 18.2). This is done in a hierarchy, which is the work breakdown structure. The scope is divided into its major parts; each major part is divided into work packages; each work package is divided into individual activities. Complex projects are broken down into many of these layers.
- Resources needed for each activity identified in the work breakdown structure.
- Relationships between the activities, including the order in which they must be done.
- The time needed for each activity, and the consequent duration of the project.
- Milestones in the project which can be used to check its progress.

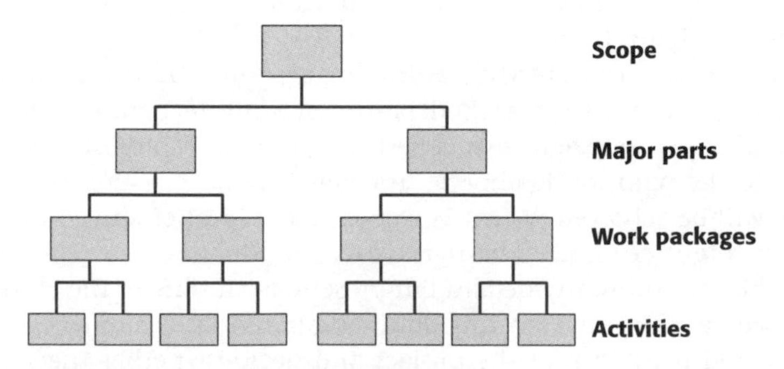

Figure 18.2 Work breakdown structure

- Costs of activities and of the whole project.
- Structure of the project team and responsibilities, including subcontracting.

4. *Execution phase*. This is the stage where the work is actually done. It implements the plans and does all the work described. Throughout its execution, the project has to be controlled. In other words, progress is monitored to make sure that everything is done according to plans, and to make changes and adjustments as needed. Projects contain a lot of uncertainty, so the initial plans are likely to change during execution.

5. *Handover*. The project is finished when all results have been achieved, any commissioning is done, and the 'deliverables' are handed over to customers. The project team has now finished its work and it is disbanded.

OPERATIONS IN PRACTICE

Peter Lutyen's retirement villa

Peter Lutyen has spent his working life in the Belgian steel industry. He is now 54 and has been offered a generous retirement package by an industry that is trying to reduce costs and capacity. Peter is using this to build a villa in the Algarve in Portugal. He looked on this as a project for his early retirement.

Peter's general plans and initial ideas for a villa formed the concept for the project. The project design included a detailed description of the villa, costs and the work needed to build this. Project planning took the project scope and broke this down into a series of related activities (such as digging foundations, laying drains, putting up main brickwork, plastering exterior, etc.). Peter developed a timetable for these activities and used these to find the overall project duration. His planning was really iterative as he kept looking for the best compromise between specifications, time and cost. During this planning, Peter worked closely with Juan Perez and Sons who were actually going to build the villa. As Peter could not be on the site all the time, he appointed a local surveyor to monitor progress and report any problems.

Assuming everything works as planned, Peter expects to be in the finished villa before his 56th birthday.

Stakeholders

We have already mentioned several people involved in a project: the project manager, the project team which does the work, customers, planners, and so on. In practice, there may be many interested people, who together form the **stakeholders**:

- *owners or customers* – the people for whom the project is done, who have to be satisfied with the results, and who pay for it;
- *sponsors or champions* – who support the project within the owners' organisation and help its progress by overcoming any problems;
- *project team* – people who do the actual work and execute the project;
- project manager – who controls the project team and is responsible for the work;
- *contractors and subcontractors* – outside organisations which are brought in to do parts of the work, often specific work packages;
- *external parties* – other people who may be affected by the project, such as local governments, environmental inspectors, residents, special interest groups, etc.

Project mangers are central figures in the operations, and it is their job to bring together all the resources and make sure the project is a success. This is a notoriously difficult job. Project managers have to work with different kinds of people, in situations where there is a lot of uncertainty, using many resources, keeping within tight constraints on budgets and schedules, and they still have to give a product that satisfies the customer. Projects usually have a matrix organisation, where people from different functions and different organisations are brought together into a team for a specific project. Project managers are generally facilitators, creating the right conditions for these people to do their jobs.

OPERATIONS IN PRACTICE

Major construction projects

In December 1990 Transmanche Link, a consortium of 10 British and French companies, finished the first continuous tunnel under the English Channel. The main tunnels were opened in 1994, and handed over to Eurotunnel to start operations. This was a significant step in a huge project.

The Channel tunnel was the world's biggest privately funded construction project, needing the largest banking syndicate ever put together, with 200 participating banks and financial institutions. By 1994 the estimated cost of the tunnel was £9 billion, and by 1998 this had risen to £15 billion, with rail companies investing another £3 billion in rolling stock and infrastructure. At its peak, the project employed 14,500 people.

The idea of a tunnel under the Channel is not new. In 1802 Albert Mathieu, one of Napoleon's engineers, drew a crude plan and several trial tunnels have been dug at various times. This project had clearly been developing for a very long time, and it was executed by very successful and experienced companies. They dug a total of 150 km of tunnels, with two main rail tunnels and a third service tunnel. By all accounts, the tunnel was a triumph of construction. None the less, its costs were several times the original estimate of £4.5 billion; the consortium was continually looking for additional funding; the opening date was delayed so much that extra interest charges, bankers' and layers' fees amounted to £1 billion; and participants were plagued by legal disputes.

It is common for major projects to overrun their budgets and schedules. In 1994 the British Library was half built after 12 years; the cost had tripled to £450 million and a House of Commons Committee reported: 'no one – ministers, library staff, building contractors, anyone at all – has more than the faintest idea when the building will be completed, when it will be open for use, or how much it will cost'. In 1995 Denver International Airport had cost $4.9 billion rather than $2 billion and it was still not finished 18 months behind schedule. In a study of 1,449 projects by the Association of Project Managers 12 came in on time and under budget.

Source: Caulkin S. (1994) 'Noah Man Who Can?', *The Observer*, 31 July

Project 18.1 *Find some examples of major projects that seem to have gone wrong. What happened and why? Could these problems have been avoided with better planning?*

Project management

The aim of project management is to complete the project successfully, giving customers the product they want, keeping within the specified time, and within the budget. Cost and time control are very important, and become a part of the product. A construction company that can build a bridge within 18 months offers a better product than a competitor taking two years to build the same bridge. Of course, decisions are rarely this simple, and the company that takes longer may offer a lower price or different specifications. This balance between cost, time and resources is a common theme in project management. If a project gets behind schedule, is it better to increase costs by using more resources? If a project gets ahead of schedule, is it better to finish it quickly and free up all resources early, or slow down and transfer some resources to other projects? Such decisions are a part of every project manager's job, which also includes:

1. using the work breakdown structure to identify all the activities in a project, together with the order in which these activities have to be done;
2. estimating the time of each activity, the total length of the project, and the time when each activity must be finished;
3. finding how much flexibility there is in the times of activities, and which activities are most critical to the completion time;
4. estimating costs and scheduling activities to minimise the overall cost;
5. allocating resources and scheduling these so the project can be completed as efficiently as possible;
6. monitoring the progress of the project, reacting quickly to any deviations from plans, and adjusting schedules as required;
7. anticipating problems and taking any actions needed to avoid them;
8. preparing regular reports on progress.

The first five of these are concerned with scheduling the project and are done in the planning phase. The last three are concerned with control of the project in the execution phase. To help with these, project managers can use a number of tools, such as Gantt charts, critical path method and project evaluation and review technique. We will look at these in the following sections.

Review questions

18.1 What is a project?

18.2 What is the purpose of project management?

18.3 Project management is only concerned with major capital projects. Do you think this is true?

18.4 What are the two main phases of a project?

Project networks

A work breakdown structure takes the project scope and forms a hierarchy of jobs. At the bottom of this hierarchy are work packages, which are themselves made up of a number of activities. These activities are the basic elements in a project, and are used for all the detailed planning. Several tools can help with this planning, but the most widely used are based on **project network analysis**.

Two groups working in the 1950s independently developed project network analysis. The first group worked on the Polaris missile project for the United States Department of Defense.[3] At that time the US government was worried about the slow progress, and **PERT (project evaluation and review technique)** was developed to control the 3,000 contractors working on the project. This reduced the overall length of the project by two years.

The second group worked for Du Pont[4] and developed **CPM (critical path method)** for planning maintenance programmes in chemical plants. PERT and CPM were always very similar, and any differences in the original ideas have disappeared over time. The one difference that remains is that PERT uses probabilistic durations of activities while CPM assumes that durations are fixed.

Drawing networks

We can represent a project by a network of activities. A project network consists of a series of alternating circles, or **nodes**, connected by arrows. There are two formats we can use:

1. *Activity on* arrow: each arrow represents an activity and each node represents the point when activities start and finish.
2. *Activity on* node: each node represents an activity and the arrows show the relationships between them.

Suppose you have a project with three activities, A, B and C, which have to be done in that order. B has to wait until A finishes before it can start, and it must then finish before C can start. We can represent this using the two formats in Figure 18.3.

The choice between these is largely a matter of personal preference. Activity on arrow networks are better at showing some relationships and the calculations are easier; activity on node networks are easier to draw and are more common in project planning software. In practice, activity on node networks are probably more common, so we will stick to this format.

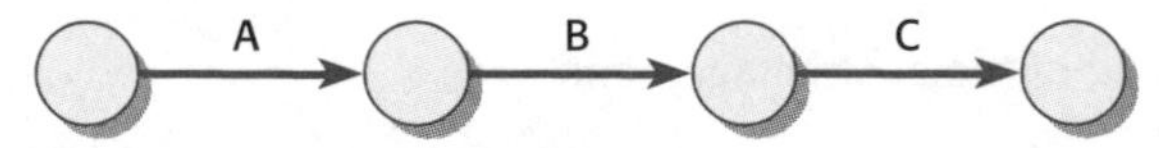

(a) Activity on arrow format

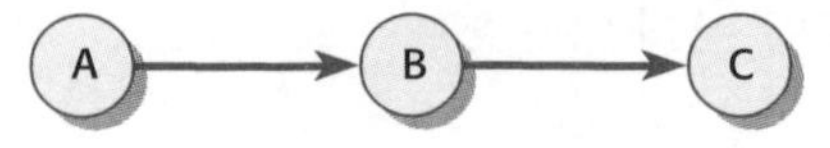

(b) Activity on node format

Figure 18.3 Alternative formats for drawing project networks

WORKED EXAMPLE

A gardener is building a greenhouse from a kit. The instructions show that this is a project with four parts:

- A, levelling the ground, which takes two days;
- B, building the base, which takes three days;
- C, building the frame, which takes two days;
- D, fixing the glass, which takes one day.

Draw a network for the project.

Solution

The project has four activities that must be done in a fixed order; levelling the ground must be done first, followed by building the base, building the frame and finally fixing the glass. We can describe this order by a **dependence table**. Here each activity is listed along with those activities that immediately precede it.

Activity	Duration (days)	Description	Immediate predecessor
A	2	Level ground	–
B	3	Build base	A
C	2	Build frame	B
D	1	Fix glass	C

Labelling the activities A, B and C is a convenient shorthand and allows us to describe activity B having activity A as its immediate predecessor. This is normally stated as 'B depends on A'. In this table only **immediate** predecessors are given. We do not need to say that C depends on A as well as B, as it follows from the other dependencies. Activity A has no immediate predecessors and can start whenever convenient.

Now we can draw a network from the dependence table, as shown in Figure 18.4.

Figure 18.4 Network for building a greenhouse

The direction of the arrows shows precedence – each preceding activity must finish before the following one starts – and following activities can start as soon as preceding ones finish. In the example above, levelling the ground must be done first, and as soon this is finished the base can be built. The frame can be built as soon as the base is finished, and the glass can be fixed as soon as the frame is built. This gives the sequence of activities, and the next stage looks at the timing.

WORKED EXAMPLE

Find the times for each activity in the last example. What happens if the base takes more than three days, or the glass is delayed, or the frame takes less than two days?

Solution

If we take a notional starting time of zero, we can finish levelling the ground by the end of day 2. Then we can start building the base, and as this takes three days we finish by the end of day 5. Then we can start building the frame, and as this takes two days we finish by the end of day 7. Finally, we can start fixing the glass, which takes one day, so we finish by the end of day 8.

If the base takes more than three days to build, or the glass is not delivered by day 7, the project is delayed. If building the frame takes less than two days, the project will finish early.

Gantt charts

Now we have a timetable for the project showing when each activity starts and finishes, and can use this to schedule resources. So we have identified the major steps in project network analysis as:

- define the activities;
- find the dependence and duration of each activity;
- draw a network of the relationships;
- analyse the timing of the project;
- schedule resources.

The timing of activities is at the core of project management, and during the execution phase we have to constantly monitor progress to make sure activities are done at the right times. The timing is not always clear from a network, and is much easier to see on a **Gantt chart**. This gives another way of representing a project, with activities listed down the left-hand side, a time scale across the bottom, and times when activities should be done blocked-off in the body of the chart. Figure 18.5 shows the Gantt chart for the last example.

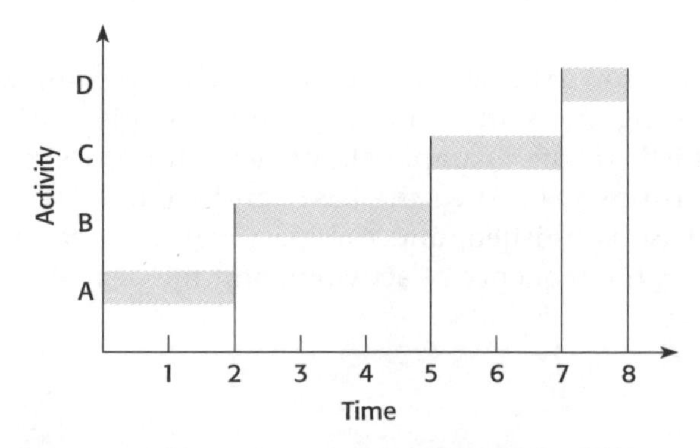

Figure 18.5 Gantt chart for building a greenhouse

Larger networks

In principle, you can draw networks of any size, simply by starting at the left-hand side with activities that do not depend on any others. Then you add activities that only depend on these first activities, then activities that only depend on the latest activities added, and so on. The network expands systematically, working from left to right, until you have added all the activities and the network is complete. There are two important rules to remember:

- before an activity can begin, all preceding activities must be finished;
- the arrows only show precedence and neither the length nor direction has any significance.

There are several other rules that make sure the network is sensible:

- to make things clear, we add one 'start' and one 'finish' activity to a network;
- every arrow must have a head and a tail connecting two activities;
- every activity (apart from the start and finish) must have at least one predecessor and at least one successor activity;
- there can be no loops in the network.

Now we can use these rules to draw networks of any size. In reality, of course, there are many specialised programs for drawing bigger networks.

WORKED EXAMPLE

Allied Commercial is opening a new office. This is a project with the following activities and dependencies:

Activity	Description	Depends on
A	Find office location	–
B	Recruit new staff	–
C	Make office alterations	A
D	Order equipment needed	A
E	Install new equipment	D
F	Train staff	B
G	Start operations	C,E,F

Draw a network of this project.

Solution

Activities A and B have no predecessors and can start as soon as convenient. As soon as activity A is finished, both C and D can start: E can start as soon as D is finished and F can start as soon as B is finished. G can only start when C, E and F have all finished. Figure 18.6 shows the resulting network.

You can see from this network that the first activities are A and B. This does not mean that these must start at the same time – only that they can both start as soon as convenient and must be finished before any following activity can start. On the other hand, activity G must wait until C, E and F are finished. This does not mean that C, E and F must finish at the same time – only that they must all finish before G can start.

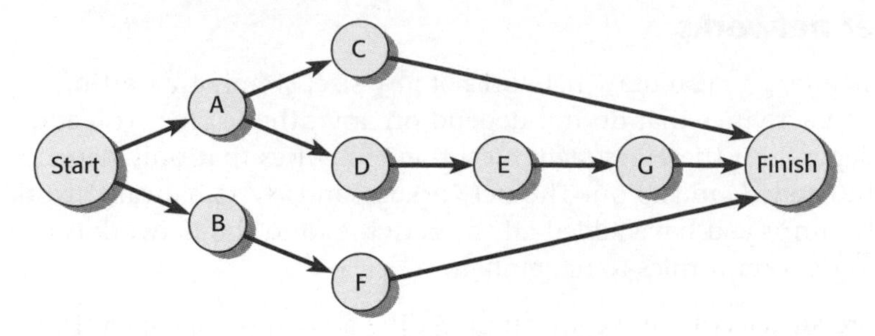

Figure 18.6 Network for Allied Commercial

WORKED EXAMPLE

The following dependence table describes a software development project. Draw a network of the project.

Activity	Depends on	Activity	Depends on
A	J	I	J
B	C,G	J	–
C	A	K	B
D	F,K,N	L	I
E	J	M	I
F	B,H,L	N	M
G	A,E,I	O	M
H	G	P	O

Solution

This may seem a difficult network, but the steps are fairly straightforward. Activity J is the only one that does not depend on anything else, so this starts the network. Then we can add activities A, E and I, which only depend on J. Then we can add activities which depend on A, E and I. Continuing this systematic addition of activities leads to the network shown in Figure 18.7.

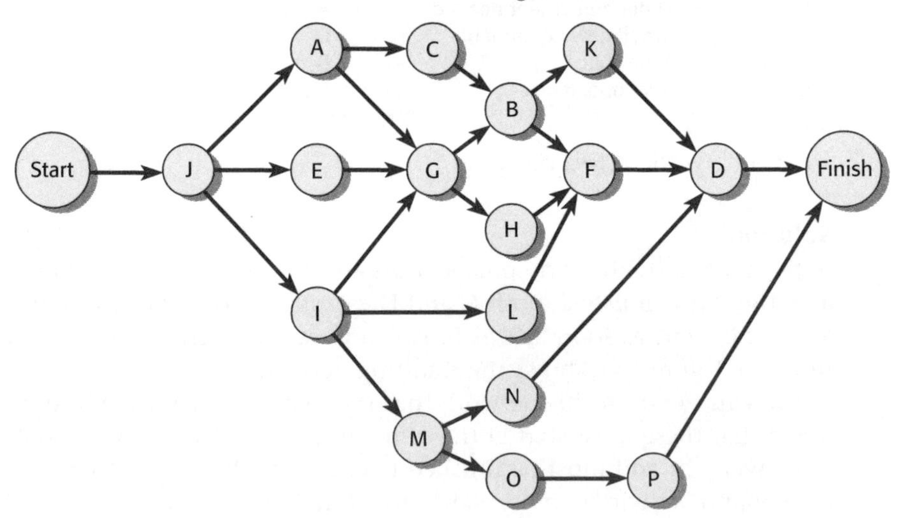

Figure 18.7 Network for software project

Bigger networks obviously take more effort to draw and analyse, even if this is done by computer. We divided our initial example of building a greenhouse into four activities. We could have used a lot more – perhaps clearing vegetation, laying hard-core, digging the foundations, and so on. As the complexity of the network increases, the significance of each activity declines. So we have to choose the best number of activities, balancing the usefulness of a network for planning with its complexity.

If we have to use a large number of activities, the network will be complicated, cover many pages, and be difficult to follow. To simplify things, we can follow the approach of the work breakdown structure. In other words, we start with a general, master network showing the major parts of the project. Then we can expand this into separate, more detailed networks covering specific areas, and so on down a hierarchy of networks. This approach is particularly useful for contractors and sub-contractors; the owner of the project can draw a master network, each contractor and subcontractor gets a network covering their own parts of the work.

OPERATIONS IN PRACTICE

Loch Moraigh Distillery

The managers of Loch Moraigh whisky distillery examined the inventory control system to find the best stock levels to meet forecast demand. They concluded that an expanded computer system was needed. This would extrapolate past demand patterns and use these to set appropriate stock levels. These stock levels are then passed to a production control module that varies the quantities bottled.

The first part of this proposed system was called DFS (Demand Forecasting System) while the second part was ICS (Inventory Control System). The introduction of these systems took about 12 months, including linking to the production control module which was already working. The introduction of DFS and ICS was a self-contained project with the following activities:

Activity	Description
A	Examine existing system and environment of ICS
B	Collect costs and other data relevant to ICS
C	Construct and test models for ICS
D	Write and test computer programs for ICS models
E	Design and print data input forms for ICS data
F	Document ICS programs and monitoring procedures
G	Examine sources of demand data and its collection
H	Construct and test models for DFS
I	Organise past demand data
J	Write and test computer programs for DFS models
K	Design and print data input forms for DFS data
L	Document DFS programs and monitoring procedures
M	Train staff in the use of DFS and ICS
N	Initialise data for ICS programs (ICS staff)
P	Initialise data for DFS programs (DFS staff)
Q	Create base files for DFS
R	Run system for trial period
S	Implement final system

A project management package gave the following results:

PROBLEM: LOCH MORAIGH DISTILLERY **Date: 09-09-1999**

o ORIGINAL NETWORK DATA

No.	Letter Code	Name	Expected Completion Time	Letter Code for Immediately Preceding Activities 1	2	3	4	5	6	7
1	A	Examine system	2.00							
2	B	Collect ICS data	1.00	A						
3	C	Test ICS models	2.00	A						
4	D	Program ICS	4.00	C						
5	E	Design ICS forms	1.00	C						
6	F	Document ICS	2.00	D	E					
7	G	Examine demand	2.00							
8	H	Test DFS models	4.00	A	G					
9	I	Organise data	2.00	G						
10	J	Program DFS	6.00	H	K					
11	K	Design DFS forms	2.00	A	G					
12	L	Document DFS	3.00	J						
13	M	Train staff	2.00	F	L					
14	N	Initialise ICS	1.00	B	M					
15	P	Initialise DFS	1.00	I	M					
16	Q	Create DFS files	1.00	P						
17	R	Trial period	4.00	N	Q					
18	S	Implement	2.00	R						

o ACTIVITY REPORT

Activity No	Code	Name	Planning Times Exp.t	ES	LS	EF	LF	Slack
1	A	Examine sys	2.0	0.0	0.0	2.0	2.0	0.0
2	B	Collect ICS	1.0	2.0	17.0	3.0	18.0	15.0
3	C	Test ICS mo	2.0	2.0	7.0	4.0	9.0	5.0
4	D	Program ICS	4.0	4.0	9.0	8.0	13.0	5.0
5	E	Design ICS	1.0	4.0	12.0	5.0	13.0	8.0
6	F	Document IC	2.0	8.0	13.0	10.0	15.0	5.0
7	G	Examine dem	2.0	0.0	0.0	2.0	2.0	0.0
8	H	Test DFS mo	4.0	2.0	2.0	6.0	6.0	0.0
9	I	Organise da	2.0	2.0	15.0	4.0	17.0	13.0
10	J	Program DFS	6.0	6.0	6.0	12.0	12.0	0.0
11	K	Design DFS	2.0	2.0	4.0	4.0	6.0	2.0
12	L	Document DF	3.0	12.0	12.0	15.0	15.0	0.0
13	M	Train staff	2.0	15.0	15.0	17.0	17.0	0.0
14	N	Initialise	1.0	17.0	18.0	18.0	19.0	1.0
15	P	Initialise	1.0	17.0	17.0	18.0	18.0	0.0
16	Q	Create DFS	1.0	18.0	18.0	19.0	19.0	0.0
17	R	Trial perio	4.0	19.0	19.0	23.0	23.0	0.0
18	S	Implement	2.0	23.0	23.0	25.0	25.0	0.0

o Expected Project Duration: 25

o The following path(s) are critical.

A H J L M P Q R S

G H J L M P Q R S

Figure 18.8 Printout for Loch Moraigh Distillery

Review questions

18.5 What are the main benefits of Gantt charts?

18.6 In the networks we have drawn, what do the nodes and arrows represent?

18.7 What information do you need to draw a project network?

18.8 What are the main rules for drawing a project network?

Timing of projects

Earlier in the chapter we said that the only real difference between critical path method (CPM) and project evaluation and review technique (PERT) is in the timing. In particular, CPM assumes that each activity has a fixed duration that is known exactly, while PERT assumes the duration can vary according to a known distribution. The basic analyses are identical, so we will start by assuming that the durations are fixed. The calculations for PERT are given in a supplement to this chapter.

Time of activities

The two most important times for an activity are the earliest time it can start, and the latest time it can finish. These define the time slot that is available for the activity. Two related times are the earliest finish (equal to the earliest start plus the duration) and the latest start (equal to the latest finish minus the duration). These are illustrated in Figure 18.9.

Earliest finish = earliest start + duration
Latest start = latest finish – duration

It is easiest to show these calculations in an example. Suppose a project has the following dependence table, where we also know the durations (in weeks).

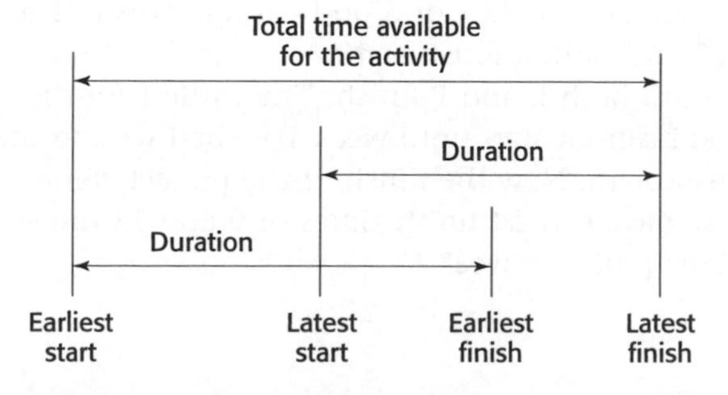

Figure 18.9 Times for an activity

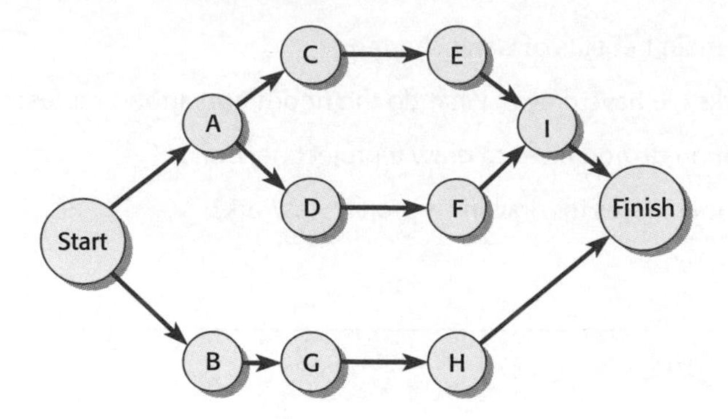

Figure 18.10 Network for timing example

Activity	Duration	Depends on
A	3	–
B	2	–
C	2	A
D	4	A
E	1	C
F	3	D
G	3	B
H	4	G
I	5	E,F

This project is shown in the network in Figure 18.10.

The first step in our analysis of times is to find the earliest possible time for starting each activity. For simplicity, we will assume a notional start time of zero for the project. The earliest start of activity B is clearly 0, and as it takes two weeks, the earliest finish is $0 + 2 = 2$. When B finishes G can start, so its earliest start is 2, and adding the duration of 3 gives an earliest finish of $2 + 3 = 5$. When G finishes H can start, so its earliest start is 5, and adding the duration of 4 gives an earliest finish of $5 + 4 = 9$.

Similarly, the earliest start of A is clearly 0, and as it takes three weeks, the earliest finish is 3. When A finishes both C and D can start, so the earliest start time for both of these is 3. Adding the durations gives earliest finish times of 5 and 7 respectively. Then E follows C, with an earliest start of 5 and earliest finish of 6; F follows D, with an earliest start of 7 and earliest finish of 10.

Activity I must wait until both E and F finish. The earliest finishes for these are 6 and 10 respectively, so I cannot start until week 10. Then we add the duration of 5 to get the earliest finish of 15. Now the finish of the project comes when both H and I are finished. These have earliest finish times of 9 and 15 respectively, so the earliest finish of the whole project is week 15.

Activity	Duration	Earliest start	Earliest finish
A	3	0	3
B	2	0	2
C	2	3	5
D	4	3	7
E	1	5	6
F	3	7	10
G	3	2	5
H	4	5	9
I	5	10	15

We can show these times on the network. The usual format makes the nodes into a box, and then puts the times in this box. We will use the notation in Figure 18.11, where the earliest start, duration and earliest finish are shown across the top of the box.

We have used this notation for the network shown in Figure 18.12.

Early start	Duration	Early finish
	Activity name	
Late start	Slack	Late finish

Figure 18.11 Node showing early and late times

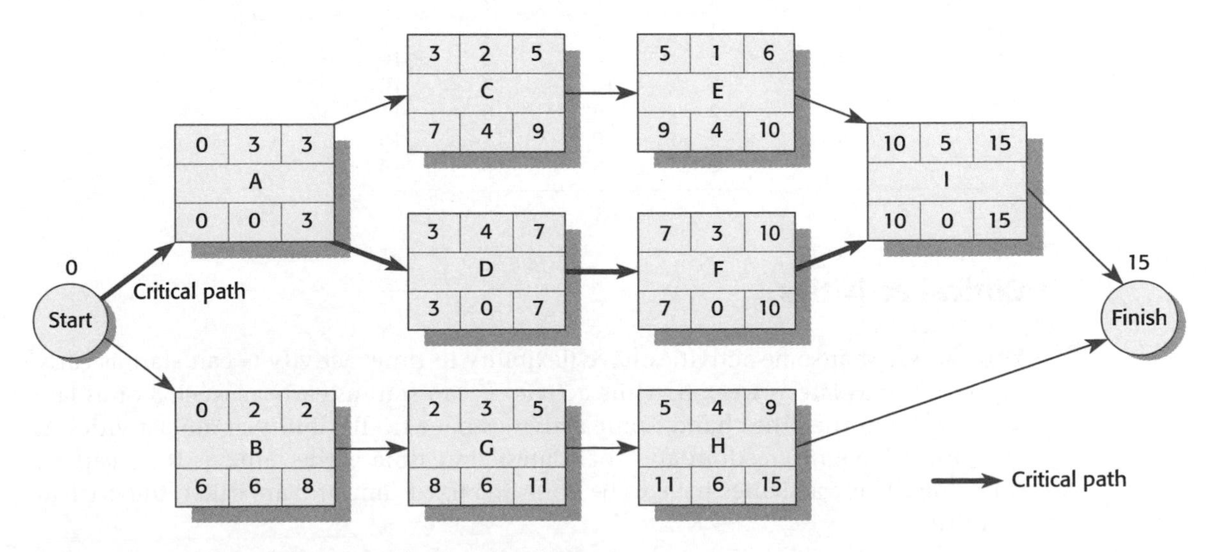

Figure 18.12 Network for example showing times

Latest times

Having worked through the network to find the earliest time for each activity, we can do a similar analysis to find the latest times. The procedure for this is almost the reverse of the procedure for finding the earliest times.

The earliest finish time for the whole project is week 15. If we want the project to finish then, we can also set this as the latest finish time. The latest finish time of activity H is clearly 15, so its latest start time is the duration 4 earlier than this at 15 – 4 = 11. Activity G must finish before this, so its latest finish is 11, and the latest start is the duration of 3 earlier at 11 – 3 = 8. Activity B must be finished before this, so its latest finish is 8, and the latest start is the duration 2 earlier at 8 – 2 = 6.

Now activity I must also finish by week 15, so its latest start is its duration of 5 earlier than this at 10. But for I to start at 10, both E and F must finish by 10, so this gives both of their latest finish times. They must start their durations earlier at time 10 – 1 = 9 and 10 – 3 = 7 respectively. Activity C must finish by time 9, so its latest start is 9 – 2 = 7, and activity D must finish by time 7 so its latest start is 7 – 4 = 3.

Activity A must finish in time for both C and D to start. Activity C has a latest start of 7 and activity D has a latest start of 3, so A must be finished for both of these, giving a latest finish of 3 and a latest start of 0. Similarly, the latest time to start the project must allow both A to start at 0 and B to start at 6, so it must start at time 0.

Activity	Duration	Earliest start	Earliest finish	Latest start	Latest finish
A	3	0	3	0	3
B	2	0	2	6	8
C	2	3	5	7	9
D	4	3	7	3	7
E	1	5	6	9	10
F	3	7	10	7	10
G	3	2	5	8	11
H	4	5	9	11	15
I	5	10	15	10	15

Critical activities

You can see that some activities have flexibility in time: activity G can start as early as week 2 or as late as week 8, while activity C can start as early as week 3 or as late as week 7. On the other hand, some activities have no flexibility at all: activities A, D, F and I have no freedom and their latest start time is the same as their earliest start time. These activities have to be done at a fixed time and are called the **critical activities**.

The **critical activities** have to be done at a fixed time.

- They form a continuous path through the network, called the **critical path**.

The length of the critical path sets the overall project duration. If one of the critical activities is extended by a certain amount, the overall project duration is extended by this amount; if one of the critical activities is delayed by some time, the overall project duration is extended by this delay. On the other hand, if one of the critical activities is made shorter, the overall project duration may be reduced.

The activities that have some flexibility in timing are the **non-critical activities** and these may be delayed or extended without necessarily affecting the overall project duration. There is, however, a limit to the amount a non-critical activity can be extended without affecting the project duration, and this is measured by the **float**. The **total float**, often called the **total slack**, is the difference between the amount of time available for an activity and the time actually used. It is the difference between the earliest and latest start times (which is the same as the difference between the earliest and latest finish times).

- Total float = latest start time – earliest start time

Or:

- Total float = latest finish time – earliest finish time

The total float is zero for critical activities and has some positive value for non-critical activities. The earliest and latest start of activity D are both 3, so the total float is 3 – 3 = 0, showing that this is one of the critical activities. The earliest and latest start of activity G are 2 and 8, so the total float is 8 – 2 = 6, showing that this is a non-critical activity. Its duration can expand by up to six weeks without affecting the duration of the project, but if it takes more than this the project is delayed. A negative total float means that an activity is late, and the project cannot be finished within the proposed time. The following table shows the calculations for other activities in the example.

Activity	Duration	Earliest time		Latest time		Total float
		Start	Finish	Start	Finish	
A	3	0	3	0	3	0
B	2	0	2	6	8	6
C	2	3	5	7	9	4
D	4	3	7	3	7	0
E	1	5	6	9	10	4
F	3	7	10	7	10	0
G	3	2	5	8	11	6
H	4	5	9	11	15	6
I	5	10	15	10	15	0

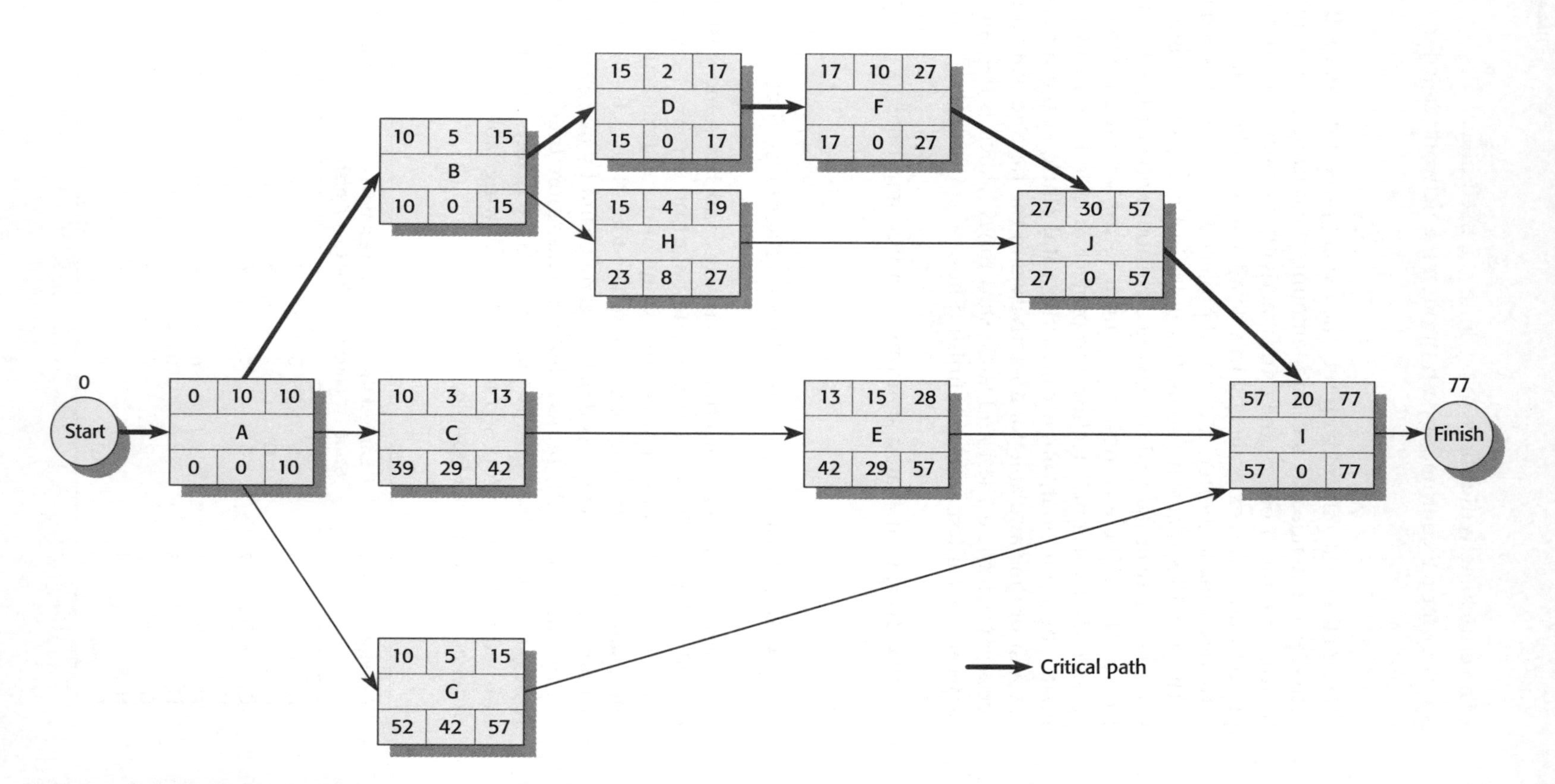

Figure 18.13 Network for building a telephone exchange

WORKED EXAMPLE

Building a small telephone exchange is planned as a project with 10 activities. Estimated durations (in days) and dependencies are shown in the following table. Draw the network for this project, find its duration and calculate the total float of each activity.

Activity	Description	Duration	Depends on
A	Design internal equipment	10	–
B	Design exchange building	5	A
C	Order parts for equipment	3	A
D	Order material for building	2	B
E	Wait for equipment parts	15	C
F	Wait for building material	10	D
G	Employ equipment assemblers	5	A
H	Employ building workers	4	B
I	Install equipment	20	E,G,J
J	Complete building	30	F,H

Solution

Figure 18.13 shows the network for this problem. Repeating the calculations described above gives the following table of results, with critical activities identified by an asterisk.

Activity	Duration	Earliest time		Latest time		Total float
		Start	Finish	Start	Finish	
A	10	0	10	0	10	0*
B	5	10	15	10	15	0*
C	3	10	13	39	42	29
D	2	15	17	15	17	0*
E	15	13	28	42	57	29
F	10	17	27	17	27	0*
G	5	10	15	52	57	42
H	4	15	19	23	27	8
I	20	57	77	57	77	0*
J	30	27	57	27	57	0*

The duration of the project is 77 days, defined by the critical path A, B, D, F, I and J.

Review questions

18.9 How do you find the earliest times for an activity?

18.10 How do you find the latest times?

18.11 What is the total float of an activity?

18.12 How big is the total float of a critical activity?

18.13 What is the significance of the critical path?

Changing project schedule

Benefits and disadvantages of network analysis

It is very difficult to plan a project and get everyone's agreement. Often the plans need revision and adjustment. There are two main reasons for this. During the planning stage, the timing, resource use or some other factor is unacceptable – typically, the initial plans take longer than the organisation has available. Alternatively, during the execution stage, an activity takes a different time to that originally planned. Project network analysis can identify such problems early, and gives ways of avoiding them. It has other benefits, as it:

- does useful analyses for time and resource planning;
- highlights areas needing special attention, particularly the critical path;
- is useful for control, identifying problems and showing how to overcome them;
- presents information in clear diagrams;
- is straightforward and easy to understand;
- is widely used, with a lot of software available.

There are also some disadvantage with network analysis, and critics identify some problems as follows:

- it is difficult to divide a project into a set of discrete activities;
- the relationships between activities are not fixed, but can take many forms;
- activity durations are subjective and can be unreliable;
- it puts too much emphasis on critical activities, and not enough on those which are nearly critical;
- managers are usually too optimistic in their plans, and schedules can be difficult to achieve in practice;
- project managers need more flexibility than their plans suggest, and only pay lip-service to the schedules.

Reducing the length of a project

One of the strengths of network analysis is that it gives ways of adjusting initial plans. Perhaps the most common adjustment is to reduce the overall length of a project. The critical path sets the length, so we can only reduce this by making the critical activities shorter. But we must also consider what happens when we reduce a critical path. Small reductions are all right, but if we keep reducing the duration of the critical path there must come a point when some other path through the network becomes critical. We can find this point from the total float on paths parallel to the critical path. Each activity on a parallel path has the same total float, and when the critical path is reduced by more than this, the parallel path itself becomes critical.

WORKED EXAMPLE

The project network shown in Figure 18.14 has a duration of 14 with A, B and C as the critical path.

If each activity can be reduced by up to 50 per cent of the original duration, how would you reduce the overall duration to: (a) 13 weeks; (b) 11 weeks; (c) 9 weeks? If reductions cost an average of $1,000 per week, what is the cost of finishing the project by week 9?

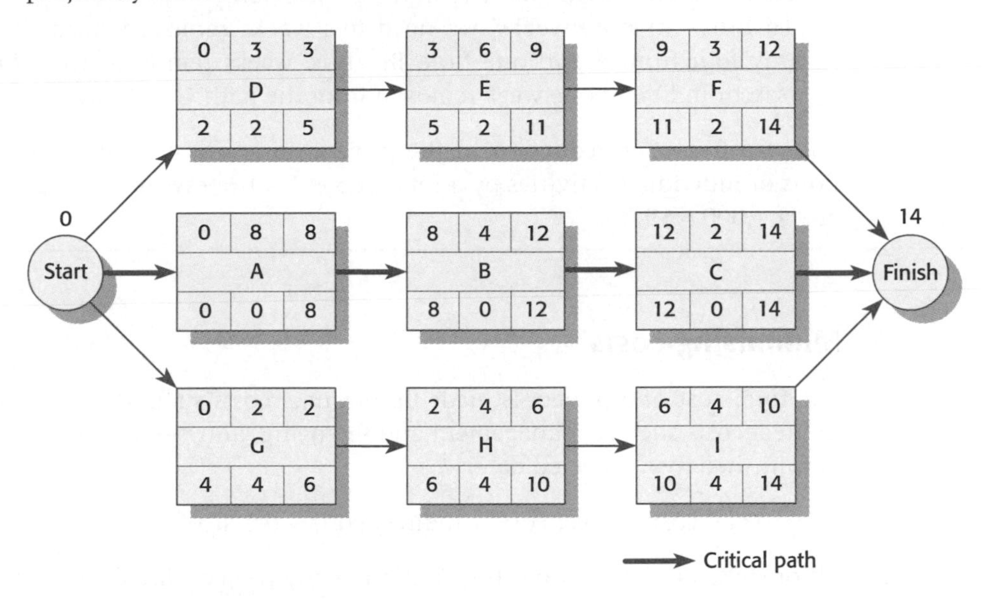

Figure 18.14 Network for worked example

Solution

The analysis of activity times for this project is as follows (critical activities are identified by an asterisk):

Activity	Duration	Earliest time		Latest time		Total float
		Start	Finish	Start	Finish	
A	8	0	8	0	8	0*
B	4	8	12	8	12	0*
C	2	12	14	12	14	0*
D	3	0	3	2	5	2
E	6	3	9	5	11	2
F	3	9	12	11	14	2
G	2	0	2	4	6	4
H	4	2	6	6	10	4
I	4	6	10	10	14	4

In this network there are three parallel paths, A-B-C, D-E-F and G-H-I. The critical path is A-B-C and these activities have zero total float. The total float of activities on the other two paths are 2 and 4 respectively. This means that we can reduce the critical path A-B-C by up to 2, but if we reduce it any more the path D-E-F becomes critical. If we reduce the critical path by more than 4, the path G-H-I also becomes critical.

(a) To finish in 13 weeks, we need a reduction of one week in the critical path. It is usually easier to find savings in longer activities, so we will reduce the duration of A to seven weeks.
(b) To finish in 11 weeks, we need a further reduction of two weeks in the critical path. We can also remove this from A, but the path D-E-F has now become critical with a duration of 12 weeks. We can remove one week from E, again chosen as the longest activity in the critical path.
(c) To finish in nine weeks, we need five weeks removed from the path A-B-C (say four from A and one from B), three weeks removed from the path D-E-F (say from E) and one week removed from the path G-H-I (say from H).

To get a five-week reduction in the project duration, we have reduced the durations of individual activities by a total of $5 + 3 + 1 = 9$ weeks. This gives a total cost of $9 \times 1{,}000 = \$9{,}000$.

Minimising costs

The total cost of a project is made up of direct costs such as labour and materials, indirect costs such as management and financing, and penalty costs if the project is not finished by a specified date.

$$\text{Total cost} = \text{direct costs} + \text{indirect costs} + \text{penalty costs}$$

All of these are affected by the duration of the project. If a project is running late, we might put in more resources to avoid the penalty costs. Sometimes a bonus is paid if a project is finished early, but this might take extra resources and increase direct costs. We really need some kind of balance between project duration and total cost. The normal method for finding this is based on two figures:

- **normal time:** the expected time to complete the activity and this has associated **normal costs**;
- **crashed time:** the shortest possible time to complete the activity and this has the higher **crashed costs**.

To simplify the analysis, we assume that the cost of completing an activity in any particular time is a linear combination of these costs. Then the cost of **crashing** an activity by a unit of time is:

$$\text{Cost of crashing by one time unit} = \frac{\text{crashed cost} - \text{normal cost}}{\text{normal time} - \text{crashed time}}$$

Now we can suggest an approach to minimising the total cost of a project. This starts by analysing the project with all activities done at their normal time and cost. Then the duration of critical activities is systematically reduced. Initially the cost of the project may fall as its duration is reduced. There comes a point, however, where any further reduction in duration makes the cost start to rise. At this point we have found the minimum cost. The formal procedure to find this minimum has the following steps:

Step 1. Draw a project network, and analyse the cost and timings assuming all activities take their normal times.
Step 2. Find the critical activity with the lowest cost of crashing per unit time. If there is more than one critical path, they must all be considered at the same time.
Step 3. Reduce the time for this activity until either:

- it cannot be reduced any further;
- another path becomes critical;
- the cost of the project begins to rise.

Step 4. Repeat steps 2 and 3 until the cost of the project begins to rise.

WORKED EXAMPLE

A project is described by the following dependence table, where times are in weeks and costs are in thousands of pounds.

Activity	Depends on	Normal Time	Normal Cost	Crashed Time	Crashed Cost
A	–	3	13	2	15
B	A	7	25	4	28
C	B	5	16	4	19
D	C	5	12	3	24
E	–	8	32	5	38
F	E	6	20	4	30
G	F	8	30	6	35
H	–	12	41	7	45
I	H	6	25	3	30
J	D,G,I	2	7	1	14

There is a penalty cost of £3,500 for every week the project finishes after week 18. When should the project be finished to minimise costs?

Solution

Using the procedure described above:

- *Step 1*. The network for this project is shown in Figure 18.15, with times based on normal durations.

The critical path is E-F-G-J which has a duration of 24 weeks, and we can find the total cost by adding the normal costs of each activity (221,000) to the 24 – 18 = 6 days of penalty costs (21,000) to give a total of £242,000.

The cost of crashing each activity (in £000 a week) is as follows:

Activity	A	B	C	D	E	F	G	H	I	J
Normal time	3	7	5	5	8	6	8	12	6	2
Crashed time	2	4	4	3	5	4	6	7	3	1
Reduction in weeks	1	3	1	2	3	2	2	5	3	1
Crashed cost	15	28	19	24	38	30	35	45	30	14
Normal cost	13	25	16	12	32	20	30	41	25	7
Cost of reduction	2	3	3	12	6	10	5	4	5	7
Cost per week	2	1	3	6	2	5	2.5	0.8	1.7	7

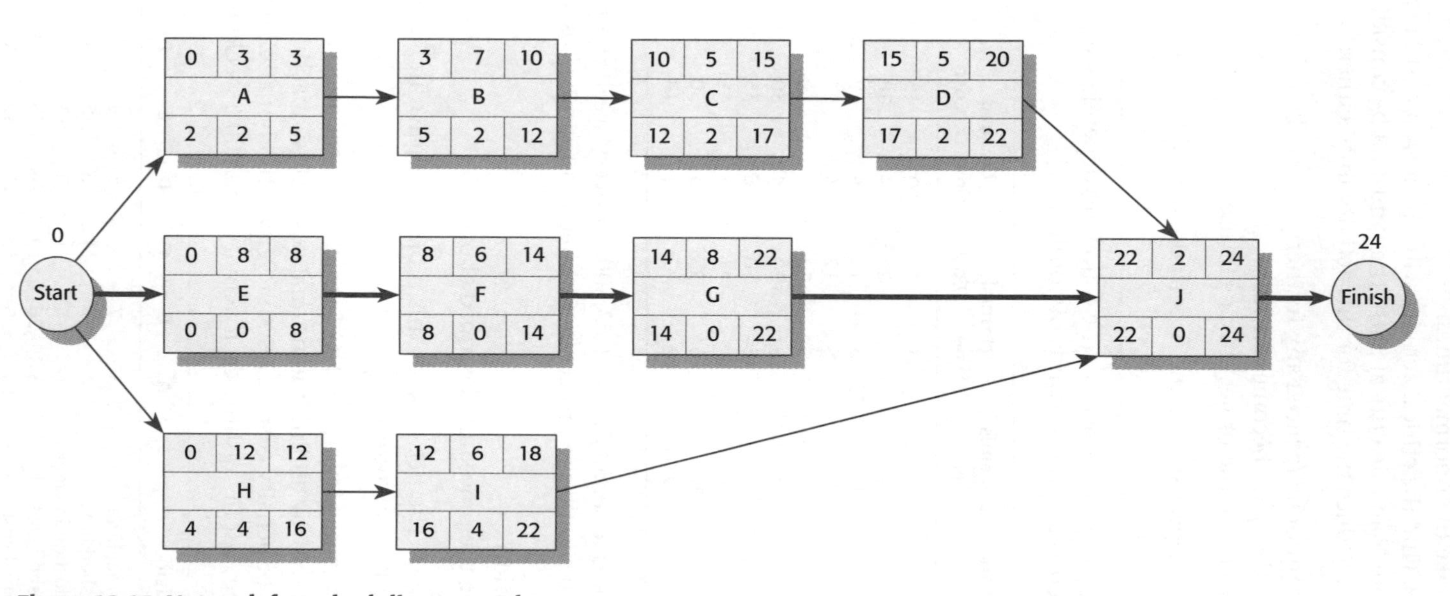

Figure 18.15 Network for scheduling example

The total float of activities on the parallel path A-B-C-D is two, so if the critical path is reduced by this amount, A-B-C-D becomes critical.

- *Step 2* finds the activity on the critical path (E-F-G-J) with lowest cost of crashing, and this is E at £2,000 a week.
- *Step 3* reduces the time for activity E by two weeks, as beyond this the path A-B-C-D-J becomes critical.

Total cost of crashing by two weeks = 2 × 2,000 = £4,000
Total savings = 2 × 3,500 = £7,000

This step has reduced the penalty cost by more than the crashing cost, so we look for more savings.

- *Step 2* finds the lowest costs in the critical paths as E in E-F-G-J and B in A-B-C-D-J.
- *Step 3* reduces the time of these activities by one week, as E is then reduced by the maximum allowed.

Total cost of crashing by one week = 2,000 + 1,000 = £3,000
Total savings = £3,500

Again, the overall cost has been reduced, so we look for more savings.

- *Step 2* finds the lowest costs in the critical paths as B in A-B-C-D-J and G in E-F-G-J.
- *Step 3* looks at reductions, but it is clear that:

Total cost of crashing by one week = 1,000 + 2,500 = £3,500
Total savings = £3,500

At this point the savings exactly match the cost, and if we make any more reductions the cost becomes greater than the savings. At this point we have found the minimum total cost.

The overall duration of the project is now 20 days, with cost of £221,000 for normal activities, £10,500 for crashing and £7,000 for penalties, giving a total of £238,500.

Levelling resources

We have already introduced the ideas of Gantt charts, and now we can use them to help with resource planning.

WORKED EXAMPLE

Draw a Gantt chart for the original data in the example on page 527 assuming each activity starts as early as possible.

Solution

The activity analysis for this example is as follows (critical activities are identified by an asterisk):

Activity	Duration	Earliest time		Latest time		Total float
		Start	Finish	Start	Finish	
A	8	0	8	0	8	0*
B	4	8	12	8	12	0*
C	2	12	14	12	14	0*
D	3	0	3	2	5	2
E	6	3	9	5	11	2
F	3	9	12	11	14	2
G	2	0	2	4	6	4
H	4	2	6	6	10	4
I	4	6	10	10	14	4

If each activity starts as early as possible, the time needed is shown by the blocked-off areas in Figure 18.16. The total float of each activity is added afterwards as a broken line. The total float shows the maximum amount an activity can expand without delaying the project, so provided each activity finishes before the end of the broken line there should be no problem keeping to the schedule.

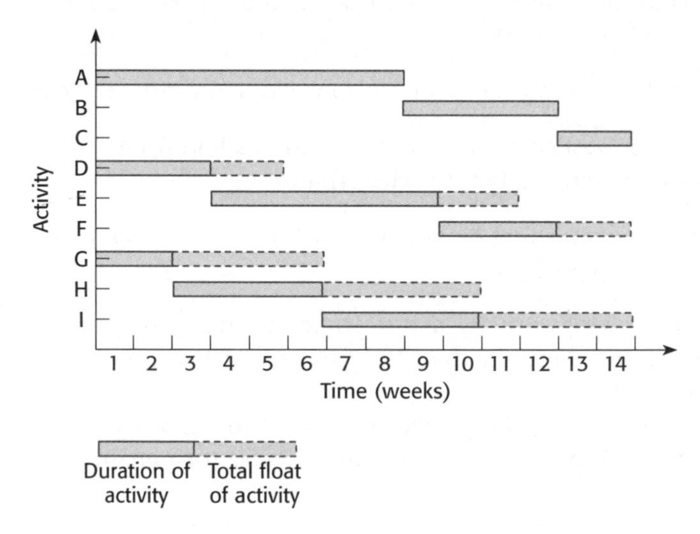

Figure 18.16 Gantt chart for scheduling example

Gantt charts have the benefit of showing clearly what should be happening at any point in the project. They show which activities should be in hand, as well as those which should be finished, and those about to start. We can add other details to the chart, perhaps showing key dates or milestones. Gantt charts are also useful for planning and allocating resources.

Consider the chart shown in Figure 18.16 and assume, for simplicity, that each activity uses one unit of a particular resource – perhaps one team of workers. If all activities start as soon as possible, we can draw a vertical bar chart to show the resources needed at any time. The project starts with activities A, D and G so three teams are needed. At the end of week 2 one team can move from G to H, but three teams are still needed. Continuing this allocation gives the graph of resources shown in Figure 18.17.

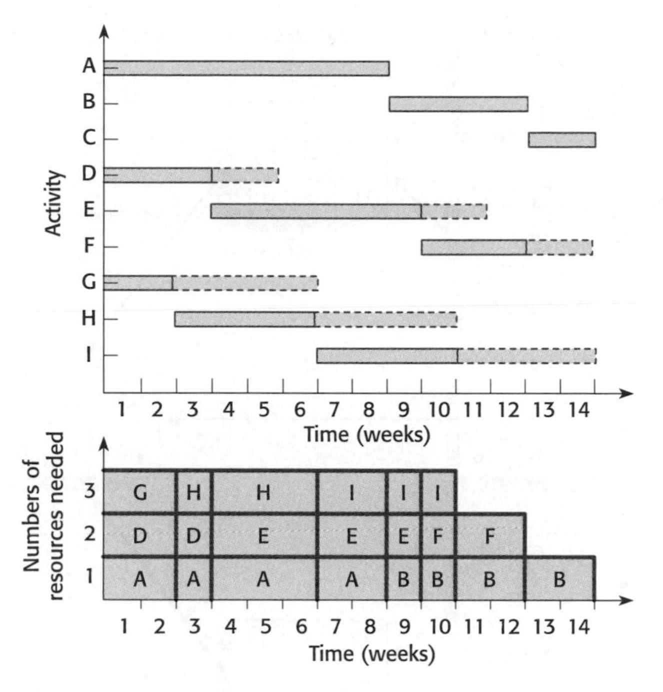

Figure 18.17 Resource use during project

In this example, the use of resources is steady for most of the project and only begins to fall near the end. In reality it is rare to get so smooth a pattern of resource use, and there are likely to be a series of peaks and troughs. It is generally preferable to have smooth operations, so we should look for ways of levelling the resources used. As critical activities are at fixed times, we have to do this levelling by rescheduling non-critical activities, and in particular by delaying those activities with large total floats.

WORKED EXAMPLE

The network shown in Figure 18.18 shows a project with 11 activities over a period of 19 months. If each activity uses one work team, how many teams will be needed at each stage of the project? Would it be possible to schedule the activities so that a maximum of three work teams are used at any time?

Solution

Figure 18.19 shows a Gantt chart for this project with the assumption that all activities start as early as possible. This uses a maximum of five work teams during months 3 to 5.

To smooth the number of work teams, we have to delay activities with large floats. One schedule delays the start of D until month 7, the start of F until month 9 and the start of H until month 10. This rescheduling reduces the maximum number of work teams needed to three and gives a smoother workload, as shown in Figure 18.20.

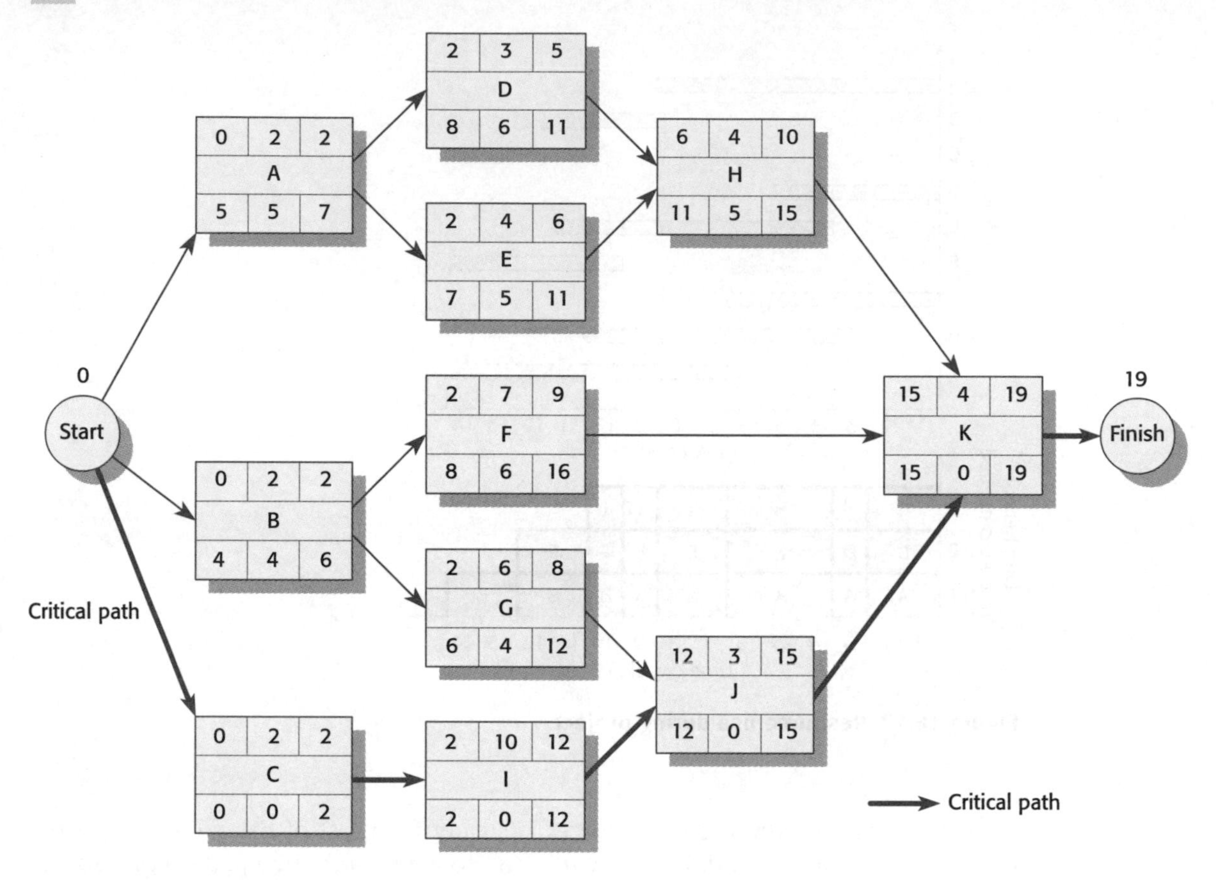

Figure 18.18 Network for worked example

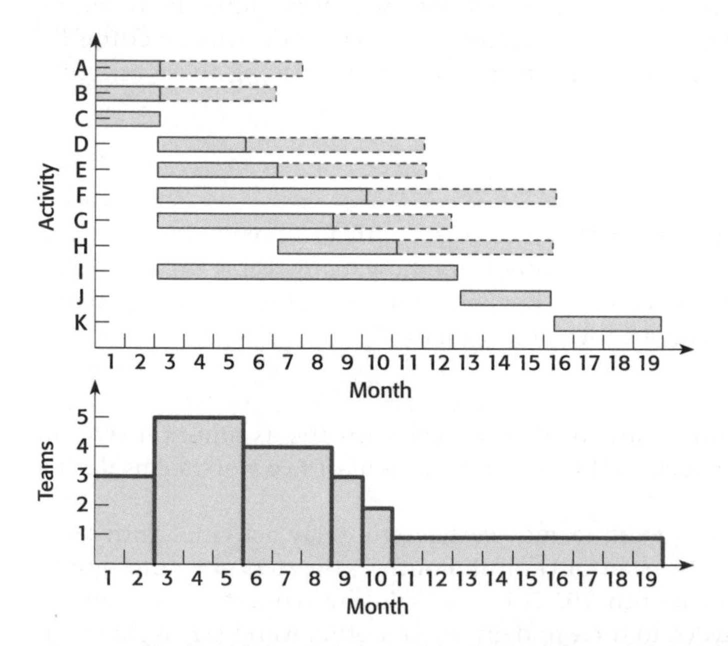

Figure 18.19 Gantt chart and work teams needed assuming all activities start as early as possible

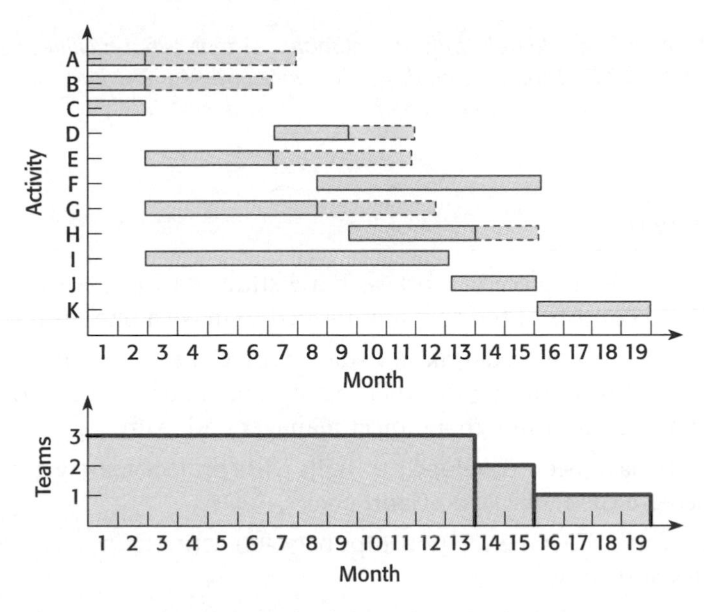

Figure 18.20 Revised schedule with smoother resource use

Review questions

18.14 Which activities must be shortened to reduce the overall duration of a project?

18.15 By how much can a critical path usefully be shortened?

18.16 By how much can a non-critical activity be expanded without affecting the project duration?

18.17 What is the crashed time of an activity?

18.18 How can the use of resources be smoothed during a project?

OPERATIONS IN PRACTICE

Planning term projects

Students are often given projects as part of their coursework. Many of these are group projects, where several students work together to solve a problem. This teaches students how to work in groups, the importance of teamwork, how to handle large jobs, and a range of planning and organisational skills. But many students find it difficult to co-ordinate their work.

Imagine that you have been given a term project. This requires four students to work together to do a literature search, conduct interviews and surveys, analyse the findings, and write a report. The final report is due 10 weeks from today.

Now suppose that you have five similar projects to do over the next 10 weeks. Each of these projects is similar in principle, but deals with different subjects. The groups have different members for each project.

How could network analysis help plan the projects?

Project 18.2 *There is a lot of software to help with project management. What facilities would you expect this to have? Find some examples of software and see how it tackles network analysis. Can you suggest improvements?*

Chapter review

- A project is a unique piece of work with a distinct start and finish. It has a finite life cycle, and consists of the activities needed to make a one-off product.
- Projects can be major undertakings that involve many resources, a long time, many organisations working together, many stakeholders, and so on. These need careful management, through a project manager and team.
- Several tools have been developed to help with project management. The most widely used are CPM, PERT and Gantt charts.
- Project networks show the relationships between activities in a network of alternating nodes and arrows.
- When the network is complete, we can analyse the timing to find the earliest and latest times for activities. The critical path identifies the critical activities that set the duration of the project. The total float measures the amount an activity can expand without affecting the project duration.
- A project can be finished earlier by reducing the durations of critical activities. If these reductions are more than the total float of a parallel path, this parallel path becomes critical.
- The costs of a project change with its duration. We can reduce the total cost to a minimum using an iterative procedure.
- Gantt charts give an alternative format that emphasises timing and can be used for resource planning.

Key terms

CASE STUDY Mediterranean Orange

Manhattan Incorporated Softdrinks is a conglomerate that owns over 350 subsidiaries around the world. One of these subsidiaries is European Softdrinks and Equipment Supply (ESES) which has headquarters in London. This company is expanding its business in southern Europe and has recently acquired Mediterranean Orange. This should markedly increase its sales in Italy, but the next plan is to open a distribution centre on the southern coast of Spain.

David Peacock is a planner in the headquarters of ESES. Last week he was invited to visit Norman Millar, the associate director of European operations. It was rare for a relatively junior planner to be called to the director's suite, but Norman Millar soon explained the problem:

Mediterranean Orange is in the late stages of planning its Villa Marbella distribution centre. Last month Mr Solstice (president of the Manhattan parent company) contacted Mr Jones (managing director of ESES) asking for details of when this centre will be ready. Mr Jones, in turn, asked the managers of Mediterranean Orange, who sent one of their planner's reports. The only problem is the report consists of a table of figures without any explanation. This means absolutely nothing to any of us. We can't go back to Mediterranean Orange – as our relations are still forming and we want to tread carefully. We also need some figures that we can pass on to Mr Solstice fairly quickly. The only thing I know for certain is that we have about 40 weeks to open the centre, and beyond that our costs start rising at 2 per cent a week. Can you look at the table and give us some information before the end of the week?

David Peacock looked at the table, which is shown below, and said he might manage something.

Act	O	M	P	DO	Manning	NC (000)	CT	CC (000)
AA	3	3	6	BW	14	8	2	10
AB	3	4	7	AG	7	7	3	9
AC	4	4	6	AB,AE,AY	12	12	3	15
AD	2	3	4	AA	3	2	1	4
AE	3	3	3	AD	2	2	3	2
AF	6	8	14	AD	6	12	4	16
AG	2	2	2	BZ	2	1	2	1
AH	6	8	14	AC,AF	10	20	5	35
AI	6	8	14	AF	12	24	6	
AJ	7	8	11	AH,AK	12	24	5	42
AK	10	14	20	BQ,BY	22	66	6	85
AL	4	5	7	AK	8	10	2	12
AM	3	3	5	AL	4	3	2	4
AN	5	6	9	AJ	6	9	3	13
AO	8	10	12	AZ	24	60	5	72

Act	O	M	P	DO	Manning	NC (000)	CT	CC (000)
AP	4	5	6	BQ	8	10	1	12
AQ	8	10	16	BO,BP	9	23	4	25
AR	3	3	3	BE	11	8	3	8
AS	4	5	6	AP,AQ,AR	3	4	3	6
AT	8	10	15	BT,BV	7	18	7	20
AU	5	6	7	AT	15	23	5	25
AV	4	6	8	AS	18	28	4	30
AW	4	5	9	AM,AN,AO	19	24	3	26
AX	4	4	4	BJ	3	3	3	3
AY	1	1	1	BY	2	1	1	2
AZ	4	5	6	AI	8	10	2	14
BA	1	1	1	–	7	2	1	2
BB	4	5	6	BK	21	27	4	30
BC	4	4	4	BJ	23	24	4	24
BD	5	7	9	AX	17	29	4	35
BE	2	2	2	BN	4	2	1	5
BF	3	5	9	BH	9	11	1	14
BG	2	2	2	BH	6	3	2	3
BH	2	4	6	–	7	7	1	9
BI	1	2	3	–	8	4	1	6
BJ	3	3	3	BK	2	2	3	2
BK	2	2	2	BA	10	5	2	5
BL	2	3	4	BA	15	11	2	15
BM	1	1	1	BI,BL	8	2	1	2
BN	2	4	8	BG,BM	12	12	2	14
BO	6	8	10	BG,BM	22	44	4	60
BP	5	7	11	BF	26	44	3	58
BQ	3	3	3	BF	15	11	3	11
BR	3	6	9	BC	15	38	3	48
BS	4	4	4	BD,BR	7	7	4	7
BT	3	4	8	BS	11	11	3	16
BU	2	2	2	BD	13	7	2	7
BV	2	2	2	BU	5	3	2	3
BW	2	3	3	–	6	5	1	12
BX	5	7	7	BW	8	14	3	18
BY	8	10	15	BX	15	38	4	42
BZ	4	5	8	BW	13	16	2	24

Question

- If you were David Peacock, what would you report to the directors of the London office?

Problems

18.1 A project has the activities shown in the following dependence table. Draw the network for this project.

Activity	Depends on	Activity	Depends on
A	–	G	B
B	–	H	G
C	A	I	E,F
D	A	J	H,I
E	C	K	E,F
F	B,D	L	K

18.2(a) An amateur dramatic society is planning its annual production and is interested in using a network to coordinate the various activities. What activities do you think should be included in the network?

18.2(b) If discussions lead to the activities listed below, what would the network look like?

- Assess resources and select play.
- Prepare scripts.
- Select actors and cast parts.
- Rehearse.
- Design and organise advertisements.
- Prepare stage, lights and sound.
- Build scenery.
- Sell tickets.
- Final arrangements for opening.

18.3 Draw a network for the following dependence table.

Activity	Depends on	Activity	Depends on
A	H	I	F
B	H	J	I
C	K	K	L
D	I,M,N	L	F
E	F	M	O
F	–	N	H
G	E,L	O	A,B
H	E	P	N

18.4 If each activity in Problem 18.3 has a duration of one week, find the earliest and latest start and finish times for each activity and the corresponding total floats.

18.5 Draw the network represented by the following dependence table and calculate the total float for each activity.

Activity	Duration (weeks)	Depends on
A	5	–
B	3	–
C	3	B
D	7	A
E	10	B
F	14	A,C
G	7	D,E
H	4	E
I	5	D

If each activity can be reduced by up to two weeks, what is the shortest duration of the project and which activities are reduced?

18.6 A project consists of ten activities with estimated durations (in weeks) and dependencies shown in the following table. What are the estimated duration of the project and the earliest and latest times for activities?

Activity	Depends on	Duration	Activity	Depends on	Duration
A	–	8	F	C,D	10
B	A	6	G	B,E,F	5
C	–	10	H	F	8
D	–	6	I	G,H,J	6
E	C	2	J	A	4

If activity B needs special equipment, when should this be hired? A check on the project at week 12 shows that activity F is running two weeks late, that activity J would now take six weeks, and that the equipment for B would not arrive until week 18. What effect does this have on the overall project duration?

18.7 Draw a Gantt chart for the project described in problem 18.5. If each activity uses one team of men, draw a graph of the manpower needed assuming each activity starts as soon as possible. How might the manpower be smoothed?

18.8 Analyse the times and resource requirements of the project described by the following data:

Activity	Depends on	Duration	Resources
A	–	4	1
B	A	4	2
C	A	3	4
D	B	5	4
E	C	2	2
F	D,E	6	3
G	–	3	3
H	G	7	1
I	G	6	5
J	H	2	3
K	I	4	4
L	J,K	8	2

18.9 In the project described in Problem 18.8 it costs £1,000 to reduce the duration of an activity by one. If there are £12,000 available to reduce the overall duration of the project, how should this be allocated and what is the shortest time in which the project can be completed? What are the minimum resources needed by the revised schedule?

Discussion questions

18.1 Project management has become very popular, with managers in many functions describing their work as a series of related projects. Are they right? What are the benefits of being a 'project manager'? Is managing a project so different to managing a continuous process?

18.2 If project management is so good, why do so many projects fail to meet expectations?

18.3 Find some examples of successful (and unsuccessful) projects. Why were these successful (or unsuccessful)? Who judges the results? Who is responsible?

18.4 Describe the matrix management structure usually found in projects. What are the advantages and drawbacks of this?

18.5 What skills does a project manager need?

18.6 What information is needed for project network analysis? Are the lists of activities, durations and dependencies little more than guesses before the project starts? How can the timings of activities be found? How accurate are these likely to be?

18.7 Large projects consist of thousands of activities. Even with the best computer support, planning and controlling this number of activities is very demanding. How do you think this can be made easier? Is there a point when it is not worth such formal planning?

References

1. Project Management Institute (1987) *The Project Management Body of Knowledge*. Drexel Hill, PA: PMI Publications.
2. *www.pmi.org/publictn/pmboktoc.htm*.
3. Special Projects Office, Bureau of Ordnance, Department of the Navy (1958) *PERT, Program Evaluation Research Task, Phase 1 Summary Report*. Washington, DC. Pp 646–669.
4. Kelley J.E. and Walker M.R. (1959) 'Critical Path Planning and Scheduling', *Proceedings of the Eastern Joint Computer Conference. Boston*. Pp 160–173.

Selected reading

Badiru A.B. and Pulat P.S. (1995) *Comprehensive Project Management*. Englewood Cliffs, NJ: Prentice-Hall.

Burke R. (1993) *Project Management Planning and Control*. 2nd edn. Chichester: John Wiley.

Cleland D.I. (1994) *Project Management*. 2nd edn. New York: McGraw-Hill.

Gido J. and Clements J.P. (1999) *Successful Project Management*. Cincinnati, OH: South-Western.

Lock D. (1996) *Project Management*. 6th edn. Aldershot: Gower Publishing.

Lockyer K.G. and Gordon J. (1996) *Project Management and Project Network Techniques*. 6th edn. London: Pitman.

Maylor H. (1996) *Project Management*. London: Pitman.

Meredith J.R. and Mantel S.J. (1995) *Project Management*. 3rd edn. New York: John Wiley.

Project Management Institute (2000) *A Guide to the Project Management Body of Knowledge*. Drexel Hill, PA: PMI Publications.

Shtub A., Bard J.F. and Globerson S. (1994) *Project Management*. Englewood Cliffs, NJ: Prentice-Hall.

Turner J.R. (1993) *The Handbook of Project Based Management*. London: McGraw-Hill.

Useful Websites

www.asterisk.co.uk/project – Association for Project Management
www.pmi.org – Project Management Institute
www.pmforum.org – Project Management Forum

SUPPLEMENT TO CHAPTER 18

Project evaluation and review technique (PERT)

In the main chapter we described the critical path method (CPM) where each activity has a fixed duration. As you know from experience, the time needed for any job can vary quite widely. PERT (project evaluation and review technique) is a useful extension to CPM that adds some uncertainty to activity durations.

The duration of an activity can often be approximated by a beta distribution. This looks like a skewed normal distribution and has one very useful property: the mean and variance can be found from three estimates of duration. In particular it needs:

- an **optimistic duration** (O), which is the shortest time an activity takes if everything goes smoothly and without any difficulties;
- a **most likely duration** (M), which is the duration of the activity under normal conditions;
- a **pessimistic duration** (P), which is the time needed if there are significant problems and delays.

Then we can calculate the expected activity duration and variance from the rule of sixths:

$$\textbf{Expected duration} = \frac{O + 4M + P}{6}$$

$$\textbf{Variance} = \frac{(O - P)^2}{36}$$

Suppose an activity has an optimistic duration of four days, a most likely duration of five days and a pessimistic duration of 12 days.

- Expected duration = $(O + 4M + P)/6 = (4 + 4 \times 5 + 12)/6 = 6$
- Variance = $(P - O)^2/36 = (12 - 4)^2/36 = 1.78$

We can use these expected durations for analysing project timing in the same way as the single estimate of CPM.

WORKED EXAMPLE

A project has nine activities with dependencies and estimated activity durations shown in the following table. Draw the network, identify the critical path and estimate the overall duration of the project.

Activity	Depends on	Duration		
		Optimistic	Most likely	Pessimistic
A	–	2	3	10
B	–	4	5	12
C	–	8	10	12
D	A,G	4	4	4
E	B	3	6	15
F	B	2	5	8
G	B	6	6	6
H	C,F	5	7	15
I	D,E	6	8	10

Solution

Using the rule of sixths for the duration of activity A:

$$\text{Expected duration} = (2 + 4 \times 3 + 10)/6 = 4$$
$$\text{Variance} = (10 - 2)^2/36 = 1.78$$

Repeating these calculations for the other activities gives the following results:

Activity	Expected duration	Variance
A	4	1.78
B	6	1.78
C	10	0.44
D	4	0
E	7	4.00
F	5	1.00
G	6	0
H	8	2.78
I	8	0.44

The network is shown in Figure 18.1s. The critical path for the project is B, G, D and I which has an expected duration of 24. The following table shows the analysis of activity times (critical activities are identified by an asterisk).

Activity	Expected duration	Earliest		Latest		Total float
		Start	Finish	Start	Finish	
A	4	0	4	8	12	8
B	6	0	6	0	6	0*
C	10	0	10	6	16	6
D	4	12	16	12	16	0*
E	7	6	13	9	16	3
F	5	6	11	11	16	5
G	6	6	12	6	12	0*
H	8	11	19	16	24	5
I	8	16	24	16	24	0*

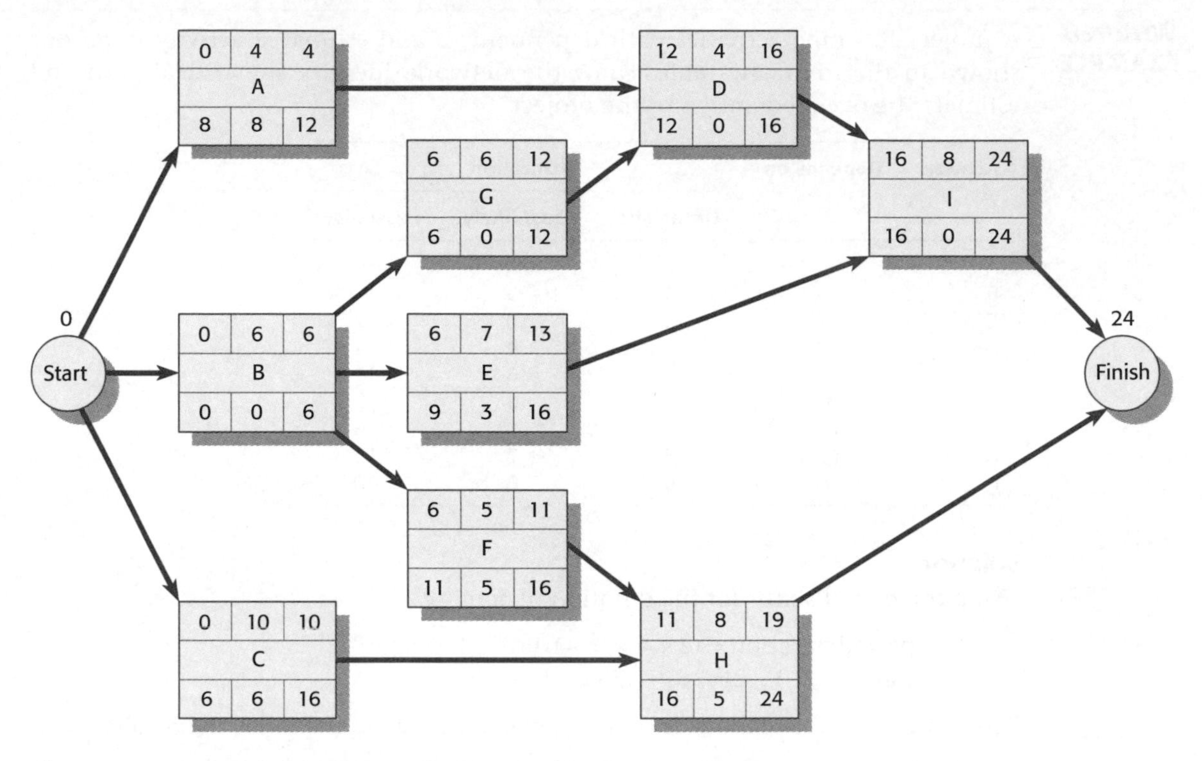

Figure 18s.1 Network for PERT worked example

The duration of the critical path is the sum of the durations of activities making up that path. If there is a large number of activities on the path, and if the duration of each activity is independent of the others, the overall duration of the project follows a normal distribution. This distribution has:

- a mean equal to the sum of the expected durations of activities on the critical path;
- a variance equal to the sum of the variances of activities on the critical path.

We can use these values to find the probability that a project will be completed by any particular time.

WORKED EXAMPLE

What are the probabilities that the project described in the last example will be finished before: (a) day 26; (b) day 20?

Solution

We have found the critical path through activities B, G, D and I with expected durations of 6, 6, 4 and 8 respectively and variances of 1.78, 0, 0 and 0.44 respectively. Although the number of activities on the critical path is small, we can assume the overall duration of the project is normally distributed. The expected duration then has mean $6 + 6 + 4 + 8 = 24$. The variance is $1.78 + 0 + 0 + 0.44 = 2.22$, so the standard deviation is $\sqrt{2.22} = 1.49$.

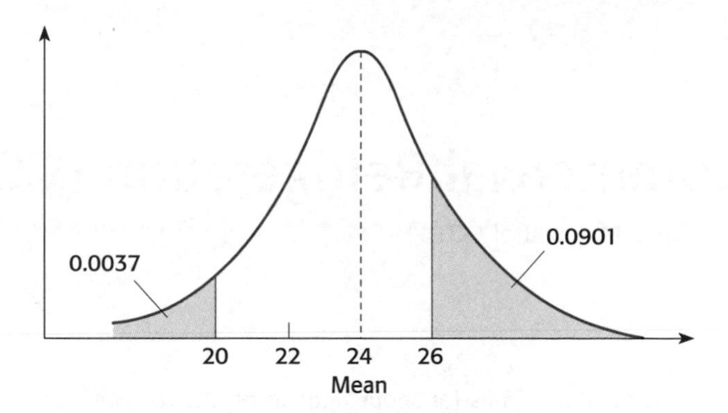

Figure 18s.2 Normal distribution for project duration

(a) Now we can find the probability that it will not be finished before day 26. Z is the number of standard deviations the point of interest is away from the mean:

$Z = (26 - 24)/1.49 = 1.34$ standard deviations

This corresponds to a probability of = 0.0901 (found from a statistical package or tables). So the probability that the project will be finished is 1 – 0.0901 = 0.9099 or almost 91 per cent.

(b) Similarly, the probability it will be finished before 20 is:

$Z = (24 - 20)/1.49 = 2.68$
Probability = 0.0037

INTEGRATING CASE STUDY

Czech Commercial Refrigeration (CCR)

by Jiri Krivsky, Production Manager of CCR

My company makes refrigeration units for shops and stores. For this we use a mixture of job shop, batch and projects. Our business is driven by customers, who demand delivery dates ranging from two days to two months. We have to meet these times to remain competitive, but they can give problems, especially as demand is seasonal with a peak in the summer.

Our planning emphasises the short term. We have some longer-term plans which show the general picture, and we add details to give detailed production plans that cover the next two weeks. As we respond to customer demands, we check these plans twice a week and make changes to allow for new orders received, materials available, technical support and capacity. Then we make minor adjustments every day. When the schedules are circulated, people working on the operations will make their own small adjustments as necessary to overcome any minor difficulties.

In general we use the following five steps to plan production:

1. Look at the planned production for next period and translate it into a demand for different types of operations. Our main concerns are the demand for product preparation (including building the frames), assembling refrigerant units (fixing components into the frames), building the electrical chassis (with switches and controls) and connecting the electrical work (connecting the terminal box to the refrigeration unit).
2. Find the total production time for all operations and translate this into overall capacity plans. Sort out any problems with overall demand.
3. Find the immediate capacity for each type of operation, by seeing how many people are available, the hours they work, etc.
4. Look at the actual orders, compare this with production plans, and find the capacities we must have. We can compare this with the capacity available, identify problems and start negotiating for late deliveries, overtime, material deliveries, etc.
5. Look for ways of adjusting the plans to give more efficient operations. We adjust ordinary operations in a number of ways, such as working overtime, delaying deliveries, hiring temporary staff, co-operating to share capacity with another factory, using stocks, increasing technology, joining operations to give more efficient processes, etc. Materials do not cause too many problems, as they are controlled by an MRP system.

At this stage we have detailed production plans for the next week or two.

We actually use three types of production process. We make relatively large numbers of small standard units in batches on an assembly line. We introduced this three years ago and it substantially increased capacity and reduced production time. The main problems here are getting the MRP system to control the supply of materials. We keep some stocks to give safety, and also help us with widely varying demand. Suppliers' lead times are all less than four weeks, which is generally satisfactory, but often determines our own delivery times.

Most of our larger, more complex units are made in a job shop. These operations are more complicated and they need more available capacity. Problems here are the supply of materials (which are usually ordered after a customer places an order), controlling production through a difficult series of operations, and technical support. When we order big and unusual parts, the lead time may be one or two months, compared with our production time of two weeks.

Sometimes we make an especially big unit, and this is managed as a project. We recently made a special booster unit with three semi-hermetic compressors for cooling and three more for freezing, with a computerised control unit that monitors food condition. This was installed in a new department store, and a simplified view of the project has the following 13 activities, as set out the table below.

Activity	Depends on	Time needed (hours)		
		Optimistic	Most likely	Pessimistic
Technical preparation				
A. Schema of refrigerant cycle	–	6	8	12
B. Design of frame construction	A	4	6	10
C. Design electrical work	A	5	6	7
Materials preparation				
D. Materials for refrigerant	A	0	0.5	2
E. Electrical materials	C	0	0.5	2
Production				
F. Produce frame	B	20	26	28
G. Paint frame	F	5	7	9
H. Assemble refrigerant cycle	D,G	35	43	50
I. Assemble other parts	G	1	2	4
J. Assemble electrical work	E	10	12	15
K. Connect electrical work	J,H	10	14	16
L. Check quality and test	K,I	1	2	3
M. Finishing	L	1	2	3

Questions

- How would you describe the approach to production planning at CCR? What are its strengths and weaknesses? Where do you think the main problems will occur?
- To what extent is the planning at CCR set by its type of operations? How could CCR improve its planning?

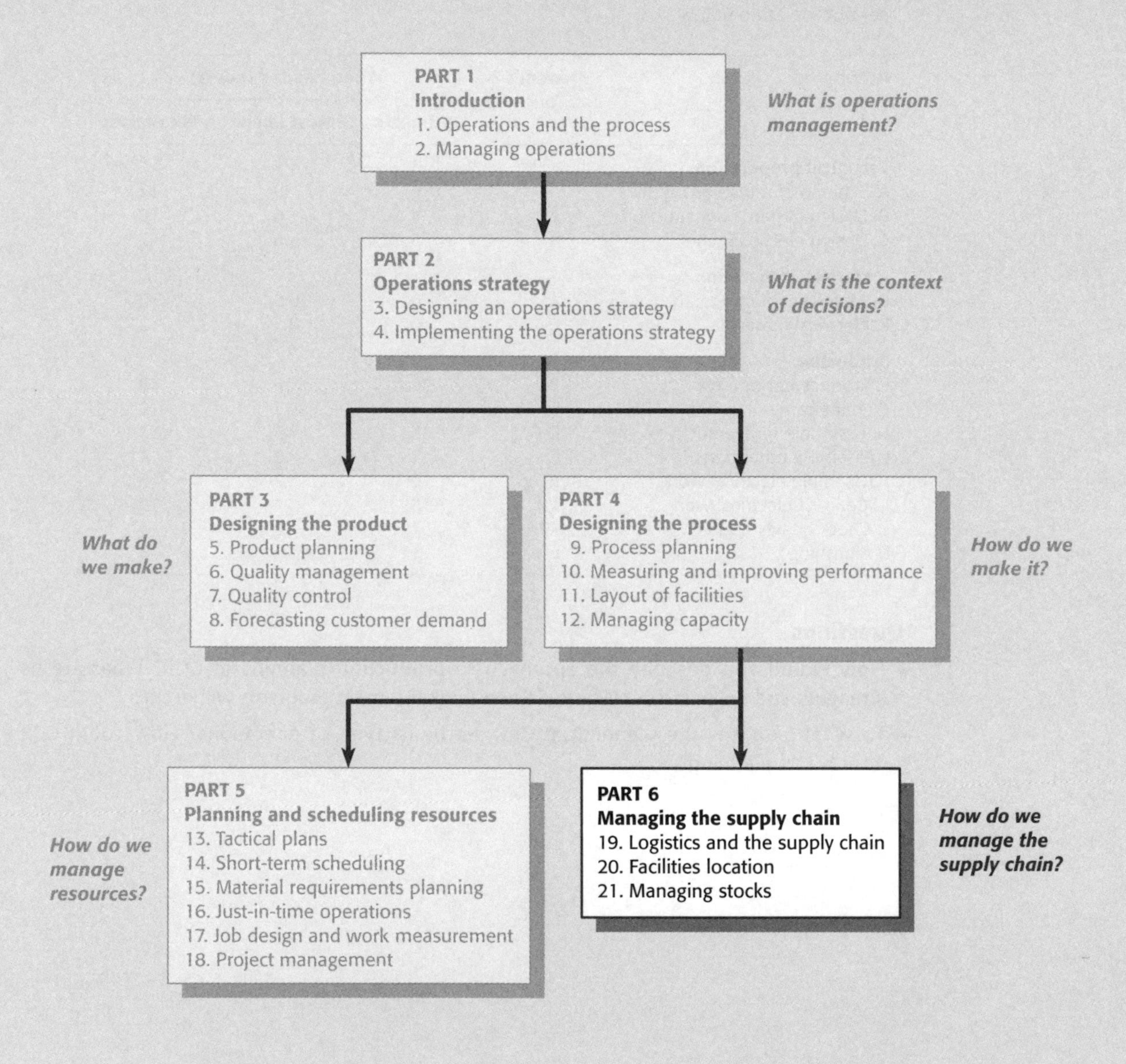
PART 1
Introduction
1. Operations and the process
2. Managing operations
What is operations management?
PART 2
Operations strategy
3. Designing an operations strategy
4. Implementing the operations strategy
What is the context of decisions?
PART 3
Designing the product
5. Product planning
6. Quality management
7. Quality control
8. Forecasting customer demand
What do we make?
PART 4
Designing the process
9. Process planning
10. Measuring and improving performance
11. Layout of facilities
12. Managing capacity
How do we make it?
PART 5
Planning and scheduling resources
13. Tactical plans
14. Short-term scheduling
15. Material requirements planning
16. Just-in-time operations
17. Job design and work measurement
18. Project management
How do we manage resources?
PART 6
Managing the supply chain
19. Logistics and the supply chain
20. Facilities location
21. Managing stocks
How do we manage the supply chain?

Part 6

MANAGING THE SUPPLY CHAIN

This book is divided into six parts. Each part describes a different aspect of operations management. Part 1 gave an introduction to the subject. Part 2 talked about strategy, emphasising the design and implementation of an operations strategy. Part 3 looked at the planning needed for a product, while Part 4 discussed the process used to make a product. Part 5 discussed the planning and scheduling of resources to support the process.

This is Part 6, which looks at some aspects of supply chain management. It shows how products and materials flow through a process. There are three chapters in this part. Chapter 19 gives an introduction to logistics and supply chain management. It defines the terms and outlines the different functions involved. Chapter 20 looks at the location of facilities in the supply chain. Earlier chapters looked at the supply of materials with material requirements planning and just-in-time. Chapter 21 looks at an alternative way of controlling stocks for independent demand systems.

Logistics and the supply chain

Under e-commerce, delivery will become the one area in which a business can truly distinguish itself.

Peter Drucker

Practice of Management, Butterworth-Heinemann, London, 1999

Contents

Aims of the chapter

After reading this chapter you should be able to:

- appreciate the role and importance of logistics;
- describe a supply chain and its organisation;
- see the benefits of integrating the functions that make up logistics;
- discuss ways in which logistics is evolving to meet new demands;
- understand the steps in procurement;
- discuss the ways procurement is changing;
- appreciate the role of transport in a supply chain.

Main themes

This chapter will emphasise:

- the **supply chain**, the series of operations that move materials between suppliers and customers;
- **logistics**, which is responsible for the movement of materials through the supply chain;
- **procurement**, which organises the purchase and supply of materials;
- **transport**, which physically moves the materials.

The supply chain

Definitions

Organisations – even those making the most intangible services – have to deliver products to customers. They also collect raw materials from suppliers and move work-in-progress through the process. In other words, they move a mixture of raw materials, goods, information, messages, consumables or anything else needed to support operations. As before, we will describe all of these as 'materials', but remember that we are talking about a wide range of things. **Materials** are all the items that move through an organisation to produce its goods and services. These movements do not happen by chance, but need careful planning, and this is done by **logistics**.

Logistics is responsible for the movement of all materials into, through and out of an organisation.

To make things easier, we often divide the materials into three different types:

- *Raw materials*: move from suppliers into the organisation. Here logistics is concerned with purchasing, inward transport, receiving and storage of goods.
- *Work-in-progress*: materials move within the organisation. Here logistics looks at retrieval of goods, handling, movement and storage of goods during operations.
- *Finished goods*: materials move from the organisation out to customers. Here logistics looks at packaging, storage and retrieval from warehouses, transport and distribution to customers.

In the past, organisations described the first two of these as **materials management** and the third as **physical distribution**. However, this is not really a useful distinction, as the final product of one organisation – or part of an organisation – becomes the raw material of another. Petrol, for example, is a final product of BP Amoco, but a raw material for Pickfords Removals; Dulux paint is a finished product for ICI, but a raw material for painters and decorators.

Most materials move through a series of organisations between the original supplier and the final customer. When you buy a toothbrush, for example, its journey starts with a company extracting crude oil, and then it passes through pipelines, refineries, chemical works, plastics companies, manufacturers, importers, wholesalers and retailers before finishing as a toothbrush in your bathroom. All of these steps taken together form the **supply chain** (illustrated in Figure 19.1).

Some people use the term **supply chain management** to mean the same thing as 'logistics'. The Institute of Logistics and Transport gives the following definitions:[1, 2]

> *Logistics is the time-related positioning of resources, or the strategic management of the total supply-chain.*

> *The supply-chain is a sequence of events intended to satisfy a customer.*

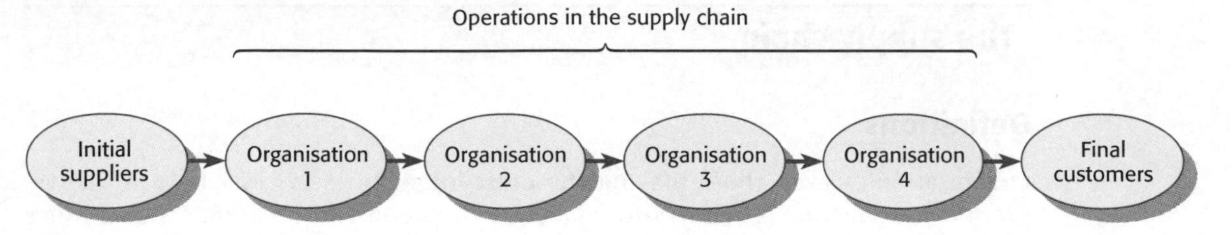

Figure 19.1 Elements in a supply chain

Movement along the supply chain

Each product has its own supply chain. Logistics is responsible for getting all materials through this chain and delivering the product to the final customer at the time it is needed. This can be very difficult, as supply chains are surprisingly complicated. The supply chain for something as simple as a sheet of paper involves many organisations (as you can imagine from Figure 19.2). A product like a cotton shirt has a long journey from the farm growing cotton to the final customer, and several chains merge as buttons, polyester, dyes and other materials arrive to join the main process. At the same time, organisations make many products – often thousands – so they are on all of these separate supply chains. Corus (formerly British Steel) supplies steel products to thousands of companies and is on a huge number of supply chains.

For a long time logistics did not receive much attention, prompting Peter Drucker to describe it as 'the economy's dark continent'.[3] More recently managers have recognised its importance, and are taking a new look at logistics as a way of both improving customer service and reducing costs. They realise that logistics is important because it:

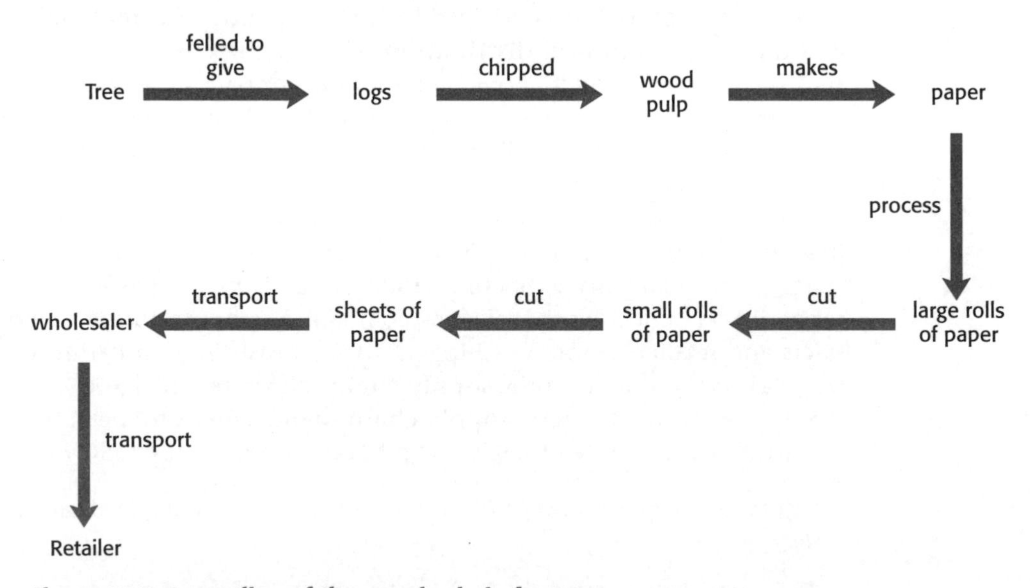

Figure 19.2 An outline of the supply chain for paper

- is essential – all organisations must move materials;
- is expensive – the costs can be high, with considerable potential savings;
- directly affects profits – it is an unavoidable overhead;
- forms a link between suppliers and customers – developing long-term relationships;
- influences lead time, reliability and other measures of customer service;
- gives public exposure – with advertising on trucks, etc.;
- can be risky, with safety considerations;
- determines the size and location of facilities;
- may prohibit some operations, such as moving excessive loads;
- can encourage development of other organisations.

OPERATIONS IN PRACTICE

Wal-Mart

In 1962 Sam Walton opened a discount store in Rogers, Arizona. He felt that customers would be attracted by his wide range of goods, low prices and friendly service. His stores succeeded, and he quickly opened other branches. In 1983 he opened a SAM'S Club warehouse for members, and in 1988 the first Supercenter selling groceries. In 1991 Wal-Mart started its international expansion, first in Mexico, Puerto Rico and Canada, and then into South America, Asia and Europe. Most of its later expansion came through buying local companies.

Wal-Mart kept the same basic operations of wide range, low prices and friendly service. By 2000 it was the world's largest retailer with 4,000 stores, serving 100 million customers a week, employing 1.2 million staff – or 'associates' – with an annual turnover of US$175 billion and profit of US$6 billion a year.

You can imagine the size of the logistics operations in Wal-Mart. In the mainland USA it has 85,000 suppliers sending $1.5 billion dollars' worth of materials a week to Wal-Mart's 62 main distribution centres, and on to over 3,000 stores (1,800 Wal-Mart stores, 800 Supercentres, 460 SAM's clubs and 13 Neighbourhood Markets). Their costs – and therefore profit – depend entirely on the quality of their logistics. This is why they use the 'industry's most efficient and sophisticated distribution system'. Their success can be judged by continuing expansion, with annual sales up 20 per cent in the first quarter of 2000, and like-for-like sales up 5 per cent.

Source: Wal-Mart reports and Website at: *www.walmartstores.com*

Functions of logistics

An organisation has to make good decisions in several related areas to get an efficient flow of materials. It has, for example, to choose reliable suppliers, negotiate terms for delivery, use appropriate transport, store materials properly until they are needed, locate facilities in the best places, and so on. Continuing with this line of reasoning, you can see that the work done in logistics forms a series of related functions. These include:

- *Procurement or purchasing* – buys the raw materials from suppliers.
- *Traffic and transport* – moves the raw materials from suppliers to the organisation's receiving area.
- *Receiving* – checks materials delivered against orders, unloads delivery vehicles, inspects goods for damage.

- *Warehousing or stores* – stores materials and takes care of them until they are needed.
- *Stock control* – sets the policies for inventory, including stock levels and order sizes.
- *Material handling* – moves materials during operations.
- *Distribution* – organises delivery of finished goods to customers.
- *Transport* – moves finished products and runs delivery vehicles.
- *Recycling and waste disposal* – reuses, returns, sells or otherwise disposes of materials not needed by the organisation.
- *Location* – decides how many facilities should be built, and where they should be.
- *Communication* – keeps and reports all records for the logistics system.

You can probably imagine these functions in a manufacturer, but the same principles apply to other organisations. When a rock band goes on tour they carry huge amounts of equipment. Purchasing buys everything that is needed on the tour, transport moves it to the next destination, receiving makes sure that everything arrives safely, warehousing keeps things until they are needed, materials handling moves things between trucks and the stage, location decides where to perform, and so on. Even the most intangible service involves these functions, as you can see when a mobile telephone company routes a message to a customer, or a university delivers its educational products to students.

Aims of logistics

Logistics has a number of objectives, which we can summarise as getting 'the right materials, to the right place, at the right time, from the right source, with the right quality, at the right price'. To be more specific, we can phrase these aims in terms of:

- finding reliable suppliers and developing business relationships;
- making purchases at lowest long-term cost;
- giving uninterrupted flows of materials into the organisation;
- maintaining the quality of materials;
- having efficient movement of work-in-progress;
- giving efficient movements of finished goods out to customers;
- protecting materials and avoiding damage;
- guaranteeing customer service and maintaining good relations;
- getting high turnover of stock and minimising the associated costs;
- making the best use of available resources.

Unfortunately, if we organise logistics as a series of distinct functions, each of them has different aims. Then different parts of an organisation will be pulling in different directions. One part will be trying to improve the routes of transport vehicles; another part will be reducing the investment in stocks of finished goods; another part will be improving the purchasing, etc. Although these are all worthy aims, this approach ignores the fact that the functions are closely related, and reducing costs in one area can increase them in another. Reducing the stock of raw materials, for example, might save costs in warehousing, but give more frequent shortages and higher costs for expediting urgent orders. Sending fewer, larger orders to suppliers reduces the administrative costs of purchasing, allows quantity discounts and gives cheaper transport, but it also increases stock levels and the associated investment and warehousing costs.

Giving different functions control over different parts of the materials flow adds artificial boundaries in logistics. You might think this does not matter, but it can lead to real inefficiencies. Imagine a wholesaler who has one fleet of vehicles run by materials management bringing raw materials in from suppliers, while a separate fleet is run by distribution to deliver the same goods out to customers. This might work, but you can imagine the duplication of effort, and waste involved in managing two separate vehicle fleets. Another organisation might have three stocks – raw materials, work-in-progress and finished goods – each run by different departments, using different standards and systems.

Dividing logistics into separate functions invites duplication of effort and wasted resources. Perhaps more importantly, different departments have different objectives, and this can lead to conflict. You can imagine some of these in a manufacturer, where:

Marketing wants:
- high stocks of finished goods to satisfy customer demands quickly;
- a wide range of finished goods always held in stock;
- locations near to customers to allow delivery with short lead times;
- production to vary output in response to customer orders;
- emphasis on an efficient distribution system.

Production wants:
- high stocks of raw materials and work-in-progress to safeguard operations;
- a narrow range of finished goods to give long production runs;
- locations near to suppliers so that they can get raw materials quickly;
- stable production to give efficient operations;
- emphasis on the efficient movement of materials through operations.

Finance wants:
- low stocks everywhere;
- few plants located to give economies of scale and minimise overall costs;
- large batch sizes to reduce unit costs;
- make-to-order operations.

The way to get around this problem is to look at the supply chain not as a series of distinct activities, but as a single integrated whole. Then the separate functions do not focus on their own operations, but join together to take a broader view of the whole chain. Then find the best compromise between conflicting objectives so that the organisation gets the best overall results.

Review questions

19.1 What is logistics?

19.2 Managing materials is best left to the people most closely involved. Do you think this is true?

19.3 What functions are usually considered part of logistics?

19.4 What is the supply chain?

19.5 Why is logistics important?

Integrating the supply chain

Integration within an organisation

If it is better to have a single integrated logistics function, how do we set about organising this? The supply chain is widely dispersed, and even if we wanted to, we could not integrate all of logistics in one step. It is more likely to be an iterative process that joins together closely related functions. A purchasing department, for example, might take over all aspects of receiving materials up to the point when they are delivered to a stock of raw materials. Most organisations moved along this path some time ago, but often stopped when there were two main functions left:

- *materials management*, aligned with production and looking after the inwards flow of raw materials and their movement through operations;
- *physical distribution*, aligned with marketing and looking at the outward flow of finished goods.

This still leaves an artificial break in what is essentially a single function. The next obvious step is to combine these two into a single logistics function responsible for all the movement of materials into, through and out of the organisation. Most well-run operations now use this approach, and they go further, integrating logistics through more of the supply chain.

Integration along the supply chain

Each organisation accounts for only one step in the supply chain. If each organises its own logistics, this still gives a fragmented flow. A more efficient approach is to co-ordinate logistics to give a smooth flow of materials along the whole supply chain. This can bring considerable benefits. Perman Frere is a small manufacturer based in Brussels. It exports most of its products and has a finished goods warehouse near the port of Ostende. Van Rijn is one of its customers, also based in Brussels. It imports most of its materials and has a raw materials warehouse near the port of Rotterdam. The two companies soon realised that parts were being made by Perman Frere in Brussels, sent to its warehouse in Ostende, delivered to van Rijn's warehouse in Rotterdam, and then sent back to Brussels. It did not take long to co-ordinate their logistics, giving a much shorter journey across Brussels, reducing costs for both companies, and reducing the lead time from days to hours.

One way of organising such co-ordination is through large integrated companies that actually own the whole, or most of, their supply chain. Some organisations can do this, such as Ford of America, which owns everything from steel mills through to distributor networks. For most organisations, however, this is clearly not possible. Even a large company, such as Heinz, cannot buy all the farmers, processors, steel mills, canners, wholesalers, retailers and other organisations in the supply chain for its baked beans. There are also many arguments – ranging from the difficulty of getting diverse skills in a single organisation, through to the ethics of market dominance – which suggest that it is not necessarily desirable.

A more realistic option is for organisations along the supply chain to co-operate. There are several ways of organising this co-operation. At the simplest level, organisations can simply work together, and over a period build up a good working relationship. Sometimes there is an informal arrangement to co-ordinate one aspect of their operations, like Perman Frere and van Rijn in Brussels. This can grow to include more functions, with other organisations included in the arrangement.

Japanese companies often extend this idea in *keiretsu*, which are groups of organisations that work together without actually forming partnerships.

More formal arrangements have 'preferred supplier' status, or organisations developing strategic alliances or partnerships. These can give obligations to work closely together over some extended period, bringing advantages to both organisations, including stability, improved operations, better service, lower costs and a range of shared benefits.

Sharing information

A fundamental part of integrating – or at least co-ordinating – operations is to connect the information flows between adjacent organisations. Then some of the information available to a customer is automatically passed to a supplier, and vice versa. You can imagine some obvious benefits of this when a customer is running out of stock of some material. Traditionally the customer notices this, and goes through all the internal procedures to raise an order, send this to a supplier, who then goes through his internal procedures for meeting an order. With co-operation and linked information systems, the supplier's system simply notes that the customer is running out of stock and organises a delivery.

Operations that link information systems and integrate activities are known by a variety of names, including **quick response** (QR) and more commonly **efficient customer response** (ECR). Early work in this area was done in the fashion industry. This had severe problems with its stocks and materials, largely caused by the traditional planning of production around four seasons. At the start of, say, the summer season shops have to be full of new products that reflect the latest styles. Shops need high stocks to give customers a wide choice, and wholesalers need high stocks to re-supply the shops at short notice. Peak manufacturing occurs some time before the start of a season, and stocks move slowly through the supply chain. Any shortages in shops cannot be met by manufacturers, who have already moved on to making their autumn and winter collections. On the other hand, if demand is lower than expected, shops cannot adjust their purchases, as they already have the stocks hanging in their shops. At the end of each season there are major sales as wholesalers and retailers try to get rid of their less popular items, and major restocking in preparation for the next season.

The industry realised that it could get huge savings if it smoothed its operations. The way to do this is not to have huge stocks sitting in the supply chain, but to move items through quickly, and respond to customer demands by more flexible manufacturing. For this, they used the approach of just-in-time operations, and linked information systems so that they could 'pull' materials through the supply chain. When a retailer sells an item, the cash register automatically sends a message to the wholesaler requesting a replacement. In turn, the wholesaler's system sends a message to the manufacturer asking for a delivery. The manufacturer is not bogged down in making excessive numbers of items that are later sold at discounts, but responds quickly to the demand and replaces the garment that has sold.

With ECR, a message passes backwards through the supply chain, and each organisation co-operates in moving materials forwards. Like JIT, ECR is a deceptively simple idea that needs substantial changes to operations – and, again, it can only be used in certain circumstances. If the supply chain starts with, say, potatoes, these are grown in a particular season, and farmers cannot suddenly grow a crop at short notice. Another problem comes with the length of the supply chain, as a single organisation that does not want to be involved – or cannot adapt – will disrupt the flow. If the supply chain crosses a slow international border, or includes an area where productivity is low, or hits other problems, the delays become unacceptable and ECR cannot work. These problems might be overcome but they need major changes in a whole range of operations.

If we bring together these ideas, you can see that the main features of ECR are:

- definition of an end-to-end supply chain from initial suppliers through to final customers;
- close collaboration of trading partners through the supply chain, each adding value to the final product;
- connected systems to move information in both directions;
- visibility, so that all organisations in the supply chain can see what is happening, and how this will affect them;
- understanding the operations of other organisations, particularly the conditions and constraints they work with;
- fast and efficient movement of materials pulled forwards through the supply chain;
- flexible operations that can deliver materials with short lead times;
- balanced resources to give a smooth flow of materials.

ECR recognises that it is not the physical transport that slows the flow of materials through a supply chain, but the associated flow of information. It might take a month for an organisation to prepare the details for a purchase, collect information, send orders, arrange payments, etc. – while delivery only takes one day. So, ECR only became feasible when a practical method of control was designed. With JIT this came with kanbans; with ECR it came with the Internet and **e-commerce**. There have only been efficient links between organisations and signals between their operations since B2B (business-to-business), B2C (business-to-customer) and other developments of e-commerce.

Other trends in logistics

There have been many developments in logistics, but none with as much impact as developments in communications, particularly e-business. DELL Computers were one of the first to recognise the importance of this, and developed 'virtual integration' that links suppliers so closely that they all seem to be part of the same company. This gives the flexibility for mass customisation. DELL no longer build computers and store them until needed by a customer, but wait until receiving an order from the DELL Website and very quickly build a computer for that specific order.

There are several other trends in logistics, some of which are direct consequences of e-business.

- **Globalisation**. Improved communications mean that physical distances disappear, increasing global competition. There are obvious impacts on logistics which have to organise the flows of information and materials across increasing distances.
- **Mass customisation**. Customers are becoming more knowledgeable and more demanding. They have access to information about all products and suppliers, and are sensitive to costs, delivery speed, innovation and service level. They increasingly insist on some customisation, and this needs fast responses from the whole supply chain.
- **Postponement**. This delays any modifications or customisation to a standard product until the last possible moment. Manufacturers of electrical equipment, such as Phillips and Hewlett-Packard, used to build the different transformers and plugs needed for different markets into their products. Then they had to assign production to markets at an early stage. By making the transformer and cables as separate, external units, they can be added to a standard product at the last minute.
- **Reduced number of suppliers**. JIT and ECR emphasise the benefits of long-term relationships between customers and suppliers. As customers agree to do more business with their favoured suppliers, this inevitably reduces the number of suppliers they use. The overall demand, however, is rising as organisations are making fewer of their own parts and buying more.
- **Cross-docking**. Traditional warehouses move goods into storage, and then move them out as they are needed. Cross-docking co-ordinates the supply and delivery, so that goods arrive at the receiving area and are transferred straight away to a loading area, where they are put onto delivery vehicles and sent to customers.
- **Drop-shipping**. This avoids delivery to a wholesaler. Usually the wholesaler receives a request for a product, and asks the manufacturer to deliver it directly to the customers.
- **Other methods of reducing the lead time**. Many methods have been suggested for reducing lead times, such as 'synchronised material scheduling'. This co-ordinates information in the supply chain, so that all organisations become aware of the needs at the same time. Rather than wait for a message to move backwards through the chain, they can all ship materials simultaneously.
- **Other stock reduction methods**. Any stocks held in the supply chain increase costs, so organisations are continually looking for ways of eliminating them. Some schemes transfer the management of stocks, such as 'Vendor Managed Inventory'. This has suppliers managing both their own stocks and those held at their customers, with improved co-ordination reducing overall costs.

In the rest of this chapter we are going to look at some of the key ideas in logistics, starting with purchasing and transport.

Review questions

19.6 Why is it better to have a single logistics function within an organisation?

19.7 What is ECR?

19.8 Why would organisations be interested in e-commerce?

OPERATIONS IN PRACTICE

Philips Semiconductors, Stadskanaal

Philips' Semiconductors plant in Stadskanaal, The Netherlands makes millions of diodes a year. These are made on a typical mass process, which is an automated assembly line. Materials (such as glass, wire and connectors) must be delivered at exactly the right time, as any delay would interrupt the process.

Over 65 per cent of the plant's cost is materials, and Philips puts exacting demands on its suppliers. It only tolerates a few defects per million parts, and typically demands decreases in price of 7 per cent a year. To monitor their performance, Philips introduced a Supplier Rating System which measures five criteria of the 12 main suppliers each month. The criteria measured are as follows.

Criteria	Performance required
Delivery performance	99.5% delivered on time, with average deliveries twice a week
Quality	less than 3–5 parts per million defective
Price	expected to fall by 7% a year
Responsiveness	supplier feedback within two hours for critical problems
Audit score	compiled score according to Philips' audit system

This system plays a key role in Philips, enabling it to keep its leading position in an increasingly competitive market.

Sources: Philips Semiconductors, *Stadskanaal* (1998) *Purchasing Annual Report* and (1998) *Supplier Rating System Manual*

Project 19.1 *Have a look at a fairly simple product, such as a coat, hamburger or CD. What does the supply chain for this look like? What do you think are likely to be the problems in this chain, and how can they be overcome?*

Procurement

Definition

In a typical manufacturer, 60 per cent of the expenditure is on raw materials. A company buying raw materials for €60, spending €40 on operations and then selling the product for €110 clearly makes a profit of €10 a unit. Now suppose it negotiates a 5 per cent discount on materials. The €3 saving goes straight to profit, which suddenly jumps to €13 – an increase of 30 per cent. This illustrates the importance of proper purchasing – it is often the biggest single element for an organisation, and one where small improvements can make a significant difference to profits.

The cost of materials in services is generally less than in manufacturing, but there is still room for substantial savings. The part of logistics that is responsible for purchasing and buying materials is generally called **procurement**.

Procurement is responsible for acquiring the materials needed by an organisation.

- It consists of all the related activities that get goods, services and any other materials from suppliers into the organisation.

Many organisations use the terms **purchasing** and procurement to mean the same thing. Usually, though, purchasing refers to the actual buying, while procurement has a broader meaning and can include purchasing, contracting, expediting, materials handling, transport, warehousing and receiving goods from suppliers. Some people prefer to talk about the 'acquisition of materials'.

How procurement works

When you buy something expensive, such as a new computer, you probably go through a number of steps. You might list the facilities that you want, search for systems that can provide these, identify suppliers, develop a short list of options, compare these and choose the best. Your aim is to find the combination of products and suppliers that best satisfies your needs. The procurement function in an organisation does exactly the same. It follows a specific procedure for purchasing materials. This procedure might aim at:

- working closely with user departments, developing relationships and understanding their needs;
- finding good suppliers, working closely with them and developing relationships;
- negotiating good prices and conditions from suppliers;
- buying the right materials from these suppliers, so that they arrive at the time and place needed for operations;
- keeping stocks low, by buying standard materials, etc.;
- expediting deliveries when necessary;
- keeping abreast of price increases, scarcities, and other changing conditions.

The procedures to achieve this are different in every organisation, and they vary with the type of thing being purchased. You would not expect an organisation such as the US army, which buys millions of items a day, to work in the same way as the directors of Real Madrid football club when it acquires a new striker. And the US army would not approach its decision to buy pencils in the same way as its decision to buy tanks. None the less, we can suggest a series of common steps in procurement.

Procurement is done in a **purchase cycle**, which starts with a user identifying a need for materials and ends when the materials are delivered. A typical cycle has the following steps, with the names of key documents underlined.

1. *In the user department*:
   - identify a need for purchased materials;
   - examine materials available and prepare specifications;
   - check departmental budgets and get clearance to purchase;
   - prepare and send a purchase request to procurement.
2. *Then procurement*:
   - receives, verifies and checks the purchase request;
   - examines the material requested, looking at current stocks, alternative products, production options, etc. – and after discussions with the user department confirms the decision to purchase;
   - makes a shortlist of possible suppliers from regular suppliers, lists of preferred suppliers or those known to meet requirements;
   - sends a request for quotations to this shortlist.

3. *Then the supplier*:
   - examines the request for quotations;
   - sees how it could best satisfy the order;
   - sends a quotation back to the organisation, giving details of products, prices and conditions.
4. *Then procurement*:
   - examines the quotations and does commercial evaluations;
   - discusses technical aspects with the user department;
   - checks budget details and clearance to purchase;
   - chooses the best supplier, based on the details supplied;
   - discusses, negotiates and finalises terms and conditions with the supplier;
   - issues a purchase order.
5. *Then the supplier*:
   - receives and processes the purchase order;
   - organises operations to supply the materials;
   - ships materials together with a shipping advice;
   - sends an invoice.
6. *Then procurement*:
   - does any necessary follow-up and expediting;
   - receives, inspects and accepts the materials;
   - notifies the user department of materials received.
7. *Then the user department*:
   - receives and checks the materials;
   - authorises transfer from budgets;
   - updates inventory records;
   - uses the materials as needed.
8. *Then procurement*
   - arranges payment of the supplier's invoice.

This formal procedure is quite complicated and time consuming. It can be even more complicated than it seems. If we take one of the steps – say, making a short-list of suitable suppliers – this itself can be very difficult. Most organisations have a list of approved suppliers who have given good service in the past, or who are otherwise known to be reliable. If there is no acceptable supplier on file, the organisation has to search for one. Suppliers for low value items can probably be found in trade journals, catalogues or through business contacts, but more expensive items need a thorough search. Normally, an organisation will look for a short list of around five potential suppliers, but it need not bother if:

- the item is low value;
- there is only one possible supplier;
- there is already a successful arrangement with a supplier;
- there is not enough time for extended negotiations;
- the organisation has a policy of selecting specific types of supplier.

One important point is that the lowest price is not necessarily the best. We saw in Chapter 6 that TQM demands some measure of quality when judging suppliers, so the 'right price' is the one that is best for all concerned: buyers, suppliers,

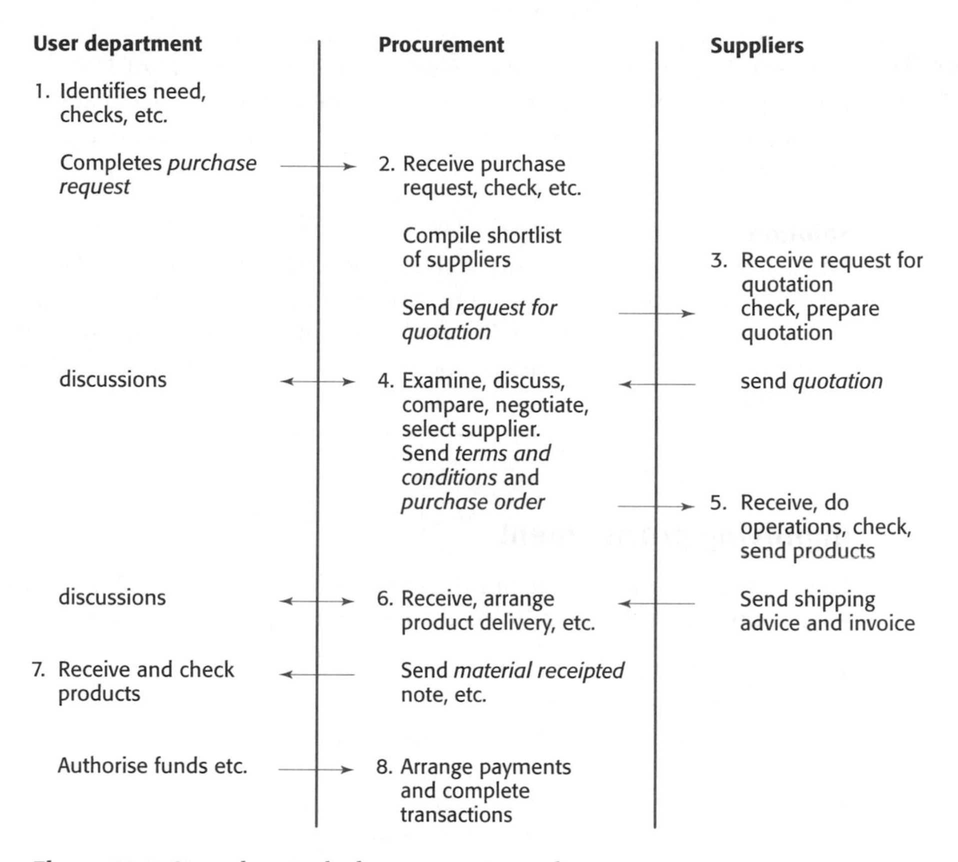

Figure 19.3 Steps in a typical procurement cycle

customers, the public and everyone else. It is certainly not in an organisation's long-term interest to save money by substituting cheap materials and hoping that nobody notices the decline in quality. Nor should it force suppliers to give the lowest possible price, or use unethical practices in negotiations. Suppliers must make a reasonable profit, or they will go out of business and not be there next time they are needed. This is, however, a complicated issue. Supermarkets in parts of the European Union, for example, have followed consumer pressure to reduce their food prices, and this has meant paying less to farmers who grow the crops. Then farmers go out of business, with a major impact on rural communities and the countryside.

Importance of procurement

You can easily see why procurement is important. Every operation relies on a supply of materials, information and other inputs, and these are obtained by procurement. Procurement is essential, and unless it is done well operations are interrupted, product quality is poor, deliveries are late, the wrong quantities are delivered, costs rise, customer service declines, and so on. As well as being essential, procurement is responsible for 60 per cent of the costs in a typical organisation.

WORKED EXAMPLE

Last year Zetafile Limited had total sales in Polish Zlotys (Ł) of 108 million. Its direct costs were Ł58 million for materials, Ł27 million for employees and Ł12 million for overheads and other costs. What would be the effect of reducing the cost of materials by 1 per cent?

Solution

The actual profit last year was = 108 – (58 + 27 + 12) = Ł11 million. If the cost of materials drops by 1 per cent, to 58 × 0.99 = Ł57.42 million, the profit rises to 108 – (57.42 + 27 + 12) = Ł11.58 million. A 1 per cent decrease in materials costs increases profits by 5.3 per cent. Profit as a percentage of sales has risen from 10.2 per cent to 10.7 per cent.

Improving procurement

The sequence of events listed in the purchase cycle can take a long time and involve a lot of documents. The traditional paper-based approach has the disadvantages of:

- taking a long time to go through the whole procedure;
- relying on a lot of paperwork;
- needing a lot of people to deal with the forms and paperwork;
- needing other people to administer the complicated procedures;
- introducing inevitable errors with so many documents and people involved;
- not giving attention to related systems, such as stock control.

There are obvious ways of improving these operations. For example, a procurement department can send out blanket orders, which cover regular orders for materials over some specified time in the future. A more obvious saving comes from replacing paper forms by electronic ones. However, this only goes some way to improving procurement, as it still leaves the same basic system. As we have already seen, there are more radical ways of improving performance by, for example, integrating information flows along the supply chain. Over three-quarters of organisations already use the Internet for procurement and this has the advantages of:

- allowing instant access to suppliers anywhere in the world;
- creating a transparent market where products and terms are readily available;
- automating procurement with standard procedures;
- outsourcing some procurement activities to suppliers or third parties;
- integrating seamlessly with suppliers' information systems.

It is obvious that **e-procurement** is growing very quickly, but it is still far from universal. Those organisations that are moving towards it start with straightforward administrative activities, such as requisitioning, ordering and payment. Later they include activities that need more human input, such as supplier selection, performance rating and even negotiation.

One major software company estimated its saving of moving to e-procurement as follows (values are in € per transaction). These substantial savings gave a return on investment of 400 per cent a year.

Process step	Original cost	Cost with e-procurement
1. Create detailed requirement	17.2	9.3
2. Approval process	5.5	2.7
3. Check requirements	20.2	0
4. Order processing	54.4	6.8
5. Receiving	10.3	2.9
6. Internal delivery	35.0	13.0
7. Payment process	23.6	0.6
Total	**166.2**	**35.3**

OPERATIONS IN PRACTICE

Accounts Payable Department at Ford

One of the early examples of *business process reengineering* was in 1988 when Ford of America looked at its Accounts Payable Department. This had 500 people working with a standard accounting system, where:

- the purchase department sent a purchase order to the vendor and a copy to Accounts Payable;
- the vendor shipped the goods ordered;
- when the goods arrived at Ford, a clerk at the receiving dock checked them, completed a form describing the goods and sent it to Accounts Payable;
- the vendor sent an invoice to Accounts Payable;
- Accounts Payable now had three descriptions of the goods: from the purchase order, receipt form and invoice. If these matched, it paid the invoice, but in a few cases there were discrepancies. These often took weeks to trace and clear up.

Ford thought that it could save perhaps 25 per cent of staffing costs by redesigning the system. In the end Ford did a radical redesign of the system so that:

- the purchase department sends a purchase order to a vendor, and enters details on a database;
- the vendor ships the goods;
- when the goods arrive at Ford, a clerk at the receiving dock checks them to see if they match the entry in the database. If they do, the clerk updates the database to show that the goods have arrived, and the system automatically sends a cheque to the supplier. If there are discrepancies, the clerk refuses to accept the delivery and sends it back to the supplier.

The 'we pay when we receive the invoice' has changed to 'we pay when we receive the right goods'. The new system takes 125 people to operate, giving a 400 per cent increase in productivity.

Source: Hammer M. and Champy J. (1993) *Reengineering the Corporation*. New York: Harper Collins

Trends in procurement

The role of procurement has changed significantly in recent years. It used to be little more than a clerical job, buying materials as they were requested. Now it is recognised as an important management function that is central to operations. Companies such as General Motors spend over $50 billion a year in purchasing materials, so it is not surprising that this is treated as a senior management role.

Procurement is still going through a period of radical change, as it moves from a ponderous paper-based function to a fast electronic one. However, there are a number of other developments in procurement that might be less revolutionary, but can still give significant benefits. **Value analysis**, for example, is a way of improving product quality and performance while reducing material cost. In effect, it uses a team of people from different functional areas to find substitute materials that are lower in price but equally as good as the original.

Review questions

19.9 What is the main aim of procurement?

19.10 Is there any difference between procurement and purchasing?

19.11 What are the stages in a typical purchasing cycle?

19.12 What trends have there been in procurement?

OPERATIONS IN PRACTICE

Amazon.com

The traditional way of buying books is to visit a bookshop or sometimes to join a book club. In 1995 Jeff Bezos went a step further and started an on-line book retailing business from his garage. His mission was 'to use the Internet to transform book buying into the fastest, easiest, and most enjoyable shopping experience possible'. He quickly developed Amazon.com into the world's largest book retailer.

At the heart of Amazon's operations is a sophisticated system to guide customers through the steps of making their purchases. This system essentially records customer orders, gets the payment and arranges delivery. However, it does far more than this and can search for material in different ways, recommend books that you might like, give reviews from other readers, authors and publishers, supply information about authors, tell you about new books that are being released, send newsletters, let you track an order, and a whole range of other functions.

Amazon allows access to huge numbers of products that are not available in local bookshops. Its efficient operations give low overheads, so it gets substantial economies of scale, and uses its size to negotiate discounts from publishers. As a result, Amazon can give discounts of up to 50 per cent on the publishers' prices of best sellers.

This combination of customer service, wide choice, efficient delivery and low costs has been successful. Amazon.com now has 25 million customers in 160 countries. Net sales for the first quarter of 2000 were US$578 million, an increase of 84 per cent. Amazon has expanded beyond its original operations in Seattle, with major operations in the UK, Germany and France, and has expanded beyond books: firstly into associated areas of CDs and videos, and then into toys, games, garden furniture, gifts, hardware, kitchen equipment, auctions, etc. It has also formed partnerships with on-line pharmacies, sporting goods suppliers, grocers, etc. As a result, Amazon offers 18 million distinct products. Its UK branch, for example, lists 1.2 million British books, 250,000 US books, 220,000 CDs and 23,000 videos and DVDs. In July 2000 when *Harry Potter and the Goblet of Fire* was published, Amazon put in the biggest-ever advance order of 410,000 copies, 250,000 of which were delivered by Federal Express on the first day of sale.

Despite its impressive performance, Amazon is not immune from the pressures and share price fluctuation of e-business. In 2000 it was making a net loss of around $200 million a quarter.

Source: company Website at: *www.amazon.com*

Project 19.2 *Describe the steps you would take when buying something relatively expensive, such as a computer. Would this differ from the way that Exxon approached buying a computer? And would it differ from the way that Exxon approached buying an oilrig for the Gulf of Mexico?*

Transport

The physical link

When we mention logistics, most people imagine lorries driving down a motorway. Transport is one of the main functions of logistics. E-commerce can deliver parts of many products, but only the intangibles such as information, software, music, and so on. Goods still have to be delivered, and they still need transport.

> **Transport** is responsible for the physical movement of materials through the supply chain from original suppliers through to final customers.

You can see where transport is needed with the view of a supply chain shown in Figure 19.4. Here materials need transport between suppliers and the start of operations, and finished goods need transport between end of operations and customers. Each organisation does, of course, have many suppliers and customers, so we get another view of transport in Figure 19.5.

You can probably imagine this kind of system used by manufacturers, but it is also used by services. Airlines use a similar system for moving passengers from pick-up points, through feeder services to major 'hub' airports, and back out to destinations. Banks collect all cheques in central clearinghouses before sending them back to branches and customers. Blood banks have regional centres which act as wholesalers. Such systems have developed because many operations are best done in locations that are some distance from both customers and suppliers. The best locations for power stations, for example, are some distance from cities and they may also be away from fuel supplies.

This pattern of logistics system has clear benefits, if the transport can be organised efficiently. Some specific benefits include:

- producers can get economies of scale by concentrating operations in central locations;
- producers do not need large stocks of finished goods;
- wholesalers can place large orders and reduce unit prices;
- wholesalers keep stocks from many suppliers, allowing retailers a choice of goods;
- wholesalers are near to retailers and have short lead times;
- retailers carry less stock as wholesalers offer reliable deliveries;
- distribution costs are reduced as large orders are moved from producers' facilities to wholesalers, rather than moving small orders directly to retailers or customers.

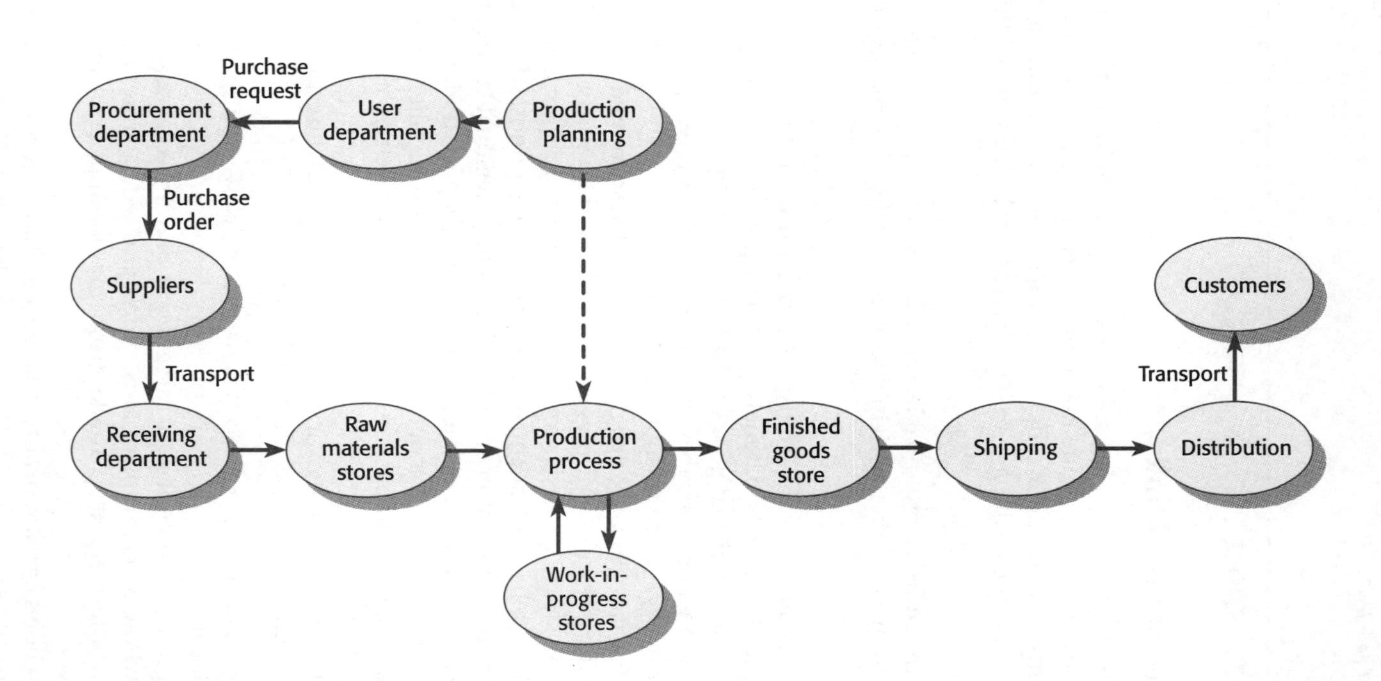

Figure 19.4 Transport in the supply chain

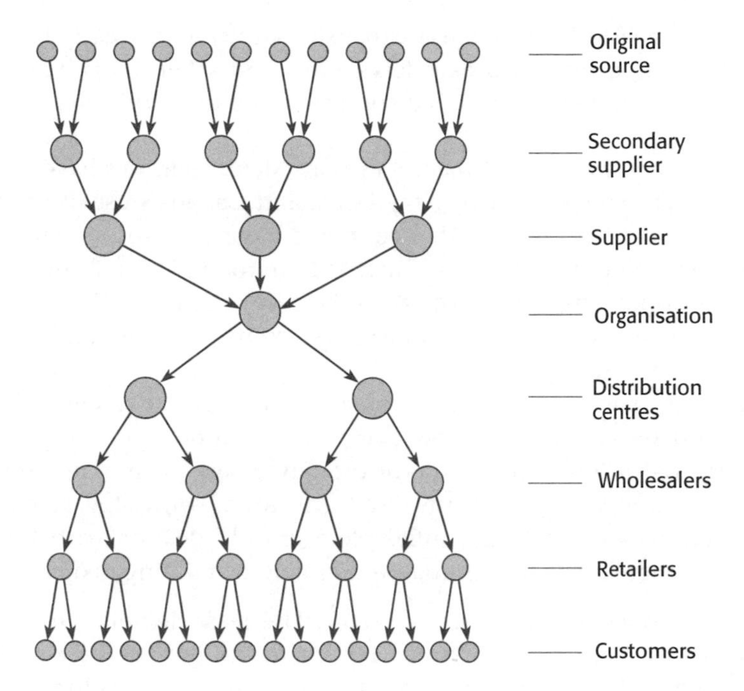

Figure 19.5 Another view of transport in the supply chain

Transport is an essential part of logistics. It is one of the most expensive parts, and needs careful organising. For this, we have to answer a series of questions. What mode of transport is best? Should we run our own transport or use a third-party carrier? How do we deal with international transport? How much will transport cost? How do we track movements? What routes should we use?

There are many of these questions. Unfortunately, the best answer will depend on the circumstances, and we can give little general advice. Here we will mention one aspect of transport, which is choosing the best mode.

Mode of transport

Most materials are moved by road, but there are five main modes of transport: road, rail, air, water and pipeline. The best in any particular circumstances depends on the type of goods to be moved, the distance, value and a whole range of other things.

- **Rail**. This has the benefit of moving heavy and bulky loads over long distances. Trains can maintain a consistent, reasonably high speed, and can link with other modes to carry containers, bulk freight, and so on. Their main disadvantage is their inflexibility. They only travel between terminals, and this often needs transfers to road at both terminals. This is worthwhile for long distances, such as across Canada, but is inefficient for small journeys, such as across The Netherlands.
- **Road**. Lorries can carry loads of reasonable size, say, 20–30 tonnes (with the European Union having a gross limit of 42 tonnes and different limits in other areas). Lorries have the advantage over rail of not having to build and maintain their own tracks, and of being flexible enough to collect and deliver door to door, but they are not so good for very long distances or high volumes.

- **Air**. This is the fastest mode, but is expensive and can only carry limited size and weight. Perhaps airlines also have less control over their costs. Fuel and landing fees are outside of their control, but competition puts a limit on the amount they can charge.
- **Water**. There are two types of water transport. Many countries have well-developed river and canal transport, such as the USA's and Canada's use of the St Lawrence Seaway and the Great Lakes. Other countries have a coastline that is suitable for international shipping, with cities such as Rotterdam, Hong Kong and New York having developed huge ports. The advantage of shipping is that it can move the biggest loads at low costs. The drawbacks are its slowness and inflexibility in being limited to using ports.
- **Pipeline**. The main uses of pipelines are for oil and gas, together with the utilities of water and sewage. They can be used for a few other types of product such as pulverised coal in oil. Pipelines have the advantage of moving large quantities over long distances. They have the disadvantages of being slow (typically moving at less than 10 km per hour), inflexible and only dealing with large volumes. In addition, there is the huge initial investment of building dedicated pipelines.

The cheapest modes of transport are usually the least flexible. Organisations can get around this by breaking a journey into stages to get the best mixture of cost and convenience. They may, for example, use the road to a rail terminal, rail to a port, ship to the nearest port, and so on. These inter-modal journeys rely on an efficient system for transferring materials between modes. The obvious way of organising this uses containers, which are standard boxes (40 feet long), which can be transferred quickly between modes at container terminals. Another option is 'piggy-back' transport, where a lorry – or usually just the trailer – is driven on to a train for fast movement over a longer distance. You can see an example of this in the Channel Tunnel, where cars and lorries are driven onto a train for this part of their journey.

The following table shows a ranking for the cost, speed, flexibility and load limits of different modes of transport. Here the modes are ranked in order, with 1 being the best performance, and 5 being the worst.

	Rail	Road	Air	Water	Pipeline
Cost	3	4	5	1	2
Speed	3	2	1	4	5
Flexibility	2	1	3	4	5
Volume/weight limits	3	4	5	1	2

Other decisions

Choosing the mode of transport is only one of a series of related questions. Suppose that an organisation decides that road transport is best. It still has to consider a whole series of alternatives. It could, for example, run its own fleet of lorries as a private carrier. You can see many lorries driving around with their company 'liveries', such as Tesco and Woolworth. Most organisations do not have the resources or skills for this, and a more common option (especially for smaller organisations) is to use specialised transport companies. There are two options for this. Firstly, public or common carriers will move materials on a one-off basis whenever asked. Companies such as TNT and Excel Logistics pick up and deliver in any location. If you want to send a parcel to Australia, you might use a parcel delivery service such as UPS, which acts as a common carrier. Secondly, contract carriers will take over the material movement for an organisation over some longer period. Tibbet & Britten, for example, are responsible for all the movement of goods for Wal-Mart in Canada.

At this point, there is still a string of decisions about transport. What are the best routes, who gives the best rates, how do we measure service and quality, what level of performance are we getting? We are, though, stepping into a specialised area which needs considerable expertise.

Review questions

19.13 What is the purpose of transport?

19.14 What are the alternative modes of transport?

19.15 What are the main questions an organisation might ask about transport?

OPERATIONS IN PRACTICE

Christian Salvesen

In 1846 Christian and Theodore Salvesen founded a shipping and fishing company in Norway. Over the years their company has been through a lot of growth, restructuring and change of focus. In 1997, the company demerged its remaining non-core activities and after restructuring in 1999 it concentrated on its role as a major European logistics business. Its aim is 'to manage client's supply chains seamlessly across Europe under the single brand of Christian Salvesen'. The company now works in partnership with manufacturers and retailers, using leading-edge systems to control stock levels, and make sure that goods are delivered to customers precisely when they are needed. To support this, it has a fleet of 2,500 vehicles, 5,500 trailers and 14,000 staff working at 160 sites.

One of Christian Salvesen's major contracts is to distribute parts for DaimlerChrysler in the UK. The problem is making sure that 300 franchised Mercedes-Benz and Chrysler dealers have adequate supplies of parts. The obvious option of having big stocks at each dealer is too expensive, so DaimlerChrysler meets demand from its European Logistics Centre at Milton Keynes, with rapid delivery guaranteed by Christian Salvesen.

At the centre of the operations is Christian Salvesen's SHARP (Shipments Handling and Reporting Programme). Every evening DaimlerChrysler enters the requirements of each dealer into this, and the parts are loaded onto large double-decked articulated lorries at Milton Keynes. These leave between 19.00 and 22.00 and travel to 11 feeder depots around the country. At the feeder depots they have an hour to transfer parts to local delivery vehicles. There are 35 of these, each of which delivers to up to 11 dealers, starting at midnight and finishing by 08.00. A key point is their ability to deliver to unmanned premises by having access to dealers' security systems.

When vehicles return to the depot, SHARP records the deliveries and prepares reports on performance. The resulting system for maintaining stocks is described as 'highly efficient and completely reliable'.

Source: company Website at: *www.salvesen.com*

Chapter review

- Logistics – or supply chain management – is responsible for the flow of materials through the supply chain. The aim is to make this flow as efficient and effective as possible.
- Logistics is essential to every organisation, and interacts with every other function. It can be viewed as a series of separate functions, ranging from procurement through to distribution.
- Better results come from combining these separate functions into an integrated logistics function. This can take advantage of e-commerce and other developments to co-ordinate activities throughout the supply chain. These methods have led to efficient customer response (ECR) and other improvements to logistics.
- Procurement is responsible for acquiring all the materials needed by an organisation. It is usually works in a purchasing cycle with a number of distinct steps.
- Procurement is changing very quickly, moving from a traditional clerical procedure towards e-commerce. Improved communications and related developments are allowing substantial improvements to procurement operations.
- Transport looks after the physical movement of materials, forming the link between suppliers and customers. This involves many related decisions about the best mode, organisation, routes and so on.

Key terms

e-commerce *p. 558*
e-procurement *p. 564*
efficient customer response (ECR) *p. 557*
logistics *p. 551*
materials *p. 551*
materials management *p. 551*
physical distribution *p. 551*
procurement *p. 560*
purchasing *p. 561*
purchasing cycle *p. 561*
quick response (QR) *p. 557*
supply chain *p. 551*
supply chain management *p. 551*
transport *p. 567*
value analysis *p. 566*

CASE STUDY Jergensen and Company

Henry Jergensen is worried. Recently his company has been late delivering some important orders. The marketing manager is also upset because his promised deliveries to customers have not been made.

When Henry asked the production manager for an explanation, he found that the shipments were late because shortages of raw materials had interrupted operations. 'But that's impossible', said Henry. 'Inventory levels have been climbing for the past six months, and they were at an all-time high last month.'

The inventory controller had an explanation for this. Inventory levels were high because purchasing had been buying some items in large quantities. This gave high stocks for most items, but there were shortages of other materials. The current high stocks were stretching the warehousing budget.

Henry then checked with the purchasing manager, Peter Schmidt, who said, 'Can I remind you that eight months ago you instructed me to reduce materials costs? I am doing this by taking advantage of quantity discounts offered by suppliers.'

Unfortunately, these large volumes of raw materials, together with the express shipping services used to bring in urgent supplies of materials in short supply, had made the transport supervisor exceed his freight budget for the past three months.

Henry now thought that he knew the problems facing his company. Then the company accountant visited to say, 'The company's inventory costs are so high that we are short of cash. We shall have to borrow money to pay the suppliers next month.' Later that day Henry found that the late customer deliveries, which had started his investigation, were actually caused by poor sales forecasts by the marketing department. The latter had seriously under-estimated monthly demand, so the planned production could not meet actual demand.

Henry knew that all his employees were trying to do their best. But somehow things were going wrong.

Questions

- Why did all the costs seem to rise at the same time?
- What are the basic problems in Jergensen and Company?
- What would you recommend that the company do?

Discussion questions

19.1 A supply chain is often seen as a single strand connecting a row of organisations. In practice, the many suppliers and customers form a complex web of interacting organisations. Does this complexity mean that supply chains are inevitably difficult to organise efficiently?

19.2 What functions are included in logistics? What are the benefits of integrating these into a single function? Are these benefits inevitable, or is it sometimes better to break logistics into smaller specialised units?

19.3 Everyone is talking about the 'revolution' that is coming with trading on the Internet. Is this realistic, or is it a passing trend with little substance? How will e-commerce affect wider operations? What other changes will there be in the future?

19.4 Is ECR really an extension of JIT? What would be the benefits of ECR? How widely is it used in practice, and what are likely to be the constraints?

19.5 Most supply chains cover several countries. What particular problems are there with international logistics?

19.6 Do you think an organisation should always negotiate hard with suppliers to get the cheapest prices and best conditions it can?

19.7 In many countries road transport is seen as offensive, as roads destroy green fields, lorries cause pollution, and so on. Why do you think this is, when we all rely on the efficient movement of goods? Are there alternative methods of transport?

19.8 How much does logistics cost a typical organisation? Do you think this is too much?

References

1. Institute for Logistics and Transport (2001) Promotional material. Corby.
2. Institute of Logistics and Transport Website at: *www.iolt.org.uk*
3. Drucker P. (1962) 'The Economy's Dark Continent', *Fortune*, April.

Selected reading

Arnold J.R.T. (1996) *Introduction to Materials Management.* 2nd edn. Englewood Cliffs, NJ: Prentice-Hall.

Baily P., Farmer D., Jessop D. and Jones D. (1998) *Purchasing Principles and Management.* 7th edn. London: Pitman.

Christopher M. (1998) *Logistics and Supply Chain Management.* London: FT Prentice-Hall.

Copacino W.C. (1997) *Supply Chain Management.* Boca Raton, FL: St Lucie Press.

Coyle J.J., Bardi E.J. and Langley C.J. (1996) *The Management of Business Logistics*. 6th edn. St Paul, MN: West Publishing.

Gattorna J.L. and Walters D.W. (1996) *Managing the Supply Chain*. New York: Palgrave.

Handfield R.B. and Nichols E.L. (1998) *Introduction to Supply Chain Management*. Englewood Cliffs, NJ: Prentice-Hall.

Hill E.R. and Fredendall L. (1999) *Basic Supply Chain Management*. Boca Raton, FL: St. Lucie Press.

Hughes J., Ralf M. and Mitchels W. (1998) *Transform your Supply Chain*. London: Thomson.

Leenders M.R. and Fearon H.E. (1996) *Purchasing and Supply Management*. New York: McGraw-Hill.

Poitier C.C. (1999) *Advanced Supply Chain Management*. New York: Berrett-Kohler.

Ptak C.A. and Schragenheim E. (1999) *ERP Tools, Techniques and Applications for Integrating the Supply Chain*. Boca Raton, FL: St. Lucie Press.

Saunders M. (1997) *Strategic Purchasing and Supply Chain Management*. 2nd edn. London: FT Prentice-Hall.

Waters C.D.J. (1999) *Global Logistics and Distribution Planning*. 3rd edn. London: Kogan Page.

Useful Websites

www.iolt.org.uk – Institute of Logistics and Transport
www.cips.org – Chartered Institute of Purchasing and Supply
www.clm.org – Council of Logistics Management
www.amsup.com – American Supplier Institute

Facilities location

The three most important things for a successful business are location, location and location.

Attributed to Lord Seif, founder of Marks & Spencer

Contents

Aims of the chapter

After reading this chapter you should be able to:

- appreciate the importance of location decisions;
- discuss factors that affect location decisions;
- describe a hierarchical approach to location decisions;
- use the centre of gravity to suggest a reasonable location;
- compare locations using costing models;
- compare locations using scoring models;
- combine available methods into an overall approach to planning.

Main themes

This chapter will emphasise:

- **facilities**, which are parts of the supply chain;
- **location**, to find the best place for operations;
- **location models**, to identify good locations.

The importance of location

Location decisions

In the last chapter we described the movement of materials along a supply chain. The supply chain for even simple products can involve a lot of movement. A simple medicine, such as Trimesterone, is manufactured in Switzerland, but the supply chain connects organisations around the world. It starts with suppliers of raw materials, and moves through exporters, importers to Switzerland, manufacturer, exporters, importers to final markets, wholesalers, pharmacies and on to patients. The chain can include other movement before reaching final customers, perhaps going through regional importers, national and local warehouses.

It is in everyone's interest to make sure that materials move smoothly through their supply chains. This is the aim of logistics. But if the main market for Trimesterone is in North America, why is it made in Switzerland? And if someone who wants to buy it is in New Zealand, why does it travel from Switzerland to The Netherlands and Australia before moving to Auckland in New Zealand and then on to local distributors? It might make sense to make products near to customers, but this raises much broader questions about the best places to put facilities. In this chapter we look for the best locations to open facilities.

Facilities location finds the best geographic location for an organisation's operations.

Importance of locations

Whenever Nissan builds a new assembly line, or Carrefour opens a new store, or Burger King opens a new restaurant, or Pfizer extends its operations in eastern Europe, these businesses have to make a decision about the best location. This is an important decision that affects the organisation's performance for many years. When Nissan opened a factory in Sunderland, it put a lot of effort into choosing the best site, and now has Europe's most productive car plant, but if Nissan had chosen a poor location, it could have had low productivity, unreliable deliveries of materials, poor-quality products and high costs. Unfortunately, once a mistake of this kind is made, and several billion euros have been invested, it is not feasible to close down such an operation and move to a better place. This is the problem that affects all organisations – if they work in the wrong location, their performance is poor, but moving can be very difficult. The only solution, of course, is to choose the best location in the first place.

The right location will not guarantee success, but the wrong location will certainly guarantee failure. This is why you do not find night clubs in residential areas where most people are retired, big petrol stations on country lanes where they cannot attract passing customers, factories in city centres where their costs are too high, or oil refineries far away from ports as their transport would cost too much.

Location decisions are invariably difficult. Families often have problems finding somewhere to live that satisfies all their needs, but this is trivial compared with a decision about where to open a new logistics centre, hospital, university, amusement park, airport, factory or any other major facility. Organisations have to examine many factors. Some of these can be measured or at least estimated, such as operating costs, wage rates, taxes, currency exchange rates, number of competitors, distance from current locations, development grants, population and reliability of supplies. Many other factors are non-quantifiable, such as the quality of infrastructure, political stability, social attitudes, industrial relations, the legal system, future developments of the economy, and so on.

Because the decisions are difficult, you can see many examples of organisations that locate in the wrong place and go out of business. Sometimes, people are reluctant to admit that a location is poor, and assume that there are other problems. This is why you can see sites that have had a string of cafés or boutiques, each of which has quickly closed down. Some organisations forget that location decisions are for the long term and are tempted by short-term benefits, such as development grants, temporary rent reductions or tax breaks. Such sweeteners can be attractive, but they rarely form the basis of good decisions. There are also examples of organisations that make the right decisions, but circumstances change. In the steel industry, for example, production has been concentrated in fewer, large facilities, so smaller sites have closed, even if they were in good locations.

OPERATIONS IN PRACTICE

Canary Wharf

London used to have large areas of docks on the River Thames. Most of these were to the east of the city on the Isle of Dogs. As ships grew larger, they could no longer get up the Thames, and new ports were built further down the river. When the London docks closed, they left large areas of unused and run-down land near the centre of the city. The land was relatively cheap, and the government gave incentives to promote development. In the late 1980s Olympia and York (a major property company based in Canada with considerable experience and office developments in many countries) decided to acquire a site and start building. The Canary Wharf site was to become the largest office development ever undertaken in Britain and among the biggest in Europe.

Unfortunately, there were drawbacks with the location and the timing of the development. Canary Wharf tried to attract companies by emphasising high quality – with corresponding high cost – but the site was some distance away from the main financial centre of the City of London. Few companies were attracted away from the City to a more distant, less convenient site that had poor transport and few facilities. Competing developers opened less prestigious – but more convenient – buildings nearer the City, and the office vacancy rate rose to 17 per cent. This had an effect on average rents, which fell by 30 per cent. At the same time, Britain was struggling through its worst recession since the 1930s, and most companies were looking for survival rather than expansion into new premises.

By March 1992 Olympia and York had serious financial difficulties, and the company's debts rose to $20 billion.

You can get more information from *www.canarywharf.com*

Project 20.1 *Find an example of an organisation that has been tempted to open in the wrong location, and see what problems it faces. There are many recent examples to start with, as well as historical ones, such as the Hillman (successively Rootes, Chrysler and Peugeot) car plant outside Glasgow, or Victorian railway stations built for towns that never developed.*

Alternatives to locating new facilities

Choosing a good location is one of the most common problems faced by organisations. There are several reasons for looking at location plans, including:

- the end of a lease on existing premises;
- expansion into new geographic areas;
- changes in the location of customers or suppliers;
- changes to operations, such as an electricity company moving from coal generators to gas;
- upgrading of facilities, perhaps to introduce new technology;
- changes to logistics, such as a switch from rail transport to road;
- changes in the transport network, such as the Channel Tunnel or the new bridge between Sweden and Denmark;
- mergers or acquisitions needing to rationalise operations.

You might think that one way of avoiding the problem of locating new facilities is simply to alter existing ones. But this is still a location decision, as it assumes the current site is the best available. In practice, when an organisation wants to change its facilities – either to expand, move or contract – it has three alternatives:

- expand or change existing facilities at the present site;
- open additional facilities at another site while keeping all existing facilities;
- close down existing operations and move.

Surveys suggest that around 45 per cent of companies expand on the same site, a similar number open additional facilities, and 10 per cent close down existing operations and move. Economies of scale can be important in this decision, as they tend to encourage expansion of existing facilities.

Expansion does not simply mean doing more of the same thing, but can give opportunities to adjust operations. Imagine a company that is expanding to work in a new market. This seems like a standard location problem of finding the best place to open more facilities. There are, however, alternatives that are not so expensive. The following list gives five options in order of increasing investment.

1. *licensing or franchising*: local organisations make and supply the company's products in return for a share of the profit;
2. *exporting*: the company makes the product in its existing facilities and sells it to a distributor working in the new market;
3. *local warehousing and sales*: the company makes the product in its existing facilities, but sets up its own warehouses and sales force to handle distribution in the new market;

4. *local assembly and finishing*: the company makes most of the product in existing facilities, but opens limited facilities in the new market to finish or assemble the final product;
5. *full local production*: the company opens complete facilities in the new market.

Local facilities give an organisation the benefits of more control over products and the supply chain, higher profits, avoidance of import tariffs and quotas, and closer links with local customers. On the other hand, they give more complex and uncertain operations. The best choice depends on many factors, such as the capital available, risk the organisation will accept, target return on investment, existing operations, time-scale, local knowledge, transport costs, tariffs, trade restrictions and available workforce.

WORKED EXAMPLE

Semantica Services is looking at five options for expansion. Each of these has a fixed annual payment (for rent, electricity, and other overheads) and a variable cost that depends on throughput (handling, depreciation, staff, etc.).

Alternative	Fixed cost	Variable cost
A. Open new medium-sized facility	£40,000	£45
B. Open two new small facilities	£120,000	£35
C. Expand current facility	£450,000	£26
D. Build large new facility and close old one	£400,000	£18
E. Build large new facility and keep old one	£600,000	£22

Over what range of throughput is each alternative most attractive?

Solution

This is an extension of the break-even analysis. You can see from Figure 20.1 that alternatives C and E are never cheapest, as they are always more expensive than D. This leaves a choice between alternatives A, B and D.

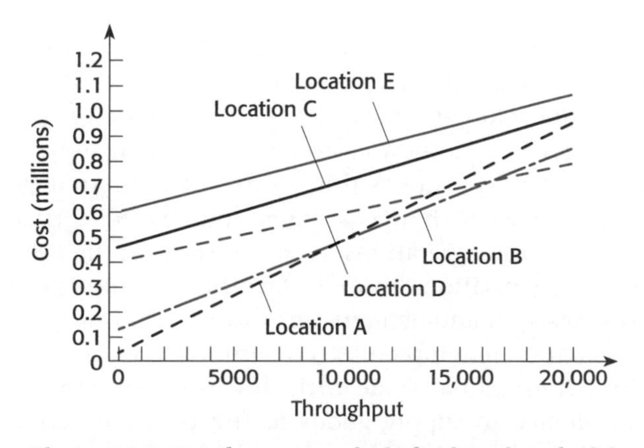

Figure 20.1 Break-even analysis for location decision

- Alternative A is the cheapest for throughput, X, from 0 until:

$$40{,}000 + 45X = 120{,}000 + 35X \quad \text{or} \quad X = 8{,}000$$

- After this alternative B is cheapest until:

$$120{,}000 + 35X = 400{,}000 + 18X \quad \text{or} \quad X = 16{,}471$$

- After this point, D remains the cheapest.

Review questions

20.1 Why are location decisions important?

20.2 When a company wants to supply products to a new market, it has to find the best location for a warehouse. Do you think this is true?

20.3 What are the three alternatives if an organisation wants to expand its facilities?

20.4 Economies of scale mean that it is always cheaper to operate a single large warehouse than a number of smaller ones. Do you think this is true?

Choosing the geographic region

Overall considerations

Facility location involves a **hierarchy of decisions**. At the top of this are the broad decisions about which geographic regions to work in. Then come more local views that consider alternative countries or areas within this region. Then we move to look more closely at alternative towns and cities within this area. Finally, we look at different sites within a preferred town (as shown in Figure 20.2). In the 1990s, for example, Marks & Spencer decided to expand its retail network in central Europe. Then it looked at various countries and decided to open branches in Poland. It looked at cities within Poland and decided to open a branch in Warsaw. After looking at available sites, it opened a store next to the Cultural Palace in the city centre.

The broad decisions about countries and geographical regions to work in are related to the business strategy. An organisation that has a strategy of expansion into new markets must make long-term decisions about the best regions to work in. Obvious choices are to get close to new customers or close to suppliers. The Marks & Spencer example in Poland illustrates this, as its business strategy in the 1990s was to expand and get closer to new customers, but by 2001 this strategy had changed and it closed European operations to concentrate on the UK.

Another trend is for organisations to open facilities in countries that can give lower operating costs. Many manufacturers, for example, do not have to be close to their final customers and are tempted to move to low-cost areas. These can give convenient bases for international trade with, for example, Japanese companies opening factories in Mexico to supply goods to the USA, or German companies opening in the Czech Republic to supply goods to the European Union.

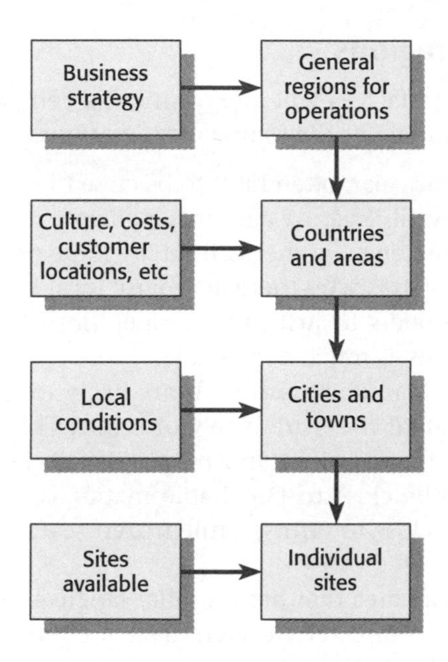

Figure 20.2 Hierarchy of decisions for location

One problem with this strategy is that costs might not be as low as expected. Transport costs are usually raised, and they may become more important than operating costs. Large, efficient steel mills in Japan, Taiwan and South Korea, for example, give low operating costs, but importing coal and iron ore is so expensive that their steel is no longer cheap. South Africa makes very good beer, but little of it is imported to Europe because of the high transportation costs.

Many people assume that low wage rates automatically mean low costs. This is not true, as low wages might be accompanied by very low productivity: there is no point in halving wage rates if labour productivity is also halved. Another important point is that many operations, particularly in manufacturing, can be automated so that wages form a very small part of overall costs. It makes little sense for a high technology company to move to a low-wage economy, when its markets are in industrial centres and wages form only 3 per cent of costs.

You also have to remember that costs may not be a dominant factor in location. A business strategy might focus on quality, flexibility and speed of response rather than lowest cost. As a result, most organisations prefer to locate in areas that are near markets, have reliable suppliers, good infrastructure, high productivity, guaranteed quality and skilled workforce, even if they appear to have higher operating costs.

One example of this came in 1980 when Tandy Corporation decided to move production of its latest computer to South Korea. Then rising shipping costs, long lead times for the sea voyage to the USA, the changing value of the dollar, and more automation in the process encouraged Tandy to reconsider its location. In 1987 it moved back to Fort Worth, Texas and reduced costs by 7.5 per cent. Quality Coils Inc. moved from Connecticut to Mexico, and then returned four years later.

Considerations in choosing regions

Organisations have to consider many factors when choosing the general regions to work in. The following list includes some of the main considerations.

- *Location of customers*. Services, in particular, often have to be close to their customers. This is why you find shops, buses, libraries, restaurants, solicitors and a range of other services in town centres. The same arguments hold for some products with a larger manufacturing element, which is why there are many local bakers, brewers and double-glazing factories. Suppliers to just-in-time operations locate near to their customers to reduce lead times as much as possible.
- *Location of suppliers and materials*. Manufacturers are more likely to locate near to supplies of raw materials, especially if these are heavy or bulky. This is why coal-burning power stations are close to coalmines and pulp mills are near to timber forests. Some operations have to be close to perishable materials, which is why fruit and vegetable processors are close to farms, while frozen seafood companies are near to fishing ports.
- *Culture*. It is easier to expand into an area that has a similar language, culture, laws and costs, than to expand into a completely foreign area. A company currently operating in Belgium would find it easier to expand into France than in, say, Korea. The decision to build Disneyland Europe near Paris gives one example where moving a successful American operation to a European culture met with less initial success than expected.
- *Government attitudes*. National and local government policies can seriously affect an area's attractiveness. Investment in Hong Kong has fallen since it returned to rule by China. Many governments offer incentive packages to encourage companies to an area, but others are less welcoming, perhaps trying to control foreign influences on the economy. Some areas encourage particular types of industry (particularly high-technology or finance companies), but are less keen on, say, nuclear, chemical or polluting industries.
- *Indirect costs*. We will look at the direct costs of operating in a given location in the next section, but there can be many less obvious costs. Perhaps the most obvious are local taxes and charges on the payroll such as social insurance and pension costs. There may also be controls on company ownership (often including a controlling local partner), currency exchange and repatriation of profits.
- *Exchange rates*. These can appear as indirect costs, but they are much less predictable. What seems like a good location one year can become much less attractive after a re-alignment of currency values.
- *Social attitudes*. Some countries put more emphasis on social welfare than others, and there is higher union membership and emphasis on individual rather than corporate benefits. Other areas do not necessarily admire high productivity, and there might be higher absenteeism and staff turnover. Cultural stereotypes often bear no relation to real conditions.
- *Organisation*. An organisation can keep a close check on new operations by controlling these from existing headquarters and giving local operations little autonomy. This is, however, inflexible, and it does not allow local organisations

to adapt operations to their specific conditions. An alternative is to devolve decisions, with three alternative approaches. An *international* organisation maintains its headquarters in the 'home' country and runs its world-wide activities from there; a *multinational* organisation opens subsidiary headquarters around the world so that each area is largely independent; a *global* company treats the whole world as a single market.

- *Operations*. If you go into a McDonald's hamburger restaurant anywhere in the world you will see virtually identical operations. It is easier to control operations in this way, but it loses the benefit of local knowledge and practices. Other organisations blend into the local environment and adapt their operations so they are more familiar to their host countries.

Review questions

20.5 Low wage rates make a country an attractive location for industry. Do you think this is true?

20.6 Name three non-economic factors that play an important part in the success of an international development.

20.7 If jobs are created in one country, they must inevitably be lost in another. Do you think this is true?

OPERATIONS IN PRACTICE — McDonald's in Moscow

In 1990 the world's largest McDonald's hamburger restaurant with 700 seats opened just off Pushkin Square in Moscow. This is operated jointly by McDonald's of Canada and local Russian companies. McDonald's had opened branches throughout the world, but this was one of the most difficult. Negotiations started with the Soviet Union 20 years before the restaurant finally opened.

The inside of the restaurant is exactly as you would expect, with the standard menu, colour scheme and decor, staff training, levels of cleanliness and cooking. Everything follows the standard McDonald's pattern, but this was only achieved with considerable effort and when conditions in Russia changed. As well as obvious political difficulties, there were major practical problems. Beef in Moscow was not readily available and the quality was poor. McDonald's had to import breeding cattle and start a beef farm to supply the restaurant. Potatoes were plentiful, but they were the wrong type to make McDonald's fries. Seed potatoes were imported and grown. Russian cheese was not suitable for cheeseburgers, so a dairy plant was opened to make processed cheese.

When the restaurant opened it was a huge success, with 27,000 people applying for a single job, 50,000 people served a day and queues half a mile long outside the restaurant. Now there are 58 outlets in Russia and a workforce of 450, but the path is still not easy. Russia suffered an economic collapse in 1998, and this has affected wages, sales and profits. The initial set-up cost was so high that the restaurant does not expect to make a profit in the foreseeable future.

Source: company reports and Cockburn P. (2000) 'Big Mac, Big Trouble', *Independent*, 14 November

Finding the best locations

After making a decision about the geographical region and country, an organisation has to look in more detail at the areas, towns, cities and individual sites. There are several ways they can approach these decisions, and the best depends on specific circumstances. One approach that is **not** recommended is personal preference. There are many examples of poor locations where managers simply chose a site they like – perhaps in the town they live or grew up in, or the area they spend their holidays. Of course, these decisions can be successful, but their main weakness is that they are unreliable. It is always safer to do some analyses than to rely on intuition and guesswork.

Two distinct approaches to location decisions are:

1. **infinite set approach** – which uses geometric arguments to find the best location when there are no restrictions on site availability;
2. **feasible set approach** – where an organisation only has a small number of feasible sites and has to choose the best.

An *infinite set approach* finds the best location in principle and then looks for a site nearby; a *feasible set approach* compares sites that are currently available and chooses the best. These approaches are often used together, with an infinite set approach finding the best location in principle, and then a feasible set approach comparing available sites near to this best location. We will start by illustrating an infinite set approach, and then move on to look at methods of comparing sites.

Infinite set approach

Infinite set approaches assume that facilities should be located near the centre of potential demands and supplies. The most common way of finding a reasonable location is to calculate the **centre of gravity** of demand. This uses an analogy from engineering, with the demand at each customer replacing the weight.

The co-ordinates of the centre of gravity are:

$$X_0 = \frac{\Sigma X_i W_i}{\Sigma W_i} \quad Y_0 = \frac{\Sigma Y_i W_i}{\Sigma W_i}$$

Where: X_0, Y_0 are the co-ordinates of the centre of gravity, which becomes the facility location;

X_i, Y_i are co-ordinates of each customer and supplier, i;

W_i is expected demand at customer i, or expected supply from source i.

WORKED EXAMPLE

Amstead Industries is building an assembly plant that will take components from three suppliers, and send finished goods to six regional warehouses. The locations of these and the amounts supplied or demanded are shown in the following table. Where would you start looking for a site for the assembly plant?

Location	*X*, *Y* co-ordinates	Supply/Demand
Supplier 1	91, 8	40
Supplier 2	93, 35	60
Supplier 3	3, 86	80
Warehouse 1	83, 26	24
Warehouse 2	89, 54	16
Warehouse 3	63, 87	22
Warehouse 4	11, 85	38
Warehouse 5	9, 16	52
Warehouse 6	44, 48	28

Solution

Figure 20.3 shows a spreadsheet for these calculations.

As you can see, the centre of gravity is $X_0 = 45.5$ and $Y_0 = 50.3$, which you can check by calculating:

$$X_0 = \frac{\Sigma X_i W_i}{\Sigma W_i} = \frac{16{,}380}{360} = 45.5$$

$$Y_0 = \frac{\Sigma Y_i W_i}{\Sigma W_i} = \frac{18{,}110}{360} = 50.3$$

A good place to start looking for locations is around (45.5, 50.3) as shown in Figure 20.4. As this is very close to warehouse 6, it might be better to expand on this site rather than look for an entirely new location.

Centre of gravity					
	X	**Y**	**Weight**	**X*Weight**	**Y*Weight**
Supplier					
1	91	8	40	3640	320
2	93	35	60	5580	2100
3	3	86	80	240	6880
Warehouse					
1	83	26	24	1992	624
2	89	54	16	1424	864
3	63	87	22	1386	1914
4	11	85	38	418	3230
5	9	16	52	468	832
6	44	48	28	1232	1344
Totals			**360**	**16380**	**18108**
Centre of			**X =**	**45.5**	
Gravity			**Y =**	**50.3**	

Figure 20.3 Calculation of the centre of gravity

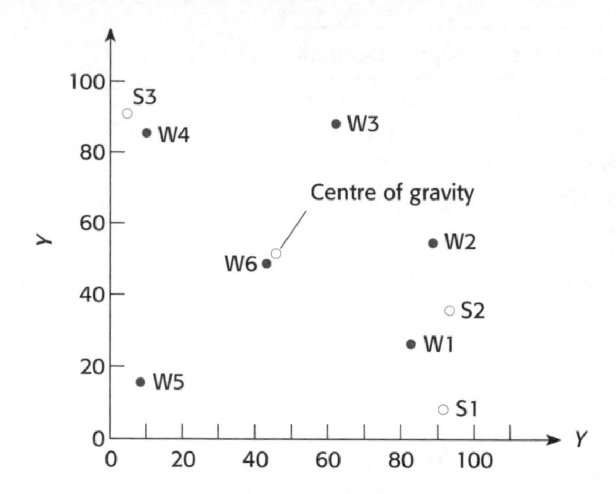

Figure 20.4 Locations for centre of gravity calculation

The centre of gravity can give a reasonably good location, but it is only a starting point. We can easily show one of its weaknesses. Suppose you work in Alberta, Canada and want to deliver 20 tonnes a day to Edmonton and 40 tonnes a day to Calgary. These two cities are connected by a straight road 300 km long (see Figure 20.5). If the costs of getting deliveries from suppliers are the same regardless of location, where would you build a warehouse to serve these two cities?

You can find the centre of gravity as being 100 km from Calgary. Then you would have to move 200×20 tonne-kilometres to Edmonton and 100×40 tonne-kilometres to Calgary, giving a total of 8,000 tonne-kilometres. But if you built the warehouse in Calgary, you would only have to move $20 \times 300 = 6{,}000$ tonne-kilometres to Edmonton. This gives one rule of thumb, which says that a good location is in the centre of highest demand.

The centre of gravity only gives guidelines for the locations, but then there may be no site available anywhere nearby, or available sites are too expensive, or it might be a long way from roads, or in an area with no workforce, or even in a river. There are many variations that improve the basic method. Often these use an iterative approach that keeps searching for a better location until it finds a reasonable location.

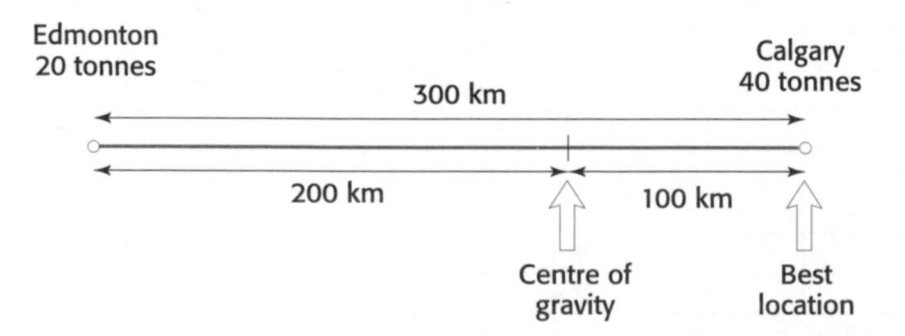

Figure 20.5 Weakness of the centre of gravity method

Feasible set approach

After using some kind of geometric model to narrow the area of search, we can now compare alternative sites. An obvious way of doing this is to look at the total costs. We consider this in the next section.

Project 20.2 *Apart from the centre of gravity, what other methods can you use to find good locations based on geometric arguments? As a starting point, you might look at some more mathematical methods, such as transportation models of linear programming, and see how these can be used. Can you find examples where organisations have used these methods?*

OPERATIONS IN PRACTICE

Kohl Transport

Kohl Transport delivers goods around western Europe, but most of its work comes from a manufacturer who wants regular deliveries from two plants to customers within Germany. A simplified view of the transportation problem is shown in the following table, which shows plant capacities, demands and unit transport costs (in euros).

	Berlin	Cologne	Dresden	Hamburg	Munich	Stuttgart	Capacity
Plant A	5.5	5.5	4.5	6.0	1.0	1.5	35,000
Plant B	1.5	6.5	3.25	2.0	6.5	7.5	40,000
Demand	22,600	4,400	9,000	8,400	13,200	7,400	

The company decided to use a quantitative model to help with its planning. It developed a linear programming model, and got the results shown in Figure 20.6. This shows the allocation of customers to plants, best plant sizes and distribution costs. As with all quantitative models, this gave one solution, which managers adjusted to see the effect of alternatives. Eventually the company decided to close down plant A and to consolidate operations in an expanded plant B.

Review questions

20.8 What exactly is the centre of gravity of customer demand?

20.9 The centre of gravity finds the optimal location for a facility. Do you think this is true?

Feasible set approaches

Costing models

Feasible set approaches look at the available sites, compare them, and identify the best. An obvious way of doing this is to look at the total costs. We could include all of the costs of running a facility, but most of them are fixed and do not vary with

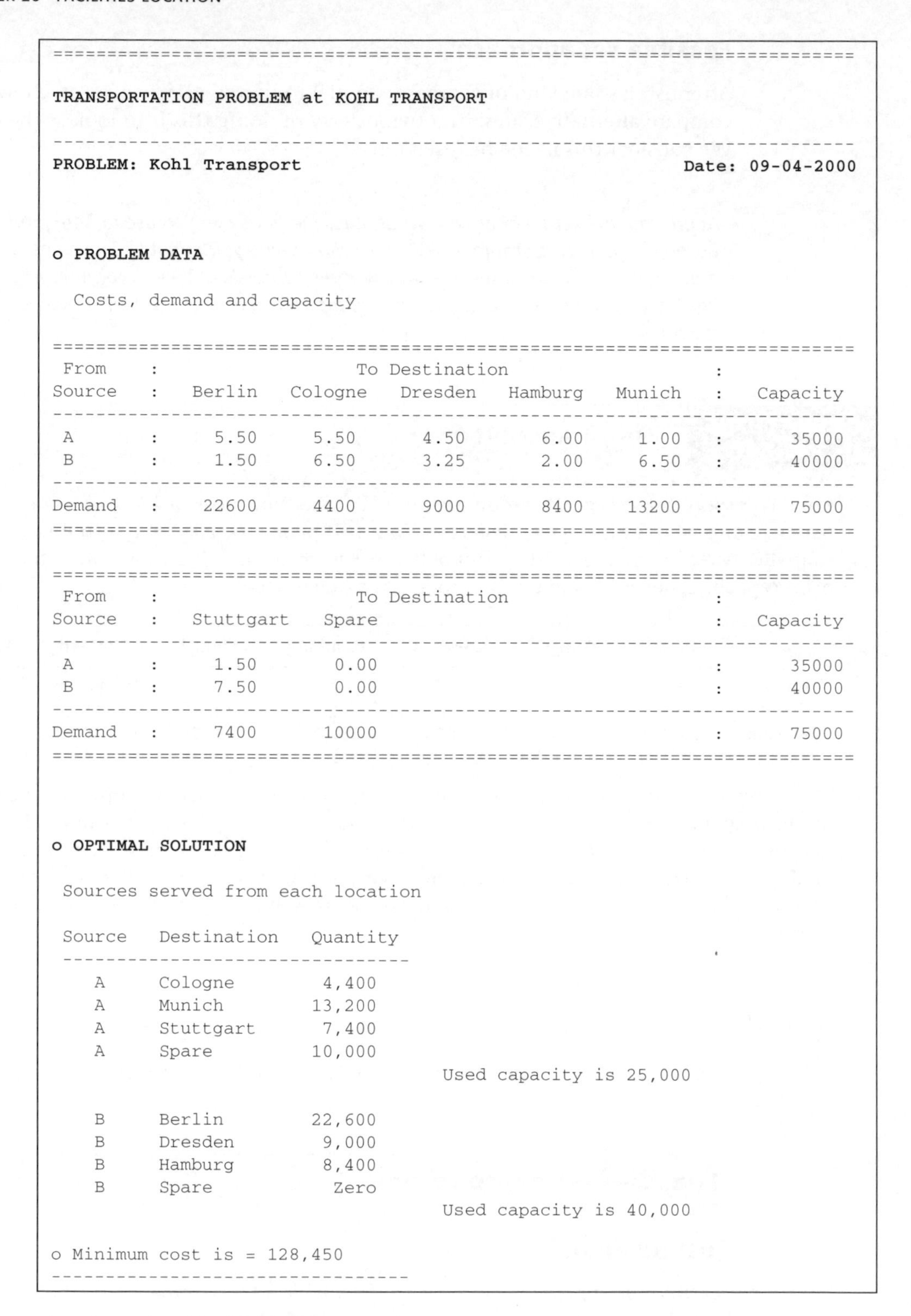

TRANSPORTATION PROBLEM at KOHL TRANSPORT

PROBLEM: Kohl Transport **Date: 09-04-2000**

o PROBLEM DATA

Costs, demand and capacity

From Source	To Destination: Berlin	Cologne	Dresden	Hamburg	Munich	Capacity
A	5.50	5.50	4.50	6.00	1.00	35000
B	1.50	6.50	3.25	2.00	6.50	40000
Demand	22600	4400	9000	8400	13200	75000

From Source	To Destination: Stuttgart	Spare	Capacity
A	1.50	0.00	35000
B	7.50	0.00	40000
Demand	7400	10000	75000

o OPTIMAL SOLUTION

Sources served from each location

Source	Destination	Quantity
A	Cologne	4,400
A	Munich	13,200
A	Stuttgart	7,400
A	Spare	10,000

Used capacity is 25,000

Source	Destination	Quantity
B	Berlin	22,600
B	Dresden	9,000
B	Hamburg	8,400
B	Spare	Zero

Used capacity is 40,000

o Minimum cost is = 128,450

Figure 20.6 Results for Kohl Transport

the location. Instead, we will concentrate on the costs that vary, and describe them as either *transport* or *operating* costs.

- **Inward transport costs** – the costs of delivering materials from suppliers to the facilities. If operations are concentrated in a few key locations, such as large factories, large deliveries are made to a few facilities and costs are low. If facilities are spread out in different locations, such as retail shops, smaller deliveries are made to more destinations and the inward transport costs are high.
- **Outward transport costs** – the costs of moving finished goods from facilities to customers. If operations are concentrated in a few large facilities they will, on average, be further away from customers and the outward transport costs are higher. If operations are spread out in more, smaller facilities, they are closer to customers and outward transport costs are low.
- **Operating costs**. Larger operations are generally more efficient than smaller ones, so operating costs are low with a few, large facilities and they rise with more, smaller ones.

We can get a direct comparison of sites by adding these three costs.

Total cost of transport facility = operating cost + inward transport cost
+ outward cost

Generally, sites near to suppliers have low costs for inward transport, but high costs of outward transport. On the other hand, sites near to customers have low costs for outward transport, but high costs for inward transport, as shown in Figure 20.7.

We can use similar reasoning to find the best number of facilities. If we plot the transport and operating costs against the number of facilities we get the pattern shown in Figure 20.8. This has a clear minimum which corresponds to the optimal number of facilities. In practice, of course, before we make such a decision we have to consider many other factors, such as management costs, communications, fixed costs, employment effects, customer service, information flows, and so on.

An obvious problem with this approach is that we do not know the real costs before we actually open a facility. How, for example, can we know the cost of

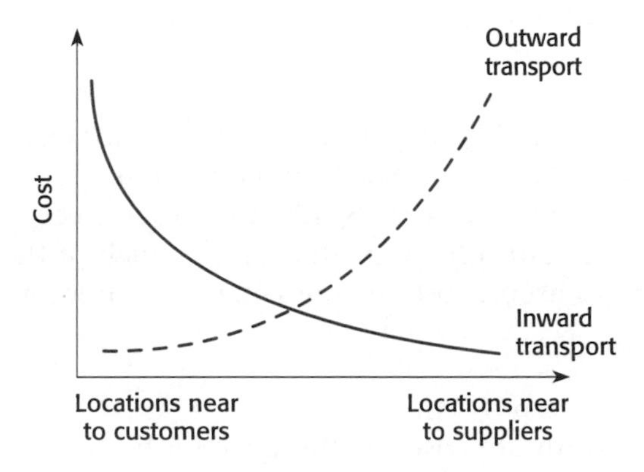

Figure 20.7 Variation in transport cost with location

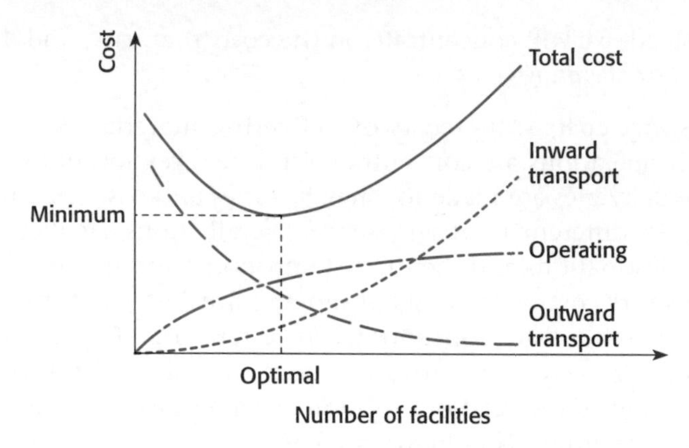

Figure 20.8 Variation in costs with number of facilities

outward transport when we do not know the customers and their demands with certainty before opening? Even if we have good forecasts of the costs, they are likely to change over time and the analysis will become outdated. As a result, these costs are useful for comparisons, and are not necessarily the costs that will actually be incurred.

If we are only using the costs for comparisons, we can make the calculations even easier. There is often little difference in operating costs between nearby locations, so we can remove these from the equation and concentrate on transport costs. It is difficult to find the exact cost of delivering to a particular customer, but we can measure the distance from the facility to the customer, and then assume that transport costs are proportional to this distance. In practice, the true costs of transport depend on more than distance, and are also affected by the type of vehicles, frequency of journeys, routes taken, ways of combining customer orders, organisation of drivers, order patterns, and so on. But we are only using these figures for comparison, so can use any reasonable approximations. A useful shortcut uses map references or co-ordinates to find the **rectilinear distance**.

$$\text{Rectilinear distance} = \text{difference in } X \text{ co-ordinates} + \text{difference in } Y \text{ co-ordinates}$$

WORKED EXAMPLE

Rondacorp Industries wants to build a depot to serve five major customers located at co-ordinates: (120, 120); (220, 120); (180, 180); (140, 160); (180, 120). Average weekly demands, in vehicle loads, are 20, 5, 8, 12 and 8 respectively. Two alternative locations are available at: (140, 120) and (180, 140). Which of these is better if operating costs and inward transport costs are the same for each location?

Solution

Figure 20.9 shows a map for this problem.

As operating and transport inward costs are the same for both locations, we only need a way of comparing the costs of local deliveries from each location, A and B. For simplicity we will use the rectilinear distance to customers. Then the distance from A to customer 1 is:

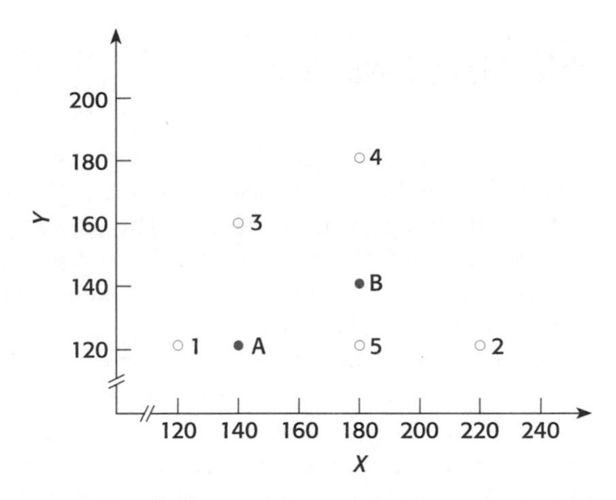

Figure 20.9 Locations for Rondacorp Industries

Difference in X co-ordinates + difference in Y co-ordinates
$= (140 - 120) + (120 - 120) = 20$

The calculations for this problem are given in the following spreadsheet, which shows that location A is clearly better.

Rondacorp Industries

Customer		A		B	
	Load	Distance	Dist*Load	Distance	Dist*Load
1	20	20	400	80	1600
2	5	80	400	60	300
3	8	100	800	40	320
4	12	40	480	60	720
5	8	40	320	20	160
Totals			**2400**		**3100**

Figure 20.10 Calculations for Rondacorp Industries

Costing models can give useful comparisons, but they have some weaknesses, including:

- it is difficult to find accurate costs;
- data depend on accounting conventions;
- costs vary over time;
- customer locations are not known in advance;
- the amount each customer will order is not known in advance;
- many factors cannot be costed.

Because of these weaknesses, it might be better to use some other methods for comparisons, such as scoring models, which are described in the next section.

OPERATIONS IN PRACTICE

Hamburg Double Glazed Windows

Hamburg Double Glazed Windows (HDGW) is one of Europe's largest manufacturers of high-quality uPVC windows. It ran three plants in Hamburg. The first plant was a plastics works where it made the uPVC and extruded the contours for window frames. The second plant was a glassworks where it made panes of glass. The third plant formed frames and glazing units, and then assembled them into finished windows. The first two plants were largely automated with little manual work, while the third plant was more labour intensive.

In 1997 the assembly works had serious labour problems, including a long strike by workers. After the strike was settled, the average wage rate in the plant was 50 per cent above the industrial average for Germany. HDGW was now a high-cost operation, and it looked for ways of increasing its competitiveness. Eventually, it decided to move the assembly works to a region with lower wage rates. After a long search, the company picked a site just outside Barcelona. The two main advantages of this site were:

- the Spanish government and European Union gave generous incentives;
- Barcelona had a pool of cheap, unskilled labour.

HDGW thought that it could save 5 million euros a year by this move.

HDGW estimated that it would take six months to move equipment from Hamburg to Barcelona, with another six months to iron out production problems. Most of the experienced managers accepted an early retirement package, 65 of the remaining 80 supervisors left the company rather than move, and all the hourly paid workers in the Hamburg assembly works were laid off.

HDGW hired 200 people in Barcelona with wages about a third of the German equivalent, but it soon hit language problems, as the unskilled workers spoke only Spanish, the managers who had moved spoke only German, and all the company's instructions and procedure manuals were in German. This language barrier caused serious problems with supervision, training and efficient operations. It soon became clear that language was only one symptom of major cultural differences. Productivity was much lower than expected and, consequently, labour costs were higher.

Some of the machines were damaged in the move, and the last phase of transfer from Hamburg was stopped rather than risk more damage. This decision was encouraged by the rising cost of oil which raised the cost of transporting materials between the plants.

Two years after the start of the relocation project there was still no end in sight to the company's problems. Its costs were even higher at a time when competitors were steadily improving their performance. The marketing department reported a continuing fall in market share.

Scoring models

There are many factors that are important to a location decision that cannot be included in a costing model. An attractive lifestyle in one location, for example, would certainly benefit employees, reduce employee turnover and assist in recruiting, but we could not assign a realistic cost to the lifestyle. There are other factors that may be important, but which are difficult to quantify:

In the region and country:

- availability, skills and productivity of workforce;
- climate;

- local and national government policies, regulations and attitudes;
- availability and conditions of development grants;
- attractiveness of locations;
- quality of life – including health, education, welfare and culture;
- location and reliability of local suppliers;
- location of local customers;
- infrastructure – particularly transport and communications;
- economic and political stability;
- culture and attitudes of people;

In the city or area:

- availability of sites and development issues;
- location of competitors;
- potential for expansion;
- local regulations and restrictions on operations;
- community feelings;
- local services, including utilities.

The easiest way of considering such non-quantifiable factors is to use a scoring model. We have already used these in Chapter 5 to compare different products, and will use exactly the same procedure for location decisions.

1. Decide the relevant factors in a decision.
2. Give each factor a maximum possible score that shows its importance.
3. Consider each location in turn and give an actual score for each factor.
4. Add the total score for each location and find the highest.
5. Discuss the result and make a final decision.

WORKED EXAMPLE

Jim Bowen is considering four alternative locations for a new electronics warehouse. After many discussions he has a list of important factors, their relative weights and the scores for each site. What is the relative importance of each factor? Which site would you recommend?

Factor	Maximum score	A	B	C	D
Climate	10	8	6	9	7
Infrastructure	20	12	16	15	8
Accessibility	10	6	8	7	9
Construction cost	5	3	1	4	2
Community attitude	10	6	8	7	4
Government views	5	2	2	3	4
Closeness to suppliers	15	10	10	13	13
Closeness to customers	20	12	10	15	17
Availability of workforce	5	1	2	4	5

Solution

The most important factors are the available infrastructure and closeness to customers. Jim has assigned up to 20 points each for these. The closeness of suppliers is a bit less important with up to 15 points, and then come climate, accessibility and community attitude with up to 10 points each. Construction cost, government views and availability of workforce are least important.

Adding the scores for each location gives:

Location	A	B	C	D
Total scores	60	63	77	69

These scores suggest that location C is the best. Jim must now consider all other relevant information before coming to a final decision.

Important factors for scoring models

The list of important factors and weight given to each obviously depends on the circumstances. Decisions about the location of a new factory, for example, are dominated by factors like:

- availability of a workforce with appropriate skills;
- labour relations and community attitudes;
- environment and quality of life for employees;
- closeness of suppliers and services;
- quality of infrastructure;
- government policies toward industry.

Manufacturers look for economies of scale by building large facilities that are often near to raw materials. On the other hand, services cannot keep stocks, so they look for locations that are near to their customers. Their decisions about location put more weight on factors like:

- population density;
- socio-economic characteristics of the nearby population;
- location of competitors and other services;
- location of retail shops and other attractions;
- convenience for passing traffic and public transport;
- ease of access and convenient parking;
- visibility of site.

The objectives in locating factories and services are clearly different, which is why town centres have shops, but no factories, while industrial estates have factories but no shops.

Review questions

20.10 What is the difference between a feasible set approach and an infinite set approach to facility location?

20.11 What costs might be included in a costing model?

20.12 What is the difference between inward transport and outward transport?

20.13 What are the benefits of using scoring models for location decisions?

20.14 Are the same factors important for locating a factory as locating a retail shop?

OPERATIONS IN PRACTICE

Intel in Costa Rica

Deloitte & Touche Fantus have listed the factors that high-tech industries consider in their location decisions. These include factors which are essential, important and desirable.

- *Essential factors*:
  - skilled and educated workforce;
  - proximity of research institutions;
  - attractive quality of life;
  - access to venture capital.
- *Important factors*:
  - reasonable cost of doing business;
  - established technology industry;
  - adequate infrastructure;
  - favourable business climate and regulations.
- *Desirable factors*:
  - established suppliers and partners;
  - community incentives.

Intel Corporation is the world's leading producer of semiconductor devices. In the mid-1990s it was planning a new expansion, and Costa Rica was keen to get the development. To encourage Intel, Costa Rica offered eight years free of income tax, followed by four years at half rate, duty-free import of materials and unrestricted movement of money into and out of the country. In addition, the country granted more licences to foreign airlines to increase the number of international flights, built a new power sub-station for the site, reduced the cost of electricity by 28 per cent, and reduced the liability for corporation tax.

Intel decided to locate a $300 million semiconductor testing and assembly plant near to San Jose, and this started work in 1998 and within two years employed 2,000 people.

Chuck Mulloy, a spokesman for Intel, said: 'When we are considering a site we use a multi-faceted set of criteria. Incentives are part of this.'

Sources: (2000) *Wall Street Journal Special Report*, September 25; Website at: *www.interactive.wsj.com*

Location planning

We have described several approaches to location, but these are by no means the only alternatives. There are many mathematical models for finding 'optimal' solutions to specific problems. Typically these will find the best location and routes through a network of roads. As the models take a simplified view of operations, they do not find the best real solution, but they give some valuable information for managers to consider. Other methods combine road maps with sophisticated databases, and give detailed analyses of locations. Route planners, such as Microsoft AutoRoute Express and Softkey Journey Planner, find the shortest road distance between two points, and specialised software extends these ideas to find locations that minimise total travel distances or achieve some other objectives. These programs often include simulation of the supply chain to show how it will work in practice.

Whichever methods are used to help with location, they need not be used in isolation. Locating facilities is a difficult problem, and organisations should look at every available analysis before reaching a conclusion.

Changing the location of facilities will clearly make changes in the supply chain. We must, therefore, fit location decisions into broader plans for the supply chain. One useful approach to this extends the planning that we met in Chapter 12. This checks what we want the supply chain to do, examines the current supply chain's performance, identifies mismatches, and designs ways of overcoming these. In more detail, we can proceed as follows:

- *Step 1. Examine the aims*, finding the aims and goals of logistics in terms of customer service, costs, speed, etc.
- *Step 2. Do a logistics audit*, describing the details of the current logistics system, including the location of facilities, network connecting these, measures of performance, and industry benchmarks.
- *Step 3. Identify mismatches*, where there are differences between the aims (from step 1) and actual performance (from step 2).
- *Step 4. Examine alternatives for overcoming the mismatch*, looking in general terms to see if the structure of the supply chain can be improved to give better performance. In particular, we identify parts of the supply chain that must be changed.
- *Step 5. Location decisions*, having set the general features of the supply chain, we look in detail at the facilities needed. Here we concentrate on alternative sizes and locations.
- *Step 6. Find the best options*, confirming the best alternatives, and making sure that the locations identified in step 5 work with the structure identified in step 4.
- *Step 7. Implement and monitor the solutions*, doing whatever is needed to execute the changes and continuing to check performance.

In this procedure step 4 designs the general features of the supply chains, while step 5 finds the best locations to fit into this. As with most plans, this is not a straightforward procedure but involves looping until a satisfactory solution is agreed (see Figure 20.11).

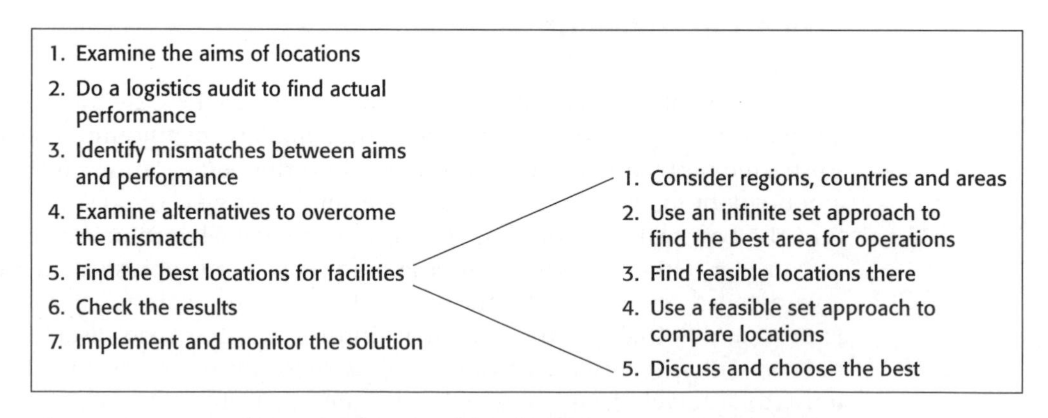

Figure 20.11 Overall approach to location decisions

The location models we have described fit into step 5. This itself is not a simple procedure, which can be tackled in several ways. We can combine these approaches to give the following approach to the specific location decisions.

1. Identify the features needed in a new location, determined by the structure of the supply chain, the business strategy, and any other factors. Look for regions and countries that can best supply these.
2. Use an infinite set approach, such as the centre of gravity or similar model, to find the best area for locating facilities.
3. Search around this area to find a feasible set of alternative locations.
4. Use a feasible set approach, such as a costing model or scoring model, to compare these alternatives.
5. Discuss all available information and come to a decision.

Review questions

20.15 What determines the best location for a facility?

20.16 Location decisions are generally strategic. Do you think this is right?

Chapter review

- Organisations often have to find the best locations for facilities. These are important, strategic decisions with long-term effects on their success.
- A location decision is needed whenever an organisation expands, contracts, or there are major changes to its operations. There are alternatives to opening new facilities, such as licensing and exporting.
- Choosing the best location involves a hierarchy of decisions. These start with a decision about the region or country to work in. Choices here are strongly influenced by the business strategy.
- After making general choices about location, an organisation has to move through decisions about the best area, town and eventually specific site.
- We described two approaches to location decisions. The first uses geometrical arguments to suggest where the best location would be in principle, regardless of site availability. We illustrated this with the centre of gravity method.
- The second approach compares a limited number of feasible locations and finds the best. We illustrated this by costing and scoring models.
- Location decisions are made within the context of the broader supply chain. We described a general approach to this planning, and showed how different models are often used together.

Key terms

centre of gravity *p. 584*
costing models *p. 587*
facilities location *p. 576*
feasible set *p. 584*
geometric models *p. 584*
hierarchy of location decisions *p. 580*
infinite set *p. 584*
new markets *p. 580*
planning the supply chain *p. 595*
rectilinear distance *p. 590*
scoring models *p. 592*

CASE STUDY Authwaite Auto Sales

Richard Authwaite worked for the same car sales firm for over 25 years before starting his own business. He saw an advertisement from an eastern European car manufacturer that wanted to start selling in Britain. Richard answered the advertisement and spent a year negotiating with the manufacturer.

The manufacturer was not keen to have all its distribution done by a new and untried company. In the end Richard agreed to set up a company called Authwaite Auto Sales, and the manufacturer agreed to give him exclusive rights to distribute its cars throughout Britain for two years. The agreement would be reviewed after a year and renegotiated after two years.

Richard invited three other directors to join the company. Their first problem is to find a location for the head office and main showroom. In the long term the company plans to open a series of facilities around Britain, but now it needs a location for its first 'flagship' site. The directors realise that their future success depends on how well this first site operates, but are finding it difficult to agree on a location.

They considered passing the problem to a firm of management consultants, but one of the directors found that similar companies paid up to £50,000 for an initial report and £125,000 for a more detailed study. The directors felt that this was too expensive and they would have to solve the problem themselves. The following summary gives an idea of their discussions.

- Gordon Mikaluk left school at 16, and worked as a car mechanic for many years before being promoted to service manager. He is now 54 years old and is looking for an opportunity to make some money for his retirement.

  Gordon argues that the location should be in Manchester. The cars could be shipped by sea to Liverpool and then brought to Manchester by train. There are good handling facilities in Manchester and the transport would be easy and efficient. In addition, Manchester is a large city that could meet the large potential market in the North of the country. The four directors all live in Manchester and they understand local conditions.
- Sarah Precik has a degree in mechanical engineering. She worked in the oil industry for many years before becoming a mining consultant in eastern Europe. She speaks fluent Hungarian and Polish, with some Russian. During her travels she became interested in the car industry and when she returned to Britain she worked on manufacturing and design problems for Ford.

  Sarah is critical of Gordon's approach as being old fashioned and relying more on where he feels at home than on any business criterion. She says that the sale of cars is likely to depend on the population so they should look at a map of Britain, see where the main centres of population are, see how many cars they expect to sell in each of these, and then do some fairly straightforward analyses to find the best location.

- Dennis MacGregor worked in banking and insurance where he specialised in fleet financing. He is now 32 years old and is ambitiously looking for a long-term career that is both challenging and financially rewarding.

  Dennis does not like the idea of opening a single location to see if it works, but suggests they set up a comprehensive distribution network as quickly as possible. This would include head offices – perhaps in London – a central receiving area near to a rail terminal, and showrooms around Britain. The fastest way of doing this is to take over an existing dealer, or several dealers, to give coverage throughout the country.
- Richard Authwaite says that Dennis MacGregor's scheme is too ambitious, while the other two put the convenience of the company above that of the customers. He says that there is only one way to sell cars and that is to give customers a product they want in a location they can get to. Richard's idea is to see where successful distributors already have their showrooms, and open-up nearby. In particular, he would look for a large dominating location that customers can see from a long way off, that they pass frequently, where they would go to buy cars, and where other distributors have traditionally been able to sell.

The time is now getting short for a decision. The directors are concerned that if they delay any longer the manufacturer will consider them indecisive, and they will not have time to give a good showing at their first year's review. To build entirely new premises could take a year. Alternatively, they could find existing premises that are empty, or they could rent temporary premises until the company finds more suitable, permanent premises.

Questions

- If you were a director of Authwaite Auto Sales, what would you do now?
- What factors are important in the location decision?
- What location – or locations – would you recommend?

Problems

20.1 George Ellison Limited manufactures 60 tonnes of goods a week in factory A and 40 tonnes a week in factory B. The map co-ordinates of these factories are (8, 9) and (52, 47) respectively. These goods are delivered to twelve main customers whose average weekly requirements and co-ordinates are shown below. The company wants to improve its customer service and decides to open a distribution centre. There are four possible locations, each with the same operating costs, located at: (20, 8); (61, 19); (29, 32); (50, 22). Which of these locations is best?

Customer	Average	Co-ordinates	Customer	Demand	Co-ordinates
1	4	(11, 16)	7	16	(12, 69)
2	11	(30, 9)	8	2	(27, 38)
3	8	(43, 27)	9	4	(51, 6)
4	7	(54, 52)	10	6	(43, 16)
5	17	(29, 62)	11	3	(54, 16)
6	10	(11, 51)	12	12	(12, 60)

20.2 A new electronics factory is planned in an area that is encouraging industrial growth. There are five alternative sites. A management team is considering these sites and has suggested the important factors, relative weights and site scores shown below. What is the relative importance of each factor? Which site appears best?

Factor	Maximum Score	Scores for sites A	B	C	D	E
Government grants	10	2	4	8	8	5
Community attitude	12	8	7	5	10	5
Availability of engineers	15	10	8	8	10	5
Experienced workforce	20	20	15	15	10	15
Nearby suppliers	8	4	3	6	3	2
Education centres	5	5	4	1	1	5
Housing	5	2	3	5	3	2

Some people prefer to fix the maximum score at 100, and then show the relative importance of each factor by multiplying the scores by a factor weight. How would the scores presented change with this format?

20.3 Find the centre of gravity of the data in question 20.1. What would be the cost of transport for a distribution centre located there? Can you find a cheaper solution?

20.4 An assembly plant is planned to take components from four suppliers and send finished goods to eight regional warehouses. The locations of these and the amounts supplied or demanded are shown in the following table. Where would you start looking for a site for the assembly plant?

Location	*X,Y* co-ordinates	Supply/Demand
Supplier 1	7, 80	140
Supplier 2	85, 35	80
Supplier 3	9, 81	120
Supplier 4	11, 62	70
Warehouse 1	12, 42	45
Warehouse 2	60, 9	65
Warehouse 3	92, 94	25
Warehouse 4	8, 79	45
Warehouse 5	10, 83	60
Warehouse 6	59, 91	35
Warehouse 7	83, 49	50
Warehouse 8	85, 30	85

Discussion questions

20.1 If a company chooses a poor site it can always move to a better one. Such change is an unavoidable part of business. To what extent is this true? If is true, should location decisions really be considered as strategic?

20.2 Which areas of the world do you think will develop most quickly over the next 20 years? What effects will this have on the world economy? How will this affect location decisions?

20.3 What costs should be considered in a location decision? Is cost always an important factor? What other factors should be considered? What factors are important in locating a professional service, such as a doctor's surgery?

20.4 What factors are most likely to affect a manufacturer's decision to locate a factory? What kind of government incentives might make an area more attractive?

20.5 Find some examples of location decisions you are familiar with. How were these locations chosen? How successful have they been?

20.6 What features would you expect to see in computer software that helps with location decisions? Do a survey of relevant packages. How do they work, and what analyses do they do?

20.7 Different cultures are the main problems of locating facilities in different countries. They make it impossible to standardise procedures, have consistent operations, compare performance, or anything else. Do you think this is true?

20.8 How does the business strategy affect location decisions?

Selected reading

Coyle J.J., Bardi E.J. and Langley C.J. (1996) *The Management of Business Logistics*. 6th edn. St Paul, MN: West.

Drezner Z. (1995) *Facility Location: a Survey of Applications and Methods*. Secausus, NJ: Springer-Verlag.

Harrington J.W. and Warf B. (1995) *Industrial Location: Principles and Practice*. London: Routledge.

Hayter R. (1997) *The Dynamics of Industrial Location*. New York: John Wiley.

Johnson J.C. and Wood D.F. (1990) *Contemporary Logistics*. 4th edn. New York: Macmillan.

Salvaneschi L. and Akin C. (eds) (1996) *Location, Location, Location: How to Select the Best Site for your Business*. Central Point, OR: Oasis Press.

Schriederjans M.J. (1999) *International Facility Acquisition and Location Analysis*. Westpoint, CT: Quorum Books.

Waters C.D.J. (1999) *Global Logistics and Distribution Planning*. London: Kogan Page.

Useful Websites

www.nam.org – National Association of Manufacturers

www.conway/wcbss – Site Selection magazine

CHAPTER 21

Managing stocks

Inventory is evil.
The sayings of Shigeo Shingo
Productivity Press, Cambridge, MA, 1985

Contents

Aims of the chapter

After reading this chapter you should be able to:

- appreciate the need for various kinds of stock;
- analyse the costs of holding stock;
- use a model for independent demand inventory systems;
- calculate economic order quantities;
- calculate associated lead times, costs and cycle lengths;
- appreciate the need for safety stock;
- define 'service level' and do related calculations;
- describe periodic review systems and calculate target stock levels;
- do ABC analyses of inventories.

Main themes

This chapter will emphasise:

- **stocks**, which are materials kept in store until they are needed;
- **stores**, which are responsible for keeping stocks;
- **inventory control**, which defines ordering policies to control stocks.

Stocks and warehouses

Reasons for holding stocks

Chapter 18 described just-in-time systems, which view any stock as a waste of resources that should be eliminated. Efficient customer response (ECR) and e-commerce can pull materials quickly through a supply chain, and eliminate most of the traditional stocks. You might get the impression that every organisation is eliminating stocks and moving to 'stockless' operations. In practice, of course, many operations cannot work in this way. Farmers grow one crop of hay a year, and then store it to feed animals throughout the year. A distiller stores barrels of whisky for at least three years before selling it. A video store buys copies of videos and keeps them in stock until people want to hire them. The aim for these organisations is not to eliminate stocks, but to control them properly. In this chapter we shall describe an approach to stock control.

Stocks are supplies of goods and materials that are held by an organisation.

- They are formed whenever the organisation's inputs or outputs are not used at the time they become available.

All organisations hold stocks of some kind. When a filling station gets a delivery of petrol from a tanker, it is put into stock until a customer buys it; when a factory moves finished goods to a warehouse, they are put into stock; when a restaurant buys vegetables, they join the inventory until delivered with a meal. There are always costs of holding stocks – to cover warehouse operations, tied-up capital, deterioration, insurance, etc. – so an obvious question is: Why do organisations hold stock? There are several answers to this, but the usual one is: To give a buffer between supply and demand.

Imagine the supplies being delivered to a supermarket. These are delivered in large quantities, perhaps a truckload at a time. But they are sold to customers in much smaller quantities. The result is a stock of goods that is replenished with every delivery, and is reduced over time to meet demand. These stocks give a cushion against unexpected variations in supply and demand. They allow the supermarket to continue working when delivery vehicles are delayed, poor quality materials are rejected, there is some disruption at the supplier – or when there is unexpectedly high demand from customers.

The main purpose of stocks is to act as a buffer between supply and demand.

- They allow operations to continue smoothly and avoid disruptions.

In more detail, stocks:

- act as a buffer between different operations;
- allow for demands that are larger than expected, or at unexpected times;

- allow for deliveries that are delayed or too small;
- take advantage of price discounts on large orders;
- allow the purchase of items when the price is low and expected to rise;
- allow the purchase of items that are going out of production or are difficult to find;
- make full loads and reduce transport costs;
- give cover for emergencies.

OPERATIONS IN PRACTICE

Stock holdings

Tesco

Tesco is the largest food retailer in the UK, where it has 16 per cent of the market. It also operates in central Europe and the Far East. Its annual report for 2000 showed:

Total sales	£20,385 million
Fixed assets	£8,527 million
Number of stores	845
Total sales area	24 million sq. feet
Stocks	£744 million

IBM

For many years IBM has been a leader in the computer industry. In 2000 IBM's revenue was $87.5 billion, and it held £3.7 billion of stocks of work-in-progress and $1.2 billion of stocks of finished goods.

ICI

ICI is a major chemical company, with four major divisions: National Starch, Quest, Industrial Specialities and Paints. In the first half of 2000 it reported a trading profit of £275 million, on a turnover of £3788 million. Its assets were valued at £7,305 million, of which £920 million were stocks.

L.T. Francis

L.T. Francis is a manufacturer of pre-cast concrete fittings for the building trade. Its 2000 annual report showed sales of £14 million and total stocks of £2.4 million.

Summary

As you can see, these organisations hold large stocks. In Tesco the stock is around 4 per cent of sales, in IBM about 7 per cent in total, in ICI it is 11 per cent for the full year, and in L.T. Francis it is 17 per cent. Many organisations have very high stocks, and it is not unusual for manufacturers to hold 25 per cent of annual sales.

Sources: annual reports and company Websites: *www.tesco.com*, *www.ICI.com* and *www.ibm.com*

Types of stock

Just about everything is held as stock somewhere, whether it is raw materials in a factory, finished goods in a shop or tins of baked beans in a pantry. We can classify these stocks as:

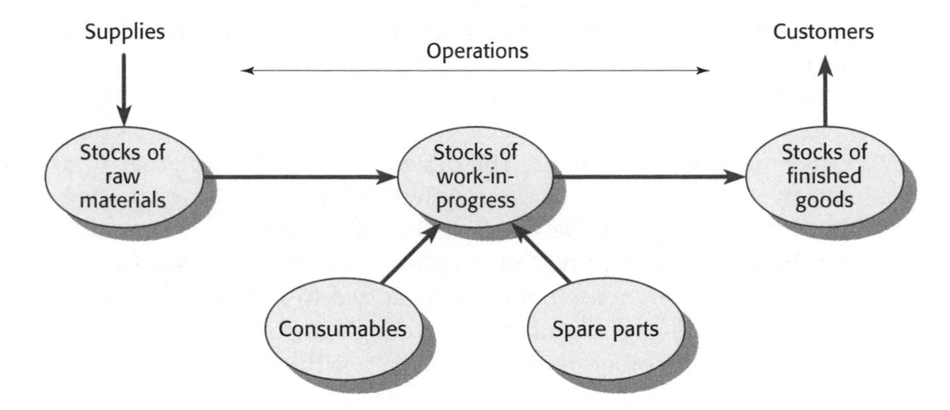

Figure 21.1 Types of stock holdings

- **raw materials**: the materials, parts and components that have been delivered to an organisation, but are not yet being used;
- **work-in-progress**: materials that have started, but not yet finished their journey through the production process;
- **finished goods**: goods that have finished the process and are waiting to be shipped out to customers.

This is a fairly arbitrary classification, as one company's finished goods are another company's raw materials. Some organisations, notably retailers and wholesalers, have stocks of finished goods only, while others, like manufacturers, have all three types in different proportions. Nationally, around 30 per cent of stocks are raw materials, 40 per cent work-in-progress and 30 per cent finished goods.[1] Some stock items do not fall easily into these categories, and we can define two additional types:

- **spare parts** for machinery, equipment, etc.;
- **consumables**, such as oil, fuel, paper, etc.

For convenience we will assume that stocks are held in **stores**. Some organisations do not have special stores, but keep stocks close to operations. Other organisations co-ordinate collections and deliveries so that they effectively have 'stock on wheels'. Some stocks, such as data and knowledge, do not involve physical storage. Despite this apparent diversity, there are many similarities, and we can describe some common principles.

In a supply chain, most stores are kept in warehouse between different stages. These warehouses are known by a variety of names, including logistics centres and distribution centres. There are several ways of organising warehousing. An organisation can obviously buy or build its own facilities. This has the advantages of greater control over stocks, tailoring the building to specific needs, and having the warehouse in the right location, but the disadvantages of high costs and needing expertise that the organisation might not have. Smaller organisations usually find private warehousing too expensive, and they use the alternative public warehousing. Then there are, again, several ways of organising this. For the short term, it is possible to rent or lease space in a public warehouse. For the longer term an organisation might use a contract provider who takes over the running of the stock. Then the organisation delivers and collects materials as it needs them, but leaves the details of storage to a specialist.

As we saw in Chapter 11, warehouses come in many different forms. Small ones have people moving small packages around; big ones have computer-controlled cranes moving heavy items. The design of a warehouse is set to achieve different objectives. The baggage-handling system at an airport is designed to move relatively light cases very quickly between planes and passengers. A wine cellar is designed to keep bottles of wine in perfect condition until they are needed, perhaps in several years' time. A warehouse might be organised to minimise the overall cost of stock, achieve a specified stock turnover, give high customer service, respond to demands quickly, or some other objective. The rest of this chapter describes an approach to this problem.

In Chapter 15 we met one way of controlling stocks of materials, which used material requirements planning (MRP). We said that this was a **dependent demand system**, where the demand for an item is found directly from a master schedule. The alternative approach looks at an **independent demand system**, where the total demand for an item is made up of lots of separate demands that are not related to each other. The overall demand for bread in a supermarket, for example, is made up of lots of demands from separate customers who (usually) act independently. Independent demand systems try to balance various costs, so we should start by taking a closer look at these.

Costs of carrying stock

The total cost of holding stock is typically around 25 per cent of its value a year. A reasonable objective is to minimise this cost. You might think, especially after the lessons of just-in-time, that minimising costs is the same as minimising stocks, but this is not necessarily true. If a shop holds no stock at all, it certainly has no inventory costs, but it also has no sales; it effectively incurs another cost of losing customers. We can divide the overall costs of holding stock into four separate components.

1. **Unit cost**: the price of an item charged by the supplier, or the cost to the organisation of acquiring one unit of the item. It may be fairly easy to find this by looking at quotations or recent invoices from suppliers, but it is more difficult when there are several suppliers offering slightly different products or offering different purchase conditions. If a company makes the item itself, it may be difficult to give a reliable production cost or set a transfer price.

2. **Reorder cost**: the cost of placing a repeat order for an item. This might include allowances for preparing an order, correspondence, receiving, unloading, checking, testing, use of equipment and follow-up. Sometimes, costs such as quality control, transport, sorting and movement of received goods are included. In practice, the best estimate for a reorder cost often comes from dividing the total annual cost of the purchasing department by the number of orders it sends out.

When a company makes an item itself, the reorder cost might be an internal transfer cost, or a batch set-up cost (including production lost while resetting machines, idle time of operators, material spoilt in test runs, time of specialist tool setters, and so on).

3. **Holding cost**: the cost of holding one unit of an item in stock for a unit period of time, for example, the cost to Air France of holding a spare engine in stock for a year. The obvious cost is tied-up money. This is either borrowed (in which case there are interest payments) or it is cash that could be put to other uses (in which case there are opportunity costs). Other holding costs are for storage space, loss, handling, special treatment (such as refrigeration), administration and insurance. It is difficult to give typical values for these, but a guideline for annual costs as a percentage of unit cost is as follows:

	Percentage of unit cost
Cost of money	10–15
Storage space	2–5
Loss	4–6
Handling	1–2
Administration	1–2
Insurance	1–5
Total	**19–35**

4. **Shortage cost**: occurs when an item is needed but it cannot be supplied from stock. In the simplest case a retailer loses direct profit from a sale, but the effects of shortages are usually more widespread and include lost goodwill, loss of reputation and loss of potential future sales. Shortages of raw materials for production can cause disruption, rescheduling of production, re-timing of maintenance periods and laying-off employees.

Shortage costs might also include payments for positive action to remedy the shortage, such as expediting orders, sending out emergency orders, paying for special deliveries, storing partly finished goods or using more expensive suppliers.

It can be difficult to get figures for any inventory costs, but shortage costs are a particular problem. These can include so many intangible factors, such as lost goodwill, that it is difficult to agree a reasonable value. Most organisations take the view that shortages are expensive, so it is generally better to avoid them. In other words, they are willing to pay the relatively lower carrying costs to avoid the relatively higher shortage costs.

WORKED EXAMPLE

Janet Long is a purchasing clerk at Overton Travel Group. She earns £14,000 a year, with other employment costs of £3,000, and has a budget of £5,200 for the telephone, stationery and postage. In a typical month Janet places 100 orders. When goods arrive there is an inspection that costs about £15 an order. The cost of borrowing money is 12 per cent, the obsolescence rate is 5 per cent and insurance and other costs average 4 per cent. How can Overton estimate its reorder and holding costs?

Solution

The total number of orders a year is 12 × 100 = 1,200 orders.

- The reorder cost includes all costs that occur for an order. These are:
  Salary = £14,000/1,200 = £11.67 an order.
  Employment costs = £3,000/1,200 = £2.50 an order.
  Expenses = £5,200/1,200 = £4.33 an order.
  Inspection = £15 an order.

So the reorder cost is 11.67 + 2.50 + 4.33 + 15 = £33.50 an order.

- Holding costs include all costs that occur for holding stock. These are:
  Borrowing = 12 per cent.
  Obsolescence = 5 per cent.
  Insurance and taxes = 4 per cent.

So the holding cost is 12 + 5 + 4 = 21 per cent of inventory value a year.

Approaches to inventory control

Inventory control looks for the best balance between these costs. It does this by answering three basic questions.

1. **What items should we stock?** No item, however cheap, should be stocked without considering the costs and benefits. This means that an organisation should stop unnecessary, new items being added to stock, and it should make regular searches to remove obsolete or dead stock.
2. **When should we place an order?** This depends on the inventory control system used, type of demand (high or low, steady or erratic, known exactly or estimated), value of the item, lead time between placing an order and receiving it into stock, supplier reliability, and a number of other factors.
3. **How much should we order?** Large, infrequent orders give high average stock level, but low costs for placing and administering orders: small, frequent orders give low average stocks, but high costs of placing and administering orders.

The first of these questions is a matter of good housekeeping, simply avoiding stock that is not needed. The following section looks for answers to the last two questions.

Review questions

21.1 What is the main reason for holding stock?

21.2 How can you classify stock holdings?

21.3 List four types of cost associated with stocks.

21.4 How do these costs vary with the amount held?

21.5 List three basic questions for inventory control systems.

Economic order quantity

Finding the order size

The **economic order quantity** (EOQ) was developed early last century[2–4] and has remained a dominant theme for stock control of independent demand systems.

Imagine a single item, held in stock to meet a constant demand of D per unit time. We will assume that unit cost (U), reorder cost (R) and holding cost (H) are all known exactly, while the shortage cost is so high that all demands must be met

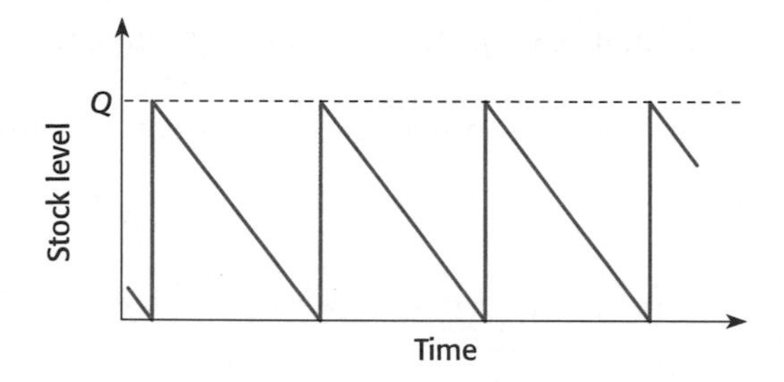

Figure 21.2 Saw-tooth pattern of stock holdings

and no shortages are allowed. The item is bought in batches from a supplier who delivers after a constant lead time. We are going to find the best order quantity, Q, and will always place orders of this size. There is no point in carrying spare stock, so we will time orders to arrive just as existing stock runs out. Then we get a series of **stock cycles**, with the saw-tooth pattern shown in Figure 21.2.

At some point an order of size Q arrives. This is used at a constant rate, D, until no stock is left. We can find the total cost for the cycle by adding the four components of cost: unit, reorder, holding and shortage. No shortages are allowed, so we can ignore this cost, and the cost of buying the item is constant regardless of the ordering policy, so we can also leave the unit cost out of the calculations. The supplement to this chapter shows that the cost per unit time is:

$$\begin{aligned} C &= \text{total reorder costs} + \text{total holding costs} \\ &= RD/Q + HQ/2 \end{aligned}$$

If we plot these two parts separately against Q, we get the results shown in Figure 21.3. From this graph you can see that:

- the total holding cost rises linearly with order size;
- the total reorder cost falls as the order quantity increases;
- large infrequent orders give high total holding costs and low total reorder costs;
- small frequent orders give low total holding costs and high total reorder costs;

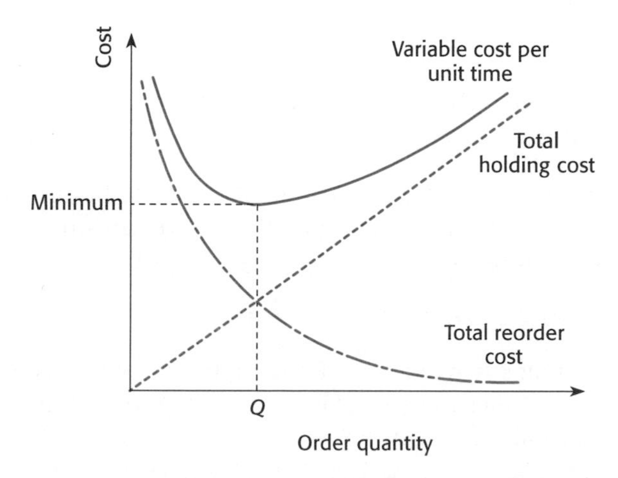

Figure 21.3 Varying cost with order quantity

- adding the two costs gives a total cost curve that is an asymmetric 'U' shape with a distinct minimum;
- this minimum cost shows the optimal order size, which is the **economic order quantity, EOQ.**

$$\text{Economic order quantity, } Q = \sqrt{\frac{2RD}{H}}$$

Where: D = demand
R = reorder cost
H = holding cost

WORKED EXAMPLE

John Pritchard buys stationery for Penwynn Motors. The demand for printed forms is constant at 20 boxes a month. Each box of forms costs £50, the cost of processing an order and arranging delivery is £60, and holding cost is £18 a box a year. What are the economic order quantity, cycle length and costs?

Solution

Listing the values we know in consistent units:

$D = 20 \times 12 = 240$ units a year
$U = £50$ a unit
$R = £60$ an order
$H = £18$ a unit a year.

- Substituting these values into the economic order quantity gives:

$$Q = \sqrt{\frac{2RD}{H}} = \sqrt{\frac{2 \times 60 \times 240}{18}} = 40 \text{ units}$$

- Then the variable cost is:

C = total reorder costs + total holding costs = $RD/Q + HQ/2$
$= 60 \times 240/40 + 18 \times 40/2 \quad = 360 + 360 \quad = £720$ a year

You can see that here the total reorder costs equal the total holding costs. This is always true if we order the economic order quantity, so we can simplify the calculation to twice the total holding cost or:

$C = HQ = 18 \times 40 = £720$

- We also have to consider the fixed cost of buying boxes, which is the number of boxes bought a year, D, times the cost of each box, U. Adding this to the variable cost above, gives the total stock cost:

Total cost = $UD + C = 50 \times 240 + 720 = £12,720$ a year

- We can find the cycle length from $Q = DT$, or $T = Q/D$:

$$T = Q/D = 40/240 = 1/6 \text{ years or two months}$$

The best policy, with total costs of £12,720 a year, is to order 40 boxes of paper every two months.

Finding the time to place orders

When an organisation buys materials, there is a **lead time** between placing the order and having them arrive in stock. This is the time taken to prepare an order, send it to the supplier, allow the supplier to make or assemble the materials and prepare them for shipment, ship the goods back to the customer, allow the customer to receive and check the materials and put them into stock. Depending on circumstances, this lead time can vary between a few minutes and months or even years. As we have seen with just-in-time systems, the trend is clearly towards shorter lead times.

Suppose the lead time, L, is constant. To make sure that a delivery arrives just as stock is running out, we have to place an order a time L earlier. The easiest way of finding this point is to monitor current stock and place an order when there is just enough left to last the lead time. With constant demand, D, this means that we place an order when the stock level falls to LD, and this point is called the **reorder level**.

Reorder level = lead time demand = lead time × demand

$$ROL = LD$$

Stock control is almost always computerised, so the computer keeps a continuous record of the stock on hand, updating this with every transaction and sending a message when it is time to place an order. Sometimes it is easier to use a manual **two-bin system**. This keeps stock in two bins: the first bin holds the reorder level and the second bin holds all the rest of the stock. Demand is met from the second bin until it is empty. At this point the stock level has fallen to the reorder level and it is time to place an order. When the order arrives, the first bin is filled to the reorder level, and all the rest of the delivery is put in the second bin.

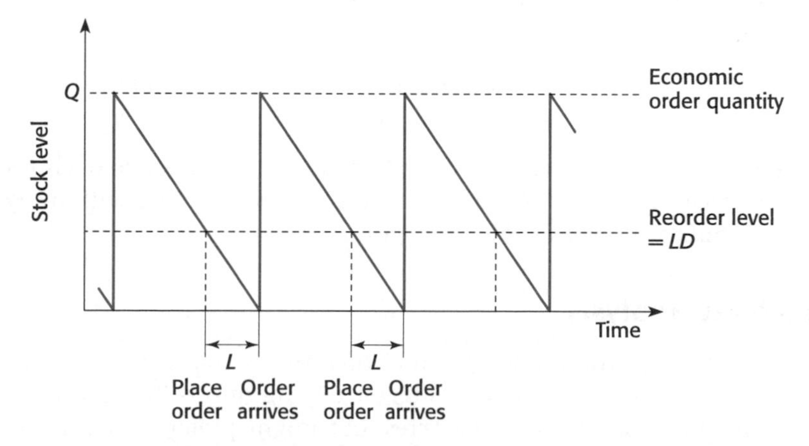

Figure 21.4 Place orders when stock falls to the reorder level

WORKED EXAMPLE

Demand for an item is constant at 20 units a week, the reorder cost is £125 an order and holding cost is £2 an unit a week. If suppliers guarantee delivery within two weeks, what is the best ordering policy for the item?

Solution

Listing the variables in consistent units:

D = 20 units a week
R = £125 an order
H = £2 a unit a week
L = 2 weeks

Substituting these gives:

$$Q = \sqrt{\frac{2RD}{H}} = \sqrt{\frac{2 \times 125 \times 20}{2}} = 50 \text{ units}$$

$$\text{Reorder level} = \text{lead time} \times \text{demand} = LD = 2 \times 20 = 40 \text{ units}$$

The best policy is to place an order for 50 units whenever stock falls to 40 units.

This calculation works well provided the lead time is less than the length of a stock cycle. In the last example the lead time was two weeks and the stock cycle was 50/20 = 2.5 weeks. Suppose the lead time is raised to three weeks. The calculation for reorder level then becomes:

$$\text{Reorder level} = \text{lead time} \times \text{demand} = LD = 3 \times 20 = 60 \text{ units}$$

The problem is that the stock level never actually rises to 60 units, but varies between 0 and 50 units. The way around this problem is to recognise that the calculated reorder level refers to both stock on hand and stock on order. Then the reorder level equals lead time demand minus any stock that is already on order. In the example above, the order quantity is 50 units, so a lead time of three weeks would have one order of 50 units outstanding when it is time to place another order. Then:

$$\begin{aligned}\text{Reorder level} &= \text{lead time demand} - \text{stock on order} = LD - Q \\ &= 3 \times 20 - 50 = 10 \text{ units}\end{aligned}$$

An order for 50 units should be placed whenever actual stock declines to 10 units. Because the lead time is longer than the stock cycle, there will always be at least one order outstanding, as shown in Figure 21.5.

Sensitivity analysis

One problem with the economic order quantity is that it can give awkward order quantities. It might, for example, suggest buying impossible figures, such as 88.39 tyres. We could round this to 88 tyres, but might prefer to order 90 or even 100. We really need to know whether this rounding has much effect on overall costs.

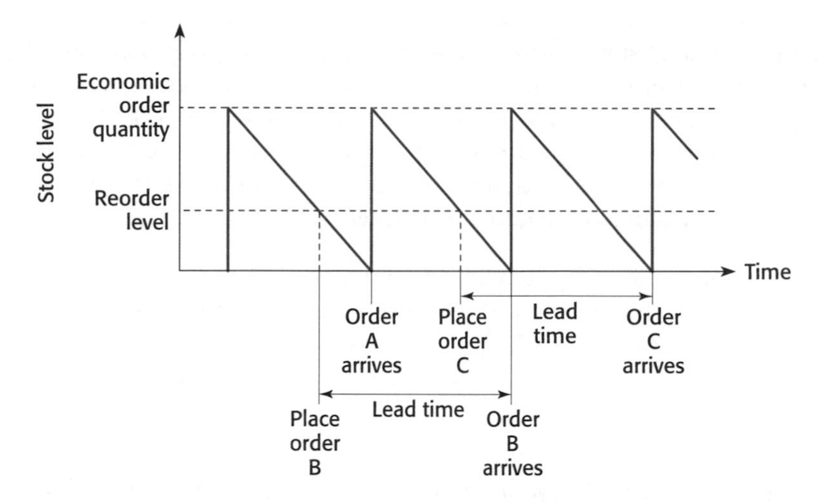

Figure 21.5 Orders when the lead time is longer than the stock cycle

In practice, the cost curve is always shallow around the economic order quantity. The amount we order can increase to 156 per cent of the economic order quantity or fall to 64 per cent and only raise variable costs by 10 per cent. Similarly, the order quantity can increase to 186 per cent of the economic order quantity or fall to 54 per cent and only raise variable costs by 20 per cent. This is one reason why the EOQ analysis is so widely used; although the calculation is based on a series of assumptions and approximations, the total cost rises slowly around the optimal. EOQ gives a good guideline for order size in a wide range of circumstances (see Figure 21.6).

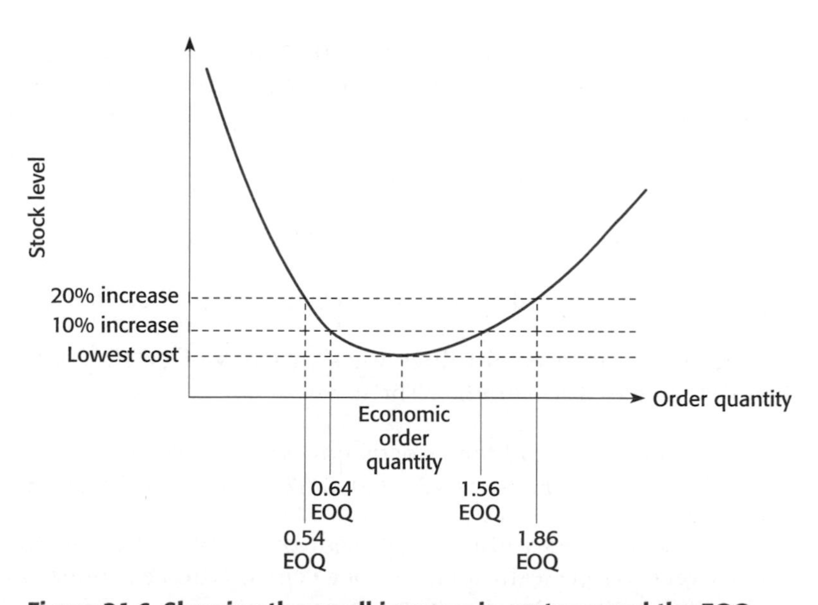

Figure 21.6 Showing the small increase in costs around the EOQ

WORKED EXAMPLE

Cheng Tau Hang notices that demand for an item his company supplies is constant at 500 units a month. Unit cost is \$100 and shortage costs are known to be very high. The purchasing department sends out an average of 3,000 orders a year, and their total operating costs are \$180,000. Any stocks have capital financing charges of 15 per cent, warehouse charges of 7 per cent and other overheads of 8 per cent a year. The lead time is constant at one week.

- Find a good ordering policy for the item.
- What is the reorder level if the lead time increases to three weeks?
- What range of order size keeps variable costs within 10 per cent of optimal?
- What is the variable cost if orders are placed for 200 units at a time?

Solution

Listing the values we know and making sure the units are consistent:

$$D = 500 \times 12 = 6{,}000 \text{ units a year}$$
$$U = \$100 \text{ a unit}$$
$$R = \frac{\text{annual cost of purchasing department}}{\text{number of orders a year}} = \frac{180{,}000}{3{,}000} = \$60 \text{ an order}$$
$$H = (15\% + 7\% + 8\%) \text{ of unit cost a year} = (0.3) \times U = \$30 \text{ a unit a year}$$
$$L = 1 \text{ week}$$

- We can find the best ordering policy by substituting these values into the equations:

  Order quantity,

$$Q = \sqrt{\frac{2RD}{H}} = \sqrt{\frac{2 \times 60 \times 6000}{30}} = 154.9 \text{ units}$$

  Cycle length, $T = Q/D = 154.9/6{,}000 = 0.026$ years or 1.3 weeks
  Variable cost a year $= HQ = 30 \times 154.9 = \$4{,}647$ a year
  Total cost a year $= UD +$ variable cost $= 100 \times 6{,}000 + 4{,}647 = \$604{,}647$ a year

- The lead time is less than the stock cycle, so:

$$\text{Reorder level} = LD = 1 \times 6{,}000/52 = 115.4 \text{ units}$$

The optimal policy is to order 154.9 units whenever stock declines to 115.4 units.

- If the lead time increases to three weeks, there will be two orders outstanding when it is time to place another. Then:

$$\text{Reorder level} = \text{lead time} \times \text{demand} - \text{stock on order}$$
$$= LD - 2Q = 3 \times 6{,}000/52 - 2 \times 154.9 = 36.4 \text{ units.}$$

- To keep variable costs within 10 per cent of optimal, the quantity ordered can vary between 64 per cent and 156 per cent of the economic order quantity, which is 99.1 units to 241.6 units.

- If fixed order sizes of 200 units are used the variable costs are:

$$C = \text{total reorder costs} + \text{total holding costs}$$
$$= RD/Q + HQ/2 = 60 \times 6{,}000/200 + 30 \times 200/2 = \$4{,}800 \text{ a year}$$

Note that we are not using the economic order quantity, so the variable costs rise and the total reorder costs no longer equal the total holding costs.

Weaknesses of this approach

The economic order quantity has been used for almost a century, and is still the basis for most independent demand inventory systems. It has a number of advantages, being:

- easy to understand and use;
- giving good guidelines for order size;
- finding other values such as costs and cycle lengths;
- easy to implement and automate;
- encouraging stability;
- easy to extend, allowing for different circumstances.

On the other hand, there are a number of drawbacks. The two most common are that the model takes too simple a view, and that it is very difficult to get reliable data. General weaknesses are that it:

- takes a simplified view of inventory systems;
- assumes demand is known and constant;
- assumes all costs are known and fixed;
- assumes a constant lead time and no uncertainty in supplies;
- gives awkward order sizes at varying times;
- assumes each item is independent of others;
- does not encourage improvement (in the way that JIT does).

We can overcome some of these problems. We can, for example, develop more complicated models that give more realistic views. In the next section we will show how to do this by allowing for some variation in demand. We can also use simulation to test how the model works in practice.

Review questions

21.6 What is the economic order quantity?

21.7 How does placing small, frequent orders (rather than large, infrequent ones) affect inventory costs?

21.8 What is the reorder level?

21.9 It is important to order exactly the economic order quantity, as even small differences will give much higher costs. Do you agree with this?

OPERATIONS IN PRACTICE

Montague Electrical Engineering

Montague Electrical Engineering (MEE) is a small electric-motor manufacturer with annual sales of £8 million. Robert Hellier is the operations manager. He read the monthly inventory report and was surprised to find total stocks had jumped from £2.2 million to £2.6 million in the past month.

Robert noticed there were very high stocks of part number XCT45, which is a 3 cm diameter bearing. MEE used these steadily, at a rate around 200 a week. The bearings cost £5 each and Robert had been buying 2,500 units at a time. There were many such items in the report, and Robert realised that he had been ordering parts without taking any notice of the inventory costs. The accountant calculated the cost of inventory as 30 per cent a year and the ordering costs were about £15 an order. Based on these figures Robert adjusted his purchase pattern, with orders for XCT45, for example, reduced to 500. One year later, stocks had fallen to less than £1 million, customer service had improved, emergency orders were almost eliminated and MEE was saving over £0.5 million a year.

Source: Robert Hellier (2000) Presentation to Western Operations Group, September

Project 21.1 *Find an organisation that stores some materials, such as a supermarket, hospital or bank. What kind of demand does it satisfy? How does it manage stocks? What technology does it use?*

Uncertain demand and safety stock

The basic economic order quantity assumes that demand is constant and known exactly. In practice, demand can vary widely and have a lot of uncertainty. A company producing a new CD, for example, does not know how many copies will sell in advance, or how sales will vary over time. When the variation is small, the EOQ model still gives useful results, but they are not so good when demand varies more widely. There are several ways we can deal with variable and uncertain demand, and we will illustrate one approach where the demand is normally distributed.

You can see easily why our previous calculations do not work with a variable demand. The reorder level is the mean demand in the lead time, *LD*. If demand in the lead time is above average, stock will run out before the next delivery arrives and there are shortages. But when demand is, say, normally distributed it is above the mean in 50 per cent of cycles. Most organisations would not be happy with shortages in 50 per cent of stock cycles.

An alternative is to hold additional stocks – above the expected needs – to add a margin of safety. Then organisations increase their holding costs by a small amount, to avoid the higher shortage costs. These **safety stocks** are used if the normal working stock runs out. They have no effect on the reorder quantity, which is still defined by the EOQ, but do affect the time when an order is placed (shown in Figure 21.7). In particular, the reorder level is raised by the amount of the safety stock to give:

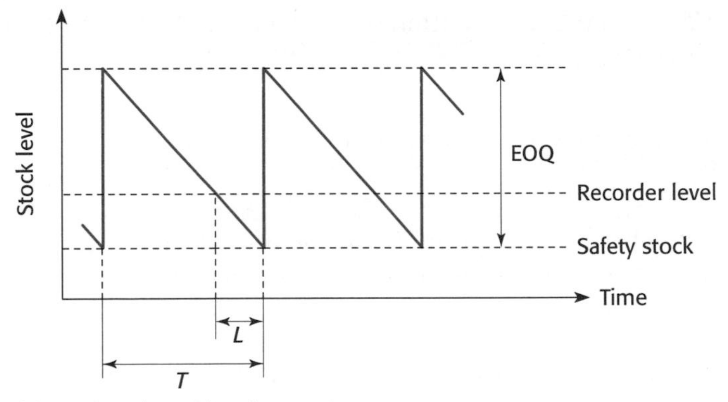

(a) Stock cycles with safety stock

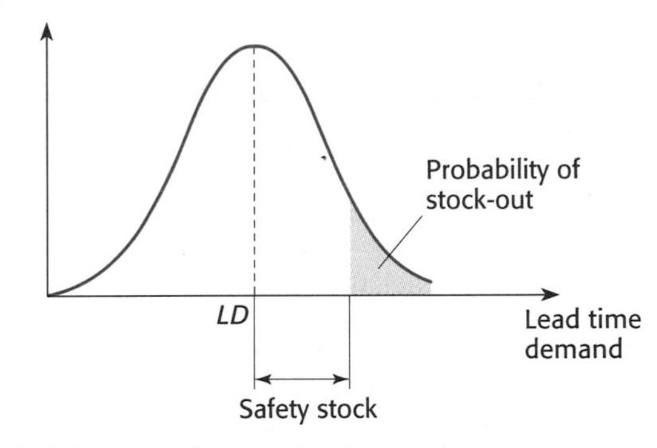

(b) Probability of stock-out with safety stock

Figure 21.7 Effects of adding a safety stock

Reorder level = lead time demand + safety stock
= LD + safety stock

Higher safety stocks obviously give a greater cushion against unexpectedly high demand, and better customer service. Of course, the costs of holding larger stocks are also higher. We have to balance these two effects. The problem is that shortage costs are so difficult to find that they are little more than guesses. An alternative approach relies more directly on managers' judgement to set an appropriate **service level**. This is the probability that a demand is met directly from stock. An organisation typically gives a service level of 95 per cent. This means that it meets 95 per cent of orders from stock, and accepts that 5 per cent of orders cannot be met from stock. The service level needs a positive decision by managers, based on their experience, objectives, competition, and knowledge of customer expectations.

There are several different ways of defining service level, but we will take it as the probability of not running out of stock in a stock cycle. This is the **cycle-service level**.

Suppose that demand for an item is normally distributed with a mean of D per unit time and standard deviation of σ. If the lead time is constant at L, the lead time demand is normally distributed with mean of LD. The lead time demand has a variance of $\sigma^2 L$ and standard deviation of $\sigma\sqrt{L}$. We get this result from the fact that variances can be added, and

If:

- demand in a single period has mean D and variance σ^2,

Then:

- demand in two periods has mean $2D$ and variance $2\sigma^2$;
- demand in three periods has mean $3D$ and variance $3\sigma^2$;

And

- demand in L periods has mean LD and variance $L\sigma^2$.

The size of the safety stock depends on the service level. To be specific, when lead time demand is normally distributed, the safety stock is:

$$\text{Safety stock} = Z \times \text{standard deviation of lead time demand} = Z\sigma\sqrt{L}$$

As usual, Z is the number of standard deviations away from the mean, and probabilities can be found from a statistics package or tables. To give some examples,

- $Z = 1$ gives a stock-out in 15.9 per cent of stock cycles;
- $Z = 2$ gives stock-outs in 2.3 per cent of stock cycles;
- $Z = 3$ gives stock-outs in 0.1 per cent of stock cycles.

If demand varies widely, the standard deviation of lead time demand is high, and very high safety stocks are needed to give a service level near to 100 per cent. This is usually too expensive and organisations set a lower level, typically around 95 per cent. Sometimes it is better to vary the service level to reflect the importance of each item. Then very important items have service levels close to 100 per cent, while less important ones are around 85 per cent.

WORKED EXAMPLE

Associated Kitchen Furnishings runs a retail shop to sell a range of kitchen cabinets. The demand for cabinets is normally distributed with a mean of 200 units a week and a standard deviation of 40 units. The reorder cost, including delivery, is £200; holding cost is £6 a unit a year; and lead time is fixed at three weeks. Describe an ordering policy that gives the shop a 95 per cent cycle-service level. What is the cost of holding the safety stock in this case? How much does the costs go up if the service level is raised to 97 per cent?

Solution

Listing the values we know:

D = 200 units a week = 10,400 units a year
σ = 40 units
R = £200 an order
H = £6 a unit a year
L = 3 weeks

- Substituting these values gives:

$$Q = \sqrt{\frac{2RD}{H}} = \sqrt{\frac{2 \times 200 \times 200 \times 52}{6}} = 833 \text{ (to the nearest integer)}$$

Reorder level = LD + safety stock = 600 + safety stock

- For a 95 per cent service level $Z = 1.64$ standard deviations from the mean. Then:

$$\text{Safety stock} = Z\sigma\sqrt{L} = 1.64 \times 40 \times \sqrt{3} = 114 \text{ (to the nearest integer)}$$

The best policy is to order 833 units whenever stock falls to 600 + 114 = 714 units. On average orders will arrive when there are 114 units left.

The safety stock is not usually used, so the holding cost is simply:

$$= \text{safety stock} \times \text{holding cost} = 114 \times 6 = £684 \text{ a year}$$

- If the service level is raised to 97 per cent, Z becomes 1.88 and:

$$\text{Safety stock} = Z\sigma\sqrt{L} = 1.88 \times 40 \times \sqrt{3} = 130$$

The cost of holding this is:

$$= \text{safety stock} \times \text{holding cost} = 130 \times 6 = £780 \text{ a year}$$

Review questions

21.10 What is a service level?

21.11 What is the purpose of safety stock?

21.12 How could you increase the service level?

OPERATIONS IN PRACTICE

Value of stocks

In April 1998 the Serious Fraud Office looked into possible false accounting at Azlan, a distributor of computer products. The problem was noticed when a projected profit of £15 million became a loss of £14.1 million. An inquiry by the auditors KPMG showed that £16.6 million of the loss was due to problems in purchasing and inventory management. The Serious Fraud Office had to see if the problems were caused by incompetence or deliberate wrongdoing.

Azlan's stock of computer products rapidly becomes obsolete, and one problem was their over-optimistic estimates of the amount of slow-moving stock that would eventually be sold.

Problems with stock are surprisingly common, and in the same week that Azlan's problems emerged Matbro, a manufacturer of tractors, also reported trading difficulties with a £46.7 million provision for loss. Trading conditions were hard, so the company offered large discounts on machines. The selling price did not cover costs and the company was trading at a loss, so it made up the difference by reclassifying stock as 'sold'. When a replacement tractor was sent out to cover one that had broken down under warranty, it was counted as another sale; when tractors were sent to dealers, they were marked as 'sold', even though they were sitting in dealers' yards.

Eventually, the company owed the Bank of Ireland more than £40 million for tractors it had never sold.

Sources: Dan Atkinson (1998) 'Fraud Office Examines Azlan's £14m Losses', *Guardian*, 15 March; Neil Bennett (1998) 'Escape Route from the Matbro Rubble', *Sunday Telegraph*, 19 April

Periodic review systems

The EOQ analysis uses a **fixed order quantity** for purchases, but there is an alternative **periodic review** approach.

- *Fixed order quantity* methods place an order of fixed size whenever stock falls to a certain level. The heating plant in your local swimming pool may order 25,000 litres of oil whenever the amount in the tank falls to 2,500 litres. Such systems need continuous monitoring of stock levels and are best suited to low, irregular demand for relatively expensive items.
- *Periodic review* methods order varying amounts at regular intervals to raise the stock level to a specified value. A supermarket may refill its shelves every evening to replace whatever it sold during the day. The operating cost of this system is generally lower and it is better suited to high, regular demand of low value items.

If the demand is constant these two systems are the same, but differences appear when demand varies. We can show this by extending the last analysis, and looking at a periodic review system where demand is normally distributed. Then we are looking for answers to two questions:

- How long should the interval between orders be?
- What should the **target stock level** be?

The interval between orders, T, can be any convenient period. It might be easiest to place an order at the end of every week, or every morning, or at the end of a month. If there is no obvious cycle we might aim for a certain number of orders a year or some average order size. One approach is to calculate an economic order

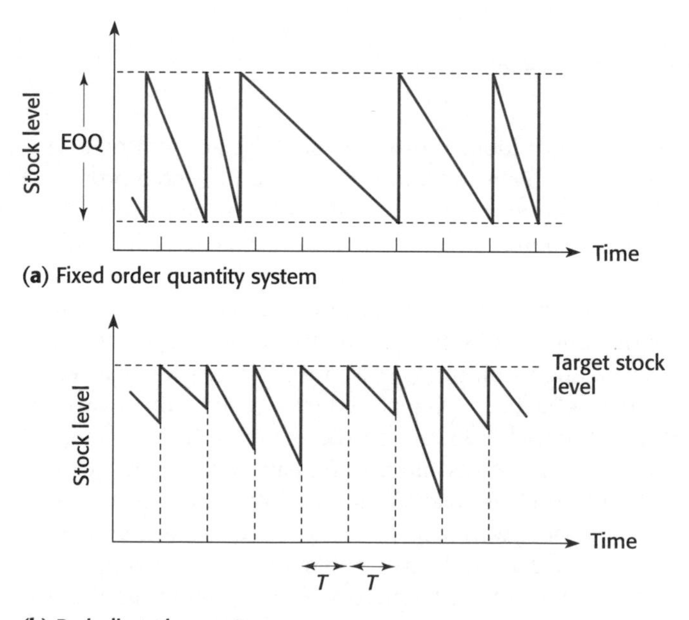

Figure 21.8 Alternative inventory policies

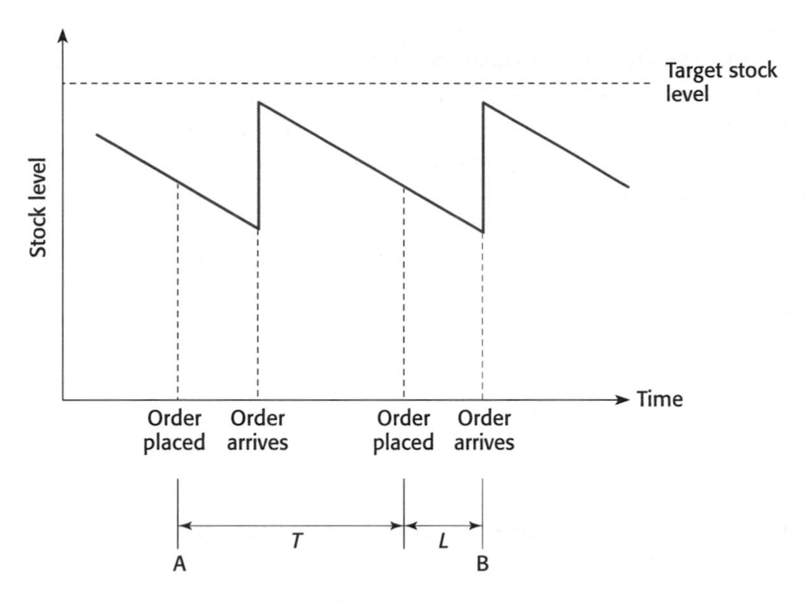

Figure 21.9 An order placed at A must cover all demand until B

quantity, and then find the period that gives orders of about this size. This decision is largely a matter for management judgement.

When we have defined the interval between orders, we can calculate an associated **target stock level**, TSL. The system works by looking at the stock on hand when an order is due, and ordering an amount that brings this up to TSL.

Order quantity = target stock level – stock on hand

Suppose the lead time is constant at L. When an order is placed, the stock on hand plus this order must last until the next order arrives. As you can see from Figure 21.9:

Next order arrives after a time = order interval + lead time = $T + L$

Now we can use the same approach as the last section to find the mean demand over this period, and then use the variance to add some safety stock to allow for the 50 per cent of cycles when demand is higher than average. We will assume that the demand each period is normally distributed with a mean D and variance σ, and that both the order period and lead time are fixed at T and L respectively. Then:

- Demand in one period has mean D and variance σ^2;
- Demand over two periods has mean $2D$ and variance $2\sigma^2$;
- Demand over $(T + L)$ periods has mean $D(T + L)$, variance of $(T + L)\sigma^2$.

The standard deviation in demand over $(T + L)$ is $\sigma\sqrt{(T + L)}$, so we can define a safety stock as:

Safety stock = $Z \times$ standard deviation of demand over $(T + L) = Z\sigma\sqrt{(T + L)}$

Then:

Target stock level = mean demand over $(T + L)$ + safety stock
$= D(T + L) + Z\sigma\sqrt{(T + L)}$

WORKED EXAMPLE

Demand for an item has a mean of 200 units a week and standard deviation of 40 units. Stock is checked every four weeks and lead time is constant at two weeks. Describe a policy that will give a 95 per cent service level. If the holding cost is £2 a unit a week, what is the cost of the safety stock with this policy? What is the effect of a 98 per cent service level?

Solution

The variables are:

D = 200 units
σ = 40 units
H = £2 a unit a week
T = 4 weeks
L = 2 weeks

- For a 95 per cent service level, Z is 1.64 (which you can find from a standard package or tables). Then:

  Safety stock = $Z\sigma\sqrt{(T + L)} = 1.64 \times 40 \times \sqrt{6} = 161$ (to the nearest integer)
  Target stock level = $D(T + L)$ + safety stock = $200 \times 6 + 161 = 1{,}361$

  When it is time to place an order, the policy is to find the stock on hand, and place an order for:

  Order size = target stock level – stock on hand = 1,361 – stock on hand

  If, for example, there are 200 units in stock, we place an order for 1,361 – 200 = 1,161 units.

- The safety stock is not normally used, so the holding cost is:

  = safety stock × holding cost = 161×2 = £322 a week.

- If the service level is increased to 98 per cent, $Z = 2.05$. Then:

  Safety stock = $Z\sigma\sqrt{(T + L)} = 2.05 \times 40 \times \sqrt{6} = 201$ units
  Target stock level = $D(T + L)$ + safety stock = $200 \times 6 + 201 = 1{,}401$ units
  Cost of the safety stock is safety stock × holding cost = 201×2 = £402 a week

In practice, there are many variations on the two basic systems: fixed order quantity and periodic review. One looks at stocks every period, but only places an order if current stocks are below a specified level. Another uses a reorder level but orders a variable amount that depends on recent demand. Such extensions to the basic analysis can give good results in a wide variety of problems.

Review questions

21.13 How is the order size calculated for a periodic review system?

21.14 Will the safety stock be higher for a fixed order quantity system or a periodic review system?

Project 21.2 *Have a look at some real stocks and see what problems they face that are missing from the analyses we have described. How could you extend the analyses? You might start by, say, adding price discounts on purchases. When Maresh Azoori tried this he found that demand for one item was 2,000 units, each order cost £10 and annual holding costs were 40 per cent of value. The basic price was £1 a unit, with a 20 per cent discount on orders over 500 units, and a 40 per cent discount on orders over 1,000 units. How could he find his best order size?*

ABC analysis of inventories

Even a simple inventory control system needs some effort to make sure that things run smoothly. For some items, especially cheap ones, this effort is not worthwhile. Very few organisations include, for example, routine stationery or nuts and bolts in their stock control system. At the other end of the scale are very expensive items that need special care above the routine calculations. Aircraft engines, for example, are very expensive, and airlines have to control their stocks of spare engines very carefully.

An **ABC analysis** puts items into categories that show the amount of effort worth spending on inventory control. This is a standard Pareto analysis or 'rule of 80/20', which suggests that 20 per cent of inventory items need 80 per cent of the attention, while the remaining 80 per cent of items need only 20 per cent of the attention. ABC analyses define:

- A items as expensive and needing special care;
- B items as ordinary ones needing standard care;
- C items as cheap and needing little care.

Typically an organisation might use an automated system to deal with all B items. The computer system might make some suggestions for A items, but decisions are made by managers after reviewing all the circumstances. C items might be excluded from the automatic system and controlled by ad hoc methods.

An ABC analysis starts by calculating the total annual use of each item by value. We find this by multiplying the number of units used in a year by the unit cost. Usually, a few expensive items account for a lot of use, while many cheap ones account for little use. If we list the items in order of decreasing annual use by value, A items are at the top of the list, B items are in the middle and C items are at the bottom. We might typically find:

Category	% of items	Cumulative % of items	% of use by value	Cumulative % of use by value
A	10	10	70	70
B	30	40	20	90
C	60	100	10	100

Figure 21.10 shows typical results of plotting the cumulative percentage of annual use against the cumulative percentage of items.

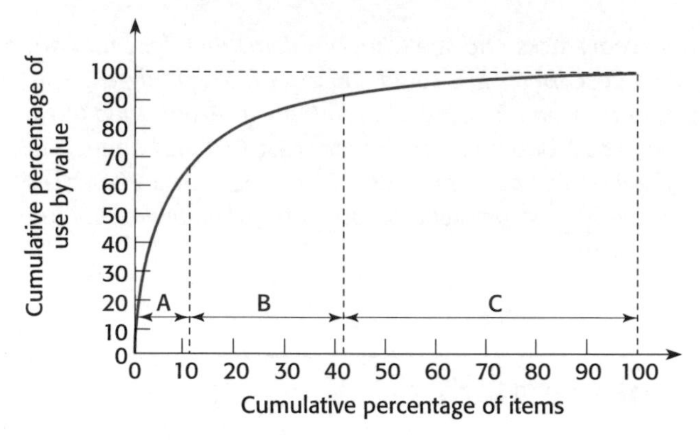

Figure 21.10 Typical ABC analysis of stock

WORKED EXAMPLE

A small store has 10 categories of product with the following costs and annual demands:

Product	P1	P2	P3	P4	P5	P6	P7	P8	P9	P0
Unit cost (€)	20	10	20	50	10	50	5	20	100	1
Annual demand (00s)	2.5	50	20	66	15	6	10	5	1	50

Do an ABC analysis of these items. If resources for inventory control are limited, which items should be given least attention?

Solution

The annual use of P1 in terms of value is $20 \times 250 =$ €5,000. Repeating this calculation for the other items gives the following results:

Item	P1	P2	P3	P4	P5	P6	P7	P8	P9	P0
% of items	10	10	10	10	10	10	10	10	10	10
Annual use (€000s)	5	50	40	330	15	30	5	10	10	5

Sorting these into order of decreasing annual use gives the following results:

Product	P4	P2	P3	P6	P5	P8	P9	P1	P7	P0
Cumulative % of items	10	20	30	40	50	60	70	80	90	100
Annual use (€000s)	330	50	40	30	15	10	10	5	5	5
Cumulative annual use	330	380	420	450	465	475	485	490	495	500
Cumulative % annual use	66	76	84	90	93	95	97	98	99	100
Category	←A→	←	B	→	←		C			→

The boundaries between categories of items are often unclear, but in this case P4 is clearly an A item, P2, P3 and P6 are B items and the rest are C items.

The C items account for only 10 per cent of annual use by value. If resources are limited, these should be given least attention.

Review questions

21.15 What is the purpose of an ABC analysis of inventories?

21.16 Which items can best be dealt with by routine, automated control procedures?

Chapter review

- Stocks are the materials that organisations keep in store until they are needed. There are many types of stocks and arrangements for their storage.
- Approaches such as JIT assume that stock serves no useful purpose, but this is not always true. The main reason for holding stocks is to give a buffer between supply and demand, allowing for uncertainty and variation. There are many other reasons in different circumstances.
- Stocks are expensive, and organisations look for ways of controlling them to achieve some specific purpose. There are several ways of approaching this, and the chapter concentrated on independent demand systems.
- The economic order quantity is the order size that minimises costs for a simple inventory system. The reorder level shows the times to place orders.
- If demand varies widely, we have to adjust the analysis by specifying a service level and adding safety stock.
- An extension of this analysis gives periodic review systems that place regular orders to bring stocks up to a target level.
- ABC analysis shows the amount of effort worth spending on controlling items of different types.

Key terms

ABC analysis *p. 623*
cost (unit, reorder, holding and shortage) *p. 606*
cycle-service level *p. 617*
dependent demand system *p. 606*
economic order quantity *p. 608*
fixed order quantity *p. 620*
independent demand system *p. 606*
inventory control *p. 608*
lead time *p. 611*
periodic review system *p. 620*
reorder level *p. 611*
safety stock *p. 616*
service level *p. 617*
stocks *p. 603*
stock cycle *p. 609*
stores *p. 605*
target stock level *p. 620*
two-bin system *p. 611*
warehouse *p. 603*

CASE STUDY Congleton Lead Refinery

Congleton Lead Refinery imports a silver-lead-zinc ore from associated companies in Australia and southern Africa, and refines it into pure metals. A team of management consultants has been advising Congleton on ways of improving productivity. Their study was drawing to a close when the project manager from the consultancy, Nigel Chatterton, visited Congleton's vice-president of operations, Beatrix de Witte. Beatrix explained the purpose of the visit.

> *We like your suggestions for rescheduling operations to meet expected demand using less plant and equipment. Now can you do one final study for us? As we will be working with less back-up equipment, it is important that this equipment continues to function. This in turn depends on our stocks of spare parts. We keep about 25,000 parts in the stores and would like some suggestions for improving performance.*

Nigel Chatterton said that his final report was already suggesting this study. He had talked to Laurens van Hooste, the supplies manager for Congleton, who described the present inventory control system as follows:

> *We stock 25,000 different items which vary from paper clips to 15-tonne buckets for ore movers. There is no such thing as a typical item. Demand ranges from zero to 100,000 units a year. Current stocks range from one (we carry a few spare engines and big earth movers) to several hundred thousand (iron balls used in the ore crushers). Lead times vary from 15 minutes for things bought in a local shop, to over a year for imported furnace bricks. The unit price ranges from almost nothing to $250,000. The reorder price varies from almost nothing for local suppliers, to very large amounts when we need a specialised piece of equipment designed and delivered. Shortage costs range from almost nothing to very large sums for things that we absolutely must keep in stock.*

The current system was installed 10 years ago and has been continually updated, with two complete revisions and many smaller adjustments. The system categorises items in a number of ways and deals with each category differently. Firstly, the system considers items' importance:

- 5 per cent of items are essential and must be kept in stock whatever the cost;
- 20 per cent of items are important and have a notional service level of 97 per cent;
- 50 per cent are ordinary items with a notional service level of 93 per cent;
- 25 per cent are low priority items with a notional service level of 80 per cent.

A second classification of items looks at how long they had been stocked:

- for new items the expected demand is suggested either by departments requesting the item, or by suppliers;
- when an item has been in stock for a few months, there is a short history of demand, and forecasts for future demand are made from average values over the past four months;
- After nine months, more historical data is available, and forecasting is switched to exponential smoothing. The parameters used for forecasting are monitored and revised every month.

A third classification of items refers to their use:

- stocks of heavily used items are reviewed at the end of every working day;
- stocks of normally used items are reviewed at the end of every week;
- stocks of lightly used items are reviewed at the end of every month;
- stocks of sporadically used items are reviewed every time there is a withdrawal;
- stocks of items that have no recorded movement in the past year are considered for removal from stock.

About 20 per cent of items are in each of these categories.

The central computer records all transactions and generates a range of reports. At the end of every working day, for example, the computer lists the heavily used items that have fallen to their reorder levels and sends suggested purchases to the procurement section. These suggestions include the economic order quantity, actual quantities to be ordered, preferred supplier, supplier reliability, lead time, quality of deliveries, probability of shortages, and a range of related information. The procurement section examines these suggestions the following day, makes any modifications it deems necessary, and gets the system to print orders, arrange payments, and update associated records. Weekly reports include comparisons of forecasts with actual demands, major errors, and suggestions for changing parameters.

Nigel feels that the system is working reasonably well. It is based on sound principles and the stocks seem to give little trouble, considering the complexity of a system containing $30 million worth of stock. His immediate problem is to prepare a proposal for an investigation of the system.

Questions

- Write the proposal that Nigel Chatterton could write for Congleton.
- Describe the current inventory control system, giving the details of the inputs, calculations and outputs. Are there any obvious weaknesses in this system? Where could you look for improvements?
- What additional information would you need for your report?

Problems

21.1 The demand for an item is constant at 100 units a year. Unit cost is £50, cost of processing an order is £20 and holding cost is £10 per unit per annum. What are the economic order quantity, corresponding cycle length and costs?

21.2 O'Sullivan (Wholesale) Limited works 50 weeks a year to meet demand for leather briefcases which is more or less constant at 100 units a week. It pays £20 for each briefcase and aims for a return of 20 per cent on capital invested. Annual storage costs are 5 per cent of the value of goods stored. The purchasing department costs £45,000 a year and sends out an average of 2,000 orders. Find the optimal order quantity for briefcases, the best time between orders and the minimum cost of stocking the item.

21.3 Demand for an item is steady at 20 units a week and the economic order quantity has been calculated at 50 units. What is the reorder level when the lead time is:

(a) one week; (b) three weeks; (c) five weeks; (d) seven weeks?

21.4 Aldous spa. forecast demand for components to average 18 a day over a 200-day working year. Any shortages disrupt production and give very high costs. The holding cost for the component is 120,000 lire a unit a year, and the cost of placing an order is 240,000 lire an order. Find the economic order quantity, the optimal number of orders a year and the total annual cost of operating the system if the interest rate is 25 per cent a year.

21.5 A company advertises a 95 per cent cycle-service level for all stock items. Stock is replenished from a single supplier who guarantees a lead time of four weeks. What reorder level should the company adopt for an item that has a normally distributed demand with mean 1,000 units a week and standard deviation of 100 units? What is the reorder level for a 98 per cent cycle-service level?

21.6 An item of inventory has a unit cost of $80, reorder cost of $100 and holding cost of $2 a unit a week. Demand for the item has a mean of 100 a week with standard deviation of 10. Lead time is constant at three weeks. Design an inventory policy for the item to give a service level of 95 per cent. How would you change this to give a 90 per cent service level? What are the costs of these two policies?

21.7 Describe a periodic review system with interval of two weeks for the company described in Problem 21.5.

21.8 Wulfgang Heinz has a small store with 10 categories of product and the following costs and annual demands:

Product	X1	X2	X3	Y1	Y2	Y3	Z1	Z2	Z3	Z4
Unit cost (Dm)	60	75	90	3	12	18	30	45	60	66
Annual demand (00s)	3	2	2	10	8	7	30	20	6	4

Do an ABC analysis of these items.

Discussion questions

21.1 Some organisations try to reduce their stocks by making to order, or guaranteeing delivery within a specified period. Do such methods really reduce inventory costs?

21.2 What costs are incurred by holding stock? How reliably can an organisation find these? Why are shortage costs so difficult to find? If there are problems finding these costs, how reliable are the resulting analyses?

21.3 What factors in real inventory control are not included in the economic order quantity model? Can you still use the EOQ, even if these real factors are omitted?

21.4 What should you consider when setting a service level? How can a hospital set a reasonable service level for its supplies of blood for transfusions?

21.5 We have now seen how stocks can be controlled by MRP, JIT and independent demand systems. When would you use each of these?

21.6 What features would you expect to see in a computerised inventory control system? Look at some commercial packages and compare the features they offer.

21.7 Stocks are an inevitable. Methods like JIT only transfer stocks from one part of the supply chain to another. To what extent do you think this is true?

References

1. Office of National Statistics (2001) *Economic Trends*. London: HMSO.
2. Harris F. (1915) *Operations and Cost*. Chicago: A. Shaw & Co.
3. Raymond F.E. (1931) *Quantity and Economy in Manufacture*. Chicago: McGraw-Hill.
4. Wilson R.H. (1934) 'A Scientific Routine for Stock Control', *Harvard Business Review*. No. XIII.

Selected reading

Fogarty D.W., Blackstone J.H. and Hoffmann T.R. (1991) *Production and Inventory Management*. 2nd edn. Cincinnati, OH: South-Western Publishing.

Greene J.H. (1997) *Production and Inventory Control Handbook*. 3rd edn. New York: McGraw-Hill.

Lewis C.D. (1997) *Demand Forecasting and Inventory Control*. London: Woodhead publishing.

Tersine R.J. (1994) *Principles of Inventory and Materials Management*. Englewood Cliffs, NJ: Prentice-Hall.

Silver E.A., Pyke D.F. and Peterson R. (1998) *Inventory Management and Production Planning and Scheduling*. 3rd edn. New York: John Wiley.

Waters C.D.J. (1992) *Inventory Control and Management*. Chichester: John Wiley.

Waters C.D.J. (1998) *A Practical Introduction to Management Science*. 2nd edn. Harlow: Addison-Wesley Longman.

Useful Websites

www.apics.org – American Production and Inventory Control Society
www.inventorymanagement.com – Centre for Inventory Management

SUPPLEMENT TO CHAPTER 21

Calculations for inventory control

Contents

Derivation of the economic order quantity

Imagine a single item, held in stock to meet a constant demand of D per unit time. We assume that unit cost (U), reorder cost (R) and holding cost (H) are all known exactly, while the shortage cost (S) is so high that all demands must be met and no shortages are allowed.

The item is bought in batches from a supplier, who delivers after a constant lead time. We are going to find the best order quantity, Q. There is no point in carrying spare stock, so we will time orders to arrive just as existing stock runs out. Then the stock level repeatedly follows the cycle shown in Figure 21s.1.

At some point an order of size Q arrives. This is used at a constant rate, D, until no stock is left. The resulting stock cycle has length T and we know:

Amount entering stock in the cycle = amount leaving stock in the cycle

So:

$$Q = DT$$

We also know that the stock level varies between Q and 0, so the average level is $(Q + 0)/2 = Q/2$.

Now we can find the total cost for the cycle by adding the four components of cost: unit, reorder, holding and shortage. We know that no shortages are allowed so we can ignore these. The cost of buying goods is constant regardless of the ordering policy, so we can also leave this out of the calculations. Then the variable cost for the cycle is:

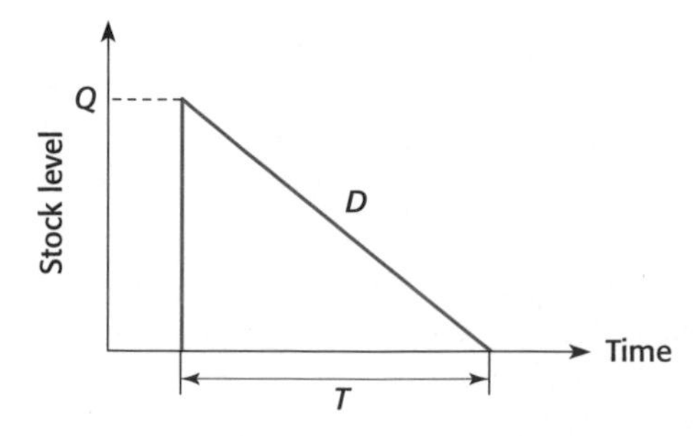

Figure 21s.1 A single stock cycle

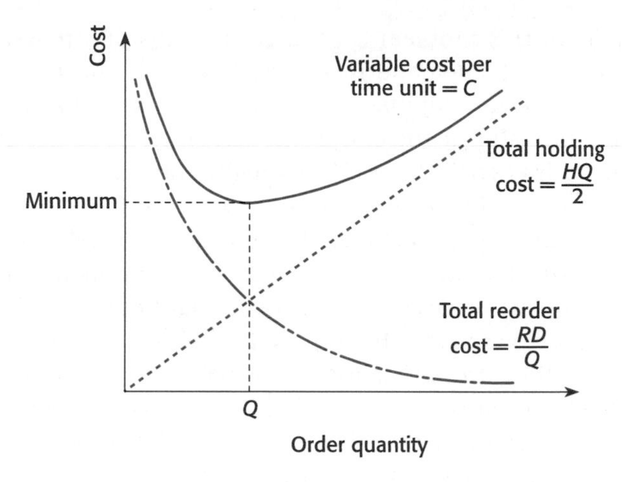

Figure 21s.2 Varying costs with order quantity

- Total reorder cost = number of orders (1) × reorder cost (R) = R
- Total holding cost = average stock level ($Q/2$) × time held (T) × holding cost (H) = $HQT/2$

Adding these two gives the total cost for the cycle, and if we divide this by the cycle length, T, we get the variable cost per unit time, C, as:

$$C = (R + HQT/2)/T = R/T + HQ/2$$

But we know that $Q = DT$, or $T = Q/D$, and substituting this gives:

$$C = RD/Q + HQ/2$$

We can plot the two parts on the right-hand side of this equation separately against Q, as shown in Figure 21s.2. The total cost curve has a distinct minimum which is the optimal order size, or economic order quantity. We can find a value for this by differentiating the equation for variable cost with respect to Q, and setting the result to equal zero.

$$0 = -RD/Q^2 + H/2$$

Or:

$$\text{Economic order quantity, } Q = \sqrt{\frac{2RD}{H}}$$

Single period models

Sometimes we are not interested in a continuing inventory, but want a policy for the short term. Suppose, for example, we have a stock of seasonal goods such as Christmas cards. We want an inventory policy that will satisfy all demand in December, but recognise that cards remaining unsold have no value in January. Effectively, we want to minimise the inventory costs over a single period.

INTEGRATING CASE STUDY

Eldon Engineering

by Mike Simpson and Tim Henry of Sheffield University Management School, University of Sheffield

Background

Eldon Engineering Limited is a small engineering company based in South Yorkshire. The company has two owner-directors, one is an engineer (Phil Muscroft) and the other (Roy Kitteringham) deals with the administration and accounts. They formed the company in 1975 as a subcontract machine shop. Now they have a turnover of £1.08 million and employ 40 people.

Nine years ago Eldon started making quick release gas line couplings, and set up a separate company, Eldon Flow Equipment Ltd, to sell these. They used a similar approach with a range of automotive tools for the garage trade, and set up Eldon Tool Company Ltd. Eldon Engineering makes the components and the subsidiaries sell them on. These two activities account for about 50 per cent of the turnover and the other 50 per cent comes from subcontract engineering work.

Purchasing

The company has about 75 suppliers of materials and components, of which eight are regarded as major suppliers. Payment is after two or three months. Eldon does not have a purchasing policy and makes no measurement of performance of its suppliers. Most purchased materials are standard items such as round and hexagonal bars. The main materials are brass bars, two types of stainless steel bars, and two types of plastic (acetyl and polypropylene rods). Other materials include springs, clips, ball bearings, seals, tools, office supplies, stationery, etc.

Purchases represent around one-third of turnover with annual costs of £420,000. All purchases are made as required for each job, so stocks of raw materials are small. The main purchasing criteria are price and especially delivery. Quality is not generally a problem with standard materials. There are finished goods stocks of about £50,000 of couplings.

The price of materials can vary by 100 per cent. For example, the price of brass varies between £1.55 and £2.00 per kilogram, but there is more variation in machine cutting costs at the suppliers. Delivered brass cut to size can vary from £0.70 per piece to £1.40 per piece. Phil Muscroft has often said: 'I would like to establish a regular order with a single supplier at a guaranteed price (say, £1.70 per kilogram for brass) since it would save a lot of time telephoning around for the best price and delivery. We have a good relationship with our suppliers and think of ourselves as collaborating as far as we can.'

Phil Muscroft and Roy Kitteringham are uncomfortable with this approach and feel vulnerable when competitors can undercut them on price. Roy Kitteringham explained: 'There are a lot of small and often struggling engineering companies in the South Yorkshire area who can do similar, if not identical, work and achieve the same results for quality, reliability, delivery, etc. as we do. What else can we do but cut our prices and make the products as cheaply as we can?'

Marketing

Marketing is ad hoc at best if not entirely absent. The brochure is very old and as Phil Muscroft explains: 'We were hoping our marketing person in Eldon Flow Equipment would help us redesign the brochure, but she left last year and we haven't got around to replacing her. We seem to be doing all right at the moment though. There is plenty of work and I don't really think we need a replacement at present.'

Some customers are small and medium-sized, local companies, and others are from France and Germany. Eldon has not done any systematic analysis of the market for its products. The work is largely obtained by phoning around and obtaining orders on price against competitors. Once Eldon found a company in Chesterfield importing gas fittings from Japan, but found that the job was too big to take on. Eldon has regular large orders from a French company for some components which any CNC equipment could make.

Research and development

Eldon did no research and development until it spent £3,000 a year (0.4 per cent of turnover) developing its gas line couplings. It did get a grant of up to £25,000 from the Department of Trade and Industry to cover 50 per cent of costs for a development project. Phil Muscroft said: 'I was surprised at how easily we obtained this grant. It was the first time we had made a grant application to the DTI. We need some new products because of the increasing competition and declining sales in our normal product range. We need a new product to replace the gas line couplings and automotive trade tools.'

Questions

- Do an operations audit of Eldon Engineering.
- What are the problems facing Eldon Engineering?
- What do you think the company should do to overcome these problems?

Appendix: Solutions to review questions

Chapter 1 Operations and the process

1.1 (a) tangible manufactured objects; (b) intangible benefits; (c) both goods and services; (d) all the operations needed to make a particular product.
1.2 To satisfy customer demand as a way of achieving their aims.
1.3 The activities directly concerned with making a product.
1.4 There are many possible answers to this.
1.5 All the operations needed to make a product.
1.6 There can be many ways, including volume, variation in demand, customer contact, balance between goods and services, objectives, etc.
1.7 No; most organisations face a range of similar problems.

Chapter 2 Managing operations

2.1 Making decisions – including planning, organising, staffing, directing, motivating, allocating, monitoring, controlling and informing.
2.2 The management function that is responsible for all aspects of operations.
2.3 There are many reasons, but increased competition is probably the most important.
2.4 Its performance declines and it becomes less competitive.
2.5 Operations, finance, marketing.
2.6 You can give many examples here.
2.7 Human resource management is not directly concerned with making the product, and when it is, it becomes part of operations management. Product design is part of operations management.
2.8 To produce goods and services that satisfy customer demand.
2.9 Examples of these are given in Table 2.2.
2.10 As a central function in an organisation, by the type of problem tackled, as a profession, or by its approach to problems.
2.11 You can give many alternatives here.
2.12 Using a defined procedure, typically describing the problem, defining your objectives, analysing data, listing alternatives, finding the best alternative, implementing the decision and monitoring progress.

Chapter 3 Designing an operations strategy

3.1 Strategic, tactical and operational.
3.2 No; operational decisions concern day-to-day running. All decisions are important.
3.3 (a) strategic; (b) operational; (c) strategic; (d) tactical.
3.4 Not really. Most decisions are based on discussion and agreement rather than orders.
3.5 A statement of its fundamental beliefs and aims.
3.6 The set of strategic decisions about the organisation as a whole.
3.7 Generally, the organisation's environment and its specific competence.

3.8 Not necessarily. They are interrelated and may develop over the same time.
3.9 All the strategic decisions made for operations.
3.10 Cost, quality, timing, flexibility, technology, customer service, etc.
3.11 No.
3.12 A general view of the products and how resources will be organised to make these.

Chapter 4 Implementing the operations strategy

4.1 Yes.
4.2 Any decisions that affect operations (Figure 4.1 shows some examples of these).
4.3 No.
4.4 Because every organisation relies on customers for its survival.
4.5 This sees how an organisation describes itself, and it can have significant effects on operations.
4.6 No.
4.7 This is unlikely as all organisations live with continual change.
4.8 Continuous improvement suggests small adjustments over time, while reengineering suggests major redesigns.
4.9 Because the best people to make decisions are often those most closely involved (see the text for benefits).
4.10 A way of treating people based on the delegation of authority and responsibility.

Chapter 5 Product planning

5.1 Any goods or services that satisfy customer demand.
5.2 To make sure that an organisation continues to supply products that satisfy customer demand.
5.3 Introduction, growth, maturity, decline and withdrawal.
5.4 Reasonable values are about: (a) one year; (b) five years; (c) ten years; (d) one day.
5.5 Costs are higher near the beginning of the life cycle and decline over time. Revenue is highest around the maturity stage. High profits can be made in the growth stage, but these generally peak with maturity.
5.6 Research driven, new product exploiters, cost reducers, etc.
5.7 Because customers have different needs.
5.8 Generation of ideas, initial screening of ideas, initial design, development and testing, market and economic analysis, final product development, launch of product.
5.9 There are many possible criteria, based on how well the product meets customer expectations and how well it fits into existing operations.
5.10 No.
5.11 Running stages in parallel to reduce the development time for new products.
5.12 No.
5.13 Functional, attractive to customers, easy to make.
5.14 It gives the general features of products, but not the detailed design.

Chapter 6 Quality management

6.1 No.
6.2 Because there are so many opinions, viewpoints and possible measures.
6.3 Generally the external view.

6.4 The function that is responsible for all aspects of quality.
6.5 Because it has implications for survival, reputation, marketing effort needed, market share, prices charged, profits, costs, liability for defects, and almost every other aspect of an organisation's operations.
6.6 No.
6.7 The sum of prevention, appraisal, internal failure and external failure costs.
6.8 Fewer defects are produced and these are found earlier, so less effort is wasted making faulty products.
6.9 By minimising the total quality cost. This is usually done by perfect quality.
6.10 Quality control inspects products to make sure they conform to designed quality; quality management is a wider function that is involved with all aspects of product quality.
6.11 No.
6.12 Everyone is responsible for passing on products of perfect quality to following operations.
6.13 Survival, high-quality products, increased productivity, low costs, reduced conflict, focused organisation, etc.
6.14 No.
6.15 Everyone in the organisation.
6.16 It doesn't – it only guarantees conformity.
6.17 Most people say that this is top management support.
6.18 A programme of continuous improvement.
6.19 No.
6.20 By asking customers how satisfied they are.

Chapter 7 Controlling quality

7.1 No.
7.2 Quality control inspects products to make sure they conform to designed quality; quality management is a wider function that is responsible for all aspects of quality.
7.3 A measure of the cost of missing target performance.
7.4 To check that designed quality is actually being achieved.
7.5 As early as possible, preferably at the product design stage, and with suppliers.
7.6 No.
7.7 Because inspecting all the products may be expensive, destructive or infeasible.
7.8 No. There are always random variations.
7.9 The distribution of means found in samples from the population.
7.10 Acceptance sampling checks that products are conforming to design quality; process control checks that the process is working properly.
7.11 Sampling by attribute classifies units as either acceptable or defective; sampling by variable measures some continuous value.
7.12 α is the highest acceptable probability of rejecting a good batch; β is the highest acceptable probability of accepting a bad batch. Sampling is always uncertain, and these put limits on acceptable risks.
7.13 Because it gives perfect differentiation between good batches (where the probability of acceptance is 1) and bad batches (where the probability of acceptance is 0).
7.14 No.
7.15 The process needs adjusting, but check for random fluctuations before doing this.

7.16 A single reading outside the control limits, a clear trend, several consecutive readings near to a control limit, several consecutive readings on the same side of the mean, a sudden change in apparent mean levels, very erratic observations.

7.17 Because *X* charts give mean values but they do not show the variation in these means.

Chapter 8 Forecasting customer demand

8.1 All decisions are affective at some point in the future, so they need information about future conditions, and this must be forecast.

8.2 No.

8.3 Judgemental, projective and causal forecasting.

8.4 Subjective views based on opinions and intuition.

8.5 Personal insight, panel consensus, market surveys, historical analogy and Delphi method.

8.6 Unreliability, conflicting views from experts, cost of data collection, lack of available expertise, and so on.

8.7 Because of the unexplained short-term variations that produce random noise.

8.8 The mean error is (Σ errors)/n. Positive and negative errors cancel each other, so the mean error has a value around zero unless the forecasts are biased.

8.9 Use alternative methods for a typical time series and calculate the errors in each. All other things being equal, the best method is the one with the smallest errors.

8.10 By finding relationships between variables and using the value of one variable to forecast the value of another.

8.11 A way of finding the line of best fit through a set of data.

8.12 The proportion of the total sum of squared error that is explained by the regression.

8.13 No.

8.14 Because older data tends to swamp more recent and more relevant data.

8.15 By using a lower value of n.

8.16 Because the weight given to data declines exponentially with its age, and it smoothes the effects of noise.

8.17 By choosing a higher value of α.

8.18 The amount a deseasonalised value must be multiplied by to allow for seasonal variations.

8.19 No.

8.20 No; it is more complicated than this.

Chapter 9 Process planning

9.1 All the operations used to make a product.

9.2 Process planning designs the best way of making a product. It is needed whenever a new product is introduced, or there is a significant change in operations.

9.3 One that concentrates on the whole process of satisfying customer demand.

9.4 Project, job shop, batch mass, production and continuous flow.

9.5 Reasonable answers are: (a) mass production (b) continuous flow; (c) batch; (d) project; (e) jobbing; (f) any depending on the number produced, etc.

9.6 The same ones as for other organisations (perhaps under different names).

9.7 Continuous flow and mass production. The processes have no time lost for set-ups, they are largely automated, use more advanced technology and specialised equipment, planning is easier, and so on.

9.8 Many factors can be important including demand pattern, flexibility, vertical integration, customer involvement and product quality.
9.9 A simplified view gives: planning uses project, introduction uses job shop, growth uses batch, maturity uses mass production.
9.10 Manual, mechanised and automated.
9.11 (a) numerically controlled; (b) computerised numerically controlled; (c) computer-aided manufacturing; (d) computer-aided design; (e) flexible manufacturing system; (f) computer-integrated manufacturing.
9.12 Generally NC, CNC, CAM, FMS and CIM.
9.13 In the same way as manufacturing: project, job shop, batch, mass production and continuous flow.
9.14 No.
9.15 It is not true. Many services are not expensive and some have extensive automation.
9.16 No.
9.17 Many things, including the list given in the text.

Chapter 10 Measuring and improving performance

10.1 There are several, including capacity, productivity, utilisation, efficiency, etc.
10.2 Capacity is the maximum amount output in a specified time; utilisation is the proportion of available capacity that is actually used; productivity is the amount produced per unit of resource; efficiency is the ratio of actual output to effective capacity.
10.3 Yes, if the efficiency decreases.
10.4 Total productivity measures the ratio of total output to total input; partial factor productivity measures the output for a single input.
10.5 Yes.
10.6 No.
10.7 Because absolute values often have little meaning.
10.8 Yes.
10.9 Because products, customers, suppliers and everything else changes over time. An organisation must respond to these changes or get left behind.
10.10 Quality, production level, processing, waiting, movement, stock or many other areas.
10.11 Business process reengineering – an approach to getting radical improvements in performance.
10.12 No.
10.13 To describe the details of a process and highlight those areas that can be improved.
10.14 They show the relationships between individual operations and are used for analysing processes.
10.15 When managers want to see what each participant in the process is doing at any time.

Chapter 11 Layout of facilities

11.1 Layout is the physical arrangement of facilities in a process. A good layout allows efficient operations: a poor layout reduces efficiency, effective capacity and utilisation.

11.2 These are set by the operations strategy, but are generally to make the process work as well as possible.
11.3 Process, product, hybrid, fixed and specialised.
11.4 No.
11.5 Yes.
11.6 Because the number of movements may not be available (particularly for new processes), the data may be too difficult to collect, or other factors are considered more important.
11.7 Yes.
11.8 To separate consecutive stages so that a short disruption to one does not affect the other.
11.9 The smallest output of any stage along the line.
11.10 To ensure a smooth flow of products, with all resources used as fully as possible.
11.11 Layouts that are a combination of process and product layouts.
11.12 An arrangement with a dominant process layout, but with some operations in a product layout. They obtain the high utilisations and other advantages of product processes in a process environment.
11.13 No, the product is in a fixed location, not the equipment.
11.14 All materials, components and people must be moved to the site, there may be limited space, scheduling is difficult, the intensity of work varies, external factors affect operations, and so on.
11.15 The size and weight of goods being stored, value of goods, demand patterns, capital available, operating costs, space available, etc.
11.16 No.

Chapter 12 Managing capacity

12.1 Because the capacity limits the output, which is related to a specific period.
12.2 Designed capacity is the maximum output in ideal circumstances; effective capacity is the maximum output that can be sustained under normal circumstances.
12.3 (a) passengers per trip; (b) customers per performance; (c) barrels a day; (d) games per day; (e) client cases; (f) acres of land.
12.4 In decreasing order, they are designed capacity, effective capacity and actual output.
12.5 Forecast demand, translate this into a capacity requirement, find available capacity, identify mismatches between these two, generate alternative plans for overcoming any mismatch, evaluate these plans and select the best.
12.6 Because it is difficult to find a solution that satisfies everyone.
12.7 It is difficult to match a discrete capacity to a continuous demand.
12.8 To minimise disruptions, get reduced costs, prepare for the future, etc.
12.9 Fixed costs are spread over more units, more efficient processes are used and there is more experience with the product.
12.10 Yes.
12.11 Demand management and capacity management.
12.12 If the first operation takes T, the second takes $0.8T$, the fourth takes 0.8^2T, the eighth takes 0.8^3T, and so on.
12.13 Experience and practice make jobs easier, short cuts are found, skills increase, routines are known, and so on.
12.14 To stop the performance of equipment falling below an acceptable level.

12.15 No.
12.16 After the period that minimises the total cost per unit time.
12.17 The probability that equipment continues to work throughout a given period.

Chapter 13 Tactical plans

13.1 In principle, strategic plans lead to capacity plans, then aggregate plans, master schedules and short-term schedules.
13.2 (a) aggregate plans; (b) master schedule; (c) short-term schedule; (d) short-term schedule.
13.3 No.
13.4 A number of sources, including forecasts, plans for previous periods, decisions at higher levels of planning, etc.
13.5 Yes.
13.6 They simplify the planning (resources this period equal resources last period, plus new arrivals, minus removals).
13.7 A schedule of monthly production for each family of products.
13.8 Monthly production over the next few months.
13.9 No.
13.10 It is easy to use, convenient, the results can be good, the process is well understood and trusted, and an experienced planner has credibility in the organisation.
13.11 The cumulative supply line should be close to the cumulative demand line, and it should have few changes in gradient.
13.12 It is relatively straightforward, easy to understand, convenient, quick to compare alternatives, etc.
13.13 To add details to the aggregate plan, and give a timetable for making individual products.
13.14 These mainly come from the aggregate plan, available capacity, actual customer orders and available resources.

Chapter 14 Short-term scheduling

14.1 Detailed timetables of jobs, equipment, people and other resources.
14.2 To meet the requirements of the master schedule while using resources efficiently.
14.3 Requirements defined by the master schedule, resources needed and available, costs, priorities, etc.
14.4 Because they are too difficult to find, and it is not worth the effort.
14.5 A simple heuristic rule that experience has found to give good solutions.
14.6 Useful rules would be: (a) most urgent first; (b) earliest due date first; (c) first-come first-served; (d) shortest first.
14.7 No.
14.8 To minimise the makespan of a set of jobs moving through two machines, one after the other
14.9 Optimised Production Technology: a package that contains procedures (based on the 'theory of constraints') for scheduling jobs.
14.10 In principle, there is no difference.
14.11 No; it depends on the circumstances.
14.12 When operators are not permanently assigned to a piece of equipment, and when they are in short supply.

14.13 Yes.
14.14 To monitor progress, make sure planned schedules are actually being achieved, warn of problems, make minor adjustments to schedules, giving feedback, etc.
14.15 No.

Chapter 15 Material requirements planning

15.1 Material requirements planning: a dependent demand system which uses the master schedule to plan the arrival of materials.
15.2 Independent demand systems assume that demands are unrelated and use forecasts, usually from historic figures; dependent demand systems assume that demands are related and find requirements from known production plans.
15.3 No.
15.4 A master schedule, bill of materials, information about current stocks, lead times, and anything else that is relevant.
15.5 By subtracting current stock and scheduled receipts from gross requirements.
15.6 There can be many of these, typically including timetables for orders, timetables for material production, changes to previous schedules, exception reports, performance information, inventory transactions, etc.
15.7 It relates demand for materials directly to a master schedule.
15.8 The requirements which limit its applicability, and the complexity of the system.
15.9 Because small orders are inconvenient and have high administration and delivery costs.
15.10 A rule which suggests how to combine small, separate orders into larger ones.
15.11 Feedback of the consequences of MRP schedules, and subsequent adjustments.
15.12 By extending the operations covered, functions, organisations, etc.
15.13 Manufacturing resources planning, which extends the MRP approach to a wide range of functions.
15.14 Yes, in common with all approaches of this type.

Chapter 16 Just-in-time operations

16.1 Operations occur just as they are needed, so materials are delivered just as they are to be used, and so on.
16.2 Traditional approaches often look for ways of overcoming the effects of problems, while JIT looks for the real cause and solves it.
16.3 They waste resources, hide problems and should be eliminated.
16.4 No; this is only one benefit.
16.5 One with a stable environment, standard products with few variations, a balanced process that uses resources fully, reliable production equipment, small batches of materials, short lead times for materials, efficient materials handling, reliable suppliers, etc.
16.6 No.
16.7 They are long-term partners who co-operate and have a mutually beneficial trading arrangement.
16.8 Stability of a long-term relationship, guaranteed supplies, mutual benefits, etc.
16.9 No.
16.10 No.
16.11 To control the flow of materials in a JIT system.

16.12 Each container has a kanban, so the number of kanbans sets the number of containers and hence the amount of work-in-progress.
16.13 No; this is just one aspect of JIT.
16.14 There are many advantages including reduced stocks, easier planning, higher quality, better control, lower costs, etc.
16.15 Not really, as JIT needs a fundamental change of attitudes, plans, procedures and operations.

Chapter 17 Job design and work measurement

17.1 Because it affects the relationships between people, the way they work together, their objectives, motivation, communications, and so on.
17.2 To some extent.
17.3 Finding the best way of doing a job.
17.4 Two groups traditionally called 'employers' and 'workers'.
17.5 Employers want to meet the economic, technical, productivity, quality and other goals of the organisation; workers want a job that is safe, satisfying and rewarding to meet their social and psychological needs.
17.6 No.
17.7 This is difficult to define, but it represents the effort that people are willing to put into their work.
17.8 Because it affects the way operations are done – and hence the performance of the organisation.
17.9 The physical environment, social environment and work methods.
17.10 Morale, and motivation, are improved by significant, identifiable and varied tasks, needing a variety of skills, and giving workers autonomy and feedback.
17.11 To find the standard time needed to do a job.
17.12 Actual time is the time a worker actually takes to do the essential parts of the job; normal time is the time a worker would take to do the job if he/she worked at standard rate; standard time is the total time that should be allowed for a job, including allowances.
17.13 Using historical data, estimation or a time study.
17.14 The standard time.

Chapter 18 Project management

18.1 A self-contained piece of work with a clear start and finish aimed at making a unique product.
18.2 To plan, schedule and control the activities in a project, finding the best balance between scope, costs, schedule and customer satisfaction.
18.3 No.
18.4 Planning and execution.
18.5 They show clearly what stage each activity in a project should have reached at any time.
18.6 Nodes represent activities; arrows show the relationships between activities.
18.7 A list of all activities in the project with their immediate predecessors.
18.8 The two main rules are: before an activity can start all preceding activities must be finished; the arrows show precedence and their length and direction have no significance.

18.9 The earliest start time is the earliest time that all preceding activities can finish; the earliest finish time is the earliest start plus the duration.
18.10 The latest finish time is the latest time that allows all following activities to start on time; the latest start time is the latest finish time minus the duration.
18.11 The amount the duration of the activity can expand without affecting the length of the project.
18.12 Zero.
18.13 The critical path is the chain of activities that sets the length of the project. If any critical activity is extended or delayed, the whole project is delayed.
18.14 The critical activities.
18.15 By the total float of activities on a parallel path.
18.16 By its total float.
18.17 The shortest time to finish it when more resources are used.
18.18 By delaying non-critical activities to times when fewer resources are needed.

Chapter 19 Logistics and the supply chain

19.1 The function responsible for the movement of all materials and products through the supply chain from initial suppliers through operations and on to final customers.
19.2 No; it should be co-ordinated.
19.3 Procurement or purchasing, traffic and transport, receiving, warehousing or stores, inventory control, material handling, shipping, distribution, location and communications.
19.4 The path taken by a product from an initial supplier through to a final customer.
19.5 Because it is essential, expensive, affects performance, etc.
19.6 Because it can co-ordinate the operations to improve overall performance.
19.7 Efficient customer response, which organises the pull of materials through a supply chain.
19.8 Because it give a fast, cheap and efficient means of communicating and exchanging information.
19.9 To get necessary materials from suppliers and into the organisation.
19.10 Purchasing is concerned with the actual buying of materials; procurement is a broader term that includes related activities.
19.11 The cycle starts when someone needs materials, moves through the work done in the procurement area and suppliers, and finishes when the item is delivered.
19.12 Procurement used to be a clerical job but now it is an essential profession – many changes come with this adjustment.
19.13 To physically move materials through a supply chain.
19.14 Road, rail, air, water and pipeline.
19.15 There are many of these including the mode, routes, types of vehicle, use of specialised logistics companies, etc.

Chapter 20 Facilities location

20.1 Because they have long-term effects, are expensive, have serious consequences for mistakes, affect all operations, etc.
20.2 No.
20.3 It can expand on the current site, open additional facilities, or close existing facilities and relocate.

20.4 No.
20.5 Not necessarily.
20.6 Culture, operation, type of organisation, etc.
20.7 No.
20.8 A measure for the centre of customer demand.
20.9 No.
20.10 A feasible set approach compares a number of feasible sites and chooses the best; an infinite set approach uses geometric arguments to show where the best site would be if there were no restrictions on site availability.
20.11 Many costs might be included, but the most important may be transport and operating costs.
20.12 Inward transport moves materials in from suppliers; outward transport moves products out to customers.
20.13 They allow a range of factors, both quantitative and qualitative, to be considered.
20.14 No.
20.15 Many factors might be important, including cost, structure of the supply chain, business strategy, etc.
20.16 Yes.

Chapter 21 Managing stocks

21.1 To act as a buffer between supply and demand.
21.2 A useful classification has raw materials, work-in-progress, finished goods, spare parts and consumables.
21.3 Unit, reorder, holding and shortage costs.
21.4 Holding cost rises with higher stocks, unit cost does not vary, and the others fall.
21.5 What items to stock, when to place orders, how much to order?
21.6 The order quantity that minimises inventory costs when a number of assumptions are made.
21.7 Total holding costs are lower, but total reorder costs (and shortage costs) are higher.
21.8 The amount of an item that is in stock when it is time to place an order.
21.9 No.
21.10 The probability that a demand can be met from stock. We used cycle-service level, which is the probability that an item remains in stock during a stock cycle.
21.11 It reduces the probability of shortages.
21.12 By increasing the amount of safety stock.
21.13 Order quantity = target stock level – current stocks (– any orders outstanding).
21.14 For a periodic review system, as there is more uncertainty over a longer period.
21.15 To show the importance of items so that appropriate effort can be spent on controlling their stocks.
21.16 B items.

Index